Robust Analytics and Reporting

©Hero Images/Getty Images

- Connect Insight® generates easy-to-read reports on individual students, the class as a whole, and on specific assignments.
- The Connect Insight dashboard delivers data on performance, study behavior, and effort. Instructors can quickly identify students who struggle and focus on material that the class has yet to master.
- Connect automatically grades assignments and quizzes, providing easy-to-read reports on individual and class performance.

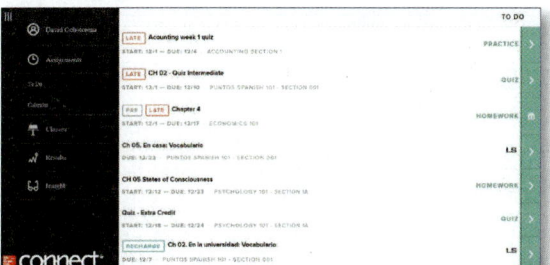

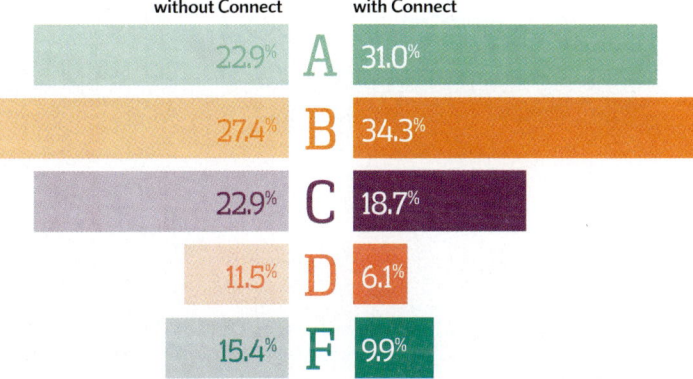

Impact on Final Course Grade Distribution

	without Connect		with Connect
A	22.9%		31.0%
B	27.4%		34.3%
C	22.9%		18.7%
D	11.5%		6.1%
F	15.4%		9.9%

More students earn **As** and **Bs** when they use **Connect**.

Trusted Service and Support

- Connect integrates with your LMS to provide single sign-on and automatic syncing of grades. Integration with Blackboard®, D2L®, and Canvas also provides automatic syncing of the course calendar and assignment-level linking.
- Connect offers comprehensive service, support, and training throughout every phase of your implementation.
- If you're looking for some guidance on how to use Connect, or want to learn tips and tricks from super users, you can find tutorials as you work. Our Digital Faculty Consultants and Student Ambassadors offer insight into how to achieve the results you want with Connect.

www.mheducation.com/connect

SOC 2018

FIFTH EDITION

Jon Witt
Central College

WITT: SOC 2018, FIFTH EDITION

Published by McGraw-Hill Education, 2 Penn Plaza, New York, NY 10121. Copyright © 2018 by McGraw-Hill Education. All rights reserved. Printed in the United States of America. Previous editions © 2016, 2015, and 2013. No part of this publication may be reproduced or distributed in any form or by any means, or stored in a database or retrieval system, without the prior written consent of McGraw-Hill Education, including, but not limited to, in any network or other electronic storage or transmission, or broadcast for distance learning.

Some ancillaries, including electronic and print components, may not be available to customers outside the United States.

This book is printed on acid-free paper.

1 2 3 4 5 6 7 8 9 LMN 21 20 19 18 17

ISBN 978-1-259-70272-3
MHID 1-259-70272-3

Author: *Jon Witt*
Field Correspondent: *Richard T. Schaefer*
Executive Portfolio Manager: *Claire Brantley*
Director, Product Development: *Meghan Campbell*
Lead Product Developer: *Dawn Groundwater*
Digital Product Developer: *Briana Porco*
Marketing Manager: *Will Walter*
Lead Content Project Manager, Core: *Susan Trentacosti*
Senior Content Project Manager, Assessment: *Katie Klochan*
Content Project Manager: *Sandy Schnee*
Senior Buyer: *Laura M. Fuller*
Design: *Matt Backhaus*
Content Licensing Specialist: *Melisa Seegmiller*
Cover Image: *©Sam Edwards/Glow Images*
Compositor: *SPi Global*

All credits appearing on page or at the end of the book are considered to be an extension of the copyright page.
Photo Credits: *Popcorn box:* © D. Hurst/Alamy RF; *Earth:* © BLOOMimage/Getty Images RF; *Hands:* © Jeff DeWeerd/Imagezoo/Getty Images RF

ISSN: 2164-0696

The Internet addresses listed in the text were accurate at the time of publication. The inclusion of a website does not indicate an endorsement by the authors or McGraw-Hill Education, and McGraw-Hill Education does not guarantee the accuracy of the information presented at these sites.

mheducation.com/highered

In memory of Megan Sloss

Sociology, Class of 2014, Central College

Be Bold. Dive Deep. Converse.

©Jon Witt

Name: Jon Witt (though my mom always called me Jonathan)

Education: I got my BA from Trinity College in Deerfield, IL, and earned my PhD from Loyola University in Chicago.

Occupations: Sociologist, father, and dog-walker

Hobbies: I like reading, writing, and messing around on computers–and I'm addicted to my iPhone and iPad.

Childhood ambition: To be a printer like my dad until I decided to become a teacher like my mom.

Family: Lori and I have been married for 33 years, and we have two daughters, Emily, 23, and Eleanor, 21.

Last book read: Grand River and Joy by Susan Messer.

Favorite film: My most recent favorite is Going in Style–mainly because Lori and I also saw the original on one of our first dates.

Favorite soundtrack: Hamilton: An American Musical (Lori and I will be co-teaching a course about it this year)

Quote: There may be fields of sociological science quite beyond the average mind, and rightly left to the learned specialist; but that is no reason why we should not learn enough of the nature and habits of society to insure a more profitable and pleasant life.
—Charlotte Perkins Gilman, Human Work, 1904

Social Media: Twitter @soc101

SOC 2018 Edition

BRIEF CONTENTS

©Duncan Walker/Getty Images RF

©Olivier Lantzendörffer/Getty Images RF

1 **The Sociological Imagination**

2 **Sociological Research**

3 **Culture**

4 **Socialization**

5 **Social Structure and Interaction**

6 **Deviance**

7 **Families**

8 **Education and Religion**

9 **Economy and Politics**

10 **Social Class**

11 **Global Inequality**

12 **Gender and Sexuality**

13 **Race and Ethnicity**

14 **Population, Health, and Environment**

15 **Social Change**

Glossary 400
References 411
Name Index 448
Subject Index 450

WHAT'S NEW IN SOC

This edition includes new statistics and data throughout to reflect 2016 research. Also, the author has revised in response to student heat-map data that pinpointed the topics and concepts with which students struggled the most. This heat-map-directed revision is reflected primarily in Chapters 5 and 14. Other content changes include the following:

> **New/updated opening vignettes:**
> > Chapter 1: Pulitzer Prize–winning sociologist Matthew Desmond's research on evictions and homelessness in Milwaukee.
> > Chapter 3: Improv Everywhere, the "prank collective."
> > Chapter 6: The Orlando mass shooting at the Pulse nightclub, as well as more recent shootings and data.
> > Chapter 7: Online dating apps and sites with a focus on Jessica Carbino, Tinder's in-house sociologist.
> > Chapter 9: The 2016 election and the role of White working-class voters in Rust Belt states.
> > Chapter 10: Research on people in the United States living on less than $2.00 per person per day.
> > Chapter 11: Inequality in Mumbai, India. Chapter 13: Cases of police killings of African American males.
> > Chapter 14: The Dakota Access Pipeline protests.
> > Chapter 15: Recent examples of student activism.

> **New topics woven into the chapter narratives:**
> > Sociology as a science, including the limits of common sense as a way of knowing and the advantages of sociology's empirical approach to explaining why we think and act as we do.

©Kim Kim Foster/The State/MCT/Getty Images

> A look at "us versus them," which connects ethnocentrism, group membership, patriotism, and prejudice.
> Henri Tajfel's work on social identity formation.
> Mass media as agents of socialization.
> The "broken window" hypothesis and its consequences for policing.
> The 1967 Supreme Court ruling in *Loving v. Virginia*.
> Research showing social and psychological benefits of remaining single.
> the index of dissimilarity, a measure of segregation.
> The "religiously unaffiliated," which includes atheists, agnostics, and those who choose "nothing in particular."
> Research on changes in global income distribution over time.
> The Bugis and their five genders as an example of cross-cultural variation in gender definitions.
> Cisgender, gender binary, and gender spectrum as new key terms.
> The likelihood of children doing better than their parents at age 30.
> The Paris Agreement regarding climate change.
> Possible impacts of technological innovation on future jobs.

> **New Did You Know? topics:** Making things from scratch; concentration of the U.S. population into a relatively small number of counties; drug arrests in the United States; favorable/unfavorable ratings of Hillary Clinton and Donald Trump leading up to the 2016 presidential election; President George Washington as a slave owner; the execution of 38 Dakota Sioux men on a single day in 1862; the amount of Brazilian rain forest lost each year.

> New PopSOC topics: The constructed language for the HBO series *Game of Thrones*; roles for African Americans and Hispanics in the top 100 films of the year.

> New SocThink: Implicit association tests.

> New graphs: U.S. Incarceration Rates, 1910–2014; Educational Attainment in the United States; College Majors by Gender, Percent Female; Net Price Cost of College; Where in the World the 767 Million People Below the international Poverty Line Live; Labor Force Participation Rates for Men and Women over Time; Gender Wage Gap by Education; Political Party Identification in the United States over Time; Income Distribution in the United States; Wealth Distribution in the United States; U.S. Uninsured Rate, 1997–2016; Complementary and Alternative Medicine Use.

©Trista Weibell/Getty Images RF

> New/revised Going Global topics: Conducting research in difficult circumstances using the annual national survey of Afghanistan as an example; the region of origin of the world's living languages contrasted with the number of speakers; time spent in unpaid labor.

> New and revised definitions for key terms to reflect current scholarship.

> New digital assets:
  > Concept Clips: Dynamic videos to help students break down key concepts and difficult themes in sociology. Assignable and assessable! Examples: Research Variables, Social Structure, Theories of Political Power.
  > Newsflash: Exercises that tie current news stories to key sociological principles and learning objectives, and assess students on their ability to make the connection between real life and research findings. Examples: Mayor of Cannes Bans Burkinis on Resort's Beaches; Finding Good Pain Treatment Is Hard. If You're Not White, It's Even Harder.

Reviewers

George Bradley, *Montgomery Community College*
Stacey Callaway, *Rowan University*
Annette Chamberlin, *Virginia Western Community College*
Lyle Foster, *Missouri State University, Springfield*
Ashley Leschyshyn, *University of North Dakota*
Shannon Little, *Southwest Tennessee Community College, Macon Campus*

Jonathan Lopez, *Old Dominion University*
Cosandra McNeal, *Jackson State University*
Kurt Olson, *Modesto Junior College*
Sammy Rastagh, *Broward College South*

©Monkey Business Images/Shutterstock.comk RF

Table of Contents

1 > The Sociological Imagination 1

WHAT IS SOCIOLOGY? 2
- The Sociological Imagination 2
- The Significance of Place 4
- A Hamburger Is a Miracle 5
- Defining Sociology 6

SOCIOLOGY'S ROOTS 8
- A Science of Society 8
- Theory and Research 9

FIVE BIG QUESTIONS 12
- How Is Social Order Maintained? 12
- How Do Power and Inequality Shape Outcomes? 13
- How Does Interaction Shape Our Worlds? 14
- How Does Group Membership Influence Opportunity? 14
- How Should Sociologists Respond? 15

THREE SOCIOLOGICAL PERSPECTIVES 15

SOCIOLOGY IS A VERB 17
- Personal Sociology 17
- Academic Sociology 18
- Applied and Clinical Sociology 19

2 > Sociological Research 23

SOCIOLOGY AS A SCIENCE 24
- Sociology and Common Sense 24
- Sociology and the Scientific Method 25

STEPS IN THE RESEARCH PROCESS 26
- Defining the Problem 26
- Reviewing the Literature 27
- Formulating the Hypothesis 28
- Collecting and Analyzing Data 29
- Developing the Conclusion 30
- In Summary: The Research Process 32

MAJOR RESEARCH DESIGNS 32
- Surveys 32
- Observation 35
- Experiments 36
- Use of Existing Sources 38

RESEARCH ETHICS 41
- Confidentiality 41
- Research Funding 41
- Value Neutrality 42
- Feminist Methodology 43

3 > Culture 47

CULTURE AND SOCIETY 48

CONSTRUCTING CULTURE 49
- Cultural Universals 49
- Innovation 50
- Diffusion 51

THREE ELEMENTS OF CULTURE 52
- Material Culture 53
- Cognitive Culture 54
- Normative Culture 59

CULTURAL VARIATION 62
- Aspects of Cultural Variation 62
- Dominant Ideology 64
- Attitudes Toward Cultural Variation 65

©Michael Zak/123RF

©Rawpixel.com/Shutterstock.com RF

4 > Socialization   70

THE ROLE OF SOCIALIZATION   71
- Internalizing Culture   71
- The Impact of Isolation   72

THE SELF AND SOCIALIZATION   74
- Sociological Approaches to the Self   74
- Us versus Them   77

AGENTS OF SOCIALIZATION   79
- Family   79
- School   80
- Peer Groups   81
- Mass Media   82
- The Workplace   85
- Religion and the State   86

SOCIALIZATION THROUGHOUT THE LIFE COURSE   86
- The Life Course   87
- Anticipatory Socialization and Resocialization   88
- Role Transitions During the Life Course   89

AGING AND SOCIETY   90
- Adjusting to Retirement   91

PERSPECTIVES ON AGING   91
- Disengagement Theory   92
- Activity Theory   92
- Ageism and Discrimination   93
- Death and Dying   94

5 > Social Structure and Interaction   98

SOCIAL INTERACTION   99
- Self and Society   99
- Social Construction of Reality   100

ELEMENTS OF SOCIAL STRUCTURE   101
- Statuses and Roles   101
- Groups   105
- Social Networks   108
- Social Institutions   111

SOCIAL STRUCTURE IN GLOBAL PERSPECTIVE   113
- *Gemeinschaft* and *Gesellschaft*   113
- Mechanical and Organic Solidarity   114
- Technology and Society   115
- Postmodern Life   117

BUREAUCRACY   118
- Characteristics of a Bureaucracy   119
- Bureaucratization as a Way of Life   121
- Bureaucracy and Organizational Culture   123

6 > Deviance   127

SOCIAL CONTROL   128
- Conformity and Obedience   128
- Informal and Formal Social Control   130
- Law and Society   131

DEVIANCE   132
- What Behavior Is Deviant?   133
- Deviance and Social Stigma   134

CRIME   135
- Official Crime Reports   135
- White-Collar Crime   137
- Victimless Crimes   138

©Rick Rycroft/AP Images

Table of Contents   •   xi

Organized Crime   138

International Crime   139

SOCIOLOGICAL PERSPECTIVES ON CRIME AND DEVIANCE   141

Functions of Crime and Deviance   141

Interpersonal Interaction and Defining Deviance   143

Conflict, Power, and Criminality   147

7 > Families   152

GLOBAL VIEW OF THE FAMILY   153

Substance: What a Family Is   153

Functions: What Families Do   156

Conflict: Who Rules?   158

MARRIAGE AND FAMILY   159

Courtship and Mate Selection   160

Parenting Patterns and Practices   162

DIVERSE LIFESTYLES   167

Cohabitation   168

Remaining Single   168

Remaining Child-Free   169

Lesbian and Gay Relationships   169

DIVORCE   170

Statistical Trends in Divorce   170

Factors Associated with Divorce   171

Impact of Divorce on Children   172

©Creatas/Getty Images RF

©Goodshoot/Alamy Stock Photo RF

8 > Education and Religion   176

EDUCATION IN SOCIETY   177

SOCIOLOGICAL PERSPECTIVES ON EDUCATION   179

Education and Social Order   179

Education and Inequality   181

SCHOOLS AS FORMAL ORGANIZATIONS   187

The Bureaucratization of Schools   187

Teaching as a Profession   188

Community Colleges   188

Homeschooling   189

DEFINING RELIGION   190

Substance: What Religion Is   190

Function: What Religions Do   191

COMPONENTS OF RELIGION   192

Beliefs   192

Rituals   193

Experience   194

Community   194

WORLD RELIGIONS   197

SOCIOLOGICAL PERSPECTIVES ON RELIGION   199

Integration   200

Social Change   200

Social Control   202

9 > Economy and Politics   207

ECONOMIC CHANGE   208

Economic Sectors   208

Deindustrialization   209

The Great Recession   210

The Changing Face of the Workforce   211

POWER AND AUTHORITY   212

©Chris Ryan/Getty Images RF

    Power   212
    Types of Authority   212

ECONOMIC SYSTEMS   214
    Capitalism   214
    Socialism   215
    The Mixed Economy   216
    The Informal Economy   217

POLITICAL SYSTEMS   218
    Monarchy   218
    Oligarchy   218
    Dictatorship and Totalitarianism   219
    Democracy   219

THE POWER STRUCTURE IN THE UNITED STATES   221
    The Pluralist Model   221
    Power Elite Models   222

POLITICAL PARTICIPATION IN THE UNITED STATES   224
    Voter Participation   224
    Race and Gender in Politics   225

WAR AND PEACE   227
    War   227
    Terrorism   229
    Peace   230

10 > Social Class   234

LIFE CHANCES   235
    Systems of Stratification   235
    Social Mobility   238

SOCIAL CLASS IN THE UNITED STATES   239
    Income and Wealth   240
    Poverty   243
    The American Dream   246

SOCIOLOGICAL PERSPECTIVES ON STRATIFICATION   250
    Marx and Material Resources   250
    Weber and Social Resources   252
    Bourdieu and Cultural Resources   253
    Material, Social, and Cultural Resources   254

11 > Global Inequality   258

THE GLOBAL DIVIDE   259

PERSPECTIVES ON GLOBAL STRATIFICATION   260
    The Rise of Modernization   261
    The Legacy of Colonialism   262
    The Growth of Multinational Corporations   265

STRATIFICATION AROUND THE WORLD   268
    Income and Wealth   268
    Poverty   270
    Social Mobility   271
    Social Stratification in Mexico   273

UNIVERSAL HUMAN RIGHTS   276
    Defining Human Rights   277
    Principle and Practice   278
    Human Rights Activism   279

©Pavel Filatov/Alamy Stock Photo RF

©The Asahi Shimbun via Getty Images

PREJUDICE AND DISCRIMINATION 316
    Prejudice 316
    Discrimination 317

SOCIOLOGICAL PERSPECTIVES ON RACE AND ETHNICITY 322
    Social Order and Inequality 322
    The Contact Hypothesis 323
    Patterns of Intergroup Relations 323
    Privilege 327

RACE AND ETHNICITY IN THE UNITED STATES 328
    Racial Groups 328
    Ethnic Groups 334

IMMIGRATION 338
    Immigration Trends 338
    Immigration Policies 340

12 > Gender and Sexuality 283

THE SOCIAL CONSTRUCTION OF GENDER 284
    Sex and Gender 284
    Gender-Role Socialization 286
    Gender Across Cultures 289
    Reimagining Sex and Gender 290

WORKING FOR CHANGE: WOMEN'S MOVEMENTS 292
    The First Wave 292
    The Second Wave 292
    The Third Wave 294

THE SOCIAL CONSTRUCTION OF SEXUALITY 295
    Sexuality and Identity 295
    Sexuality in Action 298

GENDER AND INEQUALITY 301
    Sexism and Discrimination 301
    Women in the United States 301
    Women Around the World 306

13 > Race and Ethnicity 310

RACIAL AND ETHNIC GROUPS 311
    Race 312
    Ethnicity 314

14 > Population, Health, and Environment 345

POPULATION 346
    Birth 347
    Death 348
    Migration 348
    Demographic Transition 350

©Gavriel Jecan/The Image Bank/Getty Images

SOCIOLOGICAL PERSPECTIVES ON HEALTH AND ILLNESS   353
- Culture, Society, and Health   353
- Illness and Social Order   355
- Power, Resources, and Health   356
- Negotiating Cures   358

SOCIAL EPIDEMIOLOGY   359
- Social Class   360
- Race and Ethnicity   361
- Gender   362
- Age   363

HEALTH CARE IN THE UNITED STATES   364
- A Historical View   364
- The Role of Government   365
- Complementary and Alternative Medicine   366

SOCIOLOGICAL PERSPECTIVES ON THE ENVIRONMENT   367
- Human Ecology   367
- Power, Resources, and the Environment   368
- Environmental Justice   369

ENVIRONMENTAL PROBLEMS   370
- Air Pollution   370
- Water Pollution   371
- Global Climate Change   371
- The Global Response   373

©David Crigger, Bristol Herald Courier/AP Images

15 > Social Change   377

SOCIOLOGICAL PERSPECTIVES ON SOCIAL CHANGE   378
- The Evolution of Societies   379
- Equilibrium and Social Order   380
- Resources, Power, and Change   381

TECHNOLOGY AND THE FUTURE   382
- Computer Technology   383
- Privacy and Censorship in a Global Village   384
- Biotechnology and the Gene Pool   386
- Resistance to Technology   387

SOCIAL MOVEMENTS   389
- Relative Deprivation   389
- Resource Mobilization Approach   390
- Gender and Social Movements   391
- New Social Movements   392

SOCIOLOGY IS A VERB   393
- Personal Sociology   394
- Public Sociology: Tools for Change   394
- Practicing Sociology   395

Glossary   400

References   411

Name Index   448

Subject Index   450

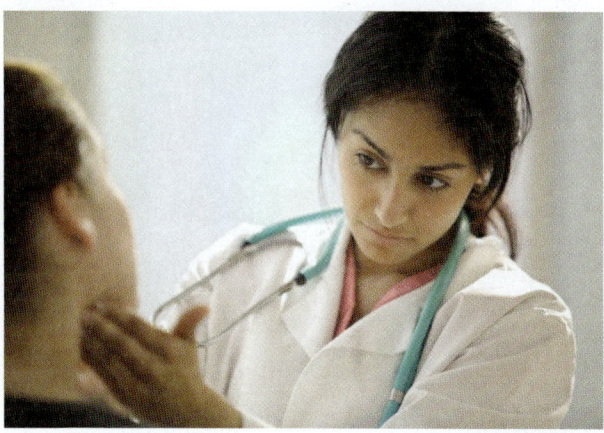
©Blend Images LLC/Getty Images RF

©Diecra Laird, The Charlotte Observer/AP Images

The Sociological Imagination

NO PLACE LIKE HOME

On a January day, with wind chills threatening to reach 40 below, Arleen Belle found herself out on the streets of Milwaukee. She and her two boys had just been evicted from their apartment due to a snowball-throwing incident that spiraled out of control, and now they had nowhere to go. They ended up staying the night at the local Salvation Army homeless shelter. Despite repeated efforts, it took until April for Arleen to find a place for her family to live. Their new rental, a four-bedroom house, had peeling paint and frequently lacked running water. They were there only a few weeks when the house was ruled "unfit for human habitation." They finally settled into an apartment in one of the worst neighborhoods in Milwaukee. The $550 they owed for rent each month took 88 percent of their monthly cash income. Even though she tried to live by the creed that, when it comes to paying the bills, "the rent eats first" (Desmond 2016:302), sometimes other expenses won out, as happened when she helped pay for the funeral of a friend who was as close as a sister. In a few months, as a result of their economic vulnerability, Arleen and her boys found themselves out on the street again.

Evictions used to be rare. Now they are commonplace. Yet relatively little is known about who gets evicted and why. Sociologist Matthew Desmond (2016) set out to learn more. To do so, he moved into low-income neighborhoods in Milwaukee, Wisconsin, first spending 5 months in a mobile home park on the city's mostly White south side, and then 10 months in a rooming house in a predominantly Black inner-city neighborhood. He joined his neighbors in their everyday activities: playing cards with neighbors and attending eviction hearings, funerals, Alcoholics Anonymous meetings, and more. To gather additional data, he also spent time with landlords, conducted a citywide survey of renters, reviewed court eviction records, and analyzed 911 calls. He learned that Arleen's story was not at all uncommon.

Desmond also uncovered the stories of those who profited from the people who lived in these communities. Tobin Charney, the owner of the 131-unit mobile home park where Desmond lived—which the city tried to shut down as a hub for drugs, prostitution, and violence—took home $447,000 per year after expenses. Sherrena Tarver, a landlord in the neighborhood where Desmond stayed in the rooming house, drove a red Camaro (though not when she was visiting her tenants), took vacations in Jamaica, and earned approximately $120,000 per year on 36 rental properties. As Sherrena put it, "The 'hood is good. There's a lot of money there" (p. 152).

Through his research, Desmond demonstrated a fundamental sociological truth. The positions we occupy—landlord or tenant, rich or poor—shape how we think, act, and feel. In this chapter, we explore how we can use the sociological imagination in order to better understand ourselves and others.

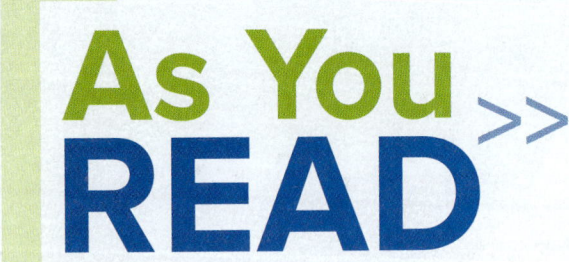

As You Read

- What is sociology?
- How do sociologists look at the world?
- How might someone practice sociology?

>> What Is Sociology?

We need one another. We may like to think that we can make it on our own, but our individualism is made possible by our interdependence. We praise the Olympic gold medalist for her impressive skill, dedicated training, and single-minded determination. Yet, if it hadn't been for her mom driving her to the pool every day, for the building manager waking up at 4:00 a.m. to make sure the pool is open, for the women working overnight to make sure the locker room is clean and safe, and so many others who fade into the background in such moments of glory, she would never have had that chance to shine.

The people upon whom we depend are often unknown and invisible to us. Even though we may never meet them, we rely on farmers, truck drivers, secretaries, store clerks, custodians, software engineers, scientists, assembly-line workers, teachers, police officers, inventors, politicians, CEOs, and a whole host of others. Yet we mostly take their contributions for granted without fully appreciating the degree to which they make our lives possible. Sociologists seek to reveal the full extent of our interdependence. They explore the intimate connection between self and society, placing that relationship at the heart of sociology's definition. **Sociology** is the systematic study of the relationship between the individual and society and of the consequences of difference. We examine the various components of that definition below, in the "Defining Sociology" section, after first considering ways in which the sociological imagination shapes how we see the world.

Sociology The systematic study of the relationship between the individual and society and of the consequences of difference.

Sociological imagination Our recognition of the interdependent relationship between who we are as individuals and the social forces that shape our lives.

THE SOCIOLOGICAL IMAGINATION

American sociologist C. Wright Mills (1959) proposed that we think of sociology as a tool that enables us to better understand why we think the way we think and act the way we act. He proposed we use our **sociological imagination** to explore the interdependent relationship between who we are as individuals and the social forces that shape our lives. To put it another way, practicing sociology involves recognizing the powerful intersection between history and biography. We are products of our times and places. Our thoughts, actions, even our feelings are shaped by our social contexts. For example, you chose to go to college, but you didn't do so in isolation. Factors such as your age, family background, geographical location, friendship networks, and available income played a role in your decision to go and what school you chose.

In addition to more immediate influences on our choices, the sociological imagination calls us to also consider the role larger social forces may play. Take unemployment as an example. A person might lose his job for a variety of reasons. A worker who is foolish, selfish, and careless may get fired because he makes a lousy employee. But it's also possible for a worker to lose her job due to factors beyond her control, regardless of how effective she may be as a worker. Unemployment levels rise and fall depending on what is happening in the larger economy. For example, when the economy nosedived in the late 2000s, unemployment rose from 4.8 percent in February 2008 to a peak of 10.1 percent in October 2010. Many wise, generous, and careful workers lost their jobs in the process.

Analyzing how rates change over time allows us to see patterns we might miss when focusing only

U.S. Employment Trends

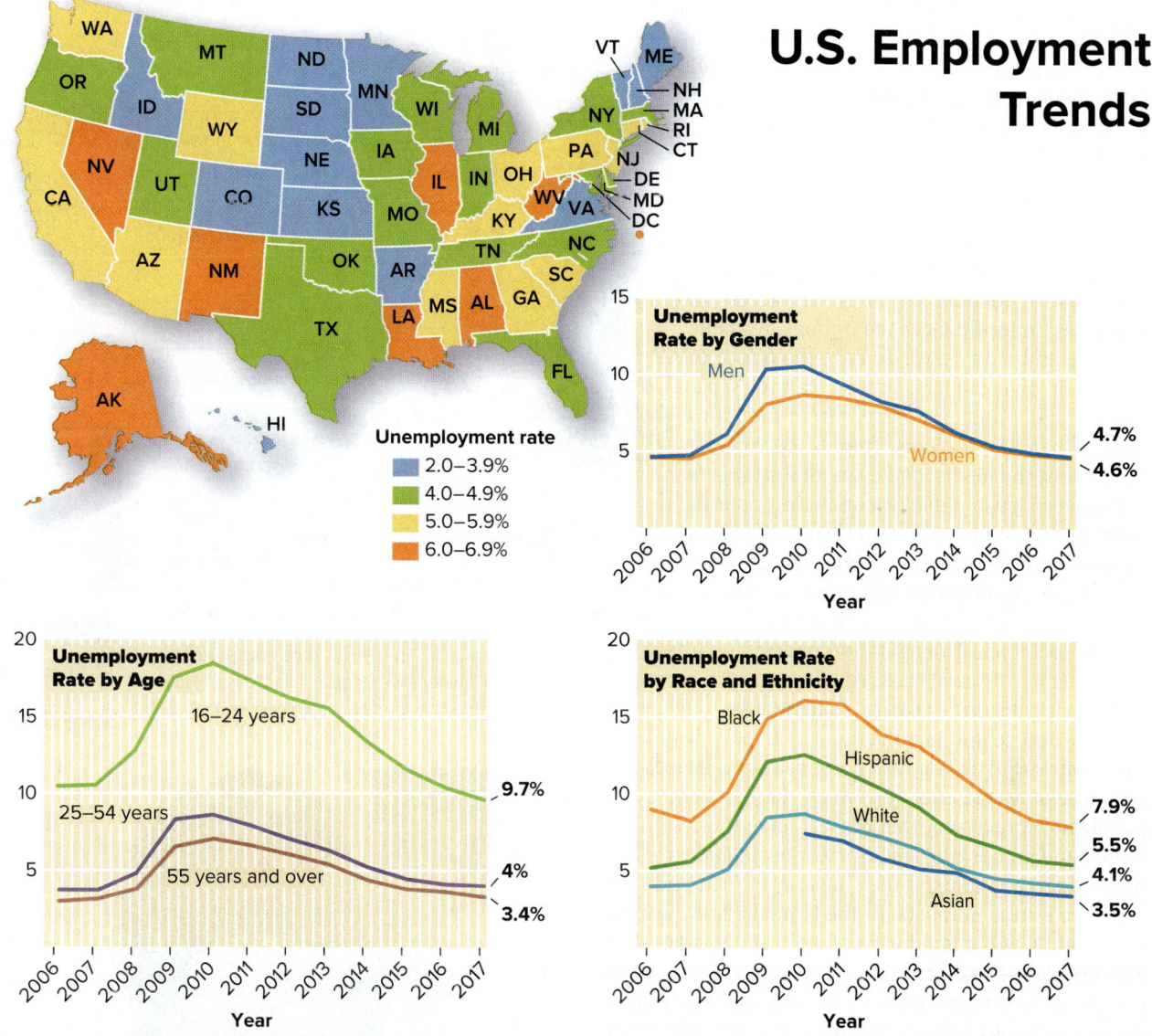

Note: The unemployment rate includes people 16 years and older who are available for work but do not have a job and who have actively looked for work within the previous four weeks.

Sources: Bureau of Labor Statistics 2016a and 2016b.

on individuals. Using the sociological imagination enables us to better recognize ways in which people in similar positions experience similar outcomes. Sticking with the unemployment example, as the accompanying "U.S. Employment Trends" map and graphs demonstrate, a person's likelihood of experiencing unemployment varies by the person's social location, which includes geographic location, age, gender, race, and ethnicity. So, as you can see, unemployment was more likely in the Southeast and West than in the Midwest. The level for young people was, and continues to be, substantially higher than for those who are older. Men experienced a more significant jump in joblessness than did women. Rates for African Americans and Latinos were, and are, significantly higher than those for Whites. Sociology teaches us that our social location matters. Understanding how different groups are affected helps policy makers decide which actions to take to address the crisis. A singular or universal solution to such a problem is unlikely to be effective in addressing the differing needs of the various groups.

To assist us in understanding the role social forces can play, Mills distinguished between private troubles and public issues. **Private troubles** are problems we face in our immediate relationships with particular individuals in our personal lives. Explanations for such troubles are particular to the individuals involved. For example, you lose your job because you failed to show up for work, disobeyed direct orders from your boss, took money from the cash register, and so forth. **Public issues** are problems we face as a consequence of the positions we occupy within the larger social structure. Private troubles are personal

> **Private troubles** Problems we face in our immediate relationships with particular individuals in our personal lives.
>
> **Public issues** Problems we face as a consequence of the positions we occupy within the larger social structure.

problems, but public issues are social problems. Analyzing data—such as unemployment rates, divorce rates, and poverty rates—enables us to see influences that might otherwise be invisible to us.

THE SIGNIFICANCE OF PLACE

To put it simply, place matters. Our position relative to others shapes our access to resources and influences the options available to us. As individuals, we do have the power to make our own choices, but we cannot separate our individual preferences from the influence of parents, teachers, friends, coworkers, politicians, the media, and even total strangers whose decisions enable or constrain opportunities for us. Where and when we were born; our parents' educational attainment, occupation, and income; our nationality; and other such factors all play major roles in shaping who we become.

The sociological imagination enables us to see the influence of social class, gender, and race, three positional categories of particular interest to sociologists due to the significance each has in our lives. Our social class position, for example, shapes our access to material resources. Researchers asked people how much they thought a chief executive officer (CEO) and an unskilled factory worker *should* earn and how much they thought they *actually* earned and then compared these numbers. In the United States, respondents said CEOs should earn about 7 times more than an unskilled worker, but they guessed that the real gap was 30 to 1. It turns out that the average yearly compensation for a CEO at a Standard & Poor's (S&P) 500 company was $12 million, approximately 354 times the $35,000 an average worker receives (Kiatpongsan and Norton 2014). This suggests that social class differences, such as that between a CEO and an unskilled worker, are even greater than we think.

Turning to gender, sociologists find a persistent wage gap between men and women. For example, when hackers attacked Sony Pictures and posted thousands of company documents and emails, it turned out that both Jennifer Lawrence (who had already won an Academy Award for her role in *Silver Linings Playbook* and had just starred in the blockbuster film *The Hunger Games: Catching Fire*) and Amy Adams (who had previously been nominated for four Academy Awards) were being paid significantly less for their roles in *American Hustle* than their three male counterparts, Christian Bale, Jeremy Renner, and Bradley Cooper, whose record of accomplishment was not as great (Kohn 2014). This pattern of unequal pay mirrors the overall wage gap in the United States. When comparing average earnings for full-time, year-round workers, women earn 80¢ for every $1 men earn (Proctor, Semega, and Kollar 2016:6). Race and ethnicity also

5 Movies on THE SOCIOLOGICAL IMAGINATION

12 Years a Slave
An 1840s African American man is kidnapped and sold into slavery.

Children of Men
A dystopian vision of society where humans can no longer reproduce.

Zootopia
A struggle against intolerance and discrimination in an animated animal kingdom.

Philomena
A mother's search for the child she gave up for adoption.

The Pursuit of Happyness
An unemployed father who becomes homeless seeks to do right by his son.

Actresses, such as Jennifer Lawrence, regularly receive less pay than do their male counterparts. Francois Duhamel/©Columbia Pictures/courtesy Everett Collection

shape likely outcomes. Being born into a White family in the United States significantly increases your odds of having access to money. In a study on the distribution of wealth, researchers found that median wealth of $141,900 for White households was 13 times greater than the $11,000 for African American households and 10 times greater than the $13,700 for Hispanic households (Kochhar and Fry 2014).

Place is important because it shapes how we think, act, and even feel. For example, when computer giant Hewlett-Packard was trying to figure out ways to get more women into upper-level management positions, it found that women applied for promotion only when they thought they met 100 percent of the qualifications for the position, whereas men applied when they believed they met 60 percent (Kay and Shipman 2014). When asked, at the end of his presidency, how Barack Obama would go down in history, 75 percent of African Americans said Obama would be remembered as outstanding or above average, compared to 38 percent among Whites (Pew Research Center 2016f). When it comes to analyzing such patterns, our tendency is to take sides, but the interesting sociological question is why such significant differences form in the first place.

A HAMBURGER IS A MIRACLE

To more fully appreciate how dependent we are on others, imagine that you have to make something completely from scratch but that you must do so without relying on any knowledge, skills, tools, or resources obtained from anyone else. How hard could that possibly be? Let's take a hamburger for example. First, you'll need beef to make the burger, which means you'll need to find a cow. But buying one from a farmer is off limits because doing so means relying on the efforts and abilities of others. So a wild cow it is. Assuming you can find one roaming around somewhere, you need to kill it, perhaps by bashing it over the head with a large rock or running it off a cliff.

Once you've got yourself a dead cow, you need to butcher it, but cowhide is tough. Imagine what it takes to produce a metal knife (finding ore, smelting, forging, tempering, and so on). Perhaps a sharp rock will do. Assuming you come up with a cutting tool, you can carve out a chunk of raw meat. Given that it's hamburger you're after (though you might be ready to settle for steak at this point), you'll need to grind up the meat. You might use a couple of those rocks to pulverize it into something of a meat mash. A meat grinder would work better, if only it weren't so hard to make one. In any event, at last you have a raw hamburger patty.

To cook your burger, you will need fire. But where does fire come from? Perhaps you could strike two rocks together or rub two sticks together. After trying this for a while, you may decide it would be easier to wait around for lightning to strike a nearby tree. However you accomplish it, after you get fire, you still have to cook the meat. No frying pans are available, so either you make one or perhaps cook it on that handy rock you used to kill the cow.

Assuming you are successful, you now have a cooked hamburger patty. But you aren't close to done. You still need to complete many other steps. You need to bake a bun, which involves figuring out how to come up with flour, water, salt, oil, sugar, yeast, and an oven. What about condiments such as ketchup, mustard, pickles, and onions? What if at the end of all that you decide to make it a cheeseburger? You killed the cow! Did you remember to milk her first?

Making something that seems so simple—that we can get for a dollar at McDonald's—turns out to be quite complicated. The resourcefulness necessary to acquire and prepare all the ingredients in a hamburger are beyond the capacity of most of us. Yet if we eat a burger, we seldom consider its complexity. If, instead,

Did You Know?

. . . Andy George explores the intricacies of the production process in his YouTube series "How to Make Things" (www.makeeverything.tv/). For example, he set out to make a grilled chicken sandwich completely from scratch. He grew his own wheat, milked a cow, evaporated ocean water for salt, slaughtered a chicken, and much more. It took him 6 months and cost him $1,500. The taste-testing verdict? Meh. Other products he makes using the raw ingredients he tracks down include chocolate bars, coffee, glass bottles, and a suit.

©G.K. & Vikki Hart/Getty Images RF

we exercise the sociological imagination, we may come to see that a hamburger is a miracle. Not literally, of course, because nothing supernatural is happening, but figuratively, as a symbolic representation of all the knowledge and skill that come together in this one meal. And it's not just hamburgers. All the products we make and use—veggie burgers, books, backpacks, shirts, cars, houses, smartphones—point toward a hidden infrastructure comprising our collective wisdom and ability.

The irony of modern society is that we depend on one another now more than ever, but we realize it less. We embrace individualism, and think we are masters of our own fates. Yet we lack the basic skills necessary for self-sufficiency. Sociology provides us with tools that enable us to more fully understand and appreciate our interdependence.

DEFINING SOCIOLOGY

Sociologists are committed to investigating, describing, and explaining such interrelationships. A more detailed breakdown of the four components of the definition of sociology helps reveal how they go about doing so.

Systematic Study Sociologists are engaged with the world, collecting empirical data through systematic research. Relying on such data means that sociologists draw their conclusions about society based on experiences or observations rather than beliefs or the authority of others. If they want to understand why the average age for first marriage keeps rising or why people commit crimes, they must gather data from those involved in these activities and base their conclusions on that information.

Agency Our freedom as individuals to think and act as we choose.

> *The function of sociology, as of every science, is to reveal that which is hidden.*
>
> — Pierre Bourdieu

Sociological research historically has involved both quantitative and qualitative approaches to data collection. Quantitative approaches emphasize counting things and analyzing them mathematically or statistically to uncover relationships between variables. The most common way to collect this type of data is through surveys. In contrast, qualitative approaches focus on listening to and observing people and allowing them to interpret what is happening in their own lives. The most common way to collect this type of data is through participant observation, in which the researcher interacts with those she or he studies. In practice, sociologists often draw on both techniques in conducting their research. We investigate these research techniques, along with others, in more detail in Chapter 2.

The Individual Although sociology is most commonly associated with the study of groups, there is no such thing as a group apart from the individuals who compose it. As individuals we are constantly choosing what to do next. Most of the time, we follow guidelines for behavior we have learned from others, but we have the ability to reject those guidelines at any time. A term sociologists use to describe this capacity is **agency**, meaning our freedom as individuals to think and act as we choose. In professional sports, for example, we use the term *free agent* to describe a player who has the power to negotiate with whatever team he or she wishes. We, too, have such freedom. We could choose not to go to class, not to go to work, not to get out of bed in the morning, not to obey traffic signals, not to respond when spoken to, not to read the next sentence in this book, and on and on.

As we saw with the significance of place, the positions we occupy relative to others shape the choices we make. In the NBA, LeBron James chose to leave the Miami Heat, where he'd won back-to-back championships, to return to his home-state Cleveland Cavaliers where he'd started his career. Signing with the NFL's Green Bay Packers or Major League Baseball's Chicago Cubs was not really an option because he lacked the kinds of skills those organizations reward. Our choices are constrained both by our abilities and by the opportunities available to us. We may have been born with amazing basketball skills, but if we live in a time and place where basketball doesn't exist, they are of limited value. We usually follow "paths of least resistance"— the accepted and expected actions and beliefs—but the choice of whether to continue to follow them is ours every second of our lives (A. Johnson 1997).

> **SOC THINK**
>
> What do you see as your biggest accomplishment in life so far? What people in your life were most directly responsible for helping make it happen? Given that we rely on others who are often unknown and invisible to us, what other people made indirect but essential contributions to your success?

As an NBA free agent, LeBron James moved from the Cleveland Cavaliers to the Miami Heat and back again. ©Christian Petersen/Getty Images

Society The study of society is at the heart of sociology. Although we will spend most of this book describing various aspects of society, we can begin by thinking of it as our social environment. **Society** consists of the structure of relationships within which culture is created and shared through regularized patterns of social interaction. The framework it provides is analogous to a building: The structure of a building both encourages and discourages different activities in different rooms (such as kitchens, bedrooms, and bathrooms), and many of the most essential operations of a building (such as heating and air conditioning) are mostly invisible to us. In the same way, the structure of our *institutions*—a term sociologists use to describe some of the major components of social structure, including economy, family, education, government, and religion—shapes what is expected of us. For example, the choices that are available to us in the context of the modern family, such as to go off and pursue our own education and career, are much different from the obligations we would face in more traditional family contexts. Nested within institutions are the groups, subgroups, and statuses that we occupy. We look at the details of these institutions in coming chapters, but it is helpful to remember that, in order to provide clear pathways for action, we construct culture and inhabit society.

The Consequences of Difference The final part of the definition of sociology involves the consequences of difference. Sociology does more than just describe our structure, culture, and interaction; it also analyzes how economic, social, and cultural resources are allocated and at the implications of these patterns in terms of the opportunities and obstacles they create for individuals and groups. Since the founding of sociology, sociologists have been concerned with the impact our social location has on our opportunities or lack thereof. As noted earlier, differential outcomes that result from class, gender, and race have been of particular interest to sociologists.

The analysis of social power deserves particular attention because it shapes how and why we think and act as we do. The simple fact is that those who have access to and control over valued material, social, and cultural resources have different options available to them than do those without such access and control. One of the main tasks of sociology is to investigate and reveal levels of **social inequality**—a condition in which members of society have differing amounts of wealth, prestige, or power. That is

> **Society** The structure of relationships within which culture is created and shared through regularized patterns of social interaction.
>
> **Social inequality** A condition in which members of society have different amounts of wealth, prestige, or power.

Chapter 1 / The Sociological Imagination • 7

Source: Library of Congress Prints and Photographs Division [LC-DIG-fsa-8b29516]

why the definition of sociology draws particular attention to the consequences of difference.

In combination, these four aspects of sociology help us understand the things that influence our beliefs and actions. Coming to terms with the reality that our choices are constrained by the positions we occupy can seem depressing, but sociology actually empowers us by providing a more complete picture of the worlds within which we live. French sociologist Pierre Bourdieu (1998a) put it this way: "Sociology teaches how groups function and how to make use of the laws governing the way they function so as to try to circumvent them" (p. 57). In other words, understanding the ways in which our thoughts and actions are determined enhances our freedom to make more effective and informed choices.

>> Sociology's Roots

Sociology, as a discipline, grew up in the midst of significant social upheaval. The advent of the Industrial Revolution and urbanization in the early 19th century led to changes in patterns of government, thought, work, and everyday life. Aristocracy was on the decline while democracy was spreading; people were moving from a primarily religious view of the world and its phenomena to a more scientific one; and life in the village and on the farm was rapidly giving way to life in the city and factory. The old rules that provided for social order no longer applied. The world seemed to be falling apart. Sociology arose as a means to understand and control the social forces that shaped our lives.

A SCIENCE OF SOCIETY

Science provided the foundation upon which sociology was built. Early scientists, such as Francis Bacon, Robert Boyle, and Isaac Newton, challenged conventional ideas about how the world worked. They didn't accept something as fact simply because others said so, choosing to reject the authority of politicians, priests, and philosophers, viewing them as insufficient sources of truth. This sometimes got them in trouble, as Galileo learned in the 1600s. He claimed that observations he'd made using his telescope, a recent invention, supported Copernicus's heliocentric theory that the earth revolved around the sun. However, because this theory contradicted the Catholic Church's geocentric teaching that the earth was the center of the universe, he was charged with heresy and kept under house arrest until his death.

Through meticulous observation and experimentation, these and other early scientists uncovered fundamental truths about the natural world. The scientific method they developed follows what we might now call the Missouri principle: don't just tell me, show me (after Missouri's nickname as the "show-me state"). In previous eras, it may have been sufficient to rely on the authority of priests or philosophers who argued that things happen due to other-worldly forces such as God's will or fate. The scientific method insists on this-worldly, empirical investigation that can be measured using our senses. If we can't see it, touch it, smell it, or in some way measure it, we shouldn't accept it as a fact. And even then we should engage in repeated experiments to protect against the possibility that our senses are fooling us. The laws of nature that resulted from these early scientific experiments, such as Newton's $F = ma$, held firm across time and place, thus providing universally true explanations about how nature operates.

©Jon Witt

The explanatory power of these laws of nature led others to explore the possibility of uncovering equally powerful laws of society. It was in this context that French sociologist and philosopher Auguste Comte (1798–1857) set out to discover laws guiding what he saw as the two most important societal forces: social stability and social change. He used the expressions "social statics" to refer to the principles by which societies hold together and order is maintained and "social dynamics" to describe the factors that bring about change and shape the nature and direction of that change. Knowledge produced by these laws could

POPSOC

Harriet Martineau ([1838] 1989) argued that we could learn a lot about a culture by analyzing the ideas, images, and themes reflected in its popular songs. She wrote, "The Songs of every nation must always be the most familiar and truly popular part of its poetry.... They present also the most prevalent feelings on subjects of the highest popular interest. If it were not so, they would not have been popular songs." What might we learn about American culture based on analysis of the lyrics of the current top-10 songs? What themes, ideas, images, and expectations are prevalent? (Lists are available at "The Billboard Hot 100" or www.top10songs.com.)

Photo: ©Kevin Mazur/WireImage/Getty Images

guide decisions that would enhance social stability while also working toward positive social change. To give this new discipline a name, Comte coined the term *sociology*—which literally means "the study of the processes of companionship" (Abercrombie, Hill, and Turner 2006:367).

English-speaking scholars learned of Comte's work largely through translations by the English sociologist Harriet Martineau (1802–1876). Seeking to systematize the research essential to conducting a science of society, Martineau ([1838] 1989) wrote the first book on sociological methods. She was also a path-breaking theorist, introducing the significance of inequality and power into the discipline. Martineau's book *Society in America* ([1837] 1962) examined religion, politics, child rearing, and immigration in the young nation. It gave special attention to social class distinctions and to such factors as gender and race. In Martineau's ([1837] 1962) view, intellectuals and scholars should not simply offer observations of social conditions; they should act on their convictions in a manner that would benefit society. Martineau spoke out in favor of the rights of women, the emancipation of slaves, and religious tolerance.

These two themes—social order and social inequality—have shaped the theoretical and research paths sociologists have pursued since this beginning. In early sociological theory, they find their fullest development in the works of Émile Durkheim and Karl Marx, respectively. As we will see throughout this book, they continue to be primary concerns for sociologists.

THEORY AND RESEARCH

French sociologist Émile Durkheim (1858–1917) was strongly influenced by Comte's dream of establishing sociology as a science. They both envisioned sociology as a conversation between theory and research. Unlike Comte, however, Durkheim gathered data to test basic sociological theories about social order. A **theory** is a set of statements that seeks to explain problems, actions, or behavior. Theories represent our attempts to make the best possible sense of the world around us. They often start out general and vague, but over time and informed by research, theories provide richer, more complete interpretations of the worlds in which we live. Durkheim provided an early model of the interplay between theory and research with his work on the impact our social connectedness has on the choices we make.

> **Theory** In sociology a set of statements that seeks to explain problems, actions, or behavior.
>
> **Social facts** Manners of acting, thinking, and feeling external to the individual with coercive power to shape how we act, think, and feel.

Formulating Sociological Theories We can better understand how theories develop in sociology by following the logic Émile Durkheim employed more than a century ago when sociology was just emerging as a social science. At the time, there were no sociology departments in universities and no academic positions for sociologists. Durkheim wanted to establish sociology's legitimacy as a distinct discipline. His theory was that social forces shape individual action. This contradicted the dominant theories of the time that biology, the individual's psyche, or God were the primary causes for our behaviors. In an attempt to create space for sociology as a discipline, he argued that factors above the level of the individual but within the domain of human society shape our actions.

Durkheim set out to prove that social facts exist and affect what we do. He defined **social facts** as manners of acting, thinking, and feeling external to the individual that have coercive power to shape how we

©Franky De Meyer/Getty Images RF

act, think, and feel. In other words, how we act, think, and feel is both enabled and constrained by social forces outside of us. But a social fact is kind of like gravity. We can't really see it or measure it directly, but we can observe its effects. Proving the power of social facts depends on demonstrating the impact they have on the choices we make.

To make the strongest case possible, Durkheim chose to study what he saw as the ultimate individual choice: suicide. He theorized that people commit suicide because they lack the social connections and obligations that prevent them from taking their own life. His hypothesis was as follows: "Suicide varies inversely with the degree of integration of the social groups of which the individual forms a part" ([1897] 1951:209). Durkheim chose religious affiliation as an indicator of social integration, arguing that Protestants are less socially integrated than Roman Catholics. He claimed that Catholicism is a traditional faith with a hierarchical system of authority in which variation in belief (on such topics as birth control, abortion, and women priests) is not up to the individual. Protestantism, in contrast, gives individual believers more power to interpret the Bible for themselves. As a result, when disagreement arises, Protestants feel freer to form new churches. Whereas there is only one Roman Catholic Church, Protestantism includes Baptist, Methodist, Reformed, Episcopalian, Presbyterian, and many other denominations. Protestants' increased individual autonomy reflects reduced levels of social integration, leading Durkheim to predict that Protestants would be more likely to commit suicide than Catholics.

Testing Sociological Theories To test his theory, Durkheim gathered data from different countries to see if suicide rates varied. Looking at France, England, and Denmark, he found that England had 67 reported suicides per million inhabitants, France had 135 per million, and Denmark had 277 per million. Durkheim concluded that Denmark's comparatively high suicide rate was due to the fact that Denmark was a more Protestant nation than either France or England. In other words, it was the social makeup of these nations that shaped their suicide rates. More recent research focusing on individual rather than national rates continues to find this same relationship.

In extending his analysis to look at other indicators of social integration, Durkheim continued to obtain results that confirmed his underlying theory: the unmarried had much higher rates of suicide than married people; and people without children were more likely to take their lives than people with children. In addition, there were higher rates in times of economic instability and recession than in times of prosperity. Durkheim concluded that his theory was correct: the suicide rate of a society reflects the extent to which people are or are not integrated into the group life of the society. Durkheim presented his results in his landmark work *Suicide,* published in 1897.

Applying Sociological Theories Built into Durkheim's theory is the presupposition that we find meaning in life through our relationships with others.

Going GLOBAL

What Makes a Country Happy?

As a flip side to the suicide research, sociologists have also shown that happiness rates vary from country to country. The five nations that score highest according to the "World Happiness Report" are Denmark, Switzerland, Iceland, Norway, and Finland. The bottom five are Benin, Afghanistan, Togo, Syria, and Burundi. The United States ranks 13th out of 157 nations (Helliwell, Layard, and Sachs 2017). The index considers indicators of both subjective well-being ("Were you happy yesterday?") and life satisfaction ("Are you happy with your life as a whole?").

Greetings from Denmark, one of the happiest nations on the planet. ©Rafael Elias/Getty Images RF

The more interconnected and interdependent we are, the less likely we are to kill ourselves. Attempting to summarize the significance of our attachment to society, Durkheim put it this way: "The individual alone is not a sufficient end for his activity. He is too little. . . . When, therefore, we have no other object than ourselves we cannot avoid the thought that our efforts will finally end in nothingness. . . . Under these conditions one would lose the courage to live, that is, to act and struggle" ([1897] 1951:210). Human beings are, at their very foundation, social beings. According to Durkheim, we cannot consider what it means to be an individual apart from our position in society. This social dimension of individual behavior is what Durkheim wants sociology to explore, elaborate, and explain.

Durkheim's work on suicide provides a classic case of sociological theory at work. He theorized that social facts shape individual actions. He tested this theory by investigating suicide as one such individual choice—perhaps the most individual of all choices—and demonstrated that the likelihood of committing suicide varied based on group membership. As the "Suicide Rates" map and graphs demonstrate, analysis of more recent data shows that suicide rates continue to vary based on social position. Durkheim concluded that if social facts are at work in this most extreme example of individual choice, they similarly shape all other individual choices. He argued that if social facts have such power in our lives, there should be a discipline dedicated to their study. As a result of Durkheim's efforts, the University of Bordeaux established Europe's first department of sociology in 1895.

Social science The systematic study of human behavior, interaction, and change.

Natural science The systematic study of the physical features of nature and the ways in which they interact and change.

Sociologists weren't the only ones who sought to apply the scientific method to social behavior. A number of additional disciplines emerged around the same time giving rise to **social science**—the systematic study of human behavior, interaction, and change—as an umbrella term to distinguish these fields of study from **natural science,** which involves the systematic study of the physical features of nature and the ways in which they interact and change. Social sciences include sociology, anthropology, psychology, economics, political science, and history. Each of these disciplines carved out its own subject matter niche and applied its version of the scientific method accordingly. Sociology's boundaries emerged over time as sociologists explored new questions about why we think and act as we do.

Suicide Rates

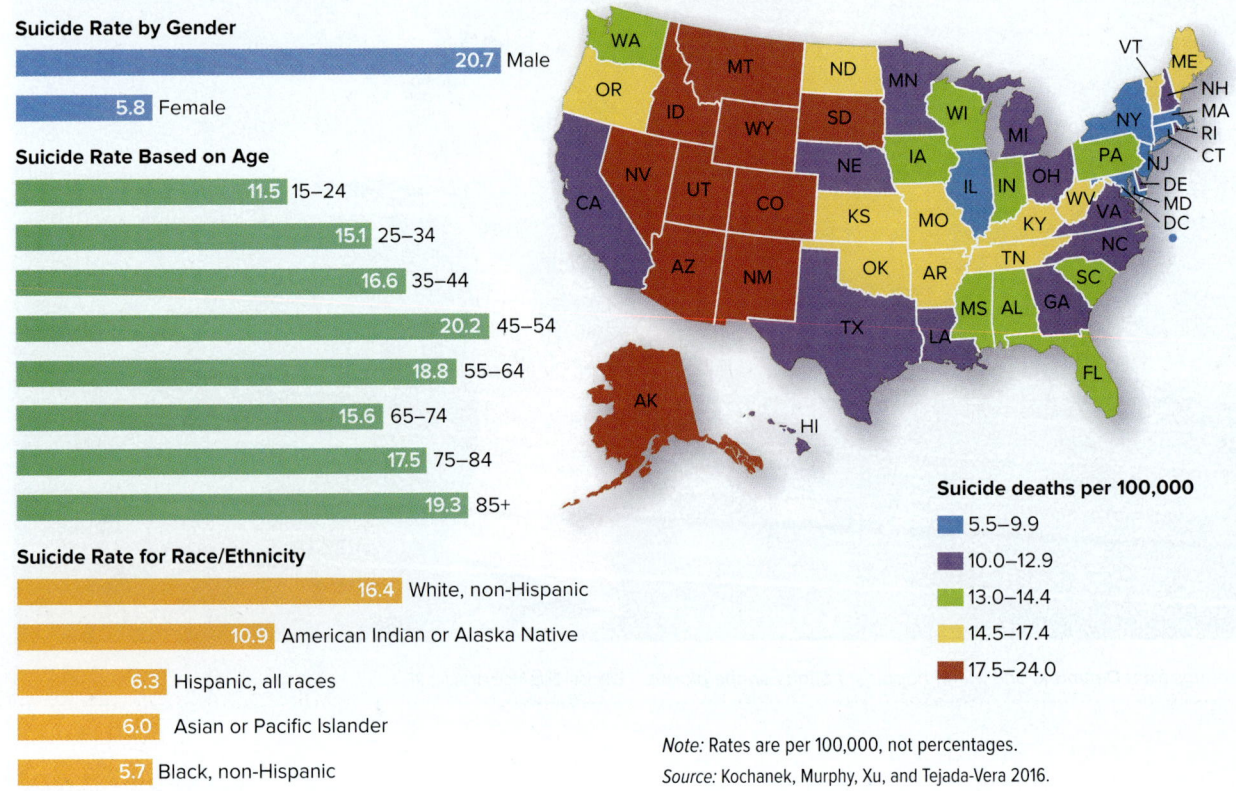

Note: Rates are per 100,000, not percentages.
Source: Kochanek, Murphy, Xu, and Tejada-Vera 2016.

SOC THINK

If Durkheim is correct and the level of social integration influences the likelihood of suicide, why do rates vary for the groups listed in the "Suicide Rates" figure? Why is the rate for men almost four times higher than that for women? Why is the rate for non-Hispanic Whites higher than that for any other racial/ethnic group? Why is there a midlife suicide peak? Why do rates vary by state and region? What might these patterns suggest about the social integration of people in these categories?

>> Five Big Questions

Given the complexity of human life, sociologists have developed a wide range of theories in which they describe and explain the diversity of social behavior. Sometimes their theories can be grand in scope, seeking to encompass the "big picture"; other times they can be more personal, intimate, and immediate. Although we spend most of the rest of this book investigating the insights sociological theories provide, here we will briefly address five big sociological questions. Each represents a significant door sociologists have opened in their quest to understand why we think and act as we do. The questions are these: How is social order maintained? How do power and inequality shape outcomes? How does interaction shape our worlds? How does group membership (especially class, race, and gender) influence opportunity? How should sociologists respond?

HOW IS SOCIAL ORDER MAINTAINED?

Because of the unsettled times within which they lived, early sociologists in general, and Émile Durkheim in particular, placed a premium on understanding how social order was achieved and maintained. As his concept of social facts demonstrates, Durkheim saw society as a real, external force existing above the level of the individual, exerting its influence over individual behavior. We act, think, and feel the way we do, according to Durkheim, largely due to the structure of society. Understanding those social forces, especially in light of changes brought on by the Industrial Revolution, was sociology's primary mission.

Durkheim theorized that the Industrial Revolution and the resulting rise in the division of labor, in which jobs became more and more specialized, meant that individuals had fewer experiences in common. Lives became increasingly segmented. This was true not only within the workplace, but within the larger community. The worlds of family, work, school, and faith, which had mostly overlapped in traditional societies, became increasingly distinct from each other. Durkheim argued that the resulting decrease in social integration put us at great risk of **anomie,** which he defined as a weak sense of social solidarity due to a lack of agreed-upon rules to guide behavior. Anomie increases the likelihood of loneliness, isolation, and despair, and thus, also, of suicide. Using Durkheim's theory, one sociological response to the problem of suicide is to build up social integration by multiplying our shared experiences across social boundaries.

Émile Durkheim. (Durkheim): ©Bettmann/Contributor/Getty Images; (frame): ©Wrangel/Getty Images RF

and shelter) to meet everyone's needs, so not all people had enough.

Social inequality for Marx, then, is determined by ownership, or lack thereof, of key material resources. The ruling class is defined by its ownership and control of the means of production—the tools and resources necessary for that transformation to happen. Members of the working class, in contrast, own only their capacity to transform raw materials into products, which requires access to the means of production controlled by the ruling class. Whereas Durkheim was concerned with anomie, Marx was concerned with **alienation,** by which he meant loss of control over our creative human capacity to produce, separation from the products we make, and isolation from our fellow workers. We consider Marx's work as it relates to capitalism as an economic system in more detail in Chapter 9's "Economic Systems" section. His influence on sociological theory, however, extends beyond social class to an analysis of additional forms of inequality, such as how gender, race, ethnicity, nationality, and age influence individual opportunity.

> **Anomie** A weak sense of social solidarity due to a lack of agreed-upon rules to guide behavior.
>
> **Alienation** Loss of control over our creative human capacity to produce, separation from the products we make, and isolation from our fellow producers.

HOW DO POWER AND INEQUALITY SHAPE OUTCOMES?

Karl Marx (1818–1883) took a different approach. He emphasized the role that power and control over resources played in how social order is established and maintained. Marx viewed our creative capacity to transform raw materials into products—for example, to take clay and make a pot, or cut down a tree and make a desk—as the key factor distinguishing humans from other animals (whose behavior is ruled by their instincts). For Marx, human history is the progressive unfolding of human creativity in the form of new technology through which we establish our relationship to the natural world and with each other. Unfortunately, for most of human history, we lacked sufficient technology to provide enough material goods (such as food, clothes,

Karl Marx. (Marx): Source: Library of Congress Prints and Photographs Division [LC-USZ62-16530]; (frame): ©mammuth/Getty Images RF

Seeking to expand sociological theory further, Max Weber (1864–1920; pronounced "VAY-ber") offered a more general theory of power that was less wedded to capitalism and ownership of the means of production. Weber argued that, although social class and its associated control over material resources may determine who has power in most instances, these are not the only possible foundations for power. Other sources he identified include social

Max Weber. (Weber): ©Hulton Archive/Getty Images; (frame): ©Visivasnc/Getty Images RF

status, in which people defer to others out of respect for their social position or prestige, and organizational resources, in which members of a group gain power through their ability to organize to accomplish some specific goal by maximizing their available resources. Weber argued that these social resources draw their power from people's willingness to obey the authority of another person, which in turn is based on their perception of the legitimacy of that person's right to rule. Marx's and Weber's models of inequality and power are considered in more detail in Chapter 10's "Sociological Perspectives on Stratification."

HOW DOES INTERACTION SHAPE OUR WORLDS?

Much of the work of Durkheim, Marx, and Weber involves **macrosociology**, which concentrates on large-scale phenomena or entire civilizations. This top-down approach focuses on society as a whole and how broad social forces shape our lives. A later school of sociologists turned away from this approach in favor of **microsociology**, which stresses the study of small groups and the analysis of our everyday experiences and interactions. Our interactions with others have a profound effect on us. Parents, siblings, friends, teachers, classmates, coworkers, and even total strangers influence how we talk, act, think, and feel. Through such interactions we learn what is appropriate and inappropriate, responding accordingly. To describe this process, sociologist W. I. Thomas established what has come to be known in sociology as the **Thomas theorem:** "If men define situations as real, they are real in their consequences" (Thomas and Thomas 1928:571–572). Or, more simply, how we see the world shapes what we do. We act on the basis of perception, and our perception is a consequence of the interactions we have had with others.

To better understand the processes at work, sociologist Erving Goffman (1922–1982) recommended studying everyday interactions as if we are all actors on a stage seeking to successfully put on a performance. In every encounter we have, he said, we all play roles, follow scripts, use props, work together, and seek to win over our audiences. The parts of ourselves that we display vary based on the roles that we perform. As a student in a class, we may project a serious image; at a party, we may want to look relaxed and friendly. The immediate context of our everyday interactions shapes who we are, what we think, and how we act. Goffman's work, along with that of other interactionists, is covered in more depth in Chapter 4's "The Self and Socialization."

Macrosociology Sociological investigation that concentrates on large-scale phenomena or entire civilizations.

Microsociology Sociological investigation that stresses the study of small groups and the analysis of our everyday experiences and interactions.

Thomas theorem What we perceive as real is real in its consequences.

HOW DOES GROUP MEMBERSHIP INFLUENCE OPPORTUNITY?

Over time, sociologists came to more fully understand and appreciate the consequences that group membership, especially class, race, and gender, has for opportunity. African American sociologist W. E. B. Du Bois (1868–1963; pronounced "dew BOYS") combined an emphasis on the analysis of the everyday lived experience with a commitment to investigating power and inequality based on race. He was critical of those who relied on common sense or on all-too-brief investigations, arguing that a researcher has to be more than just a "car-window sociologist" because true understanding demands more than "the few leisure hours of a holiday trip to unravel the snarl of centuries" (Du Bois [1903] 1994:94). Through engaged and sustained research on the lives of African Americans, Du Bois documented their relatively low status in Philadelphia and Atlanta. His research revealed the social processes that contributed to the maintenance of racial separation, which extended beyond material differences to include social separation, which he referred to as the "color line."

Similarly, feminist scholarship has broadened our understanding of social behavior by extending the analysis beyond the male point of view that dominated classic sociology. An early example of this perspective can be seen in the life and writings of Ida Wells-Barnett (1862–1931). Carrying on a tradition begun with Martineau, Wells-Barnett argued that societies can be judged based on whether the principles they claim to believe in match their actions. Wells-Barnett found that when it came to the principles of equality and opportunity for women and African Americans, America came up short. Part of the task for the sociologist, then, is to bring to light such inconsistencies that may otherwise go largely unnoticed. This is something Wells-Barnett sought to do in her groundbreaking publications in the 1890s on the practice of lynching African Americans, as well as with her advocacy of women's rights, especially the struggle to win the vote for women. Like feminist theorists

W.E.B. Du Bois. (Du Bois): Source: Library of Congress Prints and Photographs Division [LC-USZ62-16767]; *(frame):* ©Visivasnc/Getty Images RF

14 • SOC 2018

who succeeded her, Wells-Barnett used her analysis of society as a means of resisting oppression. As an African American woman, she brought attention to the overlapping impacts of race, gender, and class (Wells-Barnett [1928] 1970).

HOW SHOULD SOCIOLOGISTS RESPOND?

Throughout sociology's history, a recurring theme has been the idea that sociological theory and research should contribute to positive social change. In the early 1900s many leading sociologists in the United States saw themselves as social reformers dedicated to systematically studying and then improving a corrupt society. They were genuinely concerned about the lives of immigrants in the nation's growing cities, whether those immigrants came from Europe or from the rural American South. Early female sociologists, in particular, often took active roles in poor urban areas as leaders of community centers known as settlement houses. For example, Jane Addams (1860–1935), an early member of the American Sociological Society, cofounded the famous Chicago settlement, Hull House, which provided social, educational, and cultural programs for recent immigrants. Addams and other pioneering female sociologists commonly combined intellectual inquiry, social service work, and political activism—all with the goal of assisting the underprivileged and creating a more egalitarian society. Working with Ida Wells-Barnett, Addams successfully prevented racial segregation in the Chicago public schools, and her efforts to establish a juvenile court system and a women's trade union reflect the practical focus of her work (Addams 1910, 1930; Lengermann and Niebrugge-Brantley 1998).

Photo: ©David Paul Morris/Bloomberg via Getty Images

Did You Know?

... Former First Lady Michelle Obama received a bachelor of arts degree in sociology from Princeton University. She used that degree as a stepping-stone to law school at Harvard.

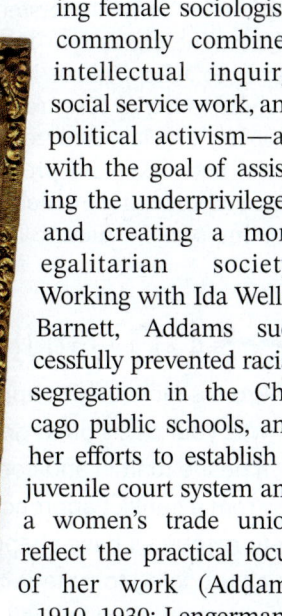

Jane Addams. (Addams): ©Hulton Archive/Getty Images; (frame): ©andipantz/Getty Images RF

This commitment to positive social change was not unique to Addams and her colleagues. From the very beginning to the present, sociologists have recognized an obligation to go beyond explaining how the world works and become actively engaged in making the world a better place. In the words of French sociologist Pierre Bourdieu, "I have come to believe that those who have the good fortune to be able to devote their lives to the study of the social world cannot stand aside, neutral and indifferent, from the struggles in which the future of that world is at stake" (1998a:11). For some this has meant publishing the results of their work so that it might enhance our understanding and inform our decisions; for others it has meant active engagement in establishing social policy or assisting in the lives of others. For example, Durkheim, who considered an educated citizenry essential to democratic success, used his appointment to the Department of Science of Education and Sociology at the Sorbonne in Paris, along with his political connections and appointments, to shape French educational policy and practice. Du Bois cofounded the National Association for the Advancement of Colored People, better known as the NAACP. In fact, one of the dominant reasons students choose to major in sociology is that they want to make a difference, and sociology provides a pathway to do just that.

>> Three Sociological Perspectives

As we will see throughout this book, the answers sociologists offer to these five questions provide a glimpse of sociology's complexity. Some theorists focus on society as a whole; others concentrate on individual interactions. Some are particularly concerned with inequality; others focus on maintaining social cohesion. Some approaches seem to overlap; others seem at odds with one another. But, regardless of their stance, all theorists share a common commitment to provide us with greater understanding of why we think and act the way we do. Each theory, whether broad or narrow, offers a way of seeing that allows us to perceive things we might have otherwise missed.

Three Sociological Perspectives

	Functionalist	Conflict	Interactionist
View of society	Stable, well integrated	Characterized by tension and struggle between groups	Active in influencing and affecting everyday social interaction
Level of analysis emphasized	Macro	Macro	Micro, as a way of understanding the larger macro phenomena
Key concepts	Social integration Institutions Anomie	Inequality Capitalism Stratification	Symbols Nonverbal communication Face-to-face interaction
View of the individual	People are socialized to perform societal functions	People are shaped by power, coercion, and authority	People manipulate symbols and create their social worlds through interaction
View of the social order	Maintained through cooperation and consensus	Maintained through force and coercion	Maintained by shared understanding of everyday behavior
View of social change	Predictable, reinforcing	Change takes place all the time and may have positive consequences	Reflected in people's social positions and their communications with others
Example	Public punishments reinforce the social order	Laws enforce the positions of those in power	People respect laws or disobey them based on their own past experience
Proponents	Émile Durkheim Talcott Parsons Robert Merton	Karl Marx W. E. B. Du Bois Ida Wells-Barnett	George Herbert Mead Charles Horton Cooley Erving Goffman

Functionalist perspective A sociological paradigm that sees society as like a living organism in which its various parts work together for the good of the whole.

Conflict perspective A sociological paradigm that focuses on power and the allocation of valued resources in society.

To simplify the rich array of sociological theories (especially for someone new to sociology), sociologists have classified various theories into three major theoretical perspectives or paradigms: functionalist, conflict, and interactionist. Each perspective offers a different set of lenses, focusing our attention in slightly different ways. Or, to put it another way, it is like three people standing on the edge of a circle looking in at the same thing but each seeing it from a different point of view, able to recognize things that others might not even see.

According to the **functionalist perspective**, society is like a living organism with its various parts working together (or functioning) for the good of the whole. Functionalists posit that society and its parts are structured to provide social order and maintain stability. Aspects of society that may appear dysfunctional, such as crime or poverty, either contribute some hidden benefits that researchers have not yet uncovered or will wither away over time. Durkheim's research into social order and its challenges, especially within modern societies, is a classic example of the functionalist perspective. Durkheim assumed that, over time, society would progress toward greater order as it came to terms with apparent threats or challenges.

Whereas the functionalist perspective emphasizes consensus and cooperation, the **conflict perspective** focuses on power and the allocation of valued resources in society. According to conflict theorists, social order cannot be fully understood apart from an analysis of how the status quo is established and maintained by those who control key resources. Such resources include material resources (such as money, land, and property), social resources (such as family connections, social networks, and prestige), and cultural resources (such as education, beliefs, knowledge, and taste). The existing social structure helps maintain the privileges

SOC THINK

From a functionalist approach, to what extent was your decision to go to college driven by a desire to fit in and contribute to society? From a conflict approach, how might access to resources have shaped your decisions about going to college? From an interactionist approach, what specific individuals influenced your decision and how did they do so?

of some groups and keep others in inferior positions. Marx's work on inequality, social class, and alienation provides a classic example of the conflict perspective.

Finally, whereas functionalist and conflict theorists both analyze large-scale, society-wide patterns of behavior, theorists who take the **interactionist perspective** maintain that society is the product of our everyday encounters (with parents, friends, teachers, or strangers) through which we establish shared meanings and thus construct order. Because it emphasizes the role we play in making sense of our interactions, this approach highlights our agency as humans. Society is dependent on this ongoing construction, making it fluid and subject to change. Goffman's research focusing on life as a performance provides an example of the interactionist perspective.

The three-perspectives model has the advantage of providing us with conceptual hooks that allow us to recall some of the key concerns and issues sociologists have raised. A disadvantage, however, is that it gives the illusion that these three are discrete categories with fundamentally different and incompatible ways of looking at the world. In practice, research rooted in one perspective almost inevitably draws on or addresses insights from the other two.

>> Sociology Is a Verb

One of the questions that students frequently ask about sociology is "What can I do with it?" This query often comes from students who really like sociology, and might want to pursue it further, but are uncertain where it leads. The good news is that there are many ways people can practice sociology.

PERSONAL SOCIOLOGY

We don't have to become professional sociologists to practice what we have learned. The sociological imagination can help all of us better understand our beliefs and actions and make more informed choices. We can all practice **personal sociology** by recognizing the impact our individual position has on who we are and how we think and act. Doing so also calls us to take responsibility for the effects our actions have on others. For example, by drawing on insights gained from sociological theory and research, we might watch the news and ask whose interests are being represented. When we walk through the mall, we might observe how people display their social status and how they are treated accordingly. When we go in for a job interview, we might abide by the largely unspoken norms of conduct that shape interaction and influence our likelihood for success. Personal sociology empowers us by allowing us to see things that were previously invisible and to act on those insights.

Personal Sociology
Hooked on Sociology

When I took "Soc 101" in college, it took me a long time to understand the sociological imagination. I still remember feeling overwhelmed by all the concepts, facts, and figures. Eventually, as we studied the impact of the media and the power of inheritance, things began to fall into place; I took another course and was hooked. I hope that after encountering sociology, you will have a new way of seeing, and be equipped to act in new and more informed ways. Ask yourself how your circumstances influence how you think, act, and feel. How might your choices be different had you been born in a different time and place?

The sociological imagination provides us with the tools necessary to respond to challenges we face today. Though the expression has become something of a cliché, it truly is a small world after all. Social, cultural, political, and economic events around the world—including, for example, the global financial meltdown and terrorist attacks—have a profound effect on how we think and what we do. The process of **globalization**—the worldwide integration of government policies, cultures, social movements, and financial markets through trade and the exchange of ideas—shows no signs of stopping. College and university campuses often provide a microcosm of this trend. Students, faculty, staff, and administrators with radically different values, political views, customs, experiences, and expectations assemble together from around the world into a relatively confined space. If the resulting interactions are to be meaningful, positive, and respectful, we must better understand the factors that shape them.

Conflicts with roommates, classmates, and professors are often chalked up to personality clashes and other individual attributes, but we cannot fully understood or deal with

> **Interactionist perspective** A sociological paradigm that maintains that society is a product of our everyday encounters with others through which we establish shared meanings and thus construct order.
>
> **Personal sociology** The practice of recognizing the impact our individual position has on who we are and how we think and act, and of taking responsibility for the impacts our actions have on others.
>
> **Globalization** The worldwide integration of government policies, cultures, social movements, and financial markets through trade and the exchange of ideas.

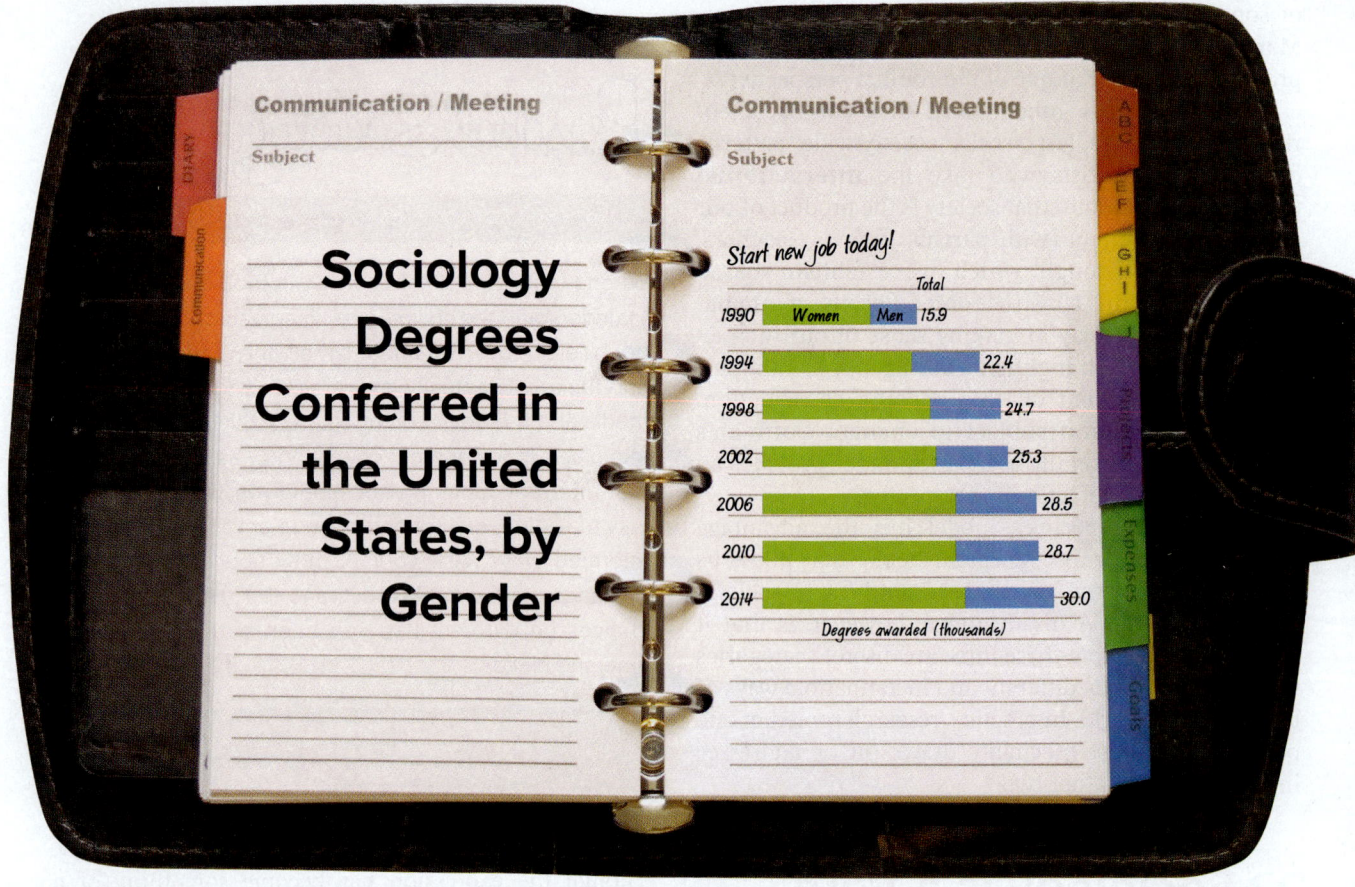

Source: National Center for Education Statistics 2016. Photo: ©Maria Suleymenova/Shutterstock.com RF

them unless we come to terms with the ways our social backgrounds have shaped how we think, act, and feel. For each of us, the social positions we occupy shape the opportunities and obstacles we face. We must learn to see the implications of this reality both for ourselves and for others. This self-knowledge necessitates a more complete appreciation of the intersection of history and biography in all of our lives.

ACADEMIC SOCIOLOGY

Many students opt to take their sociology education further, and the number of U.S. college students who have graduated with a degree in sociology has risen steadily, as the "Sociology Degrees Conferred in the United States" graph demonstrates. The American Sociological Association (ASA) conducted research on recent sociology graduates and discovered that the top reasons for choosing sociology as a major are because students found the sociological concepts interesting, sociology helped them understand the impact society has on individuals, they particularly enjoyed their first sociology course, sociology helped them understand themselves better, and they wanted to make a difference in the world (Senter, Spalter-Roth, and Van Vooren 2015). As part of their sociology education, sociology majors cultivate a variety of skills, such as using the sociological imagination, conducting data analysis, working in teams, writing reports, creating presentations, analyzing social problems, and addressing diversity. Sociology graduates who later use these skills in their jobs express the highest levels of job satisfaction (Senter 2016; Spalter-Roth and Van Vooren 2015).

The jobs that sociology majors find shortly after graduation, according to the ASA study, are in a range of fields. The most common occupational category is social services. Examples of jobs include domestic violence victims advocate, residential crisis counselor, justice and peace liaison, and teen court case manager. Researchers also found that graduates were employed in a variety of other positions, including teacher, librarian, paralegal, immigration specialist, office manager, quality assurance manager, crime scene investigator, police officer, probation officer, social media/marketing analyst, research assistant, program evaluator, statistician, and editor (Senter et al. 2015; Spalter-Roth and Van Vooren 2008).

In another ASA study looking at longer-term outcomes of sociology majors who pursued graduate school degrees, only about one-quarter did so in sociology. Instead, most used their sociology major as a stepping-stone to graduate study in social work, education, law, psychology, engineering, and business

Where Are They Now?

Occupational categories of recent sociology majors

- Social services 26.5%
- Administrative, clerical support 15.8%
- Management 14.4%
- Other (includes PR and IT) 10.2%
- Sales, marketing 10.1%
- Services 8.3%
- Education 8.1%
- Research 5.7%

Graduate school programs of recent sociology majors

- 22.4% Sociology
- 16.9% Social work
- 11.4% Education
- 10.5% Law
- 9.4% Other social sciences
- 8.6% Psychology/counseling
- 7.3% Engineering
- 5.1% Other
- 4.5% Business/management
- 3.8% Public policy/affairs

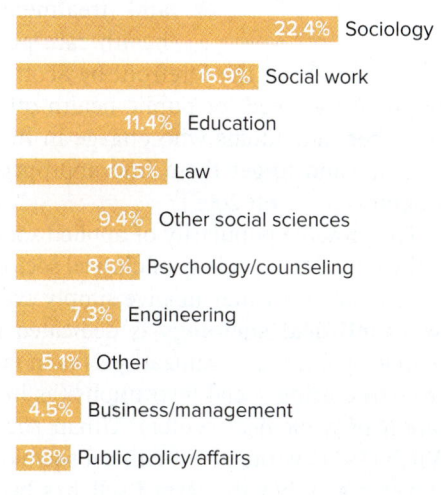

Note: Percentage based on sociology majors attending graduate school 18 months after graduation.
Source: Spalter-Roth and Van Vooren 2009. *Photo:* ©Stockbyte/Getty Images RF

> **Applied sociology** The use of the discipline of sociology with the specific intent of yielding practical applications for human behavior and organizations.

management (Spalter-Roth and Van Vooren 2009:9). Overall, 51.9 percent of the majors completed a graduate degree within four years of college graduation. Of those who pursued advanced degrees in sociology, the majority enrolled in some form of an applied sociology program (Spalter-Roth and Van Vooren 2010).

APPLIED AND CLINICAL SOCIOLOGY

Applied sociology is the use of the discipline of sociology with the specific intent of yielding practical applications for human behavior and organizations. Often, the goal of such work is to assist in resolving a social problem. For example, numerous U.S. presidents over the years have established commissions to delve into major societal concerns facing our nation. Sociologists are often asked to apply their expertise to studying such issues as violence, pornography, crime, immigration, and population.

One example of applied sociology involves the growing interest in the ways in which nationally recognized social problems manifest themselves locally. Sociologist Greg Scott and his colleagues sought to better understand the connection between illicit drug use and the spread of HIV/AIDS. By combining a variety of methods, including interviews and observation, with photo and video documentation, researchers found that across all drug users, HIV/AIDS transmission is highest among users of crystal methamphetamine. Meth users are also most likely to engage in risky sexual behavior and to have partners who do so. Fortunately, of all drug users, meth users are the ones

Sociologists found that meth users have the highest HIV/AIDS transmission rates. ©Medioimages/Photodisc/Getty Images RF

Clinical sociology The use of the discipline of sociology with the specific intent of altering social relationships or restructuring social institutions.

most closely connected to treatment programs, which allows them to receive substance abuse education and treatment from their health care providers. Their cases, brought to the forefront by Scott and his team, highlight the need for public health officials to identify other individuals who engage in high-risk sexual behavior and to get them into appropriate treatment programs (G. Scott 2005).

The growing popularity of applied sociology has led to the rise of the specialty of clinical sociology. Whereas applied sociology may involve simply evaluating social issues, **clinical sociology** is dedicated to facilitating change by altering organizations (as in family therapy) or restructuring social institutions (as in the reorganization of a medical center). Urban sociologist Louis Wirth (1931) wrote about clinical sociology more than 85 years ago, but the term itself has become popular only in recent years. The Association for Applied and Clinical Sociology was founded in 1978 to promote the application of sociological knowledge in interventions for individual and social change. This professional group has developed a procedure for certifying clinical sociologists—much as physical therapists or psychologists are certified.

Applied sociologists generally leave it to others to act on their evaluations, but clinical sociologists take direct responsibility for implementation and view those with whom they work as their clients. This specialty has become increasingly attractive to graduate students in sociology because it offers an opportunity to apply intellectual learning in practical ways. A competitive job market in the academic world has made such alternative career routes appealing.

Regardless of the level at which it is practiced, sociology is about more than the knowledge gained or career attained. Using the sociological imagination in our everyday lives enables us to understand others from their perspective and even understand ourselves through their eyes. By opening our eyes to patterns and practices that are often invisible to us, we can make more informed decisions about which pathways we choose to follow. We can also take greater responsibility for the impact that our choices have on others. Sociology provides us with tools to better understand, interpret, and respond to the world around us. Sociology is a verb; it's something you do—it's a way of life.

SOCIOLOGY IS A VERB

The Ties That Bind

Pick an object you own—maybe a pencil, a pair of shoes, or a cell phone—and trace its history. Include a diagram or map of all the people and processes it took for it to come into your possession. What is it made of? Where did all its components come from? Who contributed to its production? After it was made, who was involved in getting it into your hands? What story does it tell?

[FOR REVIEW

I. What is sociology?
- Sociology is a way of seeing that joins theory and research to investigate the relationship between the individual and society and the impact unequal distribution of resources has on opportunity.

II. How do sociologists look at the world?
- Sociologists developed theories to provide windows into our lives, including three primary perspectives: functionalist (emphasizing social order), conflict (focusing on inequality), and interactionist (highlighting the significance of our everyday relationships and exchanges).

III. How might someone practice sociology?
- Sociology can provide a pathway to a career in a related applied, clinical, or academic context. But more than that, we can practice sociology in our everyday lives by utilizing the sociological imagination to better understand ourselves and others.

SOCVIEWS on the Sociological Imagination

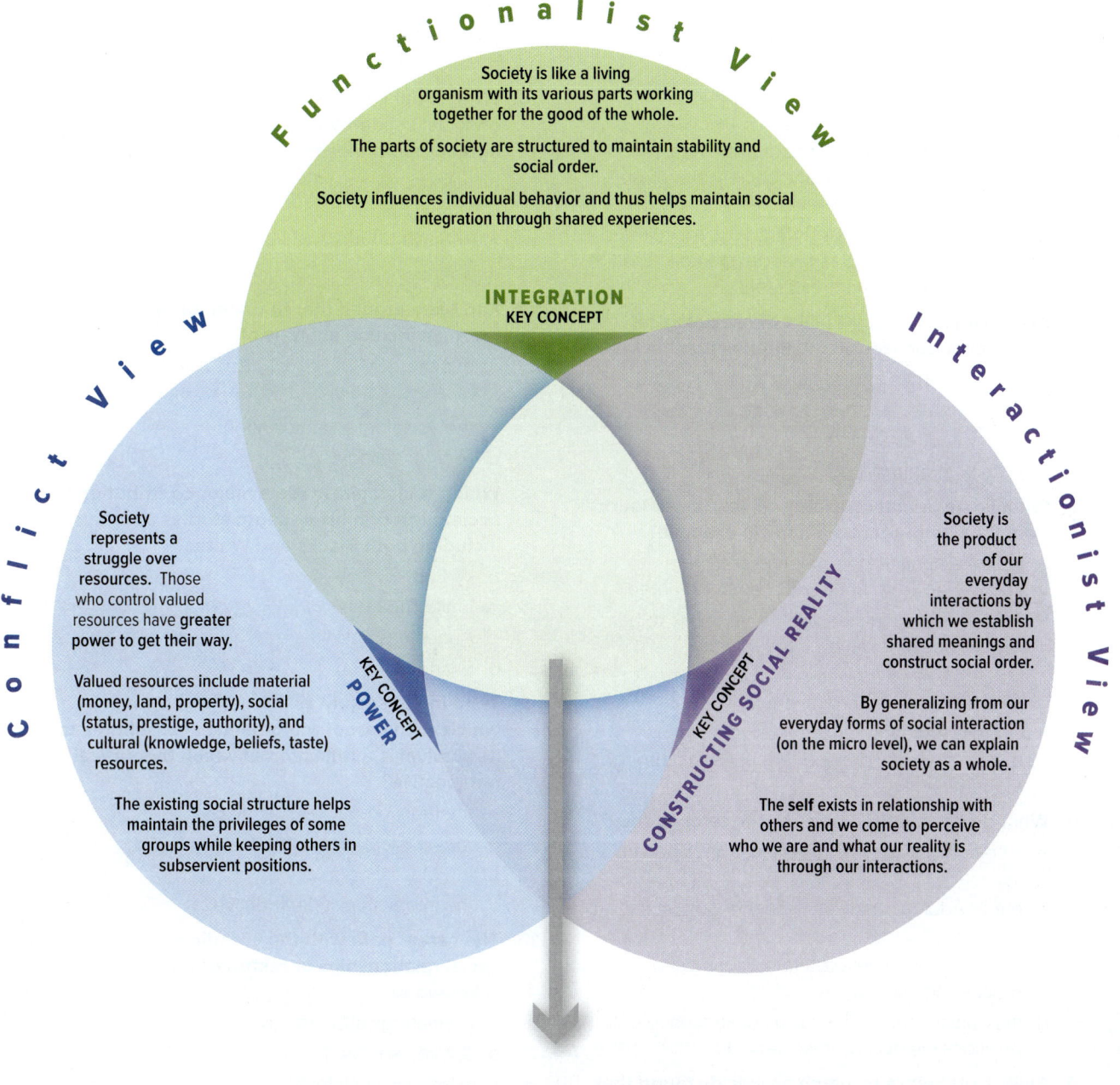

MAKE THE CONNECTION
After reviewing the chapter, answer the following questions:

1
Why might having multiple theoretical perspectives help us when we practice the sociological imagination?

2
How might each perspective differ in how it looks at what it takes to produce something (such as a hamburger, a house, a book, and so on)?

3
How might each perspective approach the study of unemployment? Of suicide?

4
How does each perspective enable you to see the way you participate in sports, either as a fan or as an athlete, in a different light?

Pop Quiz

1. **Sociology is**
   a. the analysis of individual motivations and internal struggles.
   b. concerned with predicting what particular individuals do or do not do.
   c. the systematic study of the relationship between the individual and society and of the consequences of difference.
   d. the integration of government policies, cultures, social movements, and financial markets through trade and the exchange of ideas.

2. **According to C. Wright Mills, the sociological imagination focuses on the intersection between**
   a. natural science and social science.
   b. power and access to resources.
   c. theory and research.
   d. history and biography.

3. **What is the primary sociological lesson we learn from the hamburger-as-a-miracle example?**
   a. We take our interdependence and the knowledge we collectively share for granted.
   b. An individual could easily survive on his or her own without assistance from others.
   c. Modern technology makes it difficult for us to provide for our individual needs.
   d. Interdependence is no longer necessary because we can provide for our needs through modern technology.

4. **What do sociologists mean by the term *agency*?**
   a. a company that provides clients with a particular service
   b. our freedom as individuals to think and act as we choose
   c. an organization devoted to collecting and processing information
   d. the constraints we face as a consequence of the positions we occupy in society

5. **Émile Durkheim's research on suicide found that**
   a. Catholics had much higher suicide rates than Protestants.
   b. the more socially integrated someone is the less likely he or she is to commit suicide.
   c. married people are more likely to take their lives than single people.
   d. suicide is a solitary act, unrelated to group life.

6. **What is the sociological term for the weak sense of social solidarity that arises due to a lack of agreed-upon rules to guide behavior?**
   a. suicide
   b. alienation
   c. anomie
   d. agency

7. **Karl Marx argued that to understand social order we must include analysis of**
   a. anomie.
   b. ownership of the means of production.
   c. the sociological imagination.
   d. microsociology.

8. **Which sociologist made a major contribution to society through his in-depth studies of urban life, including both Blacks and Whites?**
   a. W. E. B. Du Bois
   b. Émile Durkheim
   c. Auguste Comte
   d. Erving Goffman

9. **Thinking of society as a living organism in which each part of the organism contributes to its survival is a reflection of which theoretical perspective?**
   a. the functionalist perspective
   b. the conflict perspective
   c. the Marxist perspective
   d. the interactionist perspective

10. **The career path with the specific intent of altering social relationships or restructuring organizations is known as**
    a. dramaturgical sociology.
    b. applied sociology.
    c. academic sociology.
    d. clinical sociology.

1. (c), 2. (d), 3. (a), 4. (b), 5. (b), 6. (c), 7. (b), 8. (a), 9. (a), 10. (d)

Sociological Research

©Robert Harding Images

ASKING QUESTIONS AND FINDING ANSWERS

As a first-year college student, Alice Goffman got a job at her college cafeteria that changed her life forever. She needed a research site for her ethnography class, a course in which you embed yourself into a social setting to understand it from within, and it seemed perfect. She'd heard her fellow students refer to the cafeteria workers—most of whom were older, African American women—as lazy and rude, and she wondered what the workers thought of her, a young, White, comparatively privileged woman and her similarly privileged peers (Parry 2013). After a year filling plates and scrubbing dishes, Goffman began tutoring the grandchildren of her cafeteria boss, an African American woman in her 60s who lived in a poor Philadelphia neighborhood. Through those grandchildren, Goffman made contacts with others, and before long, a second research project was born. She moved into the neighborhood during her sophomore year to better observe and understand their social world.

She became so committed to the project and connected to the people that she continued her research project through college and graduate school and ultimately published a book telling their stories.

Goffman gained a much deeper understanding of the challenges faced by young African American males living there. As boys, they are told to run from police because, "even if it's not you [they are looking for], nine times out of ten, they'll probably book you" (Goffman 2014a:24). According to Goffman, these young men get taken away for what they see as petty offenses, contributing to suspicions that police are targeting them. Those with legal entanglements—missed court dates, unpaid court fees, parole curfew violations—face the threat of warrants for their arrest. Their fear of capture and confinement leads them to avoid beneficial social connections—visiting family, getting a job, going to the hospital when sick or injured. Such conventional social connections can be used against them, as happens when girlfriends or moms are pressured by police to inform on them. Goffman describes the resulting social fabric as "one woven in suspicion, distrust, and the paranoiac practices of secrecy, evasion, and unpredictability" (2014a:8).

At the same time, Goffman noticed that her fellow college students, who were often White and from financially secure backgrounds, engaged in similar activities—drinking, doing drugs, getting into fights—but no police raided their parties, and they walked away from their adolescence with college diplomas and good jobs instead of jail time and permanent police records (Goffman 2014b). As the sociological imagination suggests, if a lot of people in similar positions experience the same result, it likely says more about the position than the person. Through sociological research we can see patterns shaping people's outcomes that might otherwise be invisible to us.

As You READ

- What distinguishes sociology from common sense as a way of knowing?
- What steps do sociologists take when seeking to answer why people think and act the way they do?
- What techniques do sociologists use to collect data?
- What ethical concerns must sociologists consider while conducting research?

>> Sociology as a Science

By engaging directly in the lives of both cafeteria workers and inner-city African American residents in a deliberate and sustained way, Alice Goffman learned that our taken-for-granted assumptions are frequently flawed. In doing so, she carried on a tradition that goes back to sociology's founding. Early sociologists rejected explanations based on tradition ("it's always been this way"), authority ("the king says so"), or mystical insight ("God revealed it to me in a dream"). Like all scientists, sociologists are suspicious of conventional wisdom, using doubt as a tool for the advancement of knowledge.

SOCIOLOGY AND COMMON SENSE

Most of us, most of the time, think we already know why we think and act as we do. We trust our taken-for-granted knowledge as accurate. It turns out, however, that things we think we know for sure aren't necessarily so. For example, many people believe that drinking eight glasses of water per day has health benefits, that giving kids too much sugar makes them hyper, and that women's periods will synchronize when they live together, such as in a dorm. None of these beliefs hold up under careful scrutiny.

Researchers have explored all three of these claims and found each wanting. Investigators have uncovered no medical evidence of significant health benefits from drinking eight glasses of water per day. Consuming that much water doesn't reduce wrinkles, clean out toxins, improve kidney function, decrease constipation, prevent cancer, or have any other notable benefit. The best medical advice? Drink when you are thirsty (Carroll 2015; Carroll and Vreeman 2009; Negoianu and Goldfarb 2008; Valtin 2002; Williams 2013). The sugar-high hypothesis about kids has been tested repeatedly, and the results continue to find no causal link. Researchers suggest that parents' strong belief that a relationship exists leads them to notice times when the two go together and ignore times when they don't (Flora and Polenik 2013; Geggel 2016; Wolraich et al. 1994; Wolraich, Wilson, and White 1995). And when it comes to "menstrual synchrony," a reanalysis of the data used in the original scientific study to "prove" its existence showed no statistically significant relationship. And since then, additional, more rigorous, studies have found that any apparent menstrual overlap that does occur is more likely due to chance than any biological shifts in time (Fahs et al. 2014; Pettit and Vigor 2015; Strassmann 1999; Yang and Schank 2006; Ziomkiewicz 2006). Even when confronted with empirical research demonstrating that each of these claims is false, however, people still tend to trust what they call their own common sense.

©Monkey Business Images/Shutterstock.com RF

Common sense can and does serve a useful function. The knowledge it provides enables us to make it through each day. If we had to systematically investigate the best possible path for every thought and action, we might never make it out of bed in the morning. Sociologist Duncan Watts (2011) defines common sense as "the loosely organized set of facts, observations, experiences, insights, and pieces of received wisdom that each of us accumulates over a lifetime, in the course of encountering, dealing with, and learning from, everyday situations" (p. 8). Watts argues that common sense is practical and concrete. It provides us with immediate explanations, and we don't have to worry too much about where they came from, whether they are logically coherent, or whether they are generally applicable across time and place. Common sense enables us to navigate our way through our day without having to work so hard, without doubting every thought or anguishing over every action. Its primary appeal is that, on an everyday level, it just works.

As a way of knowing, however, we seldom take the time to consider the limitations of such particularistic and improvisational knowledge. Common sense consists of largely unanalyzed, and frequently incompatible, knowledge claims applied in an ad hoc manner. As a way of knowing, common sense highlights two related problems. First, we tend to apply commonsense reasoning after the fact rather than before. Once we know what we are seeking to explain, we pick an appropriate nugget of commonsense wisdom out of our toolkit of possible explanations and apply it. We typically do so without critically assessing which possible alternative explanations might be refuted had we picked those instead. For example, when two people who are very different from each other marry, we say something like "opposites attract," yet when two people who are quite similar get married, we say "birds of a feather flock together." But which is more likely? Common sense can't say for sure, and doesn't really try to, but sociology can and does, as we will see in Chapter 7.

A second major limitation of common sense is known as confirmation bias, which is our tendency to favor evidence that supports our existing beliefs while minimizing or ignoring contrary evidence. Psychologist Raymond Nickerson describes confirmation bias as "unwitting selectivity in the acquisition and use of evidence" (1998: 175). The research on the impact sugar has on children, cited above, provides a classic example. Because parents believe that consuming sugar leads to hyperactivity, they notice when the two seem to occur together and conclude that it proves the theory. But they fail to recognize the disconfirming times—that is, when their children consumed sugar but did not become hyperactive or when they became hyperactive without consuming sugar (Hoover and Millich 1994; Wolraich et al. 1995). These sugar/hyperactivity findings actually provide empirical support for sociology's Thomas theorem according to which our perceptions play a powerful role in how we respond. And that's the primary difference between common sense and sociology. Common sense may generate theories about why something happens, but it does not, in any systematic and controlled way, assess the validity of those claims.

POPSOC

We often make decisions based on common sense, but doing so can result in errors. Analyzing data reveals underlying patterns we might otherwise miss, enabling us to make more effective decisions. In the film *Moneyball,* and in the book it's based on, Michael Lewis (2003) tells the story of general manager Billy Beane, whose Oakland A's team lacked the money to afford big-money free agents. Beane goes against baseball's conventional wisdom and uses statistical analyses to make decisions about how best to produce runs; by bringing the nonobvious patterns to the surface, he turns the team into a winner.

Photo: ©Columbia Pictures/Courtesy Everett Collection

SOCIOLOGY AND THE SCIENTIFIC METHOD

Sociology puts ideas to the test. To do so, sociologists rely on the **scientific method** which is the systematic observation of empirical, this-worldly evidence to assess and refine ideas about what happens and why. If we want to know why people think and act the way they do, we need to know more about what they actually think and do. We need to observe them, ask them questions,

> **Scientific method** The systematic observation of empirical, this-worldly evidence to assess and refine ideas about what happens and why.

participate in their lives, or in other ways seek to understand their experiences from their perspective. We cannot sit back and guess.

In conducting their research, sociologists face a challenge quite different from that of researchers in the natural sciences. Even though both rely on the scientific method to guide them, the objects each studies differ greatly. Humans have agency in a way that molecules or rocks do not. Humans can choose to act in any number of ways under a variety of circumstances, whereas we can reliably predict the conditions under which two atoms of hydrogen will always bond with one atom of oxygen to form a molecule of water. To put it simply, explaining human behavior is a far more complex undertaking than deriving the physical laws of nature. And yet, behavioral patterns do exist in which we can identify causal factors influencing how we think and act. By collecting and analyzing data, we can observe such patterns and draw informed conclusions about their significance (as Durkheim's research on suicide demonstrated in in the "Theory and Research" subsection in Chapter 1). Throughout this book we will encounter a multitude of sociological insights derived from empirical research.

Sometimes sociology confirms what we all take for granted as true. Other times it clarifies the circumstances under which one thing is true as opposed to another. Yet other times, it reveals new, unanticipated truths about why we think and act as we do. Sometimes it explains what has happened in the past, whereas at other times it predicts what might happen in the future. Sociology does all this through meticulous empirical investigation, with each new investigation seeking to expand, clarify, and refine what we know.

> *In science, when human behavior enters the equation, things go nonlinear. That's why Physics is easy and Sociology is hard.*
>
> Neil de Grasse Tyson

>> Steps in the Research Process

As science developed, general principles emerged for how best to put the scientific method into practice. Because these processes have become widely accepted in both the natural and social sciences, adhering to them helps ensure the legitimacy of the results. These procedures are built on the principle that scientific exploration involves a conversation between theory and research. As such, the scientific method can be represented as an ever-turning wheel, with new ideas leading to new research, which produces new theories, and so on. Presented graphically in the accompanying "Wheel of Science," the scientific method includes five primary stages: (1) defining the problem, (2) reviewing the literature, (3) formulating the hypothesis, (4) collecting and analyzing data, and (5) developing the conclusion.

DEFINING THE PROBLEM

As we have already seen, sociology, like all sciences, explores theories about how the world works, and the initial step—defining the problem—represents the idea stage of the research process. The primary goals here are to clarify the concepts we want to learn more about and specify the nature of the relationship we suspect might exist between those concepts.

The ideas we explore can come from anywhere, including common sense, but most sociological research draws inspiration from existing sociological theories. Theories represent our most informed explanations about what happens and why. For example, as we saw in Chapter 1, Durkheim theorized that social integration shapes individual action. He set out to test

The Wheel of Science

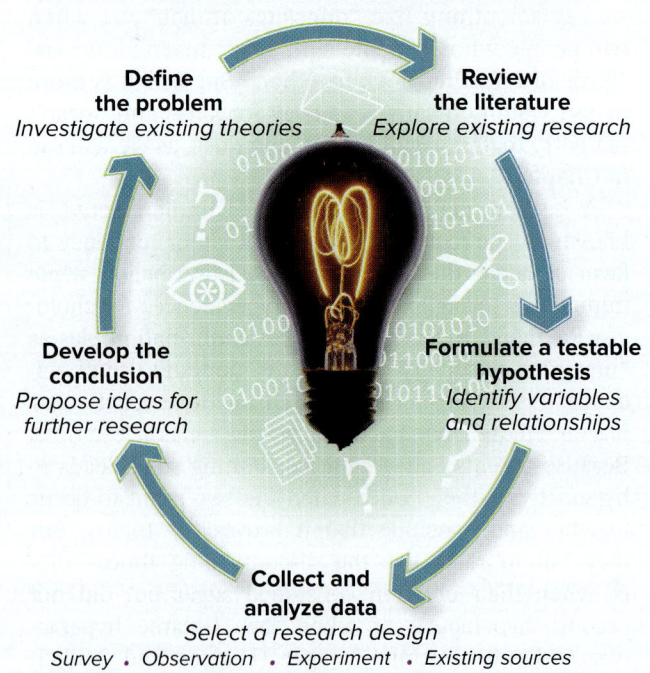

Photo: ©Digital Vision/Getty Images RF

this theory by conducting research on suicide as an example of the most extreme individual action. By clarifying possible factors to consider, existing theories help us define the new problem we want to explore, especially when we come up against something we do not yet understand.

As an example of issues we might consider when defining a problem, take the question, "Is college worth it?" The implied concepts here include college attendance and possible benefits. In asking that question, perhaps we are mostly curious about the individual benefits that might result from going to college and getting a degree. Or, drawing on the functionalist perspective in sociology, maybe we want to know how a highly educated citizenry helps society operate more effectively. Another possibility, from the conflict perspective, is that we want to know whether education reinforces the existing system of inequality, providing only the illusion of opportunity because children from wealthier families are more likely to afford and complete college. The initial question, "Is college worth it?," does not specify which of those paths was intended. If a research question is unclear or too broad, we will lack the terms and topics necessary to track down existing research in the review of the literature, the next stage in the research process.

> Without theory we are blind—we cannot see the world.
>
> Michael Burawoy

REVIEWING THE LITERATURE

After we've defined the problem, our next step is to conduct a review of existing literature to see what others have already written about our topic. Rather than starting from scratch, we can build on what they have already uncovered. Also, analyzing how others studied these concepts allows us to refine our ideas, identify additional items or relationships we want to include, clarify possible techniques for collecting data, and eliminate or reduce avoidable mistakes. We will explore some pathways to finding legitimate sources, and the accompanying "Finding Information" table offers some useful tips.

Sociological journals provide the most reliable source of existing research. Examples, among many others, include *American Sociological Review, Social Problems, Gender and Society,* and *Sociology of Education.* Most academic libraries have access to such journals in print, via digital access, or through interlibrary loan. Academic books written by recognized sociologists and published by respected presses also serve as valuable resources. Such books provide a more comprehensive account of the author's research. Examples already mentioned in this text include Matthew Desmond's *Evicted: Poverty and Profit in the American City* (2016) and Alice Goffman's *On the Run: Fugitive Life in an American City* (2014).

Secondary sources, in which others report on existing sociological research, can also be valuable. In fact, they are often the places where we encounter the research to begin with. Stories with a sociological twist frequently appear in newspapers and magazines such as *The New York Times, The Washington Post, The New Yorker, The Atlantic,* and *Contexts.* Such accounts are often more accessible, both easier to find and easier to understand, and because they may mention numerous studies, can connect us to additional research we might not otherwise know about. We can use the information included in these accounts to trace back to the original and related research.

Online sources can present a challenge for academic research because anyone anywhere can post anything without regard for the truth. The most important principle? Consider the source. Online academic databases

Finding Information

Begin with material you already have, including this text and others.

Beware of using online sources such as Wikipedia; they can be a helpful place to start, but always double-check claims with a reputable source or organization.

Use books, newspapers, magazines, and journals.

Search using the library catalog and computerized periodical indexes to find related academic journal articles.

Examine government documents (including the U.S. Census).

Contact people, organizations, and agencies related to your topic.

Consult with your instructor, teaching assistant, or reference librarian.

Photo: ©Hill Street Studios/Blend Images LLC RF

Hypothesis A testable statement about the relationship between two or more variables.

Causal logic A relationship exists between variables in which change in one brings about change in the other.

Variable A measurable trait or characteristic that is subject to change under different conditions.

Independent variable The variable in a causal relationship that causes or influences a change in a second variable.

Dependent variable The variable in a causal relationship that is subject to the influence of another variable.

Did You Know?

...U.S. government agencies regularly release reports on income, education, poverty, and health care. According to the Department of Education, 88.4 percent of people aged 25 and older have received their high school diploma or equivalent, and 32.5 percent have earned at least a bachelor's degree.

Source: National Center for Education Statistics 2016: Table 104.10. *Photo:* ©Laura Doss/Getty Images RF

provide perhaps the best way of tracking down existing research. Most academic libraries provide links to databases, such as *Academic Search, JSTOR,* and *SocINDEX*. The U.S. Census Bureau makes available numerous reports along with access to a wealth of data on income, education, gender, race, and so on. Many other sites provide annual reports and access to data, including the U.S. Department of Education, the U.S. Bureau of Labor Statistics, the Organisation for Economic Co-operation and Development (OECD), and the World Bank.

Wikipedia by itself is not considered a sufficiently legitimate academic source, but it can be a useful place to start because entries often include links to recognized academic references. Online search engines, such as Google or Bing, can turn up all kinds of interesting material, including videos of sociologists talking about their research in interviews and conference presentations. When using such search results, however, always assess the quality of the source. Professors and librarians can provide invaluable assistance when it comes to judging sources.

FORMULATING THE HYPOTHESIS

The next step in the research process, formulating the hypothesis, involves specifying exactly what we plan to observe and what outcomes to expect. A hypothesis is more than just an educated guess. In research, a **hypothesis** is a testable statement about the relationship between two or more variables. It represents an explicit attempt to indicate what we think is happening and why. It presupposes that **causal logic** is at work, meaning that a relationship exists between variables in which change in one brings about change in the other.

For example, as we saw in the "Sociology's Roots" section of Chapter 1, Durkheim hypothesized that a cause-and-effect relationship existed between religious affiliation and suicide rates.

Variables serve as the building blocks for hypotheses. A **variable** is a measurable trait or characteristic that is subject to change under different conditions. Income, religion, gender, and occupation can all serve as variables in a study. For example, among numerous possible values within each of these variables, you might be rich or poor, Buddhist or Christian, female or male, a music teacher or an astrophysicist.

Within a hypothesis, we distinguish between cause and effect variables. The causal variable that brings about change is called the **independent variable** (often referred to in equations as x). The variable that is affected is known as the **dependent variable,** because change in it depends on the influence of the independent variable (typically represented in equations as y). For example, as we saw in Chapter 1, Matthew Desmond (2016) tested the hypothesis that the availability of affordable housing (the independent variable) affects the level of homelessness in a community (the dependent variable).

SOCTHINK

To what extent do you think each of the independent variables listed in the "Causal Logic" figure would help explain variation in college grade point average? Can you think of any additional independent variables that would help explain GPA?

A generic hypothesis statement would look something like this: knowledge of the independent variable (x) allows us to better explain or predict the value or position of the dependent variable (y). We could then place variables we are interested in studying, such as those in the "Causal Logic" figure, into this statement to clearly present what we expect to find. For example, we could hypothesize that knowledge of a person's education level allows us to better explain or predict level of income.

In sociology, we are frequently interested in abstract concepts and principles, but in order to abide by our commitment to conducting empirical research—in keeping with the Missouri principle of don't just tell me, show me—we need to ensure that we can observe, measure, or otherwise demonstrate cause-and-effect relationships. That means we must create an **operational definition** for each of our variables by transforming abstract concepts into concrete indicators that are observable and measurable. Durkheim did this when he operationalized the abstract concept of social integration into the concrete indicator of religious affiliation (Protestant versus Catholic). If we were interested in studying ability, initiative, and accomplishment, we might operationalize these concepts by using educational attainment, which might concretely be measured by highest degree attained or number of years of school completed. If we wanted to know more about social inequality, we might use annual income as a concrete indicator of differential outcomes. If we wanted to create an operational definition of religiosity, we might use a combination of indicators, including attendance at religious services, time spent studying religious texts, frequency of engaging in prayer or meditation, adherence to religious beliefs, or other possible benchmarks we might combine. The goal in creating operational definitions is to indicate as clearly as possible exactly what the researcher plans to observe.

COLLECTING AND ANALYZING DATA

When we have clearly indicated which hypotheses we seek to explore, we move on to collecting and then analyzing data. Sociologists gather data via surveys, observation, experiments, and existing research. Each technique is explained in the "Major Research Designs" section later in this chapter. For now we focus on data collection issues researchers must address regardless of the research design they select.

Selecting the Sample

One of the most basic questions sociologists must answer is, "From whom shall I gather data?" For the most part, especially in the case of large-scale research projects, sociologists cannot gather information from everyone in the population they want to study. As a result, they typically include only a subset of people from that population. A **sample** is a selection from a larger population that is representative of that population. To ensure that a sample is representative, sociologists typically use some form of a **random sample**, in which every member of the entire population being studied has an equal chance of being selected. In conducting polls by telephone, for example, polling organizations often use a random digit dialing system to ensure all numbers, including those that are unlisted, have an equal likelihood of being included.

When conducted properly, such sampling allows researchers to statistically estimate how representative their results are likely to be. For example, the U.S. Census produces an annual report, titled "Income

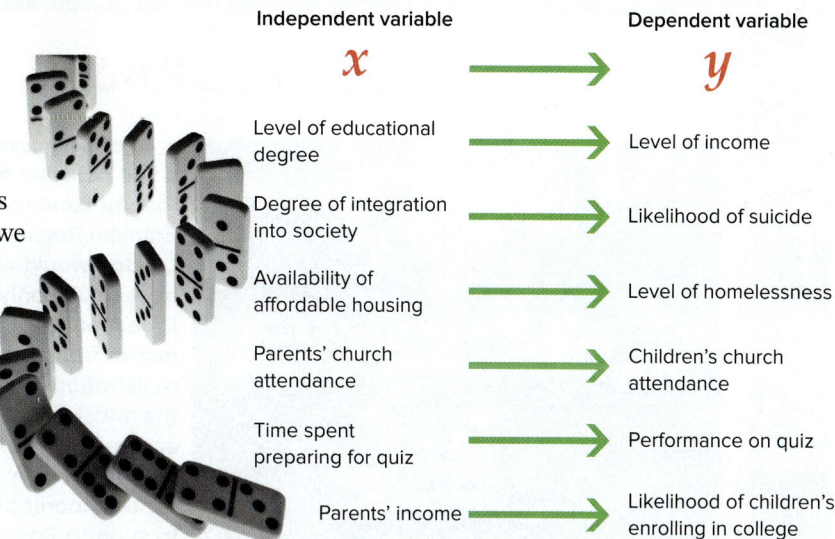

Causal Logic

Independent variable		Dependent variable
x	→	y
Level of educational degree	→	Level of income
Degree of integration into society	→	Likelihood of suicide
Availability of affordable housing	→	Level of homelessness
Parents' church attendance	→	Children's church attendance
Time spent preparing for quiz	→	Performance on quiz
Parents' income	→	Likelihood of children's enrolling in college

Photo: ©fStop Images GmbH/Shutterstock.com RF

> **Operational definition** Transformation of an abstract concept into indicators that are observable and measurable.
>
> **Sample** A selection from a larger population that is statistically representative of that population.
>
> **Random sample** A sample for which every member of an entire population has the same chance of being selected.

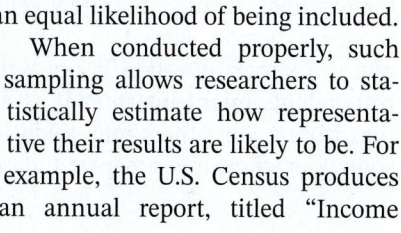

©Rubberball/Mike Kemp/Getty Images RF

Chapter 2 / Sociological Research • 29

Did You Know?

...A classic case of sampling error occurred when pollsters for *Literary Digest* declared that Alf Landon would defeat President Franklin Roosevelt in 1936. They predicted Landon would win 55 percent of the vote; he received only 37 percent. Although the *Digest* polled 2 million people, it selected names from telephone books and auto registration records. With the country in the midst of the Great Depression, phones and cars were luxuries many people could not afford. As a result, the poll underrepresented poorer people, who were more likely to support Roosevelt (Squire 1988).

Photo: ©AP Images; (frame): ©pongnathee kluaythong/123RF

and Poverty in the United States," based on a statistically representative sample of the population. Released each fall, it provides a wealth of data on, for example, types of household, regions of the country, race, ethnicity, and gender, providing statistical estimates of the margin of error for each. The same cannot be said of most online polls, such as those on Twitter, BuzzFeed, or news sites, because they rely solely on whoever logs in and chooses to participate. Although such surveys can be interesting, fun, or provocative, there is no way to tell if they are representative.

Validity The degree to which a measure or scale truly reflects the phenomenon under study.

Reliability The extent to which a measure produces consistent results.

Ensuring Validity and Reliability To have confidence in their findings, and in keeping with the scientific method, sociologists pursue research results that are both valid and reliable. **Validity** refers to the degree to which a measure or scale truly reflects the phenomenon under study. A valid measure of income, for example, would accurately represent how much money a person earned in a given year. For example, if a survey question is not written clearly, some respondents might interpret it as asking about earnings from a job; others might add income from other sources, such as investments; and others might report household income, including earnings from children or a spouse. Studies show that, even though income can be a touchy subject, people respond accurately when asked a clear and unambiguous question about how much they have earned.

Reliability refers to the extent to which a measure produces consistent results. That is, using the same instrument to collect data from the same people in similar circumstances should provide the same results. For example, if you give people the same questionnaire about income and education at two different times, unless something significant has changed between times, the responses should be approximately the same.

DEVELOPING THE CONCLUSION

In the final stage of the research process, sociologists draw conclusions about what they have learned. To do so, they must make decisions about the fate of their hypotheses and consider possible alternative explanations for their results.

Supporting Hypotheses The data provide the foundation on which we decide whether we should accept or reject our hypotheses. Whether collected from surveys, observations, experiments, or other sources, we use what we found to draw conclusions

Degree Attainment and Income

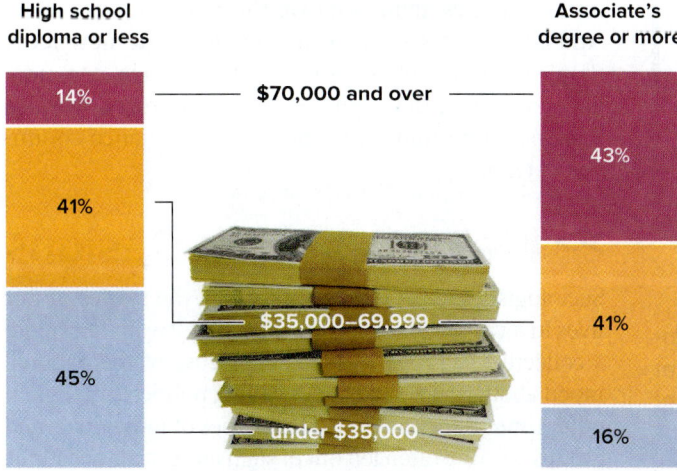

Note: Data include those aged 25–64 working full-time, year-round. High school category includes those with some college but no degree.

Source: U.S. Census Bureau 2016a:Table PINC-03. Photo: ©Comstock Images/Alamy Stock Photo RF

about possible causality between our independent and dependent variables. First, we must decide whether our variables are correlated. A **correlation** is a relationship between two variables in which change in one coincides with change in the other. For example, as a person's educational attainment rises, does income also go up? We can use existing data sources to answer that question. According to data from the Census Bureau, a person's odds of having a high income go up significantly if the person has more education. As the accompanying "Degree Attainment and Income" graphic demonstrates, only 14 percent of those who have earned at most a high school diploma reach the high-income group compared to 43 percent of those who have completed an associate's degree or more. We can also see that the correlation isn't perfect. Some people in the high school diploma category have high incomes, and others with an associate's degree or more are in the low-income group.

Assuming we find that our variables are correlated, the second decision we must make is whether that relationship is causal. One fundamental truth when interpreting results is that correlation does not equal causation. It may well be that the apparent relationship is due to chance or to the influence of some other factors. It is the task of the researcher to demonstrate—drawing on time-ordering, logical reasoning, and theory—that variation in the independent variable caused change in the dependent variable. Statistics alone are not enough.

Take, for example, the effect that divorce has on the well-being of children. Studies have shown that the two variables are correlated—children of divorce exhibit long-term adverse effects—but is that relationship causal? Before reaching a conclusion, we should consider other factors. Perhaps negative outcomes for children are due to levels of parental conflict rather than divorce itself, or to the nature of the relationship between the parents and the children, or to contextual factors such as unemployment or geographic mobility (Bhrolcháin 2001; Sun and Li 2008). In other words, we must consider the possibility that other variables besides divorce may be involved.

> **Correlation** A relationship between two variables in which a change in one coincides with a change in the other.

Correlation versus Causation

DILBERT © 2011 Scott Adams. Used By permission of Andrews McMeel.

SOC THINK

Although education plays a significant role in explaining income, some people with minimal education earn high incomes, and some with advanced degrees earn relatively little. What additional social factors do you think might explain a person's income? What effects might a person's gender, race, ethnicity, religion, age, and social background have on income?

Controlling for Other Factors Given the complexity of human behavior, it is seldom sufficient to study only one independent and one dependent variable. Although such analyses can provide us with insight, to consider additional causal factors that might influence the dependent variable, we can introduce **control variables**, which are factors the researcher holds constant to test the relative impact of an independent variable.

In exploring the relationship between education and income, for example, we should consider the possibility that variables such as parents' income or social network connections account for the correlation. In this case, perhaps "who you know" matters more than "what you know." The introduction of the control variables allows us to test how much of the variation in income that was initially assumed to be due to education is actually due to the influence of parents' income or social network connections. In later chapters we consider such additional background factors that help explain income differences, including gender, race, ethnicity, and social class.

Control variable A factor that is held constant to test the relative impact of an independent variable.

Research design A detailed plan or method for obtaining data scientifically.

Survey A predefined series of questions designed to collect information about people's particular attributes, beliefs, and actions.

IN SUMMARY: THE RESEARCH PROCESS

When our research is complete, we share our results with sociologists, policy makers, and others, primarily via presentations at professional conferences and articles in academic journals. Presenting our results in such public ways makes our research part of the literature to be reviewed for future studies. Subjecting our research to such scrutiny can uncover mistakes we made or reveal things we might have done differently,

such as including additional variables or using alternative techniques for collecting data.

Research is cyclical. Having drawn our conclusions about our hypotheses, we use those results to refine our initial theories about why we think and act as we do. And the process starts again. We generate new ideas that lead to new hypotheses, which in turn lead to more data collection. In the end we find answers, but we also have new questions, and the wheel of science continues to turn.

>> Major Research Designs

Sociologists gather information to tell the stories of our lives in a variety of ways. Sometimes they want to explore a collective story, perhaps to get a sense of the national mood about issues such as education, politics, or religion; other times they want to tell the stories of individuals and groups who are often left out of such large-scale accounts, as we saw Alice Goffman (2014a) do with her research in inner-city Philadelphia. To collect the information necessary to tell these tales, sociologists follow the guidelines set forth in a given **research design**, which is a detailed plan or method for obtaining data scientifically. There are four primary research designs in sociology: surveys, observation, experiments, and use of existing sources.

SURVEYS

Surveys represent the most commonly used research design. All of us have likely been surveyed about something: which presidential candidate we intend to vote for, what our favorite television program is, or how much time we spent studying for a course. A **survey** is a predefined series of questions designed to collect information about people's particular attributes, beliefs, and actions. Surveys become particularly commonplace during election seasons in the form of political polls. Major polling organizations include Gallup, Pew Research, SurveyUSA, ABC News/Washington Post, and Quinnipiac University. All these firms use careful techniques to ensure the accuracy of their results.

©Hill Street Studios/Getty Images RF

Issues in Designing Surveys As indicated earlier, a survey must be based on precise, representative sampling if it is to genuinely reflect a broad range of the population. We might be skeptical that feedback from just a few hundred people can provide an accurate picture of how more than 300 million people think, but properly run surveys can do just that. When it comes to presidential polling, for example, we can compare the results of such polls against actual election results. In a study of

President Obama's Approval Ratings, 2008–2017

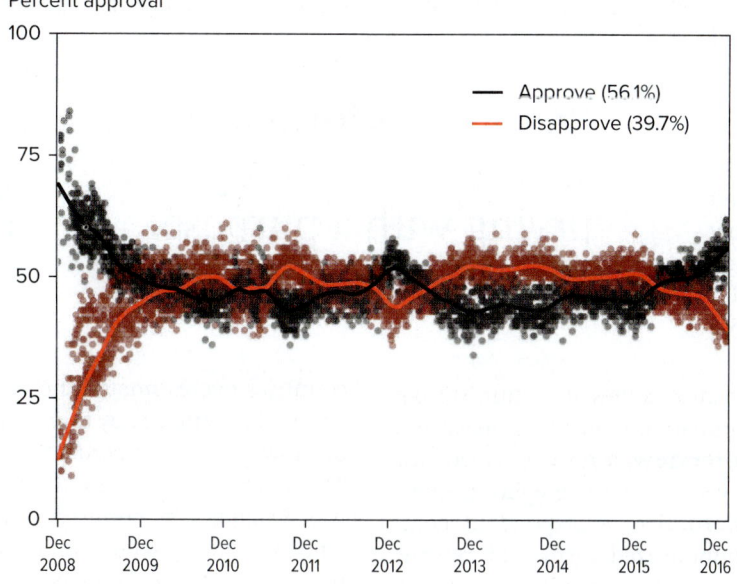

Note: Each point represents a single poll conducted by a major polling organization regarding President Obama's overall approval rating throughout his administration.

Source: www.pollster.com.

the historical accuracy of presidential polls, political scientist Costas Panagopoulos reports that the polls from 1956 to 2012 were, on average, within 2 percentage points of accurately predicting the final result (Panagopoulos 2009; Panagopoulos and Farrer 2014). Even in the 2016 presidential election, in which pollsters incorrectly predicted that Hillary Clinton would defeat Donald Trump, their projection of the popular vote was not far off. On the eve of the election, the national polling average showed Clinton 3.1 percentage points ahead of Trump and the final vote tally showed her receiving 2.1 percent more votes nationally than did Trump (Andrews, Katz, and Patel 2016; Wasserman 2016). Although pollsters sometimes fail to "get it right" (for example, mistakenly predicting that Dewey would defeat Truman in the 1948 presidential election), most often they do, and with amazing precision.

In recent years, analysts have taken to aggregating poll results, meaning they produce a single score based on averaging the results of numerous individual polls. The accompanying graph of President Obama's Approval Ratings provides an example. Each individual dot represents a single poll result, and the line represents the average. With graphs such as these, we can see that although any individual poll can vary significantly from the average, taken together they provide a much better measure of the likely result. Sites regularly producing up-to-date polling results include FiveThirtyEight.com, Pollster.com, and PollingReport.com.

In addition to ensuring samples are representative, sociologists must exercise great care in the wording of questions when conducting surveys. Failure to do so threatens the reliability and validity of their results.

An effective survey question must be simple and clear enough for people to understand. It must also be specific enough that researchers have no problems interpreting the results. Open-ended questions ("What do you think of the programming on educational television?") must be carefully phrased to solicit the type of information desired. Surveys can be indispensable sources of information, but only if the sampling is done properly and the questions are worded accurately and without bias.

Another concern involves the possible impact an interviewer's characteristics can have on survey results.

©Bettmann/Contributor/Getty Images

For example, female interviewers tend to receive more feminist responses from female subjects than do male researchers, and African American interviewers tend to receive more detailed responses about race-related issues from Black subjects than do White interviewers. The possible impact of gender and race indicates again how much care social research requires (Chun et al. 2011; D. Davis and Silver 2003).

> *Research is formalized curiosity. It is poking and prying with a purpose.*
>
> Zora Neale Hurston

Types of Surveys When it comes to administering surveys, there are two primary options: interviews and questionnaires. In an **interview,** a researcher obtains information through face-to-face or telephone questioning. With a **questionnaire,** a respondent completes a printed or computerized form and returns it to the researcher. Each of these has its advantages. An interviewer can obtain a higher response rate because people find it more difficult to turn down a personal request for an interview than to throw away a printed questionnaire. In addition, a skillful interviewer can follow up on questions to clarify a subject's underlying feelings and reasons for responding. For their part, questionnaires have the advantage of being cheaper and easier to distribute to large numbers of people. Either way, what we can learn from surveys can be amazing.

Researchers used surveys, for example, to better understand how perceptions vary between countries. They administered it to a representative sample of 11,527 people in 14 nations, asking questions about a variety of topics (Ipsos MORI 2014). For example, regarding teenage pregnancy they asked, "In your opinion, what percentage of girls aged between 15 and 19 years in [name of country] give birth each year?" In the United States, the average answer was 24 percent, whereas in Great Britain people guessed 16 percent and in Sweden it was 7. Regarding immigration they asked, "What percentage of the [name of country] population do you think are immigrants to this country?" In the United States, the average guess was 32 percent compared to guesses of 24 percent in Great Britain and 23 percent in Sweden. In addition, they asked about religion, elderly people, voting rates, unemployment rates, homicide rates, and life expectancy. The answers varied significantly from country to country.

Researchers then compared the perceptions to the actual rates for each question asked (Ipsos MORI 2014). They wondered if the degree of difference between the two varied by country. On the question of teenage pregnancy, the actual U.S. rate is 3 percent, a 21-point difference from the perceived rate. People in all 14 countries overestimated their teenage pregnancy rates. The actual percentage of immigrants in the United States is 13 percent, a 19-point difference from the perceived rate. Again, people in all 14 countries overestimated the percentage of their immigrant population. They then ranked each country based on how close their perception was to the actual data. The country that came out on top as the most accurate was Sweden. The country in last place was Italy. The United States finished in 13th place. Understanding perception is important because, as we learned from the Thomas theorem, we act on the basis of what we *think* is true, rather than what *is* true. And if our perceptions are inaccurate, our corresponding actions may prove less effective.

Quantitative and Qualitative Research Surveys typically represent an example of **quantitative research,** which collects and reports data primarily in numerical form. Analysis of these data depends on

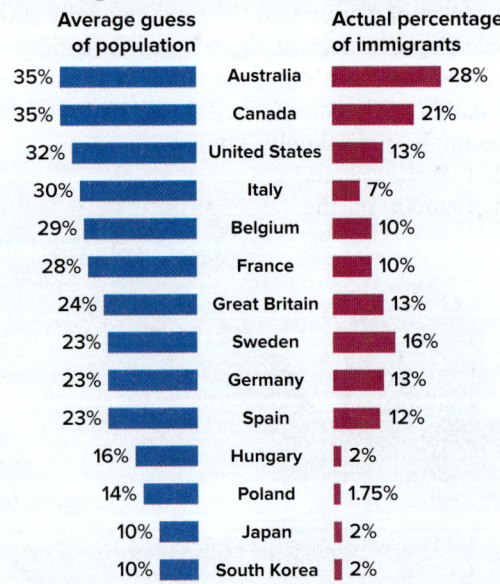

Immigration Rates: Perception versus Reality

Average guess of population	Country	Actual percentage of immigrants
35%	Australia	28%
35%	Canada	21%
32%	United States	13%
30%	Italy	7%
29%	Belgium	10%
28%	France	10%
24%	Great Britain	13%
23%	Sweden	16%
23%	Germany	13%
23%	Spain	12%
16%	Hungary	2%
14%	Poland	1.75%
10%	Japan	2%
10%	South Korea	2%

Source: Ipsos MORI 2014.

Interview A face-to-face or telephone questioning of a respondent to obtain desired information.

Questionnaire A respondent completes a printed or computerized form and returns it to the researcher.

Quantitative research Research that collects and reports data primarily in numerical form.

statistics, from the simple to the complex. Statistics can seem intimidating, but it helps to think of them as just another way of telling a story. They are tools that provide an additional window into what is happening and why. Though it takes training to understand the complex statistics used in advanced sociological research, basic descriptive statistics, such as percentages and measures of central tendency, are more familiar and are still quite helpful. The **mean,** or average, is a number calculated by adding a series of values and then dividing by the number of values. The **median,** or midpoint, is the number that divides a series of values into two groups of equal numbers of values. The median is most often used when there are extreme scores that would distort the mean. The **mode** is the most common value in a series of scores and is seldom used in sociological research. As measures of central tendency, the mean, median, and mode all provide a single score that serves as a simple summary for the whole distribution of scores.

Quantitative research proves particularly useful on familiar, well-defined topics, but when we seek to explore new concepts and contexts, researchers frequently turn to **qualitative research,** which is descriptive research that relies on narrative accounts rather than statistical procedures. Whereas quantitative research focuses on varieties of ways to count things, qualitative research seeks to make sense of the contexts within which people construct meaning through interactions with others. It focuses on small groups and communities rather than on large groups or whole nations. The most common research design for qualitative research is observation.

OBSERVATION

Investigators who collect information by participating directly and/or by closely watching a group or community are engaged in **observation.** This research design allows sociologists to examine behaviors and communities in greater depth than is possible using other methods. Though observation may seem a relatively informal method compared to surveys, researchers are careful to take detailed notes and follow appropriate procedures while observing their subjects.

An increasingly popular form of qualitative research in sociology today is **ethnography**—the study of an entire social setting through extended systematic observation. Typically, the emphasis is on how the subjects themselves view their social life in some setting. In some cases, the sociologist actually joins the group for a period to get an accurate sense of how it operates. This approach is called *participant observation.*

This is the approach Alice Goffman (2014a) took in her study in Philadelphia. As a result of embedding herself in the community, she was able to portray a fuller description of the lives of the young African American males. In addition, she describes the experience of the women in their lives (their wives, sisters, and girlfriends); the underground marketplace that emerges in which local entrepreneurs provide goods and services, such as clean urine for drug tests, faked documents, and prison guards who provide cell phones to inmates; and the lives of those living in the inner city who keep their distance from illegal activity and those involved in it. Because she used participant observation, her descriptions are deep and rich and she includes many extended quotes from the individuals involved.

> **Mean** A number calculated by adding a series of values and then dividing by the number of values.
>
> **Median** The midpoint, or number that divides a series of values into two groups of equal numbers of values.
>
> **Mode** The most common value in a series of scores.
>
> **Qualitative research** Descriptive research that relies on narrative accounts rather than statistical procedures.
>
> **Observation** A research technique in which an investigator collects information through direct participation and/or by closely watching a group or community.
>
> **Ethnography** The study of an entire social setting through extended systematic observation.

Going GLOBAL

Research Abroad

Researchers now regularly gather data from around the world, even under difficult circumstances. Since 2004, for example, researchers have conducted an annual national survey in Afghanistan. In 2015, they sent out 939 Afghani interviewers who conducted 9,586 face-to-face interviews with Afghans throughout the country. They learned that 82 percent of Afghan households owned at least one mobile phone, 62 percent owned a television, 23 percent own owned a refrigerator, 22 percent owned a car, and 21 percent had Internet access. People's optimism about the overall direction of the country reached a 10-year low in 2015 with 57 percent saying Afghanistan is moving in the wrong direction. At the same time, 75 percent say they are generally happy with their lives (Sadat et al. 2015).

SOCTHINK

What social group or setting (such as a religious group, political organization, sorority/fraternity, laboratory, or office) might you want to learn more about through in-depth participant observation? How would you go about making contact? How would you gain members' trust?

©Sally and Richard Greenhill/Alamy Stock Photo

Observation research raises questions about the appropriate nature of the relationship between researchers and their subjects. Full participation with study subjects allows for a deeper understanding of life in such social worlds (Adler and Adler 2012), but this depth must be balanced against the need for objectivity. For example, Alice Goffman's decision to become roommates with two of her informants provided her with up-close access to the reality of their everyday experiences, but it also raised questions about her capacity to remain objective. When one of those informants was later murdered, and the other wanted to go out looking for the killer, she volunteered to drive. Critics later raised questions about whether this act constituted conspiracy to commit murder (Volokh 2015). In addition to the problem of objectivity, a related concern is whether closeness to those in one part of a community may result in insufficient detail in describing another part. The depth that results from a narrow focus on a specific community, and on particular members within it, comes at the expense of breadth.

Experiment An artificially created situation that allows a researcher to manipulate variables.

Experimental group The subjects in an experiment who are exposed to an independent variable introduced by a researcher.

Control group The subjects in an experiment who are not introduced to the independent variable by the researcher.

EXPERIMENTS

Experiments represent the third major research design for collecting data. An **experiment** is a controlled procedure in which researchers assess the effect independent variables have on dependent variables. As much as possible, the goal is to isolate the dependent variable from any other influences so that any change in the dependent variable can be attributed only to the independent variable. In a classic experiment, researchers begin by dividing subjects with similar characteristics into two groups. Those in the **experimental group** are exposed to an independent variable; those in the **control group** are not. Thus, if scientists were testing a new type of antibiotic, they would administer the drug to an experimental group but not to a control group and compare the outcomes for both groups.

Experiments have become more common in sociology, but they do represent a challenge. Sociologists want to understand people's natural responses in everyday contexts. Most human behavior does not happen in isolation from other influences, so specially created experimental conditions are unlikely to exist in the real world. Sociologists also express ethical concerns about the appropriateness of deliberately manipulating people's responses.

An additional challenge with experiments, which also impacts observation research, is that the mere presence of a social scientist or other observer may affect the behavior of the people being studied.

Employees at a Westinghouse Electric and Manufacturing Company in 1925. ©Hulton Archive/Getty Images

The recognition of this phenomenon grew out of an experiment conducted during the 1920s and 1930s at the Hawthorne plant of the Western Electric Company near Chicago. A group of researchers set out to determine how to improve the productivity of workers at the plant. The investigators manipulated such variables as lighting and working hours to see what impact the changes would have on how much workers produce. To their surprise, they found that every step they took seemed to increase output. Even measures that seemed likely to have the opposite effect, such as reducing the amount of lighting in the plant down to moonlight levels, led to higher productivity (Mayo 1933).

Why did the plant's employees work harder even under less favorable conditions? The researchers initially concluded that the workers modified their behavior because they knew they were being studied. They responded positively to the novelty of being subjects in an experiment and to the fact that researchers were interested in them. Since that time, sociologists have used the term **Hawthorne effect** to describe the unintended influence that observers of experiments can have on their subjects, even though later studies show the situation there was more complex (Brannigan and Zwerman 2001). It highlights the difficulties experiments present in seeking to understand how people behave in their real-world environments.

Sociologists sometimes conduct what are called natural experiments, which seek to approximate experimental conditions in the field. For example, sociologist Devah Pager (2003, 2007) devised an experiment to assess the impact a job applicant's criminal background might have on an individual's employment opportunities. In addition, she introduced race as a control variable. She sent four polite, well-dressed young men out to look for an entry-level job in Milwaukee, Wisconsin. All four were 23-year-old college students, but they presented themselves as high school graduates with similar job histories. Two of the men were Black and two were White. One Black applicant and one White applicant claimed to have served 18 months in jail for a felony conviction—possession of cocaine with intent to distribute.

> **Hawthorne effect** The unintended influence that observers of experiments can have on their subjects.

Chapter 2 / Sociological Research • 37

White Privilege in Job Seeking

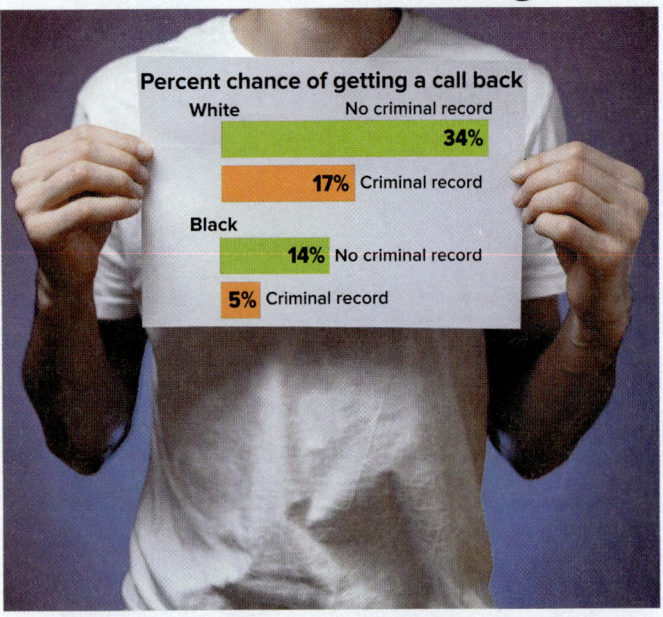

Source: Pager 2003:958. Photo: ©Dolas/Getty Images RF

Secondary analysis A variety of research techniques that make use of existing data for the purpose of new analysis.

The experiences of the four men with 350 potential employers were vastly different. The White applicant with a purported prison record received only half as many callbacks as the other White applicant—17 percent compared to 34 percent. But as dramatic as the effect of his criminal record was, the effect of his race was more significant, as is evident in the "White Privilege in Job Seeking" graphic. Despite his prison record, the White ex-con received slightly more callbacks than the Black applicant with no criminal record, 17 percent compared to 14 percent. To assess the validity of her findings, Pager and colleagues later conducted a similar experiment in New York City, and the results were the same (Pager and Pedulla 2015; Pager and Western 2012; Pager, Western, and Bonikowski 2009; Pager, Western, and Sugie 2009). This experiment revealed that when it comes to getting a job, race matters.

USE OF EXISTING SOURCES

Sociologists do not necessarily need to collect new data to conduct research. The fourth major research design,

> **SOC THINK**
>
> Imagine you are a researcher interested in the effect playing computer or console games has on a college student's grades. How might you go about setting up an experiment to measure this effect?

secondary analysis, refers to a variety of research techniques that make use of existing data for new analysis. The two major categories of secondary analysis are use of existing data sets and analysis of existing documents.

Existing data sets consist of data collected by researchers, often for other purposes, that other researchers can then use to investigate their own hypotheses. Existing data sets provide a simple record of the responses the original investigators gathered before they conducted their analysis. The U.S. Census Bureau provides a treasure trove of such data. Every 10 years, as required by the U.S. Constitution, the Bureau attempts to collect data from every household in the United States. In 2010, it ultimately gathered information from 99.62 percent of the nation's housing units. In addition to their decennial census, Census researchers also regularly collect data using representative samples of the U.S. population. Gathering data on that scale is very expensive and time-consuming, so the information the Census provides is extremely valuable to researchers.

Another invaluable existing data set comes from NORC (National Opinion Research Center) in the form of its General Social Survey (GSS). First administered in 1972, the GSS is a national survey conducted every other year, administered in both English and Spanish, of a representative sample of the U.S. adult population who are interviewed in depth on a variety of topics, including employment history, education, political preferences, religious beliefs, gun ownership, abortion rights. NORC surveyors frequently ask the same questions over multiple years, allowing for analysis of how responses change over time. The GSS Data Explorer is available online for anyone to use.

Using existing data sets can allow us to see trends or patterns that the original researchers might have never considered. For example, every year the Social Security Administration's Popular Baby Names site updates its data on the thousands of registrations it receives for newborn babies. Using these data, we can recognize shifts in

Source: U.S. Census Bureau, Public Information Office

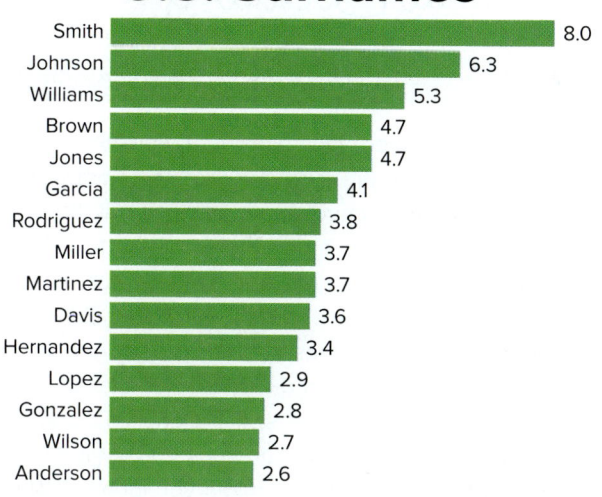

Note: Numbers are per 1,000 people in the population.
Source: Chalabi and Flowers 2014.

> **SOC THINK**
>
> "NameVoyager" at www.babynamewizard.com is an application that allows you to type in any name to trace its popularity over time. Go there and enter several names to see how their use has changed. Considering some of the names you tried, what factors might have contributed to their rise and fall? How popular is your first name? How and why has its popularity changed over time?

cultural trends. The name John was in the top five for boys from 1900 until 1972 but has since fallen to 26th. The name Mary ranked number one or two from 1900 through 1965 and now ranks 124th. By contrast, the name Juan was ranked 215th in 1900, peaked at 46th in 1999, and now ranks 114th. Maria went from 150th in 1900, peaked at 31st from 1973 to 1975, and now ranks 109th (Social Security Administration 2014). These shifts reflect the growing influence of the Latino population in the United States.

Existing data from another source, the U.S. Census Bureau, confirm this shift. Analysis of these data revealed that although Smith remained the most common surname in the United States, Garcia and Rodriguez rose into the top 10 starting in 2007 (Chalabi and Flowers 2014). This marked the first time in the nation's history that a non-Anglo name had been counted among the most common names. Such name changes reflect an overall shift in the U.S. population from a nation composed primarily of European descendants to one that is more globally diverse, a trend sociologists expect will continue (Word et al. 2007). In a statistical analysis seeking to combine first and last names, researchers estimate that James Smith is the most common name in the United States. Maria Garcia comes in at 15th (Chalabi and Flowers 2014).

In addition to using existing data sets, secondary analysis can also involve existing documents. Studying newspapers, periodicals, diaries, songs, radio and television recordings, websites, legal papers, and many other possible types of documents provides insight into how people think and act. Even better is that documents can come not only from the present, but also from the past, making historical sociology possible. We cannot conduct surveys, interviews, participant observation, or experiments with people in the 1860s, for example, but we can still learn valuable sociological lessons about them by analyzing the records they left behind.

> **Content analysis** The systematic coding and objective recording of data, guided by some rationale.

One of the most frequently used techniques when conducting such research is **content analysis,** which is the systematic coding and objective recording of data, guided by a given rationale. Erving Goffman (1979) used content analysis when he conducted a pioneering exploration of how advertisements portray women. The ads he studied typically showed women in secondary and dependent roles. Ads portrayed women using caressing and touching gestures more than men. Even when presented in leadership roles, women were likely to be shown striking seductive poses or gazing out into space. Jeanne Kilbourne's content analysis of ads in her film, *Killing Us Softly: Advertising's Image of Women* (2010), demonstrates that women continued to be portrayed as objects. She found that advertisers' primary message is that women should spend their time, energy, and money trying to attain the idealized, airbrushed image of female beauty only achievable with the assistance of Photoshop. She quotes supermodel Cindy Crawford as saying, "I wish I looked like Cindy Crawford" (Kilbourne 2010).

In addition to allowing for historical research, one of the appeals for sociologists of secondary analysis is that it is nonreactive—that is, doing this type of study does not influence how people respond. For example, Émile Durkheim's statistical analysis of existing suicide data had no impact on people's likelihood of committing suicide. In other words, secondary analysis enables researchers to avoid the problems associated with the Hawthorne effect.

Secondary analysis can also be much cheaper, both in terms of time and money, than the other research designs. But that works only if access to the data exists.

Personal Sociology

Questions & Answers

Have you ever asked yourself, "What were they thinking?" Maybe it's the music people like, the clothes they wear, the major they choose, the job they get, the person they date, the religion they practice, or the candidate they support. Although sociology cannot provide specific answers for why particular individuals think and act the way they do, it does offer insight into the social factors that influence our choices. Imagine that you had the chance to answer some specific question such as those above. Which would you choose? What independent and dependent variables might you identify? What would your hypothesis be? What research design might you select? What makes sociology fun is that we get to ask questions and find answers.

©Chirag Wakaskar/Getty Images

The biggest challenge secondary analysis faces is that the researcher relies on data collected by someone else. As a result, researchers using existing sources may not find exactly what they want or need. For example, sociologists who study family violence use data from police and social service agencies on reported cases of spouse abuse and child abuse, but not all incidents get reported to authorities. As a result, important information from nonreporters gets left out of the analysis.

Each of these research designs provides sociologists with data they need to conduct their analyses and draw their conclusions. Although most studies rely on only one type, others use a combination. By conducting both surveys and participant observation, for example, researchers benefit from the advantages both provide. In all cases, however, availability of resources, in terms of both time and money, constrain what is possible.

Major Research Designs

Method	Examples	Advantages	Limitations
Survey	Questionnaires Interviews	Detail and breadth	Depth, time, and money
Observation	Ethnography	Depth and explanation	Time and access
Experiment	Deliberate manipulation of people's social behavior	Control and specificity of cause/effect	Unnatural settings and ethical concerns
Existing sources/ Secondary analysis	Analysis of census or health data Analysis of films or TV commercials	Historical analysis, nonreactivity, and cost	Data collected for some other purpose

>> Research Ethics

Because sociological research involves studying human beings, sociologists must take special care to treat their subjects with respect and not expose them to undue harm. The American Sociological Association (1999), in its **Code of Ethics**, laid out its standards of acceptable behavior developed by and for members of a profession. It sets forth the following general principles:

- *Professional Competence:* Use appropriate research techniques in proper ways.
- *Integrity:* Be honest, respectful, and fair.
- *Professional and Scientific Responsibility:* Adhere to the highest scientific and professional standards.
- *Respect for People's Rights, Dignity, and Diversity:* Be unbiased and nondiscriminatory, respecting the dignity and worth of all people.
- *Social Responsibility:* Contribute to the public good.

Over time, these general principles have given rise to some concrete practices for researchers to follow. For example, researchers should secure informed consent from subjects, meaning that, if at all possible, the people being studied should be aware of any possible risks of participation and explicitly agree to participate. To confirm that the research does not place subjects at an unreasonable level of risk, researchers typically submit their proposals to an institutional review board.

CONFIDENTIALITY

One of the most common techniques used to protect subjects is to promise them confidentiality, shielding their identity so that others cannot know who participated. Ensuring the privacy of subjects helps protect them from potential negative effects of participation. Sometimes participation can be totally anonymous, so that not even the researcher knows who provided which responses.

Promising confidentiality may seem clear-cut in the abstract but can be difficult to adhere to in practice. For example, should a sociologist who is engaged in participant observation research protect the confidentiality of subjects who break the law? What if the sociologist is interviewing political activists and is questioned by government authorities about the research?

Like journalists, sociologists occasionally find themselves facing the ethical dilemma of whether to reveal their sources to law enforcement authorities. In May 1993 sociologist Rik Scarce was jailed for contempt of court because he declined to tell a federal grand jury what he knew—or even whether he knew anything—about a 1991 raid on a university research laboratory by animal rights activists. At the time, Scarce was doing research for a book about environmental protesters and knew at least one suspect in the break-in. Although he was chastised by a federal judge, Scarce won respect from fellow prison inmates, who regarded him as a man who "won't snitch" (Monaghan 2012; Scarce 2005).

> **SOC**THINK
>
> Under what circumstances might researchers need to deceive subjects, even if it might result in their emotional harm, in order to get genuine responses?

The ASA, in defense of the principle of confidentiality, supported Scarce's position when he appealed his sentence. Scarce maintained his silence. Ultimately, the judge ruled that nothing would be gained by further incarceration, and Scarce was released after spending 159 days in jail. The U.S. Supreme Court ultimately declined to hear Scarce's case on appeal. The Court's failure to consider his case led Scarce (1994, 1995, 2005) to argue that federal legislation is needed to clarify the right of scholars and members of the press to preserve the confidentiality of those they interview.

> **Code of ethics** The standards of acceptable behavior developed by and for members of a profession.

RESEARCH FUNDING

An additional concern of the ASA's *Code of Ethics* is the possibility that funding sources could influence research findings. Accepting funds from a private organization or even a government agency that stands to benefit from a study's results can clash with the ASA's first principle of maintaining objectivity and integrity in research. As such, all sources of funding should be disclosed.

As an example, when ExxonMobil was ordered to pay $5.3 billion in damages because its oil tanker, *Exxon Valez*, hit a reef off the coast of Alaska, spilling more than 11 million gallons of oil into Prince William Sound, it appealed the verdict and approached legal scholars, sociologists, and psychologists who might be willing to study jury deliberations. The corporation's objective was to develop academic support for its lawyers' contention that the punitive judgments in such cases result from faulty deliberations and do not deter future incidents. Some scholars have questioned the propriety of accepting funds under such circumstances, even if the source is disclosed. The scholars who accepted ExxonMobil's support deny that it influenced their work or changed their conclusions.

To date, the company has spent more than $1 million on the research, and at least one compilation of studies congenial to the corporation's point of view has been published. As ethical considerations require, the

©Siqui Sanchez/The Image Bank/Getty Images

> ## SOC THINK
> To what extent is it possible to maintain value neutrality when studying a social group with which you might disagree (such as White supremacists or convicted child molesters)? Why might sociologists choose to study such groups?

academics who conducted the studies disclosed ExxonMobil's role in funding the research. In 2006, drawing on these studies, the corporation's lawyers succeeded in persuading an appeals court to reduce the corporation's legal damages from $5.3 to $2.5 billion (Freudenburg 2005; Liptak 2008a, 2008b). In 2008, the amount was further reduced to $508 million, though in 2009 the Ninth U.S. Circuit Court of Appeals ordered ExxonMobil to pay on additional $500 million in punitive damages, court costs, and interest payments.

VALUE NEUTRALITY

The ethical considerations of sociologists lie not only in the methods they use and the funding they accept but also in the way they interpret their results. Max Weber ([1904] 1949) recognized that personal values would influence the topics that sociologists select for research. In his view, that was perfectly acceptable, but he argued that researchers should not allow their personal feelings to influence the interpretation of data. In Weber's phrase, sociologists must practice **value neutrality** in their research. As part of this neutrality, investigators have an ethical obligation to accept research findings even when the data run counter to their own personal views, to theoretically based explanations, or to widely accepted beliefs. One concern raised about Alice Goffman's research on inner-city Philadelphia was that she got too close to her subjects and lost her objectivity. The presupposition in this critique is that taking sides might undercut a researcher's capacity to accurately describe what is going on.

Value neutrality Max Weber's term for objectivity of sociologists in the interpretation of data.

Some sociologists believe that such neutrality is impossible. They worry that Weber's insistence on value-free sociology may lead the public to accept sociological conclusions without exploring researchers' biases. Others have suggested that sociologists may use objectivity as a justification for remaining uncritical of existing institutions and centers of power (Gouldner 1970). Despite the early work of W. E. B. Du Bois and Jane Addams, for example, sociologists still need to be reminded that the discipline often fails to adequately consider all people's social behavior.

Sociologists should not focus only on those in the majority but must also seek out the stories of those who are often invisible due to their relative lack of power and resources. In fact, sociologists have learned much about society by listening to the voices of those who are excluded from mainstream sources of power and denied access to valuable resources. In her book *The Death of White Sociology* (1973), Joyce

Movies on SOCIOLOGICAL RESEARCH

Kinsey
The father of modern sexual research employs individual case studies.

Thank You for Smoking
A satire about the tobacco industry, showing how statistics can lie.

Supersize Me
A reporter investigates the American fast-food industry by eating at McDonald's for one month.

56 Up
Documentary following 14 children as their lives progress from age 7 to 56.

Devil's Playground
Amish teens experiment with drinking, drugs, and sex before committing to a lifetime within the Amish community.

5

Ladner called attention to the tendency of mainstream sociologists to investigate the lives of African Americans only in the context of social problems. Similarly, feminist sociologist Shulamit Reinharz (1992) has argued that sociological research should not only include the research of sociologists who are outside the mainstream but should also be open to drawing on relevant research by nonsociologists who might provide additional depth and understanding of social life. The issue of value neutrality does not mean that sociologists can't have opinions, but it does mean that they must work to overcome any biases, however unintentional, that they may bring to their analysis of research.

FEMINIST METHODOLOGY

Although researchers must be objective, their theoretical orientation necessarily influences the questions they ask—or, just as important, the questions they fail to ask. Because their contributions have opened up so many new lines of inquiry, sociologists using the feminist perspective have had perhaps the greatest impact on the current generation of social researchers. Until the 1960s, for example, researchers frequently studied work and family separately, as if they were two discrete institutions. Feminist theorists, however, reject the notion that these are separate spheres. They were the first sociologists to look at housework as real work and to investigate the struggles people face in balancing the demands of work and family (Hochschild 1989; Lopata 1971).

Feminist theorists have also drawn attention to researchers' tendency to overlook women in sociological studies. For most of the history of sociology, researchers conducted studies of male subjects or male-led groups and organizations, then generalized their findings to all people. For many decades, for example, ethnographic studies of urban life focused on street corners, neighborhood taverns, and bowling alleys—places where men typically congregated. Although researchers gained valuable insights in this way, they did not form a true impression of city life, because they overlooked the areas where women were likely to gather, such as playgrounds, grocery stores, and front stoops. These are the arenas that the feminist perspective focuses on.

> The greatest obstacle to discovery is not ignorance—it is the illusion of knowledge.
>
> Daniel Boorstin

Feminist scholars have also contributed to a greater global awareness within sociology. To feminist theorists, the traditional distinction between industrial nations and developing countries overlooks the close relationship between these two supposedly separate worlds. Feminist theorists have called for more research on the special role that immigrant women play in maintaining their households, on the use of domestic workers from less-developed nations by households in industrial countries, and on the global trafficking of sex workers (Cheng 2003; K. Cooper et al. 2007).

Finally, feminist researchers tend to involve and consult their subjects more than other researchers, contributing to a significant increase in more qualitative and participatory research. They are also more oriented toward seeking change, raising the public consciousness, and influencing policy, which represents a return to sociology's roots (Harding 2003; Naples 2003; Sprague 2005).

Sociologists must be engaged with the world. Although there are numerous ways in which they accomplish this, first and foremost this involvement comes through research. As we have seen throughout this chapter, it is not enough for sociologists to stand back and theorize or even hypothesize about why we think and act the way we do. We must go out, collect data, and use it to inform our interpretations and explanations of human behavior. Having done so, we bear a responsibility for that knowledge, whether that means simply sharing it with other sociologists through conference presentations and journal articles or actively working for positive social change.

SOCIOLOGY IS A VERB

People Watching

As a mini-observation project, do some intentional people watching. Pick a public place, such as a mall, where people frequently walk by, and record what you observe. What characteristics stick out? How do people vary by gender, age, race, or ethnicity? To what extent do they travel individually or in groups? Record all your observations and then use your data to write up a summary of what you have learned.

[FOR REVIEW]

I. **What distinguishes sociology from common sense as a way of knowing?**
   - Sociologists conduct systematic empirical research to better understand why we think and act as we do.

II. **What steps do sociologists take when seeking to answer why people think and act the way they do?**
   - They need to define the problem, review existing literature, formulate a hypothesis, collect and analyze data, and develop a conclusion.

III. **What techniques do sociologists use to collect data?**
   - Research designs used to collect data include surveys, observation, experiments, and use of existing sources.

IV. **What ethical concerns must sociologists consider while conducting research?**
   - They have a responsibility to follow the ASA *Code of Ethics*, particularly respecting confidentiality, revealing research funding, maintaining value neutrality, and overall, treating their subjects with respect.

SOCVIEWS on Sociological Research

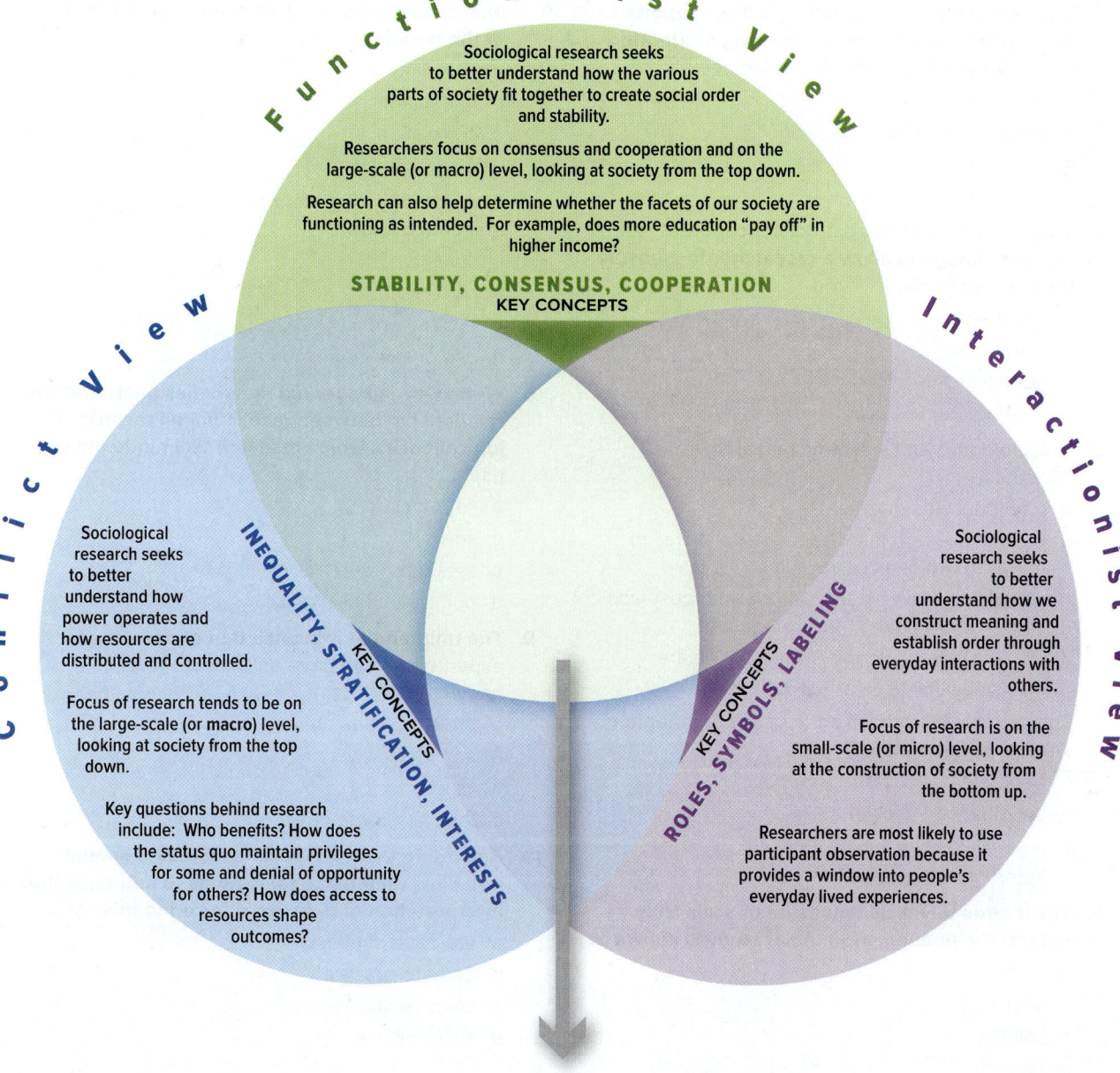

Functionalist View

Sociological research seeks to better understand how the various parts of society fit together to create social order and stability.

Researchers focus on consensus and cooperation and on the large-scale (or macro) level, looking at society from the top down.

Research can also help determine whether the facets of our society are functioning as intended. For example, does more education "pay off" in higher income?

KEY CONCEPTS: STABILITY, CONSENSUS, COOPERATION

Conflict View

Sociological research seeks to better understand how power operates and how resources are distributed and controlled.

Focus of research tends to be on the large-scale (or macro) level, looking at society from the top down.

Key questions behind research include: Who benefits? How does the status quo maintain privileges for some and denial of opportunity for others? How does access to resources shape outcomes?

KEY CONCEPTS: INEQUALITY, STRATIFICATION, INTERESTS

Interactionist View

Sociological research seeks to better understand how we construct meaning and establish order through everyday interactions with others.

Focus of research is on the small-scale (or micro) level, looking at the construction of society from the bottom up.

Researchers are most likely to use participant observation because it provides a window into people's everyday lived experiences.

KEY CONCEPTS: ROLES, SYMBOLS, LABELING

MAKE THE CONNECTION

After reviewing the chapter, answer the following questions:

1 Which perspective did Alice Goffman use in her research? Why?

2 How might each perspective study the relationship between education and income in a slightly different way?

3 How might a researcher's perspective influence the research design he or she picks? Give an example for each perspective.

4 How might each perspective interpret Devah Pager's findings in her experiment about race and job seeking?

Pop Quiz

1. One limit of common sense as a way of knowing is its tendency to favor evidence that supports our existing beliefs while minimizing or ignoring contrary evidence, which is known as
   a. operationalization.
   b. confirmation bias.
   c. correlation.
   d. value neutrality.

2. An explanation of an abstract concept that is specific enough to allow a researcher to measure the concept is a(n)
   a. hypothesis.
   b. correlation.
   c. operational definition.
   d. variable.

3. In sociological and scientific research, a hypothesis
   a. is an educated guess.
   b. is a testable statement about the relationship between two or more variables.
   c. insists that science can deal only with observable entities known directly to experience.
   d. ensures that the people being studied are representative of the population as a whole.

4. The variable hypothesized to cause or influence another is called the
   a. dependent variable.
   b. hypothetical variable.
   c. correlation variable.
   d. independent variable.

5. The degree to which a measure or scale truly reflects the phenomenon under study is known as
   a. reliability.
   b. sampling.
   c. validity.
   d. control.

6. Which research technique do sociologists use to ensure that data are statistically representative of the population being studied?
   a. sampling
   b. experiment
   c. correlation
   d. control variables

7. Ethnography is an example of which type of research design?
   a. surveys
   b. observation
   c. experiment
   d. use of existing resources

8. When Devah Pager did her studies analyzing the relationship between race, criminal records, and job callbacks, which research technique did she use?
   a. experiment
   b. survey
   c. secondary analysis
   d. participant observation

9. The unintended influence that observers of experiments can have on their subjects is known as
   a. the correlation effect.
   b. confidentiality.
   c. validity.
   d. the Hawthorne effect.

10. According to Max Weber, researchers should not allow their personal feelings to influence the interpretation of data. He referred to this as
    a. the code of ethics.
    b. content analysis.
    c. value neutrality.
    d. secondary analysis.

1. (b), 2. (c), 3. (b), 4. (d), 5. (c), 6. (a), 7. (b), 8. (a), 9. (d), 10. (c)

©Emmanuele Contini/NurPhoto via Getty Images

Culture

BREAKING RULES AND LOWERING BARRIERS

On January 8, 2017, Charlie Todd took a train ride on the New York City subway. He wasn't wearing any pants. Charlie was not alone. In fact, he was joined by more than 4,000 other pantsless riders in New York City that day. They gathered in seven locations around the city, boarded 11 different subway lines, and headed toward a rendezvous at Union Station. They spaced themselves out across many subway cars, had minimal interaction with one another, and acted as normally as possible. The event was all part of the now-annual No Pants Subway Ride coordinated by Improv Everywhere, a self-described "prank collective that causes scenes of chaos and joy in public places," which Charlie Todd founded in 2001.

Improv Everywhere has sponsored more than 150 missions, some of which may be familiar because their videos have often gone viral. The No Pants event started in 2002 with just seven participants and grew larger each year, celebrating its sixteenth anniversary in 2017 with more than 10,000 participants worldwide in 60 cities across 25 countries, including Madrid, Tokyo, and Moscow. Among other missions, in 2008, more than 200 participants ("agents") converged on Grand Central Station and simultaneously froze in place for five minutes, after which they resumed what they were doing as if nothing had happened. In 2013, agents served as "seeing eye persons" for people who were texting and walking in New York City, clearing a path while the person texting trailed behind, holding on to a leash. In 2014, 40 agents entered New York City's Fifth Avenue Gap store and pretended to be mannequins until 911 was called and police escorted them out. In 2016, they set up a fake college graduation ceremony in a park, complete with students in caps and gowns, faculty on stage, and an empty podium, while the pretend academic dean walked around with a "Commencement Speaker Needed" sign to recruit volunteers. (Videos for these and many other missions are available at ImprovEverywhere.com.)

The scenes that Improv Everywhere creates help reveal our taken-for-granted rules for behavior. In our daily lives we follow routines that are largely invisible to us, and we expect others to do likewise. When people do things differently, we tend to get uncomfortable. It disrupts our sense of order. One of the best parts of their videos is watching how people respond. Initial confusion and nervousness are often followed by smiles as people realize they are seeing a performance. We want and need the actions of others to be predictable, so we create both formal and informal rules to guide our behaviors. Such rules are an important component of culture.

As You READ

- Why do humans create culture?
- What does culture consist of?
- How does culture both enable and constrain?

>> Culture and Society

We need culture. As humans, we lack the complex instincts other species are born with that enable them to survive. Unlike birds, for example, our genes do not provide us with the knowledge to build nests (or homes) for ourselves, and we can choose whether to seek out warmer climates for the winter or cooler ones in the summer. Because our actions are not narrowly determined by such instincts, we must construct their equivalent in order to provide food, clothes, shelter, and a host of other human needs. **Culture** consists of everything humans create in establishing our relationships to nature and with each other. It includes language, knowledge, material creations, and rules for behavior. In other words, it encompasses all that we say, know, make, and do in our efforts to survive and thrive.

Culture mediates between individuals and the external world. While we experience the natural world through our senses—hearing, sight, touch, smell, and taste—we depend on culture to interpret those sensations. Our retinas may send visual images to our brains, but recognition of patterns is made possible through culture. For example, we might fail to see an image in an optical illusion until someone nudges us to "look at it this way." Nothing about the physical image changed, but our perspective on it, with the help of others, has. We do not perceive nature directly; we perceive the world around us through the lens of culture.

Culture Everything humans create in establishing our relationships to nature and with each other.

> **SOC THINK**
>
> Sometimes we can see something over and over and still not recognize patterns until someone points them out (such as the arrow in the FedEx logo . . . Hint: it's between the E and the x). What might this tell us about the importance of authorities for recognition?

Through interactions with others, we develop and share perceptions of what the world is like and how we should act within it. The shared culture that results provides us with a tool kit of similar habits, skills, and styles (Swidler 1986). For example, when someone says hello, we know how to respond. When we show up for the first day of class, we know where to sit or stand depending on whether we are the student or professor. Culture facilitates social interaction.

Over time, we take shared culture for granted. The ways we think, the rules we follow, the things we have created all seem natural to us. We pass along these expectations to others within the contexts of families, schools, places of worship, and workplaces. As a result, we know what to do, when to do it, and with whom. In so doing, we create society.

©McGraw-Hill Education/ Jill Braaten, photographer

Society consists of the structure of relationships within which culture is created and shared through regularized patterns of social interaction. Society provides the taken-for-granted structure within which we interact. It both enables and constrains the culture we construct. In a given society, some ways of thinking, acting, and making seem inevitable, whereas other ways may not even be conceivable. For example, the way our society organizes government determines our rights and responsibilities, and the way we organize education shapes how and what we learn.

Societies construct cultures in different ways, which results in significant cross-cultural variation. People often confront this reality when they travel abroad and find their taken-for-granted ideas and actions to be out of place and inappropriate. Language, gestures, marriage ceremonies, and religious doctrines vary significantly. In India, parents are accustomed to arranging marriages for their children, but in the United States, parents typically leave such choices up to their children. Lifelong residents of Cairo consider it natural to speak Arabic, whereas most Buenos Aires natives feel the same way about Spanish.

>> Constructing Culture

For humans, culture serves the function that complex instincts do for other animals. As a result, to survive as a species, our first task of culture construction is to produce sufficient food, clothes, and shelter lest we die. Working together makes providing for such needs easier, which necessitates creating culture that makes such cooperation possible. Sociologists explore how we construct and share culture with others so that we might both survive and thrive.

CULTURAL UNIVERSALS

Early sociologists explored the possibility that natural or social forces might limit the culture construction options available to us. For example, as we have already seen, Comte sought to uncover fundamental laws of society equivalent to the laws of nature. Such patterns were referred to as **cultural universals**—common practices and beliefs shared by all societies. Anthropologist George Murdock (1945) compared results from studies of hundreds of cultures and concluded that, although there are common denominators shared by all cultures, how cultures go about addressing each varies significantly. Included among his list of 70 categories were athletic sports, community organization, dancing, division of labor, folklore, funeral rites, housing, incest taboos, marriage, personal names, property rights, religious ritual, sexual restrictions, and trade. The degree of human variation we see in how we organize such activities suggests that we do not have universal laws strictly determining human behavior.

> **Society** The structure of relationships within which culture is created and shared through regularized patterns of social interaction.
>
> **Cultural universal** A common practice or belief shared by all societies.

The debate about the degree to which our behavior is determined harkens back to philosophical questions regarding nature versus nurture. According to the "nature" argument, the genes we inherit determine our outcomes, as if our fates were programmed by computer code over which we have limited

---

SOCTHINK

How does social context influence how we relate to others? If you were asked about how school is going, how might you respond differently at home with your parents compared to in a dorm with friends or at work with colleagues?

Going GLOBAL

Is Success in Life Determined by Forces Outside Our Control?

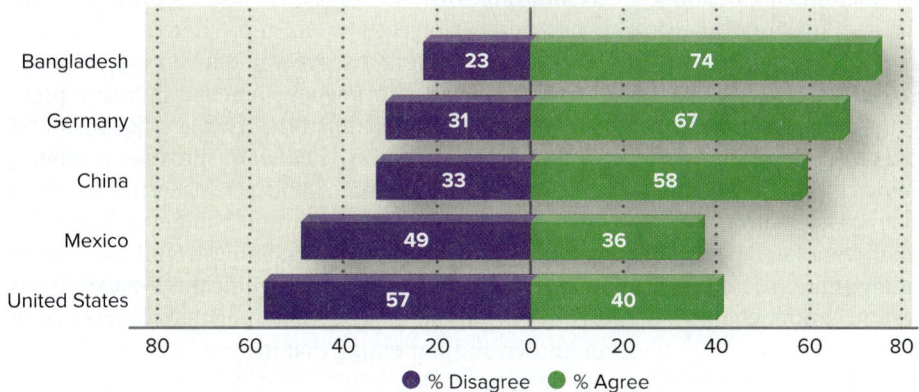

● % Disagree ● % Agree

Source: Pew Research Center 2014a.

As the graph illustrates, perceptions about the degree to which we control our fates vary by country. In a survey of 44 nations, only Venezuelans (62 percent) were more likely than people in the United States to disagree. The global median was 38 percent.

In Guatemala, Tanzania, and around the world, material culture varies across time and place.

Sociobiology The systematic study of how biology affects human social behavior.

Innovation The process of introducing a new idea or object to a culture through discovery or invention.

Discovery The process of revealing a previously unknown aspect of reality.

control. **Sociobiology** is a discipline dedicated to the systematic study of how biology affects human social behavior. On the other side, "nurture" means that our destiny is shaped primarily by the social and psychological influences of others around us (especially parents). From the nurture perspective, human nature is malleable, and we become who we are in the contexts of the societies we create. Sociologists focus primarily on the nurture side.

Sociological research reveals significant cross-cultural and cross-time variation in how we think and act. For example, in the 19th century, experts thought that, biologically speaking, women were not capable of success in college because their brains were too small and their reproductive organs made them too emotional. As a result, they denied women the opportunity to go to college, justifying it as as being in women's best interest. Over time we learned that such presuppositions are false—women now make up almost 60 percent of college graduates—but at one time these assertions were accepted as "natural" and therefore resistant to change. Similar biologically based claims have been used in the past to justify racial, ethnic, and social class inequality (claims that were later revealed to be scientifically untrue), leading many sociologists to question biological explanations for human behavior (Lucal 2010).

Over time, natural scientists have increasingly affirmed that the either-or quality of the nature-nurture argument conceals the fluid nature of the two forces. Within the scientific community, support has grown for gene-culture coevolution, in which each shapes the other through the course of human development. From this perspective, how individuals turn out isn't simply a matter of whether they inherited a set of "bad genes" or "good genes." Instead, researchers argue that an interdependent relationship exists between genes and environment. How genes are expressed (whether or not they are triggered, in other words) can depend on our natural, social, and cultural contexts. From this perspective, genes are responsive to the social context and do not inevitably trigger predetermined responses at predetermined times (Rutter 2010; Rutter, Moffitt, and Caspi 2006; Shenk 2010).

INNOVATION

Because our genes do not narrowly determine our behavior, humans have the freedom and ability to create new things. Whereas a robin's nest in the year 2018 looks very much like one in 1918 or 1018 because robins act on a nest-building instinct, human abodes vary widely. We can live in a cave, a castle, a sod house, a pueblo, a high-rise apartment, a McMansion, or a dorm room. Such variation is possible because we are free to innovate. **Innovation** is the process of introducing a new idea or object to a culture. There are two main forms of innovation: discovery and invention.

A **discovery** occurs when someone reveals a previously unknown aspect of reality. The identification of the DNA molecule and the detection of Proxima b orbiting the nearest star to our Sun, the closest Earth-like planet with the potential capacity to host life ever found, are both acts of discovery. For a claim to count as a discovery, it must be both novel and significant (Woolgar 1988). In other words, it must be something that was previously unknown and something that matters to others. Finding a hole in my sock might be news to everyone, including myself, but it's not particularly important. Attending a Shakespeare play for the first time and being blown away by how amazing it is might matter a lot to me, but it's not exactly a revelation to others. In other words, when deciding whether something counts as a discovery, we should always ask "To whom is this news?" and "How much does it matter to them?" For example, the notion

POPSOC

Comedy often draws inspiration from the sociological imagination. The website College Humor, for example, coined the term "Columbusing" to describe the process of White people taking credit for discovering things others have known about for a long time. In their satirical video, a young, White man claims to have "discovered" a bar, despite the fact that his African American friend has been going there for some time. As an example of Columbusing, some critics have suggested that the recently trendy color runs, in which participants get their shirts splashed with various colors along the running route, have their foundation in Holi, the Hindu spring festival of colors (Agrawal 2013; Salinas 2014).

Photo: ©Chelsea Lauren/Getty Images for S. C. Johnson & Son, Inc.

DIFFUSION

For innovation to succeed, others must recognize and accept the new discovery or invention. Sociologists use the term **diffusion** to refer to the process by which some aspect of culture spreads within and between societies. Historically, diffusion between societies occurred primarily through deliberate cross-cultural contact, often in the form of exploration, war, and missionary work. Today, societal boundaries that were once relatively closed have become more permeable, largely as a result of innovations in transportation and communication. Through the mass media, the Internet, immigration, and tourism, we regularly confront the people, beliefs, practices, and artifacts of other cultures.

> **Invention** The combination of existing materials to create something new.
>
> **Diffusion** The process by which a cultural item spreads within and between societies.

The global expansion of fast food chains provides a classic example of cultural diffusion. McDonald's began with a single restaurant in San Bernadino, California, in that Columbus was the one who "discovered" America would come as a surprise to the people already living there, not to mention the many generations of their ancestors who preceded them.

The second form of innovation, **invention,** combines existing materials to create something new. We are creative beings. We invent new technologies, new theories, new works of art, new ways of doing things, and so much more. The bow and arrow, the automobile, and the iPhone are all examples of inventions, as are abstract concepts such as Protestantism and democracy. Inventors are often portrayed as solitary geniuses who experience "Eureka!" moments of inspiration, but research on technological innovation, for example, reveals just how social the process is. To invent something, we must take into account existing social networks, available resources, possible sponsors, potential consumers, probable critics, and so much more. A great idea or object alone is not enough (Bijker, Hughes, and Pinch, eds. 2012). Neither discovery nor invention should be divorced from the social context within which it arises. Existing culture can both facilitate and impede possible innovation.

Did You Know?

. . . Marc Platt, producer of the Broadway play *Wicked* and numerous movies and TV series, including *Legally Blonde, Into the Woods, The Girl on the Train,* and *Empire Falls,* was a sociology major.

Photo: ©Thomas Kienzle/AP Images

Chapter 3 / Culture • 51

©Business Wire

1940, and now has 14,259 U.S. locations and 22,266 in other nations around the world (McDonald's Corporation 2016). Similarly, Starbucks, with its familiar green logo, was founded in Seattle, Washington, in 1971 but now has 24,464 stores globally. The first Starbucks in mainland China opened in 1999, and by October 2016 China had 2,359 of them. The success of Starbucks in a country where tea has always been the beverage of choice is striking. In fact, for many in China, drinking coffee has now become a status symbol of middle-class success (Christian 2009; Halper 2013; Loxcel Geomatics 2016).

Diffusion often comes at a cost. In practice, globalization has led to the cultural domination of developing nations by more affluent nations. In these encounters, people in developed nations often pick and choose the cultural practices they find intriguing or exotic, whereas people in developing nations often lose their traditional values and begin to identify with the culture of the dominant nations. They may discard or neglect their native language and dress, attempting to imitate the icons of mass-market entertainment and fashion. In this way, Western popular culture represents a threat to native cultures. For example, Walt Disney's critics have called his work "perhaps the primary example of America's cultural imperialism, supplanting the myths of native cultures with his own" (Gabler 2006). So something is gained and something is lost through diffusion, and often it is the poorer societies that sacrifice more of their culture.

>> Three Elements of Culture

The culture we create can be grouped into three general categories: material, cognitive, and normative. Each type enables us to interact more effectively with the world around us. We look at each in turn.

U.S. Wireless Subscriptions

Technology makes it possible for us to keep in touch with almost anyone anywhere, as these numbers showing the explosion in the number of wireless device subscriptions since 1985 demonstrate.
Source: CTIA 2017.

MATERIAL CULTURE

Because we lack complex instincts that determine our behavior, we must establish a relationship to the natural world in order to survive. We do so by creating **material culture,** our physical modification of the natural environment to suit our purposes. Material culture includes the clothes we wear, the books we read, the chairs we sit in, the carpets we walk on, the lights we use, the buildings we live in, the cars we drive, the roads we drive on, and so much more.

Once created, such objects become part of our lives. We lose sight of the fact that we made them, thinking of them as just natural. Take cell phones, for example. As we can see in the accompanying "U.S. Wireless Subscriptions" graph, back in 1985 there were only 340,213 total cell phone subscribers in the United States. By the end of 2016, that number rose to more than 395.9 million, now including 262 million smartphones along with 47.9 million tablets, laptops, and modems (CTIA 2017). There are now more wireless device subscriptions than people in the United States. What was once a luxury item for elites has become something that many of us can't imagine living without.

The most common term we use to refer to material culture is *technology*. **Technology** is a form of material culture in which humans convert natural resources into tools to accomplish practical ends. It includes not only high-tech items such as computers, cars, and cell phones, but low-tech items including clubs, wheels, spoons, and chalk.

Technology enhances our human abilities, giving us powers we often associate with superheroes, including X-ray vision, healing powers, flight, and more. A pivotal moment in the development of such power was the invention of the steam engine during the Industrial Revolution. It provided us with historically unprecedented strength and stamina—the ability to lift and move extremely heavy objects and to do so over sustained periods of time. It made modern coal mining practical, provided manufacturing machinery with the power needed for early factories, and powered early tractors and locomotives, setting the stage for modern global mobility (Rosen 2010).

Advances in technology, especially when it comes to the revolutions in communication and transportation, have linked more individuals in a global network than was ever possible in the past. Cell phones enable us to stay in touch with friends and family from almost anywhere. Planes, trains, and automobiles allow us to travel over long

> **Material culture** Our physical modification of the natural environment to suit our purposes.
>
> **Technology** A form of material culture in which humans convert natural resources into tools to accomplish practical ends.

©sam74100/Getty Images RF

Chapter 3 / Culture • 53

Cultural lag The general principle that technological innovation occurs more quickly than does our capacity to perceive, interpret, and respond to that change.

Cognitive culture Our mental and symbolic representations of reality.

Language A system of shared symbols; it includes speech, written characters, numerals, symbols, and nonverbal gestures and expressions.

distances in almost no time at all, reducing the historic significance of geographic separation and isolation. And laptops and iPads allow us to bring the workplace with us wherever we go.

Our knowledge, beliefs, values, and laws—core elements of cognitive and normative culture described in more detail below—cannot always keep up with the pace at which we invent new things. Sociologist William F. Ogburn (1922) coined the term **cultural lag** to describe the general principle that technological innovation occurs more quickly than does our capacity to perceive, interpret, and respond to that change. For example, the nine-month school calendar was designed with an agricultural economy in mind so that children would be home to help families in the fields during the summer months. Even though only a small percentage of jobs remain agricultural, most schools still adopt it. Another example is that global climate change has become a pressing concern. Scientists overwhelmingly point to the role carbon dioxide plays, yet we find it difficult to make the kinds of lifestyle changes that might be called for, such as driving smaller cars, using more public transportation, or reducing consumption.

POPSOC

Culture, Technology, and Superheroes

Some superheroes (Superman and the X-Men) are born that way, but others gain their powers the old-fashioned way: they invent them. Characters such as Ironman and Batman appeal to us in part because they rely on human innovation for their strength and stamina. Technology makes them faster than a speeding bullet or more powerful than a locomotive. What other seemingly superhuman powers does technology provide us?

Photo: ©Paramount/Courtesy Everett Collection

? Did You Know?

... The United States Patent and Trademark Office issued 298,407 patents in 2015 and has approved more than 9.2 million since the United States began issuing patents in 1790.

COGNITIVE CULTURE

The second component of culture, **cognitive culture**, consists of our mental and symbolic representations of reality. It is the part of culture that includes values, beliefs, knowledge, and all other representations constructed to make sense of the world around us. Its most basic component, and perhaps the most important human cultural creation and the one upon which all others depend, is language.

Language The building block of all communication and cooperation, **language** is a system of shared symbols; it includes speech, written characters, numerals, symbols, and nonverbal gestures and expressions. It provides the foundation of a common culture because it facilitates day-to-day exchanges with others, making collective action possible. According to Ethnologue, a database of all known languages around the world, 7,097 living languages exist today. Of these, 1,524 (21 percent) are classified as "in trouble," and 920 (13 percent) are "dying." There are 352 languages with fewer than 10 speakers, and 360 languages have become extinct since 1950 (Lewis, Simons, and Fennig 2016).

Language is fundamentally social in nature. Together we agree that certain sounds or shapes mean certain things, and then we act based on those shared meanings. What matters most is our shared perception rather than the actual sound or image we use. We could, for example, teach a dog the wrong meanings of commands (*fetch* means stay, *roll over* means shake, and so on). The dog would never know the difference, but we would laugh because its responses would clash with our expectations. When we start to learn a new language, we are at the mercy of those who teach us. We rely on their authority, and the only way to test our fluency is through interactions with other speakers.

Because language is socially constructed, it is open to change. We create new words and modify existing ones to suit our needs—especially in our modern global culture where innovation seems never-ending. Dictionaries are regularly modified in an effort to keep up. In 2016, the *Merriam-Webster Collegiate Dictionary* added more than 2,000 new words and phrases, including *dox, FOMO, hella, meet-cute, nomophobia,* and *trigger warning* (Steinmetz 2016). At the other end of the spectrum, words also disappear over time. The six-volume *Dictionary of American Regional English* documents

Going GLOBAL

Distribution of the World's Living Languages by Region of Origin

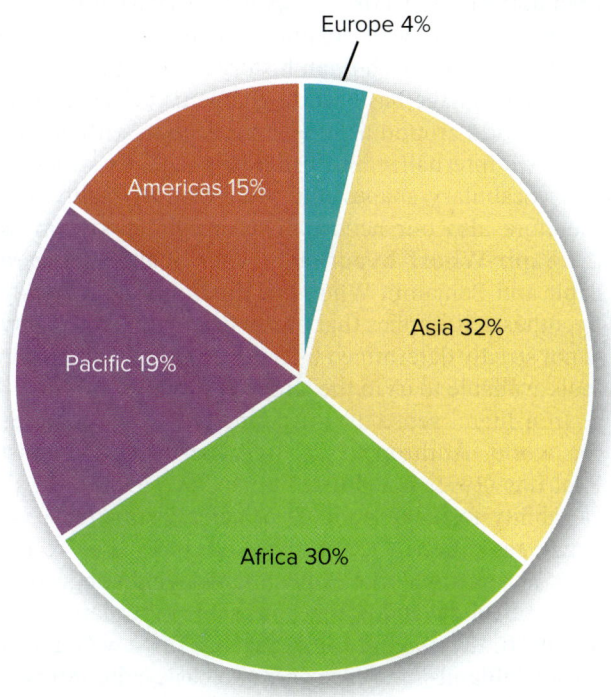

Note: A total of 7,097 languages are represented.
Source: Lewis, Simons, and Fennig 2016.

Of the 7,097 living languages around the world today, 2,139 originated in Africa. Even though 30 percent of current languages come from Africa, only 13 percent of the world's speakers use those languages as their first language. European-based languages claim 26 percent of the world's speakers, despite the fact that only 4 percent of the world's total languages originated there. This difference is due primarily to the global spread of English and Spanish (Lewis, Simons, and Fennig 2016).

---

words with meanings that seldom extend beyond their local U.S. context. Among many possible candidates are 50 words and phrases in danger of extinction, including *bonnyclabber, fleech, frog strangler, popskull,* and *winkle-hawk* (Lafrance 2016).

Some linguists, including amateurs, have seized on the socially constructed nature of language in hopes of creating whole new languages from scratch, with varying motivations (Okrent 2009; Peterson 2015). Some, inspired by the scientific revolution, were appalled by the inefficiencies and irregularities of existing languages. They invented new languages in the 17th and 18th centuries (such as Francis Lodwick's *Common Writing* or John Wilkins's *Philosophical Language*) in hopes of providing

Personal Sociology

Inventing New Words

I was reminded of our ability to create new words while on a family hiking trip in Oregon. Eleanor, who was four at the time, was riding on my shoulders along the trail while her sister, Emily, and my wife, Lori, were falling behind. Eleanor turned and yelled as loud as she could, "Stop chickenjagging!" We knew immediately what she meant and have used this word ever since. Anyone can create words, but they become meaningful only when they are shared with others. For Eleanor's new word to become part of the common language, the chickenjagging network must extend beyond our immediate family into the wider world. Have you ever done something similar with friends or family?

---

us with a logical system of communication in which the relationships between concepts were rational and everything fit together into a coherent whole. They didn't want words to be arbitrary sounds we attach to things, hoping instead to map the essence of things through language. Even though they succeeded in creating coherent systems, the languages they created were difficult to use and failed to attract widespread acceptance.

During the 20th century, other language inventors, driven in part by a desire to come to terms with globalization and increased contact across cultures, created international auxiliary languages that combined various aspects of existing languages. Their goal was to construct a relatively easy-to-learn, universally accepted language that would transcend national and ethnic differences. Rather than focus on purity of representation, such inventors emphasized pragmatic communication (Okrent 2009; Peterson 2015). The most successful language of this type was Esperanto, which continues to be used today. It was originally created by Ludwik Zamenhof in 1887 and literally means "one who hopes." It was Zamenhof's hope that his hybrid language would not only facilitate international commerce and communication but also contribute to world peace by reducing the cultural differences that separate us.

In spite of the relative success of Esperanto, none of these invented languages has achieved widespread adoption. Part of what such attempts seem to miss is that language is a community endeavor built up over generations of shared experiences that lead to common understandings of how the world works. Though it is technically possible to create a language from scratch, doing so undercuts the importance that such experiences have in shaping who we are. As linguist Arika Okrent put it in her history of invented languages, "[Languages] are the repositories of our very identities. . . . [Esperanto, along with other invented languages,] asks us to turn away from what makes our languages personal and unique and choose one that is generic and universal. It asks us to give up what distinguishes us from the rest of the world for something that makes everyone in the world the same" (Okrent 2009:112). To the extent that Esperanto has succeeded, it has done so by creating a community of shared participants who are committed to keeping the language alive.

Sapir-Whorf hypothesis The structure and vocabulary of language shapes our perception of reality and therefore also our actions.

A more recent wave of constructed languages comes mostly from hobbyists, known as "conlangers," who view the construction of a complete, functioning language as a challenge. The inspiration for these attempts often traces back to J. R. R. Tolkien's creation of Elvish for the *Lord of the Rings* book trilogy. Tolkien was a philologist—one who studies the history, structure, and criticism of language—and he used this knowledge to ensure that his constructed languages followed common linguistic patterns and practices. Due to the level of technical detail required, many recent conlangers are often similarly trained, such as Marc Okrand who created Klingon for the *Star Trek* movie franchise (see www.kli.org) and Paul Frommer who created the Na'vi language used in the film *Avatar* (see www.LearnNavi.org).

Even though it is possible to construct languages for fun, throughout human history the most basic purpose of language has been to enable us to make sense of the world around us in communication with others. After we internalize and use a language, its structure and vocabulary shapes our perception of reality and therefore also our actions. This insight is known as the **Sapir-Whorf hypothesis** (after linguists Edward Sapir and Benjamin Whorf) or the linguistic relativity hypothesis. It implies that our understanding of reality is not strictly determined by nature, but more so by the tools available to us in the languages we use.

In a literal sense, language may color how we see the world. Anthropologist Brent Berlin and linguist Paul Kay (1991) noted that humans possess the physical ability to make millions of color distinctions, yet languages differ in the number of colors they recognize. For example, the English language distinguishes between yellow and orange, but some other languages do not. In the Dugum Dani language of New Guinea's West Highlands, there are only two basic color terms—*modla* for "white" and *mili* for "black" (Roberson, Davies, and Davidoff 2000; Wierzbicka 2008).

In Japan, what people in the United States would call a green light is often called a blue light, even though it is the same color there as it is here. This practice derives from an earlier time in Japan when there was only one word, *ao* (青), to describe both green and blue (Backhaus 2013). The more recent practice of making a clear distinction between the two colors in Japan has been tied to the importation of crayons into Japan starting in 1917, which distinguished between *midori* (緑) for green and *ao* for blue. The Allied occupation of Japan after World War II reinforced this distinction in educational materials distributed throughout the country (Bhatia 2012). And yet remnants of the earlier linguistic pattern remain in the form not only of "blue" traffic lights, but also of "blue" vegetables, "blue" apples, and "blue" leaves.

Feminists have noted that gender-related language can reinforce the stereotype that some jobs are more appropriate for men than women. Each time we use a term such as *mailman, policeman,* or *fireman,* we are implying (especially to young children) that these occupations can be filled only by males. Yet many women work as *letter carriers, police officers,* and *firefighters*—a fact that has been legitimized through the increased use of such nonsexist language (Eckert and McConnell-Ginet 2003; McConnell-Ginet 2011).

Linguist Suzette Haden Elgin went so far as to invent a new language that gives voice to women's experience

POPSOC

The Dothraki language used in the HBO series *Game of Thrones* was created by linguist David J. Peterson, one of the founders of the Language Creation Society. Using just a handful of words and names coined by George R. R. Martin, the author of the book series the show is based on, Peterson built a complete language system (including grammar, syntax, and vocabulary). According to the Social Security Administration, in 2015, 341 parents named their daughters Khaleesi, the Dothraki word for "queen." An introduction to the language is available at www.livinglanguage.com/dothraki. Athchomarchomakann!

Photo: ©HBO/courtesy Everett Collection

(Elgin 1984). She argued that "existing human languages are inadequate to express the perceptions of women," which leads to inadequate perception of critical issues in the lives of women (Elgin 1988). Drawing on her expertise in the Navajo language (*Diné bizaad*), she created Láadan as a test of the Sapir-Whorf hypothesis. She argued that using Láadan would open up new dimensions of reality that are not easily accessible using such languages as English. Láadan lessons for beginners are available at www.LáadanLanguage.org.

> **SOC**THINK
>
> What are some slang terms we use to refer to men and to women? What images do such terms convey for what it means to be male or female?

Language can also transmit stereotypes related to race. Look up the meanings of the adjective *black* in dictionaries published in the United States, and you will find "dismal, gloomy or forbidding, destitute of moral light or goodness, atrocious, evil, threatening, clouded with anger." By contrast, dictionaries list "pure" and "innocent" among the meanings of the adjective *white*. Through such patterns of language, our culture reinforces positive associations with the term (and skin color) *white* and negative associations with *black*. Is it surprising, then, that a list meant to prevent people from working in a profession is called a "blacklist," and a fib that we think of as somewhat acceptable is called a "white lie"? Such examples demonstrate that language can shape how we see, taste, smell, feel, and hear (Henderson 2003; Moore 1976; Reitman 2006).

Of course, we communicate using more than just words. If you do not like the way a meeting is going, you might suddenly sit back, fold your arms, and turn down the corners of your mouth. When you see a friend in tears, you may give her a quick hug. After winning a big game, you may high-five your teammates. These are all examples of **nonverbal communication**—the use of gestures, facial expressions, and other visual images to communicate. We are not born with these expressions. We learn them, just as we learn other forms of language, from people who share our culture. We learn how to show—and to recognize—happiness, sadness, pleasure, shame, distress, and other emotional states (Burgoon, Guerrero, and Floyd 2010).

Like other forms of language, nonverbal communication is not the same in all cultures. For example, people from various cultures differ in the degree to which they touch others during the course of normal social interactions. Even experienced travelers are sometimes caught off guard by these differences. In Saudi Arabia a middle-aged man may want to hold hands with a male partner after closing a business deal. The gesture, which would surprise most Americans, is considered a compliment in that culture. The meaning of hand signals is another form of nonverbal communication that can differ from one culture to the next. For instance, in both Australia and Iraq, the thumbs-up sign is considered rude (Koerner 2003; Lefevre 2011).

> **Nonverbal communication** The use of gestures, facial expressions, and other visual images to communicate.
>
> **Value** A collective conception of what is considered good, desirable, and proper—or bad, undesirable, and improper—in a culture.

Values In addition to creating a shared language as part of our cognitive culture, we also jointly agree that some principles are at the core of who we are and what we believe. **Values** are the collective conceptions of what is considered good, desirable, and proper—or bad, undesirable, and improper—in a culture. They are typically expressed as general principles that then shape what we see as appropriate actions. Examples include family, love, opportunity, community, and freedom. Even individualism represents a collective value. As American essayist Richard Rodriguez points out, "American individualism is a communally derived value, not truly an expression of individuality. The teenager persists in rebelling against her parents, against tradition or custom, because she is shielded . . . by American culture from the knowledge that she inherited her rebellion from dead

©Echo/Getty Images RF

In Arab cultures, men sometimes hold hands as a sign of affection and friendship. ©dbimages/Alamy Stock Photo

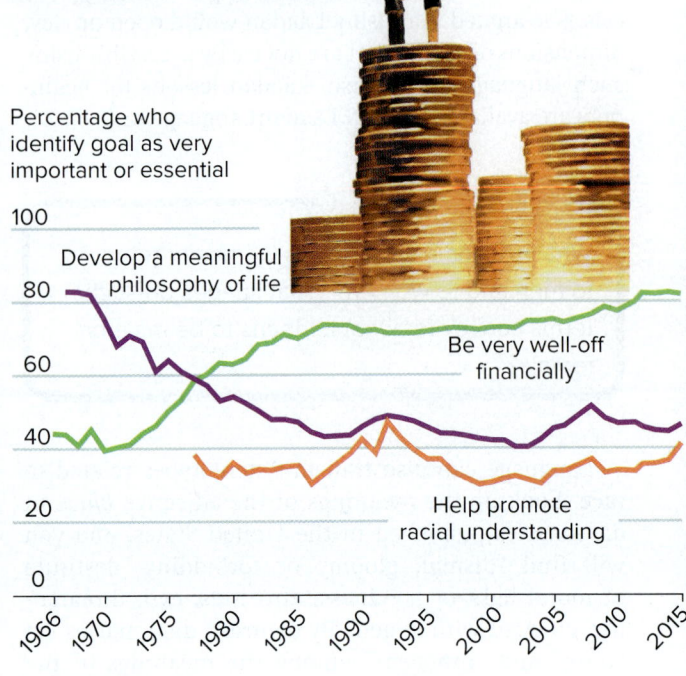

Life Goals of First-Year College Students in the United States

Source: Eagan et al. 2016. *Photo:* ©Carson Ganci/Design Pics

ancestors and living parents" (2002:130). Of course, all members of a society do not uniformly agree on its values. Angry political debates and billboards promoting conflicting causes tell us that much.

The values of a culture may change, but most remain relatively stable during any one person's lifetime. Socially shared, intensely felt values are a fundamental part of our lives in the United States. Sociologist Robin Williams (1970) offered a list of U.S. basic values. These include freedom, equality, democracy, morality, conformity, progress, humanitarianism, and material comfort. Obviously, not all 320 million people in the United States agree on all these values, but such a list serves as a starting point in defining America's national character.

Each year more than 140,000 first-year college students at approximately 200 of the nation's four-year colleges fill out a questionnaire asking them which values are most important to them. Because of its coverage, content, and scope, this survey provides a kind of barometer of the nation's values. The top value of the first-year class of 1966, the year the survey was first conducted, was "developing a meaningful philosophy of life," with 80 percent of the new students identifying it as either essential or very important. By contrast, only 44 percent chose "being very well-off financially." Since that time, the relative position of these two values has flipped, as the accompanying "Life Goals" graph demonstrates. Among the first-year class of 2015, for example, 81.9 percent identified "being very well-off financially" as a significant value compared to 46.5 percent who selected "developing a meaningful

SOC THINK

Consider Williams's list of basic values. Do you think most people value these things? How might some values, such as freedom and conformity, conflict? How do we resolve such conflicts?

©Ballyscanion/Getty Images RF

philosophy of life" (Eagan, Stolzenberg, Bates, Aragon, Suchard, and Rios-Aguilar 2016).

Researchers have also studied other family and community values among first-year students. The second-highest-rated value identified by the 2015 class was "helping others who are in difficulty," at 75 percent, although only 31 percent selected "participating in a community action program" as either essential or important. "Raising a family" came in third at 72 percent. This percentage has remained largely unchanged for 50 years. The proportion that identified "helping to promote racial understanding" rose over the previous year to 41 percent (Eagan et al. 2016). As these numbers demonstrate, a nation's values can fluctuate over time.

Because it challenges honesty as a shared value, cheating is a significant concern on college campuses. Professors who take advantage of computerized services that can identify plagiarism, such as the search engine Google or TurnItIn.com, have found that many of the papers their students hand in are plagiarized, in whole or in part. When high school students were asked about academic honesty, 32 percent admitted to copying an Internet document for a classroom assignment, 51 percent said they'd cheated during a test at school, and 74 percent had copied someone's homework, all within the past year. At the same time, 86 percent agreed that "it's not worth it to lie or cheat because it hurts your character" (Josephson Institute of Ethics 2012). Perhaps cheating has become a normal part of student culture even if it is at odds with dominant school values.

NORMATIVE CULTURE

Whereas cognitive culture highlights what we think or believe, normative culture, the third element of culture, focuses on how we act. **Normative culture** consists of the ways we establish, abide by, and enforce principles of conduct. In our everyday lives, we typically abide by **norms**—the established standards of behavior maintained by a society—both big and small, from "Thou shalt not kill" to "Chew with your mouth closed." For a norm to become significant, people must widely recognize and obey it. Most of the time, we follow norms without thinking much about them. Their power derives from our adherence.

Normative culture Consists of the ways we establish, abide by, and enforce principles of conduct.

Norm An established standard of behavior maintained by a society.

Mores Norms deemed highly necessary to the welfare of a society.

Folkways Norms governing everyday behavior, whose violation raises comparatively little concern.

Formal norm A norm that generally has been written down and that specifies strict punishments for violators.

Laws Formal norms enforced by the state.

Types of Norms Sociologists classify norms into three primary categories: mores versus folkways, formal versus informal, and ideal versus real. In practice, each pair represents a continuum along which particular norms fall. First, norms are grouped by their *centrality* to society. **Mores** (pronounced "MOR-ays") are norms deemed highly necessary to the welfare of a society, often because they embody core values. Each society demands strict obedience to its mores; violation can lead to significant penalties. Thus, the United States has strong mores against murder, treason, and child abuse, and punishes each severely. **Folkways** are norms governing everyday behavior. When we are polite—saying please and thank you, not cutting in line, and so on—we are following folkways. Such norms are less rigid in their application, and their violation raises comparatively little concern. Fashion usually represents a folkway. We have some freedom in what we choose to wear. But choosing not to wear clothes, except in clearly defined situations, violates a more.

Norms are also classified based on levels of *formality*. **Formal norms** generally have been written down and specify strict punishments for violators. In the United States we often formalize norms into **laws,** which are formal norms enforced by the state. But laws are just one example of

Movies on U.S. CULTURE

Revolutionary Road
A look at the social isolation and gender roles of 1950s America.

The Invention of Lying
What would society be like if we never told a lie?

Dawn of the Planet of the Apes
When human culture collapses and intelligent apes arise.

Brooklyn
In 1950s America, a young, Irish immigrant woman is torn between two worlds.

Good Hair
Chris Rock's documentary about the culture of hair in the African American community.

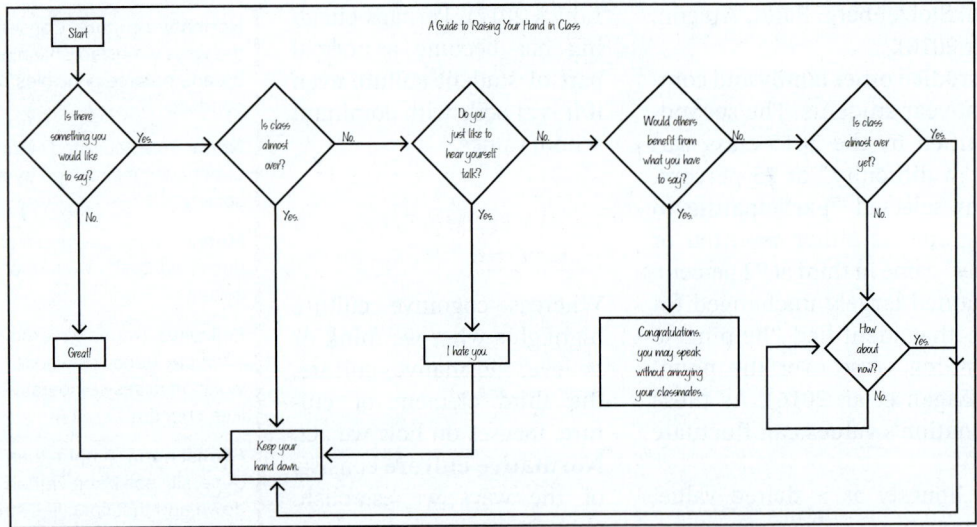

Informal norms are often unspoken and taken for granted, yet we rely on learned principles to decide how we (and we hope others) should proceed, as this cartoon humorously demonstrates.

Informal norm A norm that is generally understood but not precisely recorded.

Ideal norms Guidelines for behavior that people agree should be followed.

Real norms Rules of conduct generated from people's actual behavior.

formal norms. Any systematized set of guidelines, such as the requirements for a college major set forth in a college catalog or the rules of a card game are also considered formal norms. By contrast, **informal norms** are generally understood but not precisely recorded. We follow largely unspoken rules for all kinds of everyday interactions, such as how to ride on an elevator, how to pass someone on a sidewalk, and how to behave in a college classroom. Knowledge of such norms is often taken for granted.

The third category of norms relates to expected *adherence*. **Ideal norms** are those guidelines for behavior that people agree should be followed. **Real norms** are rules of conduct generated from people's actual behavior. Ideal norms reflect what we collectively say *ought* to be, and real norms reflect what actually *is*. Speeding provides a classic example of the contrast between the two. The posted speed limit reflects the ideal norm, but the truth is that most people exceed that limit regularly, which is a reflection of the real norm. In a bid to show the difference between the two, students, for their film festival entry, *55: A Meditation on the Speed Limit,* stuck to the speed limit while driving side-by-side on the freeway, and blocked traffic for miles with nearly disastrous results. They referred to it as "an extraordinary act of public obedience" (Five Year Plan 2006).

Breaking Norms

Although norms provide us with guidelines on how to act, we can choose not to abide by them. Sometimes we violate a norm because we face a choice between conflicting ones. For example, suppose you live in an apartment building and one night hear the screams of the woman next door, who is being beaten by her husband. If you decide to intervene by knocking on your neighbors' door or calling the police, you are violating the norm of minding your own business while at the same time following the norm of assisting a victim of domestic violence.

Sometimes we violate a norm because we belong to different societal subgroups that have clashing norms. For example, teenage drinkers may rebel against parental norms by conforming to the standards of their peer group. Similarly, business executives may reject the norms they learned in their graduate school training and choose shady accounting techniques in response to a corporate culture that demands the maximization of profits at any cost, including the deception of investors and government regulatory agencies.

Even if norms do not conflict, there are exceptions to any norm. The same action, under different circumstances, can cause one to be viewed as either a hero or a villain. For instance, secretly taping telephone conversations is normally considered not just intrusive but illegal. However, it can be done with a court order to obtain valid evidence for a criminal trial. We would heap praise on a government agent who used such methods to convict an organized crime figure. In our culture we tolerate killing another human being in self-defense, and we actually reward killing in warfare, as was evident in the celebrations that followed the death of Osama bin Laden.

Changing circumstances, such as major historical events, can also require the sudden violation of long-standing cultural norms. In Iraq, where Muslim custom strictly forbids touching by strangers for men

> **SOCTHINK**
>
> Improv Everywhere's No Pants Subway Ride calls people to do something outside their comfort zone. What factors might influence someone's decision to participate? What would it take to get you to participate?

and especially for women, the war that began in 2003 brought numerous daily violations of the norm. Outside mosques, government offices, and other facilities likely to be targeted by terrorists, visitors had to be patted down and have their bags searched by Iraqi security forces. To reduce the discomfort caused by the procedure, women were searched by female guards and men by male guards. Despite that concession, and the fact that many Iraqis admit to or even insist on the need for such measures, people still wince at the invasion of their personal privacy. In reaction to the searches, Iraqi women began to limit the contents of the bags they carry or simply to leave them at home (Rubin 2003).

Violating norms can also serve as a foundation for social change. Until the 1960s, for example, formal norms throughout much of the United States prohibited the marriage of people from different racial groups. Same-sex marriage wasn't a formally recognized right until a 2014 Supreme Court decision. Many people who initially challenged both were scorned and ridiculed.

> The past is never dead.
> It's not even past.
>
> William Faulkner

Yet if it wasn't for trailblazing norm-breakers who fought to legitimize an alternative set of norms, neither would likely have changed.

Sanctions When we violate a norm, we can usually expect a response designed to bring our behavior back into line. **Sanctions** are penalties and rewards for conduct concerning a social norm. They include both negative and positive responses to behavior; their purpose is to influence future behavior. Examples of positive sanctions include a pay raise for strong performance, a medal for winning a race, a word of gratitude for a kind deed, or a pat on the back for a job well done. Negative sanctions include fines for overdue library books, imprisonment for a crime, and stares of contempt for texting in a movie theater. Sanctions are a means of enforcing the order the norms provide. Most of the time we do not even need the external enforcement others provide to sanction our acts. Having internalized society's norms, we police

> **Sanction** A penalty or reward for conduct concerning a social norm.

Break-a-Norm Day

- Wearing formal clothes in an informal setting
- Eating with the wrong utensil or none at all
- Responding to friends or family the same as to a boss or teacher
- Having long gaps in speech when talking with someone
- Standing just a little too close to or far from someone when talking with him or her
- Facing the back of an elevator instead of getting in and turning around

Norms provide us with rules that guide our everyday behavior. All we need to do is step outside the lines even a little bit to see the influence they have over our lives. These are some examples of how people violate norms. How would you feel about violating any of these norms? How might others respond to you? Photos: (dress):—©gsermek/Getty Images RF; (jeans):—©C Squared Studios/Getty Images RF.

Agricultural strikes and boycotts in the 1960s and 1970s alerted the nation to the harsh economic plight of migrant workers.
©Rob Crandall/The Image Works

5 Movies on CULTURES OUTSIDE THE U.S.

Leviathan
A Russian man struggles for justice against an oppressive system.

Embrace of the Serpent
Worlds collide when an Amazonian shaman, the last of his tribe, encounters two scientists.

Caramel
A comedy following the lives of five women working in a Beirut beauty salon.

Persepolis
An animated coming-of-age film set during the Iranian Revolution.

Departures
An unemployed man violates Japanese norms by becoming an undertaker.

ourselves internally, using techniques such as guilt or self-satisfaction to regulate our behavior.

Every moment of our lives we face a decision. We can do what is expected, or we can set out on a different path. As social scientist Gustave Le Bon claimed, in 1895, "Civilization is impossible without traditions, and progress impossible without the destruction of those traditions. The difficulty, and it is an immense difficulty, is to find a proper equilibrium between stability and variability." Following norms provides the order we need, yet also results in a perpetuation of the status quo. Violating norms can lead to positive social change, but it also results in social disruption. And choosing to disrupt will likely result in negative sanctions. In a world of norms, we constantly face this tension: to obey or not to obey.

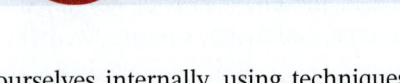

Subculture A segment of society that shares a distinctive pattern of mores, folkways, and values that differs from the pattern of the larger society.

Argot Specialized language used by members of a group or subculture.

>> Cultural Variation

Together the elements of culture provide us with social coherence and order. But culture also varies across time and place. Individuals' sense of right and wrong works well for them so long as they stay within their usual social confines, but encounters with others beyond that realm can reveal the limits of their conception of reality. Moreover, some people have more power to impose their culture on others, which highlights the importance of understanding the contexts within which culture is created and shared.

ASPECTS OF CULTURAL VARIATION

To more fully understand cultural variation, sociologists pay particular attention to differences that exist both within and between societies. Inuit tribes in northern Canada, clad in furs and dieting on whale blubber, have little in common with farmers in Southeast Asia, who dress for the heat and subsist mainly on the rice they grow in their paddies. Cultures adapt to meet specific sets of circumstances, such as climate, level of technology, population, and geography. This adaptation to different conditions shows up in differences in all elements of culture, including language, values, norms, and sanctions.

Subcultures Variation can exist within a culture. A **subculture** is a segment of society that shares a distinctive pattern of mores, folkways, and values that differs from the pattern of the larger society. Rodeo riders, residents of a retirement community, workers on an offshore oil rig—all are examples of what sociologists refer to as subcultures. The existence of many subcultures is characteristic of complex societies such as the United States.

SOCTHINK

What subcultures are common on college and university campuses? What indicators make them recognizable? Why might such subcultures be more likely to form there?

Members of a subculture participate in the dominant culture while engaging in unique and distinctive forms of behavior. Frequently, a subculture will develop its own slang, known as **argot**—specialized language that distinguishes it from the wider society. Such argot allows insiders—the members of the subculture—to understand words with special meanings, which sets them apart from outsiders. In so doing, it clarifies the boundary between "us" and "them" and reinforces a shared identity. We see something like this in the taken-for-granted words and acronyms in the text messaging and social media world. There, abbreviations come fast and furious, from the well known, such as *lol* (laughing out loud), *smh* (shaking my head), *tbt* (throwback Thursday), and *143* (I love you), to the more obscure, such as *1337* (meaning "elite" and referring to symbolic language, or "leet-speak") or *pwned* (leet term meaning "defeated").

Subculture Slang

Anime and Manga Fans

chibi eyes: the characteristic, big childlike eyes used in anime

majoko: a girl anime character with magical powers who must save the world

Con Artists & Scammers

grifter: a person who steals through deception

phishing: seeking personal information by sending out emails that appear to be from legitimate companies

Graffiti Writers

bite: to copy another graffiti writer's work

burner: a stylistically impressive, brilliantly colored piece of graffiti, usually written in a complex pattern of interlocking letters and other visual elements

toy: an inexperienced or unskilled graffiti writer

kill: to saturate an area with one's graffiti

Bikers (Motorcyclists)

brain bucket: a helmet

ink slinger: a tattoo artist

pucker factor: the degree of panic felt during a near-accident

yard shark: a dog that races out to attack passing motorcyclists

Skateboarders

deck: a skateboard platform

face plant: a face-first crash

sketchy: in reference to a trick, poorly done

Subcultures often produce their own unique jargon. The words may be appropriate in those subcultures, but they draw a line between insiders and the rest of us.
Source: Reid 2006. Photo: ©Photodisc/Getty Images RF

In India a subculture developed among employees at the international call centers established by multinational corporations. To serve customers in the United States and Europe, the young men and women who work there must be fluent speakers of English. But the corporations that employ them demand more than proficiency in a foreign language; they expect their Indian employees to adopt Western values and work habits, including the grueling pace that U.S. workers take for granted. In return, the corporations offer perks such as Western-style dinners and dances and coveted consumer goods. Ironically, they allow employees to take the day off only on such American holidays as Labor Day and Thanksgiving—not on Indian holidays such as Diwali, the Hindu festival of lights. While most Indian families are home celebrating, call center employees see mostly one another. When they have the day off, no one else is free to socialize with them. As a result, these employees have formed a tight-knit subculture based on hard work and a taste for Western luxury goods and leisure-time pursuits. Increasingly, they are the object of criticism from Indians who live a more conventional Indian lifestyle centered on family and holiday traditions (Kalita 2006).

Countercultures Sometimes a subculture can develop that seeks to set itself up as an alternative to the dominant culture. When a subculture conspicuously and deliberately opposes certain aspects of the larger culture, it is known as a **counterculture**. Countercultures typically thrive among the young, who have the least investment in the existing culture.

The 1960s, now often characterized by the phrase "sex and drugs and rock 'n' roll," provide a classic case of an extensive counterculture. Largely composed of young people, members of this counterculture were turned off by a society they believed was too materialistic and technological. It included many political radicals and "hippies" who had "dropped out" of mainstream social institutions, but its membership was extensive and diverse. The young people expressed in their writings, speeches, and songs their visions, hopes, and dreams for a new society. As was reflected in the 1966 life goals survey of first-year college students, these young women and men rejected the pressure to accumulate more expensive cars, larger homes, and an endless array of material goods. Instead, they expressed a desire to live in a culture based on more humanistic values, such as sharing, love, and coexistence with the environment. As a political force, they worked for peace—opposing U.S. involvement in the war in Vietnam and encouraging draft resistance—as well as racial and gender equality (T. Anderson 2007; Gitlin 1993).

> **Counterculture** A subculture that deliberately opposes certain aspects of the larger culture.

In the wake of the attacks of September 11, 2001, people around the United States learned of the existence of terrorist groups operating as a counterculture within their own country. Many nations have had to deal with internal counterculture groups—often rooted in long-standing national, ethnic, or political differences—whose members strongly disagree with the values and norms of the dominant culture. In most cases this does not result in violence, but in some cases, as in Northern Ireland, Israel, and France, groups have used attacks, including suicide

©Marvy! Advertising Photography

bombings, to make a statement, both symbolic and real, seeking to bring attention to their situation and an end to their repression (Juergensmeyer 2003). Terrorist cells are not necessarily fueled only by outsiders. Frequently, people become disenchanted with the policies of their own country, and a few take very violent steps (Juergensmeyer 2003).

Culture Shock Today we are more and more likely to come into contact with and even immerse ourselves in cultures unlike our own. For example, students increasingly study abroad. Even those who go through predeparture orientation sessions often have a difficult time adjusting once they arrive in-country because so many of the little things that they took for granted, things they barely noticed before, no longer apply. Anyone who feels disoriented, uncertain, out of place, or even fearful when encountering unfamiliar cultural practices may be experiencing **culture shock.** For example, a resident of the United States who visits certain areas in Cambodia and wants meat for dinner may be stunned to learn that a local specialty is rat meat. Similarly, someone from a strict Islamic culture may be shocked upon first seeing the comparatively provocative dress styles and open displays of affection that are common in the United States and other Western cultures.

Interestingly, after students who study abroad return home, they may experience a kind of reverse culture shock. Their time away has changed them, often in ways they were unaware of, and they find that they cannot so easily slip back into the old routines that those who remained at home expect of them. Culture shock reveals to us both the power and the taken-for-granted nature of culture. The rules we follow are so ingrained that we barely notice that we were following them until they are no longer there to provide the structure and order we assume as a given.

DOMINANT IDEOLOGY

When it comes to gaining cultural acceptance, a group's relative power can determine to what extent it will succeed. One way culture maintains the privileges of certain groups is through the establishment of a **dominant ideology**—the set of cultural beliefs and practices that legitimates existing powerful social, economic, and political interests. The dominant ideology, which is part of cognitive culture, helps explain and justify who gets what and why in a way that justifies and maintains the status quo. Dominant ideas

Culture shock The feelings of disorientation, uncertainty, and even fear that people experience when they encounter unfamiliar cultural practices.

Dominant ideology A set of cultural beliefs and practices that legitimates existing powerful social, economic, and political interests.

©Gavin Heller/Getty Images

©George Rinhart/Contributor/Getty Images

can even squelch alternative expressions of what might be, casting such alternatives as threats to the existing order. Karl Marx argued that the dominant ideas in society maintain the interests of the ruling class. This idea was picked up and developed by sociologists Georg Lukács (1923) and Antonio Gramsci (1929), who argued that the dominant ideology can be used as an instrument of power.

A society's most powerful groups and institutions control wealth and property. They can use their control over these resources to influence religion, education, and the media, thus providing support for the dominant ideology. Feminists argue that if all of society's most important institutions send the message that women should be subservient to men, this dominant ideology helps control and subordinate women. Images of boys and girls in toy ads typically reinforce gender stereotypes, with girls playing with pink and pastel kitchen toys while boys play with pretend power tools and video games. Similarly, women seen in magazine ads reinforce unrealistic (and usually Photoshopped) images of feminine beauty that affect how women see themselves and how men see and treat women.

ATTITUDES TOWARD CULTURAL VARIATION

Ethnocentrism Living in the modern world, especially as a result of the revolutions in transportation and communication, makes it far more likely that we will encounter people from a whole range of cultural backgrounds than we did in the past. As a result, we are also more likely to struggle with what we think about the beliefs, values, and practices of others. When we hear people talking about "our" culture versus "their" culture, we are often confronted with statements that reflect the attitude that "our" culture is best. Terms such as *underdeveloped, backward,* and *primitive* may be used to refer to other societies. What "we" believe is a religion; what "they" believe is superstition and mythology.

It is tempting to evaluate the practices of other cultures on the basis of our own perspectives. Sociologist William Graham Sumner (1906) coined the term **ethnocentrism** to refer to the tendency to assume that one's own culture and way of life represent what's normal or is superior to all others. The ethnocentric person sees his or her own group as the center or defining point of culture and views all other cultures as deviations from what is "normal." Thus, Westerners who see cattle as a food source might look down on the Hindu religion and culture, which view the cow as sacred. People in one culture may dismiss as unthinkable the mate selection or child-rearing practices of another culture.

> **Ethnocentrism** The tendency to assume that one's own culture and way of life represent what's normal or is superior to all others.

Ethnocentric value judgments complicated U.S. efforts at democratic reform of the Iraqi government. Before the 2003 war in Iraq, U.S. planners had assumed that Iraqis would adapt to a new form of government in the same way the Germans and Japanese did following World War II. But in the Iraqi culture, unlike the German and Japanese cultures, loyalty to the family and the extended clan comes before patriotism and the common good. In a country in which almost half of all people, even those in the cities, marry a first or second cousin, citizens are predisposed to favor their own kin in government and business dealings. Why trust a stranger from outside the family? What Westerners would criticize as nepotism, then, is actually an acceptable, even admirable, practice to Iraqis (J. Tierney 2003).

One of the reasons ethnocentrism develops is that it contributes to a sense of solidarity by promoting group pride. Denigrating other nations and cultures can enhance our own patriotic feelings and belief in our way of life. Yet this type of social stability is established at the expense of other peoples. One of the negative consequences of ethnocentric value judgments is that they serve to devalue groups and to deny equal opportunities.

Cultural relativism The viewing of other people's behavior from the perspective of those other people's culture.

> You never really understand a person until you consider things from his point of view . . . until you climb into his skin and walk around in it.
>
> Harper Lee, *To Kill a Mockingbird*

Cultural Relativism Whereas ethnocentrism means evaluating other cultures using the familiar culture of the observer as a standard of correct behavior, **cultural relativism** means viewing other people's behavior from the perspective of those other people's culture. As sociologists we have a responsibility to understand other cultures from their points of view, rather than imposing our own values upon them. Unlike ethnocentrists, cultural relativists seek to employ the kind of value neutrality that Max Weber saw as so important.

Cultural relativism stresses that different social contexts give rise to different norms and values. Thus, we must examine practices such as polygamy, bullfighting, and monarchy within the particular contexts of the cultures in which they are found. Cultural relativism is not the same as moral relativism, which implies that no ultimate normative standards exist. Sociologists do not have to abandon their own morals and unquestionably accept every cultural variation. But cultural relativism does require a serious and unbiased effort to evaluate norms, values, and customs in light of their distinctive culture.

Practicing the sociological imagination calls for us to be more fully aware of the culture we as humans have created for ourselves and to be better attuned to the varieties of culture other people have established for themselves. Culture shapes our everyday behaviors all the time, and we select from the tools it provides. For the most part, we are not aware of the degree to which we are immersed in a world of our own making. Whether that includes the capacity to read a book, make a meal, or hug a stranger on the street, it is through culture that we establish our relationship to the external world and with one another.

SOCIOLOGY IS A VERB

Break a Norm

Choose some minor norm of face-to-face interaction (rather than disrupting a group) and violate it. Avoid anything that would harm another person, violate policies, or break the law. Be sure to give the impression that what you are doing is perfectly normal, and record how others respond to you. In what ways do they seek to make sense of your behavior or to restore order? How did breaking the norm affect you? What lessons did you learn about our everyday actions?

For REVIEW

I. Why do humans create culture?
   - Humans lack the complex instincts present in other animals, and as such they must construct a relationship to nature and with each other. We do this through the construction of shared culture.

II. What does culture consist of?
   - There are three primary elements of culture. Material culture consists of our modification of the physical environment. Cognitive culture is the thinking part of culture, including language, values, beliefs, and knowledge. Normative culture provides rules for behavior.

III. How does culture both enable and constrain?
   - Although culture provides us with the knowledge, rules, and artifacts we need to survive, it also limits our options. Words enable us to see, and tools enable us to make things, but both are designed for particular purposes and shield us from alternative possibilities. Further, with ethnocentrism, we cut ourselves off from new possibilities from different cultures.

©Digital Vision/Getty Images RF

SOCVIEWS on Culture

Functionalist View

Sharing a culture helps define the society to which one belongs, establishing **social order**.

Society **preserves** its culture by transmitting shared language, norms, and values from one generation to the next, thus providing social **stability**.

The interests of **subgroups** within a culture are served by formation of **subcultures**.

KEY CONCEPTS: PRESERVATION, FACILITATION, COMMUNICATION

Conflict View

While a common culture helps unify a society, it also **privileges** some to the detriment of others.

The **dominant ideology** reinforces the power of the ruling class.

The existence of subcultures reflects **unequal social arrangements**, as brought to light by the civil rights and feminist movements.

Language in a culture can be a source of conflict, as in the case of **sexist** language or language that transmits **racial stereotypes**.

KEY CONCEPTS: PRIVILEGE, DOMINANCE, INEQUALITY

Interactionist View

Without social interaction, people would not be able to **construct their culture** or transmit it to others. In turn, having a common culture simplifies everyday transactions.

Cultural diffusion is enhanced by interactions involved in immigration, tourism, the Internet, and the mass media.

Both a culture's **language** and **nonverbal communication** facilitate day-to-day exchanges between people.

KEY CONCEPTS: SOCIAL CONSTRUCTION, NONVERBAL COMMUNICATION

MAKE THE CONNECTION
After reviewing the chapter, answer the following questions:

1 How would each of the three perspectives describe the lessons learned from the No Pants Subway Ride?

2 How would each perspective explain the role material, cognitive, and normative culture plays in our lives?

3 How would each perspective approach the role that dominant ideology performs in a culture?

4 How would you use the perspectives to describe one of the subcultures at your school?

Pop Quiz

1. _____ consists of everything humans create in establishing our relationships to nature and with each other.
   a. Innovation
   b. Society
   c. Ethnocentrism
   d. Culture

2. What expression did George Murdock introduce to refer to common practices and beliefs shared by all societies?
   a. norms
   b. folkways
   c. cultural universals
   d. cultural practices

3. What is an invention?
   a. introducing a new idea or object to a culture
   b. combining existing materials to create something new
   c. making known or sharing the existence of an aspect of reality
   d. the physical or technological aspects of our daily lives

4. What term do sociologists use to refer to the process by which a cultural item spreads within and between societies?
   a. diffusion
   b. globalization
   c. innovation
   d. cultural relativism

5. Which of the following statements is true according to the Sapir-Whorf hypothesis?
   a. Language simply describes reality.
   b. Language legitimates existing social, economic, and political interests.
   c. Language shapes our perception of reality.
   d. Language formation is constrained by cultural universals.

6. What do norms provide for us that we need?
   a. shared beliefs that unite us as one
   b. established standards of behavior
   c. a system of shared symbols enabling us to communicate with each other
   d. justification of existing inequality through shared beliefs and practices

7. What type of norms is deemed highly necessary to the welfare of a society, often because these norms embody the most cherished principles of a people?
   a. formal norms
   b. informal norms
   c. mores
   d. folkways

8. Terrorist groups are examples of
   a. cultural universals.
   b. subcultures.
   c. countercultures.
   d. dominant ideologies.

9. Which of the following terms describes the set of cultural beliefs and practices that help maintain powerful social, economic, and political interests?
   a. mores
   b. dominant ideology
   c. consensus
   d. values

10. What is the term used when one seeks to understand another culture from its perspective, rather than dismissing it as "strange" or "exotic"?
    a. ethnocentrism
    b. culture shock
    c. cultural relativism
    d. cultural value

1. (d), 2. (c), 3. (b), 4. (a), 5. (c), 6. (b), 7. (c), 8. (c), 9. (b), 10. (c)

Design Elements: *Going Global (Earth):* ©Studio Photogram/Alamy Stock Photo; *Personal Sociology (drawing of author):* ©McGraw-Hill Education; *5 Movies (popcorn):* ©D. Hurst/Alamy Stock Photo; *Sociology Is a Verb (overlapping hands):* ©Jeff DeWeerd/Getty Images RF

©Gareth Cattermole/Getty Images

4 Socialization

SUCCESS AND SOCIAL INFLUENCE

As an unknown author just starting out, J.K. Rowling experienced repeated rejection. Her first book, *Harry Potter and the Philosopher's Stone* (as it's known in England), was turned down by a dozen publishers. Her big break came when Nigel Newton, chair of the board for Bloomsbury Publishing, gave his eight-year-old daughter, Alice, a copy of the first chapter. She loved it. Alice insisted that her father read it and "nagged and nagged" him over the next several months, "wanting to see what came next" (Lawless 2005).

Rowling's story of initial rejection followed by award-winning success and massive sales is hardly unique. Herman Melville's *Moby Dick,* George Orwell's *Animal Farm,* Anne Frank's *The Diary of a Young Girl,* Madeleine L'Engle's *A Wrinkle in Time,* Sylvia Plath's *The Bell Jar,* Ursula K. Le Guin's *The Left Hand of Darkness,* and Meg Cabot's *The Princess Diaries* were all initially rejected by publishers. How is it possible that the widespread appeal of such works was not obvious to experts in the field who are paid to recognize such things?

Sociologist Duncan Watts, along with two colleagues, conducted an online experiment to measure the power of inherent quality versus social influence in determining artistic success (Salganik, Dodds, and Watts 2006). They presented each of their 14,341 online participants with a list of 48 new songs by unknown artists, asking them to listen to the songs, rate them, and then, if they wanted, download them for free. To test their variables, the researchers divided the participants into nine groups. One of the groups, the control group, was presented only with the name of the artist and title of the song. Participants of the eight other groups, the experimental groups, saw not only the artist and title, but also how many times each song had been downloaded by people within their group. If quality alone mattered, then the same songs should rise to the top or sink to the bottom in all nine groups. But that's not what happened. Knowing how often songs had been downloaded by others affected which songs participants in the experimental groups favored. Songs that were preferred early varied significantly between experimental groups. As a result, the songs that rose to the top also varied (D. Watts 2007, 2011). These results suggest that the popularity of songs, novels, and works of art is not determined by inherent quality alone. Social influence plays a substantial role in determining artistic success. Change that influence, especially early on, and a different outcome is likely.

As You READ >>

- How do we become ourselves?
- Who shapes our socialization?
- How does our development change over time?

>> The Role of Socialization

Babies are extremely vulnerable. Imagine what the world must look like through a newborn's eyes. Without language to give names to things, without beliefs to give things meaning, without norms to know what to do, without skills to use tools or utensils, how could we possibly survive? The good news is that babies don't have to start from scratch. They benefit from the culture created by those who came before them, learning from them how to talk, think, and act.

INTERNALIZING CULTURE

Through interactions with others, we learn what we need to know to survive and thrive. Sociologists refer to this practice of internalizing culture as **socialization,** the lifelong process through which people learn the attitudes, values, and behaviors appropriate for members of a particular culture. We absorb culture through interactions with parents, teachers, friends, coworkers, and many others. We are exposed to it in formal contexts, such as schools and workshops, and informal contexts, such as the playground or Instagram. We become who we are through our encounters with others.

> **SOC**THINK
>
> What skills that you learned before age two do you now take for granted? From whom did you learn them? In what contexts?

> **Socialization** The lifelong process through which people learn the attitudes, values, and behaviors appropriate for members of a particular culture.

Language is perhaps the most basic element of culture we need to learn. We begin teaching it to infants long before they can even understand what we are saying. We start by using baby talk with its higher and more varied pitch, longer vowel sounds, and slower speech. Infants prefer baby talk, also known as infant-directed speech, until they are about eight months old. Such speech provides important building blocks for what will later become a child's native language (Soderstrom 2007).

We can see this process at work when babies begin experimenting with sounds, mimicking what they hear even before they know any words. This was evident when a video of chattering twins went viral. In the video, available at TwinMamaRama.com, the two 17-month-olds "talked" back and

©Baltskars/Getty Images RF

forth, saying little more than "da da da." But they did so with expression, hand gestures, turn taking, and laughter in what seemed like all the right places. They knew what language sounded like—they'd learned that through interactions with family, friends, and others—and it was only a matter of time until they also learned the words that go with it.

Even though baby talk is a near cultural universal, the frequency of sounds, including both vowels and consonants, and the relationships between them vary from culture to culture. An infant in an English-speaking environment hears different combinations than one in a Swedish- or Japanese-speaking context. Such variation provides the foundation for children learning the particulars of their native tongue. For example, English has 10 vowel sounds, whereas Swedish has 16 and Japanese has 5. Baby talk in these different contexts varies accordingly, opening some linguistic pathways while closing others (Kuhl 2004).

THE IMPACT OF ISOLATION

Because socialization at a young age plays a major role in shaping who we become, missing out on such exposure can have a devastating impact on our development. We get a sense for the consequences of such deprivation through studies of children who have experienced extreme childhood isolation and research on primates who are denied care.

Extreme Childhood Isolation

Children who have been isolated or severely neglected (sometimes called *feral children* to suggest that they have reverted to a wild or untamed state) typically have a difficult time recovering from the lack of early childhood socialization. One famous case was Genie, a 13-year-old girl discovered by California authorities in 1970. Genie had been kept in extreme isolation since she was 20 months old. During the day she was strapped to a potty chair and unable to move about. At night she was bound and placed in a crib. If she made sounds, her father would

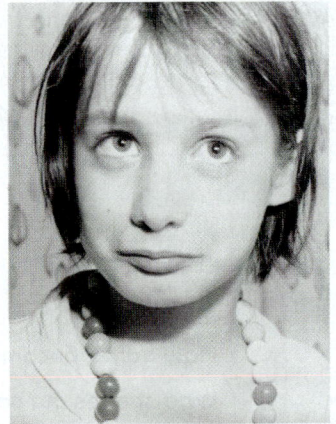

Genie at age 13. ©Bettmann/Contributor/Getty Images

growl at her, scratch her, and beat her. She was fed baby food instead of solid foods. Family members were prohibited from speaking to her. Because there was no television or radio in her home, she had never heard the sounds of normal human speech. A year after she was rescued, during which she received extensive therapy, Genie's grammar resembled that of a typical 18-month-old. Though

Cases of Children Raised in Extreme Isolation

Shamdeo, the Sultanpur Wolf Boy	He was about 4 years old when discovered playing with wolves in 1974.
Memmie LeBlanc, the Wild Girl of Champagne	About 18 to 20 years old when found, she had learned language before having been abandoned.
John Ssebunya, the Ugandan Monkey Boy	Found living with a pack of monkeys in 1991 at age 6, he now gives talks about his experience.
Ng Chhaidy of India	She disappeared in the jungle when she was 4 and, after persistent local rumors about a jungle girl, was found 38 years later in 2012.
Oxana Malaya, the Ukrainian Dog Girl	She was found living in the dog pen in her family's back yard in 1991 at the age of 8.
Vanya Yudin, the Russian Bird Boy	Found in February 2008, he was cared for by his mother but never spoken to and chirps like a bird.
The Leopard Boy of Dihungi	He was found among leopards at age 5 in 1915 after having been in the wild three years.
Kamala and Amala, the Wolf Girls of Midnapore	These two girls were found living among wolves at about the ages of 8 and 2 in 1920.
The Russian Cow Girl	This 5-year-old girl, found living with cows in 2012, communicated using mooing sounds.
Natasha, the Siberian Dog Girl	This 5-year-old Russian girl, discovered in 2009, was raised like a pet in a room full of dogs and cats.

Sources: Keith 2008; Newton 2002; www.feralchildren.com. *Photos:* ©Mary Evans Picture Library/The Image Works; *book:* ©Preto Perola/Shutterstock.com RF

she made further advances with continued therapy, she never achieved full language ability. Genie, now in her early 60s, reportedly lives in a home for adults with developmental disabilities in California (Carroll 2016; Curtiss 1977; Rymer 1993).

In a similar, more recent case, police were called to investigate a child abuse claim in Plant City, Florida, in 2005. In a trash-filled house overrun with roaches and reeking of urine and feces, they discovered an emaciated girl whose hair was crawling with lice and who had rashes and sores all over her body. She was in a room piled high with her dirty diapers. Her name was Danielle. She was almost seven years old and weighed only 46 pounds. She couldn't eat solid food. She wouldn't make eye contact. She didn't react to pain. She couldn't talk. In terms of her social, psychological, and intellectual development, she was no further along than a six-month-old baby.

The long-term consequences of extreme isolation can be substantial. Danielle was adopted in 2007 and eventually learned basic self-care skills, including how to go to the bathroom and how to feed herself using a fork and spoon, but she barely speaks and cannot read. Her family continues to work with her in hopes that she will learn to dress herself, brush her own teeth, make a sandwich, and recognize classmates. After running several medical tests, doctors determined that nothing was wrong with her physically that would explain her condition. Instead, they attributed it to extreme neglect (DeGregory 2008, 2011; Lierow 2011). When Danielle was fifteen, the Oprah Winfrey Network released a video showing both her progress and the challenges she continues to face (OWN 2015).

Cases of extreme isolation demonstrate the importance of the earliest socialization experiences for children. We now know that it is not enough to attend only to an infant's physical needs; parents must also concern themselves with children's social development. If parents severely limit their children's interaction with family, friends, and others, including strangers—even as infants and toddlers—those children miss out on social interactions with people that are critical for their social, psychological, and emotional development.

Primate Studies Our need for early socialization is reinforced by studies of animals raised in isolation. Because it would violate ethical standards of research to conduct such experiments on human babies, psychologist Harry Harlow (1971) conducted tests with rhesus monkeys so he could better understand the importance of early socialization. By studying monkeys that had been raised away from their mothers and away from contact with other monkeys, he uncovered long-term effects of extreme isolation. As was the case with Genie and Danielle, the rhesus monkeys raised in isolation were fearful and easily frightened. They did not mate, and the females, who were artificially inseminated, became abusive mothers.

©Glow Images RF

A creative aspect of Harlow's experimentation was his use of "artificial mothers." In one such experiment, Harlow presented monkeys raised in isolation with two substitute mothers—one a cloth-covered replica and one a wire-covered model that had the capacity to offer milk. Monkey after monkey went to the wire mother for the life-giving milk, yet spent much more time clinging to the more motherlike cloth model. Apparently, the infant monkeys developed greater social attachments based on their need for warmth, comfort, and intimacy than their need for food.

A cloth-covered "artificial mother" of the type used by Harry Harlow. ©Nina Leen/Time & Life Pictures/Getty Images

What we learn from cases of extreme childhood isolation and research on primates is that we lack complex instincts that will ensure our survival. Instead, we rely on the care and concern provided by others, especially when we are young. Without that early childhood socialization, we would struggle to establish working relationships with the outside world. Biology alone is not enough. The culture we create provides us with the tools we need. And through socialization, we share those tools with others.

> Self and others do not exist as mutually exclusive facts.
>
> Charles Horton Cooley

>> The Self and Socialization

We learn from others what we need to survive, yet we are not simply robots who are programmed to do what others say, whether they be parents, teachers, bosses, politicians, or religious leaders. As individuals we are engaged in an ongoing dance with the world around us. We choose what to think and how to act, but we do so within the confines of the cultural resources to which we have access.

SOCIOLOGICAL APPROACHES TO THE SELF

We come to be who we are through our relationships with others. The **self** is our sense of who we are, distinct from others and shaped by the unique combination of our social interactions. It is not a static entity; instead, it develops and changes as we seek to make sense of our life experiences. Sociologists and psychologists alike have expressed interest in how the individual develops and modifies his or her sense of self as a result of social interaction.

Self Our sense of who we are, distinct from others, and shaped by the unique combination of our social interactions.

Looking-glass self A theory that we become who we are based on how we think others see us.

Cooley: The Looking-Glass Self American sociologist Charles Horton Cooley (1864–1929), one of the founders of the interactionist perspective, argued that we become ourselves in response to reactions we receive from others. We use people's responses to the things we say and do as a mirror reflecting back to us how we should think about ourselves, both positively and negatively. Cooley used the expression the **looking-glass self** to describe his theory that we become who we are based on how we think others see us.

Our understanding of our self, according to Cooley's theory, involves a complex calculation in which we constantly read and react. This process of self-development has three phases. First, we imagine how others see us—relatives, friends, even strangers on the street. Second, we imagine how others evaluate what we think they see—as intelligent, attractive, shy, or strange. Finally, we define our self as a result of these assumptions—"I am smart" or "I am beautiful" (Cooley 1902). This process is ongoing; it happens during each and every one of our interactions. According to Cooley, we become who we are based not on how others actually see us, and not on how they judge us, but on how we think they will judge us based on what we think they perceive.

In Cooley's model, our sense of self results from our "imagination" of how others view us. Because we never truly know what others think, we can develop self-identities based on often *incorrect* perceptions of how others see us. Imagine you are on a first date or a job interview. All the cues you receive throughout the interaction are positive—your date or interviewer smiles, laughs, and nods at all the right times. You go home feeling happy, confident that things went really well. But your date never returns your call, or the expected job offer never comes. You go from a feeling of elation and confidence to a sense of disappointment, doubt, and recrimination, asking yourself, "What's wrong with me?" without ever really knowing what the date or interviewer truly thought about you. In Cooley's world, who we are is very much dependent on our interpretations of the interactions we have with others.

> **SOC**THINK
>
> What cues do you rely on to know if things are going well on a first date? How about on a job interview? To what extent do you think people can fake such cues?

Mead: Stages of the Self George Herbert Mead (1863–1931), another American sociologist and advocate of the interactionist perspective, sought to expand on Cooley's theory. Mead especially sought to clarify the relationship between our self and our environment. He argued that there are two core components

©Steve Hix/age fotostock

guesses and in so doing find the appropriate pathway to the correct solution. Similarly, in our interactions with others, pathways of appropriate action emerge over time. We become more confident that certain responses are appropriate, making our decisions about how to act in the future easier and providing us with greater self-confidence.

In developing our sense of who we are and what is appropriate, we rely on the interactions we have with our parents, friends, coworkers, coaches, and teachers. Mead used the expression **significant others** to describe the particular individuals we interact with who are most important in the development of our self. Over time, however, we begin to see that the positions these significant others occupy are part of a larger social network. Mead (1934, 1964a, 1964b) described that realization as a three-stage process of self-development: preparatory stage, play stage, and game stage.

> **I** The acting self that exists in relation to the Me.
>
> **Me** The socialized self that plans actions and judges performances based on the standards we have learned from others.
>
> **Significant other** An individual who is most important in the development of the self, such as a parent, friend, or teacher.
>
> **Symbol** A gesture, object, or word that forms the basis of human communication.

of the self: "I" and "Me." The **I** is our acting self. It is the part of us that walks, reads, sings, smiles, speaks, and performs any other action we might undertake. The **Me** is our socialized self. It draws on all our previous training and experience to plan our actions and then uses these standards to judge our performance afterward.

For Mead our self emerges through the ongoing interaction between the socialized self and the acting self. The Me plans. The I acts. The Me judges. For example, in a classroom discussion, our Me may have something to say but fears that the words won't come out right, which could lead to embarrassment. So our I stays silent. Our Me then kicks our self afterward when someone else receives praise from the professor for saying exactly what we planned to say, so our Me resolves to speak up next time.

In all our interactions, we rely on a feedback loop in which we gather information, process it, and use it to guide our reaction. In some respects, this relationship is not unlike the technique math teachers turn to when using the "guess and check" problem-solving strategy for certain types of story problems. In this approach, we try a solution to see if it works out, and if it doesn't, we try again. With each successive attempt, we use the information we've gained to make more informed

> It matters not what someone is born, but what they grow to be.
>
> J. K. Rowling

Preparatory Stage During the *preparatory stage*, which lasts until about age three, children merely imitate the people around them, especially family members with whom they continually interact. That can take the form of babbling babies, who internalize language before they even know the words, or a small child who bangs on a piece of wood while a parent is engaged in carpentry work or tries to throw a ball if an older sibling is doing so nearby. This imitation is largely mindless—simple parroting of the actions of others.

As they grow older, children begin to realize that we attach meanings to our actions, and they become more adept at using symbols to communicate with others. **Symbols** are the gestures, objects, and words that form the basis of human communication. By interacting with family and friends, as well as by watching cartoons on television and looking at picture books, children in the preparatory stage begin to develop interaction skills they will use throughout their lives. They learn that they can use symbols to get their way, such as saying please and thank you, or perhaps throwing a tantrum in the candy aisle of the local supermarket.

Play Stage As children develop skill in communicating through symbols, they gradually become more

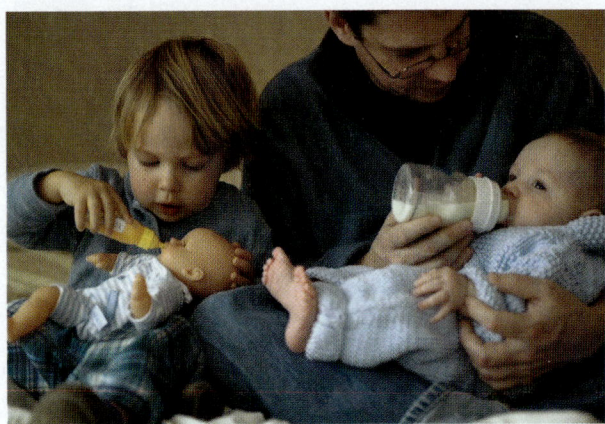
©Laurie Swope/Alamy Stock Photo RF

Role taking The process of mentally assuming the perspective of another and responding from that imagined viewpoint.

Generalized other The attitudes, viewpoints, and expectations of society as a whole that a child takes into account in his or her behavior.

Dramaturgical approach A view of social interaction in which people are seen as actors on a stage attempting to put on a successful performance.

aware of social relationships out of which those symbols grow. During the *play stage,* from about ages three through five, they begin to pretend to be other people: a doctor, parent, superhero, or teacher. Such play need not make a lot of sense or be particularly coherent to adults; children, especially when they are young, are able to move in and out of various characters with ease. For Mead, playing make-believe is more than just fun; it is a critical part of our self-development.

Mead, in fact, noted that an important aspect of the play stage is role playing. He used the expression **role taking** to describe the the process of mentally assuming the perspective of another and responding from that imagined viewpoint. Through this process a young child imagines how others might respond in particular situations and gradually learns, for example, when it is best to ask a parent for favors. If the parent usually comes home from work in a bad mood, the child might wait until after dinner, when the parent is more relaxed and approachable.

Game Stage In Mead's third stage, the *game stage,* the child of about six to nine years of age learns to more fully appreciate that he or she is involved in interconnected and interdependent relationships. Success depends upon each person playing his or her appropriate part, and each individual must often submit to the expectations of the group. The transition from play to game is evident when teaching kids to play team sports such as T-ball or soccer. When they are little, you will often see a clump of kids chasing after a ball or moving up the field together. They have yet to learn that different people play different positions and that they will be more successful as a team if everyone plays the position to which they are assigned. When they do, they can take for granted that someone will be covering a base so they can throw a runner out or that a goalie will be there to make a save if the ball gets behind them. Visualizing the map of who should be where and who should do what enables us to see a kind of blueprint for society, and internalizing it represents the final stage of development in Mead's model.

Mead uses the term **generalized other** to refer to the attitudes, viewpoints, and expectations of society as a whole that a child takes into account in his or her behavior. Simply put, this concept suggests that when an individual acts, he or she takes into account the relative positions, contributions, and expectations for an entire group of people. For example, a child comes to see that acting courteously is important not just because his or her parent says so; rather, it is a widespread norm expected in a variety of contexts, whether at home, school, religious services, or the grocery store.

At this stage, children begin to see that there really is something like a game going on with an underlying logic and shared rules and expectations for its various players. They may know their principal, Ms. Sanchez, as a significant other, but also see that the position of principal exists independent of Ms. Sanchez and that it carries with it certain expectations that make sense in the context of a school in which other positions include teacher, custodian, aide, and student. And if the individuals who come to occupy the various positions in the game fail to act accordingly, the whole thing falls apart.

Goffman: Presentation of the Self This idea that we must all play our roles as part of something larger led Erving Goffman, a Canadian sociologist and advocate of the interactionist perspective, to establish what he called the **dramaturgical approach,** which studies interaction as if we were all actors on a stage seeking to put on a successful performance. He was inspired, in part, by the William Shakespeare quote "All the world's a stage, And all the men and women merely players: They have their exits and their entrances; And one man in his time plays many parts." As we perform our roles, according to Goffman, each of us seeks to convey impressions of who we are to others, even as those others are doing the same with us.

Building on this analogy, Goffman draws our attention to various *aspects of performance,* analysis of which allows us to better understand what makes a show a success. Performances take place on a stage. *Front stage* is where we perform for our audience and includes appropriate sets and may involve other cast members with whom we work as a *team.* We largely follow *scripts* and, although some improvisation is permissible, too much may threaten the credibility of the character we are trying to portray. *Backstage* is where we prepare, including getting into costumes and gathering together appropriate *props* which help to make our performance more believable. Ultimately, the *audience* judges how

©Robbie Jack - Corbis/Contributor/Getty Images

> **SOC THINK**
>
> Imagine that going to class is like performing in a play. Who are the key players? What are some of their most-used lines? What props do people use to be convincing? How might the performance break down, and what steps might be taken to save the show?

well we did. Whether in our role as students, restaurant servers, or even lovers, we all know that we have a part to play and that if we don't say the right lines or use the correct props at the appropriate times, the show will collapse, undermining our sense of self.

Early in life, we learn to slant our presentation of self in order to create distinctive appearances and satisfy particular audiences. Goffman (1959) referred to this modifying of the presentation of the self as **impression management**. When things don't go as well as we might have hoped, we try to "save face." Goffman refers to this process as **face-work** meaning we alter our presentation of self in order to maintain a proper image and avoid public embarrassment. We often initiate some kind of face-saving behavior when we are feeling flustered or rejected. In response to a rejection at a bar, a person may engage in face-work by saying, "This place is full of losers. I'm out of here." Or, if we do poorly on an exam, we may say to a friend who did likewise, "This professor sucks." We feel the need to maintain a positive self-image if we are to continue social interaction.

In some cultures, people engage in elaborate deceptions to avoid losing face. In Japan, for example, where lifetime employment has until recently been the norm, "company men" thrown out of work during a severe economic recession may feign employment, rising as usual in the morning, donning suit and tie, and heading for the business district. But instead of going to the office, they congregate at places such as Tokyo's Hibiya Library, where they pass the time by reading before returning home at the usual hour. Many of these men are trying to protect family members, who would be shamed if neighbors discovered that the family breadwinner was unemployed. Others are deceiving their wives and families as well (French 2000).

For Goffman, Mead, and Cooley, our self is fundamentally social. Each encounter we have provides opportunities for self-assessment. Even though our sense of self may seem relatively fixed over time, it is always subject to revision as we move into and out of relationships with others. A novel interaction or experience is often all it takes to get us to question things we have taken for granted, leading to new understandings of who we really are.

> **Impression management** The altering of the presentation of the self in order to create distinctive appearances and satisfy particular audiences.
>
> **Face-work** Altering our presentation of self in order to maintain a proper image and avoid public embarrassment.

US VERSUS THEM

Through socialization, we internalize the culture of the groups to which we belong. We learn to think of our groups' norms, values, beliefs, and inventions as

©ZUMA Press, Inc./Alamy Stock Photo

as opposed to others. We adopt the group's expected cultural practices by following its norms, embracing its beliefs, using appropriate language, and otherwise seeking to fit in. By absorbing the culture of the group, membership becomes part of our identity. And, third, *social comparison* involves ranking groups in relation to each other, drawing a contrast between "us" and "them" in a way favorable to our group. In other words, we build ourselves up or show favoritism toward our group while putting down or denigrating other groups. Enhancing the status of the groups to which we belong elevates both our identity and our self-esteem by answering the questions "Who am I?" and "What am I worth?" Patriotism, which calls forth pride in flag and country, finds its roots here.

On the flip side, privileging the culture of the groups to which we belong creates a foundation for **prejudice**, which is a preconceived and unjustified judgment of individuals, whether positive or negative, based on their membership in a particular group. We elevate ourselves by viewing those who do not think or act like us as somehow lesser. Our tendency is to think of prejudice as explicit bias, in which individuals voice their opinions about "them," making the bias easy to spot. But because we are socialized to make positive and negative distinctions between groups, we become largely unaware of the degree to which we do so. Theorists refer to such judgments as **implicit bias,** the automatic and unconscious association of value, whether positive or negative, with particular groups, subgroups, or characteristics of people. Researchers have uncovered ways to measure implicit bias using a variety of assessment tools including implicit association tests (Banaji and Greenwald 2013; Staats, Capatosto, Wright, and Jackson 2016).

Implicit association tests measure participants' reaction time when presented with images, in an attempt to detect positive and negative associations. Researchers have constructed tests to assess implicit bias with regard to race, gender, age, weight, sexuality, disability, and more. Researchers can then compare results based on the test-takers' race, gender, age, region, or any other variable researchers have collected information about. A variety of these tests are available online—for example, Harvard's Project Implicit has several—for anyone to take.

not only normal for us but somewhat superior to those of others. Such ethnocentrism is a natural response, as we saw in the "Attitudes Toward Cultural Variation" section in Chapter 3. We draw lines between ourselves and others and then use those lines to define who we are in opposition to those we are not. We see such divisions in sports (Green Bay Packers fans versus Minnesota Viking fans versus New England Patriot fans), politics (Democrats versus Republicans), high school (jocks versus brains versus populars versus burnouts), the workplace (sales staff versus marketing division), religion (Christians versus Muslims versus Buddhists), and more. Such divisions solidify our identities, but they frequently do so at the expense of how we view others.

Group membership itself shapes how we think and act. Social psychologist Henri Tajfel conducted a series of experiments in which he randomly distributed people into groups. He found that even when people have no group history or common group culture, just being a member leads them to identify with each other, privilege each other, and seek to deny benefits to people in other groups (Tajfel 1981). Tajfel identified three core elements at work (Tajfel and Turner 1979). First, *social categorization* involves the simple recognition of differences between groups. Any marker can serve as the foundation for such difference, such as taste, occupation, or age. Sociologists pay particular attention to categorization based on gender, race, ethnicity, and class. Second, *social identification* occurs when we tie our sense of self with a particular group

Prejudice A preconceived and unjustified judgment of individuals, whether positive or negative, based on their membership in a particular group.

Implicit bias The automatic and unconscious association of value, whether positive or negative, with particular groups, subgroups, or characteristics of people.

> **SOC THINK**
>
> Go to the Project Implicit site and take one of the tests. To what extent do your results match your self-assessment? What factors might influence someone's score? What steps might we take to alter our implicit biases?

When considering socialization, it is easy to focus on its more positive dimensions—learning how to speak, act, and create. But through our interactions with others, we also learn how to hate and discriminate. Developing an appreciation for where such attitudes come from and why we have them, including the degree to which we may be unaware of them, enables us to take steps to change them.

>> Agents of Socialization

Sociologists refer to the various contexts within which individuals and groups shape our social identity as agents of socialization. Primary examples include family, friends, schools, peers, the mass media, the workplace, religion, and the state.

©Mark Wilson/Getty Images

FAMILY

Our families are our most important agent of socialization. Research shows that the role of the family in socializing a child cannot be overestimated (McDowell and Parke 2009). Babies are born with certain innate abilities—they can hear, see, smell, and taste, and can feel heat, cold, and pain—but they would not survive without assistance from others. Responsibility for feeding, cleaning, carrying, and comforting babies falls primarily to family members. In the context of families, we learn to talk, walk, feed ourselves, go to the bathroom, and so on—basic skills that we take for granted as natural but that we learn within families. As children grow up, they observe parents expressing affection, taking care of finances, quarreling, dealing with work stress, and so forth, which prepares them for what family life might be like in their future. We explore definitions and functions of families more fully in Chapter 7.

Children do not play a passive role in their socialization. As Mead's I implies, they choose, sometimes to the disappointment of their parents. In so doing, they are active participants in their self-creation. We can see the power of family socialization among the Amish. Children in Amish communities are raised in a highly structured and disciplined manner, but they are not immune to the temptations posed by their peers in the non-Amish world. Around the time they turn 16, Amish teens begin dating, or courtship. They refer to this phase of their lives as *rumspringa,* a word roughly translated as "running around," which lasts until they get married, usually by their early 20s. During this transitional time between childhood and adulthood, they have greater freedom and can experiment with activities that would otherwise be forbidden, ranging from wearing non-Amish clothes, owning a cell phone, buying a TV and DVD player, driving cars, smoking, drinking, even doing drugs (though most don't go that far). During this time, they must also decide whether to commit to being Amish for the rest of their lives by taking a vow and getting baptized or to pursue life outside the Amish community. Parents often react by looking the other way, sometimes literally, pretending not to notice. They remain secure in the knowledge that, after a lifetime of Amish socialization, their children almost always return to the traditional Amish lifestyle. Research shows that only about 20 percent of Amish youths leave the fold, and most of them join one of the only somewhat more modern Mennonite groups. Rarely does a baptized adult leave (Kraybill, Johnson-Weiner, and Nolt 2013; Schachtman 2006).

Cross-Cultural Variation How children are socialized within families varies significantly around the world. In Vietnam, potty training starts by the time babies are six months old. Mothers whistle to remind their children to go and children are effectively potty trained by the time they are nine months old (Duong, Jansson, and Hellström 2013). In Sweden, parents routinely leave babies asleep in strollers outside shops, even on the coldest days, while the parents go in to buy something or get something to eat, to expose their children to more fresh air. They believe that doing so makes the babies healthier and less likely to get sick (Lee 2013). In Japan, parents push their children to commute to school on their own from an early age. In cities like Tokyo, first-graders must learn to negotiate buses, subways, and long walks. To ensure their safety, parents carefully lay out rules: never talk to strangers; check with a station attendant if you get off at the wrong stop; stay on to the end of the line, then call, if you miss your stop; take stairs, not escalators; don't fall asleep. One parent acknowledges that she worries, "but

©Bjoern Kaehler/AP Images

after they are 6, children are supposed to start being independent from the mother. If you're still taking your child to school after the first month, everyone looks at you funny" (Tolbert 2000:17).

In the United States, whether out of fear for their child's safety or concern about being charged with child endangerment, few parents would consider giving their young child this much independence. Parenting norms in the United States have shifted in recent decades, resulting in greater oversight and involvement in children's lives. Reflecting on the question of whether or not parents have become overprotective, journalist Hanna Rosin (2014) points out, "Actions that would have been considered paranoid in the 70s—walking third-graders to school, forbidding your kid to play ball in the street, going down the slide with your child in your lap—are now routine." The variety of parenting practices across cultures and across time provides additional evidence that our actions are not narrowly determined by our genes.

Gender roles The normative expectations regarding proper behavior, attitudes, and activities associated with maleness and femaleness.

The Influence of Race and Gender
In the United States, social development within families includes exposure to cultural assumptions regarding gender and race. African American parents, for example, have learned that children as young as two years old can absorb negative messages about African Americans in children's books, toys, and television shows—the vast majority of which are designed primarily for White consumers. At the same time, as we will see in Chapter 13, African American families own less wealth and are more likely to experience poverty, which limits their children's access to resources such as extracurricular programs, summer camps, and specialized tutors and coaches. Because most U.S. neighborhoods are racially segregated, African American families often live in or near poor neighborhoods. As a result, their children are susceptible to exposure to gangs and drugs, despite their parents' strong family values (Benhorin and McMahon 2008; Friend, Hunter, and Fletcher 2011; Kliewar and Sullivan 2009).

Socialization within families also plays a significant role in whether we conform to conventional **gender roles,** meaning the normative expectations regarding proper behavior, attitudes, and activities associated with maleness and femaleness. In mainstream U.S. culture, for example, people traditionally identified "toughness" as masculine—and desirable only in men—while associating "tenderness" as feminine. As we will see in Chapter 12, not all societies share this model, allowing for a wider range of roles. Some societies have three or more gender categories. In the United States, people have increasingly come to see gender as a fluid concept allowing for a variety of expressions. Socialization experiences within the families play a major role in both our personal and societal acceptance of such variety.

SCHOOL
In school we typically move beyond the more sheltered confines of our family and learn to become members of the larger social groups to which we belong. Schools in the United States, for example, teach students the taken-for-granted knowledge of the broader society—not only basic skills such as reading, writing, and 'rithmatic but also shared cultural knowledge, such as the national anthem, the heroes of the American Revolution, and the pillars of good character. Like the family, schools have an explicit mandate to socialize people—and especially children—into the norms and values of the society to which they belong.

Schools teach children the values and customs of the larger society because that shared culture provides the glue that holds us together as a society. If we did not transmit our knowledge and skills from one generation to the next, society would collapse. The knowledge we gain at school, however, goes beyond the official curriculum to include the more informal lessons we learn on the playground. We do learn the facts and figures of history, science, reading, math, and more, but we also learn how to stand up for ourselves when our parents or teachers are not there to hover over us or to bail us out.

©Blue Jean Images/Getty Images RF

©Robert Daly/Caia Image/Glow Images RF

High School Behavior: Perception versus Reality

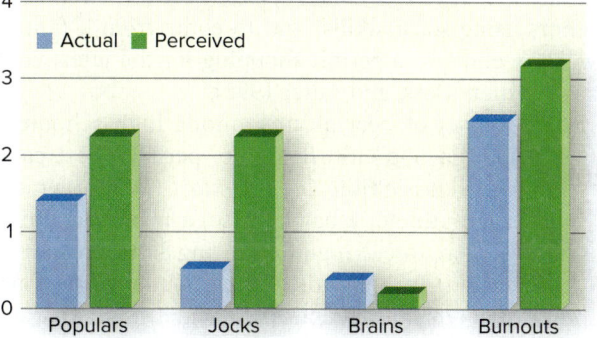

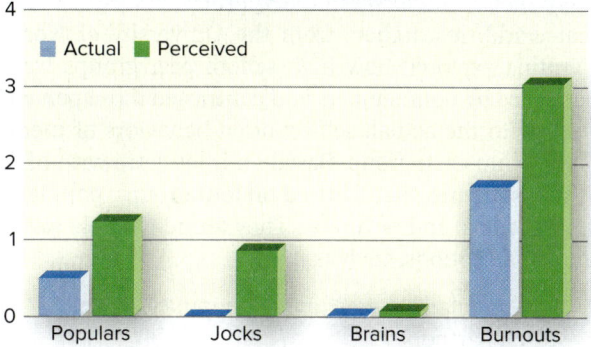

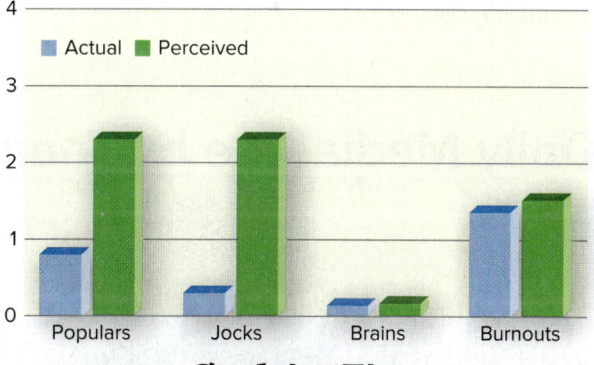

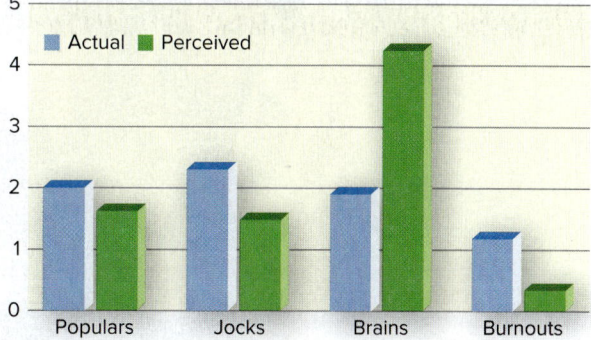

Note: Actual represents the average of self-reported practices for students within that peer group; Perceived represents responses from students outside the group.

Source: Helms et al. 2014.

In addition to reinforcing social order, schools open doors for us as individuals. We are exposed to new ways of thinking and acting that allow us to make new choices about our future. Although this can include training for careers that allow us to "get ahead," it also involves exposure to new cultures, ideas, practices, and possibilities. It might even lead us to an unexpected future such as a career in sociology!

Although schools provide both social order and individual opportunity, they can also reinforce existing inequality through the ways students are socialized. As economists Samuel Bowles and Herbert Gintis (1976) have observed, schools produce teachable students who become manageable workers. They argue that schools' primary function has less to do with transmitting academic content and more to do with socializing students to conform to, and accept, workplace authority. Schools teach students how to work for rewards, how to work in teams, how to meet deadlines, how to comply with instructions, and so on. The students who internalize these skills best are rewarded with opportunities in the workplace, whereas those who challenge authority and call for change are punished. We more fully explore various elements of education in Chapter 8.

PEER GROUPS

As we grow older, and especially in our adolescent years, our friends, schoolmates, and other peers become increasingly important in shaping how we think and act. To understand the role peers play at a relatively young age, sociologists Patricia and Peter Adler conducted observation research at elementary schools with fourth- through sixth-grade students. They found that, even this early, a pecking order is established, ranging from the "popular clique" at the top that includes the "cool kids" on down to what they call the "social isolates" at the bottom, whom other kids sometimes call "dweebs" or "nerds" (Adler and Adler 1996).

Children get the message about where they fit and how they should behave. In another study of elementary schoolchildren, the Adlers found that popularity reinforces gender stereotypes. To be popular as a boy is to be athletic, tough, and not too academic. To be popular as a girl is to be attractive, to be able to manipulate others using social skills, and to come from a family wealthy enough to permit shopping for the latest cool stuff (Adler, Kless, and Adler 1992).

The impact of peer groups among high schoolers has become a pop culture staple, perhaps best captured in the classic film *The Breakfast Club,* in which "a brain, an athlete, a basket case, a princess, and a criminal" were forced together during Saturday morning detention. In the end, the five students got past their stereotypical perceptions of each other to find common ground.

To better understand peer group culture in the real world, researchers from the University of North Carolina explored how high school peer groups were perceived by nonmembers and contrasted those perceptions with the actual, self-reported behaviors of members within each group. Based on interviews with high school students, they focused on four groups: populars, jocks, brains, and burnouts. They found a whole series of misperceptions, such as:

- Non-populars overestimated populars' number of sexual partners.
- Non-jocks overestimated jocks' amount of alcohol consumption.
- Non-brains overestimated brains' time spent studying.
- Non-burnouts overestimated burnouts' frequency of property damage.

Overall, researchers concluded that students especially tend to overestimate the degree to which students in the two most popular groups engage in sex, drugs, and property damage. In a follow-up study, the researchers found that, when analyzed over time, those students who perceived the popular kids as being more likely to engage in risky behaviors were themselves more likely to engage in those behaviors, which is consistent with what we have learned already from the Thomas theorem that perception shapes action.

MASS MEDIA

For most of human history, socialization came primarily in the form of person-to-person contact, and we had limited exposure to what was going on in the wider world. We now receive immediate accounts of incidents around the globe as they are happening. Technological innovations leading to the rise of the mass media made that possible. The word *media* is plural for *medium,* and a medium is something or someone capable of conveying or transmitting ideas or objects. For example, language, as a system of shared symbols, provides the medium through which we communicate. The term *mass media* refers to the variety of technologies that provide the capacity to easily transmit large quantities of information to large groups of people.

Daily Media Use by Teens

Time spent each day, 13- to 18-year-olds

- 2:38 Watching TV/DVDs/videos
- 1:54 Listening to music
- 1:21 Playing video, computer, or mobile games
- 1:11 Using social media
- 0:36 Browsing websites
- 0:32 Other computer/mobile device activities
- 0:28 Reading
- 0:13 Video-chatting
- 0:03 Going to movies
- 6:40 Total screen media
- 8:56 Total media

Source: Rideout 2015:20. *Photo:* ©Creatas/Getty Images RF

POPSOC

Video game designer Mike Mika's three-year-old daughter enjoys playing the classic arcade game Donkey Kong. In it, a King Kong–like ape kidnaps Pauline, and Mario's task is to save her. One day Mika's daughter asked, "How can I play as the girl? I want to save Mario!" After days spent hacking the Donkey Kong ROM, Mika (2013) fulfilled his daughter's wish to make the princess the hero.

According to Anita Sarkeesian (2013), "Damsel in Distress" plot devices are exceedingly common in video games. She concludes, "Distilled down to its essence, the plot device works by trading the disempowerment of female characters for the empowerment of male characters." With the help of more than 6,000 Kickstarter backers, she has produced a series of videos investigating the portrayal of women in video games, which are available at her website, Feminist Frequency.

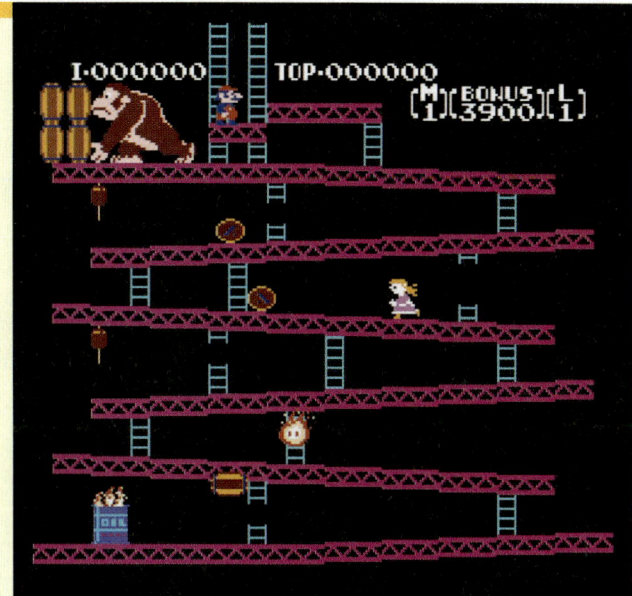

Photo: ©Mike Mika

If we think of a mass medium as the vessel through which information passes, we can identify seven types of major media (Ahonen 2008). *Print,* the first type, took off as a mass medium with Johannes Gutenberg's invention of a printing press using movable type in 1439. His press made printing many copies of materials possible, facilitating a publication explosion that continues to this day in the form of books, pamphlets, billboards, newspapers, and magazines. Access to books and pamphlets has played a significant role in historic events ever since, including the Protestant Reformation, which started in 1517, and the American Revolution, which began in 1776 (Edwards 1994; Humphrey 2013).

The second mass media type, *recordings,* got their start in the late 1800s. Since then, recordings have provided mass access to musical performances from classical music to rock and roll and beyond. In time, as a result of technological innovation, video recordings became possible. At various points, recording technology included wax cylinder recordings, vinyl records, magnetic recordings (such as reel-to-reel tape, 8-track cartridges, audio cassettes, and VHS tapes), CDs, and DVDs. Magnetic recordings were particularly transformative due to the inclusion of the "record" button, which opened the door for almost anyone to produce their own recordings, an ability we take for granted today (Marlow and Secunda 1991; Millard 2005; Milner 2009).

Cinema represents the third type of mass media. Starting in the early 1900s, movie theaters were established all over the United States. Pittsburgh's "Nickelodeon," one of the earliest, opened in 1905 with a 5 cent admission fee. Movie theaters became a shared space where people in local communities gained more immediate visual access to popular stories, news accounts, fads, and fashion from the wider world (Charney and Schartz 1995; Sklar 1994).

The fourth type, *radio,* brought mass media broadcasts directly into the home. Pittsburgh's KDKA became the first licensed commercial broadcasting station in the United States in 1920, and stations quickly spread across the country. Programming included music, news, sports, and episodic stories (soap operas, with their open and ongoing storylines originated here). Radio enabled the rapid and widespread dissemination of breaking news to entire populations, including the possibility of direct communication by political leaders. Herbert Hoover was the first presidential candidate to reach a mass audience via radio in 1928, and President Franklin Delano Roosevelt used radio to great effect with his "fireside chat" broadcasts to the nation during the Great Depression and World War II (Brands 2008; Marquis 1984).

Television, the fifth type of mass media, combined the immediacy and reach of radio with the video element of cinema. The world became a smaller place because now it was possible to bring breaking news, sporting events, variety shows, musical concerts, and more into people's living rooms. Television stations began popping up around the United States during the 1940s, and people widely adopted television as a medium in the 1950s (Edgerton 2007). The first broadcast of a presidential debate occurred in 1960 between John F. Kennedy and Richard M. Nixon. Kennedy, with a bronzed tan from campaigning in California, came across as more telegenic, and Nixon, with a pale complexion and visible sweat, appeared uncomfortable on the screen, a difference that might have swayed the election (Druckman 2003; Kraus 1996). Ever since then, candidates and campaigns have been keenly aware of the importance of optics in shaping potential outcomes. With the expansion of cable and satellite television came an explosion of available channels, though the

Did You Know?

... The average adult in the United States watches 32 hours and 32 minutes of television per week. Viewing varies substantially by age, with those aged 18–34 watching 18 hours, 32 minutes to those 50+ at 43 hours, 53 minutes.

Source: Nielsen 2016:6. Photo: ©Datacraft Co Ltd/Getty Images RF

major television networks (including ABC, CBS, FOX, and NBC), along with a select number of major cable channel corporations (especially ESPN), wield significant influence over what gets covered and how, and perhaps just as important, what gets left out.

The sixth type of mass media is referred to generally as *the Internet,* access to which expanded significantly throughout the 1990s. By linking computers through a series of networks, the World Wide Web facilitated connections between computers via web browsers (Isaacson 2014). Two core elements distinguish the Internet as a mass medium. The first is information retrieval, which provides us with access to untold amounts of data. Whether searching for sources when writing a college paper or looking for pictures of rainbows and unicorns, individuals now have more power to find information than ever before. The second core element is social networking, which provides us with historically unprecedented access to people. Sites such as Facebook, Twitter, Instagram, and Snapchat provide almost constant access to close friends, continued connections to old friends, and even connections with the rich, powerful, and famous. Getting a "like" or retweet from a celebrity can be cause for significant celebration because the distance between you and them suddenly seems so small.

SOC THINK

The average 18- to 34-year-old in the United States spends 2 hours and 48 minutes each day using a smartphone. Social networking takes up just over 1 hour of that time (Nielsen 2016). Does that total seem high or low to you? What are possible effects, both positive and negative, of such use?

Mobile phones represent the final mass media type. Although mobile phones were originally invented solely for the purpose of making calls, we now use them to send texts, take photos, access the Internet, record videos, play games, read books, get directions, listen to radio, watch movies, access our music collection, and a whole host of other actions. Smartphones can take the place of numerous devices, including watches, fitness trackers, calculators, voice recorders, compasses, flashlights, levels, alarm clocks,

Telephones and Cell Phones by Country (rates per 100 people)

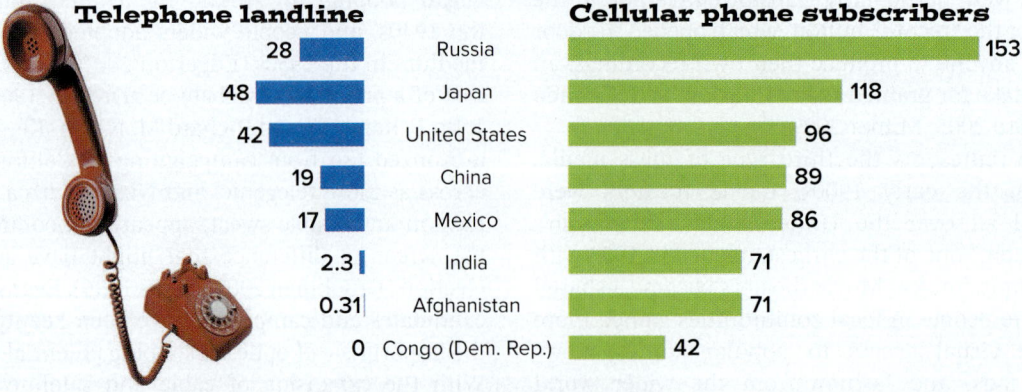

Telephone landline	Country	Cellular phone subscribers
28	Russia	153
48	Japan	118
42	United States	96
19	China	89
17	Mexico	86
2.3	India	71
0.31	Afghanistan	71
0	Congo (Dem. Rep.)	42

Source: International Telecommunications Union 2015. Photo: ©Stockbyte/Getty Images RF

calendars, portable gaming devices, and more (Agar 2013; Klemens 2010). The intersection of all these elements into a single device provides the possibility to draw on various elements of each to create something new. The game *Pokémon Go,* for example, utilized elements of the smartphone's camera, GPS, fitness tracker, gyroscope, and social networking software to create a whole new augmented reality gaming universe. Exploring the possible health benefits of such augmented reality games, researchers at Microsoft found that *Pokémon Go* increased physical activity among users by almost 1,500 steps per day, with a particular impact among low-activity populations (Althoff, White, and Horvitz 2016).

Many developing nations have essentially skipped over the use of landlines, along with the infrastructure costs they entail, and have gone directly to mobile technology. In Tunisia, for example, 88 percent of the adult population owns a cell phone; in Kenya, it's 82 percent; and in Senegal, it's 81 (Pew Research Center 2014b). Mobile phone access enables people to maintain contact with family, provides access to jobs, and expands social networks. Having a phone can be especially important to families, for example, when children leave the local village to pursue opportunities in urban areas or abroad (K. Sullivan 2006).

The key element with agents of socialization, including mass media, is that they change how we think and act. With the exposure to new cultural beliefs and practices that media have brought, we may become more accepting of others and gain a deeper understanding of ourselves. Of course, such exposure can also challenge the culture we hold dear, and the kinds of filters that might have been provided by time and distance are a thing of the past. We can see such effects in the hostility sometimes expressed in online forums and Twitter feeds. Given that these outlets for expression are relatively recent mass media creations, perhaps we will develop more effective norms for constructive exchanges in the future.

THE WORKPLACE

Learning to behave appropriately in an occupation is a fundamental aspect of human socialization. Employers and coworkers want to be confident that you know what to do and when to do it. As we saw with Mead's concept of the generalized other, the teamwork necessary for successful completion of tasks depends on everyone playing his or her part, and the workplace functions as an agent of socialization to make sure that happens.

It used to be that workplace socialization started young. Generations ago, most children began working at a young age, primarily to provide assistance with farm labor. That practice carried over past the Industrial Revolution, though laws were eventually enacted to limit child labor. Now, rates of employment for high school age students hover around 25 percent, with a peak during summer months of about 33 percent (DeSilver 2015). Adolescents generally seek jobs to earn spending money; 80 percent of high school seniors say that little or none of what they earn goes to family expenses. Moreover, these teens rarely look on their employment as a means of exploring vocational interests or getting on-the-job training (Hirschman and Voloshin 2007).

Socialization in the workplace changes when it involves a more permanent shift to full-time employment. Occupational socialization can be most intense during the transition from school to job, but it continues throughout one's work history. Technological advances and corporate reorganization may alter the requirements of the position and necessitate new training. According to the Bureau of Labor Statistics (2015f), between the ages

Did You Know?

... The National Day of Unplugging occurs on the first Friday of each March. Organizers encourage us to take a 24-hour break from the "relentless deluge of technology and information" by shutting down our computers and turning off our cell phones. Participants are urged to use the time they gain to connect with loved ones, get outside, nurture their health, find silence, and give back.

Photos: family: ©Ariel Skelley/Blend Images LLC/Getty Images RF; laptop: ©D. Hurst/Alamy Stock Photo RF

of 18 and 48, the typical person held 11.7 different jobs. We can no longer assume that we will have a job-for-life, so whether by choice or by necessity, we must be open to ongoing occupational socialization.

RELIGION AND THE STATE

Increasingly, social scientists are recognizing the growing importance of government ("the state") and the continued significance of religion as agents of socialization. Traditionally, family members served as the primary caregivers in U.S. culture, but in the 20th century, the family's protective function was steadily transferred to outside agencies, such as public schools, hospitals, mental health clinics, and child care centers, many of which are run by the state. Historically, religious groups also provided such care and protection. Despite early sociological predictions that religion would cease to play a substantial role in modern society, these groups continue to play a significant role in identity formation and collective life (Warner 2005).

Preschool children in particular are often cared for by someone other than a parent. Overall, 61 percent of children under five years old spend time in some kind of regular child care. More than 90 percent of employed mothers depend on others to care for their children, and almost 40 percent of mothers who aren't employed have regular care arrangements. Approximately one-third of children under age five are cared for by nonrelatives in nursery schools, Head Start programs, day care centers, family day care, and other providers. Children this age are also more likely to be cared for on a daily basis by grandparents than by their parents (Laughlin 2013).

Rite of passage A ritual marking the symbolic transition from one social position to another, dramatizing and validating changes in a person's status.

Although many 18-year-olds choose not to vote, voter turnout in the 2008 presidential election was the highest it had been in decades, causing long lines at some polling stations. Rates among young people declined a bit in 2012 and 2016. ©Autumn Payne/Sacramento Bee/MCT via Getty Images

Both government and organized religion act to provide markers representing significant life course transitions. For example, religious organizations continue to celebrate meaningful ritual events—such as baptism, bismillah, or bar/bat mitzvah—that often bring together all the members of an extended family, even if they never meet for any other reason. Government regulations stipulate the ages at which a person may drive a car, drink alcohol, vote in elections, marry without parental permission, work overtime, and retire. Although these regulations do not constitute strict rites of passage—most 18-year-olds choose not to vote, and most people choose their age of retirement without reference to government dictates—they do symbolize the fact that we have moved on to a different stage of our life, with different expectations regarding our behavior.

>> Socialization Throughout the Life Course

Adolescents among the Kota people of the Congo in Africa paint themselves blue. Cuban American girls go on a day-long religious retreat before dancing the night away. These are both **rites of passage**—rituals that mark the symbolic transition from one social position to another, dramatizing and validating changes in a person's status.

Leh Village, India, schoolchildren.   ©Nevada Wier/Getty Images

86 • SOC 2018

In the Kota rite the color blue—the color of death—symbolizes the death of childhood and the passage to adulthood. For adolescent girls in Miami's Cuban American community, the *quinceañera* ceremony celebrating the attainment of womanhood at age 15 supports a network of party planners, caterers, dress designers, and the Miss Quinceañera Latina pageant. For thousands of years, Egyptian mothers have welcomed their newborns to the world in the Soboa ceremony by stepping over the seven-day-old infant seven times. And Naval Academy seniors celebrate their graduation from college by hurling their hats skyward.

Milestones in the Transition to Adulthood

THE LIFE COURSE

Such specific ceremonies mark stages of development in the life course. They indicate that the process of socialization continues through all stages of the life cycle. In fact, some researchers have chosen to concentrate on socialization as a lifelong process. Sociologists and other social scientists who take such a **life course approach** look closely at the social factors, including gender and

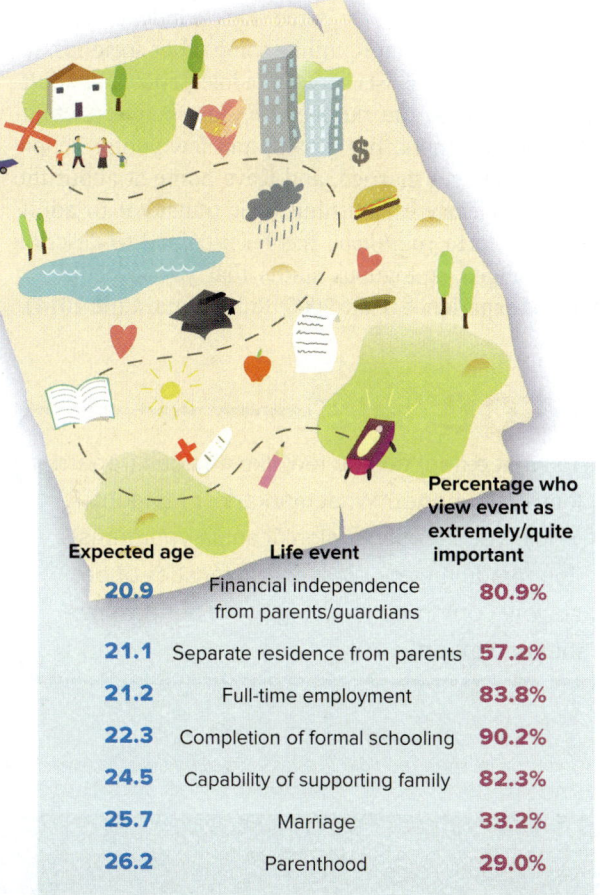

Expected age	Life event	Percentage who view event as extremely/quite important
20.9	Financial independence from parents/guardians	80.9%
21.1	Separate residence from parents	57.2%
21.2	Full-time employment	83.8%
22.3	Completion of formal schooling	90.2%
24.5	Capability of supporting family	82.3%
25.7	Marriage	33.2%
26.2	Parenthood	29.0%

Source: T. Smith 2004.

Body painting is a ritual marking the passage to puberty in some cultures. ©Thomas S. England/Science Source

income, that influence people throughout their lives, from birth to death. They recognize that biological changes help mold but do not dictate human behavior.

In the transition from childhood to adulthood, we can identify certain markers that signify the passage from one life stage to the next. These milestones vary from one society, and even one generation, to the next. In the United States, according to one national survey, completion of formal schooling has risen to the top, with 90 percent of people identifying it as an important rite of passage. On average, Americans expect this milestone to be attained by a person's 23rd birthday. Other major events in the life course, such as getting married or becoming a parent, are expected to follow three or four years later. Interestingly, the significance of these markers has declined, with only about one-third of survey respondents identifying marriage and less than one-third

> **Life course approach** A research orientation in which sociologists and other social scientists look closely at the social factors that influence people throughout their lives, from birth to death.

Chapter 4 / Socialization • 87

> **Anticipatory socialization**
> Processes of socialization in which a person "rehearses" for future positions, occupations, and social relationships.

identifying parenthood as important milestones representing adulthood (Furstenberg 2010; T. Smith 2004).

One result of these staggered steps to independence is that in the United States, unlike some other societies, no clear dividing line exists between adolescence and adulthood. Nowadays, the number of years between childhood and adulthood has grown, and few young people finish school, get married, and leave home at about the same age, clearly establishing their transition to adulthood. The term *youthhood* has been coined to describe the prolonged ambiguous status that young people in their 20s experience (Côté 2000; Roberts and Côté 2014).

> **SOC THINK**
> To what extent do you feel like an adult (regardless of your age)? What markers or moments would you identify as significant in your transition to adulthood? What characteristics of our society contribute to ambiguity in our passage into adulthood?

ANTICIPATORY SOCIALIZATION AND RESOCIALIZATION

In our journey through our lives, we seek to prepare ourselves for what is coming and to adapt to change as necessary. To prepare, we undergo **anticipatory socialization,** which refers to processes of socialization in which a person "rehearses" for future positions, occupations, and social relationships. A culture can function more efficiently and smoothly if members become acquainted with the norms, values, and behavior associated with a social position before actually assuming that status. Preparation for many aspects of adult life begins with anticipatory socialization during childhood and adolescence and continues throughout our lives as we prepare for new responsibilities (Levine and Hoffner 2006).

High school students experience a bit of anticipatory socialization when they prepare for college. They begin to imagine what college life will be like and what kind of person they will be when they get there. They may seek out information from friends and family to get a better sense of what to expect, but increasingly, they also rely on campus websites and Facebook entries. To assist in this process and to attract more students, colleges are investing more time and money in websites through which students can take "virtual"

Life in prison is highly regulated—even recreation time. ©Justin Sullivan/Getty Images

campus tours, listen to podcasts, and stream videos of everything from the school song to a sample zoology lecture.

Occasionally, assuming a new social or occupational position requires that we *unlearn* an established orientation. **Resocialization** refers to the process of discarding old behavior patterns and accepting new ones as part of a life transition. Often, resocialization results from explicit efforts to transform an individual, as happens in reform schools, therapy groups, prisons, religious conversion settings, and political indoctrination camps. The process of resocialization typically involves considerable stress for the individual—much more so than socialization in general, or even anticipatory socialization (Hart, Miller, and Johnson 2003).

Resocialization is particularly effective when it occurs within a total institution. Erving Goffman (1961) coined the term **total institution** to refer to an institution that regulates all aspects of a person's life under a single authority. Examples can be more or less extreme depending on how long it lasts and how easy it is to opt out of it, from summer camp or boarding school to prison, the military, a mental hospital, or a convent. Because the total institution is generally cut off from the rest of society, it provides for all the needs of its members. In its extreme form, so elaborate are its requirements, and so all-encompassing its activities, that the total institution represents a miniature society.

Goffman (1961) identified several common traits of total institutions:

- All aspects of life are conducted in the same place under the control of a single authority.
- Any activities within the institution are conducted in the company of others in the same circumstances—for example, army recruits or novices in a convent.
- The authorities devise rules and schedule activities without consulting the participants.
- All aspects of life within a total institution are designed to fulfill the purpose of the organization. Thus, all activities in a monastery might be centered on prayer and communion with God (Malacrida 2005; Mapel 2007; K. Williams and Warren 2009).

People often lose their individuality within total institutions. For example, a person entering prison may experience the humiliation of a **degradation ceremony** as he or she is stripped of clothing, jewelry, and other personal possessions. From that point on, scheduled daily routines allow for little or no personal initiative. The individual becomes secondary and rather invisible in the overbearing social environment (Garfinkel 1956).

> **SOC THINK**
> To what extent is summer camp, a cruise, or even life at a residential college similar to a total institution? In what ways is it different?

ROLE TRANSITIONS DURING THE LIFE COURSE

As we have seen, one of the key transitional stages we pass through occurs as we enter the adult world, perhaps by moving out of the parental home, beginning a career, or entering a marriage. As we age we move into the midlife transition, which typically begins at about age 40. Men and women often experience a stressful period of self-evaluation, commonly known as the **midlife crisis,** in which they realize that they have not achieved basic goals and ambitions and may feel they have little time left to do so. This conflict between their hopes and their outcomes causes strain. Compounding such stresses that are often associated with one's career or partner is the

Resocialization The process of discarding former behavior patterns and accepting new ones as part of a transition in one's life.

Total institution An institution that regulates all aspects of a person's life under a single authority, such as a prison, the military, a mental hospital, or a convent.

Degradation ceremony An aspect of the socialization process within some total institutions, in which people are subjected to humiliating rituals.

Midlife crisis A stressful period of self-evaluation that begins at about age 40.

Boyhood
Growing up, through the eyes of a child.

Bully
The true story of the tragic costs of peer group intimidation.

Children Underground
Documentary about children surviving in the subway systems of Romania.

The Jungle Book
The live-action remake tells the fictional story of a boy raised by animals.

Don't Think Twice
Friends in an improv group learn to adjust when one of them makes it big.

5 Movies ON SOCIALIZATION

growing responsibility for caring for two generations at once (Mortimer and Shanahan 2006; Wethington 2000).

An increasingly common midlife challenge involves becoming part of the **sandwich generation** which describes adults who simultaneously try to meet the competing needs of their parents and their children. Their caregiving goes in two directions: to children, who even as young adults may still require significant support and direction; and to aging parents, whose health and economic problems may demand intervention by their adult children. Among adults aged 40–59, 47 percent report having both a parent 65 years old or older and a minor child or are supporting a grown child (Parker and Patten 2013).

Like the role of caring for children, that of caring for aging parents falls disproportionately on women. Overall, women provide 60 percent of the care their parents receive, and even more as the demands of the role grow more intense and time-consuming. Increasingly, middle-aged women and younger are finding themselves on the "daughter track," as their time and attention are diverted by the needs of their aging mothers and fathers (Dotinga 2014; Gross 2005; P. Taylor et al. 2009).

Sandwich generation The generation of adults who simultaneously try to meet the competing needs of their parents and their children.

>> Aging and Society

Due to advances in areas such as health care, nutrition, and working conditions, life expectancy has risen significantly both in the United States and around the world. Someone born in 1900 in the United States had an average life expectancy of 47 years, but babies born in the U.S. in 2014 can anticipate living to 76.4 if they're boys and 81.2 if they're girls (National Center for Health Statistics 2016:Table 15). The proportion of the U.S. population that was 65 and older grew from 4.1 percent in 1900 to 15 percent in 2014; it is expected to rise to 24 percent by 2060 (Mather, Jacobsen, and Pollard 2015; Ortman, Velkoff, and Hogan 2014). Globally, life expectancy is 75 years in "high income nations," such as the United States, France, and Japan, but only 50 years in "low income nations," such as Afghanistan, Rwanda, and Somalia (World Bank 2016a).

How societies deal with their elderly population varies significantly across cultures. One society may treat older people with reverence, whereas another sees them as unproductive and "difficult." The Sherpas—a Tibetan-speaking Buddhist people in Nepal—live in a culture that idealizes old age. Almost all elderly members

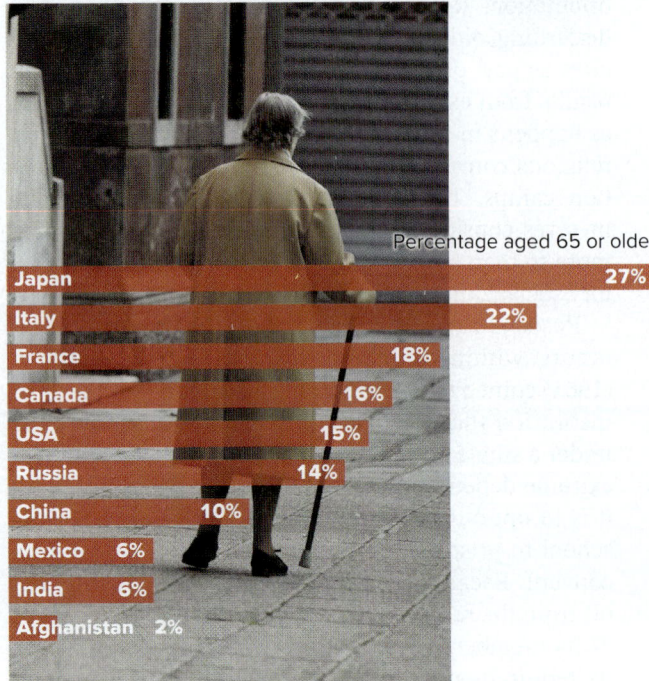

Going GLOBAL

Aging Around the World

Percentage aged 65 or older

Country	%
Japan	27%
Italy	22%
France	18%
Canada	16%
USA	15%
Russia	14%
China	10%
Mexico	6%
India	6%
Afghanistan	2%

Source: Population Reference Bureau 2016. *Photo:* ©Ingram Publishing/age fotostock RF

of the Sherpa culture own their homes, and most are in relatively good physical condition. Typically, older Sherpas value their independence and prefer not to live with their children. Among the Fulani of Africa, however, older men and women move to the edge of the family

The Sherpas in Nepal show significant respect for their elderly members. ©Paula Bronstein/Getty Images

homestead. Because that is where people are buried, the elderly sleep over their own graves, for they are viewed socially as already dead (Goldstein and Beall 1981; Stenning 1958; Tonkinson 1978).

Understandably, all societies have some system of age stratification that associates certain social roles with distinct periods in life. In the United States, children are denied certain rights, such as voting or alcohol consumption, until they reach an age when they are deemed sufficiently mature. Some of this age differentiation seems inevitable; it would make little sense to send young children off to war or to expect older citizens to handle physically demanding tasks, such as loading freight at shipyards.

ADJUSTING TO RETIREMENT

Making the role transition into retirement can be a difficult process. Retirement is a rite of passage that typically marks a transition out of active participation in the full-time labor market. Symbolic events are associated with this rite of passage, such as retirement gifts, a retirement party, and special moments on the last day on the job. The preretirement period itself can be emotionally charged, especially if the retiree is expected to train his or her successor (Reitzes and Mutran 2004).

Gerontologist Robert Atchley (1976) has identified several phases of the retirement experience:

- *Preretirement*, a period of anticipatory socialization as the person prepares for retirement.
- *The near phase*, when the person establishes a specific departure date from his or her job.
- *The honeymoon phase*, an often euphoric period in which the person pursues activities that he or she never had time for before.
- *The disenchantment phase*, in which retirees feel a sense of letdown or even depression as they cope with their new lives, which may include illness or poverty.
- *The reorientation phase*, which involves the development of a more realistic view of retirement alternatives.
- *The stability phase*, in which the person has learned to deal with life after retirement in a reasonable and comfortable fashion.
- *The termination phase*, which begins when the person can no longer engage in basic, day-to-day activities such as self-care and housework.

Retirement is not a single transition, then, but a series of adjustments that varies from one person to another. The length and timing of each phase will differ for each individual, depending on such factors as financial and health status. In fact, a person will not necessarily go through all the phases identified by Atchley. For example, people who are forced to retire or who face financial difficulties may never experience a honeymoon phase. And many retirees continue to be part of the paid labor force of the United States, often taking part-time jobs to supplement their pensions, either because they want to or because they need to.

>> Perspectives on Aging

The particular problems of older adults have become the focus of a specialized field of research and inquiry known as **gerontology**—the study of the sociological and psychological aspects of aging and the problems of aging adults. It originated in the 1930s as an increasing number of social scientists became aware of the plight of this population. Gerontologists rely heavily on sociological principles and theories to explain the effects of aging on the individual and society. They also draw on psychology, anthropology, physical education, counseling,

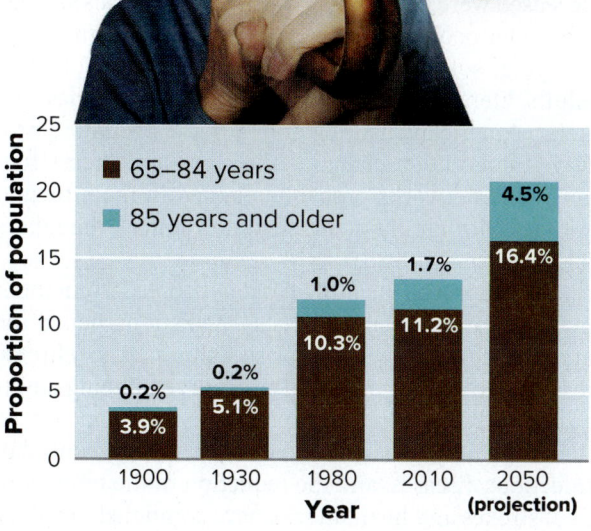

Actual and Projected Growth of the Elderly Population of the United States

[Bar chart showing Proportion of population by Year]
- 1900: 3.9% (65–84 years), 0.2% (85 years and older)
- 1930: 5.1%, 0.2%
- 1980: 10.3%, 1.0%
- 2010: 11.2%, 1.7%
- 2050 (projection): 16.4%, 4.5%

Sources: He et al. 2005:9; Ortman et al. 2014; Werner 2011. *Photo:* ©Darren Greenwood/Design Pics RF

Gerontology The study of the sociological and psychological aspects of aging and the problems of aging adults.

and medicine in their study of the aging process. Three perspectives on aging—disengagement theory, activity theory, and age discrimination—arise out of these studies.

> **SOC THINK**
>
> What age do you think counts as getting "old"? What factors influence our conception of what counts as old?

DISENGAGEMENT THEORY

After studying elderly people in good health and relatively comfortable economic circumstances, Elaine Cumming and William Henry (1961) introduced their **disengagement theory,** which implicitly suggests that society and the aging individual mutually sever many of their relationships. Highlighting the significance of social order in society, disengagement theory emphasizes that passing social roles on from one generation to another ensures social stability.

According to this theory, the approach of death forces people to drop most of their social roles—including those of worker, volunteer, spouse, hobby enthusiast, and even reader. Younger members of society then take on these functions. The aging person, it is held, withdraws into an increasing state of inactivity while preparing for death. At the same time, society withdraws from aging adults by segregating them residentially (in retirement homes and communities), educationally (in programs designed solely for senior citizens), and recreationally (in senior citizens' centers). Implicit in disengagement theory is the view that society should help older people withdraw from their accustomed social roles.

Disengagement theory has generated considerable controversy. Some gerontologists have objected to the implication that older people want to be ignored and put away—and even more to the idea that they should be encouraged to withdraw from meaningful social roles. Critics of disengagement theory insist that society forces elderly people into an involuntary and painful withdrawal from the paid labor force and from meaningful social relationships. Rather than voluntarily seeking to disengage, older employees find themselves pushed out of their jobs—in many instances, even before they are entitled to maximum retirement benefits (Boaz 1987).

ACTIVITY THEORY

Often seen as the opposite of disengagement theory, **activity theory** suggests that those elderly people who remain active and socially involved will have an improved quality of life. Proponents of this perspective acknowledge that a 70-year-old person may not have the ability or desire to perform various social roles that he or she had at age 40. Yet they contend that older people have essentially the same need for social interaction as any other group.

How important is it for older people to stay actively involved, whether at a job or in other pursuits? A tragic disaster in Chicago in 1995 showed that it can be a matter of life and death. An intense heat wave lasting more than a week—with a heat index exceeding 115 degrees on two consecutive days—resulted in 733 heat-related deaths. About three-fourths of the deceased were 65 or older. Subsequent analysis showed that older people who lived alone had the highest risk of dying, suggesting that support networks for older adults literally help save lives. Older Hispanics and Asian Americans had lower death rates from the heat wave than other racial and ethnic groups. Their stronger social networks probably resulted in more regular contact with family members and friends (Klinenberg 2002; Schaefer 1998a).

The improved health of older people—sometimes overlooked by social scientists—has strengthened the arguments of activity theorists. Illness and chronic disease are no longer quite the scourge of aging adults that they once were. The recent emphasis on fitness, the availability of better medical care, greater control of infectious diseases, and the reduction in the number of fatal strokes and heart attacks have combined to reduce the traumas of growing older.

Disengagement theory A theory of aging that suggests that society and the aging individual mutually sever many of their relationships.

Activity theory A theory of aging that suggests that those elderly people who remain active and socially involved will have an improved quality of life.

©Kelly Redinger/Design Pics RF

Rising Labor Force Participation Rates Among Older Adults

©Larry Mayer, The Billings Gazette/AP Images

Note: Data for 2024 are projections.
Source: Toossi 2015:Table 3. *Photos:* ©Lisa F. Young/Getty Images RF

Accumulating medical research also points to the importance of remaining socially involved. Among those who decline in their mental capacities later in life, deterioration is most rapid in those who withdraw from social relationships and activities. Fortunately, aging adults are finding new ways to remain socially engaged, as evidenced by their increasing use of the Internet, especially to keep in touch with family and friends (P. Taylor et al. 2009; A. Williams et al. 2010).

Older individuals continue to be involved both as volunteers and in the workforce. Many activities involve unpaid labor, for which younger adults may receive salaries. Unpaid elderly workers include hospital volunteers (versus aides and orderlies), drivers for charities such as the Red Cross (versus chauffeurs), tutors (in contrast to teachers), and craftspeople for charity bazaars (in contrast to carpenters and dressmakers). Continued engagement in the workforce has been a growing trend. In 2014, for example, 18.6 percent of those aged 65 and older worked full- or part-time (Toossi 2015:Table 3). Though many continue to work because they enjoy the social engagement work provides, others do so out of financial necessity.

AGEISM AND DISCRIMINATION

Physician Robert Butler (1990), through his research as a gerontologist in the 1970s, became concerned when he learned that a housing development near his home in metropolitan Washington, D.C., barred elderly people. Butler coined the term **ageism** to refer to prejudice and discrimination based on a person's age. For example, we may choose to assume that someone cannot handle a rigorous job because he is "too old," or we may refuse to give someone a job with authority because she is "too young."

When analyzing obstacles people face as a consequence of age, we must consider the impact of perception and denial of opportunity. Critics argue that neither disengagement nor activity theory answers the question of *why* social interaction must change or decrease for aging adults. The low status of older people is seen in prejudice and discrimination against them, in age segregation, and in unfair job practices—none of which are directly addressed by either disengagement or activity theory.

Although firing people simply because they are old violates federal law, courts have upheld the right to lay off older workers for economic reasons. Critics contend that, later, the same firms hire young, cheaper workers to replace experienced older workers. When economic growth slows and companies cut back on their workforces, the number of complaints of age bias rises sharply as older workers begin to suspect they were bearing a disproportionate share of the layoffs. For example, between 2006 and 2008, during which the U.S. economy entered into a deep economic recession, complaints of age discrimination filed with the Equal Employment Opportunity Commission rose by 49 percent (EEOC 2014).

> **Ageism** Prejudice and discrimination based on a person's age.

5 Movies ON AGING

Gran Torino
A widowed veteran confronts gang violence in his neighborhood.

Up
A cranky old man and a young boy embark on an unusual adventure.

Nebraska
An aging father and his estranged son hit the road to claim their lottery grand prize.

45 Years
On the brink of their 45th wedding anniversary, a couple confronts the past.

The Bucket List
Two men confront death by ticking off items on their to-do list.

As a whole, elderly people in the United States enjoy a standard of living that is much higher now than at any point in the nation's past. To some extent, older people owe their overall improved standard of living to a greater accumulation of wealth—in the form of home ownership, private pensions, and other financial assets. But much of the improvement is due to more generous Social Security benefits. Although modest when compared with other countries' pension programs, Social Security nevertheless provides 33 percent of all income received by older people in the United States. Still, in 2015, 8.8 percent of people aged 65 or older lived below the poverty line (Proctor et al. 2016; Social Security Administration 2016).

Members of groups who face a greater likelihood of income inequality earlier in their lives, including women and members of racial and ethnic minorities, continue to do so when they are older. For women aged 65 or older, the poverty rate is 10.3 percent compared to the rate for elderly men of 7.0 percent. Considering race and ethnicity, the 18.4 percent poverty rates for African Americans and 17.5 percent for Hispanics aged 65 or older was more than twice the 6.6 percent rate for non-Hispanic Whites of the same age (U.S. Census Bureau 2016b:Table 1 & Table 7).

Hospice care Treatment of terminally ill individuals in their own homes, or in special hospital units or other facilities, with the goal of helping them die comfortably, without pain.

DEATH AND DYING

In the film *The Bucket List,* Morgan Freeman and Jack Nicholson play the two main characters who are diagnosed with terminal cancer and have less than one year to live. They make a list of all the things they would like to do before they "kick the bucket." On the list are things they had never dared to do, such as traveling the world and skydiving, but it also includes reconciling broken relationships.

Until recently, death was a taboo topic in the United States. Death represents a fundamental disruption that cannot be undone, so we often find it easier to live with a sense of denial about our mortality. In the words of sociologist Peter Berger, "Death presents society with a formidable problem . . . because it threatens the basic assumptions of order on which society rests" (1969:23). However, psychologist Elisabeth Kübler-Ross (1969), through her pioneering book *On Death and Dying,* greatly encouraged open discussion of the process of dying. Drawing on her work with 200 cancer patients, Kübler-Ross identified five stages of the experience: denial, anger, bargaining, depression, and finally acceptance.

Although we may still be uncomfortable with the topic, *The Bucket List*'s portrayal of a "good death" represents one of the ways we have become more open about it. Gerontologist Richard Kalish (1985) laid out some of the issues people must face to prepare for a "good death." These included completing unfinished business, such as settling insurance and inheritance matters; restoring harmony to social relationships and saying farewell to friends and family; dealing with medical needs; and making funeral plans and other arrangements for survivors. In accomplishing these tasks, the dying person actively contributes to smooth intergenerational transitions, role continuity, compliance with medical procedures, and minimal disruption of the social system, despite the loss of a loved one.

We have also begun to create institutions to facilitate our wishes for a good death. The practice of **hospice care,** introduced in England in the 1960s, is devoted to easing this final transition. Hospice workers seek to improve the quality of a dying person's last days by offering comfort and by helping the person remain at home, or in a homelike setting at a hospital or other special facility, until the end. Currently, more than 6,100 hospice programs serve approximately 1.7 million people a year (NHPCO 2015).

Recent changes in the United States suggest additional ways in which people have broken through the historical taboos about death. For example, bereavement practices—once highly structured—are becoming increasingly varied and therapeutic. More and more people are actively addressing the inevitability of death by making wills, establishing "living wills" (health care proxies that explain their feelings about the use of life support equipment), donating organs, and providing instructions for family members about funerals, cremations, and burials. Given medical and technological advances and increasingly open discussion and negotiation regarding death and dying, it is possible that good deaths may become a social norm in the United States (Meier et al. 2016; Solomon 2016).

We encounter some of the most difficult socialization challenges (and rites of passage) in these later years of life. Retirement undermines the sense of self we had that was based in our occupation, a particularly significant source of identity in the United States. Similarly, taking stock of our accomplishments and disappointments, coping with declining physical abilities, and recognizing the inevitability of death may lead to painful adjustments. Part of the difficulty is that potential answers to the "Now what?" question that we might have asked in previous life stages are dwindling, and we begin to face the end of our days.

And yet, as we reflect on the story of our lives, we can look back to see all the people who shaped us into becoming who we are. Such relationships play a crucial role in our overall self-concept and self-satisfaction. As we have already seen, we are interdependent. And, though the influences of others on our life can be both a blessing and a curse, we wouldn't be who we are without them.

> Old age has its pleasures, which though different, are not less than the pleasures of youth.
>
> W. Somerset Maugham

SOCIOLOGY IS A VERB

Technology Fast

To learn more about how much we take technology and its impact for granted, go on a "technology fast." In other words, give up your cell phone, computer, television, Internet access, and so on for some preset period of time, such as a day, several days, or a week. Keep a journal. What do you miss most? What do you find yourself doing instead? How difficult was it? Did it get any easier over time? What lessons did you learn?

For REVIEW

I. How do we become ourselves?
- We are vulnerable at birth and depend on the socializing influences of others with whom we interact to provide us with the cultural tools necessary for our survival.

II. Who shapes our socialization?
- Although almost anyone with whom we interact can have a significant influence on us, particularly important to our development are family, school, peer group, mass media, religion, and the state.

III. How does our development change over time?
- We learn new things at various stages of our life course, experiencing significant transitions as we pass from childhood to adulthood and again from adulthood into old age. At each stage, the kinds of things expected of us by others shift significantly.

SOCVIEWS on Socialization

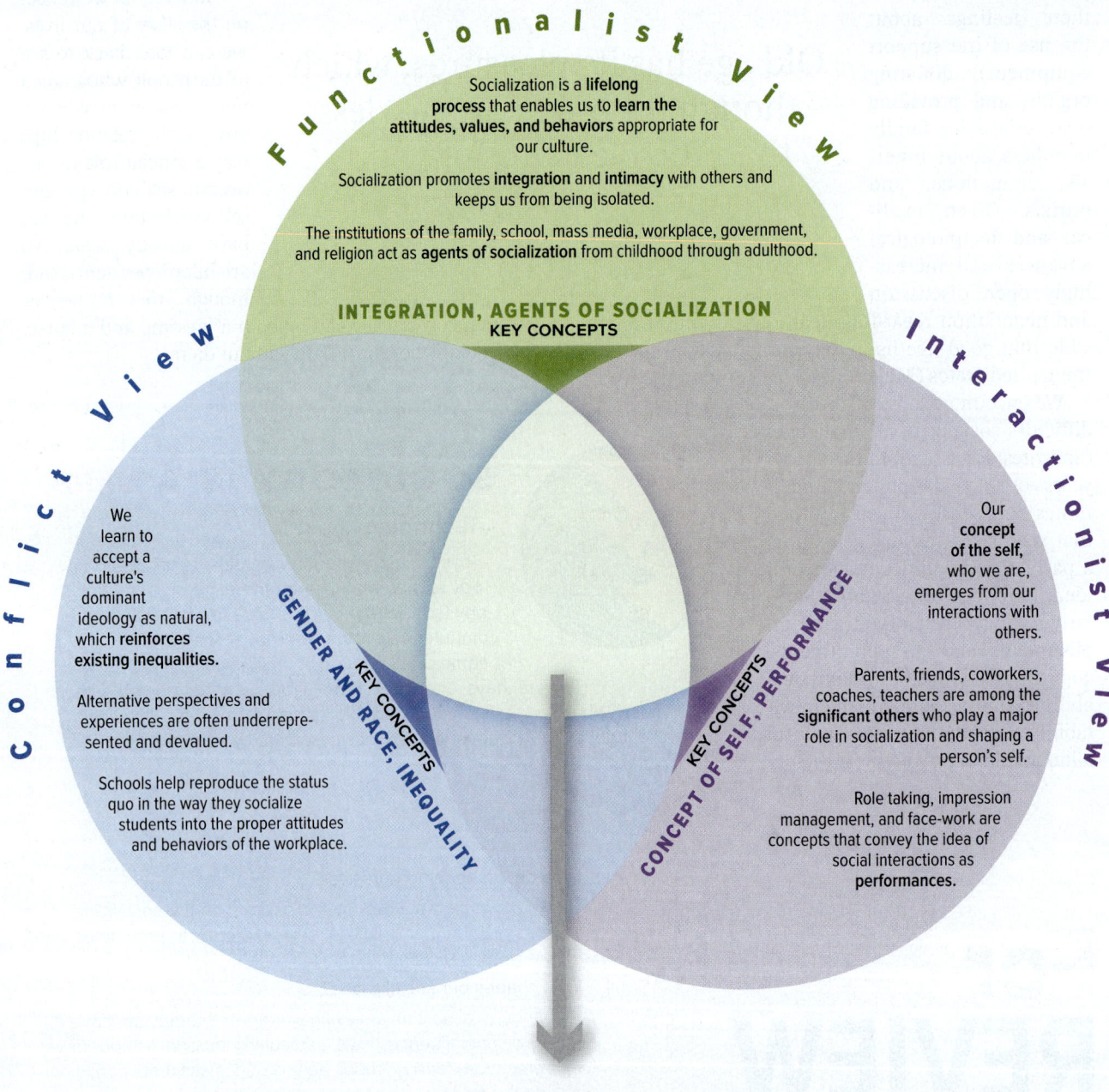

Functionalist View

Socialization is a **lifelong process** that enables us to **learn the attitudes, values, and behaviors** appropriate for our culture.

Socialization promotes **integration** and **intimacy** with others and keeps us from being isolated.

The institutions of the family, school, mass media, workplace, government, and religion act as **agents of socialization** from childhood through adulthood.

KEY CONCEPTS
INTEGRATION, AGENTS OF SOCIALIZATION

Conflict View

We learn to accept a culture's dominant ideology as natural, which **reinforces existing inequalities**.

Alternative perspectives and experiences are often underrepresented and devalued.

Schools help reproduce the status quo in the way they socialize students into the proper attitudes and behaviors of the workplace.

KEY CONCEPTS
GENDER AND RACE, INEQUALITY

Interactionist View

Our **concept of the self**, who we are, emerges from our interactions with others.

Parents, friends, coworkers, coaches, teachers are among the **significant others** who play a major role in socialization and shaping a person's self.

Role taking, impression management, and face-work are concepts that convey the idea of social interactions as **performances**.

KEY CONCEPTS
CONCEPT OF SELF, PERFORMANCE

MAKE THE CONNECTION
After reviewing the chapter, answer the following questions:

1 How would each perspective describe the impact that extreme isolation has on people?

2 How would each perspective explain the role socialization performs among children?

3 How would a functionalist look at anticipatory socialization? How might this view differ from a conflict approach?

4 Which agents of socialization have been most influential in your life? How does each perspective help shed light on those influences?

Pop Quiz

1. Babies learn to imitate the sounds of the language they hear even before they know the words. What term do sociologists use to describe the process of internalizing culture?
   a. socialization
   b. culturalization
   c. symbolization
   d. degradation

2. Which of the following terms does Charles Horton Cooley use for his model of the self as a product of how we imagine others see us?
   a. socialization
   b. the looking-glass self
   c. the I and the Me
   d. internalization

3. What term does George Herbert Mead use to refer to the attitudes, viewpoints, and expectations of society as a whole that a child takes into account in his or her behavior?
   a. play
   b. role taking
   c. dramaturgical analysis
   d. the generalized other

4. Suppose a clerk tries to appear busier than he or she actually is when a supervisor happens to be watching. Erving Goffman would say this is a form of what?
   a. degradation ceremony
   b. impression management
   c. resocialization
   d. looking-glass self

5. Which social institution is considered to be the most important agent of socialization in the United States, especially for children?
   a. family
   b. school
   c. peer group
   d. mass media

6. Which of the following terms describes the variety of technologies that provide the capacity to easily transmit large quantities of information to large groups of people?
   a. the Internet
   b. material culture
   c. print
   d. mass media

7. On the first day of basic training in the army, a male recruit has his civilian clothes replaced with army "greens," has his hair shaved off, loses his privacy, and finds that he must use a communal bathroom. All these humiliating activities are part of
   a. becoming a significant other.
   b. impression management.
   c. a degradation ceremony.
   d. face-work.

8. What do sociologists call the symbolic representations of major change in a person's status throughout his or her life course?
   a. rites of passage
   b. anticipatory socialization
   c. impression management
   d. role taking

9. The process of discarding former behavior patterns and taking on new ones is known as
   a. resocialization.
   b. impression management.
   c. anticipatory socialization.
   d. the I.

10. Which theory argues that elderly people have essentially the same need for social interaction as any other group and that those who remain active and socially involved will be best adjusted?
    a. disengagement theory
    b. institutional discrimination theory
    c. activity theory
    d. ageism theory

1. (a), 2. (b), 3. (d), 4. (b), 5. (a), 6. (d), 7. (c), 8. (a), 9. (a), 10. (c)

©B2M Productions/Getty Images

5 Social Structure and Interaction

WINNING AND LOSING

Life is like a game. Saying so has become something of a cliché, the kind of thing that appears on greeting cards and motivational posters, usually followed by some inspirational comments about how one should play. And yet, sociologically speaking, paying attention to how games operate can help us better understand what happens in our lives and why.

In the United States, players in most games start with the same basic chances—equal numbers of cards, identical amounts of cash, or the same space on the board. Card shuffling and dice throwing introduce randomness that could tilt the odds, but the presupposition is that winners and losers are determined more by skill than by anything else. In some games, however, the structure of the game itself shapes likely outcomes. One example is the traditional Chinese card game Zheng Shangyou (争上游), meaning "struggling upstream." Many variations of this game exist, including Dai Hin Min (大貧民) in Japan and Tiến Lên in Vietnam. In the United States, adaptations include Kings and Servants, the Great Dalmuti, President, and Scum.

What makes such games distinctive is that the position each player occupies conveys advantages or disadvantages. In one six-player version, positions include king, queen, jack, merchant, peasant, and servant. After all the cards have been dealt, the servant gives the king his or her best three cards, receiving the king's three worst cards in return. The peasant and queen similarly exchange two cards and the merchant and jack exchange one. Play then commences with people seeking to get rid of their cards by playing higher cards than those played by the person with the lead. At the end of each hand, after all the cards have been played, players change seats: the first person to go out, having played all his or her cards, becomes the new king, continuing until the last one out becomes the new servant. Because of the card exchanges, people at the top tend to stay at the top and those at the bottom stay at the bottom.

As a player at the top, you can easily feel good about yourself and chalk up your success to skill. As a player at the bottom, you can get discouraged, doubt your skill, and resent the unfair advantages of those at the top. There's nothing like having to give up two aces and a king only to receive worthless cards in return to make transparent the consequences of the game's unequal structure.

The choices we make do not occur in a vacuum. What these games suggest for those at the bottom is that, even if you play your cards right, you can still lose. In these games, as in life, our structural positions shape the options and opportunities available to us.

- What does society provide that we need?
- How do sociologists describe traditional versus modern societies?
- How does social structure shape individual action?

>> Social Interaction

We like to believe we are masters of our own destiny, yet the contexts within which we can make choices, such as at home, school, or the workplace, shape the choices we make. As we saw in Chapter 1, the sociological imagination calls us to consider the intersection of history and biography, and in this chapter we pay particular attention to the historical dimension by focusing on social structure. Our power to create culture demonstrates the agency we have as individuals. But the culture created by those who have gone before us constrains the options available to us, as that culture has both stood the test of time and enabled us to live orderly and meaningful lives.

To better understand the social positions we occupy, such as daughter, student, or employee, we can begin by taking a look at our everyday exchanges with others. Whether we are working together to construct culture or learning from each other through socialization, we do so via **social interaction,** a reciprocal exchange in which two or more people read, react, and respond to each other. Through this process we come to know what is expected of us. When parents discipline us or teachers praise us, we use those punishments and rewards to better inform how we might act in the future. The choices we make create patterns of behavior over time; thus our everyday interactions form the building blocks of society.

SELF AND SOCIETY

Our daily encounters with others—whether going to class, working on the job, or driving in traffic—shape who we become. Our self, as we saw in Chapter 4, must be understood as an ongoing project, constantly created and revised through our exchanges with others. Society provides the context within which that dynamic process of self-creation occurs. In the words of George Herbert Mead, "Selves can only exist in definite relationships to other selves. No hard-and-fast line can be drawn between our own selves and the selves of others" (1934:164). This social or relational conception of the self runs counter to the dominant sense of the self in the United States expressed in phrases such as "rugged individualism" or "I did it my way."

Over time, through interactions with others, we develop routine patterns of behavior that we take for granted—sitting at the same desk, having lunch with the same coworkers, traveling the same route. We do the same things and think many of the same thoughts, day after day. And so do others. Eventually such repeated practices can solidify into formal and informal norms, or become institutionalized in the form of laws. The resulting predictability allows us to know what to do most of the time.

> **Social interaction** A reciprocal exchange in which two or more people read, react, and respond to each other.

In time, the positions we occupy relative to others (such as student, boss, or traffic cop) also solidify, and we develop mutual expectations of how people in such positions should act. As these perceptions are shared with others beyond our immediate sphere of experience, it becomes possible to talk about the positions themselves—and the various relationships between them—apart from the individuals who occupy them. The end result is society—the structure of relationships within which culture is created and shared through regularized patterns of social interaction.

SOCIAL CONSTRUCTION OF REALITY

In working out the relationship between our self and society, we are engaged in the "social construction of reality." Sociologists Peter Berger and Thomas Luckmann (1966) coined this phrase to describe the interdependent relationship in which we as individuals create society through our actions and, at the same time, become products of the society we construct. They present their argument in their three-step model of world construction. The three parts include

- *Constructing culture.* Our actions are not strictly determined by biological instincts. To survive, we must establish a relationship to nature and with one another. We do so by creating tools, language, ideas, beliefs, rules for behavior, and so on to establish order and meaning. Culture enables us to make sense of our experiences and to pattern our actions. (See Chapter 3 on culture.)
- *Constructing the self.* Through socialization, we become products of the worlds we create. Anytime we enter into a new social world (for example, at birth, going away to college, the first day at a new job, marriage) we do not begin from scratch. We are shaped by the tools, ideas, and rules for action that have been constructed by others who have gone before us. We learn how we should think and act through our interactions with others, sharing ideas and experiences. Through socialization, we are constrained by the very culture we construct. (See Chapter 4 on socialization.)
- *Constructing society.* Between these first two steps is an intervening stage in which we share the culture we create with others. After it is shared, we lose control over it as individuals. It is no longer something "I" control; it is now in "our" hands. As a result of our shared acceptance, it comes to feel solid, real, or natural, even though we created it in the first place. One way to think of it is as an environment, a social world, or a structure within which we live. We come to take for granted that it simply "is."

In short, the social construction of reality involves an ongoing interaction between individuals and society. As we can see in the accompanying "World Construction" graphic, as individuals, we have the agency to create the material, cognitive, and normative culture we need to survive. At the same time, we

World Construction

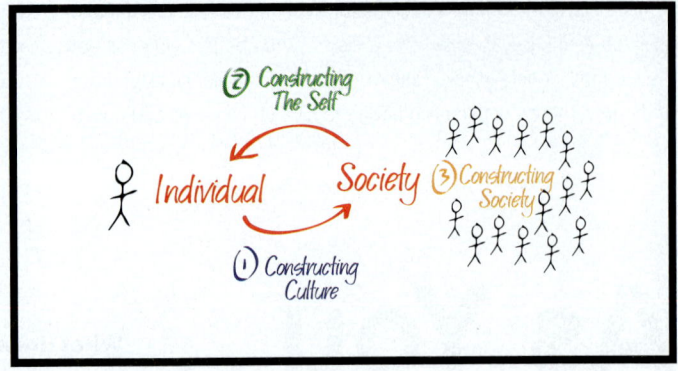

become ourselves as a consequence of the socialization we receive from those around us. That socialization seeks to reproduce and reinforce the existing relationships and expected behaviors that have been routinized and solidified over time in the form of society. The result is predictability and order that are necessary for social interaction and collective action. Through social interaction, we are always creating and being created, producers and products.

In this chapter we explore the core elements that make up society. In coming chapters we examine society's major components in greater depth. We also explore the reality that, as the patterns of relationships between us become routine, alternative ways of organizing society seem less possible. According to the conflict perspective, those taken-for-granted patterns create a power differential in which some people's values and voices are privileged over others. And, as we saw in the "Us versus Them" section in Chapter 4, we can become largely unaware that such differences exist.

When members of less powerful groups challenge existing social norms, they can raise society's collective awareness about the consequences of group membership or social position and help us perceive reality in a new way. For example, when Olympic gold medalist Muhammad Ali began his professional boxing career in the early 1960s, he was much like any other young African American fighter. He was managed and sponsored by a White boxing syndicate and went by his given name, Cassius Clay. Soon, however, the young boxer rebelled against the stereotypes of the self-effacing Black athlete and began to define his own social role. He converted to Islam, becoming a member of the U.S.-based Nation of Islam, and abandoned his "slave name" to take the name Muhammad Ali. He insisted on expressing his own political views, including refusing to fight in the Vietnam War. Ali changed the terms of social interaction for African American athletes by rebelling against racist thinking and terminology.

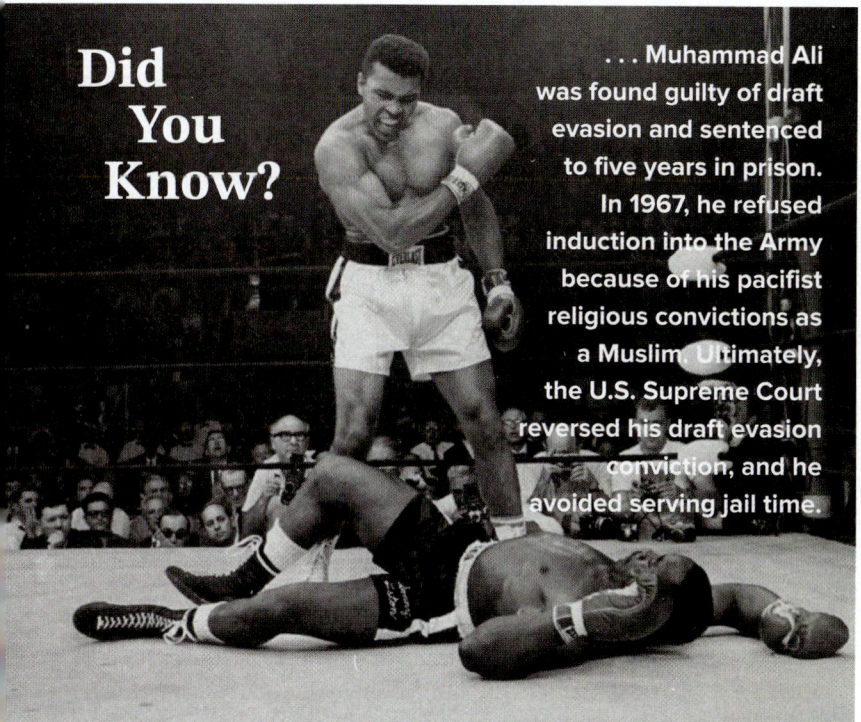

Did You Know?

...Muhammad Ali was found guilty of draft evasion and sentenced to five years in prison. In 1967, he refused induction into the Army because of his pacifist religious convictions as a Muslim. Ultimately, the U.S. Supreme Court reversed his draft evasion conviction, and he avoided serving jail time.

Photo: ©John Rooney/AP Images

In redefining culture, he helped open up new opportunities for himself and for other African Americans in the world of sports and beyond.

>> Elements of Social Structure

When it comes to games, as we saw above, the rules we invent provide us with a coherent structure. Rules specify whether to use a board, cards, dice, or tokens. They tell us what actions players can take and when they can take them. When rules change, whether in a game or in society, we must alter our actions accordingly. Game designer Zach Gage decided to mess with the rules of a classic game in his smartphone app *Really Bad Chess*. His game randomly distributes which chess pieces you receive and where they are placed. You might have five queens while your opponent has only one. As a result, the tried-and-true chess strategies and tactics that have worked for hundreds of years no longer apply. Players must adapt to the changing circumstances each time they play (Suellentrop 2016). Imagine if society was like that, if each morning we learned that the rules of the game—our material, cognitive, and normative culture—had changed and we had to adapt on the fly.

Every game has its own internal logic, the parameters within which we play. Society, though vastly more complex, functions in a similar manner. **Social structure** provides the underlying framework of society, consisting of the positions people occupy and the relationships between them. A building under construction provides a helpful analogy. Only early on can we see the framework—the girders, joists, studs, trusses, and the like—that composes the internal skeleton on which the building depends. In the same way, sociologists seek to identify and reveal society's four elemental building blocks, which include statuses and roles, groups, social networks, and social institutions. We look at each of these below.

STATUSES AND ROLES

Social structure transcends the particular people who populate it. In a college classroom, for example, from a structural perspective, the specific individuals who play the parts of student and professor matter less than the parts they play. To better understand how this works, we can begin by looking at both statuses and roles.

Achieved and Ascribed Status In sociology, **status**, which refers to the social positions we occupy relative to others, is the most basic component of social structure. In the context of families we might occupy the status of daughter, grandmother, or nephew; within the workplace, we might be an assistant manager, CEO, or salesperson. Because they emphasize the position rather than the person, statuses exist independent of the individuals who occupy them. We can occupy multiple statuses at the same time and move between a variety of statuses over the course of our lives.

Sociologists categorize statuses as either achieved or ascribed. An **achieved status** is a social position we have earned as a consequence of something we have done. Those accomplishments can be either positive or negative. For example, pianist, college graduate, sorority member, and parent are all achieved statuses. Each is realized by taking actions necessary for their attainment—practicing, studying, pledging, and having a baby. These are the kinds of accomplishments we generally celebrate.

> **Social structure** The underlying framework of society consisting of the positions people occupy and the relationships between them.
>
> **Status** The social positions we occupy relative to others.
>
> **Achieved status** A social position that is within our power to change.

Chapter 5 / Social Structure and Interaction

Social Statuses

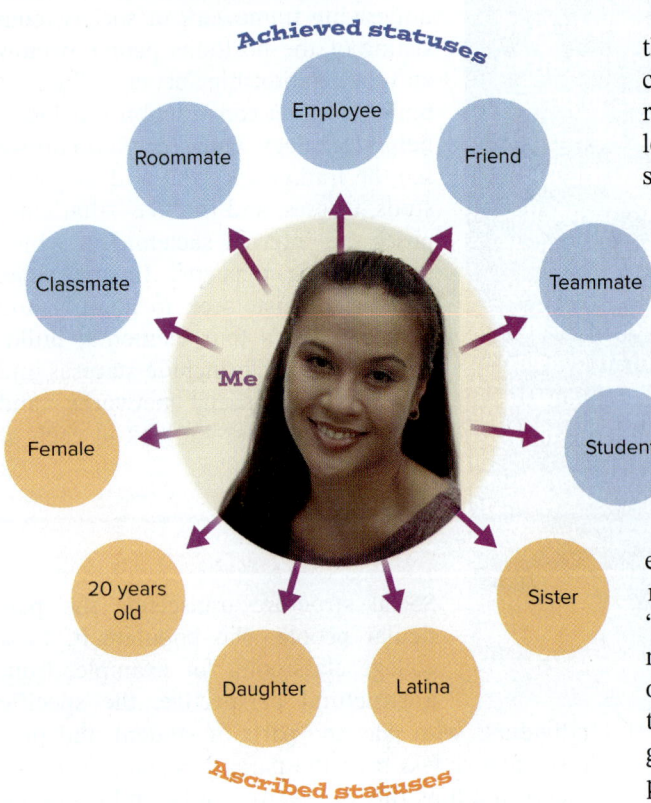

Photo: ©Amos Morgan/Getty Images RF

Ascribed status A social position assigned to a person by society without regard for the person's unique talents or characteristics.

But becoming a prisoner is also an achieved status, a consequence of committing a crime. As we explore in Chapter 10, the rags-to-riches stories that are part of the American Dream presuppose the possibility of achieving a higher social status.

By contrast, an **ascribed status** is assigned to a person by society without regard for the person's unique talents or characteristics. Whereas achieved statuses are earned, ascribed statuses are imposed. The assignment frequently takes place at birth—age, race/ethnicity, and sex are all considered ascribed statuses—but any characteristic can become an ascribed status so long as a sufficient number of people in society with the power to do so assign it significance and impose it on others. As we will see in Chapter 13, for example, conceptions of race in the United States have changed over time, which suggests that biology alone does not justify the significance attached to these statuses. Ascribed statuses are often used to justify privileges or to assign a person membership in a subordinate group.

Because statuses are social constructions we create, they are subject to change, and the line between them can become fuzzy. We see that happening now with regard to definitions of sex, gender, and sexuality. For a long time in the United States, people assumed that our sex was determined at birth, that there are only two distinct sexes, and that the one you belong to is patently obvious, a topic we will explore in more detail in Chapter 12. Furthermore, they assumed that how you think and act was largely determined by which category you were in, and that there was nothing you could do about it.

Americans have increasingly come to believe that biology is not destiny. People can make choices about what career they pursue, whether they want to have and raise children, what emotions they exhibit, what they wear, or how they express their sexuality. For example, until very recently, most Americans assumed that people's ascribed status as "male" or "female" limited their choice in marriage partners to members of the opposite sex. In 1996, 27 percent of U.S. adults supported same-sex marriage, but by 2016 that number rose to 61 percent. Perceptions vary across generations, with 83 percent of 18- to 29-year-olds supporting the right of same-sex couples to marry compared to 53 percent support among those aged 65 and older (McCarthy 2016). The 2015 Supreme Court decision to recognize the legal right of same-sex couples to marry reflected changing public sentiment on the matter. As we learned with the Thomas theorem, perception shapes action. In cases such as this, reconceptualizing our definition of status opened up new pathways.

Master Status Not all statuses are created equal. Whether achieved or ascribed, some statuses are seen as having greater significance in defining who we are

©Rob Melnychuk/Getty Images RF

than are others (Hughes 1945). Sociologists use the term **master status** to describe a status that dominates others and thereby determines a person's general position in society. This status serves as the primary lens through which people view other characteristics someone might have. Persons with disabilities frequently observe that nondisabled individuals see them only as blind, or only as wheelchair users, and so on, rather than as complex human beings with individual strengths and weaknesses whose disability is merely one aspect of their lives. In other words, their status as "disabled" receives undue weight, overshadowing their ability to hold meaningful employment and contributing to widespread discrimination (Banks and Lawrence 2006). In the United States, race, sex, and class often serve as master statuses.

Master status has consequences for opportunity. The African American activist Malcolm X (1925–1965), an eloquent and controversial advocate of Black power and Black pride in the 1960s, recalled that his feelings and perspectives changed dramatically in eighth grade. When his English teacher, a White man, advised him that his goal of becoming a lawyer was ridiculous and suggested he become a carpenter instead, Malcolm X (1964) concluded that his master status as a Black man was an obstacle to his dream of achieving the status of lawyer. Taken-for-granted conceptions of master status shape perceptions of what's possible, which can lead to systematic denial of opportunities for those in the negatively stigmatized status.

Throughout his life, Malcolm X worked to redefine the significance of race as master status. ©Burt Shavitz/Pic Inc/The LIFE Images Collection/Getty Images

a status is something you are, and a role is something you do. You occupy a status and play a role.

In some roles, our performance feels perfectly natural. We are just being ourselves. This occurs most frequently when we occupy a status within which we have a clear sense of what others expect of us and what we can expect of them. For example, we might feel this way while hanging out with close friends who can even finish our sentences. Other times, especially when we move into a new status, our actions can seem forced. The first semester at college, a first date, or the first week at a new job are all awkward times when people often fear they are

> **Master status** A status that dominates others and thereby determines a person's general position in society.
>
> **Social role** A set of expected behaviors for people who occupy a given social status.

going to be unmasked as frauds. But as we learned with Erving Goffman's dramaturgical approach, we are, all of us, always performing roles regardless of how we feel. Bruce Springsteen, reflecting back on his career as a rock and roll superstar, addressed the seeming conflict between his onstage persona as a hard-rocking hero

Roles Each status you occupy, whether it be parent, college student, social worker, or Muslim, comes with a set of actions expected of people in that status. If you are a parent, you are expected to provide food, clothes, and shelter for your child. If you are a student, you should go to class, study, and more. Sociologists use the term **social role** to describe the set of expected behaviors for people who occupy a given social status. To distinguish between the two,

©ImageDJ/Alamy Stock Photo RF

who's having nothing but a good time and the bouts of depression he experienced throughout his adult life. "I had plenty of days," he said, "where I'd go, 'Man, I wish I could be *that* guy.' And there's a big difference between what you see on stage and then my general daily, my daily existence" (NPR interview 2016).

Changing our status changes how we act, think, and feel. All of us encounter times when we feel awkward and uncomfortable. In Goffman's words, "Behind many masks and many characters, each performer tends to wear a single look, a naked unsocialized look, a look of concentration, a look of one who is privately engaged in a difficult, treacherous task" (Goffman 1959:235). The task of effectively carrying out a successful performance is compounded by the fact that we must perform for multiple, sometimes conflicting, audiences.

> **SOC THINK**
>
> List several social statuses you occupy. Which ones are ascribed, and which are achieved? What roles are you expected to play as a consequence of the positions you occupy?

Role Strain and Role Conflict Given that roles involve expected behaviors, tension can develop when we encounter role expectations that seem at odds with each other. Sociologists explore two types of such tensions: role strain and role conflict. **Role strain** occurs when role expectations within the same social status clash. For example, as a college student, it can be a challenge to balance the time you must spend studying for a sociology exam, writing a paper for a literature class, going to a work-study job washing dishes in the cafeteria, practicing clarinet for the college band, attending the big game, and managing roommate drama. **Role conflict** occurs when incompatible expectations arise from two or more social statuses held by the same person. For example, a working mom with kids at home who has returned to school to get her degree might struggle to balance the expectations tied to her multiple statuses as employee, parent, and college student. To keep the difference between strain and conflict clear, remember that role strain addresses tension within a single status, and role conflict deals with tension between statuses.

Role strain and role conflict both produce stress. They challenge our capacity to efficiently allocate our time, attention, and resources. We find ourselves forced to calculate the relative costs and benefits of fulfilling one role obligation while neglecting another. In doing so, we weigh how important each role is to us along with the possible rewards or punishments we might receive from others (Goode 1960).

Individuals sometimes cope with role strain and conflict by denying that it's a problem, redefining what counts as good-enough performance, delegating responsibilities to others, or even exiting the status altogether. One way to deal with the role strain of being a college student, for example, is to simply drop out. Sociologists point out that such solutions tend to underestimate the impact of social structure in creating role strain and conflict—and the potential benefits from reorganizing the structure. For example, among college students, reconceptualizing how institutions award financial aid might eliminate the need for work-study jobs; reorganizing the curriculum—at a handful of colleges, for example, students take only one course at a time—might alleviate the time stress of conflicting assignments; and providing only single-occupant rooms would

Role strain The difficulty that arises when role expectations within the same social status clash.

Role conflict The situation that occurs when incompatible expectations arise from two or more social statuses held by the same person.

Personal Sociology
Structure Matters

Although I love teaching, I hate grading. When I mention that to students, they say I have no one to blame but myself; if I didn't assign things, I wouldn't have to grade them. But I don't teach in a vacuum. If I didn't assign papers and tests, students would focus their time and energy on their looming chemistry test or their literature paper instead of reading for, participating in, or even attending my course. It is not that students aren't interested or sincere; it's that they are forced to budget their time for which professors compete using assignments. Because we exist in social systems, the expectations of those systems limit the amount of innovation we might desire. In what ways might the structures we are embedded within—school, work, recreation—inhibit us from making changes even if we would like to do so?

> **SOC THINK**
>
> Provide an example of both role strain and role conflict from your experience. What changes in the social structure might you propose to help alleviate each?

eliminate roommate drama. Thus, rather than focusing only on individual solutions to stress management, we should also explore the possibility that a new structure might alleviate the challenges we face.

Revising the expectations that accompany our roles and modifying the social structures they are part of can be challenging. For example, dealing with role conflict that is rooted in ascribed statuses can be particularly difficult. Lack of power to alter expectations, relationships, and access to valued resources limits an individual's opportunity to bargain with others. As we will see in Chapter 12, for example, women fought hard to alter the social structure that denied them equal access to education, jobs, promotions, and more. Any group working for change but lacking access to power in society faces an uphill challenge to revise the structure because the status quo seeks to reproduce itself.

Role Exit In addition to having to learn the social roles expected of us as we enter into new statuses, there are also steps we go through when we are leaving a status. Sociologist Helen Rose Fuchs Ebaugh (1988) used the term **role exit** to describe the process of disengagement from a role that is central to one's self-identity in order to establish a new role and identity. Drawing on interviews—with, among others, ex-convicts, divorced men and women, recovering alcoholics, ex-nuns, former doctors, retirees, and transsexuals—Ebaugh (herself a former nun) studied the process of voluntarily exiting from significant social roles.

Ebaugh has offered a four-stage model of role exit. The first stage begins with doubt. The person experiences frustration, burnout, or simply unhappiness with an accustomed status and the roles associated with that social position. The second stage involves a search for alternatives. An individual who is unhappy with his or her career may take a leave of absence; an unhappily married couple may begin what they see as a trial separation.

The third stage of role exit is the action stage, or departure. Ebaugh found that the vast majority of her respondents could identify a clear turning point when it became essential to take final action and leave their jobs, end their marriages, or engage in some other type of role exit. Only 20 percent of respondents saw their role exit as a gradual, evolutionary process that had no single turning point.

The last stage of role exit involves the creation of a new identity. Traditionally, students experience a form of role exit when they make the transition from high school to college. They may leave behind the role of a child living at home and take on the role of a somewhat independent college student living with peers in a dorm. Sociologist Ira Silver (1996) has studied the central role that material objects play in this transition. The objects students choose to leave at home (like stuffed animals and dolls) are associated with their prior identities. They

Transsexuals, such as Jenna Talackova (pictured here), often have to negotiate the four stages of role exit. ©Kevork Djansezian/Getty Images

may remain deeply attached to those objects but not want them to be seen as part of their new identities at college. The objects they bring with them symbolize how they now see themselves and how they wish to be perceived. Clothes, iPads, and wall posters, for example, are calculated to say, "This is who I am."

> **Role exit** The process of disengagement from a role that is central to one's self-identity in order to establish a new role and identity.

SOCTHINK

Whether from a sports team, a religious group, the military, or some other close-knit group, what experience, if any, have you had with role exiting? To what extent does your experience match the four stages Ebaugh describes?

GROUPS

The statuses we occupy, along with their corresponding social role expectations, are linked with other statuses to form groups, the second element of social

©Courtesy of Central College, photographer Dan Vander Beek

Primary and Secondary Groups Charles Horton Cooley (1902), whose theory of the looking-glass self we encountered in Chapter 4, coined the term **primary group** to refer to a small group characterized by intimate, face-to-face association and cooperation. Such groups often entail long-term commitment and involve more of what we think of as our whole self. Families constitute primary groups for many, although people also build close-knit, in-depth relationships with teammates, like-minded religious believers, coworkers, and fellow street gang members. In sports, for example, commitment to the cliché that there is "no 'I' in 'team'" often leads to a sense that teammates are "like family." As they work together, their level of trust and interdependence grows. Teammates come to know that the pitcher, outfielder, or catcher on the team not only will be there for them on the field, but will also have their backs when they need it off the field as well.

We also participate in many groups that are not characterized by close bonds of friendship, such as large college classes and business associations. The term **secondary group** refers to a formal, impersonal group in which there is little social intimacy or mutual understanding. Participation in such groups is typically more instrumental or goal directed, often involving only what we think of as one part of our self. Given these characteristics, we are more likely to move into and out of such groups as suits our needs. Historically, primary groups dominated in traditional societies, whereas many of our current-day groups are secondary in nature.

structure. In sociological terms, a **group** consists of two or more people, united by a shared sense of identity or purpose, who interact with each other over time in ways that distinguish them from outsiders. The members of a women's softball team, a hospital's business office, a synagogue, or a symphony orchestra constitute a group. A group can be distinguished from an aggregate, which consists of a collection of people who happen to be in the same place at the same time but who do not interact regularly or have a shared sense of purpose or common practices. Examples of aggregates include people waiting to cross the street at a busy intersection or riding together in an elevator.

We spend much of our time interacting in group settings. The type of group we are in influences our level of commitment and participation. Some groups demand our almost undivided attention and shape our core identity; others allow us to more easily accomplish specific goals.

Group Two or more people, united by a shared sense of identity or purpose, who interact with each other over time in ways that distinguish them from outsiders.

Primary group A small group characterized by intimate, face-to-face association and cooperation.

Secondary group A formal, impersonal group in which there is little social intimacy or mutual understanding.

Comparison of Primary and Secondary Groups

Primary group	Secondary group
Generally small	Usually large
Relatively long period of interaction	Relatively short duration, often temporary
Intimate, face-to-face association	Little social intimacy or mutual understanding
Some emotional depth to relationships	Relationships generally superficial
Cooperative, friendly	More formal and impersonal

In-Groups and Out-Groups The shared norms, values, and goals of group members, along with their common experiences, create a boundary distinguishing insiders and outsiders. The resulting us–them divide can lead to a strong sense of group identity, but it often does so at the expense of others, frequently serving as a basis for exclusion, especially if "they" are perceived as different either culturally or racially. Sociologists use the terms in-group and out-group to identify these two classifications.

An **in-group** consists of a category of people who share a common identity and sense of belonging. Members differentiate between themselves and everybody else (Sumner 1906). The in-group may be as narrow as a teenage clique or as broad as an entire nation. An **out-group** is defined, relative to the in-group, as a category of people who do not belong or do not fit in. Among an in-group of high school "populars" or "jocks," for example, a science "brain" might be considered an out-group member, and vice versa.

Group membership shapes our perceptions. What we see as acceptable behavior for the in-group can be simultaneously viewed as inappropriate behavior for the out-group. Sociologist Robert Merton (1968) described this process as the conversion of "in-group virtues" into "out-group vices." We can see this differential standard operating in the context of terrorism. When a group or a nation takes aggressive actions, it usually justifies them as necessary even if civilians are hurt or killed. Opponents are quick to assign the emotion-laden label of *terrorist* to such actions and to appeal to the world community for condemnation. Yet these same people may themselves retaliate with actions that hurt civilians, which the first group will then condemn as terrorist acts (Juergensmeyer 2003).

©Reza Estakhrian/Reportage/Getty Images

©Keith Srakocic/AP Images

SOC THINK

How do in-groups and out-groups function in a typical U.S. high school? What groups are common? How are boundaries separating insiders and outsiders maintained?

Reference Groups Both in-groups and primary groups can dramatically influence the way an individual thinks and behaves. Sociologists call any group that individuals use as a standard for evaluating themselves and their own behavior a **reference group**. For example, a high school student who aspires to join a social circle of hip-hop music devotees will pattern his or her behavior after that of the group. The student will begin dressing like these peers, listening to the same music, sharing "tags" on Instagram, and hanging out at the same stores and clubs.

Reference groups have two basic purposes. First, they serve a normative function by setting and enforcing standards of conduct and belief. The high school student who wants the approval of the hip-hop crowd will have to follow the group's dictates, at least to some extent. Second, reference groups perform a comparison

> **In-group** A category of people who share a common identity and sense of belonging.
>
> **Out-group** A category of people who do not belong or do not fit in.
>
> **Reference group** Any group that individuals use as a standard for evaluating themselves and their own behavior.

Chapter 5 / Social Structure and Interaction • 107

function by serving as a standard against which people can measure themselves and others. A fraternity or sorority member will evaluate himself or herself against a reference group composed of members of their "Greek" organizations (Merton and Kitt 1950).

Coalitions As groups grow larger, coalitions begin to develop. A **coalition** is an alliance, whether temporary or permanent, geared toward a common goal. Coalitions can be broad-based or narrow and can take on many different objectives. Sociologist William Julius Wilson (1999) has reported on community-based organizations in Texas that include Whites and Latinos, working-class and affluent, who banded together to work for improved sidewalks, better drainage systems, and comprehensive street paving. Out of this type of coalition building, Wilson hopes, will emerge better interracial understanding.

SOCIAL NETWORKS

These days, the term *social network* is primarily associated with our online connections through Instagram, Twitter, and the like, but it has always been possible to map the links that connect us with others. Networks represent the third element of social structure. A **social network** is a web of relationships through which people interact both directly and indirectly to accomplish formal and informal goals. Networks consist of two principal elements: nodes and relationships. In a social network, nodes consist of individuals, and relationships are the connections between them. The most basic building block of a social network is a **dyad** which consists of two connected nodes—for example, a tutor and a student or a boss and a worker. A **triad** consists of the relationships among three nodes, including both direct relationships (relationships between each of the possible pairs in the group) and indirect relationships (relationships connecting two people through the link provided by the third person). For example, a friend of a friend would constitute an indirect relationship. Beyond triads, each additional node to the network compounds the complexity of the network's interrelationships, multiplying the number of possible indirect relationships and increasing the possible distance between any two individuals to friend of a friend of a friend status and beyond. Centrality measures the degree to which any particular individual has more direct and indirect relationships than do others (Fowler and Christakis 2009). As networks become larger, centrality becomes an important additional dimension.

Sometimes social network connections are intentional and public; other times networks can develop that link us in ways that are not intentional or apparent. Sociologists Peter Bearman, James Moody, and Katherine Stovel (2004) investigated one such network, asking themselves this question: If you drew a chart of the romantic relationship network at a typical American high school, what would it look like? Using careful data-collection techniques to enhance the validity of their findings, they found that 573 of the 832 students they surveyed had been either romantically or sexually involved in the previous 18 months. Of these, 63 couples represented dyads, connected only with each other as pairs with no other partners. Other students connected directly or indirectly with a handful of partners. As we can see in the accompanying "Adolescent Sexual Networks" graphic, one larger group connected 288 students directly or indirectly into a single extended network. Such an example points to the fact that the choices we make often link us with others both known and unknown.

Research on how social networks function has produced some surprising results. For example, sociologist Scott Feld (1991) discovered that, on average, "most people have fewer friends than their friends have." This claim, which has come to be known as the friendship paradox, is somewhat counterintuitive; most people believe that the opposite is the case (Zuckerman and Jost 2001). When taking an objective look at the composition of social networks, however, it turns out that the average number of friends our friends have is elevated by the fact that, even though the number of people with many friends is relatively small, those individuals appear repeatedly in our friend's networks, driving up their averages. In other words, popular friends have a disproportionate effect because they are named as friends over and over again. Researchers at Facebook decided to put the friendship paradox to the test. They found that 93 percent of active Facebook users had fewer friends than their friends had. On average, users had 190 friends while their friends averaged 635 friends (Strogatz 2012). Overall, as mathematician Steven Strogatz (2012) put it, "Our friends are typically more popular than we are."

> I belong, therefore I am.
>
> —An old Māori proverb

Coalition A temporary or permanent alliance geared toward a common goal.

Social network A web of relationships through which people interact both directly and indirectly to accomplish formal and informal goals.

Dyad The most basic building block of a social network, it consists of two nodes and the relationship between them.

Triad Within a social network, it consists of three nodes and the direct and indirect relationships among them.

Adolescent Sexual Networks

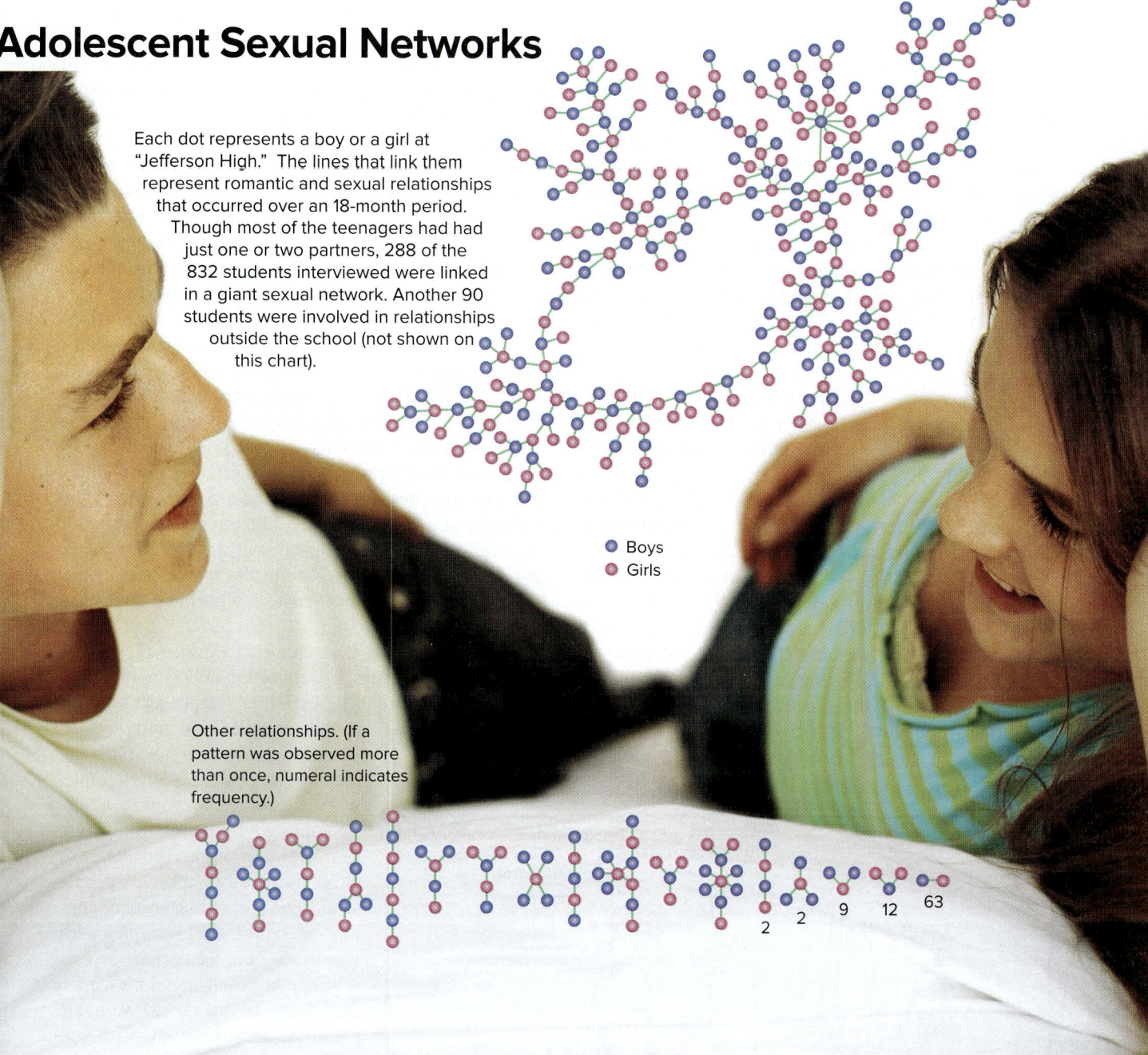

Each dot represents a boy or a girl at "Jefferson High." The lines that link them represent romantic and sexual relationships that occurred over an 18-month period. Though most of the teenagers had had just one or two partners, 288 of the 832 students interviewed were linked in a giant sexual network. Another 90 students were involved in relationships outside the school (not shown on this chart).

- Boys
- Girls

Other relationships. (If a pattern was observed more than once, numeral indicates frequency.)

Source: Bearman, Moody, and Stovel 2004:58. *Photo:* ©Stockbyte/Getty Images RF

Social network researchers, inspired by the friendship paradox, have explored a number of related phenomena. For example, in an analysis of Twitter users, and in an effort to control for the effect that outliers with high numbers of friends can have on the average, it turns out that, when analyzing the median instead of the mean, it's not just that the average number of our friend's friends is higher, it's also true that the majority of our friends have more friends than we do. This holds true for 98 percent of Twitter users (Kooti, Hodas, and Lerman 2014). Another study found that, if you are a scientist who has published a journal article, your coauthors will have more coauthors, more publications, and more citations than you (Eom and Jo 2014). It is hypothesized that the paradox is likely also true when it comes to wealth and number of sexual partners (Mullins 2014). One of the possible applications of the friendship paradox is that it can help with alerts for, and treatments of, infectious diseases by targeting friends of friends rather than simply using random samples by getting us closer to those who are most socially connected (Christakis and Fowler 2010).

Even our levels of happiness are influenced by the social networks to which we belong. Social network researchers found that our probability of being happy goes up 15 percent if someone with whom we have a direct link is happy (Fowler and Christakis 2008). The nature of the link affects the degree to which our happiness rises or falls. When considering mutual friends, those who would count each other as friends, our probability for happiness increases by 63 percent. Contrast that with the happiness of a spouse with whom we live, which increases our probability for happiness by 8 percent. Nearby siblings increase the probability of happiness by 14 percent, whereas neighbors living on the same block increase it by 34 percent. The happiness of coworkers had no significant effect. Centrality also matters. People who are more central to local networks tend to be happier than those who are at the periphery, and it is their centrality that leads to their happiness, not vice versa. In addition, happiness is more likely to spread between members of the same sex than the opposite sex. The researchers conclude, "Human happiness is not merely the province of isolated individuals" (Fowler and Christakis 2008). Again this demonstrates the significance of place. If we are to understand how we think, act, and even feel, we must take into account the social context within which we live.

Homophily Our tendency to establish close social network relationships with others who share our same knowledge, beliefs, practices, and characteristics.

It turns out that the networks we participate in can play a major role in our lives. In fact, though our closest ties to family and friends represent our strongest relationships, some of the most valuable connections can come through weaker links we have with others. Sociologist Mark Granovetter (1973) argued that we can categorize our network relationships as more or less strong using measures such as time spent together, emotional intensity, mutual confidences, and a shared sense of reciprocal obligation. In denser parts of a network, clusters of people are drawn together by strong ties that exist between them. The connections between such individuals are typically characterized by **homophily,** which literally means love of the same, a term sociologists use to describe our tendency to establish close social network relationships with others who share our same knowledge, beliefs, practices, and characteristics (McPherson, Smith-Lovin, and Cook 2001). For example, people tend to associate with others who have the same jobs, interests, education, race, ethnicity, and more. These dense clusters within a social network can be linked together through ties between individuals within two different clusters who have direct ties between each other.

In an argument that came to be known as "the strength of weak ties," Granovetter (1973) maintained that weaker ties can be extremely important because they can connect us with whole new networks of people with whom we have no direct relationships. For example, when it comes to getting a job, he reported that most jobs were found not through contacts with close friends, but through people who job seekers saw occasionally or rarely. Such people, with whom we have weak ties, serve as a bridge between social networks, providing us access to valuable resources and information.

Further support for the strength of weak ties principle emerged when Facebook researchers explored how relationships formed. They discovered that the most effective way to meet someone and start a relationship was through friends of friends. Mutual friends, in effect, serve as matchmakers. Those who played this matchmaking role have 73 percent more friends than do the people they set up. Their friendship networks are also less dense, meaning the matchmaker's friends are less likely to know each other,

TOLES © 2000 The Washington Post. Reprinted with permission of Andrews McMeel Syndication. All rights reserved.

presenting people a potential pool of possible partners. The matchmakers serve as bridges between people who might otherwise never connect (Burke, Diuk, and Friggeri 2015).

Social media theorist Clay Shirky (2008) maintains that the social networking potential of the Internet has radically transformed possibilities for collective action. In a survey of 40 nations, some of which are represented in the accompanying "Going Global—Social Networking" graphic, researchers found that 76 percent of Internet users claim to use social networking sites (Poushter 2016). Such connectedness opens up greater possibilities for widespread communication and action. Shirky argues that previous technologies inhibited collective behavior because those that allowed two-way communication (for example, the telephone) were largely limited to one-to-one conversations, and those that facilitated large-scale group formation through broadcasting were mostly limited to one-way communication (for example, television news viewers). With the Internet, he suggests, "group action just got easier" because it supports interactive, large-scale group formation. People can talk back and forth with each other and coordinate action, as occurred during the "Arab Spring" protests in countries including Egypt, Tunisia, and Libya in 2011.

SOCIAL INSTITUTIONS

Combinations of statuses, groups, and networks can coalesce to address the needs of a particular sector of society, forming what sociologists refer to as institutions, the fourth element of social structure. **Social institutions** are integrated and persistent social networks dedicated to ensuring that society's core needs are met. Sociologists have tended to focus on five major institutions that serve as key elements of the larger social structure: family, education, religion, economy, and government. Although these institutions frequently overlap and interact, taking each individually enables us to see what functions each serves within the larger social structure. We look in depth at all five in future chapters, but we begin here by considering the contributions each makes to society.

> **Social institution** An integrated and persistent social network dedicated to ensuring that society's core needs are met.

If a society is to survive, certain functions must be performed, and focusing on these institutions allows us to see how different societies fulfill these needs (Aberle et al. 1950). It is within the context of *families,* for example, that we ensure the society's continued existence by producing the next generation. Families carry out both

Going GLOBAL

Social Networking

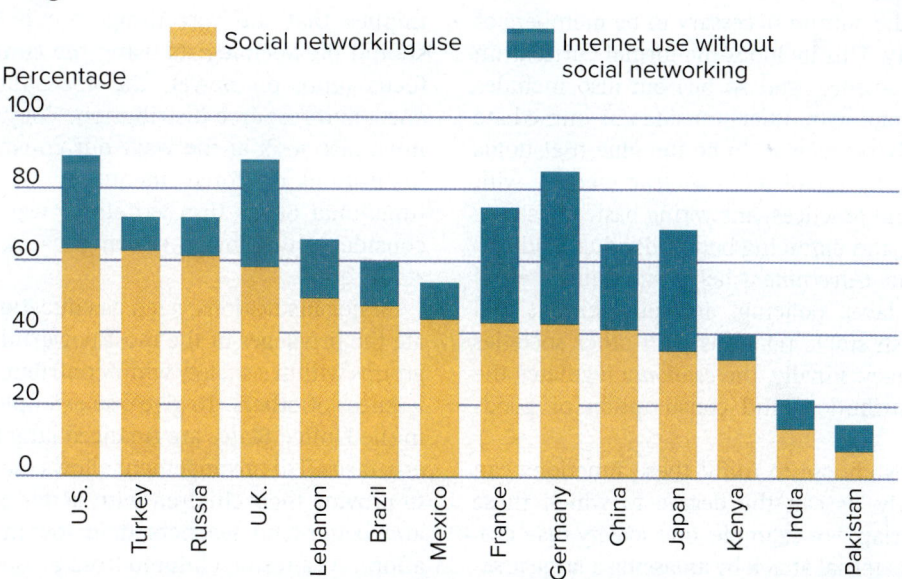

Note: Internet use includes those who use the Internet at least occasionally or report owning a smartphone.
Source: Poushter 2016.

©Amble Design/Shutterstock.com RF

biological reproduction (having children) and social reproduction (teaching them the culture they need for survival). Families also provide care and protection for members. Through *education* we teach the more formal and public culture necessary to be members of the larger society. This includes the formal curriculum (history, math, science, and so on) but also includes learning to interact with others outside our immediate families. We rely on *religion* to be the glue that holds society together by establishing a clear identity with shared beliefs and practices, answering basic questions about meaning, and enforcing both individual and collective discipline. *Government* helps maintain internal order through laws, policing, and punishment and seeks to establish stable relations with other societies through diplomacy. Finally, the *economy* regulates the production, distribution, and consumption of goods and services.

How societies choose to fulfill these functions can vary significantly, as can the degree to which these institutions overlap. For example, one society may protect itself from external attack by amassing a large arsenal of weaponry; another may make determined efforts to remain neutral in world politics and to promote cooperative relationships with its neighbors. According to the functionalist perspective, no matter what its particular strategy, any society or relatively permanent group must address all these functional prerequisites for survival.

Focusing on the functions institutions fulfill can help us better understand social order, but it often implies that the way things are is the way things should be. Sociologists using the conflict perspective focus more on power, the consequences of difference, and resource distribution. They suggest that we must also look at the ways our construction of these institutions reinforces inequality. We can meet these functional needs in a variety of ways, so we should consider why some groups might seek to maintain the status quo.

Major institutions, such as education, help perpetuate the privileges of the most powerful individuals and groups within a society while contributing to the powerlessness of others. To give one example, public schools in the United States are financed largely through property taxes. This arrangement allows more-affluent areas to provide their children with better-equipped schools and better-paid teachers than low-income areas can afford. As a result, children from prosperous communities are better prepared to compete academically than children from impoverished communities. The structure of the nation's educational system permits and even promotes such unequal treatment of schoolchildren (Kozol 2005).

©Purestock/SuperStock RF

> **SOC**THINK
> How is it possible for education to represent both a path for opportunity and an instrument for maintaining inequality? Where in your experience have you seen both at work?

By focusing on these four major elements of social structure—statuses and roles, groups, social networks, and social institutions—we gain an understanding of the building blocks of society. They clarify the factors we should consider when sociologists talk about the significance of place. We must look beyond our personal relationships with the significant others in our lives to also consider that those relationships exist as a consequence of a structure created by those who have come before us. We have the potential power to revise that structure. However, we also must recognize that we tend to reproduce the structure we have been socialized to accept as natural. Moreover, those already in power have an interest in maintaining that structure.

>> Social Structure in Global Perspective

Sociology arose as a discipline intended to illuminate and direct the transition from traditional to modern society. In the late 1800s, the taken-for-granted patterns and practices that had provided a sense of social order for hundreds of years seemed to be falling apart. Early sociologists believed that constructing a clear picture of the social structure that undergirded traditional societies would enable them to better understand the challenges faced with the rise of modern society.

GEMEINSCHAFT AND GESELLSCHAFT

Sociologist Ferdinand Tönnies (1855–1936) was appalled by the rise of industrial cities in his native Germany during the late 1800s. In his view, urban life was inferior to the close-knit community typical of rural villages. Tönnies ([1887] 1988) used the terms *Gemeinschaft* and *Gesellschaft,* typically translated as community and society, to distinguish the two.

A **Gemeinschaft** (pronounced "guh-MINE-shahft") consists of a close-knit community, often found in rural areas, in which strong personal bonds unite members. Virtually everyone knows one another, and social interactions are intimate and familiar, almost like in an extended family. Members feel a strong sense of loyalty to the group and willingly sacrifice their individual interests for the good of the whole. Social control in the *Gemeinschaft* is maintained primarily through informal means, such as moral persuasion, gossip, and even gestures. These techniques work effectively because people genuinely care how others feel about them. However, with such interpersonal intensity comes minimal privacy and a presumption of individual sacrifice. Social change is relatively limited in the *Gemeinschaft;* the lives of members of one generation may be quite similar to those of their parents, grandparents, and so on.

> **Gemeinschaft** A close-knit community, often found in rural areas, in which strong personal bonds unite members.
>
> **Gesellschaft** Consists of a large, impersonal, task-oriented society, typically urban, in which individuals have a limited commitment to the group.

In contrast, a **Gesellschaft** (pronounced "guh-ZELL-shahft") consists of a large, impersonal, task-oriented society, typically urban, in which individuals have a limited commitment to the group. Relationships here, as we saw with secondary groups, emphasize instrumental or transactional exchanges. Interactions are governed by social roles that grow out of immediate tasks, such as purchasing a product or arranging a business meeting. In such societies, most people are strangers who feel little in common with other residents. Individuals can perceive themselves as superior to other members of the society, placing their interests above those of the group. There is minimal consensus concerning shared values beyond those of maximizing self-interest. As a result, social control must rest on formal techniques, such as laws and legally defined sanctions.

Social change is a normal part of life in the *Gesellschaft,* with substantial shifts evident even within a single generation.

Sociologists use these two terms to compare social structures that stress close relationships with those that feature less personal ties. It is easy to view the *Gemeinschaft* with nostalgia, as far better than the rat race of modern life. However, the more intimate relationships of the *Gemeinschaft* come at a price. The prejudice and discrimination found there can be quite confining; ascribed statuses such as family background often outweigh a person's unique talents and achievements. In addition, the *Gemeinschaft* tends to distrust individuals who are creative or simply different (Garrett 2003). One device for keeping the two terms straight is to remember that *Gemeinschaft* focuses on personal interactions, so think "mine," and *Gesellschaft* addresses impersonal, formal interactions, such as you might buy and "sell" in the marketplace.

©Amy Sancetta/AP Images

> **SOC THINK**
> What might be appealing about living in a community characterized by *Gemeinschaft?* What are possible drawbacks?

MECHANICAL AND ORGANIC SOLIDARITY

Whereas Tönnies looked back nostalgically on the *Gemeinschaft,* Émile Durkheim was more interested in the transition to modern society, which he felt represented the birth of a new form of social order. Durkheim hoped to use sociology as a science to better understand this transition. In his book *The Division of Labor in Society* ([1893] 1933), Durkheim highlighted the seemingly inverse relationship between the division of labor and the collective conscience. As jobs became more specialized, the shared sentiments that united communities grew weaker.

Mechanical solidarity Social cohesion based on shared experiences, knowledge, and skills in which things function more or less the way they always have, with minimal change.

Organic solidarity Social cohesion based on mutual interdependence in the context of extreme division of labor.

In societies in which there is minimal division of labor, a sense of group solidarity develops because people do the same things together over time. Such societies are characterized by what Durkheim calls **mechanical solidarity,** a type of social cohesion based on shared experiences, knowledge, and skill in which social relations function more or less the way they always have. Societies with strong mechanical solidarity operate like a machine with limited change over time, which is why Durkheim chose the term *mechanical.* Most individuals perform the same basic tasks—as did their parents and grandparents before them—and they do so together. These shared experiences—whether hunting, farming, preparing meals, making clothes, or building homes—result in shared perspectives and common values. Each individual acts, thinks, and believes very much like the next. Among the Amish, for example, what you will be when you grow up is virtually set at birth. There is limited opportunity for individual variation, because deviation from expected pathways represents a threat to social solidarity (Kraybill 2001; Kraybill et al. 2013).

As societies become more advanced technologically, their division of labor expands, and jobs become increasingly specialized. A new foundation for social order emerges, which Durkheim calls **organic solidarity,** that is a type of social cohesion based on our mutual interdependence in the context of extreme division of labor. In these societies, the person who cuts down timber is no longer the same person who builds your house. In most cases, it now takes many people with diverse sets of skills to produce even a single item, such as a chair or a cell phone. As a result, the mechanical solidarity that arose through common experience breaks down as differences emerge in how the members of the society view the world and their place in it. Whereas Tönnies saw this and despaired, Durkheim suggested that organic solidarity would provide us with a new sense of unity and possibility.

In modern societies, specialization breeds interdependence, as we saw with the "a hamburger is a miracle" example in Chapter 1. The irony of modern society is that we combine extreme interdependence with a strong sense of individualism. We couldn't be self-sufficient because of our extreme division of labor, but we have a strong desire to be independent. We need one another more than ever, but we realize it less. Durkheim argued that society would evolve to address this tension and ensure social order. The various components of society would recognize how much they need one another and work together in the same way as the interdependent organs of the human body do, which is why Durkheim chose the term *organic*, each performing a vital function, but none capable of surviving alone.

TECHNOLOGY AND SOCIETY

Some sociologists focus more explicitly on technology than on social organization, expressed as division of labor, to understand distinctions between traditional and modern societies. In sociologist Gerhard Lenski's view, a society's level of technology is critical to the way it is organized (Nolan and Lenski 2006). As technology changes, new social forms arise, from preindustrial, to industrial, to postindustrial. Available technology does not narrowly determine the form that a particular society takes, but a low level of technology limits the degree to which a society can take advantage of the possibilities technology provides.

Preindustrial Societies Perhaps the earliest form of preindustrial society to emerge in human history was the **hunting-and-gathering society,** in which people simply rely on whatever foods and fibers are readily available. Such groups are typically small and widely dispersed, and technology in such societies is minimal. Organized into groups, people move constantly in search of food. There is minimal division of labor because everyone is engaged in the same basic activities. Because resources are scarce, there is relatively little inequality in terms of material goods.

In **horticultural societies,** people plant seeds and crops rather than merely subsist on available foods. Members of horticultural societies are much less nomadic than hunter-gatherers. They place greater emphasis on the production of tools and household objects. Yet technology remains rather limited in these societies, whose members cultivate crops with the aid of simple tools such as digging sticks or hoes (Wilford 1997).

The third type of preindustrial development is the **agrarian society.** As in horticultural societies, members of agrarian societies are engaged primarily in the production of food, but technological innovations such as the plow allow farmers to dramatically increase their crop yields and cultivate the same fields over generations. As a result, it becomes possible for larger, more permanent settlements to develop.

Agrarian societies continue to rely on the physical power of humans and animals (in contrast to mechanical power). Division of labor increases because technological advances free up some people from food production to focus on specialized tasks, such as the repair of fishing nets or blacksmithing. As human settlements become stabler and more established, social institutions become more elaborate and property rights more important. The comparative permanence and greater surpluses of an agrarian society allow members to specialize in creating artifacts such as

> **Hunting-and-gathering society** A preindustrial society in which people rely on whatever foods and fibers are readily available in order to survive.
>
> **Horticultural society** A preindustrial society in which people plant seeds and crops rather than merely subsist on available foods.
>
> **Agrarian society** The most technologically advanced form of preindustrial society. Members are engaged primarily in the production of food, but they increase their crop yields through technological innovations such as the plow.

Innovations in agricultural technology meant fewer people were needed to work the land. ©Ryan McVay/Getty Images RF

Industrial society A society that depends on mechanization to produce its goods and services.

Postindustrial society A society whose economic system is engaged primarily in the processing and control of information.

statues, public monuments, and art objects and to pass them on from one generation to the next.

Industrial Societies The Industrial Revolution transformed social life in England beginning in the late 1700s, and within a century its impact on society had extended around the world. An **industrial society** is one that depends on mechanization to produce its goods and services. The strength and stamina humans gained from new inventions such as the steam engine opened up a new world of possibilities by applying nonanimal (mechanical) sources of power to most labor tasks. As such, industrialization significantly altered the way people lived and worked, and it undercut taken-for-granted norms and values. It was this period of transition from traditional to modern society that led early sociologists, such as Tönnies, Durkheim, and Marx, to propose their theories of social order and change.

During the Industrial Revolution, many societies underwent an irrevocable shift from an agrarian-oriented economy to an industrial base. Specialization of tasks and manufacture of goods increasingly replaced the practice of individuals or families making an entire product in a home workshop. Workers, generally men but also women and even children, left their family homesteads to work in central locations such as urban factories.

The process of industrialization had distinctive social consequences. Families and communities could not continue to function as self-sufficient units. Individuals, villages, and regions began to exchange goods and services and to become interdependent. As people came to rely on the labor of members of other communities, the family lost its unique position as the main source of power and authority. The need for specialized knowledge led to formalized schooling, and education emerged as a social institution distinct from the family. And bureaucracies were established to manage the complex undertakings of large organizations, which we explore in more detail in the "Bureaucracy" section.

Postindustrial Societies Mechanized production continues to play a substantial role in shaping social order, relationships, and opportunities, but technological innovation again has reshaped social structure by freeing up some people from the demands of material production. This has led to the rise of the service sector of the economy in many technologically advanced countries. In the 1970s, sociologist Daniel Bell wrote about the technologically advanced **postindustrial society**, whose economic system is engaged primarily in the processing and control of information. The main output of a postindustrial society is services rather than manufactured goods. Large numbers of people become involved in occupations devoted to the teaching, generation, or dissemination of ideas. Jobs in fields such as advertising, public relations, human resources, and computer information systems are typical of a postindustrial society (Bell 1999).

Some sociologists, including Bell, view this transition from industrial to postindustrial society as largely a positive development. Others, however, point to the often hidden consequences that result from differential access to resources in postindustrial society. For example, Michael Harrington (1980), who alerted the nation to the problems of the poor in his book *The Other America,* questions the significance that Bell attaches to the growing class of white-collar workers. Harrington concedes that scientists, engineers, and economists are involved in important political and economic decisions, but he disagrees with Bell's claim that they have a free hand

Did You Know?

... One of the effects of the Industrial Revolution was that the U.S. population became increasingly urban, with more people living together in closer proximity than ever before.

144
largest counties
population: 159,524,138
50.3% of total population

2,998
smallest counties
population: 159,332,918
49% of total population

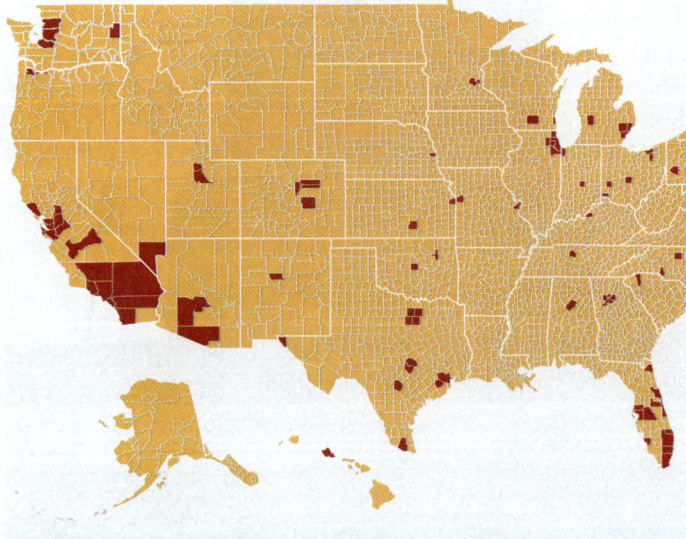

Source: Adapted from http://dadaviz.com/s/population-extremes/#4568.

in decision making, independent of the interests of the rich. Harrington follows in the tradition of Marx by arguing that conflict between social classes will continue in the postindustrial society.

POSTMODERN LIFE

Some sociologists have gone beyond discussion of the postindustrial society to contemplate the emergence of postmodern society (Best and Kellner 2001; Susen 2015). A **postmodern society** is a technologically sophisticated, pluralistic, interconnected, globalized society. Although it is difficult to summarize what a whole range of thinkers have said about postmodern life, four elements provide a sense of the key characteristics of such societies today: stories, images, choices, and networks.

Stories Because postmodern societies are pluralistic and individualistic, people hold many different, often competing, sets of norms and values. Fewer people assume that a single, all-inclusive story—whether a particular religious tradition, or an all-encompassing scientific theory of everything, or even the faith many early sociologists had in the inevitability of modern progress—can unite us all under a common umbrella. Instead, we embrace the various individual and group stories that help us make sense of the world and our place in it. We do so in the full knowledge that others out there are doing exactly the same thing and often coming to dramatically different conclusions. This multiplicity of stories undercuts the authority that singular accounts of reality, whether religious or scientific, have had in the past.

> **Postmodern society** A technologically sophisticated, pluralistic, interconnected, globalized society.

Images Postmodern society is also characterized by the explosion of the mass media, which emphasizes the importance of images. The average adult in the United States watches 4 hours and 39 minutes of television per day (Nielsen 2016). This works out to the equivalent of watching television 24 hours a day for almost 71 days per year. We are bombarded by images everywhere we turn, but in postmodern theory, the significance of the image goes much deeper than television and advertisements; it impacts our taken-for-granted notion of material reality itself. Theorists argue that we do not confront or interact with the material world directly. Just as language shapes our perception of reality according to the Sapir-Whorf hypothesis, our experience of "reality" is always mediated through representations of reality in the form of signs, symbols, and words. According to postmodernists, our images or models of reality come before reality itself. Postmodern theorists use a geography metaphor to illuminate this concept: "The map precedes the territory" (Baudrillard [1981] 1994). In other words, the images we construct draw our attention to certain features that we might not otherwise single out. A road map, for example, highlights different features, and for different purposes, than does a topographical map or political map. In so doing, it shapes what we see. We cannot step around or look through such cultural constructs to approach the thing itself, and so our knowledge of what is real is always constrained by the images we construct.

Choices In a postmodern world, reality is not simply given; it is negotiated. We pick and choose our reality from the buffet of images and experiences presented to us. In fact, we *must* choose. In contrast to societies characterized by mechanical solidarity, where one's

Going GLOBAL

International Favorability Ratings for the United States

Bottom five nations		Top five nations	
Turkey	29%	Philippines	92%
Palestinian Territories	26%	Ghana	89%
Pakistan	22%	Kenya	84%
Russia	15%	South Korea	84%
Jordan	14%	Italy	83%

Note: The numbers represent the percentage of people in each country who responded with a favorable or unfavorable opinion of the United States.
Source: Wike, Stokes, and Poushter 2015.

Because we exist in an interdependent global network, the consequences of our actions, both large and small, reverberate throughout the world. In a global survey of 39 other nations, the Pew Research Center investigated how people in those countries view the United States. In the Philippines, 92 percent of people surveyed had a favorable opinion of the United States. On the other end of the scale, only 14 percent in Jordan had a favorable view. The median favorability percentage for the 39 countries was 69 percent, with regional variation from 74 percent for the African nations surveyed to 38 percent in the Middle East.

Bureaucracy A formal organization built upon the principle of maximum efficiency.

life path is virtually set at birth, members of postmodern societies must make life choices all the time. Assuming we have access to sufficient resources, we choose what to eat, what to wear, and what to drive. Shopping, which in the past would have been viewed primarily as an instrumental necessity to provide for our basic needs, becomes an act of self-creation. As advertising professor James B. Twitchell (2000) put it, "We don't buy things, we buy meanings" (p. 47). An iPhone, a Coach purse, and a MINI Cooper are more than just a phone, a handbag, and a car. They are statements about the kind of person we are or want to be. The significance of choice goes much deeper than just consumer products. We also choose our partners, our schools, our jobs, our faith, and even our identities. As individuals, we may choose to affirm traditions, language, diet, and values we inherited from our family through socialization, but we can also choose to pursue our own path.

Networks Members of postmodern societies live in a globally interconnected world. The food we eat, the clothes we wear, the books we read, and the products we choose often come to us from the other side of the world. The computer technician we talk to for assistance in the United States may be located in India. McDonald's has even experimented with centralized drive-through attendants—who might even be located in another state—who take your order and transmit it to the restaurant you are ordering from (Richtel 2006). Increasingly, all corners of the globe are linked into a vast, interrelated social, cultural, political, and economic system. A rural Iowa farmer, for example, must be concerned with more than just the local weather and community concerns; he or she must know about international innovations in farming technology, including biotech, as well as the current and future state of international markets.

©Image Source/Getty Images RF

>> Bureaucracy

In their efforts to understand and explain the underlying structure of industrial and postindustrial societies, early sociologists anticipated the rise of bureaucracy, as evidenced by Tönnies' description of *Gesellschaft* and Durkheim's analysis of organic solidarity. A **bureaucracy** is a formal organization built on the principle of maximum efficiency. As globalization expanded and modern life became increasingly complex, the principles used to manage social order in pre–Industrial Revolution societies no longer seemed

Characteristics of a Bureaucracy

	Positive consequences	Negative consequences	
		For the individual	For the organization
Division of labor	Produces efficiency in a large-scale corporation	Limits knowledge	Creates communication barriers
Hierarchy of authority	Clarifies who is in command	Deprives employees of a voice in decision making	Permits concealment of mistakes
Written rules and regulations	Let workers know what is expected of them	Stifle initiative and imagination	Lead to goal displacement
Impersonality	Reduces bias	Contributes to feelings of alienation	Discourages loyalty to company
Employment based on technical qualifications	Discourages favoritism and reduces petty rivalries	Discourages ambition to improve oneself elsewhere	Inhibits innovative thinking

Photo: ©mevans/Getty Images RF

adequate. Modern society required the more systematic approaches to governance bureaucracy provides. According to Max Weber ([1913–1922] 1947), bureaucracy represents the most rational form of management ever devised.

CHARACTERISTICS OF A BUREAUCRACY

Bureaucratic success depends on the establishment of rational principles of organization throughout an organization. As indicated in the accompanying the company would make their contributions, including the engineers who design the product line, marketing experts who create advertising campaigns, salespersons who entice customers to buy, accountants who do the bookkeeping, mechanics who maintain the machines, custodians who clean up afterward, and a whole host of others. The justification for such complexity is that, in the context of a large firm, it would be impossible for one individual to have sufficient expertise to carry out all those tasks well.

Ideal type An abstract model of the essential characteristics of a phenomenon.

Photos: pediatric doctor: ©Arthur Tilley/Getty Images RF; butcher: ©Adam Crowley/Getty Images RF; mopping floor: ©Muntz/Taxi/Getty Images

"Characteristics of a Bureaucracy" table, Weber identified five core characteristics of bureaucracies. He did so by constructing what he called an **ideal type**, an abstract model of the essential characteristics of a phenomenon. In actuality, perfect bureaucracies do not exist. Nonetheless, Weber's model provided a useful tool for comparing and contrasting functioning bureaucracies.

Division of Labor The goal of a bureaucracy is to accomplish some specific goal in the most efficient manner possible. The most effective way to do so is to identify all the tasks necessary for success and assign specialists in each area to carry out those tasks. In traditional societies, a furniture maker might carry out every step of the production process, from cutting down the tree to finishing the table, herself. On top of that, she might have to do everything else that running a small business entails, including bookkeeping, marketing, and sales. In a modern bureaucracy, that table will likely be produced on an assembly line where each worker has responsibility for only one part of the process. In addition, workers in other parts of

Did You Know?

... In the 2010 Census, the U.S. Census Bureau identified **539** distinct occupational categories, including Chief Executive, Aerospace Engineer, Phlebotomist, Crossing Guard, and Sociologist. They organized these occupations into six major categories.

Photo: ©RT Images/Alamy Stock Photo RF

Chapter 5 / Social Structure and Interaction • 119

Goal displacement Overzealous conformity to official regulations of a bureaucracy.

The combined expertise that each specialized worker contributes produces greater efficiency than would exist if all workers were trained in every skill.

Dividing up labor in this way does have potential disadvantages. Workers who do routine tasks over and over again can feel like little more than a cog in the machine. This can produce a sense of alienation in which we experience loss of control over our creative human capacity to produce, separation from the products we make, and isolation from our fellow workers. It also can subject workers to greater job insecurity when jobs are deskilled through simplification and mechanization, making it easier to find and train a replacement worker. In addition, bureaucracy can produce what business executives refer to as "silos" in which there are limited connections between the various parts of a firm, inhibiting possible information exchange and collaboration between departments, thus resulting in greater inefficiencies (Lencioni 2006). Further, the frustration we can experience when dealing with bureaucratic red tape—whether in the workplace, at a university, or with the government—frequently results from having to deal with different segments of a bureaucratic machine.

Hierarchy of Authority Bureaucracies follow the principle of hierarchy; that is, each position is under the supervision of a higher authority. A president heads a college bureaucracy; he or she selects members of the administration, who in turn hire their own staff. In the Roman Catholic Church, the pope is the supreme authority; under him are cardinals, bishops, and so forth. In businesses, the most basic relation is between boss and worker, but in large corporations there are multiple levels of authority. To track relationships, such companies map those connections using hierarchical organizational charts that identify all the links of who answers to whom, ultimately leading up to the president or CEO at the top.

Written Rules and Regulations Through written rules and regulations, bureaucracies generally offer employees clear statements of their rights and responsibilities in the form of detailed job descriptions and comprehensive employee handbooks. If situations arise that are not covered by the rules, bureaucracies are self-correcting. They have rules in place to ensure that new rules are established that make work expectations as clear and as exhaustive as possible. Because bureaucracies are hierarchical systems of interrelated positions, such procedures provide a valuable sense of continuity for the organization. Individual workers may come and go, but the structure and past records of the organization give it a life of its own that outlives the services of any one particular person.

Of course, rules and regulations can overshadow the larger goals of an organization to the point that they

> **SOC THINK**
>
> Why do we tend to associate bureaucracies with red tape and inefficiency when they are explicitly organized to be the opposite? To what extent is our desire to be treated as an individual at odds with the principles of bureaucracies?

become dysfunctional. What if a hospital emergency room physician failed to treat a seriously injured person because he or she had no valid proof of U.S. citizenship? If blindly applied, rules no longer serve as a means to achieving an objective but instead become important (perhaps too important) in their own right. Robert Merton (1968) used the term **goal displacement** to refer to overzealous conformity to official regulations of a bureaucracy in which we lose sight of the larger principle from which the rule was created.

Impersonality Bureaucratic norms dictate that officials judge people based on performance rather than personality. So long as everyone follows the rules as written, without regard for emotion or personal preference, the greatest good will result. The intent is to ensure equal treatment for each person. But it can also contribute to the cold, uncaring feeling often associated with modern

A chief executive officer (CEO) typically rests atop the pyramid structure of bureaucratic hierarchy. Ursula Burns, pictured here, served as the CEO for Xerox Corporation from 2009 to 2016.
©Joshua Lott/AFP/Getty Images

organizations. Whether registering for college classes or getting tech support for a malfunctioning computer, most of us have had some experience of feeling like a number and longing for some personal attention. The larger the organization or society, however, the less possible such personal care becomes because attending to individual wants and needs is inefficient.

Employment Based on Technical Qualifications Within the ideal bureaucracy, hiring is based on technical qualifications rather than on favoritism, and performance is measured against specific standards. Written personnel policies dictate who gets promoted, and people often have a right to appeal if they believe that particular rules have been violated. In combination with the principle of impersonality, the driving personnel principle is supposed to be that it is "what you know, not who you know" that counts. Such procedures protect workers against arbitrary dismissal, provide a measure of security, and encourage loyalty to the organization.

Weber developed these five indicators of bureaucracy 100 years ago, and they continue to describe the ideal type. Not every formal organization will fully realize all of Weber's characteristics. The underlying logic they represent, however, points toward a way of doing things that is typical of life in modern societies.

> Bureaucracy is . . . the most rational known means of exercising authority over human beings.
>
> Max Weber

calculability, predictability, and control shape organization and decision making, in the United States and around the world. Ritzer argues that these principles, which are at the heart of the McDonald's fast-food chain's success, have been emulated by many organizations, ranging from medical care to wedding planning to education. Even sporting events reflect the influence of McDonaldization. Around the world, stadiums are becoming increasingly similar, both physically and in the way they present the sport to spectators. Swipe cards, "sports city" garages and parking lots, and automated ticket sales maximize efficiency. All seats offer spectators an unrestricted view, and a big screen guarantees them access to instant replays. Scores, player statistics, and attendance figures are updated by computers and displayed on an automated scoreboard. Spectator enthusiasm is manufactured through video displays urging applause or rhythmic chanting. At food counters, refreshments include

> **Bureaucratization** The process by which a group, organization, or social movement increasingly relies on technical-rational decision making in the pursuit of efficiency.
>
> **McDonaldization** The process by which the principles of efficiency, calculability, predictability, and control shape organization and decision making, in the United States and around the world.

BUREAUCRATIZATION AS A WAY OF LIFE

Bureaucracy for Weber was an indicator of a larger trend in modern society toward rational calculation of all decision making, using efficiency and productivity as the primary standards of success. We recognize this pattern first at the level of businesses and organizations. More companies seek greater efficiency through **bureaucratization**—the process by which a group, organization, or social movement increasingly relies on technical-rational decision making in the pursuit of efficiency. Over time, however, the technical-rational approach pervades more and more areas of our lives.

The Spread of Bureaucratization One example of the expansion of bureaucratization is found in the spread of what sociologist George Ritzer (2008) calls **McDonaldization**—the process by which the principles of efficiency,

www.buttersafe.com ©2011 Alex Culang and Raynato Castro Buttersafe.

well-known brands whose customer loyalty has been nourished by advertisers for decades. And, of course, the merchandising of teams' and even players' names and images is highly controlled.

Weber predicted that eventually even the private sphere would become rationalized. That is, we would turn to rational techniques in an effort to manage our self in order to handle the many challenges of modern life. A trip to any bookstore would seem to prove his point: we find countless self-help books, each with its own system of steps to help us solve life's problems and reach our goals.

Weber was concerned about the depersonalizing consequences of such rationalization, but he saw no way out. Because it is guided by the principle of maximum efficiency, the only way to beat bureaucratization, he thought, was to be more bureaucratic. He argued that, unfortunately, something human gets lost in the process. Culture critic Mike Daisey describes something like this through his experience working at Amazon.com. His job performance was measured based on five factors: time spent on each call, number of phone contacts per hour, time spent on each customer email, number of email contacts per hour, and the sum total of phone and email contacts per hour. Of these calculations, he writes, "Those five numbers are who you are. They are, in fact, all you are. . . . Metrics will do exactly what it claims to do: It will track everything your employees do, say, and breathe, and consequently create a measurable increase in their productivity" (Daisey 2002:114). Metrics do work, but they do so by dehumanizing the worker. "The sad thing," Daisey continues, "is that metrics work so well precisely because it strips away dignity—it's that absence that makes it possible to see precisely who is pulling his weight and who is not" (p. 114). When workers' performance is measured only in numbers, the only part of the self that counts is that part that produces those numbers. Weber predicted that those parts of the self deemed not necessary to the job, such as emotional needs and family responsibilities, would be dismissed as irrelevant.

> **Iron law of oligarchy** The principle that all organizations, even democratic ones, tend to develop into bureaucracies ruled by an elite few.

> The chains of tormented mankind are made out of red tape.
>
> Franz Kafka

From Bureaucracy to Oligarchy One of the dangers, then, is that bureaucratization overwhelms other values and principles, including the goal of greater efficiency. Sociologist Robert Michels ([1915] 1949) studied socialist parties and labor unions in Europe prior to World War I and found that such organizations were becoming increasingly bureaucratic. The emerging leaders of the organizations—even some of the most egalitarian—had a vested interest in clinging to power. If they lost their leadership posts, they would have to return to full-time work as manual laborers.

Through his research, Michels originated the idea of the **iron law of oligarchy,** the principle that all organizations, even democratic ones, tend to develop into a bureaucracy ruled by an elite few (called an oligarchy). Why do oligarchies emerge? People who achieve leadership roles usually have the skills, knowledge, or charisma to direct, if not control, others. Michels argued that the rank and file of a movement or organization look to leaders for direction and thereby reinforce the process of rule by a few. In addition, members of an oligarchy are strongly motivated to maintain their leadership roles, privileges, and power and use their control over resources to do so.

Movies ON SOCIAL STRUCTURE AND INTERACTION

Office Space
The insanity of life in a modern bureaucracy.

The Truman Show
In this postmodern tale, a man unknowingly lives his life on television.

The Square
Young Egyptians rise up together in Tahrir Square

Mona Lisa Smile
An unconventional teacher encourages her students to think outside the box.

The Social Network
The story of the founding of Facebook and the betrayals it involved.

5

Concerns about oligarchy are often raised when ideologically driven social and political movements become institutionalized. In U.S. politics, ideologically committed followers, who often represent their party's base, frequently complain that elected leaders become "Washington insiders" who look out only for their self-interests. For example, during the 2016 presidential race, conservatives on the right criticized elected Republican leaders for compromising their ideals, which contributed to the selection of outsider Donald Trump as the Republican presidential nominee. Similarly, progressive Democrats, ideologically committed to equality and opportunity, supported Bernie Sanders for president, dismissing the eventual nominee Hillary Clinton as a Wall Street–friendly, overly militaristic enemy of the progressive cause. On both sides, questions were raised about whether the craving to stay in office overshadowed politicians' willingness to do the right thing.

BUREAUCRACY AND ORGANIZATIONAL CULTURE

One of the impressions Weber's model can leave is that there is only one right, most efficient way to organize a firm. Over time, however, managers have adopted a variety of strategies in their efforts to maximize productivity. For example, according to **scientific management,** established by Frederick Winslow Taylor in the late 1800s, managers should seek to measure all aspects of the work process in an effort to eliminate any inefficiencies. One of the primary tools they used was time-motion studies, in which they used a stopwatch to measure each movement a worker would make. They then sought ways to minimize the amount of time each task took. In this system, workers were treated as objects to be managed rather than as subjects whose cares and concerns were of any relevance to the manager (Taylor 1911).

Not until workers organized unions—and forced management to recognize that they were not objects—did theorists of formal organizations begin to revise the scientific management model. Along with management and administrators, social scientists became aware that informal groups of workers have an important impact on organizations (Perrow 1986). An alternative management philosophy, the **human relations approach,** emphasizes the role of people, communication, and participation in a bureaucracy. This type of analysis reflects the significance of interaction and small-group behavior. Unlike planning under the scientific management approach, planning based on the human relations perspective focuses on workers' feelings, frustrations, and emotional need for job satisfaction (Mayo 1933). Today, many workplaces—primarily for those in higher status occupations—have been transformed to family-friendly environments (Hochschild 1997). To the extent that managers are convinced that helping workers meet all their needs increases productivity, care and concern are instituted as a result of rational calculation.

Scientific management approach Theory of management that measures all aspects of the work process to eliminate any inefficiencies.

Human relations approach An approach to the study of formal organizations that emphasizes the role of people, communication, and participation in a bureaucracy and tends to focus on the informal structure of the organization.

Whether in the form of traditional, modern, or postmodern society, social structure provides order, shaping the options that are available to us. It provides the context within which we interact with others. The statuses we occupy shape the roles we perform. Moreover, what we think and do is influenced by the relationships we have with others in the contexts of groups, networks, and institutions. Sociology as a discipline is committed to making sense of our structural context and the impact it has on our lives.

Still, society and social structure are not singular things. Though we are, in many respects, products of society, socialized to think and act in appropriate ways, we always have the option to think and act in new ways and to construct new culture. The possibility for such change may be more apparent today because our world is so pluralistic. Ours is a world not of "the" structure, "the" family, and "the" religion, but of structures, families, and religions. We have the possibility for more contact with more people who think and act in a greater diversity of ways than at any time in the past. As we become more aware of alternatives ways to think and act, we can use that knowledge to change our worlds for the better.

SOCIOLOGY IS A VERB

The Significance of Place

We occupy many statuses over the course of our lives, and they can both open and close doors for us. Ask five people in various positions—whether as parents, professors, child care providers, custodians, managers, religious leaders, and so on—how they came to be in those positions. How have the positions they occupy enabled them to accomplish their personal and collective goals? How have they been constrained by those positions?

FOR REVIEW

I. What does society provide that we need?
- Society provides a structure that is built from the statuses we occupy; the roles we perform; and the groups, networks, and institutions that connect us.

II. How do sociologists describe traditional versus modern societies?
- Sociologists highlight the impact that division of labor and technological development have on the organization of community, work, and social interaction in traditional and modern societies.

III. How does social structure shape individual action?
- The positions we occupy shape our perceptions, the resources to which we have access, and the options that are available. For example, in the context of bureaucracies, our social position, connections, and performance expectations are clearly defined.

©michaeljung/Shutterstock.com RF

SOCVIEWS on Social Structure and Interaction

Functionalist View

The elements of **social structure**—statuses, groups, social networks, and social institutions—provide order, shape our options, and give context to our lives.

Social roles create a **stable society** by allowing people to anticipate the behavior of others and to act accordingly.

Institutions contribute to **social order** by performing **vital functions**, whether it is producing children (family), teaching them (schools), establishing order (government), or distributing goods and services (economy).

STRUCTURE, ORDER
KEY CONCEPTS

Conflict View

The elements of the social structure justify and reinforce existing systems of inequality and unequal distributions of resources.

Ascribed statuses, often conferred at birth, can be used to justify **privileges** for some while limiting opportunities for others by consigning them to a **subordinate group**.

In-groups and out-groups serve to highlight **differences** between people and can foster antagonism.

KEY CONCEPTS
SUBORDINATION, INEQUALITY, PRIVILEGE

Interactionist View

It is through social interaction—the **shared experiences** through which we relate to others—that the elements of social structure are constructed.

Our social roles are governed by a set of expectations, but how we actually **perform** those roles can vary from individual to individual.

A **micro, bottom-up perspective** of social structure reinforces the significance of our actions, and helps us appreciate how we can think and act in new ways to bring about social change.

KEY CONCEPTS
SHARED EXPERIENCES, MICRO PERSPECTIVE

MAKE THE CONNECTION
After reviewing the chapter, answer the following questions:

1
How does Berger and Luckmann's social construction of reality model integrate elements of functionalist, conflict, and interactionist perspectives?

2
Briefly describe how a functionalist, a conflict theorist, and an interactionist would view social institutions.

3
Sociologists Daniel Bell and Michael Harrington have differing views of postindustrial society. Which perspectives do you think their views reflect?

4
Have you ever been part of an in- or out-group? If so, how might each perspective shed light on your experience?

Pop Quiz

1. **What are the three stages of Berger and Luckmann's model describing the interdependent relationship between the individual and society?**
   a. statuses, groups, and institutions
   b. telling stories, making choices, and establishing networks
   c. constructing culture, constructing the self, and constructing society
   d. role conflict, role strain, and role exit

2. **In the United States, we expect that cab drivers know how to get around a city. This expectation is an example of which of the following?**
   a. in-group
   b. role strain
   c. social role
   d. status

3. **What occurs when incompatible expectations arise from two or more social statuses held by the same person?**
   a. role conflict
   b. role strain
   c. role exit
   d. role playing

4. **In sociological terms, what do we call any two or more people, united by a shared sense of identity or purpose, who interact with each other over time in ways that distinguish them from outsiders?**
   a. a category
   b. a group
   c. an aggregate
   d. a society

5. **Primary groups are characterized by**
   a. a series of relationships that link individuals directly to others and, through them, indirectly to still more people.
   b. formal, impersonal relationships with minimal social intimacy or mutual understanding.
   c. social positions that are within our power to change.
   d. intimate, face-to-face association and cooperation.

6. **What is the definition of a social institution?**
   a. A series of social relationships that link individuals directly to others, and through them indirectly to still more people.
   b. An alliance, whether temporary or permanent, geared toward a common goal.
   c. An integrated and persistent social network dedicated to ensuring that society's core needs are met.
   d. A component of a formal organization that uses rules and hierarchical ranking to achieve efficiency.

7. **What type of society did Ferdinand Tönnies describe as a close-knit community in which members have strong personal bonds?**
   a. *Gesellschaft*
   b. mechanical
   c. *Gemeinschaft*
   d. organic

8. **According to Émile Durkheim, which type of solidarity is characterized by extensive division of labor?**
   a. postindustrial
   b. mechanical
   c. horticultural
   d. organic

9. **What characteristic of postmodern life emphasizes the importance of consumption on identity creation?**
   a. stories
   b. images
   c. choices
   d. networks

10. **Which characteristic of bureaucracy is carried out on the basis of performance rather than personality?**
    a. impersonality
    b. hierarchy of authority
    c. written rules and regulations
    d. division of labor

1. (c), 2. (c), 3. (a), 4. (b), 5. (d), 6. (c), 7. (c), 8. (d), 9. (c), 10. (a)

©Rick Rycroft/AP Images

Deviance

MURDER AND MAYHEM

In the early morning hours of June 12, 2016, a gunman opened fire at Pulse, Orlando, Florida's premiere gay nightclub. Approximately 320 people were inside when the shooting started, including a police officer in full uniform serving as a security guard who reportedly exchanged gunfire almost immediately with the gunman. Within minutes, two on-duty officers arrived and engaged the shooter in another firefight, and additional officers rushed into the club. Approximately 10 minutes into the incident, the gunman retreated to a bathroom, taking hostage the people hiding there. After a three-hour standoff, which ended when police shot and killed the gunman, 49 people were dead (Courvertier 2016; Stapleton and Ellis 2016).

The Orlando massacre was the deadliest public mass shooting in U.S. history. The second deadliest occurred at Virginia Tech in April 2007, when 32 people were killed, and there have been many others. In December 2015, two shooters killed 14 people at a Department of Public Health employee Christmas party in San Bernadino, California. In December 2012, a gunman forced his way into Sandy Hook Elementary School in Newtown, Connecticut, killing 20 first graders and 6 staff members. Just a few months earlier, 12 were killed and 58 were wounded in a movie theater in Aurora, Colorado, at the midnight debut of *The Dark Knight Rises*. According to the FBI, 200 active shooter incidents occurred in the United States between 2000 and 2015, killing 578 and wounding 696, and the average number of incidents per year has been rising. In 95 percent of the incidents, the shooter was male (Blair and Schweit 2014; Follman, Aronsen, and Pan 2016; Nelson 2016; U.S. Department of Justice 2016a).

After each incident, questions arise about guns and violence. The United States has the highest rate of gun ownership of any nation. Of all the civilian-owned firearms in the world, 41.5 percent are owned in the United States (India is second at 7.1 percent). In 2014, guns were used in 69 percent of all U.S. homicides, resulting in 10,945 deaths. Additionally, firearms were the cause of death in 21,334 U.S. suicides. Despite the loss of life associated with guns, as a nation we're deeply conflicted on how best to respond. On the one hand, 93 percent of Americans support requiring background checks for all gun buyers, but only 37 percent of U.S. adults rate gun control as a top priority for lawmakers, ranking it 17th out of 18 policy goals surveyed (Kochanek et al. 2016; Pew Research Center 2016a; Quinnipiac 2016; Small Arms Survey 2011; Smith and Cooper 2013).

Why do mass shootings occur? Do they result from unchecked mental illness? Gun ownership rates? Masculinity? A culture of violence? Ineffective socialization? Economic inequality? Or something else entirely? Through research, sociologists help us better understand deviance by asking such questions so that we, in turn, can better understand how to prevent it.

As You READ

- How do groups maintain social control?
- What is the difference between deviance and crime?
- How do sociologists explain deviance and crime?

>> Social Control

As individuals, we all face times when we want to rebel against what is expected of us. We may know better, having been socialized to accept the norms and values of those who surround us, yet when it comes to obedience, sometimes we would prefer not to. Or the urge to disobey may come in the form of friends and colleagues who prod us. If we give in, we are likely to encounter pushback from others in the form of **social control**, which refers to society's power to limit deviance, behavior that violates socially accepted norms, by enforcing conformity to expected norms and values. As we saw in the "Normative Culture" section in Chapter 3, those around us use positive and negative sanctions to encourage and discourage particular behaviors. The scary part about social control is the amount of power that potentially rests in the hands of those with authority over us.

CONFORMITY AND OBEDIENCE

We experience social control in a variety of forms. **Conformity** is a more horizontal form of social control that involves abiding by the norms of our peers even though they have no direct authority over us. Going along with the crowd, whether that means attending a basketball game, studying abroad, or going to a party all because your friends do, is a form of conformity. **Obedience,** on the other hand, is a vertical form of social control that involves doing what a person in a position of authority over you says you should. In this form of social control, the social status of a person whose authority we respect, whether as a teacher, religious leader, or coach, gives them power over us. We are inclined to do what they ask because we trust them and defer to their presumed knowledge and wisdom.

Curious about obedience, social psychologist Stanley Milgram (1963, 1974a) wondered how far people would go if a trusted authority figure asked them to do something harmful. He was motivated, in part, because he wanted to better understand the involvement of the German people in the murder of 6 million Jews and millions of others

©Scott Garfield/©American Movie Classics/Courtesy Everett Collection

Social control Society's power to limit deviance by enforcing conformity to expected norms and values.

Conformity Abiding by the norms of our peers even though they have no direct authority over us.

Obedience Doing what a person in a position of authority over you says you should.

during World War II. One rationalization people gave after the war was that they were "just following orders." Milgram conceived of a test to assess people's willingness to obey.

He set up a scenario in which a volunteer, recruited from the local community, was told that researchers were investigating the effects of punishment on learning. The volunteer was then brought into a lab setting and asked to serve as a "teacher" who would ask questions of a "learner." If the learner got the question wrong, the teacher was instructed by a scientist, dressed in a lab coat, to administer an electric shock to the learner. For each additional question the learner got wrong, the teacher was instructed to increase the shock's voltage. Unbeknownst to the volunteer, however, no actual shock was administered. The real purpose of the study was to see how far the teacher/volunteer would go before refusing to obey the scientist.

In a prearranged script, the learner deliberately gave incorrect answers and pretended to be in pain when "shocked." For example, at 150 volts the learner would cry out, "Get me out of here!" At 270 volts the learner would scream in agony. When the shock reached 350 volts, the learner would fall silent. If the teacher wanted to stop the experiment, the experimenter would insist that the teacher continue, using such statements as "The experiment requires that you continue" and "You have no other choice; you must go on." Milgram repeated this experiment numerous times, altering 23 different experimental conditions, such as the gender of the scientist, the number of scientists, and the presence of the scientist in the room, to see what effects they might have. In Experiment 5, the variation for which Milgram is best known, 65 percent of the volunteers continued all the way up to the 450-volt maximum (Blass 1999; Haslam, Loughnan, and Perry 2014; Milgram 1974a).

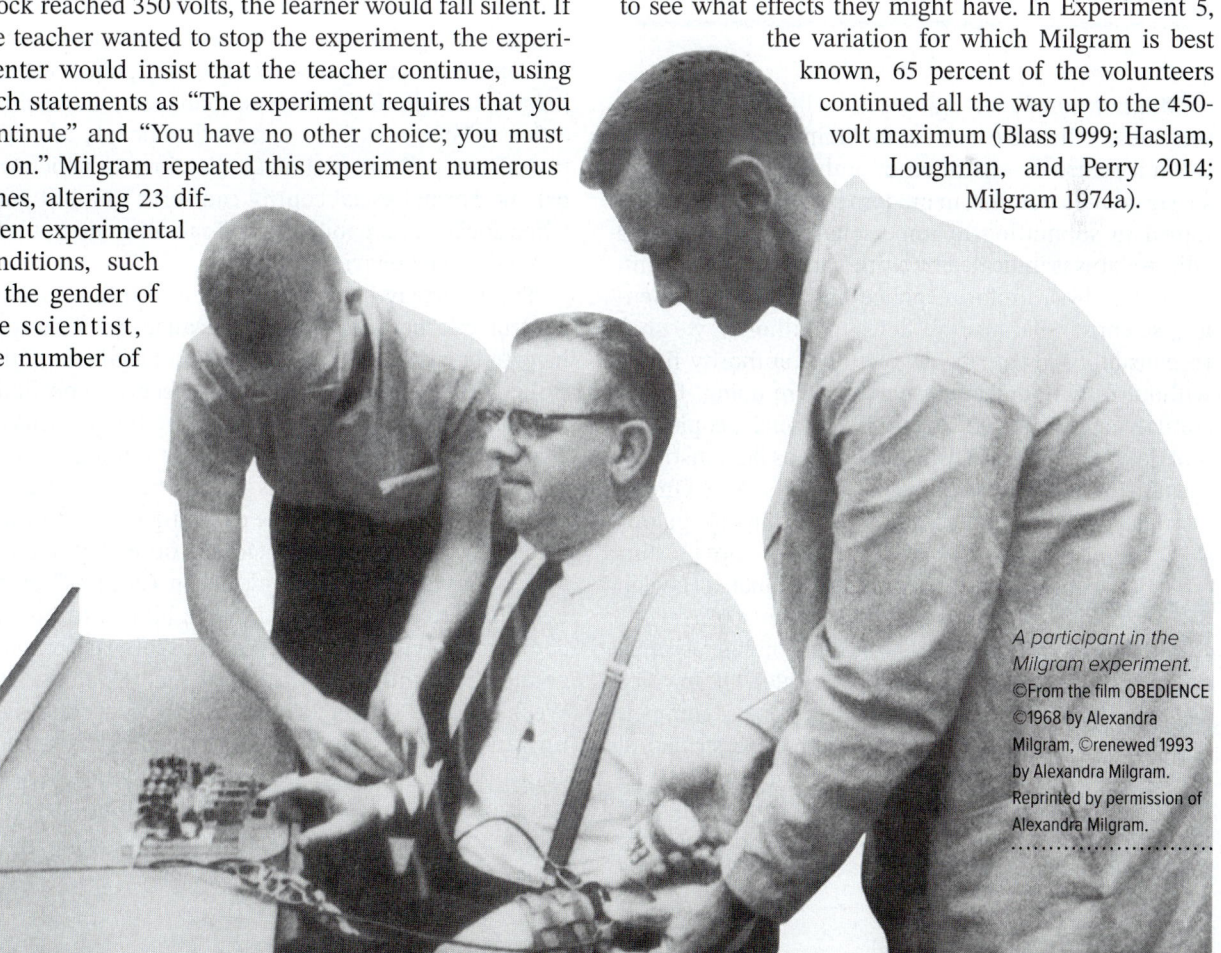

The zombie apocalypse has become a pop culture staple. Examples include George Romero's *Living Dead* films, Max Brooks's *World War Z* book and film, and *The Walking Dead* graphic novel and TV series. Such accounts often say more about humans and the breakdown of social order than they do about zombies. In the event of a zombie apocalypse, how quickly do you think social order would break down? What factors might minimize social chaos? What steps should people take to enforce social order?

POPSOC

Photo: ©Everett Collection

A participant in the Milgram experiment. ©From the film OBEDIENCE ©1968 by Alexandra Milgram, ©renewed 1993 by Alexandra Milgram. Reprinted by permission of Alexandra Milgram.

Researchers since Milgram have conducted similar demonstrations seeking to replicate his findings and have produced comparable results. The average obedience rate for 17 similar studies was 65 percent, though rates for these studies varied significantly from 28 to 91 percent (Blass 1999). Due to the potentially harmful psychological side effects on the volunteers, studies such as these ceased. In a more recent attempt, social psychologist Jerry Burger (2009) attempted to minimize the ethical concerns by, among other things, assuring volunteers they could stop at any time, guaranteeing they could keep the money they were paid for volunteering even if they stopped, and ending the experiment immediately after the 150-volt level when the "learner" asked for the experiment to stop, at which point the true nature of the experiment was revealed and the learner was shown to be unharmed. Burger found that 65 percent of his subjects continued to administer what they thought were shocks until the end.

> **SOCTHINK**
> According to the American Sociological Association *Code of Ethics*, researchers must "protect subjects from personal harm." To what extent might Milgram's subjects have experienced emotional harm? How and why might a researcher seek to justify such a risk?

Milgram concluded that we are willing to do things we would otherwise not do, including inflicting pain, when a person in a position of authority tells us to do so. He pointed out that, in modern society, we are accustomed to submitting to impersonal authority figures whose status is indicated by a title (professor, president, doctor) or by a uniform (police officer, army lieutenant, scientist). Because we defer to authority, we shift responsibility for our behavior to the authority figure without fully appreciating what we are doing. Under similar circumstances, otherwise normal people can and do treat one another inhumanely, as demonstrated by the revealing photos taken at Iraq's Abu Ghraib prison in 2004 which showed U.S. military guards humiliating, if not torturing, Iraqi prisoners (Hayden 2004; Zimbardo 2007).

Reflecting on his research, Milgram wrote, "It may be that we are puppets—puppets controlled by the strings of society. But at least we are puppets with perception, with awareness. And perhaps our awareness is the first step to our liberation" (1974b:568). We do not make choices in a vacuum. Sociology enables us to better recognize the social forces that shape our actions so that we might choose more wisely.

> **SOCTHINK**
> Do you think a person's background factors would influence how far he or she would go in Milgram's experiment? How might age, gender, religion, or education make a difference?

INFORMAL AND FORMAL SOCIAL CONTROL

In addition to being horizontal and vertical, social control can be informal and formal. **Informal social control** involves the use of interpersonal cues, either positive or negative, through everyday interaction to enforce norms. It's the kind of casual sanction parents might use when they give their child "the look" indicating they've said or done something wrong and had better stop it immediately. Other examples include smiles, laughter, crossed arms, frowns, and ridicule. We seek to read such cues in new situations, such as a first date or a job interview, so we might adjust our behavior accordingly.

Formal social control involves the imposition of sanctions, whether positive or negative, by officially recognized authorities in order to enforce norms. Examples of authorized agents are police officers, judges, school administrators, managers, and military officers. Their task is to ensure that people adhere to the official policies of the organizations to which they belong. Formal social control can serve as a last resort when socialization and informal sanctions do not bring about desired behavior.

The interplay between formal and informal social control can be complicated, because we sometimes have to balance one source of control against another. College students, for example, receive conflicting messages about the acceptability of binge drinking. On the one hand, for most college students, drinking alcohol of any kind is illegal because they are under age, and for all, binge drinking violates student codes-of-conduct policies. On the other hand, as the accompanying "Binge Drinking on Campus" graphs demonstrate, those who indulge in binge drinking are conforming with student norms, which vary based on gender, age, and living arrangements (Chauvin 2012; Wechsler and Nelson 2008). In response, colleges and universities are taking steps to exert greater social control by instituting rules banning kegs, closing fraternities and sororities that violate standards of conduct, expelling students after multiple alcohol-related

---

Informal social control The use of interpersonal cues through everyday interaction to enforce norms.

Formal social control The imposition of sanctions, whether positive or negative, by officially recognized authorities in order to enforce norms.

Binge Drinking on Campus

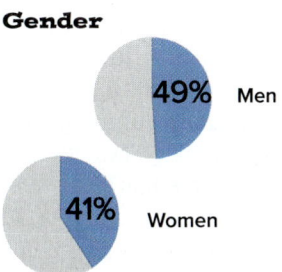

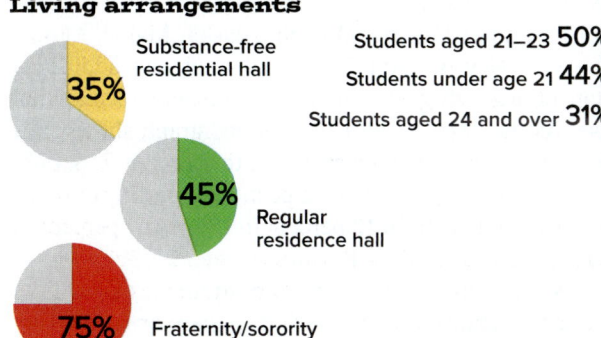

Note: Binge drinking was defined as one drinking session of at least five drinks for men or four drinks for women during the two weeks prior to the self-administered questionnaire. Based on a national survey of more than 10,000 college students.

Source: Wechsler et al. 2002:208; Wechsler and Nelson 2008.   Photo: ©Comstock/Getty Images RF

violations, and working with local liquor retailers to discourage high-volume sales to students.

LAW AND SOCIETY

Some norms are so important to a society that they are formalized into laws limiting people's behavior. **Laws**—formal norms enforced by the state—are a form of governmental social control. Some laws, such as the prohibition against murder, are directed at all members of society. Others, such as fishing and hunting regulations, primarily affect particular categories of people. Still others govern the behavior of social institutions (for instance, corporate law and laws regarding the taxing of non-profit enterprises).

Arresting, prosecuting, and convicting a person who breaks the law represents one of the most powerful means of formal social control available. In the United States, in 2014, 6.9 million adults underwent some form of correctional supervision—jail, prison, probation, or parole. Put another way, 2.8 percent, or 1 out of every 36 adult Americans, was subject to this very formal type of social control (Kaeble, Glaze, Tsoutis, and Minton 2016). As is evident from the accompanying "U.S. Incarceration Rates" graph, rates of imprisonment rose rapidly in the United States during the 1980s and remain high. Factors influencing this dramatic rise included a government crackdown on illegal drug use and the establishment of mandatory sentences. In the early 1970s, for example, President Richard Nixon declared a "war on drugs," a policy President Ronald Reagan expanded in the 1980s and that continues to shape policy today. As a result, efforts to deal with drug abuse shifted from prevention and treatment to law enforcement and punishment. The *Anti-Drug Abuse Act of 1986,* for example, put mandatory minimum sentences in place for a variety of drugs, including marijuana and cocaine.

In an effort to get tough on crime, this mandatory minimum approach was extended to other crimes. The *Sentencing Reform Act of 1984,* for example, created the United States Sentencing Commission, which establishes sentencing guidelines, including minimums, for defendants found guilty of any federal statute. Critics of the mass incarceration that resulted from these policies point out that punishment fell, and continues to fall, disproportionately on

> **Laws** Formal norms enforced by the state.

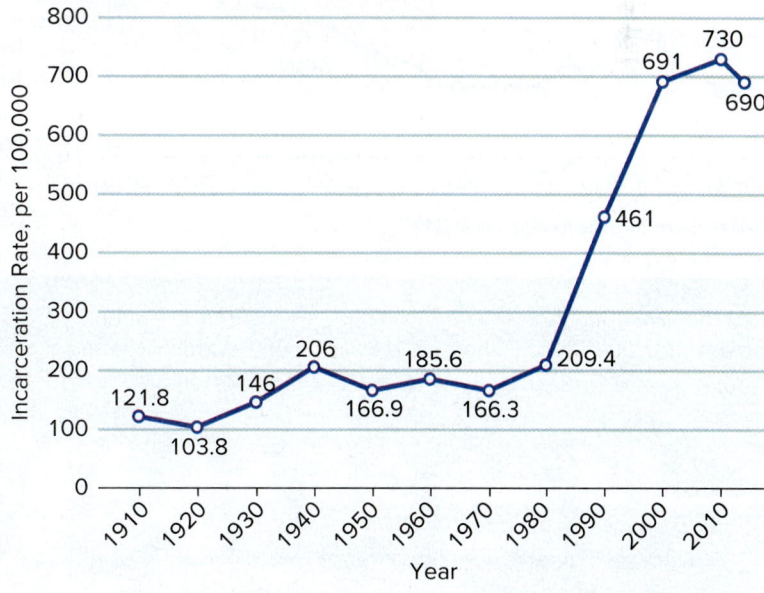

Note: Incarceration rates represent the number of persons in prison or jail per 100,000 people in the U.S. population.

Source: Justice Policy Institute 2000: 4; Kaeble et al. 2016.

Chapter 6 / Deviance • 131

African Americans and other minority groups (Alexander 2012; Davis 1998; Dufton 2012; United States Sentencing Commission 2016).

In diverse societies, the establishment of laws inevitably generates conflicts over whose values should prevail or whose interests should be protected. For example, should it be against the law to employ illegal immigrants? To have an abortion? To allow prayer in public schools? To smoke on an airplane? Such issues have been bitterly debated because they require a choice among competing interests. Not surprisingly, unpopular laws—such as the 18th Amendment, which prohibited the manufacture and sale of alcohol (ratified in 1919), or the nationwide 55-mile-per-hour speed limit that was imposed in 1974—become difficult to enforce when there is no consensus supporting the norms. In both cases the public commonly violated the stated government policy, and the laws proved unenforceable; the states repealed Prohibition in 1933, and Congress overturned the national speed-limit policy in 1987.

Deviance Behavior that violates the standards of conduct or expectations of a group or society.

The current debate over the legalization of marijuana illustrates the difficulty in crafting public laws governing private behavior. In a country where marijuana use remains illegal at the federal level, 49 percent of U.S. adults admit to having tried it, an 11-percentage-point increase since 2003. Twenty-eight states have responded by legalizing its use for medical purposes. Eight states—Washington, Colorado, Oregon, Alaska, Maine, Massachusetts, Nevada, and California—took the additional step of legalizing marijuana for personal recreational use. As the "Marijuana Legalization" graph shows, this move toward legalization matches the trend in U.S. public opinion. The percentage of people supporting outright legalization rose from 12 percent in 1969 to 57 percent in 2016 (Geiger 2016; Pew Research Center 2015c).

As individuals, each and every moment of our lives we face a choice about whether to obey or rebel. That choice gets complicated by the fact that we face competing and oftentimes incompatible options. Choosing one path may delight some of the people in our lives and enable us to pursue our own self-interests, but doing so might disappoint others and cause us to sacrifice benefits we also desire. Obedience to one group may look like deviance to another.

Marijuana Legalization, 1969–2016

Percentage saying marijuana should be . . .

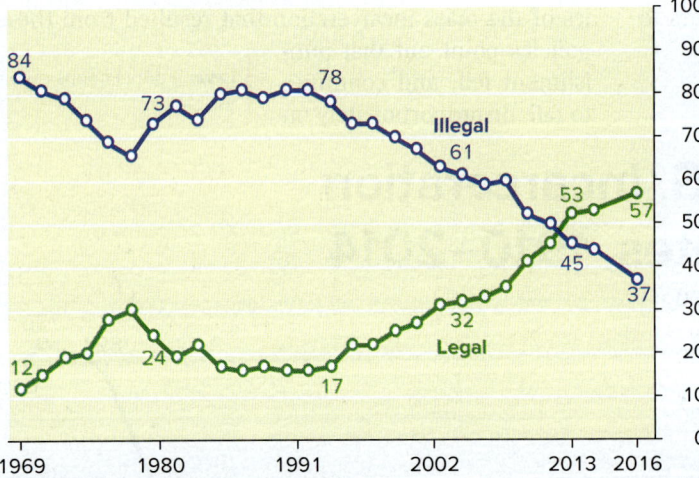

Sources: Geiger 2016; Pew Research Center 2015c.

>> Deviance

The flip side of social control is deviance. **Deviance** is behavior that violates the standards of conduct or expectations of a group or society (Wickman 1991:85). Being late for class is categorized as a deviant act, as is wearing jeans to a formal wedding. On the basis of the sociological definition, we are all deviant from time to time. Each of us violates common social norms in certain situations. As a society, we decide how deviant is *too* deviant, and sociologists provide us with tools to better understand how and why we do so.

©Leonard McLane/Getty Images RF

WHAT BEHAVIOR IS DEVIANT?

Because deviance involves violation of some group's norms, defining an act as deviant depends on the context. File sharing on the Internet—including MP3s, movies, computer games, books, and almost anything else that can be digitized—provides an example of how deviance can be in the eye of the beholder. Whenever a new film is released, online piracy groups compete with each other to see who can be the first to upload a high-definition copy. Competition to upload films nominated for an Academy Award is even more intense. On average, more than 90 percent of Academy Award–nominated films are available for illegal download before Oscar night. And because Academy Award voters typically receive DVDs to screen the films, online film pirates watch higher-definition versions of the films than voters do (Baio 2015, 2016, 2017; Van der Sar 2017). Nominated for a Best Picture Oscar in 2016, *The Revenant* was available for download six days before its U.S. release in theaters, receiving 1,145,840 downloads within a 24-hour period. The most pirated film of 2016 was *Deadpool*. The next four were *Batman v Superman: Dawn of Justice, Captain America: Civil War, Star Wars: The Force Awakens,* and *X-Men: Apocalypse* (Khatchatourian 2015; Van der Sar 2016).

©Comstock/Getty Images RF

Because the "property" these movie, music, and game files represent is not physical, it can be copied over and over again for virtually no cost. Anyone with a computer and an Internet connection can grab the files from people willing to share and pass them along to others who want them. People find it easy to justify doing so, thinking it does little harm to anyone. The entertainment companies that produce these products take a different view. In 2015, the estimated revenue lost to just the six Oscar-nominated films that had not yet been released on DVD or Blu-ray was over $40 million in the month between nominations and awards (Irdeto 2015b). These companies have actively pursued lawsuits against those who share files in part to scare those who might think of doing it. For example, William Kyle Moriarty was fined $1.12 million for stealing an advance copy of *The Revenant* and *The Peanuts Movie* and uploading them to the Internet (Spangler 2016). However, the widespread availability of these files suggests that many people do not view downloading them as particularly deviant. Some even view it as an act of protest against what they consider unfair prices charged by big corporations.

An important dimension of deviance to remember is that social change occurs when people choose to act differently. Our tendency is to go with the flow, thus reproducing the status quo. As a result, we frequently fail to see the ways in which our existing practices may violate our core principles. At times such as these, people who stand up for what they believe is right are often punished. The civil rights movement provided numerous examples of this, such as when nonviolent protestors at sit-ins and marches were met with attack dogs, fire hoses, beatings, and jail time. In the end, however, these protests led to greater political, legal, and economic opportunity for African Americans and others. Part of what makes such change difficult is that those with the greatest status have the capacity to define what is acceptable and what is deviant. It often takes a concerted effort, and the mobilization of substantial resources, to counteract such power.

Kimberley French/TM and Copyright ©20th Century Fox Film Corp. All rights reserved./Courtesy Everett Collection

DEVIANCE AND SOCIAL STIGMA

People who deviate from the norm in terms of how they think, believe, act, or look are frequently categorized as different, strange, unusual, or abnormal by people in social positions of power. Whole groups of people—whether on the basis of hair color, skin color, height, weight, clothing, nationality, physical ability, or other attributes—can be denied respect due to their presumed shortcomings. Sociologist Erving Goffman (1963) coined the term **stigma** to describe the process of labeling individuals or members of a group as less than whole persons due to some attribute that marks them as different in the eyes of others. Because our perception of others shapes how we treat them, such labels have consequences, as we learned from the Thomas theorem. As a result, stigmatizing represents a form of social control. First we label people as different using stereotypes to characterize them as "other." Then the distinction between "us" versus "them" is used to justify discrimination against those in the stigmatized group, denying them access to valued material, social, and cultural resources (Link and Phelan 2001).

Stigma Labeling individuals or members of a group as less than whole persons due to some attribute that marks them as different in the eyes of others.

Movies on DEVIANCE

Trainspotting
Scottish youths struggle with unemployment, dissatisfying relationships, and addiction.

Girl, Interrupted
A young girl enters a mental institution during the 1960s.

Compliance
When it comes to obedience, how far would you go?

The Dark Knight Rises
The Dark Knight resurfaces after eight years of hiding to protect the city of Gotham from a brutal terrorist, Bane.

Ghost World
A prank by two outcast teenagers takes an unexpected turn.

5

The pressure to conform to the norm, and thus avoid stigma, can have powerful effects. People try not to deviate too far from cultural expectations. Women, for example, can feel pressured to approximate what Naomi Wolf (1992) refers to as the "beauty myth," an exaggerated ideal of beauty, beyond the reach of all but a few females. In an effort to attain this ideal, many women undergo plastic surgery. In 2015, 279,143 women underwent breast augmentation, 196,395 chose liposuction, 174,028 had eyelid surgery, 164,731 opted for nose reshaping, and 123,003 received a tummy tuck. When it comes to less invasive procedures, 6.3 million opted for Botox, and 1.2 million received chemical peels. Overall, women received 13.9 million cosmetic procedures in 2015 alone. But it wasn't only women. Men, too, are opting for plastic surgery and accounted for 13 percent of all cosmetic procedures. Among men, 53,248 opted for nose reshaping, making it their most common surgical procedure. The estimated total cost of all U.S. cosmetic procedures in 2015 was $13.4 billion (American Society of Plastic Surgeons 2016). The desire to avoid stigma reinforces the standards of the status quo.

Often people are stigmatized for deviant behaviors that they may no longer practice. The labels "ex-convict," "formerly homeless," and "recovering alcoholic" can function like a master status, sticking to a person for life. Goffman draws a useful distinction between

POPSOC

The HBO series *The Wire* has been widely praised for its realistic portrayal of urban life in Baltimore, including its coverage of drugs, gangs, and law enforcement. A growing number of sociologists teach courses based on the show to demonstrate lessons about community, crime, poverty, and corruption. According to sociologist William Julius Wilson, who teaches such a course at Harvard, "Although *The Wire* is fiction, not a documentary, its depiction of [the] systemic urban inequality that constrains the lives of the urban poor is more poignant and compelling [than] that of any published study, including my own" (D. Bennett 2010).

Photo: ©HBO/Courtesy Everett Collection

a prestige symbol that calls attention to a positive aspect of one's identity, such as a wedding band or a police badge, and a stigma symbol that discredits or debases one's identity, such as a conviction for child molestation. Although stigma symbols may not always be obvious, they can become a matter of public knowledge. Starting in 1994, many states required convicted sex offenders to register with local police departments. Some communities publish the names and addresses and, in some instances, even the pictures, of convicted sex offenders on the web.

Being stigmatized can limit a person's opportunities. For example, even though they may be fully qualified for a job, people who are homeless often have trouble getting hired because employers are wary of applicants who cannot provide a home address. Though many hiring agencies use a telephone for contacts, cell phones are expensive, and owning one while homeless is often looked at with suspicion by others. If a homeless person has access to a telephone at a shelter, the staff generally answers by announcing the name of the institution, which discourages prospective employers from hiring the applicant. And, even if the person is hired, the stigma attached to homelessness, should the employee's past or present situation become known, can negatively impact opportunities, even in the face of positive work performance.

>> Crime

When deviance involves violating social norms administered by the state, we refer to it as crime. **Crime** is a violation of criminal law for which some governmental authority applies formal penalties. Laws divide crimes into various categories, depending on the severity of the offense, the age of the offender, the potential punishment, and the court that holds jurisdiction over the case.

OFFICIAL CRIME REPORTS

When we think of crime, the examples most likely to come to mind involve what we might think of as street crimes. The FBI breaks such crimes into two major categories: violent crimes and property crimes. They do not include all types of crime in these reports, focusing only on four major types within each category. Violent crimes include murder, forcible rape, robbery, and aggravated assault; property crimes include burglary, larceny-theft, motor vehicle theft, and arson. The FBI provides an annual account of the number of these crimes in its *Uniform Crime Reports* (UCR), which is available online. Because they are tracked so closely by the FBI and have been for a long time, these

> **Crime** A violation of criminal law for which some governmental authority applies formal penalties.

FBI Uniform Crime Reports Data

Offenses in 2015	Number reported	Rate per 100,000 inhabitants	Percentage change in rate since 2006	Clearance Rate
Violent crimes				
Murder	15,696	4.9	−15.5	62%
Forcible rape	124,047	38.6	−11.1	38%
Robbery	327,374	102	−32.1	29%
Aggravated assault	764,449	238	−18.5	54%
Total	1,197,704	373	−22.3	46%
Property crimes				
Burglary	1,579,527	491	−33	13%
Larceny-theft	5,706,346	1,775	−19.8	22%
Motor vehicle theft	707,758	220	−45	13%
Total	7,993,631	2,487	−25.7	19%

 = 10,000 Offenses

Note: Insufficient data are available on arson to estimate accurate totals. The official definition for rape changed in 2013. The percentage change data for rape uses the legacy definition to provide an appropriate comparison over time. Clearance rate refers to the percentage of crimes reported to police that were cleared by arrest or exceptional means.
Source: U.S. Department of Justice 2016b:Tables 1, 1A, & 25. *Photo:* ©D. Hurst/Alamy Stock Photo RF

Chapter 6 / Deviance • 135

Index crimes The eight types of crime reported annually by the FBI in the *Uniform Crime Reports*: murder, forcible rape, robbery, aggravated assault, burglary, larceny-theft, motor vehicle theft, and arson.

Victimization survey A questionnaire or interview given to a sample of the population to determine whether people have been victims of crime.

crimes have come to be known as **index crimes**.

As you can see in the "FBI Uniform Crime Reports Data" table, property crimes occur at a much higher rate than do violent crimes. In fact, according to the "crime clock" that the FBI provides as part of its report, a property crime occurs on average every 3.9 seconds. The most frequent property crime is larceny-theft, which includes incidents such as shoplifting and stealing items from cars. By contrast, a violent crime occurs every 26.3 seconds. Robbery, which involves the use or threat of force, is the most frequent violent crime, with one occurring every 1.6 minutes. Murder is the least frequent of the index crimes, with one occurring every 33.5 minutes (U.S. Department of Justice 2016c).

The likelihood that a crime will be "solved" varies by the type of offense. According to the FBI, an offense can be "cleared" either though arrest or exceptional means. To be cleared by arrest, at least one person must be arrested, charged with a crime, and turned over to the court for prosecution. Clearance by exceptional means includes examples such as the death of the offender or refusal of the victim to cooperate with prosecution. As the "FBI Uniform Crime Reports Data" table shows, violent crimes are more likely to be cleared than property crimes. In 2015, for example, 61.5 percent of murders were cleared compared to 12.9 percent of burglaries (U.S. Department of Justice 2016b:Table 25).

Trends in Crime Crime rates vary over time, and sociologists seek to explain factors that contribute to these changes. In the past 10 years, as indicated in the "FBI Uniform Crime Reports Data" table, crime rates have fallen in every major category. Murder rates, for example, have declined 15.5 percent since 2006 (U.S. Department of Justice 2016b: Table 1a). To explain these trends, sociologists seek to identify possible causal factors, including the potential effects of

- The overall aging of the population, because people are more likely to commit crimes when they are young.
- Changes in the economy, including the economic downturn starting in 2008.
- The expansion of community-oriented policing and crime prevention programs.
- Increased incarceration rates, removing potential offenders from the streets.
- New prison education programs designed to reduce the number of repeat offenders.

Knowledge of the impact of these and other possible factors would help us establish more effective policies designed to further reduce the crime rate in the future (Chettiar 2015; Roeder, Eisen, and Bowling 2015).

Victimization Surveys Because not all crimes that are committed are reported to the police, the UCR underestimates the actual number of crimes. In the case of larceny-theft, for example, people may conclude that, because there is little chance of getting stolen items back, it simply isn't worth the hassle. More significantly, members of racial and ethnic minority groups often distrust law enforcement agencies and may not contact the police when they are victimized. Further, many women do not report rape or spousal abuse out of fear they will be blamed for the crime.

> **SOCTHINK**
>
> The Clery Act, passed in 1990, requires schools to provide students with timely reports of campus crimes. How much do you trust official campus crime reports? Why might reports of crime on college campuses underestimate the actual number of incidents?

To address such deficiencies in official statistics, the U.S. Department of Justice conducts its annual National Crime Victimization Survey. **Victimization surveys** are questionnaires or interviews given to a sample of the population to determine whether people have been victims of crime. In their yearly report, Department of Justice officials draw on interviews with more than 160,000 people in over 90,000 households in the United States. They interview each household in their sample twice during the given year. More than 80 percent of selected households agree to participate (Truman and Morgan 2016).

Results from the National Crime Victimization Survey demonstrate significant variability in which types of crimes are reported to police. As shown in the "Crimes Reported to Police" graph, motor vehicle theft is the most likely to be reported, with 76 percent of victims contacting the authorities. Larceny-theft is the least likely at 29 percent. When it comes to violent crimes, only about one-half of victims overall contact the police (Truman and Morgan 2016:Table 4). What these numbers suggest is that a substantial amount of crime goes unreported and, as such, many offenses never see justice served within the U.S. legal system.

Another limitation of the UCR official statistics is that they exclude many offenses that we would count

Crimes Reported to Police

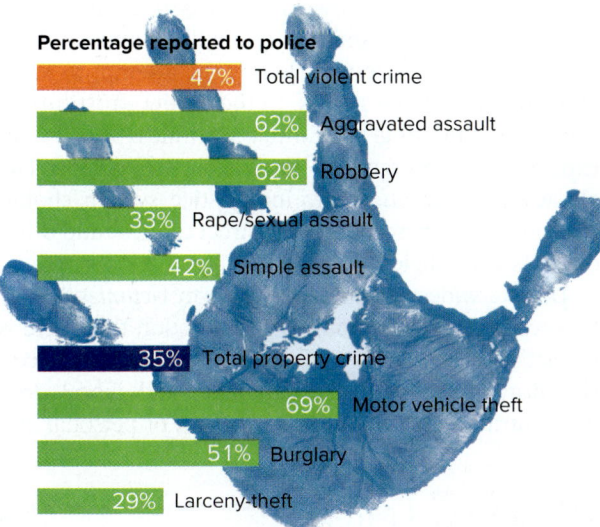

Percentage reported to police
- 47% Total violent crime
- 62% Aggravated assault
- 62% Robbery
- 33% Rape/sexual assault
- 42% Simple assault
- 35% Total property crime
- 69% Motor vehicle theft
- 51% Burglary
- 29% Larceny-theft

Note: Percentages based on the National Crime Victimization Survey for 2015.
Source: Truman and Morgan 2016:Table 4. *Photo:* ©McGraw-Hill Education

as criminal. In so doing, they minimize the degree to which we see perpetrators of other types of crime as criminal in the same way as violators of the index crimes. We turn next to several such categories, including white-collar crime, victimless crimes, and organized crime.

WHITE-COLLAR CRIME

Income tax evasion, stock manipulation, consumer fraud, bribery and extraction of kickbacks, embezzlement, and misrepresentation in advertising—these are all examples of **white-collar crime**, or illegal acts committed in the course of business activities, often by affluent, "respectable" people. Historically, we have viewed such crimes differently because they are often perpetrated through respected occupational roles (Sutherland 1949, 1983).

Sociologist Edwin Sutherland (1940) coined the term *white-collar crime* to refer to acts by individuals, but the term is now used more broadly to include offenses by businesses and corporations as well. Corporate crime, or any act by a corporation that is punishable by the government, takes many forms and includes individuals, organizations, and institutions among its victims. Corporations may engage in anticompetitive behavior, environmental pollution, medical fraud, tax fraud, stock fraud and manipulation, accounting fraud, the production of unsafe goods, bribery and corruption, and health and safety violations (Coleman 2006).

The downfall of Bernie Madoff represented the largest case of white-collar crime of its type in history. Madoff, an American businessman who managed people's financial investments, promised investors annual returns of 15 to 20 percent and delivered on that promise for years. This enabled him to attract extremely wealthy clients from around the world, even charitable organizations. In the end, he was just running a scam. Madoff had provided investors with false statements showing nonexistent trades and profits. Estimates are that he defrauded his clients out of $65 billion in purported assets. Life savings and family fortunes were gone in an instant (Gaviria and Smith 2009).

> **White-collar crime** Illegal acts committed by affluent, "respectable" individuals in the course of business activities.

The scheme collapsed in December 2008, after Madoff confessed to his sons that his investment company was a "giant Ponzi scheme." After consulting an attorney, they reported their father to the FBI. Madoff was arrested the next day. In a Ponzi scheme, the fraudulent investor uses money from new investors to pay off old ones rather than investing the money. The payoff is at higher-than-average rates of return, which encourages new investors who are attracted by the profits. The whole system topples if current investors want to pull their money out, or if there aren't enough new investors to cover profits and payouts to existing investors. Both happened with the economic collapse in late 2008. On March 12, 2009, Madoff pleaded guilty to 11 felony counts, including securities fraud, mail

5 Movies on CRIME

Dallas Buyers Club
A cowboy turned drug dealer saves lives.

The House I Live In
The war on drugs and the price we pay.

Hell or High Water
Two brothers turn to robbing banks to save their family farm.

American Hustle
Power, politics, and corruption.

Incarcerating US
An exploration of mass incarceration in the United States.

Chapter 6 / Deviance • 137

fraud, money laundering, and perjury. He was sent directly to jail and was sentenced to the maximum of 150 years in prison (Henriques and Healy 2009).

What is particularly interesting about the Madoff case is that officials at the Securities and Exchange Commission (SEC) were tipped off numerous times to the possibility that Madoff's investments were a scam. Finally, after receiving documented accusations that he was running a Ponzi scheme, the SEC launched an official investigation in 2006. Two years later they concluded that there was "no evidence of fraud." The SEC failed to see what analysts now say should have been obvious. Red flags were ignored, but why? Sociologists suggest that white-collar criminals are often given the benefit of the doubt. In fact, during each previous investigation, Madoff deliberately and successfully used his status as a respected businessman as evidence of his innocence. He might have avoided detection had it not been for his own confession (Berenson and Henriques 2008).

Victimless crime A term used by sociologists to describe the willing exchange among adults of widely desired, but illegal, goods and services.

VICTIMLESS CRIMES

Another category of crimes that raises questions about how we define deviance consists of so-called victimless crimes. **Victimless crime** refers to the willing exchange among adults of widely desired, but illegal, goods and services, such as drugs or prostitution (Schur 1965, 1985). The fact that the parties involved are willing participants has led some people to suggest that such transactions should not constitute crimes.

Some activists are working to decriminalize many of these illegal practices. For example, as the "Marijuana Laws by State" map shows, the move to legalize marijuana use has expanded nationally. Supporters of decriminalization are troubled by the attempt to legislate a moral code for adults. In their view, prostitution, drug use, gambling, and other victimless crimes are expensive to enforce and impossible to prevent. The already overburdened criminal justice system should instead devote its resources to "street crimes" and other offenses with obvious victims.

Despite widespread use of the term *victimless crime*, however, many people object to the notion that there is no victim other than the offender in such crimes. Excessive drinking, compulsive gambling, and illegal drug use contribute to an enormous amount of personal and property damage. A person with a drinking problem can become abusive to a spouse or children; a compulsive gambler or drug user may steal to pursue his or her obsession. Feminist sociologists contend that prostitution, as well as the more disturbing aspects of pornography, reinforce the misconception that women are "toys" who can be treated as objects rather than people. According to critics of decriminalization, society must not give tacit approval to conduct that has such harmful consequences (Farley and Malarek 2008; Meier and Geis 1997).

SOCTHINK

Should gambling, prostitution, and recreational drugs be legalized? What are the potential consequences, both positive and negative, of doing so?

ORGANIZED CRIME

When it comes to organized crime, images of pop culture gangsters, such as Tony Soprano from HBO's classic series *The Sopranos*, often come to mind. In real life, examples of organized crime groups go beyond the Mafia to include the Japanese Yakuza, the Russian Organization, Colombian drug cartels, and many other

Marijuana Laws by State

- 29 states have legalized the possession and use of marijuana for medical purposes.
- 8 states and the District of Columbia have legalized marijuana for personal recreational use.
- Washington, DC

Source: National Conference of State Legislatures 2016. Photo: ©Brand X Pictures/Getty Images RF

international crime syndicates. **Organized crime** is the work of a group that regulates relations among criminal enterprises involved in illegal activities, including prostitution, gambling, and the smuggling and sale of illegal drugs (National Institute of Justice 2007).

Organized crime dominates the world of illegal business, just as large corporations dominate the conventional business world. It allocates territory, sets prices for goods and services, and acts as an arbiter in internal disputes. A secret, conspiratorial activity, organized crime generally evades law enforcement. It takes over legitimate businesses, gains influence over labor unions, corrupts public officials, intimidates witnesses in criminal trials, and even "taxes" merchants in exchange for "protection" (Federal Bureau of Investigation 2016).

> You come at the king, you best not miss.
>
>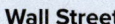
>
> Omar Little, *The Wire*

Historically, organized crime has provided a means of upward mobility for groups of people struggling to escape poverty. Sociologist Daniel Bell (1953) used the term *ethnic succession* to describe the sequential passage of leadership from Irish Americans in the early 1900s to Jewish Americans in the 1920s and then to Italian Americans in the early 1930s. Recently, ethnic succession has become more complex, reflecting the diversity of the nation's latest immigrants. Colombian, Mexican, Russian, Chinese, Pakistani, and Nigerian immigrants are among those who have begun to play a significant role in organized crime activities (Friman 2004; Kleinknecht 1996).

There has always been a global element in organized crime. However, law enforcement officials and policy makers now acknowledge the emergence of a new form of organized crime that takes advantage of advances in electronic communications. International organized crime includes drug and arms smuggling, money laundering, and trafficking in illegal immigrants and stolen goods (Lumpe 2003; National Institute of Justice 2007).

INTERNATIONAL CRIME

In the past, international crime was often limited to the clandestine shipment of goods across the border between two countries. Increasingly, however, crime is no more restricted by such borders than is legal commerce. Rather than concentrating on specific countries, international crime now spans the globe.

Transnational Crime More and more, scholars and law enforcement officials are turning their attention to **transnational crime,** or crime that occurs across multiple national borders. Historically, probably the most dreaded example of transnational crime has been slavery. At first, governments did not regard slavery as a crime but merely regulated it as they would trade in any other good. Examples of transnational crime now include human trafficking, illicit trade in firearms, sale of fraudulent medicines,

Movies on ORGANIZED CRIME/CORPORATE CRIME

Margin Call
A group of employees at an investment firm react to sensitive information in the immediate wake of the 2008 financial collapse.

Wall Street
A young stockbroker gets swept away with greed and insider trading on his ruthless climb to the top of the corporate ladder.

Inside Job
A documentary detailing the lax regulatory environment behind the 2008 recession.

The Informant!
An eccentric employee blows the whistle on his corporation's price-fixing scheme.

Eastern Promises
The inner workings of the Russian mafia.

> **Organized crime** The work of a group that regulates relations among criminal enterprises involved in illegal activities, including prostitution, gambling, and the smuggling and sale of illegal drugs.
>
> **Transnational crime** Crime that occurs across multiple national borders.

counterfeiting goods, wildlife trafficking, and migrant smuggling (Kelly and Levy 2012; Ruetschlin and Bangura 2012; UNODC 2016a).

One way to fight such crime has been through multilateral cooperation in which countries work together to pursue border-crossing crime. The first global effort to control international crime was the International Criminal Police Organization (Interpol), a cooperative network of European police forces founded to stem the movement of political revolutionaries across borders. Although such efforts to fight transnational crime may seem lofty—an activity with which any government would want to cooperate—they are complicated by sensitive legal and security issues. Most nations that have signed protocols issued by the United Nations, including the United States, have expressed concern over potential encroachments on their national judicial systems, as well as concern over their national security. Thus, they have been reluctant to share certain types of intelligence data. The terrorist attacks of September 11, 2001, increased both the interest in combating transnational crime and sensitivity to the risks of sharing intelligence data (Deflem 2005; Felson and Kalaitzidis 2005).

Going GLOBAL

International Incarceration Rates

Rank (out of 221 nations)	Country	International incarceration rates (prison population rates per 100,000 of the national population)
1	Seychelles	799
2	United States	693
8	Russian Federation	443
35	South Africa	292
44	Israel	265
66	Mexico	204
102	England and Wales	147
128	Kenya	121
134	China	118
138	Canada	114
193	Sweden	53
202	Japan	47
213	India	33

Source: Institute for Criminal Policy Research 2016. *Photo:* ©Trista Weibell/Getty Images RF

International Crime Rates Taking an international perspective on crime reinforces one of the key sociological lessons about crime and deviance: place matters. Although cross-national data comparison can be difficult, we can offer insight about how crime rates differ around the world.

Violent crimes tend to be much more common in the United States than in the nations of western Europe. Yet the incidence of other types of crime appears to be higher elsewhere. For example, France, Italy, Sweden, and New Zealand all have higher rates of reported car theft than does the United States, and rates for reported thefts are higher in the Netherlands, Denmark, Norway, and the United Kingdom. When it comes to murder, most South and Central American nations, including Honduras, El Salvador, and Venezuela, have homicide rates many times higher than does the United States (UNODC 2016b). But when comparing incarceration rates, the United States is second only to Seychelles when it comes to putting offenders behind bars. On a typical day, the United States imprisons 693 of every 100,000 adults, compared to 443 in Russia, 204 in Mexico, and 114 in Canada (Institute for Criminal Policy Research 2016).

Why are rates of violent crime so much higher in the United States than in western Europe? Sociologist Elliot Currie (1985, 1998) has suggested that U.S. society places greater emphasis on individual economic achievement than other societies. At the same time, many observers have noted that the culture of the United States has long tolerated, if not condoned, many forms of violence. Coupled with sharp disparities between poor and affluent citizens, significant unemployment, and substantial alcohol and drug abuse, these factors combine to produce a climate conducive to crime.

Violent crime remains a serious problem in nations around the world. In Mexico, for example, approximately 60 percent of the 18,146 homicides in 2013 were attributed to drug trafficking and organized crime (Heinle, Ferreira, and Shirk 2014). Attacks have been especially concentrated in the Mexican states of Chihuahua, Sinaloa, Guerrero, and Jalisco. The violence is a consequence, in part, of governmental attempts to crack down on the illegal drug trade. After his election in 2006, President Felipe Calderón sent in tens of thousands of troops to enforce the law. As a result, drug cartels fought both the authorities and one another in a struggle to maintain their local power (Camp 2010a, 2010b).

Going GLOBAL

International Gun Homicide Rates

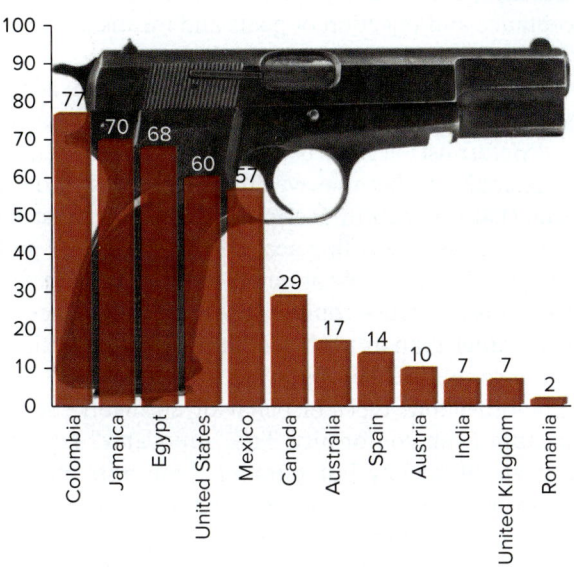

Note: The number represents the percentage of homicides committed using firearms.
Source: UNODC 2014. *Photo:* ©Stockbyte/Getty Images RF

>> Sociological Perspectives on Crime and Deviance

Why do people violate social norms? We have seen that deviant acts are subject to both informal and formal social control. The nonconforming or disobedient person may face disapproval, loss of friends, fines, or even imprisonment. Why, then, does deviance occur?

Sociologists have been interested in crime and deviance from the very beginning and have generated numerous theories of deviance and crime. Though we might wish otherwise, there is no one, simple, universal theory that explains all such acts. Here we look to just a few of the theories that sociologists have offered in order to identify significant factors that we must consider in our attempt to understand deviance and crime more fully.

FUNCTIONS OF CRIME AND DEVIANCE

Sociologists drawing on the functionalist perspective explore the ways deviance both challenges and reinforces social order. Émile Durkheim ([1895] 1964), for example, wondered why deviance, which seems to undermine order, is found in all societies. For Durkheim the answer rested with how such actions actually reinforce social order.

Durkheim's Functions of Deviance Durkheim argued that no act is inherently criminal. He put it this way: "We must not say that an action shocks the common consciousness because it is criminal, but rather that it is criminal because it shocks that consciousness" ([1895] 1964:123–24). In other words, the effect an action has on society matters more than the nature of the act itself. For example, killing another person isn't always murder. We justify killing in self-defense or in combat as legitimate but condemn killing in cold blood. But even in war, the line between acceptable and unacceptable can shift. In both Vietnam and Iraq, strong public support gave way to serious misgivings about U.S. involvement in these nations. In both cases, this was driven in part by images from the conflict, including, for example, the killing of civilians at My Lai and the treatment of prisoners at Abu Ghraib. At times such as these, our reactions clarify accepted norms of behavior, and thus help to establish social order.

No matter how much unity a society might appear to have, some individuals will always push the limits. Durkheim argued that, because some form of deviance exists in all societies, it must serve a positive social function. Collectively labeling acts as deviant clarifies our shared beliefs and values and thus brings us closer together. We say, in effect, "This is who we are, and if you want to be one of us, you cannot cross this line." Punishment, too, creates solidarity by drawing a group together in opposition to the offender. Further, seeing violators pay the price for their deviance discourages others from similar transgressions. When we see a driver receiving a speeding ticket, a department store cashier being fired for yelling at a customer, or a college student getting a failing grade for plagiarizing a term paper, we are reminded of our collective norms and values and of the consequences of their violation. Finally, Durkheim did recognize that deviant acts might also force us to recognize the limits of our existing beliefs and practices, opening up new doors and leading to positive social change.

Durkheim did, however, also recognize that some social circumstances increase the likelihood of turning toward deviance and crime. As we have already seen, Durkheim ([1897] 1951) introduced the term anomie to describe the loss of direction individuals feel when social control of their behavior becomes ineffective. Anomie is a state of normlessness that typically occurs during a period of profound social change and disorder, such as a time of economic collapse, political or social revolution, or even sudden prosperity. The power of society to constrain deviant action at such times is limited because there is no clear consensus on shared norms and values. Just as we saw with Durkheim's analysis of suicide, at times when social integration is weak, people are freer to pursue their own deviant paths.

Strain theory of deviance
Robert Merton's theory of deviance as an adaptation of socially prescribed goals or of the means governing their attainment, or both.

> **SOC THINK**
>
> Durkheim argues that increased division of labor results in fewer shared experiences and thus a weakened sense of community. What impact might a strong commitment to individualism have on our likelihood of committing crime?

Merton's Strain Theory Sociologist Robert Merton (1968) took Durkheim's theory a step further. He suggested that a disconnect can exist between a society's goals and the means people have to attain them. By *goals* he meant the dominant values that most members of a society share, and by *means* he meant the material, social, and cultural resources necessary for success. He did not assume that all people in a society would be equally committed to those values. He also did not assume that everyone would have the same opportunity to attain those goals. Putting these together, he developed the **strain theory of deviance,** which views deviance as an adaptation of socially prescribed goals or of the means governing their attainment, or both.

We can better understand Merton's model by looking at economic success as an important goal in the United States. Socially agreed upon pathways exist in order to attain that goal—go to school, work hard, do not quit, take advantage of opportunities, and so forth. Merton wondered what happened when someone who shared the goal of economic success lacked the means to attain that end. For example, a mugger and a small-business owner may share a common goal of making money, but their means of attaining it are radically different. Merton combined acceptance and rejection of goals and means to create a model with five possible adaptations.

Conformity to social norms, the most common adaptation in Merton's typology, is the opposite of deviance. The "conformist" accepts both the overall societal goal (for example, to become wealthy) and the approved means (hard work). In Merton's view, there must be some consensus regarding accepted cultural goals and the legitimate means for attaining them. Without such a consensus, societies could exist only as collectives of people rather than as unified cultures, and they might experience continual chaos.

The other four types of behavior all involve some departure from conformity. The "innovator" accepts the goals of society but pursues them with means that are regarded as improper. For instance, a safe-cracker may steal money to buy consumer goods and take expensive vacations. The "ritualist" has abandoned the goal of material success and become compulsively committed to the institutional means. Work becomes simply a way of life rather than a means to the goal of success. An example would be the bureaucratic official who blindly applies rules and regulations without remembering the larger goals of the organization. The "retreatist," as described by Merton, has basically withdrawn (or retreated) from both the goals and the means of society. In the United States, drug addicts and vagrants are typically portrayed as retreatists. Concern has been growing that adolescents who are addicted to alcohol will become retreatists at an early age.

The final adaptation identified by Merton reflects people's attempts to create a *new* social structure. The "rebel" feels alienated from the dominant means and goals and may seek a dramatically different social order. Members of a revolutionary political organization, such as a militia group, can be categorized as rebels according to Merton's model.

Merton's theory, though popular, does not fully account for patterns of

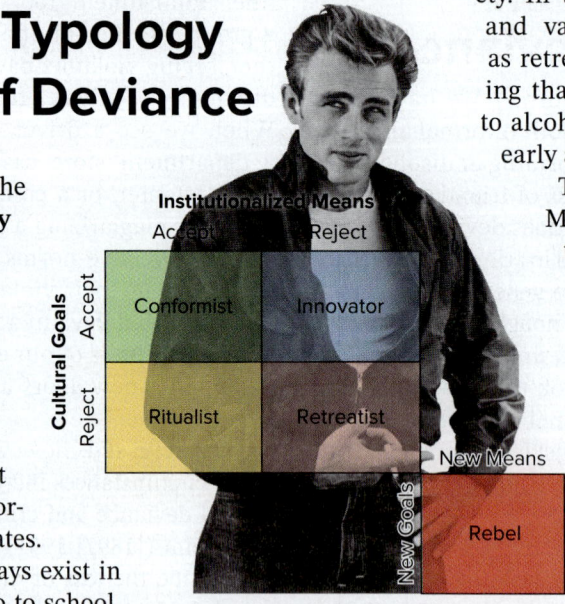

Merton's Typology of Deviance

Source: Merton, 1968. Photo: ©Kobal Foundation/Getty Images

deviance and crime. Although it is useful in explaining certain types of behavior, such as illegal gambling by disadvantaged "innovators," it fails to explain key differences in crime rates. Why, for example, do some disadvantaged groups have lower rates of reported crime than others? Why do many people in adverse circumstances reject criminal activity as a viable alternative? Merton's theory does not easily answer such questions (Clinard and Miller 1998). Exploring additional sociological perspectives on crime and deviance helps us to more fully appreciate such nuances.

Hirschi's Social Control Theory Rather than asking why people *do* commit crimes, American sociologist Travis Hirschi (1969) asked why they *don't*. He assumed that left to their own devices, people would naturally seek their own gratification, including lying, cheating, and stealing to get their way, even at the expense of others. Growing out of the functionalist perspective, the theory presupposes that society would be unable to function if people couldn't trust others to work toward common goals. As an answer, he proposed **social control theory,** which posits that the social bonds we share with other members of society lead us to conform to society's norms. According to Hirschi, deviance occurs due to lack of self-control, and self-control develops as a consequence of socialization into society's norms and values through the relationships we have with others. Even if we are tempted at times, we take into account what family, friends, and significant others might think should they find out what we did. As a result, we typically refuse to give in to temptation because we do not want to damage those relationships.

Hirschi identified four key elements involved in strengthening those social bonds. First, *attachment* refers to the emotional ties and sense of connection individuals feel toward significant others in their lives. Second, *commitment* involves the extent to which individuals view their long-term success as tied to the ongoing success of their society. In other words, investing one's time, energy, and resources in the existing system reduces the likelihood of deviance, which would jeopardize that investment. Third, *involvement* means spending time doing what is expected—for a student, that might include studying for exams, rehearsing lines, going to volleyball practice—which reduces a person's availability for deviance. If, as the old proverb goes, "Idle hands are the devil's workshop," involvement prevents deviance by keeping people busy. And fourth, *belief* involves buying into the society's core values by making them one's own. Those least integrated into society along these four dimensions are the ones most likely to commit deviant acts. Society can reduce levels of crime and deviance by socializing children effectively at a young age and building strong social ties as children develop (Brown and Jennings 2014; Hirschi 1969, 2004).

> **Social control theory** A theory of deviance that posits that the social bonds we share with other members of society lead us to conform to society's norms

INTERPERSONAL INTERACTION AND DEFINING DEVIANCE

Another approach to explaining crime and deviance grows out of insights drawn from the interactionist perspective. Rather than concentrating on the societal level and its presumed needs for social order, these theories emphasize the interpersonal level and highlight the importance of interaction in shaping how deviance occurs. Deviance here is something we learn or something attributed to us by others.

Did You Know?

... More people are arrested for drug use in the United States than for any other crime. The FBI reported 1,488,707 arrests for drug abuse violations in 2015, which constitutes 13.8% of all arrests. Regionally, the South had the highest rate. The three highest states were South Dakota, Illinois, and Mississippi, and the three lowest were Vermont, Massachusetts, and Alaska.

Source: U.S. Department of Justice 2016b:Tables 29, 30, & 69. Photo: ©ESB Professional/Shutterstock.com RF

Cultural Transmission As humans, we learn how to behave in social situations, whether properly or improperly. Sociologist Edwin Sutherland (1883–1950) proposed that, just as individuals are socialized to conform to society's basic norms and values, so also are they socialized to learn deviant acts. It's not that we are born to be wild; we learn to be wild.

Sutherland drew on the **cultural transmission** school, which emphasizes that individuals learn criminal behavior by interacting with others. Such learning includes not only the techniques of lawbreaking (for example, how to break into a car quickly and quietly), but also the motives, drives, and rationalizations of the criminal. The cultural transmission approach can also be used to explain the behavior of those who habitually abuse alcohol or drugs.

Sutherland maintained that through interactions with a primary group and significant others, people acquire definitions of proper and improper behavior. He used the term **differential association** to describe the process through which exposure to attitudes favorable to criminal acts leads to the violation of rules. Research suggests that this view of differential association also applies to noncriminal deviant acts, such as smoking, binge drinking, and cheating (Higgins, Tewksbury, and Mustaine 2007; Nofziger and Hye-Ryeon 2006; Vowell and Chen 2004).

To what extent will a given person engage in an activity that is regarded as proper or improper? For each individual, it will depend on the frequency, duration, and importance of two types of social interaction: those experiences that endorse deviant behavior and those that promote acceptance of social norms. People are more likely to engage in norm-defying behavior if they are part of a group or subculture that stresses deviant values, such as a street gang.

Sutherland offers the example of a boy who is sociable, outgoing, and athletic and who lives in an area with a high rate of delinquency. The youth is very likely to come into contact with peers who commit acts of vandalism, fail to attend school, and so forth, and he may come to adopt such behavior. However, an introverted boy who lives in the same neighborhood may stay away from his peers and avoid delinquency. In another community, an outgoing and athletic boy may join a Little League baseball team or a scout troop because of his interactions with peers. Thus, Sutherland views improper behavior as the result of the types of groups to which one belongs and the kinds of friendships one has (Sutherland, Cressey, and Luckenbill 1992).

Although the cultural transmission approach may not explain the conduct of the first-time, impulsive shoplifter or the impoverished person who steals out of necessity, it does help explain the deviant behavior of juvenile delinquents or graffiti artists. It directs our attention to the paramount role of social interaction and context in increasing a person's motivation to engage in deviant behavior (Morselli, Tremblay, and McCarthy 2006; Sutherland et al. 1992).

Social Disorganization Theory The relative strength of social relationships in a community or neighborhood influences the behavior of its members. Social psychologist Philip Zimbardo (2007) studied the effect of these communal relationships by conducting the following experiment. He abandoned a car in each of two different neighborhoods, leaving its hood up and removing its hubcaps. In one neighborhood, people started to strip the car for parts even before Zimbardo had finished setting up a remote video camera to record their behavior. In the other neighborhood, weeks passed without the car being touched, except for a pedestrian who stopped to close the hood during a rainstorm.

Social disorganization theory attributes increases in crime and deviance to the absence or breakdown

Cultural transmission A school of criminology that argues that criminal behavior is learned through social interactions.

Differential association A theory of deviance that holds that violation of rules results from exposure to attitudes favorable to criminal acts.

Social disorganization theory The theory that attributes increases in crime and deviance to the absence or breakdown of communal relationships and social institutions, such as the family, school, church, and local government.

Personal Sociology

Criminal in the Mirror

The cafeteria at the school where I teach has an all-you-can-eat policy, but you cannot take food with you when you leave. Most of my students admit they violate this policy. When I suggest that what they are doing might be criminal, they are offended. They justify their theft in any number of ways: they pay a lot for their meal plan, they sometimes miss meals, it wouldn't make sense to throw the food away, etc. Yet there are people who are in prison for having taken things costing less than the total value of food taken by the average student. Why is it that those of us, like me, who are guilty of having taken food do not view ourselves as criminal?

of communal relationships and social institutions, such as the family, school, church, and local government. The lack of such local community connections, with their associated cross-age relationships, makes it difficult to exert informal control within the community, especially of children. Without community supervision and controls, playing outside becomes an opportunity for deviance and for older violators to socialize children into inappropriate paths. Crime becomes a normal response to a local context (Shaw and McKay 1969).

The social disorganization theory gave rise to what is known as the "broken windows" hypothesis (Wilson and Kelling 1982). According to this model, physical signs of decline in a community or neighborhood, such as abandoned cars, litter, graffiti, and drug paraphernalia, indicate a corresponding breakdown of social order within which crime and deviance are likely to thrive. The analogy goes something like this, "If a window in a building is broken and is left unrepaired, all the rest of the windows will soon be broken" (Wilson and Kelling 1982). The broken window gets taken as a sign that no one cares, meaning there will be no consequences for breaking more. As that happens, a perception develops that the community is unsafe, leading people to action. Many who can will move out. As informal social controls break down, others will be more willing to display deviance publicly, including panhandling, prostitution, public intoxication, drug use, and mugging (Kelling 2015; Kelling and Coles 1996; Wilson and Kelling 1982).

The broken windows model resulted in a theory of policing premised on the idea that the metaphorical broken windows must be addressed early on before the domino effect kicked in and the neighborhood was engulfed in crime. To put this into practice, police identified some people, such as drunks or vagrants, as undesirable and dealt with them harshly in an effort to stop the first domino. The challenge arises, however, when undesirability is linked to race, ethnicity, age, and sex. The "stop and frisk" policing program, which was a direct outgrowth of this policing philosophy, empowers police to stop and search individuals for drugs, weapons, or other illegal items, even without probable cause. This technique has been criticized for unfairly targeting and denying the constitutional rights of young African American and Latino males (Gelman, Fagan, and Kiss 2007; Kochel, Wilson, and Mastrofski 2011; Sampson and Raudenbush 2004; Torres 2015), and its effectiveness in reducing crime has been questioned (Rosenfeld and Fornago 2014).

Labeling Theory Sometimes when it comes to deviance, perception dominates over reality. In the early

©Janine Wiedel Photography/Alamy Stock Photo

1970s, sociologist William Chambliss (1973) conducted what has become a classic sociological study of deviance. Using observation research at a moderate-sized suburban high school, he followed two groups of male students, which he called the Saints and Roughnecks. Those designated the Saints came from "good families," were active in school organizations, planned on attending college, and received good grades. Those designated the Roughnecks had no such aura of respectability. They drove around town in beat-up cars, were generally unsuccessful in school, and aroused suspicion no matter what they did (Chambliss 1973).

Chambliss learned that boys from both groups repeatedly engaged in excessive drinking, reckless driving, truancy, petty theft, and vandalism. However, students he identified as Saints were never arrested, whereas Roughnecks were frequently in trouble with police and townspeople. Even though their acts of deviance were largely the same, the two groups were not treated equally. The Saints hid behind a facade of respectability, and people generally viewed their delinquent acts as a few isolated cases of sowing wild oats. Consistent with the Thomas theorem, Chambliss concluded that people's perception of the students, as rooted in their social class positions, played an important role in the varying fortunes of the two groups.

Labeling theory An approach to deviance that attempts to explain why certain people are viewed as deviants while others engaged in the same behavior are not.

We can understand such discrepancies by using an approach to deviance known as **labeling theory**, which emphasizes how a person comes to be labeled as deviant or to accept that label. Unlike Sutherland's work, labeling theory does not focus on why some individuals come to commit deviant acts. Instead, it attempts to explain why society views certain people (such as the Roughnecks) as deviants, delinquents, bad kids, losers, and criminals, while it sees others whose behavior is similar (such as the Saints) in less harsh terms. Sociologist Howard Becker (1963:9; 1964), who popularized this approach, summed up labeling theory with this statement: "Deviant behavior is behavior that people so label."

Labeling theory is also called the **societal-reaction approach,** reminding us that it is the response to an act, not the act itself, that determines deviance. Traditionally, research on deviance has focused on people who violate social norms. In contrast, labeling theory focuses on police, probation officers, psychiatrists, judges, teachers, employers, school officials, and other regulators of social control. These agents, it is argued, play a significant role in creating the deviant identity by designating certain people (and not others) as deviant (Bernburg, Krohn, and Rivera 2006). An important aspect of labeling theory is the recognition that some individuals or groups have the power to define labels and apply them to others. This view ties into the conflict perspective's emphasis on the social significance of power.

The practice of racial profiling, in which people are identified as criminal suspects purely on the basis of their race, frequently occurs in stop-and-frisk policing and has come under public scrutiny. Studies confirm the public's suspicion that in some jurisdictions, police officers are much more likely to stop African American males than White males for routine traffic violations, in the expectation of finding drugs or guns in their cars. Civil rights activists refer to these cases sarcastically as DWB (Driving While Black) violations (Warren et al. 2006). The deaths of numerous young African American men, including Trayvon Martin in Sanford, Florida; Michael Brown in Ferguson, Missouri; Eric Garner in New York City; Tamir Rice in Cleveland, Ohio; and Philando Castile in Falcon Heights, Minnesota, raised substantial concerns about the life-and-death consequences of labeling young African American males as threats.

Although the labeling approach does not fully explain why certain people accept a label and others manage to reject it, labeling theorists do suggest that the power an individual has relative to others is important in determining his or her ability to resist an undesirable label. It opens the door to additional emphasis on the undeniably important actions of people with power who can shape what counts as deviance.

> Law and justice are not always the same.
>
> Gloria Steinem

Societal-reaction approach
Another name for *labeling theory.*

©EMPPhotography/Getty Images RF

CONFLICT, POWER, AND CRIMINALITY

In addition to its significance for labeling theory, the story of the Saints and Roughnecks points toward the role that power and control over valued resources can play in defining deviance. Sociologist Richard Quinney (1974, 1979, 1980) is a leading proponent of the view that the criminal justice system serves the interests of the powerful. Consistent with the conflict perspective, this approach maintains that people with power protect their own interests and define deviance to suit their own needs. Crime, according to Quinney (1970), is defined as such by legislators who may be influenced by the economic elites to advance their interests.

Race and Class Looking at crime from this perspective draws our attention to the effects that power and position might have throughout the criminal justice system in the United States. Researchers have found that the system treats suspects differently based on their racial, ethnic, or social class background. In many cases, officials using their own discretion make biased decisions about whether to press charges or drop them, whether to set bail and how much, and whether to offer parole or deny it. Researchers have found that this kind of **differential justice**, which refers to differences in the way social control is exercised over different groups, puts African Americans and Latinos at a disadvantage in the justice system, both as juveniles and as adults. On average, White offenders receive shorter sentences than comparable Latino and African American offenders, even when prior arrest records and the relative severity of the crime are taken into consideration (Brewer and Heitzeg 2008; Quinney 1974; Wakefield and Uggen 2010).

> **Differential justice** Differences in the way social control is exercised over different groups.

We see this pattern of differential justice at work with death penalty cases. Simply put, poor people cannot afford to hire the best lawyer and often must rely on court-appointed attorneys, who typically are overworked and underpaid. With capital punishment in place, these unequal resources may mean the difference between life and death for poor defendants (Kutateladze et al. 2014; National Center for Access to Justice. 2016; National Center for State Courts 2015). Indeed, the American Bar Association has repeatedly expressed concern about the limited defense

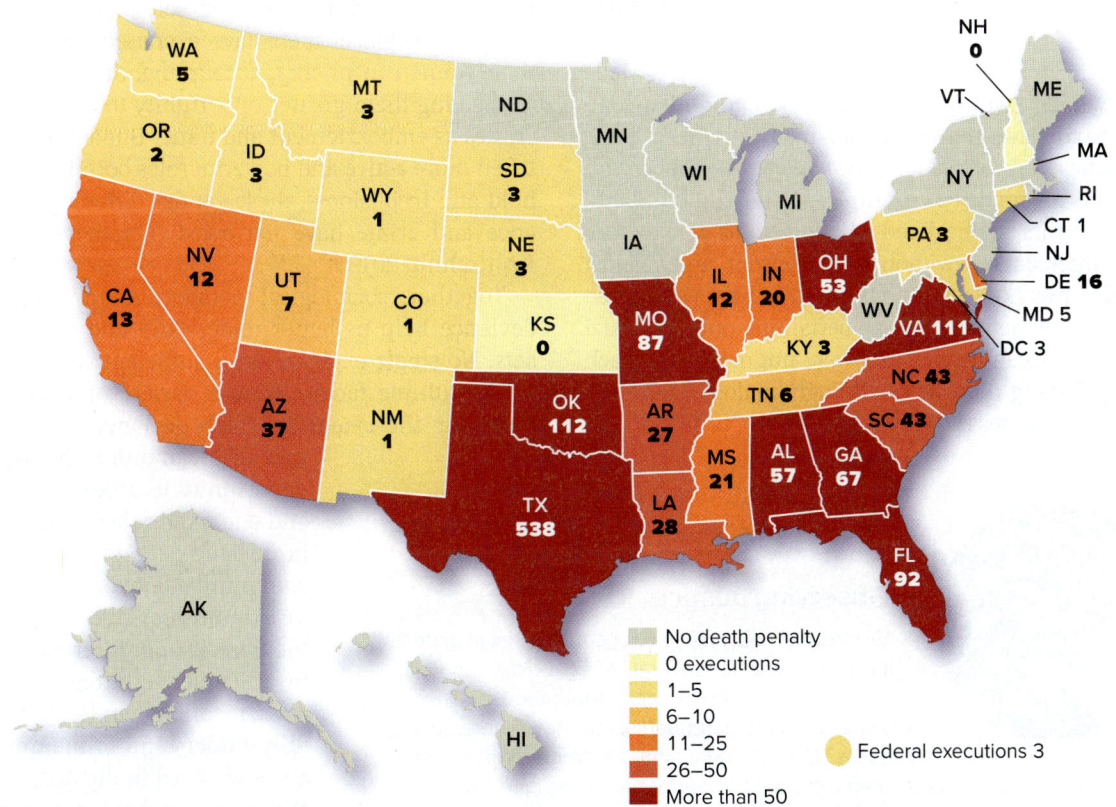

Executions by State Since 1976

Note: The death penalty was reinstated by the U.S. Supreme Court in 1976. Data current as of November 2016. New Mexico abolished the death penalty in 2009.
Source: Death Penalty Information Center 2016.

most defendants facing the death penalty receive. Through mid-2017, DNA analysis and other new technologies had exonerated 350 inmates, 20 of whom had served time on death row, with an average of 14 years served in prison. Thirty-seven of the exonerees pleaded guilty to crimes they did not commit. Overall, 62 percent of those found innocent were African American (Innocence Project 2017).

Various studies show that defendants are more likely to be sentenced to death if their victims were White rather than Black. Even though about half of all murder victims are White, 76 percent of death penalty case victims are White. Some evidence indicates that Black defendants, who constituted 42 percent of all death row inmates in 2016, are more likely to face execution than Whites in the same legal circumstances. Overall, 70 percent of those who have been exonerated by DNA testing were African American, Latino, or Asian American. Evidence exists, too, that capital defendants receive poor legal services because of the racist attitudes of their own defense counsel. Apparently, discrimination and racism do not end even when the stakes are life and death (Death Penalty Information Center 2016; Innocence Project 2016; Jacobs et al. 2007).

Gender Feminist criminologists such as Meda Chesney-Lind (with Lisa Pasko 2004) and Gillian Balfour (2006) have suggested that many of the existing approaches to deviance and crime were developed with only men in mind. For example, in the United States, for many years any husband who forced his wife to have sexual intercourse—without her consent and against her will—was not legally considered to have committed rape. The law defined rape as pertaining only to sexual relations between people who were not married to each other, reflecting the overwhelmingly male composition of state legislatures at the time.

> Whenever you find yourself on the side of the majority, it is time to pause and reflect.
>
> Mark Twain

It took repeated protests by feminist organizations to get changes in the criminal law defining rape. It was not until 1993 that husbands in all 50 states could be prosecuted under most circumstances for the rape of their wives. However, significant exceptions remain in no fewer than 30 states. For example, the husband is exempt when he does not need to use force because his wife is asleep, unconscious, or mentally or physically impaired. In such cases, the presupposition is that the husband has a right to nonconsensual sex with his wife (Bergen 2006).

When it comes to crime and to deviance in general, society tends to treat women in a stereotypical fashion. For example, consider how women who have many and frequent sexual partners are more likely to be viewed with scorn than men who are promiscuous. Cultural views and attitudes toward women influence how they are perceived and labeled. The feminist perspective also emphasizes that deviance, including crime, tends to flow from economic relationships. Traditionally, men have had greater earning power than their wives. As a result, wives may be reluctant to report acts of abuse to the authorities and thereby lose what may be their primary or even sole source of income. In the workplace, men have exercised greater power than women in pricing, accounting, and product control, giving them greater opportunity to engage in such crimes as embezzlement and fraud. But as women have taken more active and powerful roles both in the household and in business, these gender differences in deviance and crime have narrowed (Chesney-Lind 1989; Kruttschnitt 2013).

Together, sociological perspectives on crime and deviance help us better understand and explain such acts. No single explanation is sufficient. We must consider multiple factors from a variety of perspectives, including the extent to which deviance exists for the sake of social order; the degree of opportunity to attain both means and ends; the role of socialization in deviance; the strength of local community networks; the power to administer labels and make them stick; and differential access to valuable resources based on class, race, and gender. If we are to fully understand crime and deviance, we need to dig deep enough and consider what is going on from enough angles and with sufficient care, concern, and curiosity.

SOCIOLOGY IS A VERB

Observing Justice

Visit a local courthouse to observe a trial in action. If possible, stay for several cases in different courts. What do you observe about the key players, including the defendants, attorneys, judge, and witnesses? Drawing on Goffman's dramaturgical analysis, in what ways are the performances staged? What scripts and props are used? How does the trial you observed compare to trials portrayed in television dramas or on cable news channels?

For REVIEW

I. How do groups maintain social control?
   - They use positive and negative sanctions in both formal and informal ways to bring about conformity and obedience.

II. What is the difference between deviance and crime?
   - Deviance involves violating a group's expected norms, which may lead the offender to be stigmatized. Crime is a form of deviance that involves violating the formal norms administered by the state for which the offender may receive formal sanctions.

III. How do sociologists explain deviance and crime?
   - Sociologists offer a number of theories of crime, each of which provides additional factors to be considered—such as the need for social order, the significance of interpersonal relationships and local context, and the importance of power and access to resources—that help us better understand why deviance and crime occur.

©arek_malang/Shutterstock.com RF

SOCVIEWS on Deviance

Functionalist View

Agents of **social control** aim to limit deviant social behavior by enforcing norms and providing negative sanctions for disobedience. Government exerts formal social control through its **laws**.

Deviance can actually contribute to social stability by defining the limits of proper behavior and encouraging **conformity** to laws and rules.

Social **integration** constrains deviant acts because it provides a clear **consensus** on shared norms and values.

KEY CONCEPTS: CONFORMITY, OBEDIENCE, LAW, ORDER

Conflict View

In diverse societies, the process of making laws generates conflicts over whose values should prevail.

Individuals and groups with the greatest **status and power** generally define who or what is deviant in a society.

The criminal justice system **treats suspects differently** based on their racial, ethnic, or class background, which leads to distrust in the criminal system.

KEY CONCEPTS: POWER, DIFFERENTIAL JUSTICE

Interactionist View

People learn what is proper and improper behavior through their interactions with others—an idea known as **cultural transmission**.

Informal social control is achieved through casual interactions—a smile, a raised eyebrow, ridicule—that prompt us to adjust our behavior.

A breakdown in interpersonal social relationships in a local community can lead to increases in crime and deviance.

KEY CONCEPTS: LABELING, CULTURAL TRANSMISSION

MAKE THE CONNECTION

After reviewing the chapter, answer the following questions:

1 How would each perspective approach, explore, and explain mass public shootings in the United States?

2 What perspective do you think provides the best explanation for the results of Milgram's experiment on obedience? Why?

3 Describe victimless crime from the point of view of each of the three perspectives, using one of the following examples in your response: drug use, gambling, or prostitution.

4 Which perspective best describes the way you learned proper social behavior? Were social norms socialized and internalized (functionalist), imposed by powerful authority figures (conflict), or learned from observing others (interactionist)? Provide examples.

Pop Quiz

1. What term do sociologists use to describe society's power to limit deviance by enforcing conformity to expected norms and values?
   a. stigmatization
   b. labeling
   c. law
   d. social control

2. The penalties and rewards we face for conduct concerning a social norm are known as
   a. informal social controls.
   b. stigmas.
   c. sanctions.
   d. conformities.

3. What type of compliance do sociologists refer to when using the word *conformity*?
   a. Going along with peers even though they have no formal authority over us.
   b. Obedience to higher authorities in a hierarchical structure.
   c. Listening to your conscience when it tells you not to do something wrong.
   d. Acceptance of the court system's right to enforce formal sanctions.

4. Which of the following statements is true of deviance?
   a. Deviance is always criminal behavior.
   b. Deviance is behavior that violates the standards of conduct or expectations of a group or society.
   c. Deviance is perverse behavior.
   d. Deviance is inappropriate behavior that cuts across all cultures and social orders.

5. The FBI reports which two major categories of crime in its annual *Uniform Crime Reports*?
   a. violent crime and property crime
   b. organized crime and white-collar crime
   c. victimless crime and transnational crime
   d. transnational crime and victimization crime

6. Which type of crime involves the willing exchange among adults of widely desired, but illegal, goods and services?
   a. index crimes
   b. white-collar crime
   c. victimless crime
   d. organized crime

7. Which of the following is *not* one of the basic forms of adaptation specified in Robert Merton's strain theory of deviance?
   a. conformity
   b. innovation
   c. ritualism
   d. hostility

8. According to Hirschi's social control theory,
   a. deviance involves acceptance and/or rejection of society's goals and means.
   b. our social bonds with members of society lead us to conform to society's norms.
   c. we come to view ourselves as deviant based on how others view us.
   d. power and access to resources shape whose norms and values determine individual action.

9. Which of the following theories gave rise to the "broken windows" hypothesis that physical decay in a community represents a symbol of decreasing social order?
   a. labeling theory
   b. cultural transmission theory
   c. social disorganization theory
   d. strain theory

10. Even though they committed the same deviant acts, the Saints and the Roughnecks did not receive the same treatment from authorities. Sociologist William Chambliss suggests this was due to the fact that authorities viewed members of the groups differently. Which theory supports that conclusion?
    a. Merton's strain theory
    b. culture transmission theory
    c. differential association theory
    d. labeling theory

1. (d), 2. (c), 3. (a), 4. (b), 5. (a), 6. (c), 7. (d), 8. (b), 9. (c), 10. (d)

7 Families

©Danny Liao

LOOKING FOR LOVE

Swipe right or swipe left? It's a question millions of Tinder users ask and answer every day. Finding a love connection can be a tricky thing. Norms for doing so vary over time and across cultures. From arranged marriages to one-night stands, the society we live in shapes the options available to us. Smartphone technology made an app like Tinder possible, opening up a new world of possibilities for people looking for love. Tinder works by connecting people who want to find others who are also looking. When two users "like" each other, referred to as "swiping right," a match occurs, and they can then exchange messages within the app to see if anything more might develop.

Not everyone would think that sociology might have a role in making such connections possible, but Tinder did. The company hired sociologist Jessica Carbino, who earned her PhD in sociology from UCLA. Carbino collects and analyzes data using surveys, focus groups, and content analysis. What she found might be surprising. "In one of our recent surveys," claims Carbino, "we found that 80 percent of Tinder users are seeking a relationship that is not a hookup. They're looking for something more substantial" (Titlow 2016).

Carbino argues that Tinder, along with other online dating options, developed as a consequence of society's changing structure. These tools, she claims, have "replaced or supplemented a very fragmented market by which people meet. Historically, people have met through family and friends. But now given delays in marriage and childbearing generally . . . it's becoming far harder to find someone to ultimately mate with" (Titlow 2016). Based on her research, Carbino offers Tinder users some helpful advice: smile; don't use a group photo; include details in your bio that can serve as hooks for others to initiate a conversation; and include a question that might prompt others to respond (Lebowitz 2016; Titlow 2016).

It turns out that in general, men and women approach Tinder differently. Men are more likely to swipe right but not follow up with a message. Women are less likely to swipe right but more likely to send a message.

After a match occurs, meaning both parties "liked" each other, the median amount of time it took for a man to send a message was 2 minutes compared to 38 minutes for women. The median message length for men was 12 characters compared to 122 for women (Tyson et al. 2016).

When it comes to love, marriage, sex, kids, and all that, the choices people make at one time and place differ from those at another. In this chapter we explore the ways sociology enables us to understand how and why such variations occur.

As You Read >>

- What do we mean by family?
- How do people pick partners?
- How do families vary?

>> Global View of the Family

Families around the world come in many shapes and sizes. Among Tibetans, a woman may be married simultaneously to more than one man, usually brothers. This system allows sons to share the limited amount of good land. Among the Betsileo of Madagascar, a man has multiple wives, each one living in a different village where he cultivates rice. Wherever he has the best rice field, that woman is considered his first or senior wife. Among the Yanomami of Brazil and Venezuela, it is considered proper to have sexual relations with one's opposite-sex cousins if they are the children of one's mother's brother or father's sister. But if one's opposite-sex cousins are the children of one's mother's sister or father's brother, the same practice is considered to be incest (Haviland et al. 2005; Kottak 2004).

In the United States, families of today often look different than they did a century or even a generation ago. New roles, new gender distinctions, and new child-rearing patterns have all combined to create new forms of family life. These days, for example, more and more women are taking the breadwinner's role, whether as a spouse or as a single parent. Blended families—the result of divorce and remarriage—are common. Same-sex marriages have become legal across the country. And many people are seeking intimate relationships outside marriage (Fry and Cohn 2010; Patten and Parker 2012).

Because families as we experience them are varied in structure and style, we need a sociological approach that is sufficiently broad to encompass all those relationships we experience as family. Drawing insight from two distinct definitional approaches helps clarify the challenges we face. The first is a substantive definition that focuses on what a family *is*, and the second is a functional definition that focuses on what families *do*.

> **Substantive definition of the family** A definition of the family based on blood, meaning shared genetic heritage, and law, meaning social recognition and affirmation of the bond including both marriage and adoption.

SUBSTANCE: WHAT A FAMILY IS

Perhaps the most conventional approach to defining family is the **substantive definition,** which focuses on blood and law. Blood, in this case, means that people are related because they share a biological heritage passed on directly from parent to child, linking people

Did You Know?
...More than 2.1 million couples get married in the United States every year. In 2015, Nevada had the highest rate at 31 marriages per 1,000 people followed by Hawaii at 15.9. The U.S rate overall was 6.9. Perhaps not everything that happens in Vegas stays in Vegas.

Source: Centers for Disease Control and Prevention 2016a. *Photo:* ©Steve Allen/Getty Images RF

TV families in the 1950s showed very little diversity in terms of family structure, race, and ethnicity. ©NBC Television/Courtesy Getty Images

indirectly to grandparents, aunts and uncles, and other biological relatives. Law means the formal social recognition and affirmation of a bond as family, particularly in the form of marriage and adoption.

The primary advantage of this definitional approach is that boundaries are clear; we can tell who is in and who is out. This makes it easier to count such families, so perhaps it is no surprise that the U.S. Census, whose definition of family remains largely unchanged since 1930, relies on a substantive approach: "A family consists of a householder and one or more other people living in the same household who are related to the householder by birth, marriage or adoption" (Pemberton 2015). It also allows us to track who is related to whom over time.

Kinship The state of being related to others.

Bilateral descent A kinship system in which both sides of a person's family are regarded as equally important.

Patrilineal descent A kinship system in which only the father's relatives are significant.

Matrilineal descent A kinship system in which only the mother's relatives are significant.

Kinship Patterns Many of us can trace our roots by looking at a family tree or by listening to elderly family members talk about their lives—and about ancestors who lived and died long before we were born. Yet a person's lineage is more than simply a personal history; it also reflects societal traditions that govern descent. In every culture, children encounter relatives to whom they are expected to show an emotional attachment. The state of being related to others is called **kinship**. Kinship is culturally learned, however, and is not totally determined by biological or marital ties. For example, adoption creates a kinship tie that is legally acknowledged and socially accepted.

The family and the kin group are not necessarily one and the same. Whereas the family is a household unit, kin do not always live together or function as a collective body on a daily basis. Kin groups can include aunts, uncles, cousins, in-laws, and so forth. In a society such as the United States, the kinship group may come together only rarely, for a wedding or funeral. However, kinship ties frequently involve obligations and responsibilities. We may feel compelled to assist our kin, and we feel free to call on them for many types of aid, including loans and babysitting (O'Brien 2012; Rossi Del Corso and Lanz 2013).

How do we identify kinship groups? The principle of descent assigns people to kinship groups according to their relationship to a mother or father. There are three primary ways of determining descent. The United States follows the system of **bilateral descent,** which means that both sides of a person's family are regarded as equally important. For example, no higher value is given to the brothers of one's father than to the brothers of one's mother.

Historically speaking, most societies give preference to one side of the family or the other in tracing descent (Murdock 1957). In **patrilineal descent** (from the Latin *pater,* "father"), only the father's relatives are significant in terms of property, inheritance, and emotional ties. Conversely, in societies that favor **matrilineal descent** (from the Latin *mater,* "mother"), only the mother's relatives are significant.

> **SOC**THINK
>
> How important are intergenerational kinship networks and extended family members in your family? How has this changed since your parents' and grandparents' generations?

Family Types The substantive approach also shapes what we traditionally view as common family types. If we assume that we are connected through blood and law, we can analyze how we structure those relationships. Families might place greater emphasis on immediate family members or on extended family networks. They also are shaped by the number of partners deemed appropriate.

Historically, family connections served as a valuable resource, providing us with access to material, social, and cultural resources. We depended on relatives for food, shelter, opportunities, and knowledge. In fact, historian Stephanie Coontz (2005) argues that, historically, the primary reason to get married was to obtain not a partner but in-laws, thus extending one's network of cooperative relationships. This was the logic of the matchmaker tradition in which resource distribution mattered more than romantic love. The matchmaker, as a member of the community, sought to maximize social network connections for the good of the whole.

A family in which relatives—such as grandparents, aunts, or uncles—live in the same household as parents and their children is known as an **extended family.** Historically, the extended family, along with relatives living near each other, was the norm. In the pre–Industrial Revolution era before cotton gins, spinning jennies, tractors, and combines, each additional family member, whether in the form of children or in-laws, represented another producer. As the old saying goes, many hands make light work. Extending the family network provided a material advantage. The Amish, because they value the multigenerational extended family, and gain solidarity by working together, intentionally limit the use of technology that would otherwise make their work easier and more efficient (Kraybill et al. 2013). In addition to economic advantages, the extended family network has also proven to be a source of strength in times of crisis such as death, disaster, or illness.

With the advent of the Industrial Revolution, the economy shifted away from agricultural production and its corresponding small-town life and toward industrial production in urban areas. A large family went from being an asset to something of a debit. Rather than serving as producers, children primarily became consumers whom parents had to feed, clothe, and shelter, which represented a significant expense. In addition, jobs were less place specific, so the capacity to be mobile was an advantage if the company wanted to transfer you to another location. As a result, families became smaller. Conventionally, the **nuclear family** includes a married couple and their unmarried children living together. The concept of nuclear family builds on the essence or nucleus of the substantive definition of blood and law, including as it does both the parent-to-child and the marriage relationship.

Types of Marriage In the United States, the vast majority of such relationships, in keeping with the law of the land, are monogamous. The term **monogamy** describes a form of marriage in which two people are married only to each other. That does not necessarily mean a person will ever have only one marriage partner. Many people in the United States move into and out of a number of serious romantic relationships over time, what sociologist Andrew Cherlin (2009) refers to as the "marriage-go-round." Termed **serial monogamy,** a person may have several spouses in his or her lifetime, but only one spouse at a time.

Some cultures allow an individual to have several husbands or wives simultaneously. This form of marriage is known as **polygamy.** In fact, most societies throughout the world, past and present, have preferred polygamy to monogamy. Anthropologist George Murdock (1949, 1957) sampled 565 societies and found that in more than 80 percent, some type of polygamy was the preferred form. Although polygamy declined steadily through most of the 20th century, in 28 sub-Saharan African countries, at least 10 percent of men still have polygamous marriages (Fenske 2013; Tertilt 2005). In a U.S. national survey, researchers found that 16 percent of adults find polygamy to be morally acceptable, up from 7 percent in 2001 (Newport 2015).

There are two basic types of polygamy. The more common is **polygyny,** which refers to the marriage of a man to more than one woman at the same time. Less common is **polyandry,** in which a woman may have more than one husband at the same time. Such is the case, for example, in the Nyinba culture of Nepal and Tibet, in which

©Creatas/Getty ImagesRF

Extended family A family in which relatives—such as grandparents, aunts, or uncles—live in the same household as parents and their children.

Nuclear family A married couple and their unmarried children living together.

Monogamy A form of marriage in which two people are married only to each other.

Serial monogamy A form of marriage in which a person may have several spouses in his or her lifetime, but only one spouse at a time.

Polygamy A form of marriage in which an individual may have several husbands or wives simultaneously.

Polygyny A form of polygamy in which a man may have more than one wife at the same time.

Polyandry A form of polygamy in which a woman may have more than one husband at the same time.

SOC THINK

Why do you think that polygamy was the most common form of marriage historically? Why has it given way to monogamy in modern societies?

brothers share a common wife. This arrangement provides a sufficient number of physical laborers in the difficult farming environment yet minimizes the number of offspring (Zeitzen 2008).

The primary advantage of the substantive approach to defining families is that it provides clear boundaries separating who counts as family and who does not. It makes it easy, in theory at least, to trace a family tree by mapping parent-to-child relationships between generations as well as socially sanctioned relationships (such as marriage) within generations. In practice, however, we encounter limits to this substantive approach. In the case of adoption, for example, do you count the child's biological ancestors as part of the family tree? What about the ancestors of a stepfather or stepmother? And what happens when a parent and stepparent divorce? Is that stepparent, who might have played a vital role in child rearing, no longer related? What about close friends who are very much part of the family? Does Dad's college friend "Uncle" Bob count? New forms of reproductive technology, involving donated sperm and eggs and surrogate parents, also challenge the biological preconditions of this approach. Any substantive definition we might come up with runs the risk of excluding those whom we think of as family members. In response, sociologists turn toward the more inclusive functionalist definition of families to address such limitations.

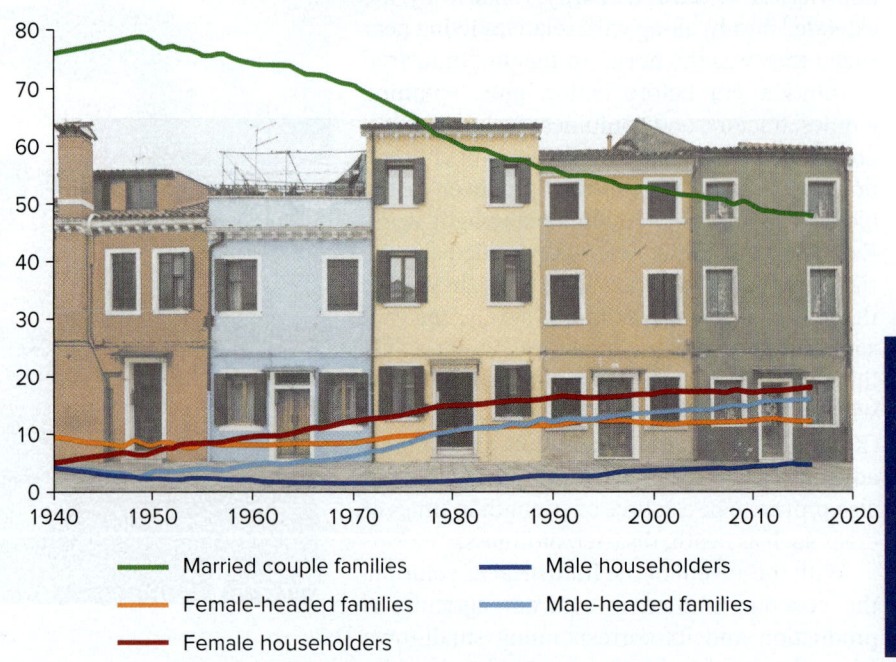

U.S. Households by Family Type, 1940–2016

— Married couple families
— Female-headed families
— Female householders
— Male householders
— Male-headed families

Note: Male and female householders include men and women living alone or exclusively with people to whom they are not related, including those in a college dormitory, homeless shelter, or military base.
Source: U.S. Census Bureau 2016c:Table HH-1.   *Photo:* ©compassandcamera/Getty Images RF

SOCstudies

FUNCTIONS: WHAT FAMILIES DO

People in the United States seem to agree that traditional definitions of family are too restrictive. When they are asked how they would define family, their conception is much more inclusive than the substantive definition implies. In one survey, only 22 percent of the respondents defined family in the same way as the U.S. Census Bureau. Instead, 74 percent considered a family to be "any group whose members love and care for one another" (Coontz 1992:21).

We need a definition of family that is inclusive enough to encompass the broad range of intimate groups that people form, such as extended families, nuclear families, single-parent families, blended or reconstituted or stepfamilies, gay and lesbian families, child-free families, racially and ethnically mixed families, commuter marriage families, surrogate or chosen families, and more. One way to avoid getting trapped into overly narrow conceptions of families and to embrace

©Ariel Skelley/Blend Images LLC RF

their diversity is to shift the emphasis away from what families *are,* which a substantive approach highlights, toward what families *do*. A **functionalist definition of families** focuses on how families provide for the physical, social, and emotional needs of individuals and of society as a whole.

Consistent with the functionalist perspective, sociologist William F. Ogburn (Ogburn and Tibbits 1934) identified six primary functions that families perform for us:

- *Reproduction.* For a society to maintain itself, it must replace dying members. Families provide the context within which biological reproduction takes place.
- *Socialization.* Parents and other family members monitor a child's behavior and transmit the norms, values, and language of their culture to the child.
- *Protection.* Unlike the young of other animal species, human infants need constant care and economic security. In all cultures, the family assumes the ultimate responsibility for the protection and upbringing of children.
- *Regulation of sexual behavior.* Sexual norms are subject to change both over time (for instance, in the customs for dating) and across cultures (compare strict Saudi Arabia to the more permissive Denmark). However, whatever the time period or cultural values of a society, standards of sexual behavior are most clearly defined within the family circle.
- *Affection and companionship.* Ideally, families provide members with warm and intimate relationships, helping them to feel satisfied and secure. Of course, a family member may find such rewards outside the family—from peers, in school, at work—and may even perceive the home as an unpleasant or abusive setting. Nevertheless, we expect our relatives to understand us, to care for us, and to be there for us when we need them.
- *Provision of social status.* We inherit a social position because of the family background and reputation of our parents and siblings. For example, the race, ethnicity, social class, education level, occupation, and religion of our parents all shape the material, social, and cultural resources to which we have access and therefore the options we might have.

From this functionalist approach, no matter how it is composed, any group that fulfills these functions is family to us. For example, members of a sports team can be family to us, as can a group of college friends who remain close for life. They are people we can count on in times of trouble, people who will have our backs. We turn to them for all kinds of support, including care and affection,

> **Functionalist definition of families** A definition of families that focuses on how families provide for the physical, social, and emotional needs of individuals and of society as a whole.

PETS AS FAMILY

When we discuss families in terms of what they do instead of what they are, my students inevitably ask, "Do pets count as family?" Some strongly agree, while others think it is the most ridiculous thing they have ever heard. Over time, more and more students have begun coming down on the side of pets as family. When Lori and I "adopted" Jessie, our Pembroke Welsh corgi, I better understood why. People develop strong emotional bonds with their pets and some refer to them as their "fur kids." Pets provide a source of comfort and companionship. When Jessie began to show symptoms of degenerative myelopathy, an inherited genetic disorder, we didn't hesitate to provide her with medical care and a set of wheels to help her get around. Pets give us someone to care about, and they care for us in their own ways. Isn't that what family is all about?

©Jon Witt

guidance in how to think and act or who to date, and sometimes even for material support, whether borrowing a car or money for pizza. Even pets can count as family. In the United States, 95 percent of pet owners think of their pets as family members, and 64 percent buy them Christmas or holiday presents. Some couples go so far as to include dogs as participants in their wedding ceremonies (Shannon-Missal 2015; Stoeckel et al. 2014; Walsh 2009a, 2009b). We may use the expression that such groups are "like family" to convey that sense of connection, or we may even refer to the significant people in our lives as a sister, brother, mom, or dad. For many people, a family *is* what a family *does*.

CONFLICT: WHO RULES?

Regardless of which definition we choose, it is inevitably the case that people living in relationship with each other will have to address the issue of power. Couples, for example, must decide where to live; how to furnish their home; who will shop, cook, and clean; which side of the family to visit on holidays; and a whole host of other decisions both big and small. Siblings may have to decide difficult end-of-life care questions regarding their parents. A society's social norms inform which family members have more or less power over such decisions, and these norms vary cross-culturally and across time.

Historically, decision-making power has largely been shaped by gender. A society that expects males to dominate in all family decision making is termed a **patriarchy.** In patriarchal societies, such as Iran, the eldest male often wields the greatest power, although wives are expected to be treated with respect and kindness. An Iranian woman's status is typically defined by her relationship to a male relative, usually as a wife or daughter. In many patriarchal societies, women find it more difficult to obtain a divorce than a man does (Farr 1999). In contrast, in a **matriarchy,** women have greater authority than men. Formal matriarchies, which are uncommon, emerged among Native American tribal societies and in nations in which men were absent for long periods because of warfare or food-gathering expeditions.

Patriarchy A society in which men dominate in family decision making.

Matriarchy A society in which women dominate in family decision making.

Egalitarian family An authority pattern in which spouses are regarded as equals.

More than a century ago, Friedrich Engels ([1884] 1959), a colleague of Karl Marx and advocate for the conflict perspective, went so far as to say that the family is the ultimate source of social inequality because of its role in the transfer of power, property, and privilege. Historically, he argues, the family has legitimized and perpetuated male dominance. It has contributed to societal injustice, denied women opportunities that are extended to men, and limited freedom in sexual expression and mate selection. In the United States, it was not until the first wave of contemporary feminism, in the mid-1800s, that there was a substantial challenge to the historical status of wives and children as the legal property of husbands and fathers.

Partly because of the efforts of women and men in similar movements over the years, we have seen the rise of a third type of authority pattern, in addition to patriarchy and matriarchy. In the **egalitarian family,** spouses are regarded as equals. This shift has been driven at least in part by occupational and financial opportunities for women that previously had been denied them (Wills and Risman 2006). In practice, this does not mean that all decisions and duties in all spheres are equally shared in such families. Wives may hold authority in some spheres, and husbands in others. For example, sociologists have found that, in terms of both paid and unpaid labor in two-parent families, the total hours worked by mothers and fathers is roughly equal at about 65 hours per week, though the distribution of tasks varies (Bianchi, Robinson, and Milkie 2006).

Historian Stephanie Coontz (2008) suggests that, when it works, marriage today is better than ever. She writes that it "delivers more benefits to its members—adults and children—than ever before. A good marriage is fairer and more fulfilling for both men and women than couples of the past could ever have imagined." She points to shared decision making and housework, increases in time spent with children, and declines in violence and sexual coercion and in the likelihood of adultery.

Although the egalitarian family has become a more common pattern in the United States in recent decades, male dominance over the family has hardly disappeared. Sociologists have found that although married men are increasing their involvement in child care, their wives still perform a disproportionate amount of it. Furthermore, with 5 million stay-at-home moms versus 209,000 stay-at-home dads, a ratio of 24 to 1, the dominant practice reinforces normative expectations (U.S. Census Bureau 2016d:Table SHP-1).

Families also provide an important conduit for maintaining the status quo within the larger society. Although the United States is widely viewed as a land of opportunity, access to valued resources is not evenly distributed to all. Family serves as the basis for transferring material, social, and cultural resources from one generation to the next. Children inherit the privileged or less-than-privileged social and economic status of their parents (and in some cases, of earlier generations as well). The socioeconomic status of a child's family has a marked influence on his or her life chances as an adult because it influences access to nutrition, health care, housing, educational opportunities, and more (Lareau 2011; Pew Research Center 2015d; Putnam 2015; Shipler 2004).

>> Marriage and Family

Despite concerns about power and inequality in the family sphere, people's faith in marriage persists. Currently, almost 80 percent of adults aged 25 and older are, or have been, married, and about half of those who have not yet married say they would like to eventually (Wang and Parker 2014). In spite of this high level of commitment to marriage, the likelihood of marriage varies over time, and the marriage rate in the United States is actually at or near a record low. In the United States, the median age of first marriage in 2016 was 27.4 for women and 29.5 for men. Contrast that with the medians in 1960, which were 20.3 for women and 22.8 for men (Cherlin 2009; Sterbenz 2014; U.S. Census Bureau 2016e:Table MS-2). Rates also vary based on a variety of factors, including income, education, race, ethnicity, and nationality.

The increased likelihood of delaying marriage is shaped by one's perception of marriage, as the Milestones in the Transition to Adulthood feature in Chapter Four demonstrated. According to one view, more common in the 1950s, marriage is a *cornerstone*, something that happens relatively early in adulthood, providing the foundation on which other adult relationships and responsibilities are built. An alternative view arose as more people in the United States waited to marry until after they had completed their educational degrees and established themselves in careers. Sociologist Andrew Cherlin (2009) argues that the symbolic significance of marriage shifted as a result. We are now more likely to view marriage as a *capstone*, something we do as a sign we have our act together and are ready to settle down and into adulthood. There are people who still adhere to the cornerstone model (Prior 2013), but as the "Median Age at First Marriage" graph demonstrates, more and more people are opting to wait.

Median Age at First Marriage, United States

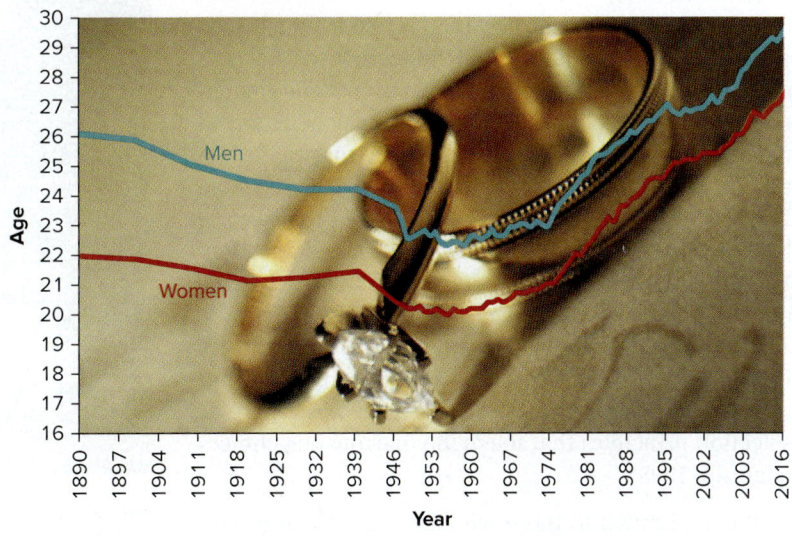

Source: U.S. Census Bureau 2015a:Table MS-2.   *Photo:* ©Janis Christie/Getty Images RF

Going GLOBAL

Percentage of People Aged 20–24 Ever Married, Selected Countries

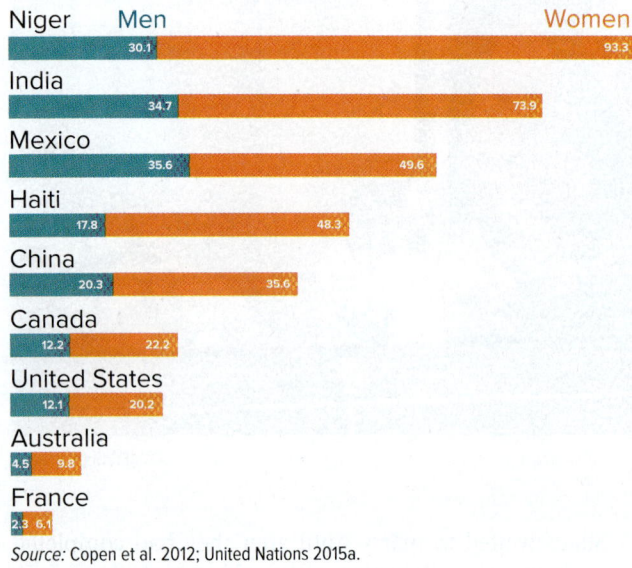

Source: Copen et al. 2012; United Nations 2015a.

SOC THINK

Some well-off professionals in the United States pay huge fees to enlist the help of matchmakers. Why might people choose to do so? What are the disadvantages of relying on one's own contacts and judgment when it comes to finding a romantic partner?

- We are heavily influenced by opinions of family, friends, and the organizations to which we belong (including religious groups and the workplace).
- We are most attracted to people like ourselves.

In the first case, our position in the social structure influences the degree to which we have the opportunity to establish a relationship with someone. Second, partner selection involves more than just the happy couple; those close to us play a significant role in shaping which characteristics we perceive as acceptable. Finally, as the saying goes, like attracts like (or at least it tends to).

When sociologists analyze social factors that shape our selection of partners, they pay particular

COURTSHIP AND MATE SELECTION

There are many ways that we might go about finding someone to marry. Historically, it was not uncommon for marriages to be arranged by families or matchmakers. This is a practice that continues in many cultures today. In the Asian nation of Uzbekistan, for example, courtship is largely orchestrated by the couple's parents. A young Uzbekistani woman is socialized to eagerly anticipate her marriage to a man whom she has met only once, at the final inspection of her dowry (Kamp 2008; Rand 2006).

When it comes to marriage in the United States, most of us assume that true love will guide the way. We can't imagine allowing others, including parents and matchmakers, to select partners for us through arranged marriages. Many are surprised to hear that this practice continues today in some subcultures within the United States. We tend to take for granted that we are best suited to make this personal and intimate selection. We may look to advice from family and friends, but the deciding factor is how we feel about the other person.

In practice, however, our pool of potential partners is substantially reduced by our social location. Sociology enables us to better recognize three basic partner selection principles that inevitably narrow our choices (Kalmijn 1998):

- We are limited to those who are available and with whom we have contact.

Marriage practices, including ceremonial customs, vary significantly across cultures.

attention to the balance between endogamy and exogamy. **Endogamy** (from the Greek *endon,* "within") specifies the groups within which a spouse must be found and prohibits marriage with outsiders. For example, in the United States, many people are expected to marry within their own racial, ethnic, or religious group and are strongly discouraged or even prohibited from marrying outside the group. Endogamy is intended to reinforce the cohesiveness of the group by suggesting that we should marry someone "of our own kind."

In contrast, **exogamy** (from the Greek *exo,* "outside") requires mate selection outside certain groups, usually one's own family or certain kinfolk. Rules for how close is too close vary across cultures and over time. The **incest taboo,** a social norm common to virtually all societies, prohibits sexual relationships between certain culturally specified relatives. In the United States, this taboo means that we must marry outside the nuclear family. We cannot marry our siblings, and in most states, we cannot marry our first cousins.

Endogamy influences a number of social location variables. We tend to pick partners who are the same age, race, ethnicity, education, and religion. Although the degree of influence of these variables has shifted over time, each continues to play a significant role. When it comes to age, for example, one-third of all married couples in the United States are within one year of each other and 77 percent are within five years. Only 9 percent of U.S. couples have an age difference of 10 or more years, and just 1.4 percent have an age difference of 20 or more (U.S. Census Bureau 2016f:Table FG3). Age is one factor for which third-party pressure can exert significant influence; people tend to look suspiciously at relationships in which the age difference is perceived to be too large.

The role of race in selecting partners demonstrates

> **Endogamy** The restriction of mate selection to people within the same group.
>
> **Exogamy** The requirement that people select a mate outside certain groups.
>
> **Incest taboo** The prohibition of sexual relationships between certain culturally specified relatives.

POPSOC

Romantic comedies are a dime a dozen, and it's easy to see why. There's the thrill of the chase and the hoped-for, and almost inevitable, happy ending. But how will the contented couple come to terms with the mundane reality of everyday life together? Film historian Jeanine Basinger (2012) argues that films about marriage are a tougher sell, because marriage is more like a merry-go-round than a roller-coaster ride. To make films about marriage viable, filmmakers use a predictable plot: begin by showing the happy couple facing the promise of eternal bliss, disrupt the relationship using one of seven common threats (money, infidelity, in-laws/children, incompatibility, class, addiction, and murder), and finally, restore order by overcoming the threat and recommitting to living happily ever after.

Photo: ©Metro-Goldwyn-Meyer/Getty Images.

Ten Questions Couples Should Ask (or Wish They Had) Before Marrying

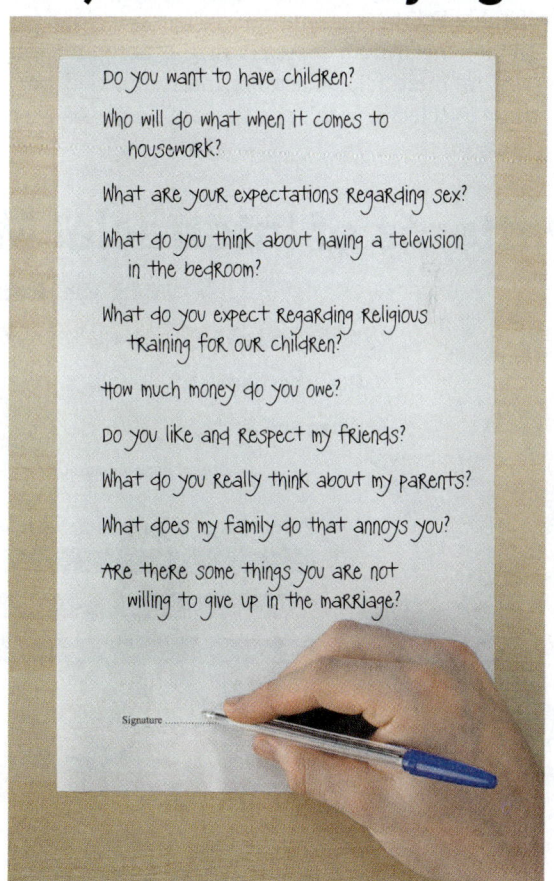

- Do you want to have children?
- Who will do what when it comes to housework?
- What are your expectations regarding sex?
- What do you think about having a television in the bedroom?
- What do you expect regarding religious training for our children?
- How much money do you owe?
- Do you like and respect my friends?
- What do you really think about my parents?
- What does my family do that annoys you?
- Are there some things you are not willing to give up in the marriage?

Source: The New York Times 2006.   *Photo:* ©Image Source, all rights reserved RF

Chapter 7 / Families • 161

how social norms can both change and remain the same. For a long time, interracial marriage was illegal in the United States. This remained true in 16 southern states until 1967 when a court case brought by Mildred and Richard Loving, an African American woman with Native American ancestry and a White man, changed the law of the land. The Lovings' home state, Virginia, banned interracial marriages, so they traveled to Washington, DC, to marry. But a month after they returned home to Virginia, in a nighttime raid on their bedroom while they were sleeping, they were arrested and taken to jail. After pleading guilty to violating Virginia's Racial Integrity Act of 1924, the Lovings avoided prison by agreeing to leave the state and not return together for 25 years. In arguing their case before the Supreme Court, their attorney relayed Richard Loving's words to the Court: "Mr. Cohen, tell the Court I love my wife, and it is just unfair that I can't live with her in Virginia." As a result of their case, the Supreme Court overturned laws banning interracial marriage in the United States (Wallenstein 2014). Since then, interracial marriages in the United States have become more common. Now, 3.1 million married couples, or 4.9 percent of the total, include partners from different racial groups (U.S. Census Bureau 2016f:Table FG3).

Homogamy The conscious or unconscious tendency to select a mate with personal characteristics and interests similar to one's own.

Despite the overall increase in the acceptance and practice of interracial marriage, most married people continue to select a partner of the same race. As we can see from the accompanying "Patterns of Interracial Marriage" table, however, there is some variation both by race and by gender. Those who are White are the most likely to practice racial endogamy; approximately 97 percent of both men and women select a marital partner of the same race. Among African Americans, men are more likely than women to be involved in interracial marriages. For those who are Asian, however, there is an even larger gender difference; women are much more likely to be in an interracial marriage than men. Still, more than 80 percent of Asian women select a partner of the same race. Such patterns demonstrate the continued significance endogamy plays in partner selection (U.S. Census Bureau 2016f:Table FG3; Wang 2012).

Even within these broader endogamous social categories, we tend to pick people like ourselves. This is known as **homogamy**—the conscious or unconscious tendency to select a mate with personal characteristics and interests similar to one's own. Most online dating services depend on this principle to help couples find matches. To help couples find homogamous partners, and long before Tinder enlisted the help of sociologist Jessica Carbino, an early online dating service hired sociologist Pepper Schwartz (2006) as a consultant to develop a 48-question survey that covered everything from decision-making style to degree of impulsivity. Based on that kind of matching, Internet dating site eHarmony claims that its site is responsible for more than 2 million marriages. Overall, researchers estimate that between a quarter and a third of couples meet online. The rate is even higher for those whose immediate pool of potential partners is smaller, including gays, lesbians, and middle-aged heterosexuals. And some evidence indicates that couples who meet online experience greater marital satisfaction and are slightly less likely to divorce (Cacioppo et al. 2013; eHarmony 2014; Rosenfeld and Thomas 2012).

In theory, Cupid's arrow could strike anyone on our behalf. But love is not blind. Love is a product of the social and cultural forces that shape the choices we make. Of course, in keeping with the sociological imagination, knowing the ways our choices are patterned frees us to decide whether to continue in those ways or decide to follow different paths.

PARENTING PATTERNS AND PRACTICES

Caring for children is a universal function of the family, yet the ways in which different societies assign this function to family members can vary significantly. The Nayars of southern India

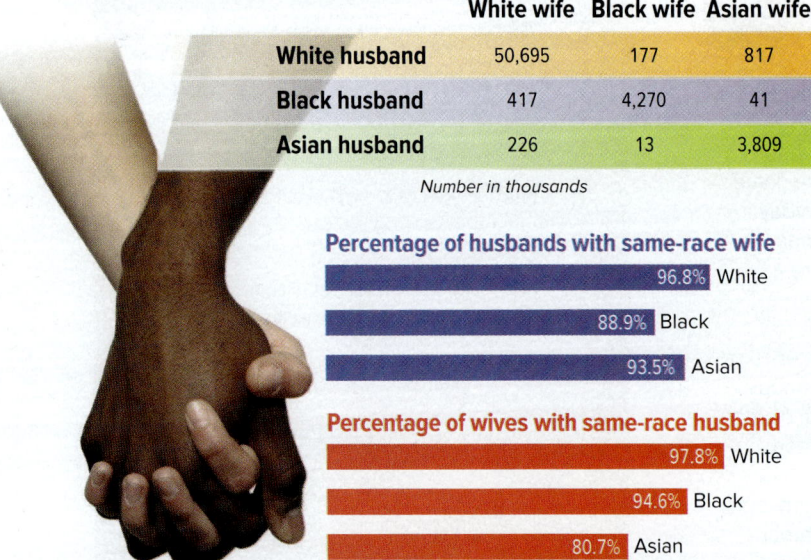

Patterns of Interracial Marriage

	White wife	Black wife	Asian wife
White husband	50,695	177	817
Black husband	417	4,270	41
Asian husband	226	13	3,809

Number in thousands

Percentage of husbands with same-race wife
- 96.8% White
- 88.9% Black
- 93.5% Asian

Percentage of wives with same-race husband
- 97.8% White
- 94.6% Black
- 80.7% Asian

Note: Numbers in thousands. Table does not show data for "Other" race husbands and wives.
Source: U.S. Census Bureau 2016f: Table FG3. *Photo:* ©alexandre zveiger/Shutterstock.com RF

SOC THINK

How important are factors such as age, education, race, ethnicity, social class, gender, and religion in your choice of someone for a serious relationship? To what extent are (were) you conscious of such influences when you pick (picked) someone to date?

acknowledge the biological role of fathers, but the mother's eldest brother is responsible for her children. In contrast, uncles play only a peripheral role in child care in the United States. Even within the United States, child-rearing patterns are varied. Just as our conception of families has changed, so also has our practice of child rearing.

Parenthood The socialization of children is essential to the maintenance of any culture. Consequently, parenthood is one of the most important (and most demanding) social roles in the United States. Sociologist Alice Rossi (1968, 1984) has identified four factors that complicate the transition to parenthood and the role of socialization. First, there is little anticipatory socialization for the social role of caregiver. The normal school curriculum gives scant attention to the subjects most relevant to successful family life, such as child care and home maintenance. Second, only limited learning occurs during the period of pregnancy itself. Third, the transition to parenthood is quite abrupt. Unlike adolescence, it is not prolonged; unlike the transition to work, the duties of caregiving cannot be taken on gradually. Finally, in Rossi's view, our society lacks clear and helpful guidelines for successful parenthood. There is little agreement on how parents can produce happy and well-adjusted offspring—or even on what it means to be well adjusted. For these reasons, socialization for parenthood involves difficult challenges for most men and women in the United States.

How we choose to parent differs based on a variety of social factors. Sociologist Annette Lareau (2003), for example, conducted an in-depth study of parenting and discovered significant social class differences. She found that middle- and upper-middle-class parents tend to see their children as a project. For them, parenting involves active engagement with their children in order to foster their growth and development. Using a gardening analogy, she labeled this parenting style *concerted cultivation,* arguing that such children are like flowers grown in a greenhouse that receive oversight, care, and protection. These children are encouraged to participate in varieties of activities, including organized sports and summer camps. They are taught to engage with adults, including physicians and teachers, and ask

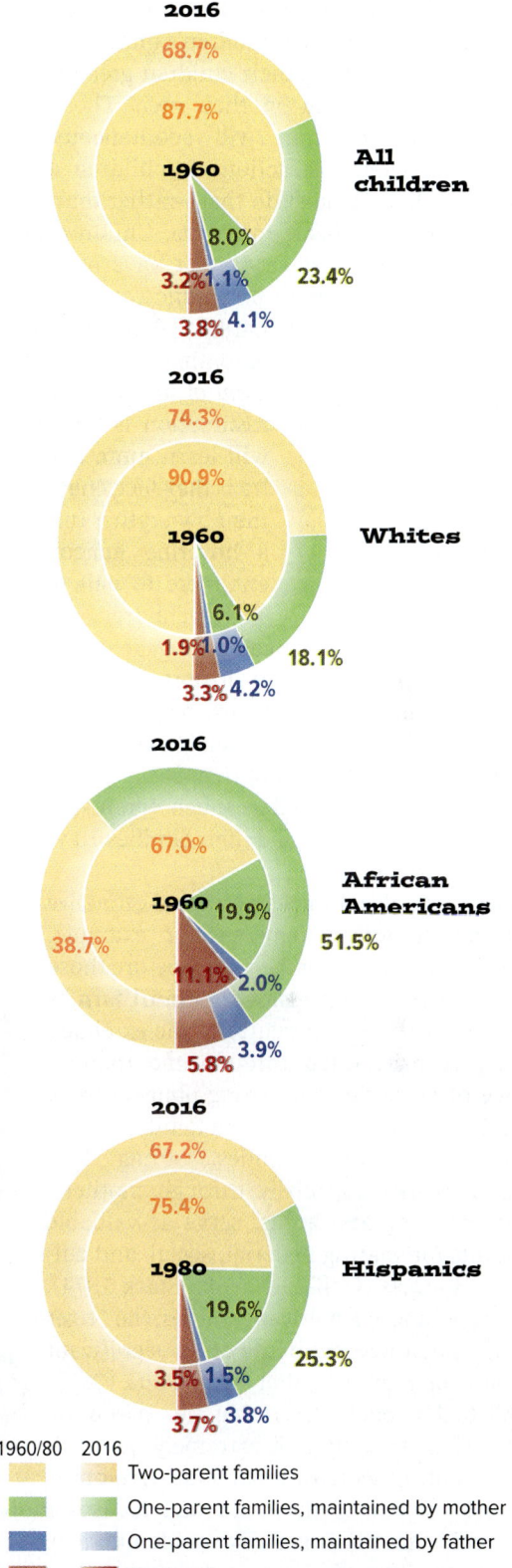

Living Arrangements of Children

Legend:
- Two-parent families (1960/80 and 2016)
- One-parent families, maintained by mother
- One-parent families, maintained by father
- No parents

Note: The "No parents" category includes children living with either other relatives or nonrelatives. Persons of Hispanic origin can be of any race.

Source: U.S. Census Bureau 2016h:Tables Ch-1, Ch-2, Ch-3, Ch-4.

Chapter 7 / Families • 163

them questions. As a result, they often grow up with a sense of entitlement.

The upper- and middle-class parenting approach differed from that found in working-class and poor families. These parents see their primary responsibility as ensuring that their children's material needs are met and then granting their children greater freedom to navigate the world on their own. These parents presume that children will spontaneously grow and thrive. Their instructions to children are more directive—do this, don't do that—rather than viewing encounters as teachable moments. Children in these families are more like seeds that have been thrown to the wind and grow to be wildflowers. As a result, Lareau labels this style of parenting the *accomplishment of natural growth*. The assumption is that children will learn more responsibility if they face challenges on their own rather than having a hovering helicopter parent there to bail them out. These children, much like their parents, were less likely to engage with authority figures such as teachers or doctors. Because children are taught interpersonal skills that grow out of their social class positions, the social class of their childhood is a strong predictor of their social class as adults. Lareau (2011) confirmed as much when she checked back with the children and their families 10 years after her initial research.

Familism Placing the interests of the family before those of the individual.

Adoption The socially recognized and affirmed transfer of the legal rights, responsibilities, and privileges of parenthood.

Parenting also differs by race and ethnicity. Among Mexican American families, for example, placing the interests of the family before those of the individual, also known as **familism**, is a core value. The importance of the extended family is manifested through the maintenance of close ties and strong obligations to kinfolk outside the immediate family. Within African American families, strong kinship networks, especially through mothers, grandmothers, and aunts, serve as valuable conduits for sharing material, social, and cultural resources (Goffman 2014a; Stack 1974). Among Chinese American families, the "tiger mom" phenomenon received a significant amount of attention after Amy Chua (2011) published a book describing her parenting style. This strict style of extremely demanding parenting worries less about developing the self-esteem of the child and focuses more on achievement, especially academic achievement. For Chua, that meant denying her daughters things other children might take for granted, such as attending sleepovers, being in school plays, watching television or playing computer games, playing any instrument other than piano or violin, or getting any grade less than an A. Research among Chinese American families, however, finds significant variation in parenting styles and suggests that the tiger mom approach is neither the most typical nor the most effective. The more common supportive parenting profile found among these families produced children with better GPAs, higher educational attainment, less depressive symptoms, and a stronger sense of family obligation (Kim et al. 2013).

In some homes, child-rearing responsibilities fall to grandparents. In 2016, 7.2 million children in the United States, 9.8 percent of all children, lived in a household with a grandparent present. Of these, 1.6 million, or 2.1 percent of all children, had no parent present to assist in child rearing (U.S. Census Bureau 2016g:Table C4). Special difficulties are inherent in such relationships, including legal custodial concerns, financial issues, and emotional problems for adults and youths alike. Perhaps not surprisingly, support groups such as Grandparents as Parents have emerged to provide assistance.

Adoption Adoption involves the socially recognized and affirmed transfer of the legal rights, responsibilities, and privileges of parenthood. It fits with the "law" part of the substantive definition of the family. In most cases, parental rights are transferred from the biological or birth parents to the adoptive parents. Approximately 1.7 percent of U.S. children live with at least one adoptive parent (U.S. Census Bureau 2015a:Table C9).

5 Movies on MARRIAGE AND FAMILIES

Loving
A couple's true love conquers all, even the Supreme Court.

Fill the Void
A marriage between a young woman and her sister's widower is arranged for the sake of family and community.

The Princess Bride
True love will follow you forever.

This Is 40
Romance confronts middle age.

Amour
An elderly couple faces the end of the road.

There are two legal methods of adopting an unrelated person: (1) the adoption may be arranged through a licensed agency, or (2) in some states it may be arranged through a private agreement sanctioned by the courts. Adopted children may come from the United States or from abroad. In 2015, parents in the United States adopted 5,648 children from other countries. The top three nations of origin for U.S. adoptions were China with 2,354, Ethiopia with 335, and South Korea with 318. The median fee for adopting a child from China was $15,825 (U.S. Department of State 2016a). Although the number of international adoptions remains substantial, it has declined substantially since it peaked in 2004, when 23,000 such adoptions occurred.

In the United States, one of the limitations historically was that only married couples could adopt. In 1995 an important court decision in New York held that a couple does not have to be married to adopt a child. Under this ruling, unmarried heterosexual couples, lesbian couples, and gay couples can all legally adopt children in New York. Writing for the majority, Chief Justice Judith Kaye argued that by expanding the boundaries of who can be legally recognized as parents, the state may be able to assist more children in securing "the best possible home." At the time, New York became the third state (after Vermont and Massachusetts) to recognize the right of unmarried couples to adopt children. Now adoption by unmarried persons is legal in all 50 states (Dao 1995; Human Rights Campaign 2009).

For every child who is adopted, many more remain the wards of state-sponsored child protective services. In 2015, 427,910 children in the United States were living in foster care. Of these children, 111,820 were waiting for adoption (U.S. Department of Health and Human Services 2016).

Dual-Income Families The mythical image of the 1950s family, idealized in TV shows such as *Father Knows Best,* portrays a breadwinner father and a homemaker wife. His job was to provide for the family's material needs by earning money, and her job was to nurture and care for her husband and their children. That image was more legend than fact for millions of American families at the time (Coontz 1992; Livingston 2015), and today even fewer families conform to it. For example, among married couples with children under age 6, 55.6 percent have both a husband and a wife in the labor force and among those with children aged 6–17, it is 64.4 percent. Among all married couples, with or without children, 21 percent of wives make $5,000-plus more than their husbands (Bureau of Labor Statistics 2016c:Table 4; Pew Research Center 2015a; U.S. Census Bureau 2016f:Table FG3).

Both opportunity and need have driven the rise in the number of dual-income couples. Women now have

Hollywood star Sandra Bullock and her son, the result of a domestic adoption. ©Marcel Thomas/FilmMagic/Getty Images

Did You Know?

... Until 1978 it was legal in the United States to fire a woman for being pregnant. The Supreme Court upheld that principle in key cases in 1974 and 1976. Two years later, in response to these rulings, Congress passed the Pregnancy Discrimination Act, which prohibited denying benefits to, firing, or refusing to hire someone for being pregnant.

Photo: ©Asia Images Group/Shutterstock.com RF

> **SOC THINK**
>
> What are the advantages and disadvantages of the dual-income model for women, for men, for children, and for society as a whole?

the chance to pursue opportunities in a way that previously had been closed due to cultural expectations regarding gender. This has resulted in increased education levels for women and increased participation in occupational fields that had been largely closed. At the same time, however, couples find it harder to make it on a single income. Even with more women entering the workforce, average income per household has remained relatively flat since the early 1970s (Proctor et al. 2016).

Single-parent family A family in which only one parent is present to care for the children.

Single-Parent Families Over time, **single-parent families,** those in which only one parent is present, have become more common and more accepted in the United States. In 2016, 27.4 percent of all children lived with only one parent. This varied by race and ethnicity with 20.4 percent of White, non-Hispanic children, 55.5 percent of African American children, 9.2 percent of Asian children, and 29.1 percent of Hispanic children living with one parent (U.S. Census Bureau 2016g:Table C3).

The life of single parents and their children is not inevitably more difficult than that of a traditional nuclear family. It is as inaccurate to assume that a single-parent family is necessarily deprived as it is to assume that a two-parent family is always secure and happy. Nevertheless, to the extent that such families have to rely on a single income or a sole caregiver, life in the single-parent family can be extremely stressful. A family headed by a single mother faces particularly difficult problems when the mother is a teenager, especially when she lacks access to significant social and economic resources. Since 2007, however, the birthrate for unmarried mothers has declined for all age groups under 35 while rising for women aged 35 to 44 (Edin and Kefalas 2005; Harris 2015; Miller 2015; Sawhill 2006).

Although 85 percent of single parents in the United States are mothers, the number of households headed by single fathers quadrupled between 1970 and 2016. Single mothers often develop social networks, but single fathers are typically more isolated. In addition, they must deal with schools and social service agencies that are more accustomed to women as custodial parents (U.S. Census Bureau 2016h:Table CH1).

Stepfamilies The most frequent image that comes to mind when thinking about stepfamilies is a stepparent

©Universal/Courtesy Everett Collection

with young step children. Approximately 5.7 percent of children under 18 live with at least one stepparent (U.S. Census Bureau 2015a:Table C9). But sociologist Susan Stewart (2007) recommends expanding our conception of stepfamilies to include cohabiting couples with children from previous relationships, families whose stepchildren do not live with them full-time, gay or lesbian couples with children from former heterosexual relationships, and stepfamilies with adult children. This expanded approach highlights the fact that stepfamily membership extends throughout the life course.

Family members in stepfamilies often deal with resocialization issues when an adult becomes a stepparent or a child becomes a stepchild and stepsibling. In evaluating these stepfamilies, some observers have assumed that children would benefit from remarriage, because they would be gaining a second custodial parent and would potentially enjoy greater economic security. However, after reviewing many studies of stepfamilies, sociologist Andrew J. Cherlin (2008:800) concluded that "the well-being of children in stepfamilies is no better, on average, than the well-being of children in divorced, single-parent households."

Stepparents can and do play valuable and unique roles in their stepchildren's lives, but their involvement does not guarantee an improvement in family life. In fact, standards may decline. Studies suggest that children raised in families with stepmothers are likely to have less health care, education, and money spent on their food than children raised by biological mothers. The measures are also negative for children raised by stepfathers, but only half as negative as in the case of stepmothers. This may be due to the stepmother holding back out of concern for seeming too intrusive or relying on the biological father to carry out parental duties (Schmeeckle 2007; Schmeeckle et al. 2006).

Multigenerational Families With the rise of the Industrial Revolution and the corresponding spread of the nuclear family model, the era of multiple generations of families living in the same household seemed largely to be over. Throughout much of the 20th century that appeared correct. The percentage of U.S. households that includes adults from at least two generations (and, if living with parents, aged 25 and older) dropped from 23.7 in 1900 to 12.1 percent in 1980. Since that time, however, the percentage of such households rose to 18.1 percent, including a marked increase since 2006 (Fry and Passel 2014; Pew Research Center 2010:Table 1).

Much of that change can be attributed to the rise in the percentage of younger adults who either continue to live with, or move back in with, their parents. This represents a change from what had been the much more common multigenerational pattern of elderly parents living with their middle-aged adult children. In 1940, 62.7 percent of adults aged 85 and older lived in a multigenerational household compared to 22.7 in 2012. Among young adults aged 25–34, the numbers were 27.7 percent in 1940 and 23.6 percent in 2012. Currently, nearly one-half of all multigenerational families include three or more generations (Fry and Passel 2014).

> What greater thing is there for human souls than to feel that they are joined for life— to be with each other in silent unspeakable memories.
>
> George Eliot

Limited job opportunities with low starting salaries, especially after the 2007 economic downturn, along with significant amounts of student loan debt, together have prompted the rise in number of students who are returning home to live with parents, though 18- to 34-year-old college graduates are half as likely to live with parents than are high school grads (Davidson 2014; DeSilver 2016; Pew Research Center 2014c). In addition, as we have already seen, the average age of first marriage has gone up, and for some percentage of young adults, opting to live with family represents a rational choice to minimize expenses (Casselman 2016). Focusing on the slightly younger 18–24 age demographic, some percentage of which includes college graduates who return home, 55.7 percent now live with their parents compared to 43 percent in 1960 (U.S. Census Bureau 2016i:Table AD-1). Just as changes in the economy helped drive the rise of the isolated nuclear family, these more recent economic events may well be contributing to the emergence of a new form of the extended family whose members leverage the material, social, and cultural resource advantages that such an arrangement provides.

>> Diverse Lifestyles

Though getting married and having children was the normative expectation for most adults throughout much of American history, significant variation existed in practice, and a wider array of options is now available.

Unmarried-Couple Households by State

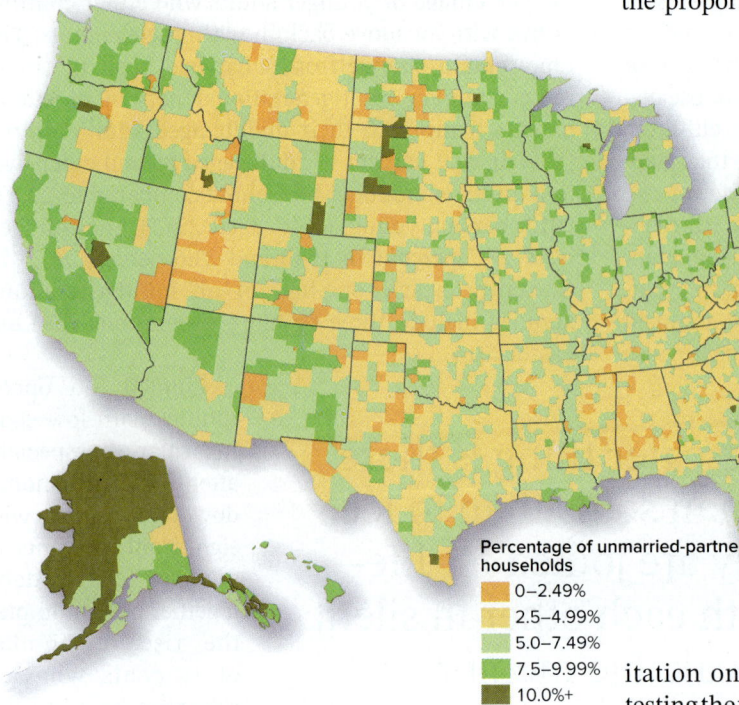

Source: U.S. Census Bureau 2015b:Table 11009.

Percentage of unmarried-partner households
- 0–2.49%
- 2.5–4.99%
- 5.0–7.49%
- 7.5–9.99%
- 10.0%+

COHABITATION

In the United States, testing the relationship waters by living together without being married is an increasingly common practice. **Cohabitation** is conventionally defined as the practice of a man and a woman living together in a sexual relationship without being married. The percentage of currently cohabiting U.S. adults aged 30–39 rose from 7 percent in 2004 to 13 percent in 2014 (Saad 2015).

Cohabitation The practice of a man and a woman living together in a sexual relationship without being married.

About half of all currently married couples in the United States say that they lived together before marriage. And this percentage is likely to increase. The number of unmarried-couple households in the United States rose sixfold in the 1960s and increased another 72 percent between 1990 and 2000. Adults aged 30–44 without a college education are more likely to cohabit than those with a college degree. Cohabitation is more common among African Americans and American Indians than among other racial and ethnic groups; it is least common among Asian Americans. The accompanying "Unmarried-Couple Households by State" map shows how cohabitation varies by region (Goodwin et al. 2010; Kreider 2010; T. Simmons and O'Connell 2003; U.S. Census Bureau 2015b:Table 11009).

In much of Europe, cohabitation is so common that the general sentiment seems to be "Love, yes; marriage, maybe." In Iceland, 62 percent of all children are born to single mothers; in France, Great Britain, and Norway, the proportion is about 40 percent. Government policies in these countries make few legal distinctions between married and unmarried couples or households. Unlike in the United States, where the best word option to describe cohabitating couple seems to be "partners," in Sweden they use the word *sambo* to refer to someone you live with but aren't married to. It combines elements of the Swedish words *samman,* meaning together, and *boende,* which means accommodation, and implies a level of commitment above that of boyfriend or girlfriend (Lyall 2002; M. Moore 2006; Thomson and Bernhardt 2010).

People commonly associate cohabitation only with younger, child-free couples who are testing the waters before marriage. Census data show that 47 percent of the 15.3 million cohabiting heterosexual individuals in the United States are aged 35 and older. Overall, 41 percent of cohabiting couples have children living with them. These cohabitants are more like spouses than dating partners. Moreover, in contrast to the common perception that people who cohabit have never been married, researchers report that about half of all people involved in cohabitation in the United States have been previously married. Cohabitation serves as a temporary or permanent alternative to matrimony for many (Jayson 2012a, 2012b).

REMAINING SINGLE

Increasingly, people are opting to remain single. In 1960, 9 percent of adults aged 25 and older had never married. It has since more than doubled to approximately 20 percent (Wang and Parker 2014). A variety of factors help explain this trend, including rising cohabitation rates and, as we saw earlier, the fact that those who do marry are waiting longer to do so. Of those who have never married, 13 percent do not want to marry compared to 45 percent of those who have been married before (Wang and Parker 2014).

There are many reasons a person may choose not to marry. Some singles do not want to limit their sexual intimacy to one lifetime partner. Some men and women do not want to become highly dependent on any one person—and do not want anyone depending heavily on them. In a society that values individuality and self-fulfillment, the single lifestyle can offer certain freedoms that marriage may not (Klinenberg 2012).

In contrast with the stereotype that single people are lonely, research shows that people who remain single have stronger social connections to parents, siblings, friends, and neighbors than do those who marry. Singles are more likely to stay in touch and to give and receive help from others in their social networks. Other research suggests that single people experience more personal growth than do their married counterparts and have a greater sense of autonomy and self-determination. By culturally privileging marriage, we may underestimate, and under-research, the benefits of singlehood (DePaulo 2014; Marks and Lambert 1998; Sarkisian and Gerstel 2016).

REMAINING CHILD-FREE

In the past, childlessness was often portrayed as a curse. Now, however, thanks in part to the development of modern birth control, an increasing number of people actively choose to remain child-free. More and more couples reject the notion that marriage inevitably leads to a baby carriage. According to census data, 16.1 percent of women aged 40–50 have never had children. Those with at least a college degree are more likely to opt out of parenthood than those who have less education. At 22.7 percent, the childless rate for women aged 40–50 who have graduate or professional degrees is nearly twice the 11.6 percent rate for those who have not completed high school. Looking to the future, nearly one-third of millennials report they do not want to have children (Monte and Ellis 2014).

Economic considerations have contributed to this shift in attitudes; having children has become quite expensive. Estimates are that middle-income parents of children born in 2015 can anticipate spending $284,570 to feed, clothe, and shelter a child from birth to age 18. If the child attends college, that amount could double, depending on the college chosen. Aware of the financial pressures, some couples are having fewer children than they otherwise might, and others are weighing the advantages of a child-free marriage (Lino et al. 2017).

LESBIAN AND GAY RELATIONSHIPS

One of the more active political debates about how we define family has involved marriage of same-sex couples. If we stick with a narrow, substantive definition that marriage necessarily involves one man and one woman, such relationships do not count as families. When we define families in terms of what functions they perform, we find growing support that such relationships do count. In 2004, 31 percent of Americans favored allowing gays and lesbians to marry. By 2016, that number rose to 55 percent who supported legalizing marriage between same-sex couples. As the accompanying "Approval of Same-Sex Marriage by Age" graph demonstrates, younger people are more supportive. Attitudes also vary by religious affiliation, political party, race, and gender (Pew Research Center 2016b).

The movement to legalize same-sex marriage in the United States crossed its first major legal hurdle in 2003 when the Massachusetts Supreme Judicial Court ruled 4–3 that, under the state's constitution, gay couples have the right to marry. In 2008 the Connecticut Supreme Court reached the same conclusion, as did Iowa's in 2009. Vermont, also in 2009, became the first state to pass a law that legalized same-sex marriage. By June 2015, 37 states and the District of Columbia provided gay and lesbian couples the same right to marry as guaranteed to heterosexual couples.

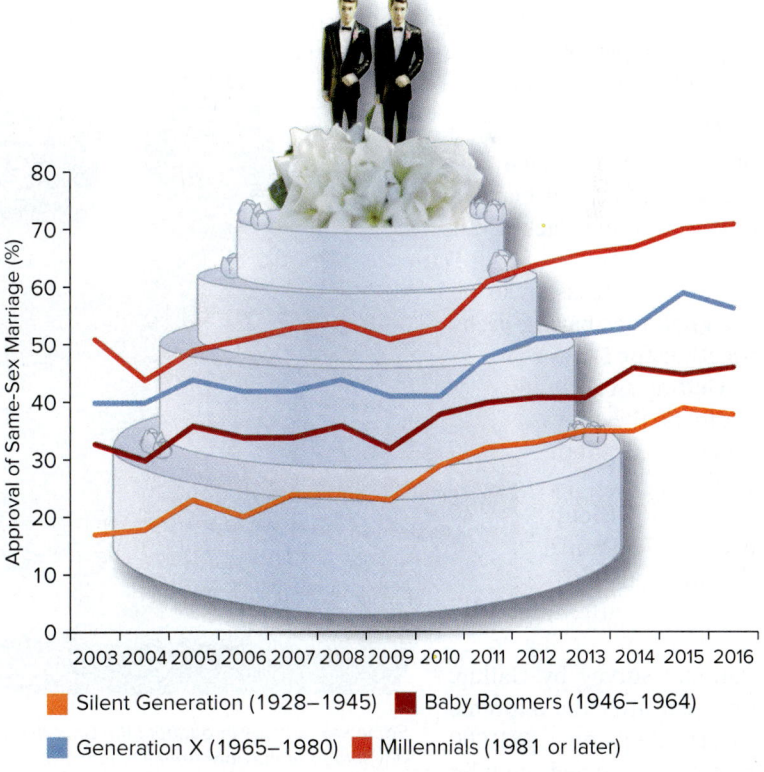

Approval of Same-Sex Marriage by Age

■ Silent Generation (1928–1945)   ■ Baby Boomers (1946–1964)
■ Generation X (1965–1980)   ■ Millennials (1981 or later)

Note: Responses are to the question, "Do you favor allowing gays or lesbians to marry legally?"
Source: Pew Research Center 2016b.   *Photo:* ©Angela Wyant/Stone/Getty Images

James Obergefell was the lead plaintiff in the Supreme Court case that affirmed same-sex couples' constitutional right to marry. ©Drew Angerer/Bloomberg via Getty Images

On June 26, 2015, same-sex marriage became legal in all 50 states as a result of a decision by the United States Supreme Court. In the ruling, Justice Anthony Kennedy, writing for the majority, declared:

> the right to marry is a fundamental right inherent in the liberty of the person, and under the Due Process and Equal Protection Clauses of the Fourteenth Amendment couples of the same-sex may not be deprived of that right and that liberty. The Court now holds that same-sex couples may exercise the fundamental right to marry.

The decision set off a celebration by same-sex marriage advocates across the land. Many got married that same day, including Jack Evans, 85, and George Harris, 82, of Dallas County, Texas, who tied the knot after having been together for 54 years.

Getting an accurate count of the prevalence of lesbian and gay families has been difficult because, up until recently, no official agencies attempted to do so. According to a national survey by Gallup, one year after the Supreme Court decision, 981,000 same-sex married couples lived in the United States, more than double the 368,000 couples when the decision was handed down (J. Jones 2016). Based on their research, the U.S. Census estimates that 16 percent of same-sex couples have their own children—biological, adopted, or step—in their households (U.S. Census Bureau 2014). On average, gay and lesbian couples have more education, a greater likelihood of both members being employed, and higher incomes than married opposite-sex couples (C. Johnson 2012; Lofquist et al. 2012). Research finds that same-sex families score above average on measures of general health and family cohesion, and the children of these families have psychosocial development comparable to that of others (Crouch et al. 2014; Tasker 2005).

>> Divorce

"Do you promise to love, honor, and cherish . . . until death do you part?" Every year, people of all social classes and racial and ethnic groups make this legally binding agreement. Yet a significant number of these promises shatter, ending in divorce.

STATISTICAL TRENDS IN DIVORCE

Just how common is divorce? Surprisingly, this is not a simple question to answer; divorce statistics are difficult to interpret. The media frequently report that one out of every two marriages ends in divorce. But that figure is misleading in that many marriages last for decades. It is based on a comparison of all divorces that occur in a single year (regardless of when the couples were married) with the number of new marriages in that same year. Sociologist Philip Cohen projects that based on current rates, 52.7 percent of people who marry today will divorce before one of the partners dies. The longer a couple is married, the more that likelihood drops. For example, a couple that makes it to year 15 has a 30 percent chance of divorcing (Cohen 2016; Steverman 2016).

We get an alternative picture by looking at marital

Same-sex couples throughout the United States took advantage of the opportunity to marry as soon as their legal right to do so was recognized. ©George Frey/Getty Images

Percentage of Marriages to Reach Milestones*

Men, year of first marriage	Anniversary (percentage still married)*							Women, year of first marriage	Anniversary (percentage still married)*						
	5th	10th	15th	20th	25th	30th	35th	40th		5th	10th	15th	20th	25th	30th	35th	40th
1960–64	94.6	83.4	74.7	70.2	66.9	64.5	62.1	60.1	1960–64	93.0	82.8	73.5	67.0	60.8	57.2	53.6	49.7
1965–69	91.7	88.0	69.9	65.8	62.7	60.5	57.9		1965–69	90.7	79.3	69.6	64.0	59.1	55.8	52.1	
1970–74	88.0	75.0	65.7	60.2	56.8	53.8			1970–74	89.2	74.5	66.1	61.3	56.2	52.6		
1975–79	88.2	73.4	63.7	58.7	54.4				1975–79	86.9	72.8	63.2	57.4	53.2			
1980–84	90.6	74.3	65.2	60.0					1980–84	87.8	71.1	62.9	56.6				
1985–89	87.7	75.4	66.6						1985–89	87.9	74.5	66.4					
1990–94	89.7	77.3							1990–94	87.1	74.5						
1995–99	89.6								1995–99	89.5							

*Counts marriages ended by divorce, separation, and death.
Source: Kreider and Ellis 2011:Table 4.

milestones people reach based on the year they first married (as shown in the accompanying "Percentage of Marriages to Reach Milestones" table). Following either the rows or the columns provides insight into both the generational effect and the effects of changing attitudes and practices over time. For example, among men married from 1960 to 1964, 94.6 percent made it to their 5th anniversary and 60.1 percent made it to their 40th. One way to see the changes in likelihood of divorce is to trace down each column to see how many couples in each cohort made it to an anniversary. For example, among women, the percentage of couples that made it to their 10th anniversary fell from 82.8 percent for those married from 1960 to 1964 to 74.5 percent for couples married between 1990 and 1994.

In the United States, overall divorce rates increased significantly in the 1960s but then leveled off; since the late 1980s the divorce rate has declined by 30 percent. This trend is due partly to the aging of the baby boomer generation and the corresponding decline in the proportion of people of marriageable age. But it also indicates an increase in marital stability in recent years (Coontz 2006; Kreider and Ellis 2011).

Getting divorced does not necessarily sour people on marriage. About 63 percent of all divorced people in the United States have remarried. The median time between their divorce and second marriage is four years. Women are less likely than men to remarry, because many retain custody of their children after a divorce, which complicates a new adult relationship (Kreider and Ellis 2011; Saad 2004).

FACTORS ASSOCIATED WITH DIVORCE

One of the major factors shaping the increase in divorce compared to 100 years ago has been the greater social acceptance of divorce. It is no longer considered necessary to endure an unhappy marriage. Even major religious groups have relaxed what were often negative attitudes toward divorce, commonly having treated it as a sin in the past.

In the United States, a variety of factors have contributed to the growing social acceptance of divorce. For instance, most states have adopted less restrictive divorce laws in the past three decades. No-fault divorce laws, which allow a couple to end their marriage without assigning blame (by specifying adultery, for instance), accounted for an initial surge in the divorce rate after they were introduced in the 1970s, though

In 2017, super couple Angelina Jolie and Brad Pitt divorced after a 12-year relationship and 2 years of marriage.
©Jaguar PS/Shutterstock.com RF

these laws appear to have had little effect beyond that. Additionally, a general increase in family incomes, coupled with the availability of free legal aid to some poor people, has meant that more couples can afford costly divorce proceedings. Also, as society provides greater opportunities for women, more and more wives are becoming less dependent on their husbands, both economically and emotionally. They may feel more able to leave a marriage if it seems hopeless (Coontz 2011).

IMPACT OF DIVORCE ON CHILDREN

Divorce is traumatic for all involved, but it has special meaning for the more than one million children whose parents divorce each year. There is significant sociological debate on the effects divorce has on children. One major study tracked 131 children of divorce over a 25-year period. It concluded that the impacts of divorce are substantial and long-lasting, including higher rates of drug and alcohol abuse, limited resources for college, and fear of intimacy in adulthood (Wallerstein, Lewis, and Blakeslee 2000). These researchers recommended that parents should stay together in a "good enough" marriage for the sake of the children. One of the limitations of this research is the relatively small sample size, raising questions about the degree to which the results can be generalized.

Other sociologists have concluded that, for many children, divorce signals the welcome end to a highly dysfunctional relationship. A national study conducted by sociologists Paul R. Amato and Alan Booth (1997) showed that in about one-third of divorces, the children actually benefited from parental separation because it lessened their exposure to conflict. Additional researchers, also using larger samples, have concluded that the long-term harmful effects of divorce affect only a minority of children (Booth and Amato 2001; Cherlin 2009; Hetherington and Kelly 2002; Sun and Li 2008).

Trends in Marriage and Divorce in the United States

Rate per 1,000 total population

Sources: Centers for Disease Control and Prevention 2015b; Tejada-Vera and Sutton 2010; U.S. Census Bureau 1975:64. *Photo:* ©TriggerPhoto/Getty Images RF

The debates surrounding issues such as divorce, cohabitation, and same-sex families highlight many of the issues sociologists seek to address in their investigation of family life. What families are, what they do, how they do it, and what obstacles they face are issues relevant for all families. In our modern, pluralistic world, the singular traditions of the past can no longer be taken for granted. People come from many different cultures with multiple taken-for-granted assumptions. Sociology investigates such complexity, providing us with tools so that we might better understand how we think and act in the context of families.

SOCIOLOGY IS A VERB

Family Counts

Interview 5 to 10 people (such as classmates) about families. Ask them questions such as: How do they define family? Does family include only those related by blood and law or does it include others? Do pets count as family? How many siblings do they have? How many siblings did their parents have? What role should parents and friends play in partner selection? Take notes on their responses. Do any patterns emerge? What conclusions can you draw from such a sample?

FOR REVIEW

I. What do we mean by family?
- Sociologists define the family in terms of both what a family is, with an emphasis on blood and law, and what families do or what functions they perform, including reproduction, socialization, protection, regulation of sexual behavior, affection and companionship, and provision of social status.

II. How do people pick partners?
- Social factors shape the pool of potential partners from which individuals select. People balance selection, favoring someone who is from within their group (endogamy) but not too close (exogamy). People tend to pick partners with similar social characteristics (homogamy), including age, education, class, race, and ethnicity.

III. How do families vary?
- There is significant variation in terms of proximity (extended versus nuclear), authority (patriarchal, matriarchal, and egalitarian), duration (divorce), and structure (dual-income, single-parent, stepfamilies, cohabitation, singlehood, child-free, and same-sex).

©Digital Vision/Getty Images RF

SOCVIEWS on Families

Functionalist View

The family contributes to **social stability** by performing important functions: reproduction, protection, socialization, regulation of sexual behavior, affection and companionship, and social status.

Kinship ties involve both obligations and responsibilities, but also serve as a source of aid in time of trouble.

Parenthood is a crucial **social role** because one of its tasks is the **socialization** of children, which is essential to maintain any culture.

STABILITY, SOCIAL ROLES, SOCIALIZATION
KEY CONCEPTS

Conflict View

A family's social position helps determine a child's opportunities in life as a result of **power, property, and privilege** that is passed from one generation to the next.

Endogamous restrictions on marriage perpetuate existing inequality and may raise **racial barriers**.

Discrimination against gay and lesbian partners is seen in bans on same-sex marriage, denial of legal rights that married couples enjoy, and restrictions on adoption of children.

KEY CONCEPTS
POWER, DISCRIMINATION

Interactionist View

Families provide the context within which we are born, **socialized**, and establish our basic identities.

We construct new family patterns—whether dual-career, single-parent, blended, or gay or lesbian—in response to social and historical changes we both experience and cause.

In egalitarian marriages, couples **interact as equals**, sharing decision making, housework, and child care.

KEY CONCEPTS
MICRO LEVEL, INTIMATE RELATIONSHIPS

MAKE THE CONNECTION

After reviewing the chapter, answer the following questions:

1
How would each perspective shed light on the use of online dating services and apps such as Tinder?

2
Take a look at the graph showing family types over time. What factors would each perspective focus on to explain the changes over the years?

3
Why does a functionalist definition of what the family does provide more insight into families today than trying to define what it is?

4
Who rules in your family? Would a functionalist, conflict, or interactionist perspective best describe your family dynamics?

Pop Quiz

1. **Which definition of the family focuses on the importance of blood and law?**
   a. functionalist
   b. matrilineal
   c. substantive
   d. extended

2. **Which system of descent is most typical in the United States?**
   a. matrilineal
   b. patrilineal
   c. bilateral
   d. unilateral

3. **Alice, age seven, lives at home with her parents, her grandmother, and her aunt. Alice's family is an example of a(n)**
   a. nuclear family.
   b. patrilineal family.
   c. extended family.
   d. polygynous family.

4. **In which form of marriage may a person have several spouses in his or her lifetime but only one spouse at a time?**
   a. serial monogamy
   b. monogamy
   c. polygamy
   d. polyandry

5. **The marriage of a woman to more than one man at the same time is referred to as**
   a. polygyny.
   b. monogamy.
   c. serial monogamy.
   d. polyandry.

6. **In what type of societies do women dominate in family decision making?**
   a. polygyny
   b. egalitarian
   c. patriarchy
   d. matriarchy

7. **Which norm requires mate selection outside certain groups, usually one's own family or certain kinfolk?**
   a. exogamy
   b. endogamy
   c. matriarchy
   d. patriarchy

8. **The principle that prohibits sexual relationships between certain culturally specified relatives is known as**
   a. monogamy.
   b. the incest taboo.
   c. polygamy.
   d. endogamy.

9. **What is the projected cost of raising a child born in 2015 until she or he is 18 years old?**
   a. $212,300
   b. $284,570
   c. $454,770
   d. $646,465

10. **Overall, how has the divorce rate in the United States changed since the late 1980s?**
    a. The divorce rate rose dramatically.
    b. The divorce rate rose slowly, but steadily.
    c. The divorce rate declined after having risen significantly in the 1960s and 1970s.
    d. Change in the divorce rate shows no clear pattern.

1. (c), 2. (c), 3. (c), 4. (a), 5. (d), 6. (d), 7. (a), 8. (b), 9. (b), 10. (c)

Design Elements: *Going Global (Earth):* ©Studio Photogram/Alamy Stock Photo; *Personal Sociology (drawing of author):* ©McGraw-Hill Education; *5 Movies (popcorn):* ©D. Hurst/Alamy Stock Photo; *Sociology Is a Verb (overlapping hands):* ©Jeff DeWeerd/Getty Images RF

©Barry Brecheisen/WireImage/Getty Images

8 Education and Religion

TRADING PLACES

Teachers Lisa Greenbaum and Angela Vassos thought it would be a good idea for the high school students at their two schools to learn a little more about each other's lives. Although their schools were located only three miles from each other in New York City, their students occupied very different social worlds. Greenbaum taught at University Heights, a public school located in a poor South Bronx neighborhood, and Vassos taught at Fieldston, an elite private school with a tuition of $47,000 per year. Greenbaum and Vassos created "Classroom Connections," a program through which their students first exchanged letters and later visited each other's schools to meet in person. Students came away with a new appreciation for the perspectives and challenges faced by students at the other school. That said, the experience appears to have been harder on students from University Heights, who could clearly see the taken-for-granted advantages available to students at Fieldston (Joffe-Walt 2015; Lovell and Pfluger 2014; Narrative 4 2015).

Years ago, Oprah Winfrey conducted a similar exchange. She had students from Chicago's Harper High School and suburban Naperville's Neuqua Valley High School visit each other's schools. The contrast was striking. At Harper, the suburban school students were surprised by the metal detectors, the leaky pool that hadn't been filled in 10 years, a music program lacking instruments, and more. At Neuqua Valley, the city school students encountered a state-of-the-art facility with an Olympic-sized pool, a well-equipped fitness center, a Grammy Award–winning music program, an up-to-date computer lab, and a wide selection of AP course offerings. As one Harper student put it, "I feel like I've been cheated" (*The Oprah Winfrey Show* 2006).

In spite of investments and upgrades at Harper since then, substantial differences remain. Harper offers only two AP courses and two languages, Spanish and American Sign Language. Neuqua Valley offers more than 20 AP courses, and the school's language options include Chinese, French, German, and Spanish. When it comes to outcomes, the average ACT score for students at Harper is 14.2 compared to 25.9 at Neuqua Valley. At Harper, 54.3 percent of students graduate in four years compared to 97 percent at Neuqua Valley. Just as was the case for New York City students from University Heights and Fieldston, these Chicago-area students come from very different situations. At Harper, 97.9 percent of students are from low-income households compared to 5.1 percent at Neuqua Valley (Illinois State Board of Education 2016). In the United States, education is seen as a pathway to opportunity for all, yet not all students have equal access to facilities, staffing, and programming. Sociology explores the consequences of such differences.

As You READ

- How does education maintain social order?
- How does education support the existing system of inequality?
- How do sociologists define religion?

>> Education in Society

We need schools. They are so important, in fact, that we often take their existence and necessity for granted. Historically, families had the primary responsibility for teaching us the knowledge and skills we needed to survive and thrive in society. With the advent of the Industrial Revolution and the rise of globalization, however, schools became essential agents of socialization. As a society, we now invest a substantial amount of time and money in **education,** a social institution dedicated to the formal process of transmitting culture from teachers to students. We do so because we believe the individual and collective benefits are worth it.

Schools provide a place where we are exposed to the knowledge of those who have gone before us, enabling us to build on their wisdom as we carve out our pathways into the future. They expose us to beauty and help us investigate the deeper meanings of life. As sociologist W. E. B. Du Bois ([1903] 1994) put it, "The true college will ever have one goal—not to earn meat, but to know the end and aim of that life which meat nourishes" (p. 51). In addition to assisting us in our search for meaning and truth, schools also provide us with the practical knowledge and skills we need as members of society, enabling us to get good jobs, become better parents, exercise our citizenship responsibilities, and more.

In the United States this commitment to education is built on a belief that our outcomes should not be determined by birth but by ability and effort. According to this value, being born to wealthy parents should not ensure economic and social privilege any more than

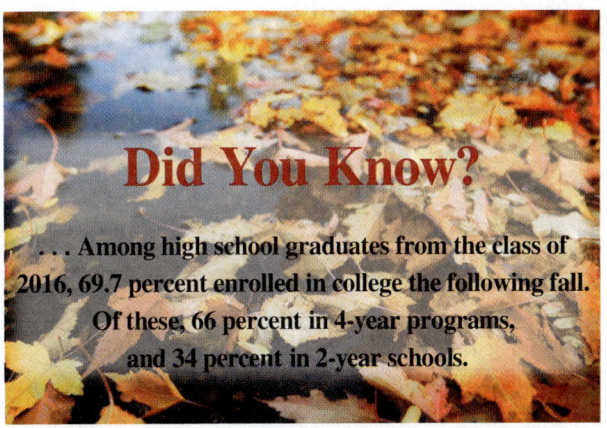

Did You Know?

. . . Among high school graduates from the class of 2016, 69.7 percent enrolled in college the following fall. Of these, 66 percent in 4-year programs, and 34 percent in 2-year schools.

Source: Bureau of Labor Statistics 2016d.   *Photo:* ©Design Pics/PunchStock

being born into meager circumstances should consign one to a life of poverty. Early American political leaders such as Benjamin Franklin and Thomas Jefferson advocated public education as an essential component of democratic societies because it provides individuals with opportunities and society with informed citizens. Horace Mann, often called the "father of American public education," wrote in 1848, "Education, beyond all other devices of human origin, is the *great equalizer* of the conditions of men" ([1848] 1957). Mann believed that building high-quality, well-staffed public schools would ensure that children without means would share the same classrooms, curriculum, and experiences with children of the well-off, thus providing everyone a chance for success.

> **Education** A social institution dedicated to the formal process of transmitting culture from teachers to students.

Educational Attainment in the United States

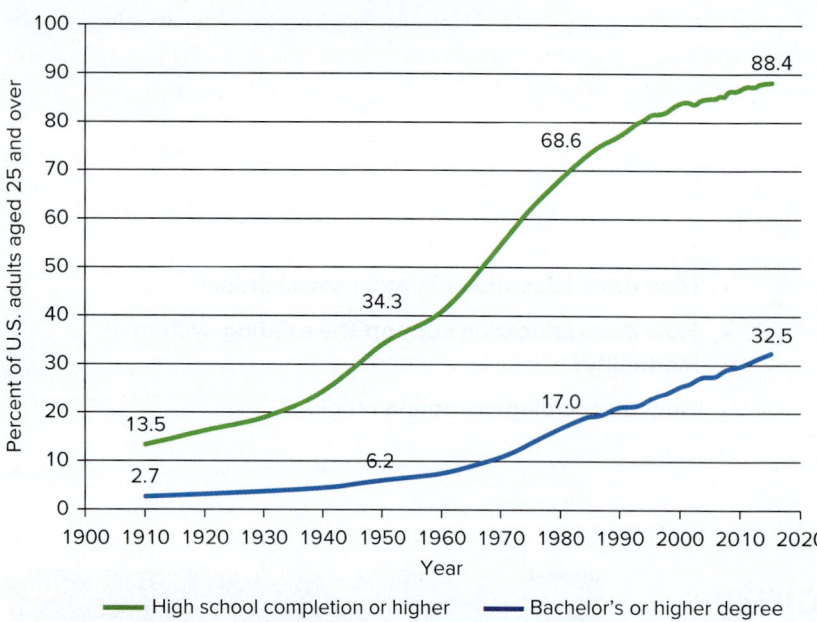

Note: Data are for adults in the United States aged 25 and over.
Source: National Center for Education Statistics 2016:Table 104.10.

which reinforced the principle of "separate, but equal." Through education reform efforts and legal decisions over two centuries, public education eventually opened up to include everyone regardless of race, ethnicity, sex, or national origin. Examples of education reformers include Emma Hart Willard, who opened the first college-level school for women in 1821, and sociologists such as Du Bois and Jane Addams, both of whom fought for racial and gender equality in the late 19th century. Legal decisions, such as *Brown v. Board of Education* in 1954, found that separate facilities are inherently unequal, and laws such as Title IX in 1972 required equal educational opportunities for both males and females as a requisite for receiving federal funding.

The rise of education as a public institution has not been limited to the United States. As the accompanying "Educational Attainment of

This societal commitment to education in the United States led to the expansion of education as a social institution. The degree of expansion is reflected in dramatically increased rates of educational attainment over the past 100 years or so. As the "Educational Attainment in the United States" graph shows, from 1910 to 2015, the proportion of people with a high school diploma rose from 13.5 to 88.4 percent, and the number with a college degree increased from 2.7 to 32.5 percent (National Center for Education Statistics 2016:Table 104.10). As education became both more available and more expected, more and more people pursued the pathway it provided.

A significant component in this expansion is the fact that education in the United States has become more inclusive over time. Initially, public schools were open only to White males. In the 19th century, education was for the most part racially segregated, a practice that was affirmed by the 1896 Supreme Court decision in *Plessy v. Ferguson*,

Going GLOBAL

Educational Attainment of 25- to 34-Year-Olds

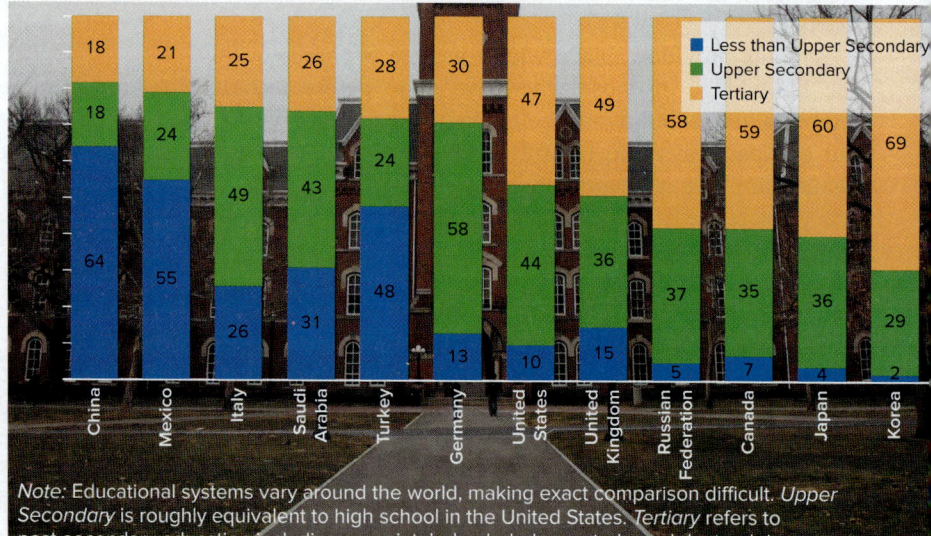

Note: Educational systems vary around the world, making exact comparison difficult. *Upper Secondary* is roughly equivalent to high school in the United States. *Tertiary* refers to post-secondary education including associate's, bachelor's, master's, and doctoral degrees.

Source: OECD 2016a:Table A1.4.   Photo: ©McGraw-Hill Education

25- to 34-Year-Olds" graph shows, countries all around the world have made a significant commitment to education, though levels of attainment vary. Increased educational attainment opens doors for individuals and produces a more educated citizenry for societies. Because education has become such a significant social institution in the world, sociologists seek to describe and explain the functions it fulfills.

>> Sociological Perspectives on Education

Fulfilling the hopes of Jefferson, Franklin, Emma Hart Willard, and Mann, the expanded educational opportunities have produced an educated citizenry equipped to take on the challenges of modern life. At the same time, however, education reinforces existing beliefs, values, and norms that justify the status quo along with its inequalities. Sociologists explore how education can do both at the same time.

EDUCATION AND SOCIAL ORDER

Society needs people with the knowledge and skills to perform the tasks necessary for society's continued existence, and individuals need this know-how to survive and prosper. Schools provide that knowledge by teaching students how to read, speak foreign languages, repair automobiles, and much more. Consistent with sociology's functionalist perspective, sociologists have identified five functions that education fulfills for both individuals and society.

Culture Transmission Each society has a common stock of cultural knowledge deemed important for its members. As a social institution, education preserves and transmits society's norms, values, beliefs, ideas, and skills, thus reinforcing society's dominant culture. This endorsed knowledge is transmitted through the formal curriculum taught in schools including "the three 'Rs" (reading, 'riting, and 'rithmetic), as well as history, science, and much more. As a result, young people of each generation learn what they need to survive and succeed.

In addition to the formal curriculum, schools create social space for children to transmit unofficial culture among their peers and to establish themselves as individuals separate from their families. Parents aren't hovering over their shoulders to ensure their children say the right things or keep their coats on at recess, and they can't protect children from getting hurt. School is the place where children learn to stand on their own and to establish relationships with their peer group (Adler and Adler 1996). As children get older, peer relationships grow stronger, and the distance from the parental world grows greater.

Social Integration Why do we need to know things such as "in 1492 Columbus sailed the ocean blue" and $a^2 + b^2 = c^2$? The answer is simple: the culture we share binds us together. Even if no one individual possesses all of it—and even if any single item seems necessary only for contestants on *Jeopardy!*—such knowledge represents who we are and what we believe is important. To put it in Durkheim's terms, it is part of our collective conscience, the social glue that holds us together; or, in Mead's terms, the shared culture we learn in schools contributes to our sense of the generalized other, the map of society we hold in our heads.

> **SOC THINK**
>
> Why do students often feel like schools teach a lot of useless facts? What might this attitude suggest about social integration in modern society?

In the past, the integrative function of education was most obvious in its emphasis on promoting a common language. Immigrant children were expected to learn English. In some instances, they were even forbidden to speak their native language on school grounds. More recently, bilingualism has been defended both for its educational value and as a means of encouraging cultural diversity. However, critics argue that bilingualism undermines the social and political integration that education traditionally has promoted.

In an effort to promote social integration, many colleges and universities have established learning communities within which students share common experiences, or they may require first- and second-year students to live on campus. Such programs become more important when students come from diverse backgrounds with different cultural expectations. The goal is to provide experiences that will unify a population composed of diverse racial, ethnic, and religious groups into a community whose members share—to some extent—a common identity. The social integration fostered by education contributes to societal stability and consensus.

Training and Social Control In schools, students learn general behaviors that are expected of them as members of society and specialized skills they will need in the workforce. In the early grades in particular, significant time and effort are spent getting students to do what

POPSOC

CALVIN AND HOBBES © 1988 Watterson. Reprinted with permission of Andrews McMeel Syndication. All rights reserved.

In the classic comic strip *Calvin and Hobbes,* Calvin is a first-grader who struggles with balancing what he wants to do versus what is expected of him. That is especially true when it comes to school. He gives voice to the experience many of us have had as we are socialized to accept the institutional expectations of the larger society at the cost of our individual freedom.

the teacher wants them to do, when and how the teacher wants them to do it. Through the exercise of **formal social control**, schools teach students various skills essential to their future positions in society. Norms provide us with the order and stability we need to make our individual and collective lives predictable, and schools help us internalize normative expectations. Students learn manners, punctuality, creativity, discipline, and responsibility—skills and abilities we need well beyond the classroom. In effect, schools serve as a transitional agent of social control, bridging the gap between childhood and entry into the labor force and wider society.

Formal social control The imposition of sanctions, whether positive or negative, by officially recognized authorities in order to to enforce norms.

In a society with a complex division of labor, we especially count on schools to select and train students so that they can become effective workers in specialized jobs. In a classic study from the functionalist perspective, sociologists Kingsley Davis and Wilbert E. Moore (1945) argued that all societies have positions that are more important for society's survival or that require greater skill or knowledge to perform and that not everyone has the ability to fill those jobs. For example, not everyone has what it takes to become a medical doctor, accountant, or lawyer. Because we value workers' knowledge, skills, abilities, and experience, which Davis and Moore referred

Education Pays

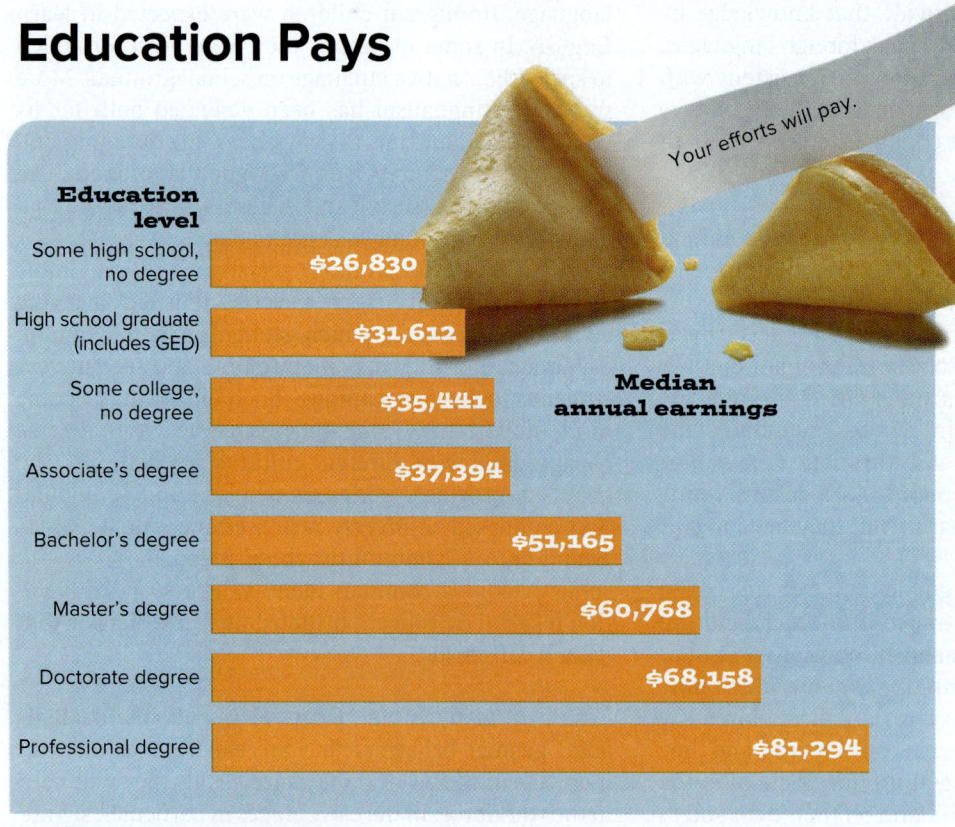

Median annual earnings

Education level	
Some high school, no degree	$26,830
High school graduate (includes GED)	$31,612
Some college, no degree	$35,441
Associate's degree	$37,394
Bachelor's degree	$51,165
Master's degree	$60,768
Doctorate degree	$68,158
Professional degree	$81,294

Note: Includes full-time, full-year wage and salary for workers aged 25–34.
Source: U.S. Census Bureau 2016a:Table PINC-03.1.3.2.1.   Photo: ©Don Farrall/Getty Images RF

to as human capital, we promise that we will reward those who take the time and effort required to develop those skills with high incomes and social esteem. We use grades as an indicator of ability and provide degrees to certify to employers that the graduate has sufficient training to perform the job well. As the accompanying "Education Pays" graph demonstrates for 25- to 34-year-olds, we deliver on the promise that making the sacrifice of increasing one's education leads to higher incomes, even relatively early on in careers.

Cultural Innovation Although schools do preserve and transmit existing culture, education can also stimulate social change. In response to the soaring pregnancy rate among teenagers, for example, public schools began to offer sex education classes. As a means of countering discrimination based on sex or race, many schools turned to affirmative action in admissions—giving priority to females or minorities. Since 1965, Project Head Start, an early-childhood program that served 1,100,000 children in 2015, has sought to compensate for the disadvantages in school readiness experienced by children from low-income families (Administration for Children and Families 2016). To ensure school readiness, it provides classes for preschool children from families below a certain income level, working with them on letter recognition, vocabulary, nutrition, and other basic skills.

Colleges and universities are particularly committed to cultural innovation. One way they do so is through faculty research, especially at large universities. Faculty members are frequently required to pursue grants, discover something new with these grants, and and publish articles and books. In so doing, they generate new technology, techniques, and knowledge. Another way cultural innovation occurs at colleges and universities is through experimentation with new ideas and practices. Campuses provide a context within which we can challenge existing values and norms. In the 1960s, for example, students and professors explored questions involving war and peace, racial inequality, gender norms, the use of recreational drugs, and more. Professors who engage in such experimentation, especially if it involves innovative or unpopular ideas, may be accused of being out of touch or out of line, but we need people to experiment with new ideas so that our culture does not stagnate.

Campuses also provide an environment in which students encounter new cultural values and norms through encounters with students from around the world. In 2015–2016, U.S. campuses hosted 1,043,839 international students, and 313,415 U.S. students studied abroad in 2014–2015 (Institute of International Education 2016). Such exposure provides opportunities for cultural innovation as people consider adopting elements of the new cultures they encounter, ranging from new foods and fashions to new folkways and faiths.

Child Care Historically, family members had the primary responsibility to teach and care for their children until adulthood. Increasingly, we expect schools and teachers to do more of the job—and at younger and younger ages. From 1970 to 2015, the percentage of 3- to 5-year-olds enrolled in preschool or kindergarten programs rose from 37.5 percent to 65.7 percent, and the number enrolled in full-day programs rose from 6.4 percent to 40.8 percent (National Center for Education Statistics 2016:Table 202.10). The movement toward day care and preschool is driven in part by changes in the economy. Although this shift does provide children with a head start in learning the skills they will need in a globally competitive world, working parents have come to depend on schools to essentially babysit their kids, making sure they are cared for and protected. Because they take responsibility for the children during the school day, schools effectively free up parents to participate in the paid labor force.

> Good schools, like good societies and good families, celebrate and cherish diversity.
>
> Deborah Meier

EDUCATION AND INEQUALITY

In the United States, faith is strong that schools can and should level the playing field by providing a fair chance for success to all. This belief grows out of a commitment to *meritocracy,* the principle that our outcomes in life should be determined by ability and effort, and a rejection of *aristocracy,* a system in which outcomes are determined by inherited position or wealth. But researchers have found that schools can and do reproduce the existing system of inequality. To better understand how that is possible, sociologists drawing on the conflict perspective explore a variety of possible factors including unequal resource distribution.

Unequal Resource Distribution As we saw at the beginning of this chapter, schools are not all the same. The facilities and programs available to students vary widely. Jonathan Kozol (1991, 2005, 2012), who has studied educational inequality for decades, argues that wealthier districts have the money to offer opportunities that poor districts cannot hope to match, including more AP (Advanced Placement) classes, high-tech labs, athletic facilities, and elective courses in art, music, and languages. This type of disparity occurs because school funding comes primarily through local property taxes. As a result, schools in wealthier areas have access to more funds than do schools in poor communities. In Chicago, for example, the public school district spent $15,378 per student in 2015. Compare that to the $24,256 per student spent by the wealthy northern suburban Highland Park/Deerfield district (Illinois State Board of Education 2016b). As a former New York City principal put it, "I'll believe money doesn't count the day the rich stop spending so much on their own children" (quoted in Kozol 2005:59).

Teacher-expectancy effect The impact that a teacher's expectations about a student's performance may have on the student's actual achievements.

Of course, money isn't the only factor shaping outcomes. We must also take into account social and cultural resources. Sociologist Annette Lareau, for example, found that a parent's level of educational attainment is a strong predictor of his or her child's educational outcome (Lareau 2011). This is due, in part, to a cultural divide between children that opens up at a young age. Researchers focusing on early childhood socialization compared language use and exposure among families from different social class positions. They found that children whose parents are professionals hear, on average, 2,153 words per hour compared to 1,251 for working-class kids, and 616 for children in families receiving welfare assistance. By the age of three, children in the professional families have a vocabulary of 1,116 words compared to 749 words in working-class families, and 525 words in families receiving welfare assistance (Hart and Risley 1995).

By the time children enter formal schooling, those with larger vocabularies are more prepared to succeed and receive more positive feedback from their teachers. Such differences carry all the way through high school. For example, as the "Effect of Parents' Education on Students' Test Performance" graph demonstrates, performance on standardized tests, in this case for math, vary based on the educational attainment of parents. Among high school seniors whose parents have graduated from college, 37 percent score at proficient or advanced levels in math. Compare that to 13 percent for those whose parents have graduated from high school (NAEP 2016). SAT scores are similarly influenced by factors such as race, ethnicity, family income, and school type (National Center for Education Statistics 2016:Tables 226.10, 226.30).

Teacher Expectancy Teacher's perceptions have powerful effects on student outcomes. Psychologist Robert Rosenthal and school principal Lenore Jacobson (1968) documented what they referred to as a **teacher-expectancy effect**—the impact that a

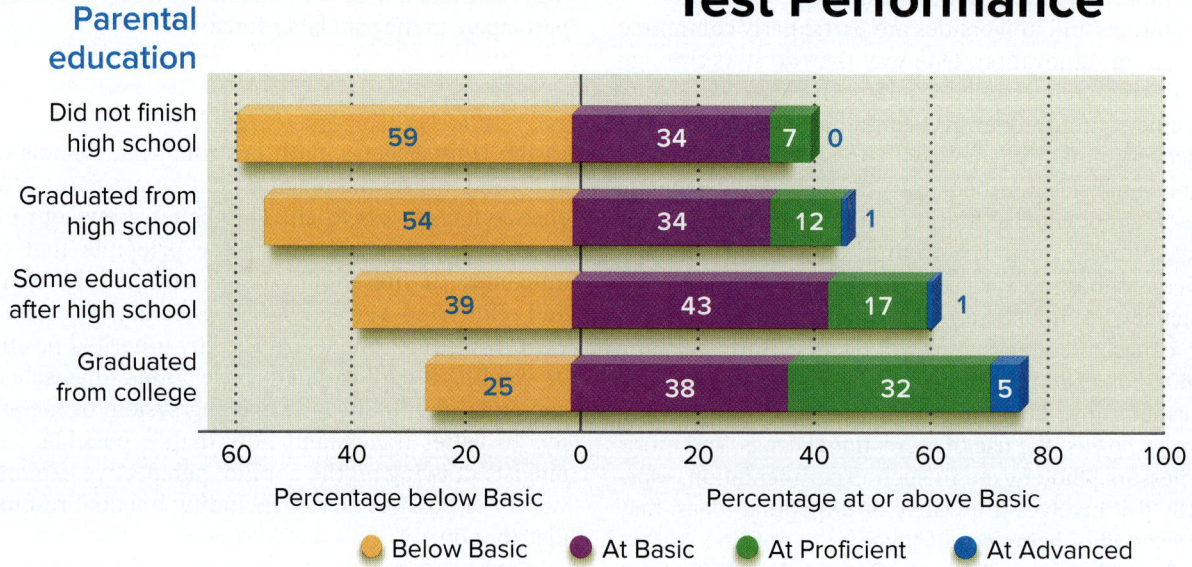

Note: Percentage distribution of 12th-grade students across NAEP mathematics achievement levels, by highest level of parental education, 2015.
Source: NAEP 2016.

Personal Sociology

Unearned Advantages

My daughters Emily and Eleanor make me proud. They get good grades, and their scores on the standardized exams are sky high. But as a sociologist, I know that they benefit from the fact that their parents are college graduates. As parents, Lori and I provided Em and El with economic, social, and cultural resources in the form of books, activities, and even vacations to historic locations. Kids from such families tend to do better in school than children who lack such opportunities. It's almost as if Emily and Eleanor are cheating. They did nothing to deserve such advantages, and yet, as a society, we act as if educational outcomes—good or bad—are solely based on merit. Looking back, what opportunities or resources did you have, or wish you had, that helped better prepare you for college success?

©Marc Romanelli/Blend Images LLC/Getty Images RF

teacher's expectations about a student's performance may have on the student's actual achievements. Drawing on sociology's interactionist perspective, they conducted experiments to document this effect.

Rosenthal and Jacobson informed teachers that they were administering a verbal and reasoning pretest to children in a San Francisco elementary school. After administering the tests, the researchers told the teachers that some of the students were "spurters"—children who showed particular academic potential. However, rather than using the actual test scores to make this determination, the researchers randomly selected the 20 percent of the students they identified as spurters. When the students were later retested, the spurters scored not only significantly higher than they had in previous tests but also significantly higher than their peers. Moreover, teachers evaluated the spurters as more interesting, more curious, and better adjusted than their classmates. As the flipside to labeling theory in criminology, these results provide a classic case of a self-fulfilling prophecy at work. Teachers expected some students to do well, and so they did. Such effects are of particular concern given that factors such as race, ethnicity, class, and gender shape teachers' perceptions (McKown and Weinstein 2008; Rubie-Davies 2010; van den Bergh et al. 2010).

Tracking As we saw in the "Training and Social Control" section, one function of education is job training. One possible unintended consequence of Davis and Moore's human capital approach, which suggests that schools simply identify those with innate ability and train them, is that people begin to assume that high pay and prestige indicate that those at the top have some superior inherent ability. Sociologists utilizing the conflict perspective suggest that the problem with Davis and Moore's model is that factors other than inherent ability, including social class, race, ethnicity, and gender, shape educational outcomes.

> **Tracking** The practice of placing students in specific curriculum groups on the basis of their test scores and other criteria.

One way schools reproduce the existing system of social inequality is by categorizing students into ability tracks. The term **tracking** refers to the practice of placing students in specific curriculum groups on the basis of their test scores and other criteria. In theory, tracking is beneficial because it allows students to be taught at a level and pace most consistent with their abilities. In practice, however, tracking often starts at a young age, and student selection for low- versus high-ability groups is often correlated with their social class, race, or ethnicity. In effect, the differences children bring with them on their first day of kindergarten shape their likely long-term educational outcomes (Oakes 2008).

SOC THINK

What experiences have you had with tracking? To what extent do you believe it was effective for both high-track and low-track students? What are its limitations in terms of equal opportunity?

Did You Know?

... The likelihood of going to college directly after high school varies by family income. For students from high-income families, 83.6 percent go directly to college, compared with 63.6 percent from middle-income families and 57.8 percent from low-income families.

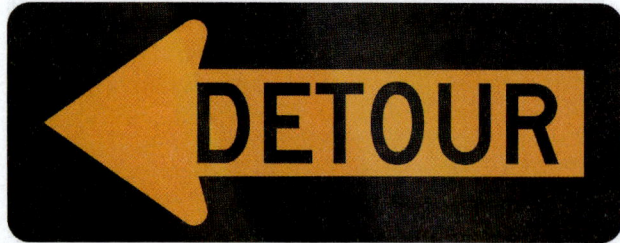

Source: National Center for Education Statistics 2016:Table 302.30.   Photo: ©Jojoo64/Shutterstock.com RF

Hidden curriculum Teaching students to submit to authority and accept society's dominant ideology.

Correspondence principle Schools' reproduction of the existing class structure through socializing students to embrace their social class position.

Credentialism An increase in the lowest level of education required to enter a field.

One consequence of such tracking is that it closes doors to students who might have the ability to succeed. For example, at a low-income school in California, all interested students were allowed to enroll in Advanced Placement (AP) courses, not just those whom the administration deemed academically worthy. Half the open-enrollment students scored high enough to qualify for college credit—a much higher proportion than in selective programs, in which only 17 percent of students qualified for college credit. When given the opportunity, otherwise-excluded students were able to succeed (Sacks 2007).

Issues such as teacher expectancy and tracking raise questions about whose interests schools really serve. Sociologists from the conflict perspective argue that, in addition to schools' formal curriculum, there is also a **hidden curriculum** through which students learn to submit to authority and accept society's dominant ideology. For example, children learn to obey orders, not to not speak until called on, to provide appropriate answers, and to regulate their behavior according to the clock. In ways such as these, schools socialize students to willingly submit to authority figures, including bosses and politicians.

Sociologists Samuel Bowles and Herbert Gintis (1976) claim that the primary function of education is to serve the interests of the ruling elite. Capitalism requires a diverse workforce with varieties of skill levels from the simple to complex. Rather than offering a pathway to opportunity for all, education in the United States follows what Bowles and Gintis call the **correspondence principle,** in which schools reproduce the existing class structure by socializing students to embrace their social class position. Thus, working-class children, assumed to be destined for subordinate positions, are likely to be placed in high school vocational and general tracks, which emphasize close supervision and compliance with authority. In contrast, young people from more affluent families are likely to be directed to college preparatory tracks, which stress leadership and decision making—the skills they are expected to need as adults.

Credentialism When issues of inequality arise, education is often presented as a pathway to opportunity. This may be true at the individual level, but there is a structural problem with that solution. The more people who get degrees, the less valuable those degrees become. If everyone has a high school diploma, it loses its power as a source of distinction. As the supply of high school graduates exceeds employers' demand, students feel compelled to pursue associate's or bachelor's degrees to stand out from the crowd. This leads to **credentialism,** the increase in the lowest level of education needed to enter a field. Many students today fear that such credential inflation means that even a college degree is not enough to ensure a good job.

Credentialism can reinforce existing patterns of social inequality. Students from poor, working-class, and middle-class families, including those in minority groups, recognize that getting ahead increasingly requires a college degree, but because they lack sufficient resources, they may have to take on significant levels of debt in the form of student loans to do so (Pew Research Center 2014d). In 2015–2016, students and parents in the United

Did You Know?

... Harvard University accepted only 5.2 percent of the 39,506 applicants to its Class of 2021. Other schools with acceptance rates below 10 percent include Stanford, Yale, Princeton, and the University of Chicago.

Source: Flanagan and Xie 2017.   Photo: ©C Squared Studios/Getty Images RF

States took out $106.8 billion in student loans. At *public* colleges and universities, 60 percent of graduates who received bachelor's degrees in 2014–2015 took out student loans with an average debt of $26,800. At *private* colleges and universities, the 63 percent who graduated with loans had an average debt of $31,400. As you might expect, students from high-income families were more likely to graduate debt-free than those from lower-income families. Forty-five percent of students from families in the top 25 percent of income earners graduated with no student debt, compared to 21 percent of debt-free students in the lowest-income quartile (College Board 2016).

Gender Women and girls in the United States experienced a long history of educational discrimination. It took until 1833 for Oberlin College to become the first institution of higher learning to admit female students—some 200 years after the founding of Harvard, the first men's college in the United States. Even so, Oberlin believed that women should aspire to become wives and mothers, not lawyers and college professors. In addition to attending classes, female students washed men's clothing, cared for their rooms, and served them meals.

In the 20th century, sexism in education showed up in many ways—in textbooks with negative stereotypes of women, in counselors' pressure on female students to prepare for "women's work," and in unequal funding for women's and men's athletic programs. In fact, throughout much of the century, only about one-third of college students were women. During that time they sat in classrooms staffed predominantly by male professors, because few college faculty members were female. Moreover, gender continues to shape the academic majors college students choose. As the "College

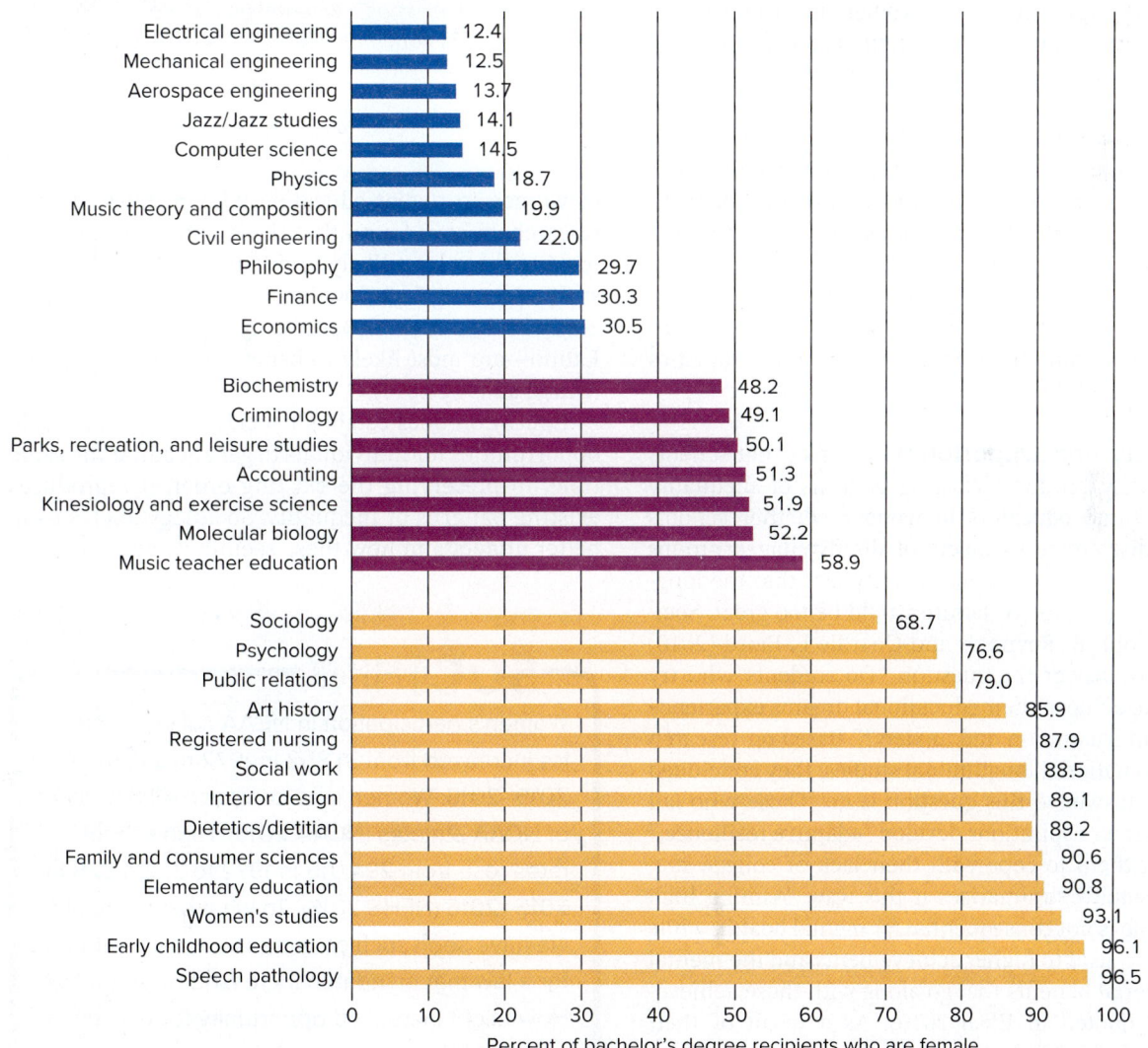

Note: Each bar represents the percentage of female bachelor's degree recipients for selected majors.

Source: National Center for Education Statistics 2016:Table 318.30.

Majors by Gender" graph demonstrates, women are more likely to graduate with bachelor's degrees in speech pathology, elementary education, or psychology than in philosophy, physics, or aerospace engineering (National Center for Education Statistics 2016:Table 318.30). As we will explore in the "Gender and Inequality" section of Chapter 12, the selection of a college major has consequences for income differences between men and women.

Today women have much greater educational opportunity, largely as a result of women's movements that worked for social change. Title IX of the Education Amendments of 1972 played a pivotal role in expanding access. It states, "No person in the United States shall, on the basis of sex, be excluded from participation in, be denied the benefits of, or be subjected to discrimination under any education program or activity receiving Federal financial assistance." Although Title IX is most commonly associated with equal opportunity for women in athletics, among other things, it also eliminated sex-segregated classes and prohibited sex discrimination in admissions. Women have made the most of this opportunity. In 1900, women received 19.1 percent of bachelor's degrees conferred. Since the 1950s, the percentage has risen dramatically so that by 2014, 57.1 percent of bachelor's degrees went to women, as the accompanying "Women in Higher Education" graph demonstrates. Women students are also more likely to be taught by women professors, who now compose 48.2 percent of total faculty (National Center for Education Statistics 2016:Table 301.20).

Inequality and Opportunity The fact that schools can actually reinforce existing patterns of inequality has led some educators to wonder whether schools should discourage members of disadvantaged groups from even attempting college. They fear that the long-term emotional toll of failure would be too great. Sociologists John R. Reynolds and Chardie L. Baird (2010) sought to answer the question "Do students who try but fail to achieve their educational dreams experience long-term frustration and anxiety?" Based on research from two national longitudinal studies, they concluded that the answer to this question is no. Those who fail to fulfill their aspirations develop "adaptive resilience," allowing them to cope with their lack of college success. Reynolds summarizes it this way: "Aiming high and failing is not consequential for mental health, while trying may lead to higher achievements and the mental and material benefits that go along with those achievements" (quoted in Elish 2010). As a result of their research, Reynolds and Baird recommend encouraging students to aim higher because it significantly increases students' chances of getting ahead, as the experience of women in higher education demonstrates. In fact, researchers have found that those with characteristics making them least likely to pursue a college degree—such as coming from low-income families, having parents with less education, or being African American or Latino—are most likely to benefit from obtaining one (Brand and Xie 2010).

Education does establish social order and provide opportunities for individuals to get ahead. At the same time, in preserving the existing order, it reproduces existing patterns of inequality. Sociology allows us to better understand how these seemingly contradictory

5 Movies ON EDUCATION

The Class
A year in the life of an inner-city classroom in Paris.

School of Rock
A substitute teacher shakes up a private grade school.

Freedom Writers
Students bond by giving voice to the stories of their lives.

Terri
An assistant principal looks out for an oversized teen misfit.

Precious
An overweight, illiterate pregnant teen finds a different path in life through an alternative school.

SOCTHINK

Women's participation in NCAA college athletics increased from 31,852 in 1972 to 211,886 in 2015–2016. Women now compose 43.5 percent of NCAA athletes (NCAA 2016). High school rates rose from 294,015 in 1972 to 3,324,326 in 2015–2016 (NFHS 2016). To what extent would we have seen such an increase had it not been for a law that mandated increased opportunity? How might increased opportunity for women in athletics have an impact on increased opportunity in other areas?

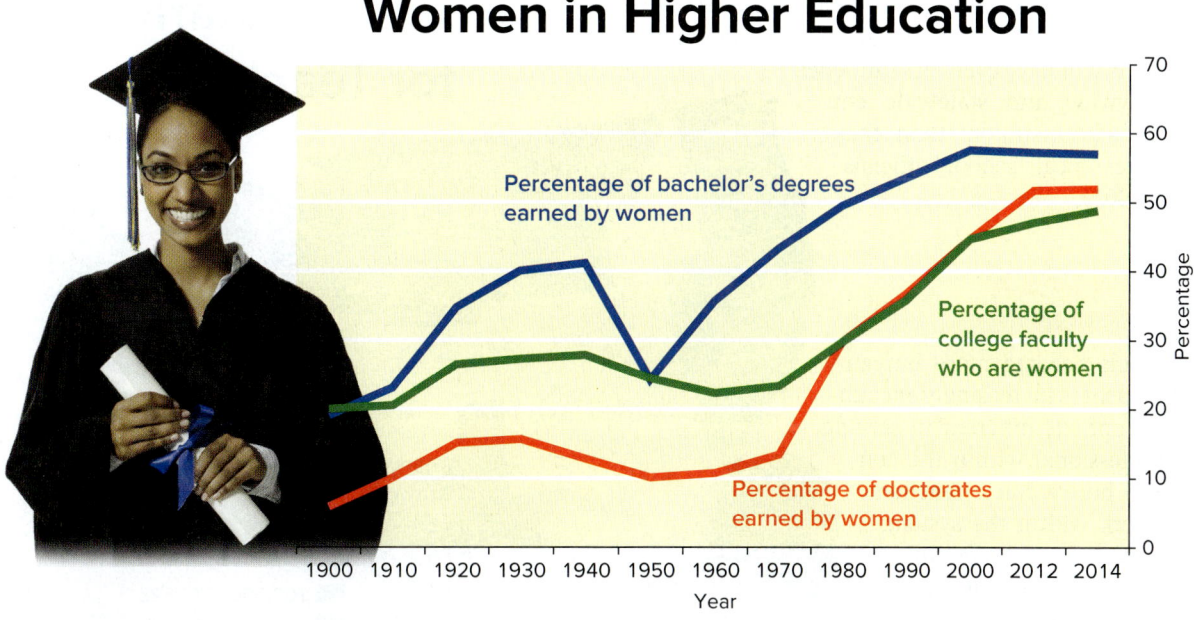

Women in Higher Education

Source: National Center for Education Statistics 2016:Table 301.20. Photo: ©Rubberball/Mike Kemp/Getty Images RF

outcomes can be accomplished through education. As the experience with Title IX demonstrates, positive social change is possible. Having a better appreciation of how education functions enables us to more effectively work toward realizing the initial goal of education: to provide opportunity and a more open society.

>> Schools as Formal Organizations

The early advocates of public education would be amazed at the scale of the education system in the United States in the 21st century. In many respects, today's schools, when viewed as an example of a formal organization, are similar to factories, hospitals, and business firms. Instead of producing cars, patients, or profits, they pump out millions of students per year. In doing so, schools must be responsive to the various constituencies outside of the student body, including parents, employers, neighborhoods, and politicians. To handle their complex mission, schools have had to become increasingly institutionalized.

THE BUREAUCRATIZATION OF SCHOOLS

It simply is not possible for a single teacher to transmit all the necessary culture and skills to children who will enter many diverse occupations. The growing number of students being served by school systems and the greater degree of specialization required within a technologically complex society have combined to bureaucratize schools.

In many respects, schools put into practice all of Max Weber's principles of bureaucracy that we considered in Chapter 5. When it comes to the division of labor, teachers specialize in particular age levels and specific subjects. Schools are hierarchically organized, with teachers reporting to principals, who are themselves answerable to the superintendent of schools and the board of education. In terms of written rules and regulations, teachers must submit written lesson plans, and students, teachers, and administrators must all adhere to established policies and procedures or face sanctions for not doing so. As schools grow, they become increasingly impersonal, and teachers are expected to treat all students in the same way, regardless of their distinctive personalities and learning needs. Finally, hiring and promotion—and even grading—are based on technical qualifications alone, and standards are established and rubrics created in an effort to ensure this practice (Vanderstraeten 2007).

The trend toward more centralized education particularly affects disadvantaged people, for whom education promises to be a path to opportunity. The standardization of educational curricula, including textbooks, generally reflects the values, interests, and lifestyles of the most powerful groups in our society and may ignore those of racial and ethnic minorities. In addition, in comparison to the affluent, the resource-poor often lack the time, financial resources, and knowledge necessary to sort through complex educational bureaucracies and to organize effective lobbying groups. As a result, low-income and minority parents will have even less influence over citywide and statewide educational administrators than they have over local school officials (Kozol 2005).

TEACHING AS A PROFESSION

As schools become more bureaucratic, teachers increasingly encounter the conflicts inherent in serving as a professional within the context of a bureaucracy. Teachers must work within the system, submitting to its hierarchical structure and abiding by its established rules. At the same time, teachers want to practice their profession with some degree of autonomy and respect for their judgment. Conflicts arise from having to serve simultaneously as instructor, disciplinarian, administrator, and employee of a school district.

As professionals, teachers feel pressure from a number of directions. First, the level of formal schooling required for teaching remains high, and the public has begun to call for new competency examinations. Second, teachers' salaries are significantly lower than those of many comparably educated professionals and skilled workers. Finally, respect for teachers as competent and responsible professionals has been challenged in the political arena. Many teachers, disappointed and frustrated, have left the educational world for careers in other professions. In fact, between a quarter and a third of new teachers quit within their first three years, and as many as half leave poor urban schools within their first five years. Even within a single year, teacher turnover is significant; in high-poverty areas, more than 20 percent of teachers did not teach in the same school the following year (Goldring et al. 2014; Planty et al. 2008; Wallis 2008).

Average Salaries for Teachers

United States (mean) 57,420
United States (median) 51,155

$60,000–$77,628
$55,000–$59,999
$50,000–$54,999
$45,000–$49,999
$40,934–$44,999

Note: Data are for 2014–2015.
Source: National Education Association 2016:Table C-11.

©Scott Olson/Getty Images

COMMUNITY COLLEGES

Community colleges exist as a testament to the ideals put forth by Jefferson, Franklin, and Mann. The GI bill in the 1940s and Pell Grants in the 1960s provided significant college financial aid for those with limited means, opening wide the doors to college. But the cost of higher education continues to rise dramatically. Community colleges, however, lower the barriers to student

The Net Price Cost of College

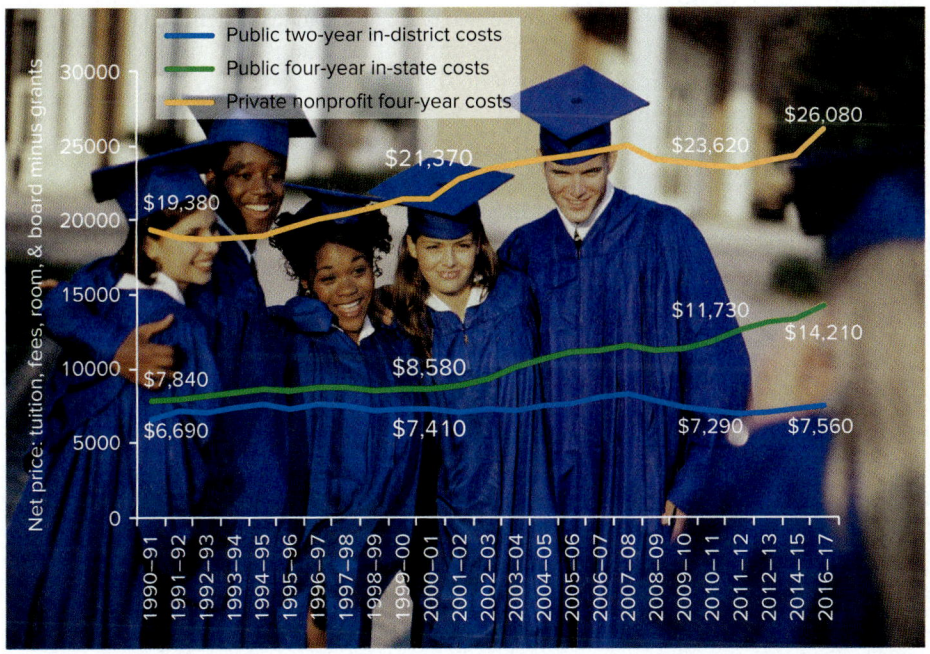

Note: Net price refers to the amount students and/or families must pay after subtracting federal, state, local, and institutional grant aid, along with education tax credits, from the institution's posted costs for tuition, fees, room, and board. Costs for all years are reported using 2016 dollars.

Source: College Board 2016b:Table 7. Photo: ©Purestock/SuperStock

success with their relatively low cost and open enrollment. As the accompanying "Net Price Cost of College" graph shows, community colleges are significantly less expensive than public in-state four-year or private four-year colleges or universities. For the sake of comparison, this graph shows the cost of tuition, fees, and room and board minus any grant aid. Choosing to not live on campus, as many community college students do, significantly lowers the cost of this option. As a result, an increasing number of students have turned to community colleges.

In 2015, 6.5 million students in the United States attended community college, almost three times as many as in 1970. They constitute 32.5 percent of all enrolled college students. These students are more likely to be older, female, Black, Hispanic, low-income, and part-time, compared to their peers at four-year schools. In fact, the more income and education a student's parents have, the less likely she or he is to attend a community college. This highlights the role these schools play in providing opportunity for those with limited resources. Enrollment at community colleges raises the aspirations of students. Whether they initially expected to take only a few courses or to finish with a two-year degree, almost one-half of these students later aspired to more education, including a four-year degree or beyond (Ginder, Kelly-Reid, and Mann 2014; National Center for Education Statistics 2016:Table 303.25; Provasnik and Planty 2008).

Community colleges do provide opportunity for many, but the likelihood of completing a degree varies significantly when comparing students at two- and four-year institutions. For students who start at two-year schools, 35.1 percent go on to earn a certificate, an associate's degree, or a bachelor's degree. Contrast that with the 64.2 percent of students who start at four-year schools and earn a degree. The likelihood of giving up also differs. Six years after they started, 46.2 percent of students from two-year schools are no longer enrolled and have no degree. Compare that to 23.6 percent of students who started at four-year schools (U.S. Department of Education 2016:Table 326.40).

Some sociologists have suggested that community colleges serve a "cooling out" function in which students who fail to complete a degree blame themselves for their lack of success. According to this theory, society has fewer good jobs than it has people who want them. Earning a degree increases one's odds of getting one of those jobs. At the level of the individual, community colleges appear to provide opportunity for everyone. Because they had the chance to get a degree, students who give up are more likely to blame themselves for failure than to develop a critique of the social structure that doesn't supply enough good jobs in the first place. In this way, community colleges can help justify the existing system of inequality (Bahr 2008; Clark 1960, 1980).

HOMESCHOOLING

Some parents view formal schooling as a path to opportunity; others have decided to opt out altogether. Almost 1.8 million students are now being educated at home—about 3.4 percent of the K–12 school population. Homeschooled families are more likely to be White, have two parents in the household with only one in the labor force, have parents with a bachelor's degree, and have three or more children (National Center for Education Statistics 2016:Table 206:10; Radford et al. 2016).

In a sense this represents a return to the pre–public school days of American education, in which the primary responsibility for teaching rested with parents.

When asked to identify the most important reason for choosing this path, 36 percent of parents said they were motivated by a desire to provide religious or moral instruction (the most common response), and 83 percent overall identified that as an important factor. A concern about the environment of schools—safety, drugs, and negative peer pressure—was most important to 21 percent, and 17 percent attributed their decision primarily to dissatisfaction with the school's academic instruction (Planty et al. 2009). In addition, some immigrants choose homeschooling as a way to ease their children's transition to a new society. For example, increasing numbers of the nation's growing Arab American population have joined the movement toward homeschooling (Cooper and Sureau 2007; MacFarquhar 2008). Other parents see it as a good alternative for children who suffer from attention deficit hyperactivity disorder (ADHD) and learning disorders (LDs). A study by the Home School Legal Defense Association (2005), a homeschool advocacy organization, found that homeschooled students score higher than others on standardized exams in every subject and in every grade.

Religion A social institution dedicated to establishing a shared sense of identity, encouraging social integration, and offering believers a sense of meaning and purpose.

The rise in homeschooling points toward a growing dissatisfaction with the institutionalized practice of education. Early public school advocates argued for the importance of a common curriculum rooted in a shared sense of values. Homeschooling, however, points toward pluralism and the desire to retain the unique subcultural values of a community. Although new forms of schooling may meet the individual needs of diverse groups in today's society, they also undermine the historical commitment to public education as a means of fostering unity within society.

SOCTHINK

What do you think are the advantages and disadvantages of being homeschooled? How might it contribute to a stronger sense of identity? How might it threaten the social order?

>> Defining Religion

Education plays a major role in socializing members of society into shared values and norms, and religion helps cement those beliefs and practices into people's hearts and minds. **Religion** is a social institution dedicated to establishing a shared sense of identity, encouraging social integration, and offering believers a sense of meaning and purpose. Though levels of religious participation vary from place to place, religion continues to be a major force both on the world stage and in the lives of individuals. To fully understand its various forms, sociologists take two basic approaches to defining religion. The first focuses on what religion is, and the second focuses on what it does.

SUBSTANCE: WHAT RELIGION IS

According to a substantive approach to studying religion, religion has a unique content or substance that separates it from other forms of knowledge and belief. Most commonly, this unique focus involves some conception of a supernatural realm, such as heaven, but it does not have to be outside the physical world. The key is that religion centers on something that goes above and beyond the mundane realities of our everyday existence, that points to something larger, and that calls for some response from us in terms of how we think and act. Sociologist Peter Berger (1969) provided a substantive definition of religion as "the human enterprise by which a sacred cosmos is established" (p. 25). The sacred here refers to that extraordinary realm that becomes the focus of religious faith and practice. It provides believers with meaning, order, and coherence. In describing that sacred realm, people might touch on concepts such as gods and goddesses, angels and demons, heaven and hell, nirvana, or other beings or realms. A society with broad agreement

©Chris Ryan/Getty Images RF

about the nature and importance of this sacred realm is, by definition, more religious.

Sociologists who follow a substantive approach focus on the ways in which religious groups rally around what they define to be sacred. The **sacred** encompasses elements beyond everyday life that inspire respect, awe, and even fear. People interact with the sacred realm through ritual practices, such as prayer or sacrifice. Because believers have faith in the sacred, they accept what they cannot understand. The sacred realm exists in contrast to the **profane,** which includes the ordinary and commonplace.

Different religious groups define their understanding of the sacred or profane in different ways. For example, who or what constitutes "god" varies among Muslims, Christians, and Hindus. Even within a group, different believers may treat the same object as sacred or profane, depending on whether it connects them to the sacred realm. Ordinarily, a piece of bread is profane, but it becomes sacred for Christians during their practice of communion because through it believers enter into connection with God. Similarly, a candelabrum becomes sacred to Jews if it is a menorah. For Confucians and Taoists, incense sticks are not mere decorative items, but highly valued offerings to the gods in religious ceremonies that mark the new and full moons.

©Michael Zak/123RF

The functional approach to defining religion has roots in the work of Émile Durkheim. He defined religion as "a unified system of beliefs and practices relative to sacred things, that is to say things set apart and forbidden—beliefs and practices which unite into a single moral community, called a 'church,' all those who adhere to them" ([1887] 1972:224). This definition points to three aspects sociologists focus on when studying religion: a unified system of beliefs and practices, sacred things, and community.

With regard to the first element—the unified system of beliefs and practices—the content of those beliefs and practices matter less than the fact that they are shared. Terms historically used to describe religious beliefs include *doctrine, dogma, creeds,* and *scripture,* all representing principles believers share through faith. Practices refer to shared rituals, such as attendance at services, prayer, meditation, and fasting. Because beliefs and practices are central to religion, we look at them in more detail below.

> **Sacred** Elements beyond everyday life that inspire respect, awe, and even fear.
>
> **Profane** The ordinary and commonplace elements of life, as distinguished from the sacred.

Unlike the substantive approach, Durkheim's emphasis on sacred things focuses less on the objects themselves than on the believers' attitude toward those objects.

FUNCTION: WHAT RELIGIONS DO

A functionalist approach focuses less on what religion is than on what religions do, with a particular emphasis on how religions contribute to social order. According to a functionalist approach to studying religion, religion unifies believers into a community through shared practices and a common set of beliefs relative to sacred things. In keeping with the functionalist perspective out of which this approach grows, the emphasis is on the unifying dimension of religion rather than on the substance of that which unifies. For functionalists, the supernatural or something like it is not an essential part of religion. Religion need not have gods or goddesses, an afterlife, or other such conventional elements. In fact, any social practices that strongly unite us, such as being a sports fan, can function like religion for the individual and for society.

©Gavriel Jecan/The Image Bank/Getty Images

©Goodshoot/Alamy Stock Photo RF

Sacred objects and sacred places convey a sense of awe, and religion calls upon believers to treat them with reverence and care. Roman Catholics, for example, treat the bread and wine of communion with respect because they believe that the sacrament transforms those elements into the body and blood of Christ. For Muslims, the Qur'an is a sacred object, and the Kaaba in Mecca is a sacred place. In the functional approach to religion, however, sacredness is in the eyes of the beholders. Any object can be sacred so long as people define it as such and treat it accordingly.

The most important component of Durkheim's definition is this third part: community. It is not the church, mosque, or temple as a building that matters, but the unification of a body of believers into a shared community. What they believe, what they practice, or what they view as sacred is less important than the fact that they have these beliefs, practices, and shared sacred things in common.

As suggested, according to this approach, religion need not look like what we conventionally think of as religion. Anything that does what Durkheim's three elements do can function as religion. Just as our understanding of what families are has expanded to include people who are "like family" to us, so also has the definition of religion expanded to include things that function like religion (Cusack and Digance 2009; Jindra 1994; Mathisen 2006). Sports provides a classic example. When it comes to beliefs and practices, sports fans—short for *fanatics,* a term that historically had religious connotations—share beliefs about the superiority of their team and regularly practice rituals in hopes that it will help their team win. They may wear the same jersey to watch the game, sit in the same chair, or do a touchdown dance after their team scores, all out of superstitious fear that failure to do so will make their team lose. In terms of sacred things, there are autographs, jerseys, balls; and the stadium where the team plays, often referred to by fans as a shrine, represents a sacred space. Finally, fans are united into a community with other fans of the team. Being a fan of the team becomes part of

Personal Sociology

Victory Dance

I confess to being a Green Bay Packers fan. I follow them religiously. Even though I know better, I practice superstitions in the hope that they will help, including wearing a lucky shirt, not talking on the phone during the game, and although I am embarrassed to admit it, doing a "touchdown dance" around the dining-room table after the Packers score, with high-fives for everyone including our dog Jessie. My wife, Lori, is an even bigger fan. We own stock in the Packers and have season tickets. We've made many pilgrimages to the "frozen tundra of Lambeau Field." Each time we go to a game, we follow the same rituals: park in the same spot, eat a pregame meal at the same restaurant, and enter the stadium early so we can soak it all in.

---

their identity. It provides them with joy, satisfaction, and even a sense of purpose. In a personal essay recounting his obsession with soccer, journalist Michael Elliott (2005) put it this way: "What does being a fan mean? It means you will never walk alone" (p. 76).

SOCTHINK

What other things function like religion for us? How about followers of bands, celebrities, TV shows, or politics? To what extent might consumerism, or even work, function as religion?

>> Components of Religion

In studying religion, regardless of which definitional approach they take, sociologists investigate components of religion that are common to most groups. Their goal is to gain a more complete picture of the role religion plays for both individuals and groups. Sociologists using both approaches focus on how religious groups organize beliefs, rituals, experience, and community.

BELIEFS

Some people believe in life after death, in supreme beings with unlimited powers, or in supernatural forces.

Religious beliefs are statements to which members of a particular religion adhere. The focus can vary dramatically from religion to religion.

In the late 1960s a significant shift occurred in the nature of religious belief in the United States. Denominations that held to relatively liberal interpretations of religious scripture (such as the Presbyterians, Methodists, and Lutherans) declined in membership, while those that held to more conservative interpretations and sought a return to the fundamentals of the faith grew in numbers. The term **fundamentalism** refers to a rigid adherence to core religious doctrines. Often, fundamentalism is accompanied by a literal application of scripture or historical beliefs to today's world. Fundamentalism grows out of a sense that the world is falling apart due to a decline in true religious belief and practice. Fundamentalists see themselves as presenting a positive vision for the future through a return to the purity of the original religious message (Aslan 2010; Juergensmeyer 2003).

The phrase "religious fundamentalism" was first applied to Protestants in the United States who took a literal interpretation of the Bible, but fundamentalism is found worldwide among most major religious groups, including Roman Catholicism, Islam, and Judaism. Fundamentalists vary immensely in their beliefs and behavior. Some stress the need to be strict in their own personal faith but take little interest in broad social issues. Others are watchful of societal actions, such as government policies, that they see as conflicting with fundamentalist doctrine (Emerson et al. 2006).

Christian fundamentalists in the United States have fought against the teaching of evolution in public schools because they believe not only that it represents a threat to their beliefs, but also that it is itself a type of religious faith in naturalism (as opposed to the supernaturalism of God). The first, and most famous, court case over the teaching of evolution in public schools occurred in 1925 and is often referred to as the "Scopes Monkey Trial." In that trial, high school biology teacher John T. Scopes was convicted of violating a Tennessee law that made it a crime to teach the scientific theory of evolution in public schools (Larson 2006). Since that time there have been numerous other court challenges, including *Kitzmiller v. Dover Area School District* in Pennsylvania in 2005. In this major case, those opposed to the teaching of evolution sought to force schools to teach the "science" of intelligent design—the idea that life is so complex that there had to be some form of intelligence behind its creation. The judge ruled that intelligent design was a variation on creationism, the teaching of which in a public school would violate the separation of church and state (Padian 2007).

Religious belief A statement to which members of a particular religion adhere.

Fundamentalism Rigid adherence to core religious doctrines, often accompanied by a literal application of scripture or historical beliefs to today's world.

Religious ritual A practice required or expected of members of a faith.

RITUALS

Religious rituals are practices required or expected of members of a faith. Rituals usually honor the divine power (or powers) worshiped by believers; they also remind adherents of their religious duties and responsibilities. Rituals and beliefs can be interdependent; rituals generally affirm beliefs, as in a public or private

Did You Know?
...Forty-eight percent of Christians in the United States believe Jesus will definitely or probably return to earth within the next 40 years.

Source: Pew Research Center 2013. *Photo:* ©DAJ/Getty Images RF

Going GLOBAL

How Often Do You Attend Religious Services?

Percentage attending religious services once a week or more

Country	%
Rwanda	70.6%
Poland	50.4%
Mexico	46.2%
Egypt	45.2%
Iraq	38.4%
United States	33.3%
South Korea	29.9%
India	24.5%
Russia	4.9%
Sweden	4.2%
China	1.9%

Source: World Values Survey 2015:V145.

statement confessing a sin. Like any social institution, religion develops distinctive norms to structure people's behavior. Moreover, sanctions are attached to religious rituals, in the form of either rewards (such as bar mitzvah gifts) or penalties (such as expulsion from a religious institution for violation of norms).

Rituals may be very simple, such as saying a prayer at a meal, meditating, or observing a moment of silence to commemorate someone's death. Other rituals, such as the *hajj*—the Muslim pilgrimage to the Grand Mosque in Mecca, Saudi Arabia—are quite elaborate. Most religious rituals in the United States focus on services conducted at houses of worship. Attendance at a service, silent and spoken prayers, communion, and the singing of hymns and chants are common forms of ritual behavior that generally take place in group settings. These rituals serve as important face-to-face encounters in which people reinforce their religious beliefs and their commitment to their faith. Religious participation varies widely from country to country.

Researchers have found that performing rituals, even apart from religious beliefs, has a significant impact on how we think and feel. For example, upon suffering loss—the death of a loved one, the breakup of a relationship, or even losing the lottery—people who engage in rituals experience lower levels of grief. This is true even for individuals who do not believe that participating in rituals would make a difference. Part of the effectiveness of rituals is the sense of control they provide (Norton and Gino 2013).

EXPERIENCE

In the sociological study of religion, the term **religious experience** refers to the feeling or perception of being in direct contact with the ultimate reality, such as a divine being, or of being overcome with religious emotion. A religious experience may be rather slight, such as the feeling of exaltation a person might receive from hearing a choir sing Handel's "Hallelujah Chorus." Many religious experiences, however, are more profound, such as a Muslim's experience on a *hajj*. In his autobiography, the late African American activist Malcolm X (1964:338) wrote of his *hajj* and how deeply moved he was by the way that Muslims in Mecca came together across racial and color lines. For Malcolm X, the color blindness of the Muslim world "proved to me the power of the One God."

Religious experience The feeling or perception of being in direct contact with the ultimate reality, such as a divine being, or of being overcome with religious emotion.

For evangelical Christians in the United States, becoming "born again" represents a profound religious experience. To do so, an unbeliever asks Jesus Christ into their hearts as their personal Lord and

Religious adherents demonstrate commitment to their faiths in various ways, including Muslim women who choose to wear the hijab. ©Patrick Baz/AFP/Getty Images

Savior. This emotionally charged experience marks a turning point in their lives when they became a Christian. According to a national survey, 35 percent of adults in the United States self-identify as "born-again or evangelical" Christians. Perhaps not surprisingly, 83 percent of Evangelical Protestants describe themselves in this way, as do 72 percent of those in historically Black Protestant churches. Only 27 percent of mainline Protestants identify as "born-again or evangelical," as do 23 percent of Mormons and 22 percent of Catholics (Pew Research Center 2015f:31). Such statistics demonstrate that what counts as a legitimate and significant religious experience, such as becoming born again, varies from group to group, which highlights the significance of the social context for religious faith.

COMMUNITY

Religious communities organize themselves in varieties of ways. Sociologists find it useful to distinguish between four basic forms of organization: the ecclesia, the denomination, the sect, and the new religious movement, or cult. We can see differences among these four forms of organization in their size, power, degree of commitment expected from members, and historical ties to other faiths (Dawson 2009).

Ecclesiae When studying how groups organize their communities, sociologists have used the term **ecclesia** (plural, *ecclesiae*) to describe a religious organization that claims to include most or all members of a society and is recognized as the national or official religion. Because virtually everyone belongs to the faith, membership is by birth rather than conscious decision. The classic example in sociology was the Roman Catholic Church in medieval Europe. Contemporary examples of ecclesiae include Islam in Saudi Arabia and Buddhism in Thailand. However, significant differences exist within this category. In Saudi Arabia's Islamic regime, leaders of the ecclesia hold vast power over actions of the state. In contrast, the historical state church in Sweden, Lutheranism, holds no such power over the Riksdag (parliament) or the prime minister.

Generally, ecclesiae are conservative in that they do not challenge the leaders of a secular government. In a society with an ecclesia, the political and religious institutions often act in harmony and reinforce each other's power in their relative spheres of influence. In the modern world, ecclesiae are declining in power.

Ecclesia A religious organization that claims to include most or all members of a society and is recognized as the national or official religion.

Denomination A large, organized religion that is not officially linked to the state or government.

Denominations A **denomination** is a large, organized religion that is not officially linked to the state or government. Like an ecclesia, it tends to have an explicit set of beliefs, a defined system of authority, and a generally respected position in society. Denominations often claim large segments of a population as members. Generally, children accept the denomination of their parents and give little thought to membership in other faiths. Although considered respectable and not viewed as a challenge to the secular government, unlike ecclesia, denominations lack the official recognition and power held by an ecclesia (Doress and Porter 1977).

The United States is home to a large number of denominations. This diversity is largely the result of the nation's immigrant heritage. Many settlers brought with them the religious commitments native to their homelands. Some Christian denominations in the United States, such as the Roman Catholics, Episcopalians, and Lutherans,

Major Religious Traditions in the United States

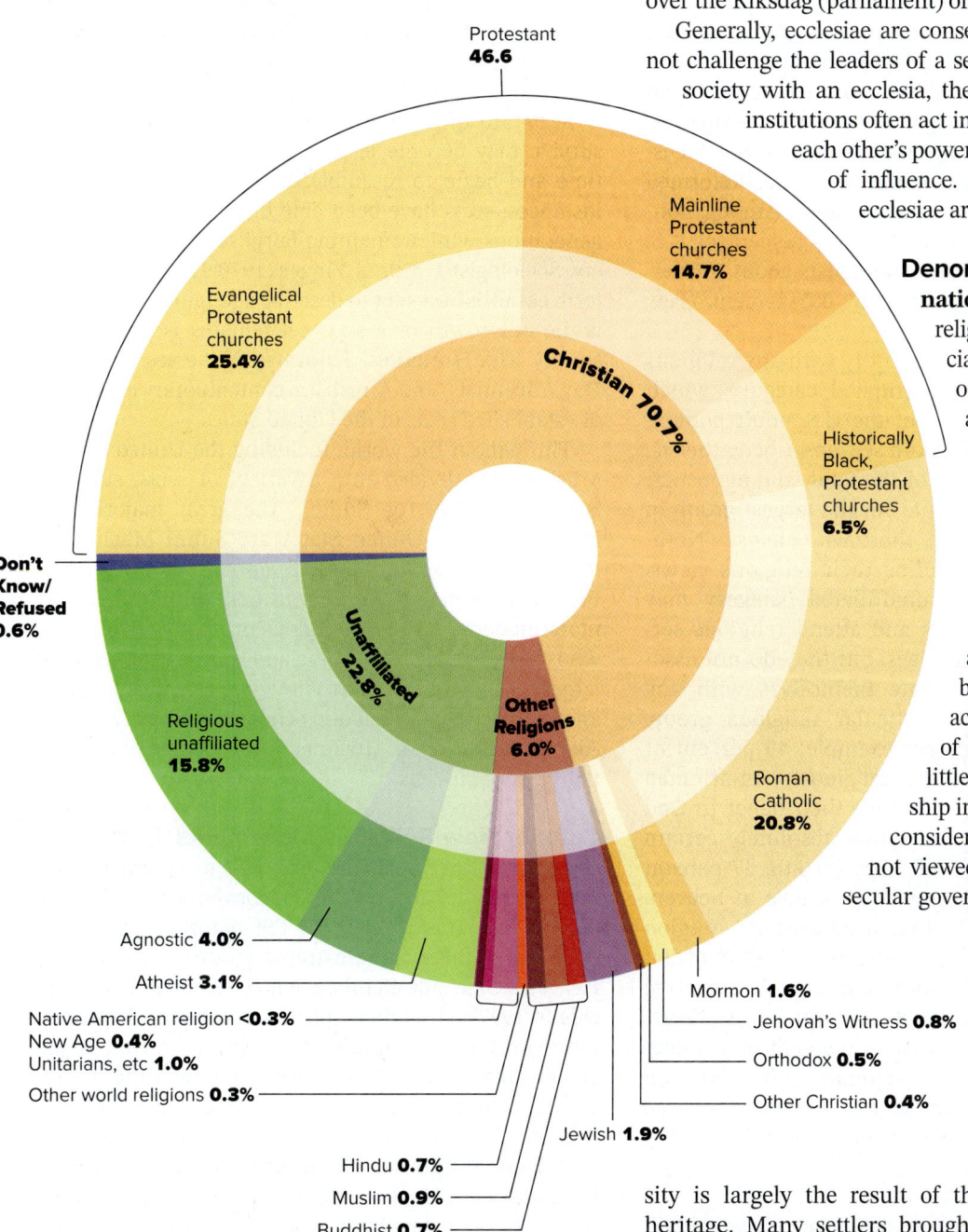

Note: Due to rounding, figures may not add to 100, and nested figures may not add to the subtotal indicated.
Source: Pew Research Center 2015f: 21.

are the outgrowth of ecclesiae established in Europe. New Christian denominations also emerged, including the Mormons and Christian Scientists. Within the last generation, immigrants have increased the number of Muslims, Hindus, and Buddhists living in the United States.

At 20.8 percent of the adult population, Roman Catholicism is by far the largest single denomination in the United States, although many other Christian faiths have one million or more members. As the "Major Religious Traditions in the United States" graphic shows, Protestants collectively account for 46.5 percent of the nation's adult population. There are a multitude of Protestant denominations in the United States, including the Southern Baptist Convention, American Baptist Association, United Methodist Church, African Methodist Episcopal, Evangelical Lutheran in America, Assemblies of God, Presbyterian Church (U.S.A.), Disciples of Christ, Church of the Nazarene, Reformed Church in America, and many others. Among non-Christian faiths, Jews account for 1.9 percent of U.S. adults, Muslims 0.9 percent, Buddhists about 0.7 percent, and Hindus approximately 0.7 percent (Pew Research Center 2015f).

Individuals who do not identify with any religious tradition fall into the unaffiliated category, which encompasses 22.8 percent of the U.S. adult population. This group includes both self-described atheists, who make up 3.1 percent of the total, and agnostics, who come in at 4.0 percent. But the largest group in this category, at 15.8%, are those who choose "Nothing in particular" to describe their religious views. Overall, people in this unaffiliated category may well hold religious beliefs and attend religious services, but they do not associate themselves with any particular religious group. For example, 49 percent of the religiously unaffiliated describe their belief in God as either absolutely certain or fairly certain, 37 percent say they believe in heaven, and 34 percent say religion is either very or somewhat important in their lives. Age plays a significant role here, with 36 percent of younger millennials, those born in 1990 and later, identifying as unaffiliated compared to 11 percent of those born from 1929 to 1945 (Pew Research Center 2015f).

Sect A relatively small religious group that has broken away from some other religious organization to renew what it considers the original vision of the faith.

Established sect A religious group that is the outgrowth of a sect, yet remains isolated from society.

New religious movement (NRM) or cult A small, alternative faith community that represents either a new religion or a major innovation in an existing faith.

Sects A **sect** can be defined as a relatively small religious group that has broken away from some other religious organization to renew what it considers the original vision of the faith. Many sects, such as that led by Martin Luther during the Reformation in the 1500s, claim to be the "true church" because they seek to cleanse the established faith of what they regard as extraneous beliefs and rituals. Max Weber ([1916] 1958b:114) termed the sect a "believer's church" because affiliation is based on conscious acceptance of a specific religious dogma.

Sects are at odds with the dominant society and do not seek to become established national religions. Unlike ecclesiae and denominations, they require intensive commitments and demonstrations of belief by members. Partly owing to their outsider status, sects frequently exhibit a higher degree of religious fervor and loyalty than more established religious groups. They actively recruit adults as new members, and acceptance comes through conversion.

Sects are often short-lived. Those that are able to survive may become less antagonistic to society over time and begin to resemble denominations. In a few instances, sects have been able to endure over several generations while remaining fairly separate from society. Sociologist J. Milton Yinger (1970:226–73) uses the term **established sect** to describe a religious group that is the outgrowth of a sect, yet remains isolated from society. The Hutterites, Jehovah's Witnesses, Seventh-Day Adventists, and Amish are contemporary examples of established sects in the United States.

Throughout the world, including the United States, Muslims are divided into a variety of sects, such as Sunni and Shia (or Shiite). The great majority of Muslims in the United States are Sunni Muslims—literally, those who follow the *Sunnah,* or way of the Prophet. Compared to other Muslims, Sunnis tend to be more moderate in their religious orthodoxy. The Shia, who come primarily from Iraq and Iran, are the second-largest group. Shia Muslims are more attentive to guidance from accepted Islamic scholars than are Sunnis. About two-thirds of Muslims in the United States are native-born citizens.

Cults or New Religious Movements Historically, sociologists have used the term *cult* to describe alternative religious groups with unconventional religious beliefs. Partly as a result of the notoriety generated by some of these more extreme groups—such as the Heaven's Gate cult members who committed mass suicide in 1997 so that their spirits might be freed to catch a ride on the spaceship hidden behind the Hale-Bopp comet—many sociologists have abandoned the use of the term. In its place they have adopted the expression "new religious movement."

A **new religious movement (NRM) or cult** is generally a small, alternative religious group that represents either a new faith community or a major innovation in an existing faith. NRMs are similar to sects in that they tend to be small and are often viewed as less respectable than more established faiths. Unlike sects, however, NRMs normally do not result from schisms or breaks with established ecclesiae or denominations. Some new religious movements, including the Church of Scientology, which was founded in 1954 by science fiction author L. Ron Hubbard, may be totally unrelated to existing faiths. Even when a cult does accept certain fundamental tenets of a dominant faith—such as a belief in Jesus as divine or in Muhammad as a messenger of God—it will offer new revelations or insights to justify its claim to being a more advanced religion (Stark and Bainbridge 1979, 1985).

Like sects, NRMs may be transformed over time into other types of religious organization. An example is the Christian Science Church, which began as a new religious movement under the leadership of Mary Baker Eddy. Today, this church exhibits the characteristics of a denomination. In fact, most major religions, including Christianity, began as cults. NRMs may be in the early stages of developing into a denomination or new religion, or they may just as easily fade away through the loss of members or weak leadership (Schaefer and Zellner 2007).

To summarize, ecclesiae are recognized as national churches. Denominations, although not officially approved by the state, are widely accepted as legitimate. On the other hand, sects are countercultures at odds with society's dominant norms and values. NRMs provide innovative, though not necessarily exclusive, types of faith. The boundaries between these four types are somewhat fluid, and it is helpful to view them as a continuum based on their level of acceptance in the larger society and the expectations they have in terms of faith and practice for their believers.

©Pierre-Philippe Marcou/AFP/Getty Images

>> World Religions

Early sociologists predicted that modern societies would experience widespread **secularization,** which involves religion's diminishing influence in the public sphere, especially in politics and the economy. In the United States, there has indeed been a dramatic increase in the number of religiously unaffiliated individuals, often referred to by researchers as "nones" because that is how they respond when asked about their religious affiliation. As a portion of the U.S. population, they have increased from 7 percent in 1972 to 16.1 percent in 2007 and 22.8 percent in 2015. That works out to 56 million individuals, an increase of 19 million between 2007 and 2015. In fact, the United States has more "nones" than Catholics (Pew Research Center 2015f; Putnam and Campbell 2012).

Globally, 1.1 billion people, or 16.4 percent of the world's population, identify themselves as religiously unaffiliated. This includes atheists and agnostics along with religious believers who do not identify with a particular religious group. The size of this unaffiliated group might suggest that those early sociologists were correct about secularization and the declining significance of religion in the modern world. Yet projections to 2050 suggest that the proportion of the global population who identify as religiously unaffiliated will actually shrink to 13.2 percent (Pew Research Center 2015g). In the United States and around the world, religion continues to exert a significant influence both individually and collectively.

Christianity is the largest single faith in the world; the second largest is Islam, as the accompanying "Major World Religions" graphic shows. Although global news events often suggest an inherent conflict between Christians and Muslims, the two faiths are similar in many ways. Both are monotheistic, meaning both claim there is only one god, and both include a belief in prophets, an afterlife, and a judgment day. In fact, Islam recognizes Jesus as a prophet, though not as the son of God. Both faiths impose a moral code on believers, which varies from fairly rigid proscriptions for fundamentalists to relatively relaxed guidelines for liberals.

Secularization Religion's diminishing influence in the public sphere, especially in politics and the economy.

The followers of Islam, called Muslims, believe that the prophet Muhammad received Islam's holy scriptures from Allah (God) nearly 1,400 years ago. They see Muhammad as the last in a long line of prophets, preceded by Adam, Abraham, Moses, and Jesus. Islam is more communal in its expression than Christianity, particularly the more individualistic Protestant denominations. Consequently, in countries that are predominantly Muslim, the separation of religion and the state is not considered necessary or even desirable. In fact, Muslim governments often reinforce Islamic practices through their laws. Muslims do vary sharply in their

Going GLOBAL

Religions of the World

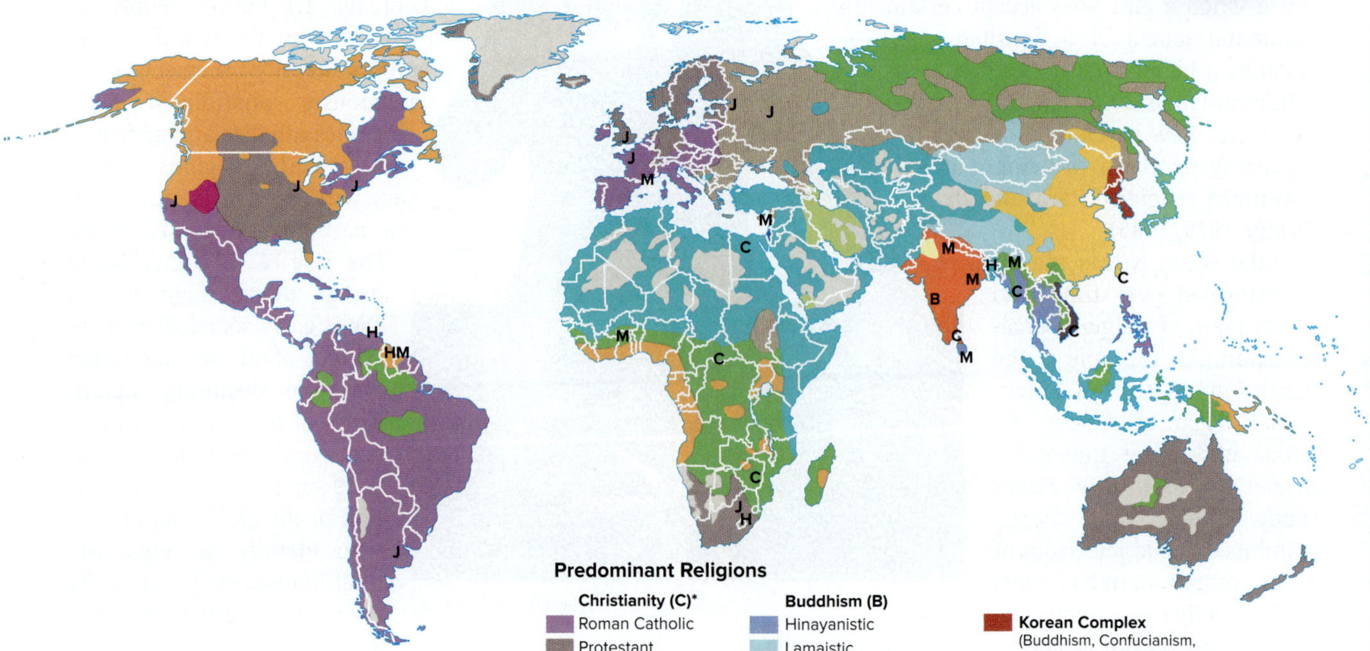

Predominant Religions

Christianity (C)*
- Roman Catholic
- Protestant
- Mormon (LDS)
- Eastern Churches
- Mixed Sects

Islam (M)
- Sunni
- Shia

Buddhism (B)
- Hinayanistic
- Lamaistic

Hinduism (H)
Judaism (J)
Sikhism
Animism (Tribal)
Chinese Complex (Confucianism, Taoism, and Buddhism)

Korean Complex (Buddhism, Confucianism, Christianity, and Chondogyo)
Japanese Complex (Shinto and Buddhism)
Vietnamese Complex (Buddhism, Taoism, Confucianism, and Cao Dai)
Unpopulated Regions

* Capital letters indicate the presence of locally important minority adherents of nonpredominant faiths.

Religious adherence is one of the defining social characteristics of a culture.
Source: Allen 2008.

---

interpretation of several traditions, some of which—such as the wearing of veils by women—are more cultural than religious in origin.

Like Christianity and Islam, Judaism is monotheistic. Jews believe that God's true nature is revealed in the Torah, which Christians know as the first five books of the Old Testament. According to these scriptures, God formed a covenant, or pact, with Abraham and Sarah, the ancestors of the twelve tribes of Israel. Even today, religious Jews believe this covenant holds them accountable to God's will. If they follow both the letter and the spirit of the Torah, a long-awaited Messiah will one day bring paradise to earth. Although Judaism has a relatively small following compared to other major faiths, it forms the historical foundation for both Christianity and Islam. That is why Jews revere many of the same sacred Middle Eastern sites as Christians and Muslims.

Two other major faiths developed in a different part of the world—India. The earliest, Hinduism, originated around 1500 BCE. Hinduism differs from Judaism, Christianity, and Islam in that it embraces a number of gods and minor gods, although most worshipers are devoted primarily to a single deity, such as Shiva or Vishnu. Hinduism is also distinguished by a belief in reincarnation, or the perpetual rebirth of the soul after death. Unlike Judaism, Christianity, and Islam, which are based largely on sacred texts, Hindu beliefs have been preserved mostly through oral tradition.

©George Doyle/Getty Images RF

198 • SOC 2018

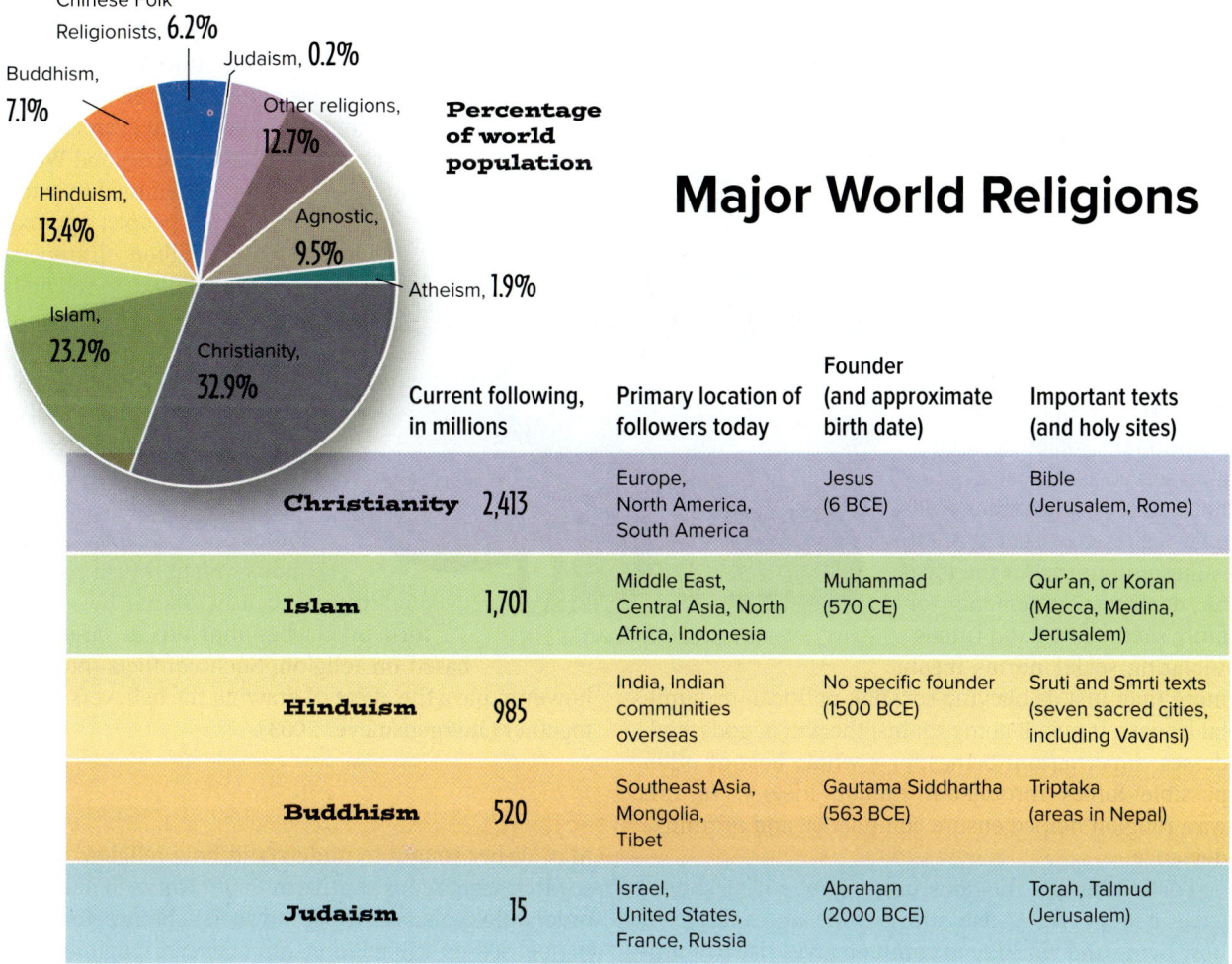

Major World Religions

Percentage of world population

- Chinese Folk Religionists, 6.2%
- Judaism, 0.2%
- Buddhism, 7.1%
- Other religions, 12.7%
- Hinduism, 13.4%
- Agnostic, 9.5%
- Atheism, 1.9%
- Islam, 23.2%
- Christianity, 32.9%

	Current following, in millions	Primary location of followers today	Founder (and approximate birth date)	Important texts (and holy sites)
Christianity	2,413	Europe, North America, South America	Jesus (6 BCE)	Bible (Jerusalem, Rome)
Islam	1,701	Middle East, Central Asia, North Africa, Indonesia	Muhammad (570 CE)	Qur'an, or Koran (Mecca, Medina, Jerusalem)
Hinduism	985	India, Indian communities overseas	No specific founder (1500 BCE)	Sruti and Smrti texts (seven sacred cities, including Vavansi)
Buddhism	520	Southeast Asia, Mongolia, Tibet	Gautama Siddhartha (563 BCE)	Triptaka (areas in Nepal)
Judaism	15	Israel, United States, France, Russia	Abraham (2000 BCE)	Torah, Talmud (Jerusalem)

Sources: Janssen 2017; Swatos 2011.

Buddhism developed in the sixth century BCE as a reaction against Hinduism. This faith is founded on the teachings of Siddhartha (later called Buddha, or "The Enlightened One"). Through meditation, followers of Buddhism strive to overcome selfish cravings for physical or material pleasures, with the goal of reaching a state of enlightenment, or nirvana. Buddhists created the first monastic orders, which are thought to be the models for monastic orders in other religions, including Christianity. Though Buddhism emerged in India, its followers were eventually driven out of that country by the Hindus. It is now found primarily in other parts of Asia.

Although the differences among religions are striking, they are exceeded by variations within faiths. Consider the differences within Christianity, from relatively liberal denominations such as Presbyterians or Episcopalians to the more conservative Mormons and Greek Orthodox Catholics. Similar divisions exist within Hinduism, Islam, and other world religions (Swatos 1998, 2011).

>> Sociological Perspectives on Religion

Sociology emerged as a discipline in the 19th century in the context of significant intellectual, political, and economic upheaval. Intellectuals at the time felt that the religious teachings that had guided society in times of crisis in the past were failing (Wilson 1999). Auguste Comte and other early sociologists sought to provide a science of society that would tap the ways of knowing built into the scientific method and apply them to the study of society. They recognized the significant role religion had played in maintaining social order in the past and believed it essential to understand how it had accomplished this. As a result, the study of religion became a significant topic for exploration in early sociology. Among classical theorists, for example, Émile Durkheim concluded that religion promoted social order; Max Weber maintained that it helped generate social change; and Karl Marx argued that it reinforced the interests of the powerful.

INTEGRATION

Durkheim, in keeping with the functionalist perspective he helped to establish, focused on religion's contribution to social integration. He argued that, in traditional societies, religion served as the social glue holding society together. Religion legitimized society's core values and norms in the form of doctrine, statements of faith, sacraments, and rituals. Violating social norms meant more than just disobeying societal, political, or familial leaders. It meant going against the will of gods, goddesses, supernatural beings, or a whole host of other possible forces throughout human history. In this way, religion helped ensure compliance and minimize deviance.

For Durkheim, religious unity grew out of shared experiences. The Amish still provide an example of how living and working in common gives rise to a unified faith (Kraybill et al. 2013). With the transition to modern society, however, especially given the rise of the division of labor, people no longer do all the same things together. We no longer possess the same knowledge and skill. As a result, religion's capacity to provide meaning and a shared sense of purpose is undercut. Yet we still see evidence of its integrating power in shared rituals today, including confessions of faith, bar and bat mitzvahs, public prayers, weddings, and funerals.

The integrative power of religion can be seen, too, in the role that churches, synagogues, and mosques have traditionally played and continue to play for immigrant groups in the United States. For example, Roman Catholic immigrants may settle near a parish church that offers services in their native language, such as Polish or Spanish. Similarly, Korean immigrants may join a Presbyterian church that has many Korean American members and follows religious practices similar to those of churches in Korea. Like other religious organizations, these Roman Catholic and Presbyterian churches help integrate immigrants into their new homeland (Peek 2005; Warner 2007).

©Pavel Filatov/Alamy Stock Photo RF

Religious integration, while unifying believers, can come at the expense of outsiders. In this sense, religion can contribute to tension and even conflict between groups or nations. During the Second World War, Nazi Germany attempted to exterminate the Jewish people; approximately 6 million European Jews were killed. In religious clashes, nations such as Lebanon (Muslims versus Christians), Israel (Jews versus Muslims, as well as Orthodox versus secular Jews), Northern Ireland (Roman Catholics versus Protestants), and India (Hindus versus Muslims and, more recently, Sikhs) have been torn by clashes that are in large part based on religion. Such conflicts often do, however, have the effect of drawing the believers closer together (Juergensmeyer 2003).

SOCIAL CHANGE

Max Weber sought to understand how religion, which so often seems conservative in that it works to maintain order, might also contribute to social change. To do so, he focused on the relationship between religious faith and the rise of capitalism. Weber's findings appeared in

Movies ON RELIGION

The Master
A charismatic religious leader recruits believers into The Cause.

Silence
Two priests face a crisis of faith while searching for their apostate mentor in Japan.

The Apostle
A Pentecostal preacher in the South seeks redemption from his sins.

Everything Is Illuminated
A young man explores his Jewish family's past.

The Tree of Life
An exploration on the meaning of life through the experiences of a 1950s Texas family.

5

his sociology classic, *The Protestant Ethic and the Spirit of Capitalism* ([1904] 2009), one of sociology's most well-known works.

Weber's Protestant Ethic Thesis Weber observed that in the European nations of his time, an overwhelming number of business leaders, owners of capital, and skilled workers were Protestant. He set out to discover why. Through his historical research, Weber concluded that this relationship between religious faith and economic success was a consequence of what he called the **Protestant ethic**—a disciplined commitment to worldly labor driven by a desire to bring glory to God that was shared by followers of Martin Luther and John Calvin starting with the Protestant Reformation in 1517. Weber argued that the Protestant combination of hard work and self-denial provided capitalism with an almost obsessive approach toward worldly labor that was essential to capitalism's development.

To explain the impact of the Protestant ethic on the rise of capitalism, Weber highlights three keys: Luther's concept of a calling, Calvin's concept of predestination, and Protestant believers' resulting experience of "salvation panic." According to Protestant reformer Martin Luther (1483–1546), God called all believers to their specific vocation in life, whether as peasant, baker, merchant, or priest. Believers wanted to work hard in their calling so as to bring glory to God, regardless of whether they were rich or poor. Protestant reformer John Calvin (1509–1564) added to this the concept of predestination, according to which God, before the beginning of time, chose who would go to heaven and who would go to hell. Before people were even born, the eternal fate of their souls was already established. Individuals could not earn salvation through good works; salvation was totally dependent on the grace of God. Complicating this was that no individual could ever know for sure that he or she was saved because none could presume to know the mind of God. Weber concluded that this created a sense of salvation panic among believers, who wanted assurance that they were going to heaven.

Weber theorized that believers would seek to resolve this uncertainty by leading the kinds of lives they thought God would expect godly people to lead. This meant hard work, humility, and self-denial, not for the sake of salvation or individual gain, but for the sake of God. Although doing so would not earn them salvation, to do otherwise would be an almost certain sign that they were not among the chosen. But they could never fully be sure, so they could never let up in their commitment to do God's will. Thus they worked hard not because they had to (either for subsistence or because they were forced) but because they wanted to

> **Protestant ethic** Max Weber's term for the disciplined commitment to worldly labor driven by a desire to bring glory to God, shared by followers of Martin Luther and John Calvin.

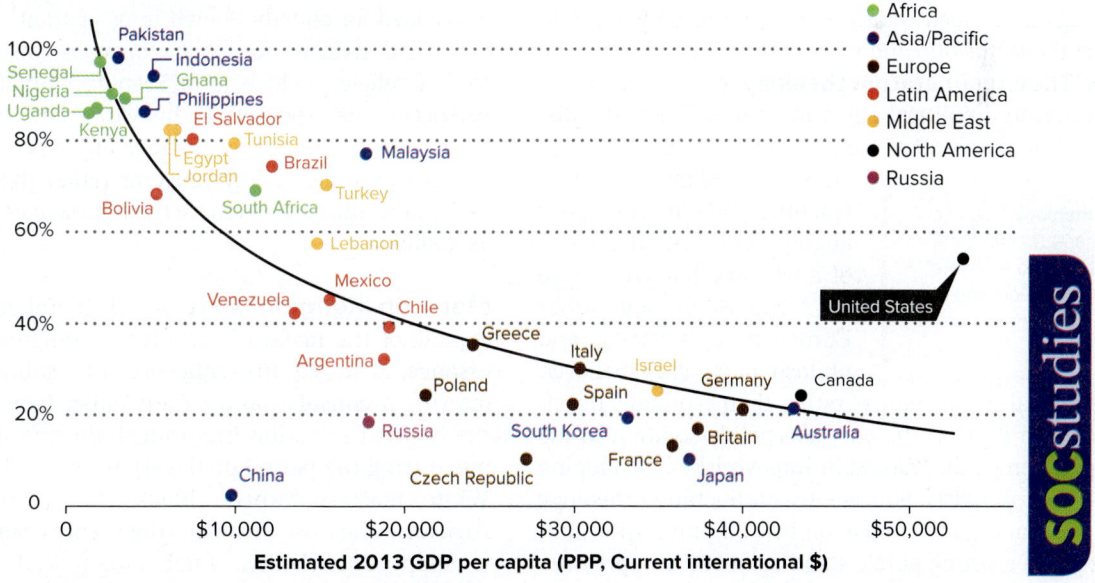

Religious Faith and Economic Well-Being

The curve represents the logarithmic relationship between GDP per capita and the percentage who say that religion plays a very important role in their lives. Notice that the United States is an outlier, falling far from the curve, when it comes to people's continued faith in religion compared to other advanced economies. What factors do you think might contribute to this difference?

Source: Gao 2015.

in response to the salvation they hoped would come from God. It was precisely this kind of worker, internally motivated to work hard and willing to show up every day even after getting paid, that capitalism needed if it was to engage in rationally planned production. This "spirit of capitalism," to use Weber's phrase, contrasted with the moderate work hours, leisurely work habits, and lack of ambition that Weber saw as typical of traditional labor.

In this way, religion, in the form of the Protestant Reformation, contributed to the rise of capitalism, one of the most significant examples of social change in human history. Weber's argument has been hailed as one of the most important theoretical works in the field and as an excellent example of macrolevel analysis. Like Durkheim, Weber demonstrated that religion is not solely a matter of intimate personal beliefs. He stressed that the collective nature of religion has consequences for society as a whole.

Liberation Theology A more contemporary example of religion serving as a force for social change came through liberation theology, which has its roots in Latin America in the 1950s and 1960s. Many religious activists, especially Roman Catholic priests, when confronted with the poverty and social injustice of the region, decided the Church had a responsibility to reject the status quo and work actively on behalf of the poor. The term **liberation theology** refers to the use of a church in a political effort to eliminate poverty, discrimination, and other forms of injustice from a secular society. Many felt Jesus' teachings about the poor aligned better with the works of Karl Marx than with those of Adam Smith and other European economists and philosophers. They believed that radical social change, rather than economic development in itself, is the only acceptable solution to the desperation of the masses in impoverished developing countries. Activists associated with liberation theology believe that organized religion has a moral responsibility to take a strong public stand against the oppression of the poor, racial and ethnic minorities, and women (Bell 2001; Rowland 2007).

The term *liberation theology* dates back to the publication in 1973 of the English translation of *A Theology of Liberation*. The book was written by a Peruvian priest, Gustavo Gutiérrez, who lived in a slum area of Lima in the early 1960s. After years of exposure to the vast poverty around him, Gutiérrez concluded that "in order to serve the poor, one had to move into political action" (R. M. Brown 1980:23; Gutiérrez 1990). Eventually, politically committed Latin American theologians came under the influence of social scientists who viewed the domination of capitalist multinational corporations as central to the hemisphere's problems. One result was a new approach to theology that built on the cultural and religious traditions of Latin America rather than on models developed in Europe and the United States.

> But the poor person does not exist as an inescapable fact of destiny.... The poor are a by-product of the system in which we live and for which we are responsible.
>
> Liberation Theologian Gustavo Gutiérrez

Liberation theology Use of a church, primarily Roman Catholic, in a political effort to eliminate poverty, discrimination, and other forms of injustice from a secular society.

SOC THINK
To what extent do you think religion can be a force for positive social change? What examples have you seen in your lifetime?

SOCIAL CONTROL

Liberation theology is a relatively recent phenomenon that signals a break with the traditional role of Durkheim envisioned for churches—that is, as guarantors of social order and stability. Karl Marx opposed this traditional role of religion, which is in keeping with the conflict perspective he espoused. In his view, religion inhibited positive social change by encouraging oppressed people to focus on otherworldly concerns rather than working in the here-and-now to relieve their immediate poverty or exploitation.

Marx on Religion Marx described religion as the "opiate of the masses." He felt that religion often, in essence, drugged the believers into submission by offering a consolation for their harsh lives on earth: the hope of salvation in an ideal afterlife. For example, during the period of slavery in the United States, White masters forbade Blacks to practice native African religions. Instead, they encouraged slaves to adopt Christianity, which taught that obedience would lead to salvation and eternal happiness in the hereafter. Viewed from this perspective, Christianity may have pacified certain slaves and blunted the rage that often fuels rebellion.

©Mireille Vautier/Alamy Stock Photo

For Marx, religion plays an important role in propping up the existing social structure. The values of religion, as already noted, tend to reinforce other social institutions and the social order as a whole. From Marx's perspective, however, religion's promotion of social stability only helps perpetuate patterns of social inequality. According to Marx, the dominant religion reinforces the interests of those in power.

From a Marxist perspective, religion keeps people from seeing their lives and societal conditions in political terms—for example, by obscuring the overriding significance of conflicting economic interests. Marxists suggest that by inducing a "false consciousness" among the disadvantaged, religion lessens the possibility of collective political action that could end capitalist oppression and transform society. Sociological analysis in this tradition seeks to reveal the ways in which religion serves the interests of the powerful at the expense of others.

Gender and Religion Drawing on the feminist approach, researchers and theorists point to the critical role women play in the functioning of religious organizations. Women are more likely than men to say religion is important in their lives, more likely to pray daily, and more likely to attend weekly services. Women also play a vital role as volunteers,

©Syracuse Newspapers/The Image Works

staff, and religious educators. Yet when it comes to positions of leadership, women have typically been relegated to a subordinate role. Indeed, most faiths have a long tradition of exclusively male spiritual leadership. Furthermore, because most religions are patriarchal, religious beliefs tend to reinforce men's dominance in secular as well as spiritual matters. Exceptions to this rule, such as the Shakers and Christian Scientists, as well as Hinduism with its long goddess heritage, are relatively rare (Pew Research Center 2009a; Schaefer and Zellner 2007).

Social institution An integrated and persistent social network dedicated to ensuring that society's core needs are met.

In the United States, women compose 20.6 percent of the clergy, even though they account for 33 percent of students enrolled in theological institutions. Female clerics typically have shorter careers than men and are often relegated to fields that do not involve congregational leadership, such as counseling. In faiths that restrict leadership positions to men, women still serve unofficially. For example, about 4 percent of Roman Catholic congregations are led by women who hold nonordained pastoral positions—a necessity in a church that faces a shortage of male priests (J. Adams 2007; Association of Theological Schools 2016; Bureau of Labor Statistics 2016e:Table 11).

Chapter 8 / Education and Religion • 203

In this chapter we have looked at both education and religion. In both cases we find **social institutions** that play a powerful role in shaping how we think and act. Each provides opportunity and reinforces the status quo, including its system of inequality. Sociologists believe that by having a better appreciation for both the opportunities and constraints such institutions present, we can better act both individually and collectively to bring about positive social change.

SOCIOLOGY IS A VERB

Exploring Faith

Pick a local religious group that is significantly different from any you may have experienced in the past. Study their history, beliefs, rituals, expectations, and structure. Interview one of their local religious leaders to gain a better understanding of their beliefs and practices from an insider's point of view. If it's okay with them, visit their services at least twice. What were your initial expectations about the group? How, if at all, did your views change?

[FOR REVIEW]

I. How does education help maintain social order?
- Education transmits culture, promotes social integration, provides training and social control, stimulates cultural innovation, and provides child care.

II. How does education support the existing system of inequality?
- Education reinforces the status quo, and therefore its existing inequalities, through the hidden curriculum, teacher expectancy, bestowal of status, and credentialism.

III. How do sociologists define religion?
- One approach focuses on the substance of what religion is, defining religion as knowledge and beliefs relating to the sacred realm. The other approach looks at what religions do for society in terms of social order and integration. Both approaches analyze common components including belief, ritual, experience, and community.

SOCVIEWS on Education and Religion

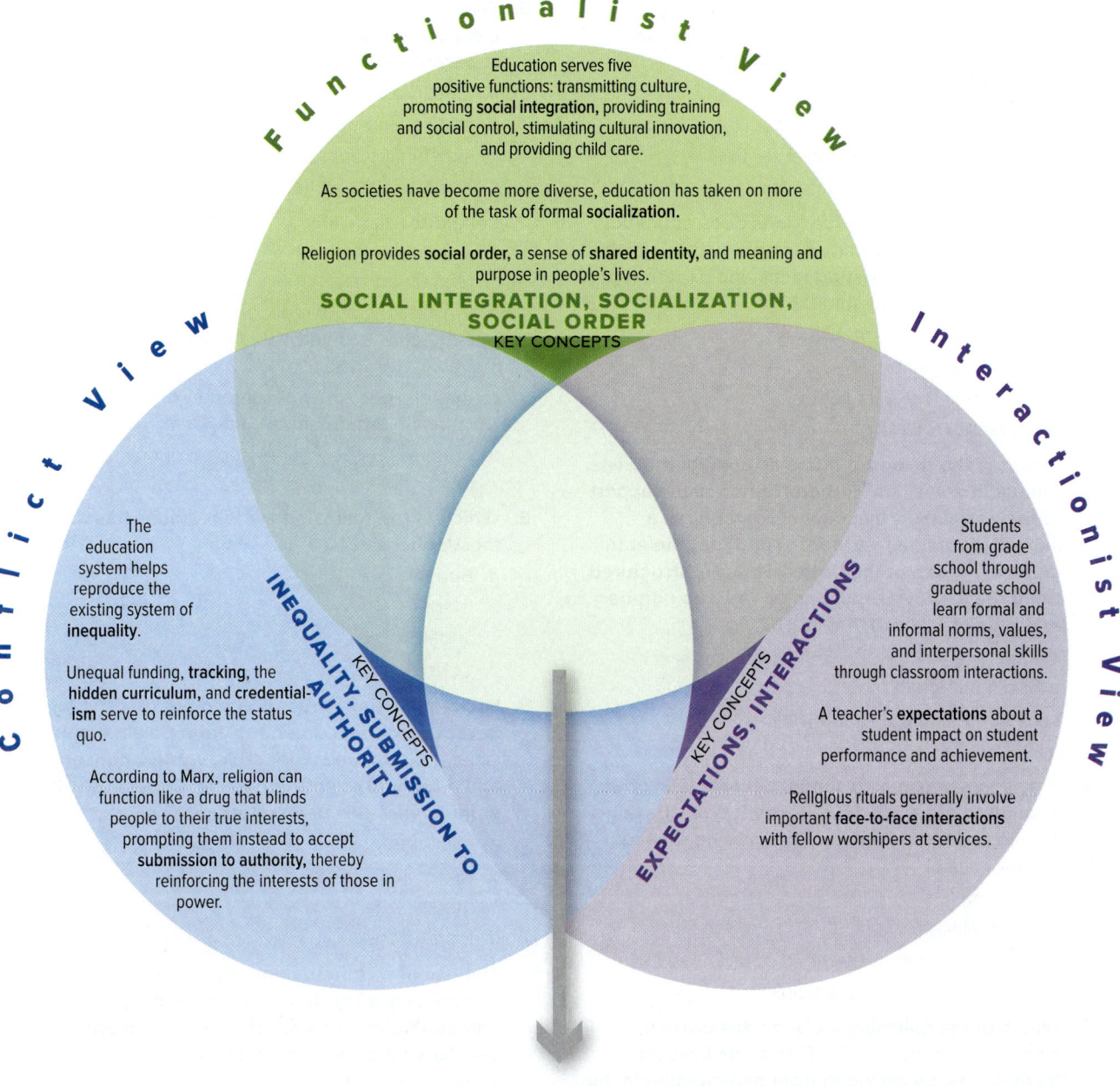

Functionalist View
Education serves five positive functions: transmitting culture, promoting **social integration**, providing training and social control, stimulating cultural innovation, and providing child care.

As societies have become more diverse, education has taken on more of the task of formal **socialization**.

Religion provides **social order**, a sense of **shared identity**, and meaning and purpose in people's lives.

SOCIAL INTEGRATION, SOCIALIZATION, SOCIAL ORDER
KEY CONCEPTS

Conflict View
The education system helps reproduce the existing system of **inequality**.

Unequal funding, **tracking**, the **hidden curriculum**, and **credentialism** serve to reinforce the status quo.

According to Marx, religion can function like a drug that blinds people to their true interests, prompting them instead to accept **submission to authority**, thereby reinforcing the interests of those in power.

KEY CONCEPTS
INEQUALITY, SUBMISSION TO AUTHORITY

Interactionist View
Students from grade school through graduate school learn formal and informal norms, values, and interpersonal skills through classroom interactions.

A teacher's **expectations** about a student impact on student performance and achievement.

Religious rituals generally involve important **face-to-face interactions** with fellow worshipers at services.

KEY CONCEPTS
EXPECTATIONS, INTERACTIONS

MAKE THE CONNECTION
After reviewing the chapter, answer the following questions:

1
The "Education Pays" graph shows higher income as one benefit of more education. Using each perspective, how else does education pay? Who benefits?

2
How do educational institutions bestow status according to both the functionalist and conflict perspectives?

3
Using the conflict perspective, describe how women experience (or have experienced) discrimination in both the educational and religious spheres.

4
Which perspective do you think best describes the dynamics of a typical classroom setting? Explain, including examples.

Chapter 8 / Education and Religion • 205

Pop Quiz

1. According to Horace Mann, often called the "father of American public education," what role does education play in society?
   a. It is the great equalizer.
   b. It is the opiate of the masses.
   c. It is an instrument for social control.
   d. It is an opportunity engine.

2. Which of the following functions does education fulfill by providing an environment within which we can challenge existing ideas and experiment with new norms and values?
   a. culture transmission
   b. social integration
   c. training and social control
   d. cultural innovation

3. Which of the following terms do conflict theorists Samuel Bowles and Herbert Gintis use in support of their argument that capitalism requires a skilled, disciplined labor force and that the educational system of the United States is structured primarily to provide companies with the number and type of workers they need?
   a. tracking
   b. credentialism
   c. the correspondence principle
   d. the teacher-expectancy effect

4. Fifty years ago, a high school diploma was often enough to get a good job. Today it typically takes a college degree or more. This change reflects the process of
   a. tracking.
   b. credentialism.
   c. the hidden curriculum.
   d. the correspondence principle.

5. Which of the following includes this provision, "No person in the United States shall, on the basis of sex, be excluded from participation in, be denied the benefits of, or be subjected to discrimination under any education program or activity receiving Federal financial assistance?"
   a. Title IX of the Education Amendments of 1972
   b. *Brown v. Board of Education of Topeka* (1954)
   c. No Child Left Behind Act of 2001
   d. Higher Education Opportunity Act of 2008

6. The approach to defining religion that emphasizes the significance of the sacred, most often supernatural, realm is known as the
   a. functionalist approach.
   b. conflict approach.
   c. substantive approach.
   d. ecclesia approach.

7. Religious rituals are
   a. statements to which members of a particular religion adhere.
   b. the feelings or perceptions of being in direct contact with the ultimate reality, such as a divine being.
   c. the religious structures through which faith communities organize themselves.
   d. practices required or expected of members of a faith.

8. Which of the following world religions has the most adherents?
   a. Buddhism
   b. Islam
   c. Judaism
   d. Christianity

9. Sociologist Max Weber pointed out that the followers of Martin Luther and John Calvin emphasized a disciplined work ethic, worldly concerns, and a rational orientation to life. Collectively, this point of view has been referred to as
   a. capitalism.
   b. the Protestant ethic.
   c. the sacred.
   d. the profane.

10. The use of a church, primarily Roman Catholic, in a political effort to eliminate poverty, discrimination, and other forms of injustice evident in a secular society is referred to as
    a. creationism.
    b. ritualism.
    c. religious experience.
    d. liberation theology.

1. (a), 2. (d), 3. (c), 4. (b), 5. (a), 6. (a), 7. (d), 8. (d), 9. (b), 10. (d)

©Bill Sikes/AP Images

9 Economy and Politics

TRUMPED

On November 8, 2016, in an election result that surprised even the winner, Donald Trump defeated Hillary Clinton to become the 45th president of the United States of America. A string of five states—Iowa, Wisconsin, Michigan, Ohio, and Pennsylvania—were decisive in tilting the results in Trump's favor. Democrat Barack Obama won all five in 2012, but in 2016 each went for the Republican candidate. In seeking an explanation, analysts pointed to the influence of White working-class (WWC) voters (Cohn 2016; Levitz 2016). But what did these voters want? Years before the 2016 election, sociologist Arlie Russell Hochschild (2016) had been pursuing the answer to that question.

Hochschild had noticed a wide chasm between her sensibilities as a White, politically liberal, upper-middle-class sociology professor living in Berkeley, California, and those of rural, White, politically conservative, working-class Americans. To better understand the world through their eyes, she headed to rural Louisiana, where over the course of five years, she conducted focus groups, carried out interviews, attended church services, and went to political rallies. She concluded that many attempts at understanding WWC voters, including those pointing toward racism or economic inequality, fall short because they do not address the emotional foundation of WWC political stances.

Most WWC members, according to Hochschild, accept competition as a normal part of life and understand that there will be winners and losers. But they also believe that those who work hard and play by the rules should receive their just reward. In recent years, however, many WWC'ers said that their progress toward the American Dream had stalled. For disrupting their progress, Hochschild's subjects blamed an increasing number of people they saw as undeserving because they broke the rules by cutting in line in front of them, including poor people who receive government assistance,

African Americans who benefit from affirmative action, immigrants from Mexico, professionals from India and China, refugees from Syria, and others who they believe receive unearned advantages, often in the form of government help. To make matters worse, the WWC heard voices from America's cultural elites dismissing them as ignorant, Bible-thumping, White trash rednecks. They felt like strangers in their own land and concluded that the system was rigged. They awaited a champion who would fix things, when along came Donald Trump.

Donald Trump's claim that "We're losing at everything" resonated with their fears about the economy. His pledge to "Make America Great Again" tapped into their hope that things can get better. As Hochschild put it, "Joined together with others like themselves, they now feel hopeful, joyous, elated" (2016:225). In Trump, they believe they have found a champion who will restore their honor and ensure their success.

By drawing on the sociological imagination, Hochschild came to understand her informants' perceptions of reality. Her work represents a classic example of sociology's fundamental commitment to clarifying why people think and act as they do. In this chapter, we explore politics and the economy so that we might know how the positions we occupy within these institutions shape us.

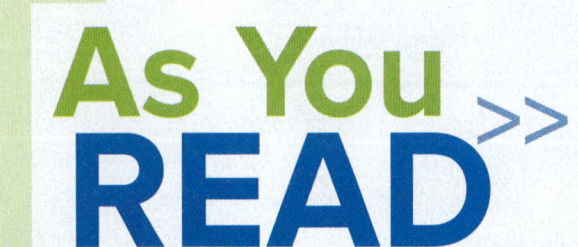

- How are economic and political power organized?
- How does power operate?
- How has the economy changed over time?

>> Economic Change

The election of Donald Trump was a manifestation of widespread frustration about the state of the economy and politics in the United States. Bernie Sanders tapped into a similar vein before losing to Hillary Clinton in the Democratic primaries, though his supporters tended to be younger, more urban, and have higher levels of educational attainment. To some extent the dissatisfaction both groups felt was a carry-over from the global recession that was triggered by a financial crisis that started in 2007 when stocks crashed, businesses went bankrupt, unemployment skyrocketed, and governments around the world struggled to figure out how to respond. Since that time, economic conditions improved, but many people felt progress was too slow and that the benefits of the recovery were unevenly distributed.

Using the sociological imagination allows us to better understand economic and political change. Doing so highlights the fact that the economic and political systems we construct influence likely outcomes for individuals. Adopting a capitalist economy or a democratic system of government leads us down different paths than we would likely have followed had we adopted alternatives. In other words, structures have consequences.

©Timothy A. Clary/AFP/Getty Images

ECONOMIC SECTORS

Focusing on the structure of the economy enables us to better see how the statuses we occupy within groups, social networks, and social institutions shape the options and opportunities available to us. As we saw in the "Sociological Imagination" section in Chapter 1, for example, high unemployment rates must be addressed as a public issue rather than as a private trouble only, because rate increases reflect changes in the economic structure. The **economy** is a social institution dedicated to the production, distribution, and consumption of goods and services. The structure of the economy varies across time and place, but we can identify three distinct sectors: primary, secondary, and tertiary.

As a species, we must provide for our subsistence needs. Without food, clothes, and shelter we will die. Throughout human history, we have most frequently ensured our survival by taking from nature the things that we need. The **primary sector** of the economy involves activities that extract products directly from the natural environment. The most important manifestation of this for us historically was the rise of agriculture, but extraction also includes activities such as fishing, hunting, forestry, and mining. The economies of the hunting-and-gathering, horticultural, and agrarian societies we encountered in the "Technology and Society" section of Chapter 5 were characterized primarily by this economic sector.

The Industrial Revolution fundamentally altered our relationship to nature. Advances in technology, including Eli Whitney's cotton gin, Cyrus McCormick's mechanical reaper, and John Deere's steel plow, all contributed to the mass production of agricultural products. As a result, fewer agricultural workers were needed to produce food, freeing them up for work in the new factories that arose due to technological innovations in industrial production. The **secondary sector** of the economy consists of activities that transform raw or intermediate materials into finished products. Workers in this sector manufacture products. The mechanization of production contributed to revolutions in transportation and communication, which effectively made the world a much smaller place. It became possible to communicate in real time with whomever we wanted, whenever we wanted, or to travel to the other side of the globe in a matter of hours. As a result, companies can now obtain raw materials from almost anywhere, transform them into products, and sell those products to customers around the world.

Technological innovation continued to the point where industrial production also became less labor intensive. The mechanization of production meant that fewer workers were needed in manufacturing, once again freeing them up for new jobs that contributed to the expansion of a third economic sector. The **tertiary sector** of the economy consists of activities that provide services rather than produce tangible goods. Put simply, the service sector involves doing things for others rather than offering them a material product. Service-sector occupations include teacher, physician, social worker, food server, hotel housekeeper, truck driver, data processor, financial adviser, investment counselor, insurance agent, real estate broker, custodian, actor, personal trainer, and life coach (U.S. Census Bureau 2013a). Most college students today are pursuing degrees in hopes of obtaining a good job in this sector.

Recent college graduates hope to find good jobs in the service sector with incomes high enough to pay off the student loans they took out to get the training necessary for those jobs. ©Tony Savino/Contributor/Getty Images

DEINDUSTRIALIZATION

When a society's economic foundation transitions from one economic sector to another, significant upheaval occurs. Moving from a traditional, agriculturally based economy to a modern, industrial economy, as happened during the Industrial Revolution, had traumatic consequences for how people lived and worked. Sociology emerged as a discipline in order to come to terms with its effects. The ongoing transition to an economy built upon the tertiary or service sector has proved no less challenging.

The consequences of this shift became apparent starting in the 1970s when the U.S. economy moved away from its manufacturing base through a process known as **deindustrialization,** which refers to the systematic and widespread reduction of investment in domestic manufacturing and material production. Two key factors play a role in its expansion. The first is the mechanization of labor. Through technological innovation, a single machine can do the job of many workers. The coordination of production in the form of the assembly line multiplied that effect, and the advent of robots and computers expanded it even further.

> **Economy** A social institution dedicated to the production, distribution, and consumption of goods and services.
>
> **Primary sector** The segment of the economy involving activities that extract products directly from the natural environment.
>
> **Secondary sector** The segment of the economy consisting of activities that transform raw or intermediate materials into finished products.
>
> **Tertiary sector** The segment of the economy consisting of activities that provide services rather than produce tangible goods.
>
> **Deindustrialization** The systematic and widespread reduction of investment in domestic manufacturing and material production.

Economist John Maynard Keynes (1930a, 1930b) referred to the resulting loss of jobs as "technological unemployment." In such a situation, productivity can remain high while the number of secondary-sector jobs, along with their level of wages, declines (Carr 2014; Rotman 2013; A. Smith and Anderson 2014). The second factor is the globalization of labor. In the United States, this began with companies moving their industrial production plants from the nation's central cities to the suburbs, then to the South where labor laws were weaker, and finally out of the country where wages were lower and health, safety, and environmental regulations were less restrictive. At the same time, many companies sought to become leaner and did so by **downsizing,** organizational restructuring to reduce the size of a company's workforce. The goal of downsizing is to increase efficiency and reduce costs in the face of worldwide competition.

©Josh Cornish/Shutterstock.com RF

> **SOC THINK**
>
> If you were the CEO of an American manufacturing company that was facing declining profits because of international competition, what would you do? Would you move your production facilities overseas to reduce labor costs? What other options might exist? To what extent does the system within which companies operate shape the choices that are available to them?

Companies are also able to leverage their economic assets by subcontracting tasks that used to be performed within the firm. Such outsourcing happens domestically, for example, when a company hires an external firm to provide security or janitorial services. Companies can take this a step further by **offshoring,** which involves outsourcing work to foreign contractors. This practice hit the manufacturing sector first, as happened when U.S. television companies contracted with Chinese manufacturing firms to produce their TVs. But it is increasingly affecting service-sector jobs as well, due to advanced telecommunications and the growth of skilled, English-speaking workers in developing nations that have relatively inexpensive labor forces. These jobs can require considerable training, such as accounting and financial analysis, computer programming, or radiology. Today, it is increasingly possible that the person reading your CT scan or MRI is located in another country (Clark, Huckman, and Staats 2013; Olofsson et al. 2014).

Downsizing Organizational restructuring to reduce the size of a company's workforce.

Offshoring Outsourcing of work to foreign contractors.

Although this shift has brought jobs and technology to nations such as India, there is a downside to offshoring for foreign workers as well. Outsourcing is a significant source of employment for India's upper-middle class, but hundreds of millions of other Indians have benefited little if at all from the trend. Most households in India do not possess any form of high technology: only about 2.3 percent have land lines and 71 percent have cell phones, and 15 percent are Internet users (International Telecommunications Union 2015). Instead of improving these people's lives, the new business centers have siphoned water and electricity away from those who are most in need. Even the high-tech workers are experiencing negative consequences. Many suffer from stress disorders such as stomach problems and difficulty sleeping; more than half quit their jobs before the end of a year (Padma et al. 2015; Waldman 2004a, 2004b, 2004c).

THE GREAT RECESSION

The process of deindustrialization was part of a larger economic shift toward a global economy consisting of complex, worldwide networks of producers and consumers. The resulting interdependent connections increased the possibility that, if one part of the system collapsed, it could have global consequences. That is precisely what happened starting in 2007 when the previously mentioned global financial collapse occurred. The resulting economic crisis, often referred to as the Great Recession, had significant and long-term consequences. People's taken-for-granted assumptions about how their lives would and should proceed—get a good education, work hard in your job, and success will follow—were called into question (Packer 2013).

The recession hit workers hard. Unemployment became a widespread problem. Rates more than doubled from February 2008 to October 2010 and did not return to their pre-recession levels until late 2016. On top of that, increasing numbers of people experienced long-term unemployment (Pew Charitable Trusts 2012). Among those who were working, wages were flat for most and fell for many. Average family income fell 17.4 percent from 2007 to 2009, the largest two-year decline since the Great Depression (Saez 2016). Incomes for young adults were particularly hard hit. The percentage of 18- to 24-year-olds *in the paid labor force* reached a record low of 54 percent, and their wages declined more than those of any other age group since the economic downturn began (Levanon, Chen, and Chang 2012; Pew Research Center 2012). A record percentage of young adults turned toward higher education, which accounts for part of their decreased employment rate (P. Taylor 2011). The hope for many was that getting a degree would bolster their employability, yet the job prospects for recent college graduates also dimmed.

Among recent college graduates, 43 percent reported they were working in jobs that did not require a college degree (Stone, Van Horn, and Zukin 2012). On top of that, most graduates had incurred substantial student loan debt to get their degrees. For college graduates in the Class of 2015, the average student loan debt was $30,100 (Project on Student Debt 2016). Among those who graduated with college debt, 27 percent had balances that were past due, and 27 percent moved in with parents or family members to save money. More than 70 percent of those with student loans who earn less than $50,000 per year worry about their ability to pay them back (Austin 2013; Brown et al. 2012; Cooper and Wang 2014; Stone et al. 2012).

SOCTHINK
What role have larger economic trends, such as rising and falling unemployment rates, had on you, your friends, and family? How might current economic trends affect your plans for the future?

For many people, bad news seemed everywhere. In the years following the Great Recession, the number of people who were working yet not earning enough to get out of poverty increased (Smiley and West 2012), as did the age at which people could expect to retire (Brandon 2012). Since then, conditions have improved. Average family incomes rose 13 percent from 2009 to 2015. But not everyone shared the benefits of a stronger economy. The number of jobs requiring more education, training, and experience has grown faster than the number requiring less, and wages for jobs requiring higher social and analytical skills have risen faster than for those requiring physical skills. Income for the top 1 percent of the population grew 37.4 percent, while the bottom 99 percent saw only a 7.6 percent increase (Pew Research Center 2016c; Saez 2016). Corporations also did well, earning record profits in part because they reduced their costs by cutting their workforce and expecting more productivity from their remaining employees (Tully 2012).

THE CHANGING FACE OF THE WORKFORCE

In the same way that the larger structure of the economy has shifted over time, the makeup of the workforce in the United States has also changed. During World War II, when men were mobilized to fight abroad, women entered the workforce in large numbers. With the coming of the civil rights movement in the 1960s, minorities found numerous job opportunities opening to them. Sociologists and labor specialists foresaw a workforce increasingly composed of women and racial and ethnic minorities. In 1970, women made up 38 percent of the civilian labor force. By 2015, that number stood at 47 percent. Overall, 57 percent of women aged 16 and up were in the paid labor force, compared to 69 percent for men (Bureau of Labor Statistics 2017b). The dynamics for minority group workers are even more dramatic,

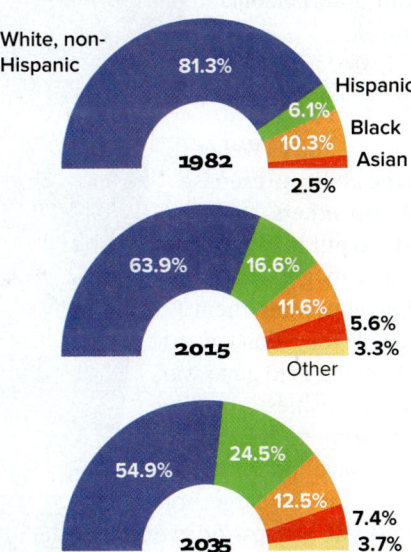

Workforce Diversity: Past, Present, and Future

Percentage of the workforce

1982:
- White, non-Hispanic: 81.3%
- Hispanic: 6.1%
- Black: 10.3%
- Asian: 2.5%

2015:
- White, non-Hispanic: 63.9%
- Hispanic: 16.6%
- Black: 11.6%
- Asian: 5.6%
- Other: 3.3%

2035:
- White, non-Hispanic: 54.9%
- Hispanic: 24.5%
- Black: 12.5%
- Asian: 7.4%
- Other: 3.7%

Note: "Other" includes American Indian and Alaska Native, Hawaiian and Other Pacific Islander, and People of Two or More Races. Numbers may not add up to 100 owing to categorization of White, non-Hispanic.
Sources: Bureau of Labor Statistics 2010, 2015c; Toossi 2004.

as the number of Black, Latino, and Asian American workers continues to increase at a faster rate than the number of White workers, owing to demographic changes, as the accompanying "Workforce Diversity" graph demonstrates (Burns, Barton, and Kerby 2012).

As the workforce has become more diverse, companies have sought ways to adapt. A sociological study of workplace programs designed to increase managerial diversity found that 39 percent of employers had diversity training programs. Researchers discovered that relying solely on education programs designed to reduce managerial bias was not particularly effective. The most successful approach is to have a point person, task force, or affirmative action plan that holds people responsible for change (Bezrukova, Jehn, and Spell 2012; Kalev, Dobbin, and Kelly 2006).

Power The ability to exercise one's will over others even if they resist.

Force The actual or threatened use of coercion to impose one's will on others.

Authority Power that is recognized as legitimate by the people over whom it is exercised.

>> Power and Authority

Sociologists have always been interested in how power is achieved and maintained. In the midst of major political and economic shifts, early sociologists developed theories of power intended to be sufficiently broad to explain the rise of democracy or the expansion of market-based capitalism yet sufficiently narrow to explain who gets their way within interpersonal relationships.

POWER

According to Max Weber, **power** is the ability to exercise one's will over others, even if they resist. To put it another way, if you can get others to do what you want them to do even if they don't want to—whether that is to go to war, coordinate a business meeting, clean their room, or even take an exam—you have power. Power relations can involve large organizations, small groups, or even people in intimate relationships.

Weber conceived of power as a continuum based on the extent to which it is accepted as legitimate by those over whom it is exercised. On one end is **force**, the actual or threatened use of coercion to impose one's will on others. When leaders imprison or execute political dissidents, they are applying force; so, too, are terrorists when they seize or bomb an embassy or assassinate a political leader. Slave-based economies typically rely on force. Such systems are not terribly efficient because of the policing costs necessary to make people do what they do not want to do.

On the other end of the continuum is what Weber calls **authority,** power that is recognized as legitimate by the people over whom it is exercised. This type of power depends on people's faith in their leader's right to rule. In a democracy, for example, the fact that people continue to obey the laws even if their candidate loses an election demonstrates their underlying faith in the legitimacy of the system. The presidential election in 2016 tested that faith when Hillary Clinton received 2,864,974 more votes nationally than did Donald Trump, yet Trump won the election.

This outcome was possible because in the U.S. system, Trump received more electoral votes, and those are the votes that determine who wins. By edging out Clinton in Wisconsin by 0.7 percent, Michigan by 0.2 percent, and Pennsylvania by 0.7 percent, Trump received all the electoral votes of those states, giving him the margin to win even though more individuals voted for Clinton nationally (Wasserman 2016). People's willingness to accept that result depends completely on their faith in the legitimacy of the electoral system in place. Weber views authority as more efficient than force because the motivation to obey comes from inside the follower rather than having to be externally imposed.

TYPES OF AUTHORITY

Weber identified three major types of authority: traditional, charismatic, and rational-legal. Often, the legitimacy of leaders depends primarily upon only one, although elements of all three can be present at the same time.

Prince William, pictured with his wife Catherine, is second in line to become king of the United Kingdom. ©Samir Hussein/WireImage/Getty Images

Traditional Authority In a political system based on **traditional authority**, legitimate power is conferred by custom and accepted practice. In other words, past practice justifies our present actions. As Weber put it, such authority rests in the belief that "everyday routine [provides] an inviolable norm of conduct" ([1922] 1958d:296). We do things the way we do because we have always done them that way. The emperor, queen, or tribal leader may be loved or hated, competent or destructive; in terms of legitimacy, that does not matter. For the traditional leader, authority depends on people's faith in custom, not in the leader's personal appeal, technical competence, or even written law. In England, for example, the right of kings and queens to rule, which people believed was ordained by God, went largely unquestioned for hundreds of years. Now, however, the power of royals to make policy has largely passed to Parliament, and the role of the Royal Family is largely ceremonial.

Charismatic Authority According to Weber's second type of authority, power can be legitimized by the charisma of an individual. **Charismatic authority** refers to power made legitimate by a leader's exceptional personal or emotional appeal to his or her followers. For example, Joan of Arc was a simple peasant girl in medieval France. Because people believed in her and the causes she represented, she was able to rally the French people and lead them into major battles against English invaders despite having no formally recognized position of power.

Charisma lets a person such as Joan of Arc lead without relying on set rules or traditions. In fact, charismatic authority is derived more from the beliefs of followers than from the actual qualities of leaders. So long as people perceive a charismatic leader such as Jesus, Joan of Arc, Mahatma Gandhi, Malcolm X, or Martin Luther King, Jr., as having qualities that set him or her apart from ordinary citizens, that leader's authority will remain secure and often unquestioned (Adair-Toteff 2005; Potts 2009). That unfortunately is also the case with malevolent figures such as Adolf Hitler, whose charismatic appeal turned people toward violent and destructive ends in Nazi Germany.

Religious and political leaders often rely on charismatic authority. For both, the power of persuasion and the ability to charm can be important assets. Religious leaders, for example, often make the bold claim that they speak on behalf of higher spiritual powers, such as gods and goddesses. They frequently call followers to make sacrifices in terms of time and money and, in extreme cases, even death. Political leaders, especially in democratic societies where they must persuade citizens to vote for them, rely on their ability to inspire. As we saw at the beginning of this chapter, a critical dimension of Donald Trump's success with White, working-class voters was his capacity to inspire hope.

People's faith in Mahatma Gandhi as a charismatic leader contributed to India's independence from Britain in 1947. ©Elliot & Fry/Hulton Archive/Getty Images

Did You Know?

...In January 2013, Hillary Clinton had a 56 percent favorable rating in national polls. By Election Day in 2016, her favorable rating fell to 42 percent, and her unfavorable rating stood at 55. Donald Trump, by contrast, had a 57 percent unfavorable rating on Election Day.

Photo: ©Brooks Kraft/Getty Images

> **Traditional authority** Legitimate power conferred by custom and accepted practice.
>
> **Charismatic authority** Power made legitimate by a leader's exceptional personal or emotional appeal to his or her followers.
>
> **Rational-legal authority** Authority based on formally agreed-upon and accepted rules, principles, and procedures of conduct that are established in order to accomplish goals in the most efficient manner possible.

Rational-Legal Authority Weber's third type of authority, **rational-legal authority,** involves formally agreed-on and accepted rules, principles, and procedures of conduct that are established to accomplish goals in the most efficient manner possible. Bureaucracies are the purest form of rational-legal authority. As we saw in the "Bureaucracy" section of Chapter 5, in a bureaucracy there's a hierarchy of authority, areas of expertise are clearly defined, rules and regulations guide decision making, people are judged

Personal Sociology

Because I Said So

I am astonished at how often my daughters, Emily and Eleanor, do what I ask. When they were little, if they disobeyed, they had to "sit in the green chair." It wasn't much of a punishment. The chair was located in our living room in full view of the television and not isolated from the rest of the family. In time, just the threat of having to sit there was enough. Eventually they simply accepted the traditional authority of "because I said so" as sufficient justification. Of course, as they grew, they began to question the legitimacy of my authority, seeking reasons for why they should obey. As a result, I often came up with rational justifications for why they should do or not do something. And yet, even now, they are usually willing to do as I say simply because I am their dad.

based on their performance, and hiring occurs based on competence. Under rational-legal authority, if something occurs for which there are no guidelines indicating how to proceed, new rules will be created to cover how to act should it happen again. As a result, rules and regulations expand, and these systems tend to get bigger and bigger. This leads to concerns about inefficiencies, dehumanization, and dysfunction.

SOCTHINK

Which of these three forms of power do parents, bosses, or professors most rely on? Do individuals in these groups sometimes use each of the three types of power?

Analyzing power using Weber's model focuses our attention in a way that allows us to better understand economic and political relationships. The degree to which we accept the legitimacy of the people who rule over us shapes the kind of power they are likely to use. For example, when police confronted civil rights protestors in the 1950s and 1960s, they sometimes used force. Protestors were made to do things that they did not otherwise want to do, and failure to do so resulted in physical injury and jail time for some of those who questioned the legitimacy of the current system. Yet the presupposition that police and political leaders had the legitimate right to act in this way was widespread. As Weber suggested, when the legitimacy to rule is internalized in the form of authority, most people will comply with the wishes of the leader and will expect others to do likewise.

Capitalism An economic system in which owners of private property compete in the marketplace in pursuit of profit.

>> Economic Systems

For the most part, we accept the legitimacy of the economic systems within which we operate. We may even find it difficult to accept the viability of alternatives. Yet people throughout history and around the world continue to provide for their needs using varieties of economic principles, such as gift exchange, bartering, or shared ownership of goods. Analyzing the characteristics of the dominant economic systems of our time allows us to better understand how and why events happen as they do.

CAPITALISM

Capitalism is an economic system in which owners of private property compete in the marketplace in pursuit of profit. Value under capitalism is determined based on what people are willing and able to pay for available goods and services. The basic principles of capitalism were laid out by Adam Smith in his book *The Wealth of Nations* ([1776], 2003) including four key concepts: pursuit of profit, competition in the market, the law of supply and demand, and laissez-faire.

- *Pursuit of profit.* One of the basic presuppositions of capitalism is that, in our exchanges with others, human beings naturally seek to get the greatest return on their investments. This extends beyond economic exchanges (i.e., making a financial profit) to include social and cultural exchanges (in which even a conversation represents an exchange of symbolic resources such as status or attention). Under capitalism, humans are seen as naturally competitive, looking out for their own interests above all others. Pursuit of profit is presented as both morally acceptable and socially desirable.
- *Competition in the market.* The marketplace is the context in which we exchange goods and services (such as shoes, cell phones, and college degrees); we do so in competition with other producers and consumers. Competition keeps prices in check. The marketplace must be open to whoever has the ability to compete so that no individual or firm controls a disproportionate share of the market.
- *Law of supply and demand.* In a competitive marketplace, a natural balance will be reached between production and consumption at the appropriate

price. If the demand for a good or service is high and the supply is low, prices will go up, and vice versa. If a producer charges too much, another producer will step in to provide the good or service at a more reasonable price. Adam Smith described this process as the "invisible hand" of the marketplace through which prices reach their natural level. Companies that don't respond to the prompting of the invisible hand—for example, by charging too much or too little—will ultimately fail.

- *Laissez-faire.* The expression **laissez-faire** means "let them do [as they please]," and in this context it means that outside entities, especially the government, should not intervene in the marketplace. Instead, the market should be allowed to function free from external influence. Ideally, markets self-correct using the invisible hand. The capitalist model presupposes that, though governments may mean well, they cannot bring about a better result for society as a whole than can individuals who are allowed to compete on their own. In capitalism, the greatest social good is attained through the competition of profit-seeking individuals.

In practice, capitalism struggles to stick to these ideals because contradictions inevitably arise. On the one hand, capitalism tends toward the establishment of **monopolies,** in which a single business firm controls the market. Although the system needs competition, capitalists, in their pursuit of profits, seek to dominate the market to the point of monopolizing it. This violates the principle of competition. To ensure that monopolies do not form, governments often respond by intervening in the marketplace—through policies such as antitrust legislation—to ensure sufficient competition, thus violating the principle of laissez-faire. In addition, some goods and services (such as police, fire protection, roads, national defense, and public education) are deemed important enough for the public good to be provided for all, even at the expense of government intervention in those spheres.

Did You Know?

... In 2016, Walmart's annual net sales exceeded $479 billion with a gross profit margin of 24.6 percent.

Source: Walmart 2016. Photo: ©J.D. Poole/Getty Images

SOCIALISM

Socialism is an economic system in which the means of production and distribution in a society are collectively rather than privately owned. Value under socialism is determined by the amount of work it takes to produce products and the use we get out of those products. The basic principles of socialism were laid out by Karl Marx in the middle to late 1800s in a variety of publications, including *The Communist Manifesto,* which he coauthored with Friedrich Engels ([1847] 1955). Marx believed socialism to be inevitable because eventually, as a result of technological innovation, we would be able to produce enough so that everyone could have more than enough. At that point we would welcome socialism as a new system of social relations because the inequality that capitalism presupposes would no longer make sense. The following five presuppositions help clarify how he reached that conclusion.

> **Laissez-faire** The principle that people should be able to compete freely, without government interference, in the capitalist marketplace.
>
> **Monopoly** Control of a market by a single business firm.
>
> **Socialism** An economic system under which the means of production and distribution are collectively owned.

- *Humans must produce.* Unlike animals, humans lack the complex instincts that direct how we provide for our basic human needs (food, shelter, and clothing) from nature. Therefore, we must fulfill those basic needs through technological innovation and culture creation.
- *Production makes us uniquely human.* Our capacity to produce distinguishes humans from the rest of the natural world. It is this free and creative productive ability, what Marx referred to as labor power, that must be protected, nourished, and valued because it is at the core of our identity as humans.
- *We pour ourselves into our products.* For Marx, when we make something, we put part of who we are into each product; this is most apparent in craft labor. For example, a handmade bookshelf inspires pride because our labor power is the difference between the original stack of lumber and the finished shelf. To put it in an equation: *Raw materials + Labor power = Products.* According to Marx, we naturally find joy in labor and take pleasure in sharing the process and exchanging the products with others.
- *Economy determines society.* Marx argued that because our capacity and need to produce is at the core of who we are, it serves as the foundation for society. In essence, how we organize the economy determines all other forms of social relations, such as government, family, education, and religion. In most agrarian societies production is rooted in the land, so ownership and control of land becomes the foundation of power. Social institutions may reinforce the privileged position of landowners, for example, by

justifying a king's "divine right" to rule using religious authority. Over time, this material foundation shifts as our capacity to produce evolves through technological innovation. Eventually, the systems of social relations that grew out of that particular set of economic relations no longer match the new economic base, and a revolution to a new set of social relations occurs. Marx contended that this shift brought about the transition from feudalism to capitalism—when the agricultural power base that gave rise to royalty gave way to the industrial power base of capitalists and corporations—and he predicted it will shift again from capitalism to communism.

- *Scarcity and distribution are obstacles to the good of society.* For Marx, the ideal society is one in which we as humans have control over, and reap the full benefits of, our labor power. Until this point in history, however, no large-scale society has fully attained this ideal because we lacked the technological capacity to produce enough for everyone. This has resulted in social systems that divide the haves and have-nots: slavery's separation between masters and slaves, feudalism's separation between lords and peasants, capitalism's separation between owners and workers. Thanks to technological innovation—a consequence of our creative capacity to produce—we can eventually solve the problem of inadequate production. In fact, Marx praised capitalism because it ultimately solves this problem by placing pressure on producers for constant innovation. After we are technically capable of producing enough for all, any continued poverty, hunger, or extreme inequality is due to how we choose to distribute the products we make, rather than to our inability to produce enough. In other words, it's a social problem, solvable by the establishment of a new set of social relations that ensures equitable distribution. According to Marx, people will eventually decide that it doesn't make sense to maintain such economic extremes in the face of material abundance; thus a revolution in social relations toward socialism is inevitable.

Mixed economy An economic system that combines elements of both capitalism and socialism.

In practice, the socialist ideal of collective ownership has been difficult to attain. The grand experiment in what was known as the Soviet Union—uniting Russia and neighboring countries as one large socialist bloc—ultimately collapsed in 1989. It did so under the weight of bureaucratic inefficiency, political corruption, and insufficient productivity—problems that seem endemic to socialist states. In addition, past crackdowns on dissidents by the totalitarian socialist governments in both the Soviet Union and communist China led to the murders of millions of their own people, purportedly for the good of the state. Surveys in most of the former Soviet-bloc nations showed that people there approved of the transition from socialism toward democracy and free markets (Pew 2009b).

THE MIXED ECONOMY

In practice, national economic systems combine elements of both capitalism and socialism. A **mixed economy** features elements of more than one economic system. Starting from a socialist ideal and moving toward a mixed economy (as China has done in recent years) involves opening up some aspects of the state-controlled economy to competition and the free market. Conversely, moving from a capitalist ideal toward a mixed economy removes some goods and services from the competitive free market and provides them for all or subsidizes them to ensure broader access. In the United States, government provides us with certain goods and services, such as police and fire protection, roads, and public schools. Most agree that we should all have access to such public goods without regard for our ability to pay. There is currently a debate under way about whether health care should be considered a similar public good.

There has long been a debate in the United States about the degree to which the government should be involved in the economy, but the economic upheaval of the Great Recession challenged people's commitment to laissez-faire principles. Government officials decided that some companies were "too big to fail," meaning that the domino effect of their failure would be greater than the cost of violating the nonintervention ideal. The George W. Bush administration, itself a strong proponent of free-market principles, took the first steps toward government intervention in the economy during this crisis. In September 2008 it pushed the Troubled Assets Relief Program (TARP) through Congress to provide up to $700 billion to buy mortgage-backed

Li Keqiang assumed office as premier of the People's Republic of China in 2013. ©Feng Li - Pool/Getty Images

securities and to prop up the financial sector. The Obama administration continued along the same lines. For example, in an effort to kick-start the U.S. economy, Congress passed the American Recovery and Reinvestment Act in February 2009, providing almost $800 billion for infrastructure projects, education and health care funding, and tax cuts. And in June 2009, General Motors, which for years was the world's largest company, went bankrupt. The U.S. government stepped in and became its majority stockholder, owning 60 percent of its shares. These funds helped many firms survive that otherwise would have failed. Now that they are back on their feet, companies have paid back the loans they received from the government. For example, General Motors paid back its $8.4 billion of government

SOC THINK

Should the U.S. government let companies fail regardless of apparent economic consequences?

loans in full, with interest, and five years early. In 2013, the U.S. Department of Treasury sold off the last of its remaining shares of GM stock.

Though critics charged that Presidents Bush and Obama were moving the nation toward socialism, most people hoped that their efforts would minimize the negative effects the economic downturn had on their lives. The majority of citizens ultimately accepted these huge government expenditures as a means to save capitalism from its own excesses. Billionaire investor Warren Buffett later reflected on the government intervention and concluded, "Only one counterforce was available, and that was you, Uncle Sam. . . . Well, Uncle Sam, you delivered" (Buffett 2010).

> Nowadays people know the price of everything and the value of nothing.
>
> Oscar Wilde

THE INFORMAL ECONOMY

An informal economy operates within the confines of the dominant macroeconomic system in many countries, whether capitalist or socialist. In this **informal economy**, transfers of money, goods, or services take place but are not reported to the government. Examples of the informal economy include bartering, in which people trade goods and services with someone (for example, exchanging a haircut for a computer lesson), selling goods on the street, and engaging in illegal transactions, such as gambling or drug deals. Participants in this type of economy avoid taxes and government regulations.

In the developing world, governments often create burdensome business regulations that overworked bureaucrats must administer. When requests for licenses and permits pile up, delaying business projects, legitimate entrepreneurs find that they need to "go underground" to get anything done. Despite its apparent efficiency, this type of informal

> **Informal economy** Transfers of money, goods, or services that are not reported to the government.

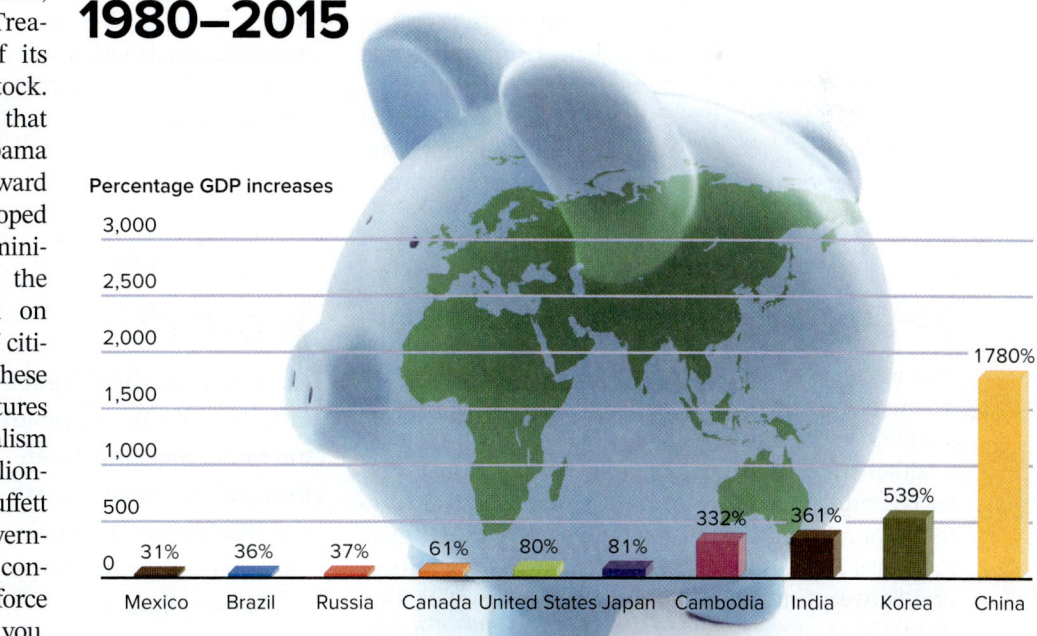

International Economic Growth, 1980–2015

Percentage GDP increases

- Mexico: 31%
- Brazil: 36%
- Russia: 37%
- Canada: 61%
- United States: 80%
- Japan: 81%
- Cambodia: 332%
- India: 361%
- Korea: 539%
- China: 1780%

Percentage Increase in per Capita GDP Growth, 1980–2015

Source: U.S. Department of Agriculture 2016. Photo: ©hidesy/Getty Images RF

economy is dysfunctional for a country's overall political and economic well-being. Because informal firms typically operate in remote locales to avoid detection, they cannot easily expand when they become profitable. And given the limited protection for their property and contractual rights, participants in the informal economy are less likely than others to save and invest their income.

> **SOC THINK**
>
> When doing jobs in the informal economy, such as babysitting, lawn mowing, housecleaning, or construction, it can be nice to get cash under the table without having to pay taxes, Social Security, and so on. What are the long-term disadvantages of doing so for the individual? What about for society? Why might someone opt to do so anyway?

Informal economies can also be dysfunctional for workers. Working conditions in these businesses are often unsafe or dangerous, and the jobs rarely provide any benefits to those who become ill or cannot continue to work. Perhaps more significant, the longer a worker remains in the informal economy, the less likely he or she is to make the transition to the regular economy. No matter how efficient or productive a worker may be, employers expect to see experience in the formal economy on a job application. Experience as a successful street vendor or self-employed cleaning person does not carry much weight with interviewers (Venkatesh 2006).

Politics The competition between individuals or groups over the allocation of valued resources.

Political system The social institution that is founded on a recognized set of procedures for implementing and achieving society's goals.

Monarchy A form of government headed by a single member of a royal family, usually a king, queen, or some other hereditary ruler.

Oligarchy A form of government in which a few individuals rule.

>> Political Systems

Just as new economic systems developed in response to broader historical changes, political systems also adapted. In all societies, someone or some group—whether it be a tribal chief, a dictator, a council, or a parliament—makes important decisions about how to use resources and allocate goods. Inevitably, the struggle for power and authority involves **politics,** the competition between individuals or groups over the allocation of valued resources. Politics takes place within the context of a **political system,** which is the social institution that is founded on a recognized set of procedures for implementing and achieving society's goals.

Government represents an institutionalized form of authority. Given the responsibilities governments have for establishing and enforcing laws and the scope of international relations and the globalization of national economies, these formal systems of authority make a significant number of critical political decisions. Such systems take a variety of forms, including monarchy, oligarchy, dictatorship, totalitarianism, and democracy.

MONARCHY

A **monarchy** is a form of government headed by a single member of a royal family, usually a king, queen, or some other hereditary ruler. In earlier times, many monarchs claimed that God had granted them a divine right to rule. Typically, they governed on the basis of traditional authority, sometimes accompanied by the use of force. By the beginning of the 21st century, however, relatively few monarchs held genuine political power. Queen Elizabeth II in England, for example, serves primarily in a ceremonial capacity.

OLIGARCHY

An **oligarchy** is a form of government in which a few individuals rule. A venerable method of governing that flourished in ancient Greece and Egypt, oligarchy now often takes the form of military rule. In developing nations in Africa, Asia, and Latin America, small factions of military officers may forcibly seize power, either

Did You Know?

. . . One of Queen Elizabeth's official duties is to appoint the prime minister. Given that political power rests with Parliament, however, this too has become largely a ceremonial duty.

Photo: ©Peter Macdiarmid/Getty Images

Sudan President Omar al-Bashir is widely considered an authoritarian dictator by the international community. ©Ashraf Shazly/AFP/Getty Images

SOCTHINK

Early in his presidency, expressing a sentiment shared by some of his predecessors, George W. Bush joked that when it came to working with Congress, "a dictatorship would be a heck of a lot easier." In what ways is the U.S. system of government intentionally inefficient? Why might that be intentional?

from legally elected regimes or from other military cliques (Michels [1915] 1949).

Strictly speaking, the term *oligarchy* is reserved for governments that are run by a few selected individuals. However, the People's Republic of China can be classified as an oligarchy if we stretch the meaning of the term. In China, power rests in the hands of a large but exclusive ruling *group,* the Communist Party. In a similar vein, we might argue that many industrialized nations of the West should be considered oligarchies (rather than democracies), because only a powerful few—leaders of big business, government, and the military—actually rule. Later in this chapter, we examine the "elite model" of the U.S. political system in greater detail.

DICTATORSHIP AND TOTALITARIANISM

A **dictatorship** is a government in which one person has nearly total power to make and enforce laws. Dictators rule primarily through the use of force, which often includes imprisonment, torture, and executions. Typically, they seize power rather than being freely elected (as in a democracy) or inheriting power (as in a monarchy). Some dictators rely on charismatic authority and manage to achieve a certain popularity, although their supporters' enthusiasm is almost certainly tinged with fear. Dictators who rely primarily on force and are often bitterly hated by their people.

Frequently, dictators develop such overwhelming control over people's lives that their governments are called totalitarian. (Monarchies and oligarchies may also achieve this type of dominance.) **Totalitarianism** involves virtually complete government control and surveillance over all aspects of a society's social and political life. Germany during Hitler's reign, the Soviet Union under Stalin in the 1930s, and North Korea today are classified as totalitarian states.

DEMOCRACY

In a literal sense, **democracy** means government by the people. The word comes from two Greek roots—*demos,* meaning "the populace" or "the common people," and *kratia,* meaning "rule." In a democracy, power is not vested in a particular person or position. Individual citizens provide the foundation for political authority, and the underlying principle of power is "one person, one vote." This principle implies that, in theory at least, everyone has equal power when it comes to decision making. Direct democracy, in which all citizens vote on all major decisions and the most votes win, provides perhaps the purest example. In large, populous nations such as the United States, direct democracy is impractical at the national level. All Americans cannot vote on every important issue. Consequently, popular rule occurs in the form of **representative democracy,** a system of government in which citizens elect political leaders to make decisions on behalf of the people.

The way representatives are chosen can vary, and the system used to select them influences the kind of politics we get. For

> **Dictatorship** A government in which one person has nearly total power to make and enforce laws.
>
> **Totalitarianism** Virtually complete government control and surveillance over all aspects of a society's social and political life.
>
> **Democracy** In a literal sense, government by the people.
>
> **Representative democracy** A system of government in which citizens elect political leaders to make decisions on behalf of the people.

Source: National Archives and Records Administration

Chapter 9 / Economy and Politics

©mikeledray/Shutterstock.com RF

©Photo by Zach D Roberts/NurPhoto via Getty Images

example, the two-party system that dominates in the United States is a consequence, in part, of how legislators are selected. To select members to the House of Representatives, the country is divided into 435 geographically distinct congressional districts. Each district has a single seat. Elections are held within each, and the winner becomes the representative for that district. As a result of this winner-take-all system, candidates have an incentive to appeal to a majority of voters, which tends to result in the creation of two parties, each vying to gain that majority. The United States has numerous "third parties." In 2016, for example, Gary Johnson was on the ballot for Libertarian Party, and Jill Stein ran for the Green Party. But the winner-take-all system makes it difficult for a minority party to break through to win a majority of votes, especially against the entrenched power and influence of the two major parties. For example, in 2016, all the third-party candidates together received 7.8 million votes, or 5.7 percent of the total.

> #### SOC THINK
> The United States is commonly classified as a representative democracy because the elected members of Congress and state legislatures make our laws. However, critics have questioned how representative our democracy really is. Do Congress and the state legislatures genuinely represent the masses? Are the people of the United States legitimately self-governing, or has our government become a forum for powerful elites?

An alternative system for selecting legislators involves proportional representation, some form of which exists in Brazil, Israel, the Netherlands, and South Africa. In such cases, a single district can be represented by multiple seats, and winners are determined based on the percentage of votes received in that district. For example, if a party receives 15 percent of the vote, that party would receive approximately 15 percent of the legislative seats. In such a system, parties that might never be able to win a majority of votes can still win seats in the legislature. In addition, the likelihood that a single party secures a majority of seats declines. As a result, parties often need to work together to create a ruling coalition, which has the effect of giving those minority parties more power than they might otherwise have.

If citizens in a democracy are unhappy with the current direction of things, they can vote to establish new policies or elect new leaders. Over time, significant changes in policy can occur in response to the changing will of the people. For example, early on in U.S. history, the "self-evident" truth that everyone was created equal and endowed with unalienable rights applied only to White, property-holding men. Slowly the definition of who counts as a citizen expanded to include others. Debates about citizenship rights in the United States continue to this day as evidenced, for example, in arguments regarding the rights of children or immigrants.

Citizenship rights involve more than just the right to vote. Sociologist T. H. Marshall (1950) identified three categories of such rights, including civil rights, political rights, and social rights:

- *Civil rights.* These citizenship rights protect individual freedoms. We find some of them articulated in the Bill of Rights, the first 10 amendments to the U.S. Constitution. Included are protections such as freedom of speech, freedom of assembly, the right to bear arms, and freedom of religion.
- *Political rights.* These ensure the right to full participation in the political process. In principle, any citizen can be involved in politics by voting or running for office. But universal political participation wasn't always guaranteed. The 15th Amendment to the U.S. Constitution extended political rights to African Americans in 1870 and the 19th Amendment secured those rights for women in 1920.

- *Social rights.* These rights provide for our welfare and security. They are based on the presupposition that a minimum standard of living is necessary to ensure the ability of all to exercise their civil and political rights. To secure these rights, some goods and services—such as public education or police and fire protection—are taken out of the marketplace, ensuring that everyone has at least a minimum amount of access regardless of their ability to pay. Substantial debates exist over the role government should play in ensuring access to basic material and social and cultural resources.

Debates over social rights—whether to guarantee health care coverage to all, for example—are due, in part, to a basic tension between core values in the United States. On the one hand is the principle of *equality,* a basic presupposition at the heart of democracy. On the other is the principle of *competition,* which is an essential premise of capitalism. A capitalist economy assumes that an economic hierarchy exists and that there will be winners and losers, but in a democracy all are created equal. Economist Arthur Okun (1975) described this tension as "the double standard of a capitalist democracy, professing and pursuing an egalitarian political and social system and simultaneously generating gaping disparities in economic wellbeing" (p. 1). The simultaneous adherence to these two principles helps explain why social policies regarding the extension of social rights go back and forth over time with one or the other becoming dominant in public discourse. Leading up to the 2016 presidential election, for example, conservative Republicans advocated strongly in favor of lower taxes and substantial cuts in federal funding for social welfare programs. Liberal Democrats, on the other hand, advocated in favor of higher taxes on the wealthy and a stronger social support safety net.

> **SOC**THINK
>
> To what extent do you think that the principles of political equality and economic competition are at odds with each other in the United States?

>> The Power Structure in the United States

The issue of power extends beyond politics and the people who occupy formally recognized offices. Over the years, sociologists repeatedly have sought to discover who really holds power in the United States. Do "we the people" genuinely run the country through our elected representatives? Or does a small elite behind the scenes control both the government and the economic system? In exploring these questions, social scientists have developed two basic models of our nation's power structure: political pluralism versus the power elite.

Pluralist model A view of society in which many competing groups within the community have access to government so that no single group is dominant.

5 Movies on ECONOMY AND POLITICS

Les Misérables
A decent man in a time of economic and political crisis.

American Winter
The Great Recession hits home.

Killing Them Softly
A parable about financial crisis and economic collapse.

Weiner
A political campaign on a crash course with destruction.

Eye in the Sky
The dilemma of drone warfare in an age of terrorism.

THE PLURALIST MODEL

According to the pluralist approach, power is widely dispersed throughout society. Though some groups may have more power in certain areas at particular times, there is no core group at the top that is able to consistently advance its interests at the expense of others. According to this **pluralist model,** many competing groups have access to government so that no single group is dominant.

To support their claims, advocates of the pluralist model point to data gathered from intensive case studies of communities collected using observation research. One of the most famous—an investigation of decision making in New Haven, Connecticut—was reported by Robert Dahl (1961). Dahl found that, although the number of people involved in any important decision was rather small, community power was nonetheless diffuse. Few political actors exercised decision-making power on all issues, and no one group got its way all the time. One individual or group might be influential in a battle over urban renewal but have little effect on educational policy.

Historically, pluralists have stressed ways in which large numbers of people can participate in or influence governmental decision making. Communications technologies, such as Facebook and Twitter, have increased the opportunity to be heard, not just in countries such as the United States but in developing countries the world over. The ability to communicate with political leaders via email, for example, increases the opportunity for the average citizen to have a voice in politics.

The pluralist model has its critics. Sociologist G. William Domhoff (1978, 2014) reexamined Dahl's study of decision making in New Haven and argued that Dahl and other pluralists had failed to trace how local elites who were prominent in decision making belonged to a larger national ruling class. In addition, studies of community power, such as Dahl's work in New Haven, can examine decision making only on issues that become part of the political agenda. They fail to address the potential power of elites to keep certain matters entirely out of the realm of political debate.

Dianne Pinderhughes (1987) has criticized the pluralist model for failing to account for the exclusion of African Americans from the political process. Drawing on her studies of Chicago politics, Pinderhughes points out that the residential and occupational segregation of Blacks and their long political disenfranchisement violate the logic of pluralism—which would hold that such a substantial minority should always have been influential in community decision making. This critique applies to many cities across the United States, where other large racial and ethnic minorities, among them Asian Americans, Puerto Ricans, and Mexican Americans, are relatively powerless.

Elite model A view of society as being ruled by a small group of individuals who share a common set of political and economic interests.

POWER ELITE MODELS

Such criticisms lend support for an alternative model of how power functions. Consistent with the conflict perspective, power elite models trace their roots back to Karl Marx, who believed that representative democracy contributed to a shared false consciousness by providing the illusion that power is in the hands of the people. Like others who hold an **elite model** of power relations, Marx believed that society is ruled by a small group of individuals who share political and economic interests. In Marx's view, government officials and military leaders essentially do the bidding of the capitalist class, who own the factories and control natural resources.

Mills's Model Sociologist C. Wright Mills, who developed the concept of the sociological imagination that we looked at in Chapter 1, put forth a model similar to

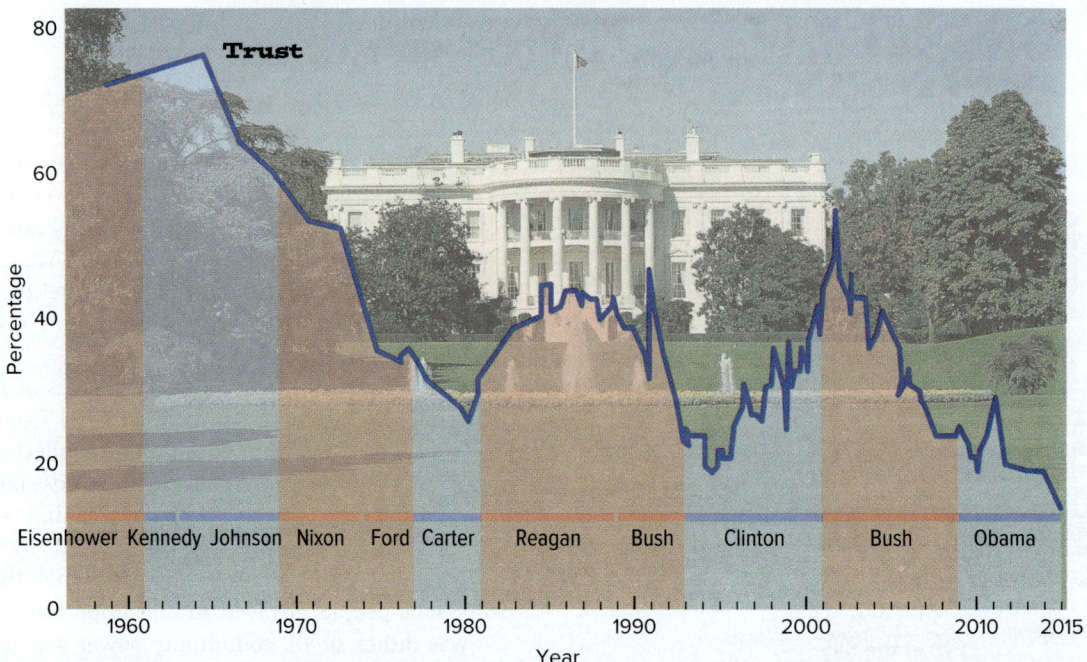

Public Trust in Government

Note: The percentage represents those who say they "can trust the government in Washington to do what is right" either "just about always" or "most of the time."
Source: Pew Research Center 2015h. Photo: ©Digital Vision/Getty Images RF

Marx's in his pioneering work *The Power Elite* ([1956] 2000). According to Mills, power rested in the hands of a few, both inside and outside government. He singled out a small group of military, industrial, and government leaders who controlled the fate of the United States—the **power elite**. A pyramid illustrates the power structure of the United States in Mills's model, as illustrated in the accompanying "Power Elite Models" graphic. The power elite rests at the top and includes the corporate rich, leaders of the executive branch of government, and heads of the military (whom Mills called the "warlords"). Directly below are local opinion leaders, members of the legislative branch of government, and leaders of special-interest groups. Mills contended that these individuals and groups basically follow the wishes of the dominant power elite. At the bottom of the pyramid are the unorganized, exploited masses.

A fundamental element in Mills's thesis is that the power elite not only includes relatively few members but also operates as a self-conscious, cohesive unit. Although not necessarily diabolical or ruthless, the elite comprises similar types of people who interact regularly with one another and have essentially the same political and economic interests. Mills's power elite represents not a conspiracy but rather a community of interest and sentiment among a small number of influential people (Jenness, Smith, and Stepan-Norris 2006).

Power elite A small group of military, industrial, and government leaders who control the fate of the United States.

Domhoff's Model Sociologist G. William Domhoff (2009, 2014) agrees with Mills that a powerful elite runs the United States. As the accompanying "Power Elite Models" graphic shows, Domhoff stresses the role played by elites from three social spheres—the corporate community, the social upper class, and policy-formation organizations such as think tanks, chambers of commerce, and labor unions. Membership in these groups overlaps, and members with connections in more than one of these spheres have more power and influence. Domhoff finds that those in this latter group are still largely White, male, and upper class, but he notes the presence of a small number of women and minority men in key positions—groups that were excluded from Mills's top echelon and are still underrepresented today (Zweigenhaft and Domhoff 2006).

> Majority rule only works if you're also considering individual rights. Because you can't have five wolves and one sheep voting on what to have for supper.
>
> —Larry Flynt

Power Elite Models

C. Wright Mills's model (pyramid, top to bottom):
- THE POWER ELITE: Corporate rich, Executive branch, Military leaders
- Interest group leaders, Legislators, Local opinion leaders
- Unorganized, exploited masses

G. William Domhoff's model (Venn diagram): Social upper class, Corporate community, Policy-formation organizations — intersection: THE POWER ELITE

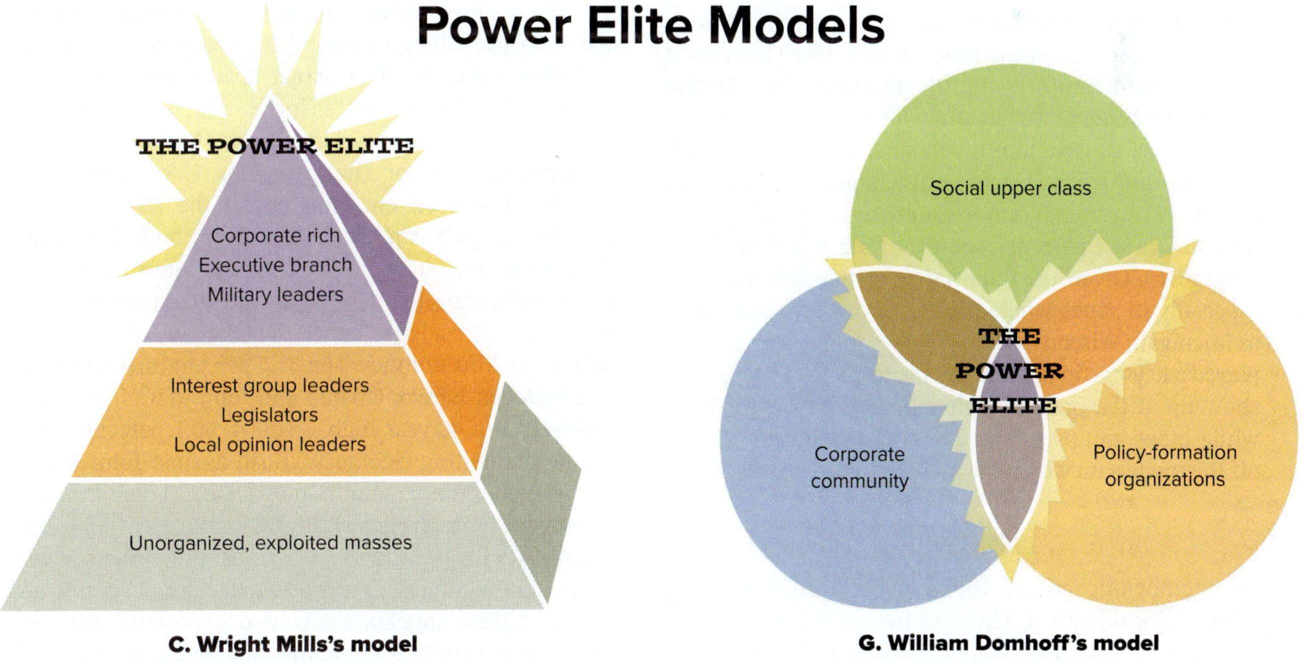

Sources: Left, based on C. W. Mills (1956) 2000; right, Domhoff 2009, 2014.

Although the three groups in Domhoff's power elite model do overlap, they do not necessarily agree on specific policies. Domhoff notes that in politics, two different coalitions have exercised influence. A corporate-conservative coalition has played a large role in both political parties, generating support for particular candidates through direct-mail and social media appeals. A liberal-labor coalition is based in unions, local environmental organizations, a segment of the minority group community, liberal churches, and the university and arts communities (Zweigenhaft and Domhoff 2006). The power this coalition wields suggests that the interests of members of the power elite are not always singular or uniform but that overall they do work together to advance their larger interests.

> **SOC THINK**
>
> Is it possible for a small and unified group of powerful people in the United States to use their power and influence to, in effect, rule the country? What obstacles exist to prevent that from happening?

>> Political Participation in the United States

Because political representatives in the United States must be elected to serve, citizens have substantial potential power to shape the nature and direction of public policy. The result for 2016's presidential election was unexpected because the national polling average on Election Day showed Clinton ahead by 3.1 percent. Among election prediction sites, Nate Silver's FiveThirtyEight.com offered the most optimistic prediction for a Trump victory at a 29 percent chance of winning. Other statistical prognosticators gave him much smaller odds, including *The New York Times,* which set his chances at 15 percent, and the Princeton Election Consortium, which posted his chances at 1 percent (Andrews, Katz, and Patel 2016; Katz 2016). Given the importance of the electoral vote, especially in states where the vote was very close, such as Michigan, Wisconsin, and Pennsylvania, voter turnout played a key role in influencing the result. If some groups show up at the polls in higher numbers than expected while other groups stay home, it systematically throws off the models on which the predictions are based.

VOTER PARTICIPATION

In a democratic system, voters have the right to select their political leaders. They are free to vote for whomever they choose, and political parties seek to persuade voters to support their positions. Political participation

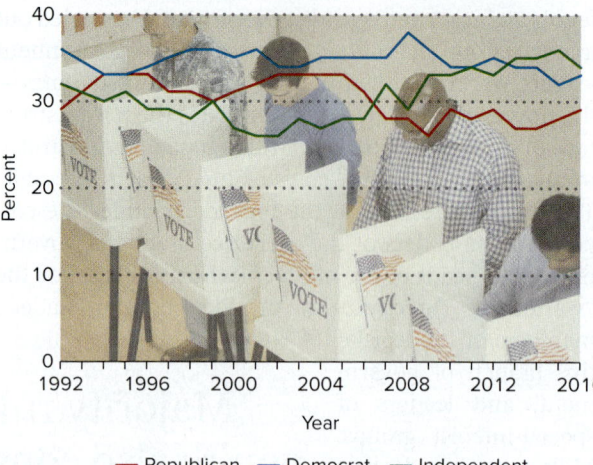

What's Your Party?

Note: Responses are to the question, "In politics today, do you consider yourself a Republican, Democrat, or independent?"
Source: Pew Research Center 2016f. Photo: ©Hill Street Studios/Blend Images LLC/Glow Images RF

makes government accountable to the voters. If participation declines, government operates with less of a sense of accountability to society. In 2016, 33 percent of registered voters in the United States self-identified as Democrats, 29 percent as Republicans, and 34 percent as independents (Pew Research Center 2016f).

Historically, voter participation rates in the United States were highest from 1848 to 1896, during which an average of about 80 percent of eligible voters participated in presidential elections. (Of course, that does not count women or African Americans, who were not legally permitted to vote.) The rate declined steadily until it reached 48.9 percent in 1928. It fluctuated throughout the rest of the 20th century, rising to more than 60 percent in 1940 and 1960 and falling to around 50 percent in 1948, 1988, and 1996. Concerns about voter apathy were expressed going into the 21st century, so increases in the new millennium were greeted as a welcome trend (McDonald 2009).

Voter turnout for the past four U.S. presidential elections has been encouraging. In the 2016 election between Republican Donald Trump and Democrat Hillary Clinton, 60.2 percent of eligible voters turned out at the polls, the same level as in the 2012 race between incumbent President Barack Obama and Republican challenger Mitt Romney. The 61.6 percent turnout in the race between Barack Obama and John McCain in 2008 represented a 40-year high. In 2004, 60.1 percent voted in the race pitting George W. Bush against John Kerry. Yet, as the accompanying "Going Global: Voter Turnout Worldwide" graph demonstrates, compared to other countries with presidential elections, the United States does not rank highest in turnout. In fact, of 113 countries for which there are data, the United States ranks 56th for voter turnout (International Institute for Democracy and Electoral Assistance 2016a; McDonald 2016).

Going GLOBAL

Voter Turnout Worldwide

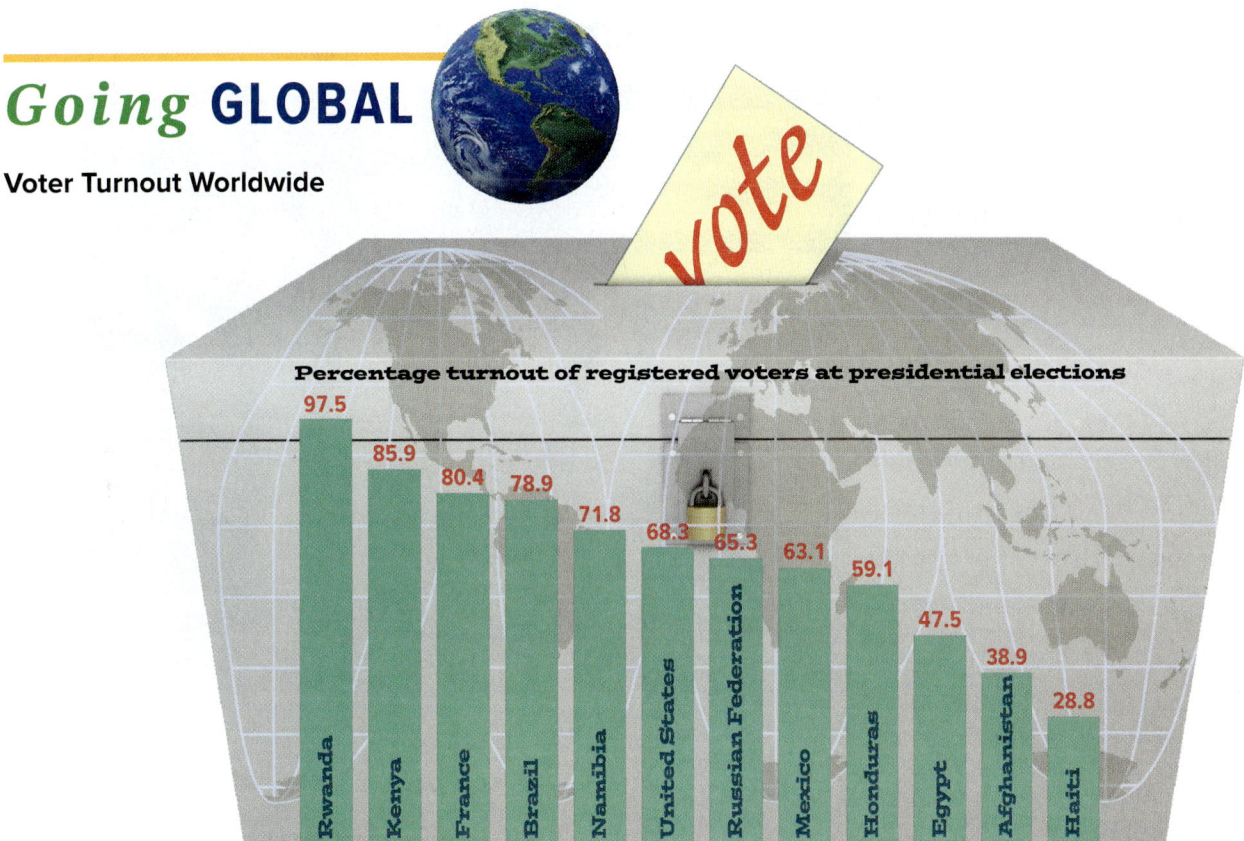

Note: Results are for the most recent presidential election. U.S. results are from 2016.
Source: International Institute for Democracy and Electoral Assistance 2016a. Photo: ©imaginima/Getty Images RF

Voting participation rates vary by social group. Younger voters have significantly lower voter participation rates than do older voters. In the 2016 presidential election, for example, only 46.1 percent of people aged 18–29 voted compared to 70.9 percent of those aged 65 and older. That difference is important because voter preferences vary by age. In 2016, 55 percent of 18- to 29-year-olds voted for Clinton and 37 percent supported Trump. Among voters 65 and older, 45 percent supported Clinton and 53 percent voted for Trump. Among African Americans, from 1996 to 2012, participation rates went up each time before falling in 2016. In 1996, 53 percent of African Americans voted. In 2012, rates jumped to 66.6 percent, overtaking non-Hispanic Whites for the first time, but then fell to 59.6 percent in 2016 (CIRCLE 2016a; File 2013; U.S. Census Bureau 2017).

RACE AND GENDER IN POLITICS

Because politics is synonymous with power and authority, we should not be surprised that marginalized groups lack political strength. Nationally, women did not get the vote until 1920. Most Chinese Americans were turned away from the polls until 1926. American Indians did not win the right to vote until 1954. And African Americans were, in practice, largely disenfranchised until 1965, when national voting rights legislation was passed. It has taken these groups some time to develop their political power and begin to exercise it fully.

Progress toward the inclusion of minority groups in government has been slow as well. As of January 2017, 21 of 100 U.S. senators were women. Three senators were African American, four were Latino, and four were Asian American or Native Hawaiian/Pacific Islander. Catherine Cortez Masto of Nevada became the first ever Latina senator. Among the 435 members of the U.S. House of Representatives, 83 were women, 46 were African Americans, 34 were Latinos, and 12 were Asian Americans or Native Hawaiian/Pacific Islanders. These numbers, though low when compared to proportions in the U.S. population, represent the most diverse Congress in U.S. history (Marcos 2016).

Many critics within minority communities decry what they term "fiesta politics." This refers to the tendency of White power brokers to visit racial and ethnic minority communities only when they need electoral support, making a quick appearance on a national or

Reasons for Not Voting, Among Young Adults

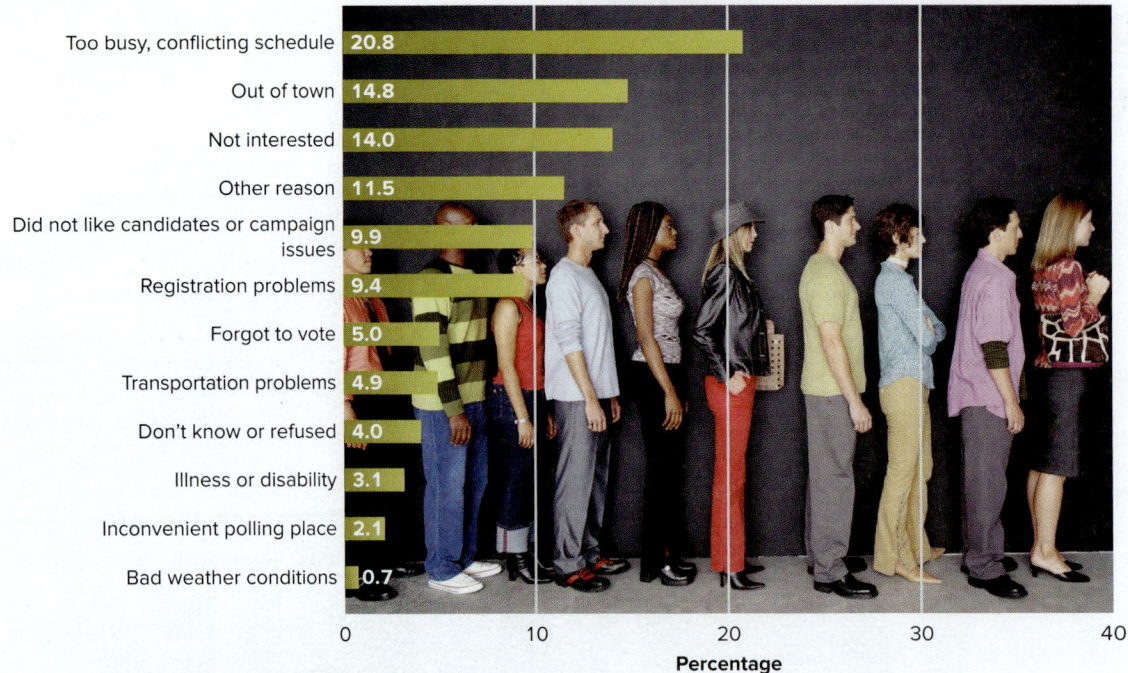

Note: Young adults include 18- to 24-year-olds. Results are for the 2012 presidential election.
Source: U.S. Census Bureau 2012:Table 10.   Photo: ©Ryan McVay/Getty Images RF

ethnic holiday to get their picture taken and then vanishing. When the election is over, they too often forget to consult the residents who supported them about community needs and concerns.

Globally, women account for at least half the members of the national legislature in only two countries. The African Republic of Rwanda ranks the highest, with 63.8 percent, and Bolivia has 53.1 percent, as shown in the accompanying "Going Global: Women in National Legislatures" graph. Overall, the United States ranked 99th among 193 nations in the proportion of women serving as national legislators in 2016 (Inter-Parliamentary Union 2016). To remedy this situation, many countries have adopted quotas for female representatives. In some, the government sets aside a certain

(Under) Representation in Congress Compared to Overall Population

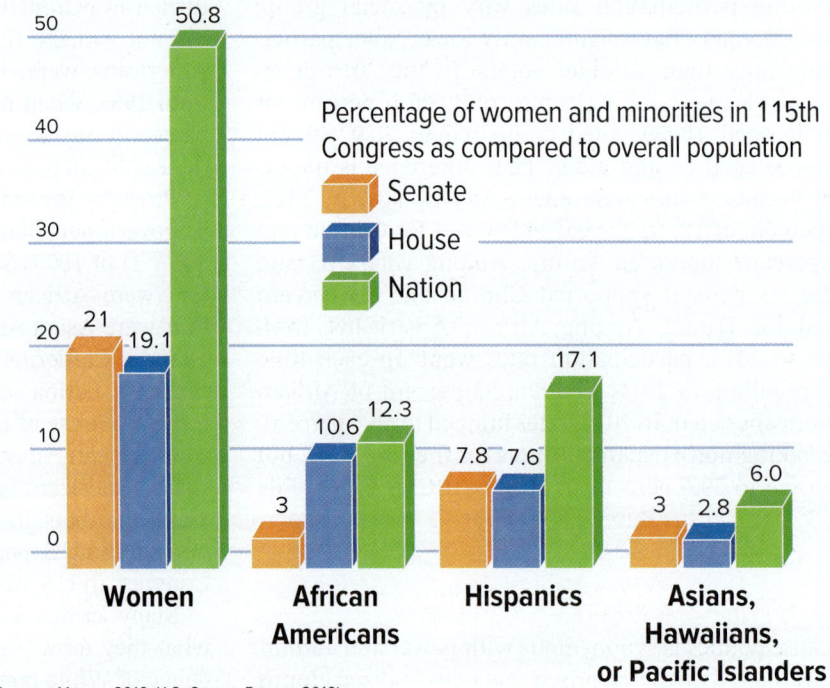

Sources: Marcos 2016; U.S. Census Bureau 2016j.

Going GLOBAL

Women in National Legislatures, Selected Countries

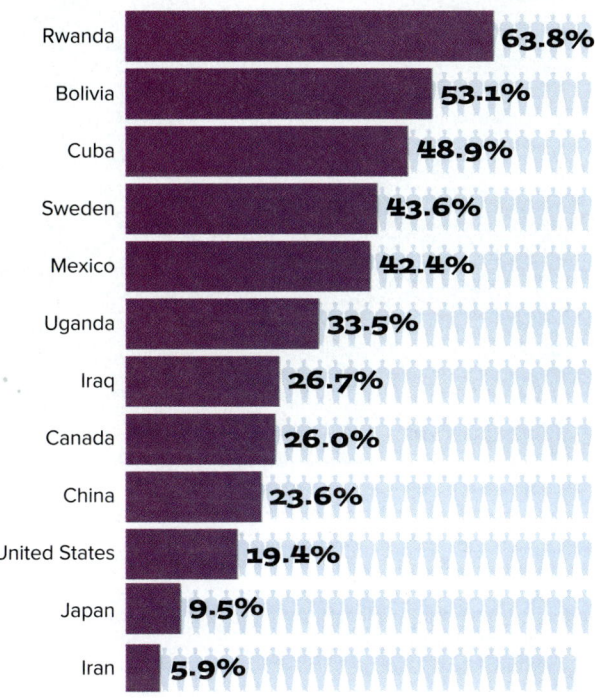

Country	Percentage
Rwanda	63.8%
Bolivia	53.1%
Cuba	48.9%
Sweden	43.6%
Mexico	42.4%
Uganda	33.5%
Iraq	26.7%
Canada	26.0%
China	23.6%
United States	19.4%
Japan	9.5%
Iran	5.9%

Note: Data are for lower legislative houses only, as of November 1, 2016; data for upper houses, such as the U.S. Senate or the UK House of Lords, are not included.
Source: Inter-Parliamentary Union 2016.

percentage of seats for women. In others, political parties have decided that a minimum percentage of their candidates should be women. Worldwide, 120 countries now have some kind of legislated or voluntary quota system in place (International Institute for Democracy and Electoral Assistance 2016b).

>> War and Peace

When it comes to political power, perhaps no decision is as weighty as the decision to go to war. Conflict is a central aspect of social relations. Sociologists Theodore Caplow and Louis Hicks (2002:3) have defined **war** as conflict between organizations that possess trained combat forces equipped with deadly weapons. This meaning is broader than the legal definition, which typically requires a formal declaration of hostilities.

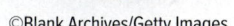
©Blank Archives/Getty Images

WAR

Sociologists approach war in three ways. Those who take a global view study how and why two or more nations become engaged in military conflict. Those who take a nation-state view stress the interaction of internal political, socioeconomic, and cultural forces. And those who take a micro view focus on the social impact of war on individuals and the groups to which they belong.

Analysis at the global level focuses on macro issues, such as the distribution of resources, struggles over political philosophies, and debates about boundaries. Often it involves nations with competing political and economic systems, as was the case in World War I, World War II, and the Cold War. Some have argued that the conflict in Iraq was about bringing freedom and democracy to the Middle East, and others argue it was motivated by oil and profits.

Sociologists have devoted much effort to studying the internal decision-making process that leads to war. During the Vietnam War, Presidents Johnson and Nixon both misled Congress, painting a falsely optimistic picture of the likely outcome. Based on their intentional distortions, Congress appropriated the military funds the two administrations requested. However, in 1971, *The New York Times* published a set of classified documents now known as "The Pentagon Papers," which revealed that many members of both administrations had knowingly distorted the real prospects for the war. Two years later—over Nixon's veto—Congress passed the War Powers Act, which requires the president to notify Congress of the reasons for committing combat troops to a hostile situation (Patterson 2003).

> **War** Conflict between organizations that possess trained combat forces equipped with deadly weapons.

Even though government leaders make the decision to go to war, public opinion plays a significant role in its execution. By 1971 the number of U.S. soldiers killed in Vietnam had surpassed 50,000, and antiwar sentiment was strong. Wars conducted by the United States since that time have tended to follow a similar pattern. Initial support both for the importance of going to war and for military spending to support it tends to give way the longer it takes to finish the job. This proved true for the conflicts in both Iraq and Afghanistan.

A major change relating to the conduct of war involves the composition of the U.S. military. Women represent a growing presence among the troops. As of October 2016, there were 207,144 women on active duty, making up 16 percent of active military personnel (Department

Chapter 9 / Economy and Politics • 227

U.S. Public Opinion on Defense Spending

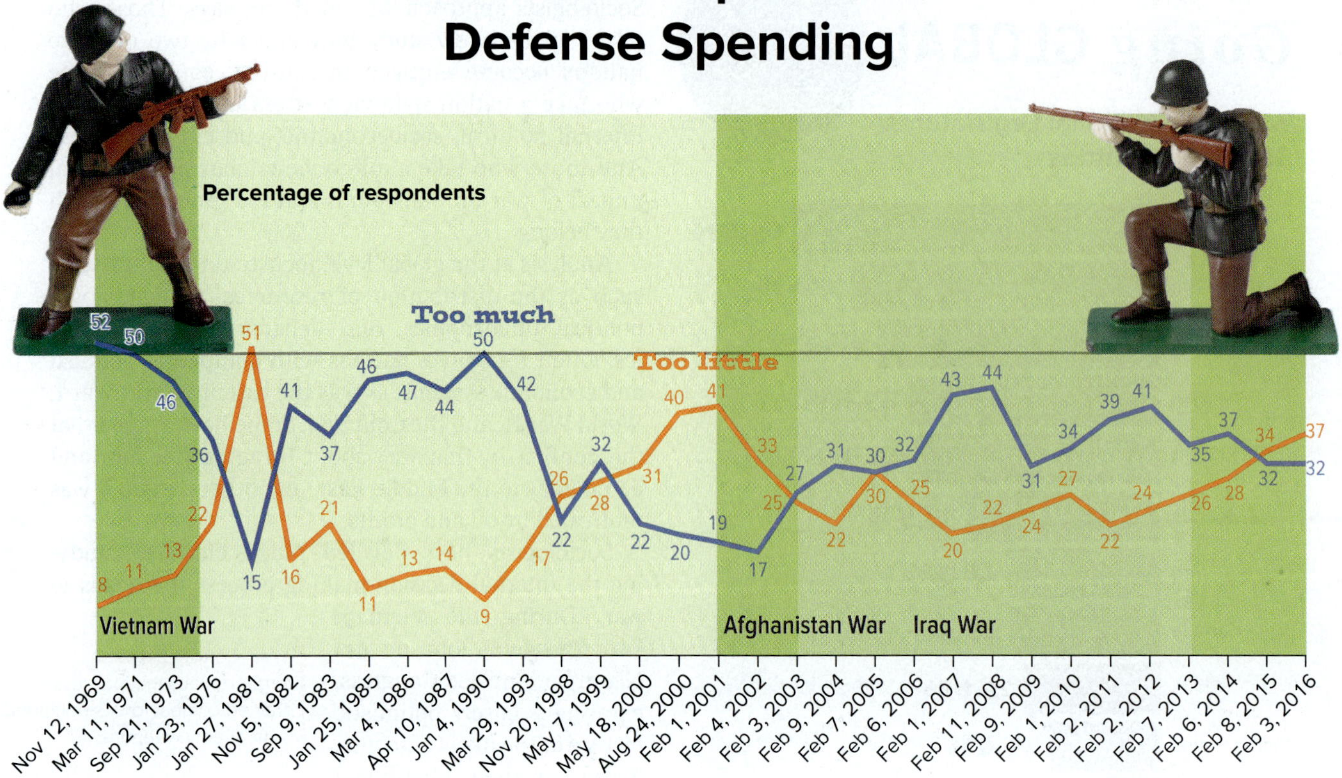

Percentage of respondents

Too much — Too little

Vietnam War | Afghanistan War | Iraq War

Too much (blue): 52, 50, 46, 36, 15, 41, 37, 46, 47, 44, 50, 42, 22, 32, 22, 20, 17, 25, 27, 31, 30, 32, 43, 44, 31, 34, 39, 41, 35, 37, 34, 32

Too little (orange): 8, 11, 13, 22, 51, 16, 21, 11, 13, 14, 9, 17, 26, 28, 31, 40, 41, 33, 22, 30, 25, 20, 27, 24, 22, 24, 22, 26, 28, 32, 37

Dates: Nov 12, 1969; Mar 11, 1971; Sep 21, 1973; Jan 23, 1976; Jan 27, 1981; Nov 5, 1982; Sep 9, 1983; Jan 25, 1985; Mar 4, 1986; Apr 10, 1987; Jan 4, 1990; Mar 29, 1993; Nov 20, 1998; May 7, 1999; May 18, 2000; Aug 24, 2000; Feb 1, 2001; Feb 4, 2002; Feb 3, 2003; Feb 9, 2004; Feb 7, 2005; Feb 6, 2006; Feb 1, 2007; Feb 11, 2008; Feb 9, 2009; Feb 1, 2010; Feb 2, 2011; Feb 2, 2012; Feb 7, 2013; Feb 6, 2014; Feb 8, 2015; Feb 3, 2016

Note: Respondents replied to the question "There is much discussion as to the amount of money the government in Washington should spend for national defense and military purposes. How do you feel about this? Do you think we are spending too little, about the right amount, or too much?"
Source: Gallup 2016a. *Photos: (left and right):* ©McGraw-Hill Education/Ken Cavanagh, photographer

of Defense 2016). Increasingly, women are serving not just as support personnel but also as an integral part of combat units. The first casualty of the war in Iraq, in fact, was Private First Class Lori Piestewa, a member of the Hopi tribe and a descendant of Mexican settlers in the Southwest.

At the level of interpersonal interaction, war can bring out the worst as well as the best in people. In 2004, graphic images of the abuse of Iraqi prisoners by U.S. soldiers at Iraq's Abu Ghraib prison shocked the world. For social scientists, the deterioration of the guards' behavior brought to mind psychology professor Philip Zimbardo's mock prison experiment at Stanford University in 1971, in which volunteer guards in a simulated prison acted sadistically toward volunteer prisoners. Zimbardo concluded it was the positions of

POPSOC

When it first came out, the film *Zero Dark Thirty*, which portrayed the capture and killing of al-Qaeda leader Osama bin Laden, seemed like a lock to win an Oscar for Best Picture. Soon, however, a negative buzz emerged because of its seemingly positive portrayal of the use of torture and questions about whether it was a propaganda film put together with assistance of the U.S. military. It ultimately lost the award to *Argo*. The controversy should not be surprising. Movies with a political agenda have been around since the beginning of Hollywood. Films such as *The Birth of a Nation, This Is the Army, Dr. Strangelove, M*A*S*H,* and *Three Kings* all had political points they sought to make.

Photo: ©Moviestore collection Ltd/Alamy Stock Photo

power the guards occupied relative to the inmates that led to their behavior, rather than the characteristics of the individuals themselves. In July 2004, the U.S. military began using a documentary film about the experiment to train military interrogators to avoid mistreatment of prisoners (Zarembo 2004; Zimbardo 2007).

TERRORISM

©Photo by Sylvain Lefevre/Getty Images

The Boston Marathon bombings in April 2013 were yet another reminder of the ability of a small number of people with a political agenda to instill fear in the hearts and minds of millions. Globally, attacks in Brussels, Belgium, where a suicide bombing at an airport killed 32; in Nice, France, where a truck plowed through a Bastille Day crowd killing 84; in Madagali, Nigeria, where a suicide bombing killed 57; and in Berlin, Germany, where a truck tore into a busy Christmas market killing and injuring many, were but a few of the major attacks of 2016. Acts of terror, whether perpetrated by a few or by many people, can be a powerful force. Formally defined, **terrorism** is the use or threat of violence against random or symbolic targets in pursuit of political aims. For terrorists, the end justifies the means. They believe that the status quo is oppressive and that desperate measures are essential to end the suffering of the deprived.

Terrorism The use or threat of violence against random or symbolic targets in pursuit of political aims.

Going GLOBAL

GLOBAL TERRORIST ATTACKS

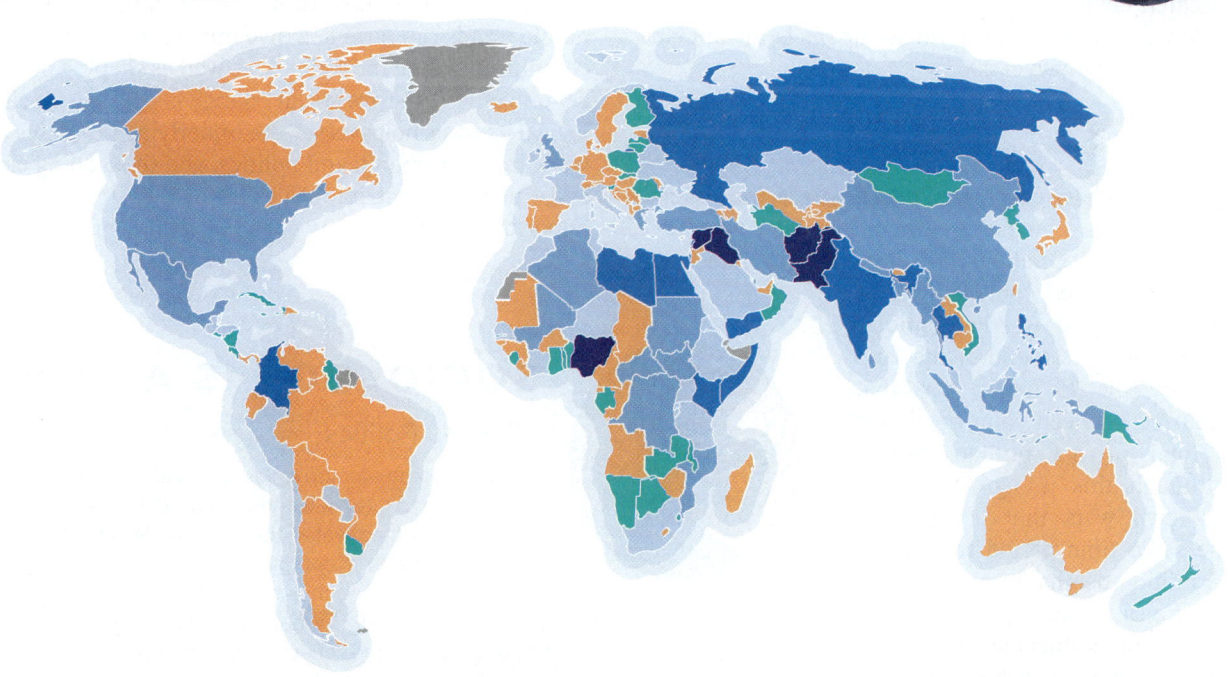

■■■ Highest impact of terrorism　■ Lowest impact of terrorism　■ No impact of terrorism　■ No records

Source: Institute for Economics and Peace 2016.

An essential aspect of contemporary terrorism involves use of the media. Terrorists may want to keep secret their individual identities, but they want their political messages and goals to receive as much publicity as possible. The purpose of many acts of terrorist violence is more symbolic than strategic or tactical. These attacks represent a statement made by people who feel that the world has gone awry, that accepted political paths to problem resolution are ineffective or blocked, and that there is a larger or cosmic struggle going on, raising the stakes and so justifying the means (Juergensmeyer 2003). Whether through calls to the media, anonymous manifestos, or other means, terrorists typically admit responsibility for and defend their violent acts.

Terrorism is a global concern. In 2015, there were 29,376 deaths from terrorist attacks around the world, 72 percent of which occurred in just five countries: Iraq, Afghanistan, Pakistan, Nigeria, and Syria. Twenty-three countries set records for the number of deaths from terrorism in 2015 (Institute for Economics and Peace 2016). Since September 11, 2001, governments around the world have renewed their efforts to fight terrorism. Even though the public generally regards increased surveillance and social control as a necessary evil, these measures have nonetheless raised governance issues. For example, some citizens in the United States and elsewhere have expressed concern that measures such as the USA PATRIOT Act of 2001 threaten civil liberties. As efforts to combat political violence illustrate, the term *terrorism* is an apt one (Howard and Sawyer 2003).

Peace The absence of war, or, more broadly, a proactive effort to develop cooperative relations among nations.

PEACE

Sociologists have considered **peace** both as the absence of war and as a proactive effort to develop cooperative relations among nations. It is important to note, however, that armed conflict involves more than just warring nations. From 1945 to the end of the 20th century, the 25 major wars that occurred between countries killed a total of 3.3 million people. Although this is significant, the 127 civil wars that occurred in the same time period resulted in 16 million deaths. In other words, five times as many people died as a result of conflicts *within* nations as died in wars *between* nations (Fearon and Laitin 2003).

Sociologists and other social scientists who draw on sociological theory and research have tried to identify conditions that deter war. One of their findings is that international trade may act as a deterrent to armed conflict. As countries exchange goods, people, and then cultures, they become more integrated and less likely to threaten each other's security. Viewed from this perspective, not just trade but also immigration and foreign exchange programs have a beneficial effect on international relations.

Another means of fostering peace is the activity of international charities and activist groups, or nongovernmental organizations (NGOs). The Red Cross and Red Crescent, Doctors Without Borders, and Amnesty International donate their services wherever they are needed, without regard to nationality. Over the past decades, these NGOs have been expanding in number, size, and scope. By sharing news of local conditions and clarifying local issues, they often prevent conflicts from escalating into violence and war. Some NGOs have initiated cease-fires, reached settlements, and even ended warfare between former adversaries.

Finally, many analysts stress that nations cannot maintain their security by threatening violence. Peace, they contend, can best be maintained by developing strong mutual security agreements among potential adversaries (Etzioni 1965; Shostak 2002). Following this path involves active diplomacy and, to the extent that it involves negotiations with countries viewed as enemies, can be controversial.

From surprising election outcomes to peace movements, stories such as these provide hope that people can make a difference. Even though large-scale economic trends can have negative impacts on companies, communities, and individuals, as well as shaping political outcomes, positive social change is possible. Sociological analysis helps us see the underlying processes at work in the economy and politics, and in so doing can assist us in recognizing places in those systems where opportunities for bringing about such change exist.

SOCIOLOGY IS A VERB

Playing Politics

Identify some elected officials—local, state, or federal—and interview them about their life in politics. What motivated them to run? What have they been able to accomplish? What frustrations do they face in getting things done? What would they change if they could? What advice would they give you? Keep notes of what they say, and reflect on the lessons learned about opportunities for, and obstacles to, change.

For REVIEW

I. **How are economic and political power organized?**
   - The two major economic systems are capitalism and socialism, though in practice most economies are some mix of the two. Political systems of government include monarchy, oligarchy, dictatorship, totalitarianism, and democracy. A debate exists when looking at formal power in the United States about the degree to which there is a small, cohesive group of power elites who effectively rule or if leadership is more diverse and pluralistic, operating through democratic processes.

II. **How does power operate?**
   - Power involves the capacity to get others to do what you want, ranging from use of force to acceptance of authority. In the case of authority, followers accept your power as legitimate, whether based on a traditional, rational-legal, or charismatic foundation.

III. **How has the economy changed over time?**
   - From the Industrial Revolution through deindustrialization to the more recent global economic crisis and recovery, the modern economy is more dynamic and the consequences of change more far reaching both for nations and for individuals. Through political engagement people have the potential to influence the direction of that change.

SOCVIEWS on Economy and Politics

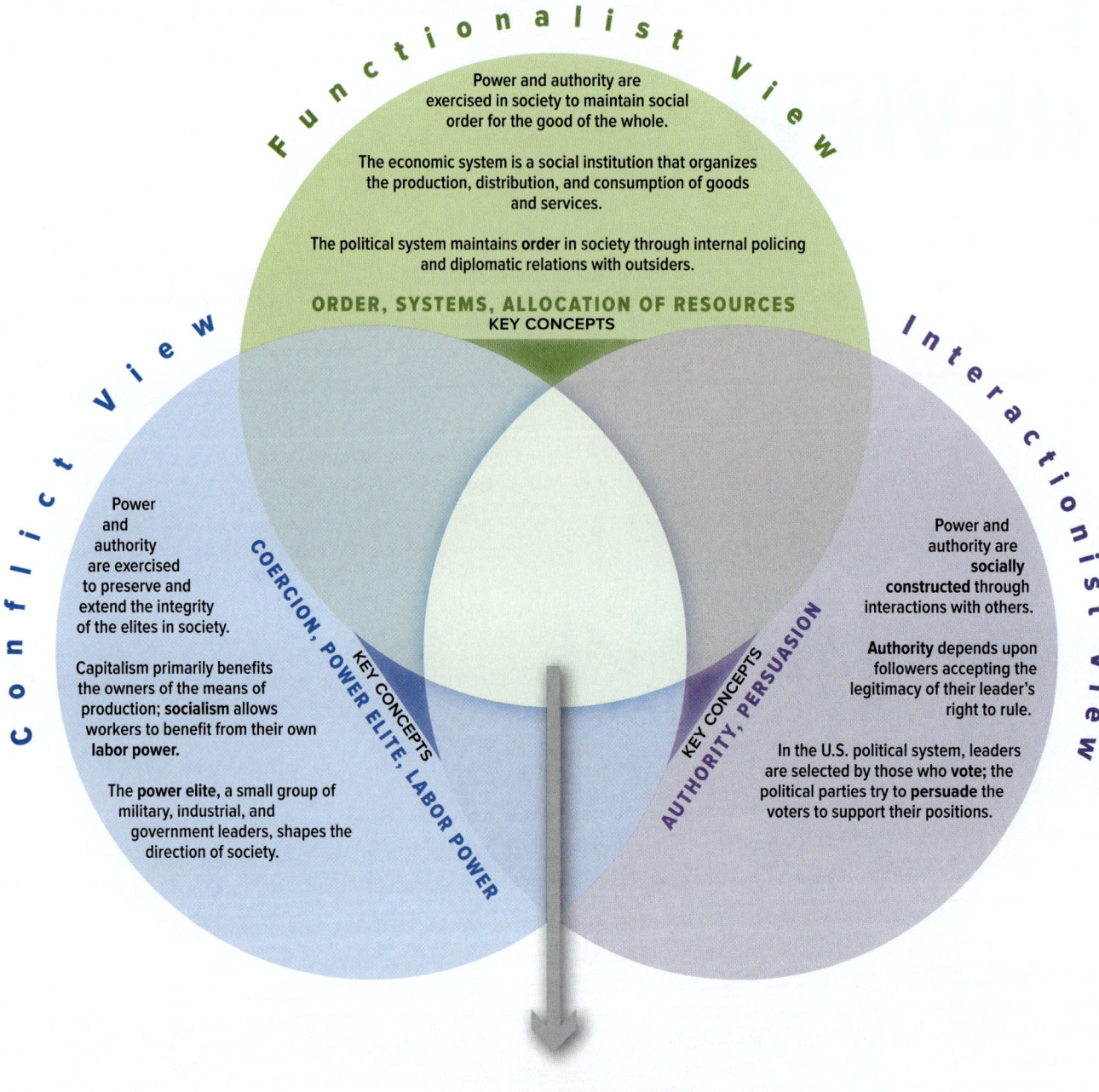

MAKE THE CONNECTION
After reviewing the chapter, answer the following questions:

1 How would each perspective explain the political stances of the White working-class workers Hochschild studied?

2 How might each perspective seek to explain charismatic authority?

3 How might theorists from each perspective explain war?

4 Are you an active or an apathetic voter? What factors influence your approach? Which perspective best describes the way you participate in the political world?

Pop Quiz

1. The systematic and widespread reduction of investment in domestic manufacturing and material production is called
   a. deindustrialization.
   b. downsizing.
   c. postindustrialization.
   d. gentrification.

2. What is the term used to describe outsourcing of work to foreign contractors?
   a. exploitation
   b. offshoring
   c. alienation
   d. downsizing

3. According to Max Weber, what is the definition of power?
   a. the recognized set of procedures for implementing and achieving society's goals
   b. the combination of strength and stamina
   c. the mechanical and electrical energy that provided the foundation for the Industrial Revolution
   d. the ability to exercise one's will over others, even if they resist

4. Which of the following is *not* part of the classification system of authority developed by Max Weber?
   a. traditional authority
   b. pluralist authority
   c. rational-legal authority
   d. charismatic authority

5. Within a capitalist economy, what does laissez-faire mean?
   a. The means of production and distribution in a society are collectively held.
   b. People should compete freely, with minimal government intervention in the economy.
   c. A single business firm controls the market.
   d. Society depends on mechanization to produce its goods and services.

6. Which of the following are primarily characterized by the transfers of money, goods, and services that are not reported to the government?
   a. globalization
   b. the mixed economy
   c. laissez-faire capitalism
   d. the informal economy

7. In which type of government do only a few individuals rule?
   a. a monarchy
   b. a democracy
   c. a dictatorship
   d. an oligarchy

8. According to the model proposed by C. Wright Mills, in whose hands does power rest?
   a. the people
   b. the power elite
   c. the aristocracy
   d. representative democracy

9. When it comes to voter turnout, where does the United States rank compared to other nations?
   a. the first, with the highest level of turnout
   b. in the top 10 internationally
   c. in about the top third of all nations
   d. just about in the middle of all nations

10. Which of the following terms best describes the threat of violence against random or symbolic targets in pursuit of political aims?
    a. politics
    b. power
    c. terrorism
    d. authority

1. (a), 2. (b), 3. (d), 4. (b), 5. (b), 6. (d), 7. (d), 8. (b), 9. (d), 10. (c)

©Spencer Platt/Getty Images

10 Social Class

JUST GETTING BY

Rae McCormick's father died of a brain aneurysm when she was 11 years old, and her mother abandoned her soon thereafter. Left to fend for herself, Rae lived on her own for a while in her hometown of Cleveland. She then moved in with her older sister for a time before Rae's mom signed custody over to a family friend. When Rae turned 18 and her Social Security survivor benefit checks stopped coming, the woman kicked Rae out, and she was on her own again. At 21, Rae met Donny, and they had a daughter named Azara. Rae and Donny lived together off and on over the next few years, but he beat her and cheated on her multiple times, so she left him. She eventually rented a room from George and Camilla, an older couple who had been friends with her father. The three of them, together with three additional boarders, pooled all their resources to get by. The house they rented lacked pipes for running water, so they hauled water up from the basement in five-gallon buckets to wash dishes, take baths, and flush toilets. Their kitchen lacked a functioning stove, so they cooked on a charcoal grill outside (Edin and Shaefer 2015).

What Rae wanted more than anything else was a good job and a place of her own to raise Azara. Just when things seemed to be looking up, she lost the job she loved at Walmart, where she'd been named "Cashier of the Month" twice in her first six months working there. She couldn't get to work one day because even though she paid George and Camilla $50 per month for gas and the use of their pickup, the tank was empty, and she'd used the rest of her paycheck for rent, diapers, and groceries. Her store manager told her that if she couldn't find a way to get to work on time, she shouldn't bother coming back. Her many attempts to find another job came up empty (Edin and Shaefer 2015).

Sociologist Kathryn Edin and social work professor Luke Shaefer (2015) told Rae's story, along with those of others like her, in their book *$2.00 a Day: Living on Almost Nothing in America*. They report that 1.5 million households, including about 3 million children, live on cash incomes of less than $2 per person, per day in the United States. Based on their observation research, the interviews they conducted, and the data they analyzed, Edin and Shaefer conclude that like millions of others facing extreme poverty, "Rae, in her current circumstances . . . basically has no shot at achieving [her] dream. . . . Housing is too expensive, the jobs she might get pay far too little, and there's too little help" (2015:91). In this chapter we explore how our position in the social class system affects our life chances.

As You READ >>

- What is social class?
- How does social class operate?
- What are the consequences of social class?

>> Life Chances

One of sociology's core lessons is that place matters. Being born to a wealthy Park Avenue family in New York City confers something quite different than being born into a poor family in Cleveland. To describe the ways in which the positions we occupy shape our outcomes, Max Weber introduced the concept of **life chances** by which he meant that our likelihood for success is shaped by our access to valued material, social, and cultural resources. The college you choose, the job you have, the money you make, the car you drive, the neighborhood you live in, the health care you receive, and many other matters are shaped by the social positions you occupy.

Our definition of sociology highlights the significance of position and power by including the phrase "the consequences of difference." This expression highlights the importance sociologists place on investigating how resources are distributed, and how we justify those distributions. In this chapter and those that follow, we take a closer look at such consequences, with particular attention paid to social class, gender, race, and ethnicity.

SYSTEMS OF STRATIFICATION

To better understand how our economic position shapes our likely outcomes, we need a better appreciation of the structures within which we find ourselves. Not all societies structure themselves in the same way, but difference exists within all societies. Sociologists call the social inequality that is built into the structure of society **stratification,** by which they mean the structured ranking of entire groups of people that perpetuates unequal economic rewards and power in a society. The *strata* in *stratification* refer to different layers or levels of power and influence built into the structure of society. Sociologists focus on four major systems of stratification: slavery, caste, estate, and social class.

> **Life chances** The likelihood that our success is shaped by our access to valued material, social, and cultural resources.
>
> **Stratification** A structured ranking of entire groups of people that perpetuates unequal economic rewards and power in a society.
>
> **Slavery** A system of enforced servitude in which some people are owned by others as property.

Slavery Slavery is a system of enforced servitude in which some people are owned by others as property. Enslaved people become objects rather than subjects. Owners are free to treat them in the same way they might their horses or cattle.

The practice of slavery has varied over time. Most of the enslaved people in ancient Greece, for example, were prisoners of war or individuals captured and sold by pirates, and slave status was not necessarily permanent. By contrast, slavery in the United States was an ascribed status, and enslaved people faced racial and legal barriers to freedom. The first African slaves in what later became the United States were brought by Dutch traders to Jamestown in 1619 and worked on the

©Bettmann/Contributor/Getty Images

Did You Know?

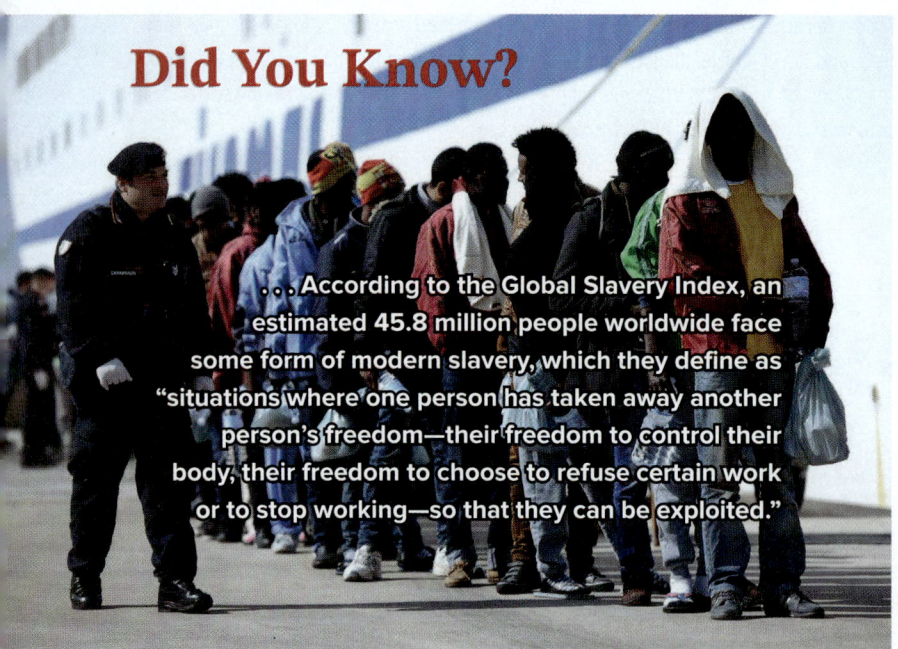

"... According to the Global Slavery Index, an estimated 45.8 million people worldwide face some form of modern slavery, which they define as "situations where one person has taken away another person's freedom—their freedom to control their body, their freedom to choose to refuse certain work or to stop working—so that they can be exploited.""

Photo: ©Photo by Tullio M. Puglia/Getty Images

recently established tobacco plantations there (Hashaw 2007). With the founding of the United States as a new nation, the U.S. Constitution established slave ownership as a legal right, and numerous founders owned people as slaves, including George Washington and Thomas Jefferson. It wasn't until 1865, with the passage of the 13th Amendment to the U.S. Constitution, that slavery was banned throughout the United States, though the amendment included the clause "except as a punishment for crime whereof the party shall have been duly convicted."

Caste A stratification system in which boundaries between strata are clear, relations between levels are regulated, and social status is ascribed.

Today, the Universal Declaration of Human Rights, which is binding on all members of the United Nations, prohibits slavery in all its forms. According to the United Nations (2010), contemporary forms of slavery include debt bondage, forced labor, child labor and child servitude, sexual slavery, sale of children, forced marriage, and the sale of wives. In many developing countries, bonded laborers are imprisoned in lifetime employment. Although slavery is outlawed in the United States and Europe, guest workers and illegal immigrants have been forced to labor for years under terrible conditions, either to pay off debts or to avoid being turned over to immigration authorities. In 2015, the National Human Trafficking Resource Center (2016) reported 5,544 incidents in the United States of potential human trafficking. Of these, 4,136 involved sex trafficking, 33 percent of which involved minors.

Castes In a stratification system based on **caste**, boundaries between strata are clear, relations between levels are regulated, and social status is ascribed. The caste into which you are born remains the same until you die. It determines your opportunities throughout life, including who your friends are, what occupation you will pursue, and whom you will marry. Caste-based systems are rigid, allowing for limited and formalized interaction between castes.

The most familiar caste-based system is based primarily in India and is associated with Hinduism. This system has four major castes, or *varnas:* priests (*Brahman*), warriors (*Kshatriya*), merchants (*Vaishya*), and artisans/farmers (*Shudra*). Within those four major castes are thousands of subcaste groupings. A fifth category, the *Dalit,* referred to in the past as untouchables, is considered to be so lowly and unclean as to have no place within this system of stratification. In 1950, after gaining independence from Great Britain, India adopted a new constitution that formally outlawed the caste system. In addition, economic changes tied to urbanization and the impact of technology have undercut its taken-for-granted status. Yet caste continues to play a powerful role in shaping patterns of social interaction throughout India.

©Andrew Aitchison/Alamy Stock Photo

Even though individuals can't change their caste, that doesn't mean change over time is impossible. Subcastes within India, for example, have been able to improve their overall standing by adopting the principles and practices of castes above them. This process is known as Sanskritization, after the language of ancient India in which most of the Hindu scriptures are written. Because the priestly Brahman caste represents the highest class, adopting that lifestyle, including becoming a vegetarian and giving up alcohol, became a marker of hoped-for higher status for the group, though this is most successful for groups that are already near the top (Bahadur 2008; Srinivas 1956; Staal 1963). Seeking to look and act like members of a higher stratum to gain social status is not unique to caste-based systems.

Estates The **estate system** divides power in society into three primary sectors: the church, the nobility, and the commoners. This stratification system was characteristic of medieval Europe, especially in England and France. French bishop Adalbéron de Laon gave names to these three estates in a poem to French king Robert the Pious around the year 1030. He identified them as *Oratores, Bellatores,* and *Laboratores,* or those who pray, those who fight, and those who work (Le Goff 1990). Members of the first estate included bishops, monks, priests, and nuns. The second estate was composed of knights, lords and ladies, dukes and duchesses, and others of noble birth. Peasants and serfs were part of the third estate, and their labor produced food for all. In this feudal system, the ruling monarch, usually the king, ruled over all, but, over time, representatives from each of these groups were granted some degree of voice in the political system. Vestiges of the estate system remain in England in the form of the Church of England, the House of Lords, and the House of Commons.

The power in this system rested primarily on the nobles' ownership of land, though the church had substantial land holdings as well. Peasants provided the nobles with their income by paying them rents, primarily in the form of produce, in exchange for the opportunity to work the land. The nobles, with help from the knights among them, pledged to maintain order and protect the peasants from bandits and rival nobles. As in the caste system, social status was largely ascribed. The nobles inherited their titles and property, and there was little commoners could do to change their lot in life. One area that did provide some degree of opportunity was the church. By the 12th century, the priesthood emerged as a distinct category in most of Europe. In addition, opportunities for local merchants and artisans began to expand. For the first time, there were groups of people whose wealth did not depend on land ownership or agriculture. Their success ultimately contributed to the demise of feudalism and the rise of capitalism.

Social Class In the final stratification system, **social class,** social position is determined primarily by socioeconomic status, both real and perceived. Social class can be assessed objectively and subjectively. Objective indicators primarily include education, occupation, and income. A college graduate who is a mechanical engineer earning $83,000 per year is higher than a high school graduate working as a dental assistant earning $32,000. Subjective class identification, the degree to which a person identifies with a particular social class category, also plays a role. It's entirely possible, for example, for a person who makes a lot of money to identify with the lower social class within which she or he was born (Rubin et al. 2014). The perceptions others have also play a significant role because, as we learned with the Thomas theorem, perception shapes action, which, in the case of social class, may well affect the degree to which we are allowed access to valued resources. Because social class can involve multiple, sometimes contradictory, indicators, settling on a universal, all-purpose model of social classes is problematic.

> **Estate system** A system of stratification that divides power in society into three primary sectors: the church, the nobility, and the commoners.
>
> **Social class** A system of stratification primarily based on socioeconomic status, both real and perceived.

Sociologists commonly use a five-class model to describe the class system in the United States, though many other models are available (Beeghley 2007; Kerbo 2011). At the top are the *upper class,* including 1–2 percent of the population who are wealthy, well-respected, and politically powerful. Just beneath them

©The British Library/The Image Works

What Class Am I?

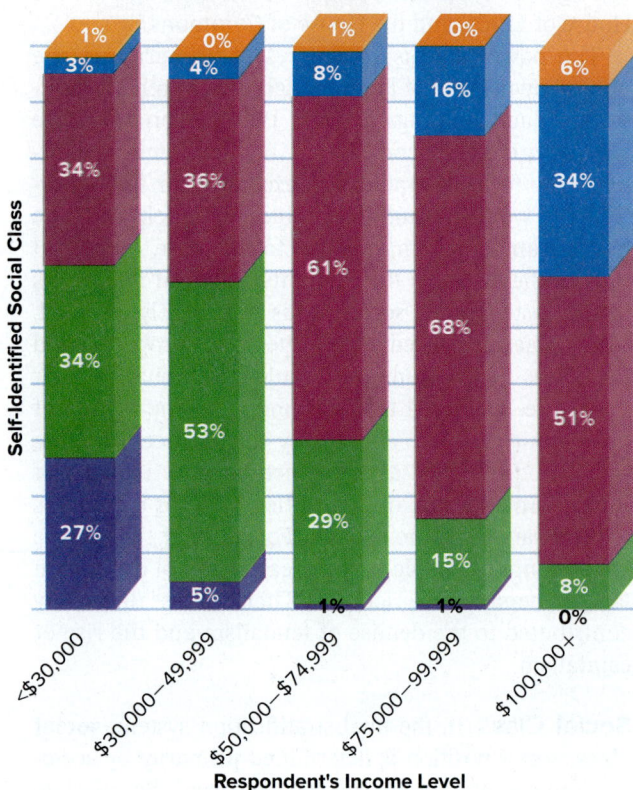

Note: Respondents were asked, "Which of the social classes would you say you belong in?" Their answers were then grouped into categories based on family income.
Source: Pew 2015a.

to categorizing themselves as either rich or poor. As a result, as the accompanying "What Class Am I?" graphic demonstrates, 51 percent of people making over $100,000 per year still identify as middle class, rejecting the available Upper-Middle and Upper options (Pew 2015a). Looked at another way, when asked how much money it takes to consider someone rich, people at different income levels have different perceptions. Among those earning less than $30,000 per year, 54 percent chose an income level of less than $100,000 to be considered rich. Among those making $100,000 or more, only 2 percent indicated a threshold that low. At this much higher income level, 46 percent said it would take $500,000 or more per year to be considered rich (Reeves 2015).

SOCIAL MOBILITY

A society's system of stratification significantly shapes one's life chances. Though the opportunity for changing position is possible in all, the likelihood of doing so varies significantly. In most cases, the story of the peasant girl who marries a prince is nothing more than a fairy tale. To better understand opportunities for are the *upper-middle class,* which is composed primarily of business executives, doctors, lawyers, architects, and other professionals; they make up about 15 percent of the population. The next 30–35 percent include members of the *middle class,* which is composed of less-affluent professionals, such as school teachers and nurses, along with owners of small businesses, clerical workers, and others who have decent jobs but a minimal amount of autonomy—that is, control over what they do and when they do it. The fourth group is the *working class,* whose jobs typically involve some degree of manual labor, including carpenters, plumbers, and factory workers, who make up another 30–35 percent of the population. The final group is the *underclass,* commonly referred to as "the poor," who make up 15–20 percent of the population. People in this class have limited and inconsistent access to resources, and membership includes a disproportionate number of African Americans, Hispanics, immigrants, and single mothers.

When asked to identify their social class, people in the United States struggle with how to respond. One of the difficulties comes from widespread assumption that social classes do not exist in the United States. Another is the difficulty people have in placing themselves in relationship to others. In particular, people seem averse

Did You Know?

. . . Six members of the Walton family, heirs of Walmart founder Sam Walton, own more wealth than the bottom 40 percent of U.S. families combined.

Photo: ©Paul Sakuma/AP Images

social mobility, meaning movement within or between society's strata, sociologists investigate the degree to which a society is open versus closed.

Open versus Closed Stratification Systems A society with an **open system** of stratification allows for social mobility between strata. Of the stratification systems discussed earlier, class-based systems have the potential to be more open than others. In principle, capitalism seeks to identify those with the greatest ability and reward them for their efforts regardless of whether their parents were rich or poor. The possibility for mobility becomes an incentive for hard work.

A society with a **closed system** of stratification does not allow for social mobility between strata. Social positions are ascribed, so the position into which you are born is the position within which you remain throughout life. Caste systems are mostly closed with limited opportunity for movement within one's lifetime. Societies with barriers to mobility, whether based on religion, gender, race, ethnicity, class, or any other positional variables, are more closed than those without such barriers.

Types of Social Mobility Sociologists also distinguish between mobility *within* a stratum versus movement *between* strata. For example, a bus driver who becomes a hotel clerk moves from one social position to another of approximately the same rank. Sociologists call this kind of movement **horizontal mobility**. However, if the bus driver were to become a lawyer, he or she would experience **vertical mobility**—the movement of an individual from one social position to another of a different rank (Sorokin [1927] 1959). Vertical mobility involves moving upward or downward in a society's stratification system.

Another contrasting pair of mobility types involves movement that occurs *between* generations versus change that occurs *within* an individual's career as an adult. **Intergenerational mobility** refers to changes in the social position of children relative to their parents. Thus, a college professor whose father was a printer provides an example of vertically upward intergenerational mobility. A plumber whose parents were both physicians illustrates vertically downward intergenerational mobility. Because education contributes significantly to upward mobility, any barrier to the pursuit of advanced degrees limits intergenerational mobility (Isaacs, Sawhill, and Haskins 2008).

Intragenerational mobility, in contrast, involves changes in social position within a person's adult life. Thus, a woman who enters the paid labor force as a teacher's aide and eventually becomes superintendent of the school district experiences vertically upward intragenerational mobility. A man who becomes a cab driver after his accounting firm goes bankrupt undergoes vertically downward intragenerational mobility.

SOC THINK

What is the story of social mobility in your family? To what extent have there been shifts both across and within generations? What factors, such as family connections or historical events, contributed to the social mobility that occurred?

In the United States one way to define the "American Dream" is as vertically upward intragenerational mobility. In other words, a person would experience a significant shift in social class position over the course of her or his career, from a relatively low-level position to one of significant wealth and power. Although this does happen, the "American reality" is that we tend to end up in positions relatively close to where we began.

>> Social Class in the United States

The stratification system in the United States is predominantly class based. Within it, three categories of resources play a major role in shaping our life chances. *Material* resources refer to economic assets that we own or control, including money, property, and land. *Social* resources include prestige based on the position we occupy and connections based on the social networks we are a part of. It turns out that the old saying "It's not what you know; it's who you know" has some truth to it. Position and connections make it possible for us to increase the likelihood of accomplishing our goals. Finally, *cultural* resources include our tastes, language, and way of looking at the world. They represent our knowledge of cognitive, normative, and material elements of culture that we can draw on when acting to accomplish our goals. A simple but classic example involves knowing which fork to use for the various courses of a formal dinner. But it also includes knowing how to respond when we are put on the spot, whether in a business meeting, at a rock concert, or in class. Viewing social class in terms of

> **Social mobility** Movement within or between society's strata.
>
> **Open system** A society with a system of stratification that allows for social mobility between strata.
>
> **Closed system** A society with a system of stratification that does not allow for social mobility between strata.
>
> **Horizontal mobility** The movement of an individual from one social position to another of the same rank.
>
> **Vertical mobility** The movement of an individual from one social position to another of a different rank.
>
> **Intergenerational mobility** Changes in the social position of children relative to their parents.
>
> **Intragenerational mobility** Changes in social position within a person's adult life.

POPSOC

Even though they like to deny that social class exists, Americans have a fascination with class as portrayed in pop culture. This curiosity is especially apparent with the appeal of British programs such as *Downton Abbey, Masterpiece Classic, Sherlock Holmes, Doctor Who,* and *Absolutely Fabulous.* Perhaps it's just the accents, but the social class dimensions of British society are often core elements of these shows. Such programs provide a window into how social stratification is practiced differently in other societies. *Downton Abbey,* for example, portrays the lives of an aristocratic family and their servants in the early 20th century.

Photo: ©Carnival Films for Masterpiece/PBS: Courtesy Everett Collection

Income Money received over some period of time.

Wealth The total value of all material assets minus debts at a single point in time.

material, social, and cultural resources enables us to better understand the degree to which living the American Dream is possible.

INCOME AND WEALTH

Income and wealth provide social class with its material foundation. **Income** refers to money received over some period of time. It often comes in the form of wages per hour or salary per year, but returns on investments, such as stock dividends or profit from the sale of property, including homes within some time period, also count. **Wealth** consists of the total value of all material assets minus debts at a single point in time. It includes savings, stocks, land, or any other material asset of value. If you were to sell everything you own and pay off all your debts, what you had left would be the value of your wealth. These material resources make our class-based lifestyles possible (Bourdieu 1986). As such, if we are to understand social classes in the United States, we need a clear picture of their distribution.

Income Income inequality is a basic characteristic of a class system. In 2015, the median household income in the United States was $56,516, a 5.2 percent increase over the previous year. In other words, half of all households had incomes higher than $56,516 in that year, and half had incomes lower than that amount. But this fact does not fully convey the income disparities in our society. We get some sense of income inequality by contrasting the median (middle) score with the mean (arithmetic average), which in 2015 was $79,263. The mean is so much higher because some people make a lot more money than others, which draws the mean up, making it a less useful statistic for describing "average" or typical income (Proctor et al. 2016).

We gain additional insight into this inequality by looking at the relative placement of households from bottom to top. One of the most common ways to present income dispersion uses quintiles. This involves lining up all income-earning households, from those who make the least to those who make the most, and then drawing a line at 20, 40, 60, and 80 percent, thus creating five groups. The United States has approximately 125 million households, so each quintile would include an equal number, or about 25 million households. Looking at things this way gives us a sense of what the average income is within each quintile, along with the percentage of the total income pie that each quintile earns.

As we can see in the "Percentage Share of Total Income" graph, even though each quintile contains 20 percent of U.S. households, some quintiles earn less than 20 percent of total income while others earn more. As a group, households in the lowest income quintile take home 3.1 percent of all income earned in the United States in 2015. Contrast that with households in the top quintile, which earn 51.1 percent of all income. In other words, the top 20 percent of households take home more than half of all income earned in the United States. When comparing the share of total income each quintile receives now to the distribution in 1970, those at the top are taking home a larger share of the overall income pie, meaning income inequality has increased over time (Proctor et al. 2016:Table A-2).

Turning from percentages to dollars, the share of income has indeed gone down for households in the four bottom quintiles, but this does not mean

©Tana Lee Alves/WireImage/Getty Images

Percentage Share of Total Income

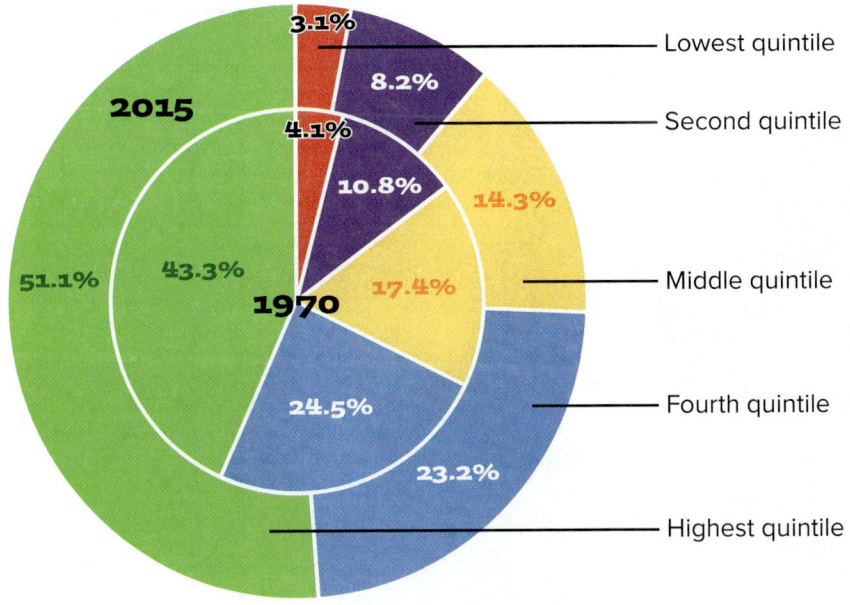

Source: Proctor et al. 2016:Table A-2.

Average Household Income by Quintile

■ 1970 ■ 2015

Note: Income for 1970 shown in 2015 dollars.
Source: Proctor et al. 2016:Table A-2. Photo: ©Stockbyte/Getty Images RF

that their average income has gone down. If total income goes up, meaning the whole pie gets bigger, it is possible for everyone's income to increase, even though the top quintile takes home a bigger slice of the pie. As the "Average Household Income by Quintile" graph shows, this is exactly what has happened. Between 1970 and 2015, the average income for all five quintiles increased, though the amount of increase varied. Income for the lowest quintile rose $1,602, or 14.8 percent. Income for the highest quintile rose $84,474, or 71.7 percent. That said, the average income of $12,457 for the lowest quintile is substantially lower than that for the highest quintile at $202,366 (Proctor et al. 2016:Table A-2). Everyone is doing better, but the gap between the top and the bottom is getting larger.

When it comes to income inequality, one focus in recent years has been the bottom 99 percent versus the top 1 percent. Economists Thomas Piketty and Emmanuel Saez found that in 2014, the average annual income for adults in the top 1 percent was $1,304,771. As the accompanying "Income Distribution in the United States" graph demonstrates, the percentage of income earned by the top 1 percent now exceeds that earned by the bottom 50 percent. Even within this top category, however, substantial income differences exist. For example, the average income for the 23,440 adults in the top 0.01 percent (the top of the top) was $28,129,418. And, according to the IRS, the top 400 U.S. households had an average income of $318 million in 2014. On the other end of the scale, 14.6 million households reported incomes under $15,000 (Internal Revenue Service 2016; Piketty, Saez, and Zucman 2016; Proctor et al. 2016).

To provide a simple measure of the distribution of anything in a population, including income and wealth, Italian sociologist and statistician

Income Distribution in the United States

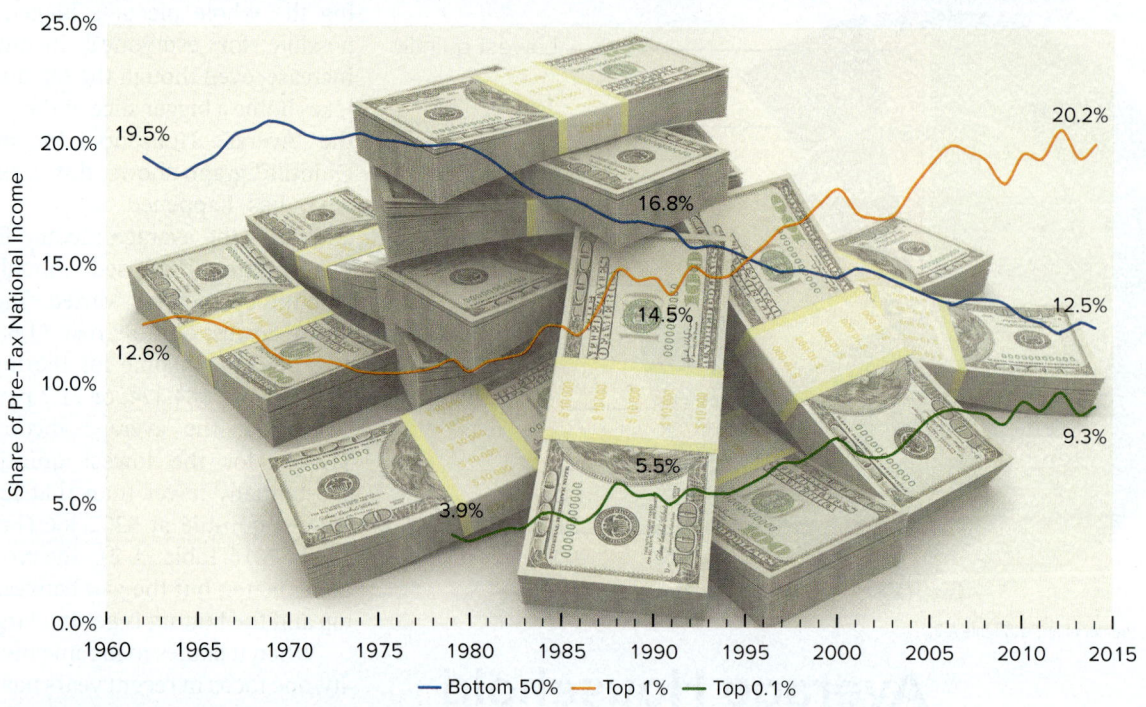

Note: Categories represent percentages of U.S. adults aged 20 and over.
Source: Piketty, Saez, and Zucman 2016.   *Photo:* ©Mmaxer/Shutterstock.com RF

Corrado Gini created the Gini index, a single number ranging between zero and one. The larger the Gini coefficient, the greater the inequality. For example, if everyone in the population earns the same income, the Gini index equals zero. If one person earns everything and everyone else earns nothing, the Gini index equals one. The real value of the Gini index is as a comparative statistic because it allows us to see whether inequality is increasing or decreasing over time. In the United States, the Gini index for income reached a low of 0.386 in 1968. Since that time it has risen fairly steadily. In 1990 it reached 0.428, and by 2015 it climbed to 0.479 (Proctor et al. 2016:Table A-2). This upswing indicates that income inequality has increased significantly during that time.

Wealth Wealth in the United States is even more unevenly distributed than income. The median wealth for households in 2013 was $63,800, but the mean was $508,700 (Wolff 2016). The large difference

Wealth Distribution in the United States

Note: Categories represent percentages of U.S. households.
Source: Saez and Zucman 2016.   *Photo:* ©C Squared Studios/Getty Images RF

Did You Know?

...Consumers in the top quintile spent, on average, $110,508 in 2015 on all items including food, clothes, and housing. To put that in perspective, people in the top quintile spend about 10 times as much in a year as those in the bottom quintile earn.

Source: Bureau of Labor Statistics 2016f. *Photo:* ©Brand X Pictures/Getty Images RF

POVERTY

In 2015, 43.1 million people in the United States—13.5 percent of the population—lived in poverty. Based on official calculations, a family consisting of two adults and two children with a combined annual income of $24,036 or less fell below the poverty line. By contrast, a single person under the age of 65 must earn less than $12,331 annually to be officially considered poor (Proctor et al. 2016).

Defining Poverty Such figures make it seem like a simple matter to define who is living in poverty: You are either above the threshold or below it. Sociologists have found, however, that our conceptions of poverty vary. For example, we can define poverty in either absolute or relative terms.

Absolute poverty refers to a minimum level of subsistence that no family should be expected to live below. According to this definition,

> **Absolute poverty** A minimum level of subsistence that no family should be expected to live below.

Going GLOBAL

The Poverty Rate in Households with Children, Selected Countries

Country	Rate
United States	20.5%
Mexico	19.7%
Italy	17.7%
Canada	16.5%
Japan	16.3%
France	11.3%
Germany	9.8%
Sweden	8.5%
Denmark	2.7%

Source: OECD 2016b:Table CO2.2. *Photo:* ©Jason R Warren/Getty Images RF

between the two is a consequence of the extreme amounts of wealth held by the richest households. The top 10 percent of households own 77.2 percent of all wealth in the United States with an average worth of $2.56 million. The bottom 90 percent own the remaining 22.8 percent with a net worth of $84,000 per household (Saez and Zucman 2016).

Breaking down that top 10 percent into smaller pieces reveals significant differences between the wealthy and the very wealthy. As the "Wealth Distribution in the United States" graph shows, the top 1 percent owns 41.8 percent of U.S. household wealth, with an average net worth of $13.8 million. At 22.8 percent, the bottom 90 percent of households collectively own about half as much wealth as that owned by the top 1 percent. Going even higher, households in the top 0.1 percent own 22 percent and are worth $72.8 million. Put another way, the 160,700 households in the top 0.1 percent own about as much wealth as do the 144,600,000 households in the bottom 90 percent. And at the very pinnacle, those in the top 0.01 percent, a total of 16,070 households, own 11.2 percent of all U.S. wealth and are worth $371 million (Saez and Zucman 2016:Table 1).

©Robyn Beck/AFP/Getty Images

Relative poverty A floating standard of deprivation by which people at the bottom of a society, whatever their lifestyles, are judged to be disadvantaged in comparison with the nation as a whole.

someone who is below the poverty level ultimately lacks sufficient resources to survive. Many nations, including the United States, use some form of this criterion as the basis of their definition of poverty. A comparatively high proportion of children in U.S. households are poor, meaning that their families are unable to afford necessary consumer goods (food, shelter, and clothing).

In contrast, **relative poverty** is a floating standard of deprivation by which people at the bottom of a society, whatever their lifestyles, are judged to be disadvantaged in comparison with the nation as a whole. For example, people who have sufficient food, clothing, and shelter might nonetheless be considered poor if they live in a wealthy nation such as the United States, because they can't afford to buy things the culture defines as important but that are not essential for survival, such as a refrigerator. Similarly, someone who would be considered poor by U.S. standards might be well-off by global standards of poverty; hunger and starvation are daily realities in many regions of the world. In addition, when viewed in historical terms, someone currently defined as poor may be better off in absolute terms than a poor person in the 1930s or 1970s.

Historically, the poverty line in the United States was first calculated based on a formula established in 1964. President Lyndon B. Johnson had declared a War on Poverty, but at the time, no official measure of poverty existed. To enact an official measure, the Johnson administration turned to the work of Mollie Orshansky, a food economist at the research bureau of the Social Security Administration. Orshansky proposed combining two facts to establish a general poverty threshold. The first came from a study that found that families spend approximately one-third of their budget on food. The second was the estimated cost of a minimally nutritious diet established by U.S. Department of Agriculture dieticians. Orshansky combined these two pieces of information to establish the poverty threshold as three times the cost of the USDA diet. She assumed that families facing poverty would cut back on both food and nonfood expenditures at approximately the same rate so that the 3-to-1 ratio would hold (Fisher 1992, 2008; Orshansky 1965).

There has been a longstanding debate about whether this approach to defining poverty in the United States measures the true nature of poverty. For example, critics argue that the measure is too simplistic, or that the multiplier should be closer to five which would have the effect of raising the poverty line. Recognizing the limits of the official definition, the U.S. government started calculating a supplemental measure of poverty in the fall of 2011. This more complex measure takes into account the actual costs of food, clothing, shelter, utilities, taxes, work expenses, and out-of-pocket medical costs. In addition to income, it counts food stamps and tax credits as available resources. And it is adjusted to reflect price differences across geographic regions (U.S. Census Bureau 2010b).

> Anyone who has ever struggled with poverty knows how extremely expensive it is to be poor.
>
> James A. Baldwin

Who Are the Poor? One of the lessons we learn by analyzing those who fall below the poverty line is that our stereotypes about poverty are flawed. For example, many people in the United States believe that the vast majority of the poor are able to work but will not. Yet, of the 43.1 million people in poverty, 43.4 percent are either under age 18 or 65 years old or older. Many working-age adults who are poor do work outside the home, although often in part-time positions. In 2015, 2.5 million people who worked full-time, year-round, and 6.9 million of those who worked part-time, were in poverty. Of those poor adults who do not work, many are ill or disabled, or are occupied in maintaining a home.

A person's likelihood of being in poverty varies based on social status. The "Who Are the Poor in the United States?" table demonstrates this by contrasting the percentage of people in a variety of status categories in the U.S. population as a whole versus the percentage in those same categories who are officially considered poor. For example, 23.1 percent of people in the United States are under 18, but 33.6 percent of people in poverty are under 18. This suggests that children are overrepresented in the poverty population when compared to the population as a whole. People who are 65 and older are underrepresented in the poverty population because their percentage within the poor population of 9.7 is smaller than their percentage in the population as a whole of 14.9 (Proctor et al. 2016:Table 3).

The type of community within which people live also plays a role. In 2015, 40.3 percent of poor people in the United States lived in big cities within metropolitan areas. These urban residents are the focus of most governmental efforts to alleviate poverty. Yet, according to many observers, the plight of the urban poor is growing worse, owing to the devastating interplay of inadequate education and limited employment prospects. Traditional employment opportunities in the industrial sector are largely closed to the unskilled poor. Past and present discrimination heightens these problems for those low-income urban residents who are Black and Hispanic (Proctor et al. 2016).

Analyses of people who are poor in general reveal that they are, however, not a static social class. The overall composition of the poor changes continually; some individuals and families move above the poverty level after a year or two, while others slip below it. In a study of economic insecurity from ages 25 to

Who Are the Poor in the United States?

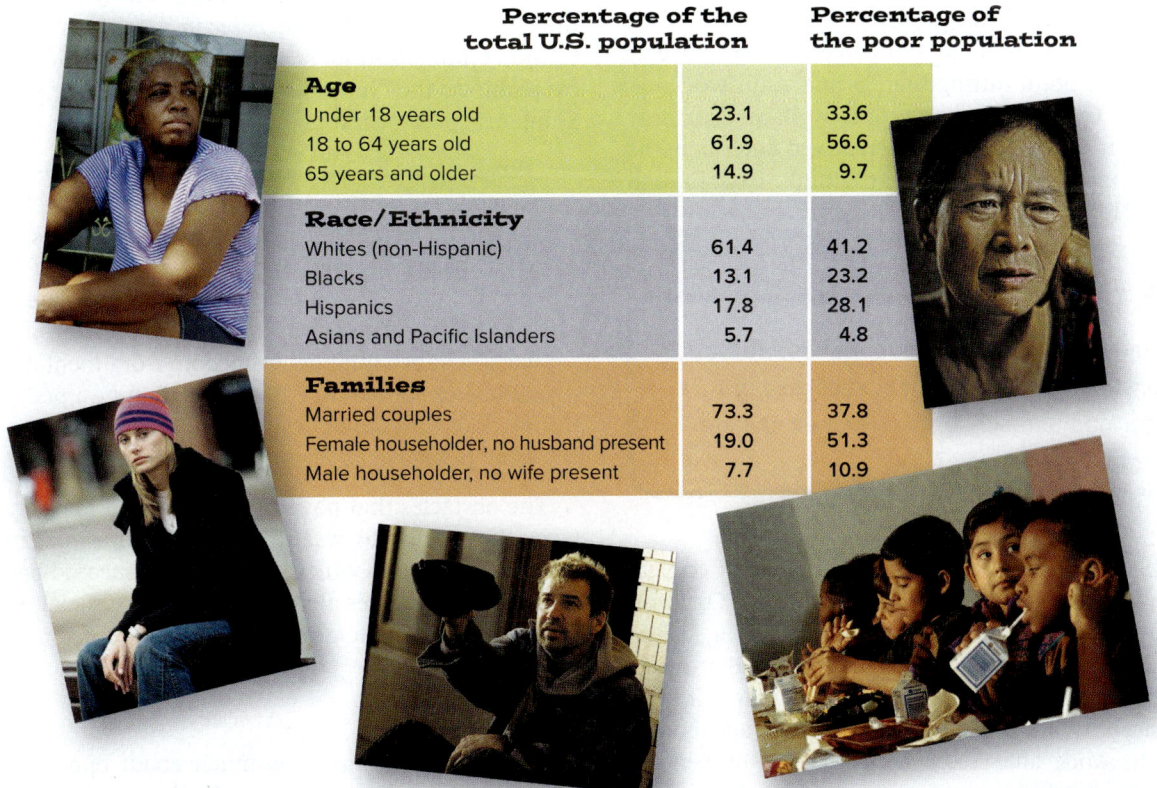

	Percentage of the total U.S. population	Percentage of the poor population
Age		
Under 18 years old	23.1	33.6
18 to 64 years old	61.9	56.6
65 years and older	14.9	9.7
Race/Ethnicity		
Whites (non-Hispanic)	61.4	41.2
Blacks	13.1	23.2
Hispanics	17.8	28.1
Asians and Pacific Islanders	5.7	4.8
Families		
Married couples	73.3	37.8
Female householder, no husband present	19.0	51.3
Male householder, no wife present	7.7	10.9

Note: Age and race/ethnicity percentages are based on total persons. Families percentages are based on total families.
Source: Proctor et al. 2016:Tables 3, 4. *Photos: (top right):* ©Wild Horse Photography/Getty Images; *(bottom right):* ©David Buffington/Getty Images RF; *(bottom center):* ©Con Tanasiuk/Design Pics RF; *(bottom left):* ©Jacobs Stock Photography/Getty Images RF; *(top left):* ©eyecrave/Getty Images RF

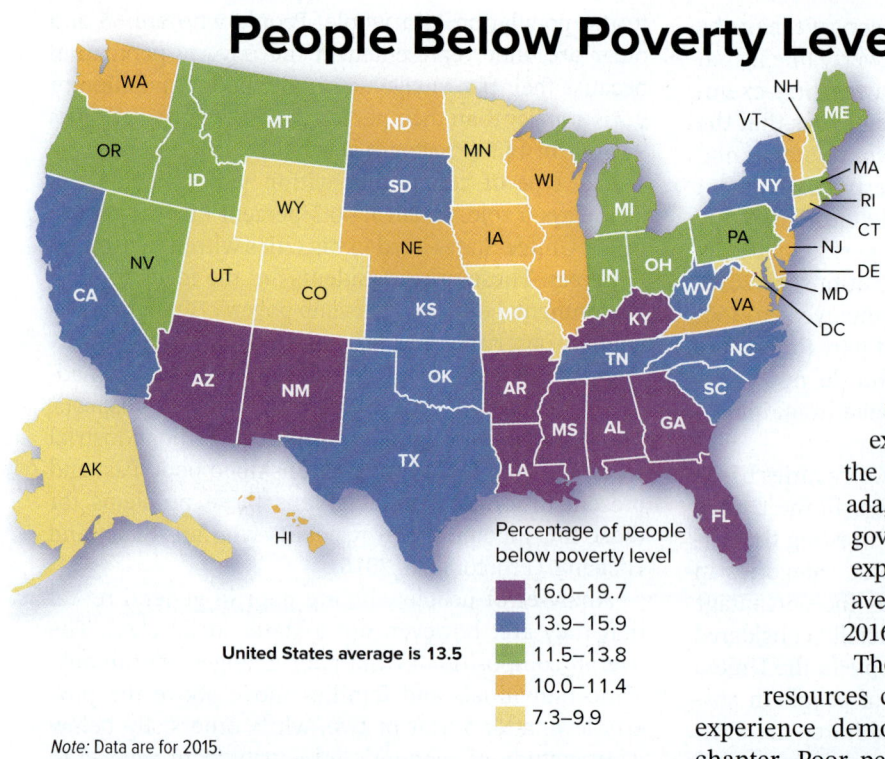

People Below Poverty Level

Percentage of people below poverty level
- 16.0–19.7
- 13.9–15.9
- 11.5–13.8
- 10.0–11.4
- 7.3–9.9

United States average is 13.5

Note: Data are for 2015.
Source: U.S. Census Bureau 2016i:Table 19.

60, sociologist Mark Rank found that 79 percent of the U.S. population experience at least one year in which they are unemployed, receive welfare benefits, or are officially poor or near poverty. Focusing just on poverty and near poverty, 54.1 percent spend a year with an income less than 150 percent of the poverty line at some point during their prime adult working-age lives. Considering long-term welfare use, only 3.8 percent of that population received such benefits for 10 or more consecutive years (Rank, Hirschl, and Foster 2014:37).

SOCTHINK

Should welfare recipients be required to work? If so, should the government subsidize preschool and afterschool care for their children while they are at work?

In 1996, in a historic shift in federal policy, Congress passed the Personal Responsibility and Work Opportunity Reconciliation Act, ending the long-standing federal guarantee of assistance to every poor family that meets eligibility requirements. The law sets a lifetime limit of five years of welfare benefits and requires all able-bodied adults to work after receiving two years of benefits (although hardship exceptions are allowed). The federal government gives block grants to the states to use as they wish in assisting poor and needy residents, and it permits states to experiment with ways to move people off welfare.

Other countries vary widely in their commitment to social service programs. But most industrialized nations devote higher proportions of their expenditures to housing, Social Security, welfare, health care, and unemployment compensation than the United States does. For example, in Cuba, the government pays for 96 percent of health care expenditures, compared to 83 percent in the United Kingdom, 71 percent in Canada, and 51.8 percent in Mexico. The U.S. government pays 48 percent of health care expenditures, ranking it behind the global average of 60.1 percent (World Bank 2016b).

The domino effects of a lack of economic resources can be severe, as Rae McCormick's experience demonstrated at the beginning of this chapter. Poor people often also lack the social network connections to help them get good jobs, not to mention having to overcome the negative status associated with being poor. When it comes to cultural resources, they also often lack the same kind of educational credentials that can serve as a valuable asset. Journalist David Shipler (2004), in his in-depth study titled *The Working Poor: Invisible in America,* referred to the combination of factors that poor people must overcome as the "interlocking deficits of poverty." As Shipler (2004:4–5) put it,

> Breaking away and moving a comfortable distance from poverty seems to require a perfect lineup of favorable conditions. A set of skills, a good starting wage, and a job with the likelihood of promotion are prerequisites. But so are clarity of purpose, courageous self-esteem, a lack of substantial debt, freedom from mental illness or addiction, a functional family, a network of upstanding friends, and the right help from private or governmental agencies.

The obstacles that poverty presents, and the advantages that access to wealth provides, raise questions about the degree to which a person can succeed based on his or her abilities alone or whether the social position people inherit determines their likely outcome.

THE AMERICAN DREAM

The American Dream is as much about opportunity as it is success. The existence of substantial levels of income and wealth inequality, and the persistence of poverty, are not themselves contrary to the American

Dream. In the United States, 62 percent of adults believe that people who want to get ahead can make it if they are willing to work hard. This belief does not vary significantly by income level (Pew Research Center 2014e, 2016d). Even though the gap between rich and poor is wide, people in the United States are less likely to see that gap as a big problem than do people in a wide variety of other nations, including England, France, Greece, Russia, China, and Pakistan (Pew Research Center 2014f). Americans want to assume that the system is fair and that both the rich and the poor are deserving of their positions (Putnam 2015).

Meritocracy Faith in opportunity manifests itself in a commitment to meritocracy. A meritocracy is a system in which a person's social status is achieved through a combination of ability and effort. To put it in terms of stratification and social mobility, a meritocracy is an open system in which your position is earned.

The commitment to meritocracy in the United States works in tandem with the principle of equality. That value is set forth within the opening lines of the Declaration of Independence: "We hold these truths to be self-evident, that all men are created equal, that they are endowed by their Creator with certain unalienable Rights, that among these are Life, Liberty and the Pursuit of Happiness." This conviction regarding our fundamental sameness implies that everyone should have a chance for success regardless of their station in life. Our outcomes should be based on something other than having had the good fortune of being born into the right family. Differences in outcomes in terms of income, wealth, and poverty are accepted, and even valued, because they provide incentives for hard work and sacrifice, so long as everyone has an opportunity to succeed (Reeves 2015).

The desire to put the principle of meritocracy into practice was apparent early on in American history in the works of people like Benjamin Franklin and Thomas Jefferson. It provided the justification for Horace Mann's commitment to public education as the great equalizer, as we saw in the "Education in Society" section in Chapter 8. One of his goals was to have schools spread a common American culture through a shared curriculum. Values, including the importance of meritocracy, were reinforced. Children in 1843, for example, in their *McGuffey's Eclectic Readers,* one of the most commonly assigned textbook series in American history, read passages such as this:

The road to wealth, to honor, to usefulness, and happiness, is open to all, and all who will, may enter upon it with the almost certain prospect of success. In this free community, there are no privileged orders. Every man finds his level. If he has talents, he will be known and estimated, and rise in the respect and confidence of society. (Quoted in Weiss 1969:33)

©Elnur Amikishiyev/123RF

Similarly, in the late 1800s, the best-selling books by Horatio Alger, including titles such as *Struggling Upward, Mark the Match Boy,* and *Rough and Ready,* reinforced the rags-to-riches ideal. In *Ragged Dick,* for example, the title character is told as a boy, "You know in this free country poverty in early life is no bar to a man's advancement" (Alger [1868] 1985:55). In Alger's stories, a person's character and values trump social position as superior resources all but ensuring certain success (Reeves 2014).

Faith in the American Dream remains strong. Former president Barack Obama reinforced the U.S. commitment to meritocracy in his second inaugural address. In it he declared, "We are true to our creed when a little girl born into the bleakest poverty knows that she has the same chance to succeed as anybody else, because she is an American; she is free, and she is equal, not just in the eyes of God but also in our own" (Obama 2013). There is, in the United States, an almost sacred aura that

©ziggymaj/Getty Images RF

(open book): ©p72/Alamy Stock Photo RF; *(title page):* ©Bettmann/Contributor/Getty Images

surrounds the principle of meritocracy. Violation of this principle would represent a betrayal of the public trust.

Aristocracy In many ways, commitment to meritocracy was the counterpoint to the rule by the British monarchy that early American colonists rebelled against. In an aristocracy, social status is ascribed and membership in the privileged or elite ranks is inherited. Unlike the sameness principle undergirding meritocracy, this system presupposes the existence of innate differences between people. Some are born to lead while others are destined to follow. *Aristocracy* literally means "rule by the best," and, over time, that came to mean the nobility. The principle of aristocracy undergirds both the caste and estate systems of stratification. Because differences are presumed to be inherited, there are limited opportunities for social mobility.

In the United States, people are less certain about the degree to which opportunities for social mobility remain possible. The 62 percent of people who believe that "anyone can get ahead if they work hard" has declined from 74 percent in 1999, and the percentage of people who now say that "hard work and determination are no guarantee of success for most people" rose from 23 to 36 percent (Pew Research Center 2016d). The likelihood of children doing better than their parents, an important marker for the American Dream, has decreased, as the accompanying "Will You Earn More Than Your Parents?" graph shows. Comparing incomes for parents and children when each reached age 30, and using constant dollars to make comparison possible, 92 percent of children born in 1940 earned more than their parents did at the same age. For those born in 1984, only 50 percent outearned their parents. In other words, the odds of doing better than your parents are now no better than a coin flip (Chetty et al. 2016).

Social mobility does occur, but most people do not move very far. For example, when comparing wealth owned by parents versus children, 36 percent of children with parents in the lowest quintile end up there themselves. Another 30 percent move up to the second quintile, but only 6 percent make the rags-to-riches journey to the top quintile. On the other end of the scale, 44 percent of children with parents in the top wealth quintile stay there, with 25 percent dropping down to the fourth quintile. Only 6 percent experience the riches-to-rags drop down into the bottom quintile (Pfeffer and Killewald 2016).

Political scientist Robert Putnam (2015) uses the expression "opportunity gap" to describe what appears to be a growing divide between the children of the well-to-do compared to children from working-class and poor families. Increased levels of neighborhood segregation, educational segregation, and social network segregation, including the increased likelihood of marrying a same-class spouse, he claims, all contribute to a growing class divide. Well-off parents provide their children with a whole host of advantages, including private schools, tutors, educational vacations, and specialized summer camps, making the divide even wider (Duncan and Murnane 2011; Finighan and Putnam 2016; Putnam 2015).

As we can see from the accompanying "Likelihood of Graduating from College" graph, a child from a high-income family who scores poorly on a standardized 8th-grade math exam is more likely to graduate from college 12 years later than a child from a low-income family who scores high on the exam. This suggests that rich kids with poor academic performance are more likely to graduate than are smart poor kids. According to sociologist Sean Reardon, "The achievement gap between children from high- and low-income families is roughly 30 to 40 percent larger among children born in 2001 than among

Will You Earn More Than Your Parents?

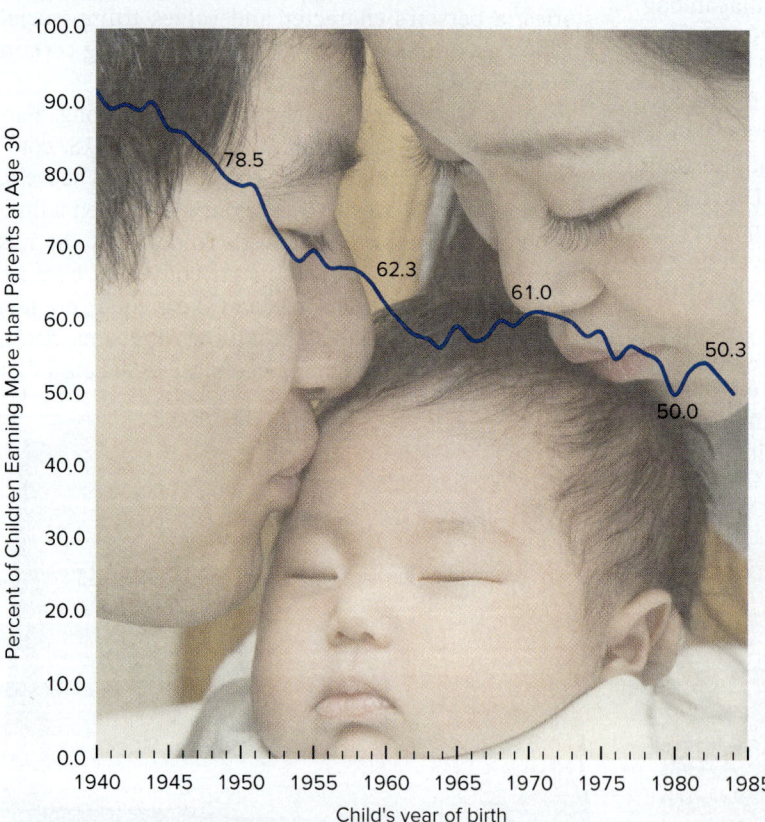

Note: Graph compares pretax income for parents and children when each reached age 30.
Source: Chetty et al. 2016. *Photo:* ©Cecilia Cartner/Getty Images RF

Likelihood of Graduating from College

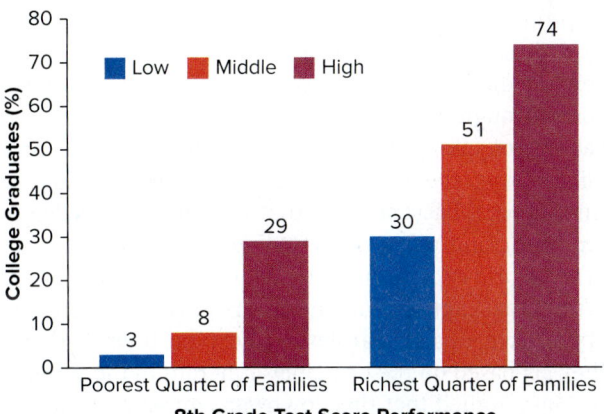

Note: Test performance is for a standardized 8th-grade math test. Family status is based on parent's education, occupation, and income. College graduation rate measure is for 12 years after the test.
Source: Putnam 2015:190.

Education Pays: Full-Time, Year-Round Workers Aged 25–64

Source: U.S. Census Bureau 2016a:Table PINC-03.   Photo: ©McGraw-Hill Education/Mark Dierker, photographer

those born twenty-five years earlier" (Reardon 2011:93). Parents' level of education, occupation, and income combined play a major role in this divide between those who are college graduates and those who are not (Lareau 2011; Putnam 2015).

The economic, social, and cultural advantages children at the top receive provide a cushion that protects these children should failure occur. Putnam writes, "Parental wealth is especially important for social mobility, because it can provide informal insurance that allows kids to take more risks in search of more reward" (Putnam 2015:36). Those who do not get the opportunity to fully develop their skills through education, for example, are less likely to share in the rewards that such accomplishment conveys, as shown in the accompanying "Education Pays" graph. Over time, as those at the top transmit increased access to resources to their children, the rungs of the mobility ladder get farther apart, making it difficult for people with limited resources to reach the next level.

When a society makes an overt commitment to meritocracy in principle, it becomes easy to minimize the degree to which inherited resources shape likely outcomes. Aristocracy in practice becomes a hidden privilege as people downplay the extent to which their advantages mattered (Chen 2016; Hayes 2012; McNamee and Miller 2014). Sociologist Thomas Shapiro provides an example of just that in his interview with Joe and Briggette Barry, a middle-class couple whose parents gave them $32,000 to help them buy a house, bought them three different cars, helped pay their daughter's tuition to a private school, helped with mortgage payments when Joe was between jobs, set up a trust fund for their daughter's college education, and provided numerous other forms of assistance. Yet when asked how they acquired their assets, Briggette responded, "we worked our butts off for what we have" (Shapiro 2004:75). It is no doubt true, but underplays the difference between those who work just as hard but lack access to similar economic resources. As Shapiro points out, the effect of such denial is particularly felt in the African American community where access to wealth is significantly lower than in the White, non-Hispanic community. The same holds true for women who, as a result of unequal treatment, wage discrimination, and occupational segregation, do not receive the same opportunities for advancement as do men. We explore gender and racial inequality in more detail in Chapters 12 and 13.

>> Sociological Perspectives on Stratification

By paying attention to the structure of the stratification system and how resources within it are distributed, we can better understand how a society committed to the principle of meritocracy might produce the practice of aristocracy. Sociologists provide us with tools to focus our attention on key resources that enable us to discern who has power and why. As noted, three categories of resources are critical: material, social, and cultural.

MARX AND MATERIAL RESOURCES

Karl Marx focuses his attention primarily on the distribution of material resources. As we saw in the "Economic Systems" section of Chapter 9, he argues that, throughout history, power was determined by ownership of the means of production. As a result, Marx's model of class has two basic categories: owners and non-owners. During feudal times, for example, the nobility owned the land, and the peasants did not. Under capitalism, the ruling class, known as the **bourgeoisie,** own the means of production, including factories and machinery. The working class, known as the **proletariat,** do not own the means of production so must sell their labor power to the capitalist in exchange for a wage.

Bourgeoisie The ruling class under capitalism due to their ownership of the means of production.

Proletariat The working class under capitalism who must sell their labor power in exchange for a wage because they lack ownership of the means of production.

Class consciousness The subjective awareness held by members of a class regarding their common vested interests and need for collective political action to bring about social change.

Marx argues that the logic of capitalism as a system determines how each group acts. The competition in the marketplace that is at the heart of capitalism initially pits capitalists against each other in their pursuit of profit. In their desire to gain greater market share, capitalists attempt to reduce the costs of production in general and labor costs in particular. They reduce these costs through mechanization (inventing new machines capable of taking over more of the labor), de-skilling (simplifying the work process by breaking it down into its most basic steps so that minimal knowledge is required), and offshoring (finding labor in other parts of the world capable of doing the work for less money). It's not that capitalists are necessarily greedier than others or have a particular desire to exploit their workers; they act based on the principles inherent in the system.

Marx argued that this downward pressure on workers' wages and working conditions is unrelenting. It ultimately leads to the development of a massive global working class of largely poor, unskilled workers competing against each other for low-wage jobs, resulting in racial, ethnic, and nationalistic conflict among the proletariat. Ironically, it is the technological innovation of capitalism that makes a better future possible. Marx praised this aspect of capitalism because it solves the problem of production like no other previous economic system. Capitalism, he writes, was "the first to show what man's activity can bring about. It has accomplished wonders far surpassing Egyptian pyramids, Roman aqueducts, and Gothic cathedrals" (Marx and Engels [1848] 1998:38). As a result, we will eventually eliminate scarcity. Even now we can produce enough so that no one in the world needs to go hungry.

Once this technological obstacle to providing for all our needs was solved, Marx felt that the only obstacle to an equitable society would be the capitalist system of social relations. Its emphasis on private property enabled the few at the top, the bourgeoisie, to own and control much more than they could ever hope to need or want while the majority at the bottom, the proletariat, struggled. Eventually, Marx argued, the proletariat would see that they had no real interest in the existing set of social relations. They would develop **class consciousness**—a subjective awareness of common vested interests and the need for collective political action to bring about social change. This would lead to the overthrow of capitalism in favor of a system of more equitable distribution in the form of socialism and then communism.

A question that often arises in response to Marx's work is this: why hasn't that revolution happened? One answer is that Marx thought capitalists would work against the development of such class consciousness by shaping society's accepted values and norms. The term dominant ideology describes a set of cultural beliefs and practices that helps to maintain powerful social, economic, and political interests. From this perspective,

Did You Know?

...The highest-paid CEO, earning $94.6 million in 2015, was Dara Khosrowshahi of Expedia, which operates numerous online travel sites, including Hotels.com, Orbitz, and Trivago. The top-earning woman CEO was Safra Catz, who earned $53.2 million with Oracle.

Photo: ©Matthew Lloyd/Bloomberg via Getty Images

©Dave Moyer

one of the possible functions of meritocracy as a value is to reinforce the belief that mobility is possible even when limited opportunity exists in practice. In addition, belief in meritocracy reinforces the idea that those at the top belong there as a consequence of ability and effort and, therefore, deserve whatever riches and power they can accumulate (Fraser 2015). As a result, workers must overcome what Marx termed **false consciousness**—an attitude held by members of a class that does not accurately reflect their objective position. A worker with false consciousness may adopt an individualistic viewpoint toward capitalist exploitation ("*I* am being exploited by *my* boss"). In contrast, the class-conscious worker realizes that all workers are being exploited by the bourgeoisie and have a common stake in revolution.

> **False consciousness** A term used by Karl Marx to describe an attitude held by members of a class that does not accurately reflect their objective position.

Because Marx paid attention to the structure of the system itself, he was able to identify inherent tensions between social classes based on their control over material resources. Much more recently, economist Thomas Piketty did something similar in his surprise best seller *Capital in the Twenty-First Century* (2014). In this expansive historical overview of economic growth, Piketty maintains that, in the long run, the rate of return on capital, including profits, rents, interest, and dividends, is greater than overall economic growth, including increased income and output. Piketty uses the formula $r > g$ to describe this relationship. One reviewer

5 Movies on SOCIAL CLASS

Snowpiercer
Class warfare breaks out on a post-apocalyptic train ride.

Winter's Bone
A teen living in the Ozarks investigates her father's criminal dealings.

Water
An Indian widow attempts to escape the social restrictions of her position.

Rich Hill
Three boys and their families struggle to get by.

The Great Gatsby
Lifestyles of the rich and famous.

Class A group of people who have a similar level of economic resources.

Status group People who share the same perceived level of prestige.

Prestige The respect and admiration that a particular status holds in society.

Socioeconomic status (SES) A measure of social class position based on a combination of education, occupation, and income.

Party The capacity to organize to accomplish some particular goal.

summarized it this way, "Simply having money is the best way to get more money" (Doctorow 2014). Yet, in the United States, the commitment to meritocracy makes it difficult to accept the consequences of this simple fact. Denial was possible, in part, because, for most of the 20th century, the economy grew faster than normal due to technological innovation, and wealth grew more slowly as a consequence of the destructive impact of both world wars and the Great Depression. According to Piketty, that anomalous period, which helped produce a prosperous middle class in the middle of the century, has come to an end. In effect, Piketty is arguing that increasing inequality is an inevitable consequence of the structure of capitalism, and this, he says, "poses a challenge to the meritocratic model" (2014:27). What we learn from both Marx and Piketty is that control over material resources conveys substantial advantages.

WEBER AND SOCIAL RESOURCES

Max Weber accepted Marx's premise that social class plays a substantial role in shaping outcomes, but he argued that Marx's conception of power was too narrow, because it focused almost exclusively on ownership of the means of production. Weber argued that, in addition to material resources, social resources mattered, too. In response, he proposed a multidimensional model of stratification that included three components: class, status, and party.

Weber used the term **class** to refer to a group of people who have a similar level of economic resources. He identified two core elements of class: material resources and skill knowledge in the marketplace. In the first instance, class is about how much you own. Like Marx, this included ownership of the means of production, but Weber argued that ownership of other economic resources, including land, savings, and stocks, also defined a person's class position. And, whereas Marx maintained that mechanization and extreme division of labor would make skilled labor less valuable under capitalism, Weber argued that, given the complexity of modern society, knowledge would continue to be a valuable commodity in the labor market, something that employers would reward. By developing our skill knowledge—for example, by going to college—we enhance our class position.

Whereas class represents a material resource, status is a social resource. Weber used the term **status group** to refer to people who share the same perceived level of prestige. The power that your status provides depends upon how others view you, including both positive and negative estimations of honor. **Prestige** refers to the respect and admiration that a particular status holds in a society. Based on national surveys, sociologists have produced the accompanying "Prestige Rankings of Occupations" table to summarize people's perceptions of the relative status of a variety of occupations. We see doctors and lawyers as more prestigious than librarians and social workers, who are higher than janitors and maids (Hout, Smith, and Marsden 2015). But prestige in a class-based system involves more than just occupation. **Socioeconomic status (SES)** is a measure of social class position that combines education, occupation, and income. Class and status are not necessarily linked. It is possible to have significant social prestige along with a low economic standing, as is the case for many clergy members who are highly regarded within their faith communities, but who often receive relatively modest incomes.

People tend to give those with high levels of socioeconomic status the benefit of the doubt and to withhold respect from those who occupy low-status positions. As we saw with white-collar crime in Chapter 6, business executives found guilty of crimes involving millions or billions of dollars frequently get less harsh punishments than people involved in common street crimes involving minimal amounts of money. In this way, status becomes a form of social power conveying advantage and disadvantage based on perceived social position. This can be particularly problematic for members of groups who historically have not been respected when it comes to social power, including women, African Americans, Hispanics, gays and lesbians, and others.

The third major element in Weber's multidimensional model of stratification focuses on organizational resources. **Party** refers to the capacity to organize to accomplish some particular goal. This is what we mean when we talk of a political party, but such organization extends beyond politics to all spheres of life. As we have seen previously with Weber, bureaucracies represent the ideal form of this resource because they are organized explicitly to maximize available resources and to accomplish their goals in the most efficient manner possible. For Weber, party was a potential resource, available to any individuals or groups who would seize it. The civil rights movement in the United States provides a classic example. With minimal class or status resources as defined by the larger society, organization was critical to the success of this movement.

Weber maintained that, in practice, these three resources work together to shape individual and group power. People who are strong in one area can leverage that power to increase resources in the others. For example, people donate material resources to political

Prestige Rankings of Occupations

Occupation	Score
Physicians and surgeons	80
Astronomers and physicists	75
College professors	74
Architects	73
Dentists	72
Chief executives	72
Psychologists	71
Lawyers	69
Clergy	66
Aircraft pilots	65
Registered nurses	64
High school teachers	64
Computer programmers	63
Sociologists	63
Chiropractors	61
Elementary and middle school teachers	61
Police officers	60
Firefighters	59
Actors	58
Dental hygienists	56
Librarians	55
Social workers	54
Chefs and head cooks	50
Electricians	49
Insurance sales agents	47
Bakers	45
Carpenters	44
Fundraisers	40
Residential advisors	39
Animal trainers	38

Occupation	Score
Tool and die makers	38
Barbers	36
Printing press operators	36
File clerks	36
Bus drivers	35
Childcare workers	35
Security guards	34
Cooks	33
Office clerks	32
Bartenders	32
Waiters and waitresses	31
Hotel desk clerks	30
Logging workers	29
Construction laborers	28
Hunters and trappers	28
Laundry and Dry-cleaning workers	26
Taxi drivers and chauffeurs	26
Janitors	24
Maids	20
Telemarketers	18

Note: 100 is the highest and 0 the lowest possible prestige score.
Source: Hout, Smith, and Marsden 2015. *Photos: (top):* ©Pixtal/age fotostock RF; *(bottom):* ©PhotoAlto RF

SOC THINK

How might a group coordinate its class, status, and party resources to accomplish its goals? Pick a group on campus or in your community that is seeking to bring about social change, and imagine how you might advise group members using Weber's principles.

causes in the hope that doing so will advance social and organizational interests. Those who already possess power in all three areas have advantages over those who do not.

BOURDIEU AND CULTURAL RESOURCES

Marx emphasized material resources, and Weber highlighted the significance of social resources in the form of both status and party. Sociologist Pierre Bourdieu (1984, 1986) added to these the significance of cultural resources. He introduced the concept of **cultural capital,** by which he meant our tastes, knowledge, attitudes, language, and ways of thinking that we exchange in interaction with others. Often associated with artistic or literary preferences, cultural capital goes much deeper than this because it is rooted in our perception of reality itself. For Bourdieu, because some culture is more highly valued than other culture, it represents a form of power.

Bourdieu argued that people in different social class positions possess different types of cultural capital. From NASCAR to Mozart, for example, the tastes of the working class typically differ from those of the upper class. Symphonic concerts, operas, and foreign films, for instance, are considered "high culture," whereas "pop culture," including popular movies, TV shows, and most music CDs, is considered "middle-brow" or below. People draw distinctions, for example, between watching *Masterpiece* on PBS versus *American Ninja Warrior* and listening to Placido Domingo versus Bruno Mars. Such judgments are based on a certain level of cultural elitism in which those at the top are able to define their preferences as apparently superior to those of the masses (C. Wilson 2007). The cultural capital of people who are working class, often disparaged as redneck or ghetto, is valued least of all—until it is claimed by others as their own, as was the case with jazz, blues, rock and roll, and rap (Gans 1971).

> **Cultural capital** Our tastes, knowledge, attitudes, language, and ways of thinking that we exchange in interaction with others.

Chapter 10 / Social Class • 253

> ### SOC THINK
>
> Paul Fussell (1992), in his book *Class: A Guide Through the American Status System,* argued that the writing on our clothes says a lot about our social class. What story do the logos, brands, and writing on your clothes tell about you? How might your clothing choices have differed had you been in a different class position?

When we interact with others, we draw on the cultural capital resources we possess. Such interaction is fairly easy with others who share the same basic set of resources. When interaction occurs with others who possess a different stock of cultural capital, however, it becomes more complex. We see these kinds of difficulties when executives try to interact casually with workers on the factory floor or when we find ourselves dining in a place where we aren't quite sure what the rules are. If this were only a matter of social difference between various subcultures, it might not be a big deal. But the cultural capital of the elite is also tied to their control over economic and social resources. As a result, cultural capital can be used as a form of exclusion from jobs, organizations, and opportunities. For example, a qualified applicant may not be hired because, during the interview, he or she used inappropriate syntax or was not adequately familiar with cultural references, such as current news events or the latest in the world of golf. Employers tend to hire people they feel comfortable with, and cultural capital plays a significant role in that process (Kanter 1993).

Compounding this problem of cultural inequality is the fact that our preferences and perceptions often pass down from parent to child in the same way that material capital is inherited. Parents teach their children linguistic patterns and cultural tastes, from the use of double negatives to the appreciation of literature (Rothstein 2009). Cultural capital is also reproduced in the next generation in the context of schools, where class distinctions within the community shape the curriculum and patterns of discipline. Sociologist Jessi Streib (2011) found that, already by age four, children had adopted cultural conventions based on their social class positions. For eight months she conducted research at a diverse preschool and found that children from upper-middle-class families were more talkative and demanding of the teacher's time and attention than were working-class kids. The linguistic style of the higher-class children was more consistent with the classroom culture, and, as a result, they were more likely to get their needs met.

Social mobility from this perspective involves more than just acquiring more money and better social connections. Winning the lottery, for example, does not transform a person at the bottom of the hierarchy into one at the top, or, as Bourdieu put it, "Having a million does not in itself make one able to live like a millionaire" (1984:374). Such movement requires a social and cultural transformation as well. For mobility to happen, individuals must earn and learn a different set of knowledge and skills, as well as a whole new lifestyle: new tastes, attitudes, language, and thoughts.

MATERIAL, SOCIAL, AND CULTURAL RESOURCES

Using these sociological tools enables us to better understand how social stratification operates. We learn that we must be particularly attentive to the type of social stratification system in place and to the categories of resources that determine positions within those systems. In closed systems, position is largely determined through inheritance at birth, and there is little you can do to change it. In the U.S. class-based system, some degree of mobility is possible. But it turns out that being rich or poor involves more than just having more or less money. We must be attentive to social and cultural resources as well.

... Researchers found that, by the age of three, children whose parents have professional jobs have heard 500,000 instances of praise and 80,000 of disapproval. In families receiving welfare, the ratio reverses; children have been praised 75,000 times and reprimanded 200,000 times.

Did You Know?

Source: Hart and Risley 1995. Photo: ©Digital Vision/Getty Images RF

When it comes to social order, it is easier for us, and for others, to continue along the same paths than to carve out new ones. In so doing, the status quo reproduces itself. Our social resources, including networks of relationships with family, friends, and coworkers, constrain the kinds of connections that might open up new pathways for us. Our cultural resources, including preferences, tastes, and knowledge, limit what we might imagine as possible or desirable. Whereas some at the top look down on those at the bottom as irresponsible and short-sighted, members of the working class may make fun of rich people's hoity-toity preference for opera and ballet and criticize their values as materialistic and selfish, lacking commitment to family and friends (MacLeod 2009).

As a result of material, social, and cultural resource differences, changing classes may involve the difficult task of changing identities, leading some to argue that the United States is more caste-like (Fussell 1992). Mobility would involve new social networks, new lifestyles, and new tastes. Complicating matters further, changing classes requires more than just changing ourselves; it also requires recognition and acceptance by others. Just as there may be interlocking deficits of poverty, there may also be interlocking advantages of wealth. One of those privileges is exclusion, denying others access to valuable social network connections. When considering the consequences of difference, implementing meritocracy and living up to the American Dream turn out to be challenging undertakings. But an understanding and appreciation for the challenges involved can empower people to take the steps necessary to succeed.

Personal Sociology

Cultural Capital

As a professor, I have seen that grades are shaped by more than just effort and inherent intellectual ability. Students with more cultural capital, including significant background educational resources, simply do not have to work as hard. Seniors in my introductory course, for example, know the rules of the game. In comparison, first-year students often have a hard time distinguishing what is essential versus what is secondary. Over time, however, most learn how to study effectively. This same principle is at work before students even arrive on campus. Students who come to college with the kinds of cultural capital that professors reward have advantages over those who lack such resources.

SOCIOLOGY IS A VERB

Sociological Autobiography

Write your sociological autobiography through the lens of class. How have your life chances been shaped by your access to material resources, such as your family income and wealth? By social resources—namely, your family and friendship network connections? By cultural resources—including taste, language, artistic and pop culture preferences, and educational attainment of family members? How might your life have been totally different if you had been born into another family with a different stock of resources?

FOR REVIEW

I. What is social class?
- Like slavery, caste, and estate, it is a stratification system in which people and groups are ranked, but it places them based primarily on economic position.

II. How does social class operate?
- Three categories of resources are key: material, including income and wealth; social, including social networks and prestige; and cultural, including tastes, education, and knowledge. Power is based on access to and control over these resources.

III. What are the consequences of social class?
- Although class-based systems are more open than the others, our life chances are shaped by our inherited class position and the material, social, and cultural resources that go with it. For most people, the social mobility that does occur, whether in terms of occupation, income, or wealth, is of a relatively short distance.

SOCVIEWS on Social Class

Functionalist View

All societies have some degree of stratification in order to ensure that all of society's needs are met.

In a society with a complex **division of labor**, some positions will inevitably be more important or require more skill than others.

Those with more talent and determination fill the higher-paid and more prestigious positions, whereas those who do not develop their talents take the low-ranking jobs.

KEY CONCEPTS
DIVISION OF LABOR, SOCIAL MOBILITY

Conflict View

Stratification systems perpetuate unequal economic rewards and facilitate exploitation.

Social class standing is largely an **ascribed status**.

People in power maintain and spread their interests and influence through their hold on the **dominant ideology** in a society.

Income and wealth are **distributed unequally** in U.S. society, and the gap between the rich and the poor is steadily increasing.

KEY CONCEPTS
STRATIFICATION, INEQUALITY, DOMINANT IDEOLOGY

Interactionist View

Social mobility results from interactions in which people attempt to better their place in the class system (for example, getting degrees, **networking**, acquiring cultural capital).

When we interact with others, we **exchange** our cultural capital resources, such as knowledge, tastes, attitudes, and ways of thinking.

Our social class helps determine our taste in clothes, food, music, TV shows, and many other everyday preferences.

KEY CONCEPTS
NETWORKING, EXCHANGE

MAKE THE CONNECTION
After reviewing the chapter, answer the following questions:

1
Analyze social mobility from the point of view of the three perspectives. In what way might mobility be functional? How would conflict theory explain it? What role does interaction play in getting ahead?

2
How do the conflict and the interactionist perspectives intersect in Marx's concept of "false consciousness"?

3
How would a theorist from each perspective explain the distribution of material, social, and cultural resources in society?

4
Think about your own "life chances." Which perspectives help you see factors that shaped your opportunities and outcomes?

Pop Quiz

1. What expression did Max Weber coin to describe the fact that our likelihood for success is shaped by our access to valued material, social, and cultural resources?
   a. *verstehen*
   b. cultural capital
   c. social mobility
   d. life chances

2. Which of the systems of stratification included "those who pray, those who fight, and those who work"?
   a. slavery
   b. caste
   c. estate
   d. class

3. A college professor whose father was a printer is an example of
   a. downward intergenerational mobility.
   b. upward intergenerational mobility.
   c. downward intragenerational mobility.
   d. upward intragenerational mobility.

4. What term describes money received over some period of time?
   a. wealth
   b. material resources
   c. assets
   d. income

5. What percentage of total income in the United States did the top quintile earn in 2015?
   a. 14.4 percent
   b. 23.0 percent
   c. 51.1 percent
   d. 77.2 percent

6. What does absolute poverty refer to?
   a. income below the 10th percentile as measured globally
   b. a minimum level of subsistence that no family should be expected to live without
   c. income below the 10th percentile within any society
   d. a level of deprivation by which people at the bottom of a society are judged to be disadvantaged in comparison with the nation as a whole

7. Approximately what percentage of the U.S. population lived in poverty in 2015?
   a. 3.2 percent
   b. 8.4 percent
   c. 13.5 percent
   d. 22.8 percent

8. According to Karl Marx, the class that owns the means of production is the
   a. nobility.
   b. proletariat.
   c. Brahman.
   d. bourgeoisie.

9. Which of the following were viewed by Max Weber as distinct components of stratification?
   a. conformity, deviance, and social control
   b. class, status, and party
   c. class, caste, and age
   d. class, prestige, and esteem

10. According to Pierre Bourdieu, our tastes, our education, the way we talk, and the things we like all represent forms of
    a. social capital.
    b. esteem.
    c. cultural capital.
    d. intelligence.

1. (d), 2. (c), 3. (b), 4. (d), 5. (c), 6. (b), 7. (c), 8. (d), 9. (b), 10. (c)

©Viviane Moos/Contributor/Getty Images

11 Global Inequality

TWO TALES OF ONE CITY

Mumbai is a city of contrasts. On the one hand, it is the entertainment and financial capital of India, home of Bollywood stars and billionaires. On the other, 5.2 million of its residents, 41 percent of the city's population, live in areas designated as slums (Abkowitz 2015; GPOBA 2014).

Nita Ambani describes Mumbai as "a city where dreams come true," and for Nita and her family, it has been (Ward 2016). Nita's husband, Mukesh Ambani, is India's wealthiest man, with a net worth of $22.7 billion. Their 27-story house—which they share with their three kids and Mukesh's mother—reportedly cost $1 billion to build, likely making it the most expensive home in the world. Named Antilia, the house contains a library, ballroom, 50-seat theater, swimming pool, spa, dance studio, terraced gardens, temple, parking garage for 160 vehicles, and reportedly even an ice-room that produces artificial snow flurries as a place to cool off on a hot day (Magnier 2010; Reginato 2012).

People at the top are doing well in Mumbai. The number of residents worth $30 million or more rose 357 percent from 2005 to 2015, producing a real estate boom (Knight Frank Research 2016). To meet the increasing demand for luxury accommodations in that city, developers launched a number of high-cost residential skyscraper projects. World One, for example, will become the tallest residential building in the world when completed, with housing units costing from $2.4 million to $16 million each. Before he became president, Donald Trump, not wanting to miss out on Mumbai's high-rise boom, also jumped in. Units at Trump Tower Mumbai start at $1.6 million apiece (Abkowitz 2015). Explaining the skyscraper boom, Babulal Varma, the managing director of yet another Mumbai developer, reports, "Everyone wants to get away from the crowd. . . . People want to go up. You're away from the noise, you're away from the pollution" (Bundhun 2016). Units in Varma's project start at $1.9 million, rising to $44 million for those near the top.

Life at street level looks very different for most people in Mumbai. In order to get by, many have to scavenge at Deonar, a massive 326-acre garbage dump that is surrounded on three sides by slums. People do this to find items they might recycle into something profitable, selling them to people such as Nawab Ali Shaikh, 61, who buys foam rubber collected from the dump, mostly from discarded furniture, cuts it into cubes, and sells it as stuffing material for toymakers. These scavenging and recycling jobs offer low pay, no security, and significant health and safety risks (Bag, Seth, and Gupta 2016; McKirdy and Kapur 2016; Shrivastava and Antony 2015; Ullah and Phadke 2016).

In India as a whole, the richest 1 percent owns 58.4 percent of the nation's wealth, up from 36.8 percent in 2000. At the other end of the scale, 224 million people live below the international poverty line of $1.90 per day (Shorrocks, Davies, and Lluberas 2016; World Bank 2016c). In this chapter we explore various dimensions of such global inequality.

As You READ

- How did the global divide develop?
- How significant is global stratification?
- Why did the global movement for universal human rights develop?

>> The Global Divide

Globally, we are more interdependent now than ever. We buy hoodies from Lesotho, blue jeans from Nicaragua, shoes from China, backpacks from the United States, coffee from Guatemala, pineapples from Thailand, tomatoes from Mexico, cars from South Korea, and a whole host of other products from places we may never have heard of before, much less visited. Our clothes are frequently more well traveled than we are. Yet, for the most part we have no real sense of the conditions under which the products we love are made (Timmerman 2012). As we saw in Chapter 1, the people upon whom we depend are often unknown and invisible to us. Sociology provides us with tools to better understand the experiences of people around the world who make the lives we lead possible.

Throughout most of human history, providing sufficient food, clothes, and shelter was a struggle for nearly everyone. Now, thanks in part to the technological

©Photofusion Picture Library/Alamy Stock Photo

Access to life's necessities, including clean drinking water, varies substantially around the world. ©B2M Productions/Getty Images RF

Going GLOBAL

Measuring Global Inequality

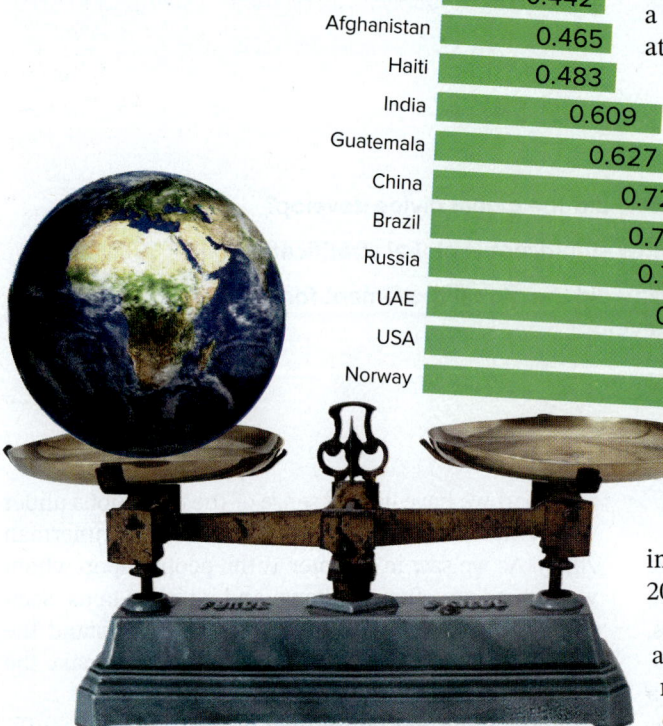

Country	HDI
Niger	0.348
Ethiopia	0.442
Afghanistan	0.465
Haiti	0.483
India	0.609
Guatemala	0.627
China	0.727
Brazil	0.755
Russia	0.798
UAE	0.835
USA	0.915
Norway	0.944

Note: The Human Development Index combines data on health, education, and income to provide a snapshot for each of 188 countries. Scores range from 0 to 1. These data are for 2014.
Source: United Nations Development Programme 2015. *Photos: (scale):* ©Ryan McVay/Getty Images RF; *(earth):* ©1xpert/123RF

---

water and modern sanitation facilities represents a daily challenge for millions of people in developing nations. And people living in the industrial nations, even though they compose a much smaller share of the total population, have higher incomes, better access to health care, and more security than people living in the developing nations. The United Nations created the Human Development Index (HDI) to assess progress along three key dimensions of human development: the ability "to lead a long and healthy life, measured by life expectancy at birth; the ability to acquire knowledge, measured by mean years of schooling and expected years of schooling; and the ability to achieve a decent standard of living, measured by gross national income per capita" (United Nations Development Programme 2015:3). As the accompanying "Going Global: Measuring Global Inequality" graph demonstrates, nations differ significantly along these dimensions. As part of their annual HDI report, the UN also explores various dimensions within these three areas, including child labor, workplace safety, labor rights, maternity leave, leisure time, child malnutrition, HIV prevalence, public expenditures on education, environmental sustainability, and gender inequality (United Nations Development Programme 2015).

When it comes to global income differences, as the accompanying "Gross National Income per Capita" map portrays, the poorest nations of the world are concentrated in sub-Saharan Africa and South Asia. The contrast between high- and low-income nations is stark. For example, in 2015, the global average for per capita **gross national income (GNI)**—which measures the total value of goods and services produced within the country plus net income from other countries—was $10,582. Industrialized countries such as the United States, Canada, Switzerland, France, and Australia had per capita GNIs more than $40,000. By comparison, more than 30 countries, including Malawi, Ethiopia, Nepal, Rwanda, and Afghanistan, had per capita GNIs of less than $1,000. Burundi had the lowest per capita GNI at $280, in stark contrast to the United States value of $56,070 (World Bank 2016d). As we saw with Mumbai in India, however, substantial differences exist not only between countries, but within them (Atkinson 2015; Milanovic 2016).

innovation brought on by the Industrial Revolution and its aftermath, a substantial percentage of the world's population no longer has to worry about providing for their subsistence needs. And yet, the resulting benefits of increased agricultural productivity and explosive economic growth have not been evenly distributed around the world. Globally, we produce enough for everyone to have enough, but we do not allocate resources in such a way that people facing hunger and starvation can gain access to the food they need to survive (International Monetary Fund 2008).

People's life chances are very much shaped by the country where they are born. For example, access to clean

Gross national income (GNI) A measure of the total monetary value of all goods and services produced within a country during some specified period of time.

>> Perspectives on Global Stratification

To better understand how today's global system developed, and how its various parts fit together, theorists have taken a step back to look at the world from a top-down, macro perspective. We focus on three major

Gross National Income per Capita

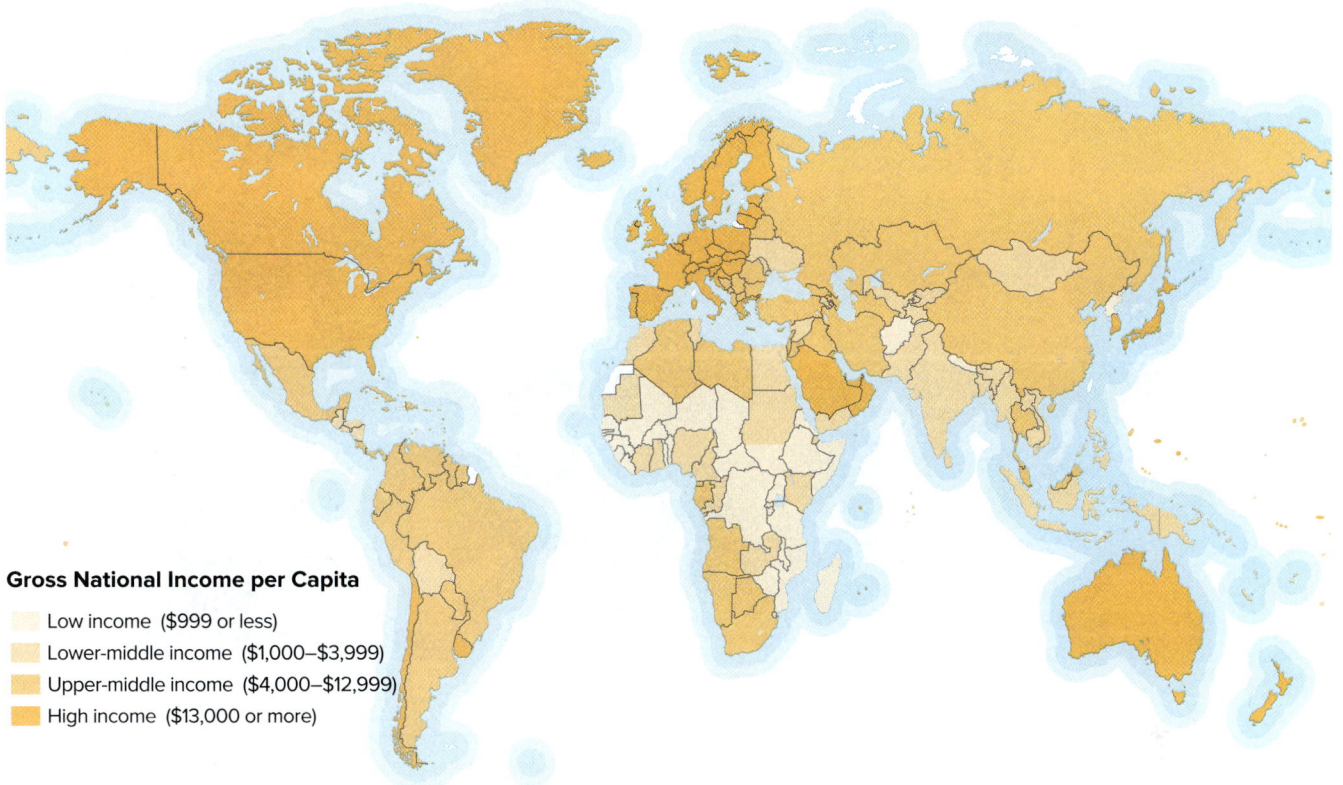

Gross National Income per Capita

- Low income ($999 or less)
- Lower-middle income ($1,000–$3,999)
- Upper-middle income ($4,000–$12,999)
- High income ($13,000 or more)

Note: Data are from 2015 with the exception of Andorra, Bermuda, and Venezuela from 2013, and Isle of Man, Puerto Rico, Gambia, Mauritania, Papua New Guinea, West Bank and Gaza, Vanuatu, and Iran from 2014.
Source: World Bank 2016d.

areas of analysis. These include the rise of modernization, the legacy of colonialism, and the growth of multinational corporations.

THE RISE OF MODERNIZATION

The desire to understand the causes and consequences of the transition from traditional to modern society played a substantial role in the founding of sociology as a discipline. Most early sociologists presumed that societies evolved along a common path from simple to complex or from primitive to advanced. Auguste Comte, for example, proposed that sociologists should be leaders, using their scientific knowledge to guide us toward a more rational, humane, and good society. Émile Durkheim envisioned a future society with a natural balance between interdependence and individual freedom. And Karl Marx anticipated a more egalitarian society in which the problem of scarcity was solved making material and social inequality a thing of the past.

This notion that the present was superior to the past, with its petty tyrannies and irrational superstitions, and that the future would be better yet, shaped how people viewed the world throughout much of the late 19th and early 20th centuries. They believed that through **modernization**, all societies would eventually progress from traditional forms of social organization—typically rural, agricultural, and religious—toward forms characteristic of post–Industrial Revolution societies. Features of the latter include a complex division of labor in which work is specialized; the separation of institutions including family, economy, government, education, and religion into specialized spheres, each with their own experts; the decline of the local and the rise of a societal or global orientation; the rise of rational decision making in the public sphere and a corresponding decline in public religious authority; and the spread of both cultural diversity, as more peoples from different backgrounds come into contact with each other, and a corresponding growth in egalitarianism as a value that embraces such diversity (Bruce 2000).

> **Modernization** The evolution of societies from traditional forms of social organization—typically rural, agricultural, and religious—toward forms characteristic of post–Industrial Revolution societies.

THE PROGRESS OF THE CENTURY.
THE LIGHTNING STEAM PRESS.   THE ELECTRIC TELEGRAPH.   THE LOCOMOTIVE.   THE STEAMBOAT.

Source: Library of Congress Prints & Photographs Division [LC-DIG-ppmsca-17563]

According to modernization theorists, countries such as China and India are in the often disruptive process of becoming modern societies. People in the United States and Europe experienced similar displacement and poverty in the early years of the Industrial Revolution, only later to lead more comfortable lives, and the same future awaits people in developing nations. Even if the transition from traditional to modern is difficult for many, the presupposition is that people in developing nations will benefit from modernization in the long term (Lipset 1959).

SOC THINK

Early sociologists were optimistic that positive social change was inevitable. To what extent do you think people today share this vision of the inevitable rise of the good society? How might cynicism about the possibility for change contribute to the maintenance of the status quo?

Critics of the modernization perspective suggest that terms such as *modernization* and even *development* contain an ethnocentric bias. They maintain that this model includes an implicit presupposition that people in "underdeveloped" nations are more "primitive" and that modern Western culture is more advanced, more "civilized." The unstated assumption of the modernization perspective, according to critics, is that what "they" (people living in developing countries) really want is to become more like "us" (people in modern industrialized nations). From this perspective, "they" want "our" economic development and our cultural values, including democracy, freedom, and consumerism. Such modernization, according to critics, represents a form of cultural imperialism. Many groups around the world reject this modernization path, viewing such "development" as an attack on their way of life and a threat to their core values and norms (Césaire 1972).

THE LEGACY OF COLONIALISM

An alternative perspective to modernization maintains that the rise of modernity has less to do with an inevitable evolution along a singular path than it has to do

Housing for people living in poverty around the world can be precarious, as shown here from Manila in the Philippines. ©John Wang/Getty Images

with power and control over resources. **Colonialism** occurs when a foreign power maintains political, social, economic, and cultural domination over a people for an extended period. In simple terms, it is rule by outsiders. The long reign of the British Empire over much of North America, parts of Africa, and India is an example of colonial domination. The same can be said of French rule over Algeria, Tunisia, and other parts of North Africa. Theorists from this perspective maintain that relations between the colonial nation and the colonized people are similar to those between the dominant capitalist class and the proletariat, as described by Marx (Fanon 1963).

By the 1980s, such global political empires had largely disappeared. Most of the nations that were colonies before World War I had achieved political independence and established their own governments. However, for many of these countries, the transition to genuine self-rule was not yet complete. Colonial domination had established patterns of economic exploitation that continued even after nationhood was achieved—in part because the former colonies were unable to develop their own industry and technology (Acemoglu and Robinson 2012). Their dependence on more-industrialized nations, including their former colonial masters, for managerial and technical expertise, investment capital, and manufactured goods kept the former colonies in a subservient position. Such continuing dependence and foreign domination are referred to as **neocolonialism.**

Analyses of colonialism and neocolonialism gave rise to **dependency theory,** which holds that poor, less-developed nations become subservient to wealthy industrial nations, which in turn use their economic and political might to maintain power. Workers in these poor nations become a source of cheap labor for major corporations based in industrialized nations. As a point of comparison, an average worker in Tokyo, Japan, would need to work 10 minutes to earn enough to buy a Big Mac, but in Nairobi, Kenya, she or he would need to work nearly three hours to afford the same thing, as the accompanying "Big Mac Index" demonstrates (Steiblin and Graef 2015). At the same time, these major corporations also exploit the raw materials of the less-developed nations by using their multinational economic might to negotiate advantageous terms. Even when developing countries advance economically, they remain dependent on powerful nations and wealthy corporations in an increasingly intertwined global economy. This interdependency allows industrialized nations to continue to exploit developing countries for their own gain.

The most widely used model of dependency comes from sociologist Immanuel Wallerstein (2000, 2004,

> **Colonialism** The maintenance of political, social, economic, and cultural dominance over a people by a foreign power for an extended period.
>
> **Neocolonialism** Continuing dependence of former colonies on foreign countries.
>
> **Dependency theory** The theory that poor, less-developed nations become subservient to wealthy industrial nations, which use their economic and political might to maintain power.

Big Mac Index

Note: Number of minutes it takes a worker with an average net wage to earn sufficient income to purchase a Big Mac based on local wages and prices. Global average is based on results from 71 cities surveyed worldwide.
Source: Steiblin and Graef 2015.   *Photo:* ©Picturenet/Blend Images LLC/Getty Images RF

2010), who views the global economic system as being divided between nations that control wealth and nations from which resources are taken. Through his **world systems analysis**, Wallerstein has described the unequal economic and political relationships in which certain industrialized nations (among them the United States, Japan, and Germany) and their global corporations dominate the core of this system. At the semiperiphery of the system are countries with marginal economic status, such as China, Ireland, and India. Wallerstein suggests that the poor developing countries of Asia, Africa, and Latin America are on the periphery of the world economic system. The key to Wallerstein's analysis is the exploitative relationship of core nations toward noncore nations. Due to the economic and political power core nations wield, it becomes difficult for nations on the periphery and semiperiphery to establish and maintain their own economic and political autonomy (Hardt and Negri 2009).

According to world systems analysis and dependency theory, a growing share of the human and natural resources of developing countries gets redistributed to the core industrialized nations. This redistribution happens in part because developing countries owe huge sums of money to industrialized nations as a result of foreign aid, loans, and trade deficits. Concerns about a potential global debt crisis have intensified the Third World dependency rooted in colonialism, neocolonialism, and multinational investment. International financial institutions can pressure indebted countries to take severe measures to meet their interest payments. The result is that developing nations may be forced to devalue their currencies, freeze workers' wages, increase privatization of industry, and reduce government services and employment (Irwin 2015; D. Lee 2015).

These trends are part of the larger process of **globalization**—the worldwide integration of government policies, cultures, social movements, and financial markets through trade and the exchange of ideas. Because the forces of world financial markets often transcend governance by conventional nation-states, international organizations such as the World Bank and the International Monetary

World systems analysis A view of the global economic system as one divided between certain industrialized nations that control wealth and developing countries that are controlled and exploited.

Globalization The worldwide integration of government policies, cultures, social movements, and financial markets through trade and the exchange of ideas.

World Systems Analysis at the Beginning of the 21st Century

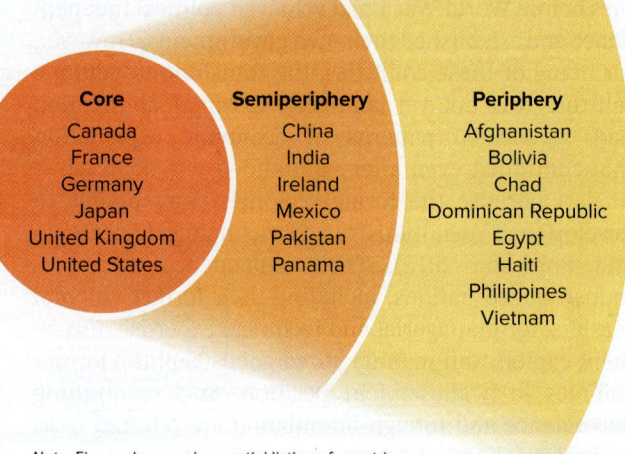

Note: Figure shows only a partial listing of countries.

Going GLOBAL

Top 10 Multinational Corporations Compared to National Economies

> ## SOC THINK
> Increasingly, we compete with workers around the world for jobs. What impact has the rise of globalization had on job prospects in your community and your country?

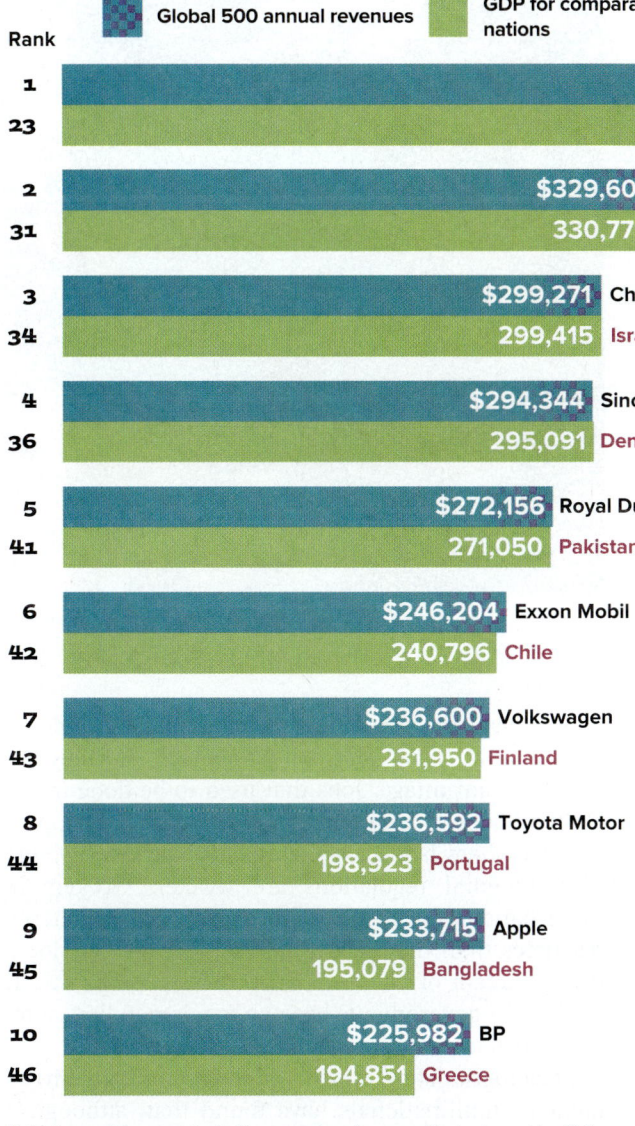

Note: Corporations are paired with economies of comparably sized countries. Dollar amounts are in millions.
Sources: For corporate data, *Fortune* 2016; for GDP data, World Bank 2016e.

environment, the loss of cultural identity, and discrimination against minority groups in periphery nations.

THE GROWTH OF MULTINATIONAL CORPORATIONS

Worldwide, corporate giants have played a key role in the rise of globalization. The term **multinational corporations** refers to commercial organizations that are headquartered in one country but do business around the world. Such private trade and lending relationships are not new; merchants have conducted business abroad for hundreds of years, trading gems, spices, garments, and other goods. Today's multinational giants are not merely buying and selling overseas; they are also producing goods all over the world (Wallerstein 1974, 2004).

These multinational corporations are huge. As the accompanying "Going Global: Top 10 Multinational Corporations Compared to National Economies" graph portrays, total revenues for these companies are equivalent to the total value of goods and services exchanged in entire nations. Foreign sales represent an important source of profit for multinational corporations, encouraging them to expand into other countries (in many cases, the developing nations). The U.S. economy is heavily dependent on foreign commerce, much of which is conducted by multinationals. In 2015 the combined value of U.S. exports and imports of goods and services was the equivalent of 28.1 percent of total economic output as measured by gross domestic product (Bureau of Economic Analysis 2016).

> **Multinational corporation** A commercial organization that is headquartered in one country but does business throughout the world.

In an effort to reduce production costs, corporate executives used deindustrialization and offshoring strategies, thus relocating production jobs around the

---

Fund have emerged as major players in the global economy. The function of these institutions, which are heavily funded and influenced by core nations, is to encourage trade and development and to ensure the smooth operation of international financial markets. As such, they are seen as promoters of globalization and defenders primarily of the interests of core nations. Critics call attention to a variety of related issues, including violations of workers' rights, the destruction of the

Chapter 11 / Global Inequality • 265

globe. Increasingly, however, it is not only production jobs that are being relocated. Today's global factories may now have the "global office" alongside them. And multinationals based in core nations have established reservation services and centers for processing data and insurance claims in the periphery nations. As service industries become a more important part of the international marketplace, many companies are concluding that the low costs of overseas operations more than offset the expense of transmitting information around the world (Rothstein 2016; Susskind and Susskind 2015; Sweet and Meiksins 2017).

> **SOC THINK**
>
> Multinational corporations have become so big that they have more economic resources than do some nations. What consequences arise from the fact that they can relocate their headquarters, offices, and production facilities anywhere in the world? How might this affect a nation's political power?

Modernization Consistent with the modernization approach, some analysts believe that the relationship between the corporation and the developing country is mutually beneficial. Multinational corporations can help the developing nations of the world by bringing industries and jobs to areas where subsistence agriculture once served as the only means of survival. Multinationals also promote rapid development through the diffusion of inventions and innovations from industrial nations. The combination of skilled technology and management provided by multinationals and the relatively cheap labor available in developing nations benefits the corporation. Multinationals can take maximum advantage of technology while reducing costs and boosting profits. Through their international ties, multinationals also make the nations of the world more interdependent. These international ties may reduce the likelihood of global conflict. A country cannot afford to sever diplomatic relations or engage in warfare with a nation that is the headquarters for its main business suppliers or a key market for its exports.

Dependency Critics of multinational expansion challenge this favorable evaluation of the impact of corporations. They argue that multinationals exploit local workers to maximize profits. For example, Starbucks—the international coffee retailer based in Seattle—gets some of its coffee beans from farms in Ethiopia. It sold its "Black Apron Exclusives" coffee in a fancy black box for $26 per pound, but it paid Ethiopian workers who picked the beans 66 cents per day (Knudson 2007).

©Siqui Sanchez/The Image Bank/Getty Images

Multinational corporations wield a significant amount of economic, social, and political power, and they use it to their advantage. Jobs that used to be done in the United States or Europe get transferred to developing nations where labor costs less and health, safety, and environmental regulations are weaker. Workers in these nations, in pursuit of better access to material resources than they would otherwise have, provide a steady stream of cheap labor for these companies. If workers or governments become too demanding, companies can up and move again.

Sociologists studying the effects of foreign investment by multinationals have found that, although it initially may contribute to a host nation's wealth, such investment eventually increases economic inequality within developing nations. This finding holds for both income and ownership. The upper and middle classes benefit most from economic expansion; the lower classes are less likely to benefit. And because multinationals invest in limited economic sectors and restricted regions of a nation, only some sectors benefit. The expansion of such sectors of the host nation's economy, such as hotels and high-end restaurants, appears to retard growth in agriculture and other economic sectors. Moreover, multinational corporations often buy out or force out local entrepreneurs and companies, thereby increasing economic and cultural dependence (Kerbo 2009; Wallerstein 1979, 2004).

In the Democratic Republic of Congo, workers mine for coltan, a key ingredient in the production of electronic circuit boards. ©Tom Stoddard Archive/Getty Images

Governments in developing nations are not always prepared to deal with the sudden influx of foreign capital and its effects on their economies. One particularly striking example of how unfettered capitalism can harm developing nations is found in the Democratic Republic of Congo (formerly Zaire). Congo has significant deposits of the metal columbite-tantalite—coltan, for short—which is used in the production of electronic circuit boards. Until the market for cell phones, pagers, and laptop computers heated up recently, U.S. manufacturers obtained most of their coltan from Australia. But at the height of consumer demand, they turned to miners in Congo to increase their supply.

Predictably, the escalating price of the metal—as much as $400 per kilogram at one point, or more than three times the average Congolese worker's yearly wages—attracted undesirable attention. Soon the neighboring countries of Rwanda, Uganda, and Burundi, at war with one another and desperate for resources to finance the conflict, were raiding Congo's national parks, slashing and burning to expose the coltan underneath the forest floor. In 2010 the U.S. Congress passed the Dodd-Frank Act, which included a provision requiring manufacturing companies to disclose whether they used any "conflict minerals," including coltan, cassiterite, gold, wolframite, or their derivatives, originating from the Democratic Republic of Congo or adjoining nations. According to a UN report, the result has been reforms in how business and government operate in Congo (Lezhnev 2011; Wyatt 2012).

POPSOC

In an analysis of more than 1,000 U.S. films, communications professor Jack Shaheen (2006, 2009, 2012) found that only 5 percent of Arab and Muslim characters were presented in a positive light. Arabs are repeatedly caricatured as Bedouin bandits, seductive belly dancers, villainous oil tycoons, or fanatical terrorists. The use of racial and ethnic stereotypes in American films and television shows is a form of symbolic power. Such portrayals reinforce the dominance of the majority groups at the expense of minorities who may lack the material, social, and cultural resources to provide alternative, more nuanced narratives to broader audiences (Allam 2016; Curiel 2016).

Photo: ©Warner Brothers/Courtesy Everett Collection

Chapter 11 / Global Inequality • 267

>> Stratification Around the World

At the same time the gap between rich and poor nations is widening, so too is the gap between rich and poor citizens within nations. As the world systems model suggests, stratification in developing nations is closely related to their relatively weak and dependent position in the global economy. Local elites work hand in hand with multinational corporations and prosper from such alliances. As a result, significant income and wealth differences arise.

INCOME AND WEALTH

Finding accurate and comparable estimates of income and wealth for countries around the world represents a challenge. To do so, Gallup—most famous for its political polls—conducted surveys. Based on its research, Gallup estimated that median household income worldwide is $9,733. When comparing countries, it found that the median incomes for the top 10 nations were 50 times higher than those for the bottom 10. For example, Norway came out on top with a median income of $51,489, and the United States was sixth at $43,585. Compare those with Rwanda's $1,101, Liberia's $781, and Burndi's $673 (Phelps and Crabtree 2013).

A more common, though less easy to understand, indicator of relative income differences between countries uses gross national income (GNI), which measures the total monetary value of all goods and services produced within a country during some specified period of time. GNI encompasses all income a country's residents and businesses earn, including net income from abroad. As we saw in the "Gross National Income per Capita" map earlier in this chapter, this indicator reveals significant differences between nations. A newer source of income data comes from the World Wealth and Income Database, which seeks to provide easily accessible information in the form of maps, graphs, and tables so that students and researchers might explore new hypotheses regarding global and national inequality (WID.world 2017).

Income differences between the haves and have-nots within nations are substantial, as the "Quintile Distribution of Income" graph displays. In South Africa, for example, the bottom quintile earns 2.5 percent of the country's total income compared to 68.9 percent for the top quintile. Compare that to Ukraine, where the bottom quintile takes home 10.5 percent of total income compared to 34.7 percent for the top. Globally, countries that consistently have substantial income inequality include, among others, Seychelles, Haiti, Colombia, Brazil, Namibia, Honduras, and Rwanda (World Bank 2015c, 2015d). As we saw with Mumbai in India, the lack of available, regular, well-paying jobs in such countries makes it extremely difficult for those at the bottom to provide for their needs.

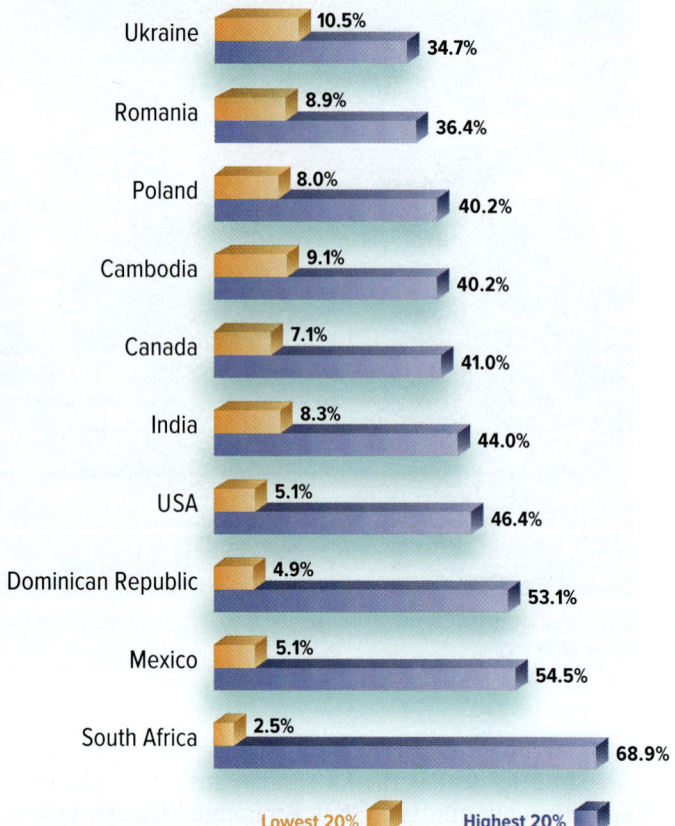

Quintile Distribution of Income

Note: Percentage of income earned by the top and bottom quintiles. Data are for the most recent year available.
Source: World Bank 2016f, 2016g.

Despite this persistent inequality, there has been good news in recent years regarding global incomes. Because the global income pie grew larger—in other words, more total income became available—average incomes in real dollars have risen for each percentile income grouping around the world. According to economist Branko Milanovic (2013, 2016), after-tax per capita household income rose significantly between 1988 and 2008 for all groups. But, as Milanovic puts it, "The gains from globalization are not evenly distributed" (2016: 10). Assuming you line up all households from those earning least to those earning most, those between the 40th and 60th percentiles did best, as their incomes rose more than 60 percent during that period. According to Milanovic, people in this middle quintile, whom he calls "the emerging global middle class," live primarily in rising Asian economies, mostly China, but also India, Thailand, Vietnam, and Indonesia (2016:19). Another group that did particularly well in terms of percentage increase included those in the top 1 percent. The group that saw the smallest increase in income during that period—whose income increased less than 10 percent—fell between the 80th and 90th percentiles globally. People in this group live primarily in richer, industrialized nations, such as the United States, Japan, and Germany, and come from the lower-half of the income distribution within those nations (Lakner and Milanovic 2015; Milanovic 2013, 2016). Milanovic sums up his findings this way: "the great [globalization] winners have been the Asian poor and middle classes; the great losers, the lower middle classes of the rich world" (2016:20).

Turning to wealth, inequality is even greater than for income. Globally, the median for household wealth is $2,222 per adult, and the mean is $52,819. The difference between the two suggests that a relatively small percentage of the world's adults own a significant amount of wealth, which is confirmed by the fact that the top 10 percent own 89.1 percent of global household wealth, and the top 1 percent own 50.8 percent. To break into the top 1 percent globally, a person must be worth a minimum of $744,396. On the other end of the spectrum, the bottom 50 percent of the world's adults combined own less than 1 percent of global wealth (Shorrocks, Davies, and Lluberas 2016).

Focusing on wealth distribution between regions and nations, as portrayed in the "Global Wealth Distribution" graph, the bulk of the world's wealth is held by countries in North America, Europe, and the rich Asia-Pacific nations. North America has 5.7 percent of the world's adult population but owns 36.1 percent of global household wealth. The United States alone commands 33.2 percent of global wealth. Contrast this with India, which has 16.7 percent of the world's population but only 1.2 percent of the world's wealth. In addition, the entire continent of Africa has 12.1 percent of the world's adult population but only 1 percent of global wealth (Shorrocks, Davies, and Lluberas 2016).

Wealth distribution within nations also varies significantly. As the accompanying "Wealth Concentration" graph shows, for example, the top 1 percent of adults in Japan owns 18.5 percent of total Japanese wealth, while in Russia the top 1 percent owns 74.5 percent of Russian wealth. In the United States, the top 1 percent owns 42.1 percent of U.S. household wealth (Shorrocks, Davies, and Lluberas 2016:Table 6-5). Ownership of significant amounts of wealth conveys substantial advantages because those who possess it do not need to rely only on their labor to produce income. Wealth can be used to produce income through various forms of investment, which can produce both more income and more wealth.

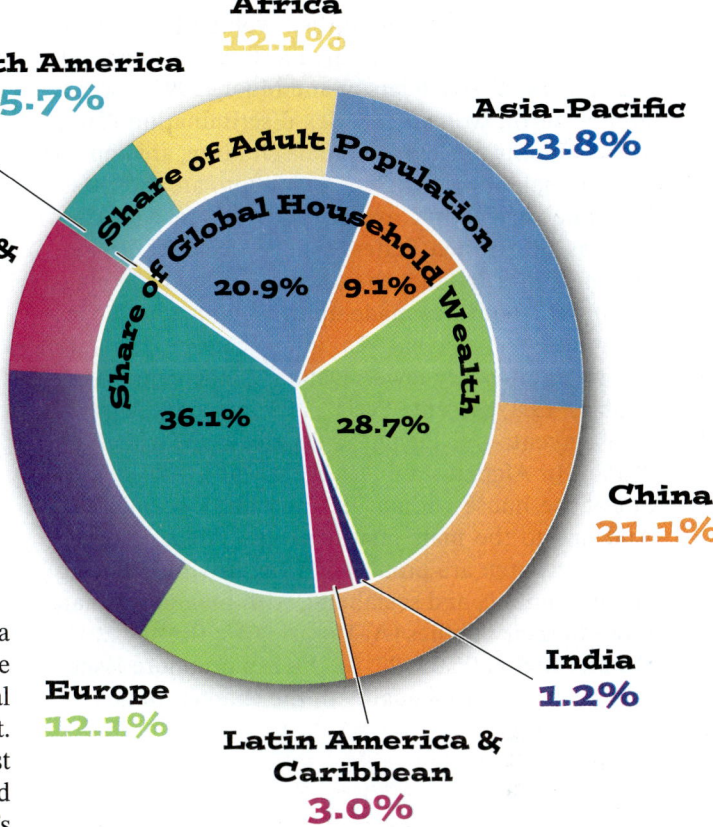

Global Wealth Distribution

Source: Shorrocks, Davies, and Lluberas 2016:Table 2-4.

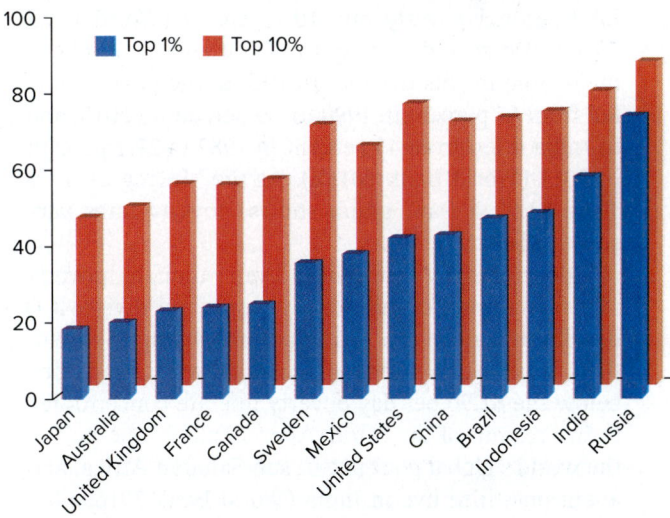

Wealth Concentration

Note: Columns represent the percentage of the country's wealth held by the top 10 percent and top 1 percent.
Source: Shorrocks, Davies, and Lluberas 2016:Table 6-5.

Women in developing countries often face significant obstacles, making it difficult for them to attain economic assets. Karuna Chanana Ahmed, a sociologist from India who has studied women in developing nations, calls women "the most exploited among the oppressed" (J. Anderson and Moore 1993). Beginning at birth, women face sex discrimination. They are commonly fed less than male children, are denied educational opportunities, and often are hospitalized only when they are critically ill. In countries such as the United States, France, Iceland, Russia, Hungary, and Ireland, the proportion of the nonagricultural labor force made up by women approaches or exceeds 50 percent. In other nations the rate can be significantly lower: Qatar, 12.6 percent; Saudi Arabia, 13.8 percent; Syria, 15.9 percent; Algeria, 17.6 percent; and Egypt, 18.6 percent (World Bank 2015e). In Afghanistan, it is illegal for a wife to step out of the house without her husband's permission. And due to the male guardianship system in Saudi Arabia, women are prohibited from driving, walking alone in public, and socializing with men other than those in their families (Al-Dosari 2016; Gorney 2016; Human Rights Watch 2016). We explore more issues related to gender inequality in the chapter on gender and sexuality.

Living on Less Than $1.90 a Day

- China: 1.9%
- Dominican Republic: 2.3%
- Pakistan: 6.1%
- Honduras: 16.0%
- Bangladesh: 18.5%
- India: 21.2%
- Kenya: 33.6%
- Nigeria: 53.5%
- Haiti: 53.9%
- Rwanda: 60.4%
- Liberia: 68.6%
- Madagascar: 77.8%

Source: World Bank 2016h. *Photo:* ©Lissa Harrison

POVERTY

In developing countries, any deterioration in the economic well-being of the least well-off threatens their very survival. The good news globally is that, driven largely by the income increases noted above, international poverty rates have fallen significantly over recent decades. In 1990, 1.85 billion people, 35 percent of the world's population, fell below the equivalent of today's international poverty line of $1.90 per day. By 2013 that number fell to 767 million, making the international poverty rate 10.7 percent (World Bank 2016c). Decreased poverty in China and India play a major role in this decline. In China, the poverty rate fell from 67 percent in 1990 to 1.9 percent in 2013, and in India it fell from 45 percent in 1987 to 21.2 percent in 2011 (World Bank 2016h). As the "Living on Less Than $1.90 a Day" graph shows, poverty rates vary substantially by country.

Geographically speaking, even though poverty affects hundreds of millions of people worldwide, it is distributed unequally. As the accompanying "Share of the Global Poor by Region" graph shows, those falling below the $1.90 per day poverty line are concentrated in two regions of the world. Approximately one-half of the world's global poor live in sub-Saharan Africa, and about one-third live in India (World Bank 2016c: 40). That does not mean poverty is absent from other parts of the world, including the United States. Instead, it reflects the effect of establishing and using a universal measure of extreme poverty that can be applied in any country.

In an effort to reduce global poverty, the United Nations passed the Millennium Declaration in 2000, promising to "spare no effort to free our fellow men, women, and children from the abject and dehumanizing conditions of extreme poverty" (United Nations 2000). The UN's General Assembly established 2015 as the target date for reaching specific, measurable goals to alleviate hunger and improve education, gender equality, and child mortality. When the targets were first established, many of the Millennium Project goals seemed extremely optimistic and likely unattainable. Yet, when 2015 arrived, substantial progress had been made.

Three Millennium Development Goals (MDGs) were met years ahead of schedule—namely, targets related to poverty, water, and slums. The goal of reducing extreme poverty by half was accomplished five years early. In developing regions, the proportion of people living on less than $1.25 a day fell from 47 percent in 1990 to 22 percent by 2010. And in China, the extreme poverty rate fell from approximately 60 percent in 1990 to 12 percent by 2010. The target of cutting in half the proportion of people without access to improved water sources was also attained, improving circumstances for more than 2 billion people between

Share of Global Poor by Region

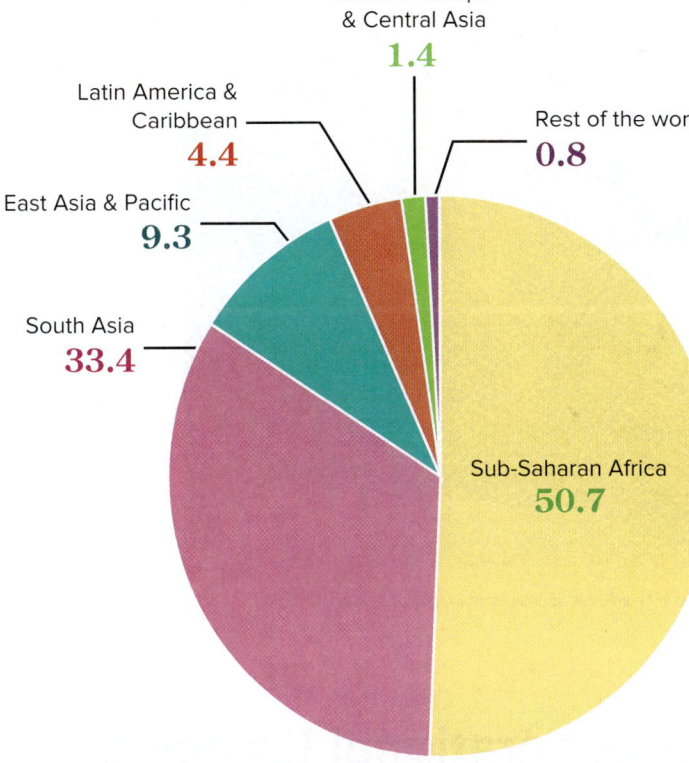

Note: Graph shows the global distribution for the world's 767 million people living on less than $1.90 per day. Numbers represent millions of people living in each region.
Source: World Bank 2016c:4.

> **SOCTHINK**
> What are the major obstacles to accomplishing the UN's Sustainable Development Goals? To what extent are the obstacles to success economic, social, and/or cultural?

to expand beyond issues faced predominantly by poor nations. As a result, the SDGs are framed to work toward a more universal and comprehensive vision of development. The SDGs include 17 goals, such as "no poverty," "no hunger," "good health," and "quality education," that in turn include 169 measurable targets to assess progress toward the goals. The goals are organized around five themes: people, planet, prosperity, peace, and partnership (L. Ford 2015; World Bank 2016i).

To accomplish the project's goals, planners estimated that industrial nations must set aside 0.7 percent of their gross national income (GNI)—the total value of a nation's goods and services—for aid to developing nations. In 2015, only three countries contributed at least that much: Sweden, United Arab Emirates, and Norway. As the following "Official Development Assistance" graph shows, although the United States contributes more aid dollars than any other nation ($30.7 billion in 2015), when measured as a percentage of gross national income, its level of contribution of 0.17 percent is well below average when compared to that of other nations. Sweden had the highest GNI rate at 1.41 percent (OECD 2016c).

1990 and 2010. More than 200 million people living in slums experienced improvements in water access, sanitation, durable housing, or less crowded living conditions, more than doubling the 2020 target. In addition to these successes, primary education reached parity between girls and boys, and there were sizable gains in access to primary schools. Considerable progress was made toward reducing child mortality, which fell by more than one-third, and maternal mortality, which was cut in half. People with HIV or AIDS now have greater access to medical treatment; rates of both tuberculosis and malaria have declined substantially saving millions of lives.

Building on the successes of goals met, and challenged by those not yet achieved, in 2015 the United Nations proposed a new program, the Sustainable Development Goals (SDGs), with a deadline of the year 2030 (United Nations 2014a). Although it celebrated the accomplishments with regard to MDG goals, it concluded that these goals failed to get at the underlying factors that give rise to the problems the MDGs addressed. The UN also asserted that the focus needed

SOCIAL MOBILITY

Although there is significant global inequality, perhaps sufficient social mobility exists to provide hope for those born without significant access to resources. As we saw in Chapter 10, mobility can and does happen in the United States, though the majority of such movement is over only short distances. Here we look at the possibility for mobility in both industrial nations and developing nations, and we consider the impact gender has on mobility.

Intergenerational Mobility Across Nations The likelihood of earning more or less than your parents varies across nations. Although Americans have more faith in their ability to get ahead than do those in other countries, their likelihood of doing so is lower than in most other industrialized nations (Corak 2016; Isaacs 2008). As the "Intergenerational Earnings Mobility by Country" figure shows, for example, when analyzing earnings, the amount of money fathers earn has

Official Development Assistance

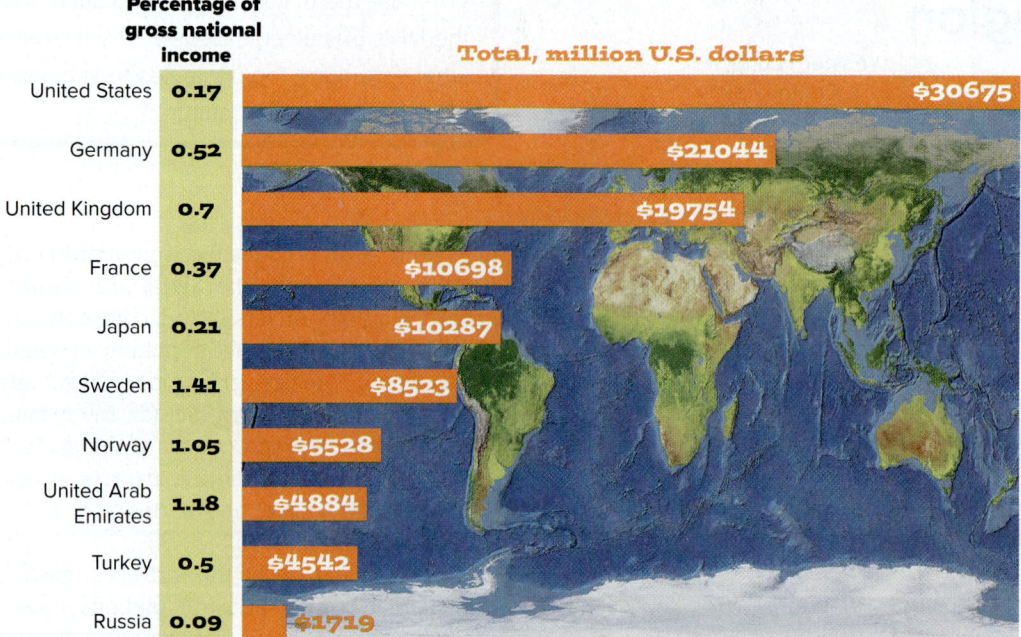

Note: Money totals represent government aid contributed to promote the economic development and welfare of developing nations. Data are from 2015.
Source: OECD 2016c. Photo: ©Jan Rysavy/Getty Images RF

a strong influence on the likely earnings of sons (Corak 2006, 2016). What this means, in contrast to the classic vision of the American Dream (see Chapter 10), is that young people in the United States have less chance for intergenerational mobility than young people in the Scandinavian countries shown.

In developing nations, macrolevel social and economic changes often overshadow microlevel movement from one occupation to another. For example, there is typically a substantial wage differential between rural and urban areas, which leads to high levels of migration to the cities. Yet the urban industrial sectors of developing countries generally cannot provide sufficient employment for all those seeking work.

In large developing nations, the most socially significant mobility is the movement out of poverty. This type of mobility is difficult to measure and confirm, however, because economic trends can differ from one area of a country to another. For instance, China's rapid income growth has been accompanied by a growing disparity in income between urban and rural areas and among different regions. Similarly, in India during the economic development

Intergenerational Earnings Mobility by Country

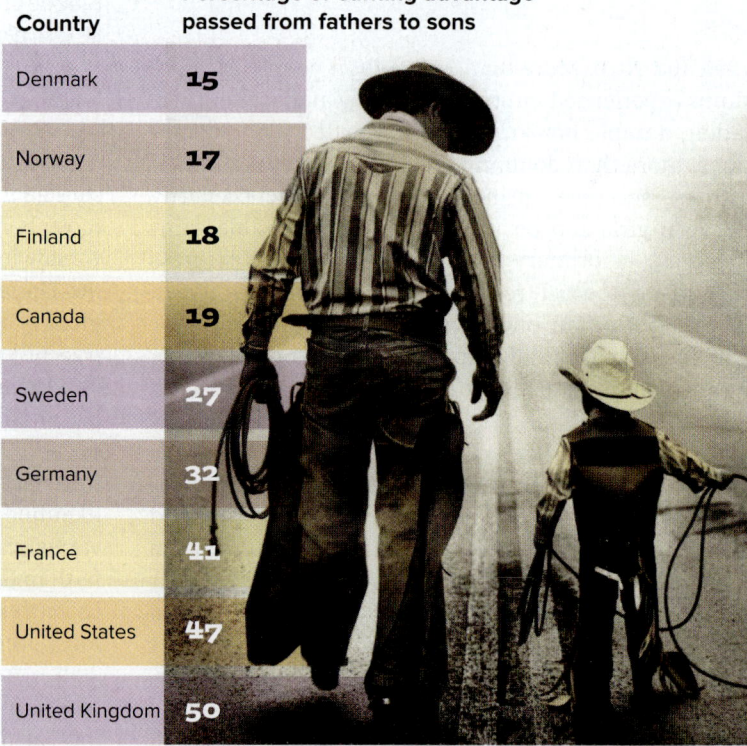

Sources: Corak 2006, 2016. Photo: ©Randolph Jay Braun/Getty Images RF

of the 1990s, poverty declined in urban areas but may have remained static at best in rural areas. Around the world, social mobility is also dramatically influenced by catastrophes such as crop failure and warfare (World Bank 2016h).

Gender Differences and Mobility Only recently have researchers begun to investigate the effect of gender on the mobility patterns of developing nations. Many aspects of the development process—especially modernization in rural areas and the rural-to-urban migration just described—may result in modification or abandonment of traditional cultural practices and even marital systems. The effects on women's social standing and mobility are not necessarily positive. As a country develops and modernizes, women's vital role in food production deteriorates, jeopardizing both their autonomy and their material well-being. Moreover, the movement of families to the cities weakens women's ties to relatives who can provide food, financial assistance, and social support.

In the Philippines, however, women have moved to the forefront of the indigenous peoples' struggle to protect their ancestral land from exploitation by outsiders. Having established their right to its rich minerals and forests, members of indigenous groups had begun to feud among themselves over the way in which the land's resources should be developed. Aided by the United Nations Partners in Development Programme, women volunteers established the Pan-Cordillera Women's Network for Peace and Development, a coalition of women's groups dedicated to resolving local disputes. The women mapped boundaries, prepared development plans, and negotiated more than 2,000 peace pacts among community members. They have also run in elections, campaigned on issues related to social problems, and organized residents to work together for the common good (United Nations Development Programme 2000:87).

SOCIAL STRATIFICATION IN MEXICO

To get a more complete picture of these global stratification issues, it helps to look at a particular case. Here we focus on the dynamics of stratification in Mexico, a country of 124 million people. As we saw in Chapter 6, drug-related homicides have become a serious problem in Mexico. Although the reasons for this are historical and complex (Camp 2010a, 2010b), economic factors play a substantial role. The same is true for the hundreds of men, women, and children who die attempting to cross into the United States each year in search of opportunity. Although solid numbers are difficult to come by, the United States Border Patrol reported 322 border deaths in 2016. The three areas with the highest numbers were Rio Grande Valley with 130, Tucson with 84, and Laredo with 68 (U.S. Customs and Border Protection 2016a).

Why do Mexicans turn to drug trafficking or risk their lives crossing the dangerous desert that lies between the two countries? The answer to this question can be found primarily in the income disparity between the two nations—one an industrial giant and the other a partially developed country still recovering from a history of colonialism and neocolonialism. Since the early 20th century, there has been a close cultural, economic, and political relationship between Mexico and the United States, one in which the United States is the dominant party. According to Immanuel Wallerstein's world systems analysis, the United States is at the core while neighboring Mexico is still on the semiperiphery of the world economic system.

Mexico's Economy If we compare Mexico's economy to that of the United States, differences in the standard of living and in life chances are quite dramatic. As we saw earlier, gross national income is a commonly used measure of an average resident's economic well-being. In 2015 the gross national income per person in the United States came to $56,070; in Mexico, it was a mere $9,830. In Mexico, 37.3 percent of adults aged 25–64 have completed high school compared to 89.3 percent in the United States. And fewer than 5.6 of every 1,000 infants in the United States die in the first year of life, compared to 11.3 per 1,000 in Mexico (National Center for Education Statistics 2016:Table 603.10; World Bank 2016d, 2016j).

Did You Know?

. . . Working 14 hours a day at 13 cents an hour, it would take seamstress Robina Akther of the Western Dresses factory in Dhaka, Bangladesh, 50 years to earn $16,200.

Photo: ©Tomohiro Ohsumi/Bloomberg via Getty Images

... The government of Mexico also has to deal with what to do about immigrants who enter that country illegally. In 2014, government authorities expelled nearly 150,000 undocumented immigrants from Central American nations, such as Guatemala, El Salvador, and Honduras.

Did You Know?

Photo: ©ALFREDO ESTRELLA/AFP/Getty Images

Not only is Mexico unquestionably a poorer country, but the gap between its richest and poorest citizens is substantial. The top quintile earns 54.5 percent of total income, whereas the bottom earns just 5.1 percent. The World Bank reports that 7.1 million, or 5.7 percent, of Mexico's population survives on less than $1.90 per day. The average amount of wealth per adult in Mexico is $21,125 compared to $344,692 in the United States. Yet, in the battle for world's richest person, in 2015, America's Bill Gates beat out Mexico's Carlos Slim Helú, $84 billion to $48.1 billion (*Forbes* 2017; Shorrocks et al. 2016; World Bank 2016f, 2016g, 2016h).

Political scientist Jorge Castañeda (1995:71), who later served as Mexico's foreign minister, called Mexico a "polarized society with enormous gaps between rich and poor, town and country, north and south, white and brown (or *criollos* and *mestizos*)." He added that the country is also divided along lines of class, race, religion, gender, and age. To better understand the nature of the stratification within Mexico, we examine race relations and the plight of Mexican Indians, the status of Mexican women, and immigration to the United States and its impact on the U.S.–Mexican borderlands.

Race Relations in Mexico: The Color Hierarchy

Mexico's indigenous Indians account for an estimated 14 percent of the nation's population. According to a United Nations report, more than 90 percent of Mexico's indigenous people (the ethnic group historically native to a region) live in extreme poverty. The literacy rate in Mexico as a whole is 92 percent, but it hovers around 50 percent among the indigenous population (Cevallos 2009; Minority Rights Group International 2007; United Nations Development Programme 2008).

The subordinate status of Mexico's Indians is but one reflection of the nation's color hierarchy, which links social class status to the appearance of racial purity. At the top of this hierarchy are the *criollos*, the 10 percent of the population who are typically White, well-educated members of the business and intellectual elites, with familial roots in Spain. In the middle is the large, impoverished *mestizo* majority, most of whom have brown skin and a mixed racial lineage as a result of intermarriage. At the bottom of the color hierarchy are the destitute, full-blooded Mexican Indian minority and a small number of Blacks, some descended from 200,000 African slaves brought to Mexico. This color hierarchy is an important part of day-to-day life—enough so that some Mexicans in the cities use hair dyes, skin lighteners, and blue or green contact lenses to appear White and European. Ironically, however, nearly all Mexicans are considered part Indian because of centuries of intermarriage (Castañeda 1995; Standish and Bell 2004).

> **SOC THINK**
>
> How might racial categories in Mexico differ from those in the United States? Why might such differences arise?

The Status of Women in Mexico Though the United Nations convened the first international conference on the status of women in Mexico in 1975, and opportunities there have improved, women still face significant obstacles. Women now constitute 37.2 percent of the labor force—an increase from 29.8 percent in 1990 (World Bank 2016k). Unfortunately, Mexican women are even more mired in the lowest-paying jobs than their counterparts in industrial nations, on average earning 51 percent of what men in similar jobs earn (World Economic Forum 2016:256). Men are still typically viewed as heads of the household, making it difficult for women to obtain credit and technical assistance in many parts of the country and to inherit land in rural areas. As for education, the literacy rate for women in Chiapas (71 percent) and Oaxaca (73 percent), states with high levels of indigenous populations, is well below the national average (INEGI 2009).

In recent decades, Mexican women have organized to address an array of economic, political, and health issues. For example, as far back as 1973, women in Monterrey—the nation's third-largest city—protested the continuing disruptions of the city's water supply. Through coordinated efforts, including delegations of politicians, rallies, and public demonstrations, they succeeded in improving Monterrey's water service, a major concern in developing nations. After being denied the opportunity to run for mayor in her hometown in 2007, Eufrosina Cruz organized QUIEGO (Queremos Unir Integrando por la Equidad y Género en Oaxaca),

Personal Sociology

Study Abroad

Central College, where I teach, started its first international program in 1965. It was a leader in establishing study abroad programs for students. It now operates programs around the world, in places such as Mérida in Mexico, Bangor in Wales, and Accra in Ghana. Central instituted these programs to provide students with a prolonged experience in another country, in hopes that such exposure would enable them to go beyond being a tourist and to achieve a deep understanding of another culture. Going abroad really does make a difference. My students are often nervous to go but come back with great stories. The experience clearly changed how they understand both the world and themselves. What factors might encourage or discourage students from studying abroad?

To ensure greater political representation by women in office, Mexico passed a series of laws setting gender quotas for candidates. First established in 1996, Mexico strengthened these laws over time, now requiring that women compose at least 40 percent of the nominees. In 2014, Mexico passed an amendment to article 41 of its Federal Constitution to cement its commitment to gender parity throughout its political system. These policy changes worked. In 1990, women accounted for 3.1 percent of seats in the Senate and 8.8 percent of seats in the Chamber of Deputies. After the 2015 elections, those numbers rose to 34 percent in the Senate and 42 percent in the Chamber of Deputies. Mexico now ranks 7th among 193 nations in female representation, substantially higher than 99th for the United States (Baldez 2004; Inter-Parliamentary Union 2016; Lucio 2014; QuotaProject 2014).

Borderlands The area of common culture along the border between Mexico and the United States.

meaning "we want to come together for equity and gender in Oaxaca") to raise awareness about political rights for women in her home state and ultimately throughout Mexico (Bennett, Dávila-Poblete, and Rico 2005; Cevallos 2009).

The Borderlands Growing recognition of the borderlands reflects the increasingly close and complex relationship between Mexico and the United States. The term **borderlands** refers to the area of common culture along the border between Mexico and the United States. Legal and illegal emigration from Mexico to the United States, day laborers crossing the border regularly to go to work in the United States, the implementation of the North American Free Trade Agreement (NAFTA), the exchange of media across

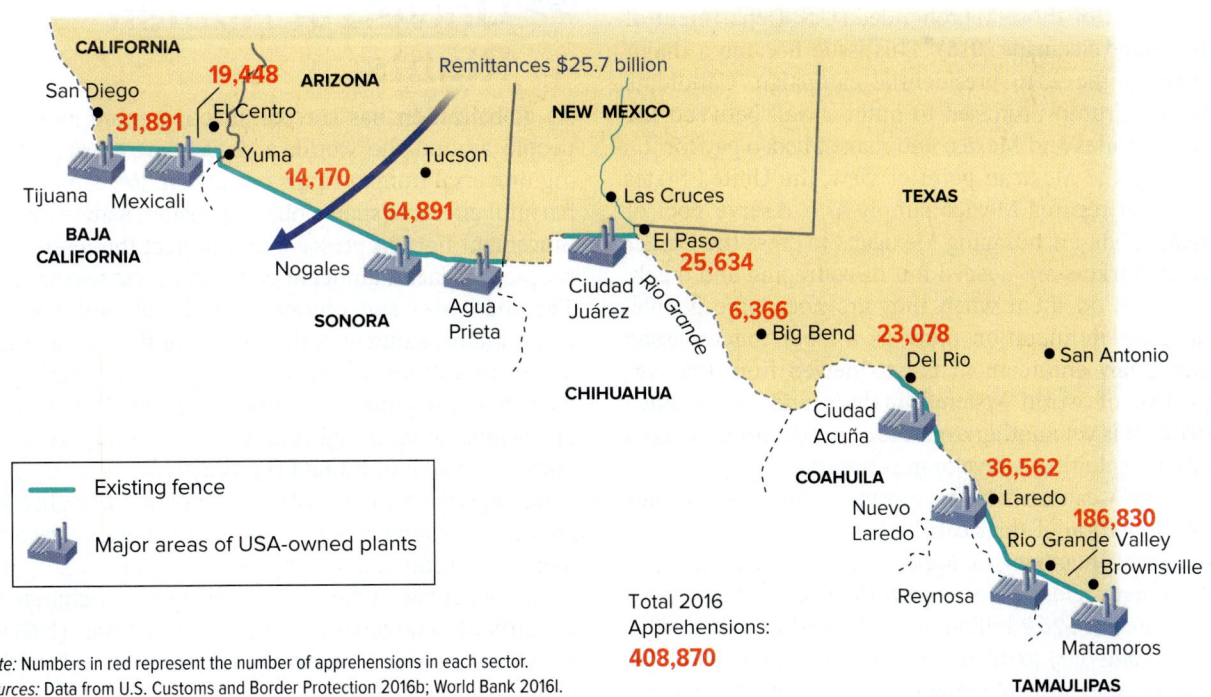

Chapter 11 / Global Inequality • 275

the border—all make the notion of separate Mexican and U.S. cultures obsolete in the borderlands.

The economic position of the borderlands is rather complicated, as demonstrated by the emergence of *maquiladoras*. These are foreign-owned factories, often located just across the border in Mexico, that are allowed to import parts and materials without tariffs. Typical jobs include manufacturing electronics, transportation equipment, electrical machinery, and textiles and apparel, as well as service jobs in call centers and coupon processing operations. The chief appeal for U.S. companies is less-expensive labor. At $514 per month, the average wages for production workers in the border region of Mexico are lower than $629 earned by similar workers in the interior of Mexico. Wages in Ciudad Juárez, just over the border from El Paso, Texas, are even lower at $422 per month (Hunt Institute 2015).

Movies on GLOBAL INEQUALITY 5

Kinyarwanda
Resilience and reconciliation in Rwanda.

Virunga
Civil war, poachers, oil reserves, and gorillas.

Güeros
Tomas gets sent to live with his brother in Mexico City.

The World Before Her
Beauty boot camp in India.

A Separation
An Iranian couple's tale of love, loss, and family.

Emigration to the United States The movement of people between Mexico and the United States significantly affects both nations. In 2015, 105,958 people who were born in Mexico became naturalized U.S. citizens, more than twice the number from India, the second leading country. Another 158,619 gained lawful permanent resident status in the United States. However, in 2015, 267,885 individuals from Mexico were apprehended and classified as "aliens" by U.S. immigration officials, which constituted 58 percent of those apprehended (U.S. Department of Homeland Security 2016). This issue became a major factor in the 2016 presidential campaign. Candidate Donald Trump promised to build a wall between the United States and Mexico and make Mexico pay for it.

Remittances The monies that immigrants return to their families of origin. Also known as *remesas*.

From the Mexican point of view, the United States too often regards Mexico simply as a reserve pool of cheap labor, encouraging Mexicans to cross the border when workers are needed but discouraging and cracking down on them when they are not. Some people, then, see immigration more as a labor market issue than a law enforcement issue. Viewed from the perspective of world systems analysis and dependency theory, it is yet another example of a core industrialized nation exploiting a developing country.

Many Mexicans who have come to the United States send a portion of their earnings back across the border to family members in Mexico. This substantial flow of money, referred to as **remittances** (or *remesas*), amounted to $25.7 billion in 2015 (World Bank 2015h). It is second only to oil as a source of foreign revenue for Mexico. After years of growth, remittances sent to Mexico fell 3.6 percent in 2008, due to the economic downturn in the United States. The decline was more dramatic in 2009, falling 15 percent for the year. Although remittances still totaled $21.5 billion, it meant a loss of $3.8 billion to the Mexican economy. As a result of the weak economy, 140,000 more Mexicans left the United States to head back to Mexico than entered the United States between 2009 and 2014, a dramatic reversal of events (Gonzalez-Barrera 2015; Stevenson 2011).

>> Universal Human Rights

As globalization has spread, affecting more and more people around the world, a movement toward ensuring universal human rights has arisen. Recognizing the harmful effects of such global expansion, activists in this movement fight to preserve and protect the interests of people who lack significant power or access to resources. The sheer size and economic might of multinational corporations, along with their freedom to move jobs and plants around the world without regard for the impact on national populations, encouraged the establishment of universal human rights as a countervailing source of power. The goal of human rights activists is to establish a nonnegotiable and inviolable foundation of rights that applies no matter where people are or which governments or multinational corporations are involved.

Many activists who work to bring about change do so through nongovernmental organizations (NGOs), which are not-for-profit groups committed to bringing about social change. These groups may be local, national,

Ongoing violence in East Timor has driven children like these to seek safety in refugee camps in the country. ©Paula Bronstein/Getty Images

or international in scope. They are frequently funded by donations and staffed by volunteers. Examples of the best-known NGOs include Amnesty International, Human Rights Watch, Red Cross, CARE International, and Oxfam.

DEFINING HUMAN RIGHTS

The term **human rights** refers to universal moral rights that all people possess by virtue of being human. The most important elaboration of human rights appears in the Universal Declaration of Human Rights, adopted by the United Nations (UN) in 1948. This declaration prohibits slavery, torture, and degrading punishment; grants everyone the right to a nationality and its culture; affirms freedom of religion and the right to vote; proclaims the right to seek asylum in other countries to escape persecution; and prohibits arbitrary interference with one's privacy and the arbitrary seizure of a person's property. It also emphasizes that mothers and children are entitled to special care and assistance.

At first the United States opposed a binding obligation to the Universal Declaration of Human Rights. The government feared loss of national sovereignty—the right to rule over its people without external interference. This concern was driven in part by the existence of racial segregation laws that were still common at the time the UN issued the Universal Declaration and that violated the human rights principles. By the early 1960s, however, the United States had begun to use the declaration to promote democracy abroad (Forsythe 1990).

In the 1990s concerns about human rights brought the term *ethnic cleansing* into the world's vocabulary as a euphemism for forcible expulsion and murder. In the former Yugoslavia, Serbs initiated a policy intended to "cleanse" Muslims from parts of Bosnia-Herzegovina and ethnic Albanians from the province of Kosovo. Hundreds of thousands of people were killed in fighting there, while many others were uprooted from their homes. Moreover, reports surfaced of Serbian soldiers raping substantial numbers of Muslim, Croatian, and Kosovar women. Regrettably, ethnic cleansing has since spread to other parts of the world, including East Timor, Iraq, Kenya, and Sudan.

An ongoing human rights concern is the transnational crime of trafficking in humans. Each year an estimated 600,000–800,000 men, women, and children are transported across international borders for slavery or sexual exploitation. In 2000, Congress passed the Trafficking Victims Protection Act, which established minimum standards for the elimination of human trafficking. The act requires the State Department to monitor other countries' efforts to vigorously investigate, prosecute, and convict individuals who participate in trafficking—including government officials. Each year the department reports its findings, dividing countries into three groups, or tiers, depending on their level of compliance. As shown in the accompanying "Human Trafficking Report" table, Tier-1 countries are thought to be largely in compliance with the act. Tier-2 nations are making a significant effort to comply, and Tier-2 "watch" nations are making efforts

> **Human rights** Universal moral rights possessed by all people because they are human.

Mass grave site in Srebrenica, Bosnia-Herzegovina. ©Marco Di Lauro/Getty Images

to comply, although trafficking remains a real concern. Tier-3 countries are not compliant (International Labour Office 2012; U.S. Department of State 2016b).

PRINCIPLE AND PRACTICE

When it comes to human rights, the balance between principle and practice can be problematic. In the wake of the terrorist attacks of September 11, 2001, increased police personnel and surveillance at U.S. airports and border crossings caused some observers to wonder whether human rights were not being jeopardized in the name of security. At the same time, thousands of noncitizens of Arab and south Asian descent were questioned for no other reason than their ethnic and religious backgrounds. A few were placed in custody, sometimes without access to legal assistance. As the war on terror moved overseas, human rights concerns escalated. In 2005, then secretary-general Kofi Annan of the UN criticized the United States and Britain for equating people who were resisting the presence of foreign troops in Afghanistan and Iraq with terrorists (A. Parker 2004; Steele 2005).

What this points to is the significance of perspective even when it comes to something that appears to be a fundamental principle. Cultural insiders and outsiders can disagree about what constitutes a violation. For example, was India's caste system an inherent violation of human rights? What about the many cultures of the world that view the subordinate status of women as an essential element in their traditions? Should human rights be interpreted differently in different parts of the world?

We can consider, as an example, female genital mutilation, a practice that is common in more than

Human Trafficking Report

Tier 1 Full Compliance	Tier 2 Significant Effort	Tier 2 Watch List Some Effort, but Trafficking Remains a Concern	Tier 3 Noncompliant, No Effort
Australia	Angola	China	Algeria
Canada	Bahrain	Cuba	Belarus
Denmark	Brazil	Hong Kong	Djibouti
France	Greece	Kuwait	Haiti
Germany	India	Malaysia	Iran
Israel	Japan	Niger	North Korea
Italy	Kenya	Pakistan	Russia
Norway	Madagascar	Rwanda	Syria
Poland	Mexico	Saudi Arabia	Uzbekistan
South Korea	Romania	Senegal	Sudan
Spain	Turkey	Thailand	Venezuela
United States	Vietnam	Ukraine	Zimbabwe

Note: Table does not include all countries; each tier lists only a sampling of nations.
Source: U.S. Department of State 2016b.

> **SOC THINK**
> To what extent do you think violations of human rights are excusable in a time of war? At such times, how might our perception of the balance between rights and security alter what we think of as universal?

30 countries around the world but that has been condemned in Western nations as a human rights abuse. This controversial practice often involves removal of the clitoris, in the belief that its excision will inhibit a young woman's sex drive, making her chaste and thus more desirable to her future husband. Though some countries have passed laws against the practice, they have gone largely unenforced. Emigrants from countries where genital mutilation is common often insist that their daughters undergo the procedure, to protect them from Western cultural norms that allow premarital sex (Religious Tolerance 2008). To what extent should outside nations have the power to dictate such internal laws? In this sense, the movement for universal human rights also represents a form of cultural imperialism.

In 1993 the United States opted for an absolute definition of human rights, insisting that the Universal Declaration of Human Rights set a single standard for acceptable behavior around the world. In practice, however, interpretation still plays a role. Some human rights activists have argued that the United States practices selective enforcement of human rights. Critics contend, for example, that officials in the United States are more likely to become concerned about human rights abuses when oil is at stake, as in the Middle East, or when military alliances come into play, as in Europe.

> **SOC THINK**
> How active should the U.S. government be in addressing violations of human rights in other countries? At what point, if any, does concern for human rights turn into ethnocentrism through failure to respect the distinctive norms, values, and customs of another culture?

HUMAN RIGHTS ACTIVISM

Efforts to protect and ensure human rights seldom come from inside governments but arise out of social movements that organize to generate economic, social, and political pressure in an effort to force change. For example, in June 2008 Human Rights Watch (www.hrw.org), a premier international human rights organization, called for other African nations to impose sanctions on Zimbabwe after what they called the sham reelection of President Robert Mugabe. They monitor human rights abuses around the world, including calling U.S. officials to end abuses against prisoners in the Guantánamo Bay detention camps.

In Sudan, the Save Darfur Coalition (www.savedarfur.org) fights for justice and relief for refugees who were attacked, driven off their land and out of the country, and often killed by the Janjaweed, a group of armed gunmen backed by the Sudanese government. Their cause was helped significantly with the release of the film *The Devil Came on Horseback*—translated from the Janjaweed—in which ex-marine Brian Steidle, who was hired as a human rights observer by the African Union, documented genocide in Darfur with photos and video. He ultimately testified before Congress and at the UN, providing his documentation to support the genocide claims. In addition to numerous other organizational efforts, the Save Darfur Coalition also coordinated an agreement on May 28, 2008, in which presidential candidates Barack Obama, John McCain, and Hillary Clinton issued a joint statement demanding an end to the violence in Darfur. Though the Sudanese government maintains that the war is officially over, violence continued. In May 2010 Ibrahim Gambari, the head of UNAMID, the joint African Union–UN Mission in Darfur, put it this way: "Results have been mixed despite our best efforts. . . . In the area of security and the protection of civilians some progress has been made, but pockets of instability remain" (UN News Service 2010). However, on July 9, 2011, the Republic of South Sudan officially became an independent, sovereign state.

Médecins Sans Frontières (Doctors Without Borders), the world's largest independent emergency medical aid organization, won the 1999 Nobel Peace Prize for its work. Founded in 1971 and based in Paris, the organization has 30,000 doctors, nurses, and other expert volunteers working around the world. In 2015 they conducted

> *There can be no peace as long as there is grinding poverty, social injustice, inequality, oppression, environmental degradation, and as long as the weak and small continue to be trodden by the mighty and powerful.*
>
> the Dalai Lama

more than 8 million outpatient consultations, treated 2.3 million malaria cases, vaccinated 326,100 people for meningitis, helped 219,300 women deliver babies, and assisted many thousands of other patients for various ailments (Doctors Without Borders 2015).

> **SOC THINK**
>
> Should other nations and the UN have the power to force the United States to change its laws to comply with human rights principles?

In the past few decades, awareness has been growing of lesbian and gay rights as an aspect of universal human rights. In 1994 Amnesty International published a pioneering report in which it examined abuses in Brazil, Greece, Mexico, Iran, the United States, and other countries, including cases of torture, imprisonment, and extrajudicial execution. Later in 1994 the United States issued an order that would allow lesbians and gay men to seek political asylum in the United States if they could prove they had suffered government persecution in their home countries solely because of their sexual orientation (Amnesty International 2009; Johnston 1994). One result of this policy change was that dozens of gay men and lesbians from Mexico and other Latin American nations were granted asylum in the United States each year. As their treatment has improved in those nations, the likelihood of receiving asylum has declined (Connolly 2008).

One of the things we learn from sociology is that we are embedded in larger networks in which decisions and events that happen far away, and about which we may know little or nothing, shape our daily life experiences. And the choices we make can have substantial consequences for the lives of others. Ethnic cleansing in Sudan, human rights violations in Iraq and Afghanistan, increased surveillance in the name of counterterrorism, violence against women inside and outside the family, governmental persecution of lesbians and gay men—all these are vivid reminders that social inequality can have life-and-death consequences. In each case, people recognized the consequences of global inequality, and individuals, groups, and nations took steps to address the problems. By developing a more fully formed sociological imagination, we can more readily see such issues and take necessary steps toward addressing them.

SOCIOLOGY IS A VERB

Global Perspectives

The world is huge, and there are so many places about which we know so little. Pick a country you are unfamiliar with, perhaps one you didn't even know existed. Find out all you can about its history, politics, economy, family structures, beliefs, and so on. If possible, contact an organization that assists immigrants from there to learn more about their experiences as first-generation immigrants here. What might you learn by trying to understand the world from their perspective?

FOR REVIEW

I. How did the global divide develop?
- Theorists emphasizing modernization argue that it is part of the natural evolution of societies as they pass through the effects of the Industrial Revolution and beyond. Dependency theorists argue that it is due to a fundamental power struggle between wealthy nations at the core and developing nations at the periphery.

II. How significant is global stratification?
- Analyses of wealth, income, poverty, and social mobility demonstrate a wide gap both within and between nations.

III. Why did the global movement for universal human rights develop?
- As global inequality became more apparent, activists worked to establish a foundational set of human rights that would protect people regardless of who or where they were.

SOCVIEWS on Global Inequality

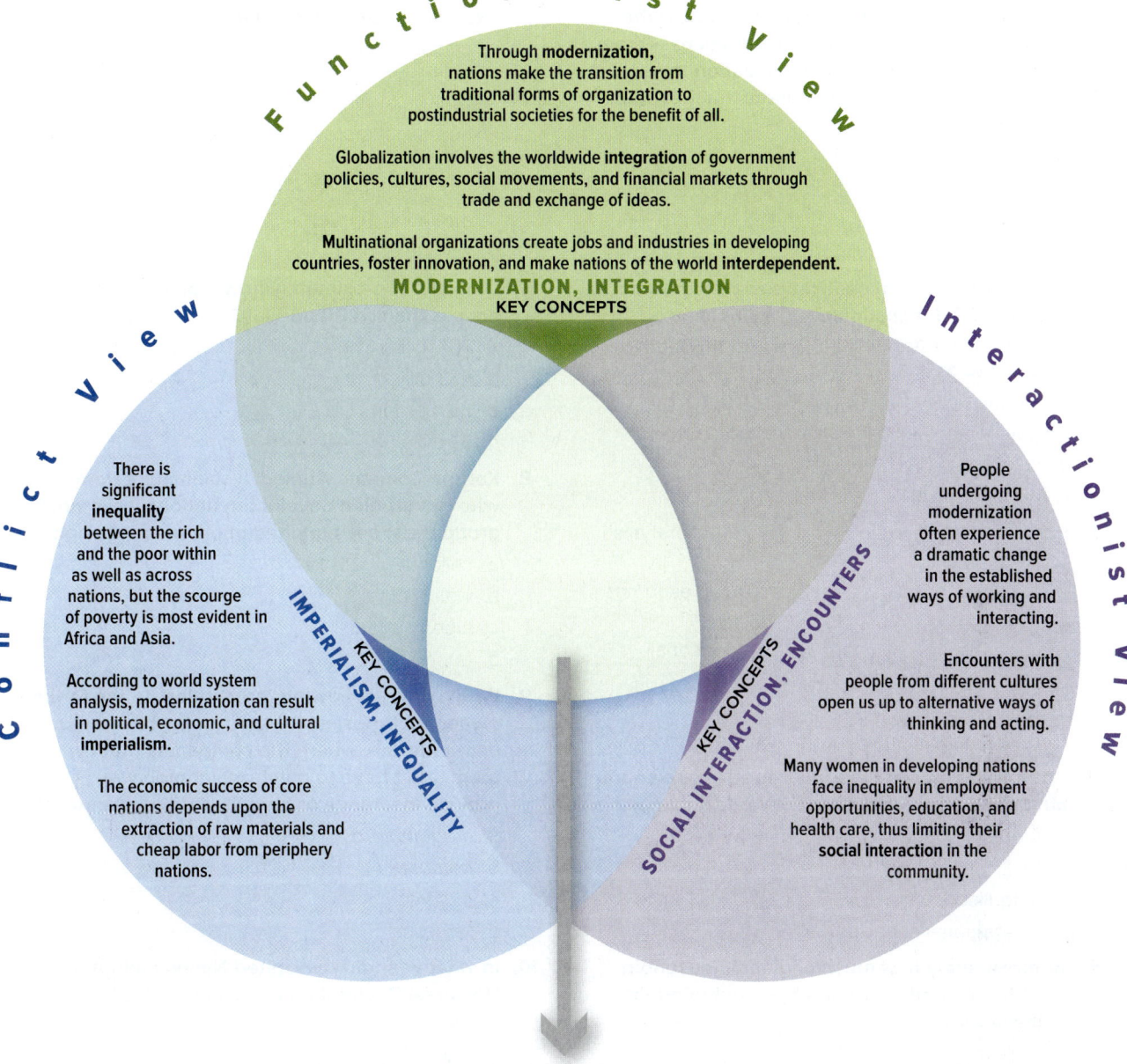

Functionalist View

Through **modernization**, nations make the transition from traditional forms of organization to postindustrial societies for the benefit of all.

Globalization involves the worldwide **integration** of government policies, cultures, social movements, and financial markets through trade and exchange of ideas.

Multinational organizations create jobs and industries in developing countries, foster innovation, and make nations of the world **interdependent**.

KEY CONCEPTS: **MODERNIZATION, INTEGRATION**

Conflict View

There is significant **inequality** between the rich and the poor within as well as across nations, but the scourge of poverty is most evident in Africa and Asia.

According to world system analysis, modernization can result in political, economic, and cultural **imperialism**.

The economic success of core nations depends upon the extraction of raw materials and cheap labor from periphery nations.

KEY CONCEPTS: **IMPERIALISM, INEQUALITY**

Interactionist View

People undergoing modernization often experience a dramatic change in the established ways of working and interacting.

Encounters with people from different cultures open us up to alternative ways of thinking and acting.

Many women in developing nations face inequality in employment opportunities, education, and health care, thus limiting their **social interaction** in the community.

KEY CONCEPTS: **SOCIAL INTERACTION, ENCOUNTERS**

MAKE THE CONNECTION
After reviewing the chapter, answer the following questions:

1 How might each perspective seek to better understand the situation in cities such as Mumbai?

2 How do the modernization and world systems theories fit with the functionalist and conflict perspectives?

3 How would each perspective provide insight into the situation of immigration between the United States and Mexico?

4 What ties do you have to a developing nation—perhaps as a tourist, or a second-generation immigrant, or an activist? Which perspective best fits those ties? Why?

Pop Quiz

1. Which of the following terms is used by contemporary social scientists to describe the far-reaching process by which nations pass from traditional forms of social organization toward those characteristic of post–Industrial Revolution societies?
   a. dependency
   b. globalization
   c. industrialization
   d. modernization

2. The maintenance of political, social, economic, and cultural domination over a people by a foreign power for an extended period of time is referred to as
   a. globalization.
   b. government-imposed stratification.
   c. colonialism.
   d. dependency.

3. Immanuel Wallerstein's world systems analysis focuses on
   a. the unequal access to and control of resources between core and periphery nations.
   b. the natural evolutionary development of all societies toward the modern ideal.
   c. the rise of multinational corporations.
   d. the global pattern of inequality faced by women.

4. Companies that are headquartered in one country but do business throughout the world are known as
   a. global corporations.
   b. multinational corporations.
   c. maquiladoras.
   d. international agencies.

5. Approximately how much of global household wealth is owned by the top 1 percent of adults in the world?
   a. 10 percent
   b. 25 percent
   c. 75 percent
   d. 90 percent

6. Which of the following Millennium Project goals has already been accomplished?
   a. cutting levels of extreme poverty around the world in half
   b. reducing by half the proportion of people without access to improved sources of water
   c. substantially improving the lives of 100,000 people living in extreme conditions in slums around the world
   d. all of the above

7. Globally, approximately how many people subsist on less than $1.90 per day?
   a. 767 million
   b. 1.53 billion
   c. 3.24 billion
   d. 5.1 billion

8. Karuna Chanana Ahmed, a sociologist from India who has studied developing nations, calls which group the most exploited of oppressed people?
   a. children
   b. women
   c. elderly people
   d. poor people

9. Which of the following terms refers to the foreign-owned factories established just across the border in Mexico, where the companies that own them don't have to pay taxes or high wages, or provide insurance or benefits for their workers?
   a. *maquiladoras*
   b. *hombres*
   c. *mujeres*
   d. *remesas*

10. In what year did the United Nations adopt the Universal Declaration of Human Rights?
    a. 1865
    b. 1919
    c. 1948
    d. 1993

1. (d), 2. (c), 3. (a), 4. (b), 5. (d), 6. (d), 7. (a), 8. (b), 9. (a), 10. (c)

©Photo by Allison Shelley/Getty Images

Gender and Sexuality

12

DREAMING BIG

When you're a child, your imagination often runs wild. When someone asks what you want to be when you grow up, almost anything seems possible—superhero, jet pilot, ballet dancer, movie star, secret agent, Olympic athlete, or maybe even president. As we get older, reality hits, and most of us narrow our choices to something more realistic. But not everyone.

When Sheryl Sandberg was young, her mom encouraged her to work hard so she could be whatever she wanted to be. She took her mom's advice, and it paid off. She earned an economics degree at Harvard, served as chief of staff at the U.S. Department of the Treasury, and worked as the vice president of global online sales and operations at Google. Now Sandberg is second in command at Facebook, a position she accepted when she was 38 years old. Hers is a classic tale of upward mobility.

Yet when she reached the top, she found that very few women had made the journey with her. It didn't start out that way. In college and in her entry-level jobs, Sandberg's peers included equal numbers of men and women. As she climbed each rung of the career ladder, men increasingly outnumbered women. One of the most staggering examples of inequity is the disparity at the very top, among corporate leaders. In fact, only 4.4 percent of CEOs at S&P 500 firms are women (Catalyst 2017).

In an effort to understand the challenges women face and help bring about change, Sandberg (2013), with research assistance from Marianne Cooper, wrote *Lean In: Women, Work, and the Will to Lead,* and founded LeanIn.Org. In her work, Sandberg highlights two key factors that have hindered women's progress in the workplace. First, women experience consistent patterns of discrimination. For example, in LeanIn.Org's 2016 annual report, which surveyed 132 companies employing 4.6 million people, researchers found that when it comes to moving up the ladder early in their careers, for every 100 women promoted to managerial jobs, 130 men are promoted. When women attempt to negotiate for a promotion or a pay increase, they are more likely than men to be told that they were "bossy," "aggressive," and "intimidating." And even though women and men are equally likely to ask for feedback on how best to improve their job performance, women are less likely to receive it (LeanIn.Org 2016).

The second obstacle Sandberg highlights involves women's own creation and acceptance of internal barriers to their success. In the 2016 annual report, LeanIn.org researchers found that fewer women aspire to become top executives. Sandberg writes, "We hold ourselves back in ways both big and small, by lacking self-confidence, by not raising our hands, and by pulling back when we should be leaning in" (p. 8). Whether the barriers are external or internal, being a woman makes success in business and politics more challenging.

As children, anything may seem possible. The truth is that the positions we occupy in society shape the choices we make. In this chapter, we explore the ways in which both gender and sexuality play roles in who we are and what we become.

As You READ >>

- How has our understanding of gender and sexuality shifted over time?
- How has opportunity for women in the United States changed over time?
- To what extent does gender still shape access to resources?

>> The Social Construction of Gender

When a baby is born, one of the first questions people ask is "Is it a boy or a girl?" The answer to this question represents one of our primary and most powerful statuses. From those earliest days, it shapes how others will interact with us as newborns. Later it influences the clothes we wear, the friends we choose, the kinds of games we play, the college majors we consider, the types of jobs we have, the amount of money we earn, and much more. Answering that question seems like such a simple thing. Yet, from a sociological perspective, understanding what it means to be a boy or a girl—and later to become men and women—involves more than anatomy alone.

Sex The biological differences between males and females.

Gender The social and cultural significance that we attach to the biological differences of sex.

SEX AND GENDER

Historically, sociologists drew a distinction between sex and gender to differentiate between biology and culture. **Sex** refers to biological differences between males and females. **Gender** involves the social and cultural significance that we attach to those presumed biological differences. Over time, even this distinction has become too limiting to fully depict our experiences as humans.

Sex emphasizes the differences between males and females that occur at the cellular, hormonal, and anatomical levels. From this perspective, we assume it is easy to tell the difference between males and females. Women have XX chromosome patterns, estrogen hormones, ovaries, and a vagina; men have XY chromosomes, androgen hormones, testicles, and a penis. The presupposition is that the dividing line is clear; there is no significant biological overlap between the sexes. This model is known as a simple two-sex, or dimorphic, model, in which the line between males and females is distinct and absolute (Fausto-Sterling 2000, 2012; Richardson 2013).

The problem with such a simplistic division is that we find many exceptions to what is assumed to be the rule. Many people exhibit physical characteristics that we presume to belong to the "opposite" sex: women with facial hair, men with high voices, tall women and short men, women with narrow hips and broad shoulders, men who are slight of build or who have "breasts," women who experience "male pattern baldness," and so on. Differences

©Rainer Elstermann/Getty Images RF

go beyond these secondary sex characteristics to include people whose cellular, hormonal, and anatomical characteristics are sexually ambiguous. As geneticist Anne Fausto-Sterling (2000) points out in a critique of the simplistic male–female model, "On close inspection, absolute dimorphism disintegrates even at the level of basic biology. Chromosomes, hormones, the internal sex structures, the gonads and the external genitalia all vary more than most people realize" (p. 20). We know, for example, that both males and females have androgen and estrogen hormones and that sex hormone levels vary by individual.

Biologically, Fausto-Sterling (1993) suggests we have at least five sexes, not just two. In addition to male and female, we exhibit at least three intersexual categories. The first category includes "true hermaphrodites," who have one testis and one ovary. In other words, they are theoretically capable of producing both sperm and eggs. The second category includes "male pseudohermaphrodites." They have testes and what appear to be female genitalia, lacking a penis and ovaries. The third category includes "female pseudohermaphrodites," who have ovaries along with some male genitalia but no testes. She later suggested that even these five sexes present an overly simplistic model of the range of biological diversity, which better resembles a continuum (Fausto-Sterling 2000, 2012).

Doctors studying what have come to be known medically as disorders of sex development (DSDs) have discovered that the basic biology of sex extends well beyond the XX and XY chromosome combinations (Davis 2014; Richardson 2013). Researchers have identified more than 25 genes involved in the development of these traits. For example, XY individuals with extra copies of the *WNT4* gene, which promotes ovarian development and suppresses testicular development, can develop a rudimentary uterus and Fallopian tubes. Individuals who are XX but with the *RSPO1* gene can develop ovotestis, a gonad incorporating both ovarian and testicular development (Ainsworth 2015). When considering the biology of sex, researcher Eric Vilain, the director of the Center for Gender-Based Biology at the University of California, Los Angeles, concludes, "Biologically, it's a spectrum" (Ainsworth 2015). Because the use of "disorder" implies something negative about people born with these naturally occurring traits, medical professionals and human rights advocates are proposing the elimination of the DSD label (Council of Europe 2015; Holmes 2011)

When babies are born presenting ambiguous indicators of maleness or femaleness, even though such conditions rarely pose a health threat, physicians typically perform surgery to make the baby fit more neatly into one category or the other. In recent years, ethical

After she won the gold medal in the 800-meter race at the 2016 Olympics in Rio, South African runner Caster Semenya again faced questions about her sex. During her career she has been ordered to submit to various psychological, gynecological, and endocrine tests (Boren 2016; Karkazis 2016; Karkazis et al. 2012; Maese 2016). ©The Asahi Shimbun via Getty Images

questions have been raised about the appropriateness of doing so, especially when the person most affected has no voice in the matter (Ainsworth 2015; Karkazis 2008). In 2013, the United Nations issued a statement condemning such nonconsensual surgeries, and in 2015 Malta became the first nation to ban such surgeries by law (Larsson 2016; Méndez 2013). Increasingly, countries have adopted policies to recognize the complexity of sex. In 2011, Australia began allowing people to select a third sex category on their passports. In 2013, Germany allowed parents to leave the gender category on their child's birth certificate blank. In 2015, Thailand was in the process of revising its constitution to formally recognize a third gender category as a human right (Commonwealth of Australia 2013; Heine 2013; Park and Dhitavat 2015).

Our biological diversity calls for a more complex model of our species than the dimorphic model of sex supplies. Gender, partnered with a more comprehensive conception of sex, enables us to capture a wider range of expressions of our humanity. Social constructions of gender vary over time and across cultures, suggesting that biology alone does not narrowly determine maleness and femaleness. Through socialization we typically internalize the cognitive, normative, and material culture deemed appropriate or natural for men and women within the context of our societies.

> **SOC THINK**
>
> Why do most women in the United States assume that shaving their legs is natural? What role does it play as a rite of passage?

GENDER-ROLE SOCIALIZATION

Because we lack complex instincts that narrowly determine our behaviors, we construct our expressions of masculinity and femininity and reinforce those gender expressions through socialization. For example, the process of becoming boys and girls begins at birth:

> During the first six months of life, mothers tend to look at and talk to girl infants more than to boy infants, and mothers tend to respond to girls' crying more immediately than they do to boys'. In fact, these behaviors tend to be greater for girls over the first two years of life. Boys, on the other hand, receive more touching, holding, rocking, and kissing than do girls in the first few months, but the situation is reversed by age six months. By one year, female infants are allowed and encouraged to spend significantly more time than males in touching and staying in close proximity to their mothers. The girls are encouraged to move away at later ages, but never as much as boys are. (Kimmel 2004:130)

As children grow, we continue to reinforce male–female differences through our actions. Male babies get blue blankets; females get pink ones. Boys are expected to play with trucks, blocks, and toy soldiers; girls receive dolls and kitchen goods. Boys must be masculine—active, aggressive, tough, daring, and dominant—but girls must be feminine—soft, emotional, sweet, and submissive. An examination of the ads in any parenting magazine shows that these traditional gender-role patterns remain influential in the socialization of children in the United States. Yet, historical and sociological research suggest that such preferences are not innate. For example, in the early 20th century, an article in *Ladies Home Journal* noted, "There has been a great diversity of opinion on the subject, but the generally accepted rule is pink for the boy and blue for the girl. The reason is that pink being a more decided and stronger color is more suitable for the boy, while blue, which is more delicate and dainty, is prettier for the girl" (quoted in Frassanito and Pettorini 2008; see also Cohen 2013; Walsh 2016a, 2016b). We learn such preferences through socialization experiences with others.

Gender Displays Gender socialization never ends. In all our interactions, we receive positive and negative feedback based on our gender performance. It is not hard to test how rigid gender-role socialization can be. Just try breaking some gender norm—say, by smoking a cigar in public if you are female, or wearing a skirt to work if you are male. Corrective feedback will likely follow. That was exactly the assignment given to sociology students at the University of Colorado and at Luther College in Iowa. Professors

Artist Nickolay Lamm used crowdfunding to release Lammily, a fashion doll (right) matching the body proportions of an average 19-year-old American woman. ©Nickolay Lamm/Rex Features/AP Images

asked students to behave in ways that they thought violated the norms of how a man or woman should act. Over the years that this ongoing experiment has been performed, students consistently received clear signals—ranging from amusement to disgust—that their actions were inappropriate and that they should instead behave in ways defined as appropriate by dominant heterosexual gender norms (Nielsen, Walden, and Kunkel 2000).

When we interact with others, we usually display our gender clearly. When we find ourselves in situations lacking explicit gender cues, we are often unsure how to proceed. For example, sociologists Candace West and Don Zimmerman (1987) provide a classic example in recounting a meeting in a computer store where the sex of the person involved remained ambiguous:

> The person who answered my questions was truly a *salesperson*. I could not categorize him/her as a woman or a man. What did I look for? (1) Facial hair: She/he was smooth skinned, but some men have little or no facial hair. (This varies by race; Native Americans and blacks often have none.) (2) Breasts: She/he was wearing a loose shirt that hung from his/her

shoulders. And, as many women who suffered through a 1950s adolescence know to their shame, women are often flat-chested. (3) Shoulders: His/hers were small and round for a man, broad for a woman. (4) Hands: Long and slender fingers, knuckles a bit large for a woman, small for a man. (5) Voice: Middle range, unexpressive for a woman, not at all the exaggerated tones some gay males affect. (6) His/her treatment of me: Gave off no signs that would let me know if I were of the same or different sex as this person. There were not even any signs that he/she knew his/her sex would be difficult to categorize and I wondered about this even as I did my best to hide these questions so I would not embarrass him/her while we talked of computer paper. I left still not knowing the sex of my salesperson, and was disturbed by that unanswered question (child of my culture that I am). (pp. 133–134)

Most of the time we do not actually see the "parts" that biologically define someone as male or female; we rely instead on other indicators, such as clothes and shapes, to be sufficient. As sociologist Judith Lorber (1994) put it, "Clothing, paradoxically, often hides the sex but displays the gender" (p. 22). We depend on established cues (such as outfits and hairstyles) to recognize someone's sex when we interact, often taking that recognition for granted.

Women's Gender Roles Parents, schools, friends, and the mass media all socialize us to internalize dominant gender norms. The positive and negative sanctions that we experience during such interactions shape the thoughts, actions, and appearances we accept as appropriate. Women, for example, continue to face pressure to be thin, beautiful, submissive, sexy, and maternal (Pai and Schryver 2015).

Films, television programs, and magazine ads all contribute to an idealized image of feminine beauty (H. Brown 2015; Kilbourne 2010, 2014). As we saw in the "Deviance and Social Stigma" section in Chapter 6, this image, dubbed the "beauty myth" by Naomi Wolf (1992), is largely unattainable for most women. It contributes to millions of cosmetic procedures each year for those seeking it. And as noted in the "Use of Existing Sources" section in Chapter 2, even supermodels such as Cindy Crawford feel they cannot achieve their own idealized images. Part of the reason is that these images are often not real. Instead, they are altered with the assistance of computer programs such as Photoshop (H. Brown 2015; Grossman 2015; Gurari, Hetts, and Strube 2006). Attaining an idealized image can be particularly problematic for those who do not match the White and heterosexual assumptions upon which it is built (Milillo 2008; Reel et al. 2008; Tate 2009).

Personal Sociology

Drawing Distinctions

When Emily and Eleanor were little, they covered our refrigerator with pictures they drew of our family. In the pictures, the girls wore dresses while I wore pants. They had long eyelashes and I did not. They had long hair, and I had what looked like a plate on my head. I asked Eleanor, "What about the women we know with short hair and the men we know with long hair?" She replied, "Yeah, but women have long hair and men have short hair." She knew there were people who didn't fit her hair theory, but she had already come to accept an image in which the line between men and women was obvious, important, and inevitable. To what extent have your hairstyles been a fairly predictable indicator of your gender?

As we increasingly recognize the impact of such artificial images, attempts have been made to offer alternative images of women in the mass media. This includes magazines that have featured images of models or

Singer Alicia Keys chose not to wear makeup as an expression of freedom and self-revelation. ©Photo by C Flanigan/Getty Images

Publishers have begun to produce more books with a diverse array of gender portrayals. ©Susan Church

conclude, "This widespread pattern of underrepresentation of females may contribute to a sense of unimportance among girls and privilege among boys" (J. McCabe et al. 2011:221). Other studies have found similar gendered patterns. Women are often shown as helpless, passive, and in need of a male caretaker. Fathers, in a study of children's picture books, were significantly less likely to touch, hug, kiss, talk to, or feed children (D. Anderson and Hamilton 2005; Etaugh 2003; Hamilton et al. 2006).

In recent years, companies have begun to respond. Mattel added Curvy Barbie, Tall Barbie, and Petite Barbie to its lineup along with a wider array of skin tones and hair types to reflect more racial and ethnic diversity (Bates 2016). Publishers of children's literature have produced a wider range of gender portrayals in books such as Robert Munsch's *The Paper Bag Princess;* Steven Lenton's *Princess Daisy, the Dragon, and the Nincompoop Knights;* and Kate Beaton's *The Princess and the Pony.* Comic book company DC Entertainment, as part of its Super Hero Girls Initiative, intends to produce more toys, TV specials, movies, and apparel for girls, a target demographic that has been largely ignored in the superhero product category (L. Brown 2016).

Men's Gender Roles Conventional gender-role expectations also exist for men. For example, stay-at-home fathers are still relatively uncommon. Among married-couple families with children under 15, there are 24 times more stay-at-home moms than stay-at-home dads (U.S. Census Bureau 2016f:Table FG-8). Although it is still rare for men to stay home to care for their children, in a nationwide survey, 53 percent of respondents said that if one parent stays home with the children, it makes no difference whether that parent is the mother or the father. Among the others responding, 45 percent still thought that the mother should be the one to stay home, and only 2 percent responded that it's better if the father stays home. Age played a significant role in the responses, with those over 65 most likely to say that the kids are better off if the mother stays home (Graf 2016).

Although attitudes toward parenting may be changing, traditional gender-role expectations continue to have a significant impact. Men, too, receive messages from family, peers, and the media about what it means to be masculine. One of the most powerful expectations is to be tough, both physically and emotionally, in sports, at work, and even in relationships. Males who fail to conform to such gender norms face criticism and even humiliation. Boys, for example, run the risk of being called a "chicken," "sissy," or

celebrities without makeup or photo retouching, as in the April 2010 issue of French *Elle,* which featured unretouched images of models and actresses without makeup. Similarly, Germany's most popular women's magazine, *Brigitte,* banned professional models from its pages. In Spain, fashion designers have established a minimum body mass index (BMI) score of 18 for runway models. And Israel passed a law banning models with a BMI less than 18.5 from fashion runways and advertisements; for example, a 5-foot, 8-inch-tall model must weigh at least 119 pounds. The law also requires publications to disclose when they have digitally altered photos to make models appear thinner. In 2016, singer Alicia Keys opted to go without makeup in appearances at the VMA and BET awards and in her role as a judge/coach in the NBC talent show *The Voice.* She did so, she said, because "I don't want to cover up anymore. Not my face, not my mind, not my soul, not my thoughts, not my dreams, not my struggles, not my emotional growth. Nothing" (Keys 2016; see also Izadi 2016).

Gendered messages about being a woman are about more than just beauty. They also project idealized images of "women's proper place," identifying some social status positions as more appropriate than others. Studies show that children's books reinforce such messages. One study of 5,618 children's books published throughout the 20th century found that male characters were represented twice as often as females. The disparity was greatest when portraying animal characters as males or females. Little Golden Books were more unequal than other series they studied. Starting in the 1970s they found a trend toward greater equity, though a significant imbalance remains. The researchers

"fag" even by fathers or brothers (Katz 1999; Pascoe 2011). Such name-calling represents a form of social control that limits the likelihood of new gender norms being established (Kimmel 2012; Pascoe and Bridges, eds. 2015).

We also see the effects of gendered expectations demonstrated by men in nontraditional occupations, such as preschool teacher or nurse. They may lie about their occupations when introduced to others in order to avoid negative reactions. For example, researchers interviewed a 35-year-old male nurse who reported that he would claim to be "a carpenter or something like that" when he "went clubbing," because women weren't interested in getting to know a male nurse. Subjects of the study made similar accommodations in casual exchanges with other men (Bagilhole and Cross 2006; Cross and Bagilhole 2002).

There may be a price to pay for such narrow conceptions of manhood. Boys who successfully adapt to cultural standards of masculinity may grow up to be inexpressive men who cannot share their feelings with others. They remain forceful and tough, but they are also closed and isolated. These traditional gender roles may be putting men at a disadvantage. Today girls outdo boys in high school, grabbing a disproportionate share of the leadership positions, from valedictorian to class president to yearbook editor—everything, in short, except captain of the boys' athletic teams. And their advantage continues after high school. In the 1980s, girls in the United States became more likely than boys to go to college. In 2015, women accounted for 57 percent of college students nationwide (National Center for Education Statistics 2016:Table 303.10). And starting in 2005–2006, more women than men in the United States earned doctoral degrees (Aud et al. 2012:284).

Increasing numbers of men in the United States have criticized the restrictive aspects of the traditional male gender role. Australian sociologist R. W. Connell (2002, 2005) has written about **multiple masculinities,** meaning that expressions of manliness can take varieties of forms beyond the culturally dominant, stereotypical construct of what it means to be a man. Masculine gender roles may include a nurturing-caring role, an effeminate-gay role, or the more traditional role (Connell and Messerschmidt 2005). Sociologist Michael Kimmel gave voice to this broader conception of what it means to be a man when he was sitting with his newborn son in the park. When a woman came up to him and said that he was expressing his "feminine side," he responded, "I'm not expressing anything of the sort, ma'am. I'm being tender and loving and nurturing toward my child. As far as I can tell, I'm expressing my *masculinity*" (Kimmel 2004:290–291).

GENDER ACROSS CULTURES

Beginning with the pathbreaking work of anthropologist Margaret Mead ([1935] 2001) and continuing through contemporary fieldwork, scholars have repeatedly shown that gender roles can vary greatly from one physical environment, economy, and political system to the next. Some cultures assume the existence of three or four gender categories. Sociologist Judith Lorber (1994) notes that "male women," biological males who live for the most part as women, and "female men," biological females who live for the most part as men, can be found in various societies. "Female men" can be found in some African and Native American societies, and in Albania, where they take on male work and family roles. "Male women" include the *berdaches,* also known as two-spirit people, of the Native Americans of the Great Plains; the *hijras* of India; and the *xanith* of Oman in the Middle East (Nanda 1997; Reddy 2005). Michael Kimmel (2004) describes the *xanith* this way:

> **Multiple masculinities** The idea that expressions of manliness can take varieties of forms beyond the culturally dominant, stereotypical construct of what it means to be a man.

> They work as skilled domestic servants, dress in men's tunics (but in pastel shades more associated with feminine colors), and sell themselves in passive homosexual relationships. They are permitted to speak with women on the street (other men are prohibited). At sex-segregated public events, they sit with the women. (p. 65)

The Bugis people, the largest ethnic group in South Sulawesi, Indonesia, identify five distinct genders: *oroané* (masculine man), *makkunrai* (feminine woman),

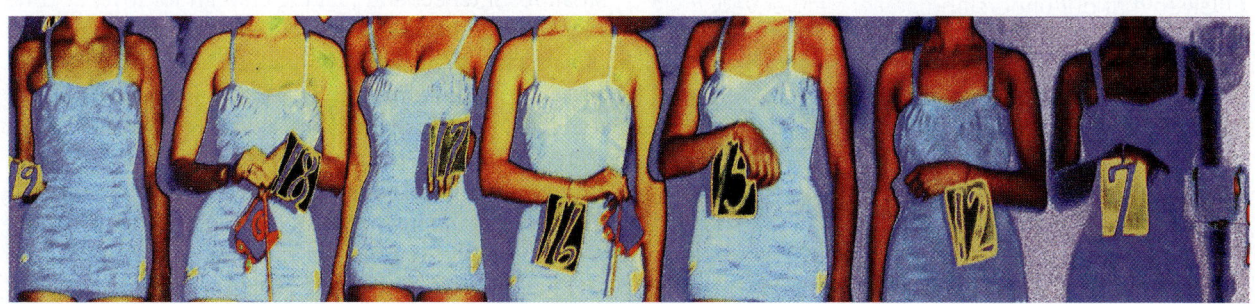
©Art Montes De Oca/Taxi/Getty Images

Thousands of hijras *gathered for a festival near Kolkata, India.* ©Salkat Paul/Pacific Press/LightRicket via Getty Images

calabai (feminine male), *calalai* (masculine female), and *bissu,* best described as a transgender shaman with physical aspects of both sexes (Davies 2007; Guy-Ryan 2016). In these societies, multiple gender categories are a well-accepted part of their social lives. Individuals who fill them are not simply tolerated or viewed as deviant. Two-spirit people and *bissu,* for example, have high status because they are thought to have special powers (Davies 2007; Kimmel 2004; Roscoe 1997).

The distribution of power based on gender also varies cross-culturally. Peggy Reeves Sanday's (2002, 2008) work in West Sumatra, Indonesia, for example, describes the 4-million-member Minangkabau society as one in which men and women are not competitors but partners for the common good. This society is characterized by a nurturing approach to the environment, blended with Islamic religious ethics. Women control the land through inheritance; in the event of a divorce, the ex-husband leaves with only his clothes. The larger community may be governed by men, women, or both men and women working together. Sanday's findings, together with Mead's, confirm the influential role of culture and socialization in gender-role differentiation.

SOCTHINK

Given that our understandings of gender vary across time and place, why are we so committed to the notion that gender differences are narrowly determined by biology?

REIMAGINING SEX AND GENDER

When it comes to gender, many people assume that the patterns we observe are a given—that biology, as the old saying goes, is destiny. Or, more specifically, that our sex defines our experience as men and women in obvious and predictable ways. We hear echoes of this sentiment in places such as John Gray's best-selling book, *Men Are from Mars, Women Are from Venus* (1992). This powerful analogy presents men and women as aliens from different planets, implying that the chasm between them is natural, inevitable, and difficult, if not impossible, to bridge (Carothers and Reis 2013; Hyde 2005). There are, however, signs that this assumption about the natural relationship between sex and gender is being called into question.

Moving beyond a simple, dimorphic model of sex opens the door to new opportunities for both men and women. It suggests that the line between what anthropologist Lisa Peattie and sociologist Martin Rein refer to as the natural and the artificial shifts over time. When we say something is *natural,* what we mean is that it should be accepted as given and cannot be changed. For example, when people contend that "men are more rational," or that "women are more nurturing," they often assume that these stereotypes are determined by our biology and thus immutable. Analysis of how gender is expressed across cultures and over time suggests, however, that such presumed-to-be inherent traits distinguishing men and women are really *artificial*—that is, they are social constructions subject to change, not inevitable determinants of who we must be (Peattie and Rein 1983).

Some major shifts in social life have been brought about by challenging the line between the natural and artificial. Even into the 20th century it was thought that women's biological makeup justified their exclusion from schools, the workplace, and politics—social locations in which women's participation is now taken for granted. For example, women were once banned from colleges and universities in the United States, because it was presumed that they were biologically incapable of succeeding. At the Jefferson Medical College in Philadelphia in 1847, Professor Charles Meigs, in a famous speech delivered to an all-male class of gynecology students, said of women, "She has a head almost too small for intellect and just big enough for love. . . . She reigns in the heart . . . the household altar is her place of worship and service" (quoted in Collins 2003:89–90). In 1874, at Harvard University, Dr. Edward Clarke, a member of its board of overseers, wrote that women were too delicate to handle the rigors of college education. The increased effort needed for thinking would sap energy from a woman's uterus and ovaries, leading these reproductive organs to shrink (Clarke 1874).

Elite schools such as Harvard, Yale, Princeton, and Dartmouth didn't formally admit women to their undergraduate programs until the late 1960s and early 1970s. In doing so, they weren't necessarily motivated by the high-minded ideals of gender equality and enhanced opportunities for women. Instead, because other prestigious schools had already made the transition to admitting women, continuing to deny access to them created a competitive disadvantage when it came to recruiting male students. In the words of Princeton's president in 1967, Princeton was "beginning to become comparatively less attractive to some applicants whom we would like to have because of lack of girls here" (Malkiel 2016:97).

... In an exploratory experiment controlling college students' knowledge of the professor's gender for an online course, students gave better teaching evaluations to professors the students thought were male. This was true even when the actual professor was a woman (MacNell, Driscoll, and Hunt 2014).

Photo: ©Asia Images/Getty Images RF

When women were finally given the opportunity to attend college, a right they had to fight hard for to win, they excelled. They now have a higher overall grade point average, and they outnumber men among college graduates. What was once thought to be natural is now recognized to have been a social construction. It turns out that the problem wasn't biology; it was the socially constructed culture that denied opportunity to women (Chee, Pino, and Smith 2005; National Center for Education Statistics 2016).

On the flip side, the notion persists that men just aren't as nurturing as women. It appears to grow out of the presumption that women, because they give birth and nurse babies, are naturally better at providing love, care, and protection. Yet research demonstrates that when men have the primary responsibility for raising children, they do the same things conventionally associated with "mothering." For example, sociologist Barbara Risman conducted research on single fathers and concluded that "when males take full responsibility for child care, when they meet expectations usually confined to females, they develop intimate and affectionate relationships with their children. Despite male sex-role training, fathers respond to the nontraditional role of single parent with strategies stereotypically considered feminine" (Risman 1986:101).

WOMAN MAY WEAR TROUSERS.

Attorney General of Kansas Rules There Is No Law Against It.

TOPEKA, Kan., April 28.—Gov. Stubbs received a letter yesterday from a widow at Oswego asking permission to wear men's trousers while at work at her home. It said she was supporting a large family, which necessitated outside work, and that in wearing skirts she was badly handicapped.

The letter was turned over to the Attorney General, who ruled there was no law prohibiting a woman from wearing men's trousers, especially if she were the head of the house.

It used to be considered unnatural for women to wear pants in the United States, but times change.
Source: Newspaper article "Woman May Wear Trousers" April 29, 1910

Similarly, researchers looking at response patterns for nearly 30,000 parents found no significant differences between North American mothers and fathers on factors including nurturance, warmth, responsiveness, encouragement, interaction, or disciplinary strictness. Thus it is not strictly biology that determines nurturing; it is the social structure and a person's position within it (Barnett and Rivers 2004; Lytton and Romney 1991; Risman and Johnson-Sumerford 1998).

Identifying some aspect of our definitions of sex and gender as artificial reveals the complex relationship between the two. Questioning our conceptions of the natural, however, is never easy, as women who have worked for the right to vote and equal opportunity in the workplace have discovered. Confronting these notions can look like an attempt to defy reality itself, but such defiance is necessary to enact significant social change.

>> Working for Change: Women's Movements

One of the lessons we learn from research on gender is that change is possible. As we saw with college education for women, past norms need not determine future practices. Change, however, seldom comes without conflict. People have fought against existing cultural assumptions about what is natural in order to advance opportunity for women in politics, the economy, and other spheres of public and private life. **Feminism** is the term for this belief in social, economic, and political equality for women.

THE FIRST WAVE

The feminist movement in the United States was born in upstate New York, in the town of Seneca Falls, in the summer of 1848. On July 19, the first women's rights convention began, attended by Elizabeth Cady Stanton, Lucretia Mott, and other pioneers in the struggle for women's rights. At the convention, members passed the "Declaration of Sentiments," which included this claim: "The history of mankind is a history of repeated injuries and usurpation on the part of man toward woman, having in direct object the establishment of an absolute tyranny over her." Echoing and expanding upon the Declaration of Independence, it called for the recognition that "all men and women are created equal." This first wave of feminists faced ridicule and scorn as they fought for legal and political equality for women. They were not afraid to risk controversy on behalf of their cause; in 1872, Susan B. Anthony was arrested for attempting to vote in that year's presidential election.

Feminism The belief in social, economic, and political equality for women.

These early feminists won many victories in health care, education, and property rights. The pinnacle accomplishment of the first wave was the passage and ratification of the 19th Amendment to the Constitution in 1920, which guaranteed women's right to vote in the United States. The amendment was initially introduced to Congress in 1878, and its wording mirrored that of the 15th Amendment, which prohibits denial of the right to vote on the basis of race. After gaining this new right, however, the movement lost momentum because various factions within it disagreed about future goals, and, for a time, the women's movement became a much less powerful force for social change (Dicker 2016; Flexner and Fitzpatrick 1996).

THE SECOND WAVE

What is called the second wave of feminism in the United States emerged in the 1960s and came into full force in the 1970s. Betty Friedan's book *The Feminine Mystique* played a crucial part, as did two other pioneering

Did You Know?

. . . When it comes to science education in the United States, the fact that boys consistently score higher than girls on standardized tests has led many to assume that the difference is related to inherent differences based on sex. Yet, in a broader study of 65 countries, girls were more likely to outperform boys. Boys tend to do better in western/northern European countries and the Americas. Girls outdo boys in Asia, eastern/southern Europe, and the Middle East.

Source: Fairfield and McLean 2012. *Photo:* ©M. Constantini/Photoalto RF

books that argued for women's rights: Simone de Beauvoir's *The Second Sex* (1952) and Kate Millett's *Sexual Politics* (1970). Friedan was an upper-middle-class, White, suburban housewife who worked part-time as a freelance journalist in the 1950s. As part of a story she planned to write, she surveyed her college classmates about their lives. What she heard repeatedly from women like her was that they shared a sense of nameless, aching dissatisfaction that she famously labeled "the problem that has no name." Even though they were living what many considered the American Dream, something was missing. They mostly blamed themselves for this feeling of emptiness or incompleteness, and when they sought help, doctors and psychiatrists prescribed charity work, community activities, or perhaps tranquilizers.

Betty Friedan's work as an organizer played a significant role in the second wave of feminism in the United States. ©B. Friedan/MPI/Getty Images

In *The Feminine Mystique,* Friedan (1963) argued that the problem was not with women as individuals, but with the position they occupied in American society at the time. Friedan's realization that this was not a private trouble but a public issue represents a classic case of using the sociological imagination. Women were cut off from the public sphere, and their lack of access to valued economic, social, and cultural resources—including money and power in the workplace—was the real problem. (Friedan herself attributed part of her own relative happiness to the fact that she retained dual status as both journalist and housewife.) To challenge this structural problem, women had to fight against the cultural assumption that the primary and most "natural" goal for women was to be a wife and mother in the private sphere. As Friedan put it, "We can no longer ignore that voice within women that says, 'I want something more than my husband and my children and my home'" (1963:32).

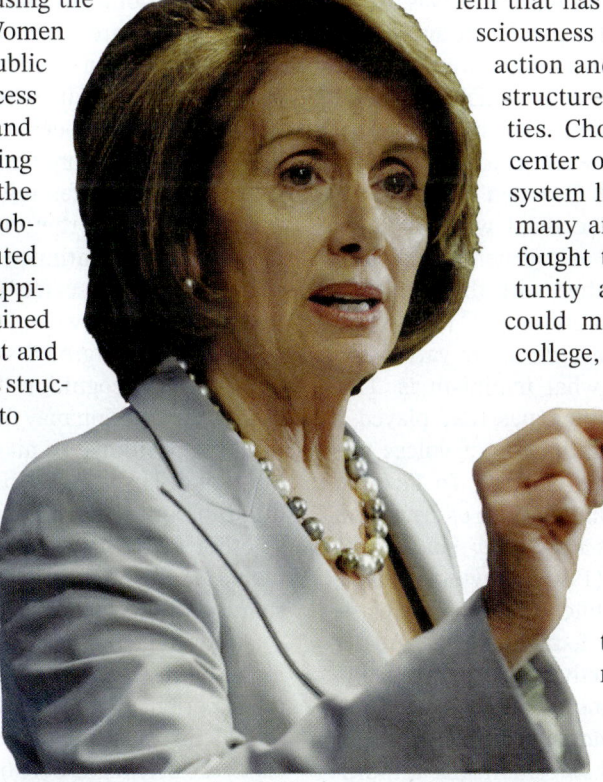

Nancy Pelosi, Democrat from California, was the first female Speaker of the U.S. House of Representatives. ©Scott J Ferrell/Getty Images

In 1966, Friedan helped found the National Organization for Women (NOW) to fight for equality for women; she served as its president until 1970. In addition to political and legal battles, one of the organization's tools was "consciousness-raising groups." Among other goals, these groups sought to elevate awareness among women regarding the degree to which they shared "the problem that has no name." This shared consciousness could then lead to collective action and the development of a new structure with enhanced opportunities. Choice was a core value at the center of these efforts. The existing system limited options for women in many areas of social life. Feminists fought to open up structural opportunity and to ensure that women could make choices about going to college, pursuing a career based on ability rather than gender expectations, getting married or staying single, having children or remaining childless, and so on.

The question of whether women should have control over their reproductive rights and their bodies has also played a significant role in this movement. In the United States, most people support a woman's right to a legal abortion, but with reservations. According to a national survey, 59 percent say it should be legal in all or most cases, while 37 percent argue it should be illegal in all or most cases. When asked about *Roe v. Wade,* the 1973 Supreme Court ruling that established the legal right to an abortion in the United States, 69 percent say it should *not* be overturned (Fingerhut 2017).

As more and more women identified existing cultural attitudes and practices as sexist—including those they themselves had accepted through socialization into traditional gender roles—they began to challenge male dominance. A sense of sisterhood, much like the class consciousness that Marx hoped would emerge in the proletariat, became evident. Individual women identified their interests with women as a whole, and they rejected the principle that their happiness depended on their acceptance of submissive and subordinate roles.

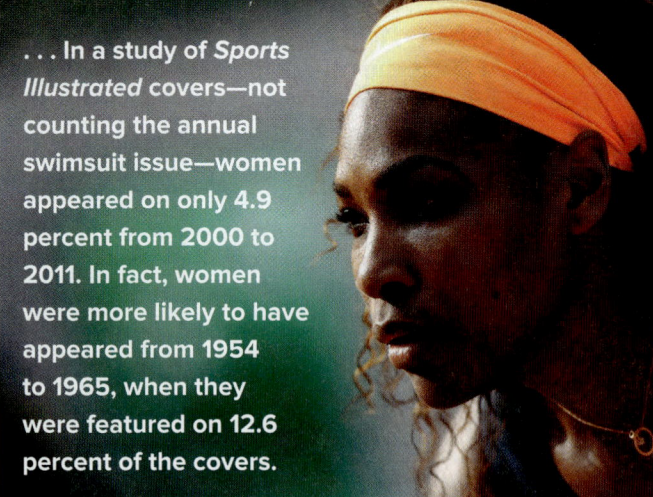

Did You Know?

...In a study of *Sports Illustrated* covers—not counting the annual swimsuit issue—women appeared on only 4.9 percent from 2000 to 2011. In fact, women were more likely to have appeared from 1954 to 1965, when they were featured on 12.6 percent of the covers.

Source: J. Weber and Carini 2013. Photo: ©Thomas Coex/Getty Images

THE THIRD WAVE

In the 1980s, partially because of second-wave successes in opening up opportunities and earning greater respect for women, a sense developed that the central goals of feminism had largely been accomplished. Some scholars argued that we had entered a postfeminist era. In the early 1990s, however, a new style of feminism arose that went beyond fighting the structural obstacles that motivated the first and second waves. It ventured into the cultural sphere to embrace a multiplicity of voices, expressions, and experiences. This third wave was part of a conceptual shift away from a singular focus on equality of persons, which it takes as a given, to a celebration of difference (Brooks 1997; Lotz 2007; Showden 2009).

Standpoint theory Because our social positions shape our perceptions, a more complete understanding of social relations must incorporate the perspectives of marginalized voices.

The third wave arose in part as a generational shift; younger women were dissatisfied with the dominant image of feminism as stodgy and uptight. It also represented a shift in message toward a more varied and pluralistic understanding of what feminism is. This was evident in two early anthologies that played a pivotal role presenting the multiplicity of voices this movement represents: Rebecca Walker's *To Be Real: Telling the Truth and Changing the Face of Feminism* (1995) and Barbara Findlen's *Listen Up: Voices from the Next Feminist Generation* (1995). Previously, feminists were characterized as White, upper-middle class, and heterosexual. Third-wave feminists place greater emphasis on agency and subjectivity; are committed to personal empowerment; are more open about sexuality and sexual exploration; and celebrate diversity of gender, race, ethnicity, and class. Embracing a multiplicity of identities led to a commitment to social justice and a global perspective so that other voices have the opportunity to be heard (Baumgardner and Richards 2000; Groeneveld 2009; Lotz 2007; Zimmerman, McDermott, and Gould 2009).

The third wave includes a bit of the postmodern idea of self-creation, which we explored in the "Postmodern Life" section in Chapter 5. According to this idea, we can choose our identities from a buffet of possibilities and also create our own realities. This fits with the notion that our sex is not narrowly determined by biology and that our expression of our gender need not be singular in nature but is open to our creativity and control. One result is a more playful or ironic element to the movement, especially when it comes to so-called girlie feminism, which seeks to reclaim things like lipstick, high heels, and more sexualized images of women as viable emblems of feminist empowerment. Critics have argued that this rhetoric of choice inappropriately minimizes the continued power of racial, sexual, and class positions in society (Munford 2007; Renegar and Sowards 2009; Showden 2009).

One of the outgrowths of this new feminist perspective was the recognition that defining others primarily by any one position may diminish the importance of the multiple positions we all occupy. To look at the social location of Hispanic women, for example, we must pay mind to both their gender and their ethnicity (as well as other factors). Two significant theoretical developments arising out of this multiple-identity approach are standpoint theory and intersectionality.

According to **standpoint theory,** our understanding of reality is shaped by the positions we occupy and the experiences we have. Given that the views of some (based on their gender, sexuality, race, ethnicity, or class) are privileged over others, this theory emphasizes the importance of listening to the voices of those who are in some way considered outsiders. Such attention provides a deeper and richer understanding of social systems (Collins 2000; Harding 2004; Hartsock 1983; D. Smith 1987).

Intersectionality represents a second major development. According to this approach, we cannot speak of gender or race or class or sexuality as if they exist in isolation from each other. Rather, these combine within us in ways that make it difficult to separate the effects of each. Thus research must analyze the intermingled effects of multiple social statuses on identity, knowledge, and outcomes. In her TED talk, "The Urgency of Intersectionality," law professor Kimberlé Crenshaw focused on the cultural frames we use to understand the world around us. In doing so, she suggested that these frames prevent us from seeing how the social justice inequalities people experience around gender, sexuality, race, ethnicity, and class overlap and cannot be dealt with in isolation from each other (Alimahomed 2010; Crenshaw 2016; Harding 2004; Shields 2008). For both standpoint theory and intersectionality, a narrative approach in research, in which we hear the voices of those who are other to us, is critical.

SOCTHINK

What do you think being a feminist means today?

how we see ourselves and what we do. **Sexuality** denotes our identities and activities as sexual beings. In terms of *identity,* our sexuality represents an expression of who we are in ways similar to how gender, race, ethnicity, and class shape us. In terms of our sexual *practices,* sexuality shapes what we do (or do not do), with whom, and how often.

SEXUALITY AND IDENTITY

Sexual expression is not simply a result of biological urges and instincts. It is situated within, and an outgrowth of, existing social, cultural, and historical processes. Though alternative expressions of sexuality have a long history in the United States, their existence and practice has not always been acknowledged (Duberman, Vicinus, and Chauncy 1989; Escoffier 1997). During the 1960s, experimentation with "free love" helped open the door to more widespread recognition of such expressions. Around the same time organizations arose, such as the Gay Liberation Front in 1969 and the Gay Activist Alliance in 1970, that

> **Intersectionality** Gender, sexuality, race, ethnicity, and class must not be studied in isolation, because they have intermingled effects on our identity, knowledge, and outcomes.
>
> **Sexuality** Denotes our identities and activities as sexual beings.

>> The Social Construction of Sexuality

The shifts that occur in how sex and gender are defined—as more complex than simple binary categories of male and female or masculine and feminine—also apply to sexuality. In the United States, as a consequence of the dimorphic model of sex, the dominant ideology presumed heterosexual relationships, in which the idealized norm was chastity until marriage, followed by lifelong faithfulness to a single partner. This vision reached perhaps its zenith in the 1950s television portrayal of families in programs such as *Leave It To Beaver* and *Father Knows Best.* Times have changed.

When considering sexuality, we should distinguish between

U.S. Attitudes About Homosexuality

Note: Responses are to the question "What about sexual relationship between two adults of the same sex—do you think it is always wrong, almost always wrong, wrong only sometimes, or wrong at all?" Data are from the General Social Survey, a regularly administered national survey of the U.S. adult population.

Sources: T. Smith 2011; T. Smith et al. 2014. *Photos: (scale):* ©Comstock/Alamy Stock Photo RF; *(two grooms):* ©Ivonne Wierink/Shutterstock.com; *(bride and groom):* ©Evgenii Zadiraka/123RF

Sexual orientation The categories of people to whom we are sexually attracted.

Heterosexual A category of sexual orientation that includes those who are sexually attracted to members of the opposite sex.

Homosexual A category of sexual orientation that includes those who are attracted to members of the same sex.

Bisexual A category of sexual orientation that includes those who are attracted to both men and women.

Gender identity People's subjective or internal sense of their own gender.

Gender expression The outward or public display of a person's gender.

raised awareness that alternatives existed and sought to establish the legitimacy of alternative sexualities in the public consciousness.

As a result of such historical events, people became more aware of the concept of **sexual orientation**—the categories of people to whom we are sexually attracted—as a form of personal and community identity. Initially, in keeping with the dimorphic model of sex, the two major subcategories included **heterosexual,** those who were sexually attracted to members of the opposite sex, and **homosexual,** those who were attracted to members of the same sex. Homosexual men were identified as gay, and homosexual women were identified as lesbian. **Bisexual** was later added to these subcategories to include those who were attracted to both men and women. Attitudes regarding sexual orientation has shifted significantly over time. As the accompanying "U.S. Attitudes About Homosexuality" graph displays, the majority of adults surveyed now believe that homosexuality is not wrong at all.

Even though this heterosexual, homosexual, bisexual model extended awareness of sexuality beyond the 1950s version, it still presents the dividing lines as clear-cut and absolute. Classifying where you or others belong is presumed to be a simple matter of identifying your sexual practices and checking the appropriate box. But people's experiences of sexuality are more complex and varied than that. For example, what about those who have had occasional homosexual experiences but are now practicing heterosexuals? Or those who engage in same-sex practices but do not identify themselves as gay, lesbian, or bisexual (Silva 2016; Ward 2015)? Over time, additional categories were added to reflect a wider array of possibilities, such as polysexual, pansexual, and asexual.

Sexual orientation, which focuses on who we choose to love, should be distinguished from **gender identity,** which refers to people's subjective or internal sense of their own gender. And this internal conception of who you are can differ from your **gender expression,** the outward or public expression of your gender, often manifested in terms of clothes, haircuts, language, and other gendered behaviors. The importance of these concepts arose largely due to greater recognition of people who are **transgender**—those whose gender identity differs from the sex they were assigned at birth. For example, a transgender person may have been born with a vagina but self-identify as male or masculine. The gender identity of those who are **cisgender,** on the other hand, aligns more closely with the cultural expectations associated with their biological sex at birth. The prefix for the two words come from Latin, with *trans-* meaning "across" and *cis-* meaning "on the same side" (Tate, Youssef, and Tate, Ledbetter, Bettergarcia 2014; and Youssef 2013; Zimmer 2015).

To represent the full range of people's lived experiences, theorists have pushed even further, suggesting that we replace the existing either/or gender dimorphism implicit within conceptions of gender with a new model. The existing **gender binary**—a model in which gender roles are represented as either masculine or feminine with a clear divide between the two—constrained both sexual orientation and gender expression. The proposed alternative model portrayed a **gender spectrum,** which presents gender as a continuum that incorporates a full range of possible combinations involving sex, gender, sexual orientation, gender identity, and gender expression. According to this model, gender is visualized as similar to

Caitlyn Jenner's coming out as a transgender woman in 2015 brought national attention to transgender issues in the United States. ©Photo by David Livingston/Getty Images

a color wheel with no clear dividing lines between shades as opposed to an either/or check box. Many have adopted the use of the term **queer** (or genderqueer), because it reflects the rejection of sexual and gender binaries and highlights the multiple varieties of possible sexual orientations, gender identities, and gender expressions.

Although awareness of the socially constructed nature of gender and sexuality has increased, a cultural expectation of heterosexuality remains dominant in the United States. Sociologists use the term **heteronormativity** to describe the cultural presupposition that heterosexuality is the appropriate standard for sexual identity and practice and that alternative sexualities are deviant, abnormal, or wrong (Chambers 2007; Jackson 2006; Warner 1993). As an example of heteronormativity, a 1957 survey found that "four out of five people believed that anyone who preferred to remain single was 'sick,' 'neurotic,' or 'immoral'" (Coontz 2005:230). Additionally, homosexuality was categorized as a psychological disorder until 1972 in the American Psychiatric Association's official *Diagnostic and Statistical Manual of Mental Disorders* (*DSM*). A new edition, *DSM-5,* came out in 2013. The category "gender identity disorders," which included those who are transgender and transsexual, was removed and replaced with "gender dysphoria." The intent was to minimize the stigma attached to the diagnosis while still recognizing its existence. Some argue for the importance of maintaining these diagnoses, because transgender people who seek gender reassignment surgery might not get proper diagnosis and treatment without such a designation (Drescher 2010, 2011; Melby 2009; Winters 2012).

Heteronormativity is a form of ethnocentrism that generalizes a particular cultural ideal (heterosexuality) onto all other populations, thus denying legitimacy to those outside it (Chambers 2007). It can be maintained in subtle, often invisible ways during our everyday interactions. The television series *Glee* captured just such a moment in an encounter between Kurt, a gay high school student, and his father, Burt, who is generally understanding and supportive of Kurt's sexuality. Kurt was saddened at the seeming ease with which his dad talked sports with Finn, the school's star quarterback. His father tries to reassure him by saying, "Kurt, I love you. And I am sympathetic to all your stuff. But come on, buddy, we've got a deal here, right? I don't try to change you; you don't try to change me. You are my son, and a little guy talk with some other kid isn't going to change that." Kurt replies, "Guy talk? I'm a guy." It is precisely at moments such as this, when a person becomes invisible as a guy because he does not conform to the dominant gender expectations, that heteronormativity is at work.

Socialization plays a key role in determining our sexual identity (R. Parker 2009). Just as was the case with gender, we face significant pressure to obey dominant norms for masculinity and femininity. In her book *Dude You're a Fag,* sociologist C. J. Pascoe (2011) set out to understand how heteronormativity is reproduced. She conducted an ethnographic study of boys in a working-class high school. She found that one of the ways they reinforced existing masculinity norms was by casually using the term *fag* to call out anyone who deviates from the dominant masculine ideal. According to Pascoe, calling someone a fag was not so much an anti-gay act (though she admits it was that, too) as it was a means of keeping guys in line. Whereas it was possible to be a homosexual and still be masculine, being a fag represented a form of failed masculinity. The threat of being a fag hangs over boys like

Transgender People whose gender identity differs from the sex they were assigned at birth.

Cisgender Persons whose gender identity aligns more closely with the cultural expectations associated with their biological sex at birth.

Gender binary A dimorphic model in which gender roles are represented as either masculine or feminine with a clear divide between the two.

Gender spectrum A model of gender as a continuum that incorporates a full range of possible combinations involving sex, gender, sexual orientation, gender identity, and gender expression.

queer A term that incorporates the multiplicity of possible sexual orientations, gender identities, and gender expressions.

Heteronormativity A term that sociologists use to describe the cultural presupposition that heterosexuality is the appropriate standard for sexual identity and practice and that alternative sexualities are deviant, abnormal, or wrong.

Kurt Hummel, an openly gay character on the television show Glee, represented a pop culture hero for many. ©Boby Bank/Getty Images

SOC THINK

How is heteronormativity reinforced in the current top-rated songs and television programs? Can you think of any exceptions?

a specter or ghost that could possess them at any time; only eternal vigilance keeps it at bay. Pascoe argues that rejecting this role also represented a repudiation of femininity. So not only did this discourse support existing heteronormative standards, it also reinforced traditional conceptions of gender. Other researchers found similar results in a study of "hogging," in which men have sex with overweight or obese women not as a means of establishing a relationship with them but as a game to prove their masculinity to other guys (Prohaska and Gailey 2010).

> **SOC THINK**
>
> How does gendered name-calling, such as joking that a guy is a fag, maintain clear-cut gender boundaries? What consequences does it have for gays, lesbians, or heterosexual girls?

Such examples point to the fact that differences in sexuality are not just matters of orientation and alternative preferences; they are connected to larger systems of power in which some statuses are privileged over others (Brickell 2009). We construct our sexual identities, making sense of who we are, within the contexts of our social structures. Within these worlds, not all paths are accepted as equally legitimate. In the United States, establishing a sexual identity as something other than heterosexual has been difficult owing to the meanings attached to such identities and the lack of broader cultural support for them. These power differences contribute to discrimination and threats of violence. According to the FBI, for example, 17.7 percent of the 6,885 hate crime offenses reported in 2015 involved sexual orientation (U.S. Department of Justice 2016d). In an effort to ensure the civil, political, and social rights of those in lesbian, gay, bisexual, and transgender (LGBT) communities around the world, a group of human rights experts worked to establish the Yogyakarta Principles (www.yogyakartaprinciples.org). They identify 29 basic principles, including the right to equality and nondiscrimination, the right to work, and the right to found a family.

In review, to better understand issues surrounding sexuality and identity, we must understand the complexity sexuality entails. Doing so necessitates taking into account sex (biology), gender (social, cultural, and psychological constructs), sexual orientation (partner preferences), gender identity (subjective sensibility), and gender expression (external displays). A variety of possible manifestations exists within each of these major variables—not only a simple dichotomy of male versus female for each. As a result, many combinations are possible. As alternative expressions of gender and sexuality become more accepted, their role as master status through which all identity is filtered may become less powerful. Instead, in keeping with the lessons learned regarding intersectionality, sexuality may become but one significant piece of identity among others, all of which we must take into account to better understand why we think and act as we do.

SEXUALITY IN ACTION

While our sexuality shapes our conception of who we are, it also has consequences for what we do. In sociological terms, as suggested by the Thomas theorem, our sexual identity is shaped by our interactions with others. We then act on the basis of those perceptions. In our everyday lives, our perceptions of ourselves and our sexual practices often reinforce each other. Working out our sexuality in practice includes the types of sex acts we perform and the types of sexual relationships we establish with others.

Because open discussions about sex are generally considered to be taboo, people are often both ignorant and curious about actual sexual practices. The Kinsey Reports (*Sexual Behavior in the Human Male* [1948] and *Sexual Behavior in the Human Female* [1953]) provided the earliest in-depth research studies on people's sexual practices. Compiled by American biologist Alfred C. Kinsey and his colleagues, the reports, particularly their finding that 8 percent of men had been in predominantly homosexual relationships for at least three years between ages 16 and 55, were considered shocking at the time. Both volumes became best sellers. Their studies opened the door for others to conduct additional research (Bullough 1998; Laumann et al. 1994; T. Smith 2006).

The National Survey of Family Growth (NSFG) provides recent data and includes detailed information on sexual practices. The survey is conducted by the National Center for Health Statistics (NCHS) and the Centers for Disease Control and Prevention (CDC) and is based on a national sample of more than 9,000 respondents (Copen, Chandra, and Febo-Vazquez 2016). Summarizing the results regarding heterosexual relationship patterns, the NSFG researchers reported that "94.2% of women and 92.0% of men aged 18–44 had ever had vaginal intercourse; 86.2% of women and 87.4% of men had ever had oral sex; and 35.9% of women and 42.3% of men had ever had anal sex" (p. 1). In an earlier wave of research they found that the median number of total opposite-sex partners was 3.6 for women and 6.1 for men (Chandra et al. 2011).

Over the years, a contentious question in such studies has involved the percentage of homosexuals in the U.S. population. A commonly reported figure (derived from the Kinsey Reports) estimates that approximately

Alfred C. Kinsey, with the help of his team of researchers, provided unprecedented insight into people's sexual practices in the United States. ©Hulton Archive/Getty Images.

10 percent of the population is homosexual. The NSFG study distinguished between having had same-sex experiences and identifying with particular sexual orientations. The researchers found that among adults aged 18–44, 6.2 percent of men and 17.4 percent of women have had same-sex sexual contact in their lifetime. Likelihoods of engaging in same-sex sexual behavior varied somewhat by age. Among women, the difference was wider: 19.4 percent of 18- to 24-year-olds compared to 13.1 percent for 35- to 44-year-olds. Among men, 6.6 percent of 18- to 24-year-olds reported having had same-sex sexual contact compared to 6.0 percent for 35- to 44-year-olds (Copen et al. 2016).

> **SOC THINK**
>
> Why are younger women more likely to have had same-sex experiences than either older women or men of any age?

Simply having had same-sex experiences does not necessarily result in a same-sex identity. The percentage of people who identify as homosexual and bisexual are lower than the percentage of those who have engaged in such practices. To explore sexual orientation, the NSFG researchers asked, "Do you think of yourself as a heterosexual, homosexual, or bisexual?" As the "Sexual Orientation Self-Identification" table indicates,

Actor Neil Patrick Harris (right) along with his husband, David Burtka. ©Jason LaVeris/FilmMagic/Getty Images

95.1 percent of men and 92.3 percent of women identify themselves as heterosexual. Overall, approximately 1.6 percent of men and women aged 18–44 in the United States identify themselves as homosexual and 3.8 percent as bisexual (Copen et al. 2016).

Sexual Orientation Self-Identification

	Men	Women
Heterosexual	95.1	92.3
Homosexual	1.9	1.3
Bisexual	2.0	5.5
Did Not Report	1.0	0.9

Note: Percentage is in response to the question "Do you think of yourself as a heterosexual, homosexual, or bisexual?" Age range of respondents was 18–44.
Source: Copen et al. 2016.

The age at which people have their first sexual experiences has historically been an additional interest of researchers. In terms of opposite-sex experiences, the percentage of teens who have had sexual intercourse rises with each subsequent year. At age 15, 13 percent of girls and 18 percent of boys have had vaginal sexual intercourse; by age 17, it is 43 percent for girls and 44 percent for boys; and at age 19, it is 68 percent for females and 69 percent for males (Martinez and Abma 2015). At the same time, teen birthrates in the United States have reached record lows, having fallen 42 percent since 2007. Rates are down significantly for all racial and ethnic groups (Patten and Livingston 2016).

One concern about those who have sex at a young age is sexual coercion. In fact, among girls who had their first sexual intercourse before age 14, 18 percent said that they really didn't want it to happen at the time. Another 52 percent had mixed feelings about whether they wanted sex or not. For boys who were the same age, 8.9 percent didn't want it to happen, and 34 percent had mixed feelings. Put another way, among those who had sex before age 20, 41 percent of females and 63 percent of males really wanted it to happen at the time (Martinez, Copen, and Abma 2011:Table 9).

When it comes to sexual activity overall, perhaps no invention in the history of human sexuality was more important than that of the birth control pill. It was approved for use in the United States in 1960 and helped spark the sexual revolution. Together with other modern forms of birth control, the pill made it possible to engage in sex without significant risk of getting pregnant. It gave women greater control over their sexuality and their careers by allowing them to control their fertility. Effective birth control also resulted in debates about how sex should be viewed, whether primarily for procreation (that is, having babies) or recreation (for pleasure, love, and commitment) or both. Religious groups, including the Roman Catholic Church, continue to struggle with these issues (Benagiano and Mori 2009).

In the United States, 61.7 percent of women of childbearing age (15–44) use some form of contraception. Of these, 26 percent use birth control pills, 25 percent opted for female surgical sterilization, and 15 percent rely on male condoms. Among those not using contraception, 11 percent have never had intercourse and 8 percent had no intercourse recently (Daniels et al. 2015).

Internationally, birth control practices vary significantly from country to country. The overall global average for use of modern forms of birth control—condoms, the pill, and sterilization—is 58 percent among women aged 15–49 who are married or in a union. For Europe as a whole, 60 percent of people use a modern form of birth control. The rate jumps to 74 percent in the countries of northern Europe (such as Norway and the United Kingdom) and 68 percent in western Europe (including France and Germany). In Asia, China's rate is 82 percent, Japan's is 51 percent, and India's is 53 percent. Compare these countries with Africa, where the overall rate is 31 percent with substantial variation between countries. Some African nations have extremely low rates—for example, South Sudan at 5.0, Chad at 5.8 percent, and Guinea at 6.5 percent. Others have rates higher than the global average—for example, Swaziland at 63 percent, South Africa at 64 percent, and Zimbabwe at 66 percent. Just as was the case for women in the United States, greater control over fertility by women internationally increases their opportunities for self-determination. It also increases the likelihood of extending basic human rights and protections to women in countries around the world (Inglehart, Norris, and Welzel 2002; Kristof and WuDunn 2009; United Nations 2016a).

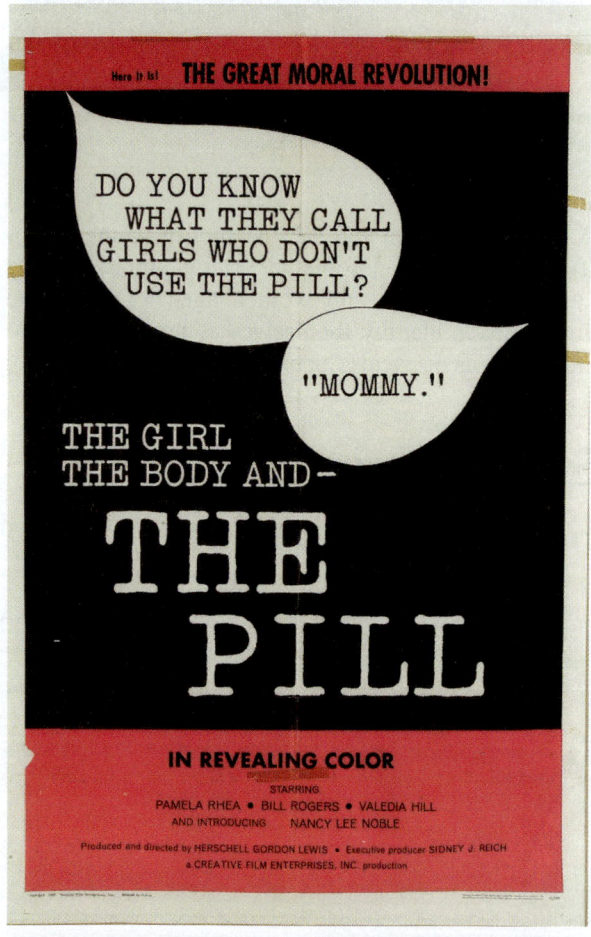

©Movie Poster Image Art/Getty Images

SOC THINK

How might economic, social, and cultural factors influence a society's pattern of birth control use? How might these factors influence a society's attitudes about gender?

>> Gender and Inequality

Although the work of early sociologists such as Harriet Martineau, Charlotte Perkins Gilman, and Ida B. Wells-Barnett highlighted the significance of gender inequality, in the 1950s sociologists Talcott Parsons and Robert Bales (1955) by and large accepted a dimorphic model of gender as natural. Drawing on the functionalist perspective, they maintained that families need both an instrumental and an expressive leader to function properly. The **instrumental leader** is the person in the family who bears responsibility for completion of tasks, focuses on distant goals, and manages the external relationship between the family and other social institutions. The **expressive leader** is the person in the family who bears responsibility for the maintenance of harmony and internal emotional affairs. Parson and Bales argued that this division of labor works well because women's interest in expressive goals frees men for instrumental tasks, and vice versa. Based on their theory, it seemed only natural that women become anchored in the family as wives, mothers, and household managers, while men become anchored in the occupational world outside the home.

As we saw above with Betty Friedan and second wave feminism, a major consequence of this supposed ideal was isolation from the public sphere's economy and politics. This separation had the effect of denying women access to financial resources and political power. Over time, as a direct consequence of activism, women have gained greater access to educational opportunities, jobs, and political positions. And yet, as we will see, women still face significant challenges.

SEXISM AND DISCRIMINATION

As is apparent in the definition of sociology, sociologists are interested in understanding the "consequences of difference"; that is, the impact the social structures we build have on the distribution of valued resources. When it comes to gender, sociologists investigate the degree of sexism that exists within social systems. **Sexism** is the ideology that claims one sex is superior to the other. The term generally refers to male prejudice and discrimination against women. It is not enough, however, to understand gender inequality only by looking at the attitudes and practices of individuals, such as sexist remarks and acts of aggression. We must analyze it as a characteristic of the social system itself.

Sociologists use the expression **institutional discrimination** to refer to patterns of treatment that, as part of a society's normal operations, systematically deny a group access to resources and opportunities. All the major institutions in the United States—including the government, the armed forces, large corporations, the media, universities, and the medical establishment—are controlled primarily by men. Analysis of patterns of distribution allow for some assessment of the degree to which institutional sexism exists.

WOMEN IN THE UNITED STATES

In 1976, 200 years after the Declaration of Independence claimed "all men are created equal," the U.S. Commission on Civil Rights (1976) concluded that the phrase had been taken literally for too long. It found that women in the United States experienced a consistent pattern of inequality. Looking at the workplace, income, housework, politics, and more, we can see that its concern is still valid.

Labor Force Participation The labor market has opened up significantly since Betty Friedan published *The Feminine Mystique* in 1963. Today, millions of women—married or single, with or without children, pregnant or recently having given birth—are in the labor force. Overall, as shown in the "Labor Force Participation Rates" graph, the percentage of U.S.

> **Instrumental leader** The person in the family who bears responsibility for the completion of tasks, focuses on distant goals, and manages the external relationship between one's family and other social institutions.
>
> **Expressive leader** The person in the family who bears responsibility for the maintenance of harmony and internal emotional affairs.
>
> **Sexism** The ideology that claims one sex is superior to the other.
>
> **Institutional discrimination** A pattern of treatment that systematically denies a group access to resources and opportunities as part of society's normal operations.

©Thomas Northcut/Digital Vision/Getty Images RF

Labor Force Participation Rates

Source: Bureau of Labor Statistics 2015b. Photo: ©kristian sekulic/Getty Images

Within the labor force, we see significant differences in the jobs men and women hold. As is evident in the "Women's Representation in U.S. Occupations" table, significant occupational gender segregation exists. For example, women account for 97 percent of all dental hygienists and 94 percent of all secretaries. Entering such sex-typed occupations often places women in "service" roles that parallel the traditional gender-role standard. At the same time, women are underrepresented in occupations historically defined as "men's jobs," which often offer much greater financial rewards and prestige than women's jobs. For example, women account for 47 percent of the paid labor force of the United States, yet they constituted only 7.2 percent of aircraft pilots, 8.8 percent of mechanical engineers, 12.4 percent of police officers, and 32.9 percent of lawyers (Bureau of Labor Statistics 2015b:Table 11).

women aged 16 and older in the labor force rose from 33.9 percent in 1950 to 57 percent in 2014. By contrast, the percentages for men were 86.3 percent in 1950 and 69.2 percent in 2014. Among women with children under age 6, 39 percent were in the labor force in 1975 compared to 64.3 percent in 2014 (Bureau of Labor Statistics 2015b:Tables 2 and 7).

Women's Representation in U.S. Occupations

Underrepresented		Overrepresented	
Occupation	Percentage female	Occupation	Percentage female
Roofer	0.5	Flight attendants	75.8
Auto mechanic	1.4	Elementary teachers	80.9
Electrician	2.4	Tellers	81.6
Firefighter	5.7	Social workers	81.9
Aircraft pilot	7.2	Librarians	84.8
Mechanical engineer	8.8	Registered nurses	90.0
Police officer	12.4	Receptionists	91.3
Printers	19.6	Occupational therapist	92.4
Computer programmer	21.4	Secretary	94.2
Architect	25.3	Hairdresser	94.6
Lawyers	32.9	Childcare workers	95.5
Physicians	36.7	Dental hygienists	97.1

Note: These data are for 2014. The elementary teacher category includes middle school teachers.
Source: Bureau of Labor Statistics 2015b:Table 11. Photo: ©JupiterImage, Creatas Image/Getty Images RF

Income Today we claim to value "equal pay for equal work," meaning that someone's sex (along with race, ethnicity, or age) shouldn't matter in determining what the person earns; the only characteristic that should matter is job performance. But in practice, women do not earn as much on average as men, even in the same occupations. When comparing individuals who worked full-time, year-round in 2015, the median income for men was $51,212, and the median for women was $40,742 (Proctor et al. 2016). In other words, women earned 80 cents for every dollar that men earned overall.

Taking occupational segregation into account does not explain away the wage gap. It's true, of course, that women are often more concentrated in occupations with lower average wages than men (child care worker or receptionist versus physician or civil engineer). However, in 2015, out of 119 specific jobs for which the Bureau of Labor Statistics provides sufficient data, in only 5 did women earn more on average than men: counselors; bookkeeping, accounting, auditing clerk; police and sheriff's patrol officers; data entry keyers; and non-farm wholesale and retail buyers. And significant wage gaps exist within occupations across the board. For example, wage gaps persist in the three occupations for which women receive the highest average pay: pharmacist

(85.5 percent of men's earnings), lawyer (89.7 percent), and chief executive officer (81.6 percent). Of course, in some occupations the wage gap is significantly wider, including securities, commodities, and financial services sales agents (52.5), personal financial advisors (59.4), advertising sales agents (63.1), and insurance sales agents (69.7) (Bureau of Labor Statistics 2016g:Table 2).

Even in occupations where women are more likely to be concentrated, they still earn less on average than do men in the same field. Examples include elementary or middle school teacher (88.9 percent), registered nurse (89.9 percent), and social worker (91.4 percent). Being a man in a predominantly female occupation seems to be an asset, whereas the reverse does not appear to be true (Bureau of Labor Statistics 2016g:Table 2).

Additional factors to explain the wage gap include education and age. When comparing women and men who have similar levels of education—for example, a woman whose highest degree is a high school diploma to a man with the same level of education—the wage gap persists. As is portrayed in the "Gender Wage Gap by Education" table, women with some college but no degree earn 72.8 percent compared to men with the same educational attainment. The wage gap is even wider for men and women with professional degrees, including medical doctors and lawyers. Within this group, women earn 67.1 percent of what men earn (U.S. Census Bureau 2016a:Table PINC-03).

When comparing women and men in similar age groups, a pattern does emerge. The wage gap between men and women narrows, at approximately 90 percent, when both are under 35 but widens for age groups older than that (Bureau of Labor Statistics 2016g:Table 1). A major factor suggested to explain this difference is that women are more likely than men to take time away from the workforce around that age to raise children. As a result, when they return to the labor force they have less seniority than men of equal age and thus receive lower wages (England et al. 2016; Erosa, Fuster, and Restuccia 2016; Golan and Hincapié 2016).

The Glass Ceiling As we saw with Sheryl Sandberg at the beginning of this chapter, the higher you look up the corporate ladder, the fewer women you see. These positions tend to have higher pay and greater power, yet women have often been passed over when it came to these jobs. The term **glass ceiling** refers to the invisible barrier that blocks the promotion of qualified individuals in a work environment because of the individual's gender, race, or ethnicity. In 1995, the federal government's Glass Ceiling Commission (1995) offered the first comprehensive study of the barriers in hiring decisions. It concluded that prejudice against women and minority group candidates plays a substantial role in hiring outcomes. It also concluded that the supply of qualified top-level candidates is limited by the cumulative effects of similar practices throughout the career path, limiting access to the training and experiences necessary to be considered for top-level jobs.

In recent years, corporations have made a concerted effort to increase their executive-level diversity, but they still have a long way to go if their goal is balanced representation between men and women. In 2015, only 3.9 percent of the chief executive officers (CEOs) and 14.1 percent of chief financial officers (CFOs) globally were women. Only 14.7 percent of board of director seats globally are occupied by women. To put it another way, men hold 85 percent of the seats on these boards, a source of a significant amount of power and influence. Board representation varies significantly between countries. In Norway, women occupy 46.7 percent of board seats; in the United States it's 16.6 percent; and in Japan women represent only 3.5 percent of board members (Dawson, Natella, and Kersley 2016).

> **Glass ceiling** An invisible barrier that blocks the promotion of a qualified individual in a work environment because of the individual's gender, race, or ethnicity.

Gender Wage Gap by Education

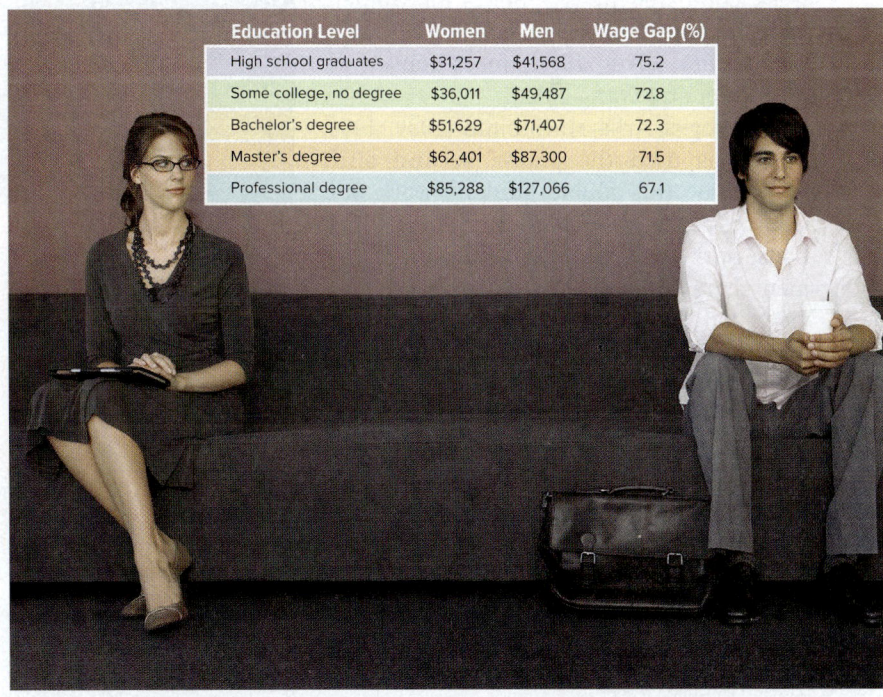

Education Level	Women	Men	Wage Gap (%)
High school graduates	$31,257	$41,568	75.2
Some college, no degree	$36,011	$49,487	72.8
Bachelor's degree	$51,629	$71,407	72.3
Master's degree	$62,401	$87,300	71.5
Professional degree	$85,288	$127,066	67.1

Note: Data based on median earnings for people ages 25 to 64 who worked full-time, year-round. High school graduates includes those with GEDs.
Source: U.S. Census Bureau 2016a:Table PINC-03.   *Photo:* ©bikeriderlondon/Shutterstock.com RF

Did You Know?

...Women spend an average of 2 hours, 15 minutes per day on housework compared to men, who spend 1 hour, 25 minutes. Food preparation represents the single largest category for both, at which women spend 37 minutes and men spend 17 minutes.

Source: Bureau of Labor Statistics 2016h.   Photo: ©Comstock Images/Getty Images RF

Home and Work Today, many women face the challenge of trying to juggle work and family. Who does the housework when women become productive wage earners? In dual-income families, fathers do an average of 9.4 hours of housework per week compared to 15.7 hours for women. Even in households where she works and he does not, wives still do more housework (K. Parker and Wang 2013).

Sociologist Arlie Hochschild (1989, 1990, 2005) has used the phrase **second shift** to describe the double burden—work outside the home followed by child care and housework—that many women face and few men share equitably. On the basis of interviews with and observations of 52 couples over an eight-year period, Hochschild reported that the wives (and not their husbands) drive home from the office while planning domestic schedules and play dates for children—and then begin their second shift. Drawing on national studies, she concluded that women spend 15 fewer hours each week in leisure activities than their husbands. In a year, these women work an extra month of 24-hour days because of the second shift; over a dozen years, they work an extra year of 24-hour days. Hochschild found that the married couples she studied were fraying at the edges, and so were their careers and their marriages. With such reports in mind, many feminists have advocated greater governmental and corporate support for child care, more-flexible family leave policies, and other reforms designed to ease the burden on the nation's families (Mann, Sullivan, and Gershuny 2011; Moen and Roehling 2005).

Politics Turning to political involvement, after years of struggle, women won the right to vote with the passage of the 19th Amendment in 1920. Looking at voter participation rates, we can see that they have taken advantage of that opportunity. In fact, a higher percentage of women turn out to vote than do men. This has been true in every presidential election since 1980 (Center for American Women and Politics 2015).

When it comes to holding elected office, however, we find the same kind of underrepresentation in positions of power by women as is evident in the workplace. Even though women make up slightly more than half of the population, they make up a significantly smaller proportion of elected officials. In 2017, for example, only 4 of the nation's 50 states had a female governor (New Mexico, Oklahoma, Oregon, and Rhode Island).

Second shift The double burden—work outside the home followed by child care and housework—that many women face and few men share equitably.

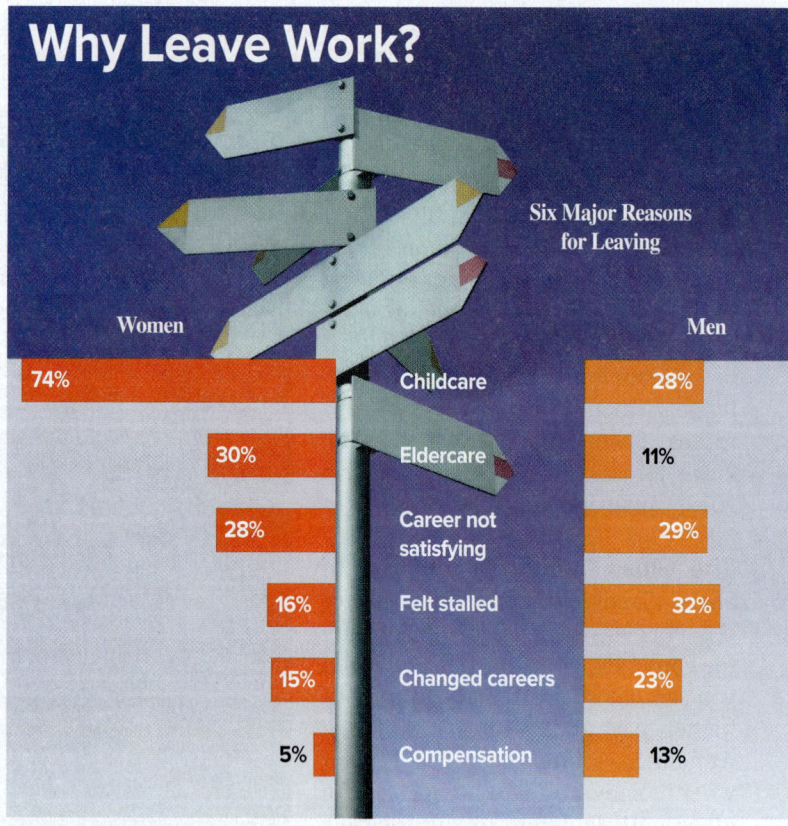

Why Leave Work?

Six Major Reasons for Leaving

Women		Men
74%	Childcare	28%
30%	Eldercare	11%
28%	Career not satisfying	29%
16%	Felt stalled	32%
15%	Changed careers	23%
5%	Compensation	13%

Note: Reasons cited as major factors in voluntarily leaving their jobs in a survey of "highly qualified" workers, aged 28–55, defined as those with a graduate degree, a professional degree, or a bachelor's degree with honors.
Source: Hewlett, Foster, Sherbin, Shiller, and Sumberg 2010.   Photo: ©narvikk/Getty Images RF

5 Movies on GENDER AND SEXUALITY

The Kids Are All Right
Two children of a lesbian couple look for their biological father.

Moonlight
An African American man movingly faces questions about love, friendship, and sexuality.

The Fits
What does being a girl mean?

Fight Club
An outsized exploration of modern masculinity.

Transamerica
A male-to-female transsexual travels the country with her son.

Women have made slow but steady progress in certain political arenas. In 1971, only 3 percent of members of Congress were women. By 2017, that number rose to 19.4 percent, a total of 104 members: 83 in the House and 21 in the Senate. In 2017, Catherine Cortez Masto of Nevada became the first Latina ever elected to the Senate. Yet even when Nancy Pelosi served as Speaker of the House from 2007 to 2011—the first woman ever to serve in that role—the membership and leadership of Congress remained overwhelmingly male (Center for American Women and Politics 2017).

At the Supreme Court, Sandra Day O'Connor became the nation's first female justice in 1981 (and retired in 2006). She was joined by Ruth Bader Ginsberg in 1993. In August 2009, Sonia Sotomayor became the third woman and first Hispanic on the Court. In August 2010 Elena Kagan was sworn in to the Court, making it the first time three women have ever served as justices on the Court at the same time. In the executive branch, no woman has ever been elected either president or vice president of the United States. Hillary Clinton challenged that barrier in 2016, winning the popular vote with 2,868,692 more votes but losing the Electoral College vote to Donald Trump.

Violence Against Women Violence against women is a global problem. The full extent of such violence, both in the United States and abroad, is unknown because such crimes often go unreported and unrecognized. Globally, the World Health Organization estimates that 35.6 percent of women have been victims of sexual or physical violence by an intimate partner. Rates vary significantly by region, including 65.6 percent in central sub-Saharan Africa and 41.7 percent in South Asia to 16.3 percent in East Asia and 19.3 percent in western Europe (World Health Organization 2013b).

Violence against women in the United States remains a significant problem. According to the National Crime Victimization Survey, women were the victims of 431,840 rapes and sexual assaults in 2015. Overall, only 32.5 percent of these rapes and sexual assaults were reported to police. Other studies suggest that the likelihood of reporting such acts to police may be significantly lower (Truman and Morgan 2016).

Research shows that women and girls of all ages are subject to acts of violence. Among high school girls, 11.7 percent had been hit, slapped, or physically hurt on purpose by their boyfriend or girlfriend in the previous year, and 15.6 percent had been kissed, touched, or forced to have sexual intercourse when they did not want to (Centers for Disease Control and Prevention 2016b:Table 21). In a survey of college women, 19 percent experienced either an attempted or completed sexual assault while in college. Overall, 3.4 percent of college women had been forcibly raped and 8.5 percent had been raped while incapacitated—drunk, passed out, drugged, or asleep. Among college women who were victims of a forced sexual assault, only 13 percent reported it to police or campus security, although 69 percent disclosed the incident to a family member or friend (Krebs et al. 2007). In a national survey of adult women in the United States, researchers found that 18 percent had been raped at some point in their lifetime. Only 16 percent of these women had reported it to law enforcement officials (Kilpatrick et al. 2007). And in the most extreme form of violence, 509 wives and 496 girlfriends were murdered by their intimate partners in 2015 according to FBI data (Truman and Morgan 2016:Table 10).

Bineta Diop, founder of Femmes Africa Solidarité, which focuses on women-led peace building, was one of Time magazine's 100 Most Influential People in the World in 2011. ©Elisabetta Villa/Getty Images

WOMEN AROUND THE WORLD

The likelihood of violence against women is shaped in part by cultural attitudes about them, along with the relative lack of power they possess in society. As Nicholas Kristof and Sherly WuDunn (2009) put it in their book *Half the Sky*, "People get away with enslaving village girls for the same reason that people got away with enslaving blacks two hundred years ago: The victims are perceived as discounted humans" (p. 24). Increased education and opportunity for women, they suggest, lead to a curtailing of violence.

Women face significant oppression, violence, and discrimination in nations around the globe. Whether in the form of sex trafficking, socially condoned rape, or denial of medical services, the simple fact of being a woman is enough to justify such practices in some countries. In the case of Woineshet Zebene, for example, a group of men came for her at 11:30 at night. She was in a deep sleep, but they took her from her home in the Ethiopian countryside and battered and raped her over the next two days. Afterward, it was expected that she would marry the man who led the assault. When she refused, she was again kidnapped, beaten, and raped. A court official to whom she pleaded for help advised her to "get over it" and marry her attacker. She was 13 years old (Kristof and WuDunn 2009).

Women are particularly vulnerable to sex trafficking, gender-based violence (including honor killings and mass rape), and death or serious injury during childbirth due to inadequate medical care. For example, in Ghana, 21 percent of women report that their first sexual experience was by rape. Regarding inadequate health care, 1 in 7 women in Nigeria, 1 in 22 in sub-Saharan Africa, and 1 in 70 in India die during childbirth, compared to 1 in 4,800 in the United States (Kristof and WuDunn 2009).

Such practices often go unnoticed because they represent "quotidian cruelties"—the everyday practice of violence and discrimination that is largely invisible and considered inevitable or even natural. Fortunately, women around the world have successfully fought to change local attitudes and practices. In India, for example, Ruchira Gupta founded Apne Aap Women Worldwide, with its mission to end sex trafficking (www.apneaap.org). In Pakistan, Mukhtar Mai used settlement money she received after having been gang raped to establish her School for Girls; she later expanded it to include a free legal clinic, a public library, and a women's shelter. And in Kenya, Myla Rodgers established the organization Mama Hope. In addition to helping build health clinics, poultry farms, drip irrigation gardens, and other projects, the group produced a number of viral videos designed to show African people as active, engaged, intelligent, and multidimensional. The videos portray the people of Kenya, Uganda, Tanzania, Ghana, and elsewhere not as objects to be manipulated or subjects to be studied, but as participants who, when given access to and control over even limited amounts of economic resources, have the vision and ability to transform their futures for the better (Kristof and WuDunn 2009).

Opportunities for women vary significantly around the world. In an attempt to quantify the degree of global gender inequality, the World Economic Forum releases an annual report ranking nations in four areas: educational attainment, health and survival, economic participation and opportunity, and political empowerment. The resulting Gender Gap Index score for each country ranges from 0 to 1, with a higher score representing greater gender equality. In 2016 only five countries—Iceland, Finland, Norway, Sweden, and Rwanda—scored at or above 0.8. The United States ranked 45th, with a score of 0.75, behind nations such as Nicaragua, South Africa, Estonia, Cuba, and Canada. Ten nations, among them Yemen, Pakistan, Syria, and Saudi Arabia, scored below 0.6. Countries in the Middle East and Africa had the lowest average rankings, primarily because of their low scores on economic and political indicators (World Economic Forum 2016).

Although people in most nations agree that women should have equal rights, significant variation exists. For example, in Tanzania, 48 percent of men agree, compared to 73 percent of women, a gap of 25 percent. In Pakistan the gap is 24 percent, and in Uganda it is 23. In Japan the gap is actually

In Kenya, Myla Rodgers established Mama Hope as an organization to provide girls a greater sense of agency and opportunity. ©Bryce Yukio Adolphson

Going GLOBAL

Time Spent in Unpaid Labor

Women (Minutes per day)	Country	Men (Minutes per day)
376.7	Turkey	116.4
373.1	Mexico	112.6
351.9	India	51.8
311.0	Australia	171.6
299.3	Japan	61.9
253.6	Canada	159.6
242.1	United States	148.6
234.0	China	91.0
232.5	France	142.7

Source: OECD 2016d. *Photo:* ©Rich Legg/Getty Images RF

"Instead of assuming what people *can't* do at work, provide opportunities for employees to prove what they can do." Norway now has the highest average percentage of female board members of any nation (Dawson et al. 2016). Setting clear workplace and political representation goals makes a difference. Looking forward, the Rockefeller Foundation (2016) has established a goal of 100 women CEOs of Fortune 500 companies by 2025, a significant increase over the current 21.

Sociology often confronts us with things that can make us uncomfortable, such as gender inequality. The point of doing so is a more complete understanding of what we do and why we do it. Such knowledge can lead us to new and better practices that provide greater understanding, fairness, equality, and opportunity. Through practicing the sociological imagination, as Betty Friedan did in the case of gender, we can make the world a better place.

reversed, with 67 percent of men versus 53 percent of women saying that it is very important for women to have the same rights as men (Zainulbhai 2016).

Change is possible. In an effort to address some of the structural inequality that exists, legislators in Norway established minimum quotas for the number of female members of boards of directors for companies. As the architects of the plan put it,

SOCIOLOGY IS A VERB

THE BECHDEL TEST

According to the Bechdel Test, developed by cartoonist Alison Bechdel, a movie fails if three criteria are not met: (1) It has to have at least two women in it, (2) who talk to each other, (3) about something besides a man. Go to BechdelTest.com to see how some of your favorite movies fared. Pick out a movie that has not been added to the site; watch and evaluate it according to the criteria, and upload your results.

FOR REVIEW

I. How has our understanding of gender and sexuality shifted over time?
- The presumption that gender and sexuality are narrowly determined by our biology has given way to an understanding of both as socially constructed, complex, and multidimensional.

II. How has opportunity for women in the United States changed over time?
- In the 1950s women's primary roles were wife and mother. Since that time, largely because of the efforts of the second wave of the women's movement, their labor force participation and income have risen significantly.

III. To what extent does gender still shape access to resources?
- Women continue to be paid less than men in the same occupations, tend to be segregated into a narrower range of female-dominated occupations, bear greater responsibility for housework, and are underrepresented as elected officials.

SOCVIEWS on Gender and Sexuality

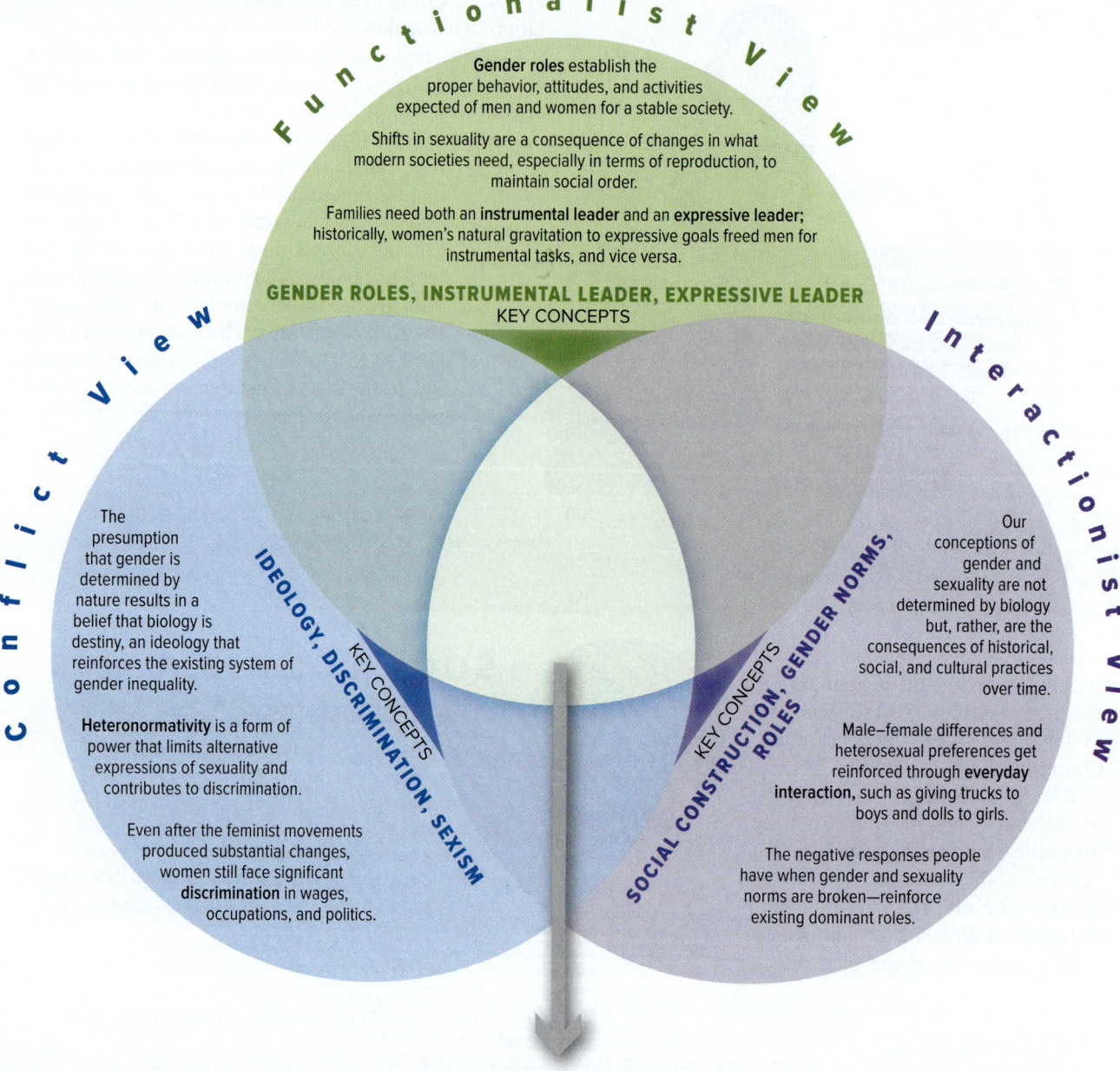

Functionalist View

Gender roles establish the proper behavior, attitudes, and activities expected of men and women for a stable society.

Shifts in sexuality are a consequence of changes in what modern societies need, especially in terms of reproduction, to maintain social order.

Families need both an **instrumental leader** and an **expressive leader**; historically, women's natural gravitation to expressive goals freed men for instrumental tasks, and vice versa.

GENDER ROLES, INSTRUMENTAL LEADER, EXPRESSIVE LEADER
KEY CONCEPTS

Conflict View

The presumption that gender is determined by nature results in a belief that biology is destiny, an ideology that reinforces the existing system of gender inequality.

Heteronormativity is a form of power that limits alternative expressions of sexuality and contributes to discrimination.

Even after the feminist movements produced substantial changes, women still face significant **discrimination** in wages, occupations, and politics.

KEY CONCEPTS
IDEOLOGY, DISCRIMINATION, SEXISM

Interactionist View

Our conceptions of gender and sexuality are not determined by biology but, rather, are the consequences of historical, social, and cultural practices over time.

Male–female differences and heterosexual preferences get reinforced through **everyday interaction**, such as giving trucks to boys and dolls to girls.

The negative responses people have when gender and sexuality norms are broken—reinforce existing dominant roles.

KEY CONCEPTS
SOCIAL CONSTRUCTION, GENDER NORMS, ROLES

MAKE THE CONNECTION
After reviewing the chapter, answer the following questions:

1
How would each of the perspectives seek to explain Sheryl Sandberg's career experiences?

2
How would each of the three perspectives look at the supposition that differences between men and women are "natural" and always have been?

3
How would the macro approaches of the conflict and functionalist perspectives study gender and sexuality differently than the micro approach of the interactionist perspective?

4
How does each perspective contribute to your understanding of your own gender-role socialization?

Pop Quiz

1. What term do sociologists use to describe the presumed biological differences between males and females?
   a. gender
   b. sexism
   c. anatomy
   d. sex

2. What term does geneticist Anne Fausto-Sterling use to describe those who have biological characteristics typically associated with both males and females?
   a. sex
   b. gender
   c. intersexual
   d. gender displays

3. When college students conducted an experiment in which they violated expected gender norms, they demonstrated the power of
   a. gender-role socialization.
   b. biological determinism.
   c. instrumental leadership.
   d. the glass ceiling.

4. What is the expression used when claiming that gender for men is not narrowly limited to traditional conceptions of masculinity?
   a. intersexual
   b. gender modification
   c. sex
   d. multiple masculinities

5. What do groups such as the *berdaches, hijras,* and *xanith* reveal about the nature of sex and gender?
   a. All societies share the same dimorphic, male–female model of sex.
   b. The number of sex and gender categories varies across cultures.
   c. Socialization plays a significant role in modern societies, but a more limited role in traditional societies.
   d. Sex categories vary across cultures, but expressions of gender are universal.

6. The primary accomplishment of the first wave of the women's movement was
   a. making women citizens.
   b. gaining the right to an abortion.
   c. earning the right to nondiscrimination in the workplace.
   d. winning the right to vote.

7. What term describes the categories of people to whom we are sexually attracted?
   a. heteronormativity
   b. sexual orientation
   c. sexuality
   d. sexual displays

8. According to early sociologists Talcott Parsons and Robert Bales, which type of leader bears responsibility for completion of tasks, focuses on more-distant goals, and manages the external relationship between the family and other social institutions?
   a. expressive
   b. charismatic
   c. instrumental
   d. traditional

9. Overall, when comparing full-time, year-round workers, how much do women earn compared to every dollar men earn?
   a. 42 cents
   b. 63 cents
   c. 80 cents
   d. 94 cents

10. The expression "second shift" refers to
    a. doing the emotional work of maintaining family relationships.
    b. maintaining the household, including housework in addition to a job outside the home.
    c. having a work shift ranging approximately between 4:00 p.m. and midnight.
    d. doing paid labor at the workplace.

1. (d), 2. (c), 3. (a), 4. (d), 5. (b), 6. (d), 7. (b), 8. (c), 9. (c), 10. (b)

13 Race and Ethnicity

©Kim Kim Foster/The State/MCT/Getty Images

#BLACKLIVESMATTER

On August 9, 2014, in Ferguson, Missouri, Michael Brown was stopped by Officer Darren Wilson because Brown matched the just-broadcast description of a suspect who stole cigarillos from a nearby convenience store. A confrontation ensued. By the time it was over, Wilson had fired 12 shots and Brown, who was unarmed, lay dead in the street. Eyewitness accounts of the encounter conflicted, some arguing Brown turned at one point and raised his hands in surrender. Wilson claimed that Brown reached for what might have been a weapon and charged at him. Huge protests broke out in the days that followed, and "Hand's up, don't shoot!" became a rallying cry.

Michael Brown's case was but one of a series of high-profile incidents involving police officers killing African American males. On November 22, 2014, Tamir Rice, 12, was playing around in a Cleveland, Ohio, park with a toy gun he'd just received from a friend. Police were called, and when Officer Timothy Loehmann arrived on the scene, he jumped out of his squad car and, within two seconds, fired shots at Rice, killing him. Loehmann claimed to have asked Rice three times to put up his hands and that Rice failed to do so.

On September 16, 2016, in Tulsa, Oklahoma, Terence Crutcher, 40, was shot and killed by police. He was unarmed. The video of the encounter shows that he had his hands in the air as he walked back to his SUV. Police claim he was acting erratically and appeared to reach into his vehicle. No weapon was found on him or in his vehicle.

On September 20, 2016, in Charlotte, North Carolina, police shot and killed Keith Scott, 43, while he was exiting his SUV. Police say he had a gun, and in video of the encounter, they can be heard shouting to Scott to "drop the gun." Family members—including his wife, who was present at the scene and cried out to the police, "Don't shoot him, don't shoot him"—claim Scott had no weapon.

When it comes to the consequences of difference, one of the lessons we learn, over and over again, is that African American men too often pay with their lives.

As You READ

- How do sociologists define race and ethnicity?
- What are prejudice and discrimination, and how do they operate?
- What are the consequences of race and ethnicity for opportunity?

>> Racial and Ethnic Groups

Race has been a vexing issue in the United States since its founding, and some groups have paid a profound price as a result. The establishment of the first permanent English settlement in the Americas at Jamestown in 1607 began a long-running rocky relationship between the European settlers and the already present Native Americans. The settlement would likely not have survived had it not been for the assistance it received, especially in the form of food, from the 25,000-member Powhatan tribe, including Pocahontas, the daughter of Chief Powhatan (Price 2003). To make money, the settlers turned toward planting tobacco—a skill taught them by the Powhatans—which resulted in their seizing more and more land, leading to a cycle of violence. In the Massacre of 1622, members of the Powhatan tribe attacked Jamestown, killing 347 English settlers. The settlers then used this attack to justify going on the offensive, setting the stage over the next centuries of back-and-forth encounters across the continent between Native Americans and European settlers (Woolley 2007).

Concurrently, African slaves were brought to Point Comfort, near Jamestown, in 1619. The Africans were purchased from Captain John Colyn Jope, a Calvinist minister and ship commander, in exchange for food "at the best and easyest rate they could [obtain]" (Sluiter 1997:396). Jope had seized the Africans from the *São João Bautista,* a Portuguese slave ship that was headed from Luanda, Angola, to Vera Cruz, one of the main ports of entry for African slaves in what is now Mexico (Hashaw 2007; Sluiter 1997). In all likelihood, the Africans were relatively recent captives from the area around Luanda (Thornton 1998). Jamestown's labor-intensive tobacco economy required many workers, and indentured servants—who worked for some established period of time to pay off their passage to the New World—made up a majority of the workforce. It is likely that at least some of these African slaves were treated as indentured servants who later gained their freedom, whereas others may have been enslaved for life (Hashaw 2007; Wood 1997).

These two examples point toward the perseverance of racial conflict throughout American history, the ramifications of which continue into the present. Sociologists, in their quest to describe and explain the consequences of difference, explore issues of race and ethnicity over time and across cultures. To better understand how they do so, we must first clarify what we mean by these two related concepts. **Race** refers to biological differences between humans, defined as socially significant and presumed to divide the population into

> **Race** Biological differences between humans, defined as socially significant and presumed to divide the population into genetically distinct subgroups.

Did You Know?

... President George Washington inherited 10 slaves when he was 11 years old. At the time of his death, he owned 123 slaves and leased another 40 from a neighbor. Martha, his wife, effectively owned another 153 through her first husband's estate.

Photo: Source: Library of Congress Prints and Photographs Division [LC-DIG-pga-02419]

Racial and Ethnic Groups in the United States

Classification	Number in Thousands	Percentage of Total Population
Racial Groups		
Whites (non-Hispanic)	197,534	61.5
Blacks/African Americans	39,598	12.3
Asian Americans	17,081	5.3
Chinese	4,134	1.3
Asian Indians	3,700	1.2
Filipinos	2,848	0.9
Vietnamese	1,739	0.5
Koreans	1,460	0.5
Japanese	757	0.2
Native Hawaiian/Pacific Islanders	503	0.2
American Indians, Alaska Natives	2,070	0.6
Ethnic Groups		
White (single or mixed, non-Hispanic)		
Germans	45,526	14.2
Irish	32,713	10.2
English	23,959	7.5
Italians	17,070	5.3
Poles	9,231	2.9
Scottish and Scotch-Irish	8,492	2.6
French	7,970	2.5
Hispanics (or Latinos)	56,496	17.6
Mexican Americans	35,797	11.1
Puerto Ricans	5,373	1.7
Cubans	2,172	0.7
Salvadorans	2,107	0.7
Dominicans	1,873	0.6
Total (all groups)	**321,419**	

Source: U.S. Census Bureau 2016j:Table S0201.

Ethnicity The cultural differences between humans, defined as socially significant and presumed to divide the population into socially distinct subgroups.

Minority group A subordinate group whose members, even if they represent a numeric majority, lack access to, and control over, valued resources in society.

genetically distinct subgroups. **Ethnicity** refers to the cultural differences between humans, defined as socially significant and presumed to divide the population into socially distinct subgroups. Racial differences typically include variations in skin color, facial features, hair texture and color, and the like, whereas ethnic differences manifest themselves through varieties of customs, languages, food preferences, and so on. A relevant third term, **minority groups,** refers to a subordinate group whose members, even if they represent a numeric majority, lack access to and control over valued resources in society.

RACE

Historically in the United States, it was presumed that racial categorization was a simple matter: Race was biologically determined in straightforward ways, and the dividing lines between groups were clear. It was also assumed that, for the most part, a person's parents would both be of the same race, so identifying a child's racial makeup was also a simple matter. Of course, there were times when people from different racial groups had children. In the 19th century, potential ambiguity was resolved in the United States by establishing the "one-drop rule." In that case, if a person had any ancestors who were Black, no matter how many generations back, the person was labeled Black, even if he or she appeared to be White.

We now know that such simplistic attempts to define race in narrowly biological terms say more about society than biology. Modern scientific research proves that no clear biological dividing lines exist between racial groups. That doesn't mean that biological variation (in things like skin color or facial features) attributed to racial difference doesn't exist; it certainly does. The key is whether such differences justify the division of the human population into distinct biological races (Desmond and Emerbayer 2009).

When it comes to genetic variation, the biological differences within what we think of as racial groups are actually greater than the differences between those groups. Genetic researchers Luca Cavalli-Sforza, Paolo Menozzi, and Alberto Piazza (1994), for example, point out that people from northeast China are genetically closer to Europeans, Eskimos, and North American Indians than they are to people from south China (p. 84). In fact, the overall degree of human genetic variation is quite small when compared with genetic variation among other large mammals—due primarily to the fact that communities of human beings have always interacted and reproduced, even across great distances (Greenwood 2013; MacEachern 2003:20). To put it in simple terms, humans have always been sleeping with people from the next tribe over.

Scientists working on the Human Genome Project (HGP) have mapped all the genes of human beings, providing us with the most detailed description of our biological makeup available. They concluded that race as we understand it does not exist. Around the globe, we simply share too many genes in common. Craig Venter (2000), one of the project's lead scientists, declared in his presentation of the HGP results that "the concept of race has no genetic or scientific basis," and in a later interview, he said, "Race is a social concept, not a scientific one" (quoted in Angier 2000). The researchers found that apparent differences, such as in skin color, represent different combinations, in greater or lesser degrees, of the same shared genes.

Social Construction of Race To understand race, we must move beyond biology to understand the ways in which we socially construct racial categories. If we look cross-culturally, we see that different groups define racial categories in different ways at different times. Each society defines which physical differences are important while ignoring other characteristics that could serve as a basis for social differentiation. In the United States, we recognize differences in both skin color and hair color, yet people learn that differences in skin color have a dramatic social and political meaning whereas differences in hair color do not.

©Rawpixel.com/Shutterstock.com RF

When observing skin color, many people in the United States tend to lump others rather casually into the traditional categories of "Black," "White," and "Asian." More-subtle differences in skin color often go unnoticed. In many nations of Central America and South America, by contrast, people recognize skin color gradients on a continuum from light to dark. Brazil has approximately 40 color groupings, and in other countries people may be described as "Mestizo Honduran," "Mulatto Colombian," or "African Panamanian." What can seem "obvious" in one cultural context may not seem so in another (Desmond and Emirbayer 2009).

We develop our understanding of racial categories through the process of what sociologists Michael Omi and Howard Winant (1994) have called **racial formation**—a sociohistorical process in which racial categories are created, inhibited, transformed, and destroyed. Omi and Winant argue that race is neither fundamentally biological nor an illusion that can simply be ignored. To understand race, one must pay careful attention to the social, economic, and political forces that have established it as a basic distinction among human beings. Historically, those in positions of power have categorized whole groups of people as fundamentally distinct from each other (for example, when the one-drop rule was instituted) and then used their control over resources to treat people differently based on those distinctions. The result is a social structure that reinforces presumed racial differences and justifies unequal treatment on the basis of race. The creation of a reservation system for Native Americans in the late 1800s is one example of racial formation. Federal officials combined what were distinctive tribes into a single racial group, which we refer to today as Native Americans.

Given that our understanding of race was rooted in particular historical circumstances, it has shifted over time as those circumstances changed. For example, the massive influx of immigrants in the 19th century, from places such as Ireland, Germany, China, Italy, and eastern Europe, complicated the supposed simplicity of the Black–White divide. These immigrant groups were often judged to be biologically beneath White citizens. For instance, both the Irish and the Italians were regarded as members of another race inferior to Whites. Many African Americans of the time regarded being Irish as lower socially than being Black. Over time, both the Irish and the Italians came to be seen as two White ethnic groups. This was accomplished in part by positioning themselves as distinct from African Americans in order to identify more closely with the White majority (Guglielmo 2003; Ignatiev 1995; Roediger 2005).

>**Racial formation** A sociohistorical process in which racial categories are created, inhibited, transformed, and destroyed.

>**SOC**THINK
>
>To what extent do race and ethnicity influence the opportunities you have and obstacles you face? How conscious are you of your race and ethnicity and their possible influences on your life?

Even though these differences are socially constructed, their consequences are no less real. Race is often used to justify unequal access to economic, social, and cultural resources based on the assumption that such inequality is somehow "natural." This can happen through the use of **stereotypes,** for example, which are unreliable generalizations about all members of a group that do not recognize individual differences within the group. Anthropologist Ashley Montagu (1997), who was at the forefront of the movement to use scientific evidence to demonstrate the socially constructed nature of race, suggested that "the very word (*race*) is racist; that the idea of 'race,' implying the existence of significant biologically determined mental differences rendering some populations inferior to others, is wholly false" (p. 35).

> **Stereotype** An unreliable generalization about all members of a group that does not recognize individual differences within the group.

Multiple Identities As the number of people who consider themselves biracial or multiracial grows, the limits of our racial categories become increasingly apparent. Prominent figures have helped bring this trend into the limelight. Golfer Tiger Woods provides a classic example. Woods created his own racial category, referring to himself as "Cablinasian," a combination of his Caucasian, Black, American Indian, and Asian (Chinese and Thai) ancestry. Other examples include former president Barack Obama, who had a Black father originally from Kenya and a White mother originally from Kansas, and Academy Award–winning actress Halle Berry, who had an African American father and a White, British-born mother (Nishime 2012).

In recognition of the growing diversity of the U.S. population, and the growing numbers of interracial marriages, for the first time in 2000 and again in 2010 the U.S. Census allowed people to select more than one category when identifying their race. People can now choose from five major race categories—White, Black, Asian, Native American, and Native Hawaiian or Other Pacific Islander—in addition to "Some other race." Considering all the combinations people might select, a total of 57 race categories are now possible (Humes et al. 2011). In the 2010 Census more than 9 million people in the United States, 2.9 percent overall, reported that they were of two or more races. Of these, 20.4 percent chose both Black and White, the most frequent combination. Within racial categories, more than half of those who chose Native Hawaiian or Other Pacific Islander also selected another race, whereas those who self-identified as White were least likely to do so (Humes et al. 2011).

This expansion of possible racial categories is part of the Census Bureau's ongoing effort to provide a snapshot of race as it is understood at various points in U.S. history. As the "U.S. Race Categories, 1790–2010" table demonstrates, racial categories used by the Census Bureau have shifted over time. The most recent expansion to allow multiracial identification is a direct consequence of the limitations of using fewer categories to reflect an increasingly diverse society. To get an accurate count, the Census Bureau needs categories that are mutually exclusive, meaning that each individual fits in one place and one place only. To do so, it must expand the number of available options beyond the three- or five-race models that historically seemed, by common sense, to be sufficient.

ETHNICITY

An ethnic group is set apart from others explicitly because of its national origin or cultural patterns. Distinctive characteristics can include language, diet, sports, and religious beliefs, along with various traditions, norms, and values. Among the ethnic groups in the United States are peoples with a Spanish-speaking background, referred to collectively as Latinos or Hispanics, such as Puerto Ricans, Mexican Americans, and Cuban Americans. Other ethnic groups in the United States include Jewish, Irish, Italian, and Norwegian Americans.

The distinction between race and ethnicity is not always clear-cut. While the conventional approach views race as biological and ethnicity as cultural, racial

Actress Maya Rudolph's mother was African American and her father was White. ©Steve Granitz/WireImage/Getty Images

U.S. Race Categories, 1790–2010

Race Categories

1790	Free white males; Free white females; All other free persons; Slaves
1890	White; Black; Mulatto; Chinese; Indian
1940	White; Negro; Indian; Chinese, Japanese, Filipino, Hindu, Korean; Other
1990	White; Black or Negro; American Indian; Eskimo; Aleut; Asian or Pacific Islander, Chinese, Filipino, Hawaiian, Korean, Vietnamese, Japanese, Asian Indian, Samoan, Guamanian, other Asian or Pacific Islander; Other race
2010	White; Black, African American, or Negro; American Indian or Alaska Native (print name of tribe); Asian: Asian Indian, Chinese, Filipino, Japanese, Korean, Vietnamese, Other Asian (print race); Native Hawaiian, Guamanian or Chamorro, Samoan, or Other Pacific Islander (print race); Some other race (print race)

Sources: Nobles 2000:1739; U.S. Census Bureau 2010c. Photo: ©Markus Mainka/Shutterstock.com RF

Puerto Rican Day Parade, New York City. ©Stephen Chernin/Getty Images

each. It treats race and ethnicity as separate items, but in its ethnicity question, the only category recognized is "Hispanic, Latino, or Spanish origin." This situation creates difficulties for groups that see themselves as a distinct ethnicity and find the race options inadequate to describe who they are. In such circumstances, many people choose "Some other race" and then write in an ethnicity or nationality (such as Mexican, Iranian, or Saudi Arabian) as their race. In the 2010 Census, of those who selected "Other," 97 percent also selected Hispanic as their ethnicity. In fact, 41 percent of those who self-identified as Hispanic also selected "Some other race" (Humes et al. 2011; U.S. Commission on Civil Rights 2009:4).

Did You Know?

... Of the Muslims in the United States, 63 percent are foreign born. Within this group of non-native immigrants, 70 percent have become U.S. citizens.

Source: Pew Research Center 2011. Photo: ©Bob Child/AP Images

groups express their identity in cultural ways (including language, norms, values, diet, and so on). Alternatively, ethnic groups may self-identify as a race. The Census Bureau runs into this difficulty in its attempt to catalog

The Census has continued to try to make these categories clear. In an attempt to clarify confusion about the relationship between race and ethnicity, the 2010 Census included the line "For this census, Hispanic origins are not races" (U.S. Census Bureau 2010c). In preparation for the 2020 Census, in keeping with the way people self-identify using elements of both biological ancestry and cultural heritage, officials are considering collapsing race and ethnicity into a single question, effectively making Hispanic into a racial category (D. Cohn 2016; Krogstad and Cohn 2014). To address the limitations of the ethnicity question, the Census also studied the possibility of expanding it to include additional options (for example, German, French, Italian) to more fully reflect people's self-identified ethnic origin (U.S. Commission on Civil Rights 2009). As currently practiced, the Census further complicates things by including some ethnic nationalities as examples within racial categories (for example, Japanese and Chinese as examples in the Asian category) but does not do so for others (for instance, White or Black). Such examples highlight the fact that race and ethnicity are more complex in practice than the commonsense models we may believe.

Members of the Ku Klux Klan, masked in white robes and hoods, used nighttime cross-burnings to instill terror. ©William Campbell/Sygma via Getty Images

>> Prejudice and Discrimination

The social significance we attach to biological and cultural differences can have life and death consequences. Defining descendants from Africa as less than fully human enabled the justification of slavery as an institution in the United States for nearly its first 100 years. In keeping with the Thomas theorem, we need to be particularly attentive to those things we perceive to be true because our perceptions shape our actions. When it comes to race and ethnicity, perception in the form of prejudice is often linked to discrimination, a type of action.

Prejudice A preconceived and unjustified judgment of individuals, whether positive or negative, based on their membership in a particular group.

Racism The belief that one race is supreme and all others are innately inferior.

PREJUDICE

Prejudice is a preconceived and unjustified judgment of individuals, whether positive or negative, based on their membership in a particular group. Defining characteristics frequently include race and ethnicity, but prejudice may also be based on gender, disability, age, or other statuses. Frequently, prejudice results from ethnocentrism—the tendency to assume that one's own culture and way of life represent the norm or are superior to all others. Ethnocentric people judge other cultures by the standards of their own group without taking into account the perspectives and experiences of others. This often leads to prejudice against cultures they view as inferior.

One important and widespread ideology that reinforces prejudice is **racism**—the belief that one race is supreme and all others are innately inferior. Such beliefs may exist even if they are not explicitly stated as part of a society's dominant values. Attitudes have changed. For example, in 1958 only 4 percent of Americans approved of marriage between Blacks and Whites, and now 87 percent approve (Newport 2013). Yet significant disagreement exists about the degree to which racism exists in the United States.

In an effort to clarify issues surrounding racism, sociologists Matthew Desmond and Mustafa Emerbayer (2009) have identified five fallacies, misunderstandings, or misconceptions about it. First, the *individualistic fallacy* is that racism springs from the "bad" ideas of a few prejudiced individuals. This approach is fallacious because it doesn't come to terms with racism's social, cultural, and institutional dimensions. Second, according to the *legalistic fallacy,* we will inevitably eliminate racism in practice by establishing the principle of racial equality in the law; for example, through the *Brown v. Board of Education* decision in 1954 or the Civil Rights Act of 1964. But the fallacy here is that principle and practice do not always align. Third, via the *tokenistic fallacy,* people assert that the success of a few individuals, such as Barack Obama, Oprah Winfrey, or Beyoncé, demonstrates that racial obstacles no longer exist. The fallacy here is that exceptions do not prove the rule. Fourth, according to the *ahistorical fallacy,* the patterns of the past, especially the legacy of slavery, do not have any significant impact on the present. But this assertion fails to fully appreciate the lessons of the sociological imagination. And, fifth, according to the *fixed fallacy,* the definition of racism is both monolithic and conspicuously horrible, such as the view expressed by those who overtly defined African Americans as less than human in order to justify slavery. But this misconception fails because manifestations of racism shift and adapt across time and place and because instances of racism occur in ways both large and small.

Some sociologists suggest that **color-blind racism,** which uses the principle of race neutrality to perpetuate a racially unequal status quo, is at work (Bonilla-Silva 2010). In such cases, commitment to the principle of equality actually serves to perpetuate inequality. In a system where inequality based on race and ethnicity is built into the structure of society, unwillingness to address these issues explicitly in those terms serves to perpetuate the status quo. Although the practice might seem counter to the principle of equality, some nations have established quotas in political representation and hiring to force the social structure to provide greater opportunity, a practice that is controversial in the United States.

DISCRIMINATION

Prejudice often leads to **discrimination,** the practice of denying equal access to opportunities and resources on the basis of group membership rather than merit or rights. As is the case with prejudice, discrimination may be based on membership in a racial or ethnic group, but can also be determined by sex, age, disability, and other statuses. Because they can be intimately linked, the line between the two can be fuzzy, but prejudice concerns what we think, whereas discrimination involves what we do.

Interpersonal Discrimination When discrimination is practiced, it is experienced on an interpersonal level. It occurs when a particular individual in a position of relative power acts to deny someone something of value—for example, a job, a promotion, an opportunity to volunteer, or a seat on a bus. Though often rooted in prejudice, the two are not always linked. A prejudiced company president who is White, for example, might choose—despite her or his prejudices—to hire a Guatemalan American because that person is the most qualified. That would be prejudice without discrimination. On the other hand, a White corporate president with a completely respectful view

Color-blind racism The use of race-neutral principles to perpetuate a racially unequal status quo.

Discrimination The practice of denying equal access to opportunities and resources on the basis of group membership rather than merit or rights.

Martin Luther King, Jr., at the March on Washington for Jobs and Freedom on August 28, 1963. ©Francis Miller/Time Life Pictures/Getty Images

Hate crime A criminal offense committed because of the offender's bias against an individual based on race, religion, ethnicity, national origin, or sexual orientation.

Racial profiling Any police-initiated action based on race, ethnicity, or national origin rather than on a person's behavior.

of Guatemalan Americans might refuse to hire them for executive posts out of fear that biased clients would take their business elsewhere. In that case, the president's action would constitute discrimination without prejudice.

Sociologist Devah Pager explored the consequences of interpersonal discrimination in her research on the hiring process, as we explored in the "Experiments" section in Chapter 2. To test the impact of both race and a criminal record on the likelihood of getting a job, Pager sent out White and Black applicants with similar characteristics and resumes, varying whether or not they reported having been convicted. In repeated experiments in a number of cities, the results consistently showed the same thing. White applicants received significantly more job callbacks than did African Americans. But what was particularly surprising was the fact that White job applicants who reported having a prison record received slightly more job callbacks than did Black applicants with no criminal record (Pager 2003, 2007; Pager and Pedulla 2015; Pager and Western 2012). Over time, the cumulative impact of such differential treatment contributes to significant differences in access to critical resources.

To better track the scope of overt racist acts in the United States, Congress passed the Hate Crime Statistics Act in 1990. A **hate crime** is a criminal offense committed because of the offender's bias against an individual based on race, religion, ethnicity, national origin, or sexual orientation. The act was amended in 2009 to also include gender and gender identity. In 2015, 6,837 hate crime offenses were reported to authorities. Overall, 58.9 percent of those crimes involved racial or ethnic bias (Department of Justice 2016d:Table 1). Offenses include crimes against individuals (including murder, rape, and assault) and crimes against property (such as vandalism, theft, and arson).

Racial Profiling Another form of discrimination involves **racial profiling**, which is any arbitrary action initiated by an authority based on race, ethnicity, or national origin rather than on a person's behavior. Generally, racial profiling occurs when law enforcement officers, including customs officials, airport security, and police, assume that people who fit a certain description are likely to engage in illegal activities. For example, whether in the form of Driving While Black covered in the "Labeling Theory" section of Chapter 6, or as we saw with police shootings of African American males at the beginning of this chapter, the possible life-and-death consequences of an encounter with police that goes bad, African American males live in fear that police officers are out to get them.

Hate Crime Offenses

- Race/Ethnicity: 58.9%
- Religion: 19.8%
- Sexual orientation: 17.8%
- Gender and gender identity: 2.2%
- Disability: 2.2%

Source: U.S. Department of Justice 2016d:Table 1. *Photo:* ©Duncan Walker/Getty Images RF

©Tom Carter/PhotoEdit

Researchers investigating arrests for marijuana use found that, even when controlling for factors such as prior arrests, prior hard drug use, prior property crimes, prior assault, prior gun carrying, and neighborhood reputation, African Americans were still substantially more likely to be arrested. As the researchers put it, "the racial disparity in drug arrests between blacks and whites cannot be explained by race differences in the *extent* of drug offending or the *nature* of drug offending. In fact, in this sample, African-Americans (and Hispanics) were no more, and often less, likely to be involved in drug offending than whites" (Mitchell and Caudy 2015:22). The strength of this relationship between race and arrest increased with age, peaking for suspects in their twenties.

After Michael Brown was killed in Ferguson, Missouri, the U.S. Justice Department conducted an investigation of the police department there. In an analysis of traffic stops, 85 percent of the stops, 90 percent of the citations, and 93 percent of the arrests involved African Americans, even though Blacks represent only 67 percent of the population. During vehicle stops, Black drivers in Ferguson were more than twice as likely to be searched, but were 26 percent less likely to have contraband. Based on the study, United States Attorney General Eric Holder concluded, "Our investigation showed that Ferguson police officers routinely violate the Fourth Amendment in stopping people without reasonable suspicion, arresting them without probable cause, and using unreasonable force against them" (U.S. Department of Justice 2015a, 2015b).

Perceptions of Discrimination

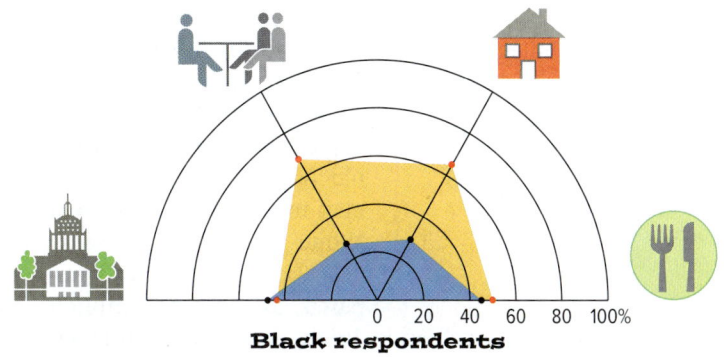

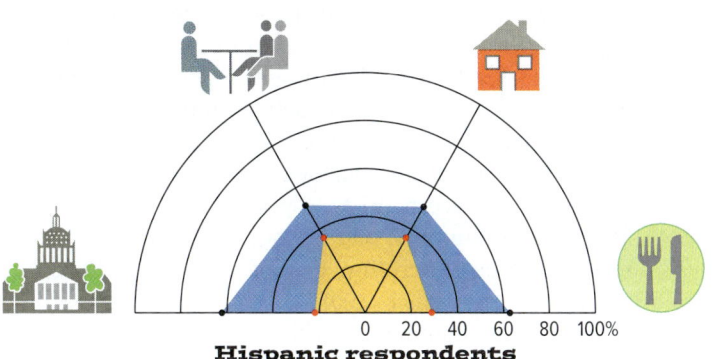

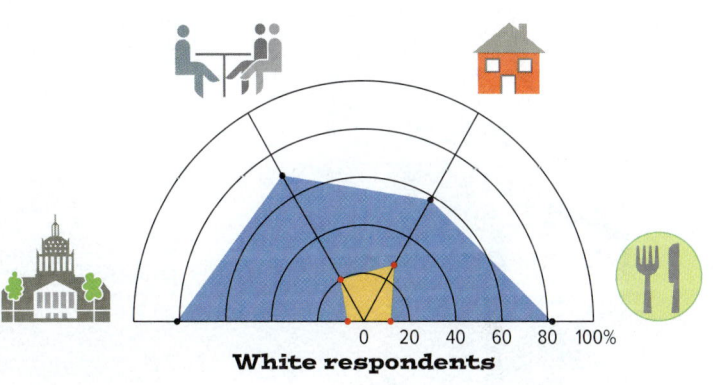

Source: Pew Research Center 2007:30.

Did You Know?

... Perception of policing varies by race. When asked if police in their community do an excellent or good job, 75 percent of Whites said they did compared to 33 percent among African Americans. When asked if local police treat racial and ethnic groups equally, only 35 percent of Blacks responded positively compared to 75 percent of Whites.

Source: Morin and Stepler 2016. *Photo:* ©Don Farrall/Getty Images RF

The protests following the deaths of Michael Brown and others sought to give voice to the persistent pattern of racial profiling experienced by African Americans in the United States. In an analysis of FBI records of 1,217 deadly police shootings from 2010 to 2012, researchers found that 15- to 19-year-old Black males were killed at a much higher rate than White males of the same age: 31.17 per million compared to 1.47 per million (Gabrielson, Grochowski Jones, and Sagara 2014). Of the 426 individuals killed by police during an arrest in 2012, 31 percent were African American, and of those not attacking police while killed, 39 percent were Black (Lind 2015). Unfortunately, these FBI records are not complete—local police department reporting of these details is voluntary—and the actual number of deadly police shootings is likely double (Banks et al. 2015).

In instances where someone dies in an encounter with police, concern exists, especially in the African American community, that the officer's actions do not receive sufficient scrutiny. Out of more than 12,000 death incidents since 2005, 54 officers have been charged after shooting and killing a suspect. Of these cases, two-thirds of the victims were African American, almost always unarmed, and 80 percent of the officers were White. Eleven of the officers were convicted, 21 were set free, and 19 were still pending. Of officers convicted in connection to these deaths, the average sentence was four years (Kindy and Kelly 2015). Given that groups differ in their experiences with law enforcement, along with other areas of differential treatment, perhaps it is not surprising that the views of African Americans, Hispanics, and Whites differ when they are asked about the degree to which African Americans face discrimination, as portrayed in the accompanying "Perceptions of Discrimination" graphic.

Institutional Discrimination Persistent patterns of inequality suggest that discrimination is practiced not only by individuals in one-to-one encounters but also by institutions in their daily operations. Social scientists are particularly concerned with the ways in which structural factors, such as employment, housing, health care, and government operations, maintain the social significance of race and ethnicity. As we saw with gender in the "Sexism and Discrimination" section in Chapter 12, **institutional discrimination** refers to the denial of opportunities and equal rights to individuals and groups that results from the normal

Institutional discrimination
A pattern of treatment that systematically denies a group access to resources and opportunities as part of society's normal operations.

Before passage of the Civil Rights Act in 1964, segregation of public accommodations was the norm throughout the South. ©Bruce Roberts/Science Source

Median Income by Race, Ethnicity, and Gender

Note: Data represent people working full-time, year-round in the United States. Race groups do not include Hispanics.
Source: U.S. Census Bureau 2016j:Table S0201. Photo: ©Comstock/Getty Images

face—varies significantly based on the group to which they belong.

The glass ceiling, which limits women's access to top-level positions in business and politics also affects opportunity for members of racial and ethnic minority groups. In 2015, for example, Hispanics held 4 percent of all board of director seats at Fortune 500 companies in spite of the fact that they make up 17.6 percent of the U.S. population. African Americans held 9.3 percent of seats, and Asians and Asian Americans held 4.8 percent. In 2016, there were five African American CEOs of Fortune 500 companies. Such underrepresentation exists in spite of the research suggesting that companies with more diverse boards are more profitable than those that remain more homogeneous (Dawson et al. 2016; Heidrick and Struggles 2016; Higginbottom 2017).

> **SOC THINK**
>
> Why might institutional discrimination be an even greater concern than interpersonal discrimination?

Attempts have been made to eradicate or compensate for discrimination in the United States. The 1960s saw the passage of many pioneering civil rights laws, including the landmark 1964 Civil Rights Act, which prohibits discrimination in public accommodations and publicly owned facilities on the basis of race, color, creed, national origin, and gender. For more than 40 years, government, schools, and industry have instituted affirmative action programs to overcome past discrimination. **Affirmative action** refers to positive efforts to recruit minority group members or women for jobs, promotions, and educational opportunities. Many people resent these programs, arguing that advancing one group's cause merely shifts the discrimination to another group. By giving priority to African Americans in admissions, for example, schools may deny more academically qualified White candidates. In many parts of the country and many sectors of the economy, affirmative action is being rolled back, even though it was never fully implemented (Hirschman et al. 2016; Pierce 2013; Stulberg and Chen 2014).

Affirmative action Positive efforts to recruit minority group members or women for jobs, promotions, and educational opportunities.

operations of a society. This kind of discrimination consistently affects certain racial and ethnic groups more than others.

A telltale sign of institutional discrimination is the ongoing presence of racial and ethnic income inequality. As we saw with the gender wage gap in the "Women in the United States" section of Chapter 12, a person's ascribed social status frequently predicts his or her income level. As the accompanying "Median Income by Race, Ethnicity, and Gender" graph demonstrates, a clear difference exists when taking race, income, and gender into account. Those who are Asian or White make more money, on average, than those from other racial and ethnic groups. A variety of factors, including educational attainment, occupation, and seniority, likely explain some of those gaps. At the very least, however, the income differences point to the fact that the lived experience of individuals—the opportunities presented to them and obstacles they

Discriminatory practices continue to pervade nearly all areas of life in the United States. In part, that is because various individuals and groups actually benefit from racial and ethnic discrimination in terms of money, status, and influence. Discrimination permits members of the majority to enhance their

©Jim West/The Image Works

wealth, power, and prestige at the expense of others. Less qualified people get jobs and promotions simply because they are members of the dominant group. Such individuals and groups will not surrender these advantages easily.

>> Sociological Perspectives on Race and Ethnicity

Sociologists seek to understand and explain why prejudice and discrimination develop and persist and what might be done to address them. As we have seen, often such negative characteristics exist because they serve certain interests. Here we also look at how prejudice and discrimination contribute to the maintenance of the existing social order by reinforcing the dominant culture.

Exploitation theory A belief that views racial subordination in the United States as a manifestation of the class system inherent in capitalism.

SOCIAL ORDER AND INEQUALITY

From the functionalist perspective in sociology, if something in society persists over long periods of time, it must contribute to social order in some positive way. If true, one possible conclusion about prejudice and discrimination is that they help us build and maintain a stronger sense of social identity and integration, even if it is at the expense of others. As we saw in the "Functions of Deviance" section in Chapter 6, the functionalist theorists suggest that crime helps to unify society through opposition to the criminal. In the same way, they maintain that the racial or ethnic "other" can unify "us" against "them," even though the consequences can be devastating for those against whom prejudice and discrimination are practiced.

According to theories rooted in the conflict perspective, when prejudice and discrimination become built into the institutional structure of society, they help preserve the existing system of inequality. **Exploitation theory,** for example, argues that such practices are a basic part of the capitalist economic system (Blauner 1972; Cox 1948; Hunter 2000). Racism keeps minorities in low-paying jobs, thereby supplying the capitalist ruling class with a pool of cheap labor. Moreover, by forcing racial minorities to accept low wages, capitalists can restrict the wages of all members of the proletariat. Business owners can always replace workers from the dominant group who demand higher wages with minorities who have no choice but to accept low-paying jobs. This increases the likelihood that working-class members of the majority group will develop racist attitudes toward working-class members of minority groups, whom they view as threats to their jobs. As a result, they direct their hostilities not toward the capitalists but toward other workers, thereby not challenging the structure of the existing system.

SOCTHINK

What are the costs and benefits of establishing hiring quotas based on race, ethnicity, or gender to ensure greater opportunity?

Maintaining these practices, however, comes at significant cost to society. For example, a society that practices discrimination fails to use the resources of all individuals. Discrimination limits the search for talent and leadership to the dominant group. Discrimination also aggravates social problems such as poverty, delinquency, and crime. Such effects require the investment of a good deal of time and money in which the primary goal is to maintain barriers to the full participation of all members (Rose 1951; Turner 2013).

Challenging prejudice and discrimination, however, involves questioning taken-for-granted views of the world in which people have invested their faith and trust. Women in the 1950s in the United States had to do just that. They challenged the idea that it was "natural"

Civil rights activist Rosa Parks being fingerprinted upon her arrest in 1955 for her act of civil disobedience in refusing to give up her seat on a bus to a White man. ©Gene Herrick/AP Images

for women to stay at home and have babies rather than get an education and enter the paid labor force. During the same time, workers in the civil rights movement faced a similar challenge in confronting social attitudes that represented barriers to the full participation of African Americans in U.S. society.

THE CONTACT HYPOTHESIS

At its heart, racism is about division, separating the human population into us versus them. As society becomes more global and interdependent, more people from diverse cultural backgrounds have increased opportunities to interact with others unlike them on a daily basis. From the interactionist perspective, when people interact with others as people, rather than as stereotypes or distant others, the possibility arises for prejudice and discrimination to decrease.

The **contact hypothesis** states that in cooperative circumstances, interracial contact between people of equal status will cause them to become less prejudiced and to abandon old stereotypes. People begin to see one another as individuals and to discard the broad generalizations characteristic of stereotyping. Note the phrases "equal status" and "cooperative circumstances." When workers from different racial or ethnic groups compete with each other for valued resources, rather than cooperate toward shared goals, hostilities can increase, highlighting the significance of power and position when it comes to the issue of racism (Allport 1979; Fine 2008).

Over time, as legal challenges to segregation and discrimination opened up greater opportunities for African Americans, Latinos, and other minorities in schools, the workplace, and politics, increased opportunities for contact became available. According to the contact hypothesis, such challenges and the resulting access may be one way of eliminating—or at least reducing—racial and ethnic stereotyping and prejudice. Another may be the establishment of interracial coalitions, an idea suggested by sociologist William Julius Wilson (1999). To work, such coalitions would obviously need to provide an equal role for all members.

> **Contact hypothesis** The theory that in cooperative circumstances interracial contact between people of equal status will reduce prejudice.

PATTERNS OF INTERGROUP RELATIONS

The possibility of equal status, however, is shaped by how societies handle racial and ethnic differences. Some societies are more open to diverse groups maintaining their cultural traditions. Others pressure groups to abandon their beliefs and practices in favor of those of the dominant society. We focus on six characteristic patterns of intergroup relations: genocide, expulsion, amalgamation, assimilation, segregation, and pluralism. Each pattern defines the dominant group's actions and the minority group's responses. The first two are relatively rare, though their consequences are extreme; the final four are more common.

Federal troops were needed to support the Supreme Court decision that led to the integration of schools in the 1950s. ©Bettmann/Contributor/Getty Images

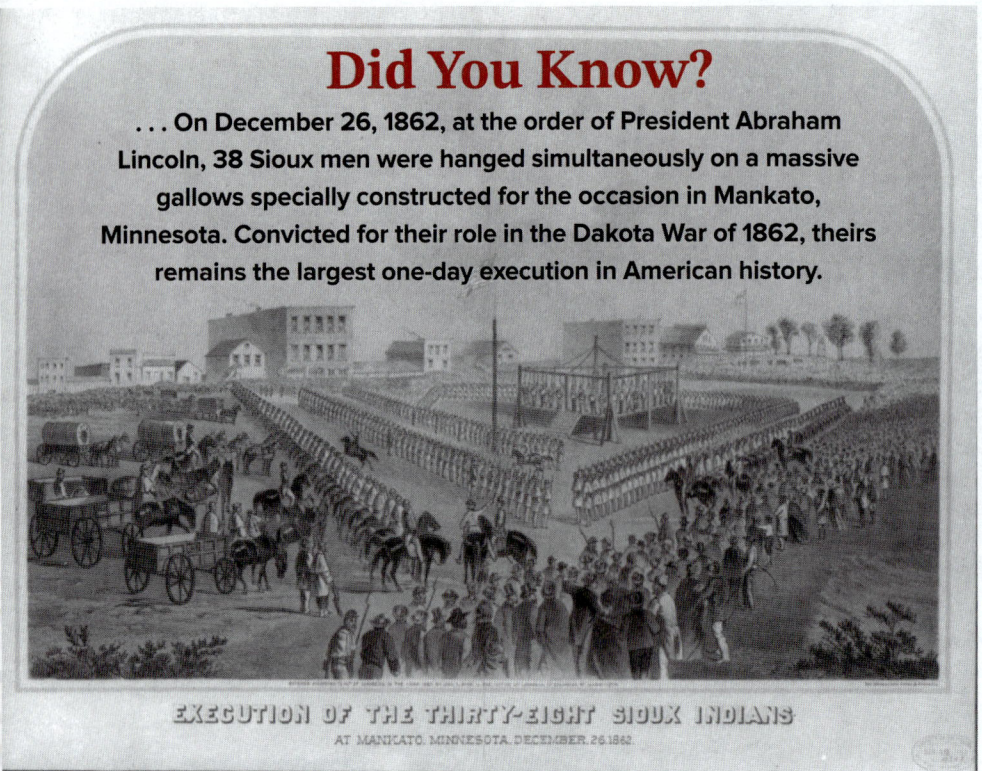

> **Did You Know?**
>
> ... On December 26, 1862, at the order of President Abraham Lincoln, 38 Sioux men were hanged simultaneously on a massive gallows specially constructed for the occasion in Mankato, Minnesota. Convicted for their role in the Dakota War of 1862, theirs remains the largest one-day execution in American history.

Photo: Source: Library of Congress, Prints and Photographs Division ([LC USZ62 193])

Genocide The most devastating pattern of intergroup relations is **genocide**—the deliberate, systematic killing of an entire people or nation. The term is most commonly associated with Nazi Germany's extermination of 6 million European Jews, along with gays, lesbians, and the Romani people ("Gypsies"), during World War II. Starting in 2003, genocide sponsored by Sudan's government led to the deaths of several hundred thousand ethnic Africans at the hands of ethnic Arab militias in the country's Darfur region. The term also describes the United States' policies toward Native Americans in the 19th century. In 1800, the Native American (or American Indian) population of the United States was about 600,000; by 1850, warfare with the U.S. Cavalry, disease, and forced relocation to inhospitable environments had reduced it to 250,000.

Genocide The deliberate, systematic killing of an entire people or nation.

Expulsion The systematic removal of a group of people from society.

Amalgamation The process through which a majority group and a minority group combine to form a new group.

Assimilation The process through which a person forsakes his or her own cultural tradition to become part of a different culture.

Expulsion Another extreme response is **expulsion**—the systematic removal of a group of people from society. In 1979, Vietnam expelled nearly 1 million ethnic Chinese, partly as a result of centuries of hostility between Vietnam and neighboring China. Similarly, Serbian forces began a program of "ethnic cleansing" in 1991, in the newly independent states of Bosnia and Herzegovina. Throughout the former Yugoslavia, the Serbs drove more than 1 million Croats and Muslims from their homes. Some they tortured and killed; others they abused and terrorized, in an attempt to "purify" the land (Cigar 1995; Petrovic 1994). More recently, the government of Sudan has pushed people off their land and out of the country in Darfur (Steidle 2007). As a result of Syria's civil war, which is a struggle involving a variety of ethnic and religious groups, 4.9 million people fled the country as refugees as of early 2017 (United Nations High Commission for Refugees 2017).

Amalgamation When a majority group and a minority group combine to form a new group, **amalgamation** results. This often occurs through intermarriage over several generations. This pattern can be expressed as $A + B + C \rightarrow D$, where A, B, and C represent different groups in a society, and D signifies the end result, a unique cultural-racial group unlike any of the initial groups (Newman 1973).

The belief in the United States as a "melting pot" became compelling in the early 20th century, particularly since that image suggested that the nation had an almost divine mission to amalgamate various groups into one people. In actuality, however, many residents were not willing to include Native Americans, Jews, Blacks, Asians, and Irish Roman Catholics in the melting pot. Therefore, this pattern does not adequately describe dominant–subordinate relations in the United States.

Assimilation In India, many Hindus complain about Indian citizens who emulate the traditions and customs of the British. In France, people of Arab and African origin, many of them Muslim, complain they are treated as second-class citizens—a charge that provoked riots in 2005. In Australia, Aborigines who have become part of the dominant society refuse to acknowledge their darker-skinned grandparents on the street. All these cases are examples of the effects of **assimilation**—the process through which a person forsakes his or her own cultural tradition to become part of a different culture. Generally, it is practiced by minority group members who want to conform to the standards of the dominant group. Assimilation can be described as a pattern in which A + B + C → A. The majority, A, dominates in such a way that members of minorities B and C imitate it and attempt to become indistinguishable from it (Newman 1973).

Assimilation can strike at the very roots of a person's identity. In the United States, some immigrants have changed their ethnic-sounding family names to names that better fit into the dominant White Protestant culture. Jennifer Anastassakis, for example, changed her name to Jennifer Aniston, Ralph Lipschitz became Ralph Lauren, Natalie Portman switched from Natalie Hershlag, and the Academy Award–winning British actress Helen Mirren gave up her birth name of Ilyena Vasilievna Mironova. Name changes, switches in religious affiliation, and the dropping of native languages can obscure one's roots and heritage. Especially across generations, assimilation can lead to the virtual death of a culture in that family's history. It is not uncommon for grandchildren of immigrants who have not learned the language or the cultural traditions of their ancestors to regret this loss.

Segregation Separate schools, separate seating on buses and in restaurants, separate washrooms, even separate drinking fountains—these were all part of the lives of African Americans in the South when segregation ruled early in the 20th century. **Segregation** refers to the physical separation of two groups of people in terms of residence, workplace, and social events. Generally, a dominant group imposes this pattern on a minority group. According to the index of dissimilarity, when looking at segregation between Blacks and Whites, Milwaukee was the most segregated urban area in the United States, with a dissimilarity index of 81.5, meaning 81.5 percent of either Blacks or Whites would have to move to a different neighborhood to completely eliminate segregation. The next four most segregated large metro areas were New York City (78.0), Chicago (76.4), Detroit (75.3), and Cleveland (74.1). When comparing counties across the United States as a whole for Whites versus African Americans, 47.2 percent of either group would have to move to a different county to eliminate segregation (Frey 2017; Lichter, Parisi, and De Valk 2016).

Segregation has consequences for social interaction between groups. In an analysis of friendship networks in the United States, researchers found that among Whites, 91 percent of their friends are White and only 1 percent are Black. Among African Americans, 83 percent of their friends are Black and 8 percent are White (Cox and Jones 2016).

From 1948 (when it received its independence) to 1990, the Republic of South Africa severely restricted the movement of Blacks and other non-Whites by means of a wide-ranging system of segregation known as **apartheid**. Apartheid even included the creation of separate homelands where Blacks were expected to live. However, decades of local resistance to apartheid, combined with international pressure, led to marked political changes in the 1990s. In 1994 a prominent Black activist, Nelson Mandela, became South Africa's president in the first election in which Blacks (the majority of the nation's population) were allowed to vote. Mandela had spent almost 28 years in South African prisons for his anti-apartheid activities. His election was widely viewed as the final blow to South Africa's oppressive policy of segregation.

Former South African President Nelson Mandela oversaw that country's transition from a segregated society. ©Daniel Berehulak/Getty Images

Segregation The physical separation of two groups of people in terms of residence, workplace, and social events; often imposed on a minority group by a dominant group.

Apartheid A former policy of the South African government, designed to maintain the separation of Blacks and other non-Whites from the dominant Whites.

Long-entrenched social patterns are difficult to change, however. An analysis of living patterns in U.S. metropolitan areas showed that despite federal laws that forbid housing discrimination, residential segregation is still the norm. The average White person lives in an area that is at least 83 percent White, whereas the average African American lives in a neighborhood that is mostly Black. The typical Latino lives in an area that is 42 percent Hispanic. And, even as U.S. suburbs have become more racially and ethnically diverse, they

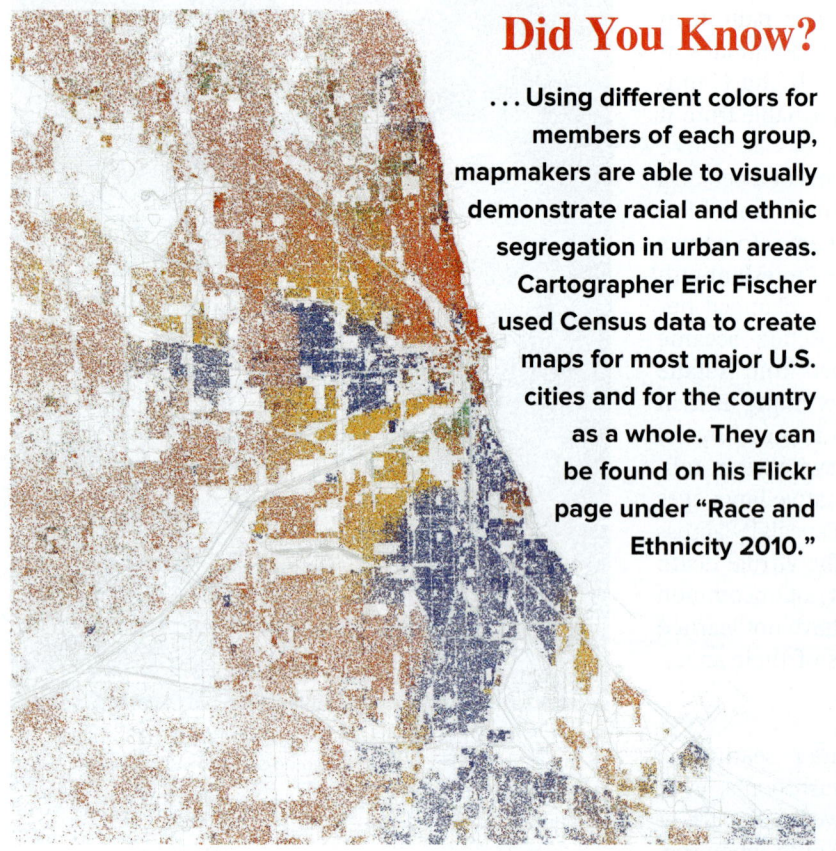

Did You Know?

...Using different colors for members of each group, mapmakers are able to visually demonstrate racial and ethnic segregation in urban areas. Cartographer Eric Fischer used Census data to create maps for most major U.S. cities and for the country as a whole. They can be found on his Flickr page under "Race and Ethnicity 2010."

Source: Fischer 2011. *Photo:* ©Bill Rankin (Yale University), www.radicalcartography.net. Color version reprinted with permission of Eric Fisher

United States wants to move up the occupational ladder, he or she cannot avoid learning English.

Switzerland exemplifies the modern pluralistic state. There the absence of both a national language and a dominant religious faith leads to a tolerance for cultural diversity. In addition, various political devices safeguard the interests of ethnic groups in a way that has no parallel in the United States. By contrast, Great Britain has had difficulty achieving cultural pluralism in a multiracial society. East Indians, Pakistanis, and Blacks from the Caribbean and Africa experience prejudice and discrimination within the dominant White society there. In 2016, the Brexit vote, in which the United Kingdom voted to exit the European Union, was motivated in part by citizens' desire to cut down on immigration (Bennett 2016; de Freytas-Tamura 2016). Similar concerns drove many voters in the United States to support Donald Trump for president, who pledged to build a wall along the border with Mexico (Corasanti 2016).

have also become more segregated (Bolt, Ozuekren, and Phillips 2010; Frey 2011; Logan 2014; Silver 2015).

Pluralism In a pluralistic society, a subordinate group does not have to forsake its lifestyle and traditions. **Pluralism** is based on mutual respect for one another's cultures among the various groups in a society. This pattern allows a minority group to express its own culture and still participate without prejudice in the larger society. Earlier, we described amalgamation as A + B + C → D, and assimilation as A + B + C → A. Using this same approach, we can conceive of pluralism as A + B + C → A + B + C; that is, all the groups coexist in the same society (Newman 1973).

In the United States, pluralism is more of an ideal than a reality. There are distinct instances of pluralism—the ethnic neighborhoods in major cities, such as Koreatown, Little Tokyo, Andersonville (Swedish Americans), and Spanish Harlem—yet there are also limits to cultural freedom. To survive, a society must promote a certain consensus among its members regarding basic ideals, values, and beliefs. Thus, if a Romanian immigrant to the

Pluralism Mutual respect for one another's cultures among the various groups in a society, which allows minorities to express their own cultures without experiencing prejudice.

As part of their annual study of the top 100 films, researchers at USC's Annenberg School for Communication and Journalism found that out of the 4,370 speaking or named roles they identified, 73.7 percent were White characters. The percentage of Black characters, at 12.2, closely approximated their proportion of the U.S. population, but Hispanics, at 5.3 percent, were significantly underrepresented in these films.

Source: Smith, Choueiti, Katherine Pieper 2016. *Photo:* Atsush Nishjima/©Paramount Pictures/Courtesy Everett Collection

POPSOC

326 • SOC 2018

Ethnic enclaves in urban areas, such as Koreatown in Los Angeles, demonstrate the vitality of cultural pluralism in the United States.
©David McNew/Getty Images

PRIVILEGE

One often-overlooked aspect of discrimination is the privileges that dominant groups enjoy at the expense of others. For instance, we tend to focus more on the difficulty women have balancing career and family than on the ease with which men avoid household chores and advance in the workplace. Similarly, we concentrate more on discrimination against racial and ethnic minorities than on the advantages members of the White majority enjoy. Indeed, most White people rarely think about their "Whiteness," taking their status for granted. However, sociologists and other social scientists are becoming increasingly interested in what it means to be "White," because White privilege is the other side of the proverbial coin of racial discrimination (Painter 2010).

Feminist scholar Peggy McIntosh (1988) became interested in White privilege after noticing that most men would not acknowledge the privileges attached to being male—even if they would agree that being female had its disadvantages. She wondered whether White people suffer from a similar blind spot regarding their own racial privilege. Intrigued, McIntosh began to list all the ways in which she benefited from her Whiteness. She soon realized that the list of unspoken advantages was long and significant.

McIntosh found that as a White person, she rarely needed to step out of her comfort zone, no matter where she went. If she wished to, she could spend most of her time with people of her own race. She could find a good place to live in a pleasant neighborhood, buy the foods she liked to eat from almost any grocery store, and get her hair styled in almost any salon. She could attend a public meeting without feeling that she did not belong or that she was different from everyone else.

McIntosh discovered, too, that her skin color opened doors for her. She could cash checks and use credit

> **Whites of course have the privilege of not caring, of being colorblind. Nobody else does.**
>
> Ursula K. Le Guin

cards without suspicion, and she could browse through stores without being shadowed by security guards. She could be seated without difficulty in a restaurant. If she asked to see the manager, she could assume he or she would be of her own race. If she needed help from a doctor or a lawyer, she could get it.

McIntosh also realized that her Whiteness made the job of parenting easier. She did not need to worry about protecting her children from people who didn't like them because of their race. She could be sure that their books would show pictures of people who looked like them and that their history texts would describe White people's achievements. She knew that the television programs they watched would include White characters.

Finally, McIntosh had to admit that others did not constantly evaluate her in racial terms. When she appeared in public, she didn't need to worry that her clothing or behavior might reflect poorly on White people. If she was recognized for an achievement, it was seen as her own accomplishment, not that of an entire race. And no one ever assumed that the personal opinions she voiced should be those of all White people. Because McIntosh blended in with the people around her, she wasn't always onstage.

5 Movies on RACE AND ETHNICITY

Selma
Marching to Montgomery for voting rights.

Zootopia
A bunny and a fox explore whether or not biology is destiny.

Fences
Segregation thwarts a man's dreams and ruins his relationships.

Hidden Figures
African American women help save NASA's space program.

13th
Slavery, in the form of imprisonment, remains legal in the United States via the 13th Amendment.

SOC THINK

McIntosh recommends that we all step back and consider unearned advantages we inherit owing to the positions we may occupy. What would be on your list? What disadvantages might you inherit?

These are not all the privileges White people take for granted as a result of their membership in the dominant racial group in the United States. As Devah Pager's study showed, White job seekers enjoy a tremendous advantage over equally well-qualified—even better-qualified—Blacks. Whiteness *does* carry privileges—to a much greater extent than most people who are White prefer to admit.

>> Race and Ethnicity in the United States

Few societies have a more diverse population than the United States. The nation is truly a multiracial, multiethnic society and is becoming more so. According to Census calculations, the number of racial or ethnic minority babies less than a year old reached 50.2 percent in July 2015 in the United States. For the U.S. population as a whole, Census projections are that the number of non-Hispanic Whites will fall below 50 percent in 2044 (Colby and Ortman 2015; Yoshinaga 2016). In the future, as marriages across racial lines and affirmation of multiracial heritage become more common, conceptions of race and ethnicity will shift, and thinking about race and ethnicity in either/or, black and white terms may become increasingly problematic (Alba 2015; Frey 2015).

RACIAL GROUPS

The three largest racial minorities in the United States currently are African Americans, Native Americans, and Asian Americans.

African Americans "I am an invisible man," wrote Black author Ralph Ellison in his novel *Invisible Man* (1952:3). "I am a man of substance, of flesh and bone, fiber and liquids—and I might even be said to possess a mind. I am invisible, understand, simply because people refuse to see me." Today, many African Americans still feel invisible. African Americans compose 13 percent of the total U.S. population, but they make up 23.2 percent of people who are officially in poverty, as we saw in the "Who Are the Poor in the United States" table in Chapter 10. Overall, 24.1 percent of African Americans were below the official poverty line, compared to 9.1 percent of non-Hispanic Whites (Proctor et al. 2016).

Racial and Ethnic Groups in the United States, 1790–2060 (Projected)

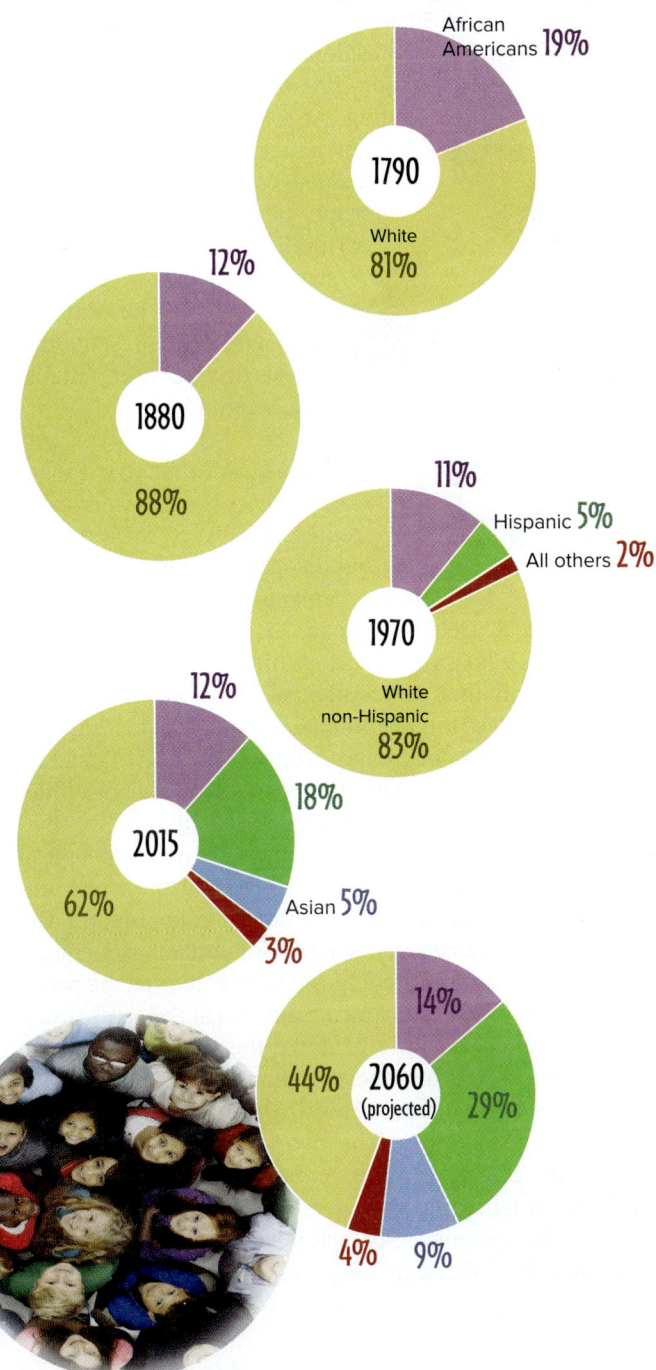

Note: U.S. Census categories vary over time.
Sources: Colby and Ortman 2016; Gibson and Jung 2002:Table 1; U.S. Census Bureau 2016j: Table S0201. Photo: ©Compassionate Eye Foundation/Jasper White/Getty Images RF

Poverty Rates by Race and Ethnicity

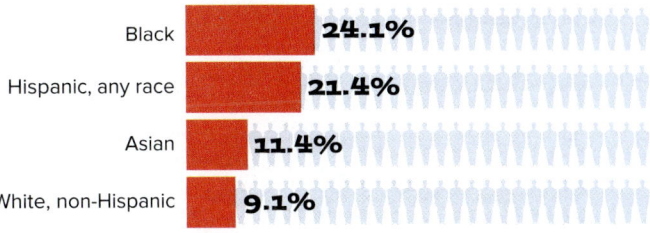

Source: Proctor et al. 2016:Table 3.

Contemporary institutional discrimination and individual prejudice against African Americans are rooted in the history of slavery in the United States. Many other subordinate groups also had little wealth and income, but as sociologist W. E. B. Du Bois (1909) and others have noted, enslaved Blacks were in an even more oppressive situation because they could not own property legally and could not pass on the benefits of their labor to their children. In spite of generations of slavery with its long-term economic consequences, African Americans never received slave reparations to compensate for the historical injustices of forced servitude (Coates 2014).

The end of the Civil War did not bring genuine freedom and equality for Blacks. Whites were able to maintain their dominance formally through legalized segregation and informally by means of vigilante terror and violence. The southern states passed "Jim Crow" laws to enforce official segregation, and the Supreme Court in the case of *Plessy v. Ferguson* upheld them as constitutional in 1896. In addition, Blacks faced the danger of lynching campaigns, often led by the Ku Klux Klan, during the late 1800s and early 1900s (Franklin and Moss 2000).

During the 1950s and 1960s, a vast civil rights movement emerged, with many competing factions and strategies for change. The Southern Christian Leadership Conference (SCLC), founded by Dr. Martin Luther King, Jr., used nonviolent civil disobedience to oppose segregation. The National Association for the Advancement of Colored People (NAACP) favored use of the courts to press for equality for African Americans. Many younger Black leaders, most notably Malcolm X, turned toward an ideology of Black power. Proponents of **Black power** rejected the goal of assimilation into White middle-class society. They defended the beauty and dignity of Black and African cultures and supported the creation of Black-controlled political and economic institutions (Glaude 2016; Ture and Hamilton 1992).

> **Black power** A political philosophy, promoted by many younger Blacks in the 1960s, that supported the creation of Black-controlled political and economic institutions.

Despite numerous courageous actions to achieve Black civil rights, Black and White citizens are still separate, still unequal. The median household income for African American households is $36,898, compared

Chapter 13 / Race and Ethnicity • 329

Life Expectancy by Race and Sex, 1950–2014

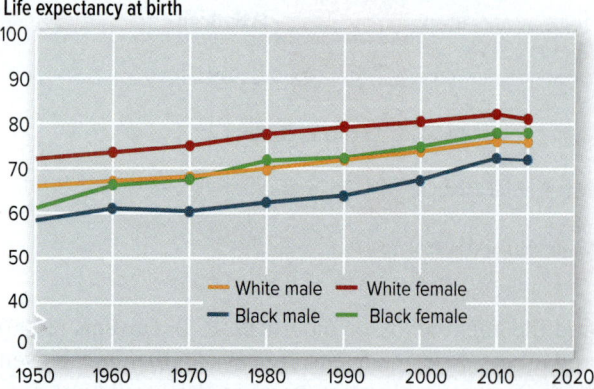

Source: National Center for Health Statistics 2016:Table 15.
Photo: ©Victoria Blackie/Getty Images RF

28 percent of bus drivers, 34 percent of postal service clerks, 38 percent of nurses' aides, and 41 percent of barbers (Bureau of Labor Statistics 2016i:Table 11).

In politics, the number of African American elected officials has increased over time. Between 1969 and 2017, the number in Congress rose from 6 to a record of 50, and the election of Barack Obama as president in 2008 represented a major breakthrough in the glass ceiling. At 9.3 percent of Congress, African Americans still are underrepresented compared to their proportion of the U.S. population. Overall, the 115th Congress, sworn in in 2017 and composed of 19 percent of non-Whites, represents the most diverse ever (Bialik and Krogstad 2017).

to $62,950 for non-Hispanic Whites (Proctor et al. 2016). Overall median wealth for African American families in 2013 was $11,184 compared to White households, which were worth $130,102 (Boshara, Emmons, and Noeth 2015). Also, when it comes to home ownership, a significant form of wealth in the United States, 41.3 percent of African American households own their own homes compared to 71.9 percent for Whites. African Americans are more likely to get turned down for a mortgage and, on average, pay a higher interest rate for the mortgages they do get (DeSilver and Bialik 2017; Fry and Brown 2016). And in part because of unequal access to health care, the life expectancy of African Americans is shorter than that of whites, although as the accompanying "Life Expectancy by Race and Sex" graph shows, the gap between the two has narrowed over time (National Center for Health Statistics 2016:Table 15).

Substantial variation exists in the types of occupations African Americans hold. Overall, African Americans make up 11.7 percent of persons employed in the labor force. Using this number as a baseline, it is possible to highlight jobs in which African Americans are over- and underrepresented. For example, African Americans compose only 2 percent of editors, 2.1 percent of aerospace engineers, 2.9 percent of dentists, 3.6 percent of CEOs, and 6.4 percent of physicians. By contrast, they constitute 22 percent of social workers,

Native Americans Today, 2.1 million Native Americans represent a diverse array of cultures distinguishable by language, family organization, religion, and livelihood (U.S. Census Bureau 2016j:Table S0201). The outsiders who came to the United States—European settlers and their descendants—came to know these native peoples' forebears as "American Indians." By the time the Bureau of Indian Affairs (BIA) was organized as part of the War Department in 1824, Indian–White relations had featured three centuries of hostility that had led to the virtual elimination of native peoples. During the 19th century, many bloody wars wiped out a significant part of the nation's Indian population. By the end of the century, schools for Indians—operated by the BIA or by church missions—prohibited the practices of Native American cultures. Yet at the same time, such schools did little to make the children effective competitors in White society (Humes et al. 2011).

Today there are 567 American Indian tribal groups in the United States. The two largest are the Navajo and the Cherokee. Life remains difficult for many Native Americans, whether they live in urban areas or on reservations. For example, median household income for American Indians is $38,248 compared to

Did You Know?

... With the release of *The Princess and the Frog* in 2009, Princess Tiana became Disney's first African American princess in a feature film. At the same time, Disney was criticized for drawing on racial stereotypes of 1920s New Orleans in the film.

Photo: ©Walt Disney Co./Courtesy Everett Collection

The Image of Diversity

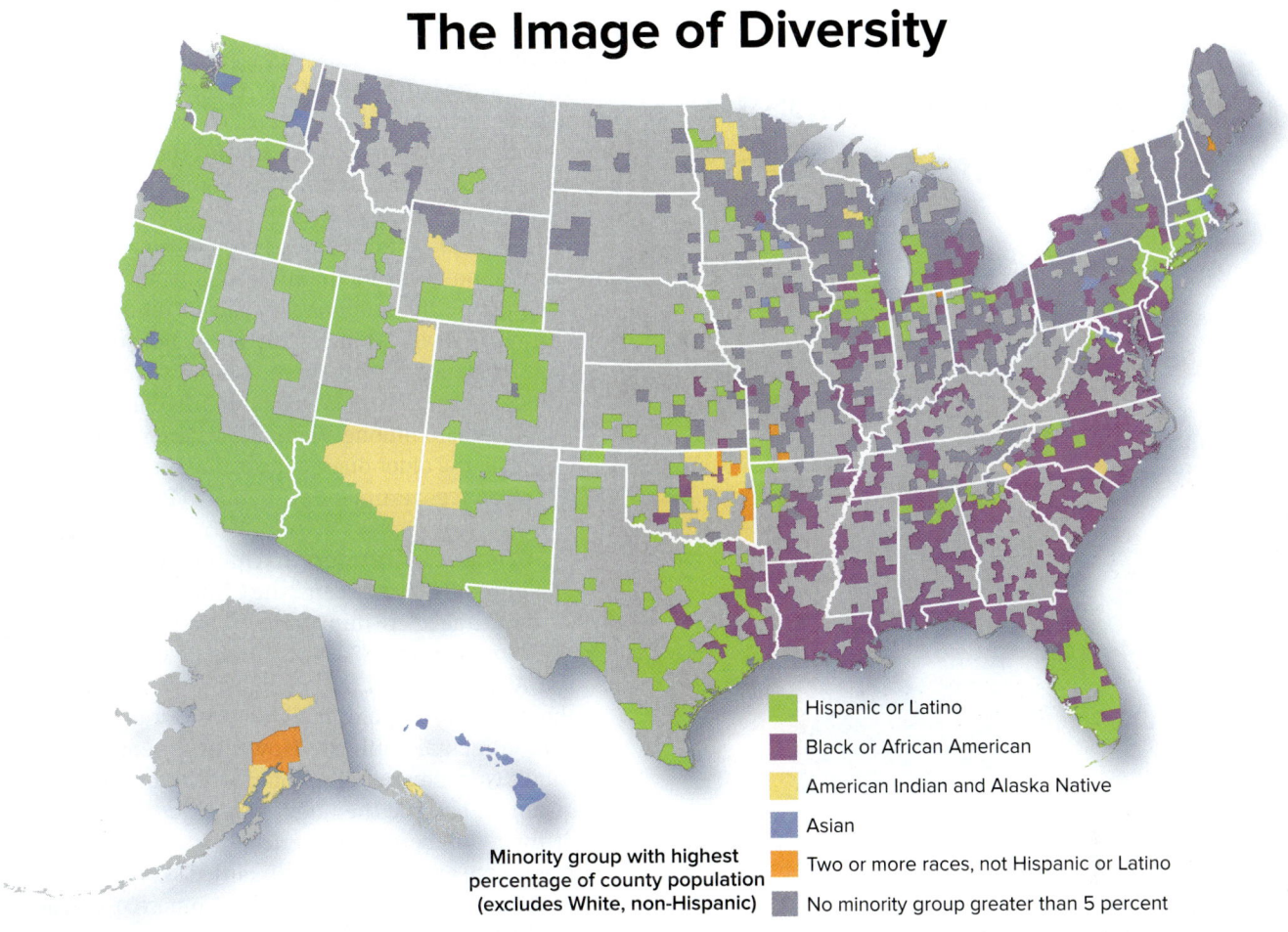

Minority group with highest percentage of county population (excludes White, non-Hispanic)

- Hispanic or Latino
- Black or African American
- American Indian and Alaska Native
- Asian
- Two or more races, not Hispanic or Latino
- No minority group greater than 5 percent

Note: Counties in gray lack sufficient data.
Source: U.S. Census 2010a:Table B03002.

$61,394 for non-Hispanic White households. Overall, 26.9 percent of American Indians fall below the official poverty line, and among American Indian children, the poverty rate is 33.4 percent. When it comes to education, 70 percent of American Indian/Alaska Native students who start ninth grade graduate from high school within four years, compared to 87 percent among non-Hispanic Whites (National Center for Education Statistics 2016:Table 219.46; U.S. Census Bureau 2016j:Table S0201, 2016l).

The introduction of gambling on Indian reservations has transformed the lives of some Native Americans. Native Americans got into the gaming industry in 1988, when Congress passed the Indian Gambling Regulatory Act. The law stipulates that states must negotiate agreements with tribes interested in commercial gaming; they cannot prevent tribes from engaging in gambling operations even if state law prohibits such ventures. The income from these lucrative operations is not evenly distributed, however. About two-thirds of recognized Indian tribes are not involved in gambling ventures. And those tribes that earn substantial revenues from gambling constitute only a small fraction of Native Americans (J. Taylor and Kalt 2005).

Asian Americans Asian Americans are a diverse group, one of the fastest-growing segments of the U.S. population. Among the many groups of Americans of Asian descent are Vietnamese Americans, Chinese Americans, Japanese Americans, and Korean Americans. The median household income for Asian Americans as a whole is $77,579, the highest for any racial or ethnic group, and the poverty rate is 12 percent. But when comparing Asian groups to each other, these numbers vary significantly (U.S. Census Bureau 2016j:Table S0201).

Asian Americans are often held up as a **model or ideal minority** group, supposedly because they have succeeded economically, socially, and educationally despite past prejudice and discrimination. Yet this representation minimizes the degree of diversity among Asian Americans. For example, 85 percent of Vietnamese aged 5 and older in the United States speak a language other than English at home, and 51 percent speak English with difficulty. Contrast this with Filipinos, 66 percent of whom speak another language at home

> **Model or ideal minority** A subordinate group whose members supposedly have succeeded economically, socially, and educationally despite past prejudice and discrimination.

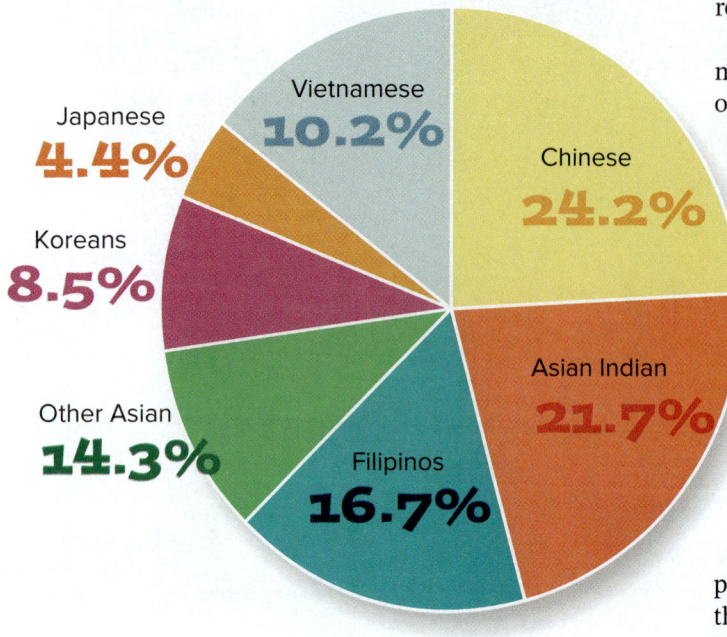

Major Asian American Groups in the United States

Source: U.S. Census Bureau 2016j:Table S0201.

and 23 percent of whom have difficulty with English. Educational attainment also varies significantly between groups. The likelihood of having completed at least a bachelor's degree among adults 25 years old and older ranges from 73.4 percent for those of Asian Indian descent and to 28.5 percent for Vietnamese. Poverty rates also vary. The rate for Asian Indians is 5.7 percent, and for Filipinos it is 6.5 percent. For Vietnamese, in contrast, it is 14.5, and for Chinese Americans it is 15.4 percent (U.S. Census Bureau 2016j: Table S0201).

> One day our descendants will think it incredible that we paid so much attention to things like the amount of melanin in our skin or the shape of our eyes or our gender instead of the unique identities of each of us as complex human beings.
>
> Franklin Thomas

Vietnamese Americans Each Asian American group has its own history and culture. Vietnamese Americans, for instance, came to the United States primarily during and after the Vietnam War—especially after the U.S. withdrawal from the region in 1975. They currently number 1.7 million, and their median household income is $60,983 (U.S. Census Bureau 2016j:Table S0201). Assisted by local agencies, refugees from communist Vietnam settled throughout the United States, tens of thousands of them in small towns. Over time, Vietnamese Americans have gravitated toward the larger urban areas, establishing ethnic enclaves featuring Vietnamese restaurants and grocery stores.

In 1995 the United States resumed normal diplomatic relations with Vietnam. Gradually, the *Viet Kieu,* or Vietnamese living abroad, began to return to their old country to visit, but usually not to take up permanent residence. Today, more than 40 years after the end of the Vietnam War, sharp differences of opinion remain among Vietnamese Americans, especially the older ones, concerning the war and the present government of Vietnam (Pfeifer 2008).

Chinese Americans Unlike African slaves and Native Americans, the Chinese were initially encouraged to immigrate to the United States. From 1850 to 1880, thousands of Chinese came to America, lured by job opportunities created by the discovery of gold, including the building of the transcontinental railroad. However, as employment possibilities decreased and competition for jobs grew, the Chinese became the target of a bitter campaign to limit their numbers and restrict their rights. Chinese laborers were exploited, then discarded (E. Lee 2015).

In 1882 Congress enacted the Chinese Exclusion Act, which prevented Chinese immigration and even forbade Chinese in the United States to send for their families. As a result, the Chinese population declined steadily until after World War II. More recently, the descendants of the 19th-century immigrants have been joined by a new influx from Hong Kong and Taiwan. These groups may contrast sharply in their degree of assimilation, desire to live in Chinatowns, and feelings about this country's relations with the communist People's Republic of China (E. Lee 2015).

Currently, 4.1 million Chinese Americans live in the United States, with an average income of $71,219 (U.S. Census Bureau 2016j:Table S0201). Some Chinese Americans have entered lucrative occupations, yet many immigrants struggle to survive under living and working conditions that belie the model minority stereotype. In major U.S. cities, including New York and San Francisco, Chinatown districts contain illegal sweatshops in which recent immigrants—many of them Chinese women—work for minimal wages. Even in legal factories in the garment industry, hours are long and rewards are limited (Greenhouse 2008; Louie 2001; Shi 2008; Shipler 2004).

Japanese Americans Approximately 757,000 Japanese Americans live in the United States with a median household income of $74,548 and a poverty rate of 8.3 percent (U.S. Census Bureau 2016j:Table S0201). As a people, they are relatively recent arrivals. In 1880 only 148 Japanese lived in the United States, but by 1920 there were more than 110,000. Japanese immigrants—called the *Issei*, or first generation—were usually males seeking employment opportunities. Many Whites saw them (along with Chinese immigrants) as a "yellow peril" and subjected them to prejudice and discrimination.

In 1941 the attack on Hawaii's Pearl Harbor by Japan had severe repercussions for Japanese Americans. The federal government decreed that all Japanese Americans on the West Coast had to leave their homes and report to "evacuation camps." Japanese Americans became, in effect, scapegoats for the anger that other people in the United States felt concerning Japan's role in World War II. By August 1943, 113,000 Japanese Americans had been forced into hastily built camps. In striking contrast, only a few German Americans and Italian Americans were sent to such camps (Neiwert 2005; Reeves 2015).

This mass detention was costly for Japanese Americans. The Federal Reserve Board estimates their total income and property losses at nearly half a billion dollars. Moreover, the psychological effect on these citizens—including the humiliation of being labeled "disloyal"—was immeasurable. Eventually, children born in the United States to the *Issei*, called *Nisei*, were allowed to enlist in the army and serve in Europe in a segregated combat unit. Others resettled in the East and Midwest to work in factories.

In 1983 a federal commission recommended government payments to all surviving Japanese Americans who had been held in detention camps. The commission reported that the detention was motivated by "race prejudice, war hysteria, and a failure of political leadership." It added that "no documented acts of espionage, sabotage, or fifth-column activity were shown to have been committed" by Japanese Americans. In 1988 President Ronald Reagan signed the Civil Liberties Act, which required the federal government to issue individual apologies for all violations of Japanese Americans' constitutional rights and established a $1.6 billion trust fund to pay reparations to the approximately 82,250 surviving Japanese Americans who had been detained (U.S. Department of Justice 1999). Each person who applied and was eligible received $20,000, with payments starting in 1990.

Korean Americans Just under 1.5 million Korean Americans live in the United States with an average household income of $63,008 and a poverty rate of 13.4 percent (U.S. Census Bureau 2016j:Table S0201). Today's Korean American community is the result of three waves of immigration. The initial wave arrived between 1903 and 1910, when Korean laborers migrated to Hawaii. The second wave followed the end of the Korean War in 1953; most of those immigrants were wives of U.S. servicemen and war orphans. The third wave, continuing to the present, has reflected the admissions priorities established by the 1965 Immigration Act. These well-educated immigrants arrive in the United States with professional skills, although they often must settle, at least initially, for positions of lower responsibility than those they held in Korea.

In the early 1990s, the apparent friction between Korean Americans and another minority racial group, African Americans, attracted nationwide attention. In New York City, Los Angeles, and Chicago, Korean American merchants confronted Blacks who were allegedly threatening them or robbing their stores. Black neighborhoods responded with hostility to what they perceived as the disrespect and arrogance of Korean American entrepreneurs. In South Central Los Angeles, the only places to buy groceries, liquor, and gas were owned by Korean immigrants, who had largely replaced White businesspeople. African Americans were well aware of the dominant role that Korean Americans played in their local retail markets. During the 1992 riots in South Central, small businesses owned by Koreans were a particular target. More than 1,800 Korean businesses were looted or burned during the riots (Kim 1999).

Conflict between the two groups was dramatized in Spike Lee's movie classic *Do the Right Thing*. The situation stems from Korean Americans' position as the latest immigrant group to cater to the needs of inner-city populations abandoned by those who have moved up the economic ladder. This type of friction is not new; generations of Jewish, Italian, and Arab

> A fully functional multiracial society cannot be achieved without a sense of history and open, honest dialogue.
>
> Cornel West

(Top left): ©Greta Gabaglio/123RF; *(top right):* ©Pitinan Piyavatin/123RF; *(bottom):* ©liquidlibrary/Getty Images

Estimates of the size of the Arab American community differ widely. According to the U.S. Census, 2 million people of Arab ancestry now reside in the United States, with a median household income of $55,117 and a poverty rate of 22.4 percent (U.S. Census Bureau 2016j:Table S0201). Iraq, Egypt, Lebanon, and Jordan were the top four Arab countries of origin for the foreign-born population in the United States (U.S. Census Bureau 2016j:Table B05006). Just as is the case for Asian Americans, there is significant variation among Arab groups in the United States based on their country of ancestry. Among those who trace their roots to Lebanon, median household income was $75,757 and the poverty rate was 10.8 percent. Contrast that with those with Iraqi backgrounds at $32,594 and 40.2 percent and Yemeni backgrounds at $32,619 and 43 percent (U.S. Census Bureau 2016j:Table S0201).

As a group, Arab Americans are extremely diverse. Many families have lived in the United States for several generations; others are foreign born. Despite the stereotype, most Arab Americans are *not* Muslim, and not all practice religion. The majority of Arab Americans are Christian. Nor can Arab Americans be characterized as having a specific family type, gender role, or occupational pattern (Arab American Institute 2008; David 2004).

ETHNIC GROUPS

Many different ethnic groups have come together in the United States resulting in a shifting mosaic of cultures. Three major groupings include Hispanics (Latinos), Jews, and White ethnics.

Hispanics At 56.5 million, Hispanics make up the largest minority group in the United States, an increase from 35.3 million in 2000. The fastest-growing subgroups are those who come from the Central American nations of El Salvador, Honduras, and Guatemala. The majority of the overall Hispanic population increase is due not to immigration. Instead, their median age is younger than the other groups—as is shown in the "Age Variation by Race and Ethnicity" graph—meaning more Hispanics are of childbearing age, and Hispanics overall have higher birthrates (Humes et al. 2011; K. Johnson and Lichter 2010; Patten 2016; U.S. Census Bureau 2016j:Table S0201).

Although the growth in the Hispanic population has been a national phenomenon, the five states with the largest Hispanic population are California, Texas, Florida, New York, and Illinois. In New Mexico, 47.7 percent of the population is Hispanic (Stepler

merchants have encountered similar hostility from another oppressed minority that to outsiders might seem an unlikely source.

Arab Americans Arab Americans are immigrants and their descendants who hail from the 22 nations of the Arab world. As defined by the League of Arab States, these are the nations of North Africa and what is commonly known as the Middle East. Not all residents of those countries are Arab; for example, the Kurds of northern Iraq are not Arab. And some Arab Americans may have immigrated to the United States from non-Arab countries such as Great Britain or France, where their families have lived for generations (Kayyali 2006; Orfalea 2006).

The Arabic language is the single most unifying force among Arabs, although not all Arabs, and certainly not all Arab Americans, can read and speak Arabic. Moreover, the language has evolved over the centuries so that people in different parts of the Arab world speak different dialects. The fact that the Muslim holy book, the Qur'an, was originally written in Arabic gives the language special importance to Muslims.

Age Variation by Race and Ethnicity

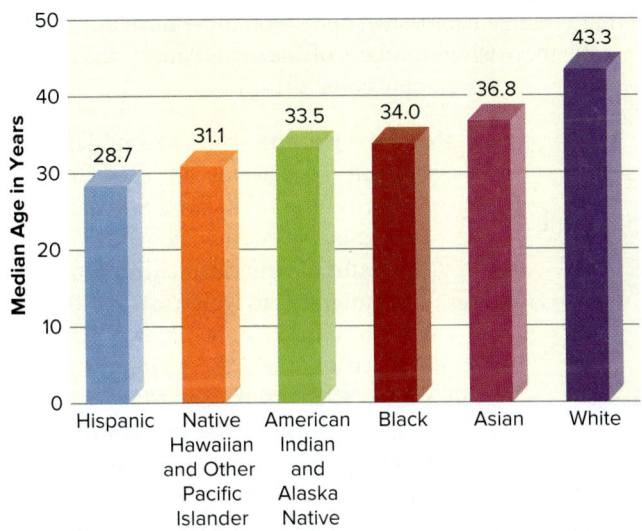

Note: The five racial group categories reported here do not include Hispanics.
Source: U.S. Census Bureau 2016j:Table S0201.

and Brown 2016:Table 44). Major urban areas have also experienced substantial expansion. As the accompanying "Hispanic Population and Percent in U.S. Metro Areas" graph depicts, Los Angeles is home to the largest number of Hispanics. Within the top metro areas, however, the population of San Antonio, at 55.7 percent, has the highest percentage of Hispanics (Pew Research Center 2016e).

The various Latino groups share a heritage of Spanish language and culture, which can cause serious problems in their assimilation. An intelligent student whose first language is Spanish may be presumed to be slow or even unruly by English-speaking schoolchildren, and frequently by English-speaking teachers as well. The labeling of Latino children as underachievers, as learning disabled, or as emotionally disturbed can act as a self-fulfilling prophecy for some children. Bilingual education aims at easing the educational difficulties experienced by Hispanic children and others whose first language is not English.

The educational challenges facing Latinos is reflected in the fact that 66 percent of Hispanics aged 25 and older have completed high school, compared to 92 percent for non-Hispanic Whites. At the college level, 34 percent of non-Hispanic Whites have a bachelor's degree, whereas only 15 percent of Hispanics have the same. The median household income for Hispanic households is $44,782, which is 73 percent as much as non-Hispanic White households. Educational attainment of Hispanics is, however, on the rise. Dropout rates for Latino youths fell dramatically from 32.4 percent in 1990 to 9.2 percent in 2015. And, the percentage of Hispanics who went directly to college exceeded the rate for non-Hispanic Whites for the first time in 2012 (Fry and Taylor 2013; National Center for Education Statistics 2016:Table 219.70.; U.S. Census Bureau 2016j:Table S0201).

Hispanic Population and Percent in U.S. Metro Areas

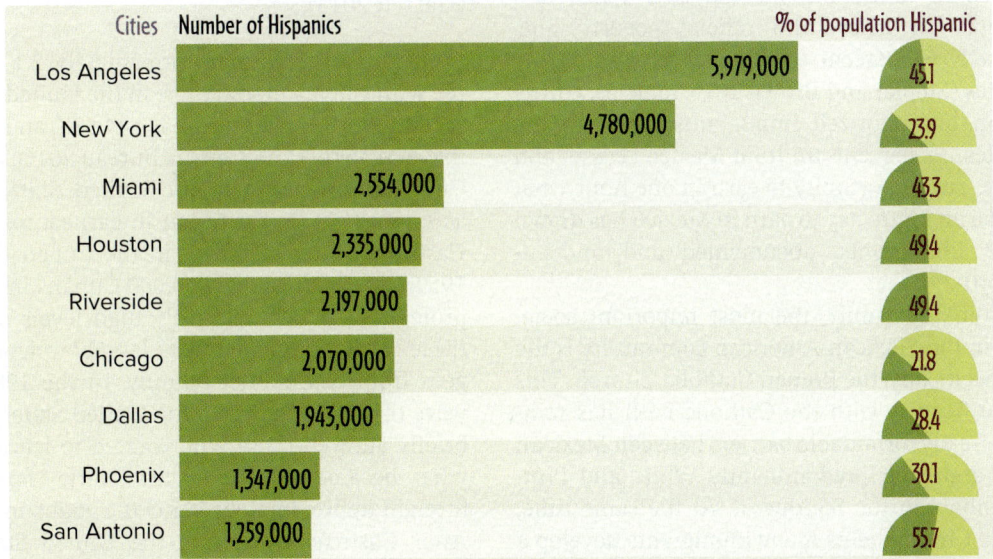

Source: Pew Research Center 2016e.

Major Hispanic Groups in the United States

Source: U.S. Census Bureau 2016j:Table S0201. Photo: ©Jack Hollingsworth/Getty Images RF

Mexican Americans The largest Hispanic population in the United States is Mexican American. Their average median household income is $44,433, and 23.5 percent fall below the official poverty line. Approximately 67 percent of them were born in the United States (Stepler and Brown 2016:Table 5). Of the 11.1 million unauthorized immigrants living in the United States, 52 percent are from Mexico (Passel and Cohn 2016). The opportunity to earn in one hour what it would take an entire day to earn in Mexico has drawn millions of immigrants, documented and undocumented, north.

Aside from the family, the most important social institution in the Mexican American community is the church—specifically, the Roman Catholic Church. This strong identification with the Catholic faith has reinforced the already formidable barriers between Mexican Americans and their predominantly White and Protestant neighbors in the Southwest. At the same time, the Catholic Church helps many immigrants develop a sense of identity and assists their assimilation into the dominant culture of the United States. The complexity of the Mexican American community is underscored by the fact that Protestant churches—especially those that endorse expressive, open worship—have attracted increasing numbers of Mexican Americans (Pew Research Center 2014g).

Puerto Ricans The second-largest segment of Latinos in the United States is Puerto Ricans. Since 1917, residents of Puerto Rico have held the status of American citizens; many have migrated to New York and other eastern cities. More Puerto Ricans now live on the U.S. mainland than in Puerto Rico itself (Krogstad, Lopez, and DeSilver 2015). With a median household income of $40,774, those who live in the continental United States earn 68 percent of what non-Hispanic White households earn and have a poverty rate of 24.6 percent (U.S. Census Bureau 2016j:Table S0201).

Politically, Puerto Ricans in the United States have not been as successful as Mexican Americans in organizing for their rights. For many mainland Puerto Ricans—as for many residents of the island—the paramount political issue is the destiny of Puerto Rico itself. Should it continue in its present commonwealth status, petition for admission to the United States as the 51st state, or attempt to become an independent nation? This question has divided Puerto Rico for decades and remains a central issue in Puerto Rican elections. In a 2012 referendum, for example, of the 1.4 million voters who expressed a preference, 61 percent supported statehood, 33 percent preferred to continue with the existing status of sovereign free association, and 5 percent supported independence; 515,000 voters, however, did not express a preference (Garrett 2013).

Cuban Americans Approximately 2.1 million people with Cuban ancestry live in the United States. Their median household income is $44,588, and 17.6 percent live in poverty (U.S. Census Bureau 2016j:Table S0201). Cuban immigration to the United States dates back as far as 1831, but it began in earnest following Fidel Castro's seizure of power in the Cuban revolution of 1959. The first wave of 200,000 Cubans included many professionals with relatively high levels of schooling; these men and women were largely welcomed as refugees from communist tyranny. In the 1980s, another wave of Cubans came to the United States when Cuba briefly allowed those who wanted to leave to do so in what became known as the Mariel boatlift, which brought approximately 125,000 Cubans to U.S. shores. After Castro's revolution, the United States severed

©Robert Nicholas/Getty Images

formal relations with Cuba, preventing all trade and banning travel. After years of softening relations, on July 20, 2015, Cuba and the United States restored official diplomatic ties (Sweig 2016).

Jewish Americans The Jewish population in the United States exceeds 6.8 million and constitutes approximately 2.1 percent of the total U.S. population; of these, 2.1 million live in the New York City metropolitan area (Sheskin and Dashefsky 2016:Table 1). They play a prominent role in the worldwide Jewish community because the United States has the world's largest concentration of Jews. Like the Japanese, many Jewish immigrants came to this country and became white-collar professionals in spite of prejudice and discrimination.

Anti-Semitism—that is, anti-Jewish prejudice—has often been vicious in the United States, although rarely so widespread and never so formalized as in Europe. In many cases, Jews have been used as scapegoats for other people's failures. Given such attitudes, Jews continue to face discrimination. Despite high levels of education and professional training, they are still conspicuously absent from the top management of large corporations (except for the few firms founded by Jews). Until the late 1960s, many prestigious universities maintained restrictive quotas that limited Jewish enrollment. Private social clubs and fraternal groups frequently limit membership to gentiles (non-Jews), a practice upheld by the Supreme Court in the 1964 case *Bell v. Maryland*.

The Anti-Defamation League (ADL) of B'nai B'rith funds an annual tally of reported anti-Semitic incidents. In 2015, the total reported incidents of harassment, threats, vandalism, and assaults came to 941, which represented a 3.1 percent increase over 2014, but a significant decrease from 1,757 in 2005 (Anti-Defamation League 2016). Some incidents were inspired and carried out by neo-Nazi skinheads—groups of young people who champion racist and anti-Semitic ideologies. Such threatening behavior only intensifies the fears of many Jewish Americans, who remember the Holocaust—the extermination of 6 million Jews by Nazi Germany during World War II.

White Ethnics Overall, 61.5 percent of the U.S. population is composed of non-Hispanic Whites. The nation's White ethnic population includes about 46 million people who claim at least partial German ancestry, 33 million Irish Americans, 24 million with English roots, 17 million Italian Americans, and 9 million Polish Americans, as well as immigrants from other European nations. Some of these people continue to live in close-knit ethnic neighborhoods, whereas others have largely assimilated and left the "old ways" behind (Hixson, Hepler, and Kim 2011; U.S. Census Bureau 2016j:Table S0201).

Anti-Semitism Anti-Jewish prejudice.

Personal Sociology

Celebrating Ethnicity

I live in Pella, Iowa, a small town with a strong Dutch heritage. The first weekend each May, Pella holds its annual Tulip Time festival (www.pellatuliptime.com). Hundreds of thousands of tourists come to the three-day celebration to watch the parades, eat the food, and see people scrub streets in their Dutch costumes. In 2015, my daughter Eleanor was crowned Pella's 80th Tulip Queen. She, along with four other girls on the Royal Court, represented Pella as goodwill ambassadors, performing at numerous locations around the region to help promote Tulip Time and celebrate Pella's Dutch heritage. Like other ethnic celebrations in other communities, Tulip Time plays a significant role in fostering a sense of community solidarity.

Communities throughout the United States celebrate their ethnic heritage with local festivals such as Cinco de Mayo, Octoberfest, and Tulip Time (shown here). ©Cyndi Atkins

Many White ethnics today identify only sporadically with their heritage. **Symbolic ethnicity** refers to an ethnic identity that emphasizes concerns such as ethnic food or political issues rather than on deeper ties to one's ethnic heritage. It is reflected in the occasional family trip to an ethnic bakery, the celebration of a ceremonial event such as St. Joseph's Day among Italian Americans, or concern about the future of Northern Ireland among Irish Americans. Except in cases in which new immigration reinforces old traditions, symbolic ethnicity tends to decline with each passing generation (Anagnostou 2009a, 2009b; Gans 2009; Waters 2009).

Symbolic ethnicity An ethnic identity that emphasizes concerns such as ethnic food or political issues rather than deeper ties to one's ethnic heritage.

Whites increasingly feel excluded and even threatened by efforts to embrace multiculturalism and expand diversity (Hochschild 2016; Plaut, Garnett, Buffardi, and Sanchez-Banks 2011). According to a national survey, 50 percent of Whites now believe that the level of anti-White discrimination is at least as common as discrimination against Blacks and other minority groups. That number rises to 60 percent among members of the White working class. When it comes to political party, 64 percent of Republicans agree and 71 percent of Democrats disagree. Researchers suggest that belief in reverse discrimination functions to bolster Whites' self-esteem (Jacobs 2016; Jones et al. 2015).

In many respects, the plight of White ethnics involves the same basic issues as that of other subordinate people in the United States. How ethnic can people be—how much can they deviate from an essentially White, Anglo-Saxon, Protestant norm—before society responds to their desire to be different? The United States does seem to reward people for assimilating. Yet, as we have seen, assimilation is no easy process. In the years to come, more and more people will face the challenge of fitting in, not only in the United States, but also around the world as the flow of immigrants from one country to another continues to increase.

>> Immigration

According to a United Nations report, there are 244 million international immigrants in the world. The United States accounts for 19 percent of that total, with 47 million migrants living there in 2015 (United Nations 2016b). Of these, 51 percent are from Latin America, 31 percent from Asia, 11 percent from Europe, and 5 percent from Africa (U.S. Census Bureau 2016j:Table DP-2). The constantly increasing numbers of immigrants and the pressure they put on employment opportunities and welfare capabilities in the countries they enter raise difficult questions for many of the world's economic powers. Who should be allowed in? At what point should immigration be curtailed? As the Brexit vote in the United Kingdom and the Trump election in the United States demonstrated, these were major concerns of voters in those countries (Bloemraad, Korteweg, and Yurdakul 2008; Hochschild 2016).

IMMIGRATION TRENDS

The migration of people is not uniform across time or space. At certain times, war or famine may precipitate large movements of people, either temporarily

Going GLOBAL

World Immigration Since 1500

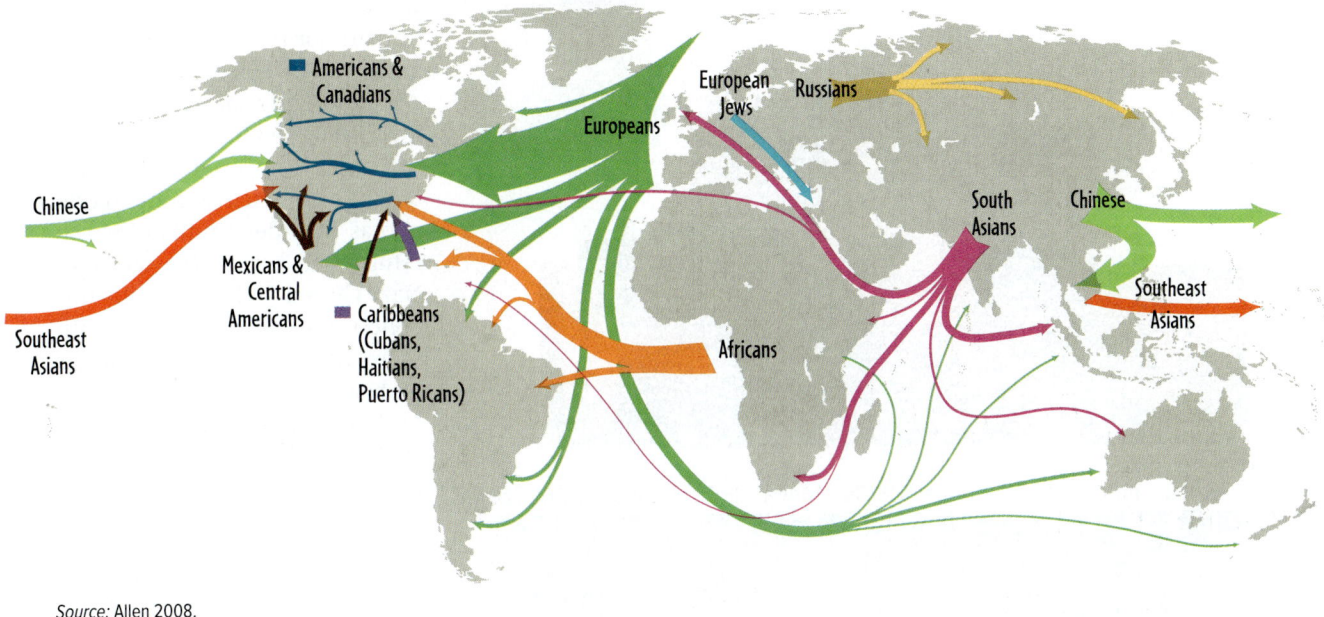

Source: Allen 2008.

or permanently. As noted earlier in the "Expulsion" section, for example, the civil war in Syria led at least 4.9 million people to leave that country. Temporary dislocations occur when people wait until it is safe to return to their home areas. However, more and more migrants who cannot eke out an adequate living at home are making permanent moves to developed nations. The major migration streams flow into North America, the oil-rich areas of the Middle East, and the industrial economies of western Europe and Asia. Currently, seven of the world's wealthiest nations (including Germany, France, the United Kingdom, and the United States) shelter about one-third of the world's migrant population but less than one-fifth of the world's total population. As long as disparities in job opportunities exist among countries, this international trend is not likely to reverse.

Even though the sending nation loses a significant source of labor and talent due to emigration, the process does contribute to its economy. For example, it reduces the size of the population that an economy with limited resources has a difficult time supporting, and it leads to an economic infusion in the form of remittances—monies that immigrants send back to their home nations. Worldwide, immigrants send more than $581 billion a year back home to their relatives—an amount that represents a major source of income for developing nations. In 2015, over $135 billion was sent from the United States to other countries in the form of remittances. The single largest recipient was Mexico with $25.7 billion, followed by China with $16.2 billion, and India at $11.7 billion (World Bank 2016l).

Immigrants continue to face obstacles owing to their relative lack of resources. Immigrant women, for example, face all the challenges that immigrant men do, plus some additional ones. Typically, they bear the responsibility for obtaining services for their families, particularly their children. Women are often left to navigate the bureaucratic tangle of schools, city services, and health care, as well as the unfamiliar stores and markets they must shop at to feed their families. Women who need special medical services or are victims of domestic violence are often reluctant to seek outside help. Finally, because many new immigrants view the United States as a dangerous place to raise a family, women must be especially watchful over their children's lives (Ruiz, Zong, and Batalva 2015).

One consequence of global immigration has been the emergence of transnationals—people or families who move across borders multiple times in search of better jobs and education. The industrial tycoons of the early 20th century, whose power outmatched that of many

Going GLOBAL

Legal Migration to the United States, 1820–2010

IMMIGRATION POLICIES

Countries that have long been a destination for immigrants, such as the United States, usually have policies to determine who has preference to enter. Often, clear racial and ethnic biases are built into these policies. In the 1920s, U.S. policy gave preference to people from western Europe while making it difficult for residents of southern and eastern Europe, Asia, and Africa to enter the country. During the late 1930s and early 1940s, the federal government refused to loosen restrictive immigration quotas in order to allow Jewish refugees to escape the terror of Nazi Germany. In line with this policy, the MS *St. Louis,* with more than 900 Jewish refugees on board, was denied permission to dock in the United States in 1939. The ship was forced to sail back to Europe, where at least a few hundred of its passengers later died at the hands of the Nazis (Morse 1967; G. Thomas and Witts 1974).

Since the 1960s U.S. policy has encouraged the immigration of relatives of U.S. residents and of people who have desirable skills. This policy has significantly altered the pattern of sending nations. Previously, Europeans dominated, but for the past 40 years, immigrants have come primarily from Latin America and Asia. Thus, an ever-growing proportion of the U.S. population will be Asian or Hispanic. To a large extent, fear and resentment of racial and ethnic diversity is a key factor in opposition to immigration. In many nations, people are concerned that the new arrivals do not reflect and will not embrace their own cultural and racial heritage. Others fear that immigrants represent an economic threat, because they increase the supply of available workers. In 1986 Congress approved the Immigration Reform and Control Act which, for the first time, outlawed the hiring of undocumented immigrants and subjected employers to fines and even imprisonment if they violated the law.

Under the George W. Bush administration, numerous high-profile workplace raids occurred to send a very public message that they were serious about

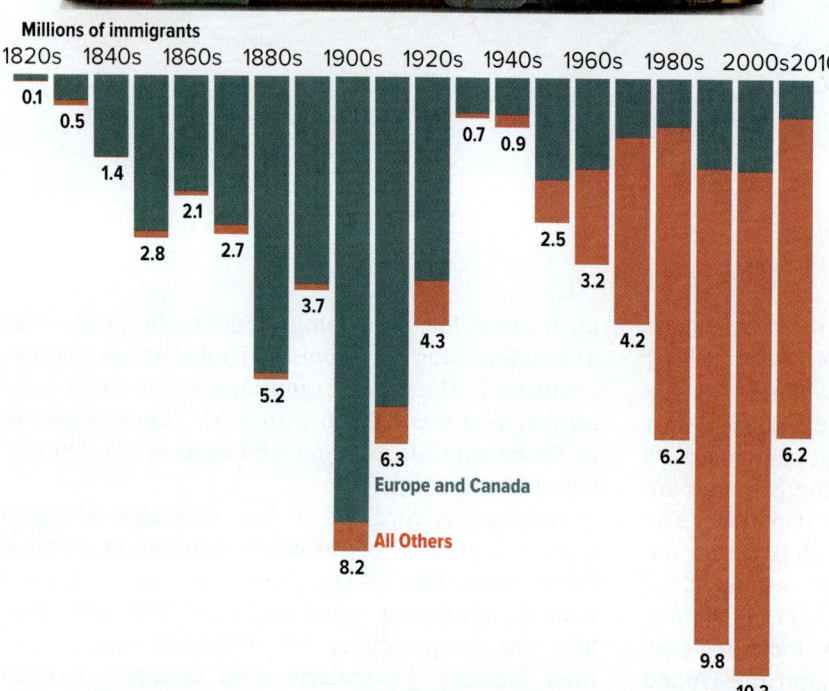

Source: Homeland Security 2016:Table 2.   *Photo:* ©pixhook/Getty Images RF

nation-states, were among the world's first transnationals. Today, however, millions of people, many of very modest means, move back and forth between countries much as commuters do between city and suburbs. More and more of these people have dual citizenship. Rather than being shaped by allegiance to one country, their identity is rooted in their struggle to survive—and in some instances prosper—by transcending international borders (Faist, Fauser, and Reisenauer 2013; Sassen 2005).

cracking down on illegal immigration. After the election of Barack Obama, the number of such raids declined, although the number of people classified as "aliens removed" from the country went up (U.S. Department of Homeland Security 2016). Workplace raids have been replaced by what are sometimes called "silent raids," in which the Immigration Customs and Enforcement (ICE) agency focuses instead on inspecting employers' hiring paperwork to see whether their workers have the legal documentation necessary for employment. In doing this, ICE targets sectors that have historically hired immigrant undocumented laborers, such as the garment industry, fast-food chains, and agricultural companies. The effect is that these workers lose their jobs. After one such raid, the clothing maker American Apparel laid off 1,500 workers, approximately a quarter of its workforce. The goal of this approach is to shut down the supply of jobs for workers who lack legal documentation, thus discouraging illegal immigration. Companies who employ these workers, however, are not entirely pleased, because it means that they will have to pay more to attract applicants to these difficult and often tedious jobs (Jordan 2011).

Battles over immigration continue. During the second week of his administration, President Donald Trump signed an Executive Order severely restricting immigration from seven predominantly Muslim nations, temporarily suspending admission of all refugees, and barring refugees from Syria indefinitely (Calamur 2017). Protesters streamed into airports around the country to make their displeasure known, and a legal battle ensued (Dolan 2017). The president justified these immigration curbs by claiming they were in the interests of national security—that is, to reduce the likelihood that a terrorist might come into the United States to stage an attack. Protesters claimed that, instead, it amounted to a Muslim ban, which ran counter to both U.S. law and values. Corporate executives claimed that these curbs would create competitive disadvantages by limiting their ability to hire talented and skilled workers from around the world (Newmyer 2017). Part of the reason that such conflicts over immigration continue is that Congress has had difficulty reaching a bipartisan compromise.

Race and ethnicity in the United States pose a challenge to the principle that everyone is created equal. The vast majority of people in the United States have rejected outright racism in which people adhere to beliefs asserting the inherent superiority of their race or ethnic group over others. But inequality in practice continues to be a significant challenge, with substantial differences in access to material, social, and cultural resources based on racial and ethnic background. This inequality of opportunity becomes especially problematic when built into the structure of society itself in the form of institutional discrimination. Sociology enables us to better see and understand such patterns so that we might make more informed decisions about what to do about them.

> **SOC THINK**
>
> Birthrates in the United States, as in many industrialized nations, are low. Populations in many states face natural decrease and will shrink without immigration to compensate for those low birthrates. Given this, why does immigration still cause such tension among many communities in the United States? Might this change as people in such states realize they need those immigrants?

> **SOCIOLOGY IS A VERB**
>
> **PRIVILEGE**
>
> As an experiment in personal sociology, and in the spirit of Peggy McIntosh's work on privilege, make a list of the unearned advantages and disadvantages that flow out of your racial and ethnic heritage. Doing so can make us more aware of both the opportunities and obstacles that are not a consequence of our individual effort or merit. How and why might such a list be more challenging for some groups than others?

For REVIEW

I. **How do sociologists define race and ethnicity?**
   - Race is defined by the social significance that groups attach to external physical characteristics. Ethnicity is rooted in cultural and national traditions that define a population. Sociologists emphasize the significance of culture and its consequences for both.

II. **What are prejudice and discrimination, and how do they operate?**
   - Prejudice involves attitudes and beliefs, whereas discrimination involves actions. In both cases, they represent a negative response to a group of people that denies them full equality as persons. Institutional discrimination is built into the structure of society itself, systematically denying some groups access to key resources.

III. **What are the consequences of race and ethnicity for opportunity?**
   - Racial and ethnic groups in the United States—including African Americans, Native Americans, Asian Americans, Hispanic Americans, Jewish Americans, and White ethnic Americans—face differing levels of opportunity based on their relative position in society. Groups within each of these categories continue to face significant structural inequality.

SOCVIEWS on Race and Ethnicity

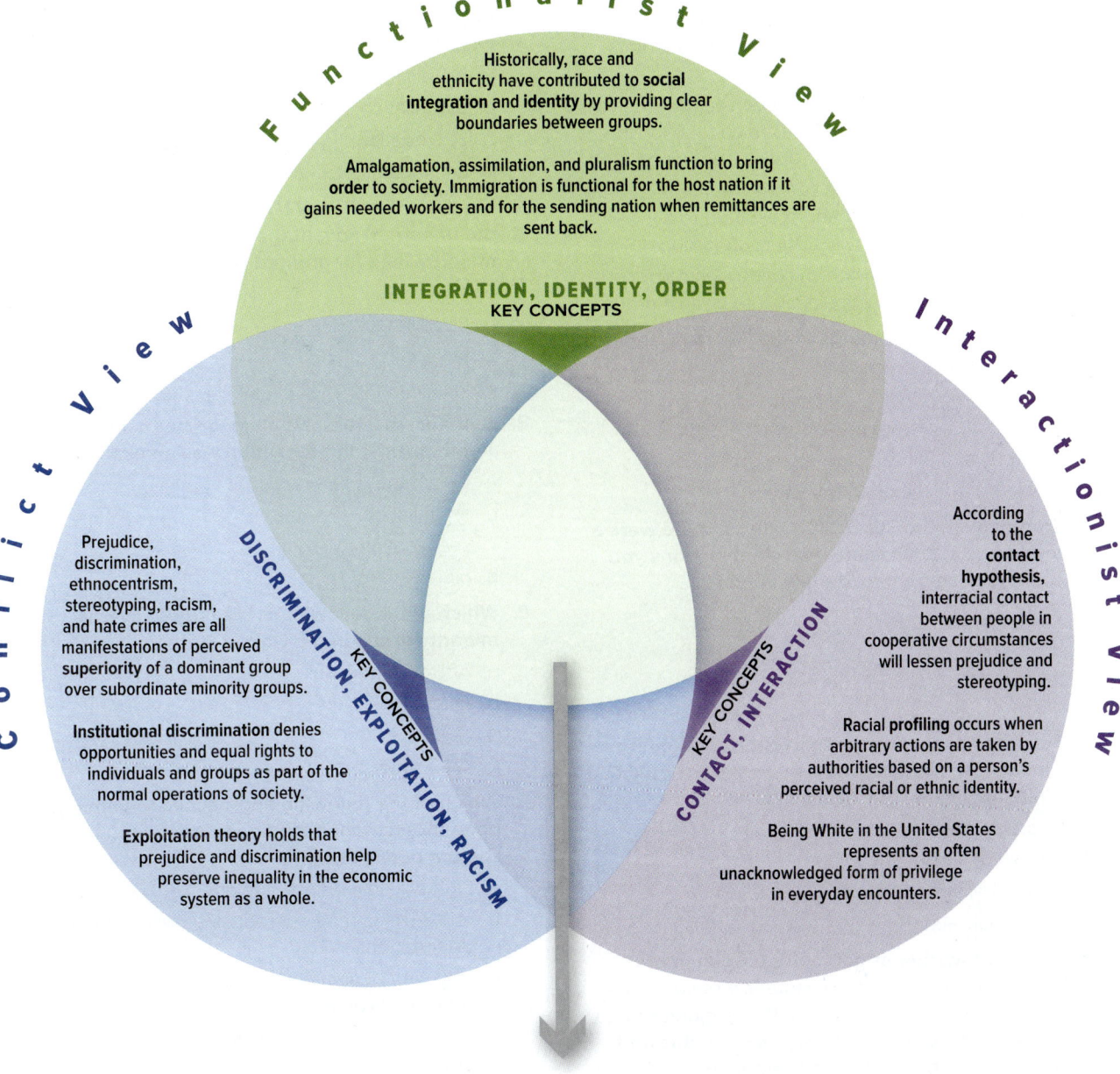

Functionalist View

Historically, race and ethnicity have contributed to **social integration** and **identity** by providing clear boundaries between groups.

Amalgamation, assimilation, and pluralism function to bring **order** to society. Immigration is functional for the host nation if it gains needed workers and for the sending nation when remittances are sent back.

INTEGRATION, IDENTITY, ORDER
KEY CONCEPTS

Conflict View

Prejudice, discrimination, ethnocentrism, stereotyping, racism, and hate crimes are all manifestations of perceived superiority of a dominant group over subordinate minority groups.

Institutional discrimination denies opportunities and equal rights to individuals and groups as part of the normal operations of society.

Exploitation theory holds that prejudice and discrimination help preserve inequality in the economic system as a whole.

KEY CONCEPTS
DISCRIMINATION, EXPLOITATION, RACISM

Interactionist View

According to the **contact hypothesis**, interracial contact between people in cooperative circumstances will lessen prejudice and stereotyping.

Racial **profiling** occurs when arbitrary actions are taken by authorities based on a person's perceived racial or ethnic identity.

Being White in the United States represents an often unacknowledged form of privilege in everyday encounters.

KEY CONCEPTS
CONTACT, INTERACTION

MAKE THE CONNECTION
After reviewing the chapter, answer the following questions:

1 How would each perspective approach the issue of African American deaths at the hands of police?

2 How would each perspective explain stereotyping?

3 How do the functionalist and conflict perspectives intersect in both color-blind racism and affirmative action?

4 Using the interactionist perspective, describe an example of interracial contact you have experienced along with its consequences.

Pop Quiz

1. **How do sociologists define race?**
   a. genetic differences between categories of humans based on clear chromosomal markers that specify a person's race
   b. the biological differences between humans, defined as socially significant and presumed to divide the population into genetically distinct subgroups
   c. the cultural differences between humans, defined as socially significant and presumed to divide the population into socially distinct subgroups
   d. levels of melatonin, which shape skin color and divide the human population into distinct groups

2. **According to the findings of the Human Genome Project, race**
   a. determines intellectual ability.
   b. is a biological, not a social, concept.
   c. explains significant social outcomes.
   d. has no genetic or scientific basis.

3. **Starting with the 2000 U.S. Census, there were a total of _____ possible race combinations you could choose from to identify yourself.**
   a. 3
   b. 6
   c. 27
   d. 57

4. **Suppose that a White employer refuses to hire a Vietnamese American and selects a less-qualified White applicant. This decision is an act of**
   a. prejudice.
   b. ethnocentrism.
   c. discrimination.
   d. stigmatization.

5. **Working together as computer programmers for an electronics firm, a Hispanic woman and a Jewish man overcome their initial prejudices and come to appreciate each other's strengths and talents. This scenario is an example of**
   a. the contact hypothesis.
   b. a self-fulfilling prophecy.
   c. amalgamation.
   d. reverse discrimination.

6. **Intermarriage over several generations, resulting in various groups combining to form a new group, would be an example of**
   a. pluralism.
   b. assimilation.
   c. segregation.
   d. amalgamation.

7. **The term that Peggy McIntosh uses to describe the unearned advantages that those in the majority take for granted is**
   a. privilege.
   b. discrimination.
   c. racism.
   d. institutional discrimination.

8. **Jennifer Anastassakis changed her name to Jennifer Aniston. Her action was an example of**
   a. expulsion.
   b. assimilation.
   c. segregation.
   d. pluralism.

9. **Which of the following is the largest overall minority group in the United States?**
   a. African Americans
   b. Asian Americans
   c. Latinos
   d. Arab Americans

10. **Which of the following approaches to immigration enforcement became most common in the Obama administration?**
    a. high-profile workplace raids
    b. relaxed enforcement reducing the number of deportations
    c. targeting of community organizations that provide services to immigrants
    d. silent raids focusing on employers and documentation

1. (b), 2. (d), 3. (d), 4. (c), 5. (a), 6. (d), 7. (a), 8. (b), 9. (c), 10. (d)

©Photo by Michael Nigro/Pacific Press/LightRocket via Getty Images

Population, Health, and Environment

WATER IS LIFE

In fall of 2016, approximately ten thousand people made their way to the Standing Rock Sioux Reservation in North Dakota to stand in solidarity against the construction of the Dakota Access Pipeline (DAPL). The proposed 1,172 mile long, $3.8 billion pipeline project would carry over 500,000 barrels of crude oil per day from North Dakota's Bakken oil fields to southern Illinois, where it would be refined and distributed. The two primary concerns for the Standing Rock Sioux were that the pipeline represented a potential threat to the reservation's water supply and that construction would desecrate ancestral lands, including tribal burial grounds and sacred cultural artifacts (Allard 2016; Bengal 2016; Healy 2016).

The protest started small. In February 2016, Jasilyn Charger, Joseph White Eyes, and a handful of friends heard about DAPL and headed to Standing Rock to see if they could make a difference. They lived about two hours away and had already founded a youth group to provide counseling, organize events, and build solidarity around issues their fellow Native American teens faced. In their meeting with representatives from Standing Rock, Ladonna Brave Bull Allard, who owned land adjacent to the pipeline project, volunteered her land and herself to the cause (Elbein 2017; Goodman 2017; Merlan 2016). Together they established Sacred Stone Camp (sacredstonecamp.org) on Allard's property as a prayer camp focused on ceremony and activism. In July, after the Army Corps of Engineers approved the easement that would allow the pipeline to cross under the Missouri River just upriver of the reservation, word spread about both the protest and the camp, and people streamed in (Elbein 2017).

The movement's rallying cry became "Mni wiconi!" (pronounced "mini we-choh-nee") which means "Water is life," and the protesters referred to themselves as water protectors (Healey and Fandos 2016). Although water served as a unifying symbol, the group conceived of this fight as part of a larger struggle for Native American culture, environmental sustainability, and the survival of the planet (Elbein 2017). As fall turned to winter, through back-and-forth legal maneuverings along with protests in which participants were subjected to tear gas, pepper spray, and rubber bullets, President Obama directed the Army Corps of Engineers on December 4, 2016, to deny the easement necessary for the project to move forward (Healey and Fandos 2016). The Standing Rock Sioux effectively declared victory and encouraged the protesters to go home. Some stayed, in part to continue the larger fight, but also because they feared that although the battle was won, the war was not over. And on February 7, 2017, the newly elected Donald Trump announced that the deputy secretary of the Army, who oversees the Army Corps of Engineers, would approve the easement enabling the project to move forward (Eilperin and Dennis 2017).

Such battles—of local versus corporate interests or cultural tradition versus social change—highlight the interdependent nature of people and interests in our world today. For the sake of our public health, we must understand the web of relationships between our natural and social environments. In this chapter we explore such interconnections in the areas of population, health, and environment.

- What role do population dynamics play in shaping our lives?
- What does sociology contribute to something as seemingly biological as health?
- What environmental lessons do we learn from sociology?

>> Population

One advantage of the sociological imagination is that it helps us understand the big picture of society and where we fit in it. It does so by contextualizing our beliefs and practices within a larger social framework, one that is often invisible to us. We have already seen this at work with regard to various components of social structure, including family, religion, education, economy, and politics. In sociology, place matters. This is no less true when it comes to the topics of population, health, and environment. Approaching these issues with a big-picture perspective allows us to see how the positions we occupy shape our individual outcomes.

Today, more than 7.4 billion people live on Earth, a number that goes up by 212,587 each day and 148 every minute, as the accompanying "World Population Clock" shows (U.S. Census Bureau 2017a). Every single one of us must live off the limited resources the planet provides. To better understand our life chances, as well as those of others, we must take into account the direction of population trends. **Demography**—the statistical study of population dynamics—is the discipline committed to studying such patterns. It focuses on how populations change over time, with particular attention to whether they are growing, shrinking, or staying the same. It also includes analysis of the composition of those populations—particularly age and sex, with special emphasis on the degree to which a group's makeup influences its likelihood for population change. For example, if the population is young, there is more potential for women to bear children, increasing the possibility for future population growth.

Demography The statistical study of population dynamics.

In their analysis, demographers begin by specifying the population to be studied. They might select a city,

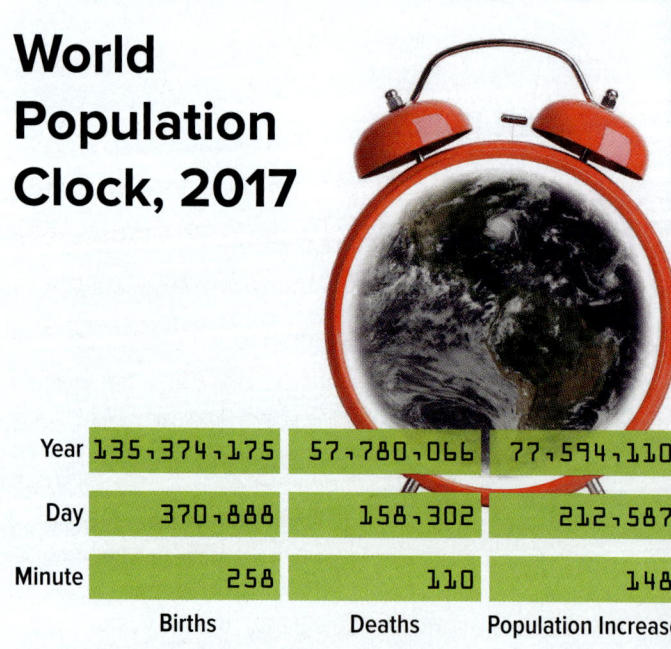

World Population Clock, 2017

	Births	Deaths	Population Increase
Year	135,374,175	57,780,066	77,594,110
Day	370,888	158,302	212,587
Minute	258	110	148

Source: U.S. Census Bureau 2017a. Photos: (clock): ©Dimedrol68/Shutterstock.com RF; (Earth): NOAA/NASA GOES Project

county, state, or, most often, a nation—although they could choose any group with a specified population boundary. They then gather data about that group over some specified period of time, usually per year, to see how many new members join and how many existing members leave. New arrivals come via birth and immigration, while departures occur through death and emigration. Demographers can then use their results to show how a population changes from one point in time to another or to contrast differences between populations.

BIRTH

Births are the primary means by which a population replaces its members from one generation to the next. Yet the likelihood of each of our births was shaped by population dynamics above and beyond the desires of our biological parents. The rate at which women give birth varies significantly over time and place. To better understand these patterns—whether studying England in the Middle Ages, the United States in the late 19th century, or Afghanistan today—demographers analyze trends in **fertility,** the number of children born in a given period of time. The two primary measures they use to do so are the crude birthrate and the total fertility rate.

A population's **crude birthrate** refers to the number of live births per 1,000 people in the population in a given year. It is described as crude because it provides a simple measure, without taking additional factors into consideration, thus allowing for straightforward comparisons between populations. In the United States, for example, the crude birthrate dropped from 23.7 in 1960 to 15.7 in 1985 to 12.4 in 2015, suggesting the long-term possibility of declining population size. Contrast this with the 2015 rates in a variety of other nations, such as Niger at 49.2, Afghanistan at 33.3, China at 12.1, Germany at 9, and a global rate of 19.1 (World Bank 2016m). One variable in isolation, however, is not sufficient to understand the full scope of population change.

A second indicator is a population's **total fertility rate,** which measures the average number of children a woman would have during her lifetime given current birthrates and assuming she survives through her childbearing years. This indicator is, in some ways, easier to understand because we may already be familiar with the notion that "the average family has 2.5 children." To provide a more precise count, rather than tying the indicator to particular family situations that are subject to change, this benchmark measures it per woman regardless of her family status. Doing so provides a more universally comparable statistic. As the accompanying "Total Fertility Rates" graph portrays, especially in the case of Iran and China, rates can vary significantly over time. In the United States

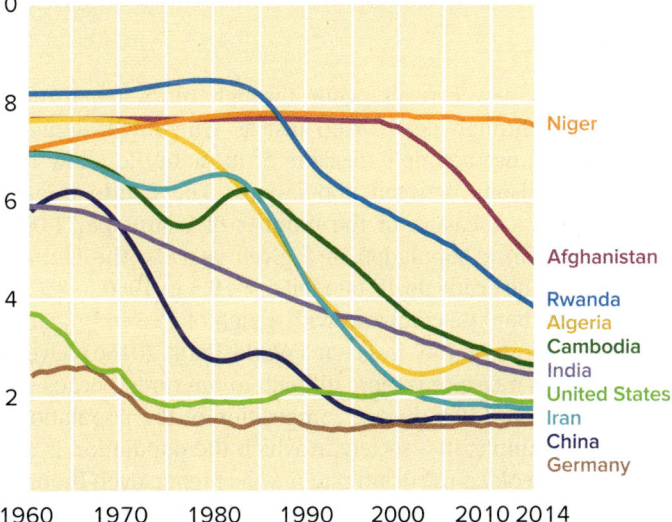

Total Fertility Rates

Average number of births per woman*

*If the woman survives to the end of her childbearing years.
Source: Google 2017a.

in 1960, the average number of children a woman had in her lifetime was 3.65. The rate fell to 1.74 in 1976 before rising again to 1.84 in 2015. This rate varies widely by country, with Niger at 7.57, Somalia at 6.36, Iraq at 4.52, and Bosnia and Herzegovina at 1.25 in 2015 (World Bank 2016n).

To sustain a population over time—apart from the addition of immigrants who join from the outside—the total fertility rate must fall no lower than approximately 2.1, which is known as the **replacement fertility rate.** This is considered the minimum number of children a woman would need to average in her lifetime to reproduce the population in the next generation. The reason for this number is fairly simple. Because men can't have babies, the average woman must have at least two children so that two parents are replaced in the next generation by two children. The number is boosted a bit to account for the fact that not all females survive through their childbearing years and because the ratio between males and females is not exactly 50/50. The global total fertility rate fell from 4.98 in 1960 to the point where the average woman now has 2.45 children in her lifetime. This decline suggests a slowing in the overall population growth rate

Fertility The number of children born in a given period of time.

Crude birthrate The number of live births per 1,000 people in the population in a given year.

Total fertility rate The average number of children a woman would have during her lifetime given current birthrates and assuming she survives through her childbearing years.

Replacement fertility rate The minimum number of children a woman would need to average in her lifetime to reproduce the population in the next generation.

Chapter 14 / Population, Health, and Environment • **347**

and, if trends continue, the possibility of zero population growth, or even global population decline, at some point in the future (World Bank 2016n).

DEATH

Just as new arrivals occur through birth, departures occur through death. And just as with birth, demographers use a simple measure of mortality to allow for comparisons between populations. The **crude death rate** is a measure of the number of deaths per 1,000 people in a population in a given year. In the United States the crude death rate fell from 9.5 in 1960 to 8.2 in 2015. That rate compares with a high of 15.3 in Bulgaria and a low of 1.49 in Qatar (World Bank 2016o). Overall, this measure is more difficult to interpret, because it is influenced by the age composition of the population. For example, in a society in which the population is on average older, the death rate may be higher, even though people are living longer. Because of this, demographers often turn to two additional measures: infant mortality and life expectancy.

A population's **infant mortality rate** measures the number of deaths in infants less than one year old per 1,000 live births per year. It is considered a major indicator of the overall well-being of a population, because it is a reflection of available health care, economic opportunity, and inequality. The fact that the numbers vary substantially also suggests that actions can be taken to improve the likelihood that a baby survives infancy. The rate in the United States in 1960 was 25.9. It fell to 10.6 by 1985 and then to 5.6 in 2015 owing to improved prenatal care and medical innovations. Internationally, the global rate fell from 121.9 in 1960 to 31.7 in 2015. Angola has the top rate at 96, followed by Central African Republic (91.5), Sierra Leone (87.1), and Somalia (85). At the other end of the scale, Luxembourg has the lowest rate at 1.5 followed by Iceland at 1.6 and Finland at 1.9 (World Bank 2016j).

The mortality statistic that is perhaps easiest for us to identify with is **life expectancy,** the projected number of years a person can expect to live based on his or her year of birth. It represents an often unwelcome reminder that factors beyond our individual control influence our life chances. For example, a baby born in Swaziland in 2015 has an average life expectancy of 48.9 years, but one born in Japan at the same time can anticipate living until the age of 83.8. The global average in 2015 was 71.7 years, a significant increase from 1960, when it was 52.5. Again, such differences point to the sociological fact that place matters. The same is true of time. In the case of Cambodia and Rwanda, for example, specific historical events, such as war and ethnic cleansing, can dramatically affect outcomes, as the accompanying "Life Expectancy" graph shows. In the United States life expectancy has increased from 69.8 in 1960 to 78.7 in 2015, owing to such factors as advances in health care, reductions in smoking rates, and increases in exercise and fitness (World Bank 2016p). As life expectancy expands, population size typically increases, because the number of people departing in any given year goes down.

Crude death rate The number of deaths per 1,000 people in a population in a given year.

Infant mortality rate The number of deaths of infants under one year old per 1,000 live births in a given year.

Life expectancy The projected number of years a person can expect to live based on his or her year of birth.

Migration The movement of people from one population group to another.

Immigration When individuals join a population group of which they were not previously a member.

Emigration When members of a population leave that group.

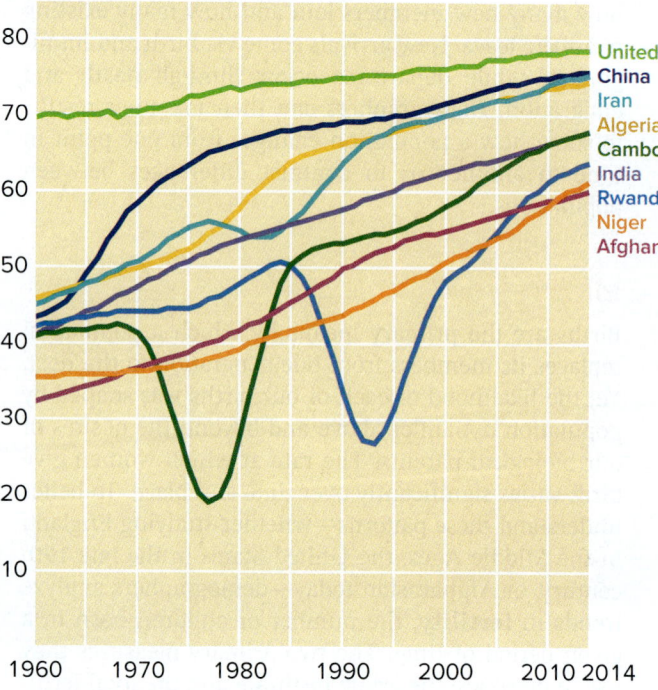

Life Expectancy
The average number of years a newborn is expected to live*

*If current mortality patterns remain the same.

Source: Google 2015b.

MIGRATION

In addition to birth and death, arrivals and departures occur through **migration,** the movement of people from one population group to another. **Immigration** occurs when someone joins a population group of which they were not previously a member. **Emigration** occurs when a member of a population leaves that group. In other words, an immigrant is someone who arrives, and an emigrant is someone who departs.

Reasons for joining or leaving a population group can be varied. Sometimes an immigrant joins a new group because of the opportunities that doing so provides.

This might include new job opportunities, connections with families, freedom of religious expression, or other factors that make migration appealing. Such influences are known as *pull* factors, because they serve as a sort of magnet attracting the immigrant to the new place. At other times people leave locations because they seek to get away from unappealing features in their home country, including violence, oppression, and lack of jobs. These are known as *push* factors, because they encourage the emigrant to leave.

> **SOCTHINK**
>
> What factors may have influenced those in your family to migrate (whether recently or generations ago)? What roles did push and pull play?

As we saw in Chapter 13, immigration is a global phenomenon. From 1950 to 2015, 102 million people departed what the United Nations classifies as less developed regions to more developed regions. As portrayed in the accompanying "Global Migration" map, those regions especially included Latin America and the Caribbean, Asia, and Africa. The nation that saw the greatest net number of departures during that period was Bangladesh with 14.7 million, followed by Mexico with 13.6 million and China with 10.7 million. The country with the most arrivals by far was the United States with 47.4 million, more than all of Europe combined (United Nations 2015b). If we control for the effect of population size by focusing on rates instead of numbers, countries most likely to lose people from 1950 to 2015 included Tonga, Grenada, and Samoa, whereas those with the highest rates of joiners included Kuwait, Qatar, and United Arab Emirates (United Nations 2015c).

In the United States, 13.5 percent of the population is foreign born. As depicted in the "U.S. Foreign-Born Population" graph, 51.1 percent were born in Latin America, and 30.6 percent came from Asia. As indicated in Chapter 13, Mexico leads the way as the source country, accounting for 27 percent, followed by India at 5.5 percent, China at 4.8, and Philippines at 4.6 percent (U.S. Census Bureau 2016j:Table S0201). California is the most common destination for these immigrants, with 10.7 million, or 24.7 percent, of the foreign-born population living there. Texas, New York, and Florida come next, each accounting for approximately 10 percent of the foreign-born population in the United States (U.S. Census Bureau 2016j:Table S0201).

Immigrants in the United States are classified into four major categories by the Department of Homeland Security (Homeland Security 2016). Lawful permanent residents, as the name suggests, are those who have been granted lawful permanent residence in the United States. Sometimes referred to as having received their "Green Card," they can legally get a job, attend public schools or colleges, and even join the military. In 2015, of the 1,051,031 such recipients, 65 percent were either immediate relatives of U.S. citizens, including spouses, children under 21 years old, and parents, or they were family-sponsored immigrants, including adult siblings, adult children and their spouses, and others (U.S. Department of Homeland Security 2016:Table 6).

Naturalized citizens, the second category of immigrants, include foreign citizens who have become U.S. citizens. In 2015 there were 730,259 new naturalized citizens. Asia accounted for 36 percent, making it the most common region of origin. Mexico was the most common country of origin, accounting for 14.5 percent of new naturalized citizens (U.S. Department of Homeland Security 2016:Table 21).

The third immigrant category consists of those seeking residence in the United States because they face persecution, or its imminent threat, in their home country. The two subgroups here are refugees and asylees. Refugees make their request for protection while located outside the United States, and those seeking asylum make the request while located within some U.S. territory. In 2015, 69,920 people living outside the country were granted refugee status, enabling admission into the United States, and another 26,124 were granted asylum status. The three top countries from which refugees came were Burma, Iraq, and Somalia. The leading sources of asylees were

Global Migration, 1950–2015

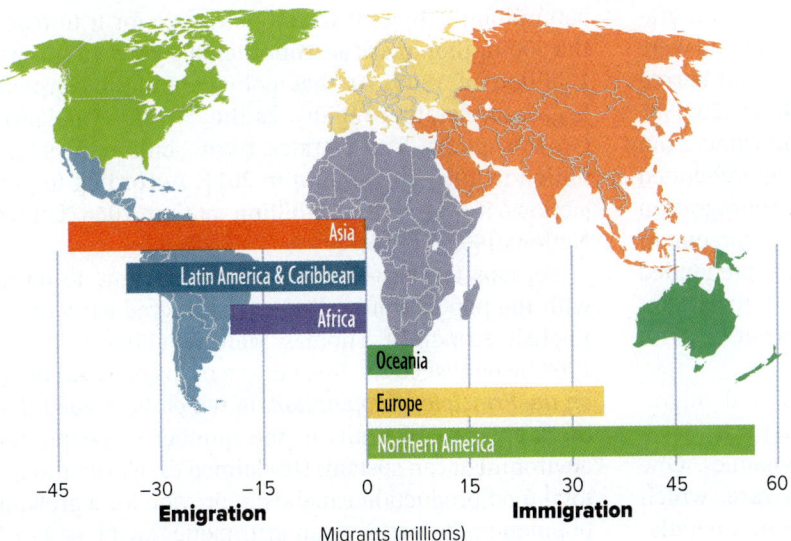

Source: United Nations 2015a.

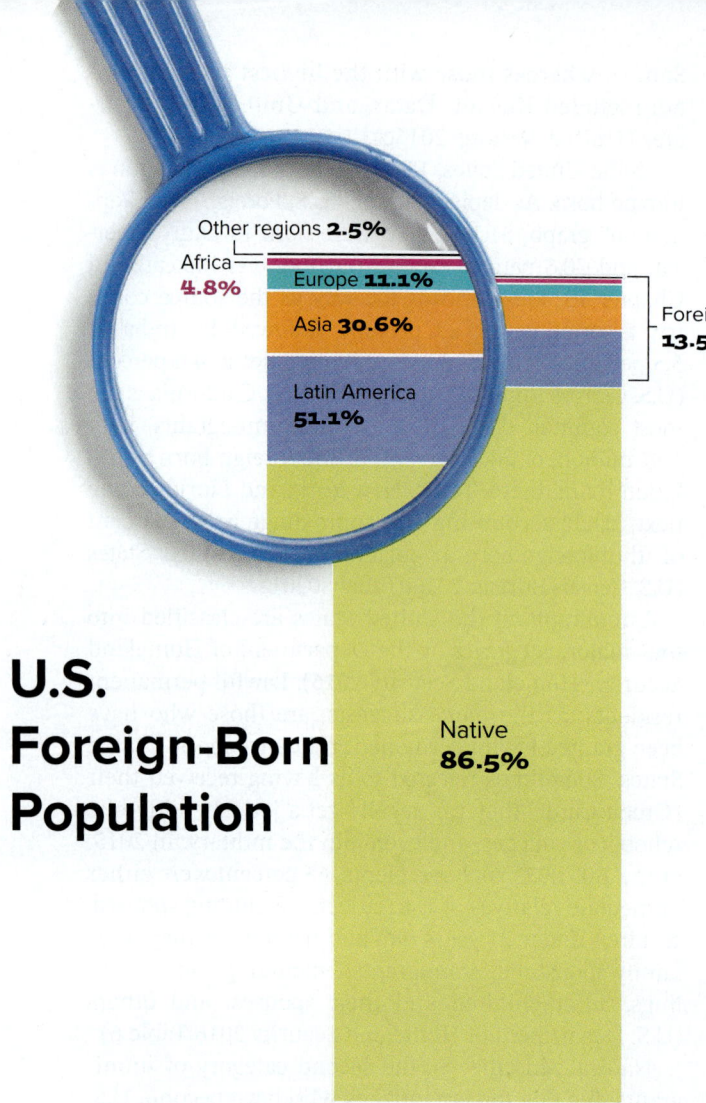

U.S. Foreign-Born Population

- Other regions 2.5%
- Africa 4.8%
- Europe 11.1%
- Asia 30.6%
- Latin America 51.1%
- Foreign 13.5%
- Native 86.5%

Source: U.S. Census Bureau 2016j:Table S0201.

China, El Salvador, and Guatemala (U.S. Department of Homeland Security 2016: Tables 14, 17, 19).

The final category of immigrants includes people entering the United States in violation of U.S. immigration laws. In 2015, a total of 462,388 individuals were apprehended by U.S. immigration officials and barred from entering the United States. Of these, 267,885 arrived from Mexico and another 66,982 came from Guatemala. U.S. Border Patrol agents apprehended 73 percent of these immigrants, and Immigration and Customs Enforcement (ICE) officials apprehended the rest (U.S. Department of Homeland Security 2016: Tables 33, 35).

Growth rate The overall percentage change in a population per year.

By combining data on births, deaths, and migration, we can create a single indicator that provides a more complete picture of population dynamics. One such measure is a population's **growth rate**, which represents the overall percentage change in a population per year. It is important to consider this overall rate in conjunction with the other measures, because the internal population dynamics at any given time can vary. For example, birthrates and death rates might both rise or fall over a given time period, or one might go up while the other goes down, and migration rates can be similarly variable. The growth rate measure provides a snapshot of whether the population as a whole is growing or shrinking. Growth rates can vary significantly from country to country. From 2010 to 2015, Oman grew by an average of 8.5 percent per year followed by Lebanon at 6 percent and Kuwait at 4.8 percent. At the other end of the scale, the population of some nations actually shrunk, including Andorra, which lost 3.6 percent per year, followed by Syria at 2.3 percent and Lithuania at 1.6 percent (United Nations 2015d).

Globally, the world's population increases each year, because the overall birthrate rate exceeds the overall death rate. From 2010 to 2015, the world's population grew an average of 1.2 percent per year. This rate represents a decline from the 2.1 percent annual increase during the late 1960s, but it is still significantly higher than the projected annual rate of 0.1 percent by the year 2100. In other words, even though the population will continue to rise by several billion over the next several decades, projections show a substantial decline in the rate of the overall population increase (United Nations 2015d). This prediction of a leveling off of total population after generations of growth is consistent with the population model known as the demographic transition.

DEMOGRAPHIC TRANSITION

The most defining characteristic of population dynamics in the past 100 years or so is its explosive growth. Throughout most of human history, global population levels were relatively stable. The world's total population 2,000 years ago was approximately 300 million people. It took 1,500 years for it to reach the 500-million mark and another 300 years to surpass 1 billion in 1804. At that point, population growth began accelerating rapidly, as the "World Population Growth" graph demonstrates, from 2 billion in 1927, 3 billion in 1960, to 7 billion in 2011. According to projections, it will top the 10-billion mark in 2056 (United Nations 1999, 2015e).

Perhaps the best-known attempt to come to terms with the population explosion was offered early on by English economist Thomas Malthus (1766–1834). In 1798 he published the first edition of his book *An Essay on the Principle of Population*, in which he argued that there are natural limits to the number of people the environment can sustain. He claimed that, even though total food production expands to provide for a growing population, it does so at an arithmetic rate ($1 \to 2 \to 3 \to 4 \to 5$). The problem is that population grows at a geometric rate (1 → 2 → 4 → 8 → 16). Ultimately, population will grow so fast there won't be sufficient land to provide enough food for everyone. Crises would inevitably occur—including poverty, famine, disease, and war—and people would die as a result, reducing the population size to a more sustainable level.

For Malthus, history is a never-ending struggle over resources in which people attempt to escape want, a battle that those who control resources are more likely to win. As a result, the burden of this misery falls more heavily on the poor. Though he did argue that people could and should exercise moral restraint to rein in population growth by delaying marriage and practicing celibacy, ultimately, Malthus's emphasis was on control of population through the increased mortality rates that result from crises over resources (Malthus 1878).

An alternative, and somewhat less dismal, model of population change is known as the **demographic transition**. According to this model, as societies transform from preindustrial to postindustrial, their population size shifts from small but stable, with high birthrates and death rates, through a period of significant population growth, to large but stable, when both birthrates and death rates are low (Notestein 1945; Thompson 1929, 1948). Unlike Malthus, theorists here do not see elevated death rates through disease and war as inevitable checks on population growth. Instead, they argue that a natural decline in fertility rates occurs owing to technological, social, and economic changes. In basic terms, they portray the transition of a population with large families but short life spans to one with small families and long life spans as virtually inevitable (Bongaarts 2009; Kirk 1996; Myrskylä, Kohler, and Billari 2009). This transition has four primary stages.

Stage 1: Preindustrial Society This is the stage humans occupied throughout most of our history. As is evident in the accompanying "World Population Growth" graph, global population size was steady for a very long time. In terms of demographic factors, nations at this stage are characterized by high fertility rates and high death rates. The economies of such nations are primarily agricultural, and more children means more workers to produce the food necessary for survival. Because infant and child mortality rates are high in this stage, having more children ensures that some will make it to adulthood. Life expectancy in such nations tends to be short. To provide a visual representation of this distribution, demographers use population pyramids to show the ratio of the population by both age groupings (usually in 5-year increments) and sex. As the accompanying "Population Pyramids" graphs portray, pyramids for nations at this stage tend to have a wide base, indicating a large percentage of children in the population, and to narrow quickly at the top, showing the relatively small percentage of those who are elderly.

> **Demographic transition** As societies transform from preindustrial to postindustrial, their population size shifts from small but stable with high birthrates and death rates, through a period of significant population growth, to large but stable, when both birthrates and death rates are low.

Stage 2: Early Industrial Society In this stage, death rates fall while birthrates remain high. More babies survive infancy and additional children make it

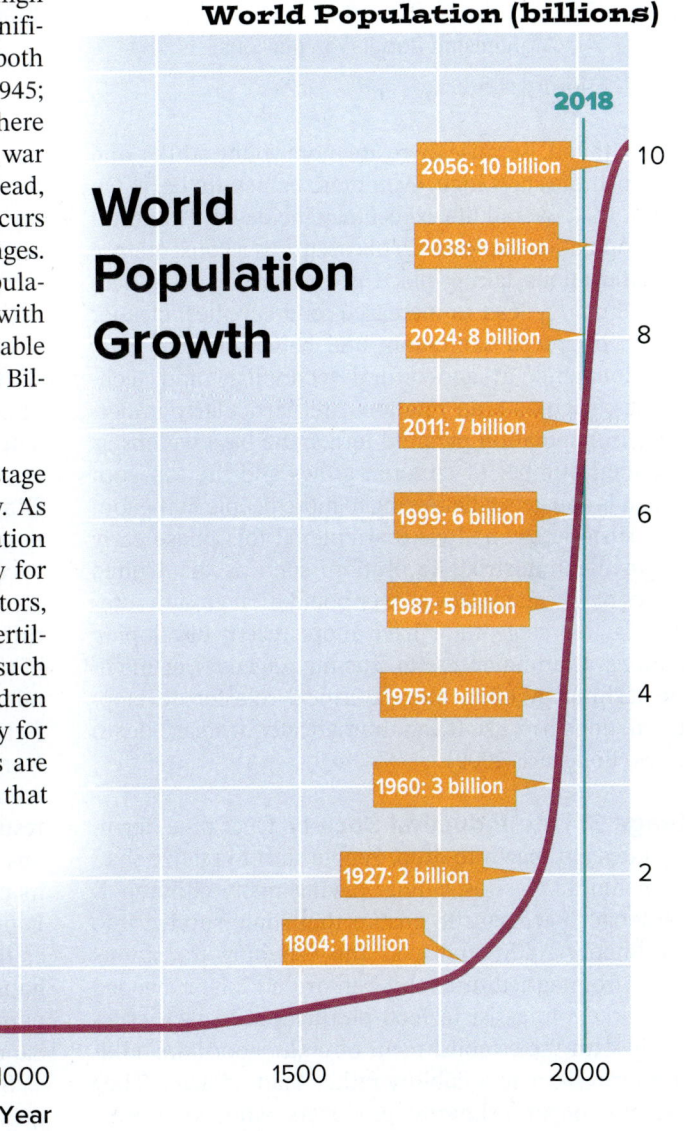

Source: United Nations 1999, 2015e.

Population Pyramids

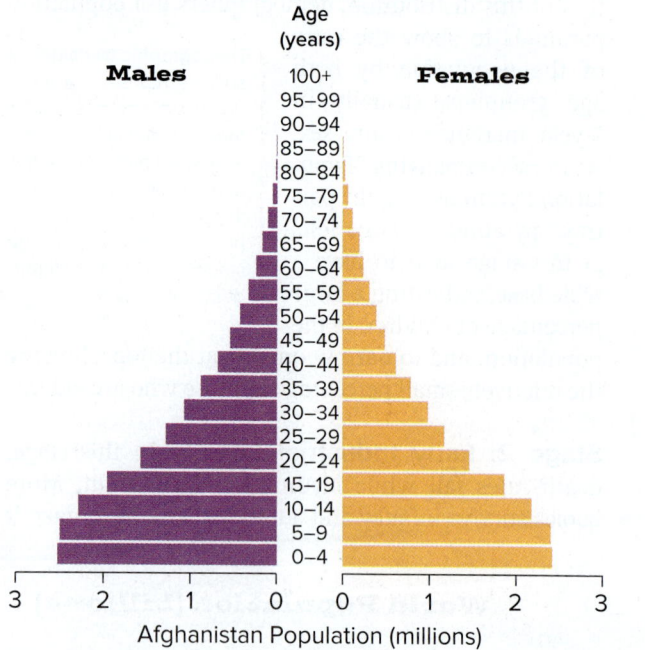
Afghanistan Population (millions)
Source: United Nations 2015f.

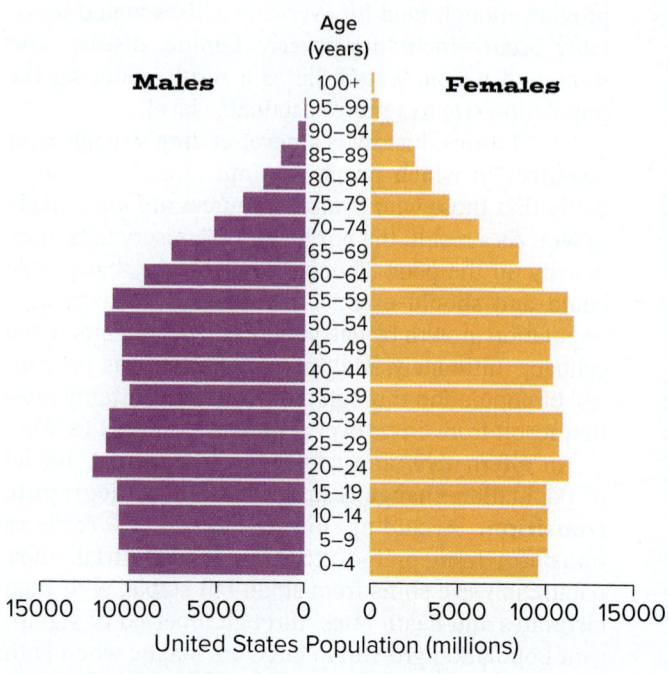
United States Population (millions)

to adulthood. Because there are more young adults, and the birthrate stays high, even more babies are born. On top of that, overall life expectancy increases. The result is a population explosion. This occurs as a consequence of innovations taking place in the society. Advances in technology lead to increased food supplies, cleaner water, improved sanitation, and better medical care. Developments in agricultural technology and techniques, such as crop rotation, are particularly important. In population pyramid terms, the base widens as the total number of children grows and the top both expands and gets taller owing to more people living longer. Historically, nations that entered this phase early on in the Industrial Revolution, such as the United States or Germany, saw slower population growth rates during this stage than have more recent developing nations. Gaining access to existing advances in medical technology often plays a critical role for developing nations because it can dramatically decrease death rates (Bongaarts 2009).

Stage 3: Late Industrial Society Over time, fertility rates also begin to drop. People start to realize that, with mortality rates falling, having many children is no longer necessary to ensure that some survive into adulthood. Additionally, as the economy transitions away from agriculture, children are no longer needed as workers to assist in food production. In fact, especially with the establishment of child labor laws, children can become a liability rather than an asset. They are no longer primarily producers who contribute, becoming instead consumers whose needs must be met. Advances in contraception technology facilitate this choice to have fewer children. One effect of declining fertility rates is increased opportunity for women. As they spend less time bearing children, women are freed up to play expanded roles in the public spheres of politics and the economy. Because the adult population is relatively young, without an overwhelming number of children or elderly people to support, the economy often thrives, creating what is sometimes referred to as a demographic dividend (Bongaarts 2009).

Stage 4: Postindustrial Society Eventually the demographic transition is complete and population size becomes stable once again. This occurs because birthrates and death rates both reach low levels. Globally this takes a long time, but within a country the amount of time can vary: longer in early industrializing nations but less time for more recent developing nations. Total fertility rates reached replacement levels in Europe and North America by 1980 and are anticipated to do so in Asia and Latin America by 2020 (Bongaarts 2009). As a result of these changes, the population pyramid develops sides that are more vertical before they angle in to its pinnacle, as portrayed in the accompanying "Global Population Pyramid" graph. According to this theory, as these trends spread it is just a matter of time, perhaps by the end of this century, until we reach a global population peak and stability (Scherbov, Lutz, and Sanderson 2011).

Some demographers have suggested that the demographic transition model needs to be extended to include additional stages to adequately describe recent

Global Population Pyramid

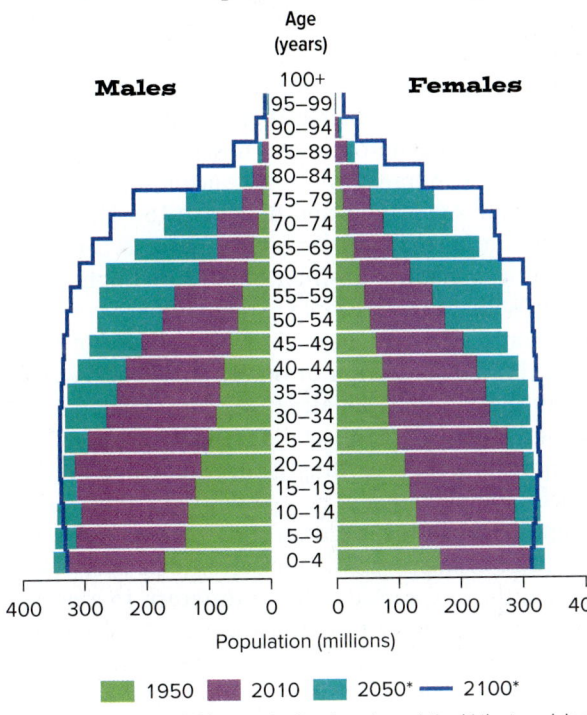

*Numbers for 2050 and 2100 are projections based on existing birthrate and death rate trends.
Source: United Nations 2015f.

Legend: 1950, 2010, 2050*, 2100*

demographic trends. In a possible Stage 5, fertility rates would continue falling below replacement levels, contributing to population decline. This has already occurred in numerous nations, including Germany and China (D. Bloom et al. 2010; Hvistendahl 2010; Myrskylä et al. 2009). In such cases, as the number of people who retire increases relative to the working-age population, questions arise about how to care for the needs of an aging population. In the United States, ongoing political struggles over health care are driven, to some extent, by concerns about the ability to pay for increased Medicare costs caused by the demographic surge in retirees in the coming years (OASDI 2011). Some countries, such as Japan, have begun taking steps to boost fertility by establishing programs, such as extended paid maternity leave and subsidized day care, that encourage people to have more children (Suzuki 2009).

? Did You Know?

... Chinese officials instituted a one-child policy in 1979 and claim their one-child policy reduced the current population by 400 million. Demographers counter that total fertility rates would have fallen substantially even without the policy, as they have in other nations.

Sources: Cai 2010; Hvistendahl 2010.

In recent years, some of these nations with below-replacement birthrates have experienced a fertility rebound, a possible Stage 6 of the demographic transition model. Demographers suggest that this is most likely to occur in countries with the highest scores on the United Nations Human Development Index (HDI). As we saw in the "Measuring Global Inequality" graph in the Chapter 11, this index ranges from 0 to 1 and is based on three societal dimensions, including health, education, and income. Countries with an HDI score of greater than 0.86, such as Norway, Netherlands, and the United States, are most likely to experience this rebound (Myrskylä et al. 2009; United Nations Development Programme 2015). Parents in such countries can worry less about having sufficient individual and collective resources to provide for the needs of their children.

SOC THINK

What factors do you think might explain the fertility rebound in countries with high HDI scores?

Studying population dynamics is important because the world into which we are born is not of our own choosing, yet it shapes our life chances. When we were born, how long we live, and our likelihood for migration are all part of larger social trends. Understanding the nature and direction of these patterns can empower us to create new pathways in hopes of a better future. Such informed innovation has contributed to advances in health care, education, and environmental protection, substantially improving the life chances of people all around the world.

>> Sociological Perspectives on Health and Illness

To understand health, we cannot focus on biology alone. We also must think beyond medicine, doctors, and hospitals. We must consider relationships, contexts, and the significance and impact of culture and society. Whether we are considered "healthy" or "ill" is not our decision alone to make. Family, friends, coworkers, physicians, and others all shape how we perceive the state of our health. A sociological understanding must take into account how society defines health and illness, what the consequences of such definitions are, and how social position and access to resources shape health outcomes.

CULTURE, SOCIETY, AND HEALTH

Our conceptions of what it means to be healthy vary over time and across cultures. In an attempt to provide a more universally applicable definition, the World

©LWA/Dann Tardif/Blend Images, LLC RF

Health Organization (WHO), in the preamble to its constitution, defined health as a "state of complete physical, mental, and social well-being, and not merely the absence of disease and infirmity" (World Health Organization 1948). Based on this absolute standard, most of us are probably not fully healthy most of the time. In practice, people fall somewhere along a continuum between this ideal at one extreme and death on the other.

Researchers have shown that diseases and disorders are rooted in the shared meanings of particular cultures. The term **culture-bound syndrome** refers to a disease or illness that cannot be understood apart from some specific social context. This means that there is something particular about the culture—how it is organized, what it believes, what is expected of members—that contributes to that malady (Burns 2013; Romans et al. 2012; Wedge 2012). Examples include amok in Malaysia, in which a knife- or spear-wielding male goes on a seemingly random and totally unanticipated rampage followed by amnesia about doing so (Carr and Tan 1976; Saint Martin 1999; Spores 1988; Williamson 2007). Another is koro, in countries such as China, India, and Malaysia, in which men come to believe their penis is shrinking and that after it fully retracts into their body, they will die (Garlipp 2008; Kumar et al. 2014).

Culture-bound syndrome A disease or illness that cannot be understood apart from some specific social context.

In our globalized world, the lines between societies have become increasingly permeable so that culture-bound syndromes can now cross boundaries, where they can transform local conceptions of disease (Ventriglio, Ayonrinde, and Bhugra 2016). This seems to have occurred with anorexia nervosa. Formally named as a medical disorder in 1873 by English physician William Gull, people in the United States now commonly associate anorexia with the fear of being fat and a misperception of one's actual body weight. But in the 1990s, psychiatrist Sing Lee wondered why he didn't see such manifestations in Hong Kong. Cases of anorexia were exceedingly rare, and when they did appear, the patients did not exhibit the same kinds of symptoms as in the West. Most did not express a fear of fatness or misperceive themselves to be overweight. In fact, they expressed a desire to return to a normal body weight. They did not obsess over food portions or suppress a strong desire to eat. They weren't enamored with pop culture visions of thinness or hooked on diet books or exercise fads. They just didn't feel hungry or said they had an upset stomach (Lee 1991; Lee, Chiu, and Chen 1989; Lee, Ho, and Hsu 1993; Watters 2010a, 2010b).

This Chinese manifestation of anorexia changed quickly, however, after 14-year-old Charlene Hsu Chi-Ying passed out and died on a busy street in downtown Hong Kong on her way home from school in 1994. She weighed 75 pounds. In an effort to make sense of what had happened, the media covering her death paid significant attention to the way anorexia nervosa was diagnosed in the West, including its emphasis on the fear of fatness and body misperception. Not long after Charlene's death, the number of Lee's patients who exhibited the symptoms more typical of the Western diagnosis rose dramatically. By the late 1990s, as many as 3 to 10 percent of Hong Kong's young women exhibited symptoms and, by 2007, 90 percent of Lee's anorexia patients reported a fear of getting fat (Watters 2010a, 2010b). Lee attributes this shift largely to the dominant power the Western medical model has attained in matters of health and illness. The legitimacy of medical books and diagnostic manuals overwhelms alternative conceptions of health and illness. In turn, such models affect what doctors perceive and what patients describe (Watters 2010a).

The fact that culture affects how anorexia nervosa presents itself doesn't make the disease any less real; people die from it. But what it does suggest is that diseases and disorders get manifested, identified, and treated through the lenses culture provides. As noted in the "Culture and Society" section of Chapter 3, we never interact with nature directly. Culture always

Did You Know?

...The average American adult woman wears a Misses size 16-18 or its equivalent, a Women's Plus size 20W. Her average waist is 39.7 inches.

Source: Christel and Dunn 2016. *Photo:* ©Alberto Pellaschiar/AP Images

When people cross the line into illness, they take on what sociologists call the **sick role,** a form of legitimate deviance in which the person who becomes ill has a corresponding set of rights and responsibilities associated with that status. A sick person can violate the norms that regularly guide their everyday actions, whether as student, parent, or employee. They have a right to expect that others will not blame them for failure to conduct their usual responsibilities and that they will be given space and time to recover. That does not mean they are exempt from social obligations. Those who are deemed legitimately sick have a responsibility to get better as soon as possible, which includes seeking competent professional care. Failure to do so can result in negative sanctions (Parsons 1951, 1975). In fact, especially in the context of competitive work environments, we often look down on those who seem to get sick too easily or frequently, suspecting that they are either lazy or weak. Such attitudes present significant difficulties for those facing chronic health problems.

> **Sick role** A form of legitimate deviance in which the person who becomes ill has a corresponding set of rights and responsibilities associated with that status.

SOC THINK

What factors shape your likelihood of doing all you can to avoid "being sick"? How might the power others have over you influence your actions? What positions do they occupy relative to you?

Physicians and nurses have the power to label people as healthy or sick and, thus, to function as gatekeepers for the sick role. For example, instructors often require

mediates, even when it comes to how we understand our bodies. Psychological or physical distress gets manifested through culture-specific symptoms recognized as available within a culture (Watters 2010a). We have no choice but to express things through culture, but we should remember that culture not only enables us to see—and Western medicine's way of seeing has produced amazing results—it also limits what we can see, or give voice to, when it comes to health and illness.

ILLNESS AND SOCIAL ORDER

From a functionalist perspective, social order is paramount and illness represents a threat to the normal processes of society. To maintain order, we place social pressure on people to continue to perform their normal roles even when they feel sick. As a result, we debate about what it means to be "sick enough" to be considered truly ill. At what point, for example, do we stay home from school or work due to illness, and who gets to decide? All of us have likely faced this dilemma, sometimes dragging ourselves out of bed and going anyway because we felt we needed to be there, whether for the sake of ourselves or for others.

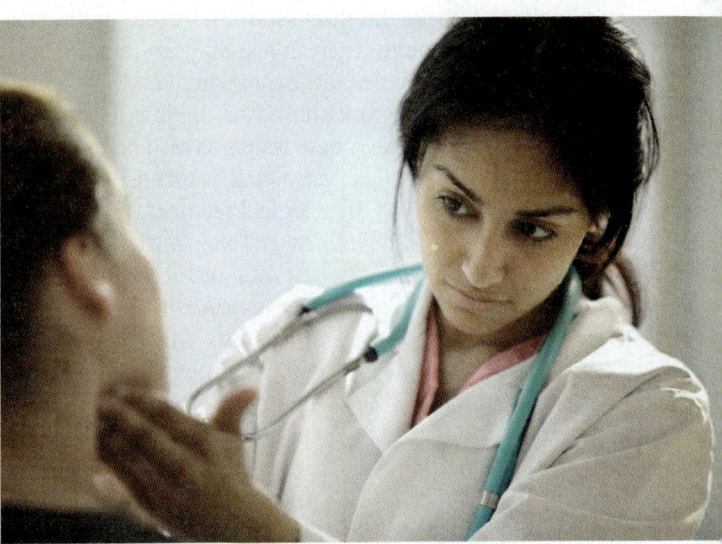

©Blend Images LLC/Getty Images RF

students to get a note from a health care professional to verify a claim of illness as a legitimate excuse for missing a paper or an exam. The ill person becomes dependent on the doctor or nurse, because physicians and nurses control the resources that patients need, whether it be a note for a professor or a prescription for medication. We look to such professionals to solve our health care needs, trusting that they have sufficient expertise and experience to diagnose and treat our problems.

POWER, RESOURCES, AND HEALTH

The faith we place in physicians to heal what ails us has helped them attain significant levels of prestige and power. Over time, the jurisdiction over which medical professionals have authority has expanded. Theorists use the phrase "medicalization of society," taking this extension of medical legitimacy into new realms thus granting medical professional greater power (Conrad 2007; Zola 1972, 1983).

The Medicalization of Society The process of **medicalization** involves redefining new areas of social life as the legitimate domain for medical expertise by converting them into treatable medical conditions. This includes aspects we used to take for granted as involving natural human processes, such as childbirth, aging, menopause, sex, diet, mental health, addictions, sexuality, and even parenting and childhood (Cacchioni and Tiefer 2012; Chavigny 2014; Fainzang 2013; Francis 2012; Shaw 2013). We accept, and even encourage, the expansion of the boundaries of medicine because we hope that these experts can provide factual and effective cures to complex human problems, as they have to various infectious diseases.

This transference of authority to medical professionals is not without consequences. The presumed expertise of these specialists—and the specialized discourse that goes with it—makes it more difficult for common people to join in the discussion and exert their influence, even though their lives may be significantly affected by decisions the experts make. In addition, the natural science orientation of this model makes it more difficult to view these issues as also being shaped by social, cultural, or psychological factors (J. Davis 2006; Starr 1982; Watters 2010a).

As medical professionals expand their authority, they also engage in boundary maintenance to ensure that only those with appropriate knowledge and training are certified to practice medicine. One of the effects historically was to place some practitioners, such as chiropractors and nurse-midwives, outside the domain of legitimate medicine. Despite the fact that midwives first brought professionalism to child delivery, they have been portrayed by doctors as having invaded the "legitimate" field of obstetrics, in both the United States and Mexico. Nurse-midwives have sought licensing as a way to achieve professional respectability, but physicians continue to exert power to ensure that midwifery remains a subordinate occupation (Scharnberg 2007; Shaw 2013).

Inequities in Health Care Another serious concern regarding power and resources in the context of contemporary medicine involves the glaring inequities that exist in health care. In 1978, at the International Conference on Primary Health Care, convened by WHO and UNICEF, global health leaders reaffirmed their commitment to health as "a fundamental human right" in the Alma-Ata Declaration. In doing so, they called on all nations to provide sufficient primary health care for all people of the world, a goal that in many respects remains aspirational (Gillam 2008; Hall and Taylor 2003). Around the world, poor areas tend to be underserved because medical services concentrate where the wealth is. The United States, for example, has 122.7 skilled health care professionals, including physicians, nurses, and midwives, per 10,000 people, whereas other nations have much lower rates, such as Sierra Leone with 2.3 per 10,000, Niger with 1.6, Somalia with 1.5, and Guinea with 1.4 (World Health Organization 2016a).

The supply of health care in poorer countries is further reduced by what is referred to as **brain drain**—the

---

Medicalization The process of redefining new areas of social life as the legitimate domain for medical expertise by converting them into treatable medical conditions.

Brain drain The immigration to the United States and other industrialized nations of skilled workers, professionals, and technicians who are needed in their home countries.

Personal Sociology

Health Care Fortunes

While working on revisions for this chapter, my retina detached, and I went blind in one eye. Fortunately, I had access to experts, especially my retina specialist Dr. Heilskov, all of whom provided me with the best possible advice and care. Three operations later, my sight has largely been restored. And (again) fortunately, I had health insurance to help pay those sizable medical bills. Had I been in the position of the majority of the world's population—lacking access to such care and coverage—I would have remained blind in that eye for life. To me, this ordeal affirmed one of the most basic lessons of sociology: The social positions we occupy shape our life chances. In what ways has your life been shaped by access, or lack thereof, to medical care?

Going GLOBAL

Infant Mortality Rates in Selected Countries

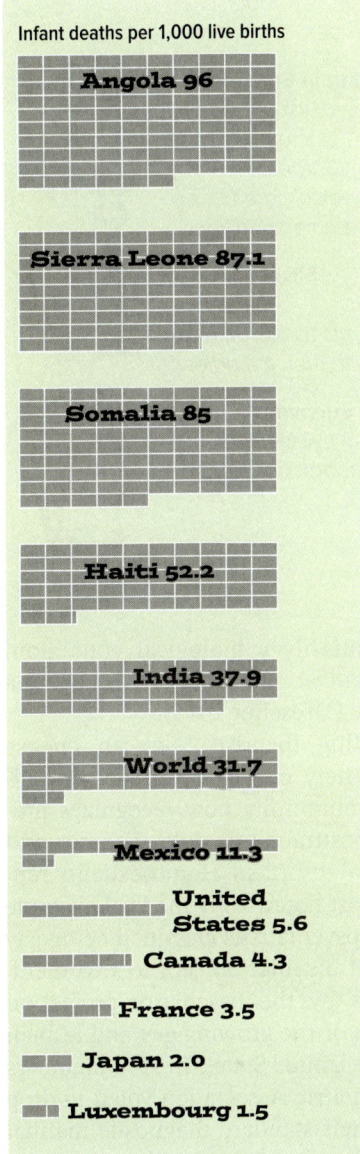

Infant deaths per 1,000 live births
- Angola 96
- Sierra Leone 87.1
- Somalia 85
- Haiti 52.2
- India 37.9
- World 31.7
- Mexico 11.3
- United States 5.6
- Canada 4.3
- France 3.5
- Japan 2.0
- Luxembourg 1.5

Source: World Bank 2016j.

industrialized nations enhance their quality of life at the expense of developing countries (Firsing 2016; List 2009).

Such inequities in health care have clear life-and-death consequences. For example, as the "Infant Mortality Rates" graph depicts, infant mortality rates in developing countries, such as Angola, Sierra Leone, and Somalia, differ dramatically from those in industrialized nations, such as Luxembourg, Japan, and France. Such differences reflect unequal distribution of health care resources based on the wealth or poverty of various nations as seen, for example, in prenatal nutrition, delivery procedures, and infant screening measures. An additional way that developing countries suffer the consequences of health care inequality is in reduced life expectancy. Average life expectancy in sub-Saharan African nations is 59 compared to 81 in European Union nations. By comparison, in the United States it is 79 years (World Bank 2016j, 2016p).

Labeling and Power Sometimes the power to label and the power to oppress go hand in hand. A historical example illustrates perhaps the ultimate extreme in labeling social behavior as a sickness. As enslavement of Africans in the United States came under increasing attack in the 19th century, medical authorities provided new rationalizations for the oppressive practice. Noted physicians published articles stating that the skin color of Africans deviated from "healthy" white skin coloring because Africans suffered from congenital leprosy. Moreover, physicians classified the continuing efforts of enslaved Africans to escape from their White masters as an example of the "disease" of drapetomania (or "crazy runaways"). In 1851 the prestigious *New Orleans Medical and Surgical Journal* suggested that the remedy for this "disease" was to treat slaves kindly, as one might treat children. Apparently, these medical authorities would not entertain the view that it was healthy and sane to flee slavery or join in a slave revolt (Szasz 1971).

When AIDS first emerged on the national stage, being labeled "HIV positive" functioned as a master status that overshadowed other aspects of a person's life, creating a stigma for the person diagnosed. Ignorance about its underlying biological causes and fear of catching the deadly disease only made things worse. The fact that a significant proportion of AIDS patients were homosexuals or drug users led critics to say that those who came down with the disease got what they deserved. People wanted to isolate and quarantine patients to keep the disease from spreading (France 2016; Shilts 1987). As a result, a person with AIDS had to deal not only with the serious medical consequences of the disease, but also with the distressing social consequences of the label.

immigration to the United States and other industrialized nations of skilled workers, professionals, and technicians who are needed in their home countries. As part of this brain drain, physicians, nurses, and other health care professionals have come to the United States from developing countries such as India, Pakistan, and various African states. Their emigration represents yet another way in which the world's core

Over time, as medical knowledge increased and social perceptions changed, the stigma associated with AIDS decreased. Today, drugs can reduce the likelihood that the disease progresses from the initial stage of HIV infection to the stage known as AIDS, in which the immune system is badly compromised (Hardin 2012). People's perceptions about its symbolic significance has also shifted. This happened in part due to public figures whose very existence called into question the stereotypes of AIDS patients, such as NBA superstar Magic Johnson and Ryan White, a 13-year-old with hemophilia who contracted HIV as a result of a blood transfusion. Attitudes also changed as a result of grassroots activists who worked hard to change the narrative, education campaigns in schools, a change in media coverage, and an overall shift in cultural values regarding homosexuality (France 2016; Shilts 1987). Our perceptions shape the labels we use to define others. As we learned with the Thomas theorem, as those perception change, the ways we respond also change. AIDS represents a case where its

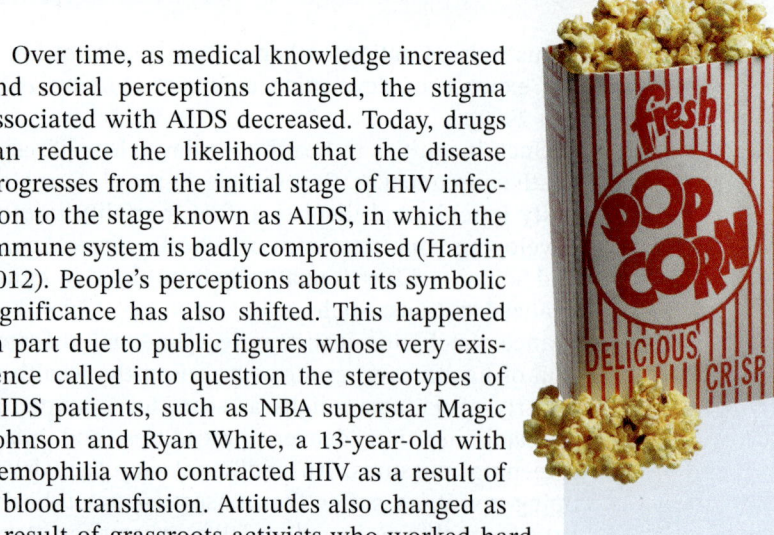

Movies on HEALTH AND MEDICINE

The Diving Bell and the Butterfly
A man suddenly becomes completely paralyzed.

Life, Animated
A story of sidekicks, heroes, and autism.

Living in Emergency
Volunteers for Doctors Without Borders provide medical care under extreme conditions.

Silver Linings Playbook
Two patients try to come to terms with their maladies.

How to Survive a Plague
Grassroots activists transform our approach to AIDS.

5

Ryan White's public battle with AIDS changed perceptions regarding the disease. ©Bettmann/Contributor/Getty Images

medicalization as primarily a biological contagion, along with its humanization, reduced the stigma attached to the disease (Drescher 2015).

According to labeling theorists, we can choose whether to view a variety of life experiences as illnesses. The medical community now recognizes premenstrual syndrome, posttraumatic stress disorder, and hyperactivity as medical disorders. Homosexuality represents perhaps the most noteworthy medical example of labeling. For years, psychiatrists classified being gay or lesbian as a mental disorder subject to treatment. This official diagnosis by the psychiatry profession became an early target of the growing gay and lesbian rights movement in the United States. In 1974 members of the American Psychiatric Association voted to drop homosexuality from their standard diagnostic manual on mental disorders (Drescher 2015).

NEGOTIATING CURES

In practice, we seek to strike a balance between the authority of the physician and the agency of the patient. Physicians use cues to reinforce their prestige and power. According to medical sociologist Brenda Beagan (2001, 2003), and consistent with Goffman's dramaturgical approach, the technical language students learn in medical school becomes the basis for the script they follow as novice physicians. The familiar white coat and stethoscope is their costume—one that helps them appear confident and professional at the same time that it identifies them as doctors to patients and other staff members. Beagan found that many medical students struggle to project the appearance of competence they think their role demands, but over time most become accustomed to expecting respect and deference.

> It is a lot harder to keep people well than it is to just get them over a sickness.
>
> DeForest Clinton Jarvis

Patients, however, are not passive. Active involvement in health care can have positive or negative consequences. Sometimes, patients play an active role in health care by choosing not to follow a physician's advice. For example, some patients stop taking medications long before they should. Some decrease or increase the dosage on purpose (because they think they know better what they need), and others never even fill their prescriptions. Such noncompliance results in part from the prevalence of self-medication in our society; many people are accustomed to self-diagnosis and self-treatment.

Patients' active involvement in their health care can have very positive consequences. Some patients consult books, magazines, and websites about preventive health care techniques, attempt to maintain a healthful and nutritious diet, carefully monitor any side effects of medication, and adjust the dosage based on perceived side effects. Recognizing this change, pharmaceutical firms are advertising their prescription drugs directly to potential customers. For their part, medical professionals are understandably suspicious of these new sources of information. Studies, including one published in the *Journal of the American Medical Association*, found that health information on the Internet can be incomplete and inaccurate, even on the best sites. Nevertheless, there is little doubt that Internet research is transforming patient–physician encounters (Adams and de Bont 2007; Arora et al. 2008; Fox and Duggan 2013).

influence our access to material, social, and cultural resources. Having enough money to afford health insurance or to purchase foods for a healthy diet; having social connections that open doors in times of crisis or concern; having knowledge about where to get medical information, what to ask the doctor, and what foods to consume are all examples of how our social position shapes our health care outcomes. And yet we tend to minimize the consequences of such differences when considering health care solutions.

To describe how widespread a disease is and how fast it is spreading, social epidemiologists report on rates of prevalence and incidence. **Prevalence** refers to the *total* number of cases of a specific disorder that exist at a given time. At the end of 2014, for example, a total of 955,081 people in the United States were living with a diagnosed HIV infection, and of these cases a total of 521,002 people had advanced to the AIDS stage of the disease (Centers for Disease Control and Prevention 2016c:Tables 18a, 21a). Rather than counting all the cases of a disease in a population, **incidence** refers only to the number of *new* cases of a specific disorder that occur within a given population during a specified period of time,

> **Social epidemiology** The study of the role social factors play in the development and distribution of disease throughout the population.
>
> **Prevalence** The total number of cases of a specific disorder that exist at a given time.
>
> **Incidence** The number of new cases of a specific disorder that occur within a given population during a stated period.

>> Social Epidemiology

By looking at patterns of health and illness throughout society, we can better understand which factors are at work in shaping health outcomes. **Social epidemiology** investigates the role social factors play in the development and distribution of disease throughout the population. The social positions we occupy shape our chances for a healthy life. Analysis of biological factors alone is insufficient. We must also consider the impact factors such as social class, ethnicity, race, and gender have on our overall health. Statuses such as these

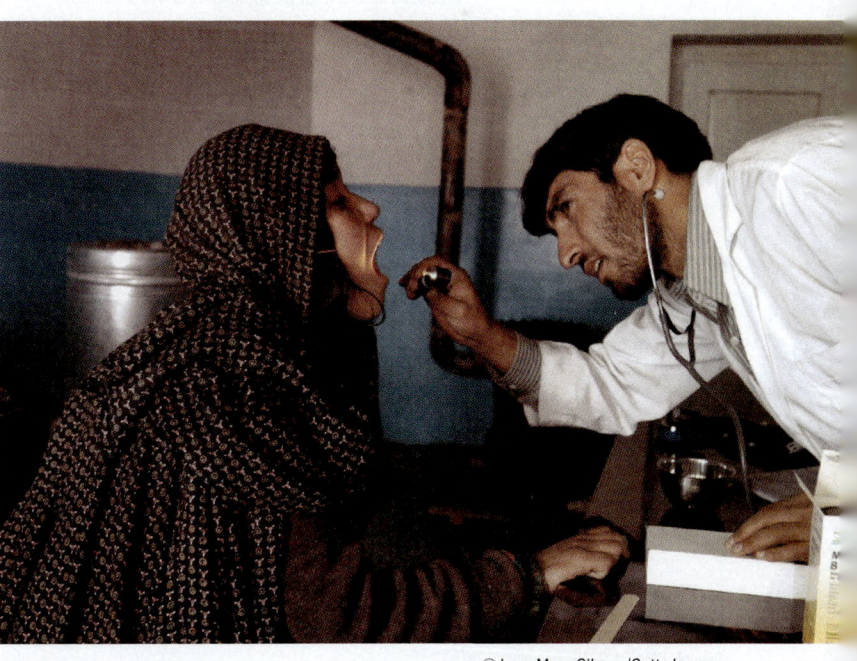

©Jean-Marc Giboux/Getty Images

usually a year. For example, 39,513 people were newly diagnosed with HIV infection in 2015 in the United States and 18,303 were people newly diagnosed with AIDS (Centers for Disease Control and Prevention 2016c:Tables 1a, 2a). Globally, in 2015, the prevalence of HIV infections amounted to an estimated 36.7 million people around the world living with the disease, as represented in the accompanying "HIV Prevalence and Mortality" graph. When it comes to incidence, there were an estimated 2.1 million new HIV cases globally in 2015 (UNAIDS 2016).

Morbidity rate The occurrences of illness in a given population over some period of time.

Mortality rate The incidence of death in a given population over some period of time.

To better understand and measure the prevalence and incidence of disease within and between cultures, researchers rely on rates to provide standardized measures. Two indicators they use to do so include morbidity and mortality. **Morbidity rates** measure the occurrences of illness in a given population over some period of time. These rates can be calculated for both prevalence and incidence. For example, when considering prevalence of HIV infections, the HIV morbidity rate is 299.5 per 100,000 people in the United States at the end of 2014. When considering incidence, the morbidity rate was 12.3 new HIV diagnoses per 100,000 people in 2015 (Centers for Disease Control and Prevention 2016c: Tables 1a, 18a). Globally, by the end of 2015, an estimated 46 percent of HIV-infected patients around the world were receiving antiretroviral therapy compared to 22.5 percent in 2010 (UNAIDS 2016).

Whereas morbidity focuses on illness, mortality deals with death. The **mortality rate** refers to the incidence of death in a given population over some period of time. In 2014, 12,333 people in the United States who had been diagnosed with AIDS died, a rate of 3.9 per 100,000 people in the population. The morbidity and mortality rates for both HIV and AIDS in the United States have declined in recent years (Centers for Disease Control and Prevention 2016c:Table 13a). Globally, as depicted in the "HIV Prevalence and Mortality" graph, 1.1 million AIDS-related deaths occurred in 2015, and the distribution of those deaths varied significantly by region (UNAIDS 2016).

SOCIAL CLASS

Morbidity and mortality rates vary significantly based on one's social positions, including factors such as social class, race, ethnicity, gender, and age (Barr 2014; Centers for Disease Control and Prevention 2013). When it comes to social class, for example, studies in the United States and other countries have consistently shown that people in the lower classes have higher rates of mortality and disability than those in higher classes. And studies of educational attainment, an indicator of

Going GLOBAL
HIV Prevalence and Mortality

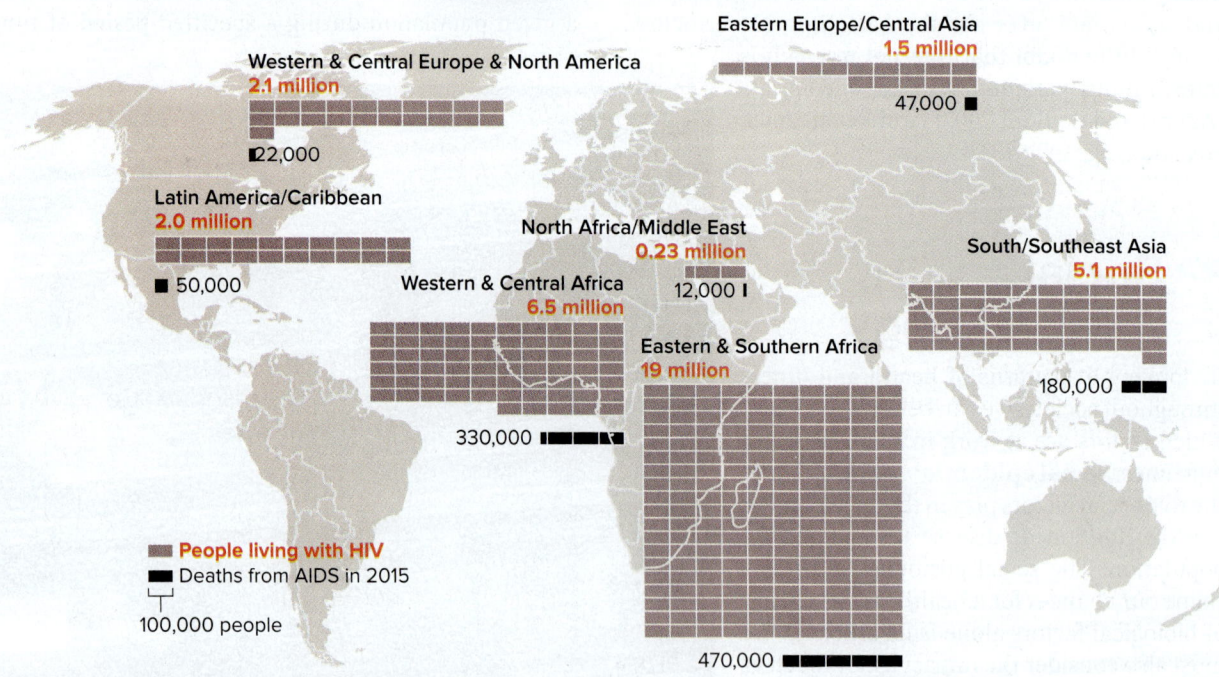

Note: Total number HIV-infected adults and children in 2015, 36.7 million; total number of AIDS-related deaths during 2015, 1.1 million.
Source: UNAIDS 2016.

People without Health Insurance

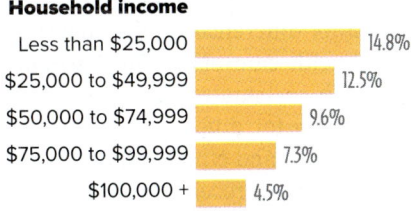

Household income
- Less than $25,000: 14.8%
- $25,000 to $49,999: 12.5%
- $50,000 to $74,999: 9.6%
- $75,000 to $99,999: 7.3%
- $100,000 +: 4.5%

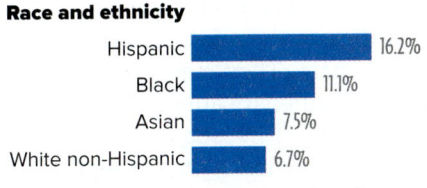

Race and ethnicity
- Hispanic: 16.2%
- Black: 11.1%
- Asian: 7.5%
- White non-Hispanic: 6.7%

Note: Numbers represent the percentage of people without health insurance for the full calendar year.
Source: Barnett and Vornovitsky 2016:Table 5.

Photo: ©UpperCut Images/SuperStock

Did You Know?

...In research looking at how social class operates, sociologist Annette Lareau (2003) found that middle-class parents and children were more likely to engage with physicians, asking questions and questioning diagnoses. Working-class patients were more deferential to the doctor's authority.

---

both income and class, show that those with with more education have significantly lower mortality rates than do those with less (Buckles et al. 2016).

A number of factors appear to influence the effect class has on health. Crowded living conditions, substandard housing, poor diet, and stress all contribute to the ill health of many low-income people in the United States. In certain instances, poor education may lead to a lack of awareness of measures necessary to maintain good health. Financial strains are certainly a major factor in the health problems of less-affluent people.

People who are poor—many of whom belong to racial and ethnic minorities—are less able than others to afford quality medical care, as the accompanying "People Without Health Insurance" graph portrays. Not surprisingly, those with high incomes are significantly more likely to have health insurance, either because they can afford it or because they have jobs that provide it (Barnett and Vornovitsky 2016). The ultimate price to pay for a lack of health insurance is the increased risk of early death.

Income level also affects likely life expectancy. Researchers found that the life expectancy for men in the top 1 percent was 14.6 years longer than men in the bottom 1 percent. For women, those in the top 1 percent lived 10.1 years longer on average. Between 2000 and 2014, life expectancy went up for virtually all income groups, but it went up faster for those nearer the top, so the life expectancy gap between the top and bottom income groups got wider over that time (Chetty et al. 2016).

Coming from the conflict perspective, Karl Marx would have argued that capitalist societies such as the United States care more about maximizing profits than they do about the health and safety of industrial workers. As a result, government agencies in the United States do not take forceful action to regulate conditions in the workplace, and workers suffer many preventable job-related injuries and illnesses. As we will see later in this chapter, research also shows that the lower classes are more vulnerable to environmental pollution, another consequence of capitalist production, than are the affluent, not only where they work but where they live as well.

RACE AND ETHNICITY

The health profiles of many racial and ethnic minorities reflect the social inequality evident in U.S. society. The poor economic and environmental conditions of groups such as African Americans, Hispanics, and Native Americans are manifested in high morbidity and mortality rates for these groups. It is true that some afflictions, such as sickle-cell anemia among African Americans, are influenced by genetics, but in most instances, environmental factors contribute to the differential rates of disease and death.

As noted in the "Population" section earlier in this chapter, infant mortality is regarded as a primary indicator of health care. There is a significant gap in the United States between the infant mortality rates of

Infant Mortality Rates in the United States

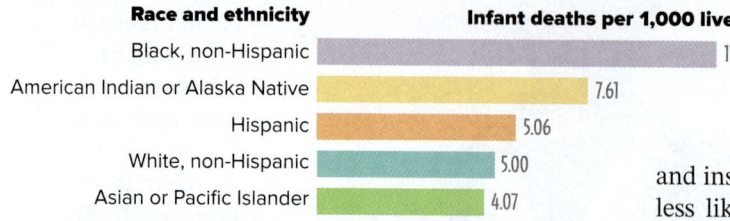

Race and ethnicity	Infant deaths per 1,000 live births
Black, non-Hispanic	11.11
American Indian or Alaska Native	7.61
Hispanic	5.06
White, non-Hispanic	5.00
Asian or Pacific Islander	4.07

Note: Rates represent the number of infant deaths per 1,000 live births.
Source: Mathews, MacDorman, and Thoma 2015.

African Americans and Whites. As the accompanying "Infant Mortality Rates" graph depicts, on average, the rate of infant death is more than twice as high among Blacks. Lack of adequate medical coverage among African Americans, which contributes to low birth weight, plays a major part in that difference (Mathews, MacDorman, and Thoma 2015).

Considering mortality rates, African Americans have higher death rates from heart disease, strokes, pneumonia, and diabetes than do Whites (Kochanek et al. 2016: Table B). Such epidemiological findings are related to the social class effects noted previously—the fact that average income for African Americans is lower than that for Whites. The effect of these factors can be seen in terms of life expectancy. According to statistics from the Centers for Disease Control and Prevention, for babies born in 2014, the life expectancy for non-Hispanic Whites is 78.8 years compared to 75.2 years for non-Hispanic Blacks (National Center for Health Statistics 2016:Table 15).

Curanderismo Latino folk medicine, a form of holistic health care and healing.

The medical establishment is not exempt from institutional discrimination. There is evidence that minorities receive inferior care even when they are insured. Despite having access to care, Blacks, Latinos, and American Indians are treated unequally as a result of differences in the quality of various health care plans. Furthermore, national clinical studies have shown that even allowing for differences in income and insurance coverage, racial and ethnic minorities are less likely than other groups to receive both standard health care and life-saving treatment (Benjamins and Whitman 2013; Cooper et al. 2012; Schroeder 2016).

Mexican Americans and many other Latinos adhere to cultural beliefs that make them less likely to use the established medical system. They may interpret their illnesses according to traditional Latino folk medicine, or **curanderismo**—a form of holistic health care and healing. *Curanderismo* influences how one approaches health care and even how one defines illness. Although most Hispanics use folk healers, or *curanderos,* infrequently, perhaps 20 percent rely on home remedies. Some define such illnesses as *susto* (fright sickness) and *atague* (fighting attack) according to folk beliefs. Because these complaints often have biological bases, sensitive medical practitioners need to deal with them carefully to diagnose and treat illnesses accurately (Hendrickson 2014; Tafur, Crowe, and Torres 2009).

Also affecting Latino morbidity rates is the fact that Latinos are much more likely to wait to seek treatment. This may be due in part, as the "People without Health Insurance" graph demonstrates, to their relative lack of health insurance. As a result, Hispanics often seek treatment for pressing medical problems at clinics and emergency rooms rather than receiving regular preventive care through a family physician. Such delays in treatments increase the severity of the consequences of illness and disease (Barnett and Vornovitsky 2016).

©Peter Frank/Getty Images RF

GENDER

Men and women do differ in their overall health. For example, women live longer than men. Girls born in 2014 can anticipate an average life expectancy of 81.2 years, compared to 76.4 for boys. The good news for men is that, although life expectancy continues to rise for both men and women, rates have been rising even faster for men. As a result, the life expectancy gap between men and women has declined from 7.6 years for those born in 1970 to 4.8 years in 2014 (National Center for Health Statistics 2016:Table 15).

Smoking Rates by Gender

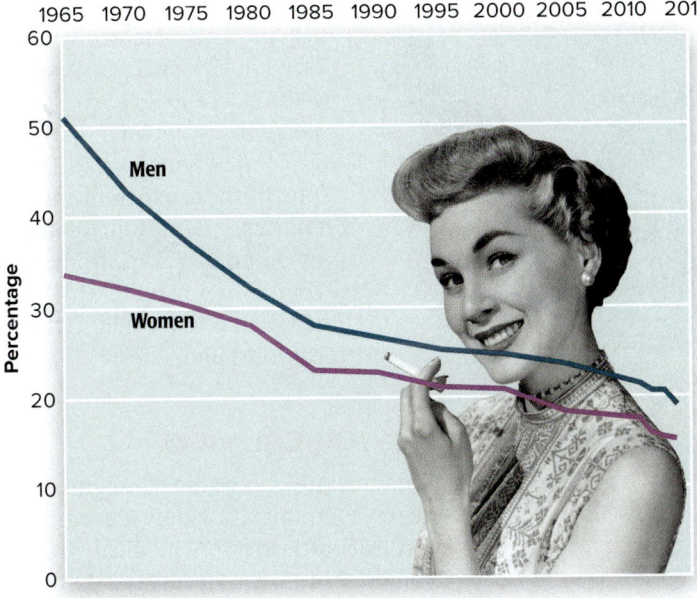

Source: National Center for Health Statistics 2016:Table 47. Photo: ©Photo by Debrocke/ClassicStock/Getty Images

Greater longevity for women appears to be tied to lifestyle differences between men and women that grow out of gendered norms. Historically, women's lower rate of cigarette smoking (reducing their risk of heart disease, lung cancer, and emphysema), lower consumption of alcohol (reducing the risk of auto accidents and cirrhosis of the liver), and lower rate of employment in dangerous occupations explain about one-third of their greater longevity than men. Researchers argue that women are much more likely than men to seek treatment, to be diagnosed as having a disease, and thus to have their illnesses reflected in the data examined by epidemiologists (National Center for Health Statistics 2016). Changes in lifestyle do matter. As the "Smoking Rates by Gender" graph shows, the gap in smoking rates between men and women has declined, accounting for some of the reduction in the difference in life expectancy between men and women.

With everything from birth to beauty being treated in an increasingly medical context, women have been particularly vulnerable to the medicalization of society. Ironically, even given the increased power of the medical establishment in women's lives, medical researchers have often excluded them from clinical studies. Female physicians and researchers charge that sexism lies at the heart of such research practices and insist there is a desperate need for studies of female subjects (Johnson et al. 2014; Pinnow et al. 2009).

AGE

Health is the overriding concern of older adults. Most older people in the United States report having at least one chronic illness, but only some of those conditions are potentially life threatening or require medical care. The quality of life among older people is of particular concern in the face of potentially escalating health problems. A substantial number of older people in the United States are troubled by arthritis and other chronic diseases, and many have visual or hearing impairments that can interfere with the performance of everyday tasks (Hootman et al. 2006; National Center for Health Statistics 2016).

Older people are also especially vulnerable to certain mental health problems. Alzheimer's disease, the leading cause of dementia in the United States, afflicts one in nine, or 11 percent, of people aged 65 years and older. In terms of prevalence, that works out to 5.4 million Americans in 2016. That number is projected to grow to 13.8 million in 2050 as the U.S. population ages (Alzheimer's Association 2016).

Because of their increased health risks, the rate at which older people in the United States (aged 75 and older) use health services is more than three times greater than that for younger people (aged 15–24). This heightened use level is tied to health insurance coverage, with people over age 65 the most likely to be covered, as the accompanying "Health Insurance Rates by Age" graph portrays. The disproportionate use of the U.S. health care system by older people is a critical factor in all discussions

Health Insurance Rates by Age

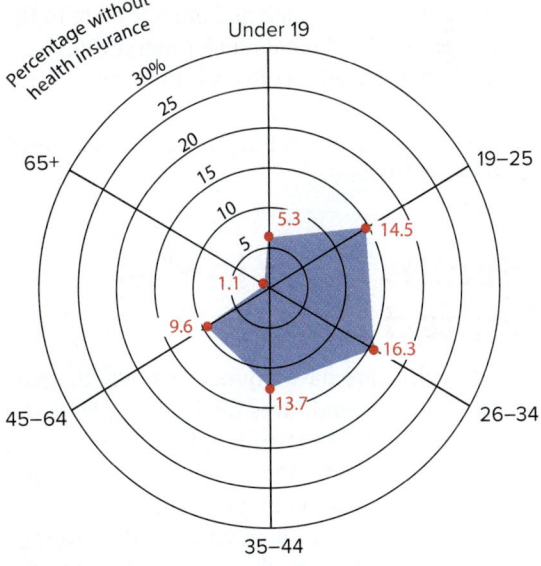

Note: Numbers represent the percentage of people without health insurance for the full calendar year.
Source: Barnett and Vornovitsky 2016:Table 2.

Availability of Physicians by State

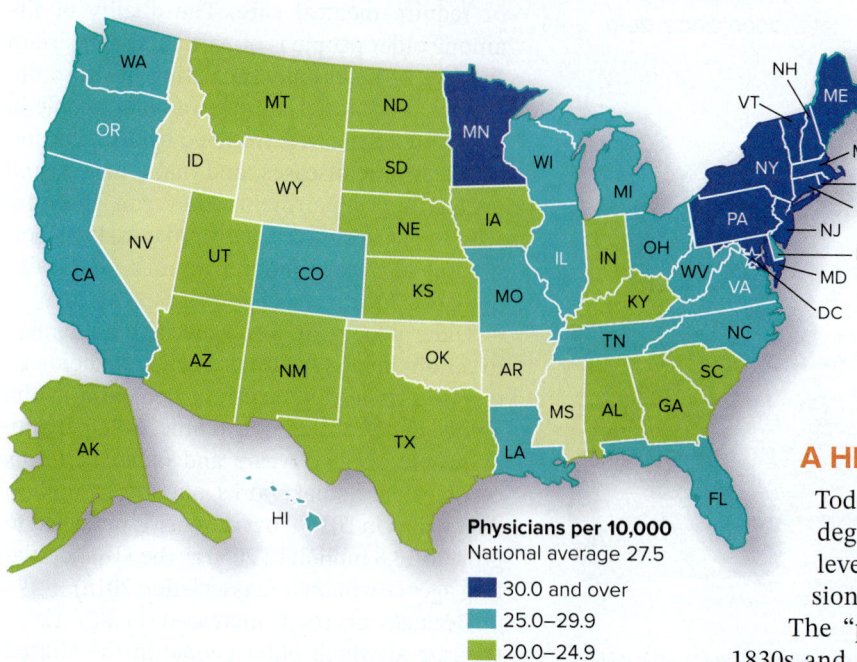

Source: National Center for Health Statistics 2014:Table 101.

17.1 percent as measured by GDP, than does any other country in the world. Contrast the U.S. rate with those of countries such as Sweden (11.9), France (11.5), Canada (10.4), Japan (10.2), or the United Kingdom (9.1). In spite of these expenditure differences, these four nations provide universal health coverage for all their people, while the United States does not (OECD 2016e; World Bank 2016q).

A HISTORICAL VIEW

Today, state licensing and medical degrees confer a widely recognized level of authority on medical professionals. This was not always the case. The "popular health movement" of the 1830s and 1840s emphasized preventive care and what is termed "self-help." It voiced strong criticism of "doctoring" as a paid occupation. New medical philosophies or sects established their own medical schools and challenged the authority and methods of traditional doctors. By the 1840s

about the cost of health care and possible reforms of the health care system. Many younger people choose not to purchase health insurance in order to save money, and their decision to opt out means fewer people paying in, which means higher costs. The Affordable Care Act, also known as ObamaCare, sought to make participation mandatory for this reason (Barnett and Vornivitsky 2016:Table 2).

A person's odds of good health are shaped by her or his class, race and ethnicity, gender, and age. Even geography matters, because there are significant differences in the number of physicians from one state to the next. Health care professionals and program advisers need to take such differential effects into account when considering what constitutes equitable health care coverage. Any attempts to do so, however, are constrained by the cost of health care.

>> Health Care in the United States

The costs of health care have skyrocketed over the past few decades. Total expenditures for health care in the United States broke the $500 million barrier in 1987. It quickly went on to reach other milestones, including $1 trillion in 1995, $2 trillion in 2005, and $3 trillion in 2014. In 2015, expenditures worked out to an average of $9,990 per person (Centers for Medicare and Medicaid Services 2016:Table 1). The United States devotes a greater proportion of its total spending to health care,

Total Health Care Expenditures in the United States

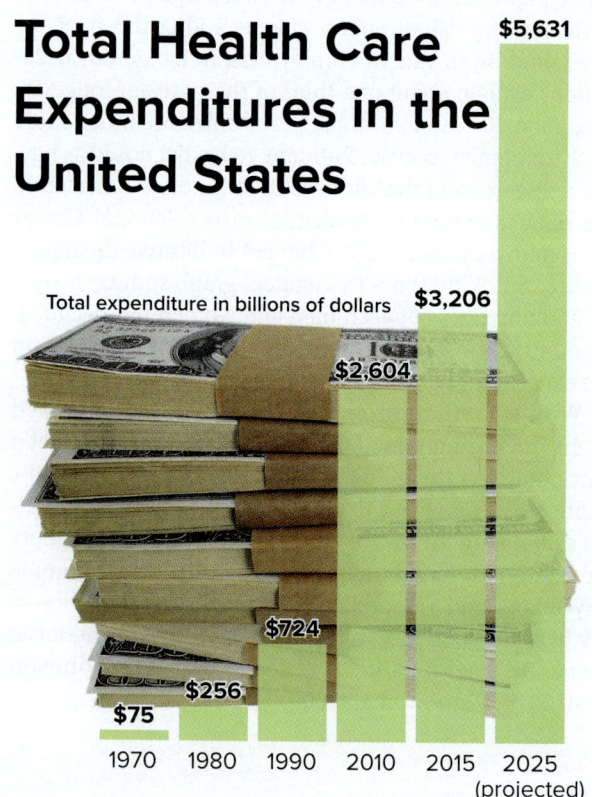

Source: Centers for Medicare and Medicaid Services 2016a, 2016b.
Photo: ©Comstock Images/Alamy Stock Photo RF

most states had repealed medical licensing laws, and the health care field was largely unregulated (Porter 1998, 2004).

In response, through the leadership of the American Medical Association (AMA), founded in 1848, "regular" doctors marginalized lay practitioners, sectarian doctors, and female physicians in general. They institutionalized their authority through standardized programs of education and licensing. Only those who successfully completed AMA programs gained legitimate authority as medical practitioners. The authority of the physician no longer depended on lay attitudes or on the person occupying the sick role; increasingly, it was built into the structure of the medical profession and the health care system.

As the institutionalization of health care proceeded, the medical profession gained control over both the market for its services and the various organizational hierarchies that govern medical practice, financing, and policy making. By the 1920s physicians controlled hospital technology, the division of labor of health personnel, and indirectly, other professional practices, such as nursing and pharmaceutical services (Coser 1984; Starr 1982; Whorton 2002).

©Jules Frazier/Getty Images RF

THE ROLE OF GOVERNMENT

Not until the 20th century did health care receive federal aid in conjunction with the expansion of medicine as a social institution. The first significant government involvement was the 1946 Hill-Burton Act, which provided subsidies for building and improving hospitals, especially in rural areas. An even more important development was the enactment in 1965 of two wide-ranging government assistance programs: Medicare and Medicaid. Medicare provides insurance primarily for those 65 and older in the United States. It is administered by the federal government and funded primarily by a payroll tax on all U.S. workers. In 2016, Medicare covered 56.5 million people. Medicaid, a joint federal and state insurance plan, provides coverage for eligible people who lack sufficient income to pay for their own health care. In 2016, Medicaid covered 71.1 million people (Centers for Medicare and Medicaid Services 2016c).

As health care costs rose, political debates about how best to provide for the public health of the nation became commonplace. In 1993 the Clinton administration proposed health care reform designed to provide universal coverage, but the legislation failed to pass. Throughout the George W. Bush administration, the United States remained the only wealthy, industrialized nation that did not provide some form of universal coverage. Then, following Barack Obama's election as president—after significant debate and against substantial Republican opposition—Congress passed, and President Obama signed, the Patient Protection and Affordable Care Act and the Health Care and Education Reconciliation Act in March 2010 (Brill 2015).

In terms of its structure, the Affordable Care Act (ACA), also referred to as ObamaCare, has three main elements and has been described as a three-legged stool, meaning if you remove any of the three, the whole thing will collapse. The first leg is known as a community rating, which means that premiums customers pay will be based on age, geographical location, size of family, and tobacco use rather than their underlying physical condition. In other words, insurance companies cannot discriminate against people with preexisting conditions by refusing them coverage or charging them higher rates. To compensate for the increased insurance costs that result from this, the second leg mandates that everyone must obtain insurance, whether through their employer, the government, or the marketplace. Those who don't are charged a penalty. The third leg involves providing subsidies to those who cannot afford to purchase insurance on their own. The combination of all three elements distributes the costs of health care across a larger pool of participants while assisting those who would otherwise lack the means to pay for it (Gruber 2010).

President Barack Obama signs the Affordable Care Act into law. ©Chip Somodevilla/Getty Images

Holistic medicine Therapies in which the health care practitioner considers the person's physical, mental, emotional, and spiritual characteristics.

To ensure that all three elements were provided for, the Affordable Care Act contained the following provisions:

- Young adults may stay on their parents' health care plans until age 26.
- Coverage for checkups and other preventive care does not require co-pays.
- Annual caps and lifetime limits on the cost of benefits patients can receive were eliminated.
- People with preexisting conditions cannot be denied coverage, and companies are no longer able to cut employees from a plan when they get sick.
- Most Americans are required to purchase some form of health insurance.
- Tax credits for the purchase of insurance are available for individuals and families between 100 and 400 percent of the poverty level.
- Companies with more than 50 employees are required to provide an employer-sponsored health plan that provides a mandated level of minimal coverage.
- Small businesses are eligible to receive tax credits to assist them in providing coverage.
- State-based insurance exchanges offer a choice of plans for small businesses and people who lack employer-supplied coverage.
- Insurance companies are required to provide greater transparency regarding spending on overhead costs.

After the Affordable Care Act was fully implemented, the rate of Americans without insurance began to fall, as the accompanying "U.S. Uninsured Rate" graph shows. This was true for people at all income levels and from all racial and ethnic groups (Barnett and Vornovitsky 2016). In spite of this, however, many Republicans continued to prefer market-based solutions, arguing that free-market capitalism would lead to greater efficiency and cost control.

In 2016, Republicans running for Congress, along with presidential candidate Donald Trump, pledged to repeal and replace ObamaCare on the first day of the new term. Once elected, however, they ran into the challenge presented by the three-legged stool. The first leg, which ensured people with preexisting conditions would not be discriminated against, was quite popular. Elimination of the second leg, the mandate requiring the purchase of insurance, a particularly unpopular element of the ACA, meant fewer people paying into the system, which would mean higher prices for those who remain. Elimination of the subsidies, the third leg, meant those without means to afford insurance drop out, again reducing the number of people participating in the system and raising costs (Gruber 2010). As noted in the discussion regarding citizenship rights in the "Democracy" section of Chapter 9, the questions regarding how best to approach health insurance hinge on the question of whether health should be considered a social right, something guaranteed for all (Marshall 1950).

COMPLEMENTARY AND ALTERNATIVE MEDICINE

In modern forms of health care, people rely on physicians and hospitals for the treatment of illness. Yet a significant proportion of adults in the United States attempt to maintain good health or respond to illness through the use of alternative health care techniques. For example, in recent decades, interest has been growing in holistic medical principles, first developed in China. **Holistic medicine** refers to therapies in which the health care practitioner considers the person's physical, mental, emotional, and spiritual characteristics. The individual is regarded as a totality rather than a collection of interrelated organ systems. Treatment methods include massage, chiropractic

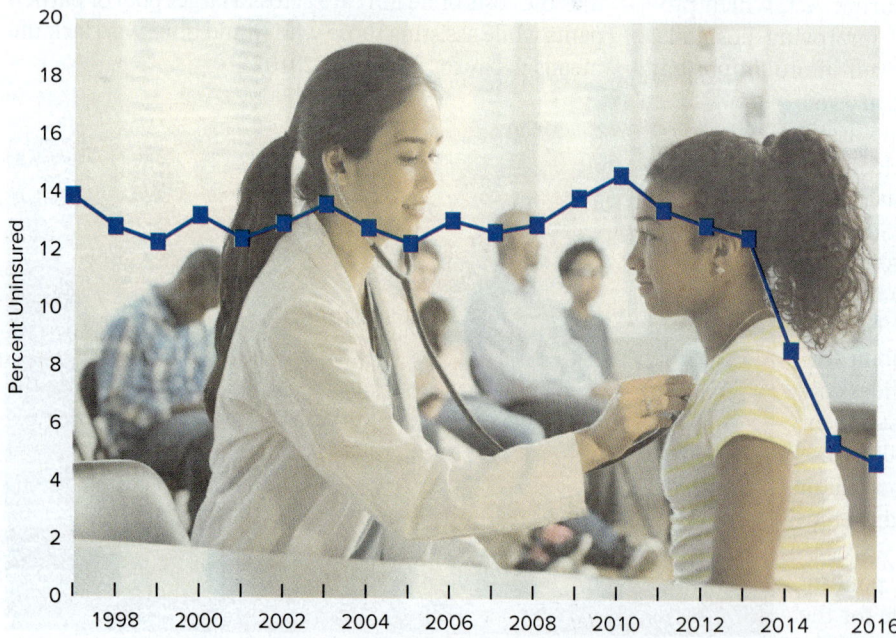

U.S. Uninsured Rate, 1997–2016

Note: Percentage of all persons without health insurance at the time of the interview. Data come from the National Health Interview Survey.
Source: Cohen, Martinez, and Zammitti 2016; Ward et al. 2016. Photo: ©KidStock/Blend Images LLC RF

medicine, acupuncture, respiratory exercises, and the use of herbs as remedies. Nutrition, exercise, and visualization may also be used to treat ailments (Barnes, Bloom, and Nahin 2008; Stratton and McGivern-Snofsky 2008).

The medical establishment—professional organizations, research hospitals, and medical schools—continues to zealously protect its authority. However, a major breakthrough occurred in 1992 when the federal government's National Institutes of Health (NIH)—the nation's major funding source for biomedical research—opened the National Center for Complementary and Alternative Medicine and empowered it to accept grant requests. A NIH-sponsored national study found that 33.2 percent of adults in the United States had used some form of complementary or alternative medicine within the previous year. As the accompanying "Complementary and Alternative Medicine Use" graph demonstrates, examples include natural dietary supplements (such as fish oil, glucosamine, echinacea, or ginseng), deep breathing, and meditation. When private or communal prayer was included as part of the NIH-sponsored 2002 study, the number rose to 62.1 percent (Barnes et al. 2004; Clarke et al. 2015).

On the international level, the WHO has begun to monitor the use of alternative medicine around the world. According to the WHO, 80 percent of people in some African and Asian countries use alternative medicine, from herbal treatments to the services of a faith healer. In most countries, these treatments are largely unregulated, even though some of them can be fatal. For example, kava kava, an herbal tea used in the Pacific Islands to relieve anxiety, can be toxic to the liver in concentrated form. Other alternative treatments have been found to be effective in the treatment of serious diseases, such as malaria and sickle-cell anemia. WHO's goal is to compile a list of such practices, as well as to encourage the development of universal training programs and ethical standards for practitioners of alternative medicine (World Health Organization 2005, 2013a).

Anthropocene A geological epoch in which human actions, even at a micro level, have global environmental consequences.

Human ecology The area of study concerned with the interrelationships between people and their environment.

Sociological analysis of health and illness suggests that if we are to understand sickness we must look beyond biology. Society and culture, family and friends, the medical profession, and social position all help shape medical outcomes. Given the increasing costs of health care, and the fact that different groups experience different outcomes, this issue becomes one of equality and fairness. Lives are at stake. It is precisely such concerns that drive debates about the expansion of health care coverage as a social right.

Complementary and Alternative Medicine Use

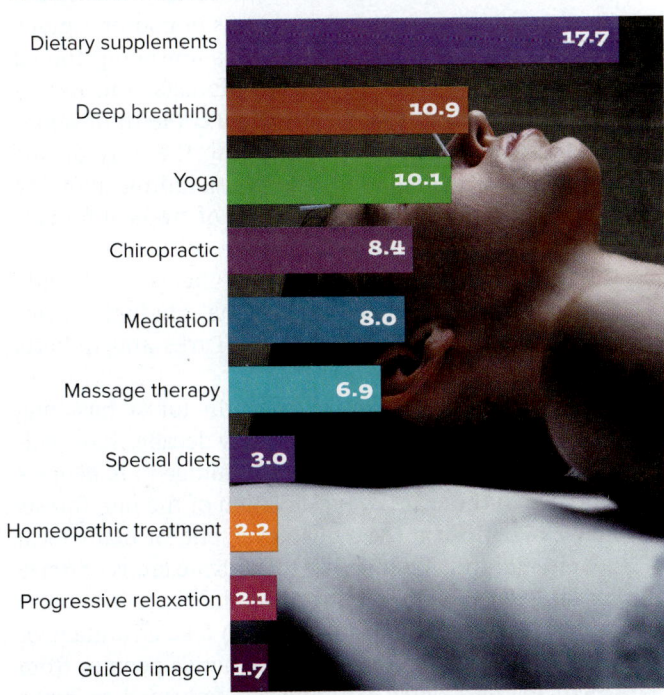

Category	Percent
Dietary supplements	17.7
Deep breathing	10.9
Yoga	10.1
Chiropractic	8.4
Meditation	8.0
Massage therapy	6.9
Special diets	3.0
Homeopathic treatment	2.2
Progressive relaxation	2.1
Guided imagery	1.7

Note: Dietary supplements include nonvitamin and nonmineral supplements such as fish oil, glucosamine, and probiotics. Special diets include vegetarian, vegan, macrobiotic, and others.
Source: Clarke et al. 2015. *Photo:* ©Anthony Saint James/Getty Images RF

>> Sociological Perspectives on the Environment

Humans' interdependent relationships with one another also extend to the natural environment. The choices we make are constrained by available natural resources. Through technology we modify nature to suit our needs, and throughout history humans have demonstrated an astonishing ability to do so, but not without consequences. The benefits of the Industrial Revolution came with costs such as air pollution, water pollution, and global climate change. We have entered an era of what some are calling the **Anthropocene**, a geological epoch in which human actions, even at a micro level, have global environmental consequences (Sample 2014).

HUMAN ECOLOGY

Human ecology is an area of study that is concerned with interrelationships between people and their environment. As biologist and environmentalist Barry Commoner (1971:39) put it during the early stages of the modern environmental movement, "Everything is connected to everything else." Human ecologists focus on how the physical environment shapes people's lives and on how people influence the surrounding environment.

In an application of the human ecological perspective, sociologists and environmentalists have identified several relationships between the environment and people. Among them are the following:

- *The environment provides the resources essential for life.* These include air, water, and materials used to create shelter, transportation, and needed products. If human societies exhaust these resources—for example, by polluting the water supply or cutting down rain forests—the consequences could be dire.
- *The environment serves as a waste repository.* More so than other living species, humans produce a huge quantity and variety of waste products—bottles, cans, boxes, paper, sewage, garbage, and so on. Various types of pollution have become more common because human societies are generating more wastes than the environment can safely absorb.
- *The environment "houses" our species.* It is our home, our living space, the place where we reside, work, and play. At times we take this truism for granted, but not when day-to-day living conditions become unpleasant and problematic. If our air is polluted, if our tap water turns brown, or if toxic chemicals seep into our neighborhood, we remember why it is vital to live in a healthful environment.

Did You Know?

. . . In 2015, Americans drank more than 11.7 billion gallons of bottled water at a total cost of $14.2 billion. That works out to 36.5 gallons per person, which was up from less than 6 gallons in 1987.

Source: Rodwan 2016. Photo: ©Digital Vision Ltd/Getty Images RF

There is no shortage of illustrations of the interconnectedness of humans and the environment. For example, scientific research has linked pollutants in the environment to people's health and behavior. The increasing prevalence of asthma, lead poisoning, and cancer has been tied to human alterations to the environment. Similarly, the rise in melanoma (skin cancer) diagnoses has been linked to global climate change. And ecological changes in our food and diet have been related to childhood obesity and diabetes (Demeneix 2017; Hill 2010).

With its view that "everything is connected to everything else," human ecology stresses the trade-offs inherent in every decision that alters the environment. In facing the environmental challenges of the 21st century, government policy makers and environmentalists must determine how they can fulfill humans' pressing needs for food, clothing, and shelter while preserving the environment as a source of resources, a waste repository, and a home.

POWER, RESOURCES, AND THE ENVIRONMENT

Analyzing environmental issues from a world systems approach allows us to better understand the global consequences of differential access to resources. This approach highlights the difference in relative power between core nations, which control wealth and so dominate the global economy, and developing countries, which lack control and whose resources are exploited. This process only intensifies the destruction of natural resources in poorer regions of the world. Less-affluent nations are being forced to exploit their mineral deposits, forests, and fisheries to meet their debt obligations. People in developing nations often end up turning to the only means of survival available to them, including plowing mountain slopes, burning sections of tropical forests, and overgrazing grasslands. The resulting reduction of the rain forest, for example, affects worldwide weather patterns, heightening the gradual warming of the earth (Jorgenson 2015; Parks and Roberts 2010; Pollini 2009).

Although destruction of the rain forest has long been a concern, only in the past few decades have policy makers begun to listen to the indigenous peoples who live in these areas. Preservation of the rain forests may make sense at the global level, but for many local peoples, it limits their ability to cultivate crops or graze cattle. Even though it harms the global environment, they feel they have no choice but to take advantage of their available resources. In 2008, native peoples from Brazil to the Congo to Indonesia convened to make the case that wealthier countries should compensate them for conservation of the tropical rain forests (Barrionuevo 2008).

Did You Know?

...An average of 7,511 square kilometers (1.9 million acres) of Brazilian rain forest was lost each year from 2007 to 2016. Since 1980, approximately 19 percent of Brazil's total has been lost to deforestation.

Source: INPE 2016; Rodwan 2016. *Photo:* ©Stockbyte/Getty Images

There is, in fact, a certain amount of ethnocentrism involved when people in industrialized countries insist that those developing nations change their practices to save the planet. In calling for the poverty-stricken and "food-hungry" populations of the world to sacrifice, they should also consider the lifestyle consequences for the "energy-hungry" nations. The industrialized nations of North America and Europe account for only 12 percent of the world's population but are responsible for 60 percent of worldwide consumption. The money their residents spend on ocean cruises each year could provide clean drinking water for everyone on the planet. Ice cream expenditures in Europe alone could be used to immunize every child in the world. The global consumer represents a serious environmental threat, but it is often difficult to look in the mirror and blame ourselves because our individual contribution to the problem seems so small. Collectively, however, the choices we make have a significant global impact (Diamond 2008; Gardner, Assadourian, and Sarin 2004).

The rise in global consumption is tied to a capitalist system that depends upon growth for its survival. Capitalism creates a "treadmill of production" (Baer 2008; Gould, Pellow, and Schnaiberg 2008). Cutting back on consumption means cutting back on purchases, which leads to reduced production and the loss of profits and jobs. This treadmill necessitates creating an increasing demand for products, obtaining natural resources at minimal cost, and manufacturing products as quickly and cheaply as possible—no matter what the long-term environmental consequences.

ENVIRONMENTAL JUSTICE

In the autumn of 1982, nearly 500 African Americans participated in a six-week protest against a hazardous waste landfill containing cancer-causing chemicals in Warren County, North Carolina. Their protests and legal actions continued until 2002, when decontamination of the site finally began. This 20-year battle can be seen as yet another "not-in-my-backyard" (NIMBY) event in which people desire the benefits of growth but want someone else to pay for its negative effects. In any event, the Warren County struggle is viewed as a transformative moment in contemporary environmentalism: the beginning of the environmental justice movement (Bullard 2000; McGurty 2007; North Carolina Department of Environment and Natural Resources 2008).

Environmental justice A legal strategy based on claims that racial minorities are subjected disproportionately to environmental hazards.

Environmental justice is a legal strategy based on claims that racial minorities are subjected disproportionately to environmental hazards. Some observers have heralded environmental justice as the "new civil rights of the 21st century" (Kokmen 2008:42). Since the advent of the environmental justice movement, activists and scholars have identified other environmental disparities that break along racial and social class lines. In general, poor people and people of color are much more likely than others to be victimized by the everyday consequences of economic development, including air pollution from expressways and incinerators (Sandler and Pezzullo 2007; Schlosberg 2013).

Sociologists Paul Mohai and Robin Saha (2007) examined more than 600 hazardous waste treatment, storage, and disposal facilities in the United States. They found that non-Whites and Latinos make up 43 percent of the people who live within one mile of these dangerous sites. There are two possible explanations for this finding. One is that racial and ethnic minorities possess less political power than others, so they cannot prevent toxic sites from being located in their backyards. The other is that they end

> ### Suburbia is where the developer bulldozes out the trees, then names the streets after them.
>
> ---
> Bill Vaughn

Public Perception of Environmental Issues

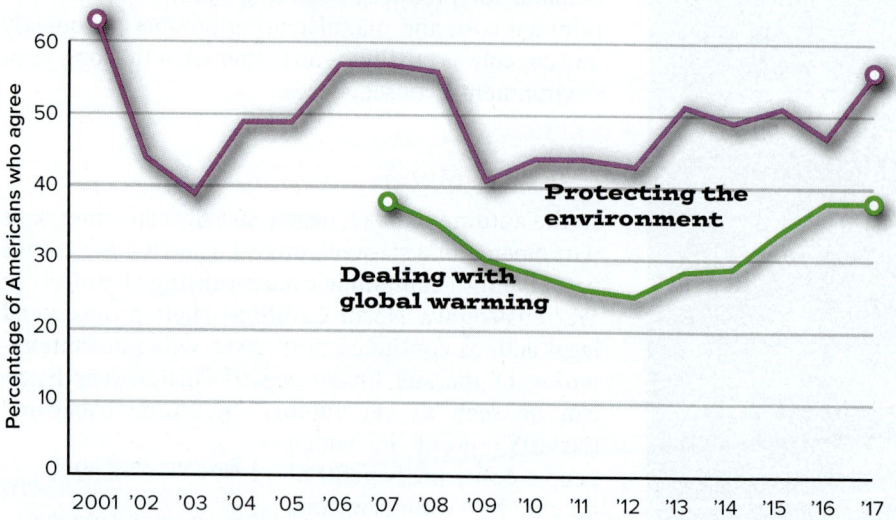

Note: When asked to identify priorities for Congress and the president, response options included top priority, important but lower priority, not too important. After 2014, wording changed from "global warming" to "global climate change."
Source: Pew Research Center 2017.

but others can last for hundreds of years and more. Some go into the air, into the water, and still more into the earth.

AIR POLLUTION

Worldwide, an estimated 3 million premature deaths occurred due to outdoor air pollution in 2012. Of these, 88 percent lived in low- and middle-income countries. Another 4.3 million died due to household air pollution (World Health Organization 2016b). Unfortunately, in cities around the world, residents have come to accept polluted air as normal. Urban air pollution is caused primarily by emissions from automobiles and secondarily by emissions from electric power plants and heavy industries. Air pollution not only limits visibility, but also can lead to health problems as uncomfortable as eye irritation and as deadly as lung cancer. Such problems are especially severe in developing countries (United Nations Environment Programme 2014).

People are capable of changing their behavior, but they are also often unwilling to make such changes permanent. During the 1984 Olympics in Los Angeles,

up settling near the sites after they are constructed, because economics and the forces of discrimination push them into the least desirable living areas (Collins, Munoz, and JaJa 2016).

When it comes to public concern about environmental issues, as the "Public Perception of Environmental Issues" graph shows, attitudes have shifted over time. People distinguish between general concern about environmental issues and global climate change more specifically. In surveys asking about future development of U.S. energy supplies, Americans showed stronger support for alternative sources than conventional ones. Given the option, 65 percent preferred wind, solar, and the like compared to 27 percent who preferred expanding production of oil, coal, and natural gas. A clear political divide existed in their responses, with 81 percent of Democrats preferring alternative sources compared to 45 percent of Republican (Kennedy 2017).

>> Environmental Problems

Until, in some distant future, humans colonize another planet, Earth is our only home. The natural environment provides for all our needs. But in consuming, we inevitably also produce waste. Some leftovers from consumption are biodegradable and some get recycled,

Movies on THE ENVIRONMENT 5

Sun Come Up
The Carteret Islands in the South Pacific are being swallowed up by the ocean.

Age of Consequences
The intersection of climate change, resource scarcity, migration, and conflict.

Food, Inc.
The effects of the food manufacturing industry on the environment.

Chasing Ice
A climate change skeptic's doubts melt through the lens of his camera.

WALL-E
A robot in the year 2700 discovers his destiny.

authorities asked residents to carpool and stagger their work hours to relieve traffic congestion and improve the quality of the air athletes would breathe. These changes resulted in a remarkable 12 percent drop in ozone levels. After the Olympics ended, however, people reverted to their normal behavior, and the ozone levels climbed again. Similarly, China took drastic action to ensure that Beijing's high levels of air pollution did not mar the 2008 Olympic Games. Construction work in the city ceased, polluting factories and power plants closed down, and workers swept roads and sprayed them with water several times a day. This temporary solution, however, has not solved China's ongoing pollution problem (*The Economist* 2008).

WATER POLLUTION

Throughout the United States, waste materials dumped by industries and local governments have polluted streams, rivers, and lakes. Consequently, many bodies of water have become unsafe for fishing and swimming, let alone drinking. Around the world, pollution of the oceans is an issue of growing concern. For example, when the Deepwater Horizon oil-well explosion occurred in the Gulf of Mexico in 2010, 4.2 million barrels of oil poured into the water. The spill affected birds, fish, mammals, and their habitats. For example,

©China Photos/Getty Images

in the two years following its occurrence, 675 dolphins were stranded in the northern Gulf of Mexico compared to an annual average of 74 before the spill; deepwater corals experienced significant stress; the nitrogen cycle for microorganisms was inhibited; and 102 species of birds were harmed (Cornwall 2015; National Geographic 2012).

This incident is one among many water-based accidents that have resulted in significant environmental harm. When the oil tanker *Exxon Valdez* ran aground in Prince William Sound, Alaska, in 1989, its cargo of 11 million gallons of crude oil spilled into the sound and washed onto the shore, contaminating 1,285 miles of shoreline. Altogether, about 11,000 people joined in a massive cleanup effort that cost more than $2 billion. Globally, oil spills occur regularly. In 2002 the oil tanker *Prestige* spilled twice as much fuel as the *Valdez*, greatly damaging coastal areas in Spain and France (ITOPF 2006).

Less dramatic than large-scale accidents or disasters, but more common in many parts of the world, are problems with the basic water supply. Worldwide, more than 663 million people lack safe and adequate drinking water, and 1.8 billion rely on a drinking water source contaminated with feces. When it comes to sanitation facilities, 2.4 billion lack access—a problem that further threatens the quality of water supplies. The health costs of unsafe water are enormous (World Health Organization 2016c, 2016d).

Given such water concerns, it should not come as a surprise that water is now a highly contested commodity in many parts of the world. In the United States, competition over water is intense, especially in the Southwest including cities such as Las Vegas. In the Middle East, the immense political challenges posed by ethnic and religious conflict are often complicated by battles over water. There, competing nations accuse each other of taking unfair advantage of existing water supplies, and water tanks are a likely target for both military forces and terrorists (Carmichael 2007).

GLOBAL CLIMATE CHANGE

The scientific evidence for global climate change is clear, consistent, and compelling, yet public opinion polls show that people remain skeptical. Global warming, one of the key indicators of global climate change, refers to the significant rise in the earth's surface temperatures that occurs when industrial gases such as carbon dioxide turn the planet's atmosphere into a virtual greenhouse. As the accompanying "Global Temperature" graph shows, the warmest global temperatures in the era for which we have detailed meteorological measurements around the world have all come in the most recent decades. Globally, 2016 was the hottest on record, topping 2015,

Global Temperature, 1850–2016

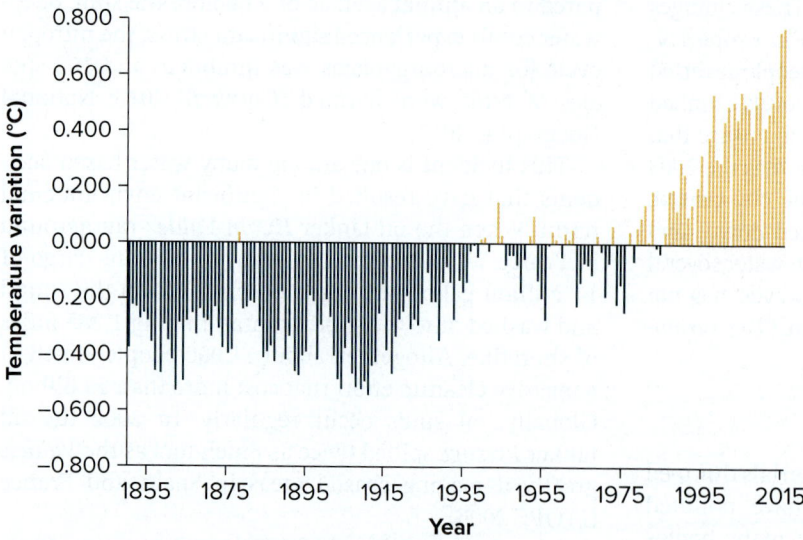

Note: The base line (0° C) is the average global air temperature from 1961–1990. Temperatures beneath that line are below that average and temperatures above that line are above that average. The hottest years on record have all occurred within the past two decades.
Source of data: Climatic Research Unit, University of East Anglia 2017.

are escalating. Ironically, many of those who are now calling for a reduction in the human activity that contributes to global climate change are located in core nations, which have contributed disproportionately to the problem. We want our hamburgers, but we decry the destruction of the rain forests to create grazing land for cattle. We want inexpensive clothes and toys, but we condemn developing countries for depending on coal-fired power plants, the number of which are expected to increase 46 percent by 2030. The challenge of global climate change, then, is closely tied to global inequality (Jenkins 2008; Leonard 2010; Roberts, Grines, and Manale 2003).

Of course, the consequences of environmental change, whether in the form of pollution or climate change, are extensive. The impacts of plastics, detergents, synthetic fibers, pesticides, herbicides, and chemical fertilizers challenge the ecosystems necessary for the survival of some species. Some environmentalists express concern that we may be entering a new age

which beat out 2014. Even one additional degree of warmth in the planet's average temperature increases the likelihood of wildfires, shrinking rivers and lakes, desert expansion, and torrential downpours, including typhoons and hurricanes (Climatic Research Unit, University of East Anglia 2017).

Scientists now track carbon dioxide emissions around the world and can map the current and projected contribution each country makes. As the accompanying "CO_2 Emissions per Capita" graph portrays, the United States produces a sizable amount of carbon dioxide per person relative to other nations, ranking 11th of 250 nations for which there are data (World Bank 2016r). Data on temperature and carbon dioxide emissions contribute to the scientific consensus regarding global climate change. In a study of 24,210 articles published in peer-reviewed scientific journals from 2013 to 2014 and written by a total of 69,406 authors, only 5 articles with a total of 4 authors rejected the conclusion that human-caused global warming is happening (Powell 2015). By contrast, when looking at public opinion, only 48 percent of Americans think that global climate change is due to human activity, and another 31 percent attribute climate change to natural causes (Funk and Kennedy 2016).

We can again draw on world systems analysis when it comes to seeing who pays the highest price for global climate changes. Historically, core nations have been the major emitters of greenhouse gases. Today, much manufacturing has moved to semiperiphery and periphery nations, where greenhouse gas emissions

Going GLOBAL

CO_2 Emissions per Capita

Country	CO_2 Emissions per Capita
Qatar	40.46
United States	16.4
Canada	13.53
Russian Federation	12.47
Japan	9.77
China	7.55
United Kingdom	7.13
World	5.0
Mexico	3.95
India	1.59
Guatemala	0.87
Haiti	0.23
Burundi	0.03

Note: Annual emissions per capita measured in metric tons.
Source: World Bank 2016r.

Threatened and Endangered Species

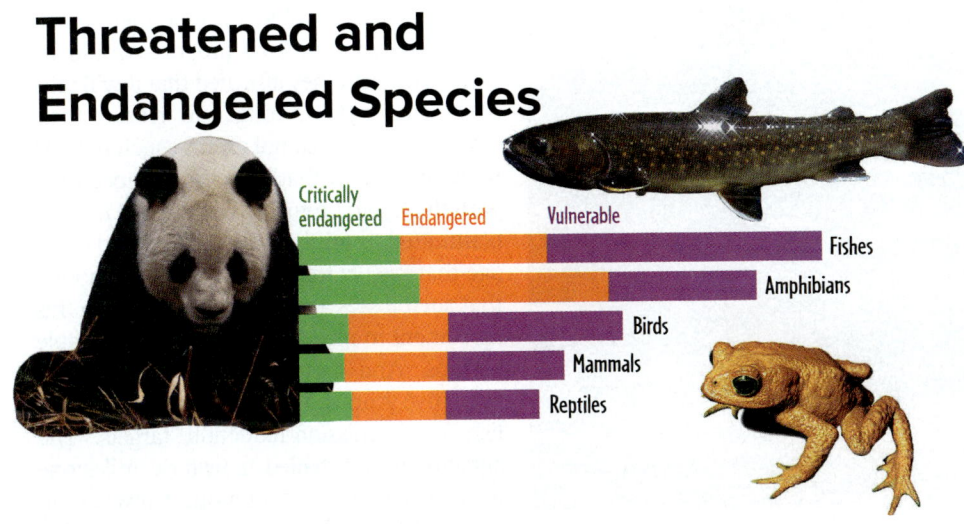

Source: IUCN 2016:Table 2. Photos: (panda): ©Fuse/Getty Images RF; (fish): Source: Bart Bammet/USFWS; (toad): Source: Charles H. Smith/USFWS

In Paris, on December 12, 2015, 195 countries agreed to a new international climate pact. Known as the Paris Agreement, it went into effect on November 4, 2016. The agreement commits the nations of the world to limiting the global temperature increase to less than 2 degrees Celsius (3.6 degrees Fahrenheit) when compared to pre–Industrial Revolution temperatures. To accomplish this goal, it includes a variety of provisions. For example, it encourages and rewards the reduction of deforestation. The nations also agreed to provide sufficient funding, including public funds, to

of extinction (Kolbert 2014). As the "Threatened and Endangered Species" graph shows, fish and amphibians are particularly vulnerable.

THE GLOBAL RESPONSE

Globalization can be both good and bad for the environment. On the negative side, it can create a race to the bottom as polluting companies relocate to countries with less stringent environmental standards. Also of concern is that globalization allows multinationals to exploit the resources of developing countries for short-term profit. From Mexico to China, the industrialization that often accompanies globalization has increased pollution of all types.

Yet globalization can have a positive impact as well. As barriers to the international movement of goods, services, and people fall, multinational corporations have an incentive to carefully consider the cost of natural resources. The Kyoto Protocol, for example, demonstrated that countries around the world can come together to take action that makes a significant difference. Established in 1997 and enacted in 2005, the Kyoto Protocol intended to provide a unified response to reducing global emissions of greenhouse gases. Nearly 200 countries ratified the accord. Collectively, the Kyoto Protocol nations met their emissions goal by the target year of 2012, and in December of that year some of the nations agreed to the Doha Amendment, which established a new set of goals to be met by 2020. The United States did not ratify the Kyoto Protocol, because U.S. political leaders feared that doing so would place the nation at a disadvantage in the global marketplace (Clark 2012; United Nations Framework Convention on Climate Change 2015a, 2015b).

Global Concern Regarding Climate Change

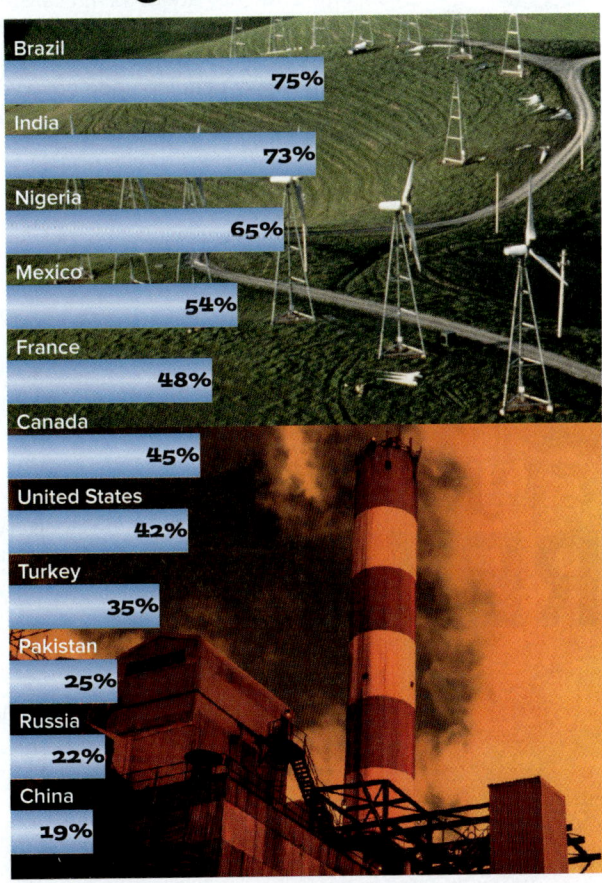

Note: Percentage of people responding that they are "very concerned" about global climate change.
Source: Carle 2015. Photos: (top): ©Kim Steele/Getty Images RF; (bottom): ©Stockbyte/Getty Images RF

Chapter 14 / Population, Health, and Environment • 373

©Jonas Marcos San Luis/Cutcaster RF

make progress possible. Further, they agreed to transparency in how progress would be measured. And they affirmed that it will take developing nations longer to reduce their emissions, but it did not exempt such nations from moving in that direction (as occurred with the Kyoto Protocol). Overall, the nations committed to minimizing the loss and damage that results from climate change, noting that such losses are inevitable even with this agreement in place, especially for vulnerable nations. And they committed to meeting every five years to review progress and establish new emission-reduction targets. The agreement was hailed a historic milestone in international cooperation. However, in June 2017, President Trump announced that the United States would withdraw from the agreement (Bradsher 2016; Davenport et al. 2015; United Nations 2016c).

Perhaps, as Émile Durkheim argued long ago, by recognizing our mutual interdependence, we will take the steps necessary to bring about positive social change. Sociology helps us better see the ways we are interconnected by highlighting the significance of the system as a whole, as well as raising awareness about the inequalities that are a consequence of the global system we have constructed. Such analysis can prepare us to more effectively respond to the global challenges we face.

SOCIOLOGY IS A VERB

Health and Environment

Conduct a mini-survey of 10 friends, family members, and/or classmates. How concerned are they about global climate change? How concerned are they about health care? What do they think are the major issues in each? What are the obstacles to positive change in each? Record their responses. How did answers vary depending upon how old they are, how much education they have, whether they are male or female, or other possible variables?

[For REVIEW]

I. **What role do population dynamics play in shaping our lives?**
   - Population dynamics provide a context within which we are born, live, move, and even die, and population trends vary significantly across time and between nations, shaping our life chances.

II. **What does sociology contribute to something as seemingly biological as health?**
   - Our understanding of what counts as health and illness is shaped by the society to which we belong. Similarly, our social position and control over resources shape our likelihood of exposure to illness and our access to health care.

III. **What environmental lessons do we learn from sociology?**
   - The natural environment represents our human home, within which all social interaction occurs, and the way we organize our social relations influences the effects we have on the environment. Countries that control a larger amount of resources have a bigger impact and therefore bear a greater responsibility for those effects.

SOCVIEWS on Population, Health, and Environment

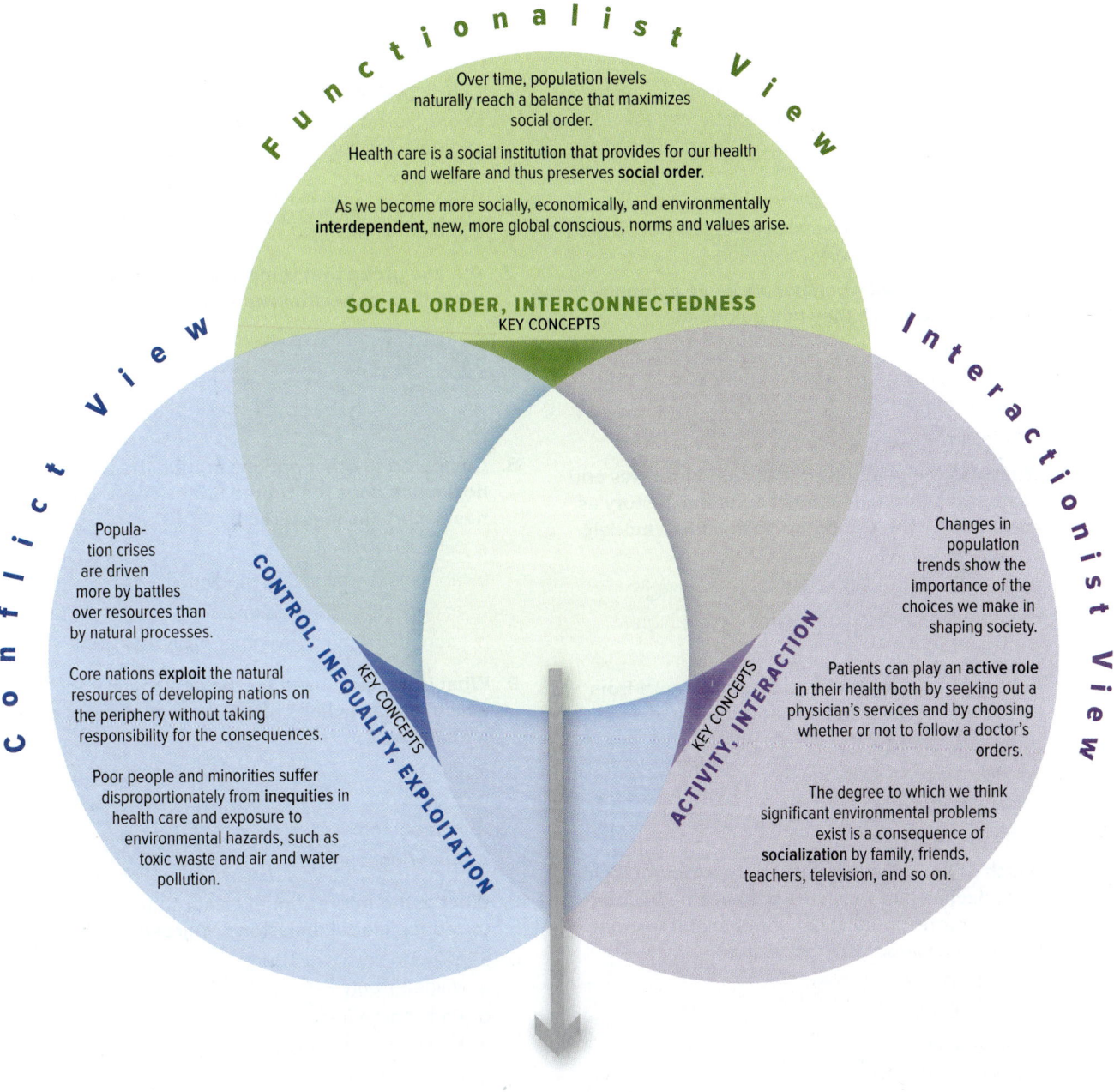

Functionalist View

Over time, population levels naturally reach a balance that maximizes social order.

Health care is a social institution that provides for our health and welfare and thus preserves **social order**.

As we become more socially, economically, and environmentally **interdependent**, new, more global conscious, norms and values arise.

KEY CONCEPTS: **SOCIAL ORDER, INTERCONNECTEDNESS**

Conflict View

Population crises are driven more by battles over resources than by natural processes.

Core nations **exploit** the natural resources of developing nations on the periphery without taking responsibility for the consequences.

Poor people and minorities suffer disproportionately from **inequities** in health care and exposure to environmental hazards, such as toxic waste and air and water pollution.

KEY CONCEPTS: **CONTROL, INEQUALITY, EXPLOITATION**

Interactionist View

Changes in population trends show the importance of the choices we make in shaping society.

Patients can play an **active role** in their health both by seeking out a physician's services and by choosing whether or not to follow a doctor's orders.

The degree to which we think significant environmental problems exist is a consequence of **socialization** by family, friends, teachers, television, and so on.

KEY CONCEPTS: **ACTIVITY, INTERACTION**

MAKE THE CONNECTION
After reviewing the chapter, answer the following questions:

1 How would each perspective approach the study of the protests over the Dakota Access Pipeline?

2 How would each of the perspectives approach the demographic transition model, and how would their insights differ?

3 What insights would we gain from each perspective regarding the current state of health care in the United States, including recent health care reform efforts?

4 Look at your experience with the medical world from an interactionist perspective. What were your interactions with the doctors and nurses like? Have you taken an active role or a passive role as a patient?

Chapter 14 / Population, Health, and Environment • 375

Pop Quiz

1. **How is the total fertility rate defined?**
   a. number of children born over a given period of time
   b. number of live births per 1,000 people in the population in a given year
   c. average number of children a woman would have during her lifetime given current birthrates and assuming she survives through her childbearing years
   d. minimum number of children a woman would need to average in her lifetime to reproduce the population in the next generation

2. **What term is used when people leave a population group to which they had belonged?**
   a. immigration
   b. replacement
   c. emigration
   d. transition

3. **What was the relationship between birthrates and death rates throughout most of human history as described by the demographic transition model?**
   a. Both were low.
   b. Death rates were low; birthrates were high.
   c. Birthrates were low; death rates were high.
   d. Both were high.

4. **A disease that cannot be understood apart from its specific social context is an example of**
   a. human ecology.
   b. culture-bound syndrome.
   c. the sick role.
   d. holistic medicine.

5. **Which of the following represents a form of legitimate deviance in which the person who becomes ill has a corresponding set of rights and responsibilities associated with that status?**
   a. medicalization
   b. the sick role
   c. brain drain
   d. social epidemiology

6. **In the area of social epidemiology, what does prevalence refer to?**
   a. the rate at which key indicators change over time
   b. the total number of cases of a specific disorder that exist at a given period of time
   c. the likelihood that a disease or illness will be labeled as such in a given cultural context
   d. the number of new cases of a specific disorder that occur within a given population during a stated period

7. **The age group that is most likely to be covered by some form of health insurance is**
   a. under 18.
   b. 18–34.
   c. 35–64.
   d. 65 and older.

8. **Compared to other nations around the world, how much does the United States spend on health care (as measured by GDP)?**
   a. near the bottom
   b. about in the middle or median
   c. at about the 75th percentile
   d. more than virtually all other nations

9. **What is the term used for the geological epoch in which human actions affect the environment on a global scale?**
   a. Jurassic
   b. Homocene
   c. demographic
   d. Anthropocene

10. **What is the international treaty that sought to reduce global emissions of greenhouse gases?**
    a. Valdez Treaty
    b. Paris Agreement
    c. Port Huron Statement
    d. Gore Accord

1. (c), 2. (c), 3. (d), 4. (b), 5. (b), 6. (b), 7. (d), 8. (d), 9. (d), 10. (b)

Social Change

©Photo by Andrew Burton/Getty Images

CHANGING THE WORLD ONE CAMPUS AT A TIME

In the summer of 1964, college students traveled to Mississippi to change the world. As volunteers in Freedom Summer, their goal was to make a difference in the lives of African Americans who had been systematically denied the right to vote, quality education, and legal and political representation. The volunteers—mostly upper-middle-class White students from northern colleges—registered Black voters, established Freedom Schools, and provided legal advice and medical assistance. By the end of the summer, they had registered 17,000 voters and taught 3,000 children. In 1964, 6.7 percent of voting-age African Americans in Mississippi were registered, but by 1967, 66.5 percent were registered (Colby 1986; McAdam 1988).

College students continue to make a difference. Concerns about global climate change, for example, have given rise to increased student activism throughout the United States. Students at Swarthmore occupied that school's investment offices; students at Mary Washington staged a 21-day sit-in outside the president's office; students at Yale were cited for trespassing and fined $92 for their sit-in; and students at Harvard blockaded the entrances to their main administration building. Consciousness-raising efforts such as these appear to be working. In 2012, Unity College became the first college in America to divest its endowment from fossil fuel holdings. It has since been joined by 26 other schools. As one student protester put it, "We are Generation Climate, because our generation will inherit the burden of the climate crisis, and . . . now is the time to take collective action to change history" (Gordon 2015).

In their annual national survey of first-year students in the United States, researchers found that a record-high 8.5 percent expected to participate in student protests while in college, and in another record high, 39.8 percent reported that they want to become community leaders (Higher Education Research Institute 2016). Activism on campus appears high. At Colgate University in Hamilton, New York, 350 students occupied the admissions hall to protest intolerance after a variety of racial and antigay incidents on campus. Students at Tufts lay down in the middle of traffic to protest police killings of African American victims, including Michael Brown and Eric Garner. In solidarity with Emma Sulkowicz's protest at Columbia University against lenient treatment of perpetrators in campus sexual assault cases, students at more than 130 colleges carried mattresses with them on campus. Students at UC-Santa Cruz, where tuition more than doubled over the previous decade, were arrested after they blocked a major highway to protest the hikes. At the University of Missouri, a series of racial incidents spurred student activism against a socially segregated and racially intolerant campus culture. After a series of protests, including a pledge by the African Americans on Missouri's football team not to play unless change occurred, the president and chancellor both resigned (Izadi 2015; Logue 2016; Wong 2015).

Society is the product of our collective action. By acting as we always have, we reproduce the status quo. By acting differently, as college students have demonstrated over and over again, we have the power to change the world.

- How and why does social change happen?
- What factors shape the success of a social movement?
- What does it mean to practice sociology?

>> Sociological Perspectives on Social Change

Social change comes in a variety of forms, from social protests to technological innovation, but all of it comes as a result of things we do. And within the past few decades, we have witnessed dramatic shifts as a consequence of human agency. Examples include the computer revolution and the explosion of Internet connectivity; the collapse of communism; major regime changes and severe economic disruptions in Africa, the Middle East, and eastern Europe; the spread of AIDS and the efforts to contain it; the cloning of complex animals; and the first major terrorist attack on U.S. soil. Today we continue to face global challenges, such as international terrorism and global climate change, and the way we respond is in our hands.

As humans, modifying our physical and social environment seems to come naturally.

Social change Shifts in how humans think and act within society that alter material, cognitive, and normative culture.

Functionalist perspective A sociological paradigm that sees society as like a living organism in which its various parts work together for the good of the whole.

Conflict perspective A sociological paradigm that focuses on power and the allocation of valued resources in society.

Interactionist perspective A sociological paradigm that maintains that society is a product of our everyday encounters with others through which we establish shared meanings and thus construct order.

We tinker, innovate, and experiment, developing new technologies, ideas, and ways of doing things. Each innovation represents an example of **social change,** which refers to shifts in how humans think and act within society that alter material, cognitive, and normative culture. Social change can occur so slowly as to be almost undetectable to those it affects, but it can also happen with breathtaking rapidity. As the accompanying "Social Change in the USA" table shows, in the past century or so, the U.S. population has more than doubled, the percentage of people finishing high school and attending college has skyrocketed, women have entered the paid labor force in significant numbers, life expectancy has risen, technological innovation has exploded, men and women have been marrying later, and family size has shrunk. At times, as we saw in this chapter's opening example about college student protests, we intentionally pursue social and political change in hopes of bringing about a better world.

From the very inception of the discipline, sociologists have sought to understand the nature and direction of social change. As we saw in the Chapter 1, Émile Durkheim, a key contributor to the **functionalist perspective,** focused on the interplay between the division of labor and the collective conscience; Karl Marx, whose work gave rise to the **conflict perspective,** emphasized the relationship between technological innovation and systems of social relations; and theorists working from the **interactionist perspective,** such as George Herbert Mead and W. I. Thomas, investigated the ways we construct culture, thus instigating social

Social Change in the USA

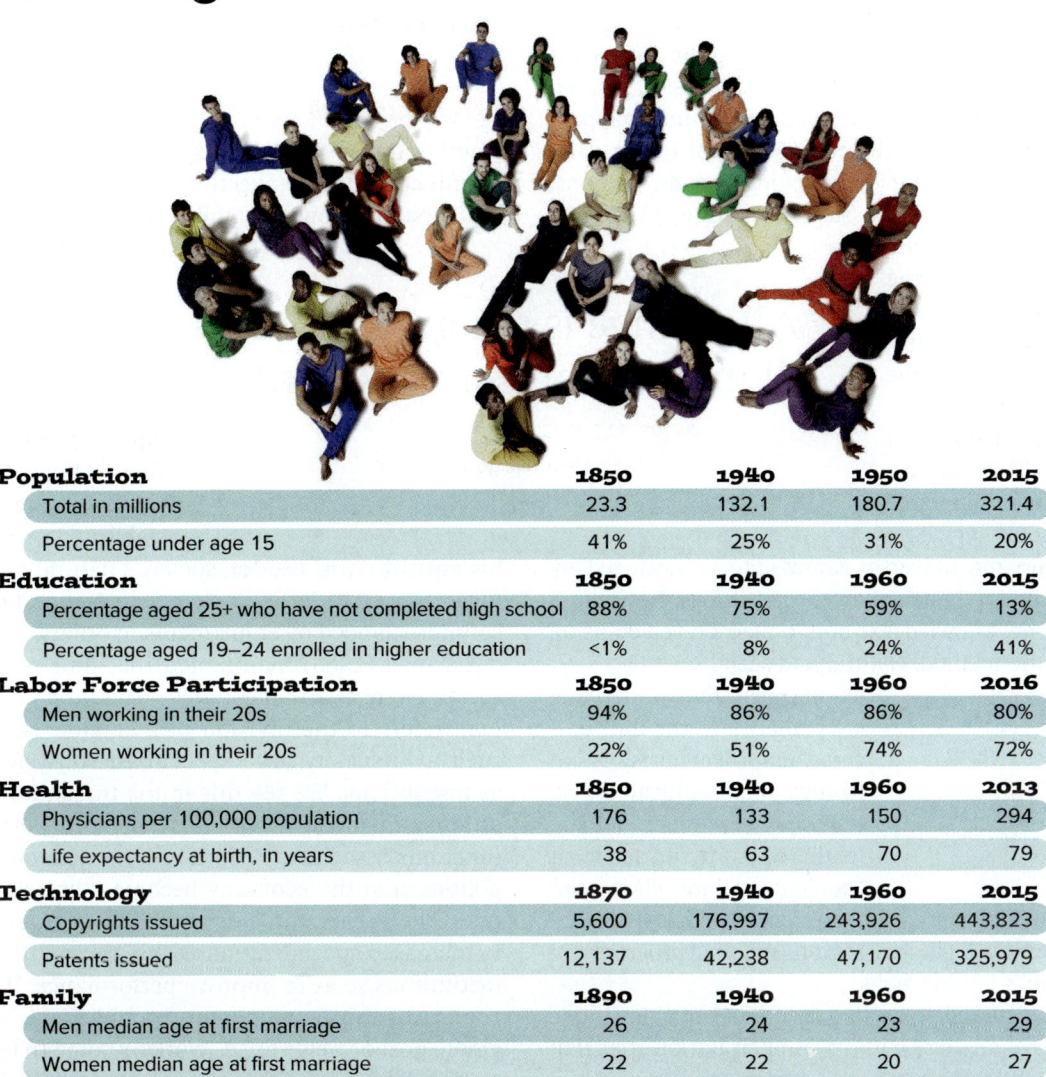

Population	1850	1940	1950	2015
Total in millions	23.3	132.1	180.7	321.4
Percentage under age 15	41%	25%	31%	20%
Education	**1850**	**1940**	**1960**	**2015**
Percentage aged 25+ who have not completed high school	88%	75%	59%	13%
Percentage aged 19–24 enrolled in higher education	<1%	8%	24%	41%
Labor Force Participation	**1850**	**1940**	**1960**	**2016**
Men working in their 20s	94%	86%	86%	80%
Women working in their 20s	22%	51%	74%	72%
Health	**1850**	**1940**	**1960**	**2013**
Physicians per 100,000 population	176	133	150	294
Life expectancy at birth, in years	38	63	70	79
Technology	**1870**	**1940**	**1960**	**2015**
Copyrights issued	5,600	176,997	243,926	443,823
Patents issued	12,137	42,238	47,170	325,979
Family	**1890**	**1940**	**1960**	**2015**
Men median age at first marriage	26	24	23	29
Women median age at first marriage	22	22	20	27
Birthrate for women aged 20–24 per 1,000	168.4	135.6	258.1	79

Note: Data are comparable, although definitions vary somewhat across time. Earliest birthrate is from 1905.

Sources: Bureau of Labor Statistics 2017a; Carter et al. 2006:vol. 1: 28–29, 401–402, 440, 541, 685, 697, 709, vol. 2: 441–442, vol. 3: 422–425, 427–428; National Center for Health Statistics 2016:Tables 3, 15, 83; National Center for Education Statistics 2016:Tables 104.10, 302.60; U.S. Census Bureau 2010a:Table 80, 2016e:Table MS-2, 2016j:Table S0201; U.S. Copyright Office 2016; U.S. Patent and Trademark Office 2016. *Photo:* ©Nisian Hughes/Getty Images

change, through everyday interactions. Sociologists who came after them and who specialize in the study of social change developed three important theoretical approaches with emphases on evolution, equilibrium, and power.

THE EVOLUTION OF SOCIETIES

Some early sociologists, inspired in part by Charles Darwin's (1859) evolutionary model of nature and rooted in the functionalist perspective, proposed a **social evolution** model of social change, according to which societies progress from simple to complex over time. From this perspective, traditional societies contain within them the essential building blocks that serve as the foundation for all societies. Analysis of "primitive" societies would reveal the indispensable tasks, or functions, that must be addressed if society is to survive. As societies become more "civilized," even though complexity increases, those core functions still need to be fulfilled. They believed that gaining a rational understanding of the laws of society would enhance our capacity to control and direct social change.

> **Social evolution** A theory of social change that holds that societies progress from simple to complex over time.

Auguste Comte, for example, whose contributions to early sociology we explored in the Sociology's Roots section of Chapter 1, posited the Law of Three Stages to describe social change over time. During the *theological* stage, people base their knowledge and decision making on religious principles. To explain why things happen, people turn toward the direct involvement in our daily lives of supernatural or divine beings—gods, demons, and the like. During this stage, according to Comte, people are irrational and superstitious. In the *metaphysical* stage, worship of concrete, active beings gives way to the belief that abstract forces guide what happens in the world. This perspective assumes that there is an underlying logic built within the universe. Knowledge is advanced by studying the fundamental essence of things. In Comte's *positive* stage, knowledge is built on facts revealed using the scientific method. Natural and social scientists seek to uncover the underlying laws that govern the universe. Empirical investigation trumps philosophical reflection, and researchers adhere to the Missouri principle of "don't just tell me, show me."

Equilibrium model The theory that society's natural tendency is toward social order with change in one part of society counterbalanced by adjustments in others.

During this stage, according to Comte, people are rational, guided by logic and reason, making progress not only possible, but inevitable.

Sociologists today are largely critical of this simple evolutionary analogy with its implicit notion that that those who adapt to changed circumstances are inherently superior. Most similarly reject the idea that all societies follow a singular path from simple to complex. Social change can happen in different ways and at different paces not only *between* societies, but also *within* societies. Within the United States, for example, many small towns are still rooted in an agricultural economy, which is reflected in their local culture. In many developing nations, cell phone service has become a normal part of everyday life. Most sociologists have also rejected the ethnocentric notion that traditional societies are primitive and that modern societies are civilized.

> **SOC**THINK
>
> Why would early theorists have thought of traditional societies as "primitive"? How is this a reflection of the evolutionary theoretical paradigm they adopted?

Traditional societies, in their adaptation to their environments, exhibit significant levels of sophistication and innovation.

EQUILIBRIUM AND SOCIAL ORDER

Another theory to explain social change, also rooted in the functionalist perspective, portrays societies as naturally tending toward stability or social order. Sociologist Talcott Parsons, an advocate of this model, maintained that even seemingly significant social disruptions, such as protests and riots, are but temporary interruptions along the pathway to enhanced social stability. According to his **equilibrium model,** society's natural tendency is toward social order with change in one part of society counterbalanced by adjustments in others.

> *All change is not growth, as all movement is not forward.*
>
> Ellen Glasgow

Parsons (1966) maintained that four processes of social change are inevitable. The first, *differentiation,* refers to the division of a singular social body, such as a society, into specialized subsystems, such as institutions. We see this in the transition from traditional to modern societies when the overlapping functions associated with family, education, religion, politics, and the economy become increasingly separate. The second process, *adaptive upgrading,* refers to increased specialization within those differentiated institutions so as to improve performance. Within the context of the economy, for example, specialists in a whole host of fields arise. Workers come to focus their time and energy within only one small sector of the larger economy. Such specialization allows for greater productivity and efficiency.

However, all that division and specialization creates the potential for social separation and disorder, which leads to Parsons's third process, *inclusion.* This process is meant to ensure that the various elements of the social system work together. In the contemporary workplace, executives frequently express concern about the development of "silos" within the organization, meaning that elements of the firm exist in relative isolation from each other. Inclusion highlights the importance of building links between those elements. Finally, as a means to enhance solidarity within the social system, Parsons contended that societies experience *value generalization*—the development of new values to legitimate the broader range of activities that arose with differentiation. All four processes identified by Parsons stress consensus—societal agreement on the nature of social organization and values (Gerhardt 2002).

SOC THINK

Why might the equilibrium model have a difficult time addressing such issues as inequality and poverty as social problems to be solved?

©Alex Brandon/AP Images

One of the sources of potential strain that can lead to such social adaptation involves technological innovation. As we saw in the "Material Culture" section of Chapter 3, sociologist William F. Ogburn (1922) distinguished between material and nonmaterial aspects of culture. **Material culture** includes inventions, artifacts, and technology; **nonmaterial culture** encompasses ideas, norms, communications, and social organization. Ogburn pointed out that technology often changes faster than do the ideas and values with which we make sense of such change. Thus, the nonmaterial culture, including values and norms, typically must respond to changes in the material culture. Ogburn introduced the term **cultural lag** to refer to the period of adjustment when the nonmaterial culture is still struggling to adapt to new material conditions. One example is the Internet, which spread quickly but now raises serious questions about personal privacy.

Parsons and other theorists would argue that those parts of society that persist, even including crime, terrorism, and poverty, do so because they contribute to social stability. Critics note, however, that his approach virtually disregards the use of coercion by the powerful to maintain the illusion of a stable, well-integrated society (Gouldner 1960). From the conflict perspective, control over resources plays a significant role in the structure of society and the maintenance of social order.

> **Material culture** Our physical modification of the natural environment to suit our purposes.
>
> **Nonmaterial culture** Ways of using material objects, as well as customs, ideas, expressions, beliefs, knowledge, philosophies, governments, and patterns of communication.
>
> **Cultural lag** The general principle that technological innovation occurs more quickly than does our capacity to perceive, interpret, and respond to that change.

5 Movies on SOCIAL MOVEMENTS AND SOCIAL CHANGE

2 Fists Up
Students fight for racial equality at the University of Missouri.

Clash
Arab Spring storylines come together in the back of a police van.

Freedom Riders
Young activists challenge segregation in the American South.

Citzenfour
A whistleblower stands up to the U.S. government.

Beasts of the Southern Wild
When you're small, you gotta fix what you can.

RESOURCES, POWER, AND CHANGE

Karl Marx, who utilized the conflict perspective, accepted the evolutionary argument that societies develop along a particular path, but argued that power and control over valued resources play a pivotal role in shaping the direction of social change. History, according to Marx, proceeds through a series of stages or epochs, and during each stage, those who control the means of production exploit an entire class of people. Thus, in ancient society owners exploited people they enslaved, under feudalism's estate system the aristocracy exploited peasants, and in modern capitalist society the bourgeoisie exploits the working class. Change happens when a revolution in social relations occurs, leading to the next stage. Ultimately, as we saw in the "Economic Systems" section of Chapter 9, Marx predicted that, after the problem of production is solved, human society would move toward the final stage of development: a classless communist society, or "community of free individuals," as Marx described it in 1867 in *Das Kapital* (Marx [1867] 2000:478).

Marx argued that conflict is a normal and desirable aspect of social change. In fact, change must be encouraged if social inequality is to be eliminated. In his view, people are not restricted to a passive role in responding to inevitable cycles or changes in the material culture. Rather, Marxist theory offers a tool for those who want to seize control of the historical process and gain their freedom from injustice. Efforts to promote social change are, however, likely to meet with resistance.

Individuals and groups in positions of power have a stake in maintaining the existing state of affairs. Social economist Thorstein Veblen (1857–1929) coined the term **vested interests** to refer to those people or groups who benefit most from the existing social, political, and economic system. They are the ones who have the most to lose should social change take place. For example, historically the American Medical Association (AMA) has taken strong stands against national health insurance and the professionalization of midwifery. National health insurance was seen as a threat to physicians' income and authority, and a rise in the status of midwives could threaten the preeminent position of doctors as deliverers of babies. In general, those with a disproportionate share of society's wealth, status, and power, such as members of the AMA, have a vested interest in preserving the status quo (Furedi 2006; Scelfo 2008; Veblen 1919).

> **Vested interests** Those people or groups who benefit most from the existing social, political, and economic structure.

Economic factors play an important role in resistance to social change. For example, it can be expensive for manufacturers to meet mandated standards for the safety of products and workers and for the protection of the environment. In the pursuit of both profit and survival, many firms seek to avoid the costs of meeting strict safety and environmental standards. If they have sufficient power in society, they can effectively pass the costs of such practices on to others who must bear the consequences. To battle against such influence requires countervailing sources of power. Government regulations, for example, force all companies to bear the common burden of such costs, and labor unions can present the unified power of workers as a group (Galbraith 1952).

Communities, too, protect their vested interests, often in the name of "protecting property values." The abbreviation NIMBY stands for "not in my backyard," a cry often heard when people protest landfills, prisons, nuclear power facilities, and even bike trails and group

©David Crigger, Bristol Herald Courier/AP Images

homes for people with developmental disabilities. The targeted community may not challenge the need for the facility, but may simply insist that it be located elsewhere. The NIMBY attitude has become so common that it is almost impossible for policy makers to find acceptable locations for facilities such as hazardous waste dumps. Unfortunately, it is often those with the fewest resources who end up on the losing end of such battles (Scally 2015; Wonjun et al. 2016).

In today's world, change is inevitable. From sociology we learn that we need to watch for the ways in which change evolves out of existing practices. We also must be aware of the ways in which societies perpetuate existing social order by seeking an acceptable level of balance between stability and change. Finally, we recognize the role that power and control over resources plays in shaping what changes do or do not occur. In all these cases, because of the ways it both enables and constrains, we must be aware of the role that technology plays in affecting the nature and direction of social change.

>> Technology and the Future

Social change also comes as transformed material culture. As discussed in the "Elements of Culture" section of Chapter 3, through technology, humans modify the natural environment to meet our wants and needs. Technological advances—the telephone, the automobile, the airplane, the television, the atomic

©Oliver Lantzendorffer/Getty Images RF

bomb, and more recently, the computer, digital media, and the cell phone—have brought striking changes to our culture, our patterns of socialization, our social institutions, and our day-to-day social interactions. Technological innovations are, in fact, emerging and being accepted with remarkable speed. In developing nations, for example, whole populations can move quite rapidly from having limited access to technologies to adopting them in their more advanced forms. An example of such leapfrogging occurs when countries skip landlines almost entirely and move directly to widespread access to cell phones, or when they go straight to e-commerce for financial transactions, such as those provided by the M-Pesa app in places such as Kenya, Afghanistan, and India (Harford 2017).

Technological change does not come without costs. Already in the mid-1800s, for example, Karl Marx predicted that technological innovation would cost people their jobs as machines took over work previously done by humans. Concerns about mechanization, computerization, and robotization continue today. Technology analysts Thomas Davenport and Julia Kirby (2016) suggest that jobs particularly susceptible to automation include those that have clearly delineated rules for performance, involve simple content transmission, require quantitative analysis, or necessitate little face-to-face contact with customers or coworkers. For example, radiologists who read x-ray images and CT scans to diagnose tumors are susceptible to replacement by technology that can draw on pattern-recognition databases to do the job. This kind of social change raises economic concerns about what happens if the supply of workers looking for good jobs exceeds the demand of employers looking to hire them (M. Ford 2015; Frey and Osborne 2017).

COMPUTER TECHNOLOGY

Although the revolutions in transportation and communication have brought us closer together since the Industrial Revolution, the Internet provides a potential for immediate global connection that previously had been virtually and physically impossible. The Internet evolved from a computer system built in 1962 by the U.S. Defense Department to enable scholars and military researchers to continue their government work, even if part of the nation's communications system were destroyed by nuclear attack. For years, it was difficult to gain access to the Internet without holding a position at a university or a government research laboratory. Today, however, virtually anyone with sufficient resources can reach the Internet with a wireless-enabled computer or a smartphone. People buy and sell cars, trade stocks, auction off items, research new medical remedies, vote, connect with friends, and coordinate social movements, to mention just a few of the thousands of possibilities (Isaacson 2014; Shirky 2008).

Driven in part by the spread of mobile phones around the world, Internet access has gone global. In 2017, the Internet reached 3.7 billion users, or 49.6 percent of the world's population (Internet World Stats 2017a). If we look at global Internet use, the regions with the greatest number of users are Asia and Europe. Asia alone represents more than 1 billion users. However, in terms of access, as the "Internet Use" graph shows, a larger proportion of the population in North America—88 percent—can connect to the Internet than in any other continent. Even though Asia has the greatest number of users, only 45.2 percent of the population there has Internet access. Another sign of the global nature of this expansion has been the increase in languages used on the Internet. As the "Internet Top 10 Languages" graph depicts, English represents the most commonly used language with 952 million users. Between 2000 and 2017, the number of users of all languages has increased dramatically. English speakers increased 576 percent, but Chinese-speaking users increased 2,263 percent and Arabic speakers increased 6,806 percent' (Internet World Stats 2017b).

Unfortunately, a digital divide persists, and not everyone can get onto the information highway, especially not the less affluent. Moreover, this pattern of inequality is global. In Africa, for example, only 27.7 percent of the population has access to the Internet (Internet World Statistics 2017a). The core nations that Immanuel Wallerstein described in his **world systems analysis** have a virtual monopoly on information technology; the peripheral nations of Asia, Africa, and Latin America depend on the core nations both for technology and for the information it provides. For example, North America, Europe, and a few industrialized nations in other regions possess almost all the world's Internet hosts—computers that are connected directly to the worldwide network.

> **World systems analysis** A view of the global economic system as one divided between certain industrialized nations that control wealth and developing countries that are controlled and exploited.

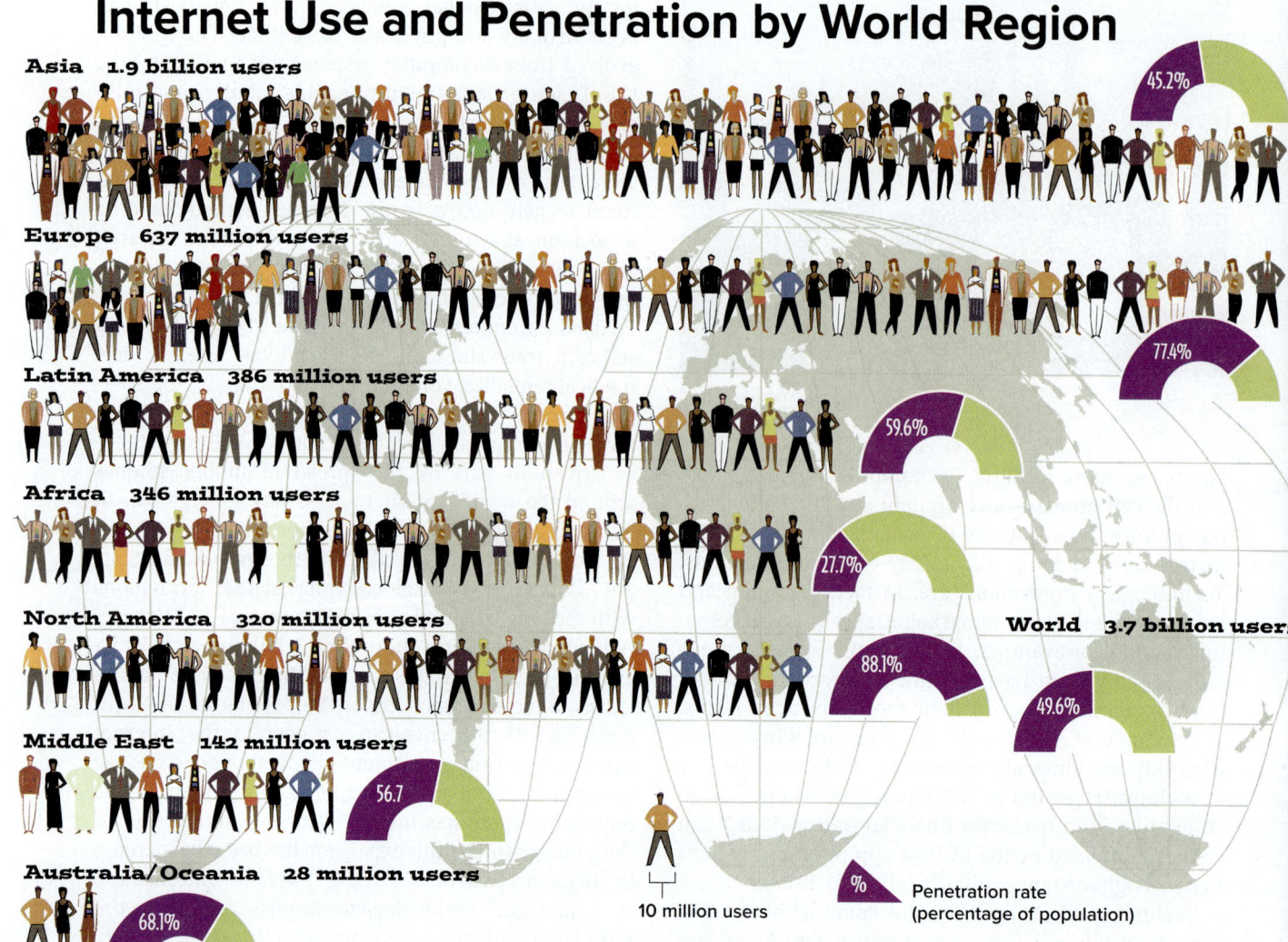

Source: Internet World Stats 2016a.

PRIVACY AND CENSORSHIP IN A GLOBAL VILLAGE

In the early days of Internet expansion, many people were concerned about sharing personal information online for fear that someone might use it against them. Now, with the advent of Facebook, Instagram, Twitter, and a whole host of other social-networking sites, many Internet users have abandoned that concern. People regularly share thoughts, feelings, and actions with others, including total strangers. But Facebook's frequent privacy-setting changes and selling of customers' personal information raised red flags for many, and others have learned the hard way that schools and employers use information they find online to make decisions about discipline and hiring (Finder 2006; Relerford et al. 2008; Solove 2008).

Concerns about who knows what extend beyond the information we deliberately share to things others can know about us without our knowledge or explicit consent. Recent advances have made it increasingly easy for business firms, government agencies, and even criminals to retrieve and store information about everything from our buying habits to our Web-surfing patterns. In public places, at work, and on the Internet, surveillance devices now track our every move, be it a keystroke or an ATM withdrawal.

As technology spreads, so does the exposure to risk. In 2013, for example, 110 million credit cards from the retail store Target were compromised. In September 2016, Yahoo! revealed the theft of account information for at least 500 million users by a hacker working on behalf of a foreign government. A few months later, Yahoo! announced that one billion user accounts had been compromised in yet another data breach. And in 2016, FriendFinder reported the theft of usernames, passwords, and email addresses for 339 million users of its AdultFriendFinder site—which describes itself as "the world's largest sex & swinger community" (Goel and Perlroth 2016; Greenberg 2016; Yang and Jayakumar 2014).

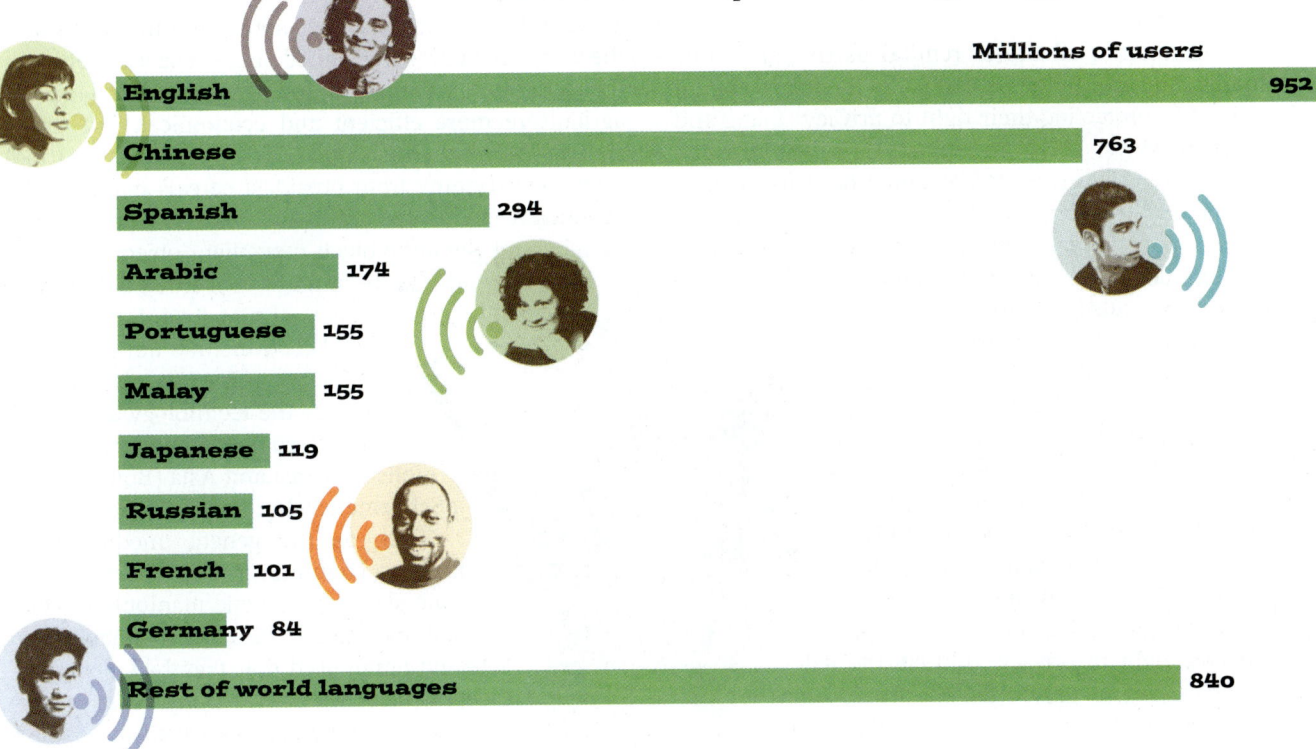

Source: Internet World Stats 2017b.

Copyright ©Matt Wuerker. Reprinted with permission.

The problem extends beyond identity theft and illegal acts by individuals. Increasingly, questions are being raised about the questionable use of technology by those in legitimate positions of power as a routine part of their jobs. In short, new technologies threaten not just our privacy but our freedom from surveillance and censorship (O'Harrow 2005). There is, for example, the danger that the most powerful groups in a society will use technology to violate the privacy of the less powerful. Indeed, officials in China block access to a range of websites, including Google, Facebook, YouTube, Twitter, and the *New York Times* (Denyer 2016; Fu 2017).

Civil liberties advocates remind us that the same abuses can occur in the United States if citizens are not vigilant in protecting their right to privacy (Liang and Lu 2010; Moyer 2010). In June 2013, it was revealed that the U.S. government's National Security Agency (NSA) was regularly and indiscriminately collecting phone records from millions of Verizon users (Greenwald 2013). The information allowed it to track who called whom, when, where, and for how long. In addition, through its PRISM program, the NSA was tapping into user data from Google, Facebook, and other sites, allowing it access to emails, chats, and other online activities (Greenwald and MacAskill 2013).

In the United States, legislation regulating the surveillance of electronic communications has not always upheld citizens' right to privacy. In 1986 the federal government passed the Electronic Communications Privacy Act, which outlawed the surveillance of telephone calls except with the permission of both the U.S. attorney general and a federal judge. Telegrams, faxes, and email did not receive the same degree of protection, however. In 2001, one month after the terrorist attacks of September 11, Congress passed the USA PATRIOT Act, which relaxed existing legal checks on surveillance by law enforcement officers. Federal agencies are now freer to gather data electronically, including credit card receipts and banking records (Etzioni 2007; Schneier 2015; Singel 2008).

BIOTECHNOLOGY AND THE GENE POOL

Another field in which technological advances have spurred global social change is biotechnology. Sex selection of fetuses, genetically engineered organisms, the cloning of animals—these have been among the significant yet controversial scientific advances in the field of biotechnology in recent years. No phase of life now seems exempt from therapeutic or medical intervention. In fact, sociologists view many aspects of biotechnology as an extension of the recent trend toward the medicalization of society. Through genetic manipulation, the medical profession is expanding its turf still further (Enriquez and Gullans 2015; Harari 2017; Kozubek 2016).

One area of genetic modification that has raised concern involves genetically modified (GM) food. This issue arose in Europe but has since spread to other parts of the world, including the United States. The idea behind the technology is to increase food production and make agriculture more efficient and economical. But critics use the term *frankenfood* (as in Frankenstein) to refer to everything from breakfast cereals made from genetically engineered grains to "fresh" GM tomatoes. Members of the antibiotech movement object to tampering with nature and are concerned about the possible health effects of GM food. Supporters of GM food include not just biotech companies but also those who see the technology as a way to help feed the growing populations of Africa and Asia (Bouis 2007; Schurman 2004).

Even as the genetic modification of plants continues to be a concern, the debate about the genetic manipulation of animals escalated in 1997 when scientists in Scotland announced that they had cloned a sheep, which they named Dolly. After many unsuccessful attempts, they were finally able to replace the genetic material of a sheep's egg with DNA from an adult sheep, creating a lamb that was a clone of the adult. Shortly thereafter, Japanese researchers successfully cloned cows. Since then many other species have been successfully cloned, as can be seen in the "Cloning Milestones" timeline. It is now

©David Toase/Getty Images RF

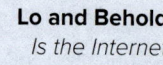

5 Movies on TECHNOLOGY AND ITS IMPACT

Lo and Behold
Is the Internet a force for good, evil, or both?

The Martian
Stranded on Mars and only technological ingenuity can save him.

Ex Machina
What happens when the line between humans and robots blurs?

The Road
Human survival in a post-apocalyptic world.

Koyaanisqaatsi
A way of life that calls for another way of living.

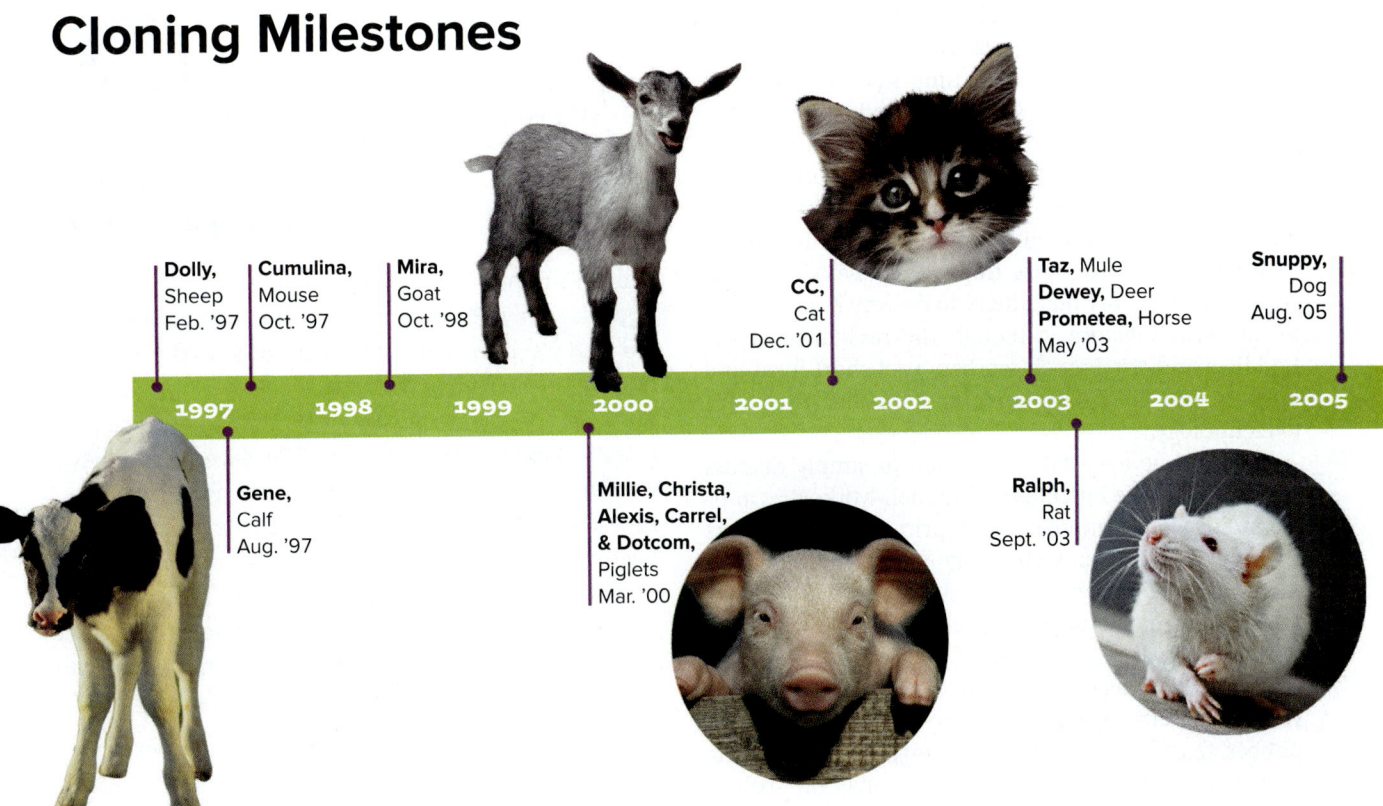

Cloning Milestones

even possible to get your pet cat or dog cloned, and scientists have begun work on "de-extinction," the cloning of extinct species such as the woolly mammoth and passenger pigeon (McCauley et al. 2016; Schultz 2016). Such accomplishments point to the possibility that in the near future, scientists may be able to clone human beings.

Manipulation that goes even further than cloning involves potentially altering species through genetic engineering. Fish and plant genes have already been mixed to create frost-resistant potato and tomato crops. More recently, human genes have been implanted in pigs to provide humanlike kidneys for organ transplants. Geneticists working with mouse fetuses have managed to disable genes that carry an undesirable trait and replace them with genes carrying a desirable trait. And in 2015, scientists announced that they had succeeded in genetically modifying human embryos. The Chinese scientists targeted a gene responsible for a potentially fatal blood disorder and they used nonviable embryos that could not have resulted in live births. These modified genes are heritable. If they were to be implanted in a baby that was born and grew to have children of his or her own, he or she could pass on these genes to the next generation, the possible consequences of which are unknown (Cyranoski and Reardon 2015).

Such advances raise ethical concerns related to applying such engineering to humans to eliminate disease or infirmities or to enhance physical abilities such as sight or strength (Avise 2004). This concern is shared by most Americans; 81 percent say cloning humans is morally wrong. And, even though cloning nonhuman mammals has become routine, 60 percent say that doing so is morally wrong (Gallup 2016b). Even William F. Ogburn could not have anticipated the extent of such scientific developments when he first proposed the problem of cultural lag in the 1920s.

SOCTHINK

If you could modify your children's genes to protect them from genetic diseases, would you do it? How about enhancing their abilities, such as eyesight, strength, or intelligence?

RESISTANCE TO TECHNOLOGY

Given such consequences, it should come as no surprise that, through the ages, there have been those who questioned whether such technological innovation equals progress. Inventions that grew out of the Industrial Revolution, for example, led to strong resistance in some countries. In England, beginning in 1811, masked

Chapter 15 / Social Change

Luddites Rebellious craft-workers in 19th-century England who destroyed new factory machinery as part of their resistance to the Industrial Revolution.

craft-workers took extreme measures: They mounted nighttime raids on factories and destroyed some of the new machinery. The government hunted these rebels, known as **Luddites,** and ultimately banished or hanged them. In a similar effort in France, angry workers threw their wooden shoes (sabots) into factory machinery to destroy it, giving rise to the term *sabotage*. Although the resistance of the Luddites and the French workers was short-lived and unsuccessful, they have come to symbolize resistance to technology.

It would be a mistake, however, to simply dismiss the actions of the Luddites and French workers as anti-technology or irrational. Their primary concern was with the impact such technology had on their employment, their communities, and their way of life. They recognized that it would undercut taken-for-granted norms and values and fought against such threats. Although it is easy to write off such groups and individuals as being against progress—or even as technophobes that fear change—their bigger concern is the impact that adoption of technologies has on society. The Amish, for example, are often dismissed as backward, when, in fact, they are quite rational and deliberative about adopting technology. They carefully weigh the benefits new technologies would provide against the potential costs adoption would have on family and community life. They do not assume that, simply because something makes work easier or faster, it is necessarily better. For the Amish, working together in community is more highly valued than working more quickly in isolation (Hostetler 1993; Hurst and McConnell 2010; Kraybill et al. 2013).

Five Questions to Ask When Adopting New Technology

- What is the problem for which this technology is the solution?
- Whose problem is it?
- What new problems might be created because we solve the problem?
- Which people and institutions might be most seriously harmed?
- Which people and institutions might acquire special economic and political power?

Source: Postman 1988.   *Photo:* ©Ariel Skelley/Blend Images LLC RF

Personal Sociology

Technology and Society

I confess to having mixed emotions about new technology. I love my iPhone and couldn't resist the appeal of the iPad. Yet I worry about the consequences such technologies have on my relationships with others. We are quick to adopt the latest gadgets, but what about the effects of abandoning old norms? I'm sure all of us have encountered that earbud-wearing cell-phone talker who barely seems to notice we exist. Technologies such as Facebook and Instagram do enable us to maintain connections with distant friends and family. But what happens to our relationships with the people right next to us when our attention is diverted to status updates and text messages?

Sociologist Jacques Ellul (1964, 1980, 1990) argued that the key factor to consider when analyzing our modern technological society is not simply the *technology,* by which he meant the physical tools we create as we modify our material environment, but what he referred to more generally as *technique*. By this he meant our systemic commitment to maximizing efficiency and increasing productivity in all areas of human endeavor. Success, whether in business, education, or love, is increasingly measured in quantitative terms. That which cannot be measured is suspect. For example, we see evidence of this at work in the No Child Left Behind education reforms. Performance on particular kinds of tests, in a narrow range of subjects, is becoming the primary indicator of learning. Although living in a technique-focused system has the advantage of technical progress, we lose something human in the process—art, beauty, and qualitative, as opposed to quantitative, values. Ellul's concerns echo those of Max Weber about the dehumanizing consequences of bureaucracy.

Most of us today automatically adopt the latest technologies without taking time to step back and ask what consequences they might have for social order and meaning. Communications professor Neil Postman (1988, 1993, 1999) argues that, instead of passively accepting technological innovations, we should critically examine whether we really need them and investigate what consequences adoption might have on ourselves, our relationships, and our society. He identified five questions we should ask whenever we consider adopting a new technology or technique, which are highlighted in the accompanying "Five Questions" feature. Postman is calling us to consciously exercise our agency rather than simply accepting the logic of the technologically dominated **social structure**. Doing so enables us to resist unconscious acceptance and exercise greater freedom in the choices we make.

>> Social Movements

We do have the power to resist change even when it seems inevitable. More than that, we also have the power to bring about positive social change. Although factors such as the physical environment, population, technology, and social inequality serve as sources of change, it is the collective effort of individuals organized in social movements that ultimately leads to change. Sociologists use the term **social movements** to refer to organized collective activities to bring about or resist fundamental change in an existing group or society. Herbert Blumer (1955:19) recognized the special importance of social movements when he defined them as "collective enterprises to establish a new order of life."

In many nations, including the United States, social movements have had a dramatic impact on the course of history and the evolution of the social structure. Consider the actions of abolitionists, suffragists, civil rights workers, and anti–Vietnam War activists. Initially, for example, people viewed the ideas of Margaret Sanger and other early advocates of birth control as radical, yet contraceptives are now widely available in the United States. Similarly, protests—whether against the practices of multinational corporations, same-sex marriage, the unethical treatment of animals, environmental destruction, or war—challenge us to question our taken-for-granted understandings of what is happening and why. This holds true even if we never formally participate ourselves or do not fully subscribe to all the beliefs and practices of the protesters.

Social movements change how we think and act. Members of each social movement stepped outside traditional channels for bringing about social change, yet they had a noticeable influence on public policy and practice. At least since the work of Karl Marx, sociologists have studied how and why social movements emerge. Obviously, one factor is that people become dissatisfied with the way things are. To explain how this develops and is transformed into action, sociologists rely on two primary explanations: relative deprivation and resource mobilization.

RELATIVE DEPRIVATION

Those members of a society who feel most frustrated with and disgruntled by social and economic conditions are not necessarily the worst off in an objective sense. Social scientists have long recognized that what is most significant is how people perceive their situation. As Marx pointed out, although the misery of the workers was important to their perception of their oppressed state, so was their position in relation to the capitalist ruling class (McLellan 2000).

The term **relative deprivation** refers to people's perception that they lack the resources necessary to lead the kind of life they believe they deserve. The relative part refers to comparing one's self to others, and the deprivation part involves resources such as money, property, or power. In other words, things aren't as good as one hoped they would be. A relatively deprived person is dissatisfied because he or she feels downtrodden relative to some appropriate reference group. Thus, blue-collar workers who live in two-family houses on small plots of land—though hardly destitute—may nevertheless feel deprived in comparison to corporate managers and professionals who live in lavish homes in exclusive suburbs (Stewart 2006).

In addition to the feeling of relative deprivation, however, two other elements

> **Social structure** The underlying framework of society consisting of the positions people occupy and the relationships between them.
>
> **Social movement** An organized collective activity to bring about or resist fundamental change in an existing group or society.
>
> **Relative deprivation** People's perception that they lack the resources necessary to lead the kind of life they believe they deserve.

Did You Know?

...In 1916 Margaret Sanger opened a family planning and birth control clinic. Nine days later, it was raided by police, and she served 30 days in jail as a result. She was undeterred and continued working to dispense birth control information.

Photo: Source: Library of Congress, Prints and Photographs Division [LC-USZ62-29808]

must be present before discontent will be channeled into a social movement. First, people must feel that they have a right to their goals, that they deserve better than what they have. For example, the struggle against European colonialism in Africa intensified when growing numbers of Africans decided that it was legitimate for them to have political and economic independence. Second, the disadvantaged group must perceive that its goals cannot be attained through conventional means. This belief may or may not be correct. In any case, the group will not mobilize into a social movement unless there is a shared perception that members can end their relative deprivation only through collective action (Walker and Smith 2002).

Critics of this approach have noted that people don't need to feel deprived to be moved to act. In addition, this approach fails to explain why certain feelings of deprivation are transformed into social movements, whereas in other, similar situations, no collective effort is made to reshape society. Consequently, sociologists have paid increasing attention to the forces needed to bring about the emergence of social movements (Finkel and Rule 1987; Ratner 2004).

> *I cannot say whether things will get better if we change; what I can say is they must change if they are to get better.*
>
> — Georg Christoph Lichtenberg

Resource mobilization The ways in which a social movement utilizes such resources as money, political influence, access to the media, and personnel.

SOCTHINK

Are there any issues on your campus or in your community that people persistently complain about? If so, what factors might inhibit them from organizing to bring about social change?

RESOURCE MOBILIZATION APPROACH

Although the desire to start a social movement is important, having access to money, political influence, the media, and personnel makes things much easier. The term **resource mobilization** refers to the ways in which a social movement utilizes such resources. The success of a movement for change will depend in good part on what resources it has and how effectively it mobilizes them. The leadership of a social movement must be able to both access valued resources and activate potential followers (McCarthy and Zald 1977, 2002).

Max Weber laid a foundation for this model with his work on social power. As we explored in the "Weber and Social Resources" section in Chapter 10, Weber argued that class, status, and party represent three types of resources. Access to each shapes relative social power within society. Class involves ownership and control of material resources. Status entails control over social resources, including both the relative perception people have of an individual or group's prestige and the power of social network connections. And party refers to the capacity to organize to accomplish some specific goal. According to Weber, groups can utilize their relative power in one of these areas to

The Women's March on Washington drew more than 500,000 participants in January 2017. Many others marched at alternative locations around the country and around the world. *(left):* ©Amanda Edwards/FilmMagic/Getty Images; *(right):* ©Jenny Anderson/FilmMagic/Getty Images

gain greater power in another. In the United States, for example, the Civil Rights Movement effectively used its organizational power to alter the relative standing of African Americans in terms of both class and status (Ling 2006).

Sociologist Anthony Oberschall (1973:199) has argued that to sustain social protest or resistance, there must be both an "organizational base and continuity of leadership." As people become part of a social movement, norms develop to guide their behavior. Members of the movement may be expected to attend regular meetings of organizations, pay dues, recruit new adherents, and boycott "enemy" products or speakers. In forming a distinct identity, an emerging social movement may give rise to special language or new words for familiar terms. In keeping with this principle, social movements advocated for the use of new labels, such as *Blacks* and *African Americans* (to replace *Negroes*), *senior citizens* (to replace *old folks*), *gays* (to replace *homosexuals*), and *people with disabilities* (to replace *the handicapped*).

Leadership is a central factor in the mobilization of the discontented into social movements. Often, a movement will be led by a charismatic figure, such as occurred in the civil rights movement with Dr. Martin Luther King, Jr. Charismatic authority alone, however, may not be enough. If a group is to succeed, coordinated action is essential. As they grow, such organizations may find they need to take advantage of the efficiency that bureaucratic structures provide. This can result in their taking on some of the characteristics of the groups they were organized to protest. For example, leaders might dominate the decision-making process without directly consulting followers.

Innovations in social-networking technologies, including Facebook, Twitter, and a variety of messaging apps, can serve as important resources, facilitating the organization of mass protests. The capacity to capture and share video of apparent brutality played an important part in the development and expansion of the Black Lives Matter movement. Text messaging and social networking also spawned the Arab Spring uprisings against repressive leaders that started in Tunisia in 2010 and spread to Egypt, Libya, Yemen, and other countries.

Many of those who participated in the Arab Spring protests were young, well educated, and technologically savvy. They sought economic and political reforms and greater opportunities for self-determination, and they used their knowledge and abilities to bring about change. As a result of the Arab Spring protests, Tunisian President Zine El Abidine Ben Ali was ousted after 23 years in power. Egyptian President Hosni Mubarak, who had been in power for nearly 30 years, resigned. Libyan leader Colonel Muammar el-Qaddafi, who ruled for 42 years, was overthrown and killed. And Yemeni President Ali Abdullah Sleh stepped down after 33 years in power (Gelvin 2012; Noueihed and Warren 2012; Raghavan 2011; Shenker et al. 2011). However, that was not the end of the story, because the capacity to mobilize resources is not limited to only one side. In many of these countries, the power struggles and civil wars that followed the ousting or challenging of leaders generated conditions that are as authoritarian, brutal, and corrupt as they were before the Arab Spring. In Egypt, for example, the army eventually seized power, and in Syria a brutal civil war continues (Worth 2016).

GENDER AND SOCIAL MOVEMENTS

Betty Friedan's publication of *The Feminine Mystique* in 1963 gave voice to a feeling shared by many women at the time that something was wrong, though they did not know that others felt the same way, as we saw in the "Second Wave" section of Chapter 12. The book alone, however, was not enough. One of the challenges faced by women's liberation activists of the late 1960s and early 1970s was to convince women that they were being deprived of their rights and of socially valued resources. Consciousness-raising groups represented a critical tool used by women's liberation activists in the 1960s and 1970s. In these groups, women gathered

Did You Know?

... Women played an active role in the antiwar and civil rights movements but were often blocked from positions of leadership. Symbolizing this exclusion perhaps better than any other example was Student Nonviolent Coordinating Committee leader Stokely Carmichael's infamous line "The only position for women in SNCC is prone." Such sexism and discrimination led women to start their own organizations to fight for women's rights.

Photo: ©Bettmann/Contributor/Getty Images

New social movement An organized collective activity that addresses values and social identities, as well as improvements in the quality of life.

to discuss topics relevant to their experience in the home, at work, in politics, and more. This helped create a popular base that contributed to significant political and social change (Morgan 2009; Sarachild 1978).

Sociologists point out that gender continues to be an important element in understanding social movements. In our male-dominated society, women continue to find themselves cut off from leadership positions in social movement organizations. Though women often serve disproportionately as volunteers in these movements, their contributions are not always recognized, nor are their voices as easily heard as men's. Gender bias causes the real extent of their influence to be overlooked. Indeed, traditional examination of the sociopolitical system tends to focus on such male-dominated corridors of power as legislatures and corporate boardrooms, to the neglect of more female-dominated domains such as households, community-based groups, and faith-based networks. But efforts to influence family values, child rearing, relationships between parents and schools, and spiritual values are clearly significant to a culture and society (Ferree and Merrill 2000; Kuumba 2001; V. Taylor 1999, 2004).

Before the June 2009 presidential election in Iran, women's social movement organizations foresaw an opportunity for change, and they organized to take advantage of it. Almost 40 equal rights groups combined to form an organization called the "Coalition of Women's Movements to Advocate Electoral Demands." Noushin Ahmadi Khorasani (2009), a key leader of the women's rights movement in Iran, described the opportunity this way: "We could grasp this relatively short and transient moment with both hands, with hope and motivation (and looking forward to tomorrow) in order to voice our demands." During the government crackdown on the protests that followed the election, women continued to fight for change. Perhaps the most visible symbol of their fight was Neda Agha-Soltan, a protestor who was shot and bled to death in the street. The violent image was caught on video and quickly spread around the world (Gheytanchi 2009; Ravitz 2009). Women continue to play a substantial role in social movements, as demonstrated by their leadership in many of the democratic uprisings during the 2011 Arab Spring protests (Ghitis 2011).

NEW SOCIAL MOVEMENTS

Beginning in the late 1960s, European social scientists observed a change in both the composition and the targets of emerging social movements. Previously, traditional social movements had focused on economic issues, often led by labor unions or by people who shared the same occupation. However, many social movements that have become active in recent decades—including the second and third waves of feminism, the peace movement, and the environmental movement—do not have the social class roots typical of the labor movements in the United States and Europe over the past century (Carty and Onyett 2006).

The term **new social movements** refers to organized collective activities that address values and social identities, as well as improvements in the quality of life. These movements may be involved in developing collective identities. Many have complex agendas that go beyond a single issue and even cross national boundaries. Educated, middle-class people are significantly represented in some of these new social movements, such as the women's movement, and the movement for lesbian and gay rights (Tilly 1993, 2004). As part of the environmental movement, for example, those with sufficient resources may find it easier to afford the latest eco-friendly lightbulbs or electric car.

New social movements generally do not view government as their ally in the struggle for a better society. They typically do not seek to overthrow the government, but they may criticize, protest, or harass public officials. Researchers have found that members of new social movements call into question the legitimacy of arguments made by established authorities. Even scientific or technical claims, they argue, do not simply represent objective facts, but often serve specific interests. This characteristic is especially evident in the environmental and anti-nuclear-power movements, whose activists present their own experts to counter those of government or big business (Clammer 2009; Jamison 2006; Rootes 2007).

Tesla, Inc., co-founded by Elon Musk (pictured), produces a line of high-performance electric cars. ©David Paul Morris/Bloomberg via Getty Images

©Stockbyte/Getty Images RF

environmental contexts do influence social change, it still takes people willing to do things differently to bring about such shifts.

Sociology is a tool that helps open up new pathways for us. By enabling us to see things we might have missed before, it helps us view ourselves and the world around us differently. Sociology allows us to recognize how the distribution of social, cultural, and material resources gives advantage to some and disadvantage to others. It helps us understand whether the things we do are consistent with what we claim to believe. It can inform our conversation of whether we are headed where we want to go. It does these things

SOC THINK

Online sites such as changemakers.net serve as information clearinghouses and networking hubs for social activists. How might the existence of such online resources shape social activism both positively and negatively?

The environmental movement is one of many new social movements with a worldwide focus. In their efforts to reduce air and water pollution, curtail global climate change, and protect endangered animal species, environmental activists have realized that strong regulatory measures within a single country are not sufficient. Similarly, labor union leaders and human rights advocates cannot adequately address exploitative sweatshop conditions in a developing country if a multinational corporation can simply move the factory to another country, where workers earn even less. Whereas traditional views of social movements tended to emphasize resource mobilization on a local level, social movement theory now offers a broader, global perspective on social and political activism (Obach 2004).

>> Sociology Is a Verb

Ultimately, social change happens because we begin to act in new ways. It involves our stepping off expected paths and, in doing so, creating new sets of norms. Although external changes in our technological and

Before his current role as host of the *Late Show* on CBS, Stephen Colbert became famous for spoofing TV talking heads on his Comedy Central show, *The Colbert Report*. He was quite serious, however, when he gave advice in a 2006 commencement speech at Knox College. He challenged students not to give in to cynicism, telling them, "Cynicism masquerades as wisdom, but it is the farthest thing from it. Because cynics don't learn anything. Because cynicism is a self-imposed blindness, a rejection of the world because we are afraid it will hurt us or disappoint us. Cynics always say 'no.' But saying 'yes' begins things. Saying 'yes' is how things grow. Saying 'yes' leads to knowledge. 'Yes' is for young people. So for as long as you have the strength to, say 'yes.'"

Photo: ©Alex Wong/Getty Images

POPSOC

Personal sociology The practice of recognizing the impact our individual position has on who we are and how we think and act, and of taking responsibility for the impacts our actions have on others.

Public sociology The process of bringing the insights gained through sociological observation and analysis into the public sphere, thereby seeking to bring about positive social change.

by getting us to pay attention to the world around us in a new way.

We need to move from thinking of sociology as only something we learn about to thinking of sociology as something we *do*. In our daily lives, sociology can help us better understand our own individual actions and the actions of those around us. In the context of our larger society and the world, it also enables us to better appreciate the forces at work shaping outcomes—knowledge that we can then use to act in ways that make the world a better place. In both our personal and public lives, we need to practice sociology in the same way that doctors practice medicine.

PERSONAL SOCIOLOGY

Sociology can help us in our everyday lives to better understand our beliefs and actions and to make more informed choices. We learn from sociology that we are in society and society is in us. Self and society are not two separate things. Being an individual necessitates understanding the importance of place, of position, of connection, and of interaction. Though we like to believe that any choice is available to us, in reality, our options are limited.

Practicing sociology means asking uncomfortable questions and not settling for easy answers. It means taking into account the significance of both the individual and society, of both action and structure, of both freedom and constraint. It means recognizing the significance of power and the impact that access to material, social, and cultural resources has on the choices available to us. In short, as we saw in Chapter 1, doing **personal sociology** means recognizing the impact our individual position has on who we are and how we think and act, and then taking responsibility for the impacts our actions have on others.

From the beginning, sociologists wanted to understand our constraints so that we might be able to change them. As sociologist Pierre Bourdieu (1998b) put it, "To those who always tax the sociologist with determinism and pessimism, I will only say that if people became fully aware of them, conscious action aimed at controlling the structural mechanisms that engender moral failure would be possible" (p. 56). In other words, we need to be honest with ourselves about the degree to which society limits our choices so that we might be empowered to make choices that are more informed and therefore more effective in helping us attain our goals.

As individuals, we need to learn to see the degree to which we follow visible and invisible rules. We need to ask whether our current paths represent the values, norms, and goals that we really want to follow. As we have seen, the movies we watch, the things we buy, our likelihood for suicide, our chances of facing a wage gap, our perception of reality, our very selves—all are shaped by the positions we occupy. Understanding these influences empowers us to change.

PUBLIC SOCIOLOGY: TOOLS FOR CHANGE

Beyond providing a more informed understanding of why we as individuals act and think the way we do, sociology calls on us to look beyond ourselves to the world around us and ask, What might we do to make the world a better place? Since the discipline was founded, sociologists have sought to understand and explain social processes for the purpose of shaping the future of society. **Public sociology** involves bringing the insights gained through sociological observation and analysis into the public sphere, thereby seeking to bring about positive social change. As Michael Burawoy, former president of the American Sociological Association, put it, public sociology seeks to speak to a wide audience, aiming to "enrich public debate about moral and political issues by infusing them with sociological theory and research" (Burawoy 2004:1603).

Did You Know?

... Martin Luther King, Jr., graduated with a BA in sociology from Morehouse College in Atlanta, Georgia, in 1948.

Photo: ©Popperfoto/Getty Images

Because we construct the existing social structures through our collective and recurring actions, we bear responsibility for their consequences. Existing systems—the structure and culture we create—are not inevitable. We can choose to change them; we can act differently, as the accompanying table "Citizen Activities in a Democratic Society" suggests. It can be difficult to step off the "paths of least resistance" that support the existing system (A. Johnson 1997), and the consequences for action and belief that run counter to the status quo can be severe. But we can do so.

Citizen Activities in a Democratic Society

PRIVATE LIFE	CIVIC LIFE	
Individual activity	**Civic engagement activities**	
	Nonpolitical activities	Political participation
Family School Work	Recycling Fellowship meetings Service activities	Voting Attending political meetings Political campaigning
Functions: Cultivates personal relationships, serves individual needs—e.g., getting an education, earning a living	Provides community services and acts as a training ground for political participation	Fulfills demands of democratic citizenship

What we cannot do is absolve ourselves of responsibility for the systems we end up with. In fact, to not act differently is to support the existing system of inequality. As sociologist Scott Schaffer (2004) points out, we can no longer ignore practices that violate our basic beliefs, trying to wash our hands of responsibility. Writes Schaffer: "Our hands are already dirty; the question I leave here is whether our hands will be dirtied through action intended to bring concrete, actual, enacted freedom into the world, or through our choice to preserve ourselves at the cost of all others in the here and now and in the future" (pp. 271–272). Our cynicism and resignation only reinforce systems of oppression and violence. To not act to bring about positive change still represents a choice, and we bear responsibility either way.

By helping us to see why we think and act as we do, by helping us clarify the relationship between belief and practice, and by helping us better understand the consequences of difference, personal and public sociology can encourage discussion that can lead to a better future. We can use the tools of sociology to allow ourselves to enter into conversations in which we share our stories with others (both positive and negative), clarifying places where we agree and disagree, and opening ourselves up to our blind spots. We often want to avoid uncomfortable conflict, opting instead for polite discourse, but to fail to be more genuinely engaged in our cultural and structural differences virtually ensures a lack of progress toward implementing our core principles (Schaffer 2004).

PRACTICING SOCIOLOGY

Change comes because people continue not only to believe that it is possible but also to act on their hopes and dreams. As ethnographer Studs Terkel (2003) put it, "In all epochs, there were at first doubts and the fear of stepping forth and speaking out, but the attribute that spurred the warriors on was hope. And then *act*" (p. xviii). We can change the world for the better. We can do so by becoming more informed about ourselves and others and then acting on that knowledge. Here are some possibilities for action:

> *Another world is not only possible; she is on her way. On a quiet day, I can hear her breathing.*
>
> —Arundhati Roy

- *Practice personal sociology.* Become more conscious of the factors that shape your beliefs and actions.
- *Become more aware of privilege.* Identify the advantages you have, especially relative to the rest of the world; you likely have sufficient food, clothes, and shelter; you can read this; you can plan for the future; and so on.
- *Become more informed.* We have access to more information about our world now than ever. Seek it out; find out what's going on.
- *Interpret what you learn.* Analyze the information you receive. Remember that data never speak for themselves; they aren't just facts but are embedded in networks and systems that have their own interests.

©20th Century Fox Film Corp. All rights reserved/Courtesy Everett Collection

- *Vote.* Elected leaders in a democracy, whether local, state, or national, are chosen by voters. It may not seem like your individual vote is significant, but the simple fact is that all those votes still add up to a winner. And even if your candidate cannot win, you can still make a statement; for example, if you don't think any of the candidates would make a good choice, write in someone who would.

> **Sociological imagination** Our exploration of the interdependent relationship between who we are as individuals and the social forces that shape our lives.

- *Participate in local politics.* Think of politics as a contact sport: Go to rallies, protests, school board meetings, city council meetings, and more. You might be surprised how much of a difference a single voice can make, especially on the local level.
- *Run for office.* Don't assume that such positions of leadership are only for others who are somehow better or more informed than you. We need more people to believe that they can lead so that we get more diversity in our leaders.
- *Volunteer.* There are local organizations in every community seeking to bring about positive social change. You might contact a local school to see if you can read to kids, work at a homeless shelter, or help build houses with Habitat for Humanity.
- *Join.* There are many organizations that provide long-term outreach opportunities, such as AmeriCorps, the Peace Corps, and the American Red Cross, in which you provide assistance to people with varieties of needs, in communities near and far.
- *Organize.* Work to bring about the world you envision; there are undoubtedly others out there who share your views. Find them and work with them, both inside and outside existing institutions, to bring about change.
- *Fight for change.* Regardless of where you are, whether in your relationships, your family, your workplace, your community, or elsewhere, work to bring about positive social change. We have the power to change the world; we can't do so in a vacuum, but if sociologists are at all correct about the social construction of reality, things could be otherwise.

As Comte wrote at sociology's very founding, "Science leads to foresight, and foresight leads to action" (quoted in Bourdieu 1998b:55). It is only by seeing those things that limit us that we can move toward freedom.

Charles Dickens expressed a fundamental sociological truth in *A Christmas Carol,* written in 1843. In it, Ebenezer Scrooge, a miserly businessman, thinks only of himself, caring little if anything for others, including his employee, his family, and the poor. But on Christmas Eve, he is visited by three ghosts: the Ghost of Christmas Past, the Ghost of Christmas Present, and the Ghost of Christmas Yet to Come. After each of these spirits shows him visions of their time, Scrooge repents, promising to live "an altered life" in which he will reaffirm relationships and reconnect to those around him. What is particularly interesting sociologically is the way he phrases his promise: "I will live in the Past, the Present, and the Future! The Spirits of all Three shall strive within me."

At its core, Scrooge's resolution represents what we are called to do by the **sociological imagination.** Just as history and biography intersect, so also do we need to understand that the past, created by the actions of ourselves and those who came before us, has shaped who we are now. As American novelist and essayist James Baldwin ([1965] 1985) wrote, "The great force of history comes from the fact that we carry it within us, are unconsciously controlled by it in many ways, and history is literally *present* in all that we do" (p. 410). Further, our present actions shape the future directions of both our lives and the lives of others in the worlds around us and of those yet to come. Like Scrooge, we can reject the myth of the isolated individual and affirm the significance of relationships and companionship (to return to one of the root word meanings of sociology). By simultaneously holding the past, present, and future together in our minds, we can act to make the world a better place to live.

Sociology is more than just a noun. Sociology is a verb. It is something we do, not something we possess. Our over-reliance on individualistic models, and our failure to appreciate the impact of social forces, presents a distorted picture of our freedom. An appreciation of the relationship between self and society and of the consequences of difference allows us to make more informed choices and to shape the future. It allows us to provide answers to the questions "Why do we think the way we think?" and "Why do we act the way we act?" Sociology shouldn't be something confined to college classrooms. It shouldn't be left only to professionals. We are all sociologists now, and there is work to be done.

SOCIOLOGY IS A VERB

Sociology as a Way of Life

Sociology is a rich and complex discipline with so much more than can possibly be covered in an introductory course. Consider exploring what else is out there and take another sociology course in an area that sparks your interest. Even if you don't, try to engage your sociological imagination every day. Investigate. Learn. Vote. Organize. Run for office. Fight for change. Practice sociology. Make a difference.

For REVIEW

I. How and why does social change happen?
- Social change evolves out of past social practices; it represents a response by those in society to maintain social order by seeking an acceptable balance between stability and change; and it is influenced by the distribution of power and control over resources, which shapes what changes do or do not occur. Technological innovation has played a powerful role causing social change.

II. What factors shape the success of a social movement?
- There needs to be a sense of relative deprivation in which people have a sense that injustice exists that can and should be challenged. In addition, people must have the capacity to mobilize resources to bring about the change they seek.

III. What does it mean to practice sociology?
- Personal sociology involves better understanding the influence social factors have on our thoughts and actions and using this information to our advantage. Public sociology means taking responsibility for the collective impacts our individual actions have in shaping society and opportunity and working for positive social change.

©Monkey Business Images/Shutterstock.comk RF

SOCVIEWS on Social Change

Functionalist View

Social change is a way for society to make adjustments in order to return to a state of **stability** or balance.

The four processes of social change identified by Parsons—differentiation, adaptive upgrading, inclusion, and value generalization—stress **consensus** in society.

Social movements and protests enable us to see the dysfunctions of the existing system, and thus facilitate positive social change.

EQUILIBRIUM, CONSENSUS, STABILITY
KEY CONCEPTS

Conflict View

Groups in society that **control** valued resources can either inhibit or facilitate social change more effectively than other groups.

Though new technology can provide tools that facilitate greater freedom, those in positions of power can use it to exert greater control and surveillance.

Social change should be encouraged as a way of eliminating **inequality** and correcting social **injustice**.

KEY CONCEPTS: **CONTROL, SURVEILLANCE, VESTED INTERESTS**

Interactionist View

Every individual has the power to change society through the everyday **choices** he or she makes and **actions** he or she takes (i.e., words we use, relationships we build, voting, volunteering, organizing for change).

Technological innovations in communication allow us to **connect** and interact with people around the world but may also cut us off from those right next to us.

Social movements consist of the **collective activities** of individuals in search of change.

KEY CONCEPTS: **ACTION, ORGANIZATION, CONNECTION**

MAKE THE CONNECTION

After reviewing the chapter, answer the following questions:

1 How would each perspective explain the activism of college students described in the opening vignette?

2 Why does "cultural lag" occur? Why might the interactionist perspective be particularly helpful to explain it?

3 According to each perspective, what effects have new communication technologies (for example, the Internet, cell phones, and so on) had on our interactions, relationships, and communities?

4 How would drawing an insight from each perspective enable you to more effectively bring about social change?

Pop Quiz

1. According to the definition, what is social change?
   a. tumultuous, revolutionary alterations that lead to changes in leadership
   b. shifts in how humans think and act within society that alter material, cognitive, and normative culture
   c. regular alterations in a consistent social frame of reference
   d. subtle alterations in any social system

2. Nineteenth-century theories of social change reflect the pioneering work in biological evolution done by
   a. Albert Einstein.
   b. Harriet Martineau.
   c. Francis Crick.
   d. Charles Darwin.

3. According to Talcott Parsons's equilibrium model, during which process do social institutions become more specialized so as to improve performance?
   a. differentiation
   b. adaptive upgrading
   c. inclusion
   d. value generalization

4. Which of the following did William F. Ogburn use to describe the period of maladjustment during which the nonmaterial culture is still struggling to adapt to new material conditions?
   a. economic shift
   b. political turmoil
   c. social change
   d. cultural lag

5. What term did sociologist Jacques Ellul use to describe our systematic commitment to maximizing efficiency and increasing human productivity in all areas of human life?
   a. technology
   b. management
   c. technique
   d. kaizen

6. You are a student and do not own a car. All your close friends who are attending your college or university have vehicles of their own. You feel downtrodden and dissatisfied. You are experiencing
   a. relative deprivation.
   b. resource mobilization.
   c. false consciousness.
   d. depression.

7. It takes more than desire to start a social movement; it helps to have money, political influence, access to the media, and workers. The ways in which a social movement uses such things are referred to collectively as
   a. relative deprivation.
   b. false consciousness.
   c. resource mobilization.
   d. economic independence.

8. What organizing technique served as a critical tool used by women's liberation activists in the 1960s and 1970s?
   a. social media campaigns using tools such as Facebook and Instagram
   b. consciousness-raising groups
   c. armed protests
   d. sit-ins at lunch counters

9. Organized collective activities that promote autonomy and self-determination, as well as improvements in the quality of life, are referred to as
   a. new social movements.
   b. social revolutions.
   c. resource mobilizations.
   d. fads.

10. Recognizing the impact our individual position has on who we are and how we think and act and then taking responsibility for the effects our actions have on others is known as
    a. resource mobilization.
    b. false consciousness.
    c. public sociology.
    d. personal sociology.

1. (b), 2. (d), 3. (b), 4. (d), 5. (c), 6. (a), 7. (c), 8. (b), 9. (a), 10. (d)

Glossary

A

Absolute poverty A minimum level of subsistence that no family should be expected to live below.

Achieved status A social position that is within our power to change.

Activity theory A theory of aging that suggests that those elderly people who remain active and socially involved will have an improved quality of life.

Adoption The socially recognized and affirmed transfer of the legal rights, responsibilities, and privileges of parenthood.

Affirmative action Positive efforts to recruit minority group members or women for jobs, promotions, and educational opportunities.

Ageism Prejudice and discrimination based on a person's age.

Agency Our freedom as individuals to think and act as we choose.

Agrarian society The most technologically advanced form of preindustrial society. Members are engaged primarily in the production of food, but they increase their crop yields through technological innovations such as the plow.

Alienation Loss of control over our creative human capacity to produce, separation from the products we make, and isolation from our fellow producers.

Amalgamation The process through which a majority group and a minority group combine to form a new group.

Anomie A weak sense of social solidarity due to a lack of agreed-upon rules to guide behavior.

Anthropocene A geological epoch in which human actions, even at a micro level, have global environmental consequences.

Anti-Semitism Anti-Jewish prejudice.

Anticipatory socialization Processes of socialization in which a person "rehearses" for future positions, occupations, and social relationships.

Apartheid A former policy of the South African government, designed to maintain the separation of Blacks and other non-Whites from the dominant Whites.

Applied sociology The use of the discipline of sociology with the specific intent of yielding practical applications for human behavior and organizations.

Argot Specialized language used by members of a group or subculture.

Ascribed status A social position assigned to a person by society without regard for the person's unique talents or characteristics.

Assimilation The process through which a person forsakes his or her own cultural tradition to become part of a different culture.

Authority Power that is recognized as legitimate by the people over whom it is exercised.

B

Bilateral descent A kinship system in which both sides of a person's family are regarded as equally important.

Bisexual A category of sexual orientation that includes those who are attracted to both men and women.

Black power A political philosophy, promoted by many younger Blacks in the 1960s, that supported the creation of Black-controlled political and economic institutions.

Borderlands The area of common culture along the border between Mexico and the United States.

Bourgeoisie The ruling class under capitalism due to their ownership of the means of production.

Brain drain The immigration to the United States and other industrialized nations of skilled workers, professionals, and technicians who are needed in their home countries.

Bureaucracy A formal organization built upon the principle of maximum efficiency.

Bureaucratization The process by which a group, organization, or social movement increasingly relies on technical-rational decision making in the pursuit of efficiency.

C

Capitalism An economic system in which owners of private property compete in the marketplace in pursuit of profit.

Caste A stratification system in which boundaries between strata are clear, relations between levels are regulated, and social status is ascribed.

Causal logic A relationship exists between variables in which change in one brings about change in the other.

Charismatic authority Power made legitimate by a leader's exceptional personal or emotional appeal to his or her followers.

Cisgender Persons whose gender identity aligns more closely with the cultural expectations associated with their biological sex at birth.

Class A group of people who have a similar level of economic resources.

Class consciousness The subjective awareness held by members of a class regarding their common vested interests and need for collective political action to bring about social change.

Clinical sociology   The use of the discipline of sociology with the specific intent of altering social relationships or restructuring social institutions.

Closed system   A society with a system of stratification that does not allow for social mobility between strata.

Coalition   A temporary or permanent alliance geared toward a common goal.

Code of ethics   The standards of acceptable behavior developed by and for members of a profession.

Cognitive culture   Our mental and symbolic representations of reality.

Cohabitation   The practice of a man and a woman living together in a sexual relationship without being married.

Colonialism   The maintenance of political, social, economic, and cultural dominance over a people by a foreign power for an extended period.

Color-blind racism   The use of race-neutral principles to perpetuate a racially unequal status quo.

Conflict perspective   A sociological paradigm that focuses on power and the allocation of valued resources in society.

Conformity   Abiding by the norms of our peers even though they have no direct authority over us.

Contact hypothesis   The theory that in cooperative circumstances interracial contact between people of equal status will reduce prejudice.

Content analysis   The systematic coding and objective recording of data, guided by some rationale.

Control group   The subjects in an experiment who are not introduced to the independent variable by the researcher.

Control variable   A factor that is held constant to test the relative impact of an independent variable.

Correlation   A relationship between two variables in which a change in one coincides with a change in the other.

Correspondence principle   Schools' reproduction of the existing class structure through socializing students to embrace their social class position.

Counterculture   A subculture that deliberately opposes certain aspects of the larger culture.

Credentialism   An increase in the lowest level of education required to enter a field.

Crime   A violation of criminal law for which some governmental authority applies formal penalties.

Crude birthrate   The number of live births per 1,000 people in the population in a given year.

Crude death rate   The number of deaths per 1,000 people in a population in a given year.

Cultural capital   Our tastes, knowledge, attitudes, language, and ways of thinking that we exchange in interaction with others.

Cultural lag   The general principle that technological innovation occurs more quickly than does our capacity to perceive, interpret, and respond to that change.

Cultural relativism   The viewing of other people's behavior from the perspective of those other people's culture.

Cultural transmission   A school of criminology that argues that criminal behavior is learned through social interactions.

Cultural universal   A common practice or belief shared by all societies.

Culture   Everything humans create in establishing our relationships to nature and with each other.

Culture shock   The feelings of disorientation, uncertainty, and even fear that people experience when they encounter unfamiliar cultural practices.

Culture-bound syndrome   A disease or illness that cannot be understood apart from some specific social context.

Curanderismo   Latino folk medicine, a form of holistic health care and healing.

D

Degradation ceremony   An aspect of the socialization process within some total institutions, in which people are subjected to humiliating rituals.

Deindustrialization   The systematic and widespread reduction of investment in domestic manufacturing and material production.

Democracy   In a literal sense, government by the people.

Demographic transition   As societies transform from preindustrial to postindustrial, their population size shifts from small but stable with high birthrates and death rates, through a period of significant population growth, to large but stable, when both birthrates and death rates are low.

Demography   The statistical study of population dynamics.

Denomination   A large, organized religion that is not officially linked to the state or government.

Dependency theory   The theory that poor, less-developed nations become subservient to wealthy industrial nations, which use their economic and political might to maintain power.

Dependent variable   The variable in a causal relationship that is subject to the influence of another variable.

Deviance   Behavior that violates the standards of conduct or expectations of a group or society.

Dictatorship   A government in which one person has nearly total power to make and enforce laws.

Differential association A theory of deviance that holds that violation of rules results from exposure to attitudes favorable to criminal acts.

Differential justice Differences in the way social control is exercised over different groups.

Diffusion The process by which some aspect of culture spreads within and between societies.

Discovery The process of revealing a previously unknown aspect of reality.

Discrimination The practice of denying equal access to opportunities and resources on the basis of group membership rather than merit or rights.

Disengagement theory A theory of aging that suggests that society and the aging individual mutually sever many of their relationships.

Dominant ideology A set of cultural beliefs and practices that legitimates existing powerful social, economic, and political interests.

Downsizing Organizational restructuring to reduce the size of a company's workforce.

Dramaturgical approach A view of social interaction in which people are seen as actors on a stage attempting to put on a successful performance.

Dyad The most basic building block of a social network, it consists of two nodes and the relationship between them.

E

Ecclesia A religious organization that claims to include most or all members of a society and is recognized as the national or official religion.

Economy A social institution dedicated to the production, distribution, and consumption of goods and services.

Education A social institution dedicated to the formal process of transmitting culture from teachers to students.

Egalitarian family An authority pattern in which spouses are regarded as equals.

Elite model A view of society as being ruled by a small group of individuals who share a common set of political and economic interests.

Emigration When members of a population leave that group.

Endogamy The restriction of mate selection to people within the same group.

Environmental justice A legal strategy based on claims that racial minorities are subjected disproportionately to environmental hazards.

Equilibrium model The theory that society's natural tendency is toward social order with change in one part of society counterbalanced by adjustments in others.

Established sect A religious group that is the outgrowth of a sect, yet remains isolated from society.

Estate system A system of stratification that divides power in society into three primary sectors: the church, the nobility, and the commoners.

Ethnicity The cultural differences between humans, defined as socially significant and presumed to divide the population into socially distinct subgroups.

Ethnocentrism The tendency to assume that one's own culture and way of life represent what's normal or is superior to all others.

Ethnography The study of an entire social setting through extended systematic observation.

Exogamy The requirement that people select a mate outside certain groups.

Experiment A controlled procedure in which researchers assess the effect independent variables have on dependent variables.

Experimental group The subjects in an experiment who are exposed to an independent variable introduced by a researcher.

Exploitation theory A belief that views racial subordination in the United States as a manifestation of the class system inherent in capitalism.

Expressive leader The person in the family who bears responsibility for the maintenance of harmony and internal emotional affairs.

Expulsion The systematic removal of a group of people from society.

Extended family A family in which relatives—such as grandparents, aunts, or uncles—live in the same household as parents and their children.

F

Face-work Altering our presentation of self in order to maintain a proper image and avoid public embarrassment.

False consciousness A term used by Karl Marx to describe an attitude held by members of a class that does not accurately reflect their objective position.

Familism Placing the interests of the family before those of the individual.

Feminism The belief in social, economic, and political equality for women.

Fertility The number of children born in a given period of time.

Folkways Norms governing everyday behavior, whose violation raises comparatively little concern.

Force The actual or threatened use of coercion to impose one's will on others.

Formal norm A norm that generally has been written down and that specifies strict punishments for violators.

Formal social control The imposition of sanctions, whether positive or negative, by officially recognized authorities in order to to enforce norms.

Functionalist definition of families A definition of families that focuses on how families provide for the physical, social, and emotional needs of individuals and of society as a whole.

Functionalist perspective A sociological paradigm that sees society as like a living organism in which its various parts work together for the good of the whole.

Fundamentalism Rigid adherence to core religious doctrines, often accompanied by a literal application of scripture or historical beliefs to today's world.

G

Gemeinschaft A close-knit community, often found in rural areas, in which strong personal bonds unite members.

Gender The social and cultural significance that we attach to the biological differences of sex.

Gender binary A dimorphic model in which gender roles are represented as either masculine or feminine with a clear divide between the two.

Gender expression The outward or public display of a person's gender.

Gender identity People's subjective or internal sense of their own gender.

Gender roles The normative expectations regarding proper behavior, attitudes, and activities associated with maleness and femaleness.

Gender spectrum A model of gender as a continuum that incorporates a full range of possible combinations involving sex, gender, sexual orientation, gender identity, and gender expression.

Generalized other The attitudes, viewpoints, and expectations of society as a whole that a child takes into account in his or her behavior.

Genocide The deliberate, systematic killing of an entire people or nation.

Gerontology The study of the sociological and psychological aspects of aging and the problems of aging adults.

Gesellschaft Consists of a large, impersonal, task-oriented society, typically urban, in which individuals have a limited commitment to the group.

Glass ceiling An invisible barrier that blocks the promotion of a qualified individual in a work environment because of the individual's gender, race, or ethnicity.

Globalization The worldwide integration of government policies, cultures, social movements, and financial markets through trade and the exchange of ideas.

Goal displacement Overzealous conformity to official regulations of a bureaucracy.

Gross national income (GNI) A measure of the total monetary value of all goods and services produced within a country during some specified period of time.

Group Two or more people, united by a shared sense of identity or purpose, who interact with each other over time in ways that distinguish them from outsiders.

Growth rate The overall percentage change in a population per year.

H

Hate crime A criminal offense committed because of the offender's bias against an individual based on race, religion, ethnicity, national origin, or sexual orientation.

Hawthorne effect The unintended influence that observers of experiments can have on their subjects.

Heteronormativity A term that sociologists use to describe the cultural presupposition that heterosexuality is the appropriate standard for sexual identity and practice and that alternative sexualities are deviant, abnormal, or wrong.

Heterosexual A category of sexual orientation that includes those who are sexually attracted to members of the opposite sex.

Hidden curriculum Teaching students to submit to authority and accept society's dominant ideology.

Holistic medicine Therapies in which the health care practitioner considers the person's physical, mental, emotional, and spiritual characteristics.

Homogamy The conscious or unconscious tendency to select a mate with personal characteristics and interests similar to one's own.

Homophily Our tendency to establish close social network relationships with others who share our same knowledge, beliefs, practices, and characteristics.

Homosexual A category of sexual orientation that includes those who are attracted to members of the same sex.

Horizontal mobility The movement of an individual from one social position to another of the same rank.

Horticultural society A preindustrial society in which people plant seeds and crops rather than merely subsist on available foods.

Hospice care Treatment of terminally ill individuals in their own homes, or in special hospital units or other facilities, with the goal of helping them die comfortably, without pain.

Human ecology The area of study concerned with the interrelationships between people and their environment.

Human relations approach An approach to the study of formal organizations that emphasizes the role of people, communication, and participation in a bureaucracy and tends to focus on the informal structure of the organization.

Glossary

Human rights Universal moral rights possessed by all people because they are human.

Hunting-and-gathering society A preindustrial society in which people rely on whatever foods and fibers are readily available in order to survive.

Hypothesis A testable statement about the relationship between two or more variables.

I

I The acting self that exists in relation to the Me.

Ideal norms Guidelines for behavior that people agree should be followed.

Ideal type An abstract model of the essential characteristics of a phenomenon.

Immigration When individuals join a population group of which they were not previously a member.

Implicit bias The automatic and unconscious association of value, whether positive or negative, with particular groups, subgroups, or characteristics of people.

Impression management The altering of the presentation of the self in order to create distinctive appearances and satisfy particular audiences.

In-group A category of people who share a common identity and sense of belonging.

Incest taboo The prohibition of sexual relationships between certain culturally specified relatives.

Incidence The number of new cases of a specific disorder that occur within a given population during a stated period.

Income Money received over some period of time.

Independent variable The variable in a causal relationship that causes or influences a change in a second variable.

Index crimes The eight types of crime reported annually by the FBI in the *Uniform Crime Reports:* murder, forcible rape, robbery, aggravated assault, burglary, larceny-theft, motor vehicle theft, and arson.

Industrial society A society that depends on mechanization to produce its goods and services.

Infant mortality rate The number of deaths of infants under one year old per 1,000 live births in a given year.

Informal economy Transfers of money, goods, or services that are not reported to the government.

Informal norm A norm that is generally understood but not precisely recorded.

Informal social control The use of interpersonal cues through everyday interaction to enforce norms.

Innovation The process of introducing a new idea or object to a culture through discovery or invention.

Institutional discrimination A pattern of treatment that systematically denies a group access to resources and opportunities as part of society's normal operations.

Instrumental leader The person in the family who bears responsibility for the completion of tasks, focuses on distant goals, and manages the external relationship between one's family and other social institutions.

Interactionist perspective A sociological paradigm that maintains that society is a product of our everyday encounters with others through which we establish shared meanings and thus construct order.

Intergenerational mobility Changes in the social position of children relative to their parents.

Intersectionality Gender, sexuality, race, ethnicity, and class must not be studied in isolation, because they have intermingled effects on our identity, knowledge, and outcomes.

Interview A face-to-face or telephone questioning of a respondent to obtain desired information.

Intragenerational mobility Changes in social position within a person's adult life.

Invention The combination of existing materials to create something new.

Iron law of oligarchy The principle that all organizations, even democratic ones, tend to develop into bureaucracies ruled by an elite few.

K

Kinship The state of being related to others.

L

Labeling theory An approach to deviance that attempts to explain why certain people are viewed as deviants while others engaged in the same behavior are not.

Laissez-faire The principle that people should be able to compete freely, without government interference, in the capitalist marketplace.

Language A system of shared symbols; it includes speech, written characters, numerals, symbols, and nonverbal gestures and expressions.

Laws Formal norms enforced by the state.

Liberation theology Use of a church, primarily Roman Catholic, in a political effort to eliminate poverty, discrimination, and other forms of injustice from a secular society.

Life chances The likelihood that our success is shaped by our access to valued material, social, and cultural resources.

Life course approach A research orientation in which sociologists and other social scientists look closely at the social factors that influence people throughout their lives, from birth to death.

Life expectancy The projected number of years a person can expect to live based on his or her year of birth.

Looking-glass self A theory that we become who we are based on how we think others see us.

Luddites Rebellious craft workers in 19th-century England who destroyed new factory machinery as part of their resistance to the Industrial Revolution.

M

Macrosociology Sociological investigation that concentrates on large-scale phenomena or entire civilizations.

Master status A status that dominates others and thereby determines a person's general position in society.

Material culture Our physical modification of the natural environment to suit our purposes.

Matriarchy A society in which women dominate in family decision making.

Matrilineal descent A kinship system in which only the mother's relatives are significant.

McDonaldization The process by which the principles of efficiency, calculability, predictability, and control shape organization and decision making, in the United States and around the world.

Me The socialized self that plans actions and judges performances based on the standards we have learned from others.

Mean A number calculated by adding a series of values and then dividing by the number of values.

Mechanical solidarity Social cohesion based on shared experiences, knowledge, and skills in which things function more or less the way they always have, with minimal change.

Median The midpoint, or number that divides a series of values into two groups of equal numbers of values.

Medicalization The process of redefining new areas of social life as the legitimate domain for medical expertise by converting them into treatable medical conditions.

Microsociology Sociological investigation that stresses the study of small groups and the analysis of our everyday experiences and interactions.

Midlife crisis A stressful period of self-evaluation that begins at about age 40.

Migration The movement of people from one population group to another.

Minority group A subordinate group whose members, even if they represent a numeric majority, lack access to, and control over, valued resources in society.

Mixed economy An economic system that combines elements of both capitalism and socialism.

Mode The most common value in a series of scores.

Model or ideal minority A subordinate group whose members supposedly have succeeded economically, socially, and educationally despite past prejudice and discrimination.

Modernization The evolution of societies from traditional forms of social organization—typically rural, agricultural, and religious—toward forms characteristic of post–Industrial Revolution societies.

Monarchy A form of government headed by a single member of a royal family, usually a king, queen, or some other hereditary ruler.

Monogamy A form of marriage in which two people are married only to each other.

Monopoly Control of a market by a single business firm.

Morbidity rate The occurrences of illness in a given population over some period of time.

Mores Norms deemed highly necessary to the welfare of a society.

Mortality rate The incidence of death in a given population over some period of time.

Multinational corporation A commercial organization that is headquartered in one country but does business throughout the world.

Multiple masculinities The idea that expressions of manliness can take varieties of forms beyond the culturally dominant, stereotypical construct of what it means to be a man.

N

Natural science The systematic study of the physical features of nature and the ways in which they interact and change.

Neocolonialism Continuing dependence of former colonies on foreign countries.

New religious movement (NRM) or cult A small, alternative faith community that represents either a new religion or a major innovation in an existing faith.

New social movement An organized collective activity that addresses values and social identities, as well as improvements in the quality of life.

Nonmaterial culture Ways of using material objects, as well as customs, ideas, expressions, beliefs, knowledge, philosophies, governments, and patterns of communication.

Nonverbal communication The use of gestures, facial expressions, and other visual images to communicate.

Norm An established standard of behavior maintained by a society.

Glossary

Normative culture Consists of the ways we establish, abide by, and enforce principles of conduct.

Nuclear family A married couple and their unmarried children living together.

O

Obedience Doing what a person in a position of authority over you says you should.

Observation A research technique in which an investigator collects information through direct participation and/or by closely watching a group or community.

Offshoring Outsourcing of work to foreign contractors.

Oligarchy A form of government in which a few individuals rule.

Open system A society with a system of stratification that allows for social mobility between strata.

Operational definition Transformation of an abstract concept into indicators that are observable and measurable.

Organic solidarity Social cohesion based on mutual interdependence in the context of extreme division of labor.

Organized crime The work of a group that regulates relations among criminal enterprises involved in illegal activities, including prostitution, gambling, and the smuggling and sale of illegal drugs.

Out-group A category of people who do not belong or do not fit in.

P

Party The capacity to organize to accomplish some particular goal.

Patriarchy A society in which men dominate in family decision making.

Patrilineal descent A kinship system in which only the father's relatives are significant.

Peace The absence of war, or, more broadly, a proactive effort to develop cooperative relations among nations.

Personal sociology The practice of recognizing the impact our individual position has on who we are and how we think and act, and of taking responsibility for the impacts our actions have on others.

Pluralism Mutual respect for one another's cultures among the various groups in a society, which allows minorities to express their own cultures without experiencing prejudice.

Pluralist model A view of society in which many competing groups within the community have access to government so that no single group is dominant.

Political system The social institution that is founded on a recognized set of procedures for implementing and achieving society's goals.

Politics The competition between individuals or groups over the allocation of valued resources.

Polyandry A form of polygamy in which a woman may have more than one husband at the same time.

Polygamy A form of marriage in which an individual may have several husbands or wives simultaneously.

Polygyny A form of polygamy in which a man may have more than one wife at the same time.

Postindustrial society A society whose economic system is engaged primarily in the processing and control of information.

Postmodern society A technologically sophisticated, pluralistic, interconnected, globalized society.

Power The ability to exercise one's will over others even if they resist.

Power elite A small group of military, industrial, and government leaders who control the fate of the United States.

Prejudice A preconceived and unjustified judgment of individuals, whether positive or negative, based on their membership in a particular group.

Prestige The respect and admiration that a particular status holds in society.

Prevalence The total number of cases of a specific disorder that exist at a given time.

Primary group A small group characterized by intimate, face-to-face association and cooperation.

Primary sector The segment of the economy involving activities that extract products directly from the natural environment.

Private troubles Problems we face in our immediate relationships with particular individuals in our personal lives.

Profane The ordinary and commonplace elements of life, as distinguished from the sacred.

Proletariat The working class under capitalism who must sell their labor power in exchange for a wage because they lack ownership of the means of production.

Protestant ethic Max Weber's term for the disciplined commitment to worldly labor driven by a desire to bring glory to God, shared by followers of Martin Luther and John Calvin.

Public issues Problems we face as a consequence of the positions we occupy within the larger social structure.

Public sociology The process of bringing the insights gained through sociological observation and analysis into the public sphere, thereby seeking to bring about positive social change.

Q

Qualitative research Descriptive research that relies on narrative accounts rather than statistical procedures.

Quantitative research Research that collects and reports data primarily in numerical form.

queer A term that incorporates the multiplicity of possible sexual orientations, gender identities, and gender expressions.

Questionnaire A respondent completes a printed or computerized form and returns it to the researcher.

R

Race Biological differences between humans, defined as socially significant and presumed to divide the population into genetically distinct subgroups.

Racial formation A sociohistorical process in which racial categories are created, inhibited, transformed, and destroyed.

Racial profiling Any police-initiated action based on race, ethnicity, or national origin rather than on a person's behavior.

Racism The belief that one race is supreme and all others are innately inferior.

Random sample A sample for which every member of an entire population has the same chance of being selected.

Rational-legal authority Authority based on formally agreed-upon and accepted rules, principles, and procedures of conduct that are established in order to accomplish goals in the most efficient manner possible.

Real norms Rules of conduct generated from people's actual behavior.

Reference group Any group that individuals use as a standard for evaluating themselves and their own behavior.

Relative deprivation People's perception that they lack the resources necessary to lead the kind of life they believe they deserve.

Relative poverty A floating standard of deprivation by which people at the bottom of a society, whatever their lifestyles, are judged to be disadvantaged in comparison with the nation as a whole.

Reliability The extent to which a measure produces consistent results.

Religion A social institution dedicated to establishing a shared sense of identity, encouraging social integration, and offering believers a sense of meaning and purpose.

Religious belief A statement to which members of a particular religion adhere.

Religious experience The feeling or perception of being in direct contact with the ultimate reality, such as a divine being, or of being overcome with religious emotion.

Religious ritual A practice required or expected of members of a faith.

Remittances The monies that immigrants return to their families of origin. Also known as *remesas*.

Replacement fertility rate The minimum number of children a woman would need to average in her lifetime to reproduce the population in the next generation.

Representative democracy A system of government in which citizens elect political leaders to make decisions on behalf of the people.

Research design A detailed plan or method for obtaining data scientifically.

Resocialization The process of discarding former behavior patterns and accepting new ones as part of a transition in one's life.

Resource mobilization The ways in which a social movement utilizes such resources as money, political influence, access to the media, and personnel.

Rite of passage A ritual marking the symbolic transition from one social position to another, dramatizing and validating changes in a person's status.

Role conflict The situation that occurs when incompatible expectations arise from two or more social statuses held by the same person.

Role exit The process of disengagement from a role that is central to one's self-identity in order to establish a new role and identity.

Role strain The difficulty that arises when role expectations within the same social status clash.

Role taking The process of mentally assuming the perspective of another and responding from that imagined viewpoint.

S

Sacred Elements beyond everyday life that inspire respect, awe, and even fear.

Sample A selection from a larger population that is statistically representative of that population.

Sanction A penalty or reward for conduct concerning a social norm.

Sandwich generation The generation of adults who simultaneously try to meet the competing needs of their parents and their children.

Sapir-Whorf hypothesis The structure and vocabulary of language shapes our perception of reality and therefore also our actions.

Scientific management approach Theory of management that measures all aspects of the work process to eliminate any inefficiencies.

Scientific method The systematic observation of empirical, this-worldly evidence to assess and refine ideas about what happens and why.

Second shift The double burden—work outside the home followed by child care and housework—that many women face and few men share equitably.

Secondary analysis A variety of research techniques that make use of existing data for the purpose of new analysis.

Secondary group A formal, impersonal group in which there is little social intimacy or mutual understanding.

Secondary sector The segment of the economy consisting of activities that transform raw or intermediate materials into finished products.

Sect A relatively small religious group that has broken away from some other religious organization to renew what it considers the original vision of the faith.

Secularization Religion's diminishing influence in the public sphere, especially in politics and the economy.

Segregation The physical separation of two groups of people in terms of residence, workplace, and social events; often imposed on a minority group by a dominant group.

Self Our sense of who we are, distinct from others, and shaped by the unique combination of our social interactions.

Serial monogamy A form of marriage in which a person may have several spouses in his or her lifetime, but only one spouse at a time.

Sex The biological differences between males and females.

Sexism The ideology that claims one sex is superior to the other.

Sexual orientation The categories of people to whom we are sexually attracted.

Sexuality Denotes our identities and activities as sexual beings.

Sick role A form of legitimate deviance in which the person who becomes ill has a corresponding set of rights and responsibilities associated with that status.

Significant other An individual who is most important in the development of the self, such as a parent, friend, or teacher.

Single-parent family A family in which only one parent is present to care for the children.

Slavery A system of enforced servitude in which some people are owned by others as property.

Social change Shifts in how humans think and act within society that alter material, cognitive, and normative culture.

Social class A system of stratification primarily based on socioeconomic status, both real and perceived.

Social control Society's power to limit deviance by enforcing conformity to expected norms and values.

Social control theory A theory of deviance that posits that the social bonds we share with other members of society lead us to conform to society's norms.

Social disorganization theory The theory that attributes increases in crime and deviance to the absence or breakdown of communal relationships and social institutions, such as the family, school, church, and local government.

Social epidemiology The study of the role social factors play in the development and distribution of disease throughout the population.

Social evolution A theory of social change that holds that societies progress from simple to complex over time.

Social facts Manners of acting, thinking, and feeling external to the individual with coercive power to shape how we act, think, and feel.

Social inequality A condition in which members of society have different amounts of wealth, prestige, or power.

Social institution An integrated and persistent social network dedicated to ensuring that society's core needs are met.

Social interaction A reciprocal exchange in which two or more people read, react, and respond to each other.

Social mobility Movement within or between society's strata.

Social movement An organized collective activity to bring about or resist fundamental change in an existing group or society.

Social network A web of relationships through which people interact both directly and indirectly to accomplish formal and informal goals.

Social role A set of expected behaviors for people who occupy a given social status.

Social science The systematic study of human behavior, interaction, and change.

Social structure The underlying framework of society consisting of the positions people occupy and the relationships between them.

Socialism An economic system under which the means of production and distribution are collectively owned.

Socialization The lifelong process through which people learn the attitudes, values, and behaviors appropriate for members of a particular culture.

Societal-reaction approach Another name for *labeling theory*.

Society The structure of relationships within which culture is created and shared through regularized patterns of social interaction.

Sociobiology The systematic study of how biology affects human social behavior.

Socioeconomic status (SES) A measure of social class position based on a combination of education, occupation, and income.

Sociological imagination Our exploration of the interdependent relationship between who we are as individuals and the social forces that shape our lives.

Sociology The systematic study of the relationship between the individual and society and of the consequences of difference.

Standpoint theory Because our social positions shape our perceptions, a more complete understanding of social relations must incorporate the perspectives of marginalized voices.

Status The social positions we occupy relative to others.

Status group People who share the same perceived level of prestige.

Stereotype An unreliable generalization about all members of a group that does not recognize individual differences within the group.

Stigma Labeling individuals or members of a group as less than whole persons due to some attribute that marks them as different in the eyes of others.

Strain theory of deviance Robert Merton's theory of deviance as an adaptation of socially prescribed goals or of the means governing their attainment, or both.

Stratification A structured ranking of entire groups of people that perpetuates unequal economic rewards and power in a society.

Subculture A segment of society that shares a distinctive pattern of mores, folkways, and values that differs from the pattern of the larger society.

Substantive definition of the family A definition of the family based on blood, meaning shared genetic heritage, and law, meaning social recognition and affirmation of the bond including both marriage and adoption.

Survey A predefined series of questions designed to collect information about people's particular attributes, beliefs, and actions.

Symbol A gesture, object, or word that forms the basis of human communication.

Symbolic ethnicity An ethnic identity that emphasizes concerns such as ethnic food or political issues rather than deeper ties to one's ethnic heritage.

T

Teacher-expectancy effect The impact that a teacher's expectations about a student's performance may have on the student's actual achievements.

Technology A form of material culture in which humans convert natural resources into tools to accomplish practical ends.

Terrorism The use or threat of violence against random or symbolic targets in pursuit of political aims.

Tertiary sector The segment of the economy consisting of activities that provide services rather than produce tangible goods.

Theory In sociology a set of statements that seeks to explain problems, actions, or behavior.

Thomas theorem What we perceive as real is real in its consequences.

Total fertility rate The average number of children a woman would have during her lifetime given current birthrates and assuming she survives through her childbearing years.

Total institution An institution that regulates all aspects of a person's life under a single authority, such as a prison, the military, a mental hospital, or a convent.

Totalitarianism Virtually complete government control and surveillance over all aspects of a society's social and political life.

Tracking The practice of placing students in specific curriculum groups on the basis of their test scores and other criteria.

Traditional authority Legitimate power conferred by custom and accepted practice.

Transgender People whose gender identity differs from the sex they were assigned at birth.

Transnational crime Crime that occurs across multiple national borders.

Triad Within a social network, it consists of three nodes and the direct and indirect relationships among them.

V

Validity The degree to which a measure or scale truly reflects the phenomenon under study.

Value A collective conception of what is considered good, desirable, and proper—or bad, undesirable, and improper—in a culture.

Value neutrality Max Weber's term for objectivity of sociologists in the interpretation of data.

Variable A measurable trait or characteristic that is subject to change under different conditions.

Vertical mobility The movement of an individual from one social position to another of a different rank.

Vested interests Those people or groups who benefit most from the existing social, political, and economic structure.

Victimization survey A questionnaire or interview given to a sample of the population to determine whether people have been victims of crime.

Victimless crime A term used by sociologists to describe the willing exchange among adults of widely desired, but illegal, goods and services.

W

War Conflict between organizations that possess trained combat forces equipped with deadly weapons.

Wealth The total value of all material assets minus debts at a single point in time.

White-collar crime Illegal acts committed by affluent, "respectable" individuals in the course of business activities.

World systems analysis A view of the global economic system as one divided between certain industrialized nations that control wealth and developing countries that are controlled and exploited.

A

Aaronson, Daniel, and Bhashkar Mazumder. 2007. "Intergenerational Economic Mobility in the U.S., 1940 to 2000." FRB Chicago Working Paper No. WP 2005–12, revised February 2007. Federal Reserve Bank of Chicago. Accessed June 21, 2008 (http://ssrn.com/abstract5869435).

Abercrombie, Nicholas, Stephen Hill, and Bryan S. Turner. 1980. *The Dominant Ideology Thesis.* London: George Allen and Unwin.

Aberle, David E., A. K. Cohen, A. K. Davis, M. J. Leng Jr., and F. N. Sutton. 1950. "The Functional Prerequisites of a Society." *Ethics* 60 (January): 100–111.

Abkowitz, Alyssa. 2015. "A High-Rise Race in Mumbai." *The Wall Street Journal,* April 2. Accessed January 14, 2017 (www.wsj.com/articles/a-high-rise-race-in-mumbai-1427988257).

Acemoglu, Daron, and James A. Robinson. 2012. *Why Nations Fail: The Origins of Power, Prosperity, and Poverty.* New York: Crown Business.

Adair-Toteff, Christopher. 2005. "Max Weber's Charisma." *Journal of Classical Sociology* 5 (2): 189–204.

Adams, Jimi. 2007. "Stained Glass Makes the Ceiling Visible: Organizational Opposition to Women in Congregational Leadership." *Gender and Society* 21 (February): 80–115.

Adams, Samantha, and Antoinette de Bont. 2007. "Information Rx: Prescribing Good Consumerism and Responsible Citizenship." *Health Care Analysis* 15 (4): 273–290.

Addams, Jane. 1910. *Twenty Years at Hull-House.* New York: Macmillan.

———. 1930. *The Second Twenty Years at Hull-House.* New York: Macmillan.

Adler, Patricia A., and Peter Adler. 1996. "Preadolescent Clique Stratification and the Hierarchy of Identity." *Sociological Inquiry* 66 (2): 111–142.

———. 2012. "Tales from the Field: Reflections on Four Decades of Ethnography." *Qualitative Sociology Review* 7 (1): 10–32.

Adler, Patricia A., Steve J. Kless, and Peter Adler. 1992. "Socialization to Gender Roles: Popularity Among Elementary School Boys and Girls." *Sociology of Education* 65 (July): 169–187.

Administration for Children and Families. 2016. "Head Start Program Facts: Fiscal Year 2015." Washington, DC: U.S. Department of Health and Human Services. Accessed December 2, 2016 (https://eclkc.ohs.acf.hhs.gov/hslc/data/factsheets/docs/head-start-fact-sheet-fy-2015.pdf).

Agar, Jon. 2013. *Constant Touch: A Global History of the Mobile Phone.* Revised and Updated. London: Icon Books, Ltd.

Agrawal, Nadya. 2013. "Dye-ing Culture: Color Run, White-washing Holi Since 2012." *Brown Girl Magazine,* April. Accessed September 30, 2016 (www.browngirlmagazine.com/2013/04/color-run-controversy/).

Ainsworth, Claire. 2015. "Sex Redefined." *Nature* 518: 288–291.

Alba, Richard. 2015. "The Myth of a White Minority." *The New York Times,* June 11. Accessed February 4, 2017 (www.nytimes.com/2015/06/11/opinion/the-myth-of-a-white-minority.html).

Al-Dosari, Hala. 2016. "Saudi Male-Guardianship Laws Treat Women as Second-Class Citizens." *The Guardian,* October 7. Accessed January 20, 2017 (www.theguardian.com/commentisfree/2016/oct/07/saudi-arabia-women-rights-activists-petition-king).

Alexander, Michelle. 2012. *The New Jim Crow: Mass Incarceration in the Age of Colorblindness.* New York: The New Press.

Alger, Horatio Jr. [1868] 1985. *Ragged Dick and Struggling Upward.* New York: Penguin Books.

Alimahomed, Sabrina. 2010. "Thinking Outside the Rainbow: Women of Color Redefining Queer Politics and Identity." *Social Identities* 16 (2): 151–168.

Allam, Hannah. 2016. "Muslim Stereotyping in Pop Culture Is Worse than Ever." *McClatchyDC,* April 26. Accessed January 18, 2017 (www.mcclatchydc.com/news/nation-world/national/article73969887.html).

Allard, Ladonna Brave Bull. 2016. "Why the Founder of Standing Rock Sioux Camp Can't Forget the Whitestone Massacre." *Yes! Magazine,* September 3. Accessed February 8, 2017 (www.yesmagazine.org/people-power/why-the-founder-of-standing-rock-sioux-camp-cant-forget-the-whitestone-massacre-20160903).

Allen, John L. 2008. *Student Atlas of World Politics,* 8th ed. New York: McGraw-Hill.

Allport, Gordon W. 1979. *The Nature of Prejudice,* 25th anniversary ed. Reading, MA: Addison-Wesley.

Althoff, Tim, Ryen W. White, and Eric Horvitz. 2016. "Influence of Pokemon Go on Physical Activity: Study and Implications." *arXiv* 1610.02085. Accessed October 24, 2016 (https://arxiv.org/pdf/1610.02085v1.pdf).

Alzheimer's Association. 2016. "2016 Alzheimer's Disease Facts and Figures." *Alzheimer's & Dementia* 12(4). Accessed February 12, 2017 (www.alz.org/facts/overview.asp).

Amato, Paul R., and Alan Booth. 1997. *A Generation at Risk.* Cambridge, MA: Harvard University Press.

American Society of Plastic Surgeons. 2016. "2015 Plastic Surgery Statistics Report." ASPS National Clearing House of Plastic Surgery Procedural Statistics. Arlington Heights, IL: ASPS. Accessed November 11, 2016 (www.plasticsurgery.org/news/plastic-surgery-statistics/).

American Sociological Association. 1999. *Code of Ethics and Policies and Procedures of the ASA Committee on Professional Ethics.* Washington, DC: American Sociological Association. Accessed May 1, 2013 (www.asanet.org/images/asa/docs/pdf/CodeofEthics.pdf).

Amnesty International. 1994. *Breaking the Silence: Human Rights Violations Based on Sexual Orientation.* New York: Amnesty International.

———. 2009. "Sexual Orientation and Gender Identity." Accessed June 15, 2009 (www.amnesty.org/en/sexual-orientation-and-gender-identity).

———. 2011. "Annual Report 2011: The State of the World's Human Rights." Accessed May 28, 2012 (www.amnesty.org/en/annual-report/2011/).

———. 2015. *Amnesty International Report 2014/15: The State of the World's Human Rights.* London: Amnesty International, Ltd. Accessed April 15, 2015 (www.amnesty.org/en/documents/pol10/0001/2015/en/).

Anagnostou, Yiorgos. 2009a. "A Critique of Symbolic Ethnicity: The Ideology of Choice?" *Ethnicities* 9 (1): 94–122.

———. 2009b. "About Facts and Fictions: Reply to Herbert Gans and Mary Waters." *Ethnicities* 9 (1).

Anderson, David, and Mykol C. Hamilton. 2005. "Gender Role Stereotyping of Parents in Children's Picture Books: The Invisible Father." *Sex Roles* 52: 145–151.

Anderson, John Ward, and Molly Moore. 1993. "Born Oppressed: Women in the Developing World Face Cradle-to-Grave Discrimination, Poverty." *The Washington Post,* February 14, p. A1.

Anderson, Terry H. 2007. *The Sixties,* 3rd ed. Englewood Cliffs, NJ: Prentice Hall.

Andrews, Wilson, Josh Katz, and Jugal Patel. 2016. "Latest Election Polls 2016." *The New York Times,* November 8. Accessed December 13, 2016 (www.nytimes.com/interactive/2016/us/elections/polls.html).

Angier, Natalie. 2000. "Do Races Differ? Not Really, Genes Show." *The New York Times,* August 22, p. F6. Accessed June 30, 2008 (http://query.nytimes.com/gst/fullpage.html?res59E07E7DF1E3EF931A1575BC0A9669C8B63&scp52&sq5natalie1angier&st5nyt).

References

Anti-Defamation League. 2016. "ADL Audit: Anti-Semitic Assaults Rise Dramatically Across the Country in 2015." Accessed February 6, 2017 (www.adl.org/press-center/press-releases/anti-semitism-usa/2015-audit-anti-semitic-incidents.html).

Arab American Institute. 2008. "Arab Americans: Demographics." Accessed July 1, 2008 (www.aaiusa.org/arab-americans/22/demographics).

Arora, Neeraj K., Bradford W. Hesse, Barbara K. Rimer, K. Viswanath, Marla L. Clayman, and Robert T. Croyle. 2008. "Frustrated and Confused: The American Public Rates Its Cancer-Related Information-Seeking Experiences."*Journal of General Internal Medicine* 23 (3): 223–228.

Aslan, Reza. 2010. *Beyond Fundamentalism: Confronting Religious Extremism in the Age of Globalization.* New York: Random House.

Association of Theological Schools. 2016. "2015–2016 Annual Data Tables." The Commission on Accrediting, Association of Theological Schools in the United States and Canada, Pittsburgh. Accessed December 7, 2016 (www.ats.edu/uploads/resources/institutional-data/annual-data-tables/2015–2016-annual-data-tables.pdf).

Atchley, Robert C. 1976. *The Sociology of Retirement.* New York: Wiley.

Atkinson, Anthony B. 2015. *Inequality: What Can Be Done?* Cambridge: Harvard University Press.

Aud, Susan, William Hussar, Grace Kena, Erin Roth, Eileen Manning, Xiaolei Wang, and Jijun Zhang. 2012. *The Condition of Education 2012.* NCES Report 2012-045. National Center for Education Statistics, U.S. Department of Education, Washington, DC, May 24. Accessed May 25, 2012 (http://nces.ed.gov/pubs2012/2012045.pdf).

Austin, Daniel A. 2013. "The Indentured Generation: Bankruptcy and Student Loan Debt." *Santa Clara Law Review* 53(2): 329–420.

Avise, John C. 2004. *The Hope, Hype, and Reality of Genetic Engineering: Remarkable Stories from Agriculture, Industry, Medicine, and the Environment.* New York: Oxford University Press.

B

Backhaus, Peter. 2013. "The Japanese Traffic Light Blues: Stop on Red, Go on What?" *The Japan Times,* February 25. Accessed January 19, 2015 (www.japantimes.co.jp/life/2013/02/25/language/the-japanese-traffic-light-blues-stop-on-red-go-on-what/#.VMgFdC6fnjY).

Baer, Drake. 2016. "English Could Use Swedish's Untranslatable Words for Relationships." *New York Magazine,* October 19. Accessed November 22, 2016 (http://nymag.com/scienceofus/2016/10/english-could-use-swedishs-words-for-relationships.html).

Baer, Hans. 2008. "Global Warming as a By-product of the Capitalist Treadmill of Production and Consumption—the Need for an Alternative Global System." *Australian Journal of Anthropology* 19 (1): 58–62.

Bag, Sugata, Suman Seth, and Anish Gupta. 2016. "A Comparative Study of Living Conditions in Slums of Three Metro Cities in India." Centre for Development Economics, Delhi School, Delhi School of Economics, Working Paper No. 253, ISSN No. 2454-1427. Accessed January 14, 2017 (https://papers.ssrn.com/sol3/papers.cfm?abstract_id=2727005).

Bagilhole, Barbara, and Simon Cross. 2006. "It Never Struck Me as Female: Investigating Men's Entry into Female-Dominated Occupations." *Journal of Gender Studies* 15 (1): 35–48.

Bahadur, Amar. 2008. "Sanskritization and Caste Opposition: A Shift from Ritual to Political-Economic Power." *Himalayan Journal of Sociology and Anthropology* 3: 1–10.

Bahr, Peter Riley. 2008. "*Cooling Out* in the Community College: What Is the Effect of Academic Advising on Students Chances of Success?" *Research in Higher Education* 49: 704–732.

Baio, Andy. 2015. "Pirating the 2015 Oscars: HD Edition." *The Message,* January 22. Accessed February 19, 2015 (https://medium.com/message/pirating-the-2015-oscars-hd-edition-6c78e0cb471d).

———. 2016. "Pirating the Oscars 2016." *Waxy,* January 19. Accessed November 11, 2016 (http://waxy.org/2016/01/pirating_the_oscars_2016/).

———. 2017. "Oscar Screener Piracy: 2003–2017." Waxy.org. Accessed May 25, 2017 (https://docs.google.com/spreadsheets/d/1H8eds6jEeBXoXIFH1Rdbgig VtWdpyc8A9gyqHUt4Do/edit#gid=0).

Baldez, Lisa. 2004. "Elected Bodies: The Gender Quota Law for Legislative Candidates in Mexico." *Legislative Studies Quarterly* 29: 231–258.

Baldwin, James. [1965] 1985. "White Man's Guilt." Pp. 409–414 in *The Price of the Ticket: Collected Nonfiction, 1948–1985.* New York: St. Martin's Press.

Balfour, Gillian. 2006. "Re-imagining a Feminist Criminology." *Canadian Journal of Criminology & Criminal Justice* 48 (5): 735–752.

Banaji, Mahzarin R., and Anthony G. Greenwald. 2013. *Blindspot: Hidden Biases of Good People.* New York: Delacorte Press.

Banks, Duren, Lance Couzens, Caroline Blanton, and Devon Cribb. 2015. "Arrest-Related Deaths Program Assessment: Technical Report." U.S. Department of Justice, Office of Justice Programs, NCJ 248543, March. Accessed April 27, 2015 (www.bjs.gov/content/pub/pdf/ardpatr.pdf).

Banks, Pauline, and Maggie Lawrence. 2006. "The Disability Discrimination Act, a Necessary, but Not Sufficient Safeguard for People with Progressive Conditions in the Workplace? The Experiences of Younger People with Parkinson's Disease." *Disability and Rehabilitation* 28 (1): 13–24.

Barnes, Patricia M., Eve Powell-Griner, Kim McFann, and Richard L. Nahin. 2004. "Complementary and Alternative Medicine Use Among Adults, United States, 2002." Advance data from *Vital and Health Statistics* 343. Hyattsville, MD: National Center for Health Statistics. Accessed July 5, 2008 (http://nccam.nih.gov/news/camsurvey_fs1.htm).

Barnes, Patricia M., Barbara Bloom, and Richard L. Nahin. 2008. "Complementary and Alternative Medicine Use Among Adults and Children: United States, 2007." *National Health Statistics Reports* 12. Hyattsville, MD: National Center for Health Statistics. Accessed May 20, 2010 (http://nccam.nih.gov/news/2008/nhsr12.pdf).

Barnett, Jessica C., and Marina S. Vornovitsky. 2016. *Health Insurance Coverage in the United States: 2015.* Current Population Reports, P60-25(RV). Washington, DC: U.S. Government Printing Office. Accessed February 11, 2017 (www.census.gov/content/dam/Census/library/publications/2016/demo/p60-257.pdf).

Barnett, Rosalind, and Caryl Rivers. 2004. *Same Difference: How Gender Myths Are Hurting Our Relationships, Our Children, and Our Jobs.* New York: Basic Books.

Barr, Donald A. 2014. *Health Disparities in the United States: Social Class, Race, Ethnicity, and Health,* 2nd ed. Baltimore, MD: Johns Hopkins University Press.

Barrionuevo, Alexei. 2008. "Amazons Forest Peoples Seek a Role in Striking Global Climate Agreements." *The New York Times,* April 6, p. 6.

Basinger, Jeanine. 2012. *I Do and I Don't: A History of Marriage in the Movies.* New York: Knopf.

Bates, Claire. 2016. "How Does 'Curvy Barbie' Compare with an Average Woman?" *BBC News,* March 3. Accessed January 30, 2017 (www.bbc.com/news/magazine-35670446).

Baudrillard, Jean. [1981] 1994. *Simulacra and Simulation.* Ann Arbor: University of Michigan Press.

Baumgardner, Jennifer, and Amy Richards. 2000. *Manifesta: Young Women, Feminism and the Future.* New York: Farrar, Straus and Giroux.

Beagan, Brenda. 2001. "Even If I Don't Know What I'm Doing I Can Make It Look Like I Know What I'm Doing: Becoming a Doctor in the 1990s." *Canadian Review of Sociology and Anthropology* 38: 275–292.

———. 2003. "Teaching Social and Cultural Awareness to Medical Students: It's All Very Nice to Talk About It in Theory, but Ultimately It Makes No Difference." *Academic Medicine* 78 (6): 605–614.

Bearman, Peter S., James Moody, and Katherine Stovel. 2004. "Chains of Affection: The Structure of Adolescent Romantic and Sexual Networks." *American Journal of Sociology* 110 (July): 44–91.

Beauvoir, Simone de. 1952. *The Second Sex.* New York: Knopf.

Becker, Howard S. 1963. *The Outsiders: Studies in the Sociology of Deviance.* New York: Free Press.

———, ed. 1964. *The Other Side: Perspectives on Deviance.* New York: Free Press.

Beeghley, Leonard. 2007. *The Structure of Social Stratification in the United States,* 5th ed. Boston: Allyn & Bacon.

Bell, Daniel. 1953. "Crime as an American Way of Life." *Antioch Review* 13 (Summer): 131–154.

———. 1999. *The Coming of Post-industrial Society: A Venture in Social Forecasting.* With new foreword. New York: Basic Books.

———. 2001. *Liberation Theology After the End of History: The Refusal to Cease Suffering.* New York: Routledge.

Benagiano, Giuseppe, and Maurizio Mori. 2009. "The Origins of Human Sexuality: Procreation or Recreation?" *Reproductive BioMedicine Online* 18 (S1): 50–59.

Bengal. Rebecca. 2016. "Standing Rock Rising: Inside the Movement to Stop the Dakota Access Pipeline." *Vogue,* November 22. Accessed February 8, 2017 (www.vogue.com/projects/13505511/standing-rock-movement-dakota-access-pipeline/).

Benhorin, Shira, and Susan D. McMahon. 2008. "Exposure to Violence and Aggression: Protective Roles of Social Support Among Urban African American Youth." *Journal of Community Psychology* 36 (6): 723–743.

Benjamins, Maureen R., and Steven Whitman. 2013. "Relationships between Discrimination in Health Care and Health Care Outcomes among Four Race/Ethnic Groups." *Journal of Behavioral Medicine* 37(3): 402–413.

Bennett, Asa. 2016. "Did Britain Really Vote Brexit to Cut Immigration?" *The Telegraph,* June 29. Accessed February 4, 2017 (www.telegraph.co.uk/news/2016/06/29/did-britain-really-vote-brexit-to-cut-immigration/).

Bennett, Drake. 2010. "This Will Be on the Midterm. You Feel Me? Why So Many Colleges Are Teaching *The Wire.*" *Slate,* March 24. Accessed April 9, 2010 (www.slate.com/id/2245788/).

Bennett, V., S. Dávila-Poblete, and M. N. Rico, eds. 2005. *Opposing Currents: The Politics of Water and Gender in Latin America.* Pittsburgh, PA: University of Pittsburgh Press.

Berenson, Alex, and Diana B. Henriques. 2008. "Look at Wall St. Wizard Finds Magic Had Skeptics." *The New York Times,* December 12. Accessed May 21, 2009 (www.nytimes.com/2008/12/13/business/13fraud.html).

Berg, Scott W. 2012. *38 Nooses: Lincoln, Little Crow, and the Beginning of the Frontier's End.* New York: Pantheon Books.

Bergen, Raquel Kennedy. 2006. *Marital Rape: New Research and Directions.* Harrisburg, PA: VAW Net.

Berger, Peter. 1969. *The Sacred Canopy: Elements of a Sociological Theory of Religion.* Garden City, NY: Anchor Books.

Berger, Peter, and Thomas Luckmann. 1966. *The Social Construction of Reality.* New York: Doubleday.

Berlin, Brent, and Paul Kay. 1991. *Basic Color Terms: Their Universality and Evolution.* Berkeley: University of California Press.

Bernburg, Jón Gunnar, Marvin D. Krohn, and Craig Rivera. 2006. "Official Labeling, Criminal Embeddedness, and Subsequent Delinquency: A Longitudinal Test of Labeling Theory." *Journal of Research in Crime & Delinquency* 43 (1): 67–88.

Best, Steven, and Douglas Kellner. 2001. *The Postmodern Adventure: Science, Technology, and Cultural Studies at the Third Millennium.* New York: The Guilford Press.

Bezrukova, Katerina, Karen A. Jehn, and Chester S. Spell. 2012. "Reviewing Diversity Training: Where We Have Been and Where We Should Go." *Academy of Management Learning & Education* 11(2): 207–227.

Bhatia, Aatish. 2012. "The Crayola-fication of the World: How We Gave Colors Names, and It Messed with Our Brains (Part I)." *Wired,* June 5. Accessed January 19, 2015 (www.wired.com/2012/06/the-crayola-fication-of-the-world-how-we-gave-colors-names-and-it-messed-with-our-brains-part-i/).

Bhrolcháin, Máire Ní. 2001. "Divorce Effects and Causality in the Social Sciences." *European Sociological Review* 17 (1): 33–57.

Bialik, Kristin, and Jens Manuel Krogstad. 2017. "115th Congress Sets New High for Racial, Ethnic Diversity." Pew Research Center January 24. Accessed February 6, 2017 (www.pewresearch.org/fact-tank/2017/01/24/115th-congress-sets-new-high-for-racial-ethnic-diversity/).

Bianchi, Suzanne M., John P. Robinson, and Melissa A. Milkie. 2006. *Changing Rhythms of American Family Life.* New York: Sage.

Bijker, Wiebe E., Thomas P. Hughes, and Trevor Pinch, eds. 2012. *The Social Construction of Technological Systems: New Directions in the Sociology and History of Technology,* Anniversary Edition. Cambridge: The MIT Press.

Blair, J. Pete, and Katherine W. Schweit. 2014. "A Study of Active Shooter Incidents, 2000–2013." Texas State University and Federal Bureau of Investigation, U.S. Department of Justice, Washington, DC. Accessed February 19, 2015 (www.fbi.gov/news/stories/2014/september/fbi-releases-study-on-active-shooter-incidents/pdfs/a-study-of-active-shooter-incidents-in-the-u.s.-between-2000-and-2013).

Blass, Thomas. 1999. "The Milgram Paradigm After 35 Years: Some Things We Now Know About Obedience to Authority." *Journal of Applied Psychology* 29: 955–978.

Blauner, Robert. 1972. *Racial Oppression in America.* New York: Harper and Row.

Bloemraad, Irene, Anna Korteweg, and Gökçe Yurdakul. 2008. "Citizenship and Immigration: Multiculturalism, Assimilation, and Challenges to the Nation-State." *Annual Review of Sociology* 34: 153–179.

Bloom, David E., David Canning, Günther Fink, and Jocelyn E. Finlay. 2010. "The Cost of Low Fertility in Europe." *European Journal of Population* 26: 141–158.

Blumer, Herbert. 1955. "Collective Behavior." Pp. 165–198 in *Principles of Sociology,* 2nd ed., ed. Alfred McClung Lee. New York: Barnes and Noble.

Boaz, Rachel Floersheim. 1987. "Early Withdrawal from the Labor Force." *Research on Aging* 9 (December): 530–547.

Bolt, Gideon, A. Sule Ozuekren, and Deborah Phillips. 2010. "Linking Integration and Residential Segregation." *Journal of Ethnic & Migration Studies* 36 (2): 169–186.

Bongaarts, John. 2009. "Human Population Growth and the Demographic Transition." *Philosophical Transactions of the Royal Society, Series B, Biological Sciences* 364: 2985–2990.

Bonilla-Silva, Eduardo. 2010. *Racism Without Racists: Color-Blind Racism and the Persistence of Racial Inequality in America,* 3rd ed. Lanham, MD: Rowman & Littlefield.

Booth, Alan, and Paul R. Amato. 2001. "Parental Predivorce Relations and Offspring Postdivorce Well-Being." *Journal of Marriage and the Family* 62: 197–212.

Boren, Cindy. 2016. "For Two Olympians, a Humiliating Journey to Rio Filled with Gender-Questioning." *The Washington Post,* August 16. Accessed January 26, 2017 (www.washingtonpost.com/news/early-lead/wp/2016/08/16/for-two-olympians-a-humiliating-journey-to-rio-filled-with-gender-questioning/).

Boshara, Ray, William R. Emmons, and Bryan J. Noeth. 2015. "Race, Ethnicity, and Wealth." The Demographics of Wealth: How Age, Education, and Race Separate Thrivers from Strugglers in Today's Economy, Essay No. 1, February. Accessed February 6, 2017 (www.stlouisfed.org/~/media/Files/PDFs/HFS/essays/HFS-Essay-1-2015-Race-Ethnicity-and-Wealth.pdf).

References

Bouis, Howarth E. 2007. "The Potential of Genetically Modified Food Crops to Improve Human Nutrition in Developing Countries." *Journal of Development Studies* 43 (1): 79–96.

Bourdieu, Pierre. 1962. *The Algerians.* Preface by Raymond Aron. Boston: Beacon Press.

———. 1984. *Distinction: A Social Critique of the Judgment of Taste.* Cambridge, MA: Harvard University Press.

———. 1986. "The Forms of Capital." Pp. 241–258 in *Handbook of Theory and Research for the Sociology of Education,* ed. J. G. Richardson. New York: Greenwood Press.

———. 1998a. *Acts of Resistance: Against the Tyranny of the Market.* New York: New Press.

———. 1998b. *On Television.* New York: New Press.

Bowles, Samuel, and Herbert Gintis. 1976. *Schooling in Capitalistic America: Educational Reforms and the Contradictions of Economic Life.* New York: Basic Books.

Bradsher, Keith. 2016. "The Paris Agreement on Climate Change Is Official. Now What?" *The New York Times,* November 3. Accessed February 13, 2017 (www.nytimes.com/2016/11/04/business/energy-environment/paris-climate-change-agreement-official-now-what.html).

Brand, Jennie E., and Yu Xie. 2010. "Who Benefits Most from College? Evidence for Negative Selection in Heterogeneous Economic Returns to Higher Education." *American Sociological Review* 75 (2): 273–302.

Brandon, Emily. 2012. "The New Ideal Retirement Age: 67." Planning to Retire, Money, *U.S. News & World Report,* May 8. Accessed May 22, 2012 (http://money.usnews.com/money/blogs/planning-to-retire/2012/05/08/the-new-ideal-retirement-age-67).

Brands, H. W. 2008. "15 Minutes that Saved America." *American History* 43 (4): 34–41.

Brannigan, Augustine, and William Zwerman. 2001. "The Real Hawthorne Effect." *Society* 38 (January/February): 55–60.

Brewer, Rose M., and Nancy A. Heitzeg. 2008. "The Racialization of Criminal Punishment." *American Behavioral Scientist* 51 (January): 625–644.

Brickell, Chris. 2009. "Sexuality and the Dimensions of Power." *Sexuality & Culture* 13 (2): 57–74.

Brill, Steven. 2015. *America's Bitter Pill: Money, Politics, Backroom Deals, and the Fight to Fix Our Broken Healthcare System.* New York: Random House.

Brooks, Ann. 1997. *Postfeminisms: Feminism, Cultural Theory, and Cultural Forms.* New York: Routledge.

Brown, Ashley. 2015. "Picture [Im]Perfect: Photoshop Redefining Beauty in Cosmetic Advertisements, Giving False Advertising a Run for the Money." *Texas Review of Entertainment and Sports Law* 16(2): 87–105.

Brown, Curt. 2015. "In Little Crow's Wake, Horrors for the Dakota." *Minneapolis Star Tribune* April 29. Accessed February 4, 2017 (www.startribune.com/in-little-crow-s-wake-horrors-for-the-dakota/166163736/).

Brown, Harriet. 2015. *Body of Truth: How Science, History, and Culture Drive Our Obsession with Weight—and What We Can Do About It.* Boston: Da Capo Press.

Brown, Luke. 2016. "Providing Role Models for Young Girls Could Make DC Super Hero Girls a Billion-Dollar Brand." *Comics Alliance,* May 25. Accessed January 30, 2017 (http://comicsalliance.com/dc-super-hero-girls-diane-nelson-billion-dollars/).

Brown, Meta, Andrew Haughwout, Donghoon Lee, Maricar Mabutas, and Wilbert van der Klaauw. 2012. "Grading Student Loans." Federal Reserve Bank of New York, March 5. Accessed May 22, 2012 (http://libertystreeteconomics.newyorkfed.org/2012/03/grading-student-loans.html).

Brown, Robert McAfee. 1980. *Gustavo Gutierrez.* Atlanta: John Knox.

Brown, Wyatt, and Wesley G. Jennings. 2014. "A Replication and an Honor-Based Extension of Hirschi's Reconceptualization of Self-Control Theory and Crime and Analogous Behaviors." *Deviant Behavior* 35: 297–310.

Bruce, Steve. 2000. *Choice and Religion: A Critique of Rational Choice Theory.* New York: Oxford University Press.

Buckles, Kasey, Andreas Hagemann, Ofer Malamud, Melinda Morrill, and Abigail Wozniak. 2016. "The Effect of College Education on Mortality." *Journal of Health Economics* 50: 99–114.

Buffett, Warren E. 2010. "Pretty Good for Government Work." *The New York Times,* November 16. Accessed June 3, 2015 (www.nytimes.com/2010/11/17/opinion/17buffett.html).

Bullard, Robert. 2000. *Dumping in Dixie: Race, Class, and Environmental Quality,* 3rd ed. Boulder, CO: Westview Press.

Bullough, Vern L. 1998. "Alfred Kinsey and the Kinsey Report: Historical Overview and Lasting Contributions." *Journal of Sex Research* 35 (2): 127–131.

Bundhun, Rebecca. 2016. "Supertall Buildings Lure Mumbai's Elite." *The New York Times,* March 3. Accessed January 14, 2017 (www.nytimes.com/2016/03/04/realestate/supertall-buildings-lure-mumbais-elite.html).

Burawoy, Michael. 2004. "Public Sociologies: Contradictions, Dilemmas, and Possibilities." *Social Forces* 82: 1603–1618.

Bureau of Economic Analysis. 2016. "Gross Domestic Product: Fourth Quarter and Annual 2015 (Third Estimate)." U.S. Department of Commerce, Washington, DC, BEA 16-16, March 25. Accessed January 18, 2017 (www.bea.gov/newsreleases/national/gdp/2016/pdf/gdp4q15_3rd.pdf).

Bureau of Labor Statistics. 2010. "Civilian Labor Force, 2019–2050."Employment Projections, Labor Force (Demographic) Data. Accessed April 20, 2010 (www.bls.gov/emp/ep_data_labor_force.htm).

———. 2015a. "Number of Jobs, Labor Market Experience, and Earnings Growth: Results from a Longitudinal Survey." Economic New Release, March 31. Accessed October 25, 2016 (www.bls.gov/news.release/nlsoy.toc.htm).

———. 2015b. "Women in the Labor Force: A Databook." U.S. Department of Labor, U.S. Bureau of Labor Statistics, Report 1059, December. Accessed December 14, 2016 (www.bls.gov/opub/reports/womens-databook/archive/women-in-the-labor-force-a-databook-2015.pdf).

———. 2015c. "Labor Force Characteristics by Race and Ethnicity, 2015." U.S. Department of Labor, U.S. Bureau of Labor Statistics, September. Accessed December 14, 2016 (www.bls.gov/opub/reports/race-and-ethnicity/2015/pdf/home.pdf).

———. 2016a. "Unemployment: Rates for States." Local Area Unemployment Statistics. Washington, DC: United States Department of Labor. Accessed July 28, 2016 (www.bls.gov/web/laus/laumstrk.htm).

———. 2016b. "Unemployment: Rates & Levels—Labor Force Statistics Including the National Unemployment Rate." Current Population Survey, Databases, Tables & Calculators by Subject. Washington, DC: United States Department of Labor. Accessed July 28, 2016 (www.bls.gov/data/#unemployment).

———. 2016c. "Employment Characteristics of Families—2015." U.S. Department of Labor, USDL-16-0795, April 22. Accessed November 22, 2016 (www.bls.gov/news.release/pdf/famee.pdf).

———. 2016d. "College Enrollment and Work Activity of 2015 High School Graduates." United States Department of Labor, USDL-16-0822, April 28. Accessed November 30, 2016 (www.bls.gov/news.release/pdf/hsgec.pdf).

———. 2016e. "2016 Employment & Earnings Online: Household Survey Data." U.S. Department of Labor. Accessed December 7, 2016 (www.bls.gov/opub/ee/2016/cps/annual.htm).

———. 2016f. "Consumer Expenditure Survey: CE Tables—Quintiles of Income before Taxes." August. Accessed December 22, 2016 (www.bls.gov/cex/tables.htm).

———. 2016g. "Highlights of Women's Earnings in 2015." U.S. Department of Labor, U.S. Bureau of Labor Statistics, Report 1064, November. Accessed December 22, 2016 (www.bls.gov/opub/reports/womens-earnings/2015/pdf/home.pdf).

———. 2016h. "Household Activities." American Time Use Survey, December 20. Accessed February 2, 2017 (www.bls.gov/tus/charts/household.htm).

———. 2016i. "Labor Force Statistics from the Current Population Survey: 2015." United States Department of Labor, Washington, DC. Accessed February 6, 2017 (www.bls.gov/cps/tables.htm).

———. 2017a. "Employment of the Civilian Noninstitutional Population by Age, Sex, and Race." Labor Force Statistics from the Current Population Survey. Washington, DC: United States Department of Labor. Accessed February 14, 2017 (www.bls.gov/cps/cpsaat03.htm).

———. 2017b. "Women in the Labor Force: A Databook." U.S. Department of Labor, U.S. Bureau of Labor Statistics, Report 1065, April. Accessed June 1, 2017 (www.bls.gov/opub/reports/womens-databook/2016/pdf/home.pdf).

Burger, Jerry M. 2009. "Replicating Milgram: Would People Still Obey Today?" *American Psychologist* 64: 1–11.

Burgoon, Judee K., Laura K. Guerrero, and Kory Floyd. 2010. *Nonverbal Communication.* New York: Allyn & Bacon.

Burke, Moira, Carlos Greg Diuk, and Adrien Friggeri. 2015. "Cupid in Your Network." Facebook Research. Accessed May 6, 2015 (https://research.facebook.com/blog/448802398605370/cupid-in-your-network/).

Burns, Corrinne. 2013. "Are Mental Illnesses Such as PMS and Depression Culturally Determined?" *The Guardian,* May 20. Accessed June 7, 2013 (www.guardian.co.uk/science/blog/2013/may/20/mental-illnesses-depression-pms-culturally-determined?CMP=twt_fd).

Burns, Crosby, Kimberly Barton, and Sophia Kerby. 2012. "The State of Diversity in Today's Workforce." Center for American Progress, Washington, DC, July. Accessed June 1, 2013 (www.americanprogress.org/wp-content/uploads/issues/2012/07/pdf/diversity_brief.pdf).

Butler, Rhett. 2016. "Calculating Deforestation Figures for the Amazon." Mongabay, January 23. Accessed February 13, 2017 (http://rainforests.mongabay.com/amazon/deforestation_calculations.html).

Butler, Robert N. 1990. "A Disease Called Ageism." *Journal of American Geriatrics Society* 38 (February): 178–180.

C

Cacchioni, Thea, and Leonore Tiefer. 2012. "Why Medicalization? Introduction to the Special Issue on the Medicalization of Sex." *Journal of Sex Research* 49: 307–310.

Cacioppo, John T., Stephanie Cacioppo, Gian C. Gonzaga, Elizabeth L. Ogburn, and Tyler J. VanderWeele. 2013. "Marital Satisfaction and Break-Ups Differ Across On-Line and Off-Line Meeting Venues." *PNAS* 110: 10135–10140.

Cai, Yong. 2010. "China's Below-Replacement Fertility: Government Policy or Socioeconomic Development?" *Population and Development Review* 36: 419–440.

Calamur, Krishnadev. 2017. "What Trump's Executive Order on Immigration Does—and Doesn't Do." *The Atlantic,* January 30. Accessed February 7, 2017 (www.theatlantic.com/news/archive/2017/01/trump-immigration-order-muslims/514844/).

Camp, Roderic Ai. 2010a. *The Metamorphosis of Leadership in a Democratic Mexico.* New York: Oxford University Press.

———. 2010b. "Armed Forces and Drugs: Public Perceptions and Institutional Challenges." Pp. 291–325 in *Shared Responsibility: U.S.–Mexico Policy Options for Confronting Organized Crime,* ed. Eric L. Olson, David A. Shirk, and Andrew Selee. San Diego: University of San Diego Trans-Border Institute.

Caplow, Theodore, and Louis Hicks. 2002. *Systems of War and Peace,* 2nd ed. Lanham, MD: University Press of America.

Carle, Jill. 2015. "Climate Change Seen as Top Global Threat." Pew Research Center, Global Attitudes & Trends July 14. Accessed February 13, 2017 (www.pewglobal.org/2015/07/14/climate-change-seen-as-top-global-threat/).

Carmichael, Mary. 2007. "Troubled Waters." *Newsweek* 149 (June 4): 52–56.

Carothers, Bobbi J., and Harry T. Reis. 2013. "Men and Women Are from Earth: Examining the Latent Structure of Gender." *Journal of Personality and Social Psychology* 104 (2): 385–407.

Carr, John E., and Eng K. Tan. 1976. "In Search of the True Amok: Amok as Viewed within the Malay Culture." *American Journal of Psychiatry* 133(11): 1295–1299.

Carr, Nicholas. 2010. *The Shallows: What the Internet Is Doing to Our Brains.* New York: Norton.

———. 2014. *The Glass Cage: Automation and Us.* New York: Norton.

Carroll, Aaron E. 2015. "No, You Do Not Have to Drink 8 Glasses of Water a Day." *The New York Times,* August 24. Accessed September 12, 2016 (www.nytimes.com/2015/08/25/upshot/no-you-do-not-have-to-drink-8-glasses-of-water-a-day.html).

Carroll, Aaron E., and Rachel C. Vreeman. 2009. *Don't Swallow Your Gum! Myths, Half-Truths and Outright Lies about Your Body and Health.* New York: St. Martin's Press.

Carroll, Rory. 2016. "Starved, Tortured, Forgotten: Genie, the Feral Child Who Left a Mark on Researchers." *The Guardian* July 14. Accessed October 17, 2016 (www.theguardian.com/society/2016/jul/14/genie-feral-child-los-angeles-researchers).

Carson, Rachel. 1962. *Silent Spring.* Boston: Houghton Mifflin.

Carter, Susan B., Scott Sigmund Gartner, Michael R. Haines, Alan L. Olmstead, Richard Sutch, and Gavin Wright. 2006. *Historical Statistics of the United States: Earliest Times to the Present, Millennial Edition.* 5 vols. Cambridge, UK: Cambridge University Press.

Carty, Victoria, and Jake Onyett. 2006. "Protest, Cyberactivism and New Social Movements: The Reemergence of the Peace Movement Post 9/11." *Social Movement Studies* 5 (3): 229–249.

Cassandra. 2015. "No Kid(ding)." Ages & Stages, Cassandra Report, Summer. Accessed November 22, 2016 (https://cassandra.co/2015/ages-and-stages/no-kidding).

Casselman, Ben. 2016. "Stuck in Your Parents' Basement? Don't Blame the Economy." *FiveThirtyEight,* May 27. Accessed November 22, 2016 (http://fivethirtyeight.com/features/stuck-in-your-parents-basement-dont-blame-the-economy/).

Castañeda, Jorge G. 1995. "Ferocious Differences." *Atlantic Monthly* 276 (July): 68–69, 71–76.

Catalyst. 2017a. "Women CEOs of the S&P 500." Catalyst Knowledge Center, January 3. Accessed January 19, 2017 (www.catalyst.org/knowledge/women-ceos-sp-500).

Cavalli-Sforza, L. Luca, Paolo Menozzi, and Alberto Piazza. 1994. *The History and Geography of Human Genes.* Princeton, NJ: Princeton University Press.

Center for American Women and Politics. 2015. "Gender Differences in Voter Turnout." Eagleton Institute of Politics, Rutgers, University, New Brunswick, NJ. Accessed February 2, 2017 (www.cawp.rutgers.edu/sites/default/files/resources/genderdiff.pdf).

———. 2017. "Women in Elective Office 2017." Eagleton Institute of Politics, Rutgers, University, New Brunswick, NJ. Accessed February 2, 2017 (www.cawp.rutgers.edu/women-elective-office-2017).

Centers for Disease Control and Prevention. 2015. "National Marriage and Divorce Rate Trends." National Center for Health Statistics, Atlanta, GA. Accessed November 23, 2016 (www.cdc.gov/nchs/nvss/marriage_divorce_tables.htm).

———. 2016a. "Marriage Rates by State: 1990, 1995, and 1999–2015." National Center for Health Statistics, Atlanta, GA. Accessed June 27, 2017 (www.cdc.gov/nchs/data/dvs/state_marriage_rates_90_95_99-15.pdf).

———. 2016b. "Youth Risk Behavior Surveillance—United States, 2015." Surveillance Summaries, June 10. *Morbidity and Mortality Weekly Report* 65(6). Accessed February 2, 2017 (www.cdc.gov/healthyyouth/data/yrbs/pdf/2015/ss6506_updated.pdf).

———. 2016c. *HIV Surveillance Report, 2015,* Vol. 25. Accessed February 11, 2017 (www.cdc.gov/hiv/pdf/library/reports/surveillance/cdc-hiv-surveillance-report-2015-vol-27.pdf).

References

Centers for Medicare & Medicaid Services. 2016a. "National Health Expenditure Data: Historical." Department of Health & Human Services. Accessed February 12, 2017 (www.cms.gov/Research-Statistics-Data-and-Systems/Statistics-Trends-and-Reports/NationalHealthExpendData/NationalHealthAccountsHistorical.html).

———. 2016b. "National Health Expenditure Data: Projected." Department of Health & Human Services. Accessed February 12, 2017 (www.cms.gov/Research-Statistics-Data-and-Systems/Statistics-Trends-and-Reports/NationalHealthExpendData/NationalHealthAccountsProjected.html).

———. 2016c. "Fast Facts: CMS Program Data—Populations." Department of Health & Human Services. Accessed February 12, 2017 (www.cms.gov/fastfacts/).

Césaire, Aimé. 1972. *Discourse on Colonialism.* New York: Monthly Review Press.

Cevallos, Diego. 2009. "Indigenous Woman Fights for Rights." *Inter Press Service,* April 1. Accessed June 15, 2009 (www.ips.org/mdg3/mexico-indigenous-woman-on-the-offensive/#more-21).

Chalabi, Mona, and Andrew Flowers. 2014. "Dear Mona, What's the Most Popular Name in America?" *FiveThirtyEight Life,* November 20. Accessed January 10, 2015 (http://fivethirtyeight.com/features/whats-the-most-common-name-in-america/).

Chambers, Samuel. 2007. "An Incalculable Effect: Subversions of Heteronormativity." *Political Studies* 55 (3): 656–679.

Chambliss, William. 1973. "The Saints and the Roughnecks." *Society* 11 (November/December): 24–31.

Chandra, Anjani, Casey E. Copen, and William D. Mosher. 2013. "Sexual Behavior, Sexual Attraction, and Sexual Identity in the United States: Data from the 2006–2010 National Survey of Family Growth." *International Handbook on the Demography of Sexuality, International Handbooks of Population* 5: 45–66.

Charney, Leo, and Vanessa R. Schwartz, eds. 1995. *Cinema and the Invention of Modern Life.* Berkeley, CA: University of California Press.

Chauvin, Chantel D. 2012. "Social Norms and Motivations Associated with College Binge Drinking." *Sociological Inquiry* 82(2): 257–281.

Chavigny, Katherine A. 2014. "An Army of Reformed Drunkards and Clergymen: The Medicalization of Habitual Drunkenness, 1857–1910." *Journal of the History of Medicine & Allied Sciences* 69: 383–425.

Chee, Kyong Hee, Nathan W. Pino, and William L. Smith. 2005. "Gender Differences in the Academic Ethic and Academic Achievement." *College Student Journal* 39 (3): 604–618.

Chen, Victor Tan. 2016. "The Spiritual Crisis of the Modern Economy." *The Atlantic,* December 21. Accessed December 22, 2016 (www.theatlantic.com/business/archive/2016/12/spiritual-crisis-modern-economy/511067/).

Cheng, Shu-Ju Ada. 2003. "Rethinking the Globalization of Domestic Service." *Gender and Society* 17 (2): 166–186.

Cherlin, Andrew. 2008. *Public and Private Families: An Introduction,* 5th ed. New York: McGraw-Hill.

———. 2009. *The Marriage-Go-Round: The State of Marriage and the Family in America Today.* New York: Knopf.

Chesney-Lind, Meda. 1989. "Girls' Crime and Woman's Place: Toward a Feminist Model of Female Delinquency." *Crime and Delinquency* 35: 5–29.

Chesney-Lind, Meda, and Lisa Pasko. 2004. *The Female Offender: Girls, Women, and Crime,* 2nd ed. Thousand Oaks, CA: Sage.

Chettiar, Inimai M. 2015. "The Many Causes of American Crime." *The Atlantic,* February 11. Accessed November 12, 2016 (www.theatlantic.com/politics/archive/2015/02/the-many-causes-of-americas-decline-in-crime/385364/).

Chetty, Raj, David Grusky, Maximilian Hell, Nathaniel Hendren, Robert Manduca, and Jimmy Narang. 2016. "The Fading American Dream: Trends in Absolute Income Mobility Since 1940." NBER Working Paper Series, Number 22910, December. Accessed December 22, 2016 (www.equality-of-opportunity.org/papers/abs_mobility_paper.pdf).

Chetty, Raj, Michael Stepner, Sarah Abraham, Shelby Lin, Benjamin Scuderi, Nicholas Turner, Augustin Bergeron, and David Cutler. 2016. "The Association between Income and Life Expectancy in the United States, 2001–2014." *JAMA* 315(16): 1750–1766.

Christakis, Nicholas A., and James H. Fowler. 2010. "Social Network Sensors for Early Detection of Contagious Outbreaks." *PLoS ONE* 5: e12948. Accessed February 11, 2015 (http://nrs.harvard.edu/urn-3:HUL.InstRepos:8852307).

Christel, Deborah A., and Susan C. Dunn. 2016. "Average American Women's Clothing Size: Comparing National Health and Nutritional Examination Surveys (1988–2010) to ASTM International Misses & Women's Plus Size Clothing." *International Journal of Fashion Design, Technology, and Education,* August: 1–8.

Christian, Joseph. 2009. "Coffee Culture: A Symbol of Middle-Class Lifestyle." *China Daily,* November 3. Accessed April 1, 2010 (www.chinadaily.com.cn/cndy/2009-11/03/content_8903174.htm).

Chua, Amy. 2011. *The Battle Hymn of the Tiger Mother.* New York: Penguin Press.

Chun, Helen, Maria I. Tavarez, Grace E. Dann, and Michael P. Anastario. 2011. "Interviewer Gender and Self-Reported Sexual Behavior and Mental Health Among Male Military Personnel." *International Journal of Public Health* 56 (2): 225–229.

Cigar, Norman. 1995. *Genocide in Bosnia: The Policy of "Ethnic Cleansing."* College Station: Texas A&M University Press.

CIRCLE. 2016. "Young People Reject Trump, But Older Voters Propel Him to Unexpected Victory." The Center for Information & Research on Civic Learning & Engagement, Medford MA, November 9. Accessed December 15, 2016 (http://civicyouth.org/too-close-to-call-young-people-reject-trump-older-voters-key-to-his-unexpectedly-strong-performance/).

Clammer, John. 2009. "Sociology and Beyond: Towards a Deep Sociology." *Asian Journal of Social Science* 37 (3): 332–346.

Clark, Burton. 1960. "The Cooling-Out Function in Higher Education." *American Journal of Sociology* 65: 569–576.

———. 1980. "The Cooling-Out Function Revisited." *New Directions for Community Colleges* 32: 15–31.

Clark, Duncan. 2012. "Has the Kyoto Protocol Made Any Difference to Carbon Emissions?" *The Guardian,* November 26. Accessed May 3, 2015 (www.theguardian.com/environment/blog/2012/nov/26/kyoto-protocol-carbon-emissions).

Clark, Jonathan R., Robert S. Huckman, and Bradley R. Staats. 2013. "Learning from Customers: Individual and Organizational Effects in Outsourced Radiological Services." *Organization Science* 24: 1539–1557.

Clarke, Edward H. 1874. *Sex in Education; or, A Fair Chance for the Girls.* Boston: James R. Osgood.

Clarke, Tainya C., Lindsey I. Black, Barbara J. Stussman, Patricia M. Barnes, and Richard L. Nahin. 2015. "Trends in the Use of Complementary Health Approaches Among Adults: United States, 2002–2012." *National Health Statistics Reports,* no. 79. Hyattsville, MD: National Center for Health Statistics, February 10. Accessed February 13, 2017 (www.cdc.gov/nchs/data/nhsr/nhsr079.pdf).

Climatic Research Unit, University of East Anglia. 2017. "Temperature: HadCRUT4 – GL." Accessed February 13, 2017 (https://crudata.uea.ac.uk/cru/data/temperature/).

Clinard, Marshall B., and Robert F. Miller. 1998. *Sociology of Deviant Behavior,* 10th ed. Fort Worth, TX: Harcourt Brace.

Coates, Ta-Nehisi. 2014. "The Case for Reparations." *The Atlantic* June. Accessed February 5, 2017 (www.theatlantic.com/magazine/archive/2014/06/the-case-for-reparations/361631/).

Cohen, Philip N. 2013. "Children's Gender and Parent's Color Preferences." *Archives of Sexual Behavior* 42(3): 393–397.

———. 2016. "Life Table Says Divorce Rate Is 52.7%." *Family Inequality,* June 8. Accessed November 23, 2016 (https://familyinequality.wordpress.com/2016/06/08/life-table-says-divorce-rate-is-52-7/).

Cohen, Robin A., Michael E. Martinez, and Emily P. Zammitti. "Health Insurance Coverage: Early Release of Estimates from the National Health Interview Survey, January–March 2016."

National Center for Health Statistics September. Accessed February 12, 2017 (www.cdc.gov/nchs/data/nhis/earlyrelease/insur201609.pdf).

Cohn, D'Vera. 2011. "Multi-Race and the 2010 Census." Pew Research Center, April 6. Accessed June 18, 2011 (http://pewresearch.org/pubs/1953/multi-race-2010-census-obama).

———. 2016. "Federal Officials May Revamp How Americans Identify Race, Ethnicity on Census and Other Forms." Pew Research Center, October 4. Accessed February 2, 2017 (www.pewresearch.org/fact-tank/2016/10/04/federal-officials-may-revamp-how-americans-identify-race-ethnicity-on-census-and-other-forms/).

Cohn, Nate. 2016. "Why Trump Won: Working-Class Whites." *The New York Times.* November 9. Accessed December 13, 2016 (www.nytimes.com/2016/11/10/upshot/why-trump-won-working-class-whites.html).

Colby, David C. 1986. "The Voting Rights Act and Black Registration in Mississippi." *Publius* 16 (Fall): 123–137.

Colby, Sandra L., and Jennifer M. Ortman. 2015. "Projections of the Size and Composition of the U.S. Population: 2014 to 2060." Current Population Reports, P25-1143, U.S. Census Bureau, March. Accessed February 4, 2017 (www.census.gov/content/dam/Census/library/publications/2015/demo/p25-1143.pdf).

Coleman, James William. 2006. *The Criminal Elite: Understanding White-Collar Crime,* 6th ed. New York: Worth.

College Board. 2016a. "Trends in Student Aid 2016." *Trends in Higher Education Series,* October. Accessed December 5, 2016 (https://trends.collegeboard.org/student-aid).

———. 2016b. "Trends in College Pricing 2016." *Trends in Higher Education Series,* October. Accessed December 6, 2016 (https://trends.collegeboard.org/college-pricingCo).

Collins, Gail. 2003. *America's Women.* New York: HarperCollins.

Collins, Mary B., Ian Munoz, and Joseph JaJa. 2016. "Linking 'Toxic Outliers' to Environmental Justice Communities." *Environmental Research Letters* 11(1): 015004.

Collins, Patricia Hill. 2000. *Black Feminist Thought,* 2nd ed. New York: Routledge.

Commoner, Barry. 1971. *The Closing Circle.* New York: Knopf.

Commonwealth of Australia. 2013. "Australian Government Guidelines on the Recognition of Sex and Gender." July. Accessed April 19, 2015 (www.ag.gov.au/Publications/Documents/AustralianGovernmentGuidelinesontheRecognitionofSexandGender/AustralianGovernmentGuidelinesontheRecognitionofSexandGender.PDF).

Connell, R. W. 2002. *Gender.* Cambridge, UK: Polity Press.

———. 2005. *Masculinities,* 2nd ed. Berkeley: University of California Press.

———, and James W. Messerschmidt. 2005. "Hegemonic Masculinity: Rethinking the Concept." *Gender & Society* 19(6): 829–859.

Connolly, Ceci. 2008. "As Latin Nations Treat Gays Better, Asylum Is Elusive." *The Washington Post,* August 12. Accessed May 28, 2010 (www.washingtonpost.com/wp-dyn/content/article/2008/08/11/AR2008081102038.html).

Conrad, Peter. 2007. *The Medicalization of Society: On the Transformation of Human Conditions into Treatable Disorders.* Baltimore, MD: Johns Hopkins University Press.

Cooley, Charles H. 1902. *Human Nature and the Social Order.* New York: Scribner.

Coontz, Stephanie. 1992. *The Way We Never Were: American Families and the Nostalgia Trap.* New York: Basic Books.

———. 2005. *Marriage, a History: From Obedience to Intimacy or How Love Conquered Marriage.* New York: Viking.

———. 2006. "A Pop Quiz on Marriage." *The New York Times,* February 19, p. 12.

———. 2008. "The Future of Marriage." *Cato Unbound,* January 14. Accessed August 2, 2010 (www.cato-unbound.org/2008/01/14/stephanie-coontz/the-future-of-marriage).

———. 2011. *A Strange Stirring: The Feminine Mystique and American Women at the Dawn of the 1960s.* New York: Basic Books.

Cooper, Bruce S., and John Sureau. 2007. "The Politics of Homeschooling: New Developments, New Challenges." *Educational Policy* 21 (January and March): 110–131.

Cooper, Daniel H., and J. Christina Wang. 2014. "Student Loan Debt and Economic Outcomes." Federal Reserve Bank of Boston, *Current Policy Perspectives* 2014–7. Accessed December 14, 2016 (www.bostonfed.org/publications/current-policy-perspectives/2014/student-loan-debt-and-economic-outcomes.aspx).

Cooper, K., S. Day, A. Green, and H. Ward. 2007. "Maids, Migrants and Occupational Health in the London Sex Industry." *Anthropology and Medicine* 14 (April): 41–53.

Cooper, Lisa A., Debra L. Roter, Kathry A. Carson, Mary Catherine Beach, Janice A. Sabin, Anthony G. Greenwald, and Thomas S. Inui. 2012. "The Associations of Clinicians' Implicit Attitudes about Race with Medical Visit Communication and Patient Ratings of Interpersonal Care." *American Journal of Public Health* 102(5): 979–987.

Copen, Casey E., Anjani Chandra, and Isaedmarie Febo-Vazquez. 2016. "Sexual Behavior, Sexual Attraction, and Sexual Orientation Among Adults Aged 18–44 in the United States: Data from the 2011–2013 National Survey of Family Growth." *National Health Statistics Reports,* No. 88. Hyattsville, MD: National Center for Health Statistics. Accessed February 1, 2017 (www.cdc.gov/nchs/data/nhsr/nhsr088.pdf).

Copen, Casey E., Kimberly Daniels, Jonathan Vespa, and William D. Mosher. 2012. "First Marriages in the United States: Data from the 2006–2012 National Survey of Family Growth." *National Health Statistics Reports* 49: March 22. Accessed November 21, 2016 (www.cdc.gov/nchs/data/nhsr/nhsr049.pdf).

Corak, Miles. 2006. "Do Poor Children Become Poor Adults? Lessons from a Cross Country Comparison of Generational Earnings Mobility." Institute for the Study of Labor (IZA) Discussion Paper No. 1993, March. Accessed June 24, 2008 (http://papers.ssrn.com/sol3/papers.cfm?abstract_id5889034).

———. 2016. "Inequality from Generation to Generation: The United States in Comparison." IZA Discussion Paper No. 9929, May. Accessed January 20, 2017 (https://papers.ssrn.com/sol3/papers.cfm?abstract_id=2786013).

Corasanti, Nick. "Donald Trump Focuses on Immigration in His First Ad of General Election." *The New York Times,* August 20. Accessed February 4, 2017 (www.nytimes.com/2016/08/21/us/politics/donald-trump-focuses-on-immigration-in-his-first-ad-of-general-election.html).

Cornwall, Warren. 2015. "*Deepwater Horizon:* After the Oil." *Science,* April 3, 22–29.

Coser, Rose Laub. 1984. "American Medicine's Ambiguous Progress." *Contemporary Sociology* 13 (January): 9–13.

Côté, James E. 2000. *Arrested Adulthood: The Changing Nature of Identity and Maturity in the Late World.* New York: New York University.

Council of Europe. 2015. *Human Rights and Intersex People.* Commissioner for Human Rights, Issue Paper, September. Accessed January 26, 2017 (https://rm.coe.int/CoERMPublicCommonSearchServices/DisplayDCTMContent?documentId=09000016806da5d4).

Courvertier, Dave. 2016. "Investigative Update Regarding Pulse Nightclub Shooting." FBI Tampa, June 20. Accessed November 4, 2016 (www.fbi.gov/contact-us/field-offices/tampa/news/press-releases/investigative-update-regarding-pulse-nightclub-shooting).

Cox, Daniel, and Robert P. Jones. 2016. "Race, Religion, and Political Affiliation of American's Core Social Networks." PRRI, Washington, DC, August 3. Accessed February 4, 2017 (www.prri.org/research/poll-race-religion-politics-americans-social-networks/).

Cox, Oliver C. 1948. *Caste, Class, and Race: A Study in Social Dynamics.* Detroit, MI: Wayne State University Press.

Crenshaw, Kimberlé. 2016. "The Urgency of Intersectionality." Video. TEDWomen, October. Accessed January 31, 2017 (www.ted.com/talks/kimberle_crenshaw_the_urgency_of_intersectionality).

Cross, Simon, and Barbara Bagilhole. 2002. "Girls' Jobs for the Boys? Men, Masculinity, and Non-Traditional Occupations." *Gender, Work, and Organization* 9: 204–226.

Crouch, Simon R., Elizabeth Waters, Ruth McNair, Jennifer Power, and Elise Davis. 2014. "Parent-Reported Measures of Child Health and Well-Being in Same-Sex Parent Families: A Cross-Sectional Survey." *BMC Public Health* 14: 636.

CTIA. 2017. "Background on CTIA's Wireless Industry Survey." CTIA—The Wireless Association. Accessed June 23, 2017 (www.ctia.org/docs/default-source/default-document-library/annual-year-end-2016-top-line-survey-results-final.pdf8).

Cumming, Elaine, and William E. Henry. 1961. *Growing Old: The Process of Disengagement.* New York: Basic Books.

Curiel, Jonathan. 2016. "A Is for Arab." *AramcoWorld* March/April. Accessed January 18, 2017 (www.aramcoworld.com/en-US/Articles/March-2016/A-Is-For-Arab).

Currie, Elliott. 1985. *Confronting Crime: An American Challenge.* New York: Pantheon Books.

———. 1998. *Crime and Punishment in America.* New York: Metropolitan Books.

Curtiss, Susan. 1977. *Genie: A Psycholinguistic Study of a Modern Day "Wild Child."* New York: Academic Press.

Cusack, Carole M., and Justine Digance. 2009. "The Melbourne Cup: Australian Identity and Secular Pilgrimage." *Sport in Society* 12 (7): 876–889.

Cyranoski, David, and Sara Reardon. 2015. "Chinese Scientists Genetically Modify Human Embryos." *Nature,* April 22. Accessed May 5, 2015 (www.nature.com/news/chinese-scientists-genetically-modify-human-embryos-1.17378).

D

Dahl, Robert A. 1961. *Who Governs?* New Haven, CT: Yale University Press.

Daisey, Mike. 2002. *21 Dog Years: Doing Time @ Amazon.com.* New York: Free Press.

Daniels, Kimberly, Jill Daugherty, Jo Jones, and William Mosher. 2015. "Current Contraceptive Use and Variation by Selected Characteristics among Women Aged 15–44: United States, 2011–2013." *National Health Statistics Reports,* No. 86, November 10. Hyattsville, MD: National Center for Health Statistics. Accessed February 1, 2017 (www.cdc.gov/nchs/data/nhsr/nhsr086.pdf).

Dao, James. 1995. "New York's Highest Court Rules Unmarried Couples Can Adopt." *The New York Times,* November 3, pp. A1, B2.

Darwin, Charles. 1859. *On the Origin of Species.* London: John Murray.

Davenport, Coral, Justin Gillis, Sewell Chan, and Melissa Eddy. 2015. "Inside the Paris Climate Deal." *The New York Times,* December 12. Accessed February 13, 2017 (www.nytimes.com/interactive/2015/12/12/world/paris-climate-change-deal-explainer.html).

Davenport, Thomas H., and Julia Kirby. 2016. *Only Humans Need Apply: Winners and Losers in the Age of Smart Machines.* New York: HarperCollins Publishers.

David, Gary. 2004. "Scholarship on Arab Americans Distorted Past 9/11." *Al Jadid* (Winter/Spring): 26–27.

Davidson, Adam. 2014. "Its Official: The Boomerang Kids Won't Leave." *The New York Times,* June 20. Accessed February 26, 2015 (www.nytimes.com/2014/06/22/magazine/its-official-the-boomerang-kids-wont-leave.html).

Davies, Sharyn Graham. 2007. *Challenging Gender Norms: Five Genders among Bugis in Indonesia.* Belmont, CA: Wadsworth, Cengage Learning.

Davis, Angela. 1998. "Masked Racism: Reflection on the Prison Industrial Complex." *Colorlines,* September 10. Accessed November 10, 2016 (www.colorlines.com/articles/masked-racism-reflections-prison-industrial-complex).

Davis, Darren W., and Brian D. Silver. 2003. "Stereotype Threat and Race of Interviewer Effects in a Survey on Political Knowledge." *American Journal of Political Science* 47(1): 33–45.

Davis, Georgiann. 2014. "The Power in a Name: Diagnostic Terminology and Diverse Experiences." *Psychology & Sexuality* 5: 15–27.

Davis, Joseph E. 2006. "How Medicalization Lost Its Way." *Society* 43 (6): 51–56.

Davis, Kingsley, and Wilbert E. Moore. 1945. "Some Principles of Stratification." *American Sociological Review* 10 (April): 242–249.

Dawson, Julia, Stefano Natella, and Richard Kersley. 2016. *The CS Gender 3000: The Reward for Change.* Zurich: Credit Suisse AG. Accessed February 2, 2017 (http://publications.credit-suisse.com/index.cfm/publikationen-shop/research-institute/cs-gender-3000/).

Dawson, Lorne. 2009. "Church-Sect-Cult: Constructing Typologies of Religious Groups." Pp. 525–544 in *The Oxford Handbook of the Sociology of Religion,* ed. Peter B. Clarke. New York: Oxford University Press.

Death Penalty Information Center. 2016. "Facts about the Death Penalty." Washington, DC, November 9. Accessed November 16, 2016 (www.deathpenaltyinfo.org/documents/FactSheet.pdf).

Deflem, Mathieu. 2005. "Wild Beasts Without Nationality: The Uncertain Origins of Interpol, 1898–1910." Pp. 275–285 in *Handbook of Transnational Crime and Justice,* ed. Philip Rerchel. Thousand Oaks, CA: Sage.

de Freytas-Tamura, Kimiko. 2016. "After 'Brexit' Vote, Immigrants Feel a Town Turn Against Them." *The New York Times,* July 9. Accessed February 4, 2017 (www.nytimes.com/2016/07/10/world/europe/brexit-immigrants-great-britain-eu.html).

DeGregory, Lane. 2008. "The Girl in the Window." *The St. Petersburg Times,* July 31. Accessed May 14, 2013 (www.tampabay.com/features/humaninterest/the-girl-in-the-window/750838).

———. 2011. "Three Years Later, The Girl in the Window Learns to Connect." *Tampa Bay Times,* August 19. Accessed May 14, 2013 (www.tampabay.com/features/humaninterest/three-years-later-the-girl-in-the-window-learns-to-connect/1186860).

Demeneix, Barbara. 2017. *Toxic Cocktail: How Chemical Pollution Is Poisoning Our Brains.* New York: Oxford University Press.

Denyer, Simon. 2016. "China's Scary Lesson to the World: Censoring the Internet Works." *The Washington Post,* May 23. Accessed February 15, 2017 (www.washingtonpost.com/world/asia_pacific/chinas-scary-lesson-to-the-world-censoring-the-intcrnet-works/2016/05/23/413afe78-fff3-11e5-8bb1-f124a43f84dc_story.html).

DeNavas-Walt, Carmen, and Bernadette D. Proctor. 2014. "Income and Poverty in the United States: 2013." *Current Population Reports,* P60-249. Washington, DC: U.S. Government Printing Office. Accessed January 7, 2015 (www.census.gov/content/dam/Census/library/publications/2014/demo/p60-249.pdf).

Department of Defense. 2016. "Active Duty Military Personnel by Service by Rank/Grade: October 2016 (Women Only)." DoD Personnel, Workforce Reports & Publications. Accessed December 16, 2016 (www.dmdc.osd.mil/appj/dwp/dwp_reports.jsp).

DePaulo, Bella. 2014. "A Singles Studies Perspective on Mount Marriage." *Psychological Inquiry* 25: 64–68.

DeSilver, Drew. 2015. "The Fading of the Teen Summer Job." Pew Research Center, June 23. Accessed October 25, 2016 (www.pewresearch.org/fact-tank/2015/06/23/the-fading-of-the-teen-summer-job/).

———. 2016. "Increase in Living with Parents Driven by Those Ages 25–34, Non-College Grads." Pew Research Center, June 8. Accessed November 22, 2016 (www.pewresearch.org/fact-tank/2016/06/08/increase-in-living-with-parents-driven-by-those-ages-25-34-non-college-grads/).

DeSilver, Drew, and Kristen Bialik. 2017. "Blacks and Hispanics Face Extra Challenges in Getting Home Loans." Pew Research Center, January 10. Accessed February 6, 2017 (www.pewresearch.org/fact-tank/2017/01/10/blacks-and-hispanics-face-extra-challenges-in-getting-home-loans/).

Desmond, Matthew. 2016. *Evicted: Poverty and Profit in the American City.* New York: Crown Publishers.

Desmond, Matthew, and Mustafa Emerbayer. 2009. "What Is Racial Domination?" *Du Bois Review* 6(2): 335–355.

Diamond, Jared. 2008. "What's Your Consumption Factor?" *The New York Times*, January 2. Accessed May 21, 2010 (www.nytimes.com/2008/01/02/opinion/02diamond.html).

Dickens, Charles. 1843. *A Christmas Carol*. London: Chapman and Hall. Accessed July 7, 2008 (www.gutenberg.org/dirs/4/46/46-h/46-h.htm).

Dicker, Rory. 2016. *A History of U.S. Feminisms*. Berkeley, CA: Seal Press.

Doctorow, Cory. 2014. "Thomas Pikettys Capital in the 21st Century." *BoingBoing*, June 24. Accessed June 8, 2015 (http://boingboing.net/2014/06/24/thomas-pikettys-capital-in-t.html).

Doctors Without Borders. 2015. *U.S. Annual Report 2015*. New York, September 12. Accessed January 20, 2017 (www.doctorswithoutborders.org/us-annual-reports).

Dolan, Maura. 2017. "A Flurry of Legal Arguments as Appeals Court Decides Whether Trump's Immigration Ban Will Be Enforced." *Los Angeles Times*, February 6. Accessed February 7, 2017 (www.latimes.com/nation/la-na-immigration-order-legal-20170206-story.html).

Domhoff, G. William. 1978. *Who Really Rules? New Haven and Community Power Reexamined*. New Brunswick, NJ: Transaction.

———. 2009. "The Power Elite and Their Challengers: The Role of Nonprofits in American Social Conflict." *American Behavioral Scientist* 52 (7): 955–973.

———. 2014. *Who Rules America?: The Triumph of the Corporate Rich*. 7th ed. New York: McGraw-Hill.

Doress, Irwin, and Jack Nusan Porter. 1977. *Kids in Cults: Why They Join, Why They Stay, Why They Leave*. Brookline, MA: Reconciliation Associates.

Dotinga, Randy. 2014. "When Parents Need Care, Daughters Carry the Burden." *CBS News*, August 19. Accessed February 2, 2015 (www.cbsnews.com/news/when-parents-need-care-daughters-carry-the-burden-study-says/).

Drescher, Jack. 2010. "Queer Diagnoses: Parallels and Contrasts in the History of Homosexuality, Gender Variance, and the *Diagnostic and Statistical Manual*." *Archives of Sexual Behavior* 39 (2): 427–460.

———. 2011. "The Removal of Homosexuality from the DSM: Its Impact on Today's Marriage Equality Debate." *Journal of Gay & Lesbian Mental Health* 16 (2): 124–135.

———. 2015. "Out of DSM: Depathologizing Homosexuality." *Behavioral Sciences* 5(4): 565–575.

Druckman, James N. 2003. "The Power of Television Images: The First Kennedy-Nixon Debate Revisited." *The Journal of Politics* 65 (2): 559–571.

Duberman, Martin Bauml, Martha Vicinus, and George Chauncey Jr., eds. 1989. *Hidden from History: Reclaiming the Gay and Lesbian Past*. New York: New American Library.

Du Bois, W. E. B. [1903] 1994. *The Souls of Black Folk*. New York: Dover.

———. [1909] 1970. *The Negro American Family*. Cambridge, MA: MIT Press.

Dufton, Emily. 2012. "The War on Drugs: How President Nixon Tied Addiction to Crime." *The Atlantic*, March 26. Accessed November 10, 2016 (www.theatlantic.com/health/archive/2012/03/the-war-on-drugs-how-president-nixon-tied-addiction-to-crime/254319/).

Duncan, Greg J., and Richard J Murnane. 2011. "Introduction: The American Dream, Then and Now." Pp. 3–23 in *Whither Opportunity?: Rising Inequality, Schools, and Children's Life Chances*, ed. Greg J. Duncan and Richard J. Murnane. New York: Russell Sage Foundation.

Duong, Thi Hoa, Ulla-Britt Jansson, and Ann-Lena Hellström. 2013. "Vietnamese Mothers Experiences with Potty Training Procedure for Children from Birth to 2 Years of Age." *Journal of Pediatric Urology* 9: 808–814.

Durkheim, Émile. [1887] 1972. "Religion and Ritual." Pp. 219–238 in *Émile Durkheim: Selected Writings*, ed. A. Giddens. Cambridge, UK: Cambridge University Press.

———. [1893] 1933. *Division of Labor in Society*, trans. George Simpson. New York: Free Press.

———. [1895] 1964. *The Rules of Sociological Method*, trans. Sarah A. Solovay and John H. Mueller. New York: Free Press.

———. [1895] 1982. *The Rules of Sociological Method and Selected Texts on Sociology and Its Method*, trans. W. D. Halls. New York: Free Press.

———. [1897] 1951. *Suicide*, trans. John A. Spaulding and George Simpson. New York: Free Press.

E

Eagan, Kevin, Ellen Bara Stolzenberg, Joseph J. Ramirez, Melissa C. Aragon, Maria Ramirez Suchard, and Cecilia Rios-Aguilar. 2016. *The American Freshman: Fifty-Year Trend, 1966–2015*. Los Angeles: Higher Education Research Institute, UCLA. Accessed October 6, 2016 (www.heri.ucla.edu/monographs/50YearTrendsMonograph2016.pdf).

Ebaugh, Helen Rose Fuchs. 1988. *Becoming an Ex: The Process of Role Exit*. Chicago: University of Chicago Press.

Eckert, Penelope, and Sally McConnell-Ginet. 2003. *Language and Gender*. New York: Cambridge University Press.

The Economist. 2008. "A Ravenous Dragon: A Special Report on China's Quest for Resources." March 15: 1–22.

Edgerton, Gary R. 2007. *The Columbia History of American Television*. New York: Columbia University Press.

Edin, Kathryn, and Maria Kefalas. 2005. *Promises I Can Keep: Why Poor Women Put Motherhood Before Marriage*. Berkeley: University of California Press.

Edin, Kathryn, and H. Luke Shaefer. 2015. *$2.00 a Day: Living on Almost Nothing in America*. Boston: Houghton Mifflin Harcourt.

Edwards, Mark U., Jr. 1994. *Printing, Propaganda, and Martin Luther*. Berkeley, CA: University of California Press.

EEOC. 2014. "Age Discrimination Employment Act (Includes Concurrent Charges with Title VII, ADA and EPA) FY 1997–FY 2014." U.S. Equal Employment Opportunity Commission. Accessed February 2, 2015 (www.eeoc.gov/eeoc/statistics/-enforcement/adea.cfm).

eHarmony. 2014. "Who We Are." Accessed February 26, 2014 (www.eharmony.com/about/eharmony/).

Eilperin, Juliet, and Brady Dennis. 2017. "Trump Administration to Approve Final Permit for Dakota Access Pipeline." *The Washington Post*, February 7. Accessed February 8, 2017 (www.washingtonpost.com/news/energy-environment/wp/2017/02/07/trump-administration-to-approve-final-permit-for-dakota-access-pipeline/).

Elbein, Saul. 2017. "The Youth Group That Launched a Movement at Standing Rock." *The New York Times Magazine*, January 31. Accessed February 8, 2017 (https://nytimes.com/2017/01/31/magazine/the-youth-group-that-launched-a-movement-at-standing-rock.html).

Elgin, Suzette Haden. 1984. *Native Tongue*. New York: Feminist Press.

———. 1988. *A First Dictionary and Grammar of Láadan*, 2nd ed. Madison, WI: Society for the Furtherance and Study of Fantasy and Science Fiction.

Elish, Jill. 2010. "Failed College Dreams Don't Spell Depression, Study Finds." *Florida State News*, March 19. Accessed April 19, 2010 (www.fsu.edu/news/2010/03/19/failed.dreams/).

Elliott, Michael. 2005. "Hopelessly Devoted: Being a Fan Is Like Having Your Own Personal Time Machine." *Time*, June 20, p. 76.

Ellison, Ralph. 1952. *Invisible Man*. New York: Random House.

Ellul, Jacques. 1964. *The Technological Society*. New York: Knopf.

———. 1980. *The Technological System*. New York: Continuum.

———. 1990. *The Technological Bluff*. Grand Rapids, MI: Eerdmans.

Emerson, Michael O., David Hartman, Karen Cook, and Douglas Massey. 2006. "The Rise of Religious Fundamentalism." *Annual Review of Sociology* 32: 127–144.

Engels, Friedrich. [1884] 1959. "The Origin of the Family, Private Property, and the State." Pp. 392–394 in *Marx and Engels: Basic Writings on Politics and Philosophy,* ed. Lewis Feuer. Garden City, NY: Anchor Books.

England, Paula, Jonathan Bearak, Michelle J. Budig, and Melissa J. Hodges. 2016. "Do Highly Paid, Highly Skilled Women Experience the Largest Motherhood Penalty?" *American Sociological Review* 81(6): 1161–1189.

Enriquez, Juan, and Steve Gullans. 2015. *Evolving Ourselves: Redesigning the Future of Humanity—One Gene at a Time.* New York: Current.

Eom, Young-Ho, and Hang-Hyun Jo. 2014. "Generalized Friendship Paradox in Complex Networks: The Case of Scientific Collaboration." *Scientific Reports* 4: 4603. Accessed February 11, 2015 (www.nature.com/srep/2014/140408/srep04603/pdf/srep04603.pdf).

Equilar. 2016. "200 Highest-Paid CEOs 2016." Redwood City, CA, May 27. Accessed December 22, 2016 (www.equilar.com/reports/38-new-york-times-200-highest-paid-ceos-2016.html).

Erosa, Andres, Luisa Fuster, and Diego Restuccia. 2016. "A Quantitative Theory of the Gender Gap in Wages." *European Economic Review* 85: 165–187.

Escoffier, Jeffrey. 1997. "Homosexuality and the Sociological Imagination: The 1950s and 1960s." Pp. 248–261 in *A Queer World: The Center for Lesbian and Gay Studies Reader,* ed. Martin Duberman. New York: New York University Press.

Etaugh, Claire. 2003. "Witches, Mothers and Others: Females in Children's Books." *Hilltopics* (Winter): 10–13.

Etzioni, Amitai. 1965. *Political Unification.* New York: Holt, Rinehart and Winston.

———. 2007. "Are New Technologies the Enemy of Privacy?" *Knowledge, Technology & Policy* 20 (2): 115–119.

F

Fahs, Breanne, Jax Gonzalez, Rose Coursey, and Stephanie Robinson-Cestaro. 2014. "Cycling Together: Menstrual Synchrony as a Projection of Gendered Solidarity." *Women's Reproductive Health* 1 (2): 90–105.

Fainzang, Sylvie. 2013. "The Other Side of Medicalization: Self-Medicalization and Self-Medication." *Culture, Medicine, & Psychiatry* 37: 488–504.

Fairfield, Hannah, and Alan McLean. 2012. "Girls Lead in Science Exam, but Not in the United States." *The New York Times,* February 4. Accessed June 5, 2013 (www.nytimes.com/interactive/2013/02/04/science/girls-lead-in-science-exam-but-not-in-the-united-states.html).

Faist, Thomas, Margit Fauser, and Eveline Reisenauer. 2013. *Transnational Migration.* Malden, MA: Polity Press.

Fanon, Frantz. 1963. *The Wretched of the Earth.* New York: Grove.

Farley, Melissa, and Victor Malarek. 2008. "The Myth of the Victimless Crime." *The New York Times,* March 12. Accessed May 20, 2009 (www.nytimes.com/2008/03/12/opinion/12farley.html).

Farr, Grant M. 1999. *Modern Iran.* New York: McGraw-Hill.

Fausto-Sterling, Anne. 1993. "The Five Sexes: Why Male and Female Are Not Enough." *The Sciences* (July/August): 18–23.

———. 2000. "The Five Sexes, Revisited." *The Sciences* (July/August): 18–23.

———. 2012. *Sex/Gender: Biology in a Social World.* New York: Routledge.

Fearon, James D., and David D. Laitin. 2003. "Ethnicity, Insurgency, and Civil War." *American Political Science Review* 97 (March): 75–90.

Federal Bureau of Investigation. 2016. "Organized Crime." U.S. Department of Justice, Washington, DC. Accessed November 15, 2016 (www.fbi.gov/investigate/organized-crime).

Feld, Scott L. 1991. "Why Your Friends Have More Friends Than You Do." *American Journal of Sociology* 96: 1464–1477.

Felson, David, and Akis Kalaitzidis. 2005. "A Historical Overview of Transnational Crime." Pp. 3–19 in *Handbook of Transnational Crime and Justice,* ed. Philip Reichel. Thousand Oaks, CA: Sage.

Fenske, James. 2013. "African Polygamy: Past and Present." Vox, The Centre for Economic Policy Research, November 9. Accessed November 21, 2016 (http://voxeu.org/article/african-polygamy-past-and-present).

Ferree, Myra Marx, and David A. Merrill. 2000. "Hot Movements, Cold Cognition: Thinking About Social Movements in Gendered Frames." *Contemporary Society* 29 (May): 454–462.

File, Thom. 2013. "The Diversifying Electorate—Voting Rates by Race and Hispanic Origin in 2012 (and Other Recent Elections)." Current Population Survey, U.S. Census Bureau, P20–568. Accessed June 1, 2013 (www.census.gov/prod/2013pubs/p20-568.pdf).

Finder, Alan. 2006. "For Some, Online Persona Undermines a Résumé." *The New York Times,* June 11. Accessed June 30, 2009 (www.nytimes.com/2006/06/11/us/11recruit.html).

Findlen, Barbara, ed. 1995. *Listen Up: Voices from the Next Feminist Generation.* Seattle, WA: Seal Press.

Fine, Gary C. 2008. "Robbers Cave." Pp. 1163–1164 in *Encyclopedia of Race, Ethnicity, and Society,* vol. 3, ed. Richard T. Schaefer. Thousand Oaks, CA: Sage.

Fingerhut, Hannah. 2017. "About Seven-in-Ten Americans Oppose Overturning Roe v. Wade." Pew Research Center, January 3. Accessed January 31, 2017 (www.pewresearch.org/fact-tank/2017/01/03/about-seven-in-ten-americans-oppose-overturning-roe-v-wade/).

Finighan, Reuban, and Robert Putnam. 2016. "A Country Divided: The Growing Opportunity Gap in America." Pp. 139–173 in *Economic Mobility: Research & Ideas on Strengthening Families, Communities, & the Economy.* St Louis, MO: Federal Reserve Bank of St. Louis. Accessed December 22, 2016 (www.stlouisfed.org/~/media/Files/PDFs/Community%20Development/EconMobilityPapers/Section2/EconMobility_2-2FinighanPutnam_508.pdf).

Finkel, Steven E., and James B. Rule. 1987. "Relative Deprivation and Related Psychological Theories of Civil Violence: A Critical Review." *Research in Social Movements* 9: 47–69.

Firsing, Scott. 2016. "How Severe Is Africa's Brain Drain?" *Quartz,* January 21. Accessed February 10, 2017 (https://qz.com/599140/how-severe-is-africas-brain-drain/).

Fischer, Eric. 2011. "Race and Ethnicity 2010." Accessed April 28, 2015 (www.flickr.com/photos/walkingsf/sets/72157626354149574/).

Fisher, Gordon M. 1992. "The Development and History of the Poverty Thresholds." *Social Security Bulletin* 55 (4): 3–14. Accessed April 25, 2010 (www.ssa.gov/history/fisheronpoverty.html).

———. 2008. "Remembering Mollie Orshansky—the Developer of the Poverty Thresholds." *Social Security Bulletin* 68 (3): 79–83. Accessed April 25, 2010 (www.ssa.gov/policy/docs/ssb/v68n3/v68n3p79.pdf).

Fisher, Max. 2012. "The Middle East Didn't Really Get Any Freer in 2011." *The Atlantic,* January 19. Accessed May 28, 2012 (www.theatlantic.com/international/archive/2012/01/the-middle-east-didnt-really-get-any-freer-in-2011/251653/).

Fishman, Charles. 2006. *The Wal-Mart Effect: How the World's Most Powerful Company Really Works—and How It's Transforming the American Economy.* New York: Penguin Books.

Five Year Plan. 2006. "55: A Meditation on the Speed Limit." Video. Campus MovieFest, Atlanta, Georgia. Accessed October 6, 2016 (www.campusmoviefest.com/movies/924-a-meditation-on-the-speed-limit).

Flanagan, William S., and Michael E. Xie. 2017. "2,056 Accepted to Harvard Class of 2021." *The Harvard Crimson,* March 31. Accessed June 1, 2017 (www.thecrimson.com/article/2017/3/31/harvard-regular-admissions-2017/).

Flexner, Eleanor, and Ellen Fitzpatrick. 1996. *Century of Struggle: The Woman's Rights Movement in the United States, Enlarged Edition.* Cambridge: The Belknap Press of Harvard University Press.

Flora, Stephen Ray, and Courtney Allyn Polenik. 2013. "Effects of Sugar Consumption on Human Behavior and Performance." *The Psychological Record* 63: 513–524.

Follman, Mark, Gavin Aronsen, and Deanna Pann. 2016. "US Mass Shootings, 1982–2016." *Mother Jones,* September 24. Accessed November 4, 2016 (www.motherjones.com/politics/2012/12/mass-shootings-mother-jones-full-data).

Forbes. 2017. "The World's Billionaires." January 20. Accessed January 20, 2017 (www.forbes.com/billionaires/).

Force, W. R. 2011. "Another Two Cents on England (and Crawley): Masculinity, Culture, and Tucson." Sociology Lens, The Society Pages, April 26. Accessed March 10, 2012 (http://thesocietypages.org/sociologylens/2011/04/26/another-two-cents-on-england-and-crawley-masculinity-culture-and-tucson/).

Ford, Liz. 2015. "Sustainable Development Goals: All You Need to Know." *The Guardian,* January 19. Accessed April 14, 2015 (www.theguardian.com/global-development/2015/jan/19/sustainable-development-goals-united-nations).

Ford, Martin. 2015. *Rise of the Robots: Technology and the Threat of a Jobless Future.* New York: Basic Books.

Forsythe, David P. 1990. "Human Rights in U.S. Foreign Policy: Retrospect and Prospect." *Political Science Quarterly* 105 (3): 435–454.

Fortune. 2016. "Global 500." *Fortune,* March 31. Accessed January 18, 2017 (http://fortune.com/global500/).

Fowler, James H., and Nicholas A. Christakis. 2008. "Dynamic Spread of Happiness in a Large Social Network: Longitudinal Analysis over 20 Years in the Framingham Heart Study." *British Medical Journal* 337: 1–9.

Fox, Susannah, and Maeve Duggan. 2013. "Health Online 2013." Pew Research Center, Internet, Science, & Tech, January 15. Accessed February 11, 2017 (www.pewinternet.org/2013/01/15/health-online-2013/).

France, David. 2016. *How to Survive a Plague: The Inside Story of How Citizens and Science Tamed AIDS.* New York: Alfred A. Knopf.

Francis, Ara. 2012. "Stigma in an Era of Medicalization and Anxious Parenting: How Proximity and Culpability Shape Middle-Class Parents Experiences of Disgrace." *Sociology of Health & Illness* 34: 927–942.

Franklin, John Hope, and Alfred A. Moss. 2000. *From Slavery to Freedom: A History of African Americans,* 8th ed. Upper Saddle River, NJ: Prentice Hall.

Fraser, Steve. 2015. *The Age of Acquiescence: The Life and Death of American Resistance to Organized Wealth and Power.* New York: Little, Brown.

Frassanito, Paolo, and Benedetta Pettorini. 2008. "Pink and Blue: The Color of Gender." *Child's Nervous System* 24(8): 881–882.

French, Howard W. 2000. "The Pretenders." *The New York Times Magazine,* December 3, pp. 86–88.

Freudenburg, William R. 2005. "Seeing Science, Courting Conclusions: Reexamining the Intersection of Science, Corporate Cash, and the Law." *Sociological Forum* 20 (March): 3–33.

Frey, Carl Benedikt, and Michael A. Osborne. 2017. "The Future of Employment: How Susceptible Are Jobs to Computerisation?" *Technological Forecasting and Social Change* 114: 254–280.

Frey, William H. 2011. "White-Black Segregation." Brookings Institution and University of Michigan Social Science Data Analysis Networks Analysis of 2010 Census Data, CensusScope. Accessed April 28, 2015 (www.censusscope.org/2010Census/index.php).

———. 2015. *Diversity Explosion: How New Racial Demographics Are Remaking America.* Washington, DC: The Brookings Institution.

———. 2017. "Race Segregation for Largest Metro Areas (Population Over 500,000): Brookings Institution and University of Michigan Social Science Data Analysis Network's Analysis of 1990, 2000, and 2010 Census Decennial Census Tract Data." Population Studies Center, Institute for Social Research, University of Michigan. Accessed February 5, 2017 (www.psc.isr.umich.edu/dis/census/segregation2010.html).

Friedan, Betty. 1963. *The Feminine Mystique.* New York: Dell.

Friend, Christian, Andrea Hunter, and Anne Fletcher. 2011. "Parental Racial Socialization and the Academic Achievement of African American Children: A Cultural-Ecological Approach." *Journal of African American Studies* 15: 40–57.

Friman, H. Richard. 2004. "The Great Escape? Globalization, Immigrant Entrepreneurship and the Criminal Economy." *Review of International Political Economy* 11 (1): 98–131.

Fry, Richard, and Anna Brown. 2016. "In a Recovering Market, Homeownership Rates Are Down Sharply for Blacks, Young Adults." Pew Research Center, Social & Demographic Trends December 15. Accessed February 6, 2017 (www.pewsocialtrends.org/2016/12/15/in-a-recovering-market-homeownership-rates-are-down-sharply-for-blacks-young-adults/).

Fry, Richard, and D'Vera Cohn. 2010. "Women, Men and the New Economics of Marriage." A Social & Demographic Trends Report, Pew Research Center, January 19. Accessed June 2, 2011 (http://pewsocialtrends.org/files/2010/11/new-economics-of-marriage.pdf).

Fry, Richard, and Jeffrey S. Passel. 2014. "In Post-Recesson Era, Young Adults Drive Continuing Rise in Multi-Generational Living." Washington, DC: Pew Research Centers Social and Demographic Trends project, July 17. Accessed February 26, 2015 (www.pewsocialtrends.org/files/2014/07/ST-2014-07-17-multi-gen-households-report.pdf).

Fry, Richard, and Paul Taylor. 2013. "Hispanic High School Graduates Pass Whites in Rate of College Enrollment." Pew Research Hispanic Center, May 9. Accessed June 6, 2013 (www.pewhispanic.org/files/2013/05/PHC_college_enrollment_2013-05.pdf).

Fu, Furio. 2017. "The List of Blocked Websites in China." *Sapore di Cina,* January 4. Accessed February 15, 2017 (www.saporedicina.com/english/list-of-blocked-websites-in-china/).

Funk, Cary, and Brian Kennedy. 2016. "The Politics of Climate." Pew Research Center, Internet, Science, & Tech October 4. Accessed February 13, 2017 (www.pewinternet.org/2016/10/04/public-views-on-climate-change-and-climate-scientists/).

Furedi, Frank. 2006. "The End of Professional Dominance." *Society* 43 (6): 14–18.

Furstenberg, Frank F., Jr. 2010. "On a New Schedule: Transitions to Adulthood and Family Change." *The Future of Children* 20 (1): 67–87.

Fussell, Paul. 1992. *Class: A Guide Through the American Status System.* New York: Touchstone.

G

Gabler, Neal. 2006. *Walt Disney: The Triumph of the American Imagination.* New York: Knopf.

Gabrielson, Ryan, Ryann Grochowski Jones, and Eric Sagara. 2014. "Deadly Force, in Black and White." *ProPublica,* October 10. Accessed April 26, 2015 (www.propublica.org/article/deadly-force-in-black-and-white).

Galbraith, John K. 1952. *American Capitalism: The Concept of Countervailing Power.* New York: Houghton Mifflin.

Gallup. 2016a. "Military and National Defense." Washington, DC: Gallup, Inc. Accessed December 16, 2016 (www.gallup.com/poll/1666/military-national-defense.aspx).

———. 2016b. "Cloning." Washington, DC: Gallup, Inc. Accessed February 15, 2017 (www.gallup.com/poll/6028/Cloning.aspx).

References

Gans, Herbert. 1971. "The Uses of Poverty: The Poor Pay All." *Social Policy,* July/August, pp. 20–24.

———. 2009. "Reflections on Symbolic Ethnicity: A Response to Y. Anagnostou." *Ethnicities* 9 (1): 123–130.

Gao, George. 2015. "How Do Americans Stand Out from the Rest of the World?" Pew Research Center, March 12. Accessed May 28, 2015 (www.pewresearch.org/fact-tank/2015/03/12/how-do-americans-stand-out-from-the-rest-of-the-world/).

Gardner, Gary, Erik Assadourian, and Radhika Sarin. 2004. "The State of Consumption Today." Pp. 3–21 in *State of the World 2004,* ed. Brian Halweil and Lisa Mastny. New York: Norton.

Garfinkel, Harold. 1956. "Conditions of Successful Degradation Ceremonies." *American Journal of Sociology* 61 (March): 420–424.

Garlipp, Petra. 2008. "Koro—A Culture-Bound Phenomenon: Intercultural Psychiatric Implications." *German Journal of Psychiatry* 11:21–28.

Garrett, R. Sam. 2013. "Puerto Rico's Political Status and the 2012 Plebiscite: Background and Key Questions." Congressional Research Service, June 25. Accessed February 6, 2017 (https://fas.org/sgp/crs/row/R42765.pdf).

Garrett, Ruth Irene. 2003. *Crossing Over: One Woman's Escape from Amish Life.* New York: HarperOne.

Gaviria, Marcela, and Martin Smith. 2009. "The Madoff Affair." *PBS Frontline,* May 12. Accessed May 21, 2009 (www.pbs.org/wgbh/pages/frontline/madoff).

Geggel, Laura. 2016. "Does Sugar Make Kids Hyper?" *LiveScience* August 15. Accessed September 12, 2016 (www.livescience.com/55754-does-sugar-make-kids-hyper.html).

Geiger, Abigail. 2016. "Support for Marijuana Legalization Continues to Rise." Pew Research Center, Fact Tank, October 12. Accessed November 10, 2016 (www.pewresearch.org/fact-tank/2016/10/12/support-for-marijuana-legalization-continues-to-rise/).

Gelman, Andrew, Jeffrey Fagan, and Alex Kiss. 2007. "An Analysis of the New York City Police Department's 'Stop-and-Frisk' Policy in the Context of Claims of Racial Bias." *Journal of the American Statistical Association* 102 (479): 813–823.

Gelvin, James L. 2012. *The Arab Uprisings: What Everyone Needs to Know.* New York: Oxford University Press.

Gerhardt, Uta. 2002. *Talcott Parsons: An Intellectual Biography.* New York: Cambridge University Press.

Gheytanchi, Elham. 2009. "Iranian Women Lead the Protests." *San Francisco Chronicle,* June 29. Accessed June 30, 2009 (www.sfgate.com/cgi-bin/article.cgi?f5/c/a/2009/06/29/ED8618EMUC.DTL).

Ghitis, Frida. 2011. "Women of Arab Spring Still Fighting for Liberation." *Salt Lake Star Tribune,* June 21. Accessed August 12, 2011 (www.startribune.com/opinion/otherviews/124292204.html).

Gibson, Campbell, and Kay Jung. 2002. "Historical Census Statistics on Population Totals by Race, 1790 to 1990, and by Hispanic Origin, 1970 to 1990, for the United States, Regions, Divisions, and States." Population Division, U.S. Census Bureau, Washington, DC, September, Working Paper Series No. 56. Accessed May 17, 2010 (www.census.gov/population/www/documentation/twps0056/twps0056.html).

Gillam, Stephen. 2008. "Is the Declaration of Alma Ata Still Relevant to Primary Health Care?" *BMJ* 336: 536–539.

Ginder, Scott, A., Janice E. Kelly-Reid, and Farrah B. Mann. 2014. *Enrollment in Postsecondary Institutions, Fall 2011; Financial Statistics, Fiscal Year 2011; and Graduation Rates, Selected Cohorts, 2003–08.* U.S. Department of Education, NCES 2012-174rev. Washington, DC: National Center for Education Statistics. Accessed May 30, 2013 (http://nces.ed.gov/pubs2012/2012174rev.pdf).

Gitlin, Todd. 1993. *The Sixties: Years of Hope, Days of Rage.* New York: Bantam Books.

Glass Ceiling Commission. 1995. "Good for Business: Making Full Use of the Nations Human Capital—the Environmental Scan." A Fact-Finding Report of the Federal Glass Ceiling Commission, Washington, DC. Accessed June 19, 2011 (www.dol.gov/oasam/programs/history/reich/reports/ceiling.pdf).

Glassner, Barry. 2010. "Still Fearful." *Chronicle of Higher Education* 56 (January 22): B11–B12.

Glaude, Eddie, Jr. 2016. *Democracy in Black: How Race Still Enslaves the American Soul.* New York: Crown Publishers.

Global Slavery Index. 2016. "About the Global Slavery Index." The Walk Free Foundation, Perth, Australia. Accessed December 21, 2016 (www.globalslaveryindex.org/about/).

Goel, Vindu, and Nicole Perlroth. 2016. "Yahoo Says 1 Billion User Accounts Were Hacked." *The New York Times,* December 14. Accessed February 15, 2017 (www.nytimes.com/2016/12/14/technology/yahoo-hack.html).

Goffman, Alice. 2014a. *On the Run: Fugitive Life in an American City.* Chicago: University of Chicago Press.

———. 2014b. "Surveillance City: The War on Drugs in Urban Neighborhoods." The 2014 Nathan Levin Lecture on Public Policy, Public Policy Forums, the Center for New York City Affairs, New School, New York City, June 18, 2014. Accessed January 10, 2015 (http://blogs.newschool.edu/cnyca/2014/05/21/surveillance-city-the-war-on-drugs-in-urban-neighborhoods/).

Goffman, Erving. 1959. *The Presentation of Self in Everyday Life.* New York: Doubleday.

———. 1961. *Asylums: Essays on the Social Situation of Mental Patients and Other Inmates.* Garden City, NY: Doubleday.

———. 1963. *Stigma: Notes on Management of Spoiled Identity.* Englewood Cliffs, NJ: Prentice Hall.

———. 1979. *Gender Advertisements.* Cambridge, MA: Harvard University Press.

Golan, Limor, and Andrés Hincapié. 2016. "Breaking Down the Gender Wage Gap by Age and Hours Worked." *The Regional Economist,* October: 6–7, 13. Accessed February 2, 2017 (www.stlouisfed.org/~/media/Publications/Regional%20Economist/2016/October/gender_wage.pdf).

Goldring, Rebecca, Soheyla Taie, Minsun Riddles, and Chelsea Owens. 2014. "Teacher Attrition and Mobility: Results from the 2012-13 Teacher Follow-Up Survey." U.S. Department of Education, National Center for Education Statistics, NCES 2014-77, September. Accessed December 6, 2016 (http://nces.ed.gov/pubs2014/2014077.pdf).

Goldstein, Melvyn C., and Cynthia M. Beall. 1981. "Modernization and Aging in the Third and Fourth World: Views from the Rural Hinterland in Nepal." *Human Organization* 40 (Spring): 48–55.

Gonzalez-Barrera, Ana. 2015. "More Mexicans Leaving than Coming to the U.S." Pew Research Center Hispanic Trends, November 19. Accessed January 20, 2017 (www.pewhispanic.org/2015/11/19/more-mexicans-leaving-than-coming-to-the-u-s/).

Goode, William J. 1960. "A Theory of Role Strain." *American Sociological Review* 25 (4): 483–496.

Goodman, Amy. 2017. "From Keystone XL Pipeline to #DAPL: Jasilyn Charger, Water Protector from Cheyenne River Reservation." Interview. *Democracy Now,* January 4. Accessed February 8, 2017 (www.democracynow.org/2017/1/4/from_keystone_xl_pipeline_to_dapl).

Goodwin, Paula Y., William D. Mosher, and Anjani Chandra. 2010. "Marriage and Cohabitation in the United States: A Statistical Portrait Based on Cycle 6 (2002) of the National Survey of Family Growth." *Vital and Health Statistics* 23 (28). National Center for Health Statistics, Washington, DC.

Google. 2017a. "Fertility Rate." World Bank Development Indicators, Public Data Visualization Program. Accessed February 8, 2017 (www.google.com/publicdata/explore?ds=d5bncppjof8f9_&ctype=l&strail=false&bcs=d&nselm=h&met_y=sp_dyn_tfrt_in&scale_y=lin&ind_y=false&rdim=country&idim=country:NER:AFG:RWA:KHM:IND:DZA:USA:IRN:CHN:DEU&ifdim=country&hl=en&dl=en&ind=false).

Google. 2017b. "Life Expectancy." World Bank Development Indicators, Public Data Visualization Program. Accessed April 30,

2015 (www.google.com/publicdata/explore?ds=d5bncppjof8f9_&ctype=l&strail=false&bcs=d&nselm=h&met_y=sp_dyn_le00_in&scale_y=lin&ind_y=false&rdim=country&idim=country:AFG:KHM:CHN:DEU:IND:IRN:DZA:USA:NER:RWA&ifdim=country&hl=en&dl=en&ind=false).

Gordon, Brian. 2015. "UMaine Students Rally for Climate Change Action." *University of Southern Maine Free Press,* April 20. Accessed May 4, 2015 (http://usmfreepress.org/2015/04/20/umaine-students-rally-for-climate-change-action/).

Gorney, Cynthia. 2016. "The Changing Face of Saudi Women." *National Geographic,* February. Accessed January 20, 2017 (http://ngm.nationalgeographic.com/2016/02/saudi-arabia-women-text).

Gould, Kenneth A., David N. Pellow, and Allan Schnaibert. 2008. *The Treadmill of Production: Injustice and Unsustainability in the Global Economy.* New York: Routledge.

Gouldner, Alvin. 1960. "The Norm of Reciprocity." *American Sociological Review* 25 (April): 161–177.

———. 1970. *The Coming Crisis of Western Sociology.* New York: Basic Books.

GPOBA. 2014. "Challenges in Formalizing the Supply of Electricity in Mumbai's Slums." The Global Parternship on Output-Based Aid, Note Number 6, October. Accessed January 16, 2017 (http://documents.worldbank.org/curated/en/594161468033306544/pdf/938370BRI0Box300MumbaiElectricity01.pdf).

Graf, Nikki. 2016. "Most Americans Say Children Are Better Off with a Parent Home." Pew Research Center October 10. Accessed January 30, 2017 (www.pewresearch.org/fact-tank/2016/10/10/most-americans-say-children-are-better-off-with-a-parent-at-home/).

Gramsci, Antonio. 1929. *Selections from the Prison Notebooks,* ed. and trans. Quintin Hoare and Geoffrey Nowell Smith. London: Lawrence and Wishort.

Granovetter, Mark S. 1973. "The Strength of Weak Ties." *American Journal of Sociology* 78: 1360–1380.

Gray, John. 1992. *Men Are from Mars, Women Are from Venus: A Practical Guide for Improving Communication and Getting What You Want in Your Relationships.* New York: HarperCollins.

Greenberg, Andy. 2016. "Hack Brief: 412M Accounts Breached on FriendFinder Sex Sites." *Wired,* November 11. Accessed February 15, 2017 (www.wired.com/2016/11/hack-brief-412m-accounts-breached-friendfinder-sex-sites/).

Greenhouse, Steven. 2008. "Queens Factory Is Found to Owe Workers $5.3 Million." *The New York Times,* July 23. Accessed June 20, 2009 (http://cityroom.blogs.nytimes.com/2008/07/23/a-queens-sweatshop-found-to-owe-workers-53-million/).

Greenwald, Glenn. 2013. "NSA Collecting Phone Records of Millions of Verizon Customers Daily." *The Guardian,* June 5. Accessed June 7, 2013 (www.guardian.co.uk/world/2013/jun/06/nsa-phone-records-verizon-court-order).

Greenwald, Glenn, and Ewen MacAskill. 2013. "NSA PRISM Program Taps in to User Data of Facebook, Yahoo and Others." *The Guardian,* June 6. Accessed June 7, 2013 (www.guardian.co.uk/world/2013/jun/06/us-tech-giants-nsa-data).

Greenwood, Veronique. 2013. "We Are All Princes, Paupers, and Part of the Human Family." Nautilus, May 17. Accessed June 6, 2013 (http://nautil.us/blog/we-are-all-princes-paupers-and-part-of-the-human-family).

Groeneveld, Elizabeth. 2009. "Be a Feminist or Just Dress Like One: BUST, Fashion and Feminism as Lifestyle." *Journal of Gender Studies* 18 (2): 179–190.

Gross, Jane. 2005. "Forget the Career. My Parents Need Me at Home." *The New York Times,* November 24, pp. A1, A20.

Grossman, Samantha. 2015. "This Time-Lapse Video Shows How Much Photoshop Is Used in High Fashion Photography." *Time* May 4. Accessed January 26, 2017 (http://time.com/3845647/high-fashion-photo-retouching-time-lapse-video/).

Gruber, Jonathan. 2010. "Health Care Reform Is a 'Three-Legged Stool': The Costs of Partially Repealing the Affordable Care Act" *Center for American Progress,* August 5. Accessed February 12, 2017 (www.americanprogress.org/issues/healthcare/reports/2010/08/05/8226/health-care-reform-is-a-three-legged-stool/).

Guglielmo, Jennifer. 2003. "White Lies, Dark Truths." Pp. 1–14 in *Are Italians White? How Race Is Made in America,* ed. Jennifer Guglielmo and Salvatore Salerno. New York: Routledge.

Gurari, Inbal, John Hetts, and Michael Strube. 2006. "Beauty in the I of the Beholder: Effects of Idealized Media Portrayals on Implicit Self-Image." *Basic & Applied Social Psychology* 28 (3): 273–282.

Gutiérrez, Gustavo. 1990. "Theology and the Social Sciences." Pp. 214–225 in *Liberation Theology at the Crossroads: Democracy or Revolution?* ed. Paul E. Sigmund. New York: Oxford University Press.

Guy-Ryan, Jessie. 2016. "In Indonesia, Non-Binary Gender Is a Centuries-Old Idea." Atlas Obscura, June 18. Accessed June 6, 2016 (www.atlasobscura.com/articles/in-indonesia-nonbinary-gender-is-a-centuriesold-idea).

H

Hall, John J., and Richard Taylor. 2003. "Health for All Beyond 2000: The Demise of the Alma-Ata Declaration and Primary Health Care in Developing Countries." *The Medical Journal of Australia* 178: 17–20.

Halper, Mark. 2013. "Hooking China on Coffee." *SmartPlanet,* May 3. Accessed May 7, 2013 (www.smartplanet.com/blog/bulletin/hooking-china-on-coffee/18742).

Hamilton, Mykol C., David Anderson, Michelle Broaddus, and Kate Young. 2006. "Gender Stereotyping and Underrepresentation of Female Characters in 200 Popular Children's Books: A Twenty-first Century Update." *Sex Roles* 55 (11/12): 757–765.

Harari, Yuval Noah. 2017. *Homo Deus: A Brief History of Tomorrow.* New York: Harper Press.

Hardin, Victoria A. 2012. *AIDS at 30: A History.* Dulles, VA: Potomac Books.

Harding, Sandra. 2004. "Introduction: Standpoint Theory as a Site of Political, Philosophic, and Scientific Debate." Pp. 1–16 in *The Feminist Standpoint Theory Reader: Intellectual and Political Controversies,* ed. Sandra Harding. New York: Routledge.

Harding, Sandra, ed. 2003. *The Feminist Standpoint Theory Reader: Intellectual and Political Controversies.* New York: Routledge.

Hardt, Michael, and Antonio Negri. 2009. *Commonwealth.* Cambridge, MA: Belknap Press.

Harford, Tim. 2017. "Money via Mobile: The M-Pesa Revolution." BBC World Service February 13. Accessed February 16, 2017 (www.bbc.com/news/business-38667475).

Harlow, Harry F. 1971. *Learning to Love.* New York: Ballantine Books.

Harrington, Michael. 1962. *The Other America: Poverty in the United States.* Baltimore: Penguin Books.

———. 1980. "The New Class and the Left." Pp. 123–138 in *The New Class,* ed. B. Bruce Briggs. New Brunswick, NJ: Transaction.

Harris, Deborah A. 2015. "'You Just Have to Look at It as a Gift': Low-Income Single Mothers' Experiences of the Child Support System." *Journal of Poverty* 19: 88–108.

Hart, Betty, and Todd R. Risley. 1995. *Meaningful Differences in the Everyday Experience of Young American Children.* Baltimore, MD: Paul H. Brookes.

Hart, Zachary P., Vernon D. Miller, and John R. Johnson. 2003. "Socialization, Resocialization and Communication Relationships in the Context of an Organizational Change." *Communication Studies* 54 (4): 483–495.

Hartsock, Nancy C. M. 1983. "The Feminist Standpoint: Developing the Ground for a Specifically Feminist Historical Materialism." Pp. 283–310 in *Discovering Reality: Feminist Perspectives in Epistemology, Methodology, and Philosophy of Science,* ed. Sandra Harding and Merrill B. Hintikka. Dordrecht, The Netherlands: Reidel.

Hashaw, Tim. 2007. *The Birth of Black America: The First African Americans and the Pursuit of Freedom at Jamestown.* New York: Carroll & Graf.

Haslam, Nick, Steve Loughnan, and Gina Perry. 2014. "Meta-Milgram: An Empirical Synthesis of the Obedience Experiments." *PLoS ONE* 9 (4): e93927. Accessed February 19, 2015 (http://journals.plos.org/plosone/article?id=10.1371/journal.pone.0093927).

Haviland, William A., Harald E. L. Prins, Dana Walrath, and Bunny McBride. 2005. *Cultural Anthropology: The Human Challenge,* 11th ed. Belmont, CA: Wadsworth.

Hayden, H. Thomas. 2004. "What Happened at Abu Ghraib." Accessed September 19, 2011 (www.military.com/NewContent/0,13190,Hayden_090704,00.html).

Hayes, Christopher. 2012. *Twilight of the Elites: America After Meritocracy.* New York: Crown.

He, Wan, Manisha Sengupta, Victoria A. Velkoff, and Kimberly A. DeBarros. 2005. "65+ in the United States: 2005." *Current Population Reports,* P23–209. Washington, DC: U.S. Government Printing Office.

Healy, Jack. 2016. "Occupying the Prairie: Tensions Rise as Tribes Move to Block a Pipeline." *The New York Times,* August 23. Accessed February 8, 2017 (www.nytimes.com/2016/08/24/us/occupying-the-prairie-tensions-rise-as-tribes-move-to-block-a-pipeline.html).

———, and Nicholas Fandos. 2016. "Protesters Gain Victory in Fight Over Dakota Access Oil Pipeline." *The New York Times,* December 4. Accessed February 8, 2017 (https://www.nytimes.com/2016/12/04/us/federal-officials-to-explore-different-route-for-dakota-pipeline.html).

Heidrick & Struggles International. 2016. *Mapping Incoming Boardroom Talent: The Heidrick & Struggles Board Monitor.* New York: Heidrick & Struggles International, Inc. Accessed February 3, 2017 (www.heidrick.com/~/media/Publications%20and%20Reports/Mapping%20incoming%20talent.pdf).

Heine, Friederike. 2013. "M, F or Blank: Third Gender Official in Germany from November." Spiegel Online International August 16. Accessed April 19, 2015 (www.spiegel.de/international/germany/third-gender-option-to-become-available-on-german-birth-certificates-a-916940.html).

Heinle, Kimberly, Octavio Rodríguez Ferreira, and David A. Shirk. 2014. *Drug Violence in Mexico: Data and Analysis Through 2013.* Justice in Mexico Project, Special Report, April. Accessed May 6, 2015 (https://justiceinmexico.files.wordpress.com/2014/04/140415-dvm-2014-releasered1.pdf).

Helms, Sarah W., Sophia Choukas-Bradley, Laura Widman, Matteo Giletta, Geoffrey L. Cohen, and Mitchell J. Prinstein. 2014. "Adolescents Misperceive and Are Influenced by High-Status Peers Health Risk, Deviant, and Adaptive Behavior." *Developmental Psychology* 50: 2697–2714.

Helliwell, John, Richard Layard, and Jeffrey Sachs. 2016. *World Happiness Report 2016, Update (Vol.I).* New York: Sustainable Development Solutions Network. Accessed July 28, 2016 (http://worldhappiness.report/ed/2016/).

Henderson, Anita. 2003. "What's in a Slur?" *American Speech* 78 (1): 52–74.

Hendrickson, Brett. 2014. *Border Medicine: A Transcultural History of Curanderismo.* New York: NYU Press.

Henriques, Diana B., and Jack Healy. 2009. "Madoff Goes to Jail After Guilty Pleas." *The New York Times,* March 12. Accessed May 21, 2009 (www.nytimes.com/2009/03/13/business/13madoff.html).

Hetherington, E. Mavis, and John Kelly. 2002. *For Better or for Worse: Divorce Reconsidered.* New York: Norton.

Hewlett, Sylvia Ann, Diana Foster, Laura Sherbin, Peggy Shiller, and Karen Sumberg. 2010. *Off-Ramps and On-Ramps Revisited.* New York: Center for Work-Life Policy.

Higginbottom, Karen. 2017. "Board Diversity Still Unusual in a Fortune 500 Firm." *Forbes,* January 30. Accessed February 3, 2017 (www.forbes.com/sites/karenhigginbottom/2017/01/30/board-diversity-still-unusual-in-a-fortune-500-firm/).

Higgins, George E., Richard Tewksbury, and Elizabeth Mustaine. 2007. "Sports Fan Binge Drinking: An Examination Using Low Self-Control and Peer Association." *Sociological Spectrum* 27 (4): 389–404.

Higher Education Research Institute. 2016. "College Students' Commitment to Activism, Political and Civic Engagement Reach All-Time Highs." UCLA Newsroom February 10. Accessed February 14, 2017 (http://newsroom.ucla.edu/releases/college-students-commitment-to-activism-political-and-civic-engagement-reach-all-time-highs).

Hill, Marquita K. 2010. *Understanding Environmental Pollution,* 3rd ed. Cambridge: Cambridge University Press.

Hirschi, Travis. 1969. *Causes of Delinquency.* Berkeley: University of California Press.

———. 2004. "Self-Control and Crime." Pp. 537–552 in *Handbook of Self-Regulation: Research, Theory, and Applications,* ed. Roy F. Baumeister and Kathleen D. Vohs. New York: Guilford Press.

Hirschman, Charles, and Irina Voloshin. 2007. "The Structure of Teenage Employment: Social Background and the Jobs Held by High School Seniors." *Research in Social Stratification and Mobility* 25: 189–203.

Hirschman, Daniel, Ellen Berrey, and Fiona Rose-Greenland. 2016. "Dequantifying Diversity: Affirmative Action and Admissions at the University of Michigan." *Theory & Society* 45(3): 265–301.

Hixson, Lindsay, Bradford B. Hepler, and Myoung Ouk Kim. 2011. "The White Population: 2010." 2010 Census Briefs, Report C2010BR-05, September. Accessed May 27, 2012 (www.census.gov/prod/cen2010/briefs/c2010br-05.pdf).

Hochschild, Arlie Russell. 1989. *The Second Shift: Working Parents and the Revolution at Home.* New York: Viking Press.

———. 1990. "The Second Shift: Employed Women Are Putting in Another Day of Work at Home." *Utne Reader* 38 (March/April): 66–73.

———. 1997. *The Time Bind: When Work Becomes Home and Home Becomes Work.* New York: Henry Holt.

———. 2005. *The Commercialization of Intimate Life: Notes from Home and Work.* Berkeley: University of California Press.

———. 2016. *Strangers in Their Own Land: Anger and Mourning on the American Right.* New York: The New Press.

Holmes, Morgan. 2011. "The Intersex Enchiridion: Naming and Knowledge." *Somatechnics* 1(2): 388–411.

Home School Legal Defense Association. 2005. "State Laws" and "Academic Statistics on Homeschooling." Accessed August 2, 2010 (www.hslda.org).

Hootman, J., J. Bolen, C. Helmick, and G. Langmaid. 2006. "Prevalence of Doctor-Diagnosed Arthritis and Arthritis-Attributable Activity Limitation—United States, 2003–2005." *Morbidity and Mortality Weekly Report* 55 (40): 1089–1092.

Hoover, Daniel W., and Richard Millich. 1994. "Effects of Sugar Ingestion Expectancies on Mother-Child Interactions." *Journal of Abnormal Child Psychology* 22 (4): 501–515.

Hostetler, John A. 1993. *Amish Society,* 4th ed. Baltimore, MD: Johns Hopkins University Press.

Hout, Michael, Tom W. Smith, and Peter V. Marsden. 2015. "Prestige and Socioeconomic Scores for the 2010 Census Codes: Supplemental File." GSS Methodological Report No. 124. Chicago: NORC. Accessed December 22, 2016 (http://gss.norc.org/Documents/other/PRESTG10SEI10_supplement.xls).

Howard, Russell D., and Reid L. Sawyer. 2003. *Terrorism and Counterterrorism: Understanding the New Security Environment.* Guilford, CT: McGraw-Hill/Dushkin.

Hughes, Everett. 1945. "Dilemmas and Contradictions of Status." *American Journal of Sociology* 50 (March): 353–359.

Human Rights Campaign. 2009. "Maps of State Laws & Policies." Accessed May 27, 2009 (www.hrc.org/about_us/state_laws.asp).

———. 2015. "Marriage Center." Human Rights Campaign, Washington, DC. Accessed February 26, 2015 (www.hrc.org/marriage-center).

Human Rights Watch. 2016. *Boxed In: Women and Saudi Arabia's Male Guardianship System.* New York, July. Accessed January 20, 2017 (www.hrw.org/sites/default/files/report_pdf/saudiarabia0716web.pdf).

Humes, Karen R., Nicholas A. Jones, and Robert R. Ramirez. 2011. "Overview of Race and Hispanic Origin: 2010." 2010 Census Briefs, C2010BR-02, March. Accessed March 25, 2015 (www.census.gov/prod/cen2010/briefs/c2010br-02.pdf).

Humphrey, Carol Sue. 2013. *The American Revolution and the Press: The Promise of Independence.* Evanston, IL: Northwestern University Press.

Hunter, Herbert M., ed. 2000. *The Sociology of Oliver C. Cox: New Perspectives: Research in Race and Ethnic Relations,* vol. 2. Stamford, CT: JAI Press.

Hunt Institute. 2015. "Paso del Norte Economic Indicator Review." Hunt Institute for Global Competitiveness, University of Texas at El Paso, Spring. Accessed April 16, 2015 (http://d31hzlhk6di2h5.cloudfront.net/20150413/d0/5b/25/92/6bd1e2c334d8287995ff5036/PASO_DEL_NORTE_ECONOMIC_INDICATOR_REVIEW.pdf).

Hurst, Charles E., and David L. McConnell. 2010. *An Amish Paradox: Diversity and Change in the World's Largest Amish Community.* Baltimore, MD: Johns Hopkins University Press.

Hvistendahl, Mara. 2010. "Has China Outgrown the One-Child Policy?" *Science* 329 (September 17): 1458–1461.

Hyde, Janet Shibley. 2005. "The Gender Similarities Hypothesis." *American Psychologist* 60 (6): 581–592.

I

Ignatiev, Noel. 1995. *How the Irish Became White.* New York: Routledge.

Illinois State Board of Education. 2016a. "eReportcard Public Site." Center for Performance. Accessed December 5, 2016 (http://webprod.isbe.net/ereportcard/publicsite/getSearchCriteria.aspx).

———. 2016b. "Illinois Report Card 2015–2016." Springfield, IL. Accessed December 5, 2016 (http://illinoisreportcard.com/Default.aspx).

INEGI. 2009. "Mujeres y Hombres en México 2005. Anexo estadístico." Instituto Nacional de Estadística y Geografía. Accessed June 14, 2009 (www.inegi.org.mx/inegi/contenidos/espanol/bvinegi/productos/integracion/sociodemografico/mujeresyhombres/2005/anexo_2005.xls).

Inglehart, Ronald, Pippa Norris, and Christian Welzel. 2002. "Gender Equality and Democracy." *Comparative Sociology* 1 (3/4): 321–346.

Innocence Project. 2017. "DNA Exonerations in the United States." Accessed May 26, 2017 (www.innocenceproject.org/free-innocent/improve-the-law/fact-sheets/dna-exonerations-nationwide).

INPE. 2016. "Taxas Anuais do Desmatamento—1988 até 2016." Projeto Prodes, Instituto Nacional de Pesquisas Espaciais, Brazil. Accessed February 13, 2017 (www.obt.inpe.br/prodes/prodes_1988_2016n.htm).

Institute for Criminal Policy Research. 2016. "Highest to Lowest—Prison Population Rate." London: World Prison Brief. Accessed November 15, 2016 (www.prisonstudies.org/highest-to-lowest/prison-population-total?field_region_taxonomy_tid=All).

Institute for Economics and Peace. 2016. *Global Terrorism Index 2016: Measuring and Understanding the Impact of Terrorism.* Sydney: Institute for Economics and Peace. Accessed December 16, 2016 (www.visionofhumanity.org/sites/default/files/Global%20Terrorism%20Index%202016_0.pdf).

Institute of International Education. 2016. "Open Doors: 2016 Fast Facts." New York City: Institute of International Education, Inc. Accessed December 2, 2016 (www.iie.org/Research-and-Insights/Open-Doors/Fact-Sheets-and-Infographics/Fast-Facts).

Internal Revenue Service. 2016. "The 400 Individual Income Tax Returns Reporting the Largest Adjusted Gross Incomes Each Year, 1992–2014." IRS Statistical Information Services, Washington, DC. Accessed December 21, 2016 (www.irs.gov/pub/irs-soi/14intop400.pdf).

International Institute for Democracy and Electoral Assistance. 2016a. "Voter Turnout Database: Voter Turnout." International IDEA, Stockholm, Sweden. Accessed December 15, 2016 (www.idea.int/themes/voter-turnout).

———. 2016b. "Quota Database." QuotaProject. Accessed December 16, 2016 (www.quotaproject.org/searchDb.cfm).

International Labour Office. 2012. "ILO Global Estimate of Forced Labour: Results and Methodology." Special Action Programme to Combat Forced Labour, Geneva. Accessed June 2, 2013 (www.ilo.org/wcmsp5/groups/public/@ed_norm/@declaration/documents/publication/wcms_182004.pdf).

International Monetary Fund. 2008. "IMF Helping Countries Respond to Food Price Crisis." *IMF Survey Magazine: In the News,* June 3. Washington, DC: IMF. Accessed August 2, 2010 (www.imf.org/external/pubs/ft/survey/so/2008/NEW060308A.htm).

International Telecommunications Union. 2015. "Explore Key ICT Statistics." ITUs ICT Eye. Accessed February 2, 2015 (www.itu.int/net4/itu-d/icteye/).

Internet World Stats. 2017a. "Internet Usage Statistics: The Internet Big Picture." Accessed June 9, 2017 (www.internetworldstats.com/stats.htm).

———. 2017b. "Internet World Users by Language: Top 10 Languages." Accessed June 9, 2017 (www.internetworldstats.com/stats7.htm).

Inter-Parliamentary Union. 2016. "Women in National Parliaments: Situation as of 1st November 2016." Geneva, Switzerland. Accessed December 16, 2016 (www.ipu.org/wmn-e/arc/classif011116.htm).

Ipsos MORI. 2014. "Perceptions Are Not Reality: Things the World Gets Wrong." Ipsos MORI Perils of Perception Survey, London, October 29. Accessed January 10, 2015 (www.ipsos-mori.com/researchpublications/researcharchive/3466/Perceptions-are-not-reality-10-things-the-world-gets-wrong.aspx).

Irdeto. 2015. "Irdeto Piracy and Business Intelligence Quick Read Report: 2015 Academy Award® Nominated Films," Irdeto Technology, Eagan, MN, February 19. Accessed February 19, 2015 (www.irdeto.com/documents/pr_quickread_oscars_piracy_and_BI_feb2015.pdf).

Irwin, Neil. 2015. "Global Debt Has Risen by $57 Trillion Since the Financial Crisis." *The New York Times,* February 5. Accessed January 17, 2017 (www.nytimes.com/2015/02/06/upshot/global-debt-has-risen-by-57-trillion-since-the-financial-crisis-heres-why-that-is-scary.html).

Isaacs, Julia B. 2008. "Economic Mobility of Black and White Families." *Economic Mobility Project,* Pew Charitable Trusts, November. Accessed July 15, 2017 (www.brookings.edu/wp-content/uploads/2016/07/02_economic_mobility_sawhill_ch6.pdf).

Isaacs, Julia B., Isabel V. Sawhill, and Ron Haskins. 2008. *Getting Ahead or Losing Ground.* Washington, DC: Economic Mobility Project, Pew Charitable Trusts.

Isaacson, Walter. 2014. *The Innovators: How a Group of Hackers, Geniuses, and Geeks Created the Digital Revolution.* New York: Simon & Schuster.

ITOPF. 2006. "Statistics: International Tanker Owners Pollution Federation Limited." Accessed May 2, 2007 (www.itopf.com/stats.html).

IUCN. 2016. "Summary Statistics." *The IUCN Red List of Threatened Species.* Cambridge, UK: International Union for Conservation of Nature and Natural Resources. Accessed February 13, 2017 (www.iucnredlist.org/about/summary-statistics).

Izadi, Elahe. 2015. "The Incidents That Led to the University of Missouri President's Resignation." *The Washington Post,* November 9. Accessed February 14, 2017 (www.washingtonpost.com/news/grade-point/wp/2015/11/09/the-incidents-that-led-to-the-university-of-missouri-presidents-resignation/).

———. 2016. "Why Alicia Keys Isn't Wearing Makeup on 'The Voice.'" *The Washington Post,* August 22. Accessed January 30, 2017 (www.washingtonpost.com/news/arts-and-entertainment/wp/2016/08/22/why-alicia-keys-isnt-wearing-makeup-on-the-voice/).

J

Jackson, Stevi. 2006. "Interchanges: Gender, Sexuality, and Heterosexuality: The Complexity (and Limits) of Heteronormativity." *Feminist Theory* 7: 105–121.

Jacobs, David, Zhenchao Qian, Jason T. Carmichael, and Stephanie L. Kent. 2007. "Who Survives on Death Row? An Individual and Contextual Analysis." *American Sociological Review* 72 (August): 610–632.

Jacobs, Tom. 2016. "Belief in Reverse Dicrimination Bolsters Whites' Self-Esteem." *Pacific Standard* March 29. Accessed February 6, 2017 (https://psmag.com/belief-in-reverse-discrimination-bolsters-whites-self-esteem-4e2890ef1699).

Jamison, Andrew. 2006. "Social Movements and Science: Cultural Appropriations of Cognitive Praxis." *Science as Culture* 15 (1): 45–59.

Janssen, Sarah, ed. 2017. *The World Almanac and Book of Facts 2017.* New York: World Almanac Books.

Jayson, Sharon. 2012a. "Young Parents, Older Adults Change Face of Cohabitation." *USA Today,* October 17. Accessed May 29, 2013 (www.usatoday.com/story/news/nation/2012/10/17/cohabitation-divorced-families-parents/1623117/).

———. 2012b. "Living Together Not Just for the Young, New Data Show." *USA Today,* October 17. Accessed May 29, 2013 (www.usatoday.com/story/news/nation/2012/10/17/older-couples-cohabitation/1630681/).

Jenkins, Matt. 2008. "A Really Inconvenient Truth." *Miller-McCure* 1 (March/April): 38–41.

Jenness, Valerie, David A. Smith, and Judith Stepan-Norris. 2006. "Pioneer Public Sociologist C. Wright Mills, 50 Years Later." *Contemporary Sociology* 35 (6): 7–8.

Jindra, Michael. 1994. "Star Trek Fandom as a Religious Phenomenon." *Sociology of Religion* 55 (1): 27–51.

Joffe-Walt, Chana. 2015. "Three Miles." *This American Life* March 13. Accessed November 29, 2016 (www.thisamericanlife.org/radio-archives/episode/550/three-miles).

Johnson, Allan G. 1997. *The Forest and the Trees: Sociology as Life, Practice, and Promise.* Philadelphia: Temple University Press.

Johnson, Chris. 2012. "Exit Poll: Gay Voters Made Up 5 Percent of 2012 Electorate." *Washington Blade,* November 7. Accessed May 29, 2013 (www.washingtonblade.com/2012/11/07/exit-poll-gay-voters-made-up-5-percent-of-2012-electorate/).

Johnson, Kenneth M., and Daniel T. Lichter. 2010. "Growing Diversity Among America's Children and Youth: Spatial and Temporal Dimensions." *Population and Development Review* 36(1): 151–176.

Johnson, Paula A., Therese Fitzgerald, Alina Salganicoff, Susan F. Wood, and Jill M. Goldstein. 2014. "Sex Specific Medical Research: Why Women's Health Can't Wait." Brigham and Women's Hospital. Accessed February 12, 2017 (www.brighamandwomens.org/Departments_and_Services/womenshealth/ConnorsCenter/Policy/ConnorsReportFINAL.pdf).

Johnston, David Cay. 1994. "Ruling Backs Homosexuals on Asylum." *The New York Times,* June 12, pp. D1, D6.

Jones, Jeffrey M. 2016. "Same-Sex Marriages Up One Year After Supreme Court Verdict." Gallup, June 22. Accessed November 23, 2016 (www.gallup.com/poll/193055/sex-marriages-one-year-supreme-court-verdict.aspx).

Jones, Robert P., Daniel Cox, Betsy Cooper, and Rachel Lienesch. 2015. *Anxiety, Nostalgia, and Mistrust: Findings from the 2015 American Values Survey.* Washington, DC: Public Religion Research Institute. Accessed February 6, 2017 (www.prri.org/wp-content/uploads/2015/11/PRRI-AVS-2015-Web.pdf).

Jordan, Miriam. 2011. "More Silent Raids over Immigration." *The Wall Street Journal,* June 16. Accessed June 21, 2011 (http://online.wsj.com/article/SB10001424052702304186404576387843087137216.html).

Jorgenson, Andrew K. 2015. "Five Points on Sociology, PEWS, and Climate Change." *Journal of World-Systems Research* 21(2): 271–275.

Josephson Institute of Ethics. 2012. "2012 Report Card on the Ethics of American Youth." Josephson Institute, Center for Youth Ethics, Los Angeles, November 20. Accessed May 8, 2013 (http://-charactercounts.org/pdf/reportcard/2012/Report-Card-2012-DataTables-HonestyIntegrityCheating.pdf).

Juergensmeyer, Mark. 2003. *Terror in the Mind of God: The Global Rise of Religious Violence,* 3rd ed. Berkeley: University of California Press.

Justice Policy Institute. 2000. "The Punishing Decade: Prison and Jail Estimates at the Millennium." Washington, DC, May. Accessed November 10, 2016 (www.justicepolicy.org/images/upload/00-05_rep_punishingdecade_ac.pdf). 16.

K

Kaeble, Danielle, Lauren Glaze, Anastasios Tsoutis, and Todd Minton. 2016. "Correctional Populations in the United States, 2014." *Bureau of Justice Statistics Bulletin,* Revised January 21, NCJ 249513. Accessed November 8, 2016 (www.bjs.gov/content/pub/pdf/cpus14.pdf).

Kalev, Alexandria, Frank Dobbin, and Erin Kelly. 2006. "Best Practices or Best Guesses? Assessing the Efficacy of Corporate Affirmative Action and Diversity Policies." *American Sociological Review* 71: 589–617.

Kalish, Richard A. 1985. *Death, Grief, and Caring Relationships,* 2nd ed. Monterey, CA: Brooks/Cole.

Kalita, S. Mitra. 2006. "On the Other End of the Line." *The Washington Post National Weekly Edition,* January 9, pp. 20–21.

Kalmijn, Matthijs. 1998. "Intermarriage and Homogamy: Causes, Patterns, Trends." *Annual Review of Sociology* 24: 395–412.

Kamp, Marianne. 2008. *The New Woman in Uzbekistan.* Seattle: University of Washington Press.

Kanter, Rosabeth Moss. 1993. *Men and Women of the Corporation.* New York: Basic Books.

Karkazis, Katrina. 2008. *Fixing Sex: Intersex, Medical Authority, and Lived Experience.* Durham, NC: Duke University Press.

———. 2016. "The Ignorance Aimed at Caster Semenya Flies in the Face of the Olympic Spirit." *The Guardian,* August 23. Accessed January 27, 2017 (www.theguardian.com/commentisfree/2016/aug/23/caster-semenya-olympic-spirit-iaaf-athletes-women).

Karkazis, Katrina, Rebecca Jordan-Youn, Georgiann Davis, and Silvia Camporesi. 2012. "Out of Bounds? A Critique of the New Policies of Hyperandrogenism in Elite Female Athletes." *American Journal of Bioethics* 12: 3–16.

Katz, Jason. 1999. *Tough Guise: Violence, Media, and the Crisis in Masculinity.* Video. Directed by Sut Jhally. Northampton, MA: Media Education Foundation.

Katz, Josh. 2016. "Who Will Be President?" *The New York Times,* November 8. Accessed December 13, 2016 (www.nytimes.com/interactive/2016/upshot/presidential-polls-forecast.html).

Kay, Katty, and Claire Shipman. 2014. "The Confidence Gap." *The Atlantic,* May. Accessed January 7, 2013 (www.theatlantic.com/features/archive/2014/04/the-confidence-gap/359815/).

Kayyali, Randa. 2006. *The Arab Americans.* Westport, CT: Greenwood Press.

Keith, Fritha. 2008. "10 Modern Cases of Feral Children." *Listverse*, March 7. Accessed October 18, 2016 (http://listverse.com/2008/03/07/10-modern-cases-of-feral-children/).

Kelling, George L. 2015. "Don't Blame My 'Broken Windows' Theory for Poor Policing". *Politico Magazine*, August 11. Accessed November 16, 2016 (www.politico.com/magazine/story/2015/08/broken-windows-theory-poor-policing-ferguson-kelling-121268).

Kelling, George L., and Catherin M. Coles. 1996. *Fixing Broken Windows: Restoring Order and Reducing Crime*. New York: Martin Kessler Books.

Kelly, Robert J., and Sharona L. Levy. 2012. "The Endangered Empire: American Responses to Transnational Organized Crime." *Journal of Social Distress and the Homeless* 21: 44–110.

Kennedy, Brian. 2017. "Two-Thirds of Americans Give Priority to Developing Alternative Energy Over Fossil Fuels." Pew Research Center, January 23. Accessed June 9, 2017 (www.pewresearch.org/fact-tank/2017/01/23/two-thirds-of-americans-give-priority-to-developing-alternative-energy-over-fossil-fuels/).

Kerbo, Harold R. 2011. *Social Stratification and Inequality: Class Conflict in Historical, Comparative, and Global Perspective*, 8th ed. New York: McGraw-Hill.

Keys, Alicia. 2016. "Alicia Keys: Time to Uncover." *Lenny*, May 31. Accessed June 6, 2017 (www.lennyletter.com/style/a410/alicia-keys-time-to-uncover/).

Keynes, John Maynard. 1930a. "Economic Possibilities for Our Grandchildren I." *The Nation and Athenaeum* 48(2): 36–37.

———. 1930b. "Economic Possibilities for Our Grandchildren II." *The Nation and Athenaeum* 48(3): 96–98.

Khatchatourian, Maane. 2015. "'Revenant,' 'Hateful Eight' Screeners Leak to Huge Piracy Before Theatrical Release." *Variety*, December 21. Accessed November 11, 2016 (http://variety.com/2015/film/news/hateful-eight-revenant-leak-watch-online-1201666010/).

Khorasani, Noushin Ahmadi. 2009. "How Social Movements Can Change Iran." *The Mark*, June 11. Accessed June 30, 2009 (www.themarknews.com/articles/290-how-social-movements-can-change-iran).

Kiatpongsan, Sorapop, and Michael I. Norton. 2014. "How Much (More) Should CEOs Make? A Universal Desire for More Equal Pay." *Perspectives on Psychological Science* 9: 587–593. Accessed January 7, 2015 (www.hbs.edu/faculty/Publication%20Files/kiatpongsan%20norton%202014_f02b004a-c2de-4358-9811-ea273d372af7.pdf).

Kilbourne, Jean. 2010. *Killing Us Softly 4: Advertisings Image of Women*. Video. Produced and directed by Sut Jhally. Northampton, MA: Media Education Foundation.

———. 2014. "The Dangerous Ways Ads See Women." TEDx Lafayette College March 25. Accessed January 27, 2017 (www.tedxlafayettecollege.com/jean-kilbourne/).

Kilpatrick, Dean G., Heidi S. Resnick, Kenneth J. Ruggiero, Lauren M. Conoscenti, and Jenna McCauley. 2007. "Drug-Facilitated, Incapacitated, and Forcible Rape: A National Study." National Institute of Justice Grant No. 2005-Wg-BX-0006. Accessed June 1, 2010 (www.ncjrs.gov/pdffiles1/nij/grants/219181.pdf).

Kim, Kwang Chung. 1999. *Koreans in the Hood: Conflict with African Americans*. Baltimore, MD: Johns Hopkins University Press.

Kim, Su Yeong, Yijie Wang, Diana Orozco-Lapray, Yishan Shen, and Mohammed Murtuza. 2013. "Does Tiger Parenting Exist? Parenting Profiles of Chinese Americans and Adolescent Developmental Outcomes." *Asian American Journal of Psychology* 4: 7–18.

Kimmel, Michael. 2004. *The Gendered Society*, 2nd ed. New York: Oxford University Press.

———. 2012. *Manhood in America: A Cultural History*. 3rd ed. New York: Oxford University Press.

Kindy, Kimberly, and Kimbriell Kelly. 2015. "Thousands Dead, Few Prosecuted." *The Washington Post*, April 11. Accessed April 26, 2015 (www.washingtonpost.com/sf/investigative/2015/04/11/thousands-dead-few-prosecuted/).

Kinsey, Alfred C., Wardell B. Pomeroy, and Clyde E. Martin. 1948. *Sexual Behavior in the Human Male*. Philadelphia: Saunders.

Kinsey, Alfred C., Wardell B. Pomeroy, and Paul H. Gebhard. 1953. *Sexual Behavior in the Human Female*. Philadelphia: Saunders.

Kirk, Dudley. 1996. "Demographic Transition Theory." *Population Studies* 50: 361–387.

Kleinknecht, William. 1996. *The New Ethnic Mobs: The Changing Face of Organized Crime in America*. New York: Free Press.

Klemens, Guy. 2010. *The Smartphone: The History and Technology of the Gadget that Changed the World*. Jefferson, NC: McFarland & Company.

Klinenberg, Eric. 2002. *Heat Wave: A Social Autopsy of Disaster in Chicago*. Chicago: University of Chicago Press.

———. 2012. *Going Solo: The Extraordinary Rise and Surprising Appeal of Living Alone*. New York: Penguin Books.

Knight Frank Research. 2016. *The Wealth Report 2016*, 10th ed. London: Knight Frank. Accessed January 17, 2017 (www.knightfrank.com/wealthreport).

Knudson, Tom. 2006. "Promises and Poverty: Starbucks Calls Its Coffee Worker-Friendly—but in Ethiopia, a Day's Pay Is a Dollar." *Sacramento Bee*, September 23. Accessed June 12, 2009 (www.sacbee.com/502/story/393917.html).

———. 2007. "Investigative Report: Promises and Poverty." *Sacramento Bee*, September 23. Accessed August 6, 2009 (www.sacbee.com/502/story/393917.html).

Kochanek, Kenneth, Sherry Murphy, Jiaquan Xu, and Betzaida Tejada-Vera. 2016. "Deaths: Final Data for 2014." *National Vital Statistics Reports* 65 (4). Hyattsville, MD: National Center for Health Statistics. Accessed July 28, 2016 (www.cdc.gov/nchs/data/nvsr/nvsr65/nvsr65_04.pdf).

Kochhar, Rakesh, and Richard Fry. 2014. "Wealth Inequality Has Widened Along Racial, Ethnic Lines Since End of Great Recession." Pew Research Center, Fact Tank: News in the Numbers, December 12. Accessed January 7, 2015 (www.pewresearch.org/fact-tank/2014/12/12/racial-wealth-gaps-great-recession/).

Kochel, Tammy Rinehart, David B. Wilson, and Stephen D. Mastrofski. 2011. "Effect of Suspect Race on Officers' Arrest Decisions." *Criminology* 49(2): 473–512.

Koerner, Brendan I. 2003. "What Does a Thumbs Up Mean in Iraq?" *Slate*, March 28. Accessed May 3, 2009 (www.slate.com/id/2080812).

Kohn, Sally. 2014. "Stop Denying the Gender Pay Gap Exists. Even Jennifer Lawrence Was Shortchanged." *The Washington Post*, December 17. Accessed January 7, 2015 (www.washingtonpost.com/posteverything/wp/2014/12/17/stop-denying-the-gender-pay-gap-exists-even-jennifer-lawrence-was-shortchanged/).

Kokmen, Leyla. 2008. "Environmental Justice for All." *Utne Reader*, March/April, pp. 42–46.

Kolbert, Elizabeth. 2014. *The Sixth Extinction: An Unnatural History*. New York: Henry Holt and Company.

Kooti, Farshad, Hathan O. Hodas, and Kristina Lerman. 2014. "Network Weirdness: Exploring the Origins of Network Paradoxes." *arXiv*: 1403.7242. Accessed February 11, 2015 (http://arxiv.org/abs/1403.7242).

Kottak, Conrad. 2004. *Anthropology: The Explanation of Human Diversity*. New York: McGraw-Hill.

Kozol, Jonathan. 1991. *Savage Inequalities: Children in Americas Schools*. New York: Crown.

———. 2005. *The Shame of the Nation: The Restoration of Apartheid Schooling in America*. New York: Crown.

———. 2012. *Fire in the Ashes: Twenty-Five Years Among the Poorest Children in America*. New York: Crown.

Kozubek, Jim. 2016. *Modern Prometheus: Editing the Human Genome with Crispr-Cas9*. Cambridge: Cambridge University Press.

Kraus, Sidney. 1996. "Winners of the First 1960 Televised Presidential Debate between Kennedy and Nixon." *Journal of Communication* 46 (4): 78–96.

Kraybill, Donald. 2001. *The Riddle of Amish Culture,* rev. ed. Baltimore, MD: Johns Hopkins University Press.

Kraybill, Donald B., Karen M. Johnson-Weiner, and Steven M. Nolt. 2013. *The Amish.* Baltimore, MD: Johns Hopkins University Press.

Krebs, Christopher P., Christine H. Lindquist, Tara D. Warner, Bonnie S. Fisher, and Sandra L. Martin. 2007. "The Campus Sexual Assault (CSA) Study, Final Report." National Institute of Justice Grant No. 2004-WG-BX-0010. Accessed June 1, 2010 (www.ncjrs.gov.pdffiles1/nij/grants/221153.pdf).

Kreider, Rose M. 2010. "Increase in Opposite-Sex Cohabiting Couples from 2009 to 2010 in the Annual Social and Economic Supplement (ASEC) to the Current Population Survey (CPS)." Housing and Household Economic Statistics Division Working Paper. Washington, DC: U.S. Bureau of the Census. Accessed June 1, 2011 (www.census.gov/population/www/socdemo/Inc-Opp-sex-2009-to-2010.pdf).

Kreider, Rose M., and Renee Ellis. 2011. "Number, Timing, and Duration of Marriages and Divorces: 2009." *Current Population Reports,* P70–125. Washington, DC: U.S. Census Bureau. Accessed September 19, 2011 (www.census.gov/prod/2011pubs/p70–125.pdf).

Kristof, Nicholas D., and Sheryl WuDunn. 2009. *Half the Sky: Turning Oppression into Opportunity for Women Worldwide.* New York: Knopf.

Krogstad, Jens Manuel. 2016. "Five Facts about Mexico and Immigration to the U.S." Pew Research Center February 11. Accessed January 20, 2017 (www.pewresearch.org/fact-tank/2016/02/11/mexico-and-immigration-to-us/).

Krogstad, Jens Manual, and D'Vera Cohn. 2014. "U.S. Census Looking at Big Changes in How It Asks About Race and Ethnicity." Pew Research Center, Fact Tank, March 14. Accessed April 26, 2015 (www.pewresearch.org/fact-tank/2014/03/14/u-s-census-looking-at-big-changes-in-how-it-asks-about-race-and-ethnicity/).

Krogstad, Jens Manuel, Mark Hugo Lopez, and Drew DeSilver. 2015. "Puerto Rico's Losses Are Not Just Economic, but in People, Too." Pew Research Center, July 1. Accessed February 6, 2017 (www.pewresearch.org/fact-tank/2015/07/01/puerto-ricos-losses-are-not-just-economic-but-in-people-too/).

Krueger, Patrick M., Melanie K. Tran, Robert A. Hummer, and Virginia W. Chang. 2015. "Mortality Attributable to Low Levels of Education in the United States." *PLoS One* 10(7): e0131809.

Kruttschnitt, Candace. "Gender and Crime." *Annual Review of Sociology* 39: 291–308.

Kübler-Ross, Elisabeth. 1969. *On Death and Dying.* New York: Macmillan.

Kuhl, Patricia K. 2004. "Early Language Acquisition: Cracking the Speech Code." *Nature Reviews Neuroscience* 5: 831–843.

Kumar, Rajesh, Hemendra Ram Phookun, and Arunya Datta. 2014. "Epidemic of Koro in North East India: An Observational Cross-Sectional Study." *Asian Journal of Psychiatry* 12: 113–117.

Kutateladze, Besike L., Nancy R. Andiloro, Brian D. Johnson, and Cassia C. Spohn. 2014. "Cumulative Disadvantage: Examining Racial and Ethnic Disparity in Prosecution and Sentencing." *Criminology* 52(3): 514–551.

Kuumba, M. Bahati. 2001. *Gender and Social Movements.* Lanham, MD: AltaMira Press.

L

Ladner, Joyce. 1973. *The Death of White Sociology.* New York: Random Books.

LaFrance, Adrienne. 2016. "A Quest to Save America's Dying Regional Slang." *The Atlantic,* September 8. Accessed October 5, 2016 (www.theatlantic.com/technology/archive/2016/09/bat-hides-and-frog-stranglers/499046/).

Lakner, Christoph, and Branko Milanovic. 2015. "Global Income Distribution: From the Fall of the Berlin Wall to the Great Recession." *World Bank Economic Review* 30(2): 203–232.

Lareau, Annette. 2003. *Unequal Childhoods: Class, Race, and Family Life.* Berkeley: University of California Press.

———. 2011. *Unequal Childhoods: Class, Race, and Family Life, 2nd ed., with an update a decade later.* Berkeley: University of California Press.

Larson, Edward J. 2006. *Summer for the Gods: The Scopes Trial and America's Continuing Debate over Science and Religion.* New York: Basic Books.

Larsson, Naomi. 2016. "Is the World Finally Waking Up to Intersex Rights?" *The Guardian,* February 10. Accessed January 26, 2017 (www.theguardian.com/global-development-professionals-network/2016/feb/10/intersex-human-rights-lgbti-chile-argentina-uganda-costa-rica).

Laughlin, Lynda. 2013. "Who's Minding the Kids? Child Care Arrangements: Spring 2011." U.S. Census Bureau, *Household Economic Studies,* pp. 70–135, April. Accessed May 20, 2013 (www.census.gov/prod/2013pubs/p70-135.pdf).

Laumann, Edward O., John H. Gagnon, Robert T. Michael, and Stuart Michaels. 1994. *The Social Organization of Sexuality: Sexual Practices in the United States.* Chicago: University of Chicago Press.

Lawless, John. 2005. "Nigel Newton: Is There Life After Harry? You Can Bet Your Hogwarts There Is." *The Independent,* July 3. Accessed February 2, 2015 (www.independent.co.uk/news/people/profiles/nigel-newton-is-there-life-after-harry-you-can-bet-your-hogwarts-there-is-296317.html).

LeanIn.Org. 2016. *Women in the Workplace: 2016.* Palo Alto, CA: LeanIn.Org. Accessed January 25, 2017 (https://womenintheworkplace.com/Women_in_the_Workplace_2016.pdf).

Le Bon, Gustav. 1895. *The Crowd: A Study of the Popular Mind.* New York: Macmillan.

Lebowitz, Shana. 2016. "Tinder's Sociologist Reveals an Easy Way to Get More People to Message You." *Business Insider,* September 19. Accessed May 31, 2017 (www.businessinsider.com/tinder-sociologist-how-to-get-more-people-to-message-you-2016-9).

Lee, Don. 2015. "Rising Global Debt Is Increasing the Risk of Another Financial Crisis." *Los Angeles Times,* July 20. Accessed January 17, 2017

Lee, Erika. 2015. *The Making of Asian America: A History.* New York: Simon & Schuster.

Lee, Helena. 2013. "The Babies Who Nap in Sub-Zero Temperatures." *BBC News Magazine,* February 21. Accessed February 2, 2015 (www.bbc.com/news/magazine-21537988).

Lee, Sing. 1991. "Anorexia Nervosa in Hong Kong: A Chinese Perspective." *Psychological Medicine* 21(3): 703–711.

Lee, Sing, H. F. K. Chiu, and Char-Nie Chen. 1989. "Anorexia Nervosa in Hong Kong: Why Not More Chinese?" *British Journal of Psychiatry* 154: 683-688.

Lee, Sing, T. P. Ho, and L. K. Hsu. 1993. "Fat Phobic and Non-Fat Phobic Anorexia Nervosa: A Comparative Study of 70 Chinese Patients in Hong Kong." *Psychological Medicine* 23(4): 999–1017.

Lefevre, Romana. 2011. *Rude Hand Gestures of the World: A Guide to Offending Without Words.* San Francisco: Chronicle Books.

Le Goff, Jacques. 1990. "Introduction: Medieval Man." Pp. 1–35 in *Medieval Callings,* ed. Jacques Le Goff. Chicago: University of Chicago Press.

Lencioni, Patrick. 2006. *Silos, Politics, and Turf Wars: A Leadership Fable About Destroying the Barriers That Turn Colleagues into Competitors.* San Francisco: Jossey-Bass.

Lengermann, Patricia Madoo, and Jill Niebrugge-Brantley. 1998. *The Women Founders: Sociology and Social Theory, 1830–1930.* Boston: McGraw-Hill.

Leonard, Annie. 2010. *The Story of Stuff: How Our Obsession with Stuff Is Trashing the Planet, Our Communities, and Our Health—and a Vision for Change.* New York: Free Press.

Levanon, Gad, Vivian Chen, and Ben Chang. 2012. "Feeling the Pain: Wage Growth in the United States During and After the Great Recession." Executive Action Series, The Conference Board, New York, April.

Levine, Kenneth J., and Cynthia A. Hoffner. 2006. "Adolescents Conceptions of Work: What Is Learned from Different Sources During Anticipatory Socialization?" *Journal of Adolescent Research* 21 (6): 647–669.

Levitz, Eric. 2016. "Trump Won a Lot of White Working-Class Voters Who Backed Obama." *New York Magazine,* November 9. Accessed December 13, 2016 (http://nymag.com/daily/intelligencer/2016/11/trump-won-a-lot-of-white-working-class-obama-voters.html).

Lewis, M. Paul, Gary F. Simons, and Charles D. Fennig, eds. 2016. *Ethnologue: Languages of the World,* 19th ed. Dallas, TX: SIL International. Accessed October 5, 2016 (www.ethnologue.com).

Lewis, Michael. 2003. *Moneyball: The Art of Winning an Unfair Game.* New York: Norton.

Lezhnev, Sasha. 2011. "New U.N. Report: U.S. Conflict Minerals Law Having Impact in Congo." *Enough,* June 16. Accessed August 8, 2011 (www.enoughproject.org/blogs/new-un-report-us-conflict-minerals-law-having-impact-congo).

Liang, Bin, and Hong Lu. 2010. "Internet Development, Censorship, and Cyber Crimes in China." *Journal of Contemporary Criminal Justice* 26 (1): 103–120.

Lichter, Daniel T., Domenico Parisi, and Helga De Valk. 2016. "Residential Segregation." *Pathways,* Special Issue, The Poverty and Inequality Report: 65–75. Accessed February 5, 2017 (http://inequality.stanford.edu/sites/default/files/Pathways-SOTU-2016.pdf).

Lierow, Diane. 2011. *Danis Story: A Journey from Neglect to Love.* Hoboken, NJ: Wiley.

Lind, Dara. 2015. "The FBI Is Trying to Get Better Data on Police Killings. Here's What We Know Now." *Vox,* April 26. Accessed April 26, 2015 (www.vox.com/2014/8/21/6051043/how-many-people-killed-police-statistics-homicide-official-black).

Ling, Peter. 2006. "Social Capital, Resource Mobilization and Origins of the Civil Rights Movement." *Journal of Historical Sociology* 19 (2): 202–214.

Link, Bruce G., and Jo C. Phelan. 2001. "Conceptualizing Stigma." *Annual Review of Sociology* 27: 363–385.

Lino, Mark, Kevin Kuczynski, Nestor Rodriguez, and TusaRebecca Schap. 2017. *Expenditures on Children by Families, 2015.* Center for Nutrition Policy and Promotion, Miscellaneous Publication No. 1528-2015. U.S. Department of Agriculture, Washington, DC. Accessed May 31, 2017 (www.cnpp.usda.gov/sites/default/files/crc2015_March2017.pdf).

Lipset, Seymour Martin. 1959. "Some Social Requisites of Demozcracy: Economic Development and Political Legitimacy." *American Political Science Review* 53: 69–105.

Liptak, Adam. 2008a. "Damages Cut Against Exxon in *Valdez* Case." *The New York Times,* June 26. Accessed April 3, 2015 (www.nytimes.com/2008/06/26/washington/26punitive.html).

———. 2008b. "From One Footnote, a Debate over the Tangles of Law, Science, and Money." *The New York Times,* June 26. Accessed April 3, 2015 (www.nytimes.com/2008/11/25/washington/25bar.html).

List, Justin M. 2009. "Justice and the Reversal of the Healthcare Worker Brain-Drain." *American Journal of Bioethics* 9 (3): 10–12.

Livingston, Gretchen. 2015. "It's No Longer a 'Leave It to Beaver' World for American Families—But It Wasn't Back Then, Either." Pew Research Center December 30. Accessed November 22, 2016 (www.pewresearch.org/fact-tank/2015/12/30/its-no-longer-a-leave-it-to-beaver-world-for-american-families-but-it-wasnt-back-then-either/).

Lofquist, Daphne, Terry Lugaila, Martin OConnell, and Sarah Feliz. 2012. "Households and Families: 2010." 2010 Census Brief, C2010BR-14, April. Washington, DC: U.S. Census Bureau. Accessed May 8, 2012 (www.census.gov/prod/cen2010/briefs/c2010br-14.pdf).

Logan, John R. 2014. "Separate and Unequal in Suburbia." Census Brief prepared for Project US2010, December 1. Accessed February 4, 2017 (https://s4.ad.brown.edu/Projects/Diversity/Data/Report/report12012014.pdf).

Logue, Josh. 2016. "A Broader Protest Agenda." *Inside Higher Ed,* April 19. Accessed February 14, 2017 (www.insidehighered.com/news/2016/04/19/student-protests-year-broaden-beyond-issues-race).

Lopata, Helena Znaniecki. 1971. *Occupation: Housewife.* New York: Oxford University Press.

Lorber, Judith. 1994. *Paradoxes of Gender.* New Haven, CT: Yale University Press.

Lotz, Amanda D. 2007. "Theorising the Intermezzo: The Contributions of Postfeminism and Third Wave Feminism." Pp. 71–85 in *Third Wave Feminism: A Critical Exploration,* expanded 2nd ed., ed. Stacy Gillis, Gillian Howie, and Rebecca Munford. New York: Palgrave Macmillan.

Louie, Miriam Ching Yoon. 2001. *Sweatshop Warriors: Immigrant Women Workers Take on the Global Factory.* Cambridge, MA: South End Press.

Lovell, Joel, and Ryan Pfluger. 2014. "The Tale of Two Schools." *The New York Times Magazine,* May 4. Accessed March 10, 2015 (www.nytimes.com/interactive/2014/05/04/magazine/tale-of-two-schools.html).

Loxcel Geomatics. 2016. "How Many Starbucks Are Out There?" July 7. Accessed October 4, 2016 (www.loxcel.com/sbux-faq.html).

Lucal, Betsy. 2010. "Better Informed, Still Skeptical: Response to Machalek and Martin." *Teaching Sociology* 38 (1): 46–49.

Lucio, José Miguel Cabrales. 2014. "Gender and Constitutionalism in Mexico: From Quotas to Parity?" ConstitutionNet, April 28. Accessed April 16, 2015 (www.constitutionnet.org/news/gender-and-constitutionalism-mexico-quotas-parity).

Lukács, Georg. 1923. *History and Class Consciousness.* London: Merlin.

Lumpe, Lora. 2003. "Taking Aim at the Global Gun Trade." *Amnesty Now* (Winter): 10–13.

Lyall, Sarah. 2002. "For Europeans, Love, Yes; Marriage, Maybe." *The New York Times,* March 24, pp. 1–8.

Lytton, Hugh, and David M. Romney. 1991. "Parents' Differential Socialization of Boys and Girls: A Meta-analysis." *Psychological Bulletin* 109 (2): 267–296.

M

MacEachern, Scott. 2003. "The Concept of Race in Anthropology." Pp. 10–35 in *Race and Ethnicity: An Anthropological Focus on the United States and the World,* ed. R. Scupin. Upper Saddle River, NJ: Prentice Hall.

MacFarquhar, Neil. 2008. "Resolute or Fearful, Many Muslims Turn to Home Schooling." *The New York Times,* March 26, p. A1.

MacLeod, Jay. 2009. *Ain't No Makin' It: Aspirations and Attainment in a Low-Income Neighborhood,* 3rd ed. Boulder, CO: Westview Press.

MacNell, Lillian, Adam Driscoll, and Andrea N. Hunt. 2014. "What's in a Name: Exposing Gender Bias in Student Ratings of Teachers." *Innovative Higher Education,* December.

References

Maese, Rick. 2016. "Whispers in Rio: Is a Female Runner Gaining an Unfair Edge from Naturally High Testosterone?" *The Washington Post,* August 17. Accessed January 26, 2017 (www.washingtonpost.com/sports/olympics/whispers-on-the-track-in-rio-does-caster-semenya-have-an-unfair-edge/2016/08/17/840cf088-6486-11e6-be4e-23fc4d4d12b4_story.html).

Magnier, Mark. 2010. "Mumbai Billionaire's Home Boasts 27 Floors, Ocean and Slum Views." *Los Angeles Times,* October 24. Accessed January 16, 2017 (http://articles.latimes.com/2010/oct/24/world/la-fg-india-rich-20101025).

Malacrida, Claudia. 2005. "Discipline and Dehumanization in a Total Institution: Institutional Survivors Descriptions of Time-Out Rooms." *Disability & Society* 20 (5): 523–537.

Malcolm X, with Alex Haley. 1964. *The Autobiography of Malcolm X.* New York: Grove.

Malkiel, Nancy Weiss. 2016. *"Keep the Damned Women Out": The Struggle for Coeducation.* Princeton, NJ: Princeton University Press.

Malthus, Thomas R. 1878. *An Essay on the Principle of Population: Or, A View of Its Past and Present Effects on Human Happiness, with an Inquiry into Our Prospects Respecting the Future Removal or Mitigation of the Evils Which It Occasions,* 8th ed. London: Reeves and Turner.

Mann, Horace. [1848] 1957. "Report No. 12 of the Massachusetts School Board." Pp. 79–97 in *The Republic and the School: Horace Mann on the Education of Free Men,* ed. L. A. Cremin. New York: Teachers College.

Mann, Yee Kan, Oriel Sullivan, and Jonathan Gershuny. 2011. "Gender Convergence in Domestic Work: Discerning the Effects of Interactional and Institutional Barriers from Large-Scale Data." *Sociology* 45 (2): 234–251.

Mapel, Tim. 2007. "The Adjustment Process of Ex-Buddhist Monks to Life After the Monastery." *Journal of Religion & Health* 46 (1): 19–34.

Marcos, Cristina. 2016. "115th Congress Will Be Most Racially Diverse in History." *The Hill,* November 17. Accessed December 16, 2016 (http://thehill.com/homenews/house/306480-115th-congress-will-be-most-racially-diverse-in-history).

Marks, Nadine F., and James David Lambert. 1998. "Marital Status Continuity and Change Among Young and Midlife Adults: Longitudinal Effects on Psychological Well-Being." *Journal of Family Issues* 19(6): 652–686.

Marlow, Eugene, and Eugene Secunda. 1991. *Shifting Time and Shifting Space: The Story of Videotape.* New York: Praeger.

Marquis, Alice Goldfarb. 1984. "Written on the Wind: The Impact of Radio during the 1930s." *Journal of Contemporary History* 19 (3): 385–415.

Marshall, T. H. 1950. *Citizenship and Social Class and Other Essays.* Cambridge, UK: Cambridge University Press.

Martineau, Harriet. [1837] 1962. *Society in America.* Edited, abridged, with an introductory essay by Seymour Martin Lipset. Garden City, NY: Doubleday.

———. [1838] 1989. *How to Observe Morals and Manners.* Philadelphia: Leal and Blanchard. Sesquicentennial ed., ed. M. R. Hill. New York: Transaction.

Martinez, Gladys M., and Joyce C. Abma. 2015. "Sexual Activity, Contraceptive Use, and Childbearing of Teenagers Aged 15–19 in the United States." *NCHS Data Brief,* No. 209, July. Hyattsville, MD: National Center for Health Statistics. Accessed February 1, 2017 (www.cdc.gov/nchs/data/databriefs/db209.pdf).

Martinez, Gladys, Casey Copen, and Joyce C. Abma. 2011. "Teenagers in the United States: Sexual Activity, Contraceptive Use, and Childbearing, 2006–2010." National Survey of Family Growth, National Center for Health Statistics. *Vital and Health Statistics* 23 (31). Accessed May 26, 2012 (www.cdc.gov/nchs/data/series/sr_23/sr23_031.pdf).

Marx, Karl. [1845] 2000. "German Ideology." Pp. 175–208 in *Karl Marx: Selected Writings,* 2nd ed., ed. David McLellan. New York: Oxford University Press.

———. [1867] 2000. "Capital." Pp. 452–546 in *Karl Marx: Selected Writings,* 2nd ed. David McLellan. New York: Oxford University Press.

Marx, Karl, and Friedrich Engels. [1847] 1955. *Selected Works in Two Volumes.* Moscow: Foreign Languages Publishing House.

———. [1848] 1998. *The Communist Manifesto: A Modern Edition.* New York: Verso.

Mather, Mark, Linda A. Jacobsen, and Kelvin M. Pollard. 2015. "Aging in the United States." Population Reference Bureau, *Population Bulletin* 70 (2). Accessed October 25, 2016 (www.prb.org/pdf16/aging-us-population-bulletin.pdf).

Mathews, T. J., Marian F. MacDorman, and Marie E. Thoma. 2015. "Infant Mortality Statistics from the 2013 Period Linked Birth/Infant Death Data Set." *National Vital Statistics Reports* 64(9): August 6. Accessed February 11, 2017 (www.cdc.gov/nchs/data/nvsr/nvsr64/nvsr64_09.pdf).

Mathisen, James A. 2006. "Sport." Pp. 285–303 in *Handbook of Religion and Social Institutions,* ed. Helen Rose Ebaugh. New York: Springer.

Mayo, Elton. 1933. *The Human Problems of an Industrial Civilization.* London: Macmillan.

McAdam, Doug. 1988. *Freedom Summer.* New York: Oxford University Press.

McCarthy, John D., and Mayer N. Zald. 1977. "Resource Mobilization and Social Movements: A Partial Theory." *AJS* 82(6): 1212–1241.

———. 2002. "The Enduring Vitality of the Resource Mobilization Theory of Social Movement." Pp. 533–565 in *Handbook of Sociological Theory,* Jonathan H. Turner, ed. New York: Academic/Plenum Publishers.

McCarthy, Justin. 2016. "American's Support for Game Marriage Remains High, at 61%." Gallup, Inc., May 19. Accessed October 29, 2016 (www.gallup.com/poll/191645/americans-support-gay-marriage-remains-high.aspx).

McCabe, Janice, Emily Fairchild, Liz Grauerholz, Bernice A. Pescosolido, and Daniel Tope. 2011. "Gender in Twentieth-Century Childrens Books: Patterns of Disparity in Titles and Central Characters." *Gender & Society* 25 (2): 197–226.

McCauley, Douglas J., Molly Hardesty-Moore, Benjamin S. Halpern, and Hillary S. Young. 2016. "A Mammoth Undertaking: Harnessing Insight from Functional Ecology to Shape De-Extinction Priority Setting." *Functional Ecology* September 12. Accessed February 15, 2017 (https://labs.eemb.ucsb.edu/young/hillary/PDF/McCauley_et_al-2016-Functional_Ecology.pdf).

McConnell-Ginet, Sally. 2011. *Gender, Sexuality, and Meaning: Linguistic Practice and Politics.* New York: Oxford University Press.

McDonald, Michael. 2009. "Election of a Century?" United States Elections Project. Accessed June 2, 2009 (http://elections.gmu.edu/Election_of_a_Century.html).

———. 2016. "2016 November General Election Turnout Rates." United States Elections Project. Accessed December 15, 2016 (www.electproject.org/2016g).

McDonald's Corporation. 2016. "2015 Annual Report." McDonald's Corporation: Oak Brook, IL. Accessed October 4, 2016 (http://corporate.mcdonalds.com/mcd/investors/financial-information/annual-report.html).

McDowell, David J., and Ross D. Parke. 2009. "Parental Correlates of Childrens Peer Relations: An Empirical Test of a Tripartite Model." *Developmental Psychology* 45 (1): 224–235.

McGurty, Eileen. 2007. *Transforming Environmentalism: Warren County, PCBs, and the Origins of Environmental Justice.* Piscataway, NJ: Rutgers University Press.

McIntosh, Peggy. 1988. "White Privilege and Male Privilege: A Personal Account of Coming to See Correspondence Through Work and Women's Studies." Working Paper No. 189, Wellesley College Center for Research on Women, Wellesley, MA.

McKirdy, Euan, and Mallika Kapur. 2016. "Poor Suffer as Mumbai Chokes on Garbage Dump Haze." *CNN,* February 5. Accessed January 16, 2017 (www.cnn.com/2016/02/05/asia/mumbai-giant-garbage-dump-fire/).

McKown, Clark, and Rhona S. Weinstein. 2008. "Teacher Expectations, Classroom Context, and the Achievement Gap." *Journal of School Psychology* 46 (3): 235–261.

McLellan, David, ed. 2000. *Karl Marx, Selected Writings,* rev. ed. New York: Oxford University Press.

McNamee, Stephen J., and Robert K. Miller Jr. 2014. *The Meritocracy Myth,* 3rd ed. Lanham, MD: Rowman & Littlefield.

McPherson, Miller, Lynn Smith-Lovin, and James M. Cook. 2001. "Birds of a Feather: Homophily in Social Networks." *Annual Review of Sociology* 27: 415–222.

Mead, George H. 1934. *Mind, Self and Society,* ed. Charles W. Morris. Chicago: University of Chicago Press.

———. 1964a. *On Social Psychology,* ed. Anselm Strauss. Chicago: University of Chicago Press.

———. 1964b. "The Genesis of the Self and Social Control." Pp. 267–293 in *Selected Writings: George Herbert Mead,* ed. Andrew J. Reck. Indianapolis: Bobbs-Merrill.

Mead, Margaret. [1935] 2001. *Sex and Temperament in Three Primitive Societies.* New York: Perennial, HarperCollins.

Meier, Emily A., Jarred V. Gallegos, Lori P. Montross Thomas, Colin A. Depp, Scott A. Irwin, and Dilip V. Jeste. 2016. "Defining a Good Death (Successful Dying): Literature Review and a Call for Research and Public Dialogue." *The American Journal of Geriatric Psychiatry* 24 (4): 261–271.

Meier, Robert F., and Gilbert Geis. 1997. *Victimless Crime? Prostitution, Drugs, Homosexuality, Abortion.* Los Angeles: Roxbury Books.

Melby, Todd. 2009. "Creating the DSM-V." *Contemporary Sexuality* 43 (3): 1, 4–6.

Méndez, Juan E. "Report of the Special Rapporteur on Torture and Other Cruel, Inhuman or Degrading Treatment or Punishment." United Nations, Human Rights Council, Twenty-Second Session, February. Accessed April 19, 2015 (http://daccess-dds-ny.un.org/doc/UNDOC/GEN/G13/105/77/PDF/G1310577.pdf).

Merlan, Anna. 2016. "Meet the Brave, Audacious, Astonishing Women Who Built the Standing Rock Movement." *Jezebel,* December 8. Accessed February 8, 2017 (http://jezebel.com/meet-the-brave-audacious-astonishing-women-who-built-1789756669).

Merton, Robert. 1968. *Social Theory and Social Structure.* New York: Free Press.

Merton, Robert K., and Alice S. Kitt. 1950. "Contributions to the Theory of Reference Group Behavior." Pp. 40–105 in *Continuities in Social Research: Studies in the Scope and Methods of the American Soldier,* ed. Robert K. Merton and Paul L. Lazarsfeld. New York: Free Press.

Michels, Robert. [1915] 1949. *Political Parties.* Glencoe, IL: Free Press.

Mika, Mike. 2013. "Why I Hacked Donkey Kong for My Daughter." *Wired,* March 11. Accessed May 20, 2013 (www.wired.com/gamelife/2013/03/donkey-kong-pauline-hack/).

Milanovic, Branko. 2013. "Global Income Inequality in Numbers: In History and Now." *Global Policy* 4(2): 198–208.

———. 2016. *Global Inequality: A New Approach for the Age of Globalization.* Cambridge: Harvard University Press.

Milgram, Stanley. 1963. "Behavioral Study of Obedience." *Journal of Abnormal and Social Psychology* 67 (October): 371–378.

———. 1974a. *Obedience to Authority: An Experimental View.* New York: Harper & Row.

———. 1974b. "We Are All Obedient." *The Listener,* October 31: 567–568.

Milillo, Diana. 2008. "Sexuality Sells: A Content Analysis of Lesbian and Heterosexual Women's Bodies in Magazine Advertisements." *Journal of Lesbian Studies* 12 (4): 381–392.

Millard, Andre. 2005. *America on Record: A History of Recorded Sound,* 2nd ed. New York: Cambridge University Press.

Miller, Claire Cain. 2015. "Single Motherhood, in Decline Over All, Rises for Women 35 and Older." *The New York Times,* May 8. Accessed November 22, 2016 (www.nytimes.com/2015/05/09/upshot/out-of-wedlock-births-are-falling-except-among-older-women.html).

Millett, Kate. 1970. *Sexual Politics.* Garden City, NY: Doubleday.

Mills, C. Wright. [1956] 2000. *The Power Elite.* New edition with afterword by Alan Wolfe. New York: Oxford University Press.

———. [1959] 2009. *The Sociological Imagination.* New York: Oxford University Press.

Milner, Greg. 2009. *Perfecting Sound Forever: An Aural History of Recorded Music.* New York: Faber and Faber.

Minority Rights Group International. 2007. "World Directory of Minorities and Indigenous Peoples—Mexico: Overview." Geneva: United Nations High Commissioner for Refugees. Accessed June 14, 2009 (www.unhcr.org/refworld/docid/4954ce409a.html).

Mitchell, Ojmarrh, and Michael S. Caudy. 2015. "Examining Racial Disparities in Drug Arrests." *Justice Quarterly* 32: 288–313.

Moen, Phyllis, and Patricia Roehling. 2005. *The Career Mystique: Cracks in the American Dream.* Lanham, MD: Rowman & Littlefield.

Mohai, Paul, and Robin Saha. 2007. "Racial Inequality in the Distribution of Hazardous Waste: A National-Level Reassessment." *Social Problems* 54 (3): 343–370.

Monaghan, Peter. 2012. "Our Storehouse of Knowledge About Social Movements . . . Is Going to Be Left Bare." *The Chronicle of Higher Education,* February 19. Accessed March 14, 2012 (http://chronicle.com/article/5-Minutes-With-a-Sociologist/130849/).

Montagu, Ashley, 1997. *Man's Most Dangerous Myth: The Fallacy of Race,* 6th ed., abridged student ed. Walnut Creek, CA: AltaMira Press.

Monte, Lindsay M., and Renee R. Ellis. 2014. "Fertility of Women in the United States: June 2012." *Current Population Reports,* P20–575, U.S. Census Bureau, Washington, DC. Accessed February 26, 2015 (www.census.gov/content/dam/Census/library/publications/2014/demo/p20-575.pdf).

Moore, Molly. 2006. "Romance, but Not Marriage." *The Washington Post National Weekly Edition,* November 27, p. 18.

Moore, Robert B. 1976. *Racism in the English Language: A Lesson Plan and Study Essay.* New York: The Racism and Sexism Resource Center for Educators.

Morgan, Philip D. 2005 "'To Get Quit of Negroes': George Washington and Slavery." *Journal of American Studies* 39(3): 403–429.

Morgan, Sue. 2009. "Theorising Feminist History: A Thirty-Year Retrospective." *Women's History Review* 18 (3): 381–407.

Morin, Rich, and Renee Stepler. 2016. "The Racial Confidence Gap in Police Performance." Pew Research Center, Social & Demographic Trends September 29. Accessed February 3, 2017 (www.pewsocialtrends.org/2016/09/29/the-racial-confidence-gap-in-police-performance/).

Morse, Arthur D. 1967. *While Six Million Died: A Chronicle of American Apathy.* New York: Ace.

Morselli, Carlo, Pierre Tremblay, and Bill McCarthy. 2006. "Mentors and Criminal Achievement." *Criminology* 44 (1): 17–43.

Mortimer, Jeylan T., and Michael J. Shanahan, eds. 2006. *Handbook of the Life Course.* New York: Springer Science and Business Media.

Moyer, Michael. 2010. "Internet Ideology War." *Scientific American* 302 (4): 14–16.

Mullins, Justin. 2014. "Can Facebook Make You Sad?" *BBC,* February 6. Accessed February 11, 2015 (www.bbc.com/future/story/20140206-is-facebook-bad-for-you).

Munford, Rebecca. 2007. "Wake Up and Smell the Lipgloss: Gender, Generation, and the (A)Politics of Girl Power." Pp. 266–279 in *Third Wave Feminism: A Critical Exploration,* expanded 2nd ed., ed. Stacy Gillis, Gillian Howie, and Rebecca Munford. New York: Palgrave Macmillan.

Murdock, George P. 1945. "The Common Denominator of Cultures." Pp. 123–142 in *The Science of Man in the World Crisis,* ed. Ralph Linton. New York: Columbia University Press.

———. 1949. *Social Structure.* New York: Macmillan.
———. 1957. "World Ethnographic Sample." *American Anthropologist* 59 (August): 664–687.
Myrskylä, Mikko, Hans-Peter Kohler, and Francesco C. Billari. 2009. "Advances in Development Reverse Fertility Declines." *Nature,* 460 (August 6): 741–743.

N

NAEP. 2016. "2015 Mathematics Assessment." NAEP Data Explorer, U.S. Department of Education, Institute of Education Sciences, National Center for Education Statistics, National Assessment of Educational Progress (NAEP). Accessed December 5, 2016 (http://nces.ed.gov/nationsreportcard/naepdata/dataset.aspx).
Nagoianu, Dan, and Stanley Goldfarb. 2008. "Just Add Water." *Journal of the American Society of Nephrology* 19 (6): 1041–1043.
Nanda, Serena. 1997. "The Hijras of India." Pp. 82–86 in *A Queer World: The Center for Lesbian and Gay Studies Reader,* ed. Martin Duberman. New York: New York University Press.
Naples, Nancy. 2003. *Feminism and Method: Ethnography, Discourse Analysis, and Activist Research.* New York: Routledge.
Narrative 4. 2015. "What We Do." New York, NY. Accessed March 10, 2015 (www.narrative4.com/mission-vision/).
National Center for Access to Justice. 2016. "The Justice Index 2016." Fordham Law School, New York. Accessed November 16, 2016 (http://justiceindex.org/).
National Center for Education Statistics. 2016. Digest of Education Statistics—Most Current Digest Tables. Washington, DC: Institute of Education Services, U.S. Department of Education. September 6, 2016 (http://nces.ed.gov/programs/digest/current_tables.asp).
National Center for Health Statistics. 2016. *Health, United States, 2015: With Special Feature on Racial and Ethnic Health Disparities.* Hyattsville, MD. Accessed October 25, 2016 (www.cdc.gov/nchs/hus.htm).
National Center for State Courts. 2015. "The Landscape of Civil Litigation in State Courts." Civil Justice Initiative, Williamsburg, Virginia. Accessed November 16, 2016 (www.ncsc.org/~/media/Files/PDF/Research/CivilJusticeReport-2015.ashx).
National Conference of State Legislatures. 2016. "State Medical Marijuana Laws." November 9. Accessed November 10, 2016 (www.ncsl.org/research/health/state-medical-marijuana-laws.aspx).
National Education Association. 2016. "Rankings & Estimates: Rankings of the States 2015 and Estimates of School Statistics 2016." NEA Research, May. Accessed December 6, 2016 (www.nea.org/assets/docs/2016_NEA_Rankings_And_Estimates.pdf).
National Geographic. 2012. "Gulf Spill Pictures: Ten New Studies Show Impact on Coast." *National Geographic,* April. Accessed May 28, 2012 (http://news.nationalgeographic.com/news/energy/2012/04/pictures/120420-gulf-oil-spill-impact-studies/).
National Human Trafficking Resource Center. 2016. "2015 NHTRC Annual Report: United States." Accessed December 21, 2016 (https://humantraffickinghotline.org/resources/2015-nhtrc-annual-report).
National Institute of Justice. 2007. "Transnational Organized Crime." U.S. Department of Justice. Accessed May 20, 2009 (www.ojp.usdoj.gov/nij/topics/crime/transnational-organized-crime/welcome.htm).
NCAA. 2016. "Student Athlete Participation 1981/82-2015/16: NCAA Sports Sponsorship and Participation Rates Report." Indianapolis, IN: The National Collegiate Athletic Association. Accessed December 5, 2016 (www.ncaapublications.com/productdownloads/PR1516.pdf).
Neiwert, David A. 2005. *Strawberry Days: How Internment Destroyed the Japanese Community.* New York: Palgrave Macmillan.
Nelson, Laura J. 2016. "The Worst Mass Shooting? A Look Back at Massacres in U.S. History." *Los Angeles Times,* June 14. Accessed November 4, 2016 (www.latimes.com/nation/la-na-mass-shooting-20160614-snap-story.html).
Newman, William M. 1973. *American Pluralism: A Study of Minority Groups and Social Theory.* New York: Harper & Row.
Newmyer, Tory. 2017. "Trump's Immigration Ban Ruptures Truce with Business, as Tech Leaders Speak Out." *Fortune,* January 29. Accessed February 7, 2017 (http://fortune.com/2017/01/28/tech-execs-criticize-trump-immigrant-ban/).
Newport, Frank. 2013. "In U.S., 87% Approve of Black-White Marriage, vs. 4% in 1958." Gallup, July 25. Accessed February 3, 2017 (www.gallup.com/poll/163697/approve-marriage-blacks-whites.aspx).
———. 2015. "Americans Continue to Shift Left on Key Moral Issues." Gallup Social Issues, May 26. Accessed November 21, 2016 (www.gallup.com/poll/183413/americans-continue-shift-left-key-moral-issues.aspx).
Newton, Michael. 2002. *Savage Girls and Wild Boys: A History of Feral Children.* London: Faber and Faber.
The New York Times. 2006. "Questions Couples Should Ask (or Wish They Had) Before Marrying." *The New York Times,* December 17. Accessed August 6, 2009 (www.nytimes.com/2006/12/17/fashion/weddings/17FIELDBOX.html).
NFHS. 2016. "2015–16 High School Athletics Participation Survey." National Federation of State High School Associations, Indianapolis, IN. Accessed December 5, 2016 (www.nfhs.org/ParticipationStatistics/PDF/2015-16_Sports_Participation_Survey.pdf).
NHPCO. 2015. "NHPCO's Facts and Figures: Hospice Care in America." National Hospice and Palliative Care Organization, September. Accessed October 25, 2016 (www.nhpco.org/sites/default/files/public/Statistics_Research/2015_Facts_Figures.pdf).
Nickerson, Raymond S. 1998. "Confirmation Bias: A Ubiquitous Phenomenon in Many Guises." *Review of General Psychology* 2 (2): 175–220.
Nielsen. 2016. "The Nielsen Comparable Metrics Report: Q2 2016." New York: The Nielsen Company. Accessed October 25, 2016 (www.nielsen.com/content/dam/corporate/us/en/reports-downloads/2016-reports/q2-comparable-metrics-report-oct-2016.pdf).
———. 2012. "State of the Media: U.S. Digital Consumer Report—Q3–Q4 2011." Accessed April 5, 2012 (www.nielsen.com/content/dam/corporate/us/en/reports-downloads/2012-Reports/Digital-Consumer-Report-Q4-2012.pdf).
Nielsen, Joyce McCarl, Glenda Walden, and Charlotte A. Kunkel. 2000. "Gendered Heteronormativity: Empirical Illustrations in Everyday Life." *Sociological Quarterly* 41 (2): 283–296.
Nishime, Leilani. 2012. "The Case for Cablinasian: Multiracial Naming from *Plessy* to Tiger Woods." *Communication Theory* 22(1): 92–111.
NOAA. 2017. "State of the Climate: Global Analysis for Annual 2016." NOAA Centers for Environmental Information, January. Accessed February 13, 2017 (www.ncdc.noaa.gov/sotc/global/201613).
Nobles, Melissa. 2000. "History Counts: A Comparative Analysis of Racial/Color Categorization in U.S. and Brazilian Censuses." *American Journal of Public Health* 90: 1738–1745.
Nofziger, Stacey, and Hye-Ryeon Lee. 2006. "Differential Associations and Daily Smoking of Adolescents: The Importance of Same-Sex Models." *Youth & Society* 37 (4): 453–478.
Nolan, Patrick, and Gerhard Lenski. 2006. *Human Societies: An Introduction to Macrosociology,* 10th ed. Boulder, CO: Paradigm.
North Carolina Department of Environment and Natural Resources. 2008. "Warren County PCB Landfill Fact Sheet." Accessed April 9, 2008 (www.wastenotnc.org/WarrenCo_Fact_Sheet.htm).
Norton, Michael I., and Francesca Gino. 2013. "Rituals Alleviate Grieving for Loved Ones, Lovers, and Lotteries." *Journal of Experimental Psychology: General* 143 (1): 266–272. Accessed

May 31, 2013 (http://francescagino.com/pdfs/norton_gino_jesp_2013.pdf).

Notestein, Frank. 1945. "Population: The Long View." Pp. 36–57 in *Food for the World,* ed. Theodore W. Schultz. Chicago: University of Chicago Press.

Noueihed, Lin, and Alex Warren. 2012. *The Battle for the Arab Spring: Revolution, Counter-Revolution and the Making of a New Era.* New Haven, CT: Yale University Press.

O

Oakes, Jeannie. 2008. "Keeping Track: Structuring Equality and Inequality in an Era of Accountability." *Teachers College Record* 110 (3): 700–712.

OASDI. 2011. "The 2011 Annual Report of the Board of Trustees of the Federal Old-Age and Survivors Insurance and Federal Disability Insurance Trust Funds." Social Security Administration, 66–327, May 13. Washington, DC: U.S. Government Printing Office. Accessed June 29, 2011 (www.ssa.gov/oact/TR/2011/).

Obach, Brian K. 2004. *Labor and the Environmental Movement: The Quest for Common Ground.* Cambridge, MA: MIT Press.

Obama, Barack. 2013. "Inaugural Address by President Barack Obama." The White House, Office of the Press Secretary, Washington, DC, January 21. Accessed March 28, 2015 (www.whitehouse.gov/the-press-office/2013/01/21/inaugural-address-president-barack-obama).

Oberschall, Anthony. 1973. *Social Conflict and Social Movements.* Englewood Cliffs, NJ: Prentice Hall.

O'Brien, Valerie. 2012. "The Benefits and Challenges of Kinship Care." *Child Care in Practice* 18: 127–146.

OECD. 2016a. *Education at a Glance 2016: OECD Indicators.* Paris: OECD Publishing. Accessed December 1, 2016 (www.oecd.org/education/skills-beyond-school/education-at-a-glance-19991487.htm).

———. 2016b. "OECD Family Database: Child Outcomes." Directorate for Employment, Labour, and Social Affairs, August. Accessed December 22, 2016 (www.oecd.org/els/family/database.htm).

———. 2016c. "Net Official Development Assistance." OECD Data. Accessed January 20, 2017 (https://data.oecd.org/oda/net-oda.htm).

———. 2016d. "Employment: Time Spend in Unpaid Work, by Sex." OECD Employment Database. Accessed February 2, 2017 (http://stats.oecd.org/index.aspx?queryid=54757).

———. 2016e. "Social Protection." *OECD Health Statistics.* Accessed February 12, 2017 (www.oecd-ilibrary.org/social-issues-migration-health/data/oecd-health-statistics/oecd-health-data-social-protection_data-00544-en).

Orfalea, Gregory. 2006. *The Arab Americans: A History.* Northampton, MA: Olive Branch Press.

Ogburn, William F. 1922. *Social Change with Respect to Culture and Original Nature.* New York: Huebsch (reprinted 1966, New York: Dell).

Ogburn, William F., and Clark Tibbits. 1934. "The Family and Its Functions." Pp. 661–708 in *Recent Social Trends in the United States,* ed. Research Committee on Social Trends. New York: McGraw-Hill.

O'Harrow, Robert Jr. 2005. "Mining Personal Data." *The Washington Post National Weekly Edition* (February 6), pp. 8–10.

Okrent, Arika. 2009. *In the Land of Invented Languages: Esperanto Rock Stars, Klingon Poets, Loglan Lovers, and the Mad Dreamers Who Tried to Build a Perfect Language.* New York: Spiegel and Grau.

Okun, Arthur. 1975. *Equality and Efficiency: The Big Tradeoff.* Washington, DC: Brookings Institution.

Olofsson, Parvin Tavakol, Peter Aspelin, Lott Bergstrand, and Lennart Blomqvist. 2014. "Patients Experience of Outsourcing and Care Related to Magnetic Resonance Examinations." *Upsala Journal of Medical Sciences* 119: 343–349.

Omi, Michael, and Howard Winant. 1994. *Racial Formation in the United States: From the 1960s to the 1990s,* 2nd ed. New York: Routledge.

The Oprah Winfrey Show. 2006. "Failing Grade." What Bill and Melinda Gates Want You to Know, April 11. Accessed March 10, 2015 (www.oprah.com/world/Failing-Grade).

Orshansky, Mollie. 1965. "Counting the Poor: Another Look at the Poverty Profile." *Social Security Bulletin* 28 (1): 3–29.

Ortman, Jennifer M., Victoria A. Velkoff, and Howard Hogan. 2014. "An Aging Nation: The Older Population in the United States." *Current Population Reports* P25-1140, May. Accessed February 2, 2015 (www.census.gov/prod/2014pubs/p25-1140.pdf).

OWN. 2015. "How 'The Girl in the Window' Is Doing 9 Years after Her Rescue from Horrific Neglect." *The Huffington Post* September 18. Accessed October 18, 2016 (www.huffingtonpost.com/2014/06/18/girl-in-the-window-danielle-oprah-lierow_n_5505079.html).

P

Packer, George. 2013. *The Unwinding: An Inner History of the New America.* New York: Farrar, Straus and Giroux.

Padian, Kevin. 2007. "The Case of Creation." *Nature* 448 (July 19): 253–254.

Padma, V., N. N. Anand, S. M. G. Swaminatha Gurukul, S. M. A. Syed Mohammed Javid, Arun Prasad, and S. Arun. 2015. "Health Problems and Stress in Information Technology and Business Process Outsourcing Employees." *Journal of Pharmacy & BioAllied Sciences* 7(S1):S9–S13.

Pager, Devah. 2003. "The Mark of a Criminal Record." *American Journal of Sociology* 108 (March): 937–975.

———. 2007 *Marked: Race, Crime, and Finding Work in an Era of Mass Incarceration.* Chicago: University of Chicago Press.

Pager, Devah, and David S. Pedulla. 2015. "Race, Self-Selection and the Job Search Process." *AJS* 120 (4): 1005–1054.

Pager, Devah, and Bruce Western. 2012. "Identifying Discrimination at Work: The Use of Field Experiments." *Journal of Social Issues* 68: 221–237.

Pager, Devah, Bruce Western, and Bart Bonikowski. 2009. "Discrimination in a Low Wage Labor Market: A Field Experiment." *American Sociological Review* 74: 777–799.

Pager, Devah, Bruce Western, and Naomi Sugie. 2009. "Sequencing Disadvantage: Barriers to Employment Facing Young Black and White Men with Criminal Records." *Annals of the American Academy of Political and Social Sciences* 623: 195–213.

Pai, Seeta, and Kelly Schryver. 2015. *Children, Teens, Media, and Body Image: A Common Sense Media Research Brief.* San Francisco: Common Sense Media. Accessed April 19, 2015 (www.commonsensemedia.org/file/csm-body-image-report-012615-interactivepdf/download).

Painter, Nell Irvin. 2010. *The History of White People.* New York: Norton.

Panagopoulos, Costas. 2009. "Polls and Elections: Preelection Poll Accuracy in the 2008 General Elections." *Presidential Studies Quarterly* 39 (4): 896–907.

Panagopoulos, Costas, and Benjamin Farrer. 2014. "*Polls and Elections:* Preelection Poll Accuracy and Bias in the 2012 General Elections." *Presidential Studies Quarterly* 44: 352–363.

Park, Madison, and Kiki Dhitavat. 2015. "Thailand's New Constitution Could Soon Recognize Third Gender." CNN, January 15. Accessed June 6, 2015 (www.cnn.com/2015/01/16/world/third-gender-thailand/index.html).

Parker, Alison. 2004. "Inalienable Rights: Can Human-Rights Law Help to End U.S. Mistreatment of Noncitizens?" *American Prospect,* October, pp. A11–A13.

Parker, Kim, and Eileen Patten. 2013. "The Sandwich Generation: Rising Financial Burdens for Middle-Aged Americans." Pew Research Center, January 30. Accessed February 2, 2015 (www.pewsocialtrends.org/2013/01/30/the-sandwich-generation/).

Parker, Kim, and Wendy Wang. 2013. "Modern Parenthood: Roles of Moms and Dads Converge as They Balance Work and Family." Pew Research Center, Washington, DC, March 14. Accessed June 6, 2013 (www.pewsocialtrends.org/files/2013/03/FINAL_modern_parenthood_03-2013.pdf).

Parker, Richard. 2009. "Sexuality, Culture and Society: Shifting Paradigms in Sexuality Research." *Culture, Health & Sexuality* 11 (3): 251–266.

Parks, Bradley C., and J. Timmons Roberts. 2010. "Climate Change, Social Theory, and Justice." *Theory, Culture, & Society* 27: 134–166.

Parry, Marc. 2013. "The American Police State: A Sociologist Interrogates the Criminal-Justice System and Tries to Stay Out of the Spotlight." *The Chronicle of Higher Education,* November 18. Accessed January 10, 2015 (http://chronicle.com/article/The-American-Police-State/142965/).

Parsons, Talcott. 1951. *The Social System.* New York: Free Press.

———. 1966. *Societies: Evolutionary and Comparative Perspectives.* Englewood Cliffs, NJ: Prentice Hall.

———. 1975. "The Sick Role and the Role of the Physician Reconsidered." *Milbank Medical Fund Quarterly Health and Society* 53 (Summer): 257–278.

Parsons, Talcott, and Robert Bales. 1955. *Family, Socialization and Interaction Process.* Glencoe, IL: Free Press.

Pascoe, C. J., and Tristan Bridges, eds. 2015. *Exploring Masculinities: Identity, Inequality, Continuity, and Change.* Cambridge, MA: Oxford University Press.

Pascoe, C. J. 2011. *Dude, You're a Fag: Masculinity in High School,* with a new preface. Berkeley, CA: University of California Press.

Passel, Jeffrey S., and D'Vera Cohn. 2016. "Overall Number of U.S. Unauthorized Immigrants Holds Steady Since 2009." Pew Research Center's Hispanic Trends Project, Washington, D.C., September 20. Accessed February 6, 2017 (http://assets.pewresearch.org/wp-content/uploads/sites/7/2016/09/31170303/PH_2016.09.20_Unauthorized_FINAL.pdf).

Patten, Eileen. 2016. "The Nation's Latino Population Is Defined by Its Youth." Pew Research Center, Hispanic Trends, April 20. Accessed February 6, 2017 (www.pewhispanic.org/2016/04/20/the-nations-latino-population-is-defined-by-its-youth/).

Patten, Eileen, and Gretchen Livingston. 2016. "Why Is the Teen Birth Rate Falling?" Pew Research Center, April 29. Accessed February 1, 2017 (www.pewresearch.org/fact-tank/2016/04/29/why-is-the-teen-birth-rate-falling/).

Patten, Eileen, and Kim Parker. 2012. "A Gender Reversal on Career Aspirations: Young Women Now Top Young Men in Valuing a High-Paying Career." A Social & Demographic Trends Report, Pew Research Center, April 19. Accessed May 2, 2012 (www.pewsocialtrends.org/2012/04/19/a-gender-reversal-on-career-aspirations/).

Patterson, Thomas E. 2003. *We the People,* 5th ed. New York: McGraw-Hill.

Paxton, Pamela, Sheri Kunovich, and Melanie M. Hughes. 2007. "Gender in Politics." Pp. 263–285 in *Annual Review of Sociology 2007.* Palo Alto, CA: Annual Reviews.

Peattie, Lisa, and Martin Rein. 1983. *Women's Claims: A Study in the Political Economy.* New York: Oxford University Press.

Peek, Lori. 2005. "Becoming Muslim: The Development of a Religious Identity." *Sociology of Religion* 66: 215–242.

Pemberton, David. 2015. "Statistical Definition of 'Family' Unchanged Since 1930." Random Samplings, Census Blogs, U.S. Census Bureau January 28. Accessed May 31, 2017 (www.census.gov/newsroom/blogs/random-samplings/2015/01/statistical-definition-of-family-unchanged-since-1930.html).

Perrow, Charles. 1986. *Complex Organizations,* 3rd ed. New York: Random House.

Peterson, David. J. 2015. *The Art of Language Invention: From Horse-Lords to Dark Elves, the Words Behind World Building.* New York: Penguin Books.

Petrovic, Drazen. 1994. "Ethnic Cleansing—an Attempt at Methodology." *EJIL* 5: 1–19.

Pettit, Michael, and Jana Vigor. 2015. "Pheromones, Feminism and the Many Lives of Menstrual Synchrony." *BioSocieties* 10 (3): 271–294.

Pew Charitable Trusts. 2012. "A Year or More: The High Cost of Long-Term Unemployment—Addendum." Pew Fiscal Analysis Initiative, May 2. Accessed May 22, 2012 (www.pewtrusts.org/uploadedFiles/wwwpewtrustsorg/Reports/-Fiscal_Analysis/Addendum_Long-Term_Unemployment_May2012.pdf).

Pew Research Center. 2007. "Optimism About Black Progress Declines: Blacks See Growing Values Gap Between Poor and Middle Class." Washington, DC: Pew Research Center. Accessed July 1, 2008 (http://pewsocialtrends.org/assets/pdf/Race.pdf).

———. 2009a. "The Stronger Sex—Spiritually Speaking." Pew Forum on Religion & Public Life, February 26. Accessed April 19, 2010 (http://pewforum.org/docs/?DocID5403).

———. 2009b. "End of Communism Cheered but Now with More Reservations: Two Decades After the Walls Fall." Pew Global Attitudes Project, November 2. Accessed April 23, 2010 (http://pewglobal.org/reports/pdf/267.pdf).

———. 2010. "The Return of the Multi-Generational Family Household." Washington, DC: Pew Research Centers Social and Demographic Trends project, March 18. Accessed February 26, 2015 (www.pewsocialtrends.org/files/2010/10/752-multi-generational-families.pdf).

———. 2011. "Muslim Americans: No Signs of Growth in Alienation or Support for Extremism." U.S. Politics & Policy, August 30. Accessed February 2, 2017 (www.people-press.org/2011/08/30/muslim-americans-no-signs-of-growth-in-alienation-or-support-for-extremism/).

———. 2012. "Young, Underemployed and Optimistic: Coming of Age, Slowly, in a Tough Economy." A Social & Demographic Trends Report, February 9. Accessed May 22, 2012 (www.pewsocialtrends.org/files/2012/02/young-underemployed-and-optimistic.pdf).

———. 2013. "U.S. Christians Views on the Return of Christ." The Pew Forum on Religion & Public Life, March 26. Accessed May 31, 2013 (www.pewforum.org/Christian/US-Christians-Views-on-the-Return-of-Christ.aspx).

———. 2014a. "Emerging and Developing Economies Much More Optimistic Than Rich Countries About the Future." Global Attitudes Project, October 9. Accessed January 22, 2015 (www.pewglobal.org/files/2014/10/Pew-Research-Center-Inequality-Report-FINAL-October-17-2014.pdf).

———. 2014b. "Emerging Nations Embrace Internet Mobile Technology." February 13. Accessed February 2, 2015 (www.pewglobal.org/files/2014/02/Pew-Research-Center-Global-Attitudes-Project-Technology-Report-FINAL-February-13-20147.pdf).

———. 2014c. "The Rising Cost of Not Going to College." Washington, DC: Social & Demographic Trends project, February 11. Accessed February 26, 2015 (www.pewsocialtrends.org/files/2014/02/SDT-higher-ed-FINAL-02-11-2014.pdf).

———. 2014d. "The Rising Cost of Not Going to College." Social & Demographic Trends, February 11. Accessed March 10, 2015 (www.pewsocialtrends.org/files/2014/02/SDT-higher-ed-FINAL-02-11-2014.pdf).

———. 2014e. "Most See Inequality Growing, but Partisans Differ over Solutions." U.S. Politics & Policy, January 23. Accessed March 26, 2015 (www.people-press.org/files/legacy-pdf/1-23-14%20Poverty_Inequality%20Release.pdf).

———. 2014f. "Global Public Downbeat about Economy." Global Attitudes & Trends, September 9. Accessed December 22, 2016 (www.pewglobal.org/2014/09/09/global-public-downbeat-about-economy/).

---. 2014g. "The Shifting Religious Identity of Latinos in the United States." Religion & Public Life, May 7. Accessed April 28, 2015 (www.pewforum.org/files/2014/05/Latinos-Religion-07-22-full-report.pdf).

---. 2015a. "Most Say Government Policies Since Recession Have Done Little to Help Middle Class, Poor." U.S. Politics & Policy Project, March 4. Accessed March 22, 2015 (www.people-press.org/files/2015/03/03-04-15-Economy-release.pdf).

---. 2015c. "In Debate Over Legalizing Marijuana, Disagreement Over Drugs Dangers." The Pew Research Center for the People & the Press April 15. Accessed November 10, 2016 (www.people-press.org/2015/04/14/in-debate-over-legalizing-marijuana-disagreement-over-drugs-dangers/).

---. 2015d. "Parenting in America." Washington, DC: Social & Demographic Trends Project, December 17. Accessed November 21, 2016 (www.pewsocialtrends.org/files/2015/12/2015-12-17_parenting-in-america_FINAL.pdf).

---. 2015e. "Raising Kids and Running a Household: How Working Parents Share the Load." Washington, DC: Social & Demographic Trends Project, November 4. Accessed November 22, 2016 (www.pewsocialtrends.org/files/2015/11/2015-11-04_working-parents_FINAL.pdf).

---. 2015f. "America's Changing Religious Landscape." Religion & Public Life, May 12. Accessed December 7, 2016 (www.pewforum.org/files/2015/05/RLS-08-26-full-report.pdf).

---. 2015g. "The Future of World Religions: Population Growth Projections, 2010–2050." Religion & Public Life, April. Accessed December 7, 2016 (www.pewforum.org/files/2015/03/PF_15.04.02_ProjectionsFullReport.pdf).

---. 2015h. "Beyond Distrust: How Americans View Their Government." U.S. Politics & Policy, November 23. Accessed December 15, 2016 (www.people-press.org/2015/11/23/beyond-distrust-how-americans-view-their-government/).

---. 2015i. "Party Identification." Accessed December 15, 2016 (www.pewresearch.org/data-trend/political-attitudes/party-identification/).

---. 2016a. "Budget Deficit Slips as Public Priority." The Pew Research Center for the People & the Press January 22. Accessed November 4, 2016 (www.people-press.org/2016/01/22/budget-deficit-slips-as-public-priority/).

---. 2016b. "Changing Attitudes on Gay Marriage." Religion & Public Life, May 12. Accessed November 22, 2016 (www.pewforum.org/2016/05/12/changing-attitudes-on-gay-marriage/).

---. 2016c. "The State of American Jobs." Social & Demographic Trends, October 6. Accessed December 14, 2016 (http://assets.pewresearch.org/wp-content/uploads/sites/3/2016/10/ST_2016.10.06_Future-of-Work_FINAL4.pdf).

---. 2016d. "Campaign Exposes Fissures Over Issues, Values, and How Life Has Changed in the U.S." U.S. Politics & Policy, March. Accessed December 22, 2016 (www.people-press.org/2016/03/31/campaign-exposes-fissures-over-issues-values-and-how-life-has-changed-in-the-u-s/).

---. 2016e. "Hispanic Population and Origin in Select U.S. Metropolitan Areas, 2014." Hispanic Trends, September 6. Accessed February 6, 2017 (www.pewhispanic.org/interactives/hispanic-population-in-select-u-s-metropolitan-areas/).

---. 2016f. "Obama Leaves Office on High Note, But Public Has Mixed Views of Accomplishments." U.S. Politics & Policy, December 14. Accessed Thursday, May 4, 2017 (http://assets.pewresearch.org/wp-content/uploads/sites/5/2016/12/14133019/12-14-16-Obama-legacy-release.pdf).

---. 2016g. "Party Identification Trends, 1992–2016." U.S. Politics & Policy, September 13. Accessed July 7, 2017 (www.people-press.org/2016/09/13/party-identification-trends-1992-2016/).

---. 2017. "After Seismic Political Shift, Modest Changes in Public's Policy Agenda." U.S. Politics and Policy, Pew Research Center, January 24. Accessed June 9, 2017 (www.people-press.org/2017/01/24/after-seismic-political-shift-modest-changes-in-publics-policy-agenda/).

Pfeffer, Carla A. 2017. *Queering Families: The Postmodern Partnerships of Cisgender Women and Transgender Men.* New York: Oxford University Press.

Pfeffer, Fabian T., and Alexdra Killewald. 2016. "Intergenerational Correlations in Wealth." Pp. 175–201 in *Economic Mobility: Research & Ideas on Strengthening Families, Communities, & the Economy.* St Louis, MO: Federal Reserve Bank of St. Louis. Accessed December 22, 2016 (www.stlouisfed.org/~/media/Files/PDFs/Community%20Development/EconMobilityPapers/Section2/EconMobility_2-3PfefferKillewald_508.pdf).

Pfeifer, Mark. 2008. "Vietnamese Americans." Pp. 1365–1368 in *Encyclopedia of Race, Ethnicity, and Society,* vol. 3, ed. Richard T. Schaefer. Thousand Oaks, CA: Sage.

Pierce, Jennifer L. 2013. "White Racism, Social Class, and the Backlash against Affirmative Action." *Sociology Compass* 7(11): 914–926.

Piketty, Thomas. 2014. *Capital in the Twenty-First Century.* Cambridge, MA: Belknap Press of Harvard University.

Piketty, Thomas, Emmanuel Saez, and Gabriel Zucman. 2016. "Distributional National Accounts: Methods and Estimates for the United States." National Bureau of Economic Research, Working Paper 22945, December. Accessed December 21, 2016 (http://gabriel-zucman.eu/usdina/).

Pinderhughes, Dianne. 1987. *Race and Ethnicity in Chicago Politics: A Reexamination of Pluralist Theory.* Urbana: University of Illinois Press.

Pinnow, Ellen, Pellavi Sharma, Ameeta Parekh, Natalie Gevorkian, and Kathleen Uhl. 2009. "Increasing Participation of Women in Early Phase Clinical Trials Approved by the FDA." *Women's Health Issues* 19 (2): 89–92.

Planty, M., W. Hussar, T. Snyder, G. Kena, A. Kewal-Ramani, J. Kemp, K. Bianco, and R. Dinkes. 2009. *The Condition of Education 2009.* NCES 2009-081. Washington, DC: National Center for Education Statistics, Institute of Education Sciences, U.S. Department of Education. Accessed May 29, 2009 (http://nces.ed.gov/pubs2009/2009081.pdf).

Planty, M., W. Hussar, T. Snyder, S. Provasnik, G. Kena, R. Dinkes, A. Kewal-Ramani, and J. Kemp. 2008. *The Condition of Education 2008.* NCES 2008-031. Washington, DC: National Center for Education Statistics, Institute of Education Sciences, U.S. Department of Education. Accessed June 14, 2008 (http://nces.ed.gov/pubs2008/2008031.pdf).

Plaut, Victoria C., Flannery G. Garnett, Laura E. Buffardi, and Jeffrey Sanchez-Burks. 2011. "What About Me? Perceptions of Exclusion and Whites Reactions to Multiculturalism." *Journal of Personality and Social Psychology* 101(2): 337–353.

Pollini, Jacques. 2009. "Agroforestry and the Search for Alternatives to Slash-and-Burn Cultivation: From Technological Optimism to a Political Economy of Deforestation." *Agriculture, Ecosystems & Environment* 133 (1/2): 48–60.

Pollster. 2016b. "Donald Trump Favorable Rating." *The Huffington Post.* Accessed December 15, 2016 (http://elections.huffingtonpost.com/pollster/donald-trump-favorable-rating).

---. 2016c. "Party Identification." *The Huffington Post.* Accessed December 15, 2016 (http://elections.huffingtonpost.com/pollster/party-identification).

Population Reference Bureau. 2016. *2016 World Population Data Sheet.* Washington, DC: Population Reference Bureau. Accessed October 25, 2016 (www.prb.org/Publications/Datasheets/2016/2016-world-population-data-sheet.aspx).

Porter, Roy. 1998. *The Greatest Benefit to Mankind: A Medical History of Humanity.* New York: HarperCollins.

---. 2004. *Blood and Guts: A Short History of Medicine.* New York: Norton.

Postman, Neil. 1988. "Questioning the Media." Video. The January Series, January 12. Grand Rapids, MI: Calvin College.
———. 1993. *Technopoly: The Surrender of Culture to Technology.* New York: Vintage Books.
———. 1999. *Building a Bridge to the 18th Century: How the Past Can Improve Our Future.* New York: Knopf.
Potts, John. 2009. *A History of Charisma.* New York: Palgrave Macmillan.
Poushter, Jacob. 2016. "Smartphone Ownership and Internet Usage Continues to Climb in Emerging Economies." Pew Research Center Global Attitudes & Trends, February 2016. Accessed October 31, 2016 (www.pewglobal.org/2016/02/22/smartphone-ownership-and-internet-usage-continues-to-climb-in-emerging-economies/).
Powell, James Lawrence. 2015. "Climate Scientists Virtually Unanimous: Anthropogenic Global Warming Is True." *Bulletin of Science, Technology, and Society* 35(5–6); 121–124.
Price, David A. 2003. *Love and Hate in Jamestown: John Smith, Pocahontas, and the Heart of a New Nation.* New York: Knopf.
Prior, Karen Swallow. 2013. "The Case for Getting Married Young." *The Atlantic,* March 22. Accessed February 26, 2015 (www.theatlantic.com/sexes/archive/2013/03/the-case-for-getting-married-young/274293/).
Proctor, Bernadette D., Jessica L. Semega, and Melissa A. Kollar. 2016. "Income and Poverty in the United States: 2015." *Current Population Reports* P60-256. Washington, DC: U.S. Government Printing Office. Accessed September 13, 2016 (www.census.gov/content/dam/Census/library/publications/2016/demo/p60-256.pdf).
Prohaska, Ariane, and Jeannine Gailey. 2010. "Achieving Masculinity Through Sexual Predation: The Case of Hogging." *Journal of Gender Studies* 19 (1): 13–25.
Project on Student Debt. 2016. "Student Debt and the Class of 2015: 11th Annual Report." The Institute for College Access and Success, Oakland, CA, October. Accessed December 14, 2016 (http://ticas.org/sites/default/files/pub_files/classof2015.pdf).
Provasnik, S., and Planty, M. 2008. *Community Colleges: Special Supplement to the Condition of Education 2008.* NCES 2008-033. Washington, DC: National Center for Education Statistics, Institute of Education Sciences, U.S. Department of Education. Accessed May 31, 2009 (http://nces.ed.gov/pubs2008/2008033.pdf).
Pryor, John H., Sylvia Hurtado, Victor B. Saenz, José Luis Santos, and William S. Korn. 2007. *The American Freshman: Forty-Year Trends.* Los Angeles: Higher Education Research Institute, UCLA.
Putnam, Robert D. 2015. *Our Kids: The American Dream in Crisis.* New York: Simon & Schuster.
Putnam, Robert D., and David E. Campbell. 2012. *American Grace: How Religion Divides and Unites Us.* New York: Simon & Schuster.

Q

Quinney, Richard. 1970. *The Social Reality of Crime.* Boston: Little, Brown.
———. 1974. *Criminal Justice in America.* Boston: Little, Brown.
———. 1979. *Criminology,* 2nd ed. Boston: Little, Brown.
———. 1980. *Class, State and Crime,* 2nd ed. New York: Longman.
Quinnipiac. 2016. "Overwhelming Support for No-Fly, No-Buy Gun Law, Quinnipiac University National Poll Finds; Support for Background Checks Tops 90 Percent Again." Quinnipiac University Poll, June 30. Accessed November 7, 2016 (https://poll.qu.edu/images/polling/us/us06302016_U37mhwbr.pdf/).
QuotaProject. 2014. "Mexico." Global Database of Quotas for Women. Accessed April 16, 2015 (www.quotaproject.org/uid/countryview.cfm?CountryCode=MX).

R

Radford, Jeremy, Danielle Battle, Stacey Bielick, and Sarah Grady. 2016. "Homeschooling in the United States: 2012." U.S. Department of Education, National Center for Education Statistics, NCES 2016-096, November. Accessed December 6, 2016 (http://nces.ed.gov/pubs2016/2016096.pdf).
Raghavan, Sudarsan. 2011. "Inspired by Tunisia and Egypt, Yemenis Join in Anti-government Protests." *The Washington Post,* January 27. Accessed May 28, 2012 (www.washingtonpost.com/wp-dyn/content/article/2011/01/27/AR2011012702081.html).
Rand, Robert. 2006. *Tamerlanes Children: Dispatches from Contemporary Uzbekistan.* Oxford: Oneworld.
Rank, Mark Robert, Thomas A. Hirschl, and Kirk A. Foster. 2014. *Chasing the American Dream: Understanding What Shapes Our Fortunes.* New York: Oxford University Press.
Ratner, Carl. 2004. "A Cultural Critique of Psychological Explanations of Terrorism." *Cross-Cultural Psychology Bulletin* 38 (1/2): 18–24.
Ravitz, Jessica. 2009. "Neda: Latest Iconic Image to Inspire." *CNN,* June 24. Accessed June 30, 2009 (www.cnn.com/2009/WORLD/meast/06/24/neda.iconic.images/).
Reardon, Sean F. 2011. "The Widening Academic Achievement Gap Between the Rich and the Poor: New Evidence and Possible Explanations." Pp. 91–115 in *Whither Opportunity?: Rising Inequality, Schools, and Childrens Life Chances,* ed. Greg J. Duncan and Richard J. Murnane. New York: Russell Sage Foundation.
Reddy, Gayatri. 2005. *With Respect to Sex: Negotiating Hijra Identity in South India.* Chicago: University of Chicago Press.
Reel, Justine J., Sonya SooHoo, Julia Franklin Summerhays, and Diane Gill. 2008. "Age Before Beauty: An Exploration of Body Image in African-American and Caucasian Adult Women." *Journal of Gender Studies* 17 (4): 321–330.
Reeves, Richard. 2015. *Infamy: The Shocking Story of the Japanese American Internment in World War II.* New York: Henry Holt and Company.
Reeves, Richard V. 2014. *Saving Horatio Alger: Equality, Opportunity, and the American Dream.* New York: Brookings Institution.
———. 2015. "Wealth, Inequality, and the Me? I'm Not Rich! Problem." *The Wall Street Journal,* February 27. Accessed March 22, 2015 (http://blogs.wsj.com/washwire/2015/02/27/wealth-inequality-and-the-me-im-not-rich-problem/).
Reginato, James. 2012. "The Talk of Mumbai." *Vanity Fair,* May 8. Accessed January 14, 2017 (www.vanityfair.com/style/2012/06/ambani-residence-photos-inside-architecture).
Reid, Luc. 2006. *Talk the Talk: The Slang of 65 American Subcultures.* Cincinnati, OH: Writers Digest Books.
Reinharz, Shulamit. 1992. *Feminist Methods in Social Research.* New York: Oxford University Press.
Reitman, Meredith. 2006. "Uncovering the White Place: Whitewashing at Work." *Social & Cultural Geography* 7 (2): 267–282.
Reitzes, Donald C., and Elizabeth J. Mutran. 2004. "The Transition to Retirement: Stages and Factors That Influence Retirement Adjustment." *International Journal of Aging & Human Development* 59 (1): 63–84.
Relerford, Patrice, Chao Xiong, Michael Rand, and Curt Brown. 2008. "42 Students Questioned, 13 Disciplined." *Minneapolis Star-Tribune,* January 10. Accessed June 30, 2009 (www.startribune.com/local/west/13663951.html).
Religious Tolerance. 2008. "Female Genital Mutilation (FGM): Informational Materials." Accessed March 1, 2008 (www.religioustolerance.org).
Renegar, Valerie R., and Stacey K. Sowards. 2009. "Contradiction as Agency: Self-Determination, Transcendence, and Counter-imagination in Third Wave Feminism." *Hypatia* 24 (2): 1–20.
Reynolds, John R., and Chardie L. Baird. 2010. "Is There a Downside to Shooting for the Stars? Unrealized Educational

Expectations and Symptoms of Depression." *American Sociological Review* 75 (1): 151–172.

Richardson, Sarah S. 2013. *Sex Itself: The Search for Male and Female in the Human Genome.* Chicago: University of Chicago Press.

Richtel, Matt. 2006. "The Long-Distance Journey of a Fast-Food Order." *The New York Times,* April 11. Accessed May 13, 2009 (www.nytimes.com/2006/04/11/technology/11fast.html).

Rideout, Victoria. 2015. *The Common Sense Census: Media Use by Tweens and Teens.* San Francisco: Common Sense. Accessed October 25, 2016 (www.commonsensemedia.org/sites/default/files/uploads/research/census_researchreport.pdf).

Risman, Barbara J. 1986. "Can Men Mother? Life as a Single Father." *Family Relations* 35 (1): 95–102.

Risman, Barbara J., and Danette Johnson-Sumerford. 1998. "Doing It Fairly: A Study of Postgender Marriages." *Journal of Marriage and Family* 60 (1): 23–40.

Ritzer, George. 2008. *The McDonaldization of Society 5.* Thousand Oaks, CA: Sage.

Roberson, Debi, Ian Davies, and Jules Davidoff. 2000. "Color Categories Are Not Universal: Replications and New Evidence from Stone Age Culture." *Journal of Experimental Psychology* 129 (3): 369–398.

Roberts, J. Timmons, Peter E. Grines, and Jodie L. Manale. 2003. "Social Roots of Global Environmental Change: A World-Systems Analysis of Carbon Dioxide Emissions." *Journal of World-Systems Research* 9 (Summer): 277–315.

Roberts, Sharon E., and James E. Côté. 2014. "The Identity Issues Inventory: Identity Stage Resolution in the Prolonged Transition to Adulthood." *Journal of Adult Development* 21: 225–238.

Rockefeller Foundation. 2016. "100x25: Achieving Gender Inclusivity in the Workplace." Accessed February 2, 2017 (www.rockefellerfoundation.org/our-work/initiatives/100x25/).

Rodriguez, Richard. 2002. *Brown: The Last Discovery of America.* New York: Penguin Books.

Rodwan, John, Jr. 2016. "Bottled Water 2013: Acceleration." *Bottled Water Reporter* 56 (July/August): 12–20. Accessed February 13, 2017 (www.bottledwater.org/newsroom/bottled-water-reporter).

Roeder, Oliver, Lauren-Brooke Eisen, and Julia Bowling. 2015. *What Caused the Crime Decline?* New York: Brennan Center for Justice at New York University School of Law. Accessed November 14, 2016 (www.brennancenter.org/publication/what-caused-crime-decline).

Roediger, David R. 2005. *Working Toward Whiteness: How Americas Immigrants Became White.* New York: Basic Books.

Romans, Sarah, Rose Clarkson, Gillian Einstein, Michele Petrovic, and Donna Stewart. 2012. "Mood and the Menstrual Cycle: A Review of Prospective Data Studies." *Gender Medicine* 9 (5): 361–384.

Rootes, Christopher. 2007. "Acting Locally: The Character, Contexts and Significance of Local Environmental Mobilisations." *Environmental Politics* 16 (5): 722–741.

Roscoe, Will. 1997. "Gender Diversity in Native North America: Notes Toward a Unified Analysis." Pp. 65–81 in *A Queer World: The Center for Lesbian and Gay Studies Reader,* ed. Martin Duberman. New York: New York University Press.

Rose, Arnold. 1951. *The Roots of Prejudice.* Paris: UNESCO.

Rosen, William. 2010. *The Most Powerful Idea in the World: A Story of Steam, Industry, and Invention.* New York: Random House.

Rosenfeld, Michael J., and Reuben J. Thomas. 2012. "Searching for a Mate: The Rise of the Internet as a Social Intermediary." *American Sociological Review* 77: 523–547.

Rosenfeld, Richard, and Robert Fornango. 2014. "The Impact of Police Stops on Precinct Robbery and Burglary Rates in New York City, 2003-2010." *Justice Quarterly* 31(1): 96–122.

Rosenthal, Robert, and Lenore Jacobson. 1968. *Pygmalion in the Classroom.* New York: Henry Holt.

Rosin, Hanna. 2014. "The Overprotected Kid." *The Atlantic,* April. Accessed February 2, 2015 (www.theatlantic.com/features/archive/2014/03/hey-parents-leave-those-kids-alone/358631/).

Rossi, Alice S. 1968. "Transition to Parenthood." *Journal of Marriage and Family* 30 (February): 26–39.

———. 1984. "Gender and Parenthood." *American Sociological Review* 49 (February): 1–19.

Rossi Del Corso, Annalisa, and Margherita Lanz. 2013. "Felt Obligation and the Family Cycle: A Study on Intergenerational Relationships." *International Journal of Psychology* 48: 1196–1200.

Rothman, Joshua. 2016. "How to Restore Your Faith in Democracy." *The New Yorker,* November 11. Accessed December 13, 2016 (www.newyorker.com/culture/persons-of-interest/how-to-restore-your-faith-in-democracy).

Rothstein, Jeffrey S. 2016. *When Good Jobs Go Bad: Globalization, De-Unionization, and Declining Job Quality in the North American Auto Industry.* New Brunswick, NJ: Rutgers University Press.

Rothstein, Richard. 2009. "Equalizing Opportunity: Dramatic Differences in Children's Home Life and Health Mean That Schools Can't Do It Alone." *American Educator* 33 (2): 4–7, 45–46. Accessed April 26, 2010 (http://archive.aft.org/pubs-reports/american_educator/issues/summer2009/equalizingopportunity.pdf).

Rotman, David. 2013. "How Technology Is Destroying Jobs." *MIT Technology Review,* June 12. Accessed March 17, 2015 (www.technologyreview.com/featuredstory/515926/how-technology-is-destroying-jobs/).

Rowland, Christopher, ed. 2007. *The Cambridge Companion to Liberation Theology,* 2nd ed. New York: Cambridge University Press.

Rubie-Davies, Christine M. 2010. "Teacher Expectations and Perceptions of Student Attributes: Is There a Relationship?" *British Journal of Educational Psychology* 80 (1): 121–135.

Rubin, Alissa J. 2003. "Pat-Down on the Way to Prayer." *Los Angeles Times,* November 25, pp. A1, A5.

Rubin, Mark, Nida Denson, Sue Kilpatrick, Kelly E. Matthews, Tom Stehlik, and David Zyngier. 2014. "I Am Working Class: Subjective Self-Definition as a Missing Measure of Social Class and Socioeconomic Status in Higher Education Research." *Educational Researcher* 43: 196–200.

Ruetschlin, Christina M., and Abdul Karim Bangura. 2012. "Transnational Organized Crime: A Global Concern." *International Journal of Diversity* 2012 (3): 94–102.

Ruiz, Ariel G., Jie Zong, and Jeanne Batalova. 2015. "Immigrant Women in the United States." Migration Policy Institute March 20. Access February 7, 2017 (www.migrationpolicy.org/article/immigrant-women-united-states).

Rutter, Michael. 2010. "Gene Environment Interplay." *Depression and Anxiety* 27: 1–4.

Rutter, Michael, Terrie E. Moffitt, and Avshalom Caspi. 2006. "Gene-Environment Interplay and Psychopathology: Multiple Varieties but Real Effects." *Journal of Child Psychology and Psychiatry* 47 (3/4): 226–261.

Rymer, Russ. 1993. *Genie: An Abused Child's Flight from Science.* New York: HarperCollins.

S

Saad, Lydia. 2004. "Divorce Doesn't Last." *Gallup Poll Tuesday Briefing,* March 30 (www.gallup.com/poll/11161/divorce-doesnt-last.aspx).

———. 2015. "Fewer Young People Say I Do—To Any Relationship." Gallup, June 8. Accessed November 22, 2016 (www.gallup.com/poll/183515/fewer-young-people-say-relationship.aspx).

Sacks, Peter. 2007. *Tearing Down the Gates: Confronting the Class Divide in American Education.* Berkeley: University of California Press.

References

Sadat, Sayed Masood, Christina Satkowski, Renard Shamim Sarabi, Sandy Feinzig, Shahim Kabuli, Charlotte Maxwell-Jones, and Zachary Warren. 2015. *Afghanistan in 2015: A Survey of the Afghan People.* San Francisco: The Asia Foundation. Accessed September 23, 2016 (https://asiafoundation.org/resources/pdfs/Afghanistanin2015.pdf).

Saez, Emmanuel. 2016. "Striking It Richer: The Evolution of Top Incomes in the United States (Updated with 2015 preliminary estimates)." Center for Equitable Growth, June 30. Accessed December 14, 2016 (http://eml.berkeley.edu/~saez/saez-UStopincomes-2015.pdf).

Saez, Emmanuel, and Gabriel Zucman. 2016. "Wealth Inequality in the United States since 1913: Evidence from Capitalized Income Tax Data." *Quarterly Journal of Economics* 131(2): 519–578. Accessed December 22, 2016 (http://gabriel-zucman.eu/uswealth/).

Saint Martin, Manuel L. 1999. "Running Amok: A Modern Perspective on a Culture-Bound Syndrome." *The Primary Care Companion to the Journal of Clinical Psychiatry* 1(3): 66–70.

Salganik, Matthew J., Peter Sheridan Dodds, and Duncan J. Watts. 2006. "Experimental Study of Inequality and Unpredictability in an Artificial Cultural Market." *Science* 311: 854–856.

Salinas, Brenda. 2014. "'Columbusing': The Art of Discovering Something That Is Not New." *NPR Code Switch,* July 6. Accessed September 30, 2016 (www.npr.org/sections/codeswitch/2014/07/06/328466757/columbusing-the-art-of-discovering-something-that-is-not-new).

Sample, Ian. 2014. "Anthropocene: Is This the New Epoch of Humans?" *The Guardian,* October 16. Accessed May 2, 2015 (www.theguardian.com/science/2014/oct/16/-sp-scientists-gather-talks-rename-human-age-anthropocene-holocene).

Sampson, Robert J., and Stephen W. Raudenbush. 2004. "Seeing Disorder: Neighborhood Stigma and the Social Construction of 'Broken Windows.'" *Social Psychology Quarterly* 67(4): 319–342.

Sanday, Peggy Reeves. 2002. *Women at the Center: Life in a Modern Matriarchy.* Ithaca, NY: Cornell University Press.

———. 2008. Homepage. Accessed March 15 (www.sas.upenn.edu/~psanday).

Sandberg, Sheryl. *Lean In: Women, Work, and the Will to Lead.* New York: Alfred A. Knopf.

Sandler, Ronald, and Phaedra C. Pezzullo, eds. 2007. *Environmental Justice and Environmentalism: The Social Justice Challenge to the Environmental Movement.* Cambridge, MA: MIT Press.

Sarachild, Kathie. 1978. "Consciousness-Raising: A Radical Weapon." Pp. 144–150 in *Feminist Revolution.* New York: Random House. Accessed June 30, 2009 (http://scriptorium.lib.duke.edu/wlm/fem/sarachild.html).

Sarkeesian, Anita. 2013. "Damsel in Distress (Part 1) Tropes vs Women." *Feminist Frequency: Conversations with Pop Culture,* March 7. Accessed May 20, 2013 (www.feministfrequency.com/2013/03/damsel-in-distress-part-1/).

Sarkisian, Natalia, and Naomi Gerstel. 2016. "Does Singlehood Isolate or Integrate? Examining the Link Between Marital Status and Ties to Kin, Friends, and Neighbors." *Journal of Social and Personal Relationships* 33(3): 361–384.

Sassen, Saskia. 2005. "New Global Classes: Implications for Politics." Pp. 143–170 in *The New Egalitarianism,* ed. Anthony Giddens and Patrick Diamond. Cambridge, UK: Polity Press.

Sawhill, Isabel V. 2006. "Teenage Sex, Pregnancy, and Nonmarital Births." *Gender Issues* 23 (4): 48–59.

Scally, Corianne Payton. 2015. "Democracy in Action?: NIMBY as Impediment to Equitable Affordable Housing Siting." *Housing Studies* 30(5): 749–69.

Scarce, Rik. 1994. "(No) Trial (but) Tribulations: When Courts and Ethnography Conflict." *Journal of Contemporary Ethnography* 23 (July): 123–149.

———. 1995. "Scholarly Ethics and Courtroom Antics: Where Researchers Stand in the Eyes of the Law." *American Sociologist* 26 (Spring): 87–112.

———. 2005a. "A Law to Protect Scholars." *Chronicle of Higher Education,* August 12, p. 324.

———. 2005b. *Contempt of Court: A Scholars Battle for Free Speech from Behind Bars.* Lanham, MD: AltaMira Press.

Scelfo, Julie. 2008. "Baby, You're Home." *The New York Times,* November 12. Accessed June 29, 2009 (www.nytimes.com/2008/11/13/garden/13birth.html).

Schachtman, Tom. 2006. *Rumspringa: To Be or Not to Be Amish.* New York: North Point Press.

Schaefer, Richard T. 1998a. "Differential Racial Mortality and the 1995 Chicago Heat Wave." Paper presented at the annual meeting of the American Sociological Association, August, San Francisco.

Schaefer, Richard T., and William W. Zellner. 2007. *Extraordinary Groups,* 8th ed. New York: Worth.

Schaffer, Scott. 2004. *Resisting Ethics.* New York: Palgrave Macmillan.

Scharnberg, Kirsten. 2007. "Black Market for Midwives Defies Bans." *Chicago Tribune,* November 25, pp. 1, 10.

Scherbov, Sergei, Wolfgang Lutz, and Warren C. Sanderson. 2011. "The Uncertain Timing of Reaching 7 Billion and Peak Population." International Institute for Applied Systems Analysis, Interim Report IR-11-002, February 21. Accessed June 29, 2011 (www.iiasa.ac.at/Admin/PUB/Documents/IR-11-002.pdf).

Schlosberg, David. 2013. "Theorising Environmental Justice: The Expanding Sphere of a Discourse." *Environmental Politics* 22(1): 37–55.

Schmeeckle, Maria. 2007. "Gender Dynamics in Stepfamilies: Adult Stepchildren's Views." *Journal of Marriage and Family* 69 (February): 174–189.

Schmeeckle, Maria, Roseann Giarrusso, Du Feng, and Vern L. Bengtson. 2006. "What Makes Someone Family? Adult Children's Perceptions of Current and Former Stepparents." *Journal of Marriage and Family* 68 (August): 595–610.

Schneier, Bruce. 2015. *Data and Goliath: The Hidden Battles to Collect Your Data and Control Your World.* New York: W. W. Norton & Company.

Schroeder, Michael O. 2016. "Racial Bias in Medicine Leads to Worse Care for Minorities." *U.S. News & World Report* February 11. Accessed February 12, 2017 (http://health.usnews.com/health-news/patient-advice/articles/2016-02-11/racial-bias-in-medicine-leads-to-worse-care-for-minorities).

Schultz, David. 2016. "Should We Bring Extinct Species Back from the Dead?" *Science* September 26. Accessed February 15, 2017 (www.sciencemag.org/news/2016/09/should-we-bring-extinct-species-back-dead).

Schur, Edwin M. 1965. *Crimes Without Victims: Deviant Behavior and Public Policy.* Englewood Cliffs, NJ: Prentice Hall.

———. 1985. "Crimes Without Victims: A 20-Year Reassessment." Paper presented at the annual meeting of the Society for the Study of Social Problems.

Schurman, Rachel. 2004. "Fighting Frankenfoods: Industry Opportunity Structures and the Efficacy of the Anti-biotech Movement in Western Europe." *Social Problems* 51 (2): 243–268.

Schwartz, Pepper. 2006. *Finding Your Perfect Match.* New York: Perigee Books.

Scott, Greg. 2005. "Public Symposium: HIV/AIDS, Injection Drug Use and Men Who Have Sex with Men." Pp. 38–39 in *Scholarship with a Mission,* ed. Susanna Pagliaro. Chicago: De Paul University.

Semigran, Hannah L., Jeffrey Linder, Courtney Gidengil, and Ateev Mehrotra. 2015. "Evaluation of Symptom Checkers for Self Diagnosis and Triage: Audit Study." *BMJ* 351: H3480.

Senter, Mary S. 2016. "Individual Salary Is Not Enough: Measuring the Well-Being of Recent College Graduates in Sociology." Bachelors and Beyond Series, August. Washington, DC: American Sociological Association. Accessed August 30, 2016 (www.asanet.

org/research-and-publications/research-sociology/research-briefs/individual-salary-not-enough).

Senter, Mary S., Roberta Spalter-Roth, and Nicole Van Vooren. 2015. "Jobs, Careers, & Sociological Skills." Bachelors and Beyond Series, February. Washington, DC: American Sociological Association. Accessed August 30, 2016 (www.asanet.org/research-and-publications/research-sociology/research-briefs/jobs-careers-sociological-skills-early-employment-experiences-2012-sociology-majors)

Shaheen, Jack. 2006. *Reel Bad Arabs: How Hollywood Vilifies a People.* Video. Directed by Sut Jhally. 50 minutes. Northampton, MA: Media Education Foundation.

———. 2009. *Reel Bad Arabs: How Hollywood Vilifies a People,* 2nd ed. New York: Olive Branch Press.

———. 2012. "The Making of the Green Menace." *The Nation,* July 2–9: 15–17.

Shannon-Missal, Larry. 2015. "More than Ever, Pets Are Members of the Family." The Harris Poll, July 16. Accessed November 21, 2016 (www.theharrispoll.com/health-and-life/Pets-are-Members-of-the-Family.html).

Shapiro, Thomas M. 2004. *The Hidden Cost of Being African American: How Wealth Perpetuates Inequality.* New York: Oxford University Press.

Sharp, Gwen. 2011. "Two News Stories About Gabrielle Giffords' Shooting . . . and Husband." *Sociological Images,* January 9. Accessed March 10, 2012 (http://thesocietypages.org/socimages/2011/01/09/two-news-stories-about-gabrielle-giffords-shooting-and-husband/).

Shaw, Clifford R., and Henry D. McKay. 1969. *Juvenile Delinquency and Urban Areas.* Chicago: University of Chicago Press.

Shaw, Jessica C. 2013. "The Medicalization of Birth and Midwifery as Resistance." *Health Care for Women International* 34: 522–536.

Shenk, David. 2010. *The Genius in All of Us: Why Everything You've Been Told About Genetics, Talent, and IQ Is Wrong.* New York: Doubleday.

Shenker, Jack, Angelique Chrisafis, Lauren Williams, Tom Finn, Giles Tremlett, and Martin Chulov. 2011. "Young Arabs Who Can't Wait to Throw Off Shackles of Tradition." *The Guardian,* February 14. Accessed May 28, 2012 (www.guardian.co.uk/world/2011/feb/14/young-arabs-throw-off-shackles-tradition).

Sheskin, Ira, and Arnold Dashefsky. 2016. "Jewish Population of the United States, 2015." *Current Jewish Population Reports* No. 13. Accessed February 6, 2017 (www.jewishdatabank.org/Studies/downloadFile.cfm?FileID=3393).

Shi, Yu. 2008. "Chinese Immigrant Women Workers: Everyday Forms of Resistance and Coagulate Politics." *Communication and Critical/Cultural Studies* 5 (4): 363–382.

Shields, Stephanie A. 2008. "Gender: An Intersectionality Perspective." *Sex Roles* 59 (5/6): 301–311.

Shilts, Randy. 1987. *And the Band Played On: Politics, People, and the AIDS Epidemic.* New York: St. Martin's Press.

Shipler, David K. 2004. *The Working Poor: Invisible in America.* New York: Knopf.

Shirky, Clay. 2008. *Here Comes Everybody: The Power of Organizing Without Organizations.* New York: Penguin Books.

Shorrocks, Anthony, James B. Davies, and Rodrigo Lluberas. 2016. *Global Wealth Databook 2016.* Zurich: Credit Suisse Research Institute. Accessed January 14, 2017 (http://publications.credit-suisse.com/tasks/render/file/index.cfm?fileid=AD6F2B43-B17B-345E-E20A1A254A3E24A5).

Shostak, Arthur B. 2002. "Clinical Sociology and the Art of Peace Promotion: Earning a World Without War." Pp. 325–345 in *Using Sociology: An Introduction from the Applied and Clinical Perspectives,* ed. Roger A. Straus. Lanham, MD: Rowman & Littlefield.

Showden, Carisa R. 2009. "What's Political About the New Feminisms?" *Frontiers: A Journal of Women Studies* 30 (2): 166–198.

Shrivastava, Bhuma, and Anto Antony. 2015. "Mumbai Is Overflowing with Garbage." Live Mint, July 27. Accessed June 2, 2017 (www.livemint.com/Politics/XUNshUdRrpzuHsV9HDd1TO/Mumbai-is-overflowing-with-garbage.html).

Silva, Tony. 2016. "Bud-Sex: Constructing Normative Masculinity among Rural Straight Men that Have Sex with Men." *Gender & Society* 31(1): 51–73.

Silver, Ira. 1996. "Role Transitions, Objects, and Identity." *Symbolic Interaction* 10 (1): 1–20.

Silver, Nate. 2015. "The Most Diverse Cities Are often the Most Segregated." *FiveThirtyEight,* May 1. Accessed February 4, 2017 (https://fivethirtyeight.com/features/the-most-diverse-cities-are-often-the-most-segregated/).

———. 2016. "Who Will Win the Presidency?" *FiveThirtyEight,* November 8. Accessed December 13, 2016 (http://projects.fivethirtyeight.com/2016-election-forecast/).

Simmons, Tavia, and Martin O'Connell. 2003. "Married-Couple and Unmarried-Partner Households: 2000." *Census 2000 Special Reports,* CENBR-5. Washington, DC: U.S. Government Printing Office.

Singel, Ryan. 2008. "FBI Tried to Cover Patriot Act Abuses with Flawed, Retroactive Subpoenas, Audit Finds." *Wired,* March 13. Accessed June 30, 2009 (www.wired.com/threatlevel/2008/03/fbi-tried-to-co).

Sklar, Robert. 1994. *Movie-Made America: A Cultural History of American Movies.* Revised and Updated. New York: Vintage Books.

Sluiter, Engel. 1997. "New Light on the 20. and Odd Negroes Arriving in Virginia, August 1619." *The William and Mary Quarterly* 54: 395–398.

Small Arms Survey. 2011. "Estimating Civilian Owned Firearms." Graduate Institute of International and Development Studies, Geneva, Switzerland, *Research Note* 9 (September). Accessed May 23, 2013 (www.smallarmssurvey.org/fileadmin/docs/H-Research_Notes/SAS-Research-Note-9.pdf).

Smiley, Tavis, and Cornel West. 2012. "America's New Working Poor." *Salon,* May 1. Accessed May 22, 2012 (www.salon.com/2012/05/01/working_in_poverty/).

Smith, Aaron. 2016. "15% of American Adults Have Used Online Dating Sites or Mobile Dating Apps." Pew Research Center February 11. Accessed November 18, 2016 (www.pewinternet.org/files/2016/02/PI_2016.02.11_Online-Dating_FINAL.pdf).

Smith, Adam. [1776] 2003. *The Wealth of Nations.* New York: Bantam Classics.

Smith, Aaron, and Janna Anderson. 2014. "AI, Robotics, and the Future of Jobs." Pew Research Center, Internet, Science & Tech, August 6. Accessed March 18, 2015 (www.pewinternet.org/files/2014/08/Future-of-AI-Robotics-and-Jobs.pdf).

Smith, Dorothy E. 1987. *The Everyday World as Problematic: A Feminist Sociology.* Boston: Northeastern University Press.

Smith, Erica L., and Alexia Cooper. 2013. "Homicide in the U.S. Known to Law Enforcement, 2011." Bureau of Justice Statistics, December, NCJ 24035. Accessed February 19, 2015 (www.bjs.gov/content/pub/pdf/hus11.pdf).

Smith, Stacy L., Marc Choueiti, and Katherine Pieper. 2016. "Race/Ethnicity in 800 Popular Films: Examining Portrayals of Gender, Race/Ethnicity, LGBT, and Disability from 2007–2015." Media, Diversity, & Social Change Initiative, Annenberg School of Communication & Journalism, September. Accessed February 4, 2017 (http://annenberg.usc.edu/pages/~/media/MDSCI/Dr%20Stacy%20L%20Smith%20Inequality%20in%20800%20Films%20FINAL.ashx).

Smith, Tom W. 2004. "Coming of Age in Twenty-first Century America: Public Attitudes Towards the Importance and Timing of Transitions to Adulthood." *Ageing International* 29 (2): 136–148.

———. 2006. "American Sexual Behavior: Trends, Socio-Demographic Differences, and Risk Behavior." National Opinion Research Center, University of Chicago, GSS Topical Report No. 25. Updated March, 2006. Accessed May 12, 2010 (www.norc.org/NR/rdonlyres/2663F09F-2E74-436E-AC81-6FFBF288E183/0/AmericanSexualBehavior2006.pdf).

———. 2011. "Public Attitudes toward Homosexuality." NORC/University of Chicago, September 2011. Accessed May 26, 2012 (www.norc.org/PDFs/2011%20GSS%20Reports/GSS_Public%20Attitudes%20Toward%20Homosexuality_Sept2011.pdf).

Smith, Tom W., Peter Marsden, Michael Hout, and Jibum Kim. 2014. *General Social Surveys, 1972–2012.* Chicago: National Opinion Research Center.

Social Security Administration. 2014. "Baby Names." Accessed September 26, 2016 (www.ssa.gov/oact/babynames/index.html).

Social Security Administration. 2016. *Fast Facts & Figures about Social Security, 2016.* Office of Retirement and Disability Policy, Office of Research, Evaluation, and Statistics, Washington, DC, SSA Publication No. 13-11785, August. Accessed October 25, 2016 (www.ssa.gov/policy/docs/chartbooks/fast_facts/2016/fast_facts16.pdf).

Soderstrom, Melanie. 2007. "Beyond Babytalk: Re-evaluating the Nature and Content of Speech Input to Preverbal Infants." *Developmental Review* 27: 501–532.

Solomon, Andrew. 2016. "'The Good Death,' 'When Breath Becomes Air,' and More." *The New York Times,* February 8. Accessed October 25, 2016 (www.nytimes.com/2016/02/14/books/review/the-good-death-when-breath-becomes-air-and-more.html).

Solove, Daniel J. 2008. "Do Social Networks Bring the End of Privacy?" *Scientific American* 299 (September): 100–106. Accessed June 30, 2009 (www.scientificamerican.com/article.cfm?id5do-social-networks-bring).

Sorokin, Pitirim A. [1927] 1959. *Social and Cultural Mobility.* New York: Free Press.

Spalter-Roth, Roberta, and Nicole Van Vooren. 2008. "What Are They Doing with a Bachelor's Degree in Sociology?" American Sociological Association Department of Research and Development. Washington, DC: ASA. Accessed March 25, 2010 (www.asanet.org/images/research/docs/pdf/What%20Are%20They%20Doing%20with%20BA%20in%20Soc.pdf).

———. 2009. "Idealists vs. Careerists: Graduate School Choices of Sociology Majors." American Sociological Association Department of Research and Development. Washington, DC: ASA. Accessed March 25, 2010 (www.asanet.org/images/research/docs/pdf/Idealist%20vs%20Careerisst.pdf).

———. 2010. "Mixed Success: Four Years of Experiences of 2005 Sociology Graduates." American Sociological Association Department of Research and Development. Washington, DC: American Sociological Association. Accessed May 5, 2011 (www.asanet.org/research/BBMixedSuccessBrief.pdf).

Spalter-Roth, Roberta, Nicole Van Vooren, Michael Kisielewski, and Mary S. Senter. 2012. "Recruiting Sociology Majors: What Are the Effects of the Great Recession?" American Sociological Association, Department of Research & Development, November. Accessed April 26, 2013 (www.asanet.org/documents/research/pdfs/Bachelors_and_Beyond_2012_Brief2_Recruiting.pdf).

Spangler, Todd. 2016. "Man Who Pirated 'The Revenant' Ordered to Pay $1.1 Million to 20th Century Fox." *Variety,* September 30. Accessed November 11, 2016 (http://variety.com/2016/digital/news/revenant-peanuts-movie-piracy-1-1-million-20th-century-fox-1201874892/).

Spores, John C. 1988. *Running Amok: An Historical Inquiry.* Athens: Ohio University Press.

Sprague, Joey. 2005. *Feminist Methodologies for Critical Research: Bridging Differences.* Lanham, MD: AltaMira Press.

Springsteen, Bruce. 2016. "On Jersey, Masculinity and Wishing to Be His Stage Persona." Interview by Terry Gross. *NPR Fresh Air* October 4. Accessed October 31, 2016 (www.npr.org/2016/10/05/496639696/bruce-springsteen-on-jersey-masculinity-and-wishing-to-be-his-stage-persona).

Squire, Peverill. 1988. "Why the 1936 *Literary Digest* Poll Failed." *Public Opinion Quarterly* 52: 125–133.

Srinivas, M. N. 1956. "A Note on Sanskritization and Westernization." *The Far Eastern Quarterly* 15: 481–496.

Staal, J. F. 1963. "Sanskrit and Sanskritization." *Journal of Asian Studies* 22: 261–275.

Staats, Cheryl, Kelly Capatosto, Robin A. Wright, and Victoria W. Jackson. 2016. *State of the Science: Implicit Bias Review,* 2016 Edition. Columbus, OH: Kirwan Institute for the Study of Race and Ethnicity, The Ohio State University. Accessed October 21, 2016 (http://kirwaninstitute.osu.edu/my-product_category/implicit-bias/).

Stack, Carol. 1974. *All Our Kin: Strategies for Survival in a Black Community.* New York: Harper & Row.

Standish, Peter, and Steven Bell. 2004. *Culture and Customs of Mexico.* Santa Barbara, CA: Greenwood Press.

Stapleton, AnneClair, and Ralph Ellis. 2016. "Timeline of Orlando Nightclub Shooting." *CNN,* June 17. Accessed November 3, 2016 (www.cnn.com/2016/06/12/us/orlando-shooting-timeline/).

Stark, Rodney, and William Sims Bainbridge. 1979. "Of Churches, Sects, and Cults: Preliminary Concepts for a Theory of Religious Movements." *Journal for the Scientific Study of Religion* 18 (June): 117–131.

———. 1985. *The Future of Religion.* Berkeley: University of California Press.

Starr, Paul. 1982. *The Social Transformation of American Medicine.* New York: Basic Books.

Steele, Jonathan. 2005. "Annan Attacks Britain and U.S. over Erosion of Human Rights." *Guardian Weekly,* March 16, p. 1.

Steiblin, Caroline, and Frank-Stephan Graef. 2015. *Prices and Earnings 2015: Do I Earn Enough for the Life I Want?* Zurich: UBS Switzerland AG. Accessed January 18, 2017 (www.ubs.com/microsites/prices-earnings/prices-earnings.html).

Steidle, Brian. 2007. *The Devil Came on Horseback: Bearing Witness to the Genocide in Darfur.* New York: PublicAffairs.

Steinmetz, Katy. 2016. "Merriam-Webster Adds 'FOMO,' 'Mx.' and About 2,000 Other Words." *Time Magazine,* April 20. Accessed October 5, 2016 (http://time.com/4299634/merriam-webster-fomo-mx-dox-update/).

Stenning, Derrick J. 1958. "Household Viability Among the Pastoral Fulani." Pp. 92–119 in *The Developmental Cycle in Domestic Groups,* ed. John R. Goody. Cambridge, UK: Cambridge University Press.

Stepler, Renee, and Anna Brown. 2016. "Statistical Portrait of Hispanics in the United States." Pew Research Center, Hispanic Trends April 19. Accessed February 6, 2017 (www.pewhispanic.org/2016/04/19/statistical-portrait-of-hispanics-in-the-united-states/).

Sterbenz, Christina. 2014. "Marriage Rates Are Near Their Lowest Levels in History—Here's Why." *Business Insider,* May 7. Accessed February 26, 2015 (www.businessinsider.com/causes-of-low-marriage-rates-2014-5).

Stevenson, Mark. 2011. "Money Sent Home by Mexican Migrants Holds Steady." *Chron,* February 1. Accessed June 13, 2011 (www.chron.com/disp/story.mpl/business/7408082.html).

Steverman, Ben. 2016. "Boomers Are Making Sure the Divorces Keep Coming." *Bloomberg,* June 17. Accessed November 23, 2016 (www.bloomberg.com/news/articles/2016-06-17/boomers-are-making-sure-the-divorces-keep-coming).

Stewart, Quincy Thomas. 2006. "Reinvigorating Relative Deprivation: A New Measure for a Classic Concept." *Social Science Research* 35 (3): 779–802.

Stewart, Susan D. 2007. *Brave New Stepfamilies: Diverse Paths Toward Stepfamily Living.* Thousand Oaks, CA: Sage.

Stoeckel, Luke E., Lori S. Palley, Randy L. Gollub, Steven M. Niemi, and Anne Eden Evins. 2014. "Patterns of Brain Activation When Mothers View Their Own Child and Dog: An fMRI Study." *PLoS ONE* 9 (10): e107205. Accessed February 26, 2015 (http://journals.plos.org/plosone/article?id = 10.1371/journal.pone.0107205).

Stone, Charley, Carl Van Horn, and Cliff Zukin. 2012. "Chasing the American Dream: Recent College Graduates and the Great Recession." WorkTrends: Americans' Attitudes About Work, Employers, and Government, John J. Heldrich Center for Workforce Development, Rutgers University, May 2012. Accessed May 22, 2012 (www.heldrich.rutgers.edu/sites/default/files/content/-Chasing_American_Dream_Report.pdf).

Strassman, Beverly I. 1999. "Menstrual Synchrony Pheromones: Cause for Doubt." *Human Reproduction* 14 (3): 579–580.

Stratton, Terry D., and Jennifer L. McGivern-Snofsky. 2008. "Toward a Sociological Understanding of Complementary and Alternative Medicine Use." *Journal of Alternative and Complementary Medicine* 14 (6): 777–783.

Streib, Jessi. 2011. "Class Reproduction by Four-Year-Olds." *Qualitative Sociology* 34 (2): 337–352.

Strogatz, Steven. 2012. "Friends You Can Count On." *The New York Times,* September 17. Accessed February 11, 2015 (http://opinionator.blogs.nytimes.com/2012/09/17/friends-you-can-count-on/).

Stulberg, Lisa M., and Anthony S. Chen. 2014. "The Origins of Race-Conscious Affirmative Action in Undergraduate Admissions: A Comparative Analysis of Institutional Change in Higher Education." *Sociology of Education* 87(1): 36–52.

Suellentrop, Chris. 2016. "Who Says Games Need to Be Fair?" *Slate,* October 14. Accessed October 27, 2016 (www.slate.com/articles/technology/gaming/2016/10/really_bad_chess_proves_that_games_don_t_need_to_be_fair.html).

Sullivan, Kevin. 2006. "In War-Torn Congo, Going Wireless to Reach Home." *The Washington Post,* July 9. Accessed May 6, 2009 (www.washingtonpost.com/wp-dyn/content/article/2006/07/08/AR2006070801063.html).

Sumner, William G. 1906. *Folkways.* New York: Ginn.

Sun, Yongmin, and Yuanzhang Li. 2008. "Stable Postdivorce Family Structures During Late Adolescence and Socioeconomic Consequences in Adulthood." *Journal of Marriage and Family* 70 (1): 129–143.

Susen, Simon. 2015. *The 'Postmodern Turn' in the Social Sciences.* London: Palgrave Macmillan.

Susskind, Richard, and Daniel Susskind. 2015. *The Future of Professions: How Technology Will Transform the Work of Human Experts.* New York: Oxford University Press.

Sutherland, Edwin H. 1940. "White-Collar Criminality." *American Sociological Review* 5 (February): 1–11.

———. 1949. *White Collar Crime.* New York: Dryden.

———. 1983. *White Collar Crime: The Uncut Version.* New Haven, CT: Yale University Press.

Sutherland, Edwin H., Donald R. Cressey, and David F. Luckenbill. 1992. *Principles of Criminology,* 11th ed. New York: Rowman & Littlefield.

Suzuki, Toru. 2009. "Fertility Decline and Governmental Interventions in Eastern Asian Advanced Countries." *Japanese Journal of Population* 7 (1): 47–56.

Swatos, William H., Jr. 2011. "Encyclopedia of Religion and Society." Hartford Institute for Religion Research, Hartford Seminary, Hartford, Connecticut. Accessed June 6, 2011 (http://hirr.hartsem.edu/ency/).

Swatos, William H., Jr., ed. 1998. *Encyclopedia of Religion and Society.* Lanham, MD: AltaMira Press.

Sweet, Stephen, and Peter Meiksins. 2017. *Changing Contours of Work: Jobs and Opportunities in the New Economy,* 3rd ed. Thousand Oaks, CA: Sage Publications, Inc.

Sweig, Julia E. 2016. *Cuba: What Everyone Needs to Know.* New York: Oxford University Press.

Swidler, Ann. 1986. "Culture in Action: Symbols and Strategies." *American Sociological Review* 51 (April): 273–286.

Szasz, Thomas S. 1971. "The Same Slave: An Historical Note on the Use of Medical Diagnosis as Justificatory Rhetoric." *American Journal of Psychotherapy* 25 (April): 228–239.

T

Tafur, Maritza Montiel, Terry K. Crowe, and Eliseo Torres. 2009. "A Review of Curanderismo and Healing Practices Among Mexicans and Mexican Americans." *Occupational Therapy International* 16 (1): 82–88.

Tajfel, Henri. 1981. *Human Groups and Social Categories: Studies in Social Psychology.* Cambridge: Cambridge University Press.

Tajfel, Henri and John Turner. 1979. "An Integrative Theory of Intergroup Conflict." Pp. 33-47 in *The Social Psychology of Intergroup Relations,* ed. W. G. Austin, & S. Worchel. Monterey, CA: Brooks/Cole.

Tasker, Fiona. 2005. "Lesbian Mothers, Gay Fathers, and Their Children: A Review." *Journal of Developmental and Behavioral Pediatrics* 26: 224–240.

Tate, Charlotte Chuck, Jay N. Ledbetter, and Cris P. Youssef. 2013. "A Two-Question Method for Assessing Gender Categories in the Social and Medical Sciences." *Journal of Sex Research* 50(8): 767–776.

Tate, Charlotte Chuck, Cris P. Youssef, and Jay N. Bettergarcia. 2014. "Integrating the Study of Transgender Spectrum and Cisgender Experiences of Self-Categorization From a Personality Perspective." *Review of General Psychology* 18(4):302-312.

Tate, Shirley Anne. 2009. *Black Beauty: Aesthetics, Stylization, Politics.* Burlington, VT: Ashgate.

Taylor, Frederick Winslow. 1911. *The Principles of Scientific Management.* New York: Harper & Brothers.

Taylor, Jonathan B., and Joseph P. Kalt. 2005. *American Indians on Reservations: A Data Book of Socioeconomic Change Between the 1990 and 2000 Censuses.* Cambridge, MA: Harvard Project on American Indian Development.

Taylor, Paul. 2011. "Is College Worth It? College Presidents, Public Assess Value, Quality and Mission of Higher Education." A Pew Research Center Social & Demographic Trends Report, May 16. Accessed May 22, 2012 (www.pewsocialtrends.org/files/2011/05/higher-ed-report.pdf).

Taylor, Paul, Rich Morin, Kim Parker, D'Vera Cohn, and Wendy Wang. 2009. *Growing Old in America: Expectations vs. Reality.* Pew Research Center Social & Demographic Trends Project, January. Accessed April 5, 2010 (http://pewsocialtrends.org/assets/pdf/Getting-Old-in-America.pdf).

Taylor, Verta. 1999. "Gender and Social Movements: Gender Processes in Womens Self-Help Movements." *Gender and Society* 13: 8–33.

———. 2004. "Social Movements and Gender." Pp. 14348–14352 in *International Encyclopedia of the Social and Behavioral Sciences,* ed. Neil J. Smelser and Paul B. Baltes. New York: Elsevier.

Tejada-Vera, Betzaida, and Paul D. Sutton. 2010. "Births, Marriages, Divorces, and Deaths: Provisional Data for 2009." *National Vital Statistics Reports* 58 (25). Hyattsville, MD: National Center for Health Statistics. Accessed May 28, 2011 (www.cdc.gov/nchs/data/nvsr/nvsr58/nvsr58_25.pdf).

Terkel, Studs. 2003. *Hope Dies Last: Keeping the Faith in Difficult Times.* New York: New Press.

Tertilt, Michèle. 2005. "Polygyny, Fertility, and Savings." *Journal of Political Economy* 113 (6): 1341–1370.

Thomas, Gordon, and Max Morgan Witts. 1974. *Voyage of the Damned.* Greenwich, CT: Fawcett Crest.

Thomas, William I., and Dorothy Swain Thomas. 1928. *The Child in America: Behavior Problems and Programs.* New York: Knopf.

Thompson, Warren S. 1929. "Population." *American Journal of Sociology* 34 (6): 959–975.

———. 1948. *Plenty of People: The World's Population Pressures, Problems and Policies and How They Concern Us,* rev. ed. New York: Ronald Press.

Thomson, Elizabeth, and Eva Bernhardt. 2010. "Education, Values, and Cohabitation in Sweden." *Marriage & Family Review* 46 (1/2): 1–21.

Thornton, John. 1998. "The African Experience of the 20. and Odd Negroes Arriving in Virginia in 1619." *The William and Mary Quarterly* 55: 421–434.

Tierney, John. 2003. "Iraqi Family Ties Complicate American Efforts for Change." *The New York Times,* September 28, pp. A1, A22.

Tilly, Charles. 1993. *Popular Contention in Great Britain 1758–1834.* Cambridge, MA: Harvard University Press.

———. 2004. *Social Movements, 1768–2004.* Boulder, CO: Paradigm.

Timmerman, Kelsey. 2012. *Where Am I Wearing?: A Global Tour of the Countries, Factories, and People That Make Our Clothes,* 2nd ed. Hoboken, NJ: John Wiley & Sons, Inc.

Titlow, John Paul. 2016. "How to Get a Match, According to Tinder's Sociologist." *Fast Company* August 3. Accessed November 19, 2016 (www.fastcompany.com/3062454/how-to-get-a-match-according-to-tinders-sociologist).

Tolbert, Kathryn. 2000. "In Japan, Traveling Alone Begins at Age 6." *The Washington Post National Weekly Edition* 17, May 15, p. 17.

Tonkinson, Robert. 1978. *The Mardudjara Aborigines.* New York: Henry Holt.

Tönnies, Ferdinand. [1887] 1988. *Community and Society.* New Brunswick, NJ: Transaction.

Toossi, Mitra. 2004. "Labor Force Projections to 2012: The Graying of the U.S. Workforce." *Monthly Labor Review,* February: 37–57.

———. 2015. "Labor Force Projections to 2024: The Labor Force Is Growing, But Slowly." *Monthly Labor Review,* Bureau of Labor Statistics, United States Department of Labor, December. Accessed October 25, 2016 (www.bls.gov/opub/mlr/2015/article/labor-force-projections-to-2024.htm).

Torres, Jose. 2015. "Race/Ethnicity and Stop-and-Frisk: Past, Present, Future." *Sociology Compass* 9(11): 931–939.

Truman, Jennifer L. and Rachel E. Morgan. 2016. "Criminal Victimization, 2015: National Crime Victimization Survey." *Bureau of Justice Statistics Bulletin* October, NCJ 250180. Accessed November 14, 2016 (www.bjs.gov/content/pub/pdf/cv15.pdf).

Tully, Shawn. 2012. "The 2011 Fortune 500: The Big Boys Rack Up Record-Setting Profits." *CNNMoney,* May 7. Accessed May 22, 2012 (www.dailyfinance.com/2012/05/07/the-2011-fortune-500-the-big-boys-rack-up-record-setting-profit/).

Ture, Kwame, and Charles Hamilton. 1992. *Black Power: The Politics of Liberation,* rev. ed. New York: Vintage Books.

Turner, Ani. 2013. "The Business Case for Racial Equity." Altarum Institute and W.K. Kellogg Foundation, October. Accessed February 4, 2017 (http://altarum.org/sites/default/files/uploaded-publication-files/The%20Business%20Case%20for%20Racial%20Equity%20FINAL.pdf).

Twitchell, James B. 2000. "The Stone Age." Pp. 44–48 in *Do Americans Shop Too Much?,* ed. Juliet Schor. Boston: Beacon Press.

Tyson, Gareth, Vasile C. Perta, Hamed Haddadi, and Michael C. Seto. 2016. "A First Look at User Activity on Tinder." *arXiv* 1607.01952. Accessed November 18, 2016 (https://arxiv.org/abs/1607.01952).

U

Ullah, Faiz, and Shilpa Phadke. 2016. "How the Deonar Garbage-Dump Fire Exposed the Self-Centredness of Mumbai's Elite." *Scroll.In,* February 5. Accessed January 16, 2017 (http://scroll.in/a/803040).

UNAIDS. 2016. *Global AIDS Update 2016.* Geneva: Joint United Nations Programme on HIV/AIDS. Accessed February 11, 2017 (www.unaids.org/sites/default/files/media_asset/global-AIDS-update-2016_en.pdf).

United Nations. 1999. "The World at Six Billion." Population Division, Department of Economic and Social Affairs, United Nations Secretariat, October. Accessed June 28, 2011 (www.un.org/esa/population/publications/sixbillion/sixbillion.htm).

———. 2000. "United Nations Millennium Declaration." United Nations General Assembly, A/RES/55/2, September 8. Accessed January 20, 2017 (www.un.org/millennium/declaration/ares552e.htm/).

———. 2014a. *The Millennium Development Goals Report 2014.* New York: United Nations. Accessed April 14, 2015 (www.un.org/millenniumgoals/2014%20MDG%20report/MDG%202014%20English%20web.pdf).

———. 2015a. *World Marriage Data 2015. Department of Economic and Social Affairs.* Accessed November 21, 2016 (www.un.org/en/development/desa/population/theme/marriage-unions/WMD2015.shtml).

———. 2015b. "Net Number of Migrants: 1950–2100." *World Population Prospect: The 2015 Revision. Department of Economic and Social Affairs,* Population Division. Accessed February 8, 2017 (https://esa.un.org/unpd/wpp/Download/Standard/Migration/).

———. 2015c. "Net Migration Rate: 1950–2100." *World Population Prospect: The 2015 Revision. Department of Economic and Social Affairs,* Population Division. Accessed February 8, 2017 (https://esa.un.org/unpd/wpp/Download/Standard/Migration/).

———. 2015d. "Annual Rate of Population Change: 1950–2100." *World Population Prospect: The 2015 Revision.* Department of Economic and Social Affairs, Population Division. Accessed February 8, 2017 (https://esa.un.org/unpd/wpp/Download/Standard/Population/).

———. 2015e. "Total Population—Both Sexes." *World Population Prospect: The 2015 Revision.* Department of Economic and Social Affairs, Population Division. Accessed February 9, 2017 (https://esa.un.org/unpd/wpp/Download/Standard/Population/).

———. 2015f. "Population by Age Groups." *World Population Prospect: The 2015 Revision.* Department of Economic and Social Affairs, Population Division. Accessed February 9, 2017 (https://esa.un.org/unpd/wpp/Download/Standard/Population/).

———. 2016a. "Model-Based Estimates and Projections of Family Planning Indicators 2016." Department of Economic and Social Affairs, Population Division. Accessed February 1, 2017 (www.un.org/en/development/desa/population/theme/family-planning/cp_model.shtml).

———. 2016b. International Migration Report 2015. Department of Economic and Social Affairs, Population Division, September. Accessed February 6, 2017 (www.un.org/en/development/desa/population/migration/publications/migrationreport/docs/MigrationReport2015.pdf).

———. 2016c. "Summary of the Paris Agreement." Climate: Get the Big Picture. Framework Convention on Climate Change. Accessed February 13, 2017 (http://bigpicture.unfccc.int/#content-the-paris-agreemen).

———. 2016d. "Total Population—Both Sexes." *World Population Prospects: The 2017.* Department of Economic and Social Affairs, Population Division. Accessed July 17, 2017 (https://esa.un.org/unpd/wpp/Download/Standard/Population/).

United Nations Development Programme. 2000. *Poverty Report 2000: Overcoming Human Poverty.* Washington, DC: UNDP.

———. 2008. *Human Development Indices: A Statistical Update 2008.* New York: UNDP. Accessed June 7, 2009 (http://hdr.undp.org/en/media/HDI_2008_EN_Complete.pdf).

———. 2015. *Human Development Report 2015: Work for Human Development.* New York: The United Nations Development Programme. Accessed January 17, 2017 (http://hdr.undp.org/en/2015-report).

United Nations Environment Programme. 2014. "Air Pollution: World's Worst Environmental Health Risk." Pp. 42–47 in *UNEP Year Book 2014: Emerging Issues in Our Environment.* Nairobi: UNEP Division of Early Warning and Assessment. Accessed February 13, 2017 (www.unep.org/yearbook/2014/PDF/UNEP_YearBook_2014.pdf).

United Nations Framework Convention on Climate Change. 2015a. "Kyoto Protocol." Accessed May 3, 2015 (http://unfccc.int/kyoto_protocol/items/2830.php).

———. 2015b. "Status of Ratification of the Kyoto Protocol." Accessed May 3, 2015 (http://unfccc.int/kyoto_protocol/status_of_ratification/items/2613.php).

United Nations High Commission for Refugees. 2017. "Syria Regional Refugee Response." Information Sharing Portal hosted by UNHCR, February 1. Accessed February 4, 2017 (http://data.unhcr.org/syrianrefugees/regional.php).

UN News Service. 2010. "Darfur: Security Council Warned of Significant Challenges to Peace Process." UN News Centre, May 20. Accessed May 28, 2010 (www.un.org/apps/news/story.asp?NewsID534761&Cr5&Crl5).

United States Sentencing Commission. 2016. *Guidelines Manual.* November. Accessed November 10, 2016 (www.ussc.gov/sites/default/files/pdf/guidelines-manual/2016/GLMFull.pdf).

UNODC. 2014. *Global Study on Homicide 2013: Trends, Contexts, Data.* United Nations Office on Drugs and Crime, 14.IV.1. Accessed February 19, 2015 (www.unodc.org/documents/gsh/pdfs/2014_GLOBAL_HOMICIDE_BOOK_web.pdf).

_____. 2016a. "Transnational Organized Crime." United Nations Office on Drugs and Crime. Accessed November 15, 2016 (www.unodc.org/toc/).

_____. 2016b. "Crime and Criminal Justice Statistics: Statistics on Crime." United Nations Office on Drugs and Crime. Accessed November 15, 2016 (www.unodc.org/unodc/en/data-and-analysis/statistics/crime.html).

U.S. Census Bureau. 1975. *Historical Statistics of the United States, Colonial Times to 1970.* Washington, DC: U.S. Government Printing Office.

_____. 2010a. "Historical Income Tables—Households." Accessed June 9, 2011 (www.census.gov/hhes/www/income/data/historical/household/index.html).

_____. 2010b. "Observations from the Interagency Technical Working Group on Developing a Supplemental Poverty Measure." Accessed April 25, 2010 (www.census.gov/hhes/www/poverty/SPM_TWGObservations.pdf).

_____. 2010c. "The Questions on the Form." Accessed May 16, 2010 (http://2010.census.gov/2010census/pdf/2010_Questionnaire_Info.pdf).

_____. 2012. "Selected Population Profile in the United States—2011 American Community Survey 1-Year Estimates." American FactFinder. Accessed June 6, 2013 (http://factfinder2.census.gov/faces/nav/jsf/pages/searchresults.xhtml).

_____. 2013a. "Services (Main)." Accessed March 17, 2015 (www.census.gov/econ/services.html).

_____. 2013b. "Detailed Tables on Wealth and Asset Ownership: 2011." Accessed June 3, 2013 (www.census.gov/people/wealth/data/dtables.html).

_____. 2014. "Same Sex Couples Main." Washington, DC: U.S. Census Bureau. Accessed February 26, 2015 (www.census.gov/hhes/samesex/).

_____. 2015a. "Families and Living Arrangements: Children." Washington, DC: U.S. Census Bureau. Accessed February 26, 2015 (www.census.gov/hhes/families/data/cps2014C.html).

_____. 2015b. "American Community Survey 5-Year Estimates: 2010–2014." American FactFinder. Accessed December 2, 2016 (http://factfinder.census.gov/faces/nav/jsf/pages/searchresults.xhtml).

_____. 2016a. "Current Population Survey Tables for Personal Income." Washington, DC: U.S. Census Bureau. Accessed September 22, 2016 (www.census.gov/data/tables/time-series/demo/income-poverty/cps-pinc.html).

_____. 2016b. "Historical Poverty Tables: People and Families—1959 to 2015." Poverty Data Tables. Accessed October 25, 2016 (www.census.gov/data/tables/time-series/demo/income-poverty/historical-poverty-people.html).

_____. 2016c. "Historical Household Tables." Washington, DC: U.S. Census Bureau. Accessed May 31, 2017 (www.census.gov/data/tables/time-series/demo/families/households.html).

_____. 2016d. "Families and Living Arrangements: Families." Washington, DC: U.S. Census Bureau. Accessed November 21, 2016 (www.census.gov/hhes/families/data/families.html).

_____. 2016e. "Families and Living Arrangements: Marital Status." Washington, DC: U.S. Census Bureau. Accessed November 21, 2016 (www.census.gov/hhes/families/data/marital.html).

_____. 2016f. "Families and Living Arrangements: Family Groups." Washington, DC: U.S. Census Bureau. Accessed November 21, 2016 (www.census.gov/hhes/families/data/cps2016FG.html).

_____. 2016g. "Families and Living Arrangements: Children." Washington, DC: U.S. Census Bureau. Accessed November 22, 2016 (www.census.gov/hhes/families/data/cps2016C.html).

_____. 2016h. "Families and Living Arrangements: Living Arrangements of Children." Washington, DC: U.S. Census Bureau. Accessed June 28, 2017 (www.census.gov/data/tables/time-series/demo/families/children.html).

_____. 2016i. "Families and Living Arrangements: Living Arrangements of Adults." Washington, DC: U.S. Census Bureau. Accessed November 22, 2016 (www.census.gov/hhes/families/data/adults.html).

_____. 2016i. "Historical Poverty Tables—People and Families—1959–2015." Accessed December 22, 2016 (www.census.gov/data/tables/time-series/demo/income-poverty/historical-poverty-people.html).

_____. 2016j. "American Community Survey 1-Year Estimates: 2015." American FactFinder. Accessed December 2, 2016 (http://factfinder.census.gov/faces/nav/jsf/pages/searchresults.xhtml).

_____. 2016l. "American Indian and Alaska Native Heritage Month: November 2016." Profile America Facts for Features, CB16-FF.22, November 2. Accessed February 6, 2017 (www.census.gov/newsroom/facts-for-features/2016/cb16-ff22.html).

_____. 2017a. "World Vital Events per Time Unit: 2017." World Vital Events, International Data Base. Accessed February 8, 2017 (www.census.gov/population/international/data/idb/worldvitalevents.php).

_____. 2017b. "Voting in America: A Look at the 2016 Presidential Election." Random Samplings, Census Blogs, May 10. Accessed June 2, 2017 (www.census.gov/newsroom/blogs/random-samplings/2017/05/voting_in_america.html).

U.S. Commission on Civil Rights. 1976. *A Guide to Federal Laws and Regulations Prohibiting Sex Discrimination.* Washington, DC: U.S. Government Printing Office.

_____. 2009. "Racial Categorization in the 2010 Census: A Briefing Before the United States Commission on Civil Rights Held in Washington, DC, April 7, 2006." Briefing Report. Accessed May 16, 2010 (www.usccr.gov/pubs/RC2010Web_Version.pdf).

U.S. Copyright Office. 2016. "Fiscal 2015 Annual Report." Library of Congress, Washington, D.C. Accessed February 14, 2017 (www.copyright.gov/reports/annual/2015/ar2015.pdf).

U.S. Customs Border and Border Protection. 2016a. "United States Border Patrol: Southwest Border Sectors—Southwest Border Deaths by Fiscal Year (Oct. 1st through Sept. 30th)." Accessed January 20, 2017 (www.cbp.gov/sites/default/files/assets/documents/2016-Oct/BP%20Southwest%20Border%20Sector%20Deaths%20FY1998%20-%20FY2016.pdf).

U.S. Customs Border and Border Protection. 2016b. "United States Border Patrol: Sector Profile—Fiscal Year 2016 (Oct. 1st through Sept. 301th)." Accessed January 20, 2017 (www.cbp.gov/sites/default/files/assets/documents/2017-Jan/USBP%20Stats%20FY2016%20sector%20profile.pdf).

U.S. Department of Agriculture. 2016. "Real Per Capita GDP (2010 Dollars) Historical." International Macroeconomic Data Set, Economic Research Service, Washington, D.C. Accessed December 15, 2016 (http://ers.usda.gov/data-products/international-macroeconomic-data-set.aspx).

U.S. Department of Education. 2015. "List of 2014 Digest Tables." Washington, DC: Institute of Education Services, U.S. Department of Education. Accessed March 10, 2015 (http://nces.ed.gov/programs/digest/2014menu_tables.asp).

_____. 2016. "Most Current Digest Tables." *Digest of Education Statistics.* Washington, DC: Institute of Education Services, U.S. Department of Education. Accessed July 17, 2017(https://nces.ed.gov/programs/digest/current_tables.asp).

U.S. Department of Health and Human Services. 2016. "The AFCARS Report." Administration for Children and Families,

Administration on Children, Youth and Families, Children's Bureau, June, No. 23. Accessed November 22, 2016 (www.acf.hhs.gov/cb/research-data-technology/statistics-research/afcars).

U.S. Department of Homeland Security. 2016. *Yearbook of Immigration Statistics: 2015.* Washington, DC: Office of Immigration Statistics. Accessed January 20, 2017 (www.dhs.gov/immigration-statistics/yearbook).

U.S. Department of Justice. 1999. "Ten-Year Program to Compensate Japanese Americans Interned During World War II Closes Its Doors." Press release No. 059, February 19. Accessed June 3, 2010 (www.justice.gov/opa/pr/1999/February/059cr.htm).

———. 2015a. "Justice Department Announces Findings of Two Civil Rights Investigations in Ferguson, Missouri." Office of Public Affairs, March 4. Accessed April 26, 2015 (www.justice.gov/opa/pr/justice-department-announces-findings-two-civil-rights-investigations-ferguson-missouri).

———. 2015b. *Investigation of the Ferguson Police Department.* Civil Rights Division, March 4. Accessed April 27, 2015 (www.justice.gov/sites/default/files/opa/press-releases/attachments/2015/03/04/ferguson_police_department_report.pdf).

———. 2016a. "Active Shooter Incidents in the United States in 2014 and 2015." Federal Bureau of Investigation. Accessed November 4, 2016 (www.fbi.gov/file-repository/activeshooterincidentsus_2014-2015.pdf/view).

———. 2016b. "Offenses Known to Law Enforcement." *Crime in the United States, 2015.* Washington, DC: United States Department of Justice, Federal Bureau of Investigation. Accessed November 12, 2016 (https://ucr.fbi.gov/crime-in-the-u.s/2015/crime-in-the-u.s.-2015/offenses-known-to-law-enforcement).

———. 2016c. "2015 Crime Clock Statistics." *Crime in the United States, 2015.* Washington, DC: United States Department of Justice, Federal Bureau of Investigation. Accessed November 12, 2016 (https://ucr.fbi.gov/crime-in-the-u.s/2015/crime-in-the-u.s.-2015/resource-pages/crime-clock).

———. 2016d. "Hate Crime Statistics 2015." *Crime in the United States, 2015.* Washington, DC: United States Department of Justice, Federal Bureau of Investigation. Accessed January 31, 2017 (https://ucr.fbi.gov/hate-crime/2015).

U.S. Department of State. 2016a. "FY 2015 Annual Report on Intercountry Adoption." United States Department of State, Washington, DC. Accessed November 22, 2016 (https://travel.state.gov/content/adoptionsabroad/en/about-us/publications.html).

———. 2016b. *Trafficking in Persons Report: June 2016.* Washington, DC. Accessed January 20, 2017 (www.state.gov/j/tip/rls/tiprpt/).

U.S. Patent and Trademark Office. 2016. "U.S. Patent Statistics Chart: Calendar Years 1963–2015." Patent Technology Monitoring Team. Accessed February 14, 2017 (www.uspto.gov/web/offices/ac/ido/oeip/taf/us_stat.htm).

V

Valtin, Heinz. 2002. "'Drink at Least Eight Glasses of Water a Day.' Really? Is There Scientific Evidence for '8 x 8.'" *American Journal of Physiology—Regulatory, Integrative and Comparative Physiology* 283 (5): R993–R1004

van den Bergh, Linda, Eddie Denessen, Lisette Hornstra, Marinus Voeten, and Rob W. Holland. 2010. "The Implicit Prejudiced Attitudes of Teachers: Relations to Teacher Expectations and the Ethnic Achievement Gap." *American Educational Research Journal,* January. doi: 10.3102/0002831209353594.

Van der Sar, Ernesto. 2016. "'Deadpool' Is the Most Torrented Movie of 2016." TorrentFreak, December 30. Accessed May 25, 2017 (https://torrentfreak.com/deadpool-torrented-movie-2016/).

———. 2017. "All Oscar Nominees Are Available on Pirate Sites." TorrentFreak, February 25. Accessed May 25, 2017 (https://torrentfreak.com/all-oscar-nominees-are-available-on-pirate-sites-170225/).

Vanderstraeten, Raf. 2007. "Professions in Organizations, Professional Work in Education." *British Journal of Sociology of Education* 28 (5): 621–635.

Veblen, Thorstein. [1899] 1964. *Theory of the Leisure Class.* New York: Macmillan.

———. 1919. *The Vested Interests and the State of the Industrial Arts.* New York: Huebsch.

Venkatesh, Sudhir. 2006. *Off the Books: The Underground Economy of the Urban Poor.* Cambridge, MA: Harvard University Press.

Venter, Craig. 2000. "Remarks at the Human Genome Announcement, at the White House." Accessed June 30, 2008 (www.celera.com/celera/pr_1056647999).

Ventriglio, Antonio, Oyedeji Ayonrinde, and Dinesh Bhugra. 2016. "Relevance of Culture-Bound Syndromes in the 21st Century." *Psychiatry and Clinical Neurosciences* 79: 3–6.

Vowell, Paul R., and Jieming Chen. 2004. "Predicting Academic Misconduct: A Comparative Test of Four Sociological Explanations." *Sociological Inquiry* 74 (2): 226–249.

W

Wakefield, Sara, and Christopher Uggen. 2010. "Incarceration and Stratification." *Annual Review of Sociology* 36: 387–406.

Waldman, Amy. 2004a. "India Takes Economic Spotlight, and Critics Are Unkind." *The New York Times,* March 7, p. 3.

———. 2004b. "Low-Tech or High, Jobs Are Scarce in India's Boom." *The New York Times,* May 6, p. A3.

———. 2004c. "What India's Upset Vote Reveals: The High Tech Is Skin Deep." *The New York Times,* May 15, p. A5.

Walker, Iain, and Heather J. Smith, eds. 2002. *Relative Deprivation: Specification, Development, and Integration.* New York: Cambridge University Press.

Walker, Rebecca. 1995. *To Be Real: Telling the Truth and Changing the Face of Feminism.* Berkeley: University of California Press.

Wallenstein, Peter. 2014. *Race, Sex, and the Freedom to Marry: Loving v. Virginia.* Lawrence, KS: The University Press of Kansas.

Wallerstein, Immanuel. 1974. *The Modern World System.* New York: Academic Press.

———. 1979. *The End of the World as We Know It: Social Science for the Twenty-first Century.* Minneapolis: University of Minnesota Press.

———. 2000. *The Essential Wallerstein.* New York: New Press.

———. 2004. *World-Systems Analysis: An Introduction.* Durham, NC: Duke University Press.

———. 2010. "Structural Crises." *New Left Review* 62 (March/April): 133–142.

Wallerstein, Judith S., Julia M. Lewis, and Sandra Blakeslee. 2000. *The Unexpected Legacy of Divorce: A 25-Year Landmark Study.* New York: Basic Books.

Wallis, Claudia. 2008. "How to Make Great Teachers." *Time,* February 25, pp. 28–34.

Walmart. 2016. "Only Walmart: 2016 Annual Report." Bentonville, AR: Wal-Mart Stores, Inc. Accessed December 15, 2016 (http://s2.q4cdn.com/056532643/files/doc_financials/2016/annual/2016-Annual-Report-PDF.pdf).

Walsh, Flora. 2016a. "Part I: The Politics of Pink." *Varsity* October 28. Accessed January 30, 2017 (www.varsity.co.uk/fashion/11099).

———. 2016b. "Part II: The Sociology of Pink." *Varsity* November 15. Accessed January 30, 2017 (www.varsity.co.uk/fashion/11290).

Walsh, Froma. 2009a. "Human Animal Bonds I: The Relational Significance of Companion Animals." *Family Process* 48: 462–480.

———. 2009b. "Human Animal Bonds II: The Role of Pets in Family Systems and Family Therapy." *Family Process* 48: 481–499.

Wang, Wendy. 2012. "The Rise of Intermarriage: Rates, Characteristics Vary by Race and Gender." A Social & Demographic Trends Report, Pew Research Center, February 16. Accessed

May 8, 2012 (www.pewsocialtrends.org/files/2012/02/SDT-Intermarriage-II.pdf).

Wang, Wendy, and Kim Parker. 2014. "Record Share of Americans Have Never Married." Pew Research Center, Social & Demographic Trends, November 20. Accessed February 26, 2015 (www.pewsocialtrends.org/files/2014/09/2014-09-24_Never-Married-Americans.pdf).

Ward, Audrey. 2016. "A Life in the Day of Nita Ambani." *The Times,* August 21. Accessed January 14, 2017 (www.thetimes.co.uk/article/a-life-in-the-day-of-nita-ambani-bq0cr2wf0).

Ward, Brian W., Tainya C. Clark, Colleen N. Nugent, and Jeannine S. Schiller. 2016. "Early Release of Selected Estimates Based on Data from the 2015 National Health Interview Survey." National Center for Health Statistics, May. Accessed February 12, 2017 (www.cdc.gov/nchs/data/nhis/earlyrelease/earlyrelease201605.pdf).

Ward, Jane. 2015. *Not Gay: Sex between Straight White Men.* New York: New York University Press.

Warner, Michael. 1993. *Fear of a Queer Planet: Queer Politics and Social Theory.* Minneapolis, MN: University of Minnesota Press.

Warner, R. Stephen. 2005. *A Church of Our Own: Disestablishment and Diversity in American Religion.* New Brunswick, NJ: Rutgers University Press.

———. 2007. "The Role of Religion in the Process of Segmented Assimilation." *Annals of the American Academy of Political and Social Science* 612 (1): 100–115.

Warren, Patricia, Donald Tomaskovic-Devey, William Smith, Matthew Zingraff, and Marcinda Mason. 2006. "Driving While Black: Bias Processes and Racial Disparity in Police Stops." *Criminology* 44 (3): 709–738.

Wasserman, David. 2016. "2016 National Popular Vote Tracker." *The Cook Political Report,* December 7. Accessed December 14, 2016 (http://cookpolitical.com/story/10174).

Waters, Mary C. 2009. "Social Science and Ethnic Options." *Ethnicities* 9 (1): 130–135.

Watters, Ethan. 2010a. *Crazy Like Us: The Globalization of the American Psyche.* New York: Free Press.

———. 2010b. "The Americanization of Mental Illness." *The New York Times Magazine,* January 8. Accessed February 10, 2017 (www.nytimes.com/2010/01/10/magazine/10psyche-t.html).

Watts, Duncan J. 2007. "Is Justin Timberlake a Product of Cumulative Advantage?" *The New York Times,* April 15. Accessed February 2, 2015 (www.nytimes.com/2007/04/15/magazine/15wwwlnidealab.t.html).

———. 2011. *Everything Is Obvious: Once You Know the Answer.* New York: Crown Business.

Weber, Jonetta D., and Robert M. Carini. 2013. "Where Are the Female Athletes in *Sports Illustrated*? A Content Analysis of Covers (2000–2011)." *International Review for the Sociology of Sport* 48 (2): 196–203.

Weber, Max. [1913–1922] 1947. *The Theory of Social and Economic Organization,* trans. A. Henderson and T. Parsons. New York: Free Press.

———. [1904] 1949. *Methodology of the Social Sciences,* trans. Edward A. Shils and Henry A. Finch. Glencoe, IL: Free Press.

———. [1904] 2009. *The Protestant Ethic and the Spirit of Capitalism,* trans. Talcott Parsons. New York: Scribner.

———. [1916] 1958a. "Class, Status, Party." Pp. 180–195 in *From Max Weber: Essays in Sociology,* ed. H. H. Gerth and C. Wright Mills. New York: Oxford University Press.

———. [1916] 1958b. *The Religion of India: The Sociology of Hinduism and Buddhism.* New York: Free Press.

———. [1921] 1958c. "Bureaucracy." Pp. 196–244 in *From Max Weber: Essays in Sociology,* ed. H. H. Gerth and C. Wright Mills. New York: Oxford University Press.

———. [1922] 1958d. "The Social Psychology of the World Religions." Pp. 267–301 in *From Max Weber: Essays in Sociology,* ed. H. H. Gerth and C. Wright Mills. New York: Oxford University Press.

Wechsler, Henry, J. E. Lee, M. Kuo, M. Seibring, T. F. Nelson, and H. Lee. 2002. "Trends in College Binge Drinking During a Period of Increased Prevention Efforts: Findings from Four Harvard School of Public Health College Alcohol Surveys: 1993–2001." *Journal of American College Health* 50 (5): 203–217.

Wechsler, Henry, and Toben F. Nelson. 2008. "What We Have Learned from the Harvard School of Public Health College Alcohol Study: Focusing Attention on College Student Alcohol Consumption and the Environmental Conditions that Promote It." *Journal of Studies on Alcohol and Drugs* 69 (4): 481–490.

Wedge, Marilyn. 2012. "Why French Kids Don't Have ADHD." *Psychology Today,* March 8. Accessed June 7, 2013 (www.psychologytoday.com/blog/suffer-the-children/201203/why-french-kids-dont-have-adhd).

Weiss, Richard. 1969. *The American Myth of Success.* New York: Basic Books.

Wells-Barnett, Ida B. [1928] 1970. *Crusade for Justice: The Autobiography of Ida B. Wells,* ed. Alfreda M. Duster. Chicago: University of Chicago Press.

Werner, Carrie A. 2011. "The Older Population: 2010." 2010 Census Briefs C2010BR-09. Washington, DC: U.S. Government Printing Office. Accessed April 6, 2012 (www.census.gov/prod/cen2010/briefs/c2010br-09.pdf).

West, Candace, and Don H. Zimmerman. 1987. "Doing Gender." *Gender and Society* 1 (June): 125–151.

Wethington, Elaine. 2000. "Expecting Stress: Americans and the Midlife Crisis." *Motivation & Emotion* 24 (2): 85–103.

Whorton, James C. 2002. *Nature Cures: The History of Alternative Medicine in America.* New York: Oxford University Press.

Wickman, Peter M. 1991. "Deviance." Pp. 85–87 in *Encyclopedic Dictionary of Sociology,* 4th ed., ed. Dushkin Publishing Group. Guilford, CT: Dushkin.

WID.world. 2017. "Average National Income per Adult." World Wealth & Income Database. Accessed January 18, 2017 (http://wid.world/world/#anninc_pall_992_i/WO/2015/us/k/p/yearly/a/false/5554.8875/20000/curve/false).

Wiencek, Henry. 2003. *An Imperfect God: George Washington, His Slaves, and the Creation of America.* New York: Farrar, Straus, and Giroux.

Wierzbicka, Anna. 2008. "Why There Are No Colour Universals in Language and Thought." *Journal of the Royal Anthropological Institute* 14 (2): 407–425.

Wike, Richard, Bruce Stokes, and Jacob Poushter. 2016. "Global Publics Back U.S. on Fighting ISIS, but Are Critical of Post-9/11 Torture." Pew Research Center, Global Attitudes and Trends June 23. Accessed November 1, 2016 (www.pewglobal.org/2015/06/23/global-publics-back-u-s-on-fighting-isis-but-are-critical-of-post-911-torture/).

Wilford, John Noble. 1997. "New Clues Show Where People Made the Great Leap to Agriculture." *The New York Times,* November 18, pp. B9, B12.

Williams, Alicia, John Fries, Jean Koppen, and Robert Prisuta. 2010. *Connecting and Giving: A Report on How Midlife and Older Americans Spend Their Time, Make Connections and Build Communities.* Washington, DC: AARP.

Williams, Caroline. 2013. "Health Myths: Drink Eight Glasses of Water per Day." *New Scientist,* August 21. Accessed September 12, 2016 (www.newscientist.com/article/mg21929310.700-health-myths-drink-eight-glasses-of-water-per-day).

Williams, Kristine N., and Carol A. B. Warren. 2009. "Communication in Assisted Living." *Journal of Aging Studies* 23 (1): 24–36.

Williams, Robin M., Jr. 1970. *American Society,* 3rd ed. New York: Knopf.

Williamson, Thomas. 2007. "Communicating Amok in Malaysia." *Identities* 14(3): 341–365.

Wills, Jeremiah B., and Barbara J. Risman. 2006. "The Visibility of Feminist Thought in Family Studies." *Journal of Marriage and Family* 68 (August): 690–700.

References

Wilson, A. N. 1999. *God's Funeral: The Decline of Faith in Western Civilization.* New York: W. W. Norton & Company.

Wilson, Carl. 2007. *Lets Talk About Love: A Journey to the End of Taste.* New York: Continuum.

Wilson, James Q., and George Kelling. 1982. "The Police and Neighborhood Safety: Broken Windows." *The Atlantic Monthly* 127:29–38.

Wilson, William Julius. 1999. *The Bridge over the Racial Divide: Rising Inequality and Coalition Politics.* Berkeley: University of California Press.

Winters, Kelley. 2012. "An Update on Gender Diagnoses, as the DSM-5 Goes to Press." GID Reform Weblog, December 5. Accessed June 5, 2013 (http://gidreform.wordpress.com/2012/12/05/an-update-on-gender-diagnoses-as-the-dsm-5-goes-to-press/).

Wirth, Louis. 1931. "Clinical Sociology." *American Journal of Sociology* 37 (July): 49–60.

Witsman, Katherine, and Ryan Baugh. 2016. "U.S. Naturalizations: 2015." Annual Flow Report, Homeland Security, November. Accessed January 20, 2017 (www.dhs.gov/immigration-statistics/naturalizations).

Wolf, Naomi. 1992. *The Beauty Myth: How Images of Beauty Are Used Against Women.* New York: Anchor.

Wolff, Edward N. 2016. "Household Wealth Trends in the United States from 1962 to 2013: What Happened over the Great Recession?" *RSF: The Russell Sage Foundation Journal of the Social Sciences* 2(6): 24–43. Accessed December 22, 2016 (www.rsfjournal.org/doi/abs/10.7758/RSF.2016.2.6.02).

Wolraich, Mark L., David B. Wilson, and Wade White. 1995. "The Effect of Sugar on Behavior or Cognition in Children: A Meta-Analysis." *JAMA* 274 (20): 1617–1621.

Wolraich, Mark L., Scott D. Lindgren, Phyllis J. Stumbo, Lewis D. Stegnik, Mark I. Applebaum, and Mary C. Kiritsy. 1994. "Effects of Diets High in Sucrose or Aspartame on the Behavior and Cognitive Performance of Children." *The New England Journal of Medicine* 330 (5): 301–307.

Wong, Alia. 2015. "The Rennaissance of Student Activism." *The Atlantic,* May 21. Accessed February 14, 2017 (www.theatlantic.com/education/archive/2015/05/the-renaissance-of-student-activism/393749/).

Wonjun, Chung, Jinbong Choi, Chang Wan Woo, Soobum Lee, and Christina E. Saindon. 2016. "Community Relations Dealing with a Not in My Back Yard (NIMBY) Context." *International Journal of Conflict Management* 27(3): 424–452.

Wood, Betty. 1997. *The Origins of American Slavery: Freedom and Bondage in the English Colonies.* New York: Hill and Wang.

Woolgar, Steve. 1988. *Science: The Very Idea.* New York: Tavistock Publications.

Woolley, Benjamin. 2007. *Savage Kingdom: Virginia and the Founding of English America.* New York: HarperPress.

Word, David L., Charles D. Coleman, Robert Nunziator, and Robert Kominski. 2007. "Demographic Aspects of Surnames from Census 2000." Accessed January 2, 2008 (www.census.gov/genealogy/www/surnames.pdf).

World Bank. 2016a. "People: Mortality." *World Development Indicators.* Accessed October 25, 2016 (http://wdi.worldbank.org/table/2.21).

———. 2016b. "Health Expenditure, Public (Percent of Total Health Expenditure)." *World Development Indicators.* Accessed December 22, 2016 (http://data.worldbank.org/indicator/SH.XPD.PUBL).

———. 2016c. *Poverty and Shared Prosperity 2016: Taking on Inequality.* Washington, DC: World Bank. Accessed January 17, 2017 (www.worldbank.org/en/publication/poverty-and-shared-prosperity).

———. 2016d. "GNI per Capita, Atlas Method (Current US$)." *World Development Indicators.* Accessed January 17, 2017 (http://data.worldbank.org/indicator/NY.GNP.PCAP.CD).

———. 2016e. "GDP (current US$)." *World Development Indicators.* Accessed January 18, 2017 (http://data.worldbank.org/indicator/NY.GDP.MKTP.CD).

———. 2016f. "Income Share Held by Highest 20%." *World Development Indicators.* Accessed January 18, 2017 (http://data.worldbank.org/indicator/SI.DST.05TH.20).

———. 2016g. "Income Share Held by Lowest 20%." *World Development Indicators.* Accessed January 18, 2017 (http://data.worldbank.org/indicator/SI.DST.FRST.20).

———. 2016h. "PovcalNet: An Online Analysis Tool for Global Poverty Monitoring." Accessed January 20, 2017 (http://iresearch.worldbank.org/PovcalNet/home.aspx).

———. 2016i. *World Development Indicators 2016.* Washington, DC: The World Bank. Accessed January 20, 2017 (https://openknowledge.worldbank.org/bitstream/handle/10986/23969/9781464806834.pdf).

———. 2016j. "Mortality Rate, Infant (per 1,000 Live Births)." *World Development Indicators.* Accessed January 20, 2017 (http://data.worldbank.org/indicator/SP.DYN.IMRT.IN).

———. 2016k. "Labor Force, Female (% of Total Labor Force)." *World Development Indicators.* Accessed January 20, 2017 (http://data.worldbank.org/indicator/SL.TLF.TOTL.FE.ZS).

———. 2016l. "Bilateral Remittance Matrix, 2015." Migration & Remittances Data. Accessed January 20, 2017 (www.worldbank.org/en/topic/migrationremittancesdiasporaissues/brief/migration-remittances-data).

———. 2016m. "Birth Rate, Crude (per 1,000 People)." *World Development Indicators.* Accessed February 8, 2017 (http://data.worldbank.org/indicator/SP.DYN.CBRT.IN).

———. 2016n. "Fertility Rate, Total (Births per Woman)." *World Development Indicators.* February 8, 2017 (http://data.worldbank.org/indicator/SP.DYN.TFRT.IN).

———. 2016o. "Death Rate, Crude (per 1,000 People)." *World Development Indicators.* Accessed February 8, 2017 (http://data.worldbank.org/indicator/SP.DYN.CDRT.IN).

———. 2016p. "Life Expectancy at Birth, Total (Years)." *World Development Indicators.* February 8, 2017 (http://data.worldbank.org/indicator/SP.DYN.LE00.IN).

———. 2016q. "Health Expenditure, Total (% of GDP)." *World Development Indicators.* February 8, 2017 (http://data.worldbank.org/indicator/SP.DYN.LE00.IN).

———. 2016r. "CO2 Emissions (Metric Tons per Capita)." *World Development Indicators.* February 13, 2017 (http://data.worldbank.org/indicator/EN.ATM.CO2E.PC).

World Economic Forum. 2016. *The Global Gender Gap Report 2016.* Geneva: World Economic Forum. Access January 20, 2017 (www3.weforum.org/docs/GGGR16/WEF_Global_Gender_Gap_Report_2016.pdf).

World Health Organization. 1948. "Preamble to the Constitution of the World Health Organization." Adopted by the International Health Conference, New York, June 19–July 22, 1946; entered into force on April 7, 1948. Accessed June 30, 2011 (http://whqlibdoc.who.int/hist/official_records/constitution.pdf).

———. 2005. *WHO Global Atlas of Traditional, Complementary, and Alternative Medicine.* Geneva: WHO Press.

———. 2013a. *WHO Traditional Medicine Strategy: 2014–2023.* Geneva: World Health Organization. Accessed February 13, 2017 (http://apps.who.int/iris/bitstream/10665/92455/1/9789241506090_eng.pdf).

———. 2013b. *Global and Regional Estimates of Violence Against Women: Prevalence and Health Effects of Intimate Partner Violence and Non-Partner Sexual Violence.* Geneva: World Health Organization. Accessed April 21, 2015 (http://apps.who.int/iris/bitstream/10665/85239/1/9789241564625_eng.pdf).

———. 2016a. *World Health Statistics, 2016: Monitoring the SDGs, Sustainable Development Goals.* Geneva: WHO Press. Accessed February 10, 2017 (http://apps.who.int/iris/bitstream/10665/206498/1/9789241565264_eng.pdf).

———. 2016b. "Ambient (Outdoor) Air Quality and Health." Media Centre, Fact Sheet No. 313, September. Accessed February 13, 2017 (www.who.int/mediacentre/factsheets/fs313/en/).

———. 2016c. "Water." Media Centre, Fact Sheet No. 391, November. Accessed February 13, 2017 (www.who.int/mediacentre/factsheets/fs391/en/).

———. 2016d. "Sanitation." Media Centre, Fact Sheet No. 392, March. Accessed February 13, 2017 (www.who.int/mediacentre/factsheets/fs392/en/).

World Values Survey. 2015. "World Values Survey Wave 6: 2010–2014." Online Data Analysis Tool. Accessed March 10, 2015 (www.worldvaluessurvey.org/WVSOnline.jsp).

Worth, Robert F. 2016. *A Rage for Order: The Middle East in Turmoil, from Tahrir Square to Isis.* New York: Farrar, Straus, and Giroux.

Wotipka, Crystal D., and Andrew C. High. 2016. "An Idealized Self or the Real Me? Predicting Attraction to Online Dating Profiles Using Selective Self-Presentation and Warranting." *Communication Monographs* 83(3): 281–302.

Wyatt, Edward. 2012. "Use of Conflict Minerals Gets More Scrutiny from U.S." *The New York Times,* March 19. Accessed May 18, 2012 (www.nytimes.com/2012/03/20/business/use-of-conflict-minerals-gets-more-scrutiny.html).

Y

Yang, Jia Lynn, and Amrita Jahakumar. 2014. "Target Says Up to 70 Million More Customers Were Hit by December Data Breach." *The Washington Post,* January 2014. Accessed February 15, 2017 (www.washingtonpost.com/business/economy/target-says-70-million-customers-were-hit-by-dec-data-breach-more-than-first-reported/2014/01/10/0ada1026-79fe-11e3-8963-b4b654bcc9b2_story.html).

Yang, Zhengwei, and Jeffrey C. Schank. 2006. "Women Do Not Synchronize Their Menstrual Cycles." *Human Nature* 17 (4): 433–447.

Yinger, J. Milton. 1970. *The Scientific Study of Religion.* New York: Macmillan.

Yogyakartaprinciples.org. 2007. *The Yogyakarta Principles: Principles on the Application of International Human Rights Law in Relation to Sexual Orientation and Gender Identity.* Accessed May 11, 2010 (www.yogyakartaprinciples.org/principles_en.pdf).

Yoshinaga, Kendra. 2016. "Babies of Color Are Now the Majority, Census Says." *NPR Ed*, July 1. Accessed February 4, 2017 (www.npr.org/sections/ed/2016/07/01/484325664/babies-of-color-are-now-the-majority-census-says).

Z

Zainulbhai, Hani. 2016. "Strong Global Support for Gender Equality, Especially Among Women." Pew Research Center, March 8. Accessed February 2, 2017 (www.pewresearch.org/fact-tank/2016/03/08/strong-global-support-for-gender-equality-especially-among-women/).

Zarembo, Alan. 2004. "A Theater of Inquiry and Evil." *Los Angeles Times,* July 15, pp. A1, A24, A25.

Zeitzen, Miriam Koktvedgaard. 2008. *Polygamy: A Cross-Cultural Perspective.* New York: Berg.

Zimbardo, Philip G. 2007. *The Lucifer Effect: Understanding How Good People Turn Evil.* New York: Random House.

Zimmer, Ben. 2015. "'Cisgender,' a Gender-Issues Buzzword, Takes Off." *The Wall Street Journal*, March 13. Accessed January 31, 2017 (www.wsj.com/articles/cisgender-a-gender-issues-buzzword-takes-off-1426278662).

Zimmerman, Amber Lynn, M. Joan McDermott, and Christina M. Gould. 2009. "The Local Is Global: Third Wave Feminism, Peace, and Social Justice." *Contemporary Justice Review* 12 (1): 77–90.

Ziomkiewicz, Anna. 2006. "Menstrual Synchrony: Fact or Artifact?" *Human Nature* 17 (4): 419–432.

Zola, Irving K. 1972. "Medicine as an Institution of Social Control." *Sociological Review* 20 (November): 487–504.

———. 1983. *Socio-Medical Inquiries.* Philadelphia: Temple University Press.

Zuckerman, Ezra W., and John T. Jost. 2001. "What Makes You Think You're So Popular?: Self-Evaluation Maintenance and the Subjective Side of the Friendship Paradox." *Social Psychology Quarterly* 64: 201–223.

Zweigenhaft, Richard L., and G. William Domhoff. 2006. *Diversity in the Power Elite: How It Happened, Why It Matters,* 2nd ed. New York: Rowman & Littlefield.

Name Index

A

Adams, A., 4
Adams, S., 31
Addams, J., 15, 42, 178
Adler, P. and P., 81–82
Agha-Soltan, N., 392
Ahmed, K. C., 270
al-Bashir, O., 219
Alger, H., 247
Ali, M., 101
Ali, Z. E. A. B., 391
Allah, 197
Allard, L. B. B., 245
Amato, P. R., 172
Ambani, N. and M., 258
Anastassakis, J., 325
Aniston, J., 325
Annan, K., 278
Anthony, S. B., 292
Atchley, R., 91

B

Bacon, F., 8
Baird, C. L., 186
Baldwin, J., 244, 396
Bale, C., 4
Bales, R., 301
Balfour, G., 148
Basinger, J., 161
Beagan, B., 358
Beane, B., 25
Bearman, P., 108
Beaton, K., 288
Bell, D., 116, 139
Belle, A., 1
Berger, P., 94, 100, 190
Berlin, B., 56
Berry, H., 314
Beyoncé, 317
bin Laden, O., 60, 228
Blumer, H., 389
Boorstin, D., 43
Booth, A., 172
Bourdieu, P., 15, 253–254, 394
Bowles, S., 81, 184
Boyle, R., 8
Brown, M., 146, 310, 319–320
Buddha, 199
Buffett, W., 217
Bullock, S., 165
Burawoy, M., 27, 394
Burger, J., 130
Burns, U., 120
Burtka, D., 299
Bush, G. W., 216–217, 219, 224, 340, 365
Butler, R., 93

C

Cabot, M., 70
Calderón, F., 140
Calvin, J., 201
Caplow, T., 227
Carbino, J., 152, 162
Carmichael, S., 391
Castañeda, J., 274
Castile, P., 146
Castro, F., 336
Catz, S., 250
Cavalli-Sforza, L., 312
Chambliss, W., 145
Charger, J., 345
Charney, T., 2
Cherlin, A., 155, 159, 167
Chesney-Lind, M., 148
Chhaidy, N., 72
Chi-Ying, C. H., 354
Chua, A., 164
Clarke, E., 290
Clay, C., 100
Clinton, B., 365
Clinton, H., 33, 123, 207–208, 212–213, 224–225, 279, 305
Cohen, P., 170
Colbert, S., 393
Commoner, B., 367
Comte, A., 8–9, 49, 199, 261, 380, 396
Connell, R. W., 289
Cooley, C. H., 16, 106, 74
Coontz, S., 154, 158
Cooper, B., 4
Cooper, M., 283
Copernicus, N., 8
Crawford, C., 40, 287
Crenshaw, K., 295
Crutcher, T., 310
Cruz, E., 274
Cumming, E., 92
Currie, E., 140

D

Dahl, R., 221–222
Daisey, M., 122
Darwin, C., 379
Davenport, T., 383
Davis, K., 180, 183
de Beauvoir, S., 292
de Laon, A., 237
Deere, J., 209
Desmond, M., 1–2, 27, 28, 316
Dewey, T. E., 33
Dickens, C., 396
Diop, B., 305f
Disney, W., 52, 330
Dolly, 386, 387
Domhoff, G. W., 222–224
Domingo, P., 253
Du Bois, W. E. B., 14, 16, 42, 177–178, 329
Durkheim, É., 9–13, 14–16, 26–28, 40, 114–116, 118, 141, 179, 191–192, 199–200, 202, 261, 374, 378

E

Ebaugh, H. R. F., 105
Eddy, M. B., 197
Edin, K., 234–235
Elgin, S. H., 56–57
Eliot, G., 167
Elliott, M., 192
Ellison, R., 328
Ellul, J., 388
el-Qaddafi, M., 391
Emerbayer, M., 316
Engels, F., 158, 215
Evans, J., 170

F

Faulkner, W., 61
Fausto-Sterling, A., 285
Feld, S., 108
Findlen, B., 294
Fischer, E., 326
Flynt, L., 223
Frank, A., 70
Franklin, B., 177, 179, 188, 247
Freeman, M., 94
Friedan, B., 292–293, 301, 307, 391
Frommer, P., 56
Fussell, P., 254

G

Gage, Z., 101
Galilei, G., 8
Gambari, I., 279
Gandhi, M., 213
Garner, E., 146
Gates, B., 274
George, A., 5
Gilman, C. P., 301
Gini, C., 241–242
Ginsberg, R. B., 305
Gintis, H., 81, 184
Glasgow, E., 380
Goffman, A., 23–24, 27, 32, 35–36, 42
Goffman, E., 14, 16t, 40, 77, 89, 103–104, 134
Gramsci, A., 65
Granovetter, M., 110–111
Gray, J., 290
Greenbaum, L., 176
Gull, W., 354
Gupta, R., 306
Gutenberg, J., 83
Gutiérrez, G., 202

H

Harlow, H., 73
Harrington, M., 116–117
Harris, G., 170
Harris, N. P., 299
Heilskov, Dr., 356
Helú, C. S., 274
Henry, W., 92
Hershlag, N., 325
Hicks, L., 227
Hirschi, T., 143
Hitler, A., 213, 219
Hochschild, A. R., 207, 304
Holder, E., 319
Hoover, H., 83
Hubbard, L. R., 197
Hummel, K., 297
Hurston, Z., 34

J

Jacobson, L., 182
James, L., 6–7
Jarvis, D. C., 359
Jefferson, T., 177, 179, 188, 236, 247
Jenner, C., 296
Jesus Christ, 194, 197, 202, 213
Joan of Arc, 213
Johnson, G., 220
Johnson, L. B., 227, 244
Johnson, M., 358
Jolie, A., 171
Jope, J. C., 311

K

Kagan, E., 305
Kalish, R., 94
Kay, P., 56
Kaye, J., 165
Kennedy, A., 170
Kennedy, J. F., 83
Keqiang, L., 216
Kerry, J., 224
Keynes, J. M., 210
Keys, A., 287–288
Khorasani, N. A., 392
Khosrowshahi, D., 250
Kilbourne, J., 40
Kimmel, M., 289
King, M. L., Jr., 213, 317, 329, 391, 394
Kinsey, A. C., 298, 299
Kirby, J., 383
Kozol, J., 182
Kristof, N., 306
Kübler-Ross, E., 94

L

L'Engle, M., 70
Ladner, J., 42–43
Lamm, N., 286
Lammily, 286
Landon, A., 30
Lareau, A., 163–164, 182, 361
Lauren, R., 325
Lawrence, J., 4, 4
Le Bon, G., 62
Le Guin, U. K., 70, 327
LeBlanc, M., 72
Lee, H., 66
Lee, S., 333, 354
Lenski, G., 115
Lenton, S., 288
Lewis, M., 25
Lichtenberg, G. C., 390
Lincoln, A., 324
Lipschitz, R., 325
Little, O., 139
Lodwick, F., 55
Loehmann, T., 310
Lorber, J., 287, 289
Loving, M. and R., 162
Luckmann, T., 100
Lukács, G., 65
Luther, M., 196, 201

M

Madoff, B., 137–138
Mai, M., 306
Malaya, O., 72

Name Index

Malcolm X, 103, 194. 213, 329
Malthus, T., 350–351
Mandela, N., 325
Mann, H., 177, 179, 188, 247
Mars, B., 253
Marshall, T. H., 220
Martin, G. R. R., 56
Martin, T., 146
Martineau, H., 9, 14, 301
Marx, K., 9, 13, 14, 16, 65, 116, 200, 202–203, 215–216, 222–223, 250–253, 261, 263, 294, 361, 378, 381–383, 389
Masto, C. C., 225, 305
Maugham, W. S., 95
McCain, J., 224, 279
McCormick, C., 209
McCormick, R., 234, 246
McIntosh, P., 327
Mead, G. H., 16, 74–77, 79, 85, 99, 179, 378
Mead, M., 289–290
Meier, D., 181
Meigs, C., 290
Melville, H., 70
Menozzi, P., 312
Merton, R., 16, 107, 120, 142–143
Michels, R., 122
Mika, M., 83
Milanovic, B., 268–269
Milgram, S., 128–130
Millett, K., 292
Mills, C. W., 2–3, 222–223
Mironova, I. V., 325
Mirren, H., 325
Mohai, P., 369
Montagu, A., 314
Moody, J., 108
Moore, W. E., 180, 183
Moriarty, W. K., 133
Mott, L., 292
Mubarak, H., 391
Mugabe, R., 279
Muhammad, 197
Munsch, R., 288
Murdock, G., 49, 155

N

Newton, I., 8
Newton, N., 70
Nicholson, J., 94
Nickerson, R., 25
Nixon, R. M., 83, 131, 227

O

O'Connor, S. D., 305
Obama, B., 33, 207, 217, 224, 247, 279, 314, 317, 330, 346, 365
Obama, M., 15
Oberschall, A., 391
Ogburn, W. F., 54, 157, 381, 387
Okrand, M., 56
Okrent, A., 56
Okun, A., 221
Omi, M., 313
Orshansky, M., 244
Orwell, G., 70

P

Pager, D., 37–38, 318, 328
Panagopoulos, C., 33
Parks, R., 323
Parsons, T., 16, 301, 380
Pascoe, C. J., 297
Peattie, L., 290
Pelosi, N., 293, 305
Peterson, D. J., 56
Piazza, A., 312
Piestewa, L., 228
Piketty, T., 241–242, 251–252
Pinderhughes, D., 222
Pitt, B., 171
Plath, S., 70
Platt, M., 51
Portman, N., 325
Postman, N., 388–389
Putnam, R., 248–249

Q

Queen Elizabeth II, 218
Quinney, R., 147

R

Rank, M., 246
Reagan, R., 131, 333
Reardon, S., 248
Rein, M., 290
Reinharz, S., 43
Renner, J., 4
Reynolds, J. R., 186
Rice, T., 146, 310
Risman, B., 291
Ritzer, G., 121
Robert the Pious, 237
Rodgers, M., 306
Rodriguez, R., 57
Romney, M., 224
Roosevelt, F. D., 30, 83
Rosenthal, R., 182
Rossi, A., 163
Rowling, J., 70, 75
Roy, A., 395
Rudolph, M., 314

S

Saez, E., 241–242
Saha, R., 369
Sanday, P. R., 290
Sandberg, S., 283–284, 303
Sanders, B., 123, 208
Sanger, M., 389
Sapir, E., 56
Sarkeesian, A., 83
Scarce, R., 41
Schaffer, S., 395
Schwartz, P., 162
Scopes, J. T., 193
Scott, G., 19–20
Scott, K., 310
Scrooge, E., 396
Semenya, C., 285
Shaefer, L., 234–235
Shaheen, J., 267
Shaikh, N. A., 259
Shakespeare, W., 77
Shapiro, T., 249
Shipler, D., 246
Shirky, C., 111
Silver, I., 105
Silver, N., 224
Sleh, A. A., 391
Smith, A., 202, 214–215
Soprano, T., 138
Sotomayor, S., 305
Springsteen, B., 103–104
Ssebunya, J., 72
Stanton, E. C., 292
Steidle, B., 279
Stein, J., 220
Steinem, G., 146
Stewart, S., 167
Stovel, K., 108
Streib, J., 254
Strogatz, S., 108
Sumner, W. G., 65
Sutherland, E., 137, 144

T

Tajfel, H., 78
Talackova, J., 105
Tarver, S., 2
Taylor, F. W., 123
Terkel, S., 395
Thomas, F., 332
Thomas, W. I., 14, 378
Todd, C., 47
Tolkien, J. R. R., 56
Truman, H. S., 33
Trump, D., 33, 123, 207–208, 212–213, 224–225, 258, 305, 326, 341, 346, 366, 374
Twain, M., 148
Twitchell, J. B., 118
Tyson, N., 26
Tönnies, F., 113–114, 116, 118

U

Uncle Sam, 217

V

Varma, B., 258
Vassos, A., 176
Vaughn, B., 369
Veblen, T., 382
Venter, C., 312
Vilain, E., 285

W

Walker, R., 294
Wallerstein, I., 263–264, 273, 383
Walton, S., 238
Washington, G., 236, 311
Watts, D., 25, 70–71
Weber, M., 13, 14, 42, 66, 119, 121–123, 187, 196, 200–202, 212–214, 235, 252–253, 388, 390
Wells-Barnett, I., 14–15, 16, 301
West, C., 286, 333
White Eyes, J., 345
White, R., 358
Whitney, E., 209
Whorf, B., 56
Wilde, O., 217
Wilkins, J., 55
Willard, E. H., 178–179
Williams, R., 58
Wilson, D., 310
Wilson, W. J., 108, 134, 323
Winant, H., 313
Winfrey, O., 73, 176, 317
Wirth, L., 20
Witt, E. and E., 55, 183, 287, 338
Witt, J. and L., 55, 183
Wolf, N., 134, 287
Woods, T., 314
WuDunn, S., 306

Y

Yinger, J. M., 196
Yudin, V., 72

Z

Zamenhof, L., 55
Zebene, W., 306
Zimbardo, P., 144, 228
Zimmerman, D., 286

Subject Index

A

ABC News/Washington Post, 32
ability tracks, schools and student, 183
abolitionists, social movement and, 389
Aborigines, Australia and assimilation of, 234
abortion, women's right to, 294
Absolutely Fabulous, 240
Abu Ghraib prison (Iraq), U.S. treatment of prisoners in, 141, 228
academic database, 28
Academic Search, 28
academic sociology, 18–19
Academy Awards, downloading nominated movies before, 133
achieved status, definition of, 101
action stage, role exit and, 105
activism, college students and, 377–378
activists, civil rights, 146
activity theory, definition of, 92
actors on a stage, interactions like, 14
acupuncture, holistic medicine and, 367
Adams, Amy, 4
Adams, Scott, 31
adaptive resilience, 186
adaptive upgrading, social change and Parson's, 380
Addams, Jane, 15, 42, 178
ADHD (attention deficit hyperactivity disorder), 190
ADL (Anti-Defamation League), 337
Adler, Patricia and Peter (sociologists), 81–82
adolescent, rites of passage, 86–87
Adolescent Sexual Network, 108–109
adoption, 164–165
AdultFriendFinder, data breach and, 384
adulthood, milestones to, 87
advanced placement (AP) courses, 176, 182, 184
affection/companionship, family function of, 157
affirmative action, definition and examples of, 321
Affordable Care Act (ACA), 364–366
African American. *See also* Blacks; race
    access to but inferior health care for, 330, 362
    Ali, Muhammad, 100–101
    Beyoncé, 317
    CEOs being, 330
    challenges faced by male, 23–24
    civil rights movement and, 133, 391
    cohabitation and, 168
    college students help voter registration for, 377
    color line, 14
    community college and, 189
    deaths of male, 147
    differential justice for, 147
    disproportionate incarceration of, 132
    driving arrests of male, 318–319
    exposure to gangs for children of, 80
    FBI racial profiling of, 320
    15th Amendment and, 220
    Goffman's study of, 35
    in Congress, 330
    infant mortality rate of, 362
    Innocence Project, 148
    interracial marriage and, 162
    interviewers and Black subjects, 34
    justification for slavery of, 317
    kinship networks, 164
    life expectancy of, 362
    living arrangements for children of, 163
    looting of Korean businesses by, 333
    lynching of, 14
    median household income/wealth of, 5, 329–330
    morbidity/mortality rates of, 361, 362
    neighborhoods, 80
    no compensation for slavery of, 329
    Obama, Barack, 330
    Obama, Michelle, 15
    parenting styles of, 164
    percentage of U.S. workforce, 211
    police killings/targeting of male, 23, 310–311
    poor neighborhoods for children of, 80
    poverty rate of, 94
    prison sentences of, 147
    protest over Warren County landfill, 369
    racial group of, 328–330
    representatives in Congress, 225, 226
    segregation and, 325–326
    sickle cell anemia and, 361
    single-parent families and, 166
    stop and frisk, 145
    U.S. Dept. of Justice investigation of deaths of, 319
    underrepresented in movies, 326
    unemployment rate of, 3
    voter participation of, 225
    voting rights legislation and, 225
    wage discrimination and, 249
    White working-class view of, 207
    Winfrey, Oprah, 73, 176, 317
Age of Consequences, 370
age, 3, 12, 360
ageism, 93. *Also see* aging; elderly
agency, 6, 17, 26, 99, 100, 378
Agha-Soltan, Neda, 392
aging, 90–92, 94, 136. *See also* elderly
agnostics, 197
agrarian society, definition of, 115
ahistorical fallacy, racism and, 317
Ahmed, Karuna Chanana, 270
aid to developing nations, 272
AIDS, 357–360
air pollution, 370–371. *See also* pollution
al-Bashir, Omar, 219
alcohol, 81, 131–132
Alcoholics Anonymous, 1
Alger, Horatio, 247
Ali, Muhammad, 100–101
Ali, Zine El Abidine Ben, 391
alienation, 13, 120
Allard, Ladonna Brave Bull, 245
Alma-Alta Declaration, 356
alternative energy, 370
Alzheimer's disease, 363
AMA (American Medical Association), 365
amalgamation, 324
Amato, Paul R., 172
Ambani, Nita and Mukesh, 258
ambiguous genitalia, 285
American Bar Association, 147
American Dream, 207, 239, 246–250, 272, 293
American Hustle, 4, 137
American Indians, 330–331. *See also* Native Americans
    access to but inferior health care for, 362
    cohabitation and, 168
    median household income of, 330
    right to vote, 225
American Medical Association (AMA), 365, 382
American Ninja Warrior, 253
American Psychiatric Association, 297, 358
American Recovery and Reinvestment Act, 217
American rite of passage, 87
American Society of Plastic Surgeons, 134
American Sociological Association (ASA), 18, 41, 130, 394
American Sociological Review, 27
American Sociological Society, 15
American Winter, 221
Ameri-Corps, volunteer opportunities with, 396
Amish, 79, 114, 196, 200, 388
Amnesty International, 230, 277, 280
amok, Malaysia males and, 354
Amour, 164
Andersonville (Swedish Americans), 326
Animal Farm, 70
anime slang, 63
Aniston, Jennifer, 325
Annan, Kofi, 278
anomie, definition of and Durkheim, 13, 141
anorexia nervosa, in the West versus China, 354
Anthony, Susan B., 292
anthropocene, 367
anticipatory socialization, 88
Anti-Defamation League (ADL), 337
Anti-Drug Abuse Act, 131
anti-nuclear power, new social movement and, 392
anti-Semitism, definition of, 337
antiwar activists, social movement and, 389
apartheid, 325
Apne Aap Women Worldwide, 306
The Apostle, 200
Arab Americans, 190, 334
Arab Spring, 8, 111, 248, 381, 391–392
argot, 62
aristocracy, 181
Army Corps of Engineers, pipeline protests and, 345–346
artificial mothers, 73
ASA (American Sociological Association), 18, 394
ascribed social positions, 239
ascribed status, definition of, 102, 235
asexual, 296
Asian Americans, 92, 225–226, 331–333
Asians, 3, 12, 162, 166, 168, 211, 324, 329
Association for Applied and Clinical Sociology, 20
atague, Latino fighting attack, 362
Atchley, Robert, 91
atheists, 197
Atlantic, 27
attachment, social bonds and, 143
attention deficit hyperactivity disorder (ADHD), 190

450

Australia, 285, 324
Authority, 120, 128, 130, 212–214
Avatar, 56

B

baby names, 38–39, 56
baby talk, 71–72
backstage, presentation of self as, 77
Bacon, Francis, 8
Baird, Chardie L., 186
Baldwin, James, 244, 396
Bale, Christian, 4
Bales, Robert, 301
Balfour, Gillian, 148
Baptist church, suicide and, 10
bar and bat mitzvahs, 200
Barbie dolls, 288
Barry, Joe and Briggette, 249
Basinger, Jeanine, 161
Batman, 54
Batman v Superman: Dawn of Justice, 133
Beagan, Brenda, 358
Beane, Billy, 25
Bearman, Peter, 108
Beaton, Kate, 288
beauty myth, 134, 287
behavior, 26, 49–50, 77, 81, 107, 133
beliefs,
    religious, 192–193
    strengthening of social bonds and, 143
The Bell Jar, 70
Bell v. Maryland, 337
Bell, Daniel, 116, 139
Belle, Arleen, 1
berdaches, 289
Berger, Peter, 94, 100, 190
Berlin, Brent, 56
Berry, Halle, 314
Beyoncé, 317
bias, 25, 78
Big Mac Index, 263, 254
bilateral descent, 154
bilingual education, 335
bilingualism, pros and cons of, 179
bin Laden, Osama, 60, 228
binge drinking, 130–131
biotechnology, 386–387
biracial identity, 314
birth control, 300, 389
The Birth of a Nation, 228
bisexual, 296, 299
Black Lives Matter, 310, 391
Blacks, 3, 12, 101, 103, 245, 329. *See also* African Americans
Blumer, Herbert, 389
body mass index (BMI), 288
body painting, as a rite of passage, 87
books, social influence of, 70–71
Boorstin, Daniel, 43
Booth, Alan, 172
borderlands, 275

born again, 194
Boston Marathon bombings, 229
Botox, 134
Bourdieu, Pierre, 15, 253–254, 394
bourgeoisie, 250, 381
Bowles, Samuel, 81, 184
boycotts and strikes, 61
Boyhood, 89
Boyle, Robert, 8
Brahman (caste system priests), 236–237
brain drain, 356
Break-a-Norm Day, 61
The Breakfast Club, 82
Brexit vote, 326, 338
Brigitte, 288
British empire, 263
British monarchy, 248
broken window hypothesis, 145
Brooklyn, 59
Brown v. Board of Education, 178, 316
Brown, Michael, 146, 310, 319–320
The Bucket List, 94
Buddhism, 199
Buffett, Warren, 217
Bugis people (Indonesia), 289–290
bullfighting, 66
Bullock, Sandra, 165
Bully, 89
Burawoy, Michael, 27, 394
bureaucracy, 118–123
    characteristics of, 118, 119–121
    definition of, 118, 187
    division of labor and, 119
    goal displacement and, 120
    impersonality and, 120–121
    metrics and, 122
    organizational culture and, 123
    rational-legal authority and, 213
    rules and regulations of, 120
    schools and, 187
bureaucratization, 121
Burger, Jerry, 130
burnouts, high school student group, 82
Burns, Ursula, 120
Burtka, David, 299
Bush, George W., 216–217, 219, 224, 340, 365
Butler, Robert, 93
BuzzFeed, 30

C

Cabot, Meg, 70
Calderón, Felipe, 140
Calvin, John, 201
campus, activism on college, 377–378
Capital in the Twenty-First Century, 251

capitalism
    definition and concepts of, 214–215
    democracy versus, 221
    environmental consequences of, 369
    Karl Marx and, 13
    mechanization and, 250
    mixed economy and, 216
Caplow, Theodore, 227
Captain American: Civil War, 133
car-window sociologist, 14
Caramel, 62
Carbino, Jessica, 152, 162
CARE International, 277
caregiver, social role of, 163
Carmichael, Stokely, 391
Castañeda, Jorge, 274
caste system, 236–237
Castile, Philando, 146
Castro, Fidel, 336
Catz, Safra, 250
causal factors, 26
causal link, 24
causal logic, 28, 29
causality, variables and, 31
causation, relationship of correlation and, 31
Cavalli-Sforza, Luca, 312
cell phones, 84
Center for Gender-Based Biology, 285
Centers for Disease Control and Prevention (CDC), 298, 362
centrality, 108
Chambliss, William, 145
Charger, Jasilyn, 345
charismatic authority, 213, 219, 391
Charney, Tobin, 2
Chasing Ice, 370
Cherlin, Andrew, 155, 159, 167
Cherokee tribal group, 330
Chesney-Lind, Meda, 148
chief executive officer (CEO), 4, 283, 303, 307, 330
child care, nonparents giving, 86
child labor laws, 352
child protective services, 165
child training, differences in, 79–80
child-free, benefits of being, 169
children
    African American, 80
    feral, 72–73
    influence of family/schools on, 80
    observation of, 81–82
    parents' income versus income of, 248
    race and living arrangements for, 163
    school pecking order in, 81
Children of Men, 4
Children Underground, 89
China, 353–354, 370–371, 385–386

Chinatown, 332
Chinese Americans, 164, 225, 332–333
Chinese Exclusion Act, 332
chiropractic medicine, 367
Chi-Ying, Charlene Hsu, 354
Christian Scientists, 196, 203
Christianity, 197, 199
Christians, 191, 194
Christmas Carol, A, 396
Chua, Amy, 164
Church of England, 237
Cinco de Mayo ethnic event, 338
cisgender, 296–297
citizenship rights, 220–221
Civil Liberties Act, 333
civil rights
    activists, 146
    citizenship and, 220
    social movements and, 389
Civil Rights Act, 316, 320
civil rights movement, 133, 323, 329, 391
    minorities and, 211
    protestors and, 214
civilized societies, 379
Clarke, Edward, 290
The Class, 186
class, 238, 252, 390
Class: A Guide through the American Status System, 254
class consciousness, 250, 294
class system, in United States, 237–238
Clay, Cassius, 100
clerics, female, 203
The Clery Act, 136
climate change, 371–373
clinical sociology/sociologist, 19–20
Clinton, Bill, 365
Clinton, Hillary, 33, 123, 207–208, 212–213, 224–225, 279, 305
cloning, 387
closed system, 239
coalition, 108
Coalition of Women's Movements to Advocate Electoral Demands (Iran), 392
Code of Ethics, 41, 130
coevolution, gene-culture, 50
cognitive culture, 54–59, 64–65
cohabitation, 168
Cohen, Philip, 170
Colbert, Stephen, 393
collective action, 390
collective ownership, socialism and, 216
College Humor (website), 51
college students, 58, 104, 130, 377–378
colleges
    community college, 188–189
    cultural innovation by, 181

Subject Index • 451

Subject Index

colleges (continued)
  discrimination in applying to, 319
  faculty research at, 181
  likelihood of going to, 184
  likelihood of graduating from, 248–249
  majors by gender in, 185, 186
  success of women in, 50
colonialism, 262–263
color-blind racism 317
color line, 14
coltan (columbite-tantalite), 267
Columbia University, student activism at, 378
Colombian drug cartels, 138
commitment, social bonds and, 143
common beliefs, research that refutes, 24
common sense, 24–25
Common Writing, 55
Commoner, Barry, 367
commoners, estate system in medieval Europe and, 237
communism, Marx and classless society of, 381–382
The Communist Manifesto, 215
Communist Party, 219
competency examination, for teachers, 188
competition, capitalism and, 214
Compliance, 134
computer technology, 383–384
Comte, Auguste, 8–9, 49, 199, 261, 380, 396
concerted cultivation, parenting style of, 163
conclusion, drawing a research, 30–32
confidentiality, maintaining a subject's, 41
confirmation bias, definition of, 25
conflict perspective, 27, 100, 112, 147, 158, 181, 183–184, 202, 222, 322, 361, 378
conformity, 128–130
Confucians, sacred/profane objects of, 191
Congress, 225, 226, 330
conlangers, 56
Connell, R. W., 289
contact hypothesis, races and, 323
content analysis, definition of, 39–40
Contexts, 27
contraception, 300, 389
control group, 36
control variable, 32
Cooley, Charles Horton, 16, 74, 106
Coontz, Stephanie, 154, 158

Cooper, Bradley, 4
Cooper, Marianne, 283
Copernicus, Nicolaus, 8
corporate crime, 137
correlation, 31
correspondence principle, 184
counterculture, definition of, 63
courtship, 160
Crawford, Cindy, 40, 287
creative capacity, Marx's view of, 13
credentialism, 184
creed, as religious belief, 191
Crenshaw, Kimberlé, 295
crime, 135–141, 252, 318, 381
Crimes Reported to Police, 137
Croats, Serbian genocide of, 324
cross-cultural variation, 49, 79
crude birthrate, 347
crude death rate, 348
Crutcher, Terence, 310
Cruz, Eufrosina, 274
Cuba, diplomatic ties with U.S., 337
Cuban Americans, 86, 336
Cubans, Mariel boatlift to U.S., 336
cult, 194, 196–197
cultural capital, 246, 253–254
cultural domination, 52
cultural innovation, by schools/colleges, 181
cultural lag, 54, 381, 387
cultural relativism, 66
cultural resources, 239–240
cultural transmission, 144
cultural universals, 49–50
cultural variation, attitudes toward, 62–66
culture, 47–69, 71, 100
  cognitive, 64
  constructing, 49–52, 100
  lens of perception and, 48
  material, 53–54, 381
culture-bound syndrome, 354
culture shock, 64
Cumming, Elaine, 92
curanderismo, Latino folk medicine, 362
curanderos, Hispanic folk healers, 362
Currie, Elliot, 140

D

Dahl, Robert, 221–222
Dai Hin Min, 98
Daisey, Mike, 122
Dakota Access Pipeline (DAPL), 345–346
Dakota War, Sioux Indians and, 324
Dallas Buyers Club, 137
Darfur, expulsion of people from, 324
The Dark Knight Rises, 134
Dartmouth, women first admitted to, 290–291
Darwin, Charles (evolutionist), 379

Das Kapital (Marx), 382
data, 29–30, 40, 384
database, online academic, 27–28
Davenport, Thomas (technology analyst), 383
Davis, Kingsley (sociologist), 180, 183
Dawn of the Planet of the Apes, 59f
day care, 181
de Beauvoir, Simone (author), 292
de Laon, Adalbéron, 237
Deadpool, 133
death and dying, 94–95
The Death of White Sociology, 42
death penalty, 147–148
Declaration of Independence, 247
decriminalization, 138
Deepwater Horizon, 371
Deere, John, 209
deforestation, 369. See also rain forest
degradation ceremony, 89
deindustrialization, 209, 265
democracy
  capitalism versus, 221
  definition of, 219
  private versus civic life of citizens in a, 395
  spread of, 8
demographic transition, 350–353
demography, 346
denomination, 194–196
Department of Homeland Security, 349
Departures, 62
dependency
  developing nations pros and cons of, 266–267
  Wallerstein's model/theory, 263
dependent variable (y), 28–29
Desmond, Matthew, 1–2, 27, 28, 316
deviance, 127–151
  definition of, 128, 132
  Durkheim's functions of, 141
  interpersonal interaction and, 143–144
  Merton's strain theory of, 142–143
  social control versus, 132
  social stigma and, 134
  societal benefit of, 141
  status quo and, 133
  typology of, 142f
The Devil Came on Horseback, 279
Devil's Playground, 42
Dewey, Thomas E., 33
Diagnostic and Statistical Manual of Mental Disorders (DSM), 297

The Diary of a Young Girl, 70
Dickens, Charles, 396
dictatorship, 219
Dictionary of American Regional English, 55
dietary supplements, 367
difference, consequences of, 7
differential association, 144
differential justice, 147
differentiation, social change and Parsons', 380
diffusion, 51
digital divide, Internet use and, 383
Diop, Bineta, 305
discovery, 50–51
discrimination, 317–322. See also prejudice; segregation
disenchantment phase, 91
disengagement theory, 92
Disney, Walt, 52, 330
disorders of sexual development (DSDs), 285
diversity training program, 212
The Division of Labor, 114
divorce, 4, 170–172
DNA testing, 148
Doctor Who, 240
Doctors Without Borders, 230
Doha Amendment, 373
Dolly, cloned sheep, 386, 387
Domhoff, G. William, 222–224
dominant ideology, 64–65, 250
domination, cultural, 52
Domingo, Placido, 253
Don't Think Twice, 89
Donkey Kong, 83
Dothraki language, 56
downsizing, 201, 210
Downtown Abbey, 240
Dr. Strangelove, 228
dramaturgical approach, 76, 103, 358
drapetomania, 357
Driving While Black (DWB), 147, 318, 368
drug cartel, 138, 140
DSM (Diagnostic and Statistical Manual of Mental Disorders), 297
Du Bois, W. E. B., 14, 16, 42, 177–178, 329
Dude You're a Fag, 297
Dugum Dani language, 56
Durkheim, Émile
  anomie and, 13
  community, 192
  deviant acts and social circumstances, 141
  French educational policy and practice shaped by, 15
  functionalist perspective, 16, 191, 378
  interdependence and individual freedom, 261

interdependence and social change, 374
knowledge and collective consciousness, 179
macrosociology, 14
maintaining social order, 12
organic solidarity, 114, 118
religion and social order, 199–200, 202
social facts and individual actions, 11
social integration, 27
sociological theory, 9
suicide, 10–11, 16, 28, 40
dyad, 108

E

earnings. *See* income; salary; wage gap
Eastern Promises, 139
Ebaugh, Helen Rose Fuchs, 105
ecclesia, 194–195, 197
economic change, 208–211
economic downturn, crime rates and 136
economic systems, 214–218
economic vulnerability, 1
economy
 definition of, 209
 social institution of, 112
 U.S. versus Mexico, 273
Eddy, Mary Baker, 197
Edin, Kathryn, 234–235
education. *See also* colleges; schools
 as social institution, 178
 bilingual, 335
 culture transmission by, 179
 definition of, 177
 father of American public, 177
 higher family income and higher, 180
 problems of Hispanics with, 335
 religion and, 176–206
 sexism and, 185
 social change in U.S. and, 379
 social institution of, 112
 social integration/social order and, 179
 sociological perspectives on, 179
 students' performance and parents' level of, 182
 system of inequality in, 181
 transmitting culture with, 177
educational attainment, 177–178

educational discrimination, gender and, 185
EEOC (Equal Employment Opportunity Commission), 93
effect, definition of Hawthorne, 37, 40
egalitarian
 family, definition of, 158
 society, 261
egalitarianism, 261
18th Amendment, 132
eHarmony, 162
elderly. *See also* age; aging
 Alzheimer's disease and, 363
 chronic disease and, 92
 fitness and, 92–93
 growth of U.S. numbers of, 91
 part-time jobs and, 91
 respect for, 90
 standard of living and, 94
 use of Internet and, 93
 volunteering and, 93
Election Consortium, election prediction by, 224
election prediction, sources of, 224
electoral votes, 212
electric shock, Milgram experiment and, 129–130
Electronic Communications Privacy Act, 386
Elgin, Suzette Haden, 56–57
Eliot, George, 167
Elle, 288
Elliott, Michael, 192
Ellison, Ralph, 328
Ellul, Jacques, 388
el-Qaddafi, Muammar, 391
Elvish language, 56
Embrace of the Serpent, 62
Emerbayer, Mustafa, 316
emigration. *See also* immigrants; immigration
 definition of, 348
 from Mexico to U.S., 276
 of health care professionals, 357
Empire Falls, 51
employee handbooks, 120
employment trends, U.S., 3
endogamy 161
Engels, Friedrich, 158, 215
environment
 genes and, 50
 new social movement for, 392
 relationship to people, 368
 social perspectives on, 367–370
environmental issues, public perception over time of, 370
environmental justice, definition of, 369
environmental problems, types of, 370–373

Episcopalian church, suicide and, 10
epochs, Marx's stages of exploitation through history, 381
Equal Employment Opportunity Commission (EEOC), 93
equality, Wells-Barnett and, 14
equilibrium, 380
error, sampling, 30
Esperanto language, 55–56
An Essay on the Principle of Population, 350–351
established sect, 196
estate system, 237
ethics, research, 41–43
ethnic cleansing, 277, 324
ethnic neighborhoods, 326
ethnic succession, 139
ethnicity, 312, 314–316
 definition of, 312
 morbidity/mortality rates vary by, 360
 names of ethnic groups, 334–338
 no health insurance based on, 361
 suicide rate, 12
 unemployment rate, 3
ethnocentrism
 advantages/disadvantages of, 66
 definition of, 65, 78, 316
 industrialized countries and, 369
 primitive versus modern societies, 380
ethnography, 35
Evans, Jack, 170
Everything is Illuminated, 200
Evicted: Poverty and Profit in the American City (Desmond), 27
eviction, 1
evolution
 social, 379
 teaching of, 193
executions of criminals, 147
exogamy, 161
Experiment 5, Milgram's, 129
experimental group, 36
exploitation, Marx's epochs of, 381
exploitation theory, 322
expressive leader, 301
expulsion, 324
extinction, 373
Exxon Valdez, 371
ExxonMobil, 41–42
Eye in the Sky, 221

F

Facebook, 108, 111
 China blocks access to, 386
 governmental decision making and, 222
 information privacy and, 384

 mass protests organized by, 391
 NSA collects user data from, 386
 social networking and, 84
face-work, definition of, 77
faith healer, 367
false consciousness, 251
familism, 164
family, 152–175
 blended, 153
 breadwinner's role in the, 153
 definition of egalitarian, 158
 definition of extended, 155
 definition of nuclear, 155
 dual-income, 165
 functions and types of, 154, 157
 functionalist definition of, 157
 gay/lesbian, 156
 households by type of, 156
 multigenerational, 167
 power and decisions in the, 157
 racially mixed, 156
 related by blood, 153
 related by law, 154
 single-parent, 156
 social change in the U.S. and the, 379
 social institution of, 111–112
 socialization by, 79
 society's status quo and, 158
 substantive definition of, 153
 U.S. Census Bureau definition of, 156
family network, 155
family therapy, 20
family tree, 156
fanatics, religion and sports, 192
fasting, as religious practice, 191
Father Knows Best, 165, 295
Faulkner, William, 61
Fausto-Sterling, Anne, 285
FBI
 African American racial profiling and, 320
 crime clock, 136
 sexual orientation and hate crimes and, 297
 statistics on rape and murder of women, 305
 Uniform Crime Reports, 135
feedback loop, interactions and, 75
Feld, Scott, 108
female. *See also* woman; women

Subject Index • 453

Subject Index

female genital mutilation, 278–279
female interviewers, 34
female sociologists, 15
female-dominated domains, 392
The Feminine Mystique, 292–293, 301, 391
feminism. *See also* gender; women
    definition of, 292
    first wave, 292
    in the mid-1800s, 158
    labor market and, 301
    multiple-identity approach, 294
    second wave, 292–293
    third wave, 294
    women's right to vote, 292
feminist methodology, 43
feminist theorists, 43
feminists, dominant ideology and, 65
Femmes Africa Solidarité, 305
Fences, 328
fertility, 347
feudalism, 216, 237, 381
Fieldston private school, 176
fiesta politics, 225–226
55: A Meditation on the Speed Limit, 60
56 Up, 42
Fight Club, 305
Fill the Void, 164
film pirates, 133
Findlen, Barbara, 294
Fischer, Eric, 326
The Fits, 305
FiveThirtyEight.com, 33, 224
fixed fallacy, 317
Flynt, Larry, 223
folkways
    definition of, 181
    mores versus, 59
food production, 386
food stamps, 244
Food, Inc., 370
force
    dictatorship and, 219
    Weber's definition of, 212
formal norms, 59–60
formal social control, 180
45 Years, 94
Frank, Anne, 70
Franklin, Benjamin, 177, 179, 188, 247
fraternity and sorority, 109
free agent (sports), 6
Freedom Schools, 377
Freedom Summer, 377
Freedom Writers, 186
Freeman, Morgan, 94
free-market principles, 216
Friedan, Betty, 292–293, 301, 307, 391
friendship networks, 325
friendship paradox, 108–109
Frommer, Paul, 56
front stage, 76
functionalist definition of family, 157
functionalist perspective, 27, 112, 141, 143, 157, 179, 180, 181, 191, 301, 322, 355, 378
functionalist sociological view 15
fundamentalism, 193
Fussell, Paul, 254

G

Gage, Zach, 101
Galilei, Galileo, 8
Gallup, 32, 268
Gambari, Ibrahim, 279
gambling, 331
Game of Thrones, 56
game stage of self, 76
games, 98–99
Gandhi, Mahatma, 213
Garner, Eric, 146
Gates, Bill, 274
Gay Activist Alliance, 295
gay/lesbian people, 296, 391. *See also* gender; homosexuality
    adoption by couples who are, 165
    new social movement for rights of, 392
    same-sex marriage, 169
Gay Liberation Front, 295
Gemeinschaft, 113
gender. *See also* gender role
    birth certificate category, 285
    clothing and hair cues, 287
    college majors, 185, 186
    colors and toys, 286
    definition, 284
    educational discrimination, 185
    federal educational funding, 178
    female men, 289
    hate crimes for gender identity, 318
    labor force participation by, 302
    male women, 289
    morbidity/mortality rates, 360
    number of sociology degrees, 18
    rape, 148
    suicide rate, 12
    unemployment rates, 3
Gender and Society, 27
gender bias, women overlooked due to, 392
gender binary model, 296–297
gender dysphoria, 297
gender expression, 296
Gender Gap Index score, 306
gender identity, 296, 318
gender inequality, 301–307
gender role
    effeminate-gay masculine, 289
    expectations for, 288
    nurturing-caring masculine, 289
    traditional masculine/feminine, 289
    gender spectrum, definition, 296–297
gender-related language, 56
gender-role socialization, 286–289
gene mapping, 312
gene pool, biotechnology and, 386–387
gene-culture coevolution, 50
General Motors, 217
General Social Survey (GSS), 38
generalized other, 76, 85, 179
Generation Climate, 377
generation, sandwich, 90
genes, 49–50
genetic modification, 386
genetics, 312
genocide, 128–129, 200, 279, 324
gentile (non-Jew), 337
George, Andy (YouTube), 5
Germans, 66, 128–129
gerontology, 91
Gesellschaft, 113, 118
gestures, 57–58
Ghost World, 134
GI bill, 188
Gilman, Charlotte Perkins, 301
Gini index, 242
Gini, Corrado, 241–242
Ginsberg, Ruth Bader, 305
Gintis, Herbert, 81, 184
Girl, Interrupted, 134
The Girl on the Train, 51
Glasgow, Ellen, 380
glass ceiling, 303, 321, 330
Glass Ceiling Commission, 303
Glee, 297, 297
global climate change, 371–373
global divide, 256–260
global financial collapse, 210
globalization
    definition and examples of, 17, 118, 264–265
    of labor, 210
    pros and cons, 373
global perspective, social structure and, 113–118
global recession, 208
Global Slavery Index, 236
GM (genetically modified) food, 386
GNI (gross national income), 260, 268, 271
goal displacement, 120
goals, 142
God, 247
Goffman study, 35
Goffman, Alice, 23–24, 27, 32, 35–36, 42
Goffman, Erving, 14, 39, 16, 76–77, 89, 103–104, 134
Good Hair, 59

Google, 28, 59, 386
government
    health care reform, 365–366
    public trust in, 222
    social institution, 112
graffiti artist/writers, 63, 144
Gramsci, Antonio, 65
grandparents, 164
Granovetter, Mark, 110–111
Gran Torino, 94
Gray, John, 290
Great Dalmuti (game), 98
Great Depression, 211, 252
The Great Gatsby, 251
Great Recession, 210–211, 216
Green Card, 349
Green Party, 220
Greenbaum, Lisa, 176
greenhouse, effect and gases, 371–373
gross national income (GNI), 260, 268, 271
groups, 6, 14, 36, 66, 82, 105–108, 113, 208
growth rate, 350
GSS (General Social Survey), 38
Guantánamo Bay detention camps, 279
Güeros, 276
Gull, William, 354
guns, 127–128, 139, 141
Gupta, Ruchira, 306
Gutenberg, Johannes, 83
Gutiérrez, Gustavo, 202

H

Habitat for Humanity, 396
hajj, Muslim pilgrimage to Mecca, 194
Half the Sky, 306
happiness, 10–11, 109–110
Harlow, Harry, 73
Harrington, Michael, 116–117
Harris, George, 170
Harris, Neil Patrick, 299
Harry Potter, 70
Harvard University, 78, 184, 290–291, 318, 377
hate crimes, 318
Hawthorne effect, 37, 40
Head Start program, 86
health, 356, 359, 379
health care
    African Americans access to, 330
    costs in U.S., 364–367
    inequality of, 357
    countries that provide universal coverage, 364
    social rights and coverage, 221
Health Care and Education Reconciliation Act, 365
health care professionals, 356
health care reform, 365
health insurance, 361, 363, 365
Heaven's Gate cult, 196

Subject Index

Heilskov, Dr., 356
Hell or High Water, 137
Helú, Carlos Slim, 274
Henry, William, 92
heteronormativity, 297
heterosexual, 296, 299. *See also* gender
Hicks, Louis, 227
hidden curriculum, 184
Hidden Figures, 328
hierarchy of authority, 120
high culture, 253
hijras, 289
Hill-Burton Act, 365
Hindu Spring Festival (Holi), 51
Hinduism, 65, 198–199, 236–237
hip-hop crowd, 107
hippies, 63
Hirschi, Travis, 143
Hispanics. *See also* Latinos
    community college, 189
    folk healers, 362
    in Los Angeles, 335
    largest U.S. minority group, 334
    living arrangements for children, 163
    major groups in U.S., 336
    median household wealth, 5
    morbidity/mortality rates, 361
    numbers in U.S. cities, 335
    percentage of U.S. workforce, 211
    poverty and low-income urban, 245
    poverty rates, 94, 329
    social network, 92
    Spanish-speaking ethnic group, 314–315
    suicide rate, 12
    unemployment rate, 3
    underrepresented in movies, 326
Hitler, Adolf, 213, 219
HIV/AIDS, 357–360
Hochschild, Arlie Russell, 207, 304
Holder, Eric, 319
holistic medicine, 366
Holocaust, 337
Home School Legal Defense Association, 190
homeless, 135
homeschooling, 189–190
homicides, use of guns in U.S., 127
homogamy, 162
homophily, 110–111
homosexuality, 296–297, 299, 358. *See also* gay/lesbian people
honesty, value of, 59
Hoover, Herbert, 83
horizontal mobility, 239
hormones, 284
horticultural society, 115
hospice, 94
The House I Live In, 137
housing, discrimination in, 319, 325
"How to Make Things Happen" (YouTube), 5
Hubbard, L. Ron, 197
Hull House, 15
Human Development Index (HDI), 260
human ecology, 367
Human Genome Project (HGP), 312
human relations approach, 123
human rights, 276–280
    cultural imperialism and, 279
    definition and examples of, 277
    female genital mutilation and, 278–279
    global security versus, 278
    Guantánamo Bay detention camps, 279
    India's caste system, 278
Human Rights Watch, 277, 279
human trafficking, 139, 277–278
The Hunger Games: Catching Fire, 4
hunting-and-gathering society, 115
Hurston, Zora N., 34
Hutterites, sect of, 196
Hypothesis, 28
    broken window, 145
    linguistic relativity, 56
    Sapir-Whorf, 56–57, 117

I

I (acting self), definition of, 75, 79
ICE (Immigration and Customs Enforcement) agency, 341, 350
ideal norms, 60
ideal type, 119
identity theft, 385. *See also* data breach; information privacy
ideology, dominant, 64–65
immigrants. *See also* emigration; immigration
    illegal from Mexico to U.S., 274
    categories of, 349–350
    illegal, 336, 350
    nationalities of, 139
    nationalities of current, 139
    not legal to hire undocumented, 340
    religious integration and, 200
    silent raids and illegal, 341
    viewed as inferior to Whites, 313
immigration. *See also* emigration
    around the world, 338–339
    Bush and Obama administrations and illegal, 341
    definition of, 348
    from Latin American and Asia, 340
    illegal, 336, 350
    labor versus law enforcement issue, 276
    legal to the U.S., 340
    perception versus reality of rates of, 34
    policies for, 340
    remittances and, 339
    societal boundaries affected by, 51
    trends in, 338–339
    Trump administration and Muslim ban on, 341
    U.S. policy on relatives and, 340
    U.S. refused Jews, 340
Immigration Act, 333
Immigration Customs and Enforcement (ICE) agency, 341, 350
Immigration Reform and Control Act, 240
impersonality, 120–121
implicit association tests, 78
implicit bias, 78
impression management, 77
Improv Everywhere
    No Pants Subway Ride, 60
    prank collective, 47–48
Incarcerating US, 137
incarceration. *See also* prison
    international rates of, 140
    of African American disproportionate, 132
    rates in U.S. versus other countries, 140
    U.S. rates of, 131
incest taboo, 161
incidence, 359
inclusion, 380
income. *See also* salary; wage discrimination; wage gap
    attaining a degree and resulting, 31
    definition of, 240
    gross national (GNI), 260, 268, 271
    household (by quintile), 241
    life expectancy and, 361
    no health insurance based on, 361
    parents' income versus child's projected, 248
    per capita gross national, 261
    teachers' average, 188
    total (by quintile), 241
income dispersion, 240, 241
income inequality, 241, 268–269, 321
income per capita, 260, 261
independent variable (x), 28–29
index crimes, 136
India, 210, 236–237, 289
Indian Gambling Regulatory Act, 331
individualism, 2, 6
    American, 57
    rugged, 99
individualistic fallacy, 316
industrialization, 116
Industrial Revolution, 8, 12, 116, 209, 260–262, 383
    air pollution and climate change during, 367
    education and, 177
    emergence of sociology and, 209
    population and, 352
    resistance to, 387–388
    urban population growth and, 116
industrial society, 116
inequality. *See also* income inequality; gender inequality; wage discrimination
    global, 258–282
    Karl Marx and, 14
    Max Weber and, 14
    of education system, 181
    of health care, 357
    schools reinforce, 81
    social order and, 322.
infant mortality rate, 348
informal economy, 217–218
informal norms, 59–60, 181
The Informant, 139
information privacy, 384
information, how to find, 27
innovation, definition of, 50–51, 378
Inside Job, 139
Instagram, 71, 84, 107–108, 384
Institution, 7, 89. *See also* social institution
institutional discrimination, 301, 320–322, 329
instrumental leader, 301
integration, immigrants and religious, 200
integrity, 41
interaction, social structure, 98–126
interactional perspective, 74
interactionist perspective, 17, 76, 143, 183, 323, 378
interactionist sociological view, 15–16
interdependence on others, 2
intergenerational mobility, 271–272, 239
intergroup relations, types of, 323
internalizing culture, 71

Subject Index • 455

Subject Index

International Conference on Primary Health Care, 356
International Monetary Fund, 264–265
international students, 181
Internet
    as type of mass media, 84
    collection action and, 111
    elderly use of, 93
    global use of, 111, 383–384
    global village, 384
    health information, 359
    languages used on, 383, 385
    origin of, 383
    privacy, 384
    societal boundaries, 51
interpersonal discrimination, 317
interracial marriage, 314, 316, 328
interrelationships, 6
intersectionality, 295
interview, 33–34
Into the Woods, 51
intragenerational mobility, 239
Inuit tribes, 62
invention, 51
The Invention of Lying, 59
Invisible Man (Ellison), 328
Iran, 158, 392
Iraqi government, democratic reform, 65–66
Iraq's Abu Ghraib prison, 130
Irish American immigrants, 139
iron law of oligarchy, 122
Ironman, 54
Islam, 101, 195, 197, 199
isolation, extreme childhood, 72–73
Italian American immigrants, 139

J

Jacobson, Lenore, 182
James, LeBron, 6–7
Jamestown, European settlers at, 311
Japan, 66, 79–80
Japanese Americans, 333
Jarvis, DeForest Clinton, 359
Jefferson, Thomas, 177, 179, 188, 236, 247
Jehovah's Witnesses, 196
Jenner, Caitlyn, 296
Jesus Christ, 194, 197, 202, 213
Jewish American immigrants, 139, 337
Jewish people, 128–129, 191, 200, 324, 337, 340
Jim Crow laws, 329
Joan of Arc, 213
job training, 183, 179–180
jobs, 18–19, 85–86, 209, 253, 319
Johnson, Gary, 220
Johnson, Lyndon B., 227, 244
Johnson, Magic, 358
Jolie, Angelina, 171
Jope, John Colyn, 311
Journal of the American Medical Association, 359
Judaism, 198–199
The Jungle Book, 89

K

Kagan, Elena, 305
Kalish, Richard, 94
Kay, Paul, 56
Kaye, Judith, 165
KDKA, first radio station, 83
Kennedy, Anthony, 170
Kennedy, John F., 83
Kenya, cells phones in, 85
Keqiang, Li, 216
Kerry, John, 224
Keynes, John Maynard, 210
Keys, Alicia, 287–288
Khorasani, Noushin Ahmadi, 392
Khosrowshahi, Dara, 250
The Kids Are All Right, 305
Kilbourne, Jeanne, 39
Killing Them Softly, 221
Killing Us Softly: Advertising's Image of Women, 39
Kimmel, Michael, 289
King, Martin Luther, Jr., 213, 317, 329, 391, 394
Kings and Servants (game), 98
Kinsey, Alfred C., 298, 299
Kinsey, 42
Kinsey Reports, 298–299
kinship, 154
Kinyarwanda, 276
Kitzmiller v. Dover Area School District, 193
Korean Americans, 333
Koreatown, 326
koro, 354
Kota (Congo) rite of passage, 86–87
Kozol, Jonathan, 182
Kristof, Nicholas, 306
Ku Klux Klan, 316f, 329
Kübler-Ross, Elisabeth, 94
Kurds, 334
Kyoto Protocol, 373

L

labeling theory, 145, 183
labels, 134
labor, 119, 209–210, 307
labor force, and women, 301–302
labor unions, 122–123, 382
Ladies' Home Journal, 286
Ladner, Joyce, 42–43
laissez-faire, 215
Lamm, Nickolay, 286
landlords and tenants, 1–2
Landon, Alf, 30
language
    components of, 54–55
    creation of Láadan, 57
    definition of, 54
    dictionaries and changes in, 55
    Dothraki, 56f
    Dugum Dani, 56
    Elvish, 56
    gender-related, 56
    hybrid, 55
    international auxiliary, 55
    Internet's top, 385
    Navajo (Diné bizaad), 57
    Na'vi, 56
    nonsexist, 56
    region of origin of a living, 54
    social nature of, 55
    stereotypes in and transmitted by, 56–57
    symbolic, 62
    words for colors in different, 56
Language Creation Society, 56
Lareau, Annette, 163–164, 182, 361
Latinos
    access to but inferior health care for, 362
    community coalition of Whites and, 108
    differential justice and, 147
    educational problems of, 335
    median household income of, 335
    prison sentences of, 147
    proximity to hazardous waste facilities, 369
    reluctance to seek medical care, 362
    representatives in Congress, 225, 226
    single-parent family and, 166
    Spanish-speaking ethnic group, 314–315
    stop and frisk, 145
    unemployment rate and, 3
Lauren, Ralph, 325
law of supply and demand, 214
Law of Three Stages, 380
Lawrence, Jennifer, 4
laws
    definition of, 99
    formal norms and, 59–60
    nature and, 49
    of society, 8
    society and, 49, 131
    versus regulations, 131
lawsuits, file sharing on Internet and, 133
League of Arab States, 334
Lean in: Women, Work, and the Will to Lead (Cooper), 283
Leanin.org, 284
leapfrogging, technology and, 383
learning disorder, 190
Leave It to Beaver, 295
Lee, Harper, 66
Lee, Sing, 354
Lee, Spike, 333
The Left Hand of Darkness (Le Guin), 70
legalistic fallacy, racism and, 316
legalization, of marijuana, 132
Legally Blond, 51
L'Engle, Madeleine, 70
Lenski, Gerhard, 115
Lenton, Steven, 288
Les Misérables, 221
lesbian, gay, bisexual, and transgender (LGBT), 298
lesbian/gay people, 296
    adoption by couples who are, 165
    new social movement for rights of, 392
    same-sex marriage, 169
Le Bon, Gustave, 62
Le Guin, Ursula K., 70, 327
Leviathan, 62
Lewis, Michael, 25
LGBT (lesbian, gay, bisexual, and transgender), 298
liberation theology, 202
Libertarian Party, 220
Lichtenberg, Georg Christoph, 390
life chances, 159, 235–239, 260, 346
life course, 86–87
life cycle, 87
life expectancy
    by race and sex, 330
    definition of, 348
    income and, 361
    reasons for women's longer, 363
    women versus men, 362
life goals, college students and, 58
life satisfaction, 10
lifestyles, 167–168
Lincoln, Abraham, 324
linguistic relativity hypothesis, 56
Listen Up: Voices from the Next Feminist Generation (Findlen), 294
Literary Digest, 30
literature, types of research, 27
Little Golden Books, gender inequality in, 288
Little Tokyo, 326
Little, Omar, 139
living will, 95
Lodwick, Francis, 55
Loehmann, Timothy, 310
looking-glass self, 74, 106
Lorber, Judith, 287, 289
Lord of the Rings (Tolkien), 56
Loving, 164
Loving, Mildred and Richard, 162
Luckmann, Thomas, 100
Luddites, 388

Lukács, Greg, 65
Luther, Martin, 196, 201
lynching, 14

M

macrosociology, 14
Madoff, Bernie, 137–138
Mai, Mukhtar, 306
makkunrai (Indonesia), 289
malaria, 367
Malcolm X, 103, 194, 213, 329
male-dominated domains, 392
Malthus, Thomas, 350–351
Mama Hope, 306
mandatory sentences, 131
Mandela, Nelson, 325
Mann, Horace, 177, 179, 188, 247
maquiladoras, 276
Margin Call, 139
marijuana, 81, 132, 138
Mark the Match Boy (Alger), 247
Marriage, 159–160
    global views of, 153
    interracial, 162, 314, 316, 328
    milestones to reach, 171
    parental-arranged, 49
    questions to ask before, 161
    same-sex, 61, 153, 169–170
    Supreme Court and interracial, 162
    trends in, 172
    types of, 155
Mars, Bruno, 253
Marshall, T. H., 220–221
Martin, George R. R., 56
Martin, Trayvon, 146
Martineau, Harriet, 9, 14, 301
Marx, Karl
    capitalism and, 13, 250
    class consciousness, 294
    classless communist society, 381–382
    conflict perspective, 361, 378
    egalitarian society, 261
    elite model of power, 222–223
    false consciousness, 251
    material resources and class tension, 251–253
    power and social order, 13
    religion and the powerful, 200, 203
    ruling class, 65
    social order and change, 116
    socialism and, 215–216
    sociological perspective, 16*t*
    sociological theory, 9
    stages of exploitation, 381
    technology and loss of jobs, 383
masculinity, 289

M*A*S*H, 228
mass media, 51, 82–83
mass shootings, 127–128
Massacre of 1622, 311
The Master, 200
master status, 103, 134, 298, 357
Masterpiece, 253
Masterpiece Classic, 240
Masto, Catherine Cortez, 225, 305
matchmaker, 154, 160
mate selection, 160–161
material culture, 50, 53–54, 381
material resources, 239, 250
matriarchy, 158
matrilineal descent, 154
Maugham, W. Somerset, 95
McCain, John, 224, 279
McCormick, Cyrus, 209
McCormick, Rae, 234, 246
McDonaldization, 121–122
McGuffey's Eclectic Readers, 247
McIntosh, Peggy, 327
Me (socialized self), 75
Mead, George Herbert, 16, 74–77, 79, 85, 99, 179, 378
Mead, interactionist perspective of, 74–75
Mead, Margaret, 74–75, 78, 85, 289–290
mean, 35, 109
means, 142
mechanization, 250
Médecins Sans Frontières (Doctors Without Borders), 279
median, 35, 109
Medicaid, 365
medicalization, 356, 358
Medicare, 353, 365
medicine, 366–367
Meier, Deborah, 181
Meigs, Charles, 290
melting pot, 324
Melville, Herman, 70
Men Are from Mars, Women Are from Venus (Gray), 290
Menozzi, Paolo, 312
meritocracy, 181, 247
Merriam-Webster Collegiate Dictionary, 55
Merton, Robert, 16*t*, 107, 120, 142–143
methodology, feminist, 43
metrics, bureaucracy and, 122
Mexican Americans, 164, 336, 362
Mexican immigrants, White working-class view of, 207
Mexican Indians, status of indigenous, 274
Mexico
    emigration to U.S. from, 276
    homicides in, 140
    illegal immigrants to U.S. from, 274
    income and status of women in, 274–275
    women and politics in, 274–275

Michels, Robert, 122
microsociology, 14
middle-brow, 253
middle class, U.S., 238
midlife crisis, 89
midwifery, 382
migrants, smuggling of, 140
migration, 348–350
Milanovic, Branko, 268–269
Milgram, Stanley, 128–130
military rule, oligarchy and, 218–219
Millennium Declaration, 270
Millett, Kate, 292
Mills, C. Wright, 2–3, 222–223
Minangkabau society, 290
minority group, 312
Mirren, Helen, 325
Miss Quinceañera Latina pageant, 87
Missouri principle, "Don't just tell me, show me," 8, 380
mixed economy, 216
mobility, 271–272
Moby Dick (Melville), 70
mode, 35
model or ideal minority, 331
modernization, 261, 266
Mohai, Paul, 369
Mona Lisa Smile, 122
monarchy, 66, 218
monastic orders, 199
Moneyball, 25
monogamy, 155
monopoly, 215
monotheistic, 191
Montagu, Ashley, 314
Moody, James, 108
Moonlight, 305
Moore, Wilbert E., 180, 183
morbidity rate, 360
mores, 59
Moriarty, William Kyle, 133
Mormon, 196
mortality rate, 260
Mott, Lucretia, 292
M-Pesa app, 383
Mubarak, Hosni, 391
Mugabe, Robert, 279
multinational corporations, 265–266
multiple masculinities, 289
multiracial identity, 314
Mumbai (India), inequality in, 258–259
Munsch, Robert, 288
murder, 141, 305. *See also* genocide; mass shootings
Murdock, George, 49, 155
Muslim people, 192, 194, 267, 315, 324, 341

N

NAACP (National Association for the Advancement of Colored People), 15, 329
name-calling, 288–289, 297
names, most popular baby, 38–39

National Association for the Advancement of Colored People (NAACP), 15, 329
National Center for Complementary and Alternative Medicine, 367
National Center for Health Statistics (NCHS), 298
National Crime Victimization Survey, 136, 305
national health insurance, resistance of AMA to, 382
National Human Trafficking Resource Center, 236
National Institutes of Health (NIH), 367
National Opinion Research Center (NORC), 38
National Organization for Women (NOW), 293
National Security Agency (NSA), collection of user data by, 386
National Survey of Family Growth (NSFG), 298–299
Native Americans
    family authority of women, 158
    female men, 289
    gambling on reservations, 331
    male women (berdaches), 289
    morbidity/mortality rates of, 361
    reservations for, 313
    schools prohibited cultural practices of, 330
    U.S. genocide of, 324
native culture, 52
natural growth, 164
natural science, 12, 50
naturalism, 193
nature, 49–50
Navajo, 57, 330
Na'vi language, 56
Nayar (India), parenting patterns, 162–163
Nazi Germany, 128–129, 200, 324, 337
NCHS (National Center for Health Statistics), 298
near phase, 91
Nebraska, 94
neocolonialism, 263
neo-Nazi skinheads, 337
networks, 108, 117, 155
Neuqua Valley High School (suburban), 176
new religious movement (NRM), 196–197
new social movements, 392–393
Newton, Isaac, 8
Newton, Nigel, 70
NGOs (nongovernmental organizations), 230, 276–277
Nicholson, Jack, 94
Nickerson, Raymond, 25
NIH (National Institutes of Health), 367

Subject Index

NIMBY (not in my backyard), 369, 382
nirvana, state of enlightenment, 190, 199
Nixon, Richard M., 83, 131, 227
No Child Left Behind, 388
No Pants Subway Ride, 47–48
Nobel Peace Prize, 279
nongovernmental organizations (NGOs), 230, 276–277
nonmaterial culture, definition and examples of, 381
nonsexist language, 56
nonverbal communication, 57–58
NORC (National Opinion Research Center), 38
normative culture, 59
norms
    breaking, 60–61
    definition of, 59, 99, 100, 194, 287, 393
    exceptions to, 60
    following versus violating, 62
    formal versus informal, 59–60
    ideal versus real, 59, 60
    informal, 181
    real, 60
    religion and, 194
    types of, 59
    values and, 128
    violation of cultural, 60–61
not in my backyard (NIMBY), 369, 382
NOW (National Organization for Women), 293
NRM (new religious movement), 196–197
NSA (National Security Agency), collection of user data by, 386
NSFG (National Survey of Family Growth), 298–299
Nyinba (Nepal, Tibet), polyandry and the, 155–156

O

O'Connor, Sandra Day, 305
Obama administration, illegal immigration and, 341
Obama, Barack
    African Americans versus Whites view of, 5
    approval ratings for, 33
    breaking glass ceiling, 330
    commitment to meritocracy, 247
    Dakota Access Pipeline and, 346
    interracial marriage of parents of, 314
    ObamaCare and, 365
    presidential election and voter turnout, 207, 224
    socialism and, 217
    statement on violence in Darfur, 279
    success and, 317
Obama, Michelle, 15
ObamaCare (Affordable Care Act), 364–365
obedience, 128
Oberlin College, 185
Oberschall, Anthony, 391
observation, 6, 35–36, 81–82, 145, 221
occupational gender segregation, 302
occupational socialization, 85
occupations, 209, 253
OECD (Organisation for Economic Co-operation and Development), 28
Office Space, 122
offshoring, 210, 265–266
Ogburn, William F., 54, 157, 381, 387
Okrand, Marc, 56
Okrent, Arika, 56
Okun, Arthur, 221
older adults, 93, 363
oligarchy, 122, 218–219
Omi, Michael, 313
On Death and Dying (Kübler-Ross), 94
On the Run: Fugitive Life in an American City (Goffman), 27
one-child policy, China, 353
one-drop rule, 312
online dating services, 152–153, 162
online polls, 30
open system, 239
operational definition, 29
opportunity gap, 248
organic solidarity, 118
Organisation for Economic Co-operation and Development (OECD), 28
organized crime, 138–139
oroané (Indonesia), 289
Orwell, George, 70
The Other America, 116

P

Pager, Devah, 37–38, 318, 328
Pan-Cordillera Women's Network for Peace and Development, 273
panhandling, 145
pansexual, 296
The Paper Bag Princess, 288
parent, 156, 166
parenting, 162–167
Paris Agreement, 373–374
Parks, Rosa, 323
Parsons, Talcott, 16, 301, 380
participant observation, 35
Partners in Development Programme, 273
Pascoe, C. J., 297
patriarchy, 158
patrilineal descent, 154
peace, 230
Peace Corps, 396
The Peanuts Movie, 133
Peattie, Lisa, 290
peer groups, 81–82
Pell Grants, 188
Pelosi, Nancy, 293, 305
"The Pentagon Papers," 227
Persepolis, 62
Personal Responsibility and Work Opportunity Reconciliation Act, 246
personal sociology, 17, 394
personal values, 42
Peterson, David J., 56
pets, as part of family, 157
Pew Research Center, 32, 117
Philomena, 4
Philosopher's Stone (Rowling), 70
Philosophical Language (Wilkin), 55
physicians, 356, 357–359, 361, 364–365
Piazza, Alberto, 312
Piestewa, Lori, 228
Piketty, Thomas, 241–242, 251–252
Pinderhughes, Dianne, 222
Pitt, Brad, 171
place, significance of, 4–5
plagiarism, 59
Plath, Sylvia, 70
Platt, Marc, 51
play stage of self, 75
Plessy v. Ferguson, 178, 329
pluralism, 326
pluralist model, 221
Pocahontas, 311
Pokémon, Pokémon Go (game), 85
policy makers, 3
political rights, 220
political system, 218
politics
    definition of, 218
    ethnocentrism and, 78
    participation, 224, 396
polls, 30, 32–33, 224, 268,
pollution, 368, 392. *See also* air pollution; water pollution
polyandry, 155
polygamy, 66, 155
polygyny, 155
polysexual, 296
Ponzi scheme, Madoff and, 137
pop culture, 253
population
    dynamics, 350, 353
    growth of world's, 351
    pyramid, 351–352, 352, 353
    social change in U.S., 379
    world clock of, 346
Portman, Natalie, 325
postindustrial society, 116
Postman, Neil, 388–389
postmodern society, 117–118
poverty, 245–246
    American Indians and, 331
    contribution to social stability, 381
    definition of absolute and relative, 243–246
    global, 270
    housing in Manila (Philippines), 263
    rates by race/ethnicity, 329
    regions and the global, 271
poverty line, 246, 259, 270
poverty rate, 4, 94, 243
poverty threshold, 244
power
    definition of, 252, 390
    family issue of decisions and, 157
    Weber's definition of, 212
power elite, 222–223
The Power Elite (Mills), 223
power structure, models of U.S., 221–224
Powhatan Indians, 311
Precious, 186
predestination, 201
preexisting conditions, 365
Pregnancy Discrimination Act, 165
preindustrial society, 115
prejudice, 78, 316–317, 329. *See also* discrimination; segregation
preparatory stage of self, 75
President (game), 98
presidential debate, 83
presidential elections, 30, 32–33, 224
Prestige ship, oil spill, 371
prestige, 252
prevalence, 359
primitive societies, 379
The Princess and the Frog, 330
The Princess and the Pony, 288
The Princess Bride, 164
Princess Daisy, the Dragon, and the Nincompoop Knights, 288
Princess Diaries, 70
Princess Tiana, 330
PRISM program, NSA collects user data with, 386
prison, 136, 228. *See also* incarceration
private trouble, 3, 209, 293
privilege, 38, 327–328, 395
profane (common), 191
profit, capitalism and, 214
Prohibition, 132
Project Head Start, 181
proletariat, 250
proportional representation, 220
prostitution, deviant behavior and, 145

Protestant ethic, 201
Protestant Reformation, 196, 201–202
protests/riots, 380
public issues, 3, 209, 293
public policy, 389
public sociology, 394–396
Puerto Ricans, 336
The Pursuit of Happyness, 4
Putnam, Robert, 248–249

Q

qualitative approach, data collection and, 6
quantitative research, 34–35
Queen Elizabeth II, 218
Questionnaire, 34
quinceañera rite of passage, 87
Quinney, Richard, 147
quotidian cruelties, 306
Qur'an, Muslim holy book, 192, 334

R

race, 312–314. *See also* ethnicity
    as a word is racist, 314
    categories of, 314–315
    definition of, 311
    life expectancy by, 330
    morbidity/mortality rates vary by, 360
    no genetic or scientific basis for, 312
    no health insurance based on, 361
    relations in Mexico, 274
    skin color and, 313
    suicide rate by, 12
    unemployment rate by, 3
racial formation, definition of, 313
racial groups, 312, 328–334
racial minorities, 328–334
racial profiling, 146, 318
racial stereotypes, in films, 330
racism, 316–317
Ragged Dick (Alger), 247
rain forest, 358, 368. *See also* deforestation
random digit dialing, 29
random sample, 29
Rank, Mark, 246
rape, 148, 305–306
rational-legal authority, 213
Reagan, Ronald, 131, 333
real norms, 60
Really Bad Chess (game), 101
Reardon, Sean, 248
Red Crescent, 230
Red Cross, 230, 277
red tape, bureaucratic, 120
redneck, 253
reference group, 107
refugees and asylees, 349
Rein, Martin, 290
reincarnation, 198
Reinharz, Shulamit, 43
relative deprivation, 389–390

reliability, 30, 33
religion
    beliefs and, 192–193
    components of, 192–197
    definition of, 190
    Durkheim's definition of, 191
    education and, 176–206
    ethnocentrism and, 78
    rituals and, 193
    sacred objects and, 192
    sacred realm of, 190
    sanctions and, 194
    social change and, 200–202
    social control and, 202–203
    social institution and, 112, 193
    socialization and, 86
    sociological perspectives on, 199–204
    sports fans as a, 191
    unaffiliated category of, 196
    woman's role in, 203–204
religious beliefs, 193
religious events, 86
religious experience, 194
religious ritual, 193
religious services, 193
religious tolerance, 9
religious traditions, U.S., 195
remittances, 276, 339
Renner, Jeremy, 4
reorientation phase, retirement and, 91
representative democracy, 219
representative sampling, 32
reproduction, 157
Republic of South Africa, apartheid and, 325
Republic of South Sudan, 279
research
    definition of qualitative and quantitative, 34–35
    presentation of findings of, 32
    sociological, 23–46
research design, 32, 40
research ethics, 41–43
research funding, 41
research process, 26
residents, 349
resocialization, 89
resource mobilization, 390
resourcefulness, 5
resources
    categories of, 239–230
    economic/social/cultural, 7
responsibility, professional/scientific/social, 41
retirement, 91
The Revenant, 133
reverse culture shock, 64
Revolutionary Road, 59
Reynolds, John R., 186

Rice, Tamir, 146, 310
Rich Hill, 251
Risman, Barbara, 291
rite of passage, 86–87, 91
Ritzer, George, 121
Rodgers, Myla, 306, 306
Rodriguez, Richard, 57
Roe v. Wade, 294
role conflict, 104
role exit, 105
role strain, 104
role taking, 76
Roman Catholic Church, 8, 10, 120, 192, 195, 300, 336
Romney, Mitt, 224
Roosevelt, Franklin Delano, 30, 83
Rosenthal, Robert, 182
Rossi, Alice, 163
Rough and Ready (Alger), 247
Rowling, Jo K., 70, 75
Roy, Arundhati, 395
Rudolph, Maya, 314
rules and regulations, 120
ruling class, 13
rumspringa, Amish, 79
Russian mafia, 139
Russian Organization (organized crime), 138
Rwanda, 226

S

sabotage, 388
sacred objects, 191–192
sacred realm, 190–191
Sacred Stone Camp, Sioux, 345
Saez, Emmanuel, 241–242
Saha, Robin, 369
Salvation Army homeless shelter, 1
salvation panic, 201
sampling error, 30
San Bernadino, mass shooting, 127
sanction, 61–62, 130, 194, 287, 355
Sanday, Peggy Reeves, 290
Sandberg, Sheryl, 283–284, 303
Sanders, Bernie, 123, 208
sandwich generation, 90
Sandy Hook Elementary School mass shooting, 127
Sanger, Margaret, 389
Sapir, Edward, 56
Sapir-Whorf hypothesis, 56–57, 117
Sarkeesian, Anita, 83
Save Darfur Coalition, 279
Scarce, Rik, 41
Schaffer, Scott, 395
school calendar, 54
School of Rock, 186
school readiness, 181
schools, 80–81, 179–182, 187, 377
Schwartz, Pepper, 162
scientific management, 123
scientific method, 11, 25–26
scientific responsibility, 41

SCLC (Southern Christian Leadership Conference), 329
Scopes Monkey Trial, 193
Scopes, John T., 193
Scott, Greg, 19–20
Scott, Keith, 310
Scum (game), 98
SEC (Securities and Exchange Commission), 138
The Second Sex, 292
second shift, 304
secondary analysis, 38, 40, 113, 209
secondary sex characteristics, 285
second-class citizens, 324
sects, 194, 196, 200
secularization, 197
Securities and Exchange Commission (SEC), 138
segregation, 248, 320, 325–326
self, 74, 99
    connection of society and, 2
    constructing, 100
    Cooley's looking-glass, 74
    dramaturgical approach, 76
    Goffman's presentation, 76–77
    interactionist presentation, 76
    looking-glass, 106
    Mead's stages, 74–77
    socialization and, 74–79
    society and, 99–101
Selma, 328
Semenya, Caster, 285
Sentencing Reform Act, 131
A Separation, 276
September 11, 2001, 130
service industry, 116
service-sector occupations, 209
SES (socioeconomic status), 252
settlement houses, 15
Seventh-Day Adventists, 196
sex, 284–285
sex education classes, 181
sexism, 301, 185
sex offenders, 135
sex trafficking, 306
sexual coercion, 300
sexuality, 295–299. *See also* gender; sex
sexually ambiguous, 285
sexual orientation, 296, 299
Sexual Politics (Millett), 292
sexual violence, 305
Shaefer, Luke, 234–235
Shaheen, Jack, 267
Shaikh, Nawab Ali, 259
Shakers, female leadership in, 203
Shakespeare, William, 76
Shapiro, Thomas, 249
Sherlock Holmes, 240
Sherpas (Nepal), 90
Shia/Shiite, Muslim sect of, 196

Subject Index

Shirky, Clay, 111
Shiva, 198
sick role, 355
sickle cell anemia, 361, 367
Siddhartha, 199
significant other, definition of, 75, 113
Silence, 200
Silver Linings Playbook, 4
Silver, Ira, 105
Silver, Nate, 224
single people, 168–169
Sioux Indians, 324, 345–346
slang, 62–63
slavery, 235–236
slaves, 9, 236, 311, 357
Sleh, Ali Abdullah (Yemen), 391
Smith, Adam, 202, 214–215
Snapchat, 84
SNCC (Student Nonviolent Coordinating Committee), 391
Snowpiercer, 251
social behavior, 11
social bonds, 143
social categorization, 78
social change. *See also* social movement
    as a societal force, 8
    commitment to, 15
    conflict desirable for, 382
    definition and examples of, 378
    in the U.S., 379
    Parsons' four processes of, 380
    reasons for resistance to, 382
    religion and, 200–202
    sociological perspectives on, 378
    stimulated by schools, 181
    violating norms and, 62
social class, 237–238
social coherence, 62
social comparison, 78
social context, genes and, 50
social control
    definition of, 128
    definition of formal and informal, 130–131
    deviance versus, 132
    Hirschi's theory of, 143
    name-calling and, 289
    religion and, 202–203
social disorganization theory, 144–145
social disruption, violating norms and, 62
social dynamics, 8
social environment, 7
social epidemiology, definition of, 359
social evolution, functionalist perspective and, 379
social fabric, distrust and evasion as part of, 23–24
social facts, definition of, 9–10, 12

social forces, 2, 9
social identification, 78
social inequality. *See also* gender; global inequality; race
    definition of, 7
    Marx's view of, 13
    stratification and, 235
social influence, artistic success and, 71
social institutions, 111–112, 178–179, 193, 204, 208
social integration
    Durkheim and, 27
    education and, 179
    suicide and, 10
    traditional societies and, 13
social interactions, 48–99
socialism, 215–216
socialization, 70–97
    agents of, 79
    anticipatory, 88
    by family, 79
    definition of, 71, 100, 286
    family function of, 157
    gender and, 80
    gender-role, 286–289
    movies on, 89
    occupational, 85
    peer groups and, 81–82
    race/ethnicity and, 80
    role of, 71
    schools and, 80
    self and, 74–79
    workplace, 85
socialized, definition of, 128
social location, 7, 160
social media, 82, 384
social mobility
    definition and types of, 238–239
    gender differences and, 273
    intergenerational across nations, 271–272
    wealth and, 249
social movement. *See also* new social movement
    abolitionists and suffragists, 389
    Arab Spring, 391
    Black Lives Matter, 391
    charismatic authority and, 391
    civil rights and antiwar, 389
    definition and example, 389
    feminism and, 391
    leadership and, 391
    use of new words in a, 391
    utilization of resources, 390
    women in leadership, 392
    women's role, 389, 392
social nature, language and, 55

The Social Network, 122
social networking, 84, 111
social networks, 92, 108–111, 208, 248
social order
    education and, 179
    equilibrium and, 380
    how to maintain, 12, 13
    inequality and, 322
    theories of, 9
social power, 7, 13, 390
Social Problems, 27
social reformers, U.S. sociologists as, 15
social resources, 239, 390
social responsibility, 41
social rights, citizenship and, 221
social role, 103
social science, 11–12
social separation, 14
social stability, 8
    equilibrium model, and, 380
    Parson says crime and poverty aid, 381
social statics, 8
social status, 13–14, 157
social stigma, deviance and, 134
social stratification, U.S. versus Mexico, 273–274
social structure
    definition of, 101, 389
    elements of, 101–113
    global perspective and, 113–118
    institutions and, 7
    interaction and, 98–126
    movies on interaction and, 122f
societal boundaries, 51
societal-reaction approach, definition of, 146
society
    aging and, 90–91
    constructing, 100
    culture and, 48–49
    definition of, 7, 49, 100
    demographic transition from preindustrial, 351
    evolution of, 379–380
    laws of, 8, 49
    postmodern, 117
    pre- to postindustrial, 351–352
    science of, 8
    self and, 99–101
    structure and organization of, 49
    technology and, 115–117
    types of, 115
Society in America (Martineau), 9
SocINDEX, 28
sociobiology, 50
socioeconomic status (SES), 252
sociological imagination, 1–22
    definition of, 99, 162, 208, 293, 317, 346, 396

Mills and, 222
sociological journals, list of, 27
sociological perspectives, 15–17
    crime and deviance, 141
    education and, 179
    on the environment, 367–370
sociological research, 23–46
sociological theorists, 15
sociological theory, 9, 12, 26
sociologist, 6, 15, 20
sociology
    academic, 18–19
    applied, 19
    clinical, 19
    coining of the word, 9
    common sense and, 24
    definition of, 2, 6, 235, 301
    definition of personal, 17, 394
    definition of public, 394
    degrees by gender and number, 18
    empowerment by, 8
    first university department of, 11
    function of, 6
    gender and college degrees in, 18
    jobs for majors in, 18–19
    main task of, 7
    Martin Luther King, Jr., 394
    science of, 24
    scientific method and, 25
    roots of, 8
Sociology of Education, 27
Solidarity, 114–118
songs, 9
The Sopranos, 138
Sotomayor, Sonia, 305
Southeast Asian farmers, 62
Southern Christian Leadership Conference (SCLC), 329
Spanish Harlem, 326
spirit of capitalism, 202
sports, 78, 191
Springsteen, Bruce, 103–104
The Square, 122
stability phase, 91
Standing Rock Sioux Reservation, 345–346
standpoint theory, 294
Stanton, Elizabeth Cady, 292
Star Wars: The Force Awakens, 133
Starbucks, 52, 266
statistics, use of, 35
status
    achieved and ascribed, 101–102
    definition, 101, 208, 284
    master, 134, 102–103
    roles and, 101–105
    social power and, 390
status group, 252
status quo, 133, 395

Steidle, Brian, 279
Stein, Jill, 220
Steinem, Gloria, 146
stepfamily, 166–167
stereotypes, 56–57, 101, 314
Stewart, Susan, 167
stigma, 134–135, 357–358
Stovel, Katherine, 108
strain theory of deviance, Merton's, 142–143
stratification, 235–238, 250–255, 260–276
Streib, Jessi, 254
Strogatz, Steven, 108
Struggling Upward (Alger), 247
student culture, 59
student loans and debt, 185, 211
Student Nonviolent Coordinating Committee (SNCC), 391
student outcomes, 182–183
subcultures, 62–63
substantive definition of family, 153, 164
Sudan, genocide of Africans, 324
suffragists, 389
suicide, 10–13, 26–27, 127
Suicide (Durkheim), 10
suicide bombings, counterculture and, 63–64
Sumner, William Graham, 65
Sun Come Up, 370
Super Hero Girls Initiative, DC entertainment comic books, 288
Superman, 54
Supersize Me, 42
surnames, 39
surveillance, 385–386
surveys, 6, 32–34
SurveyUSA (polling), 32
Sustainable Development Goals (SDG), 271
Sutherland, Edwin, 137, 144
Sweden, 79, 195
Switzerland, 326
symbols, 75, 135
Syria, 207, 324

T

tags on Instagram, 107
Tajfel, Henri, 78
Talackova, Jenna, 105
Tarver, Sherrena, 2
Taylor, Frederick Winslow, 123
teacher, 188
teacher-expectancy effect, 182
technological unemployment, Keynes and, 210
technology
    computer, 383–384
    definition of, 53, 367
    dehumanizing consequences of, 388
    increasing productivity, 388
    material culture, 53
    problems for social order, 388
    questions to ask when adopting new, 388
    resistance to, 387–389
    social change in U.S., 379
    society and, 115–117
    the future and, 382–389
TED talk, "The Urgency of Intersectionality," 295
teen birth rates, 300
teenage clique, 107
telephones, 84, 386
television, 83–84, 117
temperature, increasing global, 371, 372
tenants and landlords, 1–2
Terkel, Studs, 395
Terri, 186
terrorism
    contribution to social stability, 381
    definition and examples of 229–230
    global attacks of, 229
    terrorist attack, on September 11, 2001, 130
    terrorist cells/groups, 63–64
tertiary sector, economy and definition of, 209
text messaging, 62
Thank You for Smoking, 42
A Theology of Liberation (Gutiérrez), 202
theory
    activity, 92
    definition of, 9
    deviance and Merton's strain, 142–143
    disengagement, 92
    exploitation, 322
    Hirschi's, 143
    labeling, 145, 183
    Merton's strain, 142–143
    social control, 143
    social disorganization, 144–145
    sociological, 9, 12, 26
    standpoint, 294
    Wallerstein's model, 263
Third World dependency, 264
13th, 328
This Is 40, 164
This Is the Army, 228
Thomas theorem, 14, 25, 34, 82, 102, 134, 145, 237, 298, 316
Thomas, Franklin, 332
Thomas, W. I., 14, 378
Three Kings, 228
the three R's, 179
Tibetans, marriage view of, 153
Tiên Lên (Vietnamese game), 98
tiger mom, 164
time-motion studies, 123
Tinder, 152–153
Title IX, 178, 186, 187
To Be Real: Telling the Truth and Changing the Face of Feminism, 294
Todd, Charlie, 47
tokenistic fallacy, racism and, 316–317
Tolkien, J. R. R., 56
Tönnies, Ferdinand, 113–114, 116, 118
Torah, 198
total fertility rate, 347
totalitarianism, 219
tracking, 83–184
traditional authority, 213, 218
trafficking
    human and wildlife, 139–140
    sex, 236
Trafficking Victims Protection Act, 277
Trainspotting, 134
Transamerica, 305
transgender, 296–297
transnational crime, 139
transnationals, 339
transsexuals, 105
The Tree of Life, 200
triad, 108
tribal groups, 330
Troubled Assets Relief Program (TARP), 216–217
Truman, Harry S., 33
The Truman Show, 122
Trump, Donald
    Dakota Access Pipeline and, 346
    election of, 207–208
    electoral votes received by, 212, 305
    "Make America Great Again" election slogan, 208
    ObamaCare repeal and replace election promise, 366
    pollsters said Clinton would defeat, 33
    Republican selection of outsider, 123
    restriction of immigration from Muslim nations, 338, 341
    Trump Tower (Mumbai), 258
    unfavorable rating on Election Day, 213
    voter turnout for election of, 224–225
    wall with Mexico election pledge, 326
    withdrawal from Paris Agreement by, 374
TurnItIn.com, 59
12 Years as a Slave, 4
Twain, Mark, 148
Twitchell, James B., 118
Twitter, 30, 84, 108–109, 222, 384, 391
$2.00 a Day: Living on Almost Nothing in America, 234
Tyson, Neil de Grasse, 26

U

UCR (*Uniform Crime Reports*), 135
UNAMID (African Union–UN Mission in Darfur), 279
Uncle Sam, 217
underclass, U.S., 238
unemployment, 2–4, 210–211
UNICEF, 356
Uniform Crime Reports (UCR), 135
United Nations, 260, 270–271, 273, 277, 285, 353
United States Border Patrol, immigration and, 273
United States Patent and Trademark Office, 54
United States Sentencing Commission, 131
Universal Declaration of Human Rights, 236, 277
unmarried couples, 165, 168. *See also* cohabitation
Up, 94
upper class, U.S., 237
upper-middle class, U.S., 238
U.S. Border Patrol, 349
U.S. Bureau of Labor Statistics, 28, 85–86
    U.S. Census Bureau, 28–30, 31, 38, 119, 170, 314–316
U.S. Commission on Civil Rights, 301
U.S. Defense Department, 383
U.S. Department of Education, 28
U.S. Department of Homeland Security, 276
U.S. Department of Justice, 136, 319
U.S. Supreme Court, 165
    Bell v. Maryland, 337
    Brown v. Board of Education, 178, 316
    case of draft evasion of Muhammad Ali, 101
    declines to hear case of Rik Scarce, 41
    interracial marriages and, 162
    Plessy v. Ferguson, 178, 329
    Roe v. Wade, 294
    same-sex marriage and, 170
    school integration decision, 323
USA PATRIOT Act, 203, 386
us versus them, 77–79, 134, 262, 322

V

Vaishya (caste system merchants), 236

Subject Index

validity, 30, 33
value, 57, 177, 181
value generalization, social change and Parson's, 380
values, 57–59
variables, 28–29, 32
variation
    cross-cultural, 49–50
    cross-time, 50
    cultural, 62–66
Varma, Babulal, 258
varnas (India), 236
Vassos, Angela, 176
Vaughn, Bill, 369
Veblen, Thorstein, 382
Venter, Craig, 312
vertical mobility, 239
vested interests, 382
victimization survey, 136
victimless crime, 138
video games, 82
Vietnam, 79, 324
Vietnamese Americans, 332
Vilain, Eric, 285
Virginia Tech, mass shooting, 127
Virginia's Racial Integrity Act, 162
Virunga, 276
Vishnu, 198
volunteers, 93, 392, 396
voter participation, 86, 207, 224–226, 304, 396

W

wage gap, 4, 249, 302–303, 321
Walker, Rebecca, 294
Wall Street, 139
WALL-E, 370
Wallerstein, Immanuel, 263–264, 273, 383
Walmart, sales and profit margin, 215
Walton, Sam, 238
War, definition, 227
warlords, Mills and power elite, 223
war on drugs, 131
War on Poverty, 244
War Powers Act, The, 227
Washington, George, 236, 311
Washington insiders, 123
Washington Post, 27, 32
Water, 251
water is life, 345–346
water pollution, by oil, 371
Watts, Duncan, 25, 70–71
wealth
    concentration of in nations, 269
    definition of, 240
    distribution of, 242–243
    global distribution of, 269
    median household, 5
The Wealth of Nations, 214
Weber, Max
    authority and legitimacy to rule, 214
    bureaucracy and rational management, 119, 121
    class, status, and party, 252–253, 390
    concept of life chances, 235
    definition and continuum of power, 212
    dehumanizing consequences of bureaucracy, 388
    influence of personal values on research topics, 42
    model and three components of stratification, 252–253, 390
    rationalization, 122
    theory of power and social status, 13–14
    importance of value neutrality, 66
    Protestant ethic and "salvation panic," 201
    social change, 200
    social power, 390
    spirit of capitalism, 202
    traditional authority belief, 213
    true church and dogma, 196
Weiner, 221
Wells-Barnett, Ida B., 14–15, 16, 301
West, Candace, 286
West, Cornel, 333
Western Electric Company, Hawthorne plant, 37
Westinghouse Electric and Manufacturing Company, 37
White ethnics, immigrants to U.S., 337–338
White Eyes, Joseph, 345
White, Ryan, 358
white-collar workers, 116
Whiteness, 327–328
Whites
    life expectancy for, 362
    living arrangements for children, 163
    median household wealth, 5
    poverty rate of, 94
    privilege and job seeking, 38
    suicide rate for, 12
    unemployment rate for, 3
    white-collar crime, definition and types of, 137, 252
Whitney, Eli, 209
WHO (World Health Organization), 353–354, 356, 367
Whorf, Benjamin, 56
Wicked, 51
Wikipedia, 28
Wilde, Oscar, 217
wildlife, trafficking of, 140
Wilkins, John, 55
Willard, Emma Hart, 178–179
Williams, Robin, 58
Wilson, Darren, 310
Wilson, William Julius, 108, 134, 323
Winant, Howard, 313
Winfrey, Oprah, 73, 176, 317
Winter's Bone, 251
The Wire, 134
Wirth, Louis, 20
Witt, Emily and Eleanor, 55, 183, 287, 338
Witt, Jon and Lori, 55, 183
Wolf, Naomi, 134, 287
women
    abortion right of, 294
    blocked from leadership, 391
    CEOs percentage of, 283, 307
    college success and, 50
    higher education and, 185, 187
    housework done by men versus, 304
    images in mass media of, 287
    in legislature in other countries, 226–227
    in Mexican politics, 274–275
    in the military, 227–228
    life expectancy of men versus, 362–363
    movements for, 292–295
    19th Amendment and right to vote for, 220, 292
    not included in clinical studies, 363
    not suited for college, 290–291
    representatives in Congress, 226–227
    rights of, 9, 14
    second shift and, 304
    sexual or physical violence against, 305
    urban migration effect on, 273
    voter participation rates of, 304
    wage discrimination and, 249
    workforce and, 211
Women's March on Washington, 390
women's movement, 292–295
Woods, Tiger, 314
Workforce, 211–212
working class, 13, 238
working mother, 104
The Working Poor: Invisible in America (Shipler), 246
workplace socialization, 85
World Bank, 264–265
The World Before Her, 276
World Construction, 100
World Economic Forum, 306
World Health Organization (WHO), 305, 353–354, 367
World One skyscraper, 258
world systems analysis, 264, 273, 372, 383
World Wealth and Income Database, 268
World Wide Web, 84
A Wrinkle in Time (L'Engle), 70
WuDunn, Sherly, 306

X

xanith, 289
X-Men, 54
X-Men: Apocalypse, 133

Y

Yakuza, 138
Yale University, 290–291, 377
Yinger, J. Milton, 196
Yogyakarta Principles, 298
YouTube, 386

Z

Zamenhof, Ludwik, 55
Zebene, Woineshet, 306
Zero Dark Thirty, 228
Zimbardo, Philip, 144, 228
Zimmerman, Don, 286
Zootopia, 4, 328